# Contents

| | |
|---|---|
| II | European driving: cut through the confusion |
| IV | Driving regulations |
| VIII | Ski resorts |
| X | Sights of Europe |
| XXIV | European politics and economics |

## 1 Route planning maps

1 Key to route planning map pages

## 24 Road maps

24 Key to road map pages · Distance table

## 201 City plans and approach maps

| | | | | | |
|---|---|---|---|---|---|
| Alicante C | 201 | | Luxembourg C | 215 |
| Amsterdam C U | 202 | | Lyon C U | 215 |
| Antwerpen C | 201 | | Madrid U C | 215 |
| Athina U C | 202 | | Málaga C | 216 |
| Barcelona C U | 203 | | Marseille C | 216 |
| Basel C | 203 | | Milano C U | 217 |
| Beograd C | 205 | | Moskva C U | 218 |
| Berlin C U | 204 | | München C U | 218 |
| Bordeaux C U | 205 | | Nápoli C U | 219 |
| Bruxelles U C | 205 | | Oslo U C | 219 |
| Budapest C U | 206 | | Paris C U | 220 |
| Dublin C U | 207 | | Praha C U | 222 |
| Düsseldorf C U | 207 | | Roma C U | 223 |
| Edinburgh C | 207 | | Rotterdam C | 222 |
| Firenze Florence C | 209 | | Sankt Peterburg U | 222 |
| Frankfurt C | 209 | | Sevilla C | 224 |
| Genève Geneva C | 209 | | Stockholm C U | 225 |
| Génova Genoa C | 209 | | Strasbourg C U | 224 |
| Göteborg C | 210 | | Stuttgart C | 224 |
| Granada C | 210 | | Torino U C | 226 |
| Hamburg C U | 210 | | Venézia C | 226 |
| Helsinki C U | 211 | | Warszawa C U | 227 |
| İstanbul U | 211 | | Wien U C | 227 |
| København C U | 212 | | Zagreb C | 228 |
| Köln Cologne C | 212 | | Zürich C | 228 |
| Lisboa C U | 213 | | C City street plan | |
| London C U | 213 | | U Urban area map | |

## 229 Index to road maps

www.philips-maps.co.uk

First published in 2007 as *Philip's EasyRead Europe* by
Philip's, a division of Octopus Publishing Group Ltd
www.octopusbooks.co.uk
Endeavour House, 189 Shaftesbury Avenue, London WC2H 8JY
An Hachette UK Company · www.hachette.co.uk

Fourth edition 2013, first impression 2013

Ordnance Survey® This product includes mapping
data licensed from Ordnance
Survey®, with the permission of
the Controller of Her Majesty's Stationery Office © Crown
copyright 2013. All rights reserved. Licence number 100011710.

is a registered Trade Mark of the Northern Ireland
Department of Finance and Personnel.
This product includes mapping data licensed from
Ordnance Survey of Northern Ireland®, reproduced with the
permission of Land and Property Services under delegated
athority from the Controller of Her Majesty's Stationery Office,
© Crown Copyright 2013.

All rights reserved. Apart from any fair dealing for the purpose of
private study, research, criticism or review, as permitted under
the Copyright Designs and Patents Act, 1988, no part of this
publication may be reproduced, stored in a retrieval system, or
transmitted in any form or by any means, electronic, electrical,
chemical, mechanical, optical, photocopying, recording, or
otherwise, without prior written permission.

All enquiries should be addressed to the Publisher.

While every reasonable effort has been made to ensure that the
information compiled in this atlas is accurate, complete and

up-to-date at the time of publication, some of this information
is subject to change and the Publisher cannot guarantee its
correctness or completeness.

The information in this atlas is provided without any
representation or warranty, express or implied and the Publisher
cannot be held liable for any loss or damage due to any use
or reliance on the information in this atlas, nor for any errors,
omissions or subsequent changes in such information.

The representation in this atlas of any road, drive or track is not
evidence of the existence of a right of way.

The mapping on page 214 and the town plans of Edinburgh and
London are based on mapping data licenced from Ordnance
Survey with the permission of the Controller of Her Majesty's
Stationery Office, © Crown Copyright 2013. All rights reserved.
Licence number 100011710.

The maps of Ireland on pages 26 to 30 and the urban area
map and town plan of Dublin are based on Ordnance Survey
Ireland by permission of the Government Permit Number 8847
© Ordnance Survey Ireland and Government of Ireland, and
Land and Property Services under delegated authority from the
Controller of Her Majesty's Stationery Office © Crown Copyright
2013. Permit Number 130042

Cartography by Philip's, Copyright © Philip's 2013

**Photographic acknowledgements:** Page II top left, *joyfull /
Shutterstock*; top right *Tjurunga / Dreamstime*; bottom right
*mladn61 / iStockphoto* · Page III centre *zstock / Shutterstock*;
bottom *Lya_Cattel /iStockphoto* · Page VII *Ingmar Wesemann /
iStockphoto.com* · Page VIII *Jivko Kazakov / iStockphoto.com*

Printed in China

---

## Legend to route planning maps pages 2–23

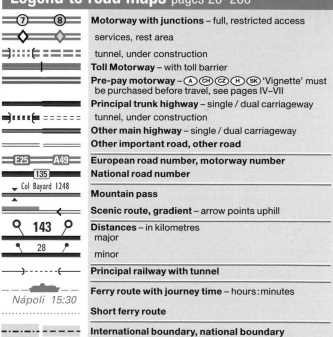

| | |
|---|---|
| | Motorway with selected junctions |
| | tunnel, under construction |
| | Toll motorway, pre-pay motorway |
| | Main through route, other major road, other road |
| 25   56 | European road number, motorway number |
| 55 | National road number |
| 56 | Distances – in kilometres |
| | International boundary, national boundary |
| LE HAVRE | Car ferry and destination |
| ✈ 1089 ▲ | Mountain pass, international airport, height (metres) |

**Town** – population
| | | | |
|---|---|---|---|
| MOSKVA | 5 million + | Gävle | 50000–100000 |
| BERLIN | 2–5 million | Nybro | 20000–50000 |
| MINSK | 1–2 million | Ikast | 10000–20000 |
| Oslo | 500000–1million | Skjern | 5000–10000 |
| Århus | 200000–500000 | Lillesand | 0–5000 |
| Turku | 100000–200000 | | |

The green version of the symbol indicates towns with
Low Emission Zones

### Scale · pages 2–23

**1:3200000**
1 in = 50.51 miles
1 cm = 32km

0  10  20  30  40  50  60  70  80  90  100  110 miles
0  20  40  60  80  100  120  140  160  180 km

## Legend to road maps pages 26–200

| | |
|---|---|
| ⑦   ⑧ | Motorway with junctions – full, restricted access |
| ◇   ◇ | services, rest area |
| | tunnel, under construction |
| | Toll Motorway – with toll barrier |
| | Pre-pay motorway – (A) (CH) (CZ) (H) (SK) 'Vignette' must be purchased before travel, see pages IV–VII |
| | Principal trunk highway – single / dual carriageway |
| | tunnel, under construction |
| | Other main highway – single / dual carriageway |
| | Other important road, other road |
| E25   A49 | European road number, motorway number |
| 135 | National road number |
| Col Bayard 1248 | Mountain pass |
| | Scenic route, gradient – arrow points uphill |
| 143 | Distances – in kilometres major |
| 28 | minor |
| | Principal railway with tunnel |
| Nápoli 15:30 | Ferry route with journey time – hours : minutes |
| | Short ferry route |
| | International boundary, national boundary |
| | National park, natural park |

| | | | |
|---|---|---|---|
| 🛬 Airport | | 🎿 Ski resort | |
| 🏛 Ancient monument | | 🎡 Theme park | |
| 🏖 Beach | | ◉ World Heritage site | |
| 🏰 Castle or house | | 1754▲ Spot height | |
| 🕳 Cave | | Sevilla World Heritage town | |
| ✦ Other place of interest | | Verona Town of tourist interest | |
| ❀ Park or garden | | ■ ◉ City or town with Low Emission Zone | |
| ✠ Religious building | | | |

### Scale · pages 26–181

**1:753800**
1 inch = 12 miles
1 cm = 7.5km

0  2  4  6  8  10  12  14  16  18  20  22  24  26 miles
0  4  8  12  16  20  24  28  32  36  40km

### Scale · pages 182–200

**1:1507600**
1 inch = 24 miles
1 cm = 15km

0  4  8  12  16  20  24  28  32  36  40  44  48  52 miles
0  8  16  24  32  40  48  56  64  72  80km

# European driving:
## cut through the confusion
### Stay safe with GEM Motoring Assist

● Are you confused about European driving laws? ● Do you need advice about equipment requirements and which documents to take? ● Are you new to driving on the right hand side? ● How will you know what speed limits apply? ● Who do you call if you have an accident or break down?

**M**illions of us drive abroad on holiday each year. Perhaps it's a long motorway trip to the Mediterranean, a selection of historic cities and sites or a gentle tour along quiet country lanes. Whatever the purpose, it makes sense to ensure that both we and our vehicles are properly prepared for the journey.

It's not easy getting to grips with the finer points of driving in other countries, however experienced you may be as a motorist. Whether you have notched up thousands of miles of European driving or are preparing to make your first journey, the chances are you will always manage to find some road sign or legal requirement that will cause confusion.

What's more, 'driving in Europe' covers such a huge area. With the inclusion of Croatia (July 2013), there are 28 countries in the European Union alone, each with its own set of road traffic laws and motoring customs. Driving in Europe can mean a spectacular and sunny coastal road that's within sight of Africa, or a snowy track amid the biting cold of the Arctic Circle, where the only others on the road are reindeer. Add to this some of the world's most congested cities, dense clusters of motorways (many with confusing numbers) and a big variation in safety standards and attitudes to risk. No wonder we often risk getting lost, taking wrong turnings or perhaps stopping where we shouldn't.

Depending on the country we're in, our errors at the wheel or our lack of familiarity with the rules of the road can sometimes bring unwelcome consequences. In any country, foreign drivers are subject to the same traffic rules as residents, enforceable in many situations by hefty on-the-spot fines and other sanctions. The situation across Europe is complex, simply because of the number of different sets of rules. For example, failure to carry a specific piece of breakdown equipment may be an offence in one country, but not in another. It's easy to see why the fun and excitement of a road trip in Europe could be spoilt by a minefield of regulations.

But we want to ensure that doesn't happen. Preparation and planning are key to a great holiday. It certainly pays to do a bit of research before you go, just to ensure you and your vehicle are up to the journey, your documents are in order and you're carrying the correct levels of equipment to keep the law enforcers happy.

## BEFORE YOU GO
Some sensible planning will help make sure your European journey is enjoyable and, we hope, stress-free. So take some time before departure to ensure everything is in good shape: and that includes you, your travelling companions and your vehicle.

### For you:
Try to become familiar with the driving laws of your holiday desti-nation, including the local speed limits and which side of the road to drive on. You will be subject to these laws when driving abroad and if you are stopped by the police, it is not an excuse to say that you were unaware of them. Police officers in many countries have the power to impose (and collect) substantial on-the-spot fines for motoring offences, whether you are a resident of that country or a visitor. GEM Motoring Assist can link you direct with up-to-date information on driving in 27 different European countries. For each country, you will find a downloadable three-page PDF document containing detailed information on driving facts, traffic laws, document and equipment requirements – and even a few simple, emergency phrases to help you if you're in difficulty.
Go to www.motoringassist.com/europe

The Foreign and Commonwealth Office also gives country-specific travel and driving advice www.gov.uk/driving-abroad.

### Passports
Check everyone's passport to make sure they are all valid.
Don't wait for your passport to expire. Unused time, rounded up to whole months (minimum one month, maximum nine months), will usually be added to your new passport. New passports usually take two weeks to arrive. The Passport Office (0300 222 0000, www.gov.uk/government/organisations/hm-passport-office) offers a faster service if you need a replacement passport urgently, but you'll have to pay a lot more.

### Driving Licence
The new style photocard driving licence is valid in all European Union countries. However, you must ensure you carry both parts: the credit card-size photocard and paper licence. The previously used pink EU format UK licence is also valid but may not be recognized in some areas so it is advisable to carry an International Driving Permit as well. These cost £5.50 and are available from Post Offices (www.postoffice.co.uk/international-driving-permit).

### Travel Insurance
Travel insurance is vital as it covers you against medical emergencies, accidents, thefts and cancellations, and repatriation. Ask for details before buying any travel insurance policy. Find out what it covers you for, and to what value. More important, check what's not covered. One of the key benefits of GEM membership is the excellent discount you can get on travel insurance.
For more details, please visit our website:
www.motoringassist.com/philipsmaps

### European Breakdown Cover
Don't risk letting a breakdown ruin your European trip. Ensure you purchase a policy that will cover you for roadside assistance, emergency repair and recovery of your vehicle to the UK, wherever in Europe you may be heading. Once again, GEM members enjoy a specially discounted rate. You'll find the details at www.motoringassist.com/philipsmaps

### EHIC
The E111 medical treatment form is no longer valid. Instead, you need an EHIC card for everyone travelling. These are free and cover you for any medical treatment you may need during a trip to another EU country or Switzerland. However, do check at the time of requiring assistance that your EHIC will be accepted. Apply online (www.ehic.org.uk), by telephone (0845 606 2030) or complete an application form, available from a Post office. Allow up to 14 days for the cards to arrive.

### For your vehicle:

### Service
It makes sense to get your car serviced before you travel. As a minimum, ensure the tyres have plenty of tread left and that water and oil levels are checked and topped up if required. Check them regularly during your time away.

## STOP AND GIVE WAY

### Who has priority?
Make sure you keep a watchful eye on signs telling you who has priority on the road. Look for a yellow diamond sign, which tells you that traffic already on the road has priority. If you see the yellow diamond sign crossed out, then you must give way to traffic joining the road.

### Priorité a droite
Despite the use of the yellow diamond signs, be aware that on some French and Belgian roads (especially roundabouts in Paris), the traditional 'priorité a droite' practice is followed, even though it may no longer be legal. In theory these days, the rule no longer applies unless it is clearly signed. In practice, though, it makes sense to anticipate a driver pulling out in front of you, even though the priority may be yours.

### Stop means stop!
If you come to a solid white line with an octagonal 'STOP' sign, then you must come to a complete stop. In other words your wheels must stop turning. Adherence to the 'STOP' sign is gener-ally more rigorously enforced in European countries than you may be used to here.

### Headlight flash
Bear in mind that the practice of flashing headlights at a junction in France does not mean the same thing as it might in the UK. If another motorists flashes his headlights at you, he's telling you that he has priority and will be coming through in front of you.

### Vehicle Registration Document
Police in many countries can demand that you prove you have the right to be driving your car. That means you need to show the registration document, or a suitable letter of authorization if the registration document is not in your name. Remember you should never leave the registration document in the car.

### Nationality plate
Your vehicle must display a nationality plate of an approved pattern, design and size.

### MOT
If your car is more than three years old, make sure you take its current MOT test certificate with you.

### Insurance
If you are planning a trip to Europe, you should find that your car insurance policy provides the minimum amount of cover you need. But it's important to contact your insurer before you go, to confirm exactly what level of cover you have and how long it will be valid, especially if you plan to venture outside the EU (see also page IV).

### Mechanical adjustments
Check the adjustments required for your headlights before you go. Beam deflectors are a legal requirement if you drive in Europe. They are generally sold at the ports, on ferries and in the Folkestone Eurotunnel terminal, but be warned – the instructions can be a little confusing! The alternative is to ask a local garage to do the job for you before you go. If you choose this, then make sure you shop around as prices for this simple task vary enormously.

### Equipment check-list
This checklist represents GEM's suggestions for what you should take with you in the car. Different countries have different rules about what's compulsory and these rules change from time to time. So it's important to check carefully before you set out. For country-by-country guidance, visit www.motoringassist.com/europe or see page IV of this atlas.
- Fire extinguisher
- First aid kit
- High-visibility jacket – one for each occupant
- Two warning triangles
- Replacement bulbs and fuses
- Spare spectacles (if worn) for each driver
- Snow chains for winter journeys into the mountains
- Disposable camera and notebook to record any collisions or damage for insurance purposes (if it is safe).

### Contact details
Make sure you have all relevant emergency helpline numbers with you, including emergency services, breakdown assistance, the local British consulate and your insurance company. There are links to embassies and consulates around the world from the Foreign Office website. (www.fco.gov.uk) For information, the European emergency telephone number (our equivalent of 999) is 112.

## TOP TIPS FOR STAYING SAFE

**Collisions abroad occur not just because of poor driving conditions locally, but also because we do not always take the same safety precautions as we might expect to take at home, for example by not wearing a seatbelt or by drinking and driving.**

**1. Plan your route before you go.** That includes the journey you make to reach your destination (with sufficient breaks built in) and any excursions or local journeys.

**2. Remember that you will be subject to the same laws as local drivers.** Ignorance will not be accepted as an excuse.

**3. Take extra care at junctions** when you're driving on the 'right side' of the road. If driving in a family group, involve everyone in a quick 'junction safety check' to help reduce the risk of a collision. Having everybody in the car call out a catchphrase such as "DriLL DriLL DriLL" (Driver Look Left) on the approach to junctions and roundabouts is a small but potentially life-saving habit.

**4. Take fatigue seriously.** The excellent European motorway network means you can cover big distances with ease but you must also make time for proper breaks (experts recommend at least 15 minutes every two hours). If possible, share the driving and set strict daily limits to the number of hours.

**5. Drink-driving limits across Europe are lower than those in the UK.** The only exception is Malta, where the limit is the same (0.8mg per ml). Bear this in mind if you're flying to a holiday or business destination and plan to have a drink on the plane, as the combination of unfamiliar roads and alcohol in your bloodstream is not a safe one. It's also worth remembering that drivers who cause collisions because they were drinking are likely to find their insurance policy will not cover them.

**6. Expect the unexpected.** Styles of driving in your destination country are likely to different from those you know in the UK. Drive defensively and don't get involved in any altercations on the road.

**7. Don't overload your car** while away, however tempting the local bargains may appear. Also, make sure you have good all-round visibility by ensuring you don't pile up items on the parcel shelf or boot, and keep your windscreen clear of dirt and dust.

**8. Always wear a seatbelt** and ensure everyone else on board wears one. Check specific regulations regarding the carriage of children: in some countries children under the age of 12 are not permitted to travel in the front of the car.

**9. Don't use your phone while driving.** Even though laws on phone use while driving differ from country to country, the practice is just as dangerous wherever you are.

**10. When you're exploring on foot, be wise to road safety as a pedestrian.** You may get into trouble for 'jay-walking', so don't just wander across a road. Use a proper crossing, but remember that drivers may not stop for you! And don't forget that traffic closest to you approaches from the LEFT.

## WORTH KNOWING

**You will need a separate GB sticker** in EU countries unless your car has a registration plate containing the GB euro-symbol. In non-EU countries the euro-plate is not valid so you will need the separate sticker as well.

**Fuel is generally most expensive at motorway service areas and cheapest at supermarkets.** However, these are usually shut on Sundays and Bank Holidays. So-called '24 hour' regional fuel stations in France seldom accept payment by UK credit card, so don't rely on them if to fill up during a night-time journey.

**If you see several fuel stations in short succession** before a national border, it's likely that fuel on the other side will be more expensive, so take the opportunity to fill up.

**Radar speed camera detectors** are illegal in most European countries.

**The insurance 'green card'** is no longer required for journeys in the EU but it is advisable to carry one anyway. It is also important to make sure you have contact details for your insurer in case of an accident or claim.

**Speed limits in France are enforced vigorously.** An additional 400 fixed cameras were installed across France in early 2012. Radar controls are frequent, and any driver (including non-residents) detected at more than 25km/h above the speed limit can have their licence confiscated on the spot. Furthermore, if you are caught exceeding the speed limit by 50km/h, even on a first offence, you will face a term of imprisonment.

**New legislation introduced in France in 2012 required every driver to carry a self-breathalyser test kit.** However, the imposition of a €11 fine for failing to produce a breathalyser when required has been postponed indefinitely. So, in theory, you are required to carry a breathalyser kit, but no fine can be imposed if you don't.

**Luxembourg has specific rules relating to how you fix a sat nav device to your windscreen.** Get it wrong and you could be fined on the spot.

**Norway and Sweden have low drink-driving limits:** just 20mg per 100ml of blood (compared to 80 in the UK). In Slovakia, the limit is zero.

**In Hungary, the limit is also zero.** If you are found to be drink-driving, your driving licence will be withdrawn by police officers on the spot.

### Other laws and motoring advice to be aware of across Europe:

**Austria** Recent rules require the mandatory use of winter tyres between 1 November and 15 April.

**Belgium** You will have to pay to use most public toilets – including those at motorway service stations • You are not permitted to use cruise control on motorways when traffic is heavy • There are also specific penalties for close-following on motorways • Roadside drug-testing of drivers (using oral fluid testing devices) was introduced late in 2010 and now forms a regular part of any police controls.

**Cyprus** There have been important changes in how speeding and drink-driving are sanctioned. Cyprus now has a graduated system of speeding fines, ranging from one euro per km/h over the limit in marginal cases through to fines of up to €5,000 and a term of imprisonment for the most severe infringements. There are also graduated fines for drink-driving, ranging from fixed penalties for being slightly over the limit to terms of imprisonment and fines of up to 5,000 for the most severe.

**Denmark** Cars towing caravans and trailers are prohibited from overtaking on motorways at certain times of day.

**Finland** If you hit an elk or deer, you must report the collision to the police. • Speeding fines are worked out according to your income. Access to a national database allows police at the roadside to establish a Finnish resident's income and number of dependants. Officers then impose a fine based on a specific number of days' income. A 'ticket calculator' on the Finnish Police website (www.poliisi.fi) allows you to work out the fine before committing the offence! The minimum speeding fine is 115 euros.

**France** As of 1 July 2012, any driver must be in possession of a valid breathalyser (displaying a 'BF' number), either electronic or chemical, to be shown to a police officer in case of control. • The banning of radar detectors, with fines of €1500 for anyone using them • Increased penalties for driving while using a mobile phone • Legislation requiring motorcyclists and their passengers to wear high-visibility clothing may be reintroduced.

**Germany** Check your fuel level regularly as it's an offence to run out of fuel on a German motorway. If you run out, you face an on-the-spot fine • It's also an offence to make rude signs to other road users.

**Greece** has Europe's highest accident rate in terms of the number of crashes per vehicle. Take extra care at traffic light junctions, as red lights are frequently ignored. • Since 2 April 2012 all drivers detected with more than 1.10 g/l of alcohol in blood, or more than 0.60mg/l in breath will be prosecuted for the offence. • Carrying a petrol can in a vehicle is forbidden.

**Ireland** The alcohol limit was reduced in 2011 from 0.8 mg per ml to 0.5mg • Beware of rural three-lane roads, the middle overtaking lane is used by traffic travelling in both directions • On wider rural roads it's the accepted practice for slower vehicles to pull over to let faster traffic through.

**Italy** Police can impound your vehicle if you cannot present the relevant ownership documents when requested. • You will need a red and white warning sign if you plan to use any rear-mounted luggage rack such as a bike rack • Zero alcohol tolerance is now applied for drivers who have held a driving licence for less than three years, as well as to drivers aged 18 to 21, professional drivers, taxi drivers and truckers.

**Norway** Under new legislation, police officers can perform roadside drug impairment saliva tests. There are specific limits set for the presence of 20 common non-alcohol drugs • You'll find what amounts to a zero tolerance where drinking and driving is concerned. Only 0.1mg of alcohol per millilitre of blood is permitted • Speeding fines are high. For example, a driver caught at 25 km/h over the 80 km/h speed limit on a national road could expect a fine of around £600.

**Portugal** If you are towing a caravan, you must have a current inventory of the caravan's contents to show a police officer if requested.

**Slovakia** It is now mandatory to use dipped headlights on every road journey, regardless of the time of day, season or weather conditions.

**Spain** Motorway speed limits in Spain are 120km/h. • If you need glasses for driving, then the law requires you to carry a spare pair with you in the car. • It's compulsory to carry two spare warning triangles, spare bulbs for your car and reflective jackets.

**Turkey** Take great caution if you're driving at dusk. Many local drivers put off using their lights until it's properly dark, so you may find oncoming traffic very hard to spot • During the time of Ramadan, many people will do without food and water between the hours of sunrise and sunset. This can seriously reduce levels of alertness, especially among people driving buses, trucks and taxis.

## MOTORWAY VIGNETTES

**Some countries require you to purchase (and in some cases display) a vignette before using motorways.**

In **Austria** you will need to purchase and display a vignette on the inside of your windscreen, they are available at border crossings and petrol stations. More details from **www.austria.info**

**Bulgaria** operates a vignette system for travel on all state roads. Vignettes can only be purchased in Bulgaria (not before you get there). A seven-day vignette costs €5 for a car. The penalty for not displaying is €60.

In the **Czech Republic**, you can buy a vignette at the border and at petrol stations. Make sure you write your vehicle registration number on the vignette before displaying it. The roads without toll are indicated by a traffic sign saying "Bez poplatku". More details from **www.motorway.cz**

In **Hungary** an e-vignette system was introduced in 2008. It is therefore no longer necessary to display the vignette, though you should make doubly sure the information you give on your vehicle is accurate. Vignettes are sold at petrol stations throughout the country. Buy online at **www.motorway.hu.**

In **Slovakia**, a vignette also must be purchased before using the motorways. This is sold in two kinds at the border and petrol stations. You will need to write your vehicle registration plate on the vignette before displaying it. More details from **www.slovensko.com**

In **Switzerland**, you will need to purchase and display a 'vignette' before you drive on the motorway. Bear in mind you will need a separate vignette if you are towing a caravan. Purchase the Swiss vignette in advance from **www.autobahnen.ch.**

## FREQUENTLY ASKED QUESTIONS

**Do I need to use dipped headlights all the time?** It is currently mandatory to use dipped headlights for daytime journeys in 15 of the 27 EU countries. Additionally, an European directive now requires all new cars to be fitted with daytime running lights.

**Do German motorways still not have speed limits?** Speed limits apply to around 30% of German motorways. A further 10% of motorway in Germany is subject to variable speed limits, determined by motorway control rooms. Across other stretches there is a recommended speed limit of 130km/h. It is worth remembering that whereas exceeding this limit is not an offence, the penalties for a high-speed driver being involved in an accident are considerably higher.

**Why do European motorways all seem to have two numbers on the map and the road signs?** This is because the roads form the international network of 'E-roads'. In most countries maps and signs will have the European road number (shown in white on green) alongside the appropriate national road number. However, in Sweden and Belgium only the E-road number will be shown.

**As a visitor to a country, rather than a resident, am I exempt from speeding fines?** No. Different countries have different mechanisms for dealing with traffic offences committed by non-resident drivers. If, for example, you are stopped for speeding, then expect to receive a fine which you can usually pay 'on the spot' by credit card. A number of bilateral agreements exist, allowing police to obtain non-resident driver details and issue penalties for offences recorded by automatic enforcement cameras. Interestingly, 'foreign' drivers make up only about 5% of traffic on Europe's roads, yet they account for 15% of all speeding offences. A wider European cross-border enforcement directive is expected to be brought into law in 2014. This will cover not only speeding but also other offences, such as non-wearing of seatbelts and crossing red traffic lights.

**If I hire a car in one country, am I allowed to take it into another country?** The issue is most likely to be with insurance, so check with the hiring company before setting off. Ask to see something in writing so you are sure that you are getting the right information. Often, when hiring, you will find you have only the minimum cover required for driving in the country where you hired the car. If you plan to take it into other countries, then make sure your insurance will cover you and purchase a top-up policy if necessary.


**GEM MOTORING ASSIST**

Since its foundation in 1932, GEM Motoring Assist has been at the forefront of road safety in the UK. Now one of the largest member-led road safety organisations, GEM provides a wide range of discounts and benefits for its 74,000+ members, including the UK's best-value range of breakdown recovery insurance products for motorists, motorcyclists and caravanners. GEM members also benefit from discounts on European breakdown cover and travel insurance, as well as enjoying free access to GEM's Accident Management Service, which provides free-of-charge legal help following any road traffic collision. Members receive *Good Motoring*, a free quarterly magazine and access to an excellent line-up of road safety leaflets and web-based advice. Why not make GEM Motoring Assist your one-stop shop for trouble-free motoring! Visit **www.motoringassist.com/philipsmaps** today.

# Driving regulations

A national vehicle identification plate is always required when taking a vehicle abroad. It is important for your own safety and that of other drivers to fit headlamp converters or beam deflectors when taking a right-hand drive car to a country where driving is on the right (every country in Europe except the UK and Ireland). When the headlamps are dipped on a right-hand drive car, the lenses of the headlamps cause the beam to shine upwards to the left – and so, when driving on the right, into the eyes of oncoming motorists.

Where compulsory visibility vests should be kept in the passenger compartment and put on before exiting the vehicle in breakdowns or emergencies. All countries require that you carry a driving licence, green card/insurance documentation, registration document or hire certificate, and passport.

The penalties for infringements of regulations vary considerably from one country to another. In many countries the police have the right to impose on-the-spot fines (you should always request a receipt for any fine paid). Penalties can be severe for serious infringements, particularly for drinking when driving which in some countries can lead to immediate imprisonment. Insurance is important, and you may be forced to take out cover at the frontier if you cannot produce acceptable proof that you are insured. Please note that driving regulations often change.

## Symbols

| | | | |
|---|---|---|---|
| 🏛 Motorway | | △ Warning triangle | |
| ⚠ Dual carriageway | | ✛ First aid kit | |
| ▲ Single carriageway | | ☒ Spare bulb kit | |
| 🚗 Surfaced road | | 🜂 Fire extinguisher | |
| 🚗 Unsurfaced / gravel road | | ⊖ Minimum driving age | |
| 🏭 Urban area | | 🖼 Additional documents required | |
| ⊙ Speed limit in kilometres per hour (kph) | | 📱 Mobile phones | |
| 🎀 Seat belts | | **LEZ** Low Emission Zone | |
| 🎎 Children | | ★ Other information | |
| ♟ Blood alcohol level | | | |

The publishers have made every effort to ensure that the information given here was correct at the time of going to press. No responsibility can be accepted for any errors or their consequences.

## Andorra (AND)

| | 🏛 | ⚠ | ▲ | 🏭 |
|---|---|---|---|---|
| ⊙ | n/a | 90 | 60/90 | 50 |

🎎 Compulsory

🎎 Under 10 and below 150 cm must travel in an EU-approved restraint system adapted to their size in the rear

♟ 0.05%  △ Compulsory

✛ Recommended  ☒ Compulsory

🜂 Recommended  ⊖ 18

📱 Not permitted whilst driving

★ Dipped headlights compulsory for motorcycles during day and for other vehicles during poor daytime visibility.

★ On-the-spot fines imposed

★ Visibility vests compulsory

★ Winter tyres or snow chains compulsory in poor conditions or when indicated by signs

## Austria (A)

| | 🏛 | ⚠ | ▲ | 🏭 |
|---|---|---|---|---|
| ⊙ | 130 | 100 | 100 | 50 |
| **If towing trailer under 750kg / over 750 kg** | | | | |
| ⊙ | 100 | 100 | 100/80 | 50 |

🎎 Compulsory

🎎 Under 12 and under 150cm cannot travel as a front or rear passenger unless they use a suitable child restraint; under 12 over 150cm must wear adult seat belt

♟ 0.049%; 0.01% if licence held less than 2 years

△ Compulsory

✛ Compulsory

☒ Recommended

🜂 Recommended

⊖ 18 (16 for mopeds)

📱 Only allowed with hands-free kit

**LEZ** LEZ On A12 motorway non-compliant vehicles banned and certain substances banned, night-time speed restrictions; Steermark province has LEZs affecting lorries

★ Dipped headlights must be used during the day by all road users. Headlamp converters compulsory

★ Radar detectors prohibited

★ Snow chains recommended in winter. Winter tyres compulsory 1 Nov–15 Apr in poor driving conditions

★ To drive on motorways or expressways, a motorway sticker must be purchased at the border or main petrol station. These are available for 10 days, 2 months or 1 year. Vehicles 3.5 tonnes or over must display an electronic tag.

★ Visibility vests compulsory

## Belarus (BY)

| | 🏛 | ⚠ | ▲ | 🏭 |
|---|---|---|---|---|
| ⊙ | 110 | 90 | 90 | 60* |
| **If towing trailer under 750kg** | | | | |
| ⊙ | 90 | 70 | 70 | |

*In residential areas limit is 20 km/h
• Vehicle towing another vehicle 50 kph limit • If full driving licence held for less than two years, must not exceed 70 kph

---

🎀 Compulsory in front seats, and rear seats if fitted

🎎 Under 12 not allowed in front seat and must use appropriate child restraint

♟ 0.00%  △ Compulsory

✛ Compulsory  ☒ Recommended

🜂 Compulsory

⊖ 18

🖼 Visa, vehicle technical check stamp, international driving permit, green card, health insurance. Even with a green card, local third-party insurance may be imposed at the border

📱 Use prohibited

★ A temporary vehicle import certificate must be purchased on entry and driver must be registered

★ Dipped headlights are compulsory during the day Nov–Mar and at all other times in conditions of poor visibility or when towing or being towed.

★ Fees payable for driving on highways

★ It is illegal for vehicles to be dirty

★ Radar-detectors prohibited

★ Winter tyres and snow chains recommended

## Belgium (B)

| | 🏛 | ⚠ | ▲ | 🏭 |
|---|---|---|---|---|
| ⊙ | 120* | 120* | 90 | 50** |
| **If towing trailer** | | | | |
| ⊙ | 90 | 90 | 60 | 50 |
| **Over 3.5 tonnes** | | | | |
| ⊙ | 90 | 90 | 60 | 50 |

*Minimum speed of 70kph may be applied in certain conditions on motorways and some dual carriageways
**Near schools, hospitals and churches the limit may be 30kph

🎀 Compulsory

🎎 All under 19s under 135 cm must wear an appropriate child restraint. Airbags must be deactivated if a rear-facing child seat is used in the front

♟ 0.05%

△ Compulsory

✛ Recommended

🜂 Recommended

🜂 Compulsory

⊖ 18

📱 Only allowed with a hands-free kit

★ Cruise control is not permitted on motorways

★ Dipped headlights mandatory at all times for motorcycles and advised during the day in poor conditions for other vehicles

★ On-the-spot fines imposed

★ Radar detectors prohibited

★ Sticker indicating maximum recommended speed for winter tyres must be displayed on dashboard if using them

★ Visibility vest compulsory

## Bosnia and Herzegovina (BIH)

| | 🏛 | ⚠ | ▲ | 🏭 |
|---|---|---|---|---|
| ⊙ | 130 | 100 | 80 | 50 |

🎀 Compulsory if fitted

🎎 Under 12 not allowed in front seat; under 5 must use appropriate child restraint

♟ 0.03%  △ Compulsory

✛ Compulsory  🜂 Compulsory

⊖ 18

🖼 Visa, International Driving Permit

📱 Prohibited

★ Dipped headlights compulsory for all vehicles at all times

★ GPS must have fixed speed camera function deactivated; radar detectors prohibited.

★ On-the-spot fines imposed

★ Visibility vest compulsory

★ Winter tyres compulsory 15 Nov–15 Apr; snow chains recommended

## Bulgaria (BG)

| | 🏛 | ⚠ | ▲ | 🏭 |
|---|---|---|---|---|
| ⊙ | 130 | 90 | 90 | 50 |
| **If towing trailer** | | | | |
| ⊙ | 100 | 70 | 70 | 50 |

🎀 Compulsory in front and rear seats

🎎 Under 3s not permitted in vehicles with no child restraints; 3–10 year olds must sit in rear

♟ 0.05%  △ Compulsory

✛ Compulsory  🜂 Recommended

🜂 Compulsory  ⊖ 18

🖼 Photo driving licence with translation and International Driving Permit; vehicle insurance specific to Bulgaria

📱 Only allowed with a hands-free kit

★ Dipped headlights compulsory

★ Fee at border

★ GPS must have fixed speed camera function deactivated; radar detectors prohibited

★ On-the-spot fines imposed

★ Road tax stickers (annual, monthly or weekly) must be purchased at the border and displayed prominently with the vehicle registration number written on them.

★ Visibility vest compulsory

## Croatia (HR)

| | 🏛 | ⚠ | ▲ | 🏭 |
|---|---|---|---|---|
| ⊙ | 130 | 110 | 90 | 50 |
| **Under 24** | | | | |
| ⊙ | 120 | 100 | 80 | 50 |
| **If towing** | | | | |
| ⊙ | 110 | 80 | 80 | 50 |

🎀 Compulsory if fitted

🎎 Children 2–12 not permitted in front seats and must use appropriate child restraint. Under 2 permitted in front only in appropriate rear-facing seat with any airbags disabled

♟ 0.05%, 0.00% for drivers of vehicles over 3.5 tonnes and under-25s

△ Compulsory

✛ Compulsory

🜂 Compulsory

⊖ 18

📱 Only allowed with hands-free kit

★ Dipped headlights compulsory

★ In winter, snow chains compulsory in the mountains; snow tyres compulsory everywhere else Nov–Apr

★ On-the-spot fines imposed

★ Radar detectors prohibited

★ Tow bar and rope compulsory

★ Visibility vest compulsory

## Czech Republic (CZ)

| | 🏛 | ⚠ | ▲ | 🏭 |
|---|---|---|---|---|
| ⊙ | 130 | 130 | 90 | 50 |
| **If towing** | | | | |
| ⊙ | 80 | 80 | 80 | 50 |

🎀 Compulsory in front seats and, if fitted, in rear

🎎 Children: Children under 36 kg and 150 cm must use appropriate child restraint. Only front-facing child retraints are permitted in the front in vehicles with airbags fitted.

♟ 0.00%  △ Compulsory

✛ Compulsory  🜂 Compulsory

🜂 Compulsory

⊖ 18 (17 for motorcycles under 125 cc)

📱 Only allowed with a hands-free kit

**LEZ** Two-stage LEZ in Prague for vehicles over 3.5 and 6 tonnes. Permit system.

★ Dipped headlights compulsory at all times

★ GPS must have fixed speed camera function deactivated; radar detectors prohibited

★ On-the-spot fines imposed

★ Vignette needed for motorway driving, available for 1 year, 60 days, 15 days. Toll specific to lorries introduced 2006, those over 12 tonnes must buy an electronic tag

★ Visibility vest compulsory

- ★ Spectacles or contact lens wearers must carry a spare pair in their vehicle at all times
- ★ Winter tyres or snow chains compulsory between Nov and Apr

## Denmark (DK)

| | 🛣 130 | ⑂ 80 | ⚠ 80 | 🏘 50 |
|---|---|---|---|---|
| **If towing** | | | | |
| ⏱ | 80 | 70 | 70 | 50 |

- 🦺 Compulsory front and rear
- 👶 Under 135cm must use appropriate child restraint; in front permitted only in an appropriate rear-facing seat with any airbags disabled.
- 🍷 0.05% △ Compulsory
- ✚ Recommended 🔦 Recommended
- 🔺 Recommended ⊖ 17
- 📱 Only allowed with a hands-free kit
- LEZ Aalborg, Arhus, Copenhagen, Frederiksberg and Odense. Proofs of emissions compliance/compliant filter needed to obtain sticker. Non-compliant vehicles banned.
- ★ Dipped headlights must be used at all times
- ★ Radar detectors prohibited
- ★ Tolls apply on the Storebaeltsbroen and Oresundsbron bridges.
- ★ Visibility vest recommended

## Estonia (EST)

| | 🛣 n/a | ⑂ 90* | ⚠ 90 | 🏘 50 |
|---|---|---|---|---|
| **If full driving licence held for less than two years** | | | | |
| ⏱ | 90 | 90 | 90 | 50 |

*In summer, the speed limit on some dual carriageways may be raised to 100/110 kph

- 🦺 Compulsory if fitted
- 👶 Children too small for adult seatbelts must wear a seat restraint appropriate to their size. Rear-facing safety seats must not be used in the front if an air bag is fitted, unless this has been deactivated.
- 🍷 0.00% △ Compulsory
- ✚ Compulsory 🔦 Recommended
- 🔺 Compulsory ⊖ 18
- 📱 Only allowed with a hands-free kit
- ★ A toll system is in operation in Tallinn
- ★ Dipped headlights compulsory at all times
- ★ Winter tyres are compulsory from Dec–Mar. Studded winter tyres are allowed from 15 Oct–31 Mar, but this can be extended to start 1 October and/or end 30 April

## Finland (FIN)

| | 🛣 120 | ⑂ 100 | ⚠ 80* | 🏘 30/60 |
|---|---|---|---|---|
| **If towing** | | | | |
| ⏱ | 80 | 80 | 80 | 30/60 |

*100 in summer • If towing a vehicle by rope, cable or rod, max speed limit 60 kph.
•Maximum of 80 kph for vans and lorries
•Speed limits are often lowered in winter

- 🦺 Compulsory in front and rear
- 👶 Below 135 cm must use a child restraint or seat
- 🍷 0.05% △ Compulsory
- ✚ Recommended 🔦 Recommended
- 🔺 Recommended
- ⊖ 18 (motorbikes below 125cc 16)
- 📱 Only allowed with a hands-free kit
- ★ Dipped headlights must be used at all times
- ★ On-the-spot fines imposed
- ★ Radar-detectors are prohibited
- ★ Visibility vest compulsory
- ★ Winter tyres compulsory Dec–Feb

## France (F)

| | 🛣 130 | ⑂ 110 | ⚠ 90 | 🏘 50 |
|---|---|---|---|---|
| **On wet roads or if full driving licence held for less than 2 years** | | | | |
| ⏱ | 110 | 100 | 80 | 50 |
| **If towing below / above 3.5 tonnes gross** | | | | |
| ⏱ | 110/90 | 100/90 | 90/80 | 50 |

50kph on all roads if fog reduces visibility to less than 50m • Licence will be lost and driver fined for exceeding speed limit by over 40kph

- 🦺 Compulsory in front seats and, if fitted, in rear
- 👶 In rear, 4 or under must have a child safety seat (rear facing if up to 9 months); if 5–10 must use an appropriate restraint system. Under 10 permitted in the front only if rear seats are fully occupied by other under 10s or there are no rear safety belts. In front, if child is in rear-facing child seat, any airbag must be deactivated.
- 🍷 0.05%. If towing or with less than 2 years with full driving licence, 0.00% • All drivers/motorcyclists must carry 2 unused breathalysers to French certification standards, showing an NF number.
- △ Compulsory
- ✚ Recommended 🔦 Recommended
- ⊖ 18 (16 for motorbikes under 80 cc)
- 📱 Use not permitted whilst driving
- LEZ An LEZ operates in the Mont Blanc tunnel
- ★ Dipped headlights compulsory in poor daytime visibility and at all times for motorcycles
- ★ GPS must have fixed speed camera function deactivated; radar-detection equipment is prohibited
- ★ It is compulsory to carry a French-authority-recognised (NF) breathalyser.
- ★ On-the-spot fines imposed
- ★ Tolls on motorways. Electronic tag needed if using automatic tolls.
- ★ Visibility vests must be carried in the passenger compartment; legislation making visibility vests compulsory for motorcyclists and passengers may be reintroduced.
- ★ Winter tyres recommended. Carrying snow chains recommended in winter as these may have to be fitted if driving on snow-covered roads, in accordance with signage.

## Germany (D)

| | 🛣 * | ⑂ * | ⚠ 100 | 🏘 50 |
|---|---|---|---|---|
| **If towing** | | | | |
| ⏱ | 80 | 80 | 80 | 50 |

*no limit, 130 kph recommended

- 🦺 Compulsory
- 👶 Under 150 cm and 12 or under must use an appropriate child seat or restraint. In front if child is in rear-facing child seat, airbags must be deactivated.
- 🍷 0.05%, 0.0% for drivers 21 or under or with less than two years full licence
- △ Compulsory
- ✚ Compulsory 🔦 Recommended
- 🔺 Recommended
- ⊖ 18 (motorbikes: 16 if under 50cc)
- 📱 Use permitted only with hands-free kit – also applies to drivers of motorbikes and bicycles
- LEZ More than 60 cities have or are planning LEZs. Proof of compliance needed to acquire sticker. Non-compliant vehicles banned.
- ★ Dipped headlights compulsory in poor weather conditions and tunnels; recommended at other times
- ★ GPS must have fixed speed camera function deactivated; radar detectors prohibited

---

- ★ Motorcyclists must use dipped headlights at all times; other vehicles must use dipped headlights during poor daytime visibility.
- ★ On-the-spot fines imposed
- ★ Tolls on autobahns for lorries
- ★ Winter tyres compulsory in all winter weather conditions; snow chains recommended

## Greece (GR)

| | 🛣 120 | ⑂ 110 | ⚠ 110 | 🏘 50 |
|---|---|---|---|---|
| **Motorbikes, and if towing** | | | | |
| ⏱ | 90 | 70 | 70 | 40 |

- 🦺 Compulsory in front seats and, if fitted, in rear
- 👶 Under 12 or below 135cm must use appropriate child restraint. In front if child is in rear-facing child seat, any airbags must be deactivated.
- 🍷 0.05%, 0.00% for drivers with less than 2 years' full licence and motorcyclists
- △ Compulsory
- ✚ Compulsory 🔦 Recommended
- 🔺 Compulsory ⊖ 17
- 📱 Not permitted.
- ★ Dipped headlights compulsory during poor daytime visibility and at all times for motorcycles
- ★ On-the-spot fines imposed
- ★ Radar-detection equipment is prohibited
- ★ Tolls on several newer motorways.

## Hungary (H)

| | 🛣 130 | ⑂ 110 | ⚠ 90 | 🏘 50 |
|---|---|---|---|---|
| **If towing** | | | | |
| ⏱ | 80 | 70 | 70 | 50 |

- 🦺 Compulsory in front seats and if fitted in rear seats
- 👶 Under 150cm and over 3 must be seated in rear and use appropriate child restraint. Under 3 allowed in front only in rear-facing child seat with any airbags deactivated.
- 🍷 0.00% △ Compulsory
- ✚ Compulsory 🔦 Compulsory
- 🔺 Recommended ⊖ 17
- 📱 Only allowed with a hands-free kit
- LEZ Budapest has vehicle restrictions on days with heavy dust and is planning an LEZ.
- ★ All motorways are toll and operate electronic vignette system with automatic number plate recognition, tickets are available for 4 days, 7 days, 1 month, 1 year
- ★ During the day dipped headlights compulsory outside built-up areas; compulsory at all times for motorcycles
- ★ Electronic vignette system in use for tolls on several motorways
- ★ On-the-spot fines issued
- ★ Snow chains compulsory where conditions dictate
- ★ Visibility vest compulsory

## Iceland (IS)

| | 🛣 n/a | 🚗 90 | 🚗 80 | 🏘 50 |
|---|---|---|---|---|

- 🦺 Compulsory in front and rear seats
- 👶 Under 12 or below 150cm not allowed in front seat and must use appropriate child restraint.
- 🍷 0.05% △ Compulsory
- ✚ Compulsory 🔦 Compulsory
- 🔺 Compulsory
- ⊖ 18; 21 to drive a hire car; 25 to hire a jeep
- 📱 Only allowed with a hands-free kit
- ★ Dipped headlights compulsory at all times
- ★ Driving off marked roads is forbidden
- ★ Highland roads are not suitable for ordinary cars
- ★ On-the-spot fines imposed
- ★ Winter tyres compulsory c.1 Nov–14 Apr (variable)

## Ireland (IRL)

| | 🛣 120 | ⑂ 100 | ⚠ 80 | 🏘 50 |
|---|---|---|---|---|
| **If towing** | | | | |
| ⏱ | 80 | 80 | 80 | 50 |

- 🦺 Compulsory where fitted. Driver responsible for ensuring passengers under 17 comply
- 👶 Children 3 and under must be in a suitable child restraint system. Airbags must be deactivated if a rear-facing child seat is used in the front. Those under 150 cm and 36 kg must use appropriate child restraint in cars with seatbelts.
- 🍷 0.05%, 0.02% for novice and professional drivers
- △ Compulsory
- ✚ Recommended
- 🔦 Recommended
- 🔺 Recommended
- ⊖ 17 (16 for motorbikes up to 125cc; 18 for over 125cc; 18 for lorries; 21 bus/minibus)
- 📱 Only allowed with a hands-free kit
- ★ Dipped headlights are compulsory during daylight hours
- ★ Dipped headlights compulsory for motorbikes at all times and in poor visibility for other vehicles
- ★ Driving is on the left
- ★ GPS must have fixed speed camera function deactivated; radar detectors prohibited
- ★ On-the-spot fines imposed
- ★ Tolls are being introduced on some motorways; the M50 Dublin has barrier-free tolling with number-plate recognition.

## Italy (I)

| | 🛣 130 | ⑂ 110 | ⚠ 90 | 🏘 50 |
|---|---|---|---|---|
| **If towing** | | | | |
| ⏱ | 80 | 70 | 70 | 50 |
| **Less than three years with full licence** | | | | |
| ⏱ | 100 | 90 | 90 | 50 |
| **When wet** | | | | |
| ⏱ | 100 | 90 | 80 | 50 |

Some motorways with emergency lanes have speed limit of 150 kph

- 🦺 Compulsory in front seats and, if fitted, in rear
- 👶 Under 12 not allowed in front seats except in child safety seat; children under 3 must have special seat in the back
- 🍷 0.05%, but 0.00% for professional drivers or with less than 3 years full licence
- △ Compulsory
- ✚ Recommended
- 🔦 Compulsory
- 🔺 Recommended
- ⊖ 18 (14 for mopeds, 16 up to 125cc, 20 up to 350cc)
- 📱 Only allowed with hands-free kit
- LEZ Most northern and several southern regions operate seasonal LEZs and many towns and cities have various schemes that restrict access. There is an LEZ in the Mont Blanc tunnel
- ★ Dipped headlights compulsory outside built-up areas, in tunnels, on motorways and dual carriageways and in poor visibility; compulsory at all times for motorcycles
- ★ On-the-spot fines imposed
- ★ Radar-detection equipment is prohibited
- ★ Snow chains compulsory where signs indicate Nov–April
- ★ Tolls on motorways. Blue lanes accept credit cards; yellow lanes restricted to holders of Telepass pay-toll device.
- ★ Visibility vest compulsory

## Kosovo (RKS)

| 🛣 | ⛟ | ▲ | 🏭 |
|---|---|---|---|
| 120 | 100 | 100 | 60 |

- 🔵 Compulsory
- 👶 Under 12 must sit in rear seats
- 🍷 0.03%, 0.00% for professional, business and commercial drivers
- △ Compulsory
- ⊡ Compulsory
- 💡 Compulsory
- 🧯 Compulsory
- ⊖ 18 (16 for motorbikes less than 125 cc, 14 for mopeds)
- 🪪 International driving permit, locally purchased third-party insurance (green card is not recognised), documents with proof of ability to cover costs and valid reason for visiting. Visitors from many non-EU countries require a visa.
- 📱 Only allowed with a hands-free kit
- ★ Dipped headlights compulsory at all times
- ★ Winter tyres or snow chains compulsory in poor winter weather conditions

## Latvia (LV)

| 🛣 | ⛟ | ▲ | 🏭 |
|---|---|---|---|
| 90/100 | 90 | 90 | 50 |
| **If towing** | | | |
| 90/100 | 90 | 90 | 50 |

In residential areas limit is 20kph • If full driving licence held for less than two years, must not exceed 80 kph

- 🔵 Compulsory in front seats and, if fitted, in rear
- 👶 If under 12 years and 150cm must use child restraint in front and rear seats
- 🍷 0.05%, 0.02% with less than 2 years experience
- △ Compulsory
- ⊡ Compulsory
- 💡 Recommended
- 🧯 Compulsory
- ⊖ 18 (14 for mopeds, 16 up to 125cc, 21 up to 350cc)
- 📱 Only allowed with hands-free kit
- ★ Dipped headlights must be used at all times all year round
- ★ On-the-spot fines imposed
- ★ Pedestrians have priority
- ★ Visibility vests compulsory
- ★ Winter tyres compulsory for vehicles up to 3.5 tonnes Dec–Feb, but illegal May–Sept

## Lithuania (LT)

| 🛣 | ⛟ | ▲ | 🏭 |
|---|---|---|---|
| 130 | 110 | 90 | 50 |
| **If towing** | | | |
| n/a | 70 | 70 | 50 |

In winter speed limits are reduced by 10–20 km/h

- 🔵 Compulsory in front seats and if fitted in rear seats
- 👶 Under 12 not allowed in front seats unless in a child safety seat; under 3 must use appropriate child seat and sit in rear
- 🍷 0.04%, 0.02% for those with less than 2 years' full licence
- △ Compulsory
- ⊡ Compulsory
- 💡 Recommended
- 🧯 Compulsory
- ⊖ 18 (14 for mopeds)
- 📱 Only allowed with a hands-free kit
- ★ Dipped headlights must be used at all times
- ★ On-the-spot fines imposed
- ★ Visibility vest compulsory
- ★ Winter tyres compulsory 10 Nov–1 Apr

## Luxembourg (L)

| 🛣 | ⛟ | ▲ | 🏭 |
|---|---|---|---|
| 130/110 | 90 | 90 | 50 |
| **If towing** | | | |
| 90 | 75 | 75 | 50 |

If full driving licence held for less than two years, must not exceed 75 kph • In 20 km/h zones, pedestrians have right of way.

- 🔵 Compulsory
- 👶 Children under 3 must use an appropriate restraint system. Airbags must be disabled if a rear-facing child seat is used in the front. Children 3 to 18 and / or under 150 cm must use a restraint system appropriate to their size. If over 36kg a seatbelt may be used in the back only
- 🍷 0.05%, 0.02 for young drivers, drivers with less than 2 years experience and drivers of taxis and commercial vehicles
- △ Compulsory
- ⊡ Compulsory (buses)
- 💡 Compulsory
- 🧯 Compulsory (buses, transport of dangerous goods)
- ⊖ 18
- 📱 Use permitted only with hands-free kit
- ★ Dipped headlights compulsory for motorcyclists and in poor visibility for other vehicles
- ★ On-the-spot fines imposed
- ★ Visibility vest compulsory
- ★ Winter tyres compulsory in winter weather

## Macedonia (MK)

| 🛣 | ⛟ | ▲ | 🏭 |
|---|---|---|---|
| 120 | 100 | 60 | 60 |
| **Newly qualified drivers** | | | |
| 100 | 80 | 60 | 60 |
| **If towing** | | | |
| 80 | 70 | 50 | 50 |

- 🔵 Compulsory in front seats; compulsory if fitted in rear seats
- 👶 Under 12 not allowed in front seats
- 🍷 0.05%, 0.00% for business, commercial and professional drivers and with less than 2 years experience
- △ Compulsory
- ⊡ Compulsory 💡 Compulsory
- 🧯 Recommended; compulsory for LPG vehicles
- ⊖ 18 (mopeds 16)
- 🪪 International driving permit; visa
- 📱 Use not permitted whilst driving
- ★ Dipped headlights compulsory at all times
- ★ GPS must have fixed speed camera function deactivated; radar detectors prohibited
- ★ Novice drivers may only drive between 11pm and 5am if there is someone over 25 with a valid licence in the vehicle.
- ★ On-the-spot fines imposed
- ★ Tolls apply on many roads
- ★ Visibility vest must be kept in the passenger compartment and worn to leave the vehicle in the dark outside built-up areas
- ★ Winter tyres or snow chains compulsory 15 Nov–15 Mar

## Moldova (MD)

| 🛣 | ⛟ | ▲ | 🏭 |
|---|---|---|---|
| 90 | 90 | 90 | 60 |
| **If towing or if licence held under 1 year** | | | |
| 70 | 70 | 70 | 60 |

- 🔵 Compulsory in front seats and, if fitted, in rear seats
- 👶 Under 12 not allowed in front seats
- 🍷 0.00%
- △ Compulsory
- ⊡ Compulsory
- 💡 Recommended
- 🧯 Compulsory
- ⊖ 18 (mopeds and motorbikes, 16; vehicles with more than eight passenger places, taxis or towing heavy vehicles, 21)

## [Netherlands intro symbols]

- 🪪 International Driving Permit (preferred), visa
- 📱 Only allowed with hands-free kit
- ★ Motorcyclists must use dipped headlights at all times
- ★ Winter tyres recommended Nov–Feb

## Montenegro (MNE)

| 🛣 | ⛟ | ▲ | 🏭 |
|---|---|---|---|
| n/a | 100 | 80 | 80 |

80kph speed limit if towing a caravan

- 🔵 Compulsory in front and rear seats
- 👶 Under 12 not allowed in front seats
- 🍷 0.05% △ Compulsory ⊡ Compulsory
- 💡 Compulsory 🧯 Compulsory
- ⊖ 18 (16 for motorbikes less than 125cc; 14 for mopeds)
- 📱 Prohibited
- ★ An 'eco' tax vignette must be obtained when crossing the border and displayed in the upper right-hand corner of the windscreen
- ★ Dipped headlights must be used at all times
- ★ From mid-Nov to March, driving wheels must be fitted with winter tyres
- ★ On-the-spot fines imposed
- ★ Tolls on some primary roads and in the Sozina tunnel between Lake Skadar and the sea
- ★ Visibility vest compulsory

## Netherlands (NL)

| 🛣 | ⛟ | ▲ | 🏭 |
|---|---|---|---|
| 120/100 | 80/100 | 80/100 | 50 |

- 🔵 Compulsory in front seats and, if fitted, rear
- 👶 Under 135cm must use appropriate child restraint; if no seat belts, under 3s not permitted in vehicle; rear-facing child seat permitted in the front only if airbags deactivated
- 🍷 0.05%, 0.02% with less than 5 years experience or moped riders under 24
- △ Recommended
- ⊡ Recommended 💡 Recommended
- 🧯 Recommended ⊖ 18
- 📱 Only allowed with a hands-free kit
- **LEZ** About 20 cities operate or are planning LEZs. A national scheme is planned.
- ★ Dipped headlights compulsory for motorcycles and recommended in poor visibility and on open roads for other vehicles.
- ★ Radar-detection equipment is prohibited

## Norway (N)

| 🛣 | ⛟ | ▲ | 🏭 |
|---|---|---|---|
| 90/100 | 80 | 80 | 30/50 |
| **If towing trailer with brakes** | | | |
| 80 | 80 | 80 | 50 |
| **If towing trailer without brakes** | | | |
| 60 | 60 | 60 | 50 |

- 🔵 Compulsory in front seats and, if fitted, in rear
- 👶 Children less than 150cm tall must use appropriate child restraint. Children under 4 must use child safety seat or safety restraint (cot)
- 🍷 0.01% △ Compulsory ⊡ Recommended
- 💡 Recommended 🧯 Recommended
- ⊖ 18 (heavy vehicles 18/21)
- 📱 Only allowed with a hands-free kit
- **LEZ** Planned for Bergen, Oslo and Trondheim
- ★ Dipped headlights must be used at all times
- ★ On-the-spot fines imposed
- ★ Radar-detectors are prohibited
- ★ Tolls apply on some bridges, tunnels and access roads into Bergen, Oslo, Trondheim and Stavangar. Several use electronic fee collection only.
- ★ Visibility vest compulsory
- ★ Winter tyres or summer tyres with snow chains compulsory for snow- or ice-covered roads

## Poland (PL)

| 🛣 | ⛟ | ▲ | 🏭 |
|---|---|---|---|
| **Motor-vehicle only roads[1], under/over 3.5 tonnes** | | | |
| 130[2]/80[2] | 110/80 | 100/80 | n/a |
| **Motor-vehicle only roads[1] if towing** | | | |
| n/a | 80 | 80 | n/a |
| **Other roads, under 3.5 tonnes** | | | |
| n/a | 100 | 90 | 50/60[3] |
| **Other roads, 3.5 tonnes or over** | | | |
| n/a | 80 | 70 | 50/60[3] |
| **Other roads, if towing** | | | |
| n/a | 60 | 60 | 30 |

[1]Indicated by signs with white car on blue background. [2]Minimum speed 40 kph.
[3]50 kph 05.00–23.00; 60 kph 23.00–05.00; 20 kph in marked residential areas

- 🔵 Compulsory in front seats and, if fitted, in rear
- 👶 Under 12 not allowed in front seats unless in a child safety seat; in rear seats children under 12 and less than 150 cm must use child safety seat. Rear-facing child seats not permitted in vehicles with airbags.
- 🍷 0.02%
- △ Compulsory
- ⊡ Recommended
- 💡 Recommended
- 🧯 Compulsory
- ⊖ 18 (mopeds and motorbikes – 16)
- 📱 Only allowed with a hands-free kit
- ★ Dipped headlights compulsory for all vehicles
- ★ On-the-spot fines imposed
- ★ Radar-detection equipment is prohibited

## Portugal (P)

| 🛣 | ⛟ | ▲ | 🏭 |
|---|---|---|---|
| 120* | 100 | 90 | 50 |
| **If towing** | | | |
| 100* | 90 | 80 | 50 |

*40kph minimum; 90kph maximum if licence held under 1 year

- 🔵 Compulsory in front seats; compulsory if fitted in rear seats
- 👶 Under 12 and below 150cm must travel in the rear in an appropriate child restraint; rear-facing child seats permitted in front only if airbags deactivated
- 🍷 0.05%
- △ Compulsory
- ⊡ Recommended
- 💡 Recommended
- 🧯 Recommended
- ⊖ 18 (motorcycles under 50cc 17)
- 🪪 MOT certificate for vehicles over 3 years old, photographic proof of identity (e.g. driving licence or passport) must be carried at all times.
- 📱 Only allowed with hands-free kit
- **LEZ** An LEZ prohibits vehicles without catalytic converters from certain parts of Lisbon. There are plans to extend the scheme to the whole of the city
- ★ Dipped headlights compulsory for motorcycles, compulsory for other vehicles in poor visibility and tunnels
- ★ It is recommended that spectacles or contact lens wearers carry a spare pair.
- ★ On-the-spot fines imposed
- ★ Radar-detectors prohibited
- ★ Tolls on motorways; do not use green lanes, these are reserved for auto-payment users. Some motorways require an automatic toll device.
- ★ Visibility vest compulsory

## Romania (RO)

| | 🛣️ | ⛟ | 🚗 | 🏭 |
|---|---|---|---|---|
| **Cars and motorcycles** | | | | |
| ⏱️ | 120/130 | 100 | 90 | 50 |
| **Vans** | | | | |
| ⏱️ | 110 | 90 | 80 | 50 |
| **Motorcycles** | | | | |
| ⏱️ | 100 | 80 | 80 | 50 |

For motor vehicles with trailers or if full driving licence has been held for less than one year, speed limits are 20kph lower than those listed above •Jeep-like vehicles: 70kph outside built-up areas but 60kph in all areas if diesel

- Compulsory in front seats and, if fitted, in rear
- Under 12 not allowed in front seats
- 0.00% △ Compulsory
- Compulsory 🔦 Compulsory
- Compulsory ⊖ 18
- Only allowed with hands-free kit
- ★ Dipped headlights compulsory outside built-up areas, compulsory everywhere for motorcycles
- ★ Electronic road tax system; price depends on emissions category and length of stay
- ★ It is illegal for vehicles to be dirty
- ★ On-the-spot fines imposed
- ★ Tolls on motorways
- ★ Visibility vest compulsory
- ★ Winter tyres compulsory Nov–Mar if roads are snow- or ice-covered, especially in mountainous areas

## Russia (RUS)

| | 🛣️ | ⛟ | 🚗 | 🏭 |
|---|---|---|---|---|
| ⏱️ | 110 | 90 | 90 | 60 |
| **If licence held for under 2 years** | | | | |
| ⏱️ | 70 | 70 | 70 | 60 |

- Compulsory in front seats
- Under 12 permitted in front seat only in an appropriate child restraint
- 0.00% △ Compulsory
- Compulsory 🔦 Compulsory
- Compulsory ⊖ 18
- International Driving Permit with Russian translation, visa, green card endorsed for Russia, International Certificate for Motor Vehicles
- Only allowed with a hands-free kit
- ★ Dipped headlights compulsory during the day
- ★ On-the-spot fines imposed
- ★ Picking up hitchhikers is prohibited
- ★ Radar detectors/blockers prohibited
- ★ Road tax payable at the border

## Serbia (SRB)

| | 🛣️ | ⛟ | 🚗 | 🏭 |
|---|---|---|---|---|
| ⏱️ | 120 | 100 | 80 | 60 |

- Compulsory in front and rear seats
- Age 3–12 must be in rear seats and wear seat belt or appropriate child restraint; under 3 in rear-facing child seat permitted in front only if airbag deactivated
- 0.03% △ Compulsory 🔲 Compulsory
- Compulsory 🔦 Compulsory
- ⊖ 18 (16 for motorbikes less than 125cc; 14 for mopeds)
- International Driving Permit, green card or locally bought third-party insurance
- No legislation
- ★ 3-metre tow bar or rope
- ★ 80km/h speed limit if towing a caravan
- ★ Dipped headlights compulsory
- ★ Radar detectors prohibited
- ★ Tolls on motorways and some primary roads
- ★ Visibility vest compulsory
- ★ Winter tyres compulsory Nov–Apr for vehicles up to 3.5 tonnes. Carrying snow chains recommended in winter as these may have to be fitted if driving on snow-covered roads, in accordance with signage.

## Slovak Republic (SK)

| | 🛣️ | ⛟ | 🚗 | 🏭 |
|---|---|---|---|---|
| ⏱️ | 130 | 90 | 90 | 60 |

- Compulsory in front seats and, if fitted, in rear
- Under 12 or below 150cm must be in rear in appropriate child restraint
- 0.0 △ Compulsory
- Compulsory 🔦 Compulsory
- Recommended
- ⊖ 18 (15 for mopeds)
- International driving permit, proof of health insurance
- Only allowed with a hands-free kit
- ★ Dipped headlights compulsory at all times
- ★ On-the-spot fines imposed
- ★ Radar-detection equipment is prohibited
- ★ Tow rope recommended
- ★ Vignette required for motorways, car valid for 1 year, 30 days, 7 days; lorry vignettes carry a higher charge.
- ★ Visibility vests compulsory
- ★ Winter tyres compulsory

## Slovenia (SLO)

| | 🛣️ | ⛟ | 🚗 | 🏭 |
|---|---|---|---|---|
| ⏱️ | 130 | 100* | 90* | 50 |
| **If towing** | | | | |
| ⏱️ | 80 | 80* | 80* | 50 |

*70kph in urban areas

- Compulsory in front seats and, if fitted, in rear
- Under 12 and below 150cm must use appropriate child restraint; babies must use child safety seat
- 0.05% △ Compulsory 🔲 Compulsory
- Compulsory 🔦 Recommended
- ⊖ 18 (motorbikes up to 125cc – 16, up to 350cc – 18)
- Only allowed with hands-free kit
- ★ Dipped headlights must be used at all times
- ★ Snow chains or winter tyres compulsory mid-Nov to mid-March, and in wintery conditions at other times
- ★ Vignettes valid for variety of periods compulsory for vehicles below 3.5 tonnes for toll roads. Write your vehicle registration number on the vignette before displaying it. For heavier vehicles electronic tolling system applies; several routes are cargo-traffic free during high tourist season.
- ★ Visibility vest compulsory

## Spain (E)

| | 🛣️ | ⛟ | 🚗 | 🏭 |
|---|---|---|---|---|
| ⏱️ | 110 | 100 | 90 | 50 |
| **If towing** | | | | |
| ⏱️ | 80 | 80 | 70 | 50 |

- Compulsory in front seats and if fitted in rear seats
- Under 135cm and below 12 must use appropriate child restraint
- 0.05%, 0.03% if less than 2 years full licence or if vehicle is over 3.5 tonnes or carries more than 9 passengers
- △ Two compulsory (one for in front, one for behind)
- 🔲 Recommended 🔦 Compulsory
- Recommended
- ⊖ 18 (18/21 heavy vehicles; 18 for motorbikes over 125cc; 16 for motorbikes up to 125cc; 14 for mopeds up to 75cc)
- Only allowed with hands-free kit
- ★ Dipped headlights compulsory for motorcycles and in poor daytime visibility for other vehicles.
- ★ It is recommended that spectacles or contact lens wearers carry a spare pair.
- ★ Radar-detection equipment is prohibited
- ★ Snow chains recommended for mountainous areas in winter
- ★ Spare tyre compulsory
- ★ Tolls on motorways
- ★ Visibility vest compulsory

## Sweden (S)

| | 🛣️ | ⛟ | 🚗 | 🏭 |
|---|---|---|---|---|
| ⏱️ | 110–120 | 80 | 70–100 | 30–60 |
| **If towing trailer with brakes** | | | | |
| ⏱️ | 80 | 80 | 70 | 50 |

- Compulsory in front and rear seats
- Under 16 or below 135cm must use appropriate child restraint; below 140cm may travel in front only if airbag deactivated; rear-facing child seat permitted only if airbag deactivated.
- 0.02%
- △ Compulsory
- 🔲 Recommended
- 🔦 Recommended
- Recommended
- ⊖ 18
- No legislation
- **LEZ** Gothenberg, Helsingborg, Lund, Malmo, Mölndal and Stockholm have LEZs, progressively prohibiting vehicles 6 or more years old.
- ★ 1 Dec–31 Mar winter tyres, anti-freeze and shovel compulsory
- ★ Dipped headlights must be used at all times
- ★ On-the-spot fines imposed
- ★ Radar-detection equipment is prohibited

## Switzerland (CH)

| | 🛣️ | ⛟ | 🚗 | 🏭 |
|---|---|---|---|---|
| ⏱️ | 120 | 80 | 80 | 50/30 |
| **If towing up to 1 tonne / over 1 tonne** | | | | |
| ⏱️ | 80 | 80 | 60/80 | 30/50 |

- Compulsory in front and, if fitted, in rear
- Up to 12 years and below 150 cm must use an appropriate child restraint
- 0.05%
- △ Compulsory
- 🔲 Recommended
- 🔦 Recommended
- Recommended
- ⊖ 18 (mopeds up to 50cc – 16)
- Only allowed with a hands-free kit
- ★ Dipped headlights compulsory
- ★ GPS must have fixed speed camera function deactivated; radar detectors prohibited
- ★ Motorways are all toll and for vehicles below 3.5 tonnes a vignette must be purchased at the border. The vignette is valid for one calendar year. Vehicles over 3.5 tonnes must have an electronic tag for travel on any road.
- ★ On-the-spot fines imposed
- ★ Pedestrians have right of way
- ★ Picking up hitchhikers is prohibited on motorways and main roads
- ★ Spectacles or contact lens wearers must carry a spare pair in their vehicle at all times
- ★ Winter tyres recommended Nov–Mar; snow chains compulsory in designated areas in poor winter weather

## Turkey (TR)

| | 🛣️ | ⛟ | 🚗 | 🏭 |
|---|---|---|---|---|
| ⏱️ | 120 | 90 | 90 | 50 |
| **If towing** | | | | |
| ⏱️ | 70 | 70 | 70 | 40 |

- Compulsory in front seats
- Under 150 cm and below 36kg must use suitable child restraint. If above 136 cm may sit in the back without child restraint. Under 3s can only travel in the front in a rear facing seat if the airbag is deactivated. Children 3–12 may not travel in the front seat.
- 0.05%, 0.00% if towing
- △ Two compulsory (one in front, one behind)
- 🔲 Compulsory
- Compulsory
- 🔦 Compulsory
- ⊖ 18
- International driving permit advised; note that Turkey is in both Europe and Asia, green card/UK insurance that covers whole of Turkey or locally bought insurance, visa bought at the point of entry
- Prohibited
- ★ Dipped headlights compulsory in daylight hours
- ★ On-the-spot fines imposed
- ★ Several motorways, and the Bosphorus bridges are toll roads
- ★ Tow rope and tool kit must be carried

## Ukraine (UA)

| | 🛣️ | ⛟ | 🚗 | 🏭 |
|---|---|---|---|---|
| ⏱️ | 130 | 90 | 90 | 60 |
| **If towing** | | | | |
| ⏱️ | 80 | 80 | 80 | 60 |

Speed limit in pedestrian zone 20 kph

- Compulsory in front and rear seats
- Under 12 and below 145cm must sit in rear
- 0.02% – if use of medication can be proved. Otherwise 0.00%
- △ Compulsory
- 🔲 Compulsory
- Optional
- 🔦 Compulsory
- ⊖ 18 cars; 16 motorbikes
- International Driving Permit, visa, International Certificate for Motor Vehicles, green card
- No legislation
- ★ A road tax is payable on entry to the country.
- ★ Dipped headlights compulsory in poor daytime visibility
- ★ Tow rope and tool kit recommended
- ★ Winter tyres compulsory Nov–Apr in snowy conditions

## United Kingdom (GB)

| | 🛣️ | ⛟ | 🚗 | 🏭 |
|---|---|---|---|---|
| ⏱️ | 112 | 112 | 96 | 48 |
| **If towing** | | | | |
| ⏱️ | 96 | 96 | 80 | 48 |

- Compulsory in front seats and if fitted in rear seats
- Under 3 not allowed in front seats except with appropriate restraint, and in rear must use child restraint if available; in front 3–12 or under 135cm must use appropriate child restraint, in rear must use appropriate child restraint (or seat belt if no child restraint is available, e.g. because two occupied restraints prevent fitting of a third).
- 0.08% (may change to 0.05% in Scotland)
- △ Recommended
- 🔲 Recommended
- Recommended
- 🔦 Recommended
- ⊖ 17 (16 for mopeds)
- Only allowed with hands-free kit
- **LEZ** London's LEZ operates by number-plate recognition; non-compliant vehicles face hefty daily charges. Foreign-registered vehicles must register.
- ★ Driving is on the left
- ★ On-the-spot fines imposed
- ★ Smoking is banned in all commercial vehicles
- ★ Some toll motorways and bridges

# VIII

# Ski resorts

The resorts listed are popular ski centres, therefore road access to most is normally good and supported by road clearing during snow falls. However, mountain driving is never predictable and drivers should make sure they take suitable snow chains as well as emergency provisions and clothing. Listed for each resort are: the atlas page and grid square; the resort/minimum piste altitude (where only one figure is shown, they are at the same height) and maximum altitude of its own lifts; the number of lifts and gondolas (the total for lift-linked resorts); the season start and end dates (snow cover allowing); whether snow is augmented by cannon; the nearest town (with its distance in km) and, where available, the website and/or telephone number of the local tourist information centre or ski centre ('00' prefix required for calls from the UK).

The ❄ symbol indicates resorts equipped with snow cannon.

## Andorra
### Pyrenees

**Pas de la Casa / Grau Roig 146 B2** ❄
2050–2640m · 65 lifts · Dec–Apr
· Andorra La Vella (30km)
💻 www.pasdelacasa-andorra.com
*Access via Envalira Pass (2407m), highest in Pyrenees, snow chains essential.*

## Austria
### Alps

**Bad Gastein 109 B4** ❄ 50 lifts · Dec–Mar
1050/1100–2700m · St Johann im Pongau
(45km) 📞+43 6432 3393 0
💻 www.gastein.com

**Bad Hofgastein 109 B4** ❄ 860–2295m ·
50 lifts · Dec–Mar · St Johann im Pongau
(40km) 📞+43 6432 3393260 💻 www.
gastein.com/en/bad-hofgastein-austria

**Bad Kleinkirchheim 109 C4** ❄ 27 lifts
1070–2310m Dec–Mar ·Villach (35km)
💻 www.badkleinkirchheim.at
📞+43 4240 8212

**Ehrwald 108 B1** ❄ 1000–2965m · 24 lifts
Dec–Apr · Imst (30km) 📞+43 512 5351 553
💻 www.tiscover.at/ehrwald

**Innsbruck 108 B2** ❄ 574/850–3200m ·
78 lifts Dec–Apr ·Innsbruck
💻 www.innsbruck-pauschalen.com
📞+ 43 512 56 2000 *Motorway normally clear. The motorway through to Italy and through the Arlberg Tunnel are both toll roads.*

**Ischgl 107 B5** ❄ 1340/1380–2900m
42 lifts · Dec–May · Landeck (25km)
📞+43 50990 100 💻 www.ischgl.com
*Car entry to resort prohibited between 2200hrs and 0600hrs.*

**Kaprun 109 B3** ❄ 885/770–3030m,
53 lifts · Nov–Apr · Zell am See (10km)
💻 www.zellamsee-kaprun.com
📞+43 6542 770

**Kirchberg in Tirol 109 B3** ❄ 860–2000m
60 lifts · Nov–Apr · Kitzbühel (6km)
💻 www.kitzbuehel-alpen.com
📞+43 5357 2000 *Easily reached from Munich International Airport (120 km)*

**Kitzbühel (Brixen im Thale) 109 B3** ❄
800/1210–2000m · 60 lifts · Dec–Apr
· Wörgl (40km) 📞+ 43 5357 2000
💻 www.kitzbuehel-alpen.com

**Lech/Oberlech 107 B5** ❄ 1450–2810m ·
62 lifts · Dec–Apr · Bludenz (50km)
📞+43 5583 21610 💻 www.lech-zuers.at
*Roads normally cleared but keep chains accessible because of altitude.*

**Mayrhofen 108 B2** ❄ 630–2500m
75 lifts · Dec–Apr · Jenbach (35km)
📞+43 5285 6760 💻 www.mayrhofen.at
*Chains rarely required.*

**Obertauern 109 B4** ❄ 1740/1640–2350m
· Dec–Apr · Radstadt (20km) 📞+43 6456
7252 💻 www.obertauern.com *Roads normally cleared but chain accessibility recommended. Camper vans and caravans not allowed; park these in Radstadt*

**Saalbach Hinterglemm 109 B3** ❄
1030/1100–2100m · 52 lifts · Nov–Apr
· Zell am See (19km) 📞+43 6541 6800 68
💻 www.saalbach.com *Both village centres are pedestrianised and there is a good ski bus service during the daytime*

**St Anton am Arlberg 107 B5** ❄
1300–2810m · 84 lifts · Dec–Apr
·Innsbruck (104km) 📞+43 5446 22690
💻 www.stantonamarlberg.com

**Schladming 109 B4** ❄ 745–1900m
88 lifts · Dec–Mar · Schladming
💻 www.schladming-dachstein.at
📞+ 43 36 87 233 10

**Serfaus 108 B1** ❄ 1427/1200–2820m
70 lifts Dec–Apr · Landeck (30km)
💻 www.serfaus-fiss-ladis.at 📞+43 5476
6239 *Private vehicles banned from village. Use Dorfbahn Serfaus, an underground funicular which runs on an air cushion.*

**Sölden 108 C2** ❄ 1380–3250m · 33 lifts ·
Sep–Apr (glacier) · Nov–Apr (main area)
· Imst (50km) 📞+43 572 000 200
💻 www.soelden.com *Roads normally cleared but snow chains recommended because of altitude. The route from Italy and the south over the Timmelsjoch via Obergurgl is closed Oct–May and anyone arriving from the south should use the Brenner Pass motorway.*

**Zell am See 109 B3** ❄ 750–1950m
53 lifts · Dec–Mar · Zell am See
💻 www.zellamsee-kaprun.com
📞+43 6542 770 *Low altitude, so good access and no mountain passes to cross.*

**Zell im Zillertal (Zell am Ziller) 109 B3** ❄
580/930–2410m · 22 lifts · Dec–Apr
· Jenbach (25km) 📞+43 5282 7165–226
💻 www.zillertalarena.com

**Zürs 107 B5** ❄ 1720/1700–2450m
· 62 lifts · Dec–Apr · Bludenz (30km)
📞+43 5583 2245 💻 www.lech-zuers.at
*Roads normally cleared but keep chains accessible because of altitude. Village has garage with 24 hour self service gas/petrol, breakdown service and wheel chains supply.*

## France
### Alps

**Alpe d'Huez 118 B3** ❄ 1860–3330m
85 lifts · Dec–Apr · Grenoble (63km)
💻 www.alpedhuez.com
📞+33 4 76 11 44 44 *Snow chains may be required on access road to resort.*

**Avoriaz 118 A3** ❄ 1800/1100–2280m
35 lifts · Dec–May · Morzine (14km)
📞+33 4 50 74 02 11 💻 www.avoriaz.com
*Chains may be required for access road from Morzine. Car-free resort, park on edge of village. Horse-drawn sleigh service.*

**Chamonix-Mont-Blanc 119 B3** ❄
49 lifts · 1035–3840m · Dec–Apr
· Martigny (38km) 📞+33 4 50 53 00 24
💻 www.chamonix.com

**Chamrousse 118 B2** ❄ 1700–2250m
26 lifts · Dec–Apr · Grenoble (30km)
💻 www.chamrousse.com 📞+33 4 76 89
92 65 *Roads normally cleared, keep chains accessible because of altitude.*

**Châtel 119 A3** ❄ 1200/1110–2200m
41 lifts · Dec–Apr · Thonon-Les-Bains
(35km) 📞+33 4 50 73 22 44
📧 info.chatel.com/english-version.html

**Courchevel 118 B3** ❄ 1750/1300–2470m
67 lifts · Dec–Apr · Moûtiers (23km)
💻 www.courchevel.com · *Roads normally cleared but keep chains accessible. Traffic 'discouraged' within the four resort bases.*

**Flaine 118 A3** ❄ 1600–2500m · 26 lifts
·Dec–Apr ·Cluses (25km) 📞+33 4 50 90 80
💻 www.flaine.com *Keep chains accessible for D6 from Cluses to Flaine. Car access for depositing luggage and passengers only. 1500-space car park outside resort. Near Sixt-Fer-á-Cheval.*

**La Clusaz 118 B3** ❄ 1100–2600m
·55 lifts ·Dec–Apr ·Annecy (32km)
💻 www.laclusaz.com *Roads normally clear but keep chains accessible for final road from Annecy.*

**La Plagne 118 B3** ❄ 2500/1250–3250m
109 lifts · Dec–Apr · Moûtiers (32km)
📞+33 4 79 09 79 79 💻 www.la-plagne.com
*Ten different centres up to 2100m altitude. Road access via Bozel, Landry or Aime normally cleared. Linked to Les Arcs by cablecar*

**Les Arcs 119 B3** ❄ 1600/1200–3230m
77 lifts ·Dec–May ·Bourg-St-Maurice
(15km) 📞+33 4 79 07 12 57
💻 www.lesarcs.com · *Four base areas up to 2000 metres; keep chains accessible. Pay parking at edge of each base resort. Linked to La Plagne by cablecar*

**Les Carroz d'Araches 118 A3** ❄ 80 lifts
·1140–2500m · Dec–Apr · Cluses (13km)
📞+33 4 50 90 00 04 💻 www.lescarroz.com

**Les Deux-Alpes 118 C3** ❄ 1650/1300–
3600m · 55 lifts · Grenoble (75km) 📞+33 4
76 79 22 00 💻 www.les2alpes.com · *Roads normally cleared, however snow chains recommended for D213 up from valley road.*

**Les Gets 118 A3** ❄ 1170/1000–2000m
52 lifts · Dec–Apr · Cluses (18km)
📞+33 4 50 75 80 80 💻 www.lesgets.com

**Les Ménuires 118 B3** ❄ 40 lifts
Dec–Apr · 1815/1850–3200m ·
Moûtiers (27km) 📞+33 4 79 00 73 00
💻 www.lesmenuires.com *Keep chains accessible for D117 from Moûtiers.*

**Les Sept Laux Prapoutel 118 B3** ❄
1350–2400m · 24 lifts · Dec–Apr
· Grenoble (38km) 📞+33 4 76 08 17 86
💻 www.les7laux.com · *Roads normally cleared but keep chains accessible for mountain road from the A41 motorway. Near St Sorlin d'Arves.*

**Megève 118 B3** ❄ 1100/1050–2350m
79 lifts · Dec–Apr · Sallanches (12km)
📞+ 33 4 50 21 28 💻 www.megeve.com
*Horse-drawn sleigh rides available.*

**Méribel 118 B3** ❄ 1400/1100–2950m
61 lifts · Dec–May · Moûtiers (18km)
📞+33 4 79 08 60 01 💻 www.meribel.net
*Keep chains accessible for 18km to resort on D90 from Moûtiers.*

**Morzine 118 A3** ❄ 1000–2460m
· 67 lifts Dec–Apr · Thonon-Les-Bains
(30km) 📞+33 4 50 74 72 72
💻 www.morzine-avoriaz.com

**Pra Loup 132 A2** ❄ 1600/1500–2500m
53 lifts · Dec–Apr · Barcelonnette (10km)
📞+33 4 92 84 10 04 💻 www.praloup.com
*Roads normally cleared but chains accessibility recommended.*

**Risoul 118 C3** ❄ 1850/1650–2750m
51 lifts · Dec–Apr · Briançon (40km)
💻 www.risoul.com *Keep chains accessible. Near Guillestre. Linked with Vars Les Claux*

**St-Gervais Mont-Blanc 118 B3** ❄
27 lifts · 850/1150–2350m Dec–Apr
·Sallanches (10km) 📞+33 4 50 47 76 08
💻 www.st-gervais.com

**Serre Chevalier 118 C3** ❄ 77 lifts
Dec–Apr 1350/1200–2800m
· Briançon (10km) 📞+ 33 4 92 24 98 98
💻 www.serre-chevalier.com
*Made up of 13 small villages along the valley road, which is normally cleared.*

**Tignes 119 B3** ❄ 2100/1550–3450m
· 97 lifts · Jan–Dec · Bourg St Maurice
(26km) 📞+33 4 79 40 04 40
💻 www.tignes.net
*Keep chains accessible due to altitude.*

**Val d'Isère 119 B3** ❄ 1850/1550–3450m
· 97 lifts · Dec–Apr · Bourg-St-Maurice
(30km) 📞+33 4 79 06 06 60
💻 www.valdisere.com *Roads normally cleared but keep chains accessible.*

**Val Thorens 118 B3** ❄ 29 lifts · Dec–Apr
2300/1850–3200m · Moûtiers (37km)
📞+33 4 79 00 08 08 💻 www.valthorens.
com *Chains essential – Europe highest ski resort. Obligatory paid parking.*

**Valloire 118 B3** ❄ 1430–2600m · 34 lifts
Dec–Apr · Modane (20km) 📞+33 4 79 59
03 96 💻 www.valloire.net · *Road normally clear up to the Col du Galbier, to the south of the resort, which is closed from 1st Nov to 1st Jun. Linked to Valmeinier.*

**Valmeinier 118 B3** ❄ 1500–2600m
· 34 lifts · Dec–Apr · St Michel de
Maurienne (47km) 📞+33 4 79 59 53 69
💻 www.valmeinier.com · *Access from north on D1006 / D902. Col du Galbier, to the south of the resort closed from 1st November to 1st June. Linked to Valloire.*

**Valmorel 118 B3** ❄ 1400–2550m
· 90 lifts · Dec–Apr · Moûtiers (15km)
📞+33 4 79 09 85 55 💻 www.valmorel.com
*Near St Jean-de-Belleville. · Linked with ski areas of Doucy-Combelouvière and St François-Longchamp.*

**Vars Les Claux 118 C3** ❄ 51 lifts · Dec–
Apr · 1850/1650–2750m · Briançon (40km)
📞+33 4 92 46 51 31 💻 www.vars-ski.com
*Four base resorts up to 1850 metres. Keep chains accessible. Linked with Risoul.*

**Villard de Lans 118 B2** ❄
1050/1160–2170m · 28 lifts · Dec–Apr
· Grenoble (32km) 📞+33 4 76 95 10 38
💻 www.villarddelans.com

### Pyrenees

**Font-Romeu 146 B3** ❄ Nov–Apr · 25 lifts
1800/1600–2200m · Perpignan (87km)
💻 www.font-romeu.fr 📞+33 4 68 30 68 30
*Roads normally cleared but keep chains accessible.*

**Saint-Lary Soulan 145 B4** ❄ Dec–Mar
· 830/1650/1700–2515m · 31 lifts · Tarbes
(75km) 💻 www.saintlary.com 📞+33 5 62
39 50 81 *Access roads constantly cleared.*

### Vosges

**La Bresse-Hohneck 106 A1** ❄ Dec–Mar
500/900–1350m ·33 lifts ·Cornimont (6km)
📞+33 3 29 25 41 29 💻 www.labresse.net

# Germany

## Alps

**Garmisch-Partenkirchen 108 B2** ✷
700–2830m · 38 lifts · Dec–Apr · Munich
(95km) *i* +49 8821 180 700
🖥 www.gapa.de · *Roads usually clear,
chains rarely needed.*

**Oberaudorf 108 B3** ✷ 480–1850m
30 lifts · Dec–Apr · Kufstein (15km)
*i* +49 8033 301 20 🖥 www.oberaudorf.de
*Motorway normally kept clear.
Near Bayrischzell.*

**Oberstdorf 107 B5** 815m · 26 lifts
· Dec–Apr · Sonthofen (15km)
*i* +49 8322 7000 🖥 http://oberstdorf.de

## Rothaargebirge

**Winterberg 81 A4** ✷ 700/620–830m
19 lifts · Dec–Mar · Brilon (30km)
*i* +49 2981 925 00 🖥 www.winterberg.de
*Roads usually cleared, chains rarely needed.*

# Greece

## Central Greece

**Mount Parnassos: Kelaria-Fterolakka
182 E4** 1640–2260m · 14 lifts · Dec–Apr
· Amfiklia *i* Kelaria +30 22340 22693–5,
Fterolakka 22340 22373
🖥 www.parnassos-ski.gr (Greek only)

**Mount Parnassos: Gerondovrahos 182
E4** 1800–1900m · 14 lifts · Dec–Apr
· Amfiklia *i* +30 29444 70371

## Peloponnisos

**Mount Helmos: Kalavrita Ski Centre
184 A3** 1650–2100m · 7 lifts · Dec–Mar
· Kalavrita *i* +30 2692 2261
🖥 www.kalavrita-ski.gr (Greek only)

**Mount Menalo: Ostrakina 184 B3**
1500–1600m · 4 lifts · Dec–Mar · Tripoli
*i* +30 27960 22227

## Macedonia

**Mount Falakro: Agio Pneuma 183 B6**
1720/1620–2230m · 7 lifts · Dec–Apr
· Drama *i* +30 25210 23691
🖥 www.falakro.gr (Greek only)

**Mount Vasilitsa: Vasilitsa 182 C3**
1750/1800–2113m · 3 lifts · Dec–Mar
· Konitsa *i* +30 24620 26100
🖥 www.vasilitsa.com (Greek only)

**Mount Vermio: Seli 182 C4** 1500–1900m
· 8 lifts · Dec–Mar · Kozani *i* +30 23320
71234 🖥 www.seli-ski.gr (in Greek)

**Mount Vermio: Tria-Pente Pigadia
182 C3** 1420–2005m · 7 lifts · Dec–Mar
· Ptolemaida *i* +30 23320 44464
🖥 www.3-5pigadia.gr

**Mount Verno: Vigla 182 C3** 1650–1900m
· 5 lifts · Dec–Mar · Florina *i* +30 23850
22354 🖥 www.vigla-ski.gr (in Greek)

**Mount Vrondous: Lailias 183 B5**
1600–1850m · 4 lifts · Dec–Mar · Serres
*i* +30 23210 53790

## Thessalia

**Mount Pilio: Agriolefkes 183 D5** · 5 lifts
1300–1500m · Dec–Mar · Volos *i* +30
24280 73719 🖥 www.skipilio.gr (Greek)

# Italy

## Alps

**Bardonecchia 118 B3** ✷ 1312–2750m
21 lifts · Dec–Apr · Bardonecchia
🖥 www.bardonecchiaski.com
*i* + 39 0122 99137 · *Resort reached through
the 11km Frejus tunnel from France, roads
normally cleared.*

**Bórmio 107 C5** ✷ 1200/1230–3020m
24 lifts Dec–Apr · Tirano (40km)
*i* +39 342 903300 🖥 www.bormio.com
*Tolls payable in Ponte del Gallo Tunnel,
open 0800hrs–2000hrs.*

**Breuil-Cervinia 119 B4** ✷ 2050–3500m
21 lifts Jan–Dec · Aosta (54km)
*i* +39 166 949136 🖥 www. cervinia.it
*Snow chains strongly recommended.
Bus from Milan airport.*

**Courmayeur 119 B3** ✷ 1200–2760m
21 lifts Dec–Apr · Aosta (40km)
🖥 www.courmayeur.com *Access through
the Mont Blanc tunnel from France.
Roads constantly cleared.*

**Limone Piemonte 133 A3** ✷ Dec–Apr
1000/1050–2050m 29 lifts · Cuneo (27km)
🖥 www.limonepiemonte.it
*i* + 39 171 925281 *Roads normally cleared,
chains rarely required.*

**Livigno 107 C5** ✷ 1800–3000m 31 lifts
Nov–May · Zernez (CH) (27km)
*i* + 39 342 996379 🖥 www.livigno.com
*Keep chains accessible. The direction of
traffic through Munt la Schera Tunnel to/
from Zernez is regulated on Saturdays.
Check in advance.*

**Sestrière 119 C3** ✷ 2035/1840–2840m
92 lifts Dec–Apr · Oulx (22km)
*i* +39 122 799411 🖥 http://www.comune.
sestriere.to.it *One of Europe's highest
resorts; although roads are normally cleared
keep chains accessible.*

## Appennines

**Roccaraso – Aremogna 169 B4** ✷
1285/1240–2140m 39 lifts Dec–Apr
· Castel di Sangro (7km) *i* +39 864 62210
🖥 www.roccaraso.net (in Italian)

## Dolomites

**Andalo – Fai della Paganella 121 A3** ✷
1042/1050/2125m 19 lifts Dec–Apr
· Trento (40km) 🖥 www.paganella.com
*i* +39 0461 585836

**Arabba 108 C2** ✷ 1600/1450–2950m
29 lifts Dec–Mar · Brunico (45km)
*i* +39 436 780019 🖥 www.arabba.it *Roads
normally cleared but keep chains accessible.*

**Cortina d'Ampezzo 108 C3** ✷ Dec–Apr
1224/1050–2930m 37 lifts · Belluno (72km)
🖥 www.cortina.dolomiti.org *Access from
north on route 51 over the Cimabanche Pass
may require chains.*

**Corvara (Alta Badia) 108 C2** ✷ 52 lifts
1568–2500m Dec–Apr · Brunico (38km)
*i* +39 471 836176 🖥 www.altabadia.it
*Roads normally clear but keep chains
accessible.*

**Madonna di Campiglio 121 A3** ✷
1550/1500–2600m 72 lifts Dec–Apr
· Trento (60km) *i* +39 465 447501
🖥 www.campigliodolomiti.it *Roads
normally cleared but keep chains accessible.
Linked to Folgarida and Marilleva.*

**Moena di Fassa (Sorte/Ronchi) 108
C2** ✷ 1184/1450–2520m 8 lifts Dec–Apr
· Bolzano (40km) *i* +39 462 609500
🖥 www.fassa.com

**Selva di Val Gardena/Wolkenstein
Groden 108 C2** ✷ 1563/1570–2450m
84 lifts Dec–Apr · Bolzano (40km) *i* +39
471 777777 🖥 www.valgardena.it *Roads
normally cleared but keep chains accessible.*

# Norway

**Hemsedal 47 B5** ✷ 700/640–1450m
24 lifts Nov–May · Honefoss (150km)
🖥 www.hemsedal.com
*i* +47 32 055030 *Be prepared for extreme
weather conditions.*

# Slovak Republic

**Chopok (Jasna-Chopok) 99 C3** ✷
900/950–1840m 17 lifts Dec–Apr · Jasna
*i* +421 907 886644 🖥 www.jasna.sk

**Donovaly 99 C3** ✷ 913–1360m 17 lifts
Nov–Apr · Ruzomberok *i* +421 48
4199900 · www.parksnow.sk/zima

**Martinské Hole 98 B2** 1250/1150–1456m
8 lifts Nov–May · Zilina *i* +421 43 430 6000
🖥 www.martinky.com (in Slovak only)

**Plejcy 99 C4** 470–912m 9 lifts Dec–Mar
· Krompachy *i* +421 53 429 8015
🖥 www.plejsy.com

**Strbske Pleso 99 B4** 1380–1825m 7 lifts
Dec–Mar · Popra *i* +421 52 449 2455
🖥 www.vt.sk

# Slovenia

## Julijske Alpe

**Kanin (Bovec) 122 A2** 460/1600–2389m
5 lifts Dec–Apr · Bovec *i* + 386 5 3896444
🖥 www.boveckanin.si

**Kobla (Bohinj) 122 A2** 512/530–1495m
6 lifts Dec–Mar · Bohinjska Bistrica *i* +386
4 5747 100 🖥 www.bohinj.si/kobla

**Kranjska Gora 122 A2** ✷ 800–1210m
19 lifts Dec–Mar · Kranjska Gora *i* +386 4
5809 440 🖥 www.kranjska-gora.si

**Vogel 122 A2** 570–1800m 8 lifts Dec–Apr
· Bohinjska Bistrica *i* +386 4 5729 712
🖥 www.vogel.si

## Kawiniške Savinjske Alpe

**Krvavec 122 A3** ✷ 1450–1970m 10 lifts
Dec–Apr · Kranj *i* 386 4 25 25 911
🖥 www.rtc-krvavec.si

## Pohorje

**Rogla 123 A4** 1517/1050–1500m
13 lifts Dec–Apr · Slovenska Bistrica
*i* +386 3 75 76 000 🖥 www.rogla.eu

# Spain

## Pyrenees

**Baqueira-Beret/Bonaigua 145 B4** ✷
1500–2500m 33 lifts Dec–Apr · Vielha
(15km) *i* +34 973 639010
🖥 www.baqueira.es *Roads normally clear
but keep chains accessible. Near Salardú.*

## Sistema Penibetico

**Sierra Nevada 163 A4** ✷ 2100–3300m
24 lifts Dec–May · Granada (32km)
🖥 http://sierranevada.es *i* +34 902 70 80
90–3 *Access road designed to be
avalanche-safe and is snow cleared.*

# Sweden

**Idre Fjäll 199 D9** 590–890m 33 lifts
Nov–Apr · Mora (140km) *i* +46 253
41000 🖥 www.idrefjall.se *Be prepared for
extreme weather conditions.*

**Sälen 49 A5** 360m 100 lifts
Nov–Apr · Malung (70km)
🖥 www.skistar.com/salen *Be prepared
for extreme weather conditions.*

# Switzerland

## Alps

**Adelboden 106 C2** 1353m Dec–Apr
55 lifts · Frutigen (15km) *i* +41 33 673 80 80
🖥 www.adelboden.ch *Linked with Lenk.*

**Arosa 107 C4** 1800m 16 lifts Dec–Apr
· Chur (30km) *i* +41 81 378 70 20
🖥 www.arosa.ch *Roads cleared but keep
chains accessible due to high altitude.*

**Crans Montana 119 A4** ✷ 1500–3000m
34 lifts Dec–Apr, Jul–Oct · Sierre (15km)
*i* +41 27 485 04 04 🖥 www.crans-mon-
tana.ch *Roads normally cleared but keep
chains accessible for ascent from Sierre.*

**Davos 107 C4** ✷ 1560/1100–2840m
38 lifts Nov–Apr · Davos *i* +41 81 415 21 21
🖥 www.davos.ch

**Engelberg 106 C3** ✷ 1000/1050–3020m
26 lifts Nov–May · Luzern (39km)
*i* +41 41 639 77 77 🖥 www.engelberg.ch
*Straight access road normally cleared.*

**Flums (Flumserberg) 107 B4** ✷
1400/1000–2220m 17 lifts Dec–Apr
· Buchs (25km) *i* +41 81 720 18 18
🖥 www.flumserberg.ch
*Roads normally cleared, but 1000-metre
vertical ascent; keep chains accessible.*

**Grindelwald 106 C3** ✷ 1050–2950m
39 lifts Dec–Apr · Interlaken (20km)
*i* +41 33 854 12 12
🖥 www.jungfrauregion.ch

**Gstaad – Saanenland 106 C2** ✷
1050/950–3000m 74 lifts Dec–Apr
· Gstaad *i* +41 33 748 81 81
🖥 www.gstaad.ch *Linked to Anzère.*

**Klosters 107 C4** ✷ 1191/1110–2840m
52 lifts Dec–Apr · Davos (10km)
*i* +41 81 410 21 21 🖥 www.klosters.ch
*Roads normally clear but keep chains
accessible.*

**Leysin 119 A4** ✷ 2263/1260–2330m
16 lifts Dec–Apr · Aigle (6km)
🖥 www.leysin.ch

**Mürren 106 C2** ✷ 1650–2970m
12 lifts Dec–Apr · Interlaken (18km)
*i* +41 33 856 86 86 🖥 www.mymuerren.
ch *No road access. Park in Strechelberg
(1500 free places) and take the two-stage
cable car.*

**Nendaz 119 A4** ✷ 1365/1400–3300m
20 lifts Nov–Apr · Sion (16km)
*i* +41 27 289 55 89 🖥 www.nendaz.ch
*Roads normally cleared, however keep
chains accessible for ascent from Sion.
Near Vex.*

**Saas-Fee 119 A4** ✷ 1800–3500m
23 lifts Jan–Dec · Brig (35km)
*i* +41 27 958 18 58 🖥 www.saas-fee.ch
*Roads normally cleared but keep chains
accessible because of altitude.*

**St Moritz 107 C4** ✷ 1856/1730–3300m
24 lifts Nov–May · Chur (89km)
*i* +41 81 837 33 33 🖥 www.stmoritz.ch
*Roads normally cleared but keep chains
accessible.*

**Samnaun 107 C5** ✷ 1846/1400–2900m
40 lifts Dec–May · Scuol (30km) *i* +41 81
868 58 58 🖥 www.engadin.com *Roads
normally cleared but keep chains accessible.*

**Verbier 119 A4** ✷ 1500–3330m
17 lifts Nov–Apr · Martigny (27km)
*i* +41 27 775 38 88 🖥 www.verbier.ch
*Roads normally cleared.*

**Villars-Gryon 119 A4** ✷ 1253/1200–
2100m 16 lifts Dec–Apr, Jun–Jul
· Montreux (35km) *i* +41 24 495 32 32
🖥 www.villars.ch *Roads normally cleared
but keep chains accessible for ascent from
N9. Near Bex.*

**Wengen 106 C2** ✷ 1270–2320m 39 lifts
Dec–Apr · Interlaken (12km) *i* +41 33 856
85 85 🖥 http://wengen.ch *No road access.
Park at Lauterbrunnen and take railway.*

**Zermatt 119 A4** ✷ 1620–3900m 40 lifts,
all year · Brig (42km) *i* +41 27 966 81 19
🖥 www.zermatt.ch *Cars not permitted in
resort, park in Täsch and take shuttle train.*

# Turkey

## North Anatolian Mountains

**Uludag 186 B4** 1770–2320m 13 lifts
Dec–Mar · Bursa (36km)
🖥 skiingturkey.com/resorts/uludag.html
*i* +90 224 285 21 11

# 300 greatest sights of Europe

## Albania Shqipëria

www.albaniantourism.com

### Berat

Fascinating old town with picturesque Ottoman Empire buildings and traditional Balkan domestic architecture. www.berat.info **182 C1**

### Tirana Tiranë

Capital of Albania. Skanderbeg Square has main historic buildings. Also: 18c Haxhi Ethem Bey Mosque; Art Gallery (Albanian); National Museum of History. Nearby: medieval Krujë; Roman monuments. www.tirana.gov.al **182 B1**

## Austria Österreich

www.austria.info

### Bregenz

Lakeside town bordering Germany, Liechtenstein, Switzerland. Locals, known as Vorarlbergers, have their own dialect. The Martinsturm Roman to 17c tower, 17c town hall and Seekapelle, Kunsthaus modern art museum, Vorarlberger Landesmuseum, Festspielhaus. www.bregenz.travel **107 B4**

### Graz

University town, seat of imperial court to 1619. Historic centre around Hauptplatz. Imperial monuments: Burg; mausoleum of Ferdinand II; towers of 16c schloss; 17c Schloss Eggengerg (with Old Gallery). Also: 16c Town Hall; Zeughaus; 15c cathedral; New Gallery (good 19–20c); Kunsthaus (modern art). www.graztourismus.at **110 B2**

### Innsbruck

Old town is reached by Maria-Theresien-Strasse with famous views. Buildings: Goldenes Dachl (1490s); 18c cathedral; remains of Hofburg imperial residence; 16c Hofkirche (tomb of Maximilian I). www.innsbruckaustria.co.uk **108 B2**

### Krems

On a hill above the Danube, medieval quarter has Renaissance mansions. Also: Gothic Piaristenkirche; Museumkrems; Kunsthalle (modern art). www.krems.gv.at **97 C3**

### Linz

Port on the Danube. Historic buildings are concentrated on Hauptplatz below the imperial 15c schloss. Notable: Baroque Old Cathedral; 16c Town Hall; Old Castle Museum; Lentos Art Museum. www.linz.at **96 C2**

▲ Maholicahaus, Vienna, Austria

### Melk

Set on a rocky hill above the Danube, the fortified abbey is the greatest Baroque achievement in Austria – particularly the Grand Library and abbey church. www.stiftmelk.at **110 A2**

### Salzburg

Set in subalpine scenery, the town was associated with powerful 16–17c prince-archbishops. The 17c cathedral has a complex of archiepiscopal buildings: the Residence and its gallery (19c); the 13c Franciscan Church (notable altar). Also: Mozart's birth-place; Schloss Mirabell; Salzburg Museum; the Hohensalzburg fortress; the Collegiate Church of St Peter (cemetery, catacombs); Museum of Modern Art at the Mönschberg and Rupertinum. www.salzburg.info/en **109 B4**

### Salzkammergut

Natural beauty with 76 lakes (Wolfgangersee, Altersee, Traunsee, Grundlsee) in mountain scenery. Attractive villages (St Wolfgang) and towns (Bad Ischl, Gmunden) include Hallstatt, famous for Celtic remains. www.salzkammergut.at **109 B4**

### Vienna Wien

Capital of Austria, the historic centre lies within the Ring. Churches: Gothic St Stephen's Cathedral; 17c Imperial Vault; 14c Augustine Church; 14c Church of the Teutonic Order (treasure); 18c Baroque churches (Jesuit Church, Franciscan Church, St Peter, St Charles). Imperial residences: Hofburg; Schönbrunn. Architecture of Historicism on Ringstrasse (from 1857). Art Nouveau: station pavilions, Secession Building, Postsparkasse, Looshaus, Majolicahaus. Museums: Art History Museum (antiquities, old masters), Cathedral and Diocesan Museum (15c), Albertina (graphic arts), Liechtenstein Museum (old masters), Museum of Applied Arts, Museum of Modern Art (MUMOK), Leopold Museum, Belvedere (Gothic, Baroque, 19–20c); AzW (architecture); Vienna Museum. www.wien.info **111 A3**

## Belgium Belgique

www.visitbelgium.com

### Antwerp Antwerpen

City with many tall gabled Flemish houses on the river. Heart of the city is Great Market with 16–17c guildhouses and Town Hall. Charles Borromeus Church (Baroque). 14–16c Gothic

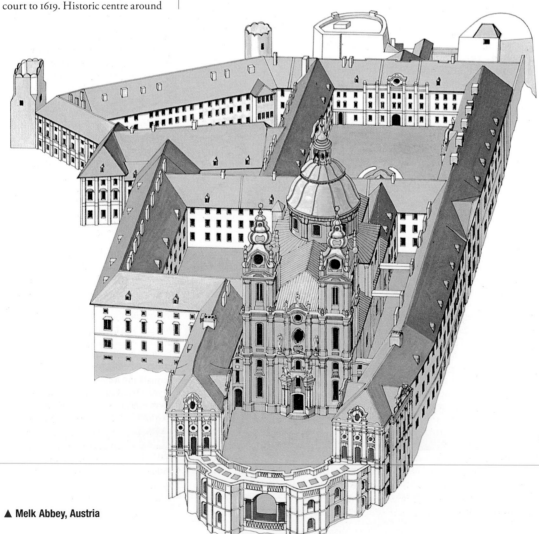

▲ Melk Abbey, Austria

▼ Town Hall, Antwerp, Belgium

cathedral has Rubens paintings. Rubens also at the Rubens House and his burial place in St Jacob's Church. Excellent museums: Mayer van den Bergh Museum (applied arts); Koninklijk Museum of Fine Arts (Flemish, Belgian); MAS (ethnography, folklore, shipping); Muhka (modern art). www.antwerpen.be **79 A4**

### Bruges Brugge

Well-preserved medieval town with narrow streets and canals. Main squares: the Market with 13c Belfort and covered market; the Burg with Basilica of the Holy Blood and Town Hall. The collections of Groeninge Museum and Memling museum in St Jans Hospital include 15c Flemish masters. The Onze Lieve Vrouwekerk has a famous *Madonna and Child* by Michelangelo www.brugge.be **78 A3**

### Brussels Bruxelles

Capital of Belgium. The Lower Town is centred on the enormous Grand Place with Hôtel de Ville and rebuilt guildhouses. Symbols of the city include the 'Manneken Pis' and Atomium (giant model of a molecule). The 13c Notre Dame de la Chapelle is the oldest church. The Upper Town contains: Gothic cathedral; Neoclassical Place Royale; 18c King's Palace; Royal Museums of Fine Arts (old and modern masters) Magritte Museum; MRAH (art and historical artefacts); BELvue museum (in the Bellevue Residence). Also: much Art Nouveau (Horta Museum, Hôtel Tassel, Hôtel Solvay); Place du Petit Sablon and Place du Grand Sablon; 19c Palais de Justice. http://visitbrussels.be **79 B4**

### Ghent Gent

Medieval town built on islands surrounded by canals and rivers. Views from Pont St-Michel. The Graslei and Koornlei quays have Flemish guild houses. The Gothic cathedral has famous Van Eyck altarpiece. Also: Belfort; Cloth Market; Gothic Town Hall; Gravensteen. Museums: STAM Museum in Bijloke Abbey (provincial and applied art); Museum of Fine Arts (old masters). www.visitgent.be **79 A3**

### Namur

Reconstructed medieval citadel is the major sight of Namur, which also has a cathedral and provincial museums. www.namurtourisme.be/index.php **79 B4**

### Tournai

The Romanesque-Gothic cathedral is Belgium's finest (much excellent art). Fine Arts Museum has a good collection (15–20c). www.tournai.be/en/officiel **78 B3**

## Bulgaria Bulgariya

www.bulgariatravel.org

### Black Sea Coast

Beautiful unspoiled beaches (Zlatni Pyasŭtsi). The delightful resort Varna is popular. Nesebŭr is famous for Byzantine churches. Also: Danube Delta in Hungary. **17 D7**

### Koprivshtitsa

Beautiful village known both for its half-timbered houses and links with the April Rising of 1876. Six house museums amongst which the Lyutov House and the Oslekov House, plus the birthplaces of Georgi Benkovski, Dimcho Debelyanov, Todor Kableshkov, and Lyuben Karavelov. www.eng.koprivshtitza.com

### Plovdiv

City set spectacularly on three hills. The old town has buildings from many periods: 2c Roman stadium and amphitheatre; 14c Dzumaiya Mosque; Archaeological Museum; 19c Ethnographic Museum. Nearby: Bačkovo Monastery (frescoes). www.plovdiv.org **183 A6**

### Rila

Bulgaria's finest monastery, set in the most beautiful scenery of the Rila mountains. The church is richly decorated with frescoes. www.rilamonastery.pmg-blg.com **183 A5**

### Sofia Sofiya

Capital of Bulgaria. Sights: exceptional neo-Byzantine cathedral; Church of St Sofia; St Alexander Nevsky Cathedral; Boyana church; 4c rotunda of St George (frescoes); Byzantine Boyana Church (frescoes) on panoramic Mount Vitoša. Museums: National Historical Museum (particularly for Thracian artefacts); National Art Gallery (icons, Bulgarian art). www.sofia.bg **17 D5**

### Veliko Tŭrnovo

Medieval capital with narrow streets. Notable buildings: House of the Little Monkey; Hadji Nicoli Inn; ruins of medieval citadel; Baudouin Tower; churches of the Forty Martyrs and of SS Peter and Paul (frescoes); 14c Monastery of the Transfiguration. www.veliko.co.uk **17 D6**

## Croatia Hrvatska

http://croatia.hr

### Dalmatia Dalmacija

Exceptionally beautiful coast along the Adriatic. Among its 1185 islands, those of the Kornati Archipelago and Brijuni Islands are perhaps the most spectacular. Along the coast are several attractive medieval and Renaissance towns, most notably Dubrovnik, Split, Šibenik, Trogir, Zadar. www.dalmacija.net **138 B2**

### Dubrovnik

Surrounded by medieval and Renaissance walls, the city's architecture dates principally from 15–16c. Sights: many churches and monasteries including Church of St Blaise and Dominican monastery (art collection); promenade street of Stradun, Dubrovnik Museums; Renaissance Rector's Palace; Onofrio's fountain; Sponza Palace. The surrounding area has some 80 16c noblemen's summer villas. www.tzdubrovnik.hr **139 C4**

### Islands of Croatia

There are over 1,000 islands off the coast of Croatia among which there is Brač, known for its white marble and the beautiful beaches of Bol (www.bol.hr); Hvar (www.tzhvar.hr/en/) is beautifully green with fields of lavender, marjoram, rosemary, sage and thyme; Vis (www.tz-vis.hr) has the beautiful towns of Komiža and Vis Town, with the Blue Cave on nearby Biševo. **123 & 137–138**

### Istria Istra

Peninsula with a number of ancient coastal towns (Rovinj, Poreč, Pula, Piran in Slovene Istria) and medieval hill-top towns (Motovun). Pula has Roman monuments (exceptional 1c amphitheatre). Poreč has narrow old streets; the mosaics in 6c Byzantine basilica of St Euphrasius are exceptional. See also Slovenia. www.istra.hr **122 B2**

### Plitvička Jezera

Outstandingly beautiful world of water and woodlands with 16 lakes and 92 waterfalls interwoven by canyons. Archaeological museums; art gallery; Gallery of Ivan Meštrović. www.tzplitvice.hr **123 C4**

### Split

Most notable for the exceptional 4c palace of Roman Emperor Diocletian, elements of which are incorporated into the streets and buildings of the town itself. The town also has a cathedral (11c baptistry) and a Franciscan monastery. www.split.info **138 B2**

### Trogir

The 13–15c town centre is surrounded by medieval city walls. Romanesque-Gothic cathedral includes the chapel of Ivan the Blessed. Dominican and Benedictine monasteries house art collections; Ćipiko palace; Lučić palace. http://tztrogir.hr **138 B2**

### Zagreb

Capital city of Croatia with cathedral and Archbishop's Palace in Kaptol and to the west Gradec with Baroque palaces. Donji Grad - The Lower Town - is home to the Archaeological Museum, Art Pavilion, Museum of Arts and Crafts, Ethnographic Museum, Mimara Museum and National Theatre; Modern Gallery; Museum of Contemporary Art. www.zagreb-touristinfo.hr **124 B1**

## Czech Republic Česká Republica

www.czechtourism.com

### Brno

Capital of Moravia. Sights: Vegetable Market and Old Town Hall; Capuchin crypt decorated with bones of dead monks; hill of St Peter with Gothic cathedral; Church of St James; Mies van der Rohe's buildings (Bata, Avion Hotel, Togendhat House). Museums: Moravian Museum; Moravian Gallery; City Art Gallery; Brno City Museum in Spilberk Castle. www.brno.cz **97 B4**

### České Budějovice

Famous for Budvar beer, the medieval town is centred on náměsti Přemysla Otokara II. The Black Tower gives fine views. Nearby: medieval Český Krumlov. www.c-budejovice.cz/en **96 C2**

### Kutná Hora

A town with strong silver mining heritage shown in the magnificent Cathedral of sv Barbara which was built by the miners. See also the ossuary with 40,000 complete sets of bones moulded into sculptures and decorations. **97 B3**

### Olomouc

Well-preserved medieval university town of squares and fountains. The Upper Square has the Town Hall. Also: 18c Holy Trinity; Baroque Church of St Michael. http://tourism.olomouc.eu **98 B1**

### Plzeň

Best known for Plzeňský Prazdroj (Pilsener Urquell), beer has been brewed here since 1295. An industrial town with eclectic architecture shown in the railway stations and the namesti Republiky (main square). http://web.zcu.cz/plzen/ **96 B1**

### Prague Praha

Capital of Czech Republic and Bohemia. The Castle Quarter has a complex of buildings behind the walls (Royal Castle; Royal Palace; cathedral). The Basilica of St George has a fine Romanesque interior. The Belvedere is the best example of Renaissance architecture. Hradčani Square has aristocratic palaces and the National Gallery. The Little Quarter has many Renaissance (Wallenstein

Palace) and Baroque mansions and the Baroque Church of St Nicholas. The Old Town has its centre at the Old Town Square with the Old Town Hall (astronomical clock), Art Nouveau Jan Hus monument and Gothic Týn church. The Jewish quarter has 14c Staranova Synagogue and Old Jewish Cemetery. The Charles Bridge is famous. The medieval New Town has many Art Nouveau buildings and is centred on Wenceslas Square. www.prague.cz **84 B2**

## Spas of Bohemia

Spa towns of Karlovy Vary (Carlsbad: www.karlovyvary.cz), Márianske Lázně (Marienbad: www.marianskel-azne.cz) and Frantiskovy Lázně **83 B4**

## Denmark Danmark

www.visitdenmark.com

### Århus

Second largest city in Denmark with a mixture of old and new architecture that blends well, Århus has been dubbed the culture capital of Denmark with the Gothic Domkirke; Latin Quarter; 13th Century Vor Frue Kirke; Den Gamle By, open air museum of traditional Danish life; ARoS (art museum). www.visitaarhus.com **59 B3**

### Copenhagen København

Capital of Denmark. Old centre has fine early 20c Town Hall. Latin Quarter has 19c cathedral. 18c Kastellet has statue of the Little Mermaid nearby. The 17c Rosenborg Castle was a royal residence, as was the Christianborg (now government offices). Other popular sights: Nyhavn canal; Tivoli Gardens. Excellent art collections: Ny Carlsberg Glypotek; National Gallery; National Museum. www.visitcopenhagen.dk **61 D2**

### Hillerød

Frederiskborg (home of the national history museum) is a fine red-brick Renaissance castle set among three lakes. www.hillerod.dk www.dnm.dk **61 D2**

### Roskilde

Ancient capital of Denmark. The marvellous cathedral is a burial place of the Danish monarchy. The Viking Ship Museum houses the remains of five 11c Viking ships excavated in the 1960s. www.visitroskilde.com **61 D2**

## Estonia Eesti

www.visitestonia.com

### Kuressaare

Main town on the island of Saaremaa with the 14c Kuressaare Kindlus. www.kuressaare.ee **8 C3**

### Pärnu

Sea resort with an old town centre. Sights: 15c Red Tower; neoclassical Town Hall; St Catherine's Church. www.visitparnu.com **8 C4**

### Tallinn

Capital of Estonia. The old town is centred on the Town Hall Square. Sights: 15c Town Hall; Toompea Castle; Three Sisters houses. Churches: Gothic St Nicholas; 14c Church of the Holy Spirit; St Olaf's Church; Kumu Art Museum. www.tourism.tallinn.ee **8 C4**

### Tartu

Historic town with 19c university. The Town Hall Square is surrounded by neoclassical buildings. Also: remains of 13c cathedral; Estonian National Museum. www.visittartu.com **8 C5**

## Finland Suomi

www.visitfinland.com

### Finnish Lakes

Area of outstanding natural beauty covering about one third of the country with thousands of lakes, of which Päijänne and Saimaa are the most important. Tampere, industrial centre of the region, has numerous museums, including the Tampere Art Museum (modern). Savonlinna has the medieval Olavinlinna Castle. Kuopio has the Orthodox and Regional Museums. **8 A5**

### Helsinki

Capital of Finland. The 19c neoclassical town planning between the Esplanade and Senate Square includes the Lutheran cathedral. There is also a Russian Orthodox cathedral. The Constructivist Stockmann Department Store is the largest in Europe. The main railway station is Art Nouveau. Gracious 20c buildings in Mannerheimintie avenue include Finlandiatalo by Alvar Aalto. Many good museums: Art Museum of the Ateneum (19–20c); National Museum; Design Museum; Helsinki City Art Museum (modern Finnish); Open Air Museum (vernacular architecture); 18c fortress of Suomenlinna has several museums. www.visithelsinki.fi **8 B4**

### Lappland (Finnish)

Vast unspoiled rural area. Lappland is home to thousands of nomadic Sámi living in a traditional way. The capital, Rovaniemi, was rebuilt after WWII; museums show Sámi history and culture. Nearby is the Arctic Circle with the famous Santa Claus Village. Inari is a centre of Sámi culture. See also Norway and Sweden. www.lapland.fi/en/travel **192–193**

## France

http://us.franceguide.com

### Albi

Old town with rosy brick architecture. The vast Cathédrale Ste-Cécile (begun 13c) holds some good art. The Berbie Palace houses the Toulouse-Lautrec museum. www.albi-tourisme.fr **130 B1**

### Alps

Grenoble, capital of the French Alps, has a good 20c collection in the Museum of Grenoble. The Vanoise Massif has the greatest number of resorts (Val d'Isère, Courchevel). Chamonix has spectacular views on Mont Blanc, France's and Europe's highest peak. www.thealps.com **118 B2**

### Amiens

France's largest Gothic cathedral has beautiful decoration. The Museum of Picardy has unique 16c panel paintings. www.visit-amiens.com **90 B2**

### Arles

Ancient, picturesque town with Roman relics (1c amphitheatre), 11c cathedral, Archaeological Museum (Roman art); Van Gogh centre. www.arlestourisme.com **131 B3**

### Avignon

Medieval papal capital (1309–77) with 14c walls and many ecclesiastical buildings. Vast Palace of the Popes has stunning frescoes. The Little Palace has fine Italian Renaissance painting. The 12–13c Bridge of St Bénézet is famous. www.ot-avignon.fr **131 B3**

### Bourges

The Gothic Cathedral of St Etienne, one of the finest in France, has a superb sculptured choir. Also notable is the House of Jacques Coeur. www.bourgestourisme.com **103 B4**

▲ Abbaye aux Hommes, Caen, France

▼ Château de Chenonceaux, Châteaux of the Loire, France

### Burgundy Bourgogne

Rural wine region with a rich Romanesque, Gothic and Renaissance heritage. The 12c cathedral in Autun and 12c basilica in Vézelay have fine Romanesque sculpture. Monasteries include 11c L'Abbaye de Cluny (ruins) and L'Abbaye de Fontenay. Beaune has beautiful Gothic Hôtel-Dieu and 15c Nicolas Rolin hospices. www.burgundy-tourism.com **104 B3**

## Brittany Bretagne

Brittany is famous for cliffs, sandy beaches and wild landscape. It is also renowned for megalithic monuments (Carnac) and Celtic culture. Its capital, Rennes, has the Palais de Justice and good collections in the Museum of Brittany (history) and Museum of Fine Arts. Also: Nantes; St-Malo. www.bretagne.com **100–101**

## Caen

City with two beautiful Romanesque buildings: Abbaye aux Hommes; Abbaye aux Dames. The château has two museums (15–20c painting; history). The *Bayeux Tapestry* is displayed in nearby Bayeux. www.tourisme.caen.fr **89 A3**

## Carcassonne

Unusual double-walled fortified town of narrow streets with an inner fortress. The fine Romanesque Church of St Nazaire has superb stained glass. www.carcassonne.fr **130 B1**

## Chartres

The 12–13c cathedral is an exceptionally fine example of Gothic architecture (Royal Doorway, stained glass, choir screen). The Fine Arts Museum has a good collection. www.chartres.com **90 C1**

## Clermont-Ferrand

The old centre contains the cathedral built out of lava and Romanesque basilica. The Puy de Dôme and Puy de Sancy give spectacular views over some 60 extinct volcanic peaks (*puys*). www.clermont-ferrand.fr **116 B3**

## Colmar

Town characterised by Alsatian half-timbered houses. The Unterlinden Museum has excellent German religious art including the famous Isenheim altarpiece. The Dominican church also has a fine altarpiece. Espace André Malraux (contemporary arts). www.ot-colmar.fr **106 A2**

## Corsica Corse

Corsica has a beautiful rocky coast and mountainous interior. Napoleon's birthplace of Ajaccio has: Fesch Museum with Imperial Chapel and a large collection of Italian art; Maison Bonaparte; cathedral. Bonifacio, a medieval town, is spectacularly set on a rock over the sea. www.visit-corsica.com **180**

## Côte d'Azur

The French Riviera is best known for its coastline and glamorous resorts. There are many relics of artists who worked here: St-Tropez has Musée de l'Annonciade; Antibes has 12c Château Grimaldi with the Picasso Museum; Cagnes has the Renoir House and Mediterranean Museum of Modern Art; St-Paul-de-Vence has the excellent Maeght Foundation and Matisse's Chapelle du Rosaire. Cannes is famous for its film festival. Also: Marseille, Monaco, Nice. www.frenchriviera-tourism.com **133 B3**

## Dijon

Great 15c cultural centre. The Palais des Ducs et des Etats is the most notable monument and contains the Museum of Fine Arts. Also: the Charterhouse of Champmol. www.visitdijon.com **105 B4**

## Disneyland Paris

Europe's largest theme park follows in the footsteps of its famous predecessors in the United States. www.disneylandparis.com **90 C2**

## Le Puy-en-Velay

Medieval town bizarrely set on the peaks of dead volcanoes. It is dominated by the Romanesque cathedral (cloisters). The Romanesque chapel of St-Michel is dramatically situated on the highest rock. www.ot-lepuyenvelay.fr **117 B3**

## Loire Valley

The Loire Valley has many 15–16c châteaux built amid beautiful scenery by French monarchs and members of their courts. Among the most splendid are Azay-le-Rideau, Chenonceaux and Loches. Also: Abbaye de Fontévraud. www.lvo.com **102 B2**

## Lyon

France's third largest city has an old centre and many museums including the Museum of the History of Textiles and the Museum of Fine Arts (old masters). www.lyon-france.com **117 B4**

## Marseilles Marseille

Second lagest city in France. Spectacular views from the 19c Notre-Dame-de-la-Garde. The Old Port has 11–12c Basilique St Victor (crypt, catacombs). Cantini Museum has major collection of 20c French art. Château d'If was the setting of Dumas' *The Count of Monte Cristo*. www.marseille-tourisme.com **131 B4**

## Mont-St-Michel

Gothic pilgrim abbey (11–12c) set dramatically on a steep rock island rising from mud flats and connected to the land by a road covered by the tide. The abbey is made up of a complex of buildings. www.ot-montsaintmichel.com **101 A4**

## Nancy

A centre of Art Nouveau. The 18c Place Stanislas was constructed by dethroned Polish king Stanislas. Museums: School of Nancy Museum (Art Nouveau furniture); Fine Arts Museum. www.ot-nancy.fr **92 C2**

## Nantes

Former capital of Brittany, with the 15c Château des ducs de Bretagne. The cathedral has a striking interior. www.nantes-tourisme.com **101 B4**

## Nice

Capital of the Côte d'Azur, the old town is centred on the old castle on the hill. The seafront includes the famous 19c Promenade des Anglais. The aristocratic quarter of the Cimiez Hill has the Marc Chagall Museum and the Matisse Museum. Also: Museum of Modern and Contemporary Art (especially neo-Realism and Pop Art). www.nicetourism.com **133 B3**

## Paris

Capital of France, one of Europe's most interesting cities. The Île de la Cité area, an island in the River Seine has the 12–13c Gothic Notre Dame (wonderful stained glass) and La Sainte-Chapelle (1240–48), one of the jewels of Gothic art. The Left Bank area: Latin Quarter with the famous Sorbonne university; Museum of Cluny housing medieval art; the Panthéon; Luxembourg Palace and Gardens; Montparnasse, interwar artistic and literary centre; Eiffel Tower; Hôtel des Invalides with Napoleon's tomb. Right Bank: the great boulevards (Avenue des Champs-Élysées joining the Arc de Triomphe and Place de la Concorde); 19c Opéra Quarter; Marais, former aristocratic quarter of elegant mansions (Place des Vosges); Bois de Boulogne, the largest park in Paris; Montmartre, centre of 19c bohemianism, with the Basilique Sacré-Coeur. The Church of St Denis is the first gothic church and the mausoleum of the French monarchy. Paris has three of the world's greatest art collections: The Louvre (to 19c, *Mona Lisa*), Musée d'Orsay (19–20c) and National Modern Art Museum in the Pompidou Centre. Other major museums include: Orangery Museum; Paris Museum of Modern Art; Rodin Museum; Picasso Museum. Notable cemeteries with graves of the famous: Père-Lachaise, Montmartre, Montparnasse. Near Paris are the royal residences of Fontainebleau and Versailles. www.parisinfo.com **90 C2**

## Pyrenees

Beautiful unspoiled mountain range. Towns include: delightful sea resorts of St-Jean-de-Luz and Biarritz; Pau, with access to the Pyrenees National Park; pilgrimage centre Lourdes. www.pyrenees-online.fr **144–145**

## Reims

Together with nearby Epernay, the centre of champagne production. The 13c Gothic cathedral is one of the greatest architectural achievements in France (stained glass by Chagall). Other sights: Palais du Tau with cathedral sculpture, 11c Basilica of St Rémi; cellars on Place St-Niçaise and Place des Droits-des-Hommes. www.reims-tourisme.com **91 B4**

## Rouen

Old centre with many half-timbered houses and 12–13c Gothic cathedral and the Gothic Church of St Maclou with its fascinating remains of a dance macabre on the former cemetery of Aître St-Maclou. The Fine Arts Museum has a good collection. www.rouentourisme.com **89 A5**

## St-Malo

Fortified town (much rebuilt) in a fine coastal setting. There is a magnificent boat trip along the river Rance to Dinan, a splendid well-preserved medieval town. www.saint-malo-tourisme.com **101 A3**

## Strasbourg

Town whose historic centre includes a well-preserved quarter of medieval half-timbered Alsatian houses, many of them set on the canal. The cathedral is one of the best in France. The Palais Rohan contains several museums. www.otstrasbourg.fr **93 C3**

## Toulouse

Medieval university town characterised by flat pink brick (Hôtel Assézat). The Basilique St Sernin, the largest Romanesque church in France, has many art treasures. Marvellous Church of the Jacobins holds the body of St Thomas Aquinas. www.toulouse-tourisme.com **129 C4**

## Tours

Historic town centred on Place Plumereau. Good collections in the Guilds Museum and Fine Arts Museum. www.tours-tourisme.fr **102 B2**

## Versailles

Vast royal palace built for Louis xiv, primarily by Mansart, set in large formal gardens with magnificent fountains. The extensive and much-imitated state apartments include the famous Hall of Mirrors and the exceptional Baroque chapel. www.chateauversailles.fr **90 C2**

## Vézère Valley Caves

A number of prehistoric sites, most notably the cave paintings of Lascaux (some 17,000 years old), now only seen in a duplicate cave, and the cave of Font de Gaume. The National Museum of Prehistory is in Les Eyzies. www.tourisme-vezere.com **129 B4**

## Germany Deutschland

www.germany.travel

### Northern Germany

## Aachen

Once capital of the Holy Roman Empire. Old town around the Münsterplatz with magnificent cathedral. An exceptionally rich treasure is in the Schatzkammer. The Town Hall is on the medieval Market. www.aachen.de **80 B2**

## Berlin

Capital of Germany. Sights include: the Kurfürstendamm avenue; Brandenburg Gate, former symbol of the division between East and West Germany; Tiergarten; Unter den Linden; 19c Reichstag. Berlin has many excellent art and history collections. Museum Island: Pergamon Musem (classical antiquity, Near and Far East, Islam; Bode Museum (sculpture, Byzantine art); Altes Museum (Greek and Roman);

New National Gallery (20th-c European); Old National Gallery (19th-c German); New Museum (Egyptian, prehistoric). Dahlem: Museum of Asian Art; Museum of European Cultures; Mueseum of Ethnology; Die Brücke Museum (German Expressionism). Tiergarten: Picture Gallery (old masters); Decorative Arts Museum (13–19c); New National Gallery (19–20c); Bauhaus Archive. Kreuzberg: Gropius Building with Jewish Museum and Berlin Gallery; remains of Berlin Wall and Checkpoint Charlie House. Unter den Linden: German Guggenheim (commissioned contemporary works). http://visitberlin.de **74 B2**

### Cologne Köln

Ancient city with 13–19c cathedral (rich display of art). In the old town are the Town Hall and many Romanesque churches (Gross St Martin, St Maria im Kapitol, St Maria im Lyskirchen, St Ursula, St Georg, St Severin, St Pantaleon, St Apostolen). Museums: Diocesan Museum (religious art); Roman-German Museum (ancient history); Wallraf-Richartz and Ludwig Museum (14–20c art). www.cologne.de **80 B2**

### Dresden

Historic centre with a rich display of Baroque architecture. Major buildings: Castle of the Electors of Saxony;

**Gothic cathedral, Cologne, Germany**

18c Hofkirche; Zwinger Palace with fountains and pavilions (excellent old masters); Albertinum with excellent Gallery of New Masters; treasury of Grünes Gewölbe. The Baroque-planned New Town contains the Japanese Palace and Schloss Pillnitz. www.dresden.de **84 A1**

### Frankfurt

Financial capital of Germany. The historic centre around the Römerberg Square has 13–15c cathedral, 15c Town Hall, Gothic St Nicholas Church, Saalhof (12c chapel). Museums: Museum of Modern Art (post-war); State Art Institute. www.frankfurt-tourismus.de **81 B4**

### Hamburg

Port city with many parks, lakes and canals. The Kunsthalle has Old Masters and 19-20c German art. Buildings: 19c Town Hall; Baroque St Michael's Church. www.hamburg-tourism.de **72 A3**

### Hildesheim

City of Romanesque architecture (much destroyed). Principal sights: St Michael's Church; cathedral (11c interior, sculptured doors, St Anne's Chapel); superb 15c Tempelhaus on the Market Place. **72 B2**

### Lübeck

Beautiful old town built on an island and characterised by Gothic brick architecture. Sights: 15c Holsten Gate; Market with the Town Hall and Gothic brick St Mary's Church; 12–13c cathedral; St Ann Museum. www.luebeck-tourism.de **65 C3**

### Mainz

The Electoral Palatinate schloss and Market fountain are Renaissance. Churches: 12c Romanesque cathedral; Gothic St Steven's (with stained glass by Marc Chagall). www.mainz.de **93 A4**

### Marburg

Medieval university town with the Market Place and Town Hall, St Elizabeth's Church (frescoes, statues, 13c shrine), 15–16c schloss. www.marburg.de **81 B4**

### Münster

Historic city with well-preserved Gothic and Renaissance buildings: 14c Town Hall; Romanesque-Gothic cathedral. The Westphalian Museum holds regional art. www.munster.de **71 C4**

### Potsdam

Beautiful Sanssouci Park contains several 18–19c buildings including: Schloss Sanssouci; Gallery (European masters); Orangery; New Palace; Chinese Teahouse. www.potsdam.de **74 B2**

### Rhein Valley Rheintal

Beautiful 80km gorge of the Rhein Valley between Mainz and Koblenz with rocks (Loreley), vineyards

(Bacharach, Rüdesheim), white medieval towns (Rhens, Oberwesel) and castles. Some castles are medieval (Marksburg, Rheinfles, island fortress Pfalzgrafenstein) others were built or rebuilt in the 19c (Stolzenfles, Rheinstein). **80 B3**

### Weimar

The Neoclassical schloss, once an important seat of government, now houses a good art collection. Church of SS Peter and Paul has a Cranach masterpiece. Houses of famous people: Goethe, Schiller, Liszt. The famous Bauhaus was founded at the School of Architecture and Engineering. www.weimar.de **82 B3**

## Southern Germany

### Alpine Road
Deutsche Alpenstrasse

German Alpine Road in the Bavarian Alps, from Lindau on Bodensee to Berchtesgaden. The setting for 19c fairy-tale follies of Ludwig II of Bavaria (Linderhof, Hohenschwangau, Neuschwanstein), charming old villages (Oberammergau) and Baroque churches (Weiss, Ottobeuren). Garmisch-Partenkirchen has views on Germany's highest peak, the Zugspitze. **108 B2**

### Augsburg

Attractive old city. The Town Hall is one of Germany's finest Renaissance buildings. Maximilianstrasse has several Renaissance houses and Rococo Schaezler Palace (good art collection). Churches: Romanesque-Gothic cathedral; Renaissance St Anne's Church. The Fuggerei, founded 1519 as an estate for the poor, is still in use. www.augsburg.de **94 C2**

### Bamberg

Well-preserved medieval town. The island, connected by two bridges, has the Town Hall and views of Klein Venedig. Romanesque-Gothic cathedral (good art) is on an exceptional square of Gothic, Renaissance and Baroque buildings – Alte Hofhalttung; Neue Residenz with State Gallery (German masters); Ratstube. **94 B2**

### Black Forest Schwarzwald

Hilly region between Basel and Karlsruhe, the largest and most picturesque woodland in Germany, with the highest summit, Feldberg, lake resorts (Titisee), health resorts (Baden-Baden) and clock craft (Triberg). Freiburg is the regional capital. www.schwarzwald.de **93 C4**

### Freiburg

Old university town with system of streams running through the streets. The Gothic Minster is surrounded by the town's finest buildings. Two towers remain of the medieval walls. The Augustine Museum has a good collection. www.freiburg.de **106 B2**

## Heidelberg

Germany's oldest university town, majestically set on the banks of the river and romantically dominated by the ruined schloss. The Gothic Church of the Holy Spirit is on the Market Place with the Baroque Town Hall. Other sights include the 16c Knight's House and the Baroque Morass Palace with the Museum of the Palatinate.
www.heidelberg-marketing.de **93 B4**

## Lake Constance Bodensee

Lake Constance, with many pleasant lake resorts. Lindau, on an island, has numerous gabled houses. Birnau has an 18c Rococo church. Konstanz (Swiss side) has the Minster set above the Old Town. www.bodensee.eu **107 B4**

## Munich München

Old town centred on the Marienplatz with 15c Old Town Hall and 19c New Town Hall. Many richly decorated churches: St Peter's (14c tower); Gothic red-brick cathedral; Renaissance St Michael's (royal portraits on the façade); Rococo St Asam's. The Residenz palace consists of seven splendid buildings holding many art objects. Schloss Nymphenburg has a palace, park, botanical gardens and four beautiful pavilions. Superb museums: Old Gallery (old masters), New Gallery (18–19c), Lenbachhaus (modern German). Many famous beer gardens.
www.muenchen.de **108 A2**

## Nuremberg Nürnberg

Beautiful medieval walled city dominated by the 12c Kaiserburg. Romanesque-Gothic St Sebaldus Church and Gothic St Laurence Church are rich in art. On Hauptmarkt is the famous 14c Schöner Brunnen. Also notable is 15c Dürer House. The German National Museum has excellent German medieval and Renaissance art.
www.nuernberg.de/internet/portal_e **94 B3**

## Regensburg

Medieval city set majestically on the Danube. Views from 12c Steinerne Brücke. Churches: Gothic cathedral; Romanesque St Jacob's; Gothic St Blaisius; Baroque St Emmeram. Other sights: Old Town Hall (museum); Haidplatz; Schloss Thurn und Taxis; State Museum. www.regensburg.de **95 B4**

## Romantic Road
### Romantische Strasse

Romantic route between Aschaffenburg and Füssen, leading through picturesque towns and villages of medieval Germany. The most popular section is the section between Würzburg and Augsburg, centred on Rothenburg ob der Tauber. Also notable are Nördlingen, Harburg Castle, Dinkelsbühl, Creglingen.
www.romantischestrasse.de **94 B2**

## Rothenburg ob der Tauber

Attractive medieval walled town with tall gabled and half-timbered houses on narrow cobbled streets. The Market Place has Gothic-Renaissance Town Hall, Rattrinke-stubbe and Gothic St Jacob's Church (altarpiece).
www.tourismus.rothenburg.de **94 B2**

## Speyer

The 11c cathedral is one of the largest and best Romanesque buildings in Germany. 12c Jewish Baths are well-preserved. **93 B4**

## Stuttgart

Largely modern city with old centre around the Old Schloss, Renaissance Alte Kanzlei, 15c Collegiate Church and Baroque New Schloss. Museums: Regional Museum; Old and New State Galleries. The 1930s Weissenhofsiedlung is by several famous architects.
www.stuttgart.de **94 C1**

## Trier

Superb Roman monuments: Porta Nigra; Aula Palatina (now a church); Imperial Baths; amphitheatre. The Regional Museum has Roman artefacts. Also, Gothic Church of Our Lady; Romanesque cathedral.
www.trier-info.de **92 B2**

## Ulm

Old town with half-timbered gabled houses set on a canal. Gothic 14–19c minster has tallest spire in the world (161m). www.tourismus.ulm.de **94 C1**

## Würzburg

Set among vineyard hills, the medieval town is centred on the Market Place with the Rococo House of the Falcon. The 18c episcopal princes' residence (frescoes) is magnificent. The cathedral is rich in art. Work of the great local Gothic sculptor, Riemenschneider, is in Gothic St Mary's Chapel, Baroque New Minster, and the Mainfränkisches Museum.
www.wuerzburg.de/en/index.html **94 B1**

# Greece Ellas

www.visitgreece.gr

## Athens Athina

Capital of Greece. The Acropolis, with 5c bc sanctuary complex (Parthenon, Propylaia, Erechtheion, Temple of Athena Nike), is the greatest architectural achievement of antiquity in Europe. The Agora was a public meeting place in ancient Athens. Plaka has narrow streets and small Byzantine churches (Kapnikarea). The Olympeum was the largest temple in Greece. Also: Olympic Stadium; excellent collections of ancient artefacts (Museum of Cycladic and Ancient Greek Art; New Acropolis Museum; National Archeological Museum; Benaki Museum).
www.visitgreece.gr **185 B4**

## Corinth Korinthos

Ancient Corinth (ruins), with 5c bc Temple of Apollo, was in 44 bc made capital of Roman Greece by Julius Caesar. Set above the city, the Greek-built acropolis hill of Acrocorinth became the Roman and Byzantine citadel (ruins). **184 B3**

## Crete Kriti

Largest Greek island, Crete was home to the great Minoan civilization (2800–1100 bc). The main relics are the ruined Palace of Knossos and Malia. Gortys was capital of the Roman province. Picturesque Rethimno has narrow medieval streets, a Venetian fortress and a former Turkish mosque. Matala has beautiful beaches and famous caves cut into cliffs. Iraklio (Heraklion), the capital, has a good Archeological Museum. **185 D6**

## Delphi

At the foot of the Mount Parnassos, Delphi was the seat of the Delphic Oracle of Apollo, the most important oracle in Ancient Greece. Delphi was also a political meeting place and the site of the Pythian Games. The Sanctuary of Apollo consists of: Temple of Apollo, led to by the Sacred Way; Theatre; Stadium. The museum has a display of objects from the site (5c bc Charioteer). www.delphi.gr **182 E4**

## Epidavros

Formerly a spa and religious centre focused on the Sanctuary of Asclepius (ruins). The enormous 4c bc theatre is probably the finest of all ancient theatres. www.ancientepidavros.com **184 B4**

## Greek Islands

Popular islands with some of the most beautiful and spectacular beaches in Europe. The many islands are divided into various groups and individual islands: The major groups are the Kiklades and Dodekanisa in the Aegean Sea, the largest islands are Kerkyra (Corfu) in the Ionian Sea and Kriti. **182–185 & 188**

## Meteora

The tops of bizarre vertical cylinders of rock and towering cliffs are the setting for 14c Cenobitic monasteries, until recently only accessible by baskets or removable ladders. Mega Meteoro is the grandest and set on the highest point. Roussánou has the most extraordinary site. Varlaám is one of the oldest and most beautiful, with the Ascent Tower and 16c church with frescoes. Aghiou Nikolaou also has good frescoes.
www.meteora-greece.com **182 D3**

## Mistras

Set in a beautiful landscape, Mistras is the site of a Byzantine city, now in ruins, with palaces, frescoed churches, monasteries and houses. **184 B3**

## Mount Olympus
### Oros Olymbos

Mount Olympus, mythical seat of the Greek gods, is the highest, most dramatic peak in Greece. **182 C4**

## Mycenae Mikines

The citadel of Mycenae prospered between 1950 bc and 1100 bc and consists of the royal complex of Agamemnon: Lion Gate, royal burial site, Royal Palace, South House, Great Court. **184 B3**

## Olympia

In a stunning setting, the Panhellenic Games were held here for a millennium. Ruins of the sanctuary of Olympia consist of the Doric temples of Zeus and Hera and the vast Stadium. There is also a museum (4c bc figure of Hermes). **184 B2**

## Rhodes

One of the most attractive islands with wonderful sandy beaches. The city of Rhodes has a well-preserved medieval centre with the Palace of the Grand Masters and the Turkish Süleymaniye Mosque www.rhodestravels.com **188 C2**

## Salonica Thessaloniki

Largely modern city with Byzantine walls and many fine churches: 8c Aghia Sofia; 11c Panaghia Halkeo; 14c Dodeka Apostoli; 14c Aghios Nikolaos Orfanos; 5c Aghios Dimitrios (largest in Greece, 7c Mosaics). **183 C5**

# Hungary Magyarország

http://itthon.hu

## Balaton

The 'Hungarian sea', famous for its holiday resorts: Balatonfüred, Tihany, Badasconytomaj, Keszthely.
http://gotohungary.com **111 C4**

## Budapest

Capital of Hungary on River Danube, with historic area centring on the Castle Hill of Buda district. Sights include: Matthias church; Pest district with late 19c architecture, centred on Ferenciek tere; neo-Gothic Parliament Building on river; Millennium Monument. The Royal Castle houses a number of museums: Hungarian National Gallery, Budapest History Museum; Ludwig Collection. Other museums: National Museum of Fine Arts (excellent Old and Modern masters); Hungarian National Museum (Hungarian history). Famous for public thermal baths: Király and Rudas baths, both made under Turkish rule; Gellért baths, the most visited.
www.budapestinfo.hu **112 B3**

## Esztergom

Medieval capital of Hungary set in scenic landscape. Sights: Hungary's largest basilica (completed 1856); royal palace ruins. www.esztergom.hu **112 B2**

## Pécs

Attractive old town with Europe's fifth oldest university (founded 1367). Famous for Turkish architecture

(Mosque of Gazi Kasim Pasha, Jakovali Hassan Mosque).
http://varoslako.pecs.hu **125 A4**

## Sopron

Beautiful walled town with many Gothic and Renaissance houses. Nearby: Fertöd with the marvellous Eszergázy Palace.
http://portal.sopron.hu **111 B3**

## Ireland

www.discoverireland.com

### Aran Islands

Islands with spectacular cliffs and notable pre-Christian and Christian sights, especially on Inishmore.
www.aranislands.ie **26 B2**

### Cashel

Town dominated by the Rock of Cashel (61m) topped by ecclesiastical ruins including 13c cathedral; 15c Halls of the Vicars; beautiful Romanesque 12c Cormac's Chapel (fine carvings). www.cashel.ie **29 B4**

### Connemara

Beautiful wild landscape of mountains, lakes, peninsulas and beaches. Clifden is the capital.
www.connemara.net **28 A1**

### Cork

Pleasant city with its centre along St Patrick's Street and Grand Parade lined with fine 18c buildings. Churches: Georgian St Anne's Shandon (bell tower); 19c cathedral.
www.corktourist.com **29 C3**

### County Donegal

Rich scenic landscape of mystical lakes and glens and seascape of cliffs (Slieve League cliffs are the highest in Europe). The town of Donegal has a finely preserved Jacobean castle.
www.govisitdonegal.com **26 B2**

### Dublin

Capital of Ireland. City of elegant 18c neoclassical and Georgian architecture with gardens and parks (St Stephen's Green, Merrion Square with Leinster House – now seat of Irish parliament). City's main landmark, Trinity College (founded 1591), houses in its Old Library fine Irish manuscripts (7c Book of Durrow, 8c Book of Kells). Two Norman cathedrals: Christ Church; St Patrick's. Other buildings: originally medieval Dublin Castle with State Apartments; James Gandon's masterpieces: Custom House; Four Courts. Museums: National Museum (archaeology, decorative arts, natural history); National Gallery (old masters, Impressionists); Museum of Modern Art; Dublin Writers' Museum.
www.visitdublin.com **30 A2**

### Glendalough

Impressive ruins of an important early Celtic (6c) monastery with 9c cathedral, 12c St Kevin's Cross, oratory of St Kevin's Church. www.glendalough.ie **30 A2**

### Kilkenny

Charming medieval town, with narrow streets dominated by 12c castle (restored 19c). The 13c Gothic cathedral has notable tomb monuments.
www.kilkennytourism.ie **30 B1**

### Newgrange

Part of a complex that also includes the sites of Knowth, Dowth, Fourknocks, Loughcrew and Tara, Newgrange is one of the best passage graves in Europe, the massive 4500-year-old tomb has stones richly decorated with patterns.
www.knowth.com/newgrange.htm **30 A2**

### Ring of Kerry

Route around the Iveragh peninsula with beautiful lakes (Lough Leane), peaks overlooking the coastline and islands (Valencia Island, Skelling). Also: Killarney; ruins of 15c Muckross Abbey.
www.ringofkerrytourism.com **29 B2**

## Italy Italia

www.italia.it

### Northern Italy

### Alps

Wonderful stretch of the Alps running from the Swiss and French borders to Austria. The region of Valle d'Aosta is one of the most popular ski regions, bordered by the highest peaks of the Alps. www.thealps.com **108–109 & 119–120**

### Arezzo

Beautiful old town set on a hill dominated by 13c cathedral. Piazza Grande is surrounded by medieval and Renaissance palaces. Main sight: Piero della Francesca's frescoes in the choir of San Francesco.
www.arezzocitta.com **135 B4**

### Assisi

Hill-top town that attracts crowds of pilgrims to the shrine of St Francis of Assisi at the Basilica di San Francesco, consisting of two churches, Lower and Upper, with superb frescoes.
www.assisionline.com **136 B1**

### Bologna

Elegant city with oldest university in Italy. Historical centre around Piazza Maggiore and Piazza del Nettuno with the Town Hall, Palazzo del Podestà, Basilica di San Petronio. Other churches: San Domenico; San Giacomo Maggiore. The two towers (one incomplete) are symbols of the city. Good collection in the National Gallery (Bolognese).
www.bolognawelcome.com **135 A4**

## Italy Italia

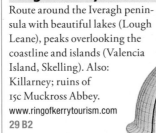

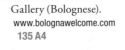

▲ Il Redentore (cutaway), Venice, Italy

### Dolomites Dolomiti

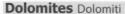

Part of the Alps, this mountain range spreads over the region of Trentino-Alto Adige, with the most picturesque scenery between Bolzano and Cortina d'Ampezzo. www.dolomiti.it **121 A4**

### Ferrara

Old town centre around Romanesque-Gothic cathedral and Palazzo Communale. Also: Castello Estense; Palazzo Schifanoia (frescoes); Palazzo dei Diamanti housing Pinacoteca Nazionale. www.ferraraterraeacqua.it **121 C4**

### Florence Firenze

City with exceptionally rich medieval and Renaissance heritage. Piazza del Duomo has: 13–15c cathedral (first dome since antiquity); 14c campanile; 11c baptistry (bronze doors). Piazza della Signoria has: 14c Palazzo Vecchio (frescoes); Loggia della Signoria (sculpture); 16c Uffizi Gallery with one of the world's greatest collections (13–18c). Other great paintings: Museo di San Marco; Palatine Gallery in 15–16c Pitti Palace surrounded by Boboli Gardens. Sculpture: Cathedral Works Museum; Bargello Museum; Academy Gallery (Michelangelo's *David*). Among many other Renaissance palaces: Medici-Riccardi; Rucellai; Strozzi. The 15c church of San Lorenzo has Michelangelo's tombs of the Medici. Many churches have richly frescoed chapels: Santa Maria Novella, Santa Croce, Santa Maria del Carmine. The 13c Ponte Vecchio is one of the most famous sights. www.firenzeturismo.it **135 B4**

### Italian Lakes

Beautiful district at the foot of the Alps, most of the lakes with holiday resorts. Many lakes are surrounded by aristocratic villas (Maggiore, Como, Garda). **120–121**

### Mantua Mántova

Attractive city surrounded by three lakes. Two exceptional palaces: Palazzo Ducale (Sala del Pisanello; Camera degli Sposi, Castello San Giorgio); luxurious Palazzo Tè (brilliant frescoes). Also: 15c Church of Sant'Andrea; 13c law courts. **121 B3**

### Milan Milano

Modern city, Italy's fashion and design capital (Corso and Galleria Vittoro Emmanuelle II). Churches include: Gothic cathedral (1386–1813), the world's largest (4c baptistry); Romanesque St Ambrose; 15c San Satiro; Santa Maria delle Grazie with Leonardo da Vinci's *Last Supper* in the convent refectory. Great art collections, Brera Gallery, Ambrosian Library, Museum of Modern Art. Castello Sforzesco (15c, 19c) also has a gallery. The famous La Scala opera house opened in 1778. Nearby: monastery at Pavia.
www.visitamilano.it/turismo **120 B2**

## Padua Pádova

Pleasant old town with arcaded streets. Basilica del Santo is a place of pilgrimage to the tomb of St Anthony. Giotto's frescoes in the Scrovegni chapel are exceptional. Also: Piazza dei Signori with Palazzo del Capitano; vast Palazzo della Ragione; church of the Eremitani (frescoes). www.turismopadova.it **121 B4**

## Parma

Attractive city centre, famous for Correggio's frescoes in the Romanesque cathedral and church of St John the Evangelist, and Parmigianino's frescoes in the church of Madonna della Steccata. Their works are also in the National Gallery. www.turismo.comune.parma.it **120 C3**

## Perúgia

Hill-top town centred around Piazza Quattro Novembre with the cathedral, Fontana Maggiore and Palazzo dei Priori. Also: Collegio di Cambio (frescoes); National Gallery of Umbria; many churches. www.perugiaonline.com **136 B1**

## Pisa

Medieval town centred on the Piazza dei Miracoli. Sights: famous Romanesque Leaning Tower, Romanesque cathedral (excellent façade, Gothic pulpit); 12–13c Baptistry; 13c Camposanto cloistered cemetery (fascinating 14c frescoes). www.turismo.pisa.it **134 B3**

## Ravenna

Ancient town with exceptionally well-preserved Byzantine mosaics. The finest are in 5c Mausoleo di Galla Placidia and 6c Basilica di San Vitale. Good mosaics also in the basilicas of Sant'Apollinare in Classe and Sant'Apollinare Nuovo. www.turismo.ravenna.it **135 A5**

▼ Romanesque cathedral, Pisa, Italy

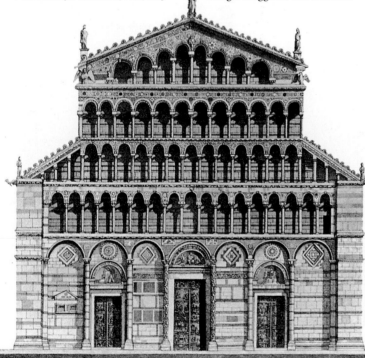

## Siena

Outstanding 13–14c medieval town centred on beautiful Piazza del Campo with Gothic Palazzo Publico (frescoes of secular life). Delightful Romanesque-Gothic Duomo (Libreria Piccolomini, baptistry, art works). Many other richly decorated churches. Fine Sienese painting in Pinacoteca Nazionale and Museo dell'Opera del Duomo. www.sienaonline.com **135 B4**

## Turin Torino

City centre has 17-18c Baroque layout dominated by twin Baroque churches. Also: 15c cathedral (holds Turin Shroud); Palazzo Reale; 18c Superga Basilica; Academy of Science with rich Egyptian Museum. www.comune.torino.it **119 B4**

## Urbino

Set in beautiful hilly landscape, Urbino's heritage is mainly due to the 15c court of Federico da Montefeltro at the magnificent Ducal Palace (notable Studiolo), now also a gallery. www.turismo.pesarourbino.it **136 B1**

## Venice Venezia

Stunning old city built on islands in a lagoon, with some 150 canals. The Grand Canal is crossed by the famous 16c Rialto Bridge and is lined with elegant palaces (Gothic Ca'd'Oro and Ca'Foscari, Renaissance Palazzo Grimani, Baroque Rezzonico). The district of San Marco has the core of the best known sights and is centred on Piazza San Marco with 11c Basilica di San Marco (bronze horses, 13c mosaics); Campanile (exceptional views) and Ducal Palace (connected with the prison by the famous Bridge of Sighs). Many churches (Santa Maria Gloriosa dei Frari, Santa Maria della Salute, Redentore, San Giorgio Maggiore, San Giovanni e Paolo) and scuole (Scuola di San Rocco, Scuola di San Giorgio degli Schiavoni) have excellent works of art. The Gallery of the Academy houses superb 14–18c Venetian art. The Guggenheim Museum holds 20c art. www.comune.venezia.it **122 B1**

## Verona

Old town with remains of 1c Roman Arena and medieval sights including the Palazzo degli Scaligeri; Arche Scaligere; Romanesque Santa Maria Antica; Castelvecchio; Ponte Scaliger. The famous 14c House of Juliet has associations with *Romeo and Juliet*. Many churches with fine art works (cathedral; Sant'Anastasia; basilica di San Zeno Maggiore). www.tourism.verona.it **121 B4**

## Vicenza

Beautiful town, famous for the architecture of Palladio, including the Olympic Theatre (extraordinary stage), Corso Palladio with many of his palaces, and Palazzo Chiericati. Nearby: Villa Rotonda, the most influential of all Palladian buildings. www.vicenzae.org **121 B4**

## Southern Italy

## Naples Napoli

Historical centre around Gothic cathedral (crypt). Spaccanapoli area has numerous churches (bizarre Cappella Sansevero, Gesù Nuovo, Gothic Santa Chiara with fabulous tombs). Buildings: 13c Castello Nuovo; 13c Castel dell'Ovo; 15c

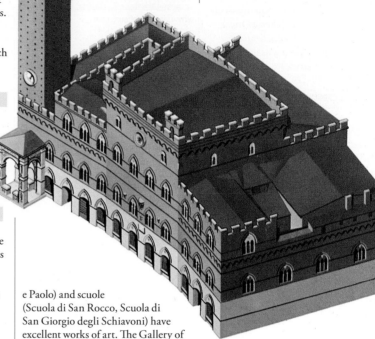

▼ Palazzo Publico, Siena, Italy

Palazzo Cuomo. Museums: National Archeological Museum (artefacts from Pompeii and Herculaneum); National Museum of Capodimonte (Renaissance painting). Nearby: spectacular coast around Amalfi; Pompeii; Herculaneum. www.inaples.it **170 C2**

## Orvieto

Medieval hill-top town with a number of monuments including the Romanesque-Gothic cathedral (façade, frescoes). www.inorvieto.it/en **168 A2**

## Rome Roma

Capital of Italy, exceptionally rich in sights from many eras. Ancient sights: Colosseum; Arch of Constantine; Trajan's Column; Roman and Imperial fora; hills of Palatino and Campidoglio (Capitoline Museum shows antiquities); Pantheon; Castel Sant' Angelo; Baths of Caracalla). Early Christian sights: catacombs (San Calisto, San Sebastiano, Domitilla); basilicas (San Giovanni in Laterano, Santa Maria Maggiore, San Paolo Fuori le Mura). Rome is known for richly decorated Baroque churches: il Gesù, Sant'Ignazio, Santa Maria della Vittoria, Chiesa Nuova. Other churches, often with art treasures: Romanesque Santa Maria in Cosmedin, Gothic Santa Maria Sopra Minerva, Renaissance Santa Maria del Popolo, San Pietro in Vincoli. Several Renaissance and Baroque palaces and villas house superb art collections (Palazzo Barberini, Palazzo Doria Pamphilj, Palazzo Spada, Palazzo Corsini, Villa Giulia, Galleria Borghese) and are beautifully frescoed (Villa Farnesina). Fine Baroque public spaces with fountains: Piazza Navona; Piazza di Spagna with the Spanish Steps; also Trevi Fountain. Nearby: Tivoli; Villa Adriana. Rome also contains the Vatican City (Città del Vaticano). www.turismoroma.it **168 B2**

## Volcanic Region

Region from Naples to Sicily. Mount Etna is one of the most famous European volcanoes. Vesuvius dominates the Bay of Naples and has at its foot two of Italy's finest Roman sites, Pompeii and Herculaneum, both destroyed by its eruption in 79 AD. Stromboli is one of the beautiful Aeolian Islands.

## Sardinia Sardegna

Sardinia has some of the most beautiful beaches in Italy (Alghero). Unique are the nuraghi, some 7000 stone constructions (Su Nuraxi, Serra Orios), the remains of an old civilization (1500–400 BC). Old towns include Cagliari and Sássari.
www.sardi.it **178–179**

## Sicily Sicilia

Surrounded by beautiful beaches and full of monuments of many periods, Sicily is the largest island in the Mediterranean. Taormina with its Greek theatre has one of the most spectacular beaches, lying under the mildly active volcano Mount Etna. Also: Agrigento; Palermo, Siracusa.
www.sicilytourism.com **176–177**

## Agrigento

Set on a hill above the sea and famed for the Valley of the Temples. The nine originally 5c bc Doric temples are Sicily's best-preserved Greek remains.
www.agrigento-sicilia.it **176 B2**

## Palermo

City with Moorish, Norman and Baroque architecture, especially around the main squares (Quattro Canti, Piazza Pretoria, Piazza Bellini). Sights: remains of Norman palace (12c Palatine Chapel); Norman cathedral; Regional Gallery (medieval); some 8000 preserved bodies in the catacombs of the Cappuchin Convent. Nearby: 12c Norman Duomo di Monreale.
www.palermotourism.com **176 A2**

## Syracuse Siracusa

Built on an island connected to the mainland by a bridge, the old town has a 7c cathedral, ruins of the Temple of Apollo; Fountain of Arethusa; archaeological museum. On the mainland: 5c BC Greek theatre with seats cut out of rock; Greek fortress of Euralus; 2c Roman amphitheatre; 5–6c Catacombs of St John. **177 B4**

## Latvia Latvija

www.latvia.travel/en

## Riga

Well-preserved medieval town centre around the cathedral. Sights: Riga Castle; medieval Hanseatic houses; Great Guild Hall; Gothic Church of St Peter; Art Nouveau buildings in the New Town. Nearby: Baroque Rundale Castle. www.riga.lv **8 D4**

## Lithuania Lietuva

http://lietuva.lt/en/tourism

## Vilnius

Baroque old town with fine architecture including: cathedral; Gediminas Tower; university complex; Archbishop's Palace; Church of St Anne. Also: remains of Jewish life; Vilnius Picture Gallery (16–19c regional); Lithuanian National Museum. www.vilnius.com **13 A6**

## Luxembourg

www.visitluxembourg.com

## Luxembourg

Capital of Luxembourg, built on a rock with fine views. Old town is around the Place d'Armes. Buildings: Grand Ducal Palace; fortifications of Rocher du Bock; cathedral. Museum of History and Art holds an excellent regional collection.
www.visitluxembourg.com **92 B2**

## Macedonia Makedonija

www.exploringmacedonia.com

## Ohrid

Old town, beautifully set by a lake, with houses of wood and brick, remains of a Turkish citadel, many churches (two cathedrals; St Naum south of the lake). www.ohrid.org.mk **182 B2**

## Skopje

Historic town with Turkish citadel, fine 15c mosques, oriental bazaar, ancient bridge. Superb Byzantine churches nearby.
www.skopjeonline.com.mk **182 A3**

## Malta

www.visitmalta.com

## Valletta

Capital of Malta. Historic walled city, founded in 16c by the Maltese Knights, with 16c Grand Master's Palace and a richly decorated cathedral. www.visitmalta.com **175 C3**

## Monaco

www.visitmonaco.com

## Monaco

Major resort area in a beautiful location. Sights include: Monte Carlo casino, Prince's Palace at Monaco-Ville; 19c cathedral; oceanographic museum. www.visitmonaco.com **133 B3**

## Netherlands Nederland

http://holland.com

## Amsterdam

Capital of the Netherlands. Old centre has picturesque canals lined with distinctive elegant 17–18c merchants' houses. Dam Square has 15c New Church and Royal Palace. Other churches include Westerkerk. The Museumplein has three world-famous museums: the newly restored Rijksmuseum (several art collections including 15–17c painting); Van Gogh Museum; Municipal Museum (art from 1850 on). Other museums: Anne Frank House; Jewish Historical Museum; Rembrandt House; Hermitage Museum (exhibitions). http://holland.com **70 B1**

## Delft

Well-preserved old Dutch town with gabled red-roofed houses along canals. Gothic churches: New Church; Old Church. Famous for Delftware (two museums). www.delft.nl **70 B1**

## Haarlem

Many medieval gabled houses centred on the Great Market with 14c Town Hall and 15c Church of St Bavon. Museums: Frans Hals Museum; Teylers Museum.
www.haarlemmarketing.co.uk **70 B1**

## The Hague Den Haag

Seat of Government and of the royal house of the Netherlands. The 17c Mauritshuis houses the Royal Picture Gallery (excellent 15–18c Flemish and Dutch). Other museums: Escher Museum; Meermanno Museum (books); Municipal Museum. Museum www.denhaag.nl **70 B1**

## Het Loo

Former royal palace and gardens set in a vast landscape (commissioned by future the future King and Queen of England, William and Mary).
www.paleishetloo.nl **70 B2**

## Keukenhof

In spring, landscaped gardens, planted with bulbs of many varieties, are the largest flower gardens in the world. www.keukenhof.nl **70 B1**

▼ Westerkerk, Amsterdam, Netherlands

## Leiden

University town of beautiful gabled houses set along canals. The Rijksmuseum Van Oudheden is Holland's most important home to archaeological artefacts from the Antiquity. The 16c Hortus Botanicus is one of the oldest botanical gardens in Europe. The Cloth Hall with van Leyden's *Last Judgement*.
http://leidenholland.com **70 B1**

## Rotterdam

The largest port in the world. The Boymans-van Beuningen Museum has a huge and excellent decorative and fine art collection (old and modern). Nearby: 18c Kinderdijk with 19 windmills. www.rotterdam.info **79 A4**

## Utrecht

Delightful old town centre along canals with the Netherlands' oldest university and Gothic cathedral. Good art collections: Central Museum; National Museum.
www.utrecht.nl **70 B2**

## Norway Norge

www.visitnorway.com

### Bergen
Norway's second city in a scenic setting. The Quay has many painted wooden medieval buildings. Sights: 12c Romanesque St Mary's Church; Bergenhus fortress with 13c Haakon's Hall; Rosenkrantz Tower; Grieghallen; Bergen Art Museum (Norwegian art); Bryggens Museum. www.visitbergen.com **46 B2**

### Lappland (Norwegian)
Vast land of Finnmark is home to the Sámi. Nordkapp is the northern point of Europe. Also Finland, Sweden. **192–193**

### Norwegian Fjords
Beautiful and majestic landscape of deep glacial valleys filled by the sea. The most thrilling fjords are between Bergen and Ålesund. www.fjords.com **46 & 198**

### Oslo
Capital of Norway with a modern centre. Buildings: 17c cathedral; 19c city hall, 19c royal palace; 19c Stortinget (housing parliament); 19c University; 13c Akershus (castle); 12c Akerskirke (church). Museums: National Gallery; Munch Museum; Viking Ship Museum; Folk Museum (reconstructed buildings). www.visitoslo.com **48 C2**

### Stavkirker
Wooden medieval stave churches of bizarre pyramidal structure, carved with images from Nordic mythology. Best preserved in southern Norway.

### Tromsø
Main arctic city of Norway with a university and two cathedrals. www.visittromso.no **192 C3**

### Trondheim
Set on the edge of a fjord, a modern city with the superb Nidaros cathedral (rebuilt 19c). Also: Stiftsgaard (royal residence); Applied Arts Museum. www.trondheim.com **199 B7**

## Poland Polska

www.poland.travel/en-gb

### Częstochowa
Centre of Polish Catholicism, with the 14c monastery of Jasna Góra a pilgrimage site to the icon of the Black Madonna for six centuries. www.jasnagora.pl **86 B3**

### Gdańsk
Medieval centre with: 14c Town Hall (state rooms); Gothic brick St Mary's Church, Poland's largest; Long Market has fine buildings (Artus Court); National Museum. **69 A3**

### Kraków
Old university city, rich in architecture, centred on superb 16c Marketplace with Gothic-Renaissance Cloth Hall containing the Art Gallery (19c Polish), Clock Tower, Gothic red-brick St Mary's Church (altarpiece). Czartoryski Palace has city's finest art collection. Wawel Hill has the Gothic cathedral and splendid Renaissance Royal Palace. The former Jewish ghetto in Kazimierz district has 16c Old Synagogue, now a museum. **99 A3**

### Poznań
Town centred on the Old Square with Renaissance Town Hall and Baroque mansions. Also: medieval castle; Gothic cathedral; National Museum (European masters). www.poznan.pl **76 B1**

### Tatry
One of Europe's most delightful mountain ranges with many beautiful ski resorts (Zakopane). Also in Slovakia. **99 B3**

### Warsaw Warszawa
Capital of Poland, with many historic monuments in the Old Town with the Royal Castle (museum) and Old Town Square surrounded by reconstructed 17–18c merchants' houses. Several churches including: Gothic cathedral; Baroque Church of the Nuns of Visitation. Richly decorated royal palaces and gardens: Neoclassical Łazienki Palace; Baroque palace in Wilanów. The National Museum has Polish and European art. www.um.warszawa.pl/en **77 C6**

### Wrocław
Historic town centred on the Market Square with 15c Town Hall and mansions. Churches: Baroque cathedral; St Elizabeth; St Adalbert. National Museum displays fine art. Vast painting of Battle of Racławice is specially housed. www.wroclaw.pl **85 A5**

## Portugal

www.visitportugal.com

### Alcobaça
Monastery of Santa Maria, one of the best examples of a Cistercian abbey, founded in 1147 (exterior 17–18c). The church is Portugal's largest (14c tombs). http://whc.unesco.org/en/list/505 **154 A1**

### Algarve
Modern seaside resorts among picturesque sandy beaches and rocky coves (Praia da Rocha). Old towns: Lagos; Faro. www.algarve-information.com **160 B1**

### Batalha
Abbey is one of the masterpieces of French Gothic and Manueline architecture (tombs, English Perpendicular chapel, unfinished pantheon). http://whc.unesco.org/en/list/264 **154 A2**

### Braga
Historic town with cathedral and large Archbishop's Palace. **148 A1**

### Coimbra
Old town with narrow streets set on a hill. The Romanesque cathedral is particularly fine (portal). The university (founded 1290) has a fascinating Baroque library. Also: Museum of Machado de Castro; many monasteries and convents. **148 B1**

### Évora
Centre of the town, surrounded by walls, has narrow streets of Moorish character and medieval and Renaissance architecture. Churches: 12–13c Gothic cathedral; São Francisco with a chapel decorated with bones of some 5000 monks; 15c Convent of Dos Lóis. The Jesuit university was founded in 1559. Museum of Évora holds fine art (particularly Flemish and Portugese). http://whc.unesco.org/en/list/361 **154 B3**

### Guimarães
Old town with a castle with seven towers on a vast keep. Churches: Romanesque chapel of São Miguel; São Francisco. Alberto Sampaio Museum and Martins Sarmento Museum are excellent. http://whc.unesco.org/en/list/1031 **148 A1**

### Lisbon Lisboa
Capital of Portugal. Baixa is the Neoclassical heart of Lisbon with the Praça do Comércio and Rossío squares. São Jorge castle (Visigothic, Moorish, Romanesque) is surrounded by the medieval quarters. Bairro Alto is famous for *fado* (songs). Monastery of Jerónimos is exceptional. Churches: 12c cathedral; São Vicente de Fora; São Roque (tiled chapels); Torre de Belém; Convento da Madre de Deus. Museums: Gulbenkian Museum (ancient, oriental, European), National Museum of Ancient Art; Design Museum; Modern Art Centre; Azulego Museum (decorative tiles). Nearby: palatial monastic complex Mafra; royal resort Sintra. www.visitlisboa.com **154 B1**

### Porto
Historic centre with narrow streets. Views from Clérigos Tower. Churches: São Francisco; cathedral. Soares dos Reis Museum holds fine and decorative arts (18–19c). The suburb of Vila Nova de Gaia is the centre for port wine. www.portoturismo.pt **148 A1**

### Tomar
Attractive town with the Convento de Cristo, founded in 1162 as the headquarters of the Knights Templar (Charola temple, chapter house, Renaissance cloisters). **154 A2**

## Romania

www.romaniatourism.com

### Bucovina
Beautiful region in northern Romanian Moldova renowned for a number of 15–16c monasteries and their fresco cycles. Of particular note are Moldovita, Voroneţ and Suceviţa. **17 B6**

### Bucharest Bucureşti
Capital of Romania with the majority of sites along the Calea Victoriei and centring on Piaţa Revoluţei with 19c Romanian Athenaeum and 1930s Royal Palace housing the National Art Gallery. The infamous 1980s Civic Centre with People's Palace is a symbol of dictatorial aggrandisement. www.romaniatourism.com/bucharest.html **17 C7**

### Carpathian Mountains Carpaţii
The beautiful Carpathian Mountains have several ski resorts (Sinaia) and peaks noted for first-rate mountaineering (Făgă raşuiui, Rodnei). Danube Delta Europe's largest marshland, a spectacular nature reserve. Travel in the area is by boat, with Tulcea the starting point for visitors. The Romanian Black Sea Coast has a stretch of resorts (Mamaia, Eforie) between Constantaţ and the border, and well-preserved Roman remains in Histria. **17 B6**

### Transylvania Transilvania
Beautiful and fascinating scenic region of medieval citadels (Timişoara, Sibiu) provides a setting for the haunting image of the legendary Dracula (Sighişoara, Braşov, Bran Castle). Cluj-Napoca is the main town. **17 B5**

## Russia Rossiya

www.russia-travel.com

### Moscow Moskva
Capital of Russia, with many monuments. Within the Kremlin's red walls are: 15c Cathedral of the Dormition; 16c Cathedral of the Archangel; Cathedral of the Annunciation (icons), Armour Palace. Outside the walls, Red Square has the Lenin Mausoleum and 16c St Basil's Cathedral. There are a number of monasteries (16c Novodevichi). Two superb museums: Tretiakov Art Gallery (Russian); Pushkin Museum of Fine Art (European). Kolomenskoe, once a royal summer retreat, has the Church of the Ascension. The VDNKh is a symbol of the Stalinist era. www.russia-travel.com **9 E10**

### Novgorod
One of Russia's oldest towns, centred on 15c Kremlin with St Sophia Cathedral (iconostasis, west door). Two other cathedrals: St Nicholas; St George. Museum of History, Architecture and Art has notable icons and other artefacts. http://visitnovgorod.com **9 C7**

### Petrodvorets
This is a grand palace with numerous pavilions (Monplaisir) set in beautiful parkland interwoven by a system of fountains, cascades and waterways connected to the sea. www.peterhofmuseum.ru **9 C6**

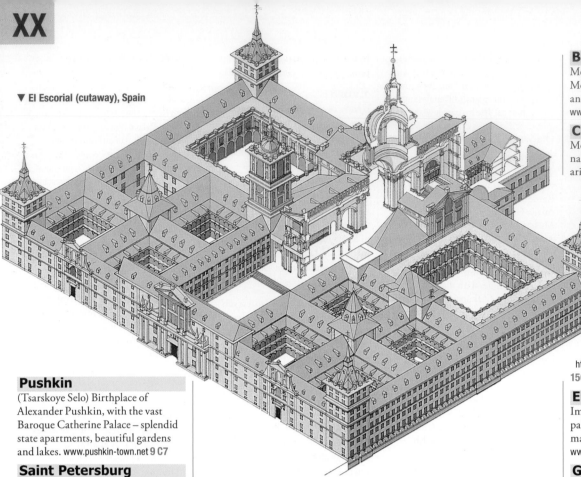

▼ El Escorial (cutaway), Spain

## Pushkin

(Tsarskoye Selo) Birthplace of Alexander Pushkin, with the vast Baroque Catherine Palace – splendid state apartments, beautiful gardens and lakes. www.pushkin-town.net **9 C7**

## Saint Petersburg
Sankt Peterburg

Founded in 1703 with the SS Peter and Paul Fortress and its cathedral by Peter the Great, and functioning as seat of court and government until 1918. Many of the most famous sights are around elegant Nevski Prospekt. The Hermitage, one of the world's largest and finest art collections is housed in several buildings including the Baroque Winter and Summer palaces. The Mikhailovsky Palace houses the Russian Museum (Russian art). Other sights: neoclassical Admiralty; 19c St Isaac's Cathedral and St Kazan Cathedral; Vasilievsky Island with 18c Menshikov Palace; Alexander Nevsky Monastery; 18c Smolny Convent. www.saint-petersburg.com **9 C7**

## Sergiev Posad

(Zagorsk) Trinity St Sergius monastery with 15c cathedral. **9 D11**

## Serbia Srbija

www.serbia.travel

## Belgrade Beograd

Capital of Serbia. The largely modern city is set between the Danube and Sava rivers. The National Museum holds European art. To the south there are numerous fascinating medieval monasteries, richly embellished with frescoes. www.beograd.rs **127 C2**

## Slovak Republic
Slovenska Republika

www.slovakia.travel

## Bratislava

Capital of Slovakia, dominated by the castle (Slovak National Museum, good views). Old Town centred on the Main Square with Old Town Hall

and Jesuit Church. Many 18–19c palaces (Mirbach Palace, Pálffy Palace, Primate's Palace), churches (Gothic cathedral, Corpus Christi Chapel) and museums (Slovak National Gallery). http://visit.bratislava.sk/en **111 A4**

## Košice

Charming old town with many Baroque and neoclassical buildings and Gothic cathedral. www.kosice.info **12 D4**

## Spišské Podhradie

Region, east of the Tatry, full of picturesque medieval towns (Levoča, Kežmarok, Prešov) and architectural monuments (Spišský Castle). **99 B4**

## Tatry

Beautiful mountain region. Poprad is an old town with 19c villas. Starý Smokovec is a popular ski resort. See also Poland. www.tatry.sk **99 B3**

## Slovenia Slovenija

www.slovenia.info

## Istria Istra

Two town centres, Koper and Piran, with medieval and Renaissance squares and Baroque palaces. See also Croatia. www.slovenia.info **122 B2**

## Julian Alps Julijske Alpe

Wonderfully scenic section of the Alps with lakes (Bled, Bohinj), deep valleys (Planica, Vrata) and ski resorts (Kranjska Gora, Bohinjska Bistrica). **122 A2**

## Karst Caves

Numerous caves with huge galleries, extraordinary stalactites and stalagmites, and underground rivers. The most spectacular are Postojna (the

most famous, with Predjamski Castle nearby) and Škocjan. www.postojna-cave.com **123 B3**

## Ljubljana

Capital of Slovenia. The old town, dominated by the castle (good views), is principally between Prešeren Square and Town Hall (15c, 18c), with the Three Bridges and colonnaded market. Many Baroque churches (cathedral, St Jacob, St Francis, Ursuline) and palaces (Bishop's Palace, Seminary, Gruber Palace). Also: 17c Križanke church and monastery complex; National Gallery and Modern Gallery show Slovene art. www.visitljubljana.si **123 A3**

## Spain España

www.spain.info

## Ávila

Medieval town with 2km-long 11c walls. Pilgrimage site to shrines to St Teresa of Ávila (Convent of Santa Teresa, Convent of the Incarnation). www.avila.com/avila_tourism **150 B3**

## Barcelona

Showcase of Gothic ('Barri Gòtic': cathedral; Santa María del Mar; mansions on Carrer de Montcada) and *modernista* architecture ('Eixample' area with Manzana de la Discòrdia; Sagrada Familia, Güell Park, La Pedrera). Many elegant boulevards (La Rambla, Passeig de Gràcia). Museums: Modern Catalan Art, Catalan Archaeology, Picasso Museum, Miró Museum, Tàpies Museum. Nearby: monastery of Montserrat (Madonna); Figueres (Dali Museum). www.barcelonaturisme.com **147 C3**

## Burgos

Medieval town with Gothic cathedral, Moorish-Gothic Royal Monastery and Charterhouse of Miraflores. www.turismoburgos.org **143 B3**

## Cáceres

Medieval town surrounded by originally Moorish walls and with several aristocratic palaces with solars. http://en.turismo.ayto-caceres.es **155 A4**

## Córdoba

Capital of Moorish Spain with a labyrinth of streets and houses with tile-decorated patios. The 8–10c Mezquita is the finest mosque in Spain. A 16c cathedral was added at the centre of the building and a 17c tower replaced the minaret. The old Jewish quarter has 14c synagogue http://english.turismodecordoba.org **156 C3**

## El Escorial

Immense Renaissance complex of palatial and monastic buildings and mausoleum of the Spanish monarchs. www.patrimonionacional.es **151 B3**

## Granada

The Alhambra was hill-top palace-fortress of the rulers of the last Moorish kingdom and is the most splendid example of Moorish art and architecture in Spain. The complex has three principal parts: Alcazaba fortress (11c); Casa Real palace (14c, with later Palace of Carlos V); Generalife gardens. Also: Moorish quarter; gypsy quarter; Royal Chapel with good art in the sacristy. www.turgranada.es **163 A4**

## León

Gothic cathedral has notable stained glass. Royal Pantheon commemorates early kings of Castile and León. www.leon.es **142 B1**

## Madrid

Capital of Spain, a mainly modern city with 17–19c architecture at its centre around Plaza Mayor. Sights: Royal Palace with lavish apartments; Descalzas Reales Convent (tapestries and other works); Royal Armoury museum. Spain's three leading galleries: Prado (15–18c); Queen Sofia Centre (20c Spanish, Picasso's *Guernica*); Thyssen-Bornemisza Museum (medieval to modern). www.esmadrid.com **151 B4**

## Oviedo

Gothic cathedral with 12c sanctuary. Three Visigoth (9c) churches: Santullano, Santa María del Naranco, San Miguel de Lillo. www.turismoviedo.es **141 A5**

## Palma

Situated on Mallorca, the largest and most beautiful of the Balearic islands, with an impressive Gothic cathedral. www.palmademallorca.es **166 B2**

## Picos de Europa

Mountain range with river gorges and peaks topped by Visigothic and Romanesque churches. **142 A2**

## Pyrenees

Unspoiled mountain range with beautiful landscape and villages full of Romanesque architecture (cathedral of Jaca). The Ordesa National Park has many waterfalls and canyons. **144–145**

## Salamanca

Delightful old city with some uniquely Spanish architecture: Renaissance Plateresque is famously seen on 16c portal of the university (founded 1215); Baroque Churrigueresque on 18c Plaza Mayor; both styles at the Convent of San Esteban. Also: Romanesque Old Cathedral; Gothic-Plateresque New Cathedral; House of Shells. www.salamanca.es **150 B2**

## Santiago di Compostela

Medieval city with many churches and religious institutions. The famous pilgrimage to the shrine of St James the Apostle ends here in the magnificent cathedral, originally Romanesque with many later elements (18c Baroque façade). www.santiagodecompostela.org **140 B2**

## Segovia

Old town set on a rock with a 1c Roman aqueduct. Also: 16c Gothic cathedral; Alcázar (14–15c, rebuilt 19c); 12-sided 13c Templar church of Vera Cruz. **151 B3**

## Seville Sevilla

City noted for festivals and flamenco. The world's largest Gothic cathedral (15c) retains the Orange Court and minaret of a mosque. The Alcazar is a fine example of Moorish architecture. The massive 18c tobacco factory, now part of the university, was the setting for Bizet's *Carmen*. Barrio de Santa Cruz is the old Jewish quarter with narrow streets and white houses. Casa de Pilatos (15–16c) has a fine domestic patio. The Museum of Fine Arts is in a former convent. Nearby: Roman Italica with amphitheatre. www.sevillatourist.com **162 A2**

## Tarragona

The city and its surroundings have some of the best-preserved Roman heritage in Spain. Also: Gothic cathedral; Archaeological Museum. www.tarragonaturisme.cat **147 C2**

## Toledo

Historic city with Moorish, Jewish and Christian sights. The small 11c mosque of El Cristo de la Luz is one of the earliest in Spain. Two synagogues have been preserved: Santa María la Blanca; El Tránsito. Churches: San Juan de los Reyes; Gothic cathedral (good artworks). El Greco's *Burial of the Count of Orgaz* is in the Church of Santo Tomé. More of his works are in the El Greco house and, with other art, in Hospital de Santa Cruz. **151 C3**

## Valencia

The old town has houses and palaces with elaborate façades. Also: Gothic cathedral and Lonja de la Seda church. www.turisvalencia.es **159 B3**

## Zaragoza

Town notable for Moorish architecture (11c Aljafería Palace). The Basilica de Nuestra Señora del Pilar, one of two cathedrals, is highly venerated www.zaragoza.es/turismo **153 A3**

## Sweden Sverige

www.visitsweden.com/sweden

## Abisko

Popular resort in the Swedish part of Lapland set in an inspiring landscape of lakes and mountains. www.abisko.nu **194 B9**

## Gothenburg Göteborg

Largest port in Sweden, the historic centre has 17–18c Dutch architectural character (Kronhuset). The Art Museum has interesting Swedish works. www.goteborg.com **60 B1**

## Gotland

Island with Sweden's most popular beach resorts (Ljugarn) and unspoiled countryside with churches in Baltic Gothic style (Dahlem, Bunge). Visby is a pleasant walled medieval town. www.gotland.info **57 C4**

## Lappland (Swedish)

Swedish part of Lappland with 18c Arvidsjaur the oldest preserved Sámi village. Jokkmokk is a Sámi cultural centre, Abisko a popular resort in fine scenery. Also Finland, Norway. www.kirunalapland.se **192–193**

## Lund

Charming university city with medieval centre and a fine 12c Romanesque cathedral (14c astronomical clock, carved tombs). www.lund.se **61 D3**

## Malmö

Old town centre set among canals and parks dominated by a red-brick castle (museums) and a vast market square with Town Hall and Gothic Church of St Peter. www.malmo.se/english **61 D3**

## Mora

Delightful village on the shores of Siljan Lake in the heart of the Dalarna region, home to folklore and traditional crafts. **50 A1**

## Stockholm

Capital of Sweden built on a number of islands. The Old Town is largely on three islands with 17–18c houses, Baroque Royal Castle (apartments and museums), Gothic cathedral, parliament. Riddarholms church has tombs of the monarchy. Museums include: National Museum; Modern Museum (one of world's best modern collections); Nordiska Museet (cultural history); open-air Skansen (Swedish houses). Baroque Drottningholm Castle is the residence of the monarchy. http://international.stockholm.se **57 A4**

▼ Château de Chillon, Switzerland

## Swedish Lakes

Beautiful region around the Vättern and Vänern Lakes. Siljan Lake is in the Dalarna region where folklore and crafts are preserved (Leksand, Mora, Rättvik). **55 B4**

## Uppsala

Appealing university town with a medieval centre around the massive Gothic cathedral. www.uppsala.se **51 C4**

## Switzerland Schweiz

www.myswitzerland.com

## Alps

The most popular Alpine region is the Berner Oberland with the town of Interlaken a starting point for exploring the large number of picturesque peaks (Jungfrau). The valleys of the Graubünden have famous ski resorts (Davos, St Moritz). Zermatt lies below the most recognizable Swiss peak, the Matterhorn. www.thealps.com **119 A4**

## Basle Basel

Medieval university town with Romanesque-Gothic cathedral (tomb of Erasmus). Superb collections: Art Museum; Museum of Contemporary Art. www.basel.com/en **106 B2**

## Bern

Capital of Switzerland. Medieval centre has fountains, characteristic streets (Spitalgasse) and tower-gates. The Bärengraben is famed for its bears. Also: Gothic cathedral; good Fine Arts Museum. www.berninfo.com **106 C2**

## Geneva Genève

The historic area is centred on the Romanesque cathedral and Place du Bourg du Four. Excellent collections: Art and History Museum; new Museum of Modern and Contemporary Art. On the lake shore: splendid medieval Château de Chillon. www.geneve-tourisme.ch **118 A3**

## Interlaken

Starting point for excursions to the most delightful part of the Swiss

Alps, the Bernese Oberland, with Grindelwald and Lauterbrunnen – one of the most thrilling valleys leading up to the ski resort of Wengen with views on the Jungfrau. www.interlaken.ch **106 C2**

## Lucerne Luzern

On the beautiful shores of Vierwaldstättersee, a charming medieval town of white houses on narrow streets and of wooden bridges (Kapellbrücke, Spreuerbrücke). It is centred on the Kornmarkt with the Renaissance Old Town Hall and Am Rhyn-Haus (Picasso collection). www.luzern.com **106 C1**

## Zürich

Set on Zürichsee, the old quarter is around Niederdorf with 15c cathedral. Gothic Fraumünster has stained glass by Chagall. Museums: Swiss National Museum (history); Art Museum (old and modern masters); Rietberg Museum (non-European cultures). www.zuerich.com **107 B3**

## Turkey Türkiye

www.gototurkey.co.uk

## Istanbul

Divided by the spectacular Bosphorus, the stretch of water that separates Europe from Asia, the historic district is surrounded by the Golden Horn, Sea of Marmara and the 5c wall of Theodosius. Major sights: 6c Byzantine church of St Sophia (converted first to a mosque in 1453 and then a museum in 1934); 15c Topkapi Palace; treasury and Archaeological Museum; 17c Blue Mosque; 19c Bazaar; 16c Süleymaniye Mosque; 12c Kariye Camii; European district with Galata Tower and 19c Dolmabahçe Palace. http://english.istanbul.com **186 A3**

## Ukraine Ukraina

www.ukraine.com

### Kiev Kyïv

Capital of Ukraine, known for its cathedral (11c, 17c) with Byzantine frescoes and mosaics. The Monastery of the Caves has churches, monastic buildings and catacombs.
www.kiev.info **13 C9**

## United Kingdom

www.visitbritain.com

## England

www.visitengland.com

### Bath

Elegant spa town with notable 18c architecture: Circus, Royal Crescent, Pulteney Bridge, Assembly Rooms; Pump Room. Also: well-preserved Roman baths; superb Perpendicular Gothic Bath Abbey. Nearby: Elizabethan Longleat House; exceptional 18c landscaped gardens at Stourhead. http://visitbath.co.uk **43 A4**

### Brighton

Resort with a sea-front of Georgian, Regency and Victorian buildings, Palace Pier and old town of narrow lanes. The main sight is the Oriental-style Royal Pavilion. Nearby: South Downs National Park.
www.brighton.co.uk **44 C3**

### Bristol

Old port city with the fascinating Floating Harbour. Major sights include Gothic 13–14c Church of St Mary Redcliffe and Brunel's Clifton Suspension Bridge.
http://visitbristol.co.uk **43 A4**

### Cambridge

City with university founded in the early 13c. Peterhouse (1284) is the oldest college. Most famous colleges were founded in 14–16c: Queen's, King's (with the superb Perpendicular Gothic 15–16c King's College Chapel), St John's (with famous 19c Bridge of Sighs), Trinity, Clare, Gonville and Caius, Magdalene. Museums: excellent Fitzwilliam Museum (classical, medieval, old masters). Kettle's Yard (20c British).
www.visitcambridge.org **45 A4**

### Canterbury

Medieval city and old centre of Christianity. The Norman-Gothic cathedral has many sights and was a major medieval pilgrimage site (as related in Chaucer's *Canterbury Tales*). St Augustine, sent to convert the English in 597, founded St Augustine's Abbey, now in ruins.
www.canterbury.co.uk **45 B5**

### Chatsworth

One of the richest aristocratic country houses in England (largely 17c) set in a large landscaped park. The palatial interior has some 175 richly furnished rooms and a major art collection.
www.chatsworth.org **40 B2**

### Chester

Charming medieval city with complete walls. The Norman-Gothic cathedral has several abbey buildings.
www.visitchester.com **38 A4**

### Cornish Coast

Scenic landscape of cliffs and sandy beaches with picturesque villages (Fowey, Mevagissey). St Ives has the Tate Gallery with work of the St Ives Group. St Michael's Mount is reached by causeway at low tide.
www.visitcornwall.com **42 B1**

### Dartmoor

Beautiful wilderness area in Devon with tors and its own breed of wild pony as well as free-ranging cattle and sheep.
www.dartmoor-npa.gov.uk **42 B3**

### Durham

Historic city with England's finest Norman cathedral and a castle, both placed majestically on a rock above the river. www.thisisdurham.com **37 B5**

### Eden Project

Centre showing the diversity of plant life on the planet, built in a disused clay pit. Two biomes, one with Mediterranean and Southern African focus and the larger featuring a waterfall, river and tropical trees plants and flowers. Outdoors also features plantations including bamboo and tea.
www.edenproject.com **42 B2**

### Hadrian's Wall

Built to protect the northernmost border of the Roman Empire in the 2c AD, the walls originally extended some 120km with castles every mile and 16 forts. Best-preserved walls around Hexam; forts at Housesteads and Chesters. www.hadrians-wall.org **37 A4**

### Lake District

Beautiful landscape of lakes (Windermere, Coniston) and England's high peaks (Scafell Pike, Skiddaw, Old Man), famous for its poets, particularly Wordsworth.
www.lakedistrict.gov.uk **36 B3**

### Leeds Castle

One of the oldest and most romantic English castles, standing in the middle of a lake. Most of the present appearance dates from 19c. www.leeds-castle.com **45 B4**

### Lincoln

Old city perched on a hill with narrow streets, majestically dominated by the Norman-Gothic cathedral and castle.
www.visitlincolnshire.com **40 B3**

### Liverpool

City on site of port founded in 1207 and focused around 1846 Albert Dock, now a heritage attraction. Croxteth Hall and Country Park; Speke Hall; Sudley House; Royal Liver Building; Liverpool Cathedral; Walker Art Gallery; Tate Liverpool; University of Liverpool Art Gallery.
www.visitliverpool.com **38 A4**

### London

Capital of UK and Europe's largest city. To the east of the medieval heart of the city – now the largely modern financial district and known as the City of London – is the Tower of London (11c White Tower, Crown Jewels) and 1880s Tower Bridge. The popular heart of the city and its entertainment is the West End, around Piccadilly Circus, Leicester Square and Trafalgar Square (Nelson's Column). Many sights of political and royal power: Whitehall (Banqueting House, 10 Downing Street, Horse Guards); Neo-Gothic Palace of Westminster (Houses of Parliament) with Big Ben; The Mall leading to Buckingham Palace (royal residence, famous ceremony of the Changing of the Guard). Numerous churches include: 13–16c Gothic Westminster Abbey (many tombs, Henry VII's Chapel); Wren's Baroque St Paul's Cathedral, St Mary-le-Bow, spire of St Bride's, St Stephen Walbrook. Museums of world fame: British Museum (prehistory, oriental and classical antiquity, medieval); Victoria and Albert Museum (decorative arts); National Gallery (old masters to 19c); National Portrait Gallery (historic and current British portraiture); Tate – Britain and Modern; Science Museum; Natural History Museum. Madame Tussaud's waxworks museum is hugely popular. Other sights include: London Eye, Kensington Palace; Greenwich with Old Royal Observatory (Greenwich meridian), Baroque Royal Naval College, Palladian Queen's House; Tudor Hampton Court Palace; Syon House. Nearby: Windsor Castle (art collection, St George's Chapel).
www.visitlondon.com **44 B3**

◄ Salisbury Cathedral, England

## Longleat

One of the earliest and finest Elizabethan palaces in England. The palace is richly decorated. Some of the grounds have been turned into a pleasure park, with the Safari Park, the first of its kind outside Africa. www.longleat.co.uk **43 A4**

## Manchester

Founded on a Roman settlement of 79 AD and a main player in the Industrial Revolution. Victorian Gothic Town Hall; Royal Exchange; Cathedral. Many museums including Imperial War Museum North, Lowry Centre and Manchester Art Gallery. www.visitmanchester.com **40 B1**

## Newcastle upon Tyne

A key player in the Industrial Revolution with 12th century cathedral and many museums as well as strong railway heritage. www.newcastlegateshead.com **37 B5**

## Norwich

Medieval quarter has half-timbered houses. 15c castle keep houses a museum and gallery. Many medieval churches include the Norman-Gothic cathedral. www.visitnorwich.co.uk **41 C5**

## Oxford

Old university city. Earliest colleges date from 13c: University College; Balliol; Merton. 14–16c colleges include: New College; Magdalen; Christ Church (perhaps the finest). Other buildings: Bodleian Library; Radcliffe Camera; Sheldonian Theatre; cathedral. Good museums: Ashmolean Museum (antiquity to 20c); Museum of the History of Science; Museum of Modern Art; Christ Church Picture Gallery

(14–17c). Nearby: outstanding 18c Blenheim Palace. www.visitoxfordandoxfordshire.com **44 B2**

## Petworth

House (17c) with one of the finest country-house art collections (old masters), set in a huge landscaped park. www.nationaltrust.org.uk **44 C3**

## Salisbury

Pleasant old city with a magnificent 13c cathedral built in an unusually unified Gothic style. Nearby: Wilton House. www.visitwiltshire.co.uk **44 B2**

## Stonehenge

Some 4000 years old, one of the most famous and haunting Neolithic monuments in Europe. Many other Neolithic sites are nearby. www.english-heritage.org.uk **44 B2**

## Stourhead

Early 18c palace famous for its grounds, one of the finest examples of neoclassical landscaped gardening, consisting of a lake surrounded by numerous temples. www.nationaltrust.org.uk **43 A4**

## Stratford-upon-Avon

Old town of Tudor and Jacobean half-timbered houses, famed as the birth and burial place of William Shakespeare and home of the Royal Shakespeare Company. www.shakespeare-country.co.uk **44 A2**

## Wells

Charming city with beautiful 12–16c cathedral (west facade, scissor arches, chapter house, medieval clock). Also Bishop's Palace; Vicar's Close. www.wellssomerset.com **43 A4**

## Winchester

Historic city with 11–16c cathedral. Also: 13c Great Hall, Winchester College, St Cross almshouses. Western gateway to the South Downs National Park. www.visitwinchester.co.uk **44 B2**

## York

Attractive medieval city surrounded by well-preserved walls with magnificent Gothic 13–15c Minster. Museums: York City Art Gallery (14–19c); Jorvik Viking Centre. Nearby: Castle Howard. www.visityork.org **40 B2**

### Northern Ireland
www.discovernorthernireland.com

## Antrim Coast

Spectacular coast with diverse scenery of glens (Glenarm, Glenariff), cliffs (Murlough Bay) and the famous Giant's Causeway, consisting of some 40,000 basalt columns. Carrickefergus Castle is the largest and best-preserved Norman castle in Ireland. www.causewaycoastandglens.com **27 A4**

## Belfast

Capital of Northern Ireland. Sights: Donegall Square with 18c Town Hall; neo-Romanesque Protestant cathedral; University Square; Ulster Museum (European painting). http://visit-belfast.com **27 B5**

## Giant's Causeway

Spectacular and unique rock formations in the North Antrim coast, formed by volcanic activity 50–60 million years ago. World Heritage Site. www.nationaltrust.org.uk **27 A4**

### Scotland
www.visitscotland.com

## Edinburgh

Capital of Scotland, built on volcanic hills. The medieval Old Town is dominated by the castle set high on a volcanic rock (Norman St Margaret's Chapel, state apartments, Crown Room). Holyrood House (15c and 17c) has lavishly decorated state apartments and the ruins of Holyrood Abbey (remains of Scottish monarchs). The 15c cathedral has the Crown Spire and Thistle Chapel. The New Town has good Georgian architecture (Charlotte Square, Georgian House). Excellent museums: Scottish National Portrait Gallery, National Gallery of Scotland; Scottish National Gallery of Modern Art. www.edinburgh.org **35 C4**

## Glamis Castle

In beautiful, almost flat landscaped grounds, 14c fortress, rebuilt 17c, gives a fairy-tale impression. www.strathmore-estates.co.uk **35 B5**

## Glasgow

Scotland's largest city, with centre around George Square and 13–15c Gothic cathedral. The Glasgow School of Art is the masterpiece of Charles Rennie Mackintosh. Fine art collections: Glasgow Museum and Art Gallery; Hunterian Gallery; Burrell Collection; Kelvingrove Art Gallery and Museum. www.visitscotland.com **35 C3**

## Loch Ness

In the heart of the Highlands, the lake forms part of the scenic Great Glen running from Inverness to Fort William. Famous as home of the fabled Loch Ness Monster (exhibition at Drumnadrochit). Nearby: ruins of 14–16c Urquhart Castle. www.lochness.com **32 D2**

### Wales
www.visitwales.com

## Caernarfon

Town dominated by a magnificent 13c castle, one of a series built by Edward I in Wales (others include Harlech, Conwy, Beaumaris, Caerphilly). www.visitcaernarfon.com **38 A2**

## Cardiff

Capital of Wales, most famous for its medieval castle, restored 19c in Greek, Gothic and Oriental styles. Also: National Museum and Gallery. www.visitcardiff.com **39 C3**

### Vatican City
www.vatican.va

## Vatican City
### Città del Vaticano

Independent state within Rome. On Piazza San Pietro is the 15–16c Renaissance-Baroque Basilica San Pietro (Michelangelo's dome and *Pietà*), the world's most important Roman Catholic church. The Vatican Palace contains the Vatican Museums with many fine art treasures including Michelangelo's frescoes in the Sistine Chapel. www.vatican.va **168 B2**

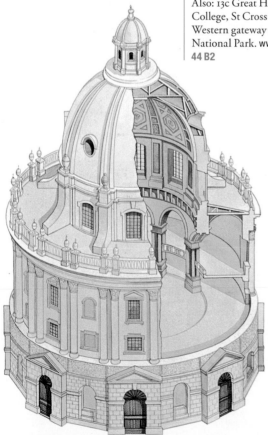

◀ Radcliffe Camera), Oxford, England

▼ The facade of Basilica San Pietro, Vatican City

# European politics and economics

## EUROPEAN UNION MEMBERSHIP

**1957** Founder members, Belgium, France, Italy, West Germany, Luxembourg, Netherlands

**1973** Denmark, Ireland, UK

**1981** Greece

**1986** Portugal, Spain

**1990** East Germany, following German reunification

**1995** Austria, Finland, Sweden

**2004** Czech Republic, Cyprus, Estonia, Hungary, Latvia, Lithuania, Malta, Poland, Slovakia, Slovenia

**2007** Bulgaria, Romania

**2013** Croatia

Future candidates for EU membership

Eurozone countries are outlined in yellow

## Albania Shqipëria

**Area** 28,748 km² (11,100 mi²)
**Population** 2,995,000
**Capital** Tirana / Tiranë (764,000)
**Languages** Albanian (official), Greek, Vlach, Romani and Slavic
**GDP** (2012) US$8,052
**Currency** Lek = 100 Quindars
**Government** multiparty republic
**Head of state** Bujar Nishani, 2012
**Head of government**
Prime Minister Edi Rama, Socialist Party, 2013
**Website** www.km.gov.al/?gj=gj2
**Events** In the 2005 general elections, the Democratic Party and its allies won a decisive victory on pledges of reducing crime and corruption, promoting economic growth and decreasing the size of government. The party retained power by a narrow margin in 2009, amid disputes over electoral procedure. After three years of talks, a Stabilisation and Association Agreement was signed with the EU in June 2006, and the country formally applied for membership in April 2009, the same month as it became a member of NATO. Protests at alleged official corruption and vote-rigging led to violent clashes in 2011. The Socialist Party won 53% of the vote in 2013 elections.
**Economy** Although economic growth has begun, Albania is still one of the poorest countries in Europe. 56% of the workforce are engaged in agriculture. Private ownership of land has been encouraged since 1991 and foreign investment is encouraged.

## Andorra
### Principat d'Andorra

**Area** 468 km² (181 mi²)
**Population** 86,000
**Capital** Andorra la Vella (22,884)
**Languages** Catalan (official), French, Castilian and Portuguese
**GDP** (2010) US$44,900
**Currency** Euro = 100 cents
**Government** independent state and co-principality

**Head of state** co-princes: Joan Enric Vives i Sicilia, Bishop of Urgell, 2003 and François Hollande (see France), 2012
**Head of government** Chief Executive Antoni Martí Petit, Democrats for Andorra, 2011
**Website** http://visitandorra.com
**Events** In 1993 a new democratic constitution was adopted that reduced the roles of the President of France and the Bishop of Urgell to constitutional figureheads. In 2010, the OECD removed Andorra from its list of uncooperative tax havens.
**Economy** About 80% of the work force are employed in the services sector, but tourism accounts for about 80% of GDP with an estimated 9 million visiting annually, attracted by its duty-free status and its summer and winter resorts. Agricultural production is limited (2% of the land is arable) and most food has to be imported. The principal livestock activity is sheep rearing. Manufacturing output consists mainly of cigarettes, cigars and furniture.

## Austria Österreich

**Area** 83,859 km² (32,377 mi²)
**Population** 8,414,000
**Capital** Vienna / Wien (2,419,000)
**Languages** German (official)
**GDP** (2012) US$42,409
**Currency** Euro – 100 cents
**Government** federal republic
**Head of state** President Heinz Fischer, 2004
**Head of government** Federal Chancellor Werner Faymann, Social Democratic Party, 2008
**Website** www.austria.gv.at
**Events** In general elections in 1999, the extreme right Freedom Party, under Jörg Haider, made gains at the expense of the Social Democrats. In July 2004 President Fischer's predecessor Thomas Klestil died of a heart attack one day before Heinz Fischer was due to take his place. The grand coalition between the Social Democrats collapsed in the summer of 2008, but after snap parliamentary elections in September, was reinstated in December, although with a reduced share of the vote. Far right parties gained 29% of the vote, 3% more than the People's Party. Austria

became a non-permanent member of the UN General Security Council in January 2009.
**Economy** Has a well-developed market economy and high standard of living. The economy grew marginally in 2012. The leading economic activities are the manufacture of metals and tourism. Dairy and livestock farming are the principal agricultural activities.

## Belarus

**Area** 207,600 km² (80,154 mi²)
**Population** 9,457,000
**Capital** Minsk (2,101,000)
**Languages** Belarusian, Russian (both official)
**GDP** (2012) US$15,633
**Currency** Belarussian ruble = 100 kopek
**Government** Republic
**Head of state**
President Alexander Lukashenko, 1994
**Head of government** Prime Minister Mikhail Myasnikovich, independent, 2010
**Website** www.belarus.by/en/government
**Events** Belarus attained its independence in 1991. As a result of a referendum in 1996 the president increased his power at the expense of parliament. In 1997, Belarus signed a Union Treaty committing it to political and economic integration with Russia. Since his election in July 1994 as the country's first president, Alexander Lukashenko, has steadily consolidated his power through authoritarian means. Government restrictions on freedom of speech, the press and religion continue and in early 2005, the US listed Belarus as an outpost of tyranny. Belarus joined the EU's Eastern Partnership in 2009. In 2010, it signed a customs union with Russia and Kazakhstan. Alexander Lukashenko was declared to have won a fourth term as president in December 2010 in elections, described internationally as flawed, which provoked protests. The arrests and beatings of opposition candidates and protesters led to EU sanctions, but clamp-downs on personal and political freedoms have continued.
**Economy** Belarus has faced problems in the transition to a free-market economy. After relaxation of currency rules in early 2011, the value of the ruble dropped sharply and the

country's large foreign debts and lack of hard currency led to negotiations with Russia over substantial loans. Agriculture, especially meat and dairy farming, is important. In 2011, the country was forced to apply to the IMF for funds and for a Russian-led bailout.

## Belgium Belgique

**Area** 30,528 km² (11,786 mi²)
**Population** 11,036,000
**Capital** Brussels/Bruxelles (1,830,000)
**Languages** Dutch, French, German (all official)
**GDP** (2012) US$37,883
**Currency** Euro = 100 cents
**Government** federal constitutional monarchy
**Head of state** Philippe I, 2013
**Head of government** Prime Minister Elio Di Rupo, Socialist Party, 2011
**Website** www.belgium.be/en
**Events** In 1993 Belgium adopted a federal system of government. Elections in June 2007 led to the Christian Democrats gaining almost 30% of the vote in Flanders. An uneasy coalition was eventually formed in March 2008, but negotiations for constitutional reform stalled. Former PM Leterme replaced Herman van Rompuy when the latter became President of the European Council. The coalition collapsed in April 2010. Elections in June resulted in gains for the pro-separatist New Flemish Alliance and the Socialist Party in Wallonia. Protracted negotiations about the exact make up of a coalition government , lasted until December 2011. Albert II abdicated in favour of his son Philippe in 2013.
**Economy** Belgium is a major trading nation with a modern, private-enterprise economy, which grew slightly in 2012. The leading activity is manufacturing i.e. steel and chemicals. With few natural resources, it imports substantial quantities of raw materials and export a large volume of manufactures.

## Bosnia-Herzegovina
### Bosna i Hercegovina

**Area** 51,197 km² (19,767 mi²)
**Population** 3,840,000
**Capital** Sarajevo (669,000)
**Languages** Bosnian/Croatian/Serbian
**GDP** (2012) 4,461
**Currency**
Convertible Marka = 100 convertible pfenniga
**Government** federal republic
**Head of state** Chairman of the Presidency – rotates between Presidency members Bakir Izetbegović (Party of Democratic Action), Željko Komšić (Social Democratic Party) and Nebojša Radmanović (Political party Alliance of Independent Social Democrats)
**Head of government** Prime Minister Vjekoslav Bevanda, Croatian Democratic Union of Bosnia and Herzegovina, 2012
**Website**
www.fbihvlada.gov.ba/english/index.php
**Events** In 1992 a referendum approved independence from the Yugoslav federation. The Bosnian Serb population was against independence and in the resulting war occupied over two-thirds of the land. Croat forces seized other parts of the area. The 1995 Dayton Peace Accord ended the war and set up the Bosnian Muslim/Croat Federation and the Bosnian Serb Republic, each with their own president, government, parliament, military and police. There is also a central Bosnian government and rotating presidency. The office of High Representative has the power to impose decisions where the authorities are unable to agree or where political or economic interests are affected; the current incumbent, Valentin Inzko took charge in 2009. EUFOR troops took over from the NATO-led force in 2004. In late 2005, agreement was reached to set up state-wide police defence and security forces, a state court and state taxation system, and the EU initiated its Stabilisation and Association Agreement with Bosnia in 2007. Application for full EU membership has been delayed. In December 2006 Bosnia joined NATO's Partnership for Peace programme and in April 2010 received its Membership Action Plan. Elections in 2010 resulted in a 14-month stalemate before a new government could be agreed.
**Economy** Excluding Macedonia, Bosnia was the least developed of the former republics of Yugoslavia. Currently receiving substantial aid, though this will be reduced. The country attracts considerable foreign direct investment and the Convertible Marka is Euro-pegged. Per capita GDP shrank in 2012.

## Bulgaria Bulgariya

**Area** 110,912 km² (42,822 mi²)
**Population** 7,365,000
**Capital** Sofia (1,302,000)
**Languages** Bulgarian (official), Turkish
**GDP** (2012) US$14,312
**Currency** Lev = 100 stotinki
**Government** multiparty republic
**Head of state** President Rosen Asenov Plevneliev, Citizens for European Development of Bulgaria GERB, 2012
**Head of government** Prime Minister Plamen Oresharski, independent, 2013
**Website** www.government.bg/fce/index.shtml?p=0023&s=001
**Events** In 1990 the first non-communist president for 40 years, Zhelyu Zhelev, was elected. A new constitution in 1991 saw the adoption of free-market reforms. Bulgaria joined NATO in 2004. The president was re-elected in 2006. Bulgaria joined the EU in January 2007, but lack of progress in tackling corruption has led to the delay, then scrapping of a large proportion of EU funding. The GERB-led coalition fell in early 2012 after street protests and was replaced in May 2013 by a technocratic government.
**Economy** The Lev has been pegged to the Euro since 2002 and the country may adopt the latter by 2012. The economy has begun to attract significant amounts of foreign direct investment. Bulgaria experienced macroeconomic stability and strong growth from 1996 to early 2008, and after a sharp decline in GDP in 2009, the economy returned to slight growth from 2010. Manufacturing is the leading economic activity but has outdated technology. The main products are chemicals, metals, machinery and textiles. The valleys of the Maritsa are ideal for winemaking, plums and tobacco. Tourism is increasing rapidly.

## Croatia Hrvatska

**Area** 56,538 km² (21,829 mi²)
**Population** 4,285,000
**Capital** Zagreb (1,212,000)
**Languages** Croatian
**GDP** (2011) US$18,191
**Currency** Kuna = 100 lipa
**Government** multiparty republic
**Head of state** President Ivo Josipović, SDP, 2010
**Head of government** Prime Minister Zoran Milanović, Social Democratic Party of Croatia (SDP), 2011.
**Website** www.vlada.hr/en
**Events** A 1991 referendum voted overwhelmingly in favour of independence from Yugoslavia. Serb-dominated areas took up arms to remain in the federation. Serbia armed Croatian Serbs, war broke out between Serbia and Croatia, and Croatia lost much territory. In 1992 United Nations peacekeeping troops were deployed. Following the Dayton Peace Accord of 1995, Croatia and Yugoslavia established diplomatic relations. An agreement between the Croatian government and Croatian Serbs provided for the eventual reintegration of Krajina into Croatia in 1998. PM Kosor leads a minority government with the support of many smaller parties, promising to continue the policies of her predecessor.Croatia applied for EU membership in 2003. Parliamentary elections in 2011 saw the centre-left return to power for the first time since 2003. After a referendum in January 2012, Croatia's accession to the EU was set for July 2013. The earliest date for accession is 2013. Croatia joined NATO in 2009 and the EU in July 2013.
**Economy** The wars badly disrupted Croatia's economy but it emerged from a mild recession in 2000, with tourism, banking and public investment leading the way. The economy continues to struggle and unemployment is high.

## Czech Republic Česka Republica

**Area** 78,864 km² (30,449 mi²)
**Population** 10,513,000
**Capital** Prague/Praha (2,300,000)
**Languages** Czech (official), Moravian
**GDP** (2012) US$27,190
**Currency** Czech Koruna = 100 haler
**Government** multiparty republic
**Head of state** President Milos Zeman, 2013
**Head of government** Prime Minister Petr Nečas (outgoing), Civic Democratic Party, 2010
**Website** www.vlada.cz/en/
**Events** In 1992 the government agreed to the secession of the Slovak Republic, and on 1 January 1993 the Czech Republic was created. The Czech Republic was granted full membership of NATO in 1999 and joined the EU in May 2004. Governments have been characterized by short-lived coalitions. PM Petr Nečas was forced to resign in June 2013 over allegations of corruption. His interim replacement, Jiří Rusnok, had a month to prepare for a statutory vote of no confidence.
**Economy** The country has deposits of coal, uranium, iron ore, tin and zinc. Industries include chemicals, beer, iron and steel. Private ownership of land is gradually being restored. Agriculture employs 12% of the workforce. Inflation is under control. Intensified restructuring among large enterprises, improvements in the financial sector and effective use of available EU funds served to strengthen output growth until the onset of the worldwide economic downturn, because of reduced exports. Prague is now a major tourist destination.

## Denmark Danmark

**Area** 43,094 km² (16,638 mi²)
**Population** 5,580,000
**Capital** Copenhagen/København (1,954,000)
**Languages** Danish (official)
**GDP** (2012) US$37,657
**Currency** Krone = 100 øre
**Government** parliamentary monarchy
**Head of state** Queen Margrethe II, 1972
**Head of government** Prime Minister Helle Thorning-Schmidt, Social Democrats, 2011.
**Website** www.denmark.dk/en
**Events** In 1992 Denmark rejected the Maastricht Treaty, but refersed the decision in a 1993 referendum. In 1998 the Amsterdam Treaty was ratified by a further referendum. In 2009 Greenland assumed responsibility for many domestic competencies. The government is a coalition formed by the Social Democrats, Danish Social Liberal Party and the Socialist People's Party, which narrowly beat the rightwing coalition led by Lars Lokke Rasmussen in 2011.
**Economy** Danes enjoy a high standard of living with a thoroughly modern market economy featuring high-tech agriculture, up-to-date small-scale and corporate industry, comfortable living standards and a stable currency, which is pegged to the Euro, but still independent. Economic growth gained momentum in 2004, but slowed in 2007. GDP grew slightly in 2012. Denmark is self-sufficient in oil and natural gas. Services, including tourism, form the largest sector (63% of GDP). Farming employs only 4% of the workforce but is highly productive. Fishing is also important.

## Estonia Eesti

**Area** 45,100 km² (17,413 mi²)
**Population** 1,287,000
**Capital** Tallinn (543,000)
**Languages** Estonian (official), Russian
**GDP** (2012) US$21,713
**Currency** Euro = 100 cents
**Government** multiparty republic
**Head of state** President Toomas Hendrik Ilves, 2006
**Head of government** Prime Minister Andrus Ansip, Reform Party 2005
**Website** http://valitsus.ee/en/government
**Events** In 1992 Estonia adopted a new constitution and multiparty elections were held. Estonia joined NATO in March 2004 and the EU in May 2004. In 2005 a treaty defining the border with Russia was signed, but Russia refused to ratify it after Estonia introduced a reference to the Russian occupation of Estonia. Parliamentary elections in 2007 resulted in Andrus Ansip retaining his position at the head of a coalition, a situation consolidated in 2011. Estonia joined the OECD in 2010 and adopted the Euro in January 2011. Manufactures include petrochemicals, fertilisers and textiles.Strict language laws are regarded by Russian-speakers as discriminatory.
**Economy** Privatisation and free-trade reforms have increased foreign investment and trade with the EU. Chief natural resources are oil shale and forests. The economy benefits from strong electronics and telecommunications sectors. The economy rebounded from the economic crisis in 2010, and growth was strong in 2011. Manufactures include petrochemicals, fertilisers and textiles. Growth continued in 2012.

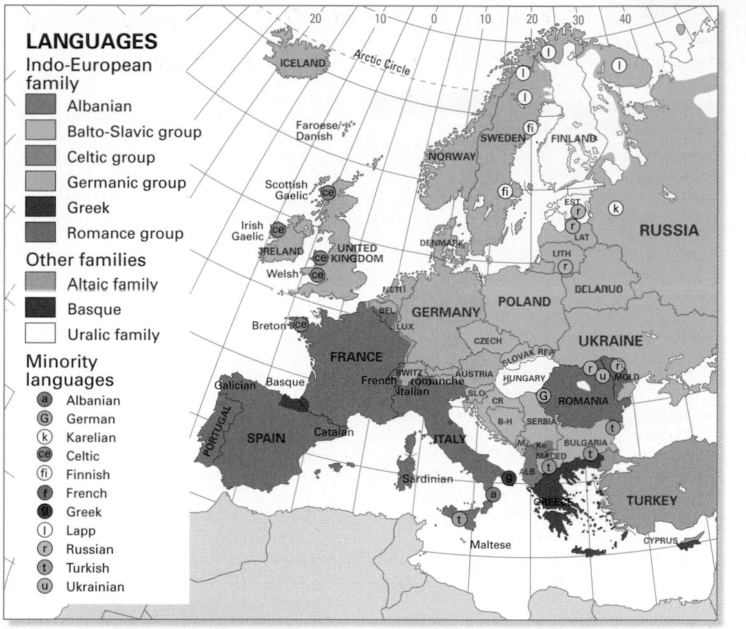

LANGUAGES
Indo-European family
Albanian
Balto-Slavic group
Celtic group
Germanic group
Greek
Romance group
Other families
Altaic family
Basque
Uralic family
Minority languages
Albanian
German
Karelian
Celtic
Finnish
French
Greek
Lapp
Russian
Turkish
Ukrainian
ICELAND
Arctic Circle
Faroese/Danish
NORWAY
SWEDEN
FINLAND
RUSSIA
Scottish Gaelic
Irish Gaelic
IRELAND
UNITED KINGDOM
Welsh
DENMARK
EST
LAT
LITH
NETH
BEL
LUX
GERMANY
POLAND
BELARUS
Breton
CZECH
SLOVAK REP
UKRAINE
FRANCE
SWITZ
French
Romanche
Italian
AUSTRIA
HUNGARY
MOLD
SLO
CR
B-H
SERBIA
ROMANIA
Galician
Basque
PORTUGAL
SPAIN
Catalan
ITALY
BULGARIA
MACED
ALB
Sardinian
GREECE
TURKEY
Maltese
CYPRUS


## Finland Suomi

**Area** 338,145 km² (130,557 mi²)
**Population** 5,422,000
**Capital** Helsinki (1,362,000)
**Languages** Finnish, Swedish (both official)
**GDP** (2012) US$36,395
**Currency** Euro = 100 cents
**Government** multiparty republic
**Head of state** President Sauli Niinistö, National Coalition Party, 2012
**Head of government** Prime Minister Jyrki Katainen, National Coalition Party, 2011
**Website** http://government.fi/etusivu/en.jsp
**Events** In 1986 Finland became a member of EFTA and in 1995 joined the EU. A new constitution was established in March 2000. The Finnish Parliament voted for the EU constitution in 2006. Successive governments have been in the form of multi-party coalitions. In the presidential election of 2012, Sauli Niinistö defeated Pekka-Haavisto of the Green Party.
**Economy** Forests are Finland's most valuable resource, with wood and paper products accounting for 35% of exports. Engineering, shipbuilding and textile industries have grown. Finland excels in high-tech exports and is a leading light in the telecoms industry. Farming employs 9% of the workforce. Unemployment remains high, although the economy returned to growth in 2011.

## France

**Area** 551,500 km² (212,934 mi²)
**Population** 65,350,000
**Capital** Paris (12,162,000)
**Languages** French (official), Breton, Occitan
**GDP** (2012) US$35,548
**Currency** Euro = 100 cents
**Government** multiparty republic
**Head of state** President François Hollande, Socialist Party. 2012
**Head of government** Prime Minister Jean-Marc Ayrault, Socialist Party, 2012
**Website** www.diplomatie.gouv.fr/en/
**Events** France was a founder member of both the EU and NATO. Its post-war governments have swung between socialist and centrist/right. Widespread dissatisfaction with François Sarkozy's austerity measures led to a return to' power for the Socialist Party in 2012.
**Economy** France is a leading industrial nation. Industries include chemicals and steel. It is the leading producer of farm products in western Europe. Livestock and dairy farming are vital sectors. The French economy was badly affected by the global financial turndown. In May 2013 it entered its second recession in four years. It is the world's second largest producer of cheese and wine. Tourism is a major industry.

## Germany Deutschland

**Area** 357,022 km² (137,846 mi²)
**Population** 80,328,000
**Capital** Berlin (6,000,000)
**Languages** German (official)
**GDP** (2012) US$39,028
**Currency** Euro = 100 cents
**Government** federal multiparty republic
**Head of state** President Joachim Gauck, independent, 2012
**Head of government** Chancellor Angela Merkel, Christian Democratic Union, 2005
**Website** www.bundesregierung.de
**Events** Germany is a major supporter of the European Union, and former chancellor Helmut Köhl was the driving force behind the creation of the Euro. The grand coalition government formed in 2005 between the CDU, CSU and Social Democrats was replaced by one of the CDU, CSU and FDP after elections in 2009. Repeated calls upon German funds in support of weaker Eurozone economies have caused widespread anger. In 2012, after Christian Wulff was forced to resign because of corruption charges the consensus candidate former Lutheran pastor and civil rights activist Joacham Glauk was elected president.
**Economy** Germany has long been one of the world's greatest economic powers. In 2010–12, it underwent strong, export-led growth. Services form the largest economic sector. Machinery and transport equipment account for 50% of exports. It is the world's third-largest car producer. Other major products include ships, iron, steel, petroleum and tyres. It has the world's second-largest lignite mining industry. Other minerals are copper, potash, lead, salt, zinc and aluminium. Germany is the world's second-largest producer of hops and beer, and fifth-largest of wine. Other products are cheese and milk, barley, rye and pork.

## Greece Ellas

**Area** 131,957 km² (50,948 mi²)
**Population** 10,815,000
**Capital** Athens / Athina (3,753,000)
**Languages** Greek (official)
**GDP** (2012) US$24,505
**Currency** Euro = 100 cents
**Government** multiparty republic
**Head of state** President Karolos Papoulias, Panhellenic Socialist Movement (PASOK), 2005
**Head of government** Prime Minister Antonis Samaris, New Democracy
**Website** www.primeminister.gr/english
**Events** In 1981 Greece joined the EU and Andreas Papandreous became Greece's first Socialist prime minister. His son was re-elected in 2009, but lost power in 2012 as a result of his handling of the economic crisis and the deep unpopularity of the austerity measures imposed by the Eurozone and IMF as a condition of bailout funds. After inconclusive election results, the president asked Antonis Samaris to form a government, resulting in continued uncertainty about Greece's remaining within the Eurozone. Strikes and protests continued through 2012 and 2013.
**Economy** Greece is one of the poorest members of the European Union. Manufacturing is important. Products: textiles, cement, chemicals, metallurgy. Minerals: lignite, bauxite, chromite. Farmland covers 33% of Greece, grazing land 40%. Major crops: tobacco, olives, grapes, cotton, wheat. Livestock are raised. Tourism provides 15% of GDP. Severely hit by the global turndown, from 2010 it was repeatedly in danger of defaulting on debt repayments, forcing

multiple bailouts by other Eurozone countries and the IMF and putting extreme pressure on the Euro. In 2013 the economy continued to contract rapidly.

## Hungary Magyarorszàg

**Area** 93,032 km² (35,919 mi²)
**Population** 9,938,000
**Capital** Budapest (3,285,000)
**Languages** Hungarian (official)
**GDP** (2012) US$19,637
**Currency** Forint = 100 filler
**Government** multiparty republic
**Head of state**
President János Áder, Fidesz, 2012.
**Head of government** Prime Minister
Viktor Orban, Fidesz, 2010
**Website** www.kormany.hu/en
**Events** In 1990 multiparty elections were held for the first time. In 1999 Hungary joined NATO and in 2004 it acceded to the EU. In 2012 attempts to change the electoral system led to widespread protests, as have austerity measures imposed by successive governments. Relations with the EU bodies and IMF remain fractious because of the effect of terms imposed for Euro accession and financial bailouts.
**Economy** Since the early 1990s, Hungary has adopted market reforms and partial privatisation programmes. High levels of public debt meant that Hungary had to appeal for repeated loans from the IMF and EU to prevent economic collapse when the world economic crisis struck. The manufacture of machinery and transport is the most valuable sector. Hungary's resources include bauxite, coal and natural gas. Major crops include grapes for wine-making, maize, potatoes, sugar beet and wheat. Tourism is a growing sector.

## Iceland Ísland

**Area** 103,000 km² (39,768 mi²)
**Population** 322,000
**Capital** Reykjavik (202,000)
**Languages** Icelandic
**GDP** (2013) US$39,223
**Currency** Krona = 100 aurar
**Government** multiparty republic
**Head of state** President Sigmundur Gunnlaugsson, Progressive Party, 2013
**Head of government** Prime Minister Johanna Sigurdardottir, Social Democratic Alliance, 2009
**Website** www.government.is/
**Events** In 1944, a referendum decisively voted to sever links with Denmark, and Iceland became a fully independent republic. In 1946 it joined NATO. In 1970 Iceland joined the European Free Trade Association. The last post-war US military personnel left in September 2006, the same year that the government voted to resume commercial whaling. There are concerns among environmentalists about the impact of major new industrial complexes powered by Iceland's abundant thermal energy. Even though Sigurdardottir's Social Democratic Alliance had returned some stability to the economy, the Social Democrats were defeated in 2013 parliamentary elections.
**Economy** The economy has long been sensitive to declining fish stocks as well as to fluctuations in world prices for its main exports: fish and fish products, aluminum and ferrosilicon. There has traditionally been low unemployment, and remarkably even distribution of income. Risky levels of investment in overseas companies left Iceland's banks with high debts when the global credit crunch hit, and the government had to apply for IMF funding.

## Ireland Eire

**Area** 70,273 km² (27,132 mi²)
**Population** 4,588,000
**Capital** Dublin (1,804,000)
**Languages** Irish, English (both official)
**GDP** (2012) US$41,920
**Currency** Euro = 100 cents
**Government** multiparty republic
**Head of state** President Michael Higgins, Independent (formerly Labour Party), 2011
**Head of government**
Taoiseach Enda Kenny, Fine Gael, 2011
**Website** www.gov.ie/en/
**Events** In 1948 Ireland withdrew from the British Commonwealth and joined the European Community in 1973. The Anglo-Irish Agreement (1985) gave Ireland a consultative role in the affairs of Northern Ireland. Following a 1995 referendum, divorce was legalised. Abortion remains a contentious political issue.

In the Good Friday Agreement of 1998 the Irish Republic gave up its constitutional claim to Northern Ireland and a North-South Ministerial Council was established. Sinn Fein got its first seats in the European elections of June 2004. In 2008, long-standing PM Bertie Ahern stood down and Brian Cowen of Fianna Fáil formed a coalition. This fell in early 2011 because of public anger at the bailout from the EU and IMF.
**Economy** Ireland benefited greatly from its membership of the European Union. It joined in circulating the Euro in 2002. Grants have enabled the modernisation of farming, which employs 14% of the workforce. Major products include cereals, cattle and dairy products, sheep, sugar beet and potatoes. Fishing is important. Traditional sectors, such as brewing, distilling and textiles, have been supplemented by high-tech industries, such as electronics. Tourism is the most important component of the service industry. The economy also benefited from a rise in consumer spending, construction and business investment, but growth slowed in 2007 and the country went into recession in 2008, and the joint banking and debt crisis eventually led to the government of Brian Cowen requesting a bailout from the EU and IMF. The economy returned to recession in 2013.

## Italy Italia

**Area** 301,318 km² (116,338 mi²)
**Population** 60,000,000
**Capital** Rome / Roma (2,778,000)
**Languages** Italian (official)
**GDP** (2012) US$30,136
**Currency** Euro = 100 cents
**Government** social democracy
**Head of state** Enrico Letta, Democratic Party, 2013
**Head of government**
Silvio Berlusconi, Forza Italia, 2008
**Website** www.italia.it
**Events** Since World War II Italy has had a succession of unstable, short-lived governments. Silvio Berlusconi regain control in 2008, but was forced to resign in late 2011 because of the ongoing economic crisis and alleged personal scandals. His successor, Mario Monti, was defeated in 2013 elections that resulted in a coalition between the Democrats and Berlusconi's Freedom Party.
**Economy** Italy's main industrial region is the north-western triangle of Milan, Turin and Genoa. It is the world's eighth-largest car and steel producer. Machinery and transport equipment account for 37% of exports. Agricultural production is important. Italy is the world's largest producer of wine. Tourism is a vital economic sector. Per capita GDP fell in 2012, and unemployment remains at a high level.

## Kosovo (Republika e Kosoves/Republika Kosovo)

**Area** 10,887 km2 (4203 mi2)
**Population** 1,734,000
**Capital** Pristina (198,000)
**Languages** Albanian, Serbian (both official), Bosnian, Turkish, Roma
**GDP** (2011) US$7,043
**Currency** Euro (Serbian dinar in Serb enclaves)
**Government** Multiparty republic
**Head of state** President Atifete Jahjaga (2011)
**Head of government**
Prime Minister Hashim Thaci (2008)
**Website** www.kryeministri-ks.net/?page=2,1
**Events** An autonomous province with a mainly ethnic Albanian Muslim popluation, Kosovo first declared independence from Serbia in 1990, leading to years of increased ethnic tension and violence. In 1998 conflict between Serb police and the Kosovo Liberation Army led to a violent crackdown by Serbia, which ceased only after more than two months' aerial bombardment by Nato in 1999, during which hundreds of thousands of Kosovo Albanians were massacred or expelled before Serbia agreed to withdraw and a UN peacekeeping force and administration were sent in, which remained in place until 2008. Talks on the status of the province took place in 2003 and 2006. In 2008, independence was declared again and a new constitution was adopted that transferred power from the UN to the ethnic Albanian government, a move that was rejected by Serbia and Russia but recognised by the US and major European countries. The UN referred Kosovo's declaration of independence to the International Court of Justice, which declared in 2010 that it was not illegal. In March 2011, direct talks between Serbia and

Kosovo began. In 2013, the EU brokered an agreement on policing for the Serb minority.
**Economy** Kosovo is one of the poorest areas of Europe, with a high proportion of the population classed as living in poverty. It possesses some mineral resources but the chief economic activity is agriculture.

## Latvia Latvija

**Area** 64,589 km² (24,942 mi²)
**Population** 2,070,000
**Capital** Riga (1,018,000)
**Languages** Latvian (official), Russian
**GDP** (2012) US$18,254
**Currency** Lats = 100 santims.
From 1 Jan 2014 Euro = 100 cents
**Government** multiparty republic
**Head of state** President Andris Bērziņš, Independent, 2011, Independent, 2011
**Head of government** Prime Minister Valdis Dombrovskis, Unity, 2009
**Website** www.mk.gov.lv/en
**Events** Latvia became a member of NATO and the EU in spring 2004. People applying for citizenship are now required to pass a Latvian language test, which has caused much upset amongst the one third of the population who are Russian speakers. After Ivars Godmanis resigned in February 2009 over his handling of the economic crisis, including having to apply for aid from the IMF, a 6-party coalition was approved by parliament. After the previous coalition government fell in May 2011, elections resulted in the formation of a new coalition, again led by Valdis. Latvia's date for adopting the Euro was set for 1 January 2014.
**Economy** Latvia has to import many of the materials needed for manufacturing. It produces only 10% of the electricity it needs, and the rest has to be imported from Belarus, Russia and Ukraine. Manufactures include electronic goods, farm machinery and fertiliser. Farm exports include beef, dairy products and pork. The majority of companies, banks, and real estate have been privatised. Unemployment remains very high.

## Liechtenstein

**Area** 157 km² (61 mi²)
**Population** 36,281
**Capital** Vaduz (5,109)
**Languages** German (official)
**GDP** (2012) US$98,432
**Currency** Swiss franc = 100 centimes
**Government** independent principality
**Head of state** Adrian Hasler, Progressive Citizens Party, 2013
**Head of government** Prime Minister Klaus Tschütsher, Patriotic Union, 2009
**Website** www.liechtenstein.li/index.php?id=54&L=1
**Events** Women finally got the vote in 1984. The principality joined the UN in 1990. In 2003 the people voted in a referendum to give Prince Hans Adam II new political powers, rendering the country Europe's only absolute monarchy with the prince having power of veto over the government. Its status as a tax haven has been criticised as it has been alleged that many billions are laundered there each year. The law has been reformed to ensure that anonymity is no longer permitted when opening a bank account. In August 2004 Prince Hans Adam II transferred the day-to-day running of the country to his son Prince Alois, though he did not abdicate and remains titular head of state. The OECD removed Liechtenstein from its list of uncooperative tax havens in 2010. In 2013, the Progressive Citizens Party came first in parliamentary elections.
**Economy** Liechtenstein is the fourth-smallest country in the world and one of the richest per capita. Since 1945 it has rapidly developed a specialised manufacturing base. It imports more than 90% of its energy requirements. The economy is widely diversified with a large number of small businesses. Tourism is increasingly important.

## Lithuania Lietuva

**Area** 65,200 km² (25,173 mi²)
**Population** 3,043,000
**Capital** Vilnius (839,000)
**Languages** Lithuanian (official), Russian, Polish
**GDP** (2012) US$21,615
**Currency** Litas = 100 centai
**Government** multiparty republic
**Head of state** Algirdas Butkevicius, Social Democratic Party, 2012

**Head of government** Prime Minister Andrius Kubilius, Homeland Union – Lithuanian Christian Democrats, 2008
**Website** www.lrvk.lt/en
**Events** The Soviet Union recognised Lithuania's independence in September 1991. Lithuania joined NATO in March 2004 and the EU that May. Elections in autumn 2012 led to a change in the make-up of the ruling coalition. Entry to the Euro has been put back to at least 2015.
**Economy** Lithuania is dependent on Russian raw materials. Manufacturing is the most valuable export sector and major products include chemicals, electronic goods and machine tools. Dairy and meat farming and fishing are also important activities. More than 80% of enterprises have been privatised. The economy was badly hit by the 2008 global economic crisis.

## Luxembourg

**Area** 2,586 km² (998 mi²)
**Population** 538,000
**Capital** Luxembourg (metropolitan 94,000)
**Languages** Luxembourgian / Letzeburgish (official), French, German
**GDP** (2012) US$79,785
**Currency** Euro = 100 cents
**Government** constitutional monarchy (or grand duchy)
**Head of state** Grand Duke Henri, 2000
**Head of government** Prime Minister Jean-Claude Juncker, Christian Social People's Party, 1995
**Website** www.gouvernement.lu
**Events** Governments have mostly been coalitions led by the Christian Social People's Party under Jean-Claude Juncker. In July 2013, the Social Workers Party withdrew from the latest coalition, provoking early elections.
**Economy** It has a stable, high-income economy, benefiting from its proximity to France, Germany and Belgium. Per capita GDP rose in 2012. The city of Luxembourg is a major centre of European administration and finance. In 2009, it implemented stricter laws on transparency in the banking sector. There are rich deposits of iron ore, and is a major producer of iron and steel. Other industries include chemicals, textiles, tourism, banking and electronics.

## Macedonia Makedonija

**Area** 25,713 km² (9,927 mi²)
**Population** 2,059,000
**Capital** Skopje (metropolitan 507,000)
**Languages** Macedonian (official), Albanian
**GDP** (2012) US$10,718
**Currency** Denar = 100 deni
**Government** multiparty republic
**Head of state** President Gjorge Ivanov, VMRO-DPMNE, 2009
**Head of government** Nikola Gruevski, VMRO-DPMNE, 2006
**Website** www.vlada.mk/?language=en-gb
**Events** In 1993 the UN accepted the new republic as a member. It formally retains the FYR prefix because of Greek fears that the name implies territorial ambitions towards the Greek region named Macedonia. In August 2004, proposed expansion of rights and local autonomy for Albanians provoked riots by Macedonian nationalists, but the measures went through. In December 2005, EU leaders agreed that Macedonia should become a candidate for membership, if corruption was stamped out, but in February 2007 expressed alarm at political developments during 2006 and continuing problems about rights for ethnic Albanians. In 2008 Greece vetoed NATO's invitation of membership to Macedonia, in a move ruled illegal by the International Court of Justice in 2011. After he called early elections in the latter year, Gruevski's VMRO-DPMNE win, but fail to get a majority.
**Economy** Macedonia is a developing country. The poorest of the six former republics of Yugoslavia, its economy was devastated by UN trade damaged by sanctions against Yugoslavia and by the Greek embargo. Per capita GDP rose slightly overall in 2012. Manufactures, especially metals, dominate exports. Agriculture employs 17% of the workforce. Major crops include cotton, fruits, maize, tobacco and wheat.

## Malta

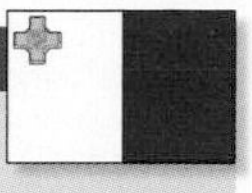

**Area** 316 km² (122 mi²)
**Population** 453,000
**Capital** Valetta (metropolitan 7,000)
**Languages** Maltese, English (both official)
**GDP** (2012) US$27,022
**Currency** Euro = 100 cents
**Government** multiparty republic
**Head of state** President George Abela, Labour Party, 2009
**Head of government** Prime Minister Joseph Muscat, Labour Party, 2013
**Website** www.gov.mt

**Events** In 1990 Malta applied to join the EU. In 1997 the newly elected Malta Labour Party pledged to rescind the application. The Christian Democratic Nationalist Party, led by the pro-European Edward Fenech Adami, regained power in 1998 elections and won again by a narrow margin in March 2008. Malta joined the EU in May 2004 and adopted the Euro on 1 January 2008. In 2013, the Labour Party defeated Lawrence Gonzi's Nationalists to return to power for the first time in 15 years.
**Economy** Malta produces only about 20% of its food needs, has limited fresh water supplies and has few domestic energy sources. Machinery and transport equipment account for more than 50% of exports. Malta's historic naval dockyards are now used for commercial shipbuilding and repair. Manufactures include chemicals, electronic equipment and textiles. The largest sector is services, especially tourism. The economy remains at risk from the Eurozone crisis.

## Moldova

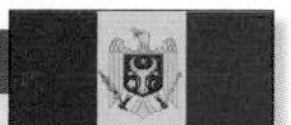

**Area** 33,851 km² (13,069 mi²)
**Population** 3,500,000
**Capital** Chisinau (metropolitan 801,000)
**Languages** Moldovan / Romanian (official)
**GDP** (2012) US$3,415
**Currency** Leu = 100 bani
**Government** multiparty republic
**Head of state** President Nicolae Timofti, independent, 2012.
**Head of government** Prime Minister Iurie Leancă, Liberal Democratic Party, 2013
**Website** www.moldova.md

**Events** In 1994 a referendum rejected reunification with Romania and Parliament votes to join the CIS. A new constitution established a presidential parliamentary republic. The Transnistria region mainly inhabited by Russian and Ukrainian speakers declared independence in 1990. This independence has never been recognised and a regional referendum in Transnistria in 2006 that supported eventual union of the region with Russia is similarly being ignored. Relations between Chisinau and Moscow remain strained. Moldova joined the EU's Eastern Partnership in 2009. In September 2010, a referendum on the appointment of a president failed because of a low turnout. It took nearly 18 months to appoint a new president before Parliament elected Nicolae Timofti in March 2012. Iurie Leancă was confirmed as PM some two months after Vlad Filat was dismissed by a vote of no confidence in April 2013.
**Economy** There is a favourable climate and good farmland but no major mineral deposits. Agriculture is important and major products include fruits and grapes for wine-making. Farmers also raise livestock, including dairy cattle and pigs. Moldova has to import materials and fuels for its industries. Exports include food, wine, tobacco and textiles. The economy remains vulnerable to high fuel prices and poor agricultural weather. Per capita GDP rose slightly in 2012.

## Monaco

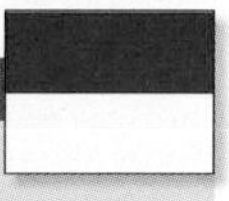

**Area** 1.5 km² (0.6 mi²)
**Population** 36,000
**Capital** Monaco-Ville (1150)
**Languages** French (official), Italian, Monegasque
**GDP** (2012) US$132,571
**Currency** Euro = 100 cents
**Government** principality
**Head of state** Prince Albert II, 2005
**Head of government** Minister of State Michel Roger, independent, 2010
**Website** www.gouv.mc

**Events** Monaco has been ruled by the Grimaldi family since the end of the 13th century and been under the protection of France since 1860.
**Economy** The chief source of income is tourism. The state retains monopolies in tobacco, the telephone network and the postal service. There is some light industry, including printing, textiles and postage stamps. Also a major banking centre, residents live tax free. Prince Albert wishes to attract high-tech industries and to prove that Monaco is not a haven for money-launderers, and in 2010 the OECD removed Monaco from its list of uncooperative tax havens.

## Montenegro
Crna Gora

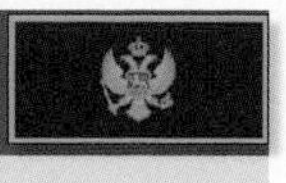

**Area** 13,812 km² (5,333 mi²)
**Population** 625,000
**Capital** Podgorica (metropolitan 186,000)
**Languages** Serbian (of the Ijekavian dialect)
**GDP** (2012) US$11,800
**Currency** Euro = 100 cents
**Government** federal republic
**Head of state** President Filip Vujanovic, 2003
**Head of government** Prime Minister Milo Djukanovich, Democratic Party of Socialists, 2012
**Website** www.gov.me/en/homepage

**Events** In 1992 Montenegro went into federation with Serbia, first as Federal Republic of Yugoslavia, then as a looser State Union of Serbia and Montenegro. Montenegro formed its own economic policy and adopted the Deutschmark as its currency in 1999. It currently uses the Euro, though it is not formally part of the Eurozone. In 2002, Serbia and Montenegro came to a new agreement regarding continued cooperation. On 21 May 2006, the status of the union was decided as 55.54% of voters voted for independence of Montenegro, narrowly passing the 55% threshold needed to validate the referendum under rules set by the EU. On 3 June 2006 the Parliament of Montenegro declared independence. Montenegro was rapidly admitted to the UN, the World Bank and the IMF, joined NATO's Partnership for Peace and applied for EU membership. It was formally named as an EU candidate country in 2010, with accession negotiations due to start in 2012. It joined the WTO in April 2012.
**Economy** A rapid period of urbanisation and industrialisation was created within the communism era of Montenegro. During 1993, two thirds of the Montenegrin population lived below the poverty line. Financial losses under the effects of the UN sanctions on the economy of Montenegro are estimated to be $6.39 billion. Today there is faster and more efficient privatisation, introduction of VAT and usage of the Euro.

## The Netherlands
Nederland

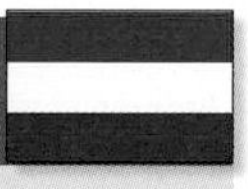

**Area** 41,526 km² (16,033 mi²)
**Population** 16,789,000
**Capital** Amsterdam (metropolitan 2,333,000); administrative capital 's-Gravenhage (The Hague) (metropolitan 1,406,000)
**Languages** Dutch (official), Frisian
**GDP** (2012) US$42,193
**Currency** Euro = 100 cents
**Government** constitutional monarchy
**Head of state** King Willem-Alexander, 2013
**Head of government** Prime Minister Mark Rutte, People's Party for Freedom and Democracy, 2010
**Website** www.government.nl

**Events** A founding member of NATO and the EU. Jan Peter Balkenende's coalition cabinet with the Labour Party and the Christian Union collapsed in early 2010 after Labour refused to sanction continued military deployment in Afghanistan. In 2010 the former junior coalition partner, the Party for Freedom and Democracy, took power, winning again in 2012. In 2013, Queen Beatrix abdicated.
**Economy** The Netherlands has prospered through its close European ties. Private enterprise has successfully combined with progressive social policies. It is highly industrialised. Products include aircraft, chemicals, electronics and machinery. Agriculture is intensive and mechanised, employing only 5% of the workforce. Dairy farming is the leading agricultural activity. It continues to be one of the leading European nations for attracting foreign direct investment.

## Norway Norge

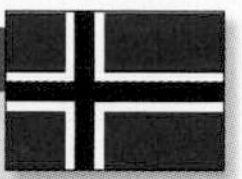

**Area** 323,877 km² (125,049 mi²)
**Population** 5,064,000
**Capital** Oslo (metropolitan 1,442,000)
**Languages** Norwegian (official), Lappish, Finnish **GDP** (2012) US$53,470
**Currency** Krone = 100 øre
**Government** constitutional monarchy
**Head of state** King Harald V, 1991
**Head of government** Prime Minister Jens Stoltenberg, Labour, 2005
**Website** www.norway.org.uk

**Events** In referenda in 1972 and 1994 Norway rejected joining the EU. A centre-left coalition, the Labour-led 'Red-Green Alliance' won closely contested elections in September 2005, and retained power in 2009.
**Economy** Norway has one of the world's highest standards of living. Discovery of oil and gas in adjacent waters in the late 1960s boosted its economic fortunes, with its chief exports now oil and natural gas. Per capita, it is the world's largest producer of hydroelectricity. It is possible oil and gas will begin to run out in Norway in the next two decades but it has been saving its oil budget surpluses and is invested abroad in a fund, valued at more than $250 billion at its height, although this fell rapidly as a result of the global financial crisis. Major manufactures include petroleum products, chemicals, aluminium, wood pulp and paper.

## Poland Polska

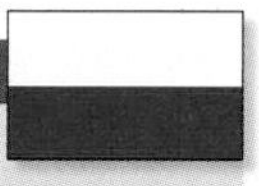

**Area** 323,250 km² (124,807 mi²)
**Population** 38,501,000
**Capital** Warsaw / Warszawa (metropolitan 2,666,000) **Languages** Polish (official)
**GDP** (2012) US$21,000
**Currency** Zloty = 100 groszy
**Government** multiparty republic
**Head of state** President Bronislaw Komorowski, Civic Platform, 2010
**Head of government** Prime Minister Donald Tusk, Civic Platform, 2007
**Website** http://en.poland.gov.pl

**Events** Poland joined the OECD in 1996, NATO in 1999 and the EU in 2004. The death of President Lech Kaczynski and large numbers of the country's military and civilian leadership in a plane crash in April 2010 brought forward presidential elections to June. The first round was inconclusive, with Mr Komorowski gaining more votes than the ex-president's brother, Jaroslaw, but in the second round, he gained 53% of the vote to secure a mandate.
**Economy** Of the workforce, 27% is employed in agriculture and 37% in industry. Poland is the world's fifth-largest producer of lignite and ships. Copper ore is also a vital resource. Manufacturing accounts for 24% of exports. Agriculture remains important. The economic outlook remains uncertain.

## Portugal

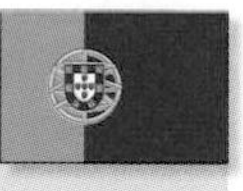

**Area** 88,797 km² (34,284 mi²)
**Population** 10,582,000
**Capital** Lisbon/Lisboa (metropolitan 2,815,000)
**Languages** Portuguese (official)
**GDP** (2012) US$23,385
**Currency** Euro = 100 cents
**Government** multiparty republic
**Head of state** President Anibal Cavaco Silva, Social Democratic Party, 2006
**Head of government** Pedro Passos Coelho, social Democratic Party, 2011
**Website** www.portugal.gov.pt/en.aspx

**Events** In 1986 Portugal joined the EU. In 2002 the Social Democrat Party won the election and formed a coalition government with the Popular Party. The opposition Socialist Party were clear victors in European elections of June 2004, a result attributed in part to the ruling party's support for the war in Iraq. The Socialist Party's minority government collapsed in 2011 when Parliament rejected further austerity measures. Since their return to power they have instigated several further tranches, leading to instability in both the coalition and the country.
**Economy** Portugal was hit by the economic downturn and in April 2011 it became the third Eurozone country to ask for a financial bailout. Public debt rose above the 3% threshold allowed by Eurozone regulations and in March 2010 the government introduced further budget cuts. Manufacturing accounts for 33% of exports. Textiles, footwear and clothing are major exports. Portugal is the world's fifth-largest producer of tungsten and eighth-largest producer of wine. Olives, potatoes and wheat are also grown. Tourism is very important.

## Romania

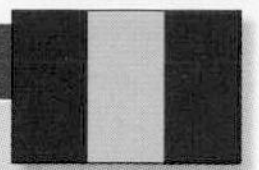

**Area** 238,391 km² (92,042 mi²)
**Population** 19,044,000
**Capital** Bucharest / Bucuresti (metropolitan 2,822,000)
**Languages** Romanian (official), Hungarian
**GDP** (2012) US$12,808
**Currency** Romanian leu = 100 bani
**Government** multiparty republic
**Head of state** President Traian Basescu, 2004
**Head of government** Prime Minister Victor-Viorel Ponta, Social Liberal Union, 2012
**Website** www.gov.ro

**Events** A new constitution was introduced in 1991. Ion Iliescu, a former communist official, was re-elected in 2000, but barred from standing again in 2004, when he was replaced by Traian Basescu. After losing a vote of no confidence after just 10 months as PM, Boc was reappointed in December 2009. Romania joined NATO in 2004 and joined the EU in January 2007 after making progress towards tackling corruption, although because of this issue France and Germany blocked its Schengen area accession in December 2010. Protests in 2012 led to PM Emil Boc's resignation, Interim PM Ungureanu was toppled in weeks and electionsin September were won by Victor Ponta. Euro adoption is set for 2015 at the earliest. The Romany minority still suffers from discrimination.
**Economy** The currency was re-valued in 2005. Despite a period of strong economic growth, Romania's large public debt led to the need for substantial IMF loans in 2009, necessitating severe cuts in public services.

## Russia Rossiya

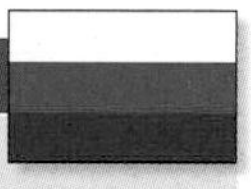

**Area** 17,075,000 km² (6,592,800 mi²)
**Population** 143,400,000
**Capital** Moscow / Moskva (metropolitan 11,511,000)
**Languages** Russian (official), and many others
**GDP** (2012) US$23,549
**Currency** Russian ruble = 100 kopeks
**Government** federal multiparty republic
**Head of state** President Vladimir Putin 2012
**Head of government** Prime Minister Dimitry Medvedev, 2012
**Website** http://government.ru/eng/#

**Events** In 1992 the Russian Federation became a co-founder of the CIS (Commonwealth of Independent States). A new Federal Treaty was signed between the central government and the autonomous republics within the Russian Federation, Chechnya refused to sign and declared independence. In December 1993 a new democratic constitution was adopted. From 1994 to 1996, Russia fought a civil war in Chechnya which flared up again in 1999. Putin's chosen successor, Medvedev, was elected by a landslide in elections that were criticised by outside observers for biased media coverage. In 2011 Putin was re-elected as President, after the law that prevented serving a third term was revoked. He appointed former president Medvedev as PM. Critics allege that freedom of speech and dissent are being repressed amid crackdowns on NGOs and opponents of the ruling party. Russia joined the WTO in 2012.
**Economy** In 1993 mass privatisation began. By 1996, 80% of the Russian economy was in private hands. A major problem remains the size of Russia's foreign debt. It is reliant on world oil prices to keep its economy from crashing and the sudden fall in oil prices in the second half of 2008 forced it to devalue the ruble several times. Industry employs 46% of the workforce and contributes 48% of GDP. Mining is the most valuable activity. Russia is the world's leading producer of natural gas and nickel, the second largest producer of aluminium and phosphates. and the third-largest of crude oil, lignite and brown coal. Most farmland is still government-owned or run as collectives, with important products barley, oats, rye, potatoes, beef and veal. In 2006, the ruble became a convertable currency.

## San Marino

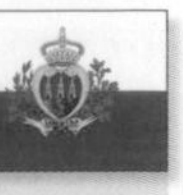

**Area** 61 km² (24 mi²)
**Population** 33,000
**Capital** San Marino (4,500)
**Languages** Italian (official)
**GDP** (2012) US$35,928
**Currency** Euro = 100 cents
**Government** multiparty republic
**Head of state** co-Chiefs of State: Antonella Muralini and Denis Amici
**Head of government** Secretary of State for Foreign and Political Affairs and Economic Planning Pasquale Valentini, 2012
**Website** www.visitsanmarino.com
**Events** World's smallest republic and perhaps Europe's oldest state, San Marino's links with Italy led to the adoption of the Euro. Its 60-member Great and General Council is elected every five years and headed by two captains regent, who are elected by the council every six months.
**Economy** The economy is largely agricultural. Tourism is vital to the state's income, contributing over 50% of GDP. Per capita GDP grew slightly in 2012.

## Serbia Srbija

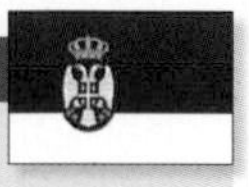

**Area** 88,412 km² (34,137 mi²), including Kosovo
**Population** 7,187,000
**Capital** Belgrade / Beograd (metropolitan 1,659,000)
**Languages** Serbian
**GDP** (2012) US$13,004
**Currency** Dinar = 100 paras
**Government** federal republic
**Head of state** President Tomislav Nikolić, Serbian Progresssive Party,
**Head of government** Prime Minister Ivica Dacic, Socialist Party, 2012
**Website** www.srbija.gov.rs
**Events** Serbian attempts to control the Yugoslav federation led to the secession of Slovenia and Croatia in 1991 and to Bosnia-Herzegovina's declaration of independence in 1992 and the three-year war that ended only with the signing of the Dayton Peace Accord. Slobodan Milosovic became president of Yugoslavia in 1997. Kostunica won the elections of September 2000: Milosevic refused to hand over power, but was ousted after a week. From 2003 to 2006, Serbia was part of the State Union of Serbia and Montenegro, After a referendum in May 2006, the Parliament of Montenegro declared Montenegro independent. Serbia assumed the State Union's UN membership. In 2006 Serbia joined the NATO Partnership for Peace programme and in 2008 signed a Stability and Association Agreement with the EU, to which it applied formally for membership in December 2009. Serbia became a candidate member of the EU in 2012, with accession talks due to begin in 2014. In May 2012 the Serbian Progressive Party made gains in Parliament and took the presidency. It is a junior member in the Socialist-led coalition.
**Economy** The lower-middle income economy was devastated by war and economic sanctions. Industrial production collapsed. Natural resources include bauxite, coal and copper. There is some oil and natural gas. Manufacturing includes aluminium, cars, machinery, plastics, steel and textiles. Agriculture is important. In 2008 Serbia and Russia signed an energy deal, and in October 2009 the latter granted the former a 1 billion Euro loan to ease its budgetary problems.

## Slovak Republic Slovenska Republika

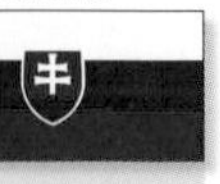

**Area** 49,012 km² (18,923 mi²)
**Population** 5,411,000
**Capital** Bratislava (metropolitan 660,000)
**Languages** Slovak (official), Hungarian
**GDP** (2012) US$24,284
**Currency** Euro = 100 cents
**Government** multiparty republic
**Head of state** President Ivan Gasparovic, 2004
**Head of government** Prime Minister Robert Fico, Direction - Social Democracy (Smer), 2012.
**Website** www.government.gov.sk
**Events** In 1993 the Slovak Republic became a sovereign state, breaking peaceably from the Czech Republic, with whom it maintains close relations. In 1996 the Slovak Republic and Hungary ratified a treaty confirming their borders and stipulating basic rights for the 560,000 Hungarians in the country. The Slovak Republic joined NATO in March 2004 and the EU two months later. There is still a problem with the Romany population. The country adopted the Euro in January 2009. In elections in April 2012 Smer returned to power with a parliamentary majority
**Economy** The transition from communism to private ownership was initially painful with industrial output falling, unemployment and inflation rising, but the economy has become more stable. Manufacturing employs 33% of the workforce. Bratislava and Košice are the chief industrial cities. Major products include ceramics, machinery and steel. Farming employs 12% of the workforce. Crops include barley and grapes. Tourism is growing.

## Slovenia Slovenija

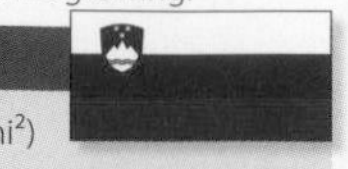

**Area** 20,256 km² (7,820 mi²)
**Population** 2,055,000
**Capital** Ljubljana (metropolitan 273,000)
**Languages** Slovene
**GDP** (2012) US$28,195
**Currency** Euro = 100 cents
**Government** multiparty republic
**Head of state** President Borut Pahor, Social Democratic Party, 2012
**Head of government** Prime Minister Alenka Bratusek Liberal Party, 2013
**Website** www.gov.si
**Events** In 1990 Slovenia declared itself independent, which led to brief fighting between Slovenes and the federal army. In 1992 the EU recognised Slovenia's independence. Janez Drnovsek was elected president in December 2002. Slovenia joined NATO in March 2004 and the EU two months later. In June 2004 the value of the Tolar was fixed against the Euro, which it joined in 2007. The 2008 general election resulted in a coalition government led by the Social Democratic Party. A referendum in June 2010 narrowly approved the settlement of the border dispute with Croatia. After two years of political instability, Ivan Janša was appointed PM in February 2012, leading a centre-right coalition, but his government fell the following year.
**Economy** The transformation of a centrally planned economy and the fighting in other parts of former Yugoslavia caused problems for Slovenia but the economy eventually experienced strong growth in per capita GDP until this was badly hit by the gobal financial crisis. Manufacturing is the leading activity. Major manufactures include chemicals, machinery, transport equipment, metal goods and textiles. Major crops include maize, fruit, potatoes and wheat.

## Spain España

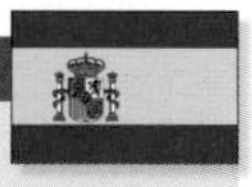

**Area** 497,548 km² (192,103 mi²)
**Population** 47,265,000
**Capital** Madrid (metropolitan 6,369,000)
**Languages** Castilian Spanish (official), Catalan, Galician, Basque
**GDP** (2012) US$30,557
**Currency** Euro = 100 cents
**Government** constitutional monarchy
**Head of state** King Juan Carlos I, 1975
**Head of government** Prime Minister Mariano Rajoy, Spanish People's Party, 2011
**Website** www.lamoncloa.gob.es/home.htm
**Events** From 1959-98 the militant Basque organisation ETA waged a campaign of terror. Its first ceasefire was broken in 2000 and a second - declared in 2006 - with a bomb attack on Madrid airport at the end of the year. A third ceasefire was declared in September 2010. In March 2004 Al qaeda-related bombers killed 191 people in Madrid, resulting in an election win for the opposition Socialist Party. In the 2008 elections, the socialists increased their numbers in Parliament, but did not gain a majority. Austerity measures brought in to tackle public debt, and as condition of the country's financial bailout, changes to pensions and benefits and rising unemployment led to widespread protests in 2010 and 2011. Local and regional elections in May 2011 resulted in heavy losses for the socialists and the Popular Party won a sweeping majority in general elections in November
**Economy** Spain's transformation from a largely poor, agrarian society to a prosperous nation came to an end with the economic downturn of 2008. The country's debt burden became untenable and financial bailouts from the international community in 2010 and the Eurozone in 2012 were necessary. Unemployment is more than double the European average. Agriculture now employs only 10% of the workforce and the sector is shrinking further because of recurrent droughts. Spain is the world's third-largest wine producer. Other crops include citrus fruits, tomatoes and olives. Industries: cars, ships, chemicals, electronics, metal goods, steel, textiles.

## Sweden Sverige

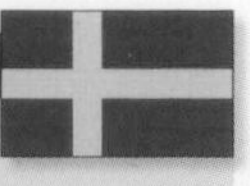

**Area** 449,964 km² (173,731 mi²)
**Population** 9,556,000
**Capital** Stockholm (metropolitan 2,121,000)
**Languages** Swedish (official), Finnish
**GDP** (2012) US$40,393
**Currency** Swedish krona = 100 ore
**Government** constitutional monarchy
**Head of state** King Carl Gustaf XVI, 1973
**Head of government** Prime Minister Fredrik Reinfeldt, Moderate Party, 2006
**Website** www.sweden.gov.se
**Events** In 1995 Sweden joined the European Union. The cost of maintaining Sweden's extensive welfare services has become a major political issue. In 2003 Sweden rejected adoption of the Euro. The elections of 2010 saw a rise in votes for the far right.
**Economy** Sweden is a highly developed industrial country. It has rich iron ore deposits. Privately owned firms account for about 90% of industrial output. Steel is a major product, used to manufacture aircraft, cars, machinery and ships. Forestry and fishing are important. Agriculture accounts for 2% of GDP and jobs. The Swedish central bank focuses on price stability with its inflation target of 2%.

## Switzerland Schweiz

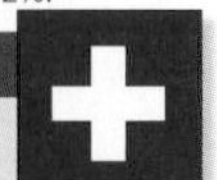

**Area** 41,284 km² (15,939 mi²)
**Population** 7,955,000
**Capital** Bern (metropolitan 126,000)
**Languages** French, German, Italian, Romansch (all official)
**GDP** (2012) US$45,417
**Currency** Swiss Franc = 100 centimes/rappen
**Government** federal republic
**Head of government** President Ueli Maurer, 2013.
**Website** www.admin.ch
**Events** Priding themselves on their neutrality, Swiss voters rejected membership of the UN in 1986 and the EU in 1992 and 2001. However, Switzerland finally became a partner country of NATO in 1997 and joined the organisation in 2002, when it also joined the UN. The federal council is made up of seven federal ministers from whom the president is chosen on an annual basis. A 2005 referendum backed membership of EU Schengen and Dublin agreements, bringing Switzerland into the European passport-free zone and increasing co-operation on crime and asylum seekers. Immigration is becoming an increasingly divisive issue.
**Economy** Switzerland is a wealthy and stable modern market economy with low unemployment, and per capita GDP grew slightly in 2012. Manufactures include chemicals, electrical equipment, machinery, precision instruments, watches and textiles. Livestock, notably dairy farming, is the chief agricultural activity. Tourism is important, and Swiss banks remain a safe haven for investors. In November 2011, the government announced that the Swiss franc would be pegged to the Euro.

## Turkey Türkiye

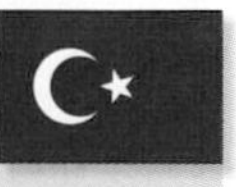

**Area** 774,815 km² (299,156 mi²)
**Population** 75,627,000
**Capital** Ankara (metropolitan 4,966,000)
**Languages** Turkish (official), Kurdish
**GDP** (2012) US$17,651
**Currency** New Turkish lira = 100 kurus
**Government** multiparty republic
**Head of state** President Abdullah Gül, Justice and Development Party (AK), 2007
**Head of government** Prime Minister Recep Tayyip Erdogan, Justice and Development Party (AK), 2003
**Website** www.mfa.gov.tr/default.en.mfa
**Events** The Kurdistan Workers Party (PKK) carried out terrorist activities throughout the 1980s and 1990s, but declared a ceasefire in 1999, changed their name to Congress for Freedom and Democracy in Kurdistan (KADEK) and said they wanted to campaign peacefully for Kurdish rights. In September 2003 they ended a 4-year ceasefire, but declared another in 2006, although this did not hold. In October 2005, the EU opened accession negotiations with Ankara. Membership of the EU is an aim but human rights, the Cyprus issue and the hostility of successive French and Austrian governments are barriers. The PM and President are both former Islamists, although they say they are committed to secularism. The escalating civil war in Syria has caused a refugee crisis on the border. In 2013, the proposed introduction of laws seen as being anti-secular and the proposed development of one of Istanbul's few green spaces led to widespread protests and calls for the resignation of the government.
**Economy** Turkey is a lower-middle income developing country. Agriculture employs 47% of the workforce, but is becoming less important to the economy. Turkey is a leading producer of citrus fruits, barley, cotton, wheat, tobacco and tea. It is a major producer of chromium and phosphate fertilisers. Tourism is a vital source of foreign exchange. In January 2005, the New Turkish lira was introduced at a rate of 1 to 1,000,000 old Turkish lira. The country's economy grew slightly in 2012.

## Ukraine Ukraina

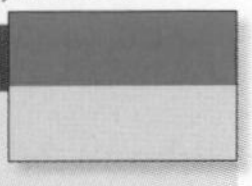

**Area** 603,700 km² (233,088 mi²)
**Population** 44,854,000
**Capital** Kiev / Kyyiv (metropolitan 3,648,000)
**Languages** Ukrainian (official), Russian
**GDP** (2012) US$7,598
**Currency** Hryvnia = 100 kopiykas
**Government** multiparty republic
**Head of state** President Viktor Yanukovic, Party of the Regions, 2010
**Head of government** Prime Minister (acting) Mykola Azarov, Party of the Regions, 2010
**Website** www.kmu.gov.ua/control/en
**Events** The Chernobyl disaster of 1986 contaminated large areas of Ukraine. Independence was achieved in 1991 with the dissolution of the USSR. Leonid Kuchma was elected president in 1994. He continued the policy of establishing closer ties with the West and sped up the pace of privatisation. In 2010, the coalition governent of Yulia Tymoshenko fell, and the Party of the Regions formed a coalition with the Communists and the centrist Lytvyn Bloc. Former PM Victor Yanukovic beat Tymoshenko in the presidential elections. Ukraine joined the EU?s Eastern Partnership in 2009, but has abandoned plans to join NATO. Continued political oppression and the arrest and imprisonment of opponents of the President led to international condemnation.
**Economy** Ukraine is a lower-middle-income economy. Agriculture is important. It is the world's leading producer of sugar beet, the second-largest producer of barley, and a major producer of wheat. Ukraine has extensive raw materials, including coal (though many mines are exhausted), iron ore and manganese ore. Ukraine is reliant on oil and natural gas imports. The economy's dependence on steel exports made it vulnerable to the 2008 global economic downturn and it was offered a massive loan by the IMF.

## United Kingdom

**Area** 241,857 km² (93,381 mi²)
**Population** 63,182,000
**Capital** London (metropolitan 15,011,000)
**Languages** English (official), Welsh (also official in Wales), Gaelic
**GDP** (2012) US$35,728
**Currency** Sterling (pound) = 100 pence
**Government** constitutional monarchy
**Head of state** Queen Elizabeth II, 1952
**Head of government** Prime Minister David Cameron, Conservative Party, 2010
**Website** www.gov.uk
**Events** The United Kingdom of Great Britain and Northern Ireland is a union of four countries – England, Northern Ireland, Scotland and Wales. Since 1997, Scotland and Wales have had their own legislative assemblies. The Good Friday Agreement of 1998 offered the best change of peace in Northern Ireland for a generation. In 2005 the IRA anounced a permanent cessation of hostilities and the Northern Ireland Assembly was finally reinstated in early 2007. Right-wing political parties have gained some ground, fuelled by warnings of rising levels of immigration and anti- EU rhetoric.
**Economy** The UK is a major industrial and trading nation. A producer of oil, petroleum products, natural gas, potash, salt and lead. Financial services and tourism are the leading service industries. The economic downturn of 2008 led to the government effectively nationalising several banks and bailing out others with massive loans. Although the economy emerged from recession in late 2009, economic recovery remains weak.

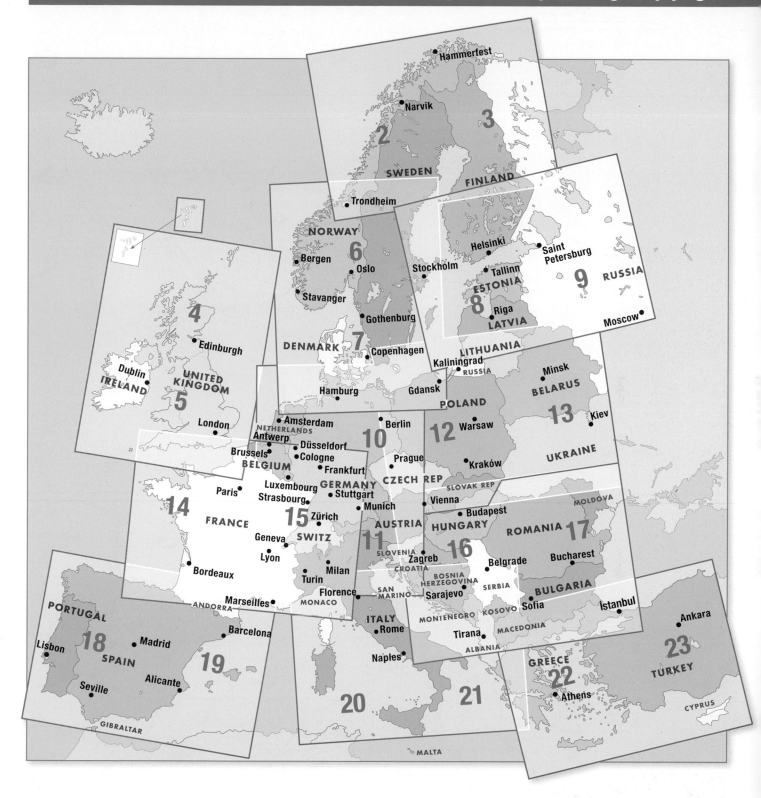

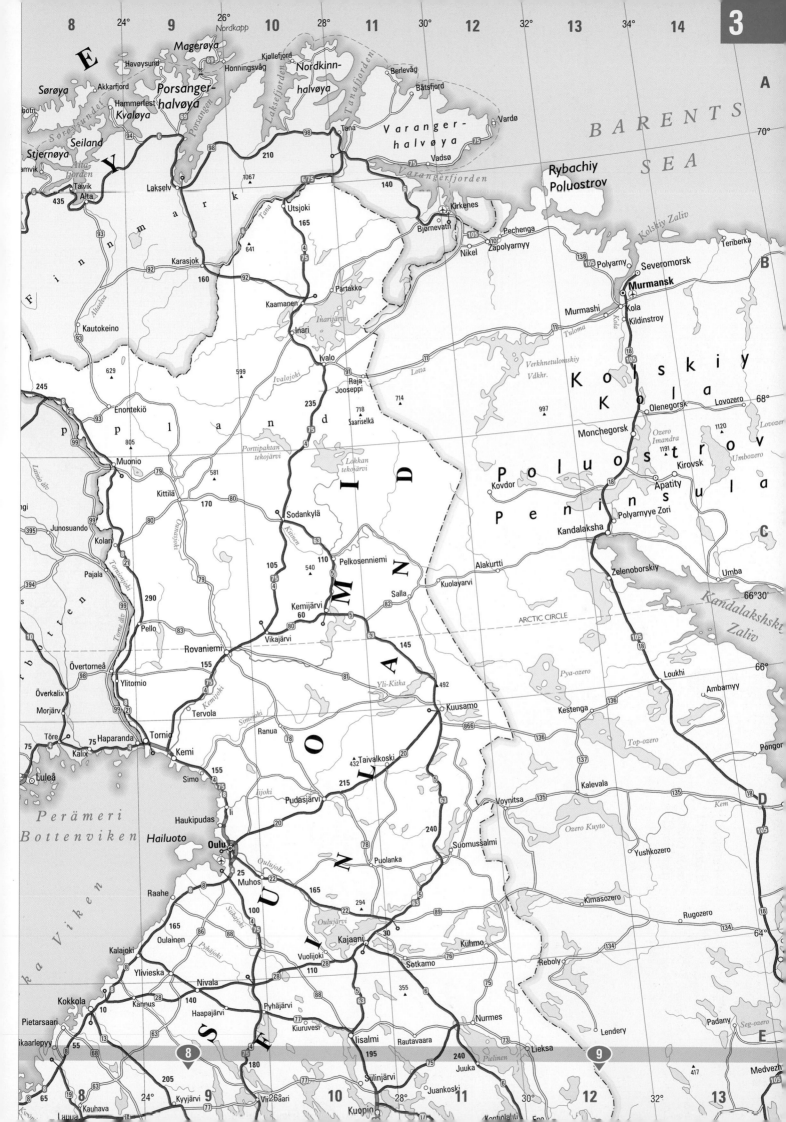

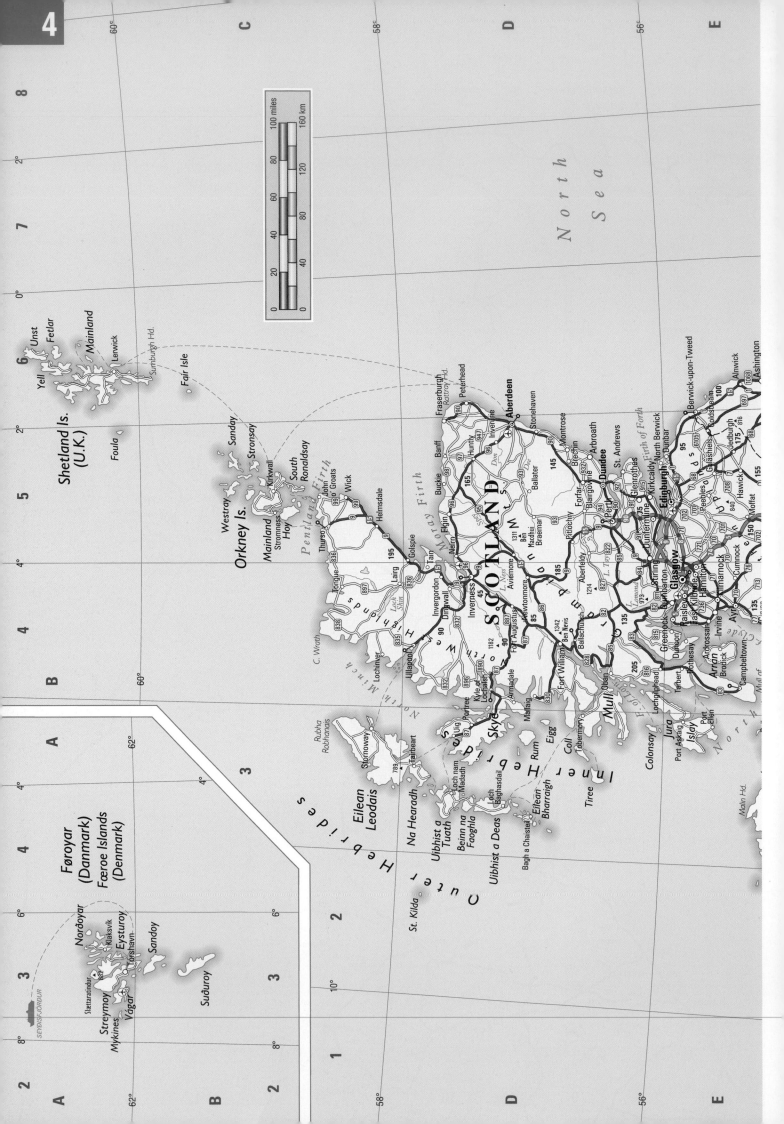

**4**

Shetland Is.
(U.K.)

Unst
Fetlar
Mainland
Yell
Lerwick
Foula
Sumburgh Hd.
Fair Isle

100 miles
80
60
40
20
0
160 km
120
80
40
0

*N o r t h*

*S e a*

Westray
Sanday
Stronsay
Orkney Is.
Kirkwall
South Ronaldsay
Mainland
Stromness
Hoy
John o'Groats
Wick
*Pentland Firth*

Fraserburgh
Rattray Hd.
Peterhead
Banff
**Aberdeen**
Inverurie
Stonehaven
Huntly
90
Montrose
Brechin
Arbroath
**Dundee**
St. Andrews
Forfar
Blairgowrie
Firth of Forth
North Berwick
Glenrothes
Dunbar
**Edinburgh**
Kirkcaldy
Peebles
Berwick-upon-Tweed
Coldstream
Galashiels
Jedburgh
Alnwick
Hawick
Moffat
Ashington
**100**
816
1068
175
68
**155**

Helmsdale
Golspie
195
Tongue
Lairg
*Loch Shin*
Dingwall
Invergordon
Tain
Elgin
Nairn
Buckie
165
Aviemore
Newtonmore
Fort Augustus
85
Ben Nevis
1342
Fort William
Ballachulish
**185**
Aberfeldy
Pitlochry
Ballater
Braemar
Madhui
Ben
1311
145
*Don*
*Dee*
947
98
Inverness
*L. Ness*
45
90
Thurso
C. Wrath
838
836
15
9
Ullapool
Lochinver
835
896
890
*North Minch*
836
887
*Highlands*
Rubha Robhanais
Stornoway
789
Tarbert
Na Hearaidh
*Eilean Leodais*
Loch nam Madadh
Uibhist a Tuath
Beinn na Faoghla
*Outer Hebrides*
Uibhist a Deas
Bagh a Chaisteil
Loch Baghasdail
Eilean Bharraigh
St. Kilda
Portree
Uig
Skye
Kyle of Lochalsh
Armadale
Mallaig
Eigg
Rum
Coll
Tiree
Tobermory
Mull
*Inner Hebrides*
Colonsay
Jura
Islay
Port Askaig
Port Ellen
Oban
Lochgilphead
Tarbert
Campbeltown
Mull of
Ardrossan
Arran
Brodick
Port
205
816
83
828
830
135
Ben
973
*L. Lomond*
822
84
**SCOTLAND**
*Grampian Mts.*
1214
93
932
915
Perth
**75**
702
80
82
Stirling
Dunfermline
Dumbarton
**Glasgow**
Greenock
Paisley
Hamilton
East Kilbride
Kilmarnock
Ayr
Cumnock
Irvine
77
70
150
135
713
708
840
701

**A**

*Føroyar (Danmark)*
*Færoe Islands (Denmark)*

Norðoyar
Klaksvik
Eysturoy
Streymoy
Tórshavn
882
Slættaratindur
Vágar
Mykines
Sandoy
Suðuroy
*SEYÐISFJØRÐUR*

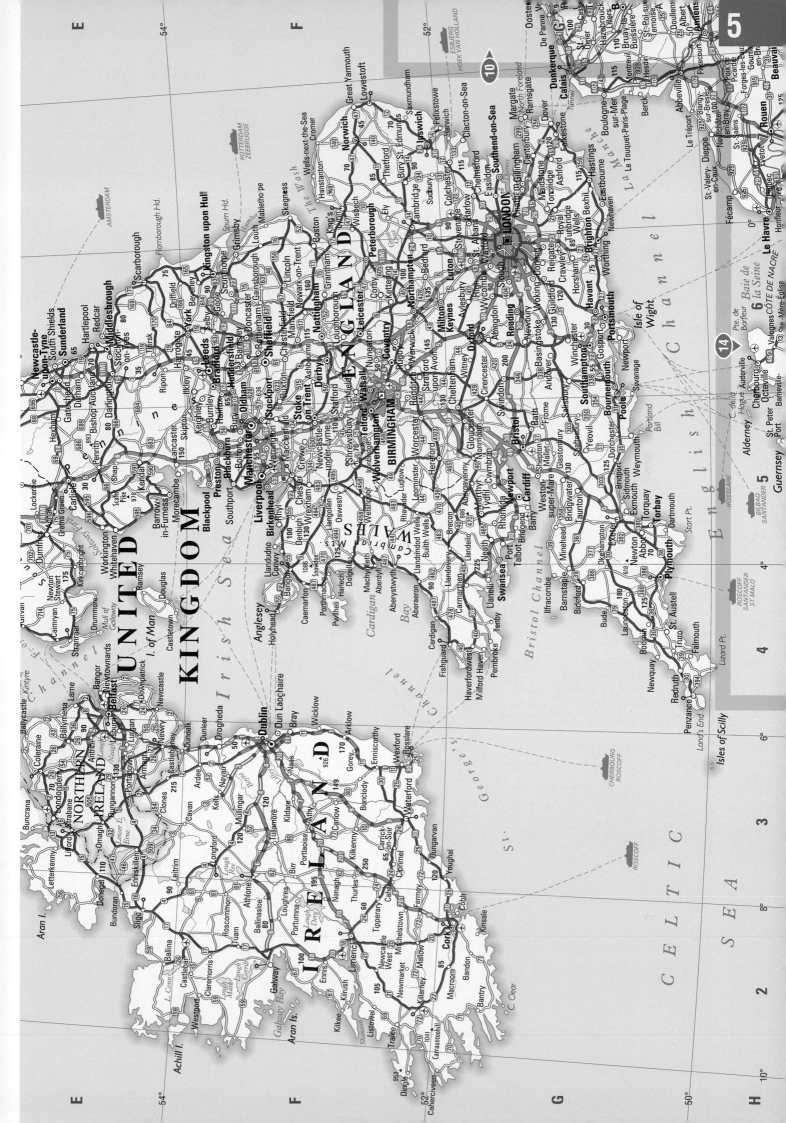

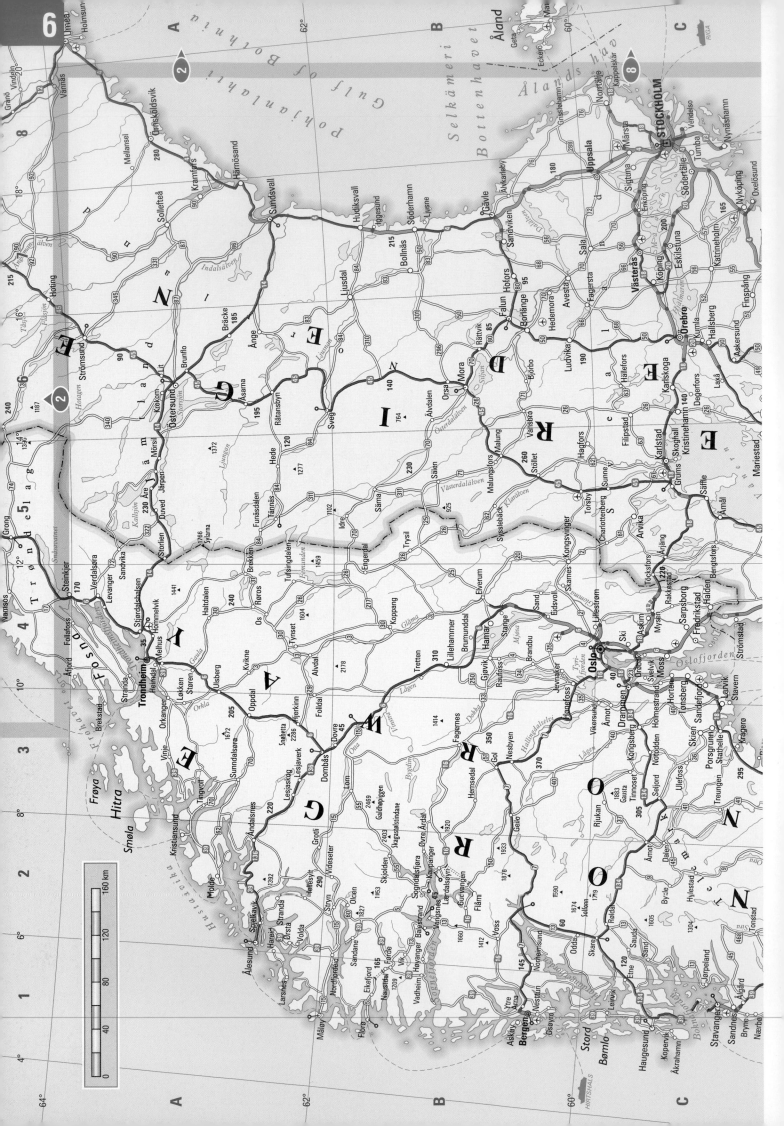

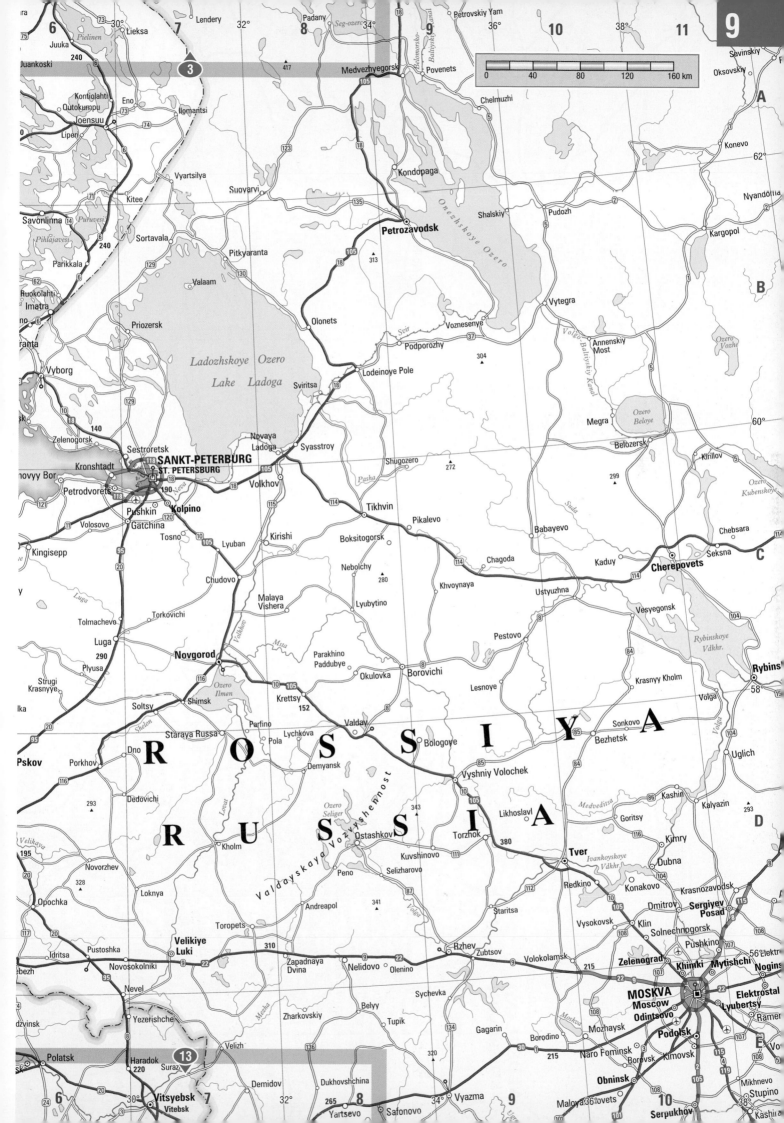

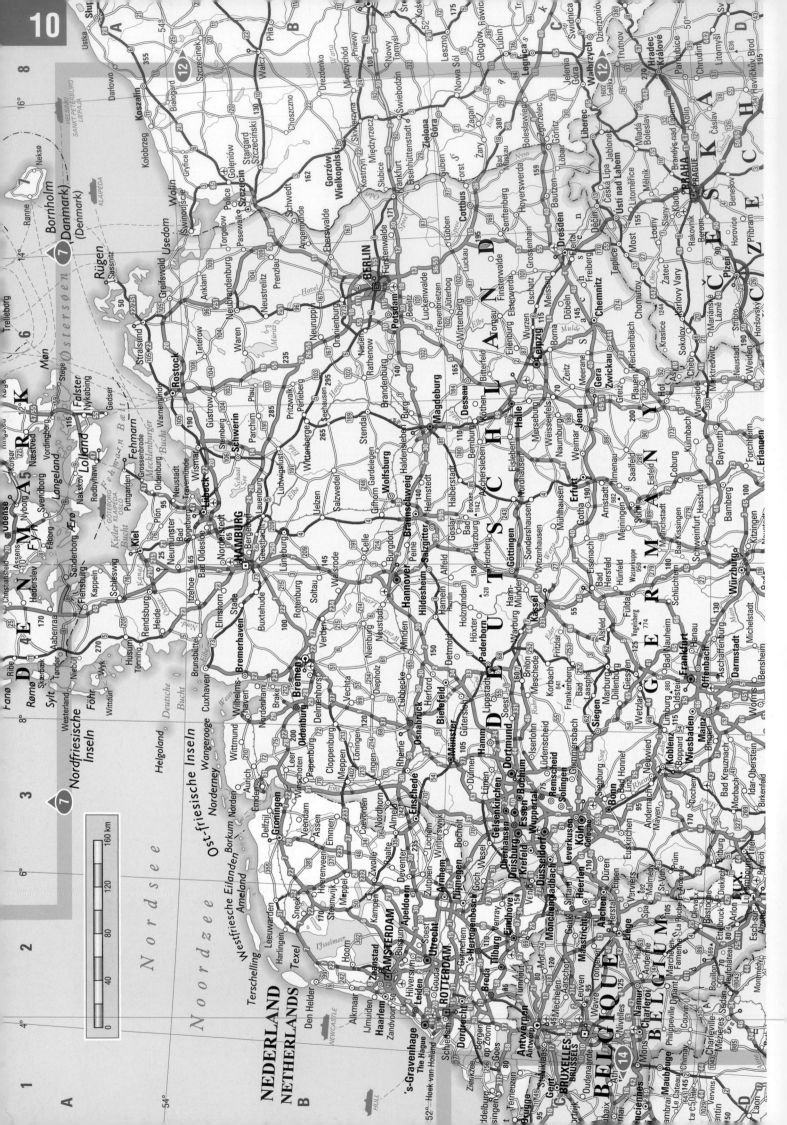

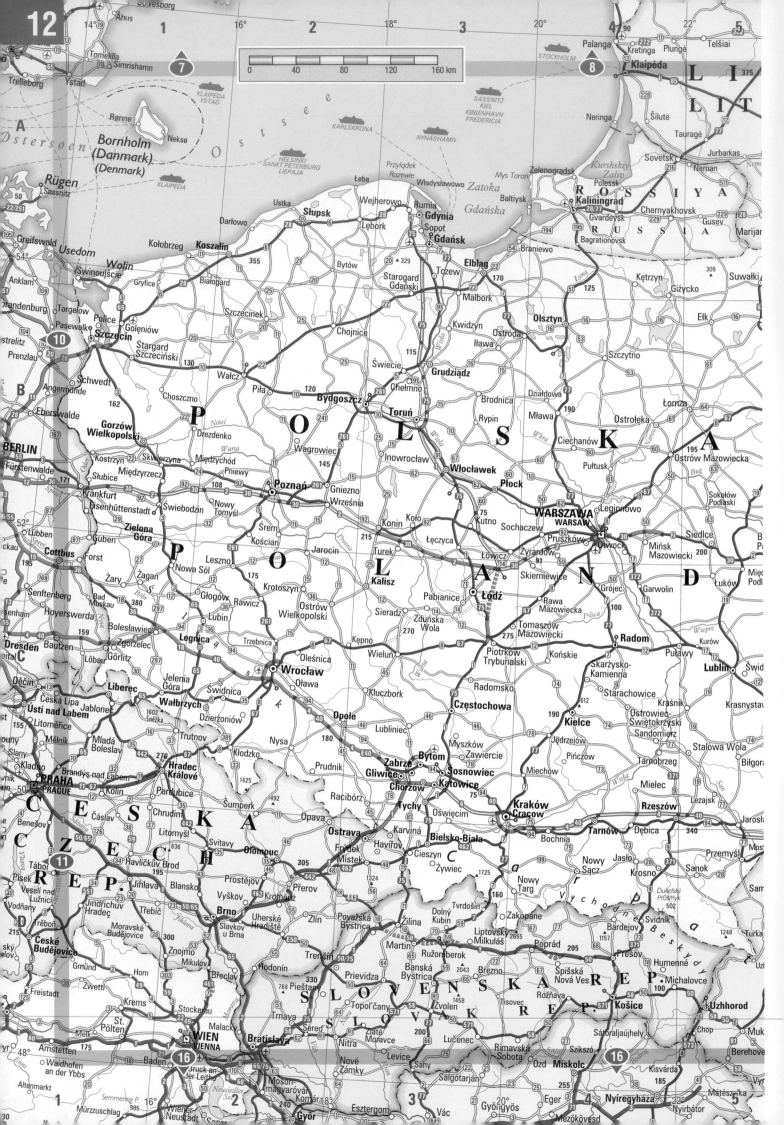

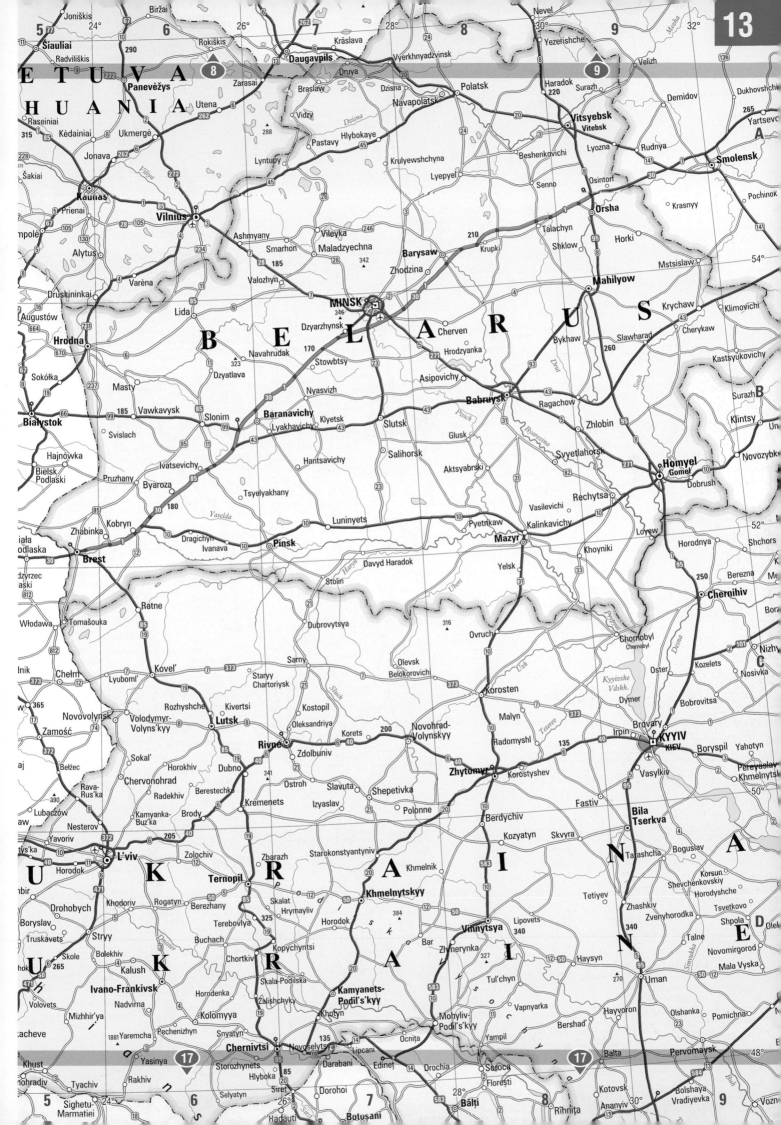

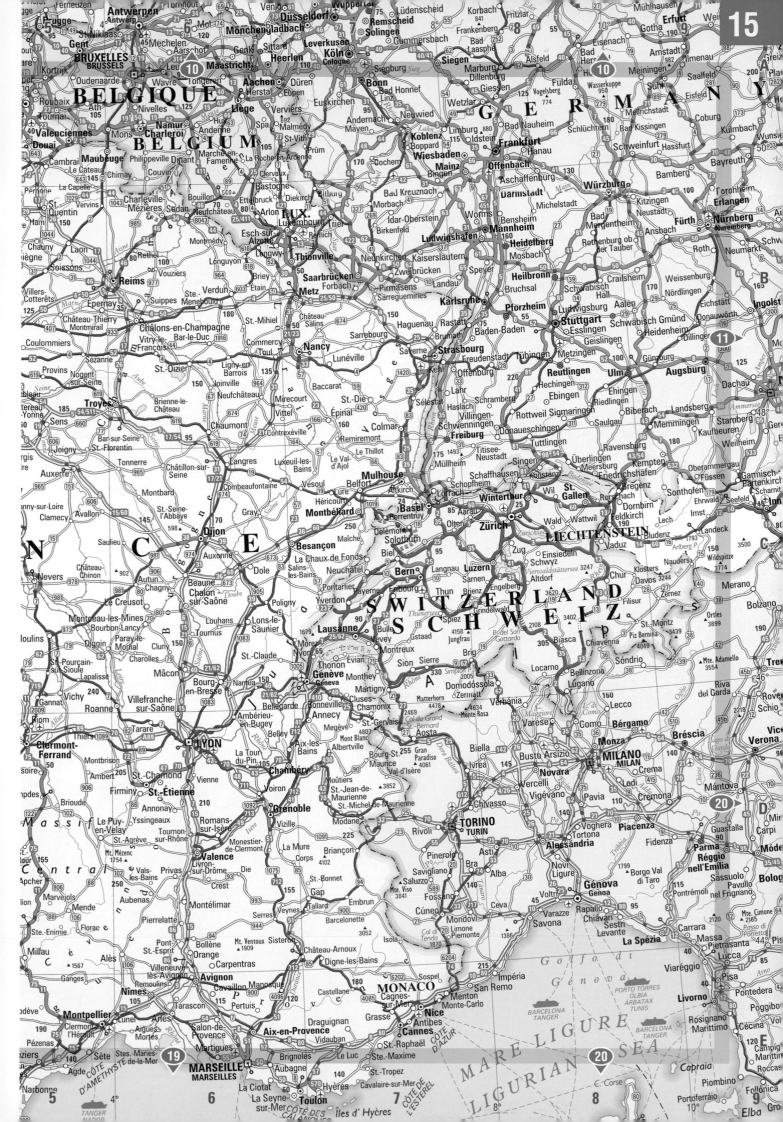

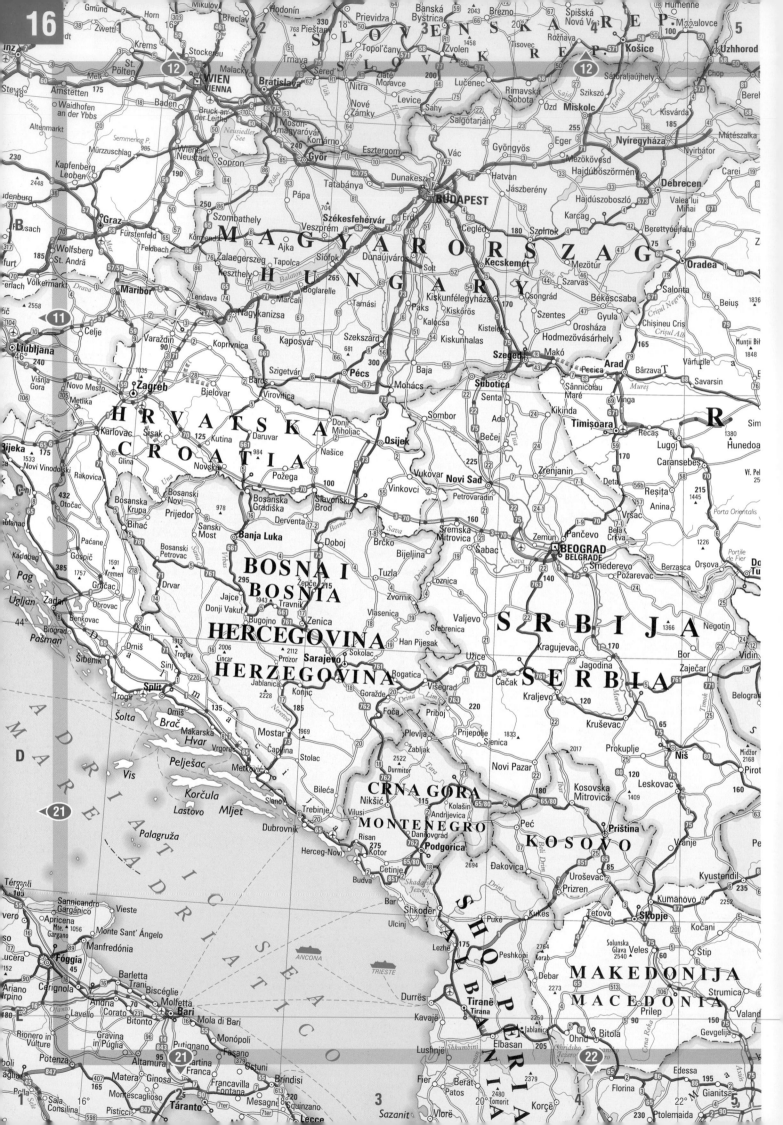

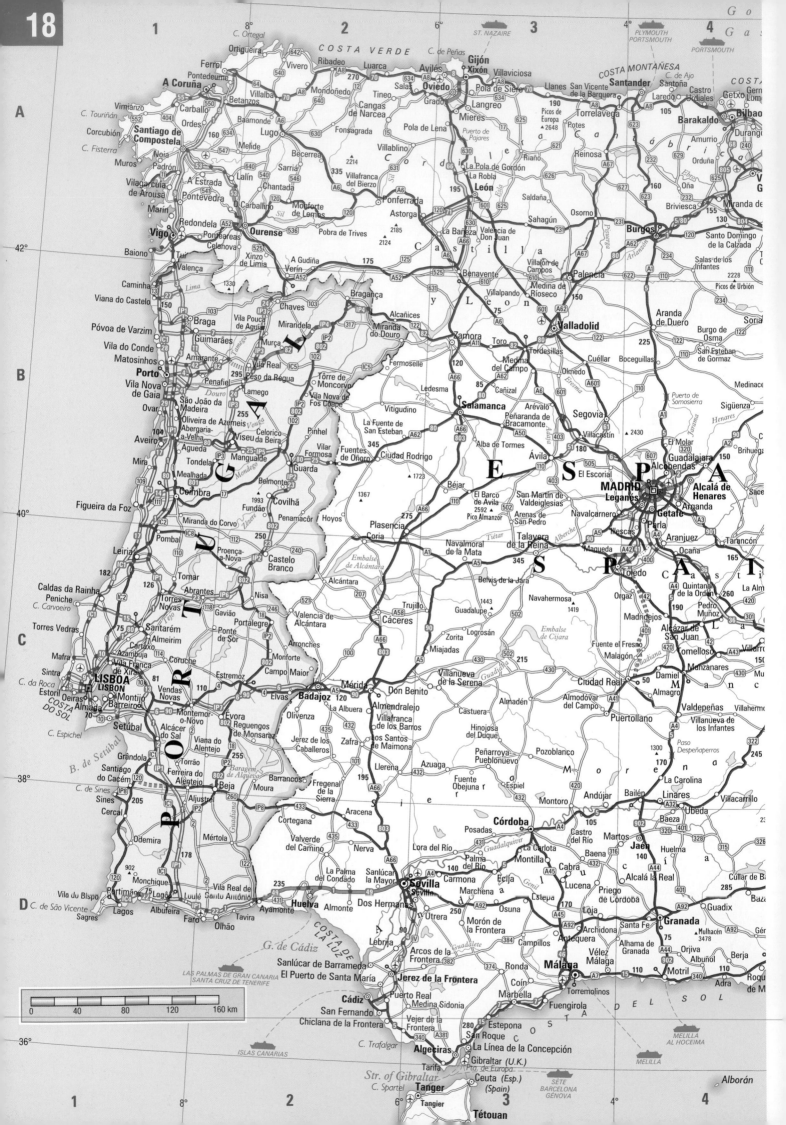

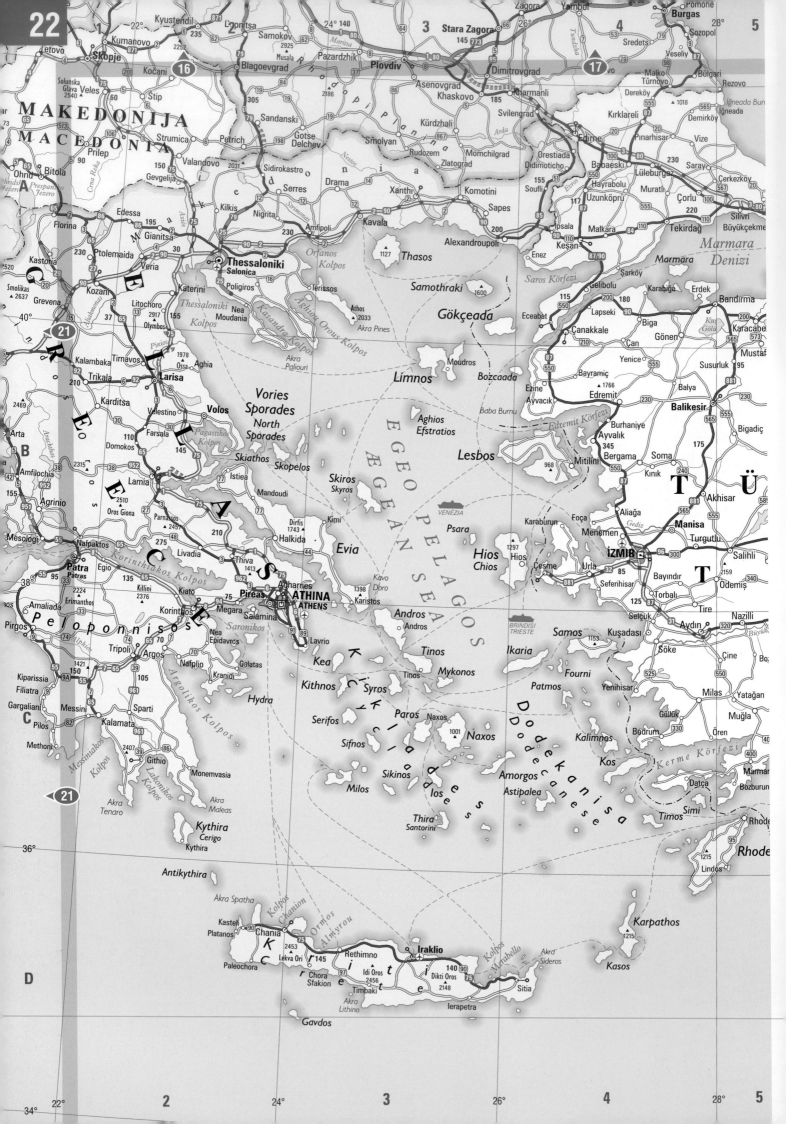

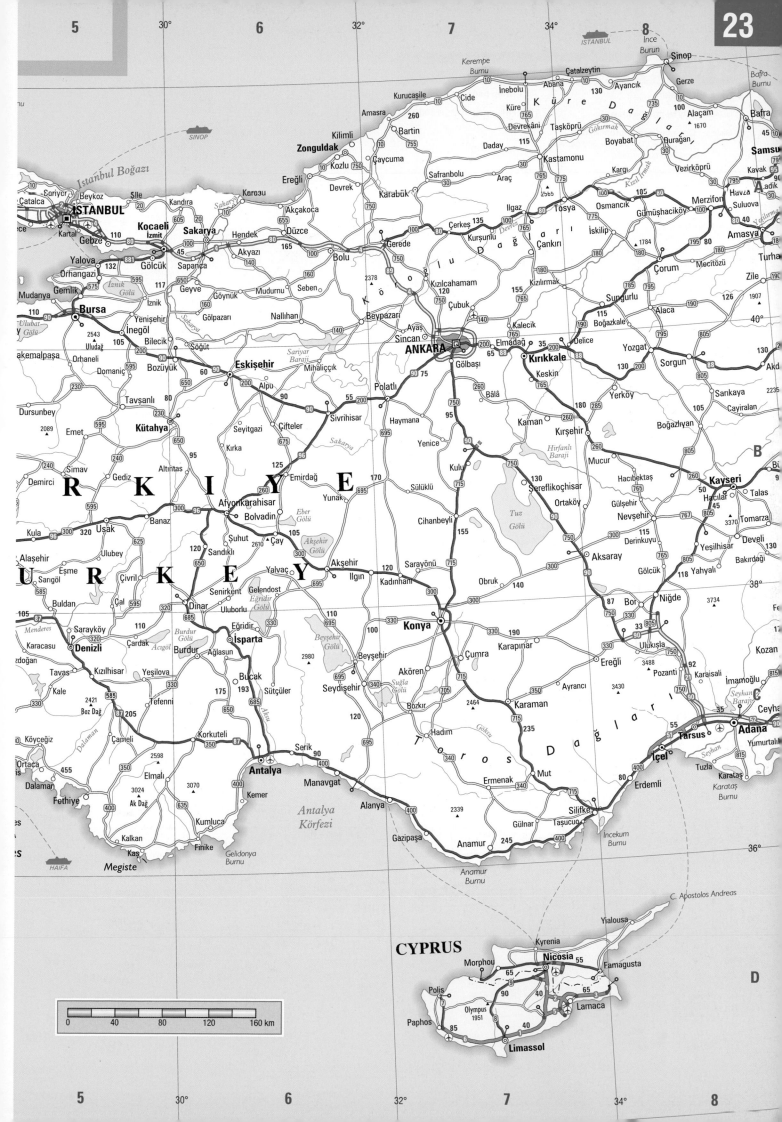

## Key to road map pages

- ● Florence *Firenze* — City plan
- ☐ İstanbul — City approach map
- ■ Milan *Milano* — City plan and approach map
  See pages 201–228 for city plans and approach maps
- **97** Map pages at 1:750 000
- **182** Map pages at 1:1 500 000

# Distance table

**Amsterdam**

2945 **Athina**

1505 3192 **Barcelona**

1484 3742 2803 **Bergen**

650 2412 1863 1309 **Berlin**

197 2895 1308 1586 764 **Bruxelles**

2245 1219 2644 3037 1707 2181 **Bucuresti**

1420 1530 1999 2212 882 1358 852 **Budapest**

367 3100 1269 1783 956 215 2398 1573 **Calais**

533 3630 1817 270 1504 763 3021 2196 548 **Dublin**

1093 3826 1995 176 1696 941 3124 2299 726 346 **Edinburgh**

441 2499 1313 1508 550 383 1804 979 575 1123 1301 **Frankfurt**

1029 3080 2362 819 668 1145 1734 1550 1342 477 176 1067 **Göteborg**

447 2719 1780 1023 286 563 2014 1189 760 477 1486 485 582 **Hamburg**

1560 2539 2338 1063 475 1239 1834 1009 1431 1318 1236 1598 505 1113 **Helsinki**

2756 1145 2990 3653 2223 2706 690 1341 2911 3537 3657 2314 2891 2530 2350 **İstanbul**

965 2782 2090 1103 370 1081 2077 1252 1278 752 479 795 284 518 803 2593 **København**

256 2684 1376 1427 566 198 1983 1158 390 938 1116 180 986 404 1517 2499 714 **Köln**

2331 4460 1268 3723 2869 3141 3917 3222 2069 2617 2795 2400 3282 2700 3817 4342 3014 2339 **Lisboa**

480 3200 1387 458 1074 333 2591 1766 118 430 608 693 122 878 1991 3107 1188 508 2187 **London**

406 2661 1190 1613 749 209 2052 1227 424 972 1150 240 1172 590 1703 2472 900 186 2160 542 **Luxembourg**

1790 3809 617 3183 2364 1600 3262 2622 1528 1634 2254 1930 2742 2160 3276 3589 2473 1798 651 1646 1628 **Madrid**

1210 2683 509 2435 1541 1030 2154 1505 1063 1588 1789 1023 1994 1412 2525 2479 1722 1006 1777 1182 822 1126 **Marseille**

1085 2182 1038 2141 1060 890 1668 992 1072 1620 1798 683 1700 1118 1535 1993 1428 868 2315 1190 679 1655 538 **Milano**

2457 2930 3655 2223 1821 2585 1761 2099 2800 3348 3526 2312 1665 2115 1160 2605 2325 2387 4875 2918 2852 4224 3270 3027 **Moskva**

839 2106 1340 1788 594 789 1497 672 994 1524 1720 398 1347 765 1069 1907 969 580 2545 1094 555 2010 1011 473 2305 **München**

1347 3372 2680 503 960 1463 2667 1842 1660 773 729 1385 316 900 697 3089 590 1304 3604 1778 1490 3063 2312 2018 1823 1559 **Oslo**

510 2917 988 1922 1051 320 2307 1482 281 829 1007 591 1481 899 2012 2727 1209 495 1821 399 351 1280 782 857 2903 810 1799 **Paris**

950 2067 1750 1675 345 888 1362 537 1097 1635 1816 512 1013 652 770 1878 715 690 2870 1205 753 2329 1399 853 1853 388 1305 1061 **Praha**

1691 1140 1385 2706 1502 1520 1904 1263 1678 2226 2404 1289 2265 1683 1977 2237 1993 1474 2653 1796 1285 2002 876 606 3362 918 2583 1389 1309 **Roma**

2347 4223 1031 3736 2894 2150 3709 3010 2078 2626 2804 2344 3295 2713 3826 4034 3023 2318 401 2196 2178 550 1540 2078 4774 2371 3613 1830 2781 2446 **Sevilla**

2206 828 2453 3103 1673 2156 391 790 2361 2891 3087 1764 2341 1980 1800 550 2043 1949 3706 2461 1922 3037 1929 1443 2252 1367 2632 2177 1328 1687 3484 **Sofiya**

1393 3418 2726 1063 1006 1509 2713 1888 1673 2254 1069 1431 505 946 167 3185 590 1350 3650 1824 1536 3109 2358 2064 1228 1600 530 1845 1351 2629 3659 2679 **Stockholm**

1256 2128 2366 1909 606 1350 1473 648 1542 2110 2268 1136 1274 886 361 1989 956 1152 3480 1680 1345 2960 2015 1469 1245 996 1506 1677 616 1853 3397 1439 1612 **Warszawa**

1168 1772 1856 1970 640 1114 1067 242 1308 1954 2034 731 1308 947 1088 1583 1010 916 3100 1524 993 2473 1353 818 2137 430 1600 1240 295 1126 2876 1033 1646 727 **Wien**

816 2426 1030 1938 863 619 1810 985 804 1352 1530 464 1497 915 2164 2323 1433 589 2296 922 410 1647 699 292 2552 303 1815 592 691 898 2061 1173 1861 1307 743 **Zürich**

---

548 **Dublin** — Dublin ▶ Göteborg = 477 km

726 346 **Edinburgh**

575 1123 1301 **Frankfurt**

1342 477 176 1067 **Göteborg**

760 477 1486 485 582 **Hamburg**

**Distances shown in blue involve at least one ferry journey**

RUSSIA
ROSSIYA

Moscow
Moskva

Kiev
Kyyiv

UKRAINE
UKRAINA

MOLDOVA

İstanbul

Ankara

186  187

TURKEY
TÜRKIYE

İzmir

Antalya

188  189

181
Nicosia  CYPRUS
KYPROS

# km

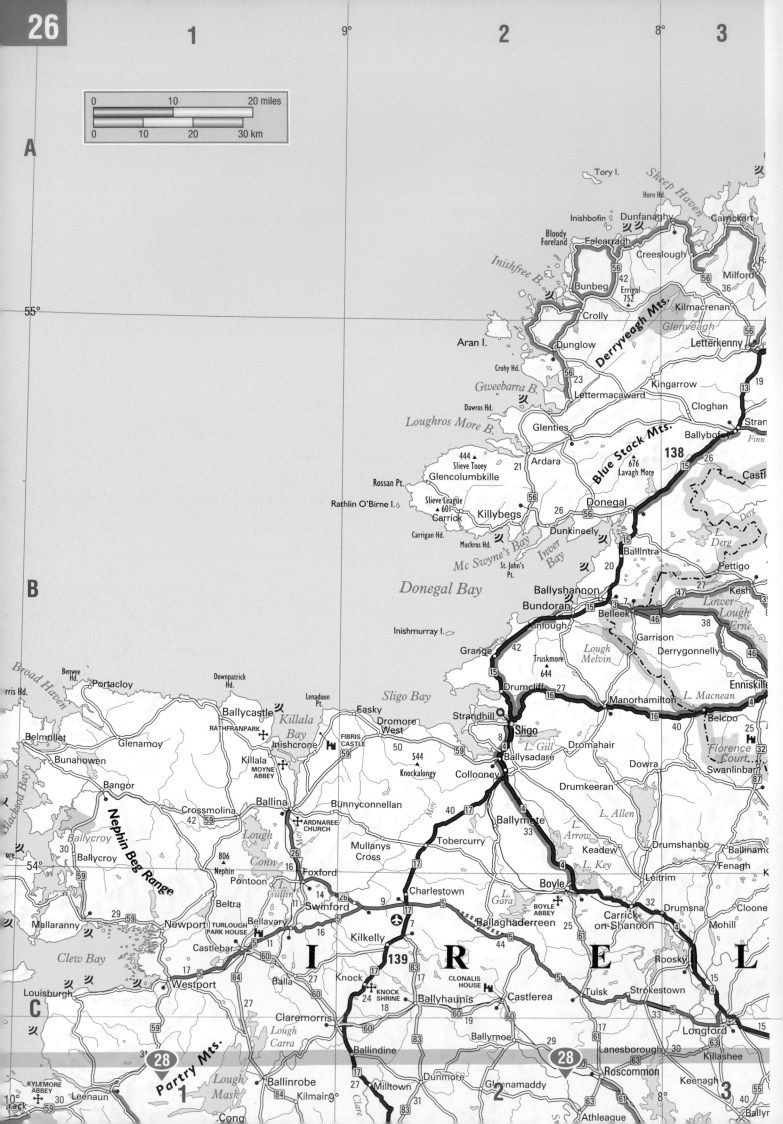

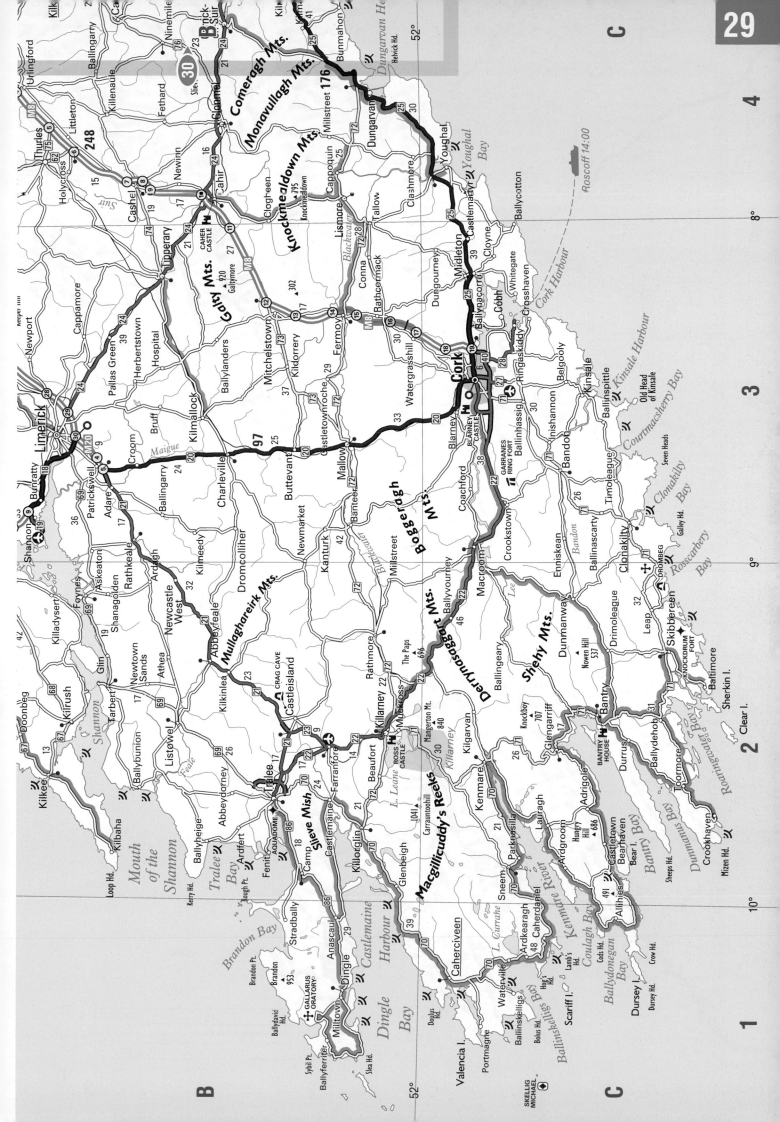

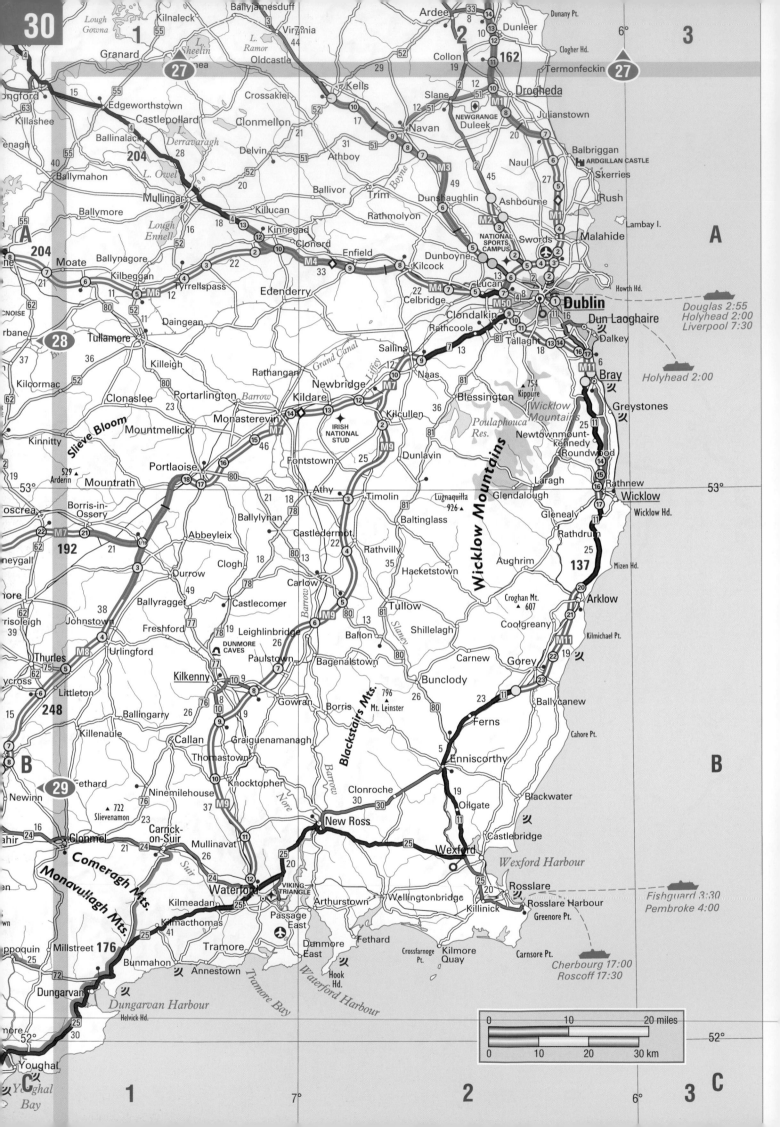

**1**   7°   **2**   6°   **3**

Butt of Lewis
Port Nis
Dail bho Dheas
857   24

**A**

Barabhas
Tolastadh bho Thuath
857   Tolsta Hd.
Siabost   16   Bac
858   Broad Bay
Carlabhagh
292   Tiumpan Hd.
Great   Ben   Port Nan Giuran
Gallan Hd.   Bernera   Mholach
Timsgearraidh   Calanais   51   Newmarket   16   866
Stornoway   Mealabost
**L e w i s**   Chicken Hd.
574
Mealisval   Giosla
Crosbost
Scarp   859
48
Kintarvie
Leumrabhagh   Grabhair
Husinish   572   Kebock Hd.

58°   **58°**

799   Beinn Mhor
Clisham
*West L. Tarbert*   Ardhasig
Taransay
Aird Asaig   Shiant Is.
Tairbeart
859   38   Scalpay
Toe Hd.   *East L. Tarbert*
Sgarasta Mhor
Pabbay   An t-Ob   1:40
*Sd. of Pabbay*   Roghadal
Berneray   Renish Pt.

Rubha Hunish   DUNTULM CASTLE
Vaternish Pt.
855   Staffin
Geary   *Trotternish*
L. Snizort   Uig
Stein   51
Dunvegan Hd.
87   23   The Storr
DUNVEGAN   719
CASTLE   850   32   Carbost
Lephin   Dunvegan   855
Roskhill   863   34   Portree
Bracadale
*L. Bracadale*   15   Clachan
Carbost   Drynoch   Sconser
Glenbrittle   **Cuillin Hills**   Broadford
Kylerhea
*The Cuillin Hills*   851
Soay   Elgol
KNOCK CASTLE
Teangue
Armadale
ARMADALE GARDENS
Pt. of Sleat

*Hebrides*

**North Minch**

Pt. of Stoer

Stoer

*Enard B.*
Rubha Coigeach

Achiltibuie
HYDROPONICUM GARDENS
32
*Gruinard B.*
Greenstone Pt.   Gruinard B.
Cove   Aultbea   62
L. Ewe
Melvaig   *Fionn Loch*
INVEREWE GARDEN
Longa I.   Poolewe   *Wester*
Port Henderson   Gairloch   L. Maree   Ross
Red Point   Kerrysdale   L. Gairloch
Talladale   29   832
L. Torridon
Kinlochewe
24
Rona   Torridon
Shieldaig   896
Achnashellach
Applecross   Coulags
27
Ardarroch   Lochcarron
890   20
Stromeferry
WOODLAND GARDEN
Auchtertyre
8   Dornie
L. Carron   Kyle of Lochalsh
CASTLE MOIL   L. Alsh   87   18
28   L. Alsh   Shiel
12   Kyleakin
Glenelg   Kir
*Sd. of Sleat*   L. Hourn   *Knoydart*

**1**   **2**   **3**

*Sound of Monach*
Monach Is.   Solas   48   865   Loch nam   1:45
North Uist   Madadh   1:00
865   867
Clachan na Luib
Baleshare   Ronay
Benbecula   Wiay
Creag Ghoraidh   865
53
Tobha Mor
*South Uist*   **South**
*Machair*   **Uist**
865   Dalabrog
Loch Baghasdail
Pol a Charra   5:20
*Sound of Barra*   0:40   1:40
Barra   888
18
Bagh a Chaisteil
Vatersay   4:50
Sandray
Mingulay

**B**   **B**

**C**

*Outer Hebrides*   H   *Little Minch*   *Inner Hebrides*

Canna
Sanday
Rùm   Kinloch
Eigg
Galmisdale
Muck
*The Small Isles*
*Sound of Rùm*

Mallaig   0:30   L. Nevis
Arisaig   *L. Morar*
830   26   Lochailort
882   Rhois-Bheinn
LOCH NAN   Kinlochmoidart
UAMH CAIRN
861

57°   **57°**

Achosnich   Acharacle   Salen   *Loch Shiel*
MINGARY CASTLE   46   861   Strontian
Kilchoan
Sorisdale
Coll   Ballyhaugh
Arinagour   2:55   0:35   34
Arileod   Tobermory
Calgary   Dervaig   848
Tiree   1:00   6°   Claggan
Lochaline

861   Kinlochmoidart
*Morar, Moidart & Ardnamurchan*
884   30
*Loch Linnhe*

**1**   7°   **2**   6°   **3**

Scale:
0   10   20 miles
0   10   20   30 km

Ullapool 2:45

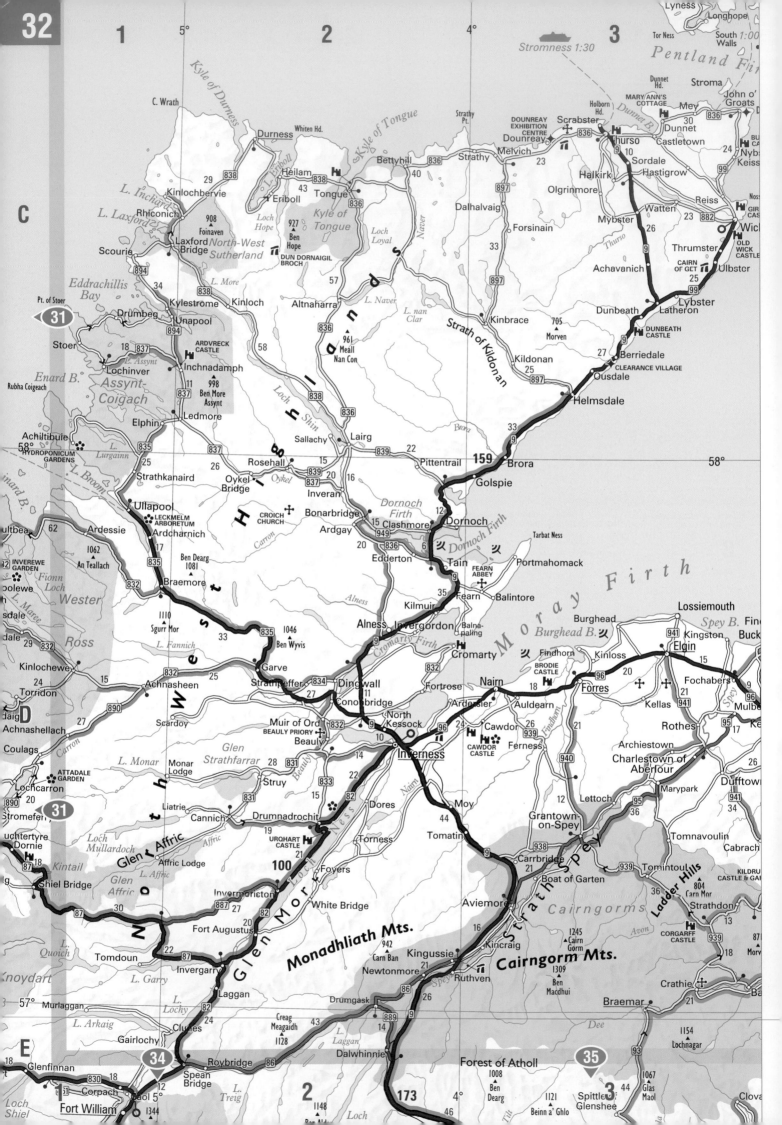

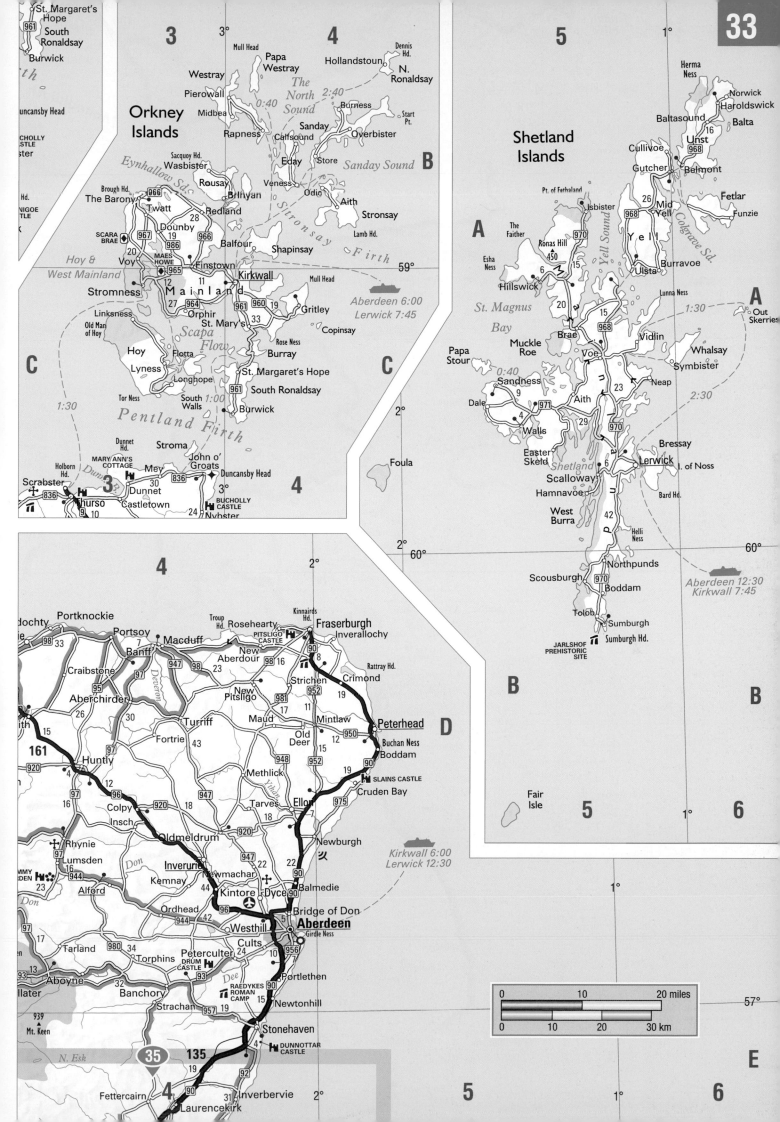

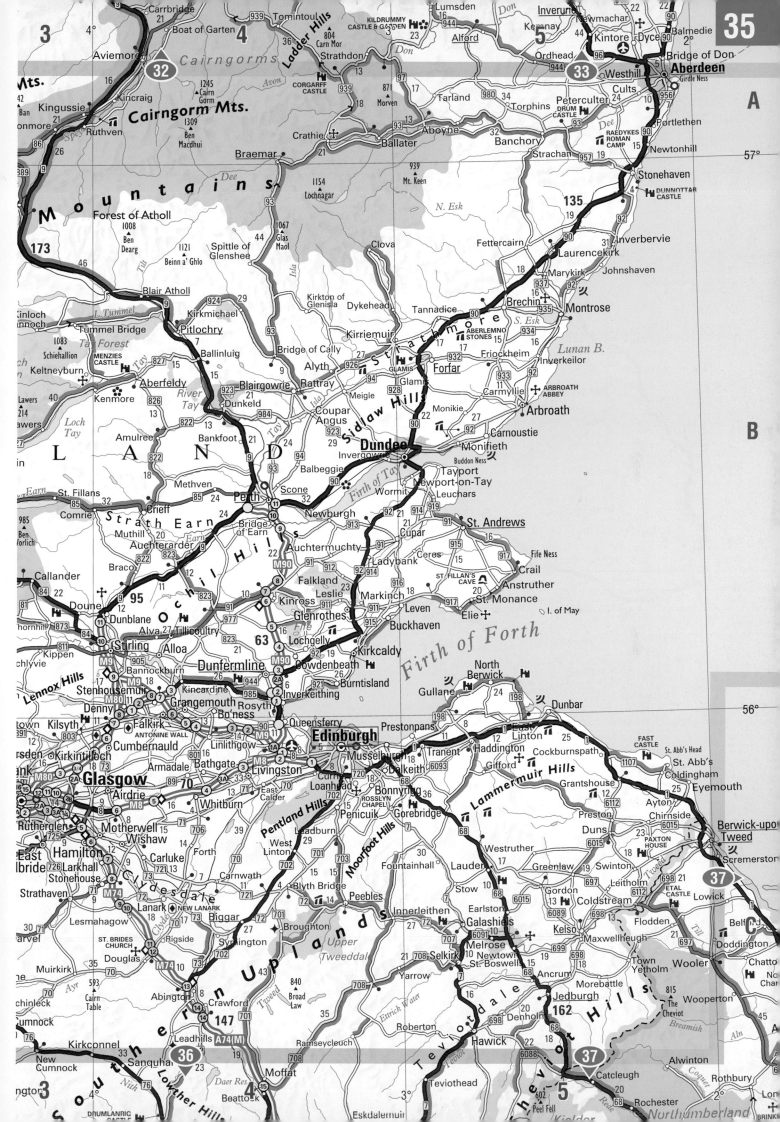

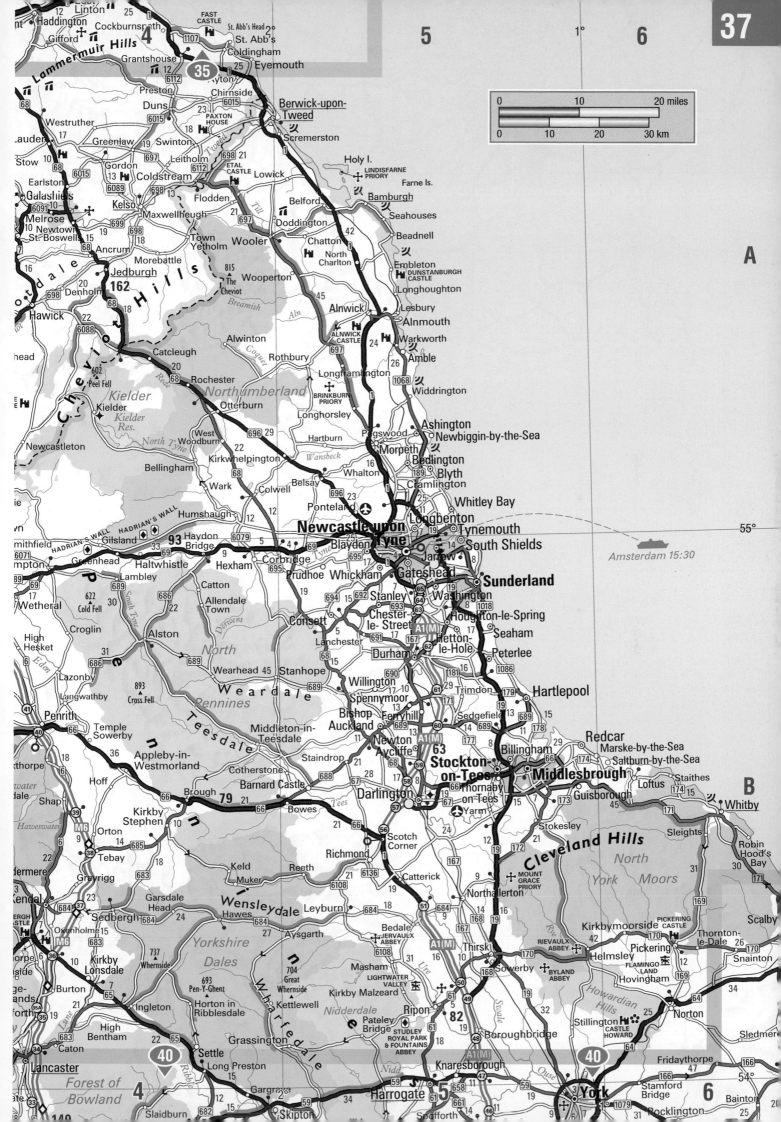

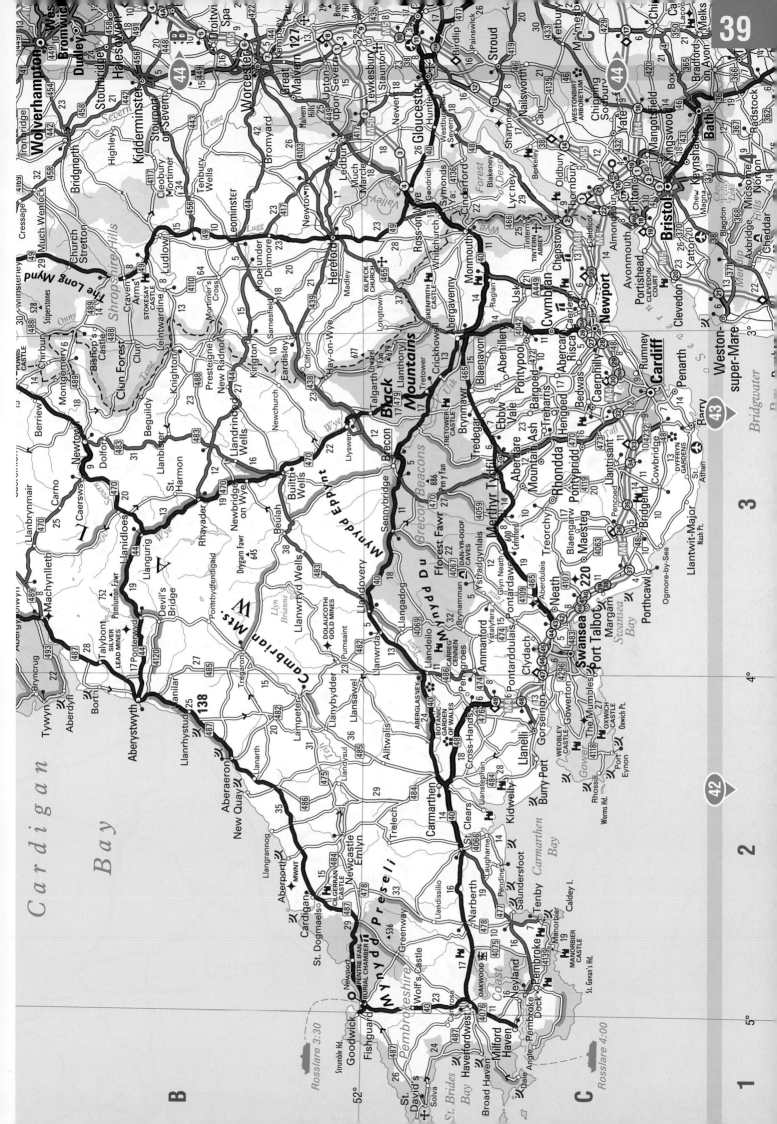

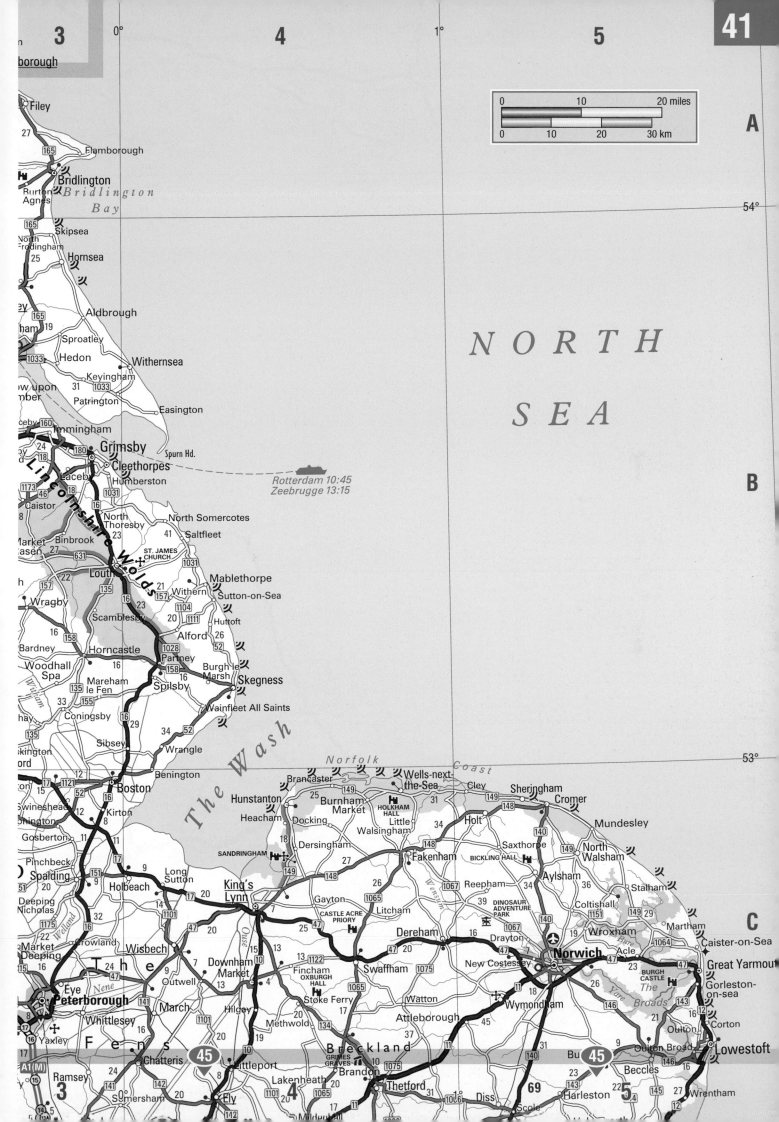

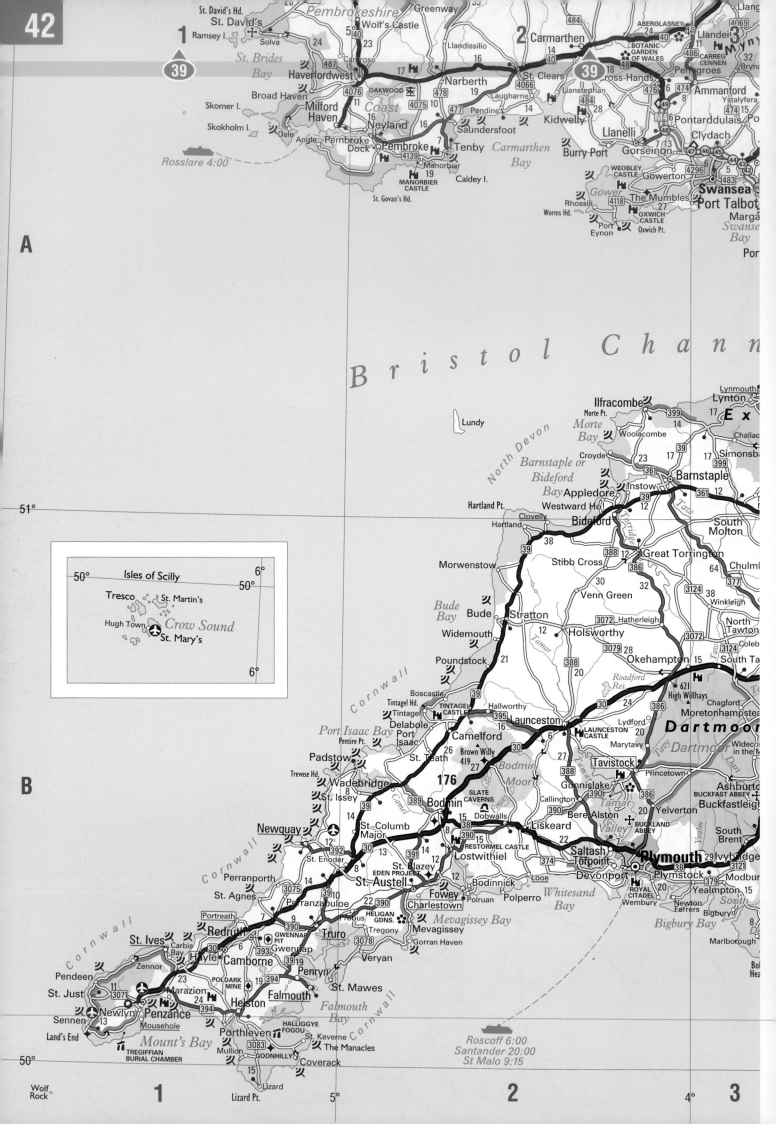

St. David's Hd.
St. David's
Ramsey I.
Solva
**Pembrokeshire**    Greenway
Wolf's Castle
Llandissilio
Carmarthen
Llandei

**1**
39

Haverfordwest
Broad Haven
Milford
Haven
Neyland
Dale
Angle Pembroke
Dock
Pembroke

Skomer I.
Skokholm I.

Rosslare 4:00

Narberth
Laugharne
Pendine
Saundersfoot
Tenby
Manorbier
MANORBIER
CASTLE
Caldey I.
St. Govan's Hd.

St. Clears
Llanstephan
Kidwelly

Carmarthen
Bay

Burry Port
Llanelli

Botanic
Garden
of Wales
39
Cross-Hands
Pontarddulais
Gorseinon

Aberglasney
Llandei
Carreg
Cennen
Ammanford
Ystalyfera

**3**
Mynydd

WEOBLEY
CASTLE    Gowerton
Gower
Rhossili
The Mumbles
Worms Hd.    Port
Eynon    OXWICH
CASTLE    Oxwich Pt.

Swansea
Port Talbot
Marga
Swanse
Bay
Por

**A**

**Bristol Chann**

Lundy

Ilfracombe
Morte Pt.
Morte
Bay
North Devon
Barnstaple or
Bideford
Bay
Hartland Pt.
Hartland
Clovelly
Morwenstow

Woolacombe
Croyde
Appledore
Instow
Westward Ho!
Bideford

Lynmouth
Lynton
Ex
399
17
Challac
399
361
Barnstaple
Simonsba
South
Molton

Bude
Bay    Bude
Widemouth
Poundstock
Boscastle
Tintagel Hd.
Tintagel
Delabole
Port Isaac Bay    Port
Pentire Pt.    Isaac
St. Teath
Padstow
Trevose Hd.    Wadebridge
St. Issey
Newquay

Stratton
Holsworthy
Hatherleigh
Okehampton
Hallworthy
Launceston
LAUNCESTON
CASTLE
Camelford
Brown Willy
419
Bodmin
Moor
SLATE
CAVERNS
Dobwalls
Bodmin
Liskeard
St. Columb
Major
St. Enoder
RESTORMEL CASTLE
Lostwithiel
Callington
Gunnislake
Tavistock

Great Torrington
Stibb Cross
Venn Green
North
Tawton
Roadford
Res.
High Willhays
621
Lydford
Marytavy
Princetown
BUCKFAST ABBEY

Chumle
Winkleigh
Chagford
Moretonhampstea
**Dartmoor**
Dartmoor
Widecc
in the
Ashbur
Buckfastleigh

**51°**

**Isles of Scilly**
Tresco    St. Martin's
Hugh Town    Crow Sound
St. Mary's
**50°**    **6°**
**50°**
**6°**

Cornwall

**B**

Cornwall

Perranporth
St. Agnes
Portreath
Redruth
St. Ives
Carbis
Bay
Zennor
Pendeen
St. Just
Sennen
Land's End
Mousehole
Newlyn
Penzance
TREGIFFIAN
BURIAL CHAMBER
Marazion
Helston
Wolf
Rock    Lizard
Lizard Pt.

Perranzabuloe
Truro
Gwennap
GWENNAP
PIT
Gwennap
Camborne
POLDARK
MINE
Penryn
Falmouth
St. Mawes
Falmouth
Bay
Mullion
TREGIFFIAN
HALLIGGYE
FOGOU
St. Keverne
GOONHILLY
Coverack
The Manacles
Porthleven

Eden Project
St. Blazey
St. Austell
Charlestown
HELIGAN GDNS.
Probus
Tregony
Veryan
Gorran Haven
Mevagissey
Mevagissey Bay

Bodmin
St. Columb
St. Blazey
Fowey
Bodinnick
Polruan
Looe
Polperro
Whitesand
Bay

Liskeard
Saltash
Torpoint
Devonport
Bere Alston
BUCKLAND
ABBEY
Tamar
Valley
Yelverton

Plymouth
Plymstock
ROYAL
CITADEL
Wembury
Newton
Ferrers

South
Brent
Ivybridge
Yealmpton
Modbur
Bigbury
Bigbury Bay
Marlborough
Bol
Hea
D

Roscoff 6:00
Santander 20:00
St Malo 9:15

Mount's Bay

**50°**

**1**    **5°**    **2**    **4°**    **3**

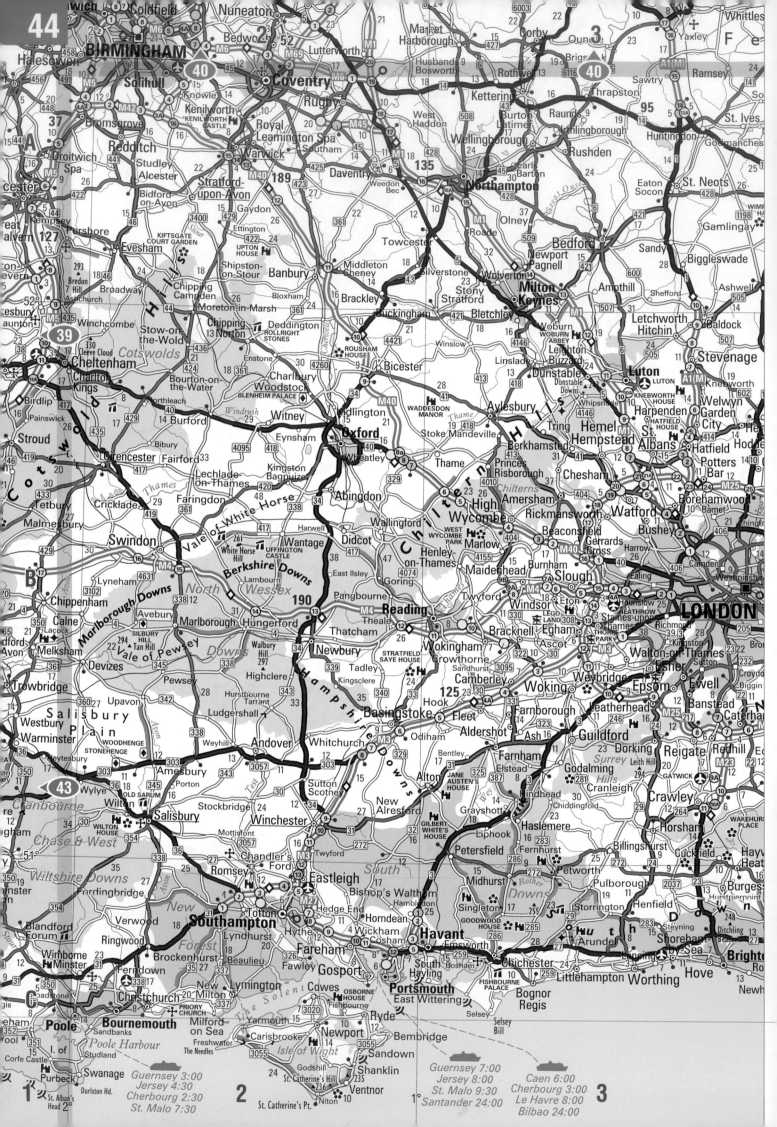

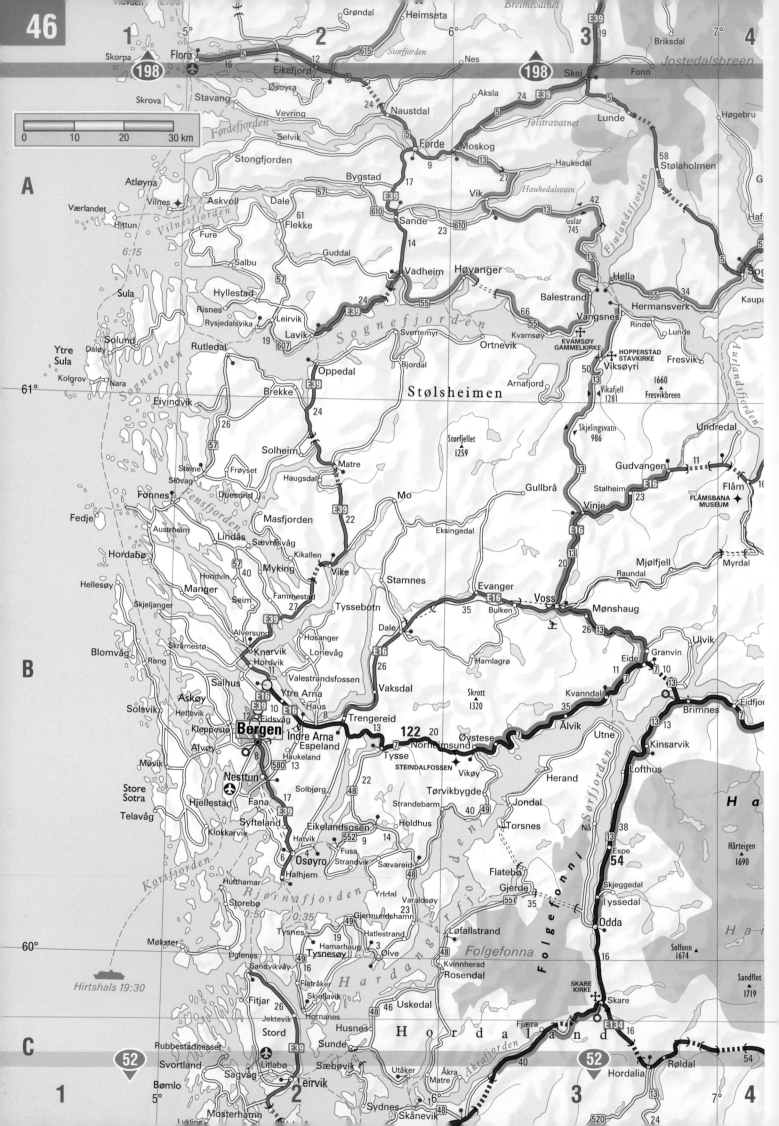

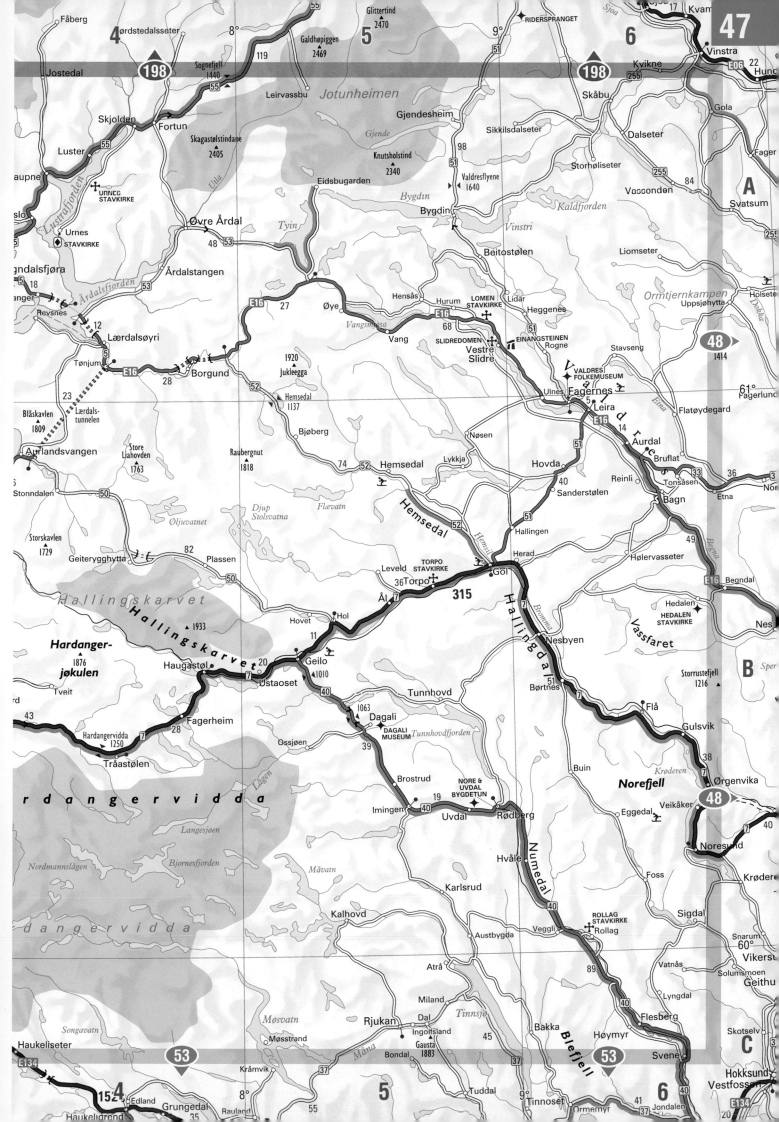

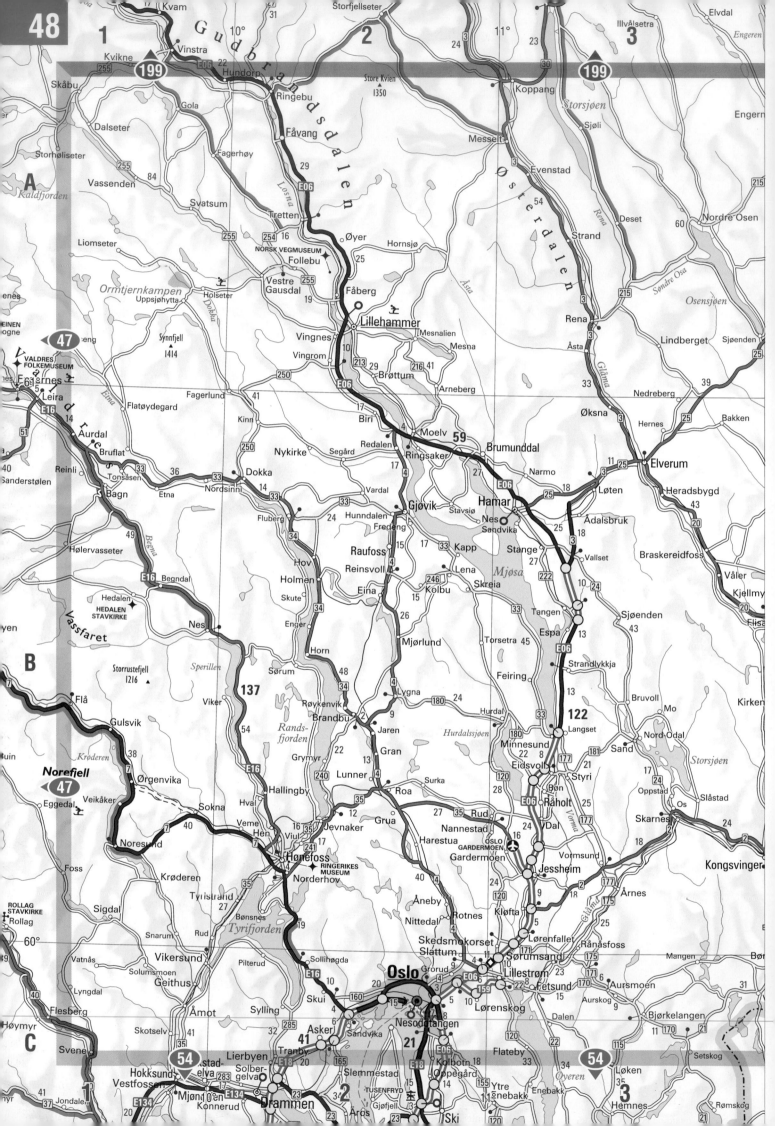

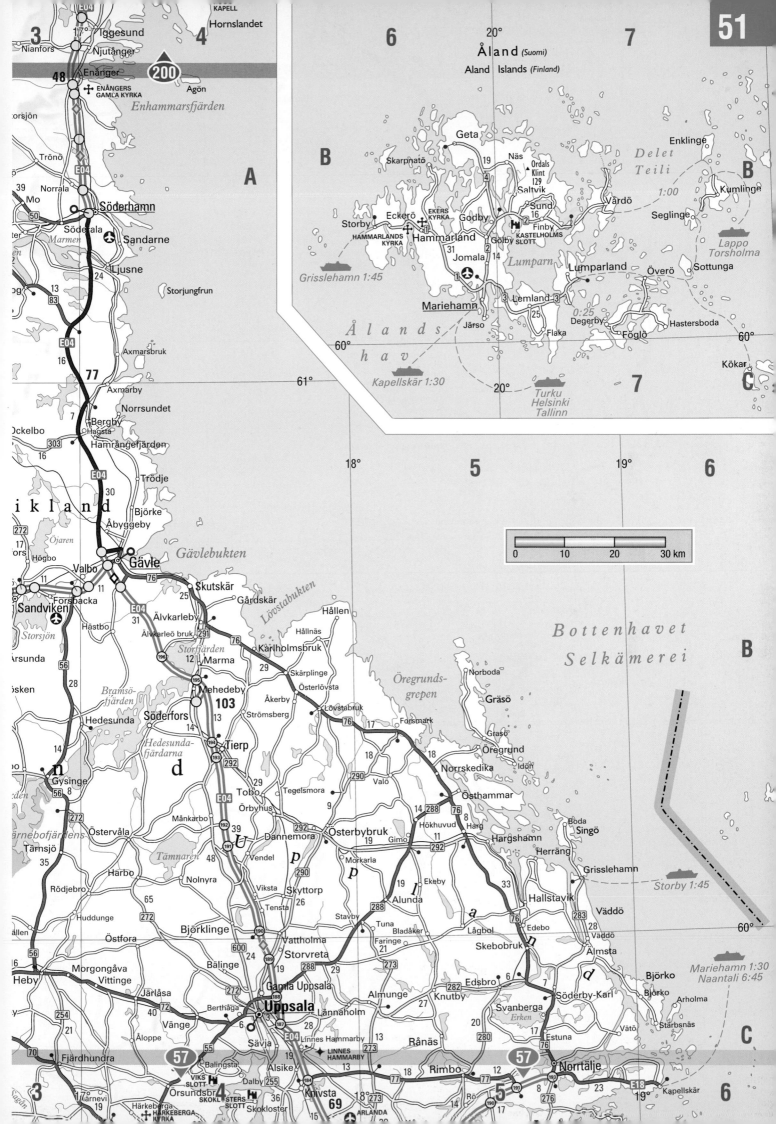

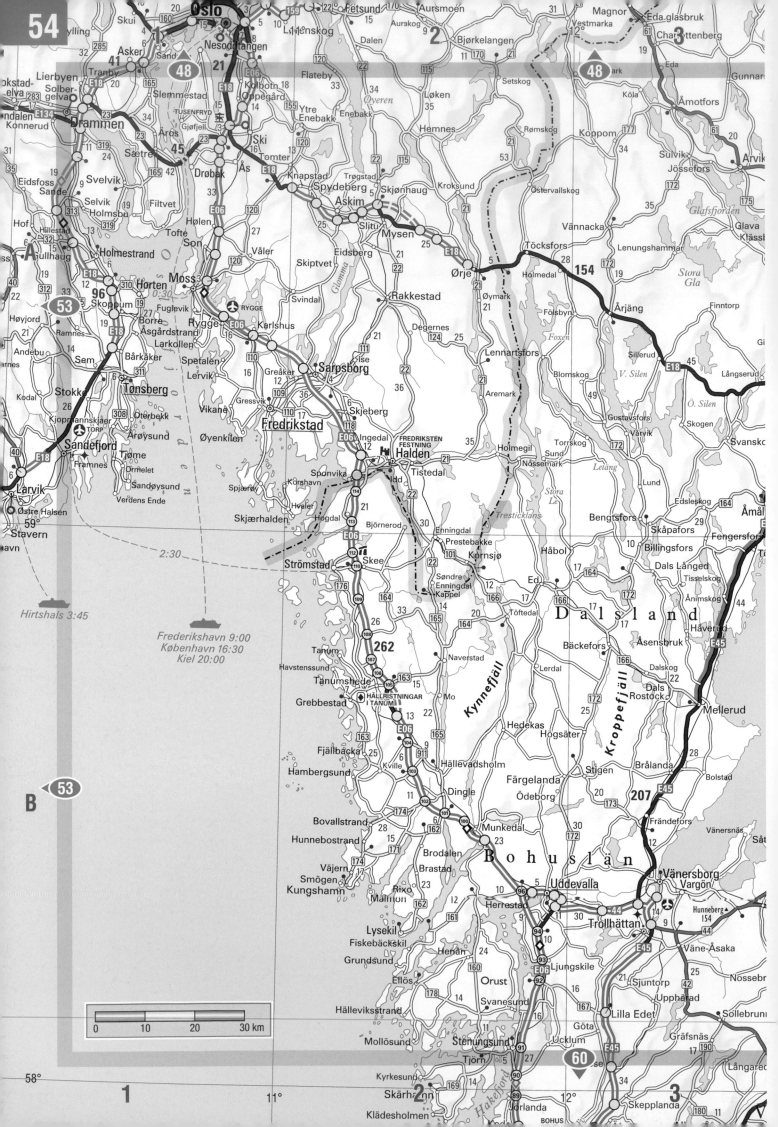

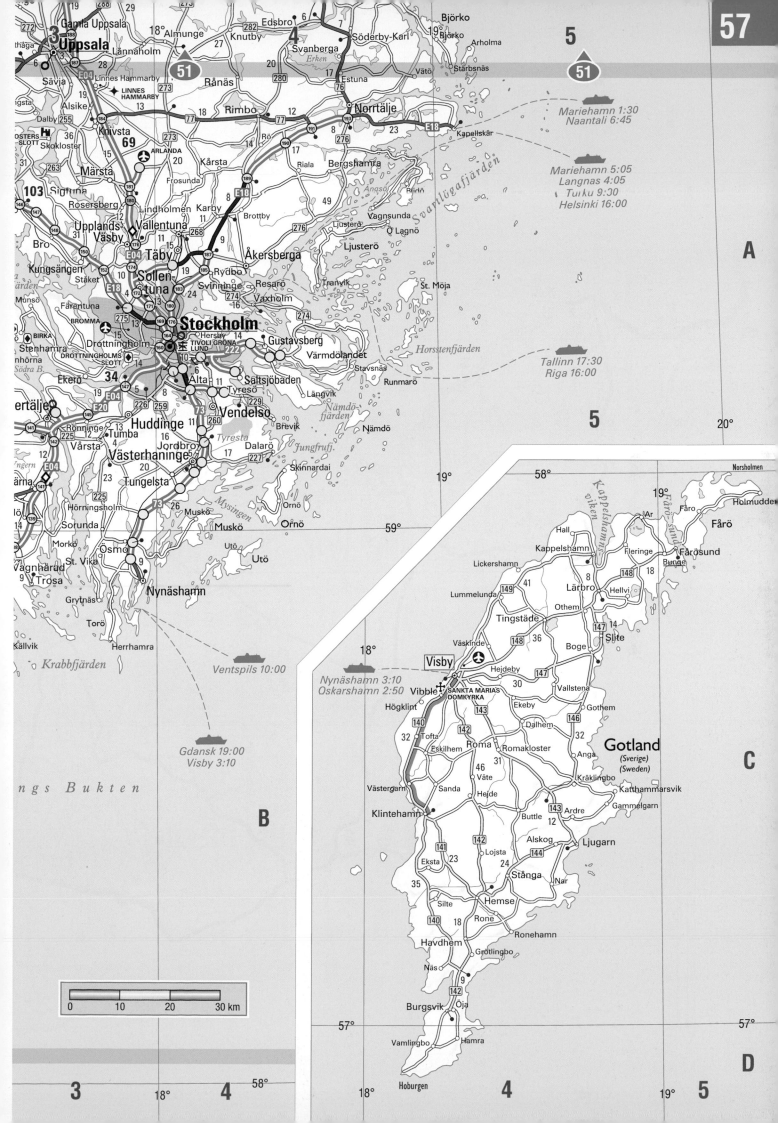

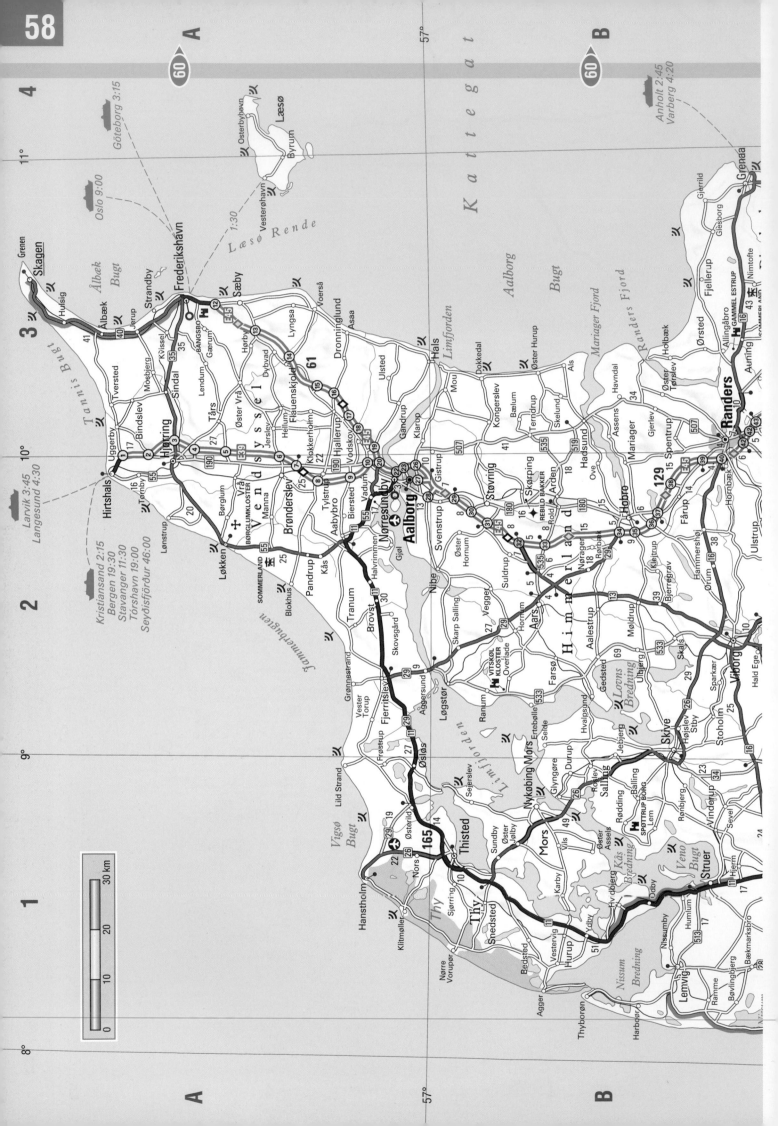

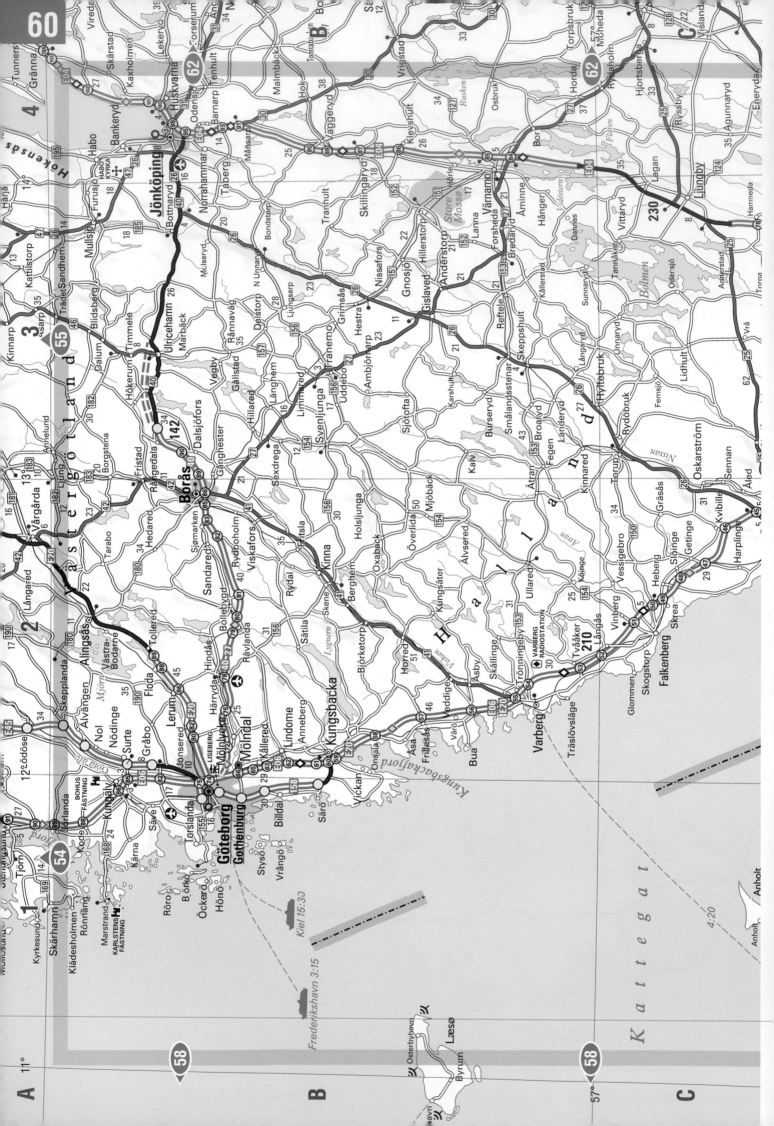

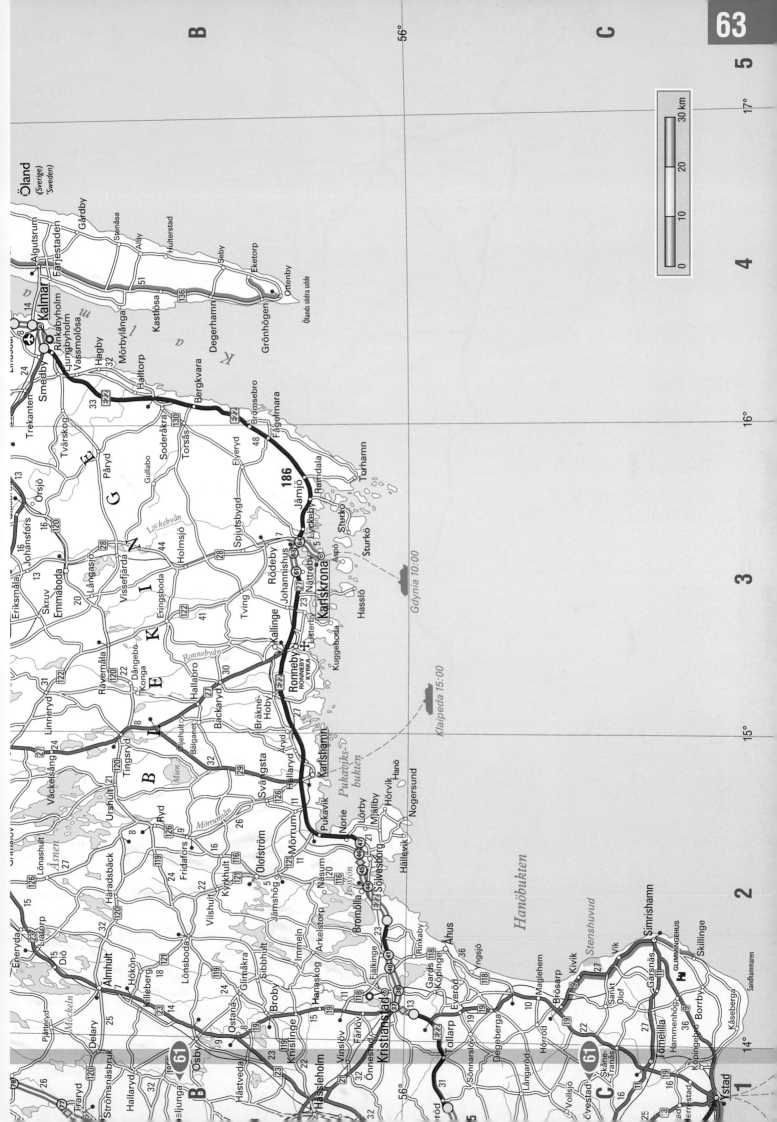

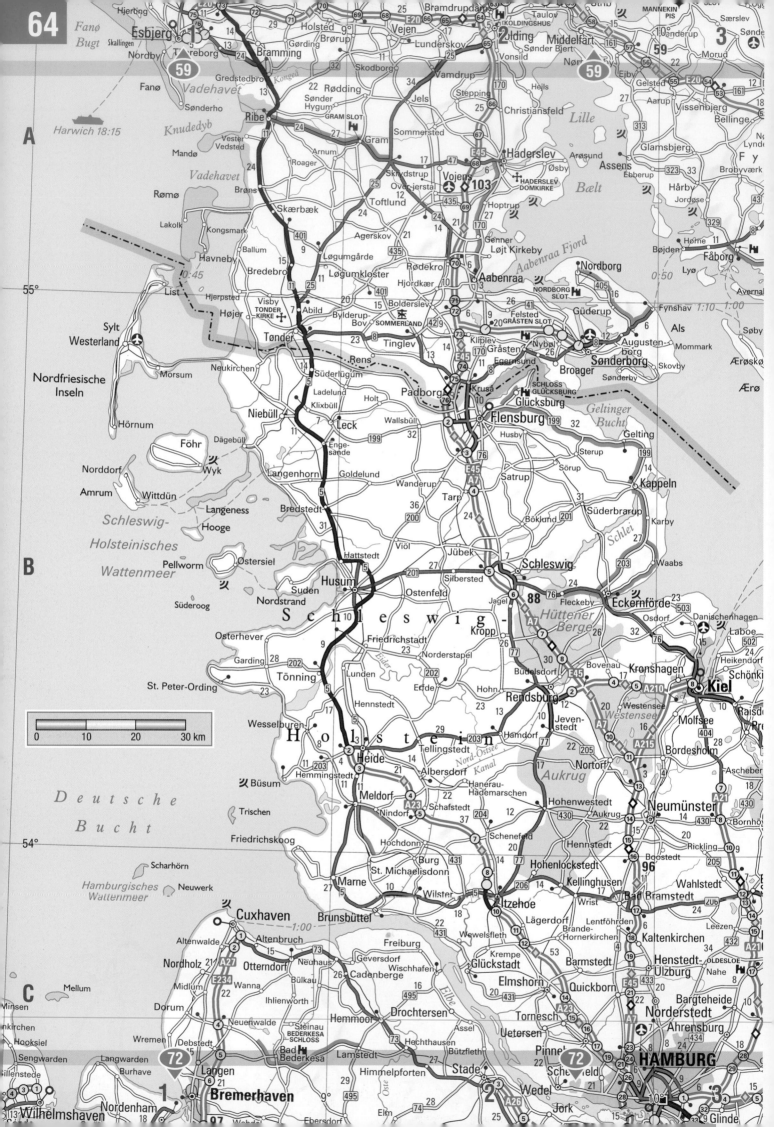

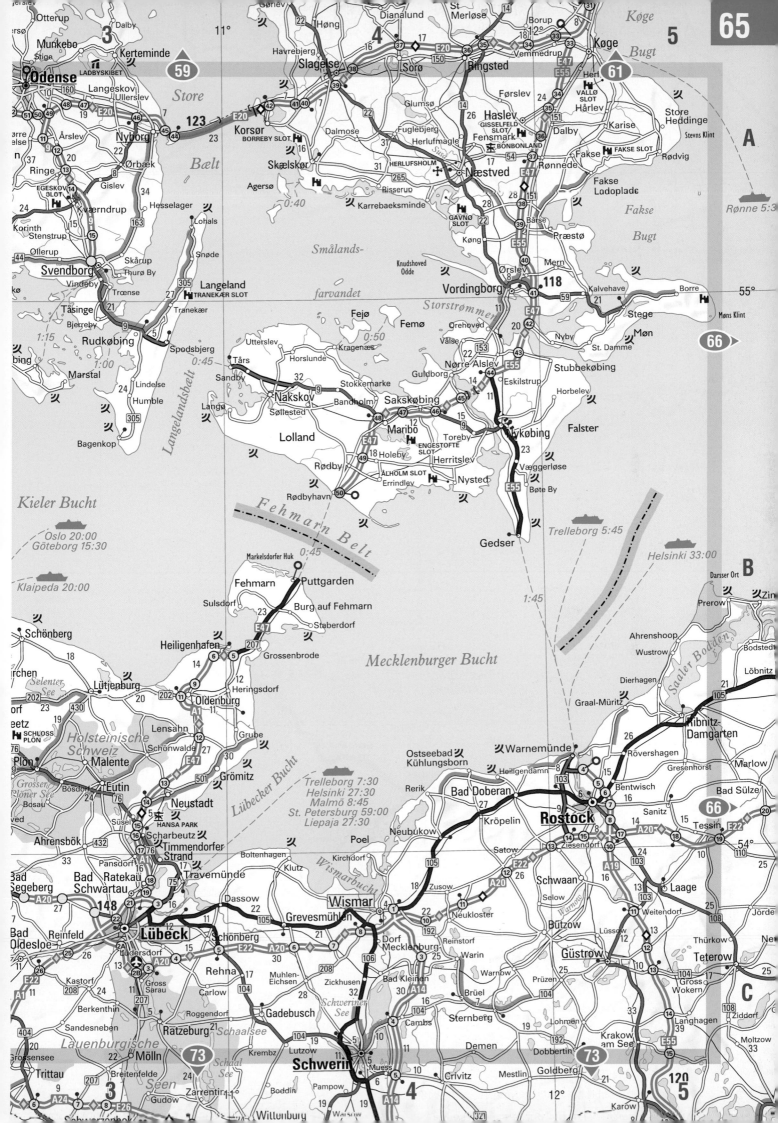

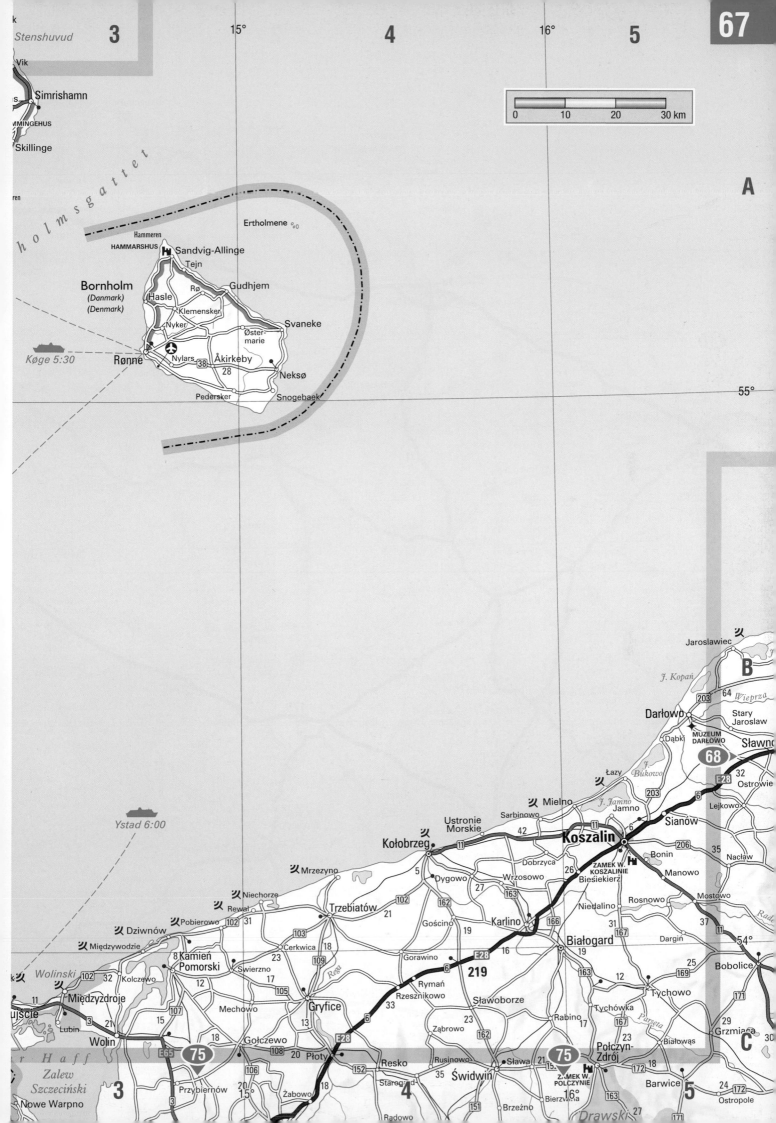

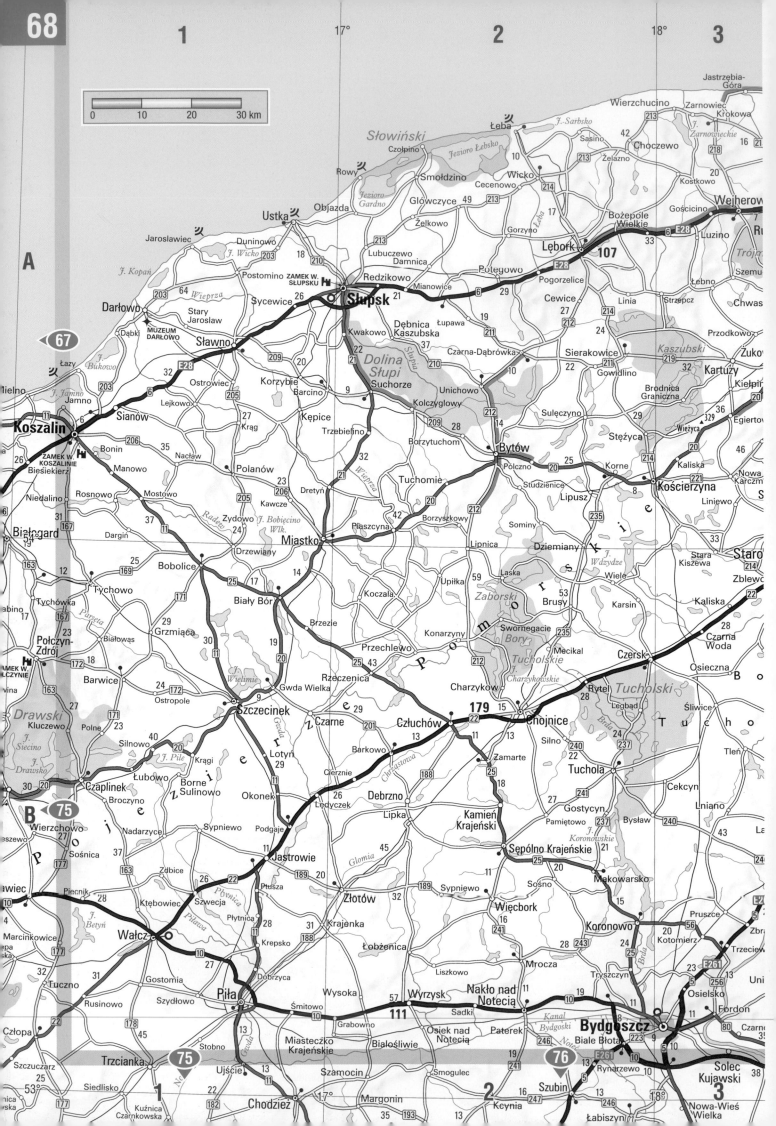

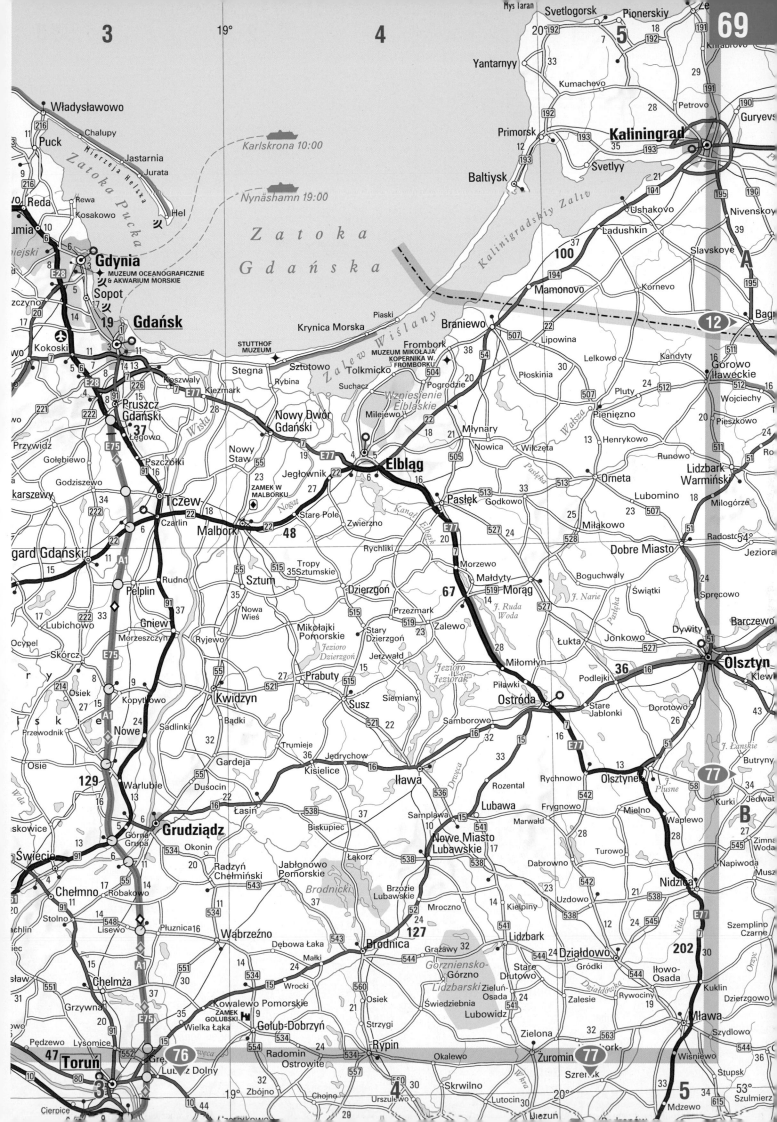

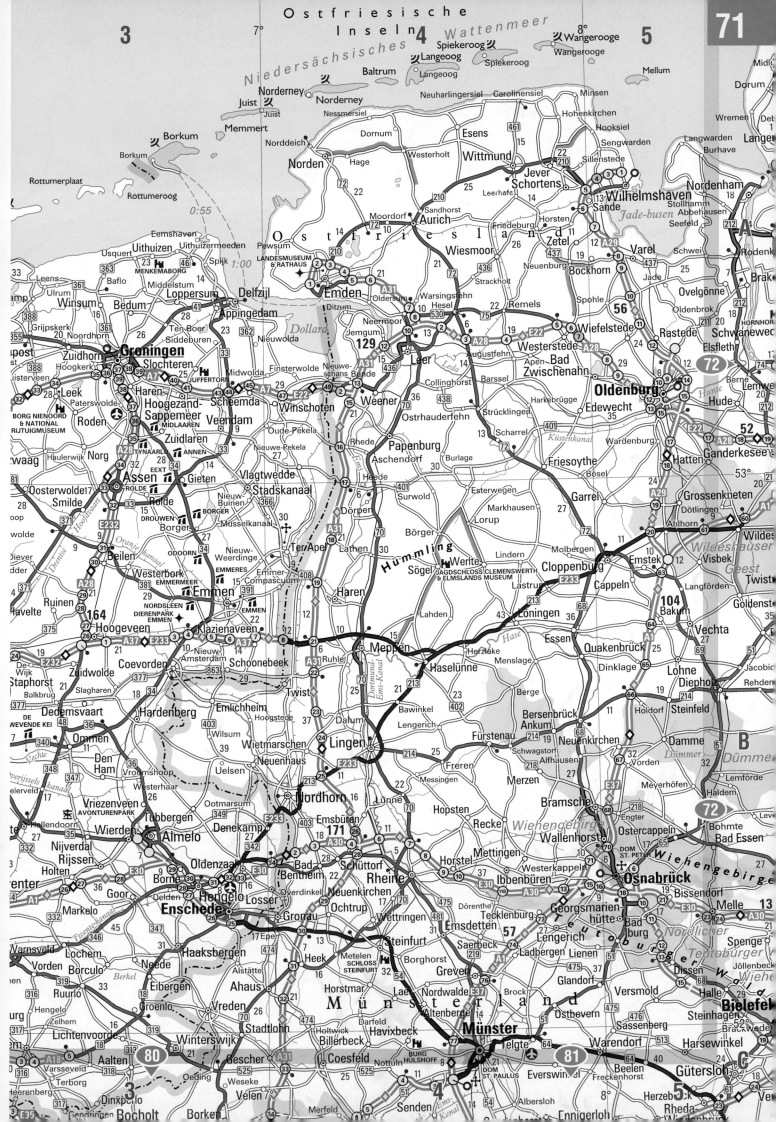

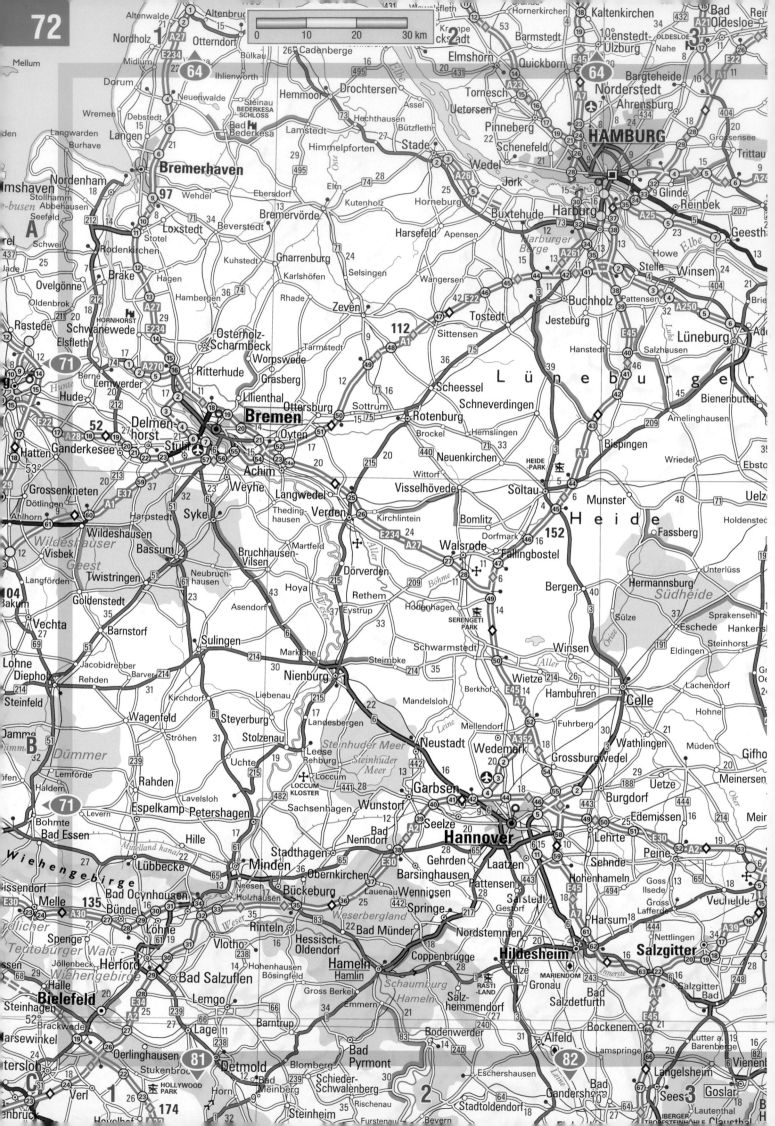

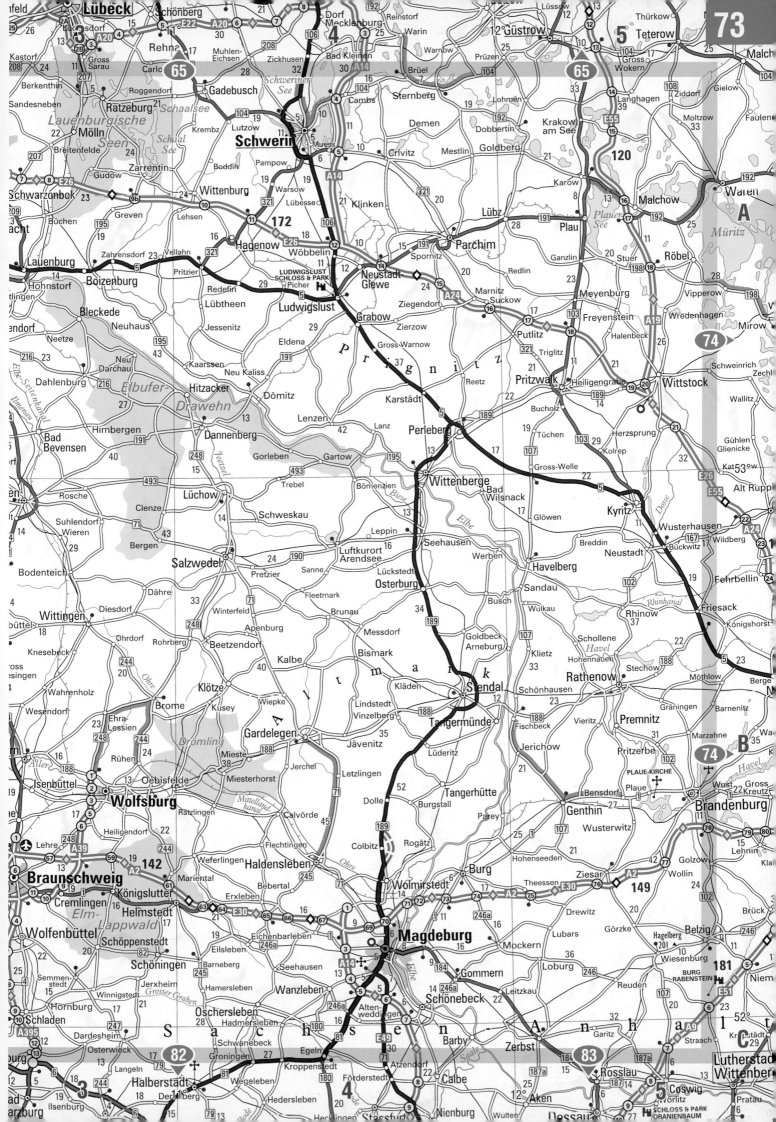

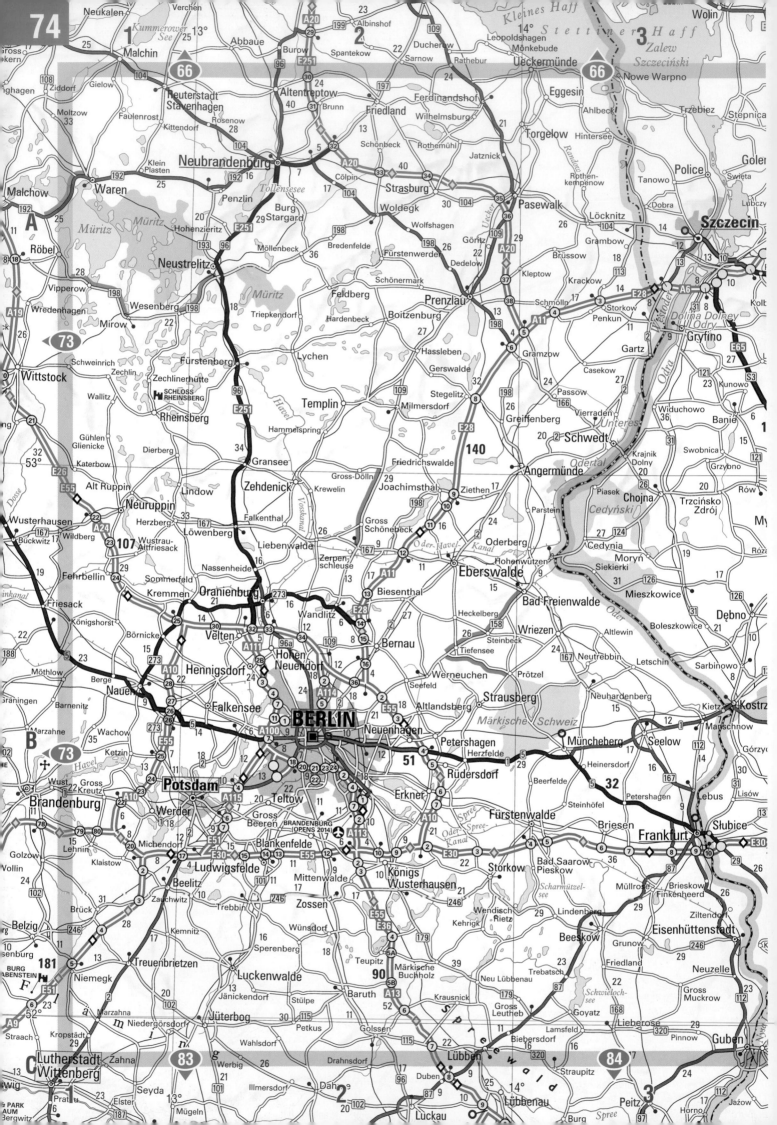

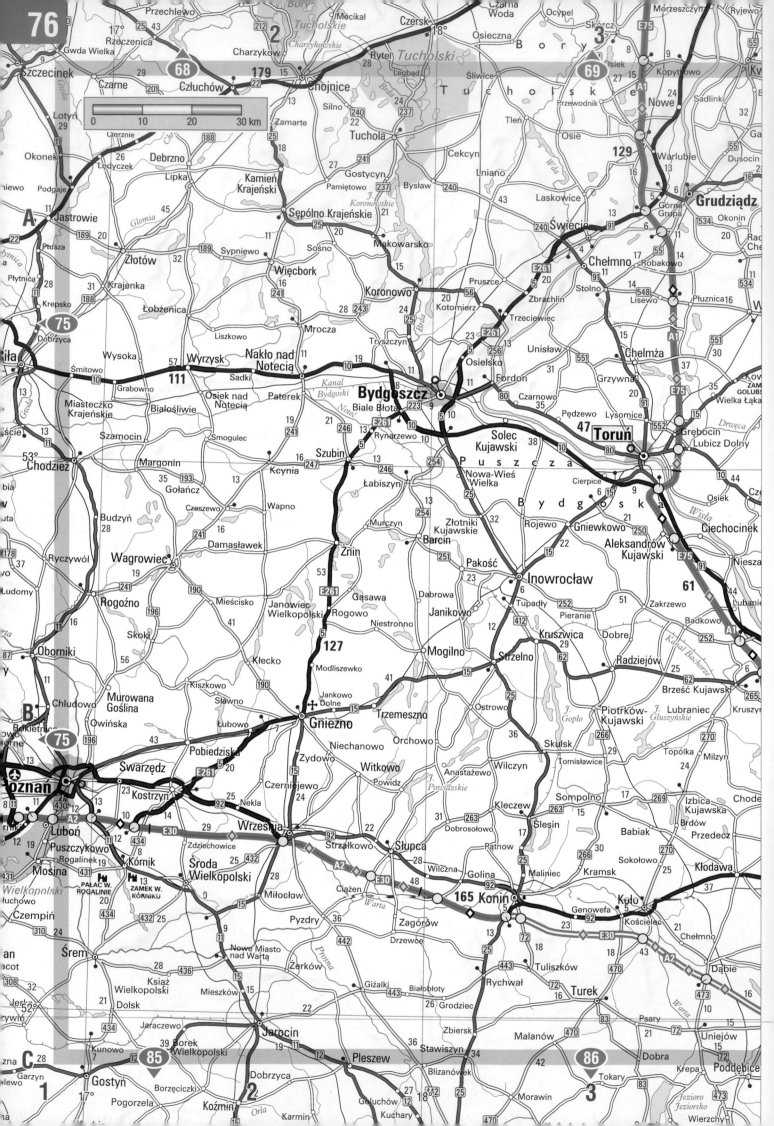

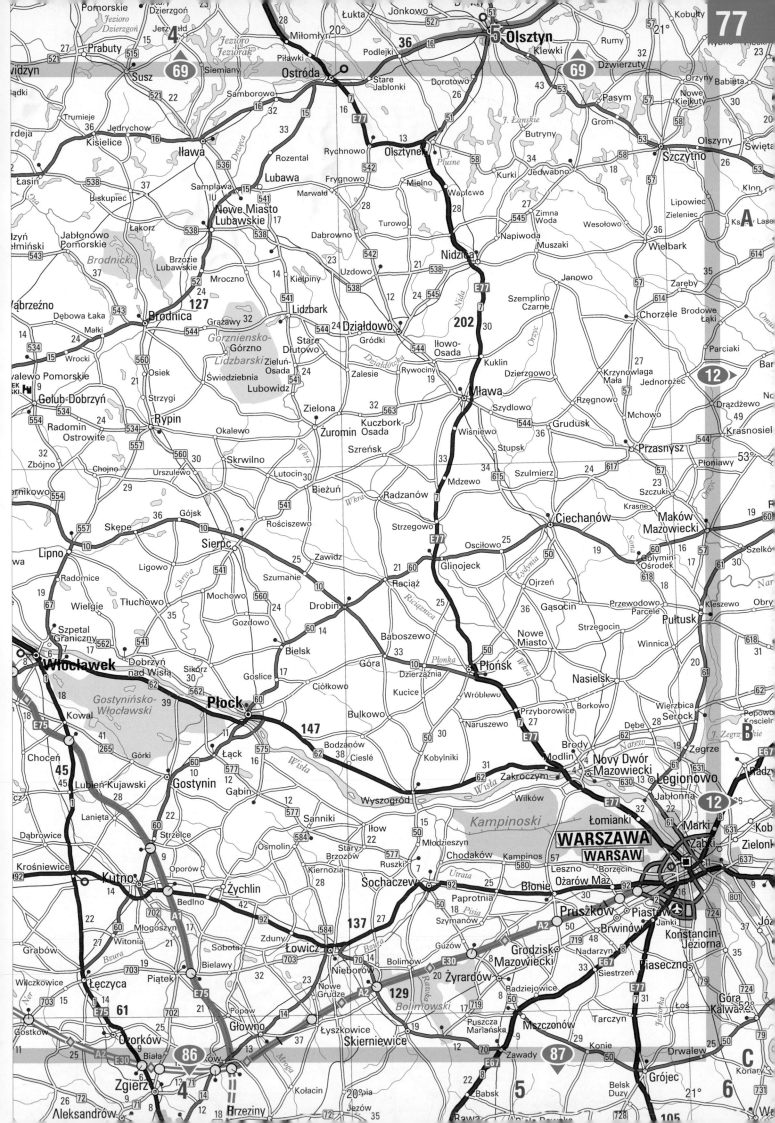

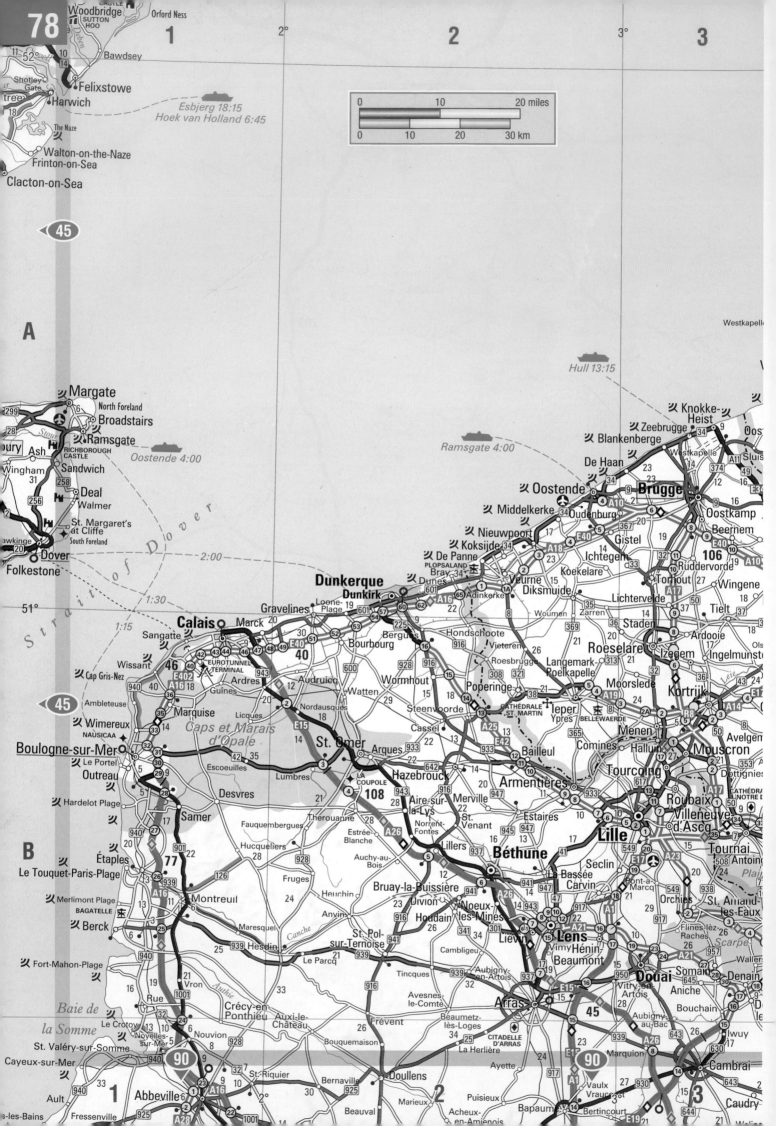

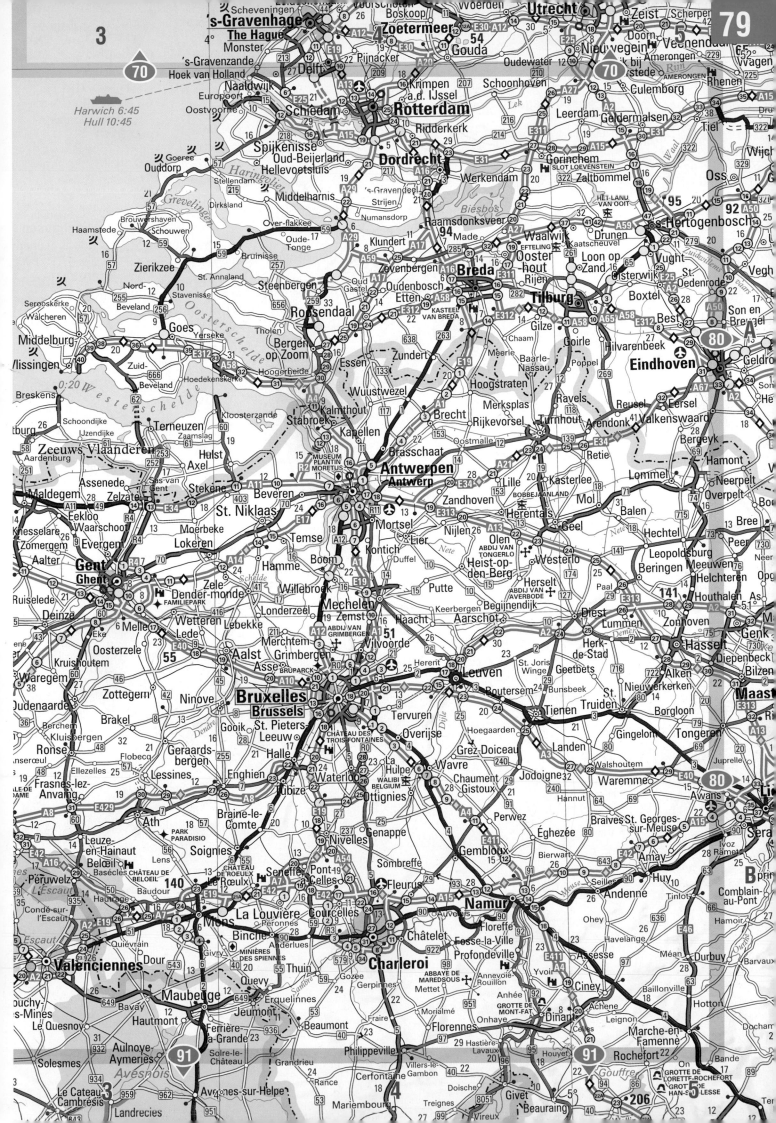

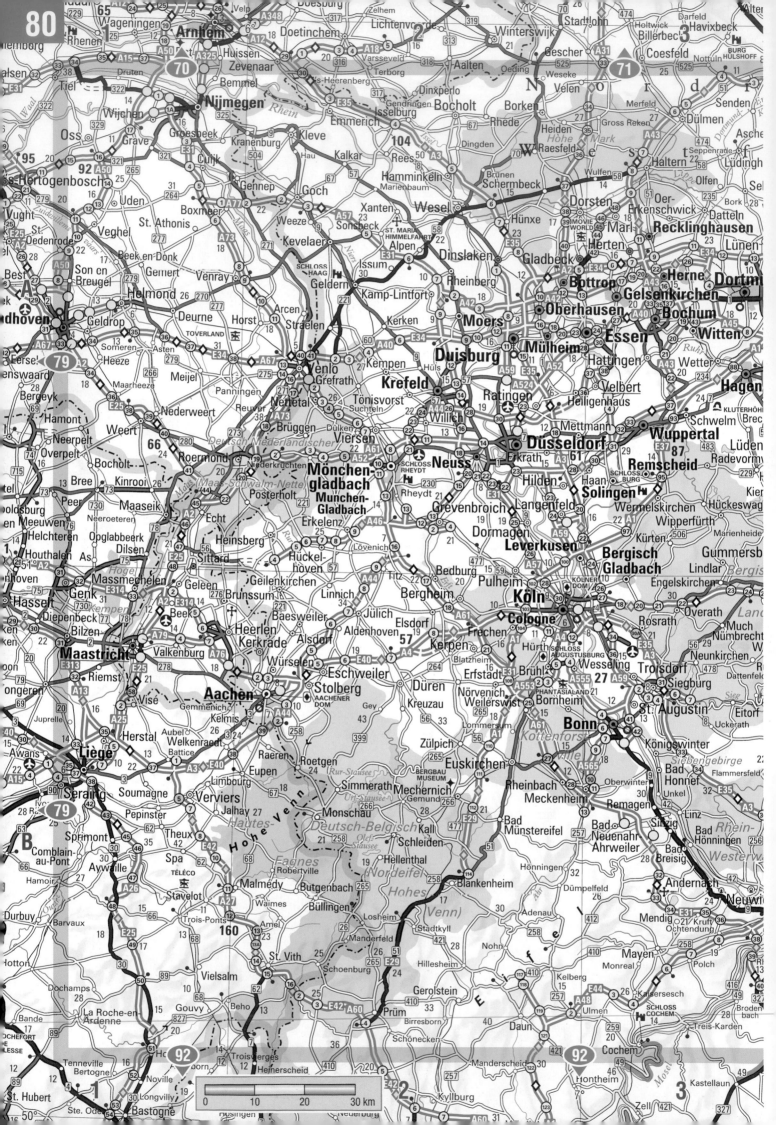

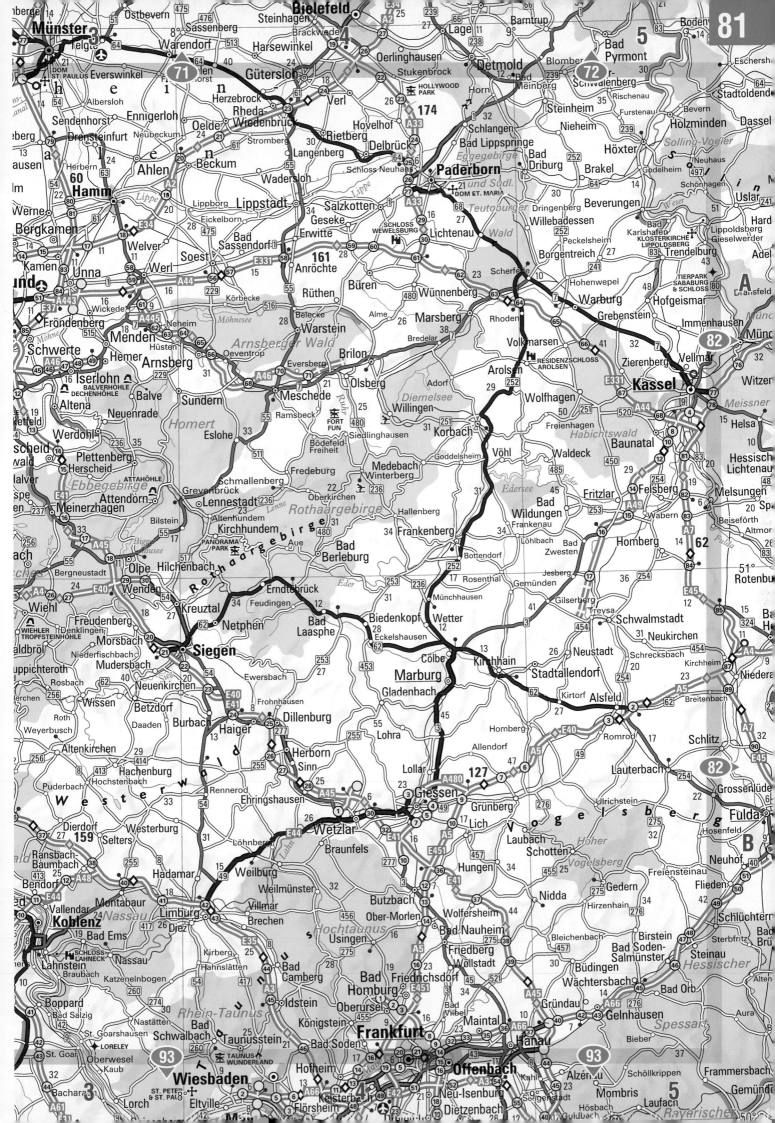

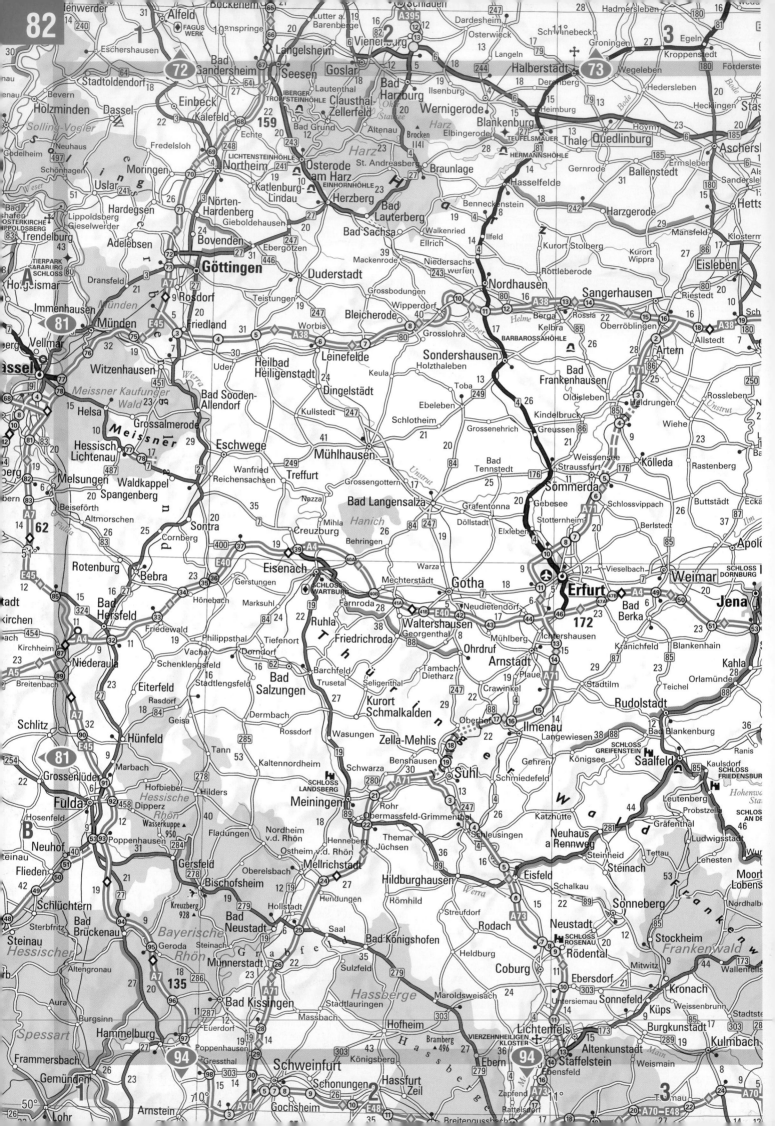

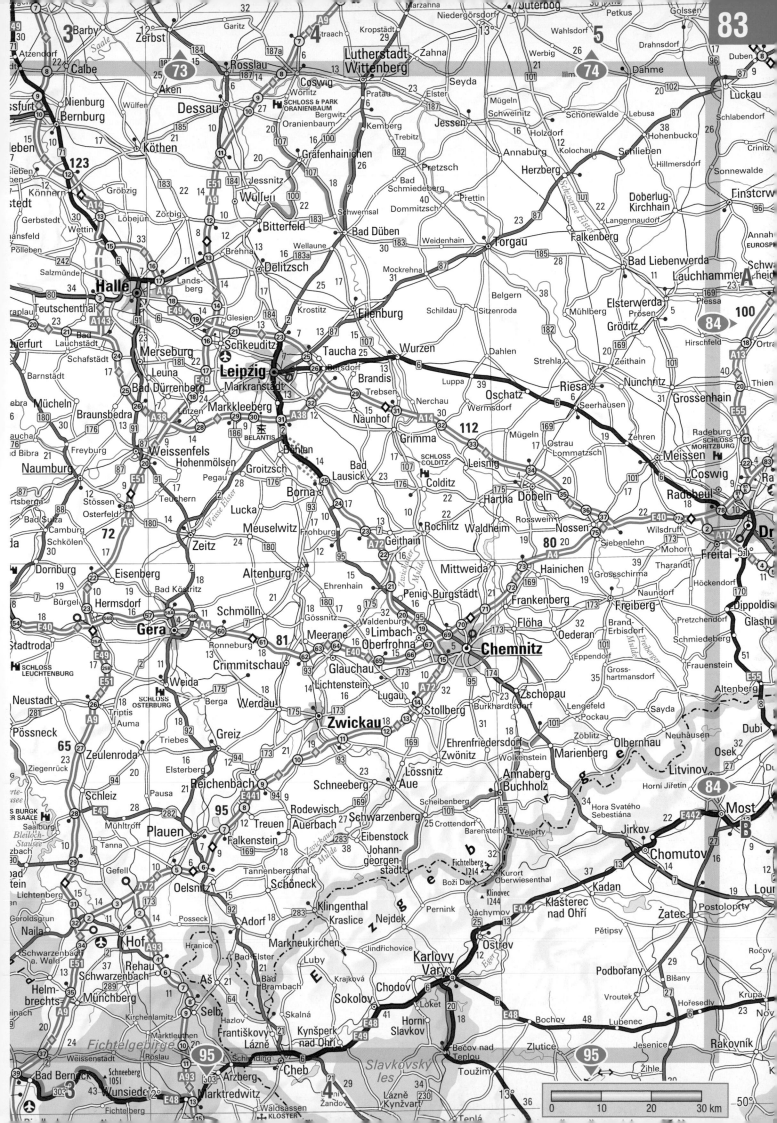

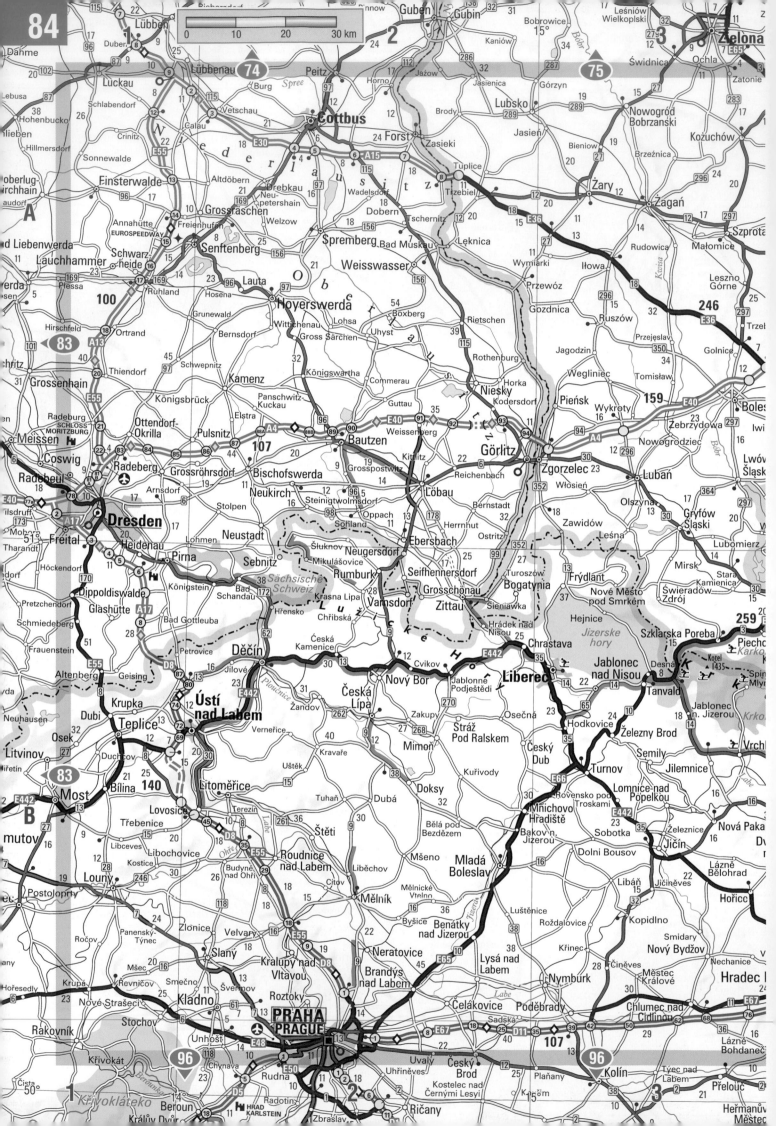

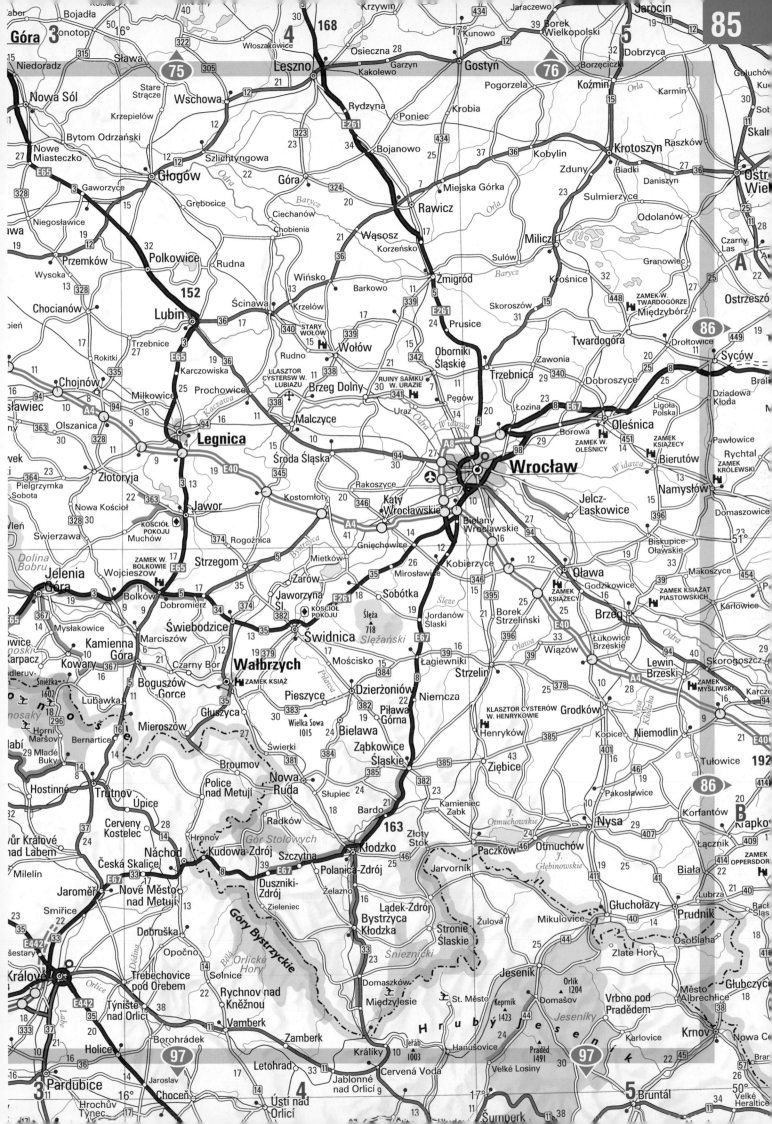

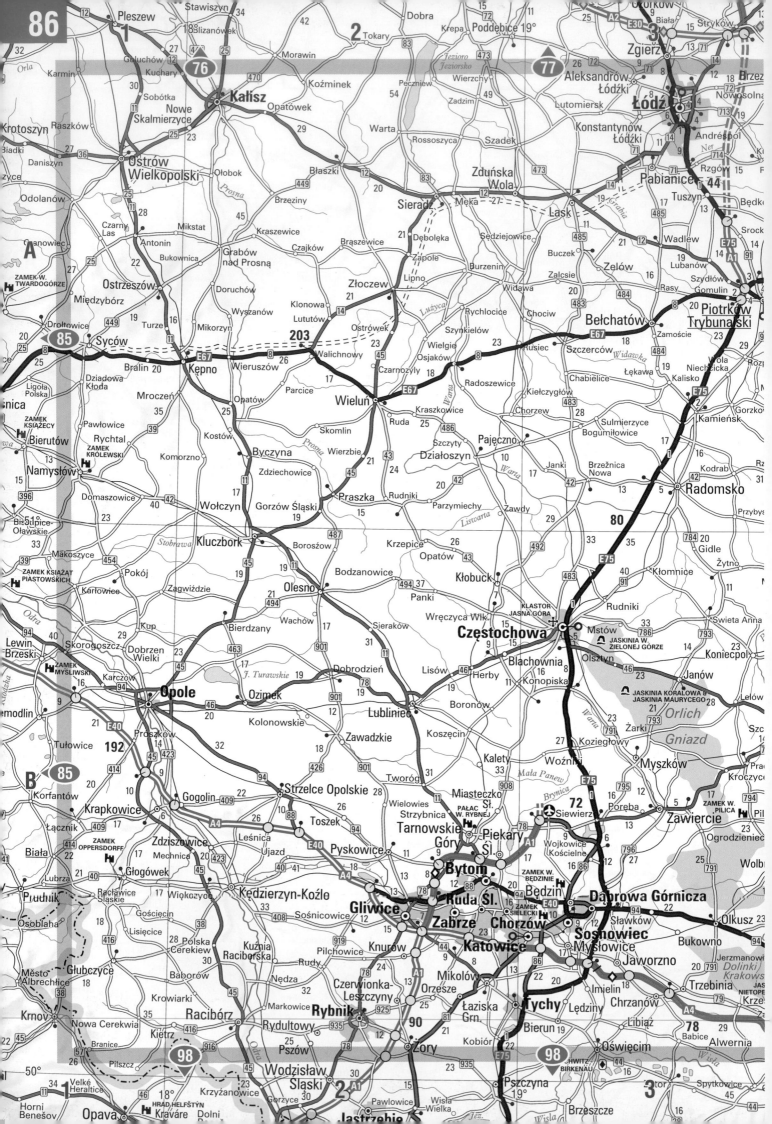

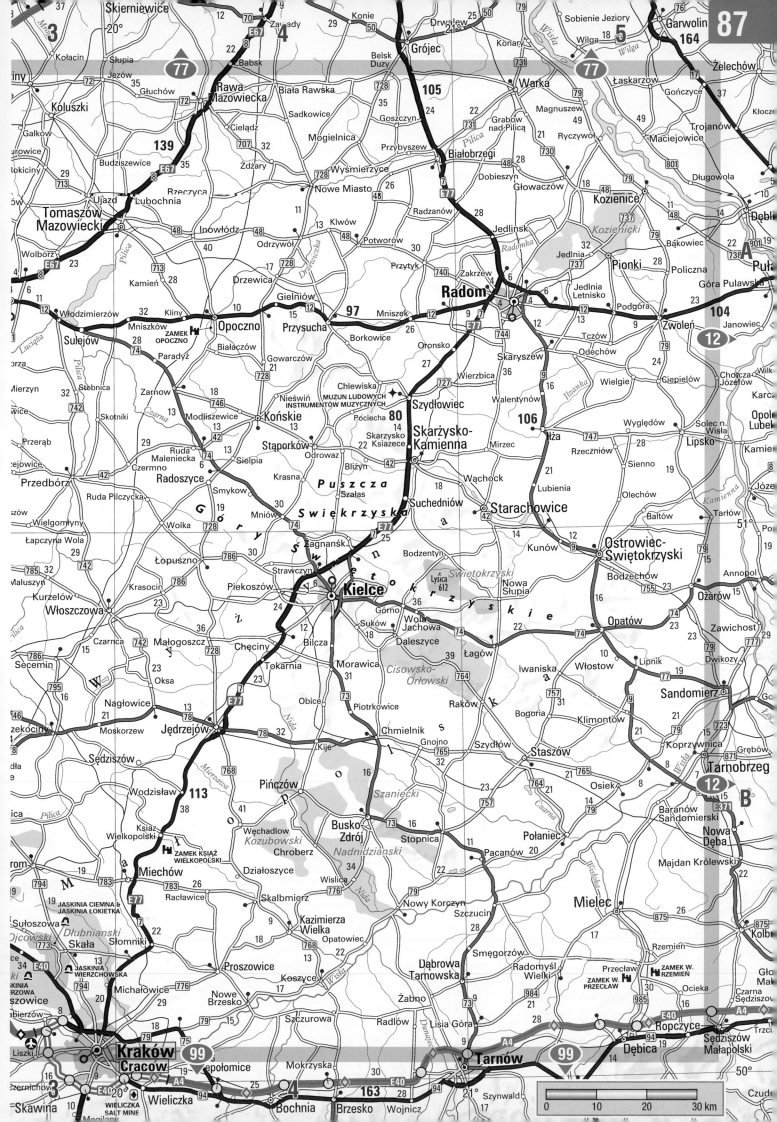

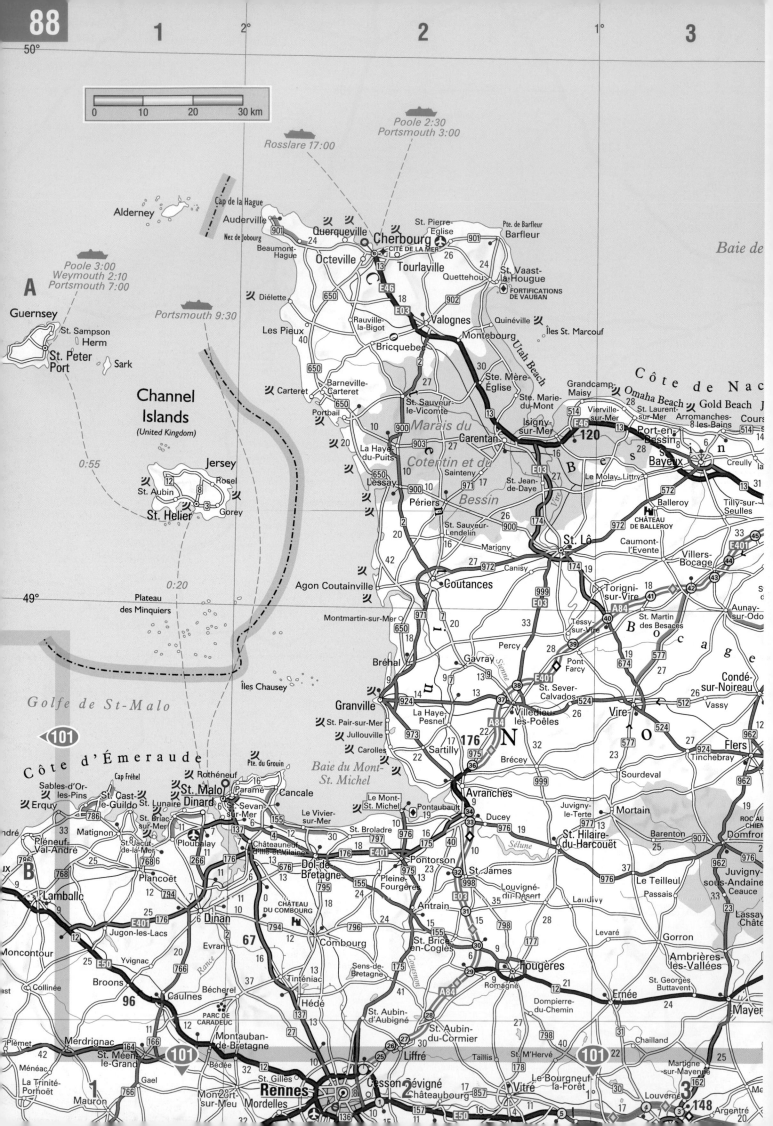

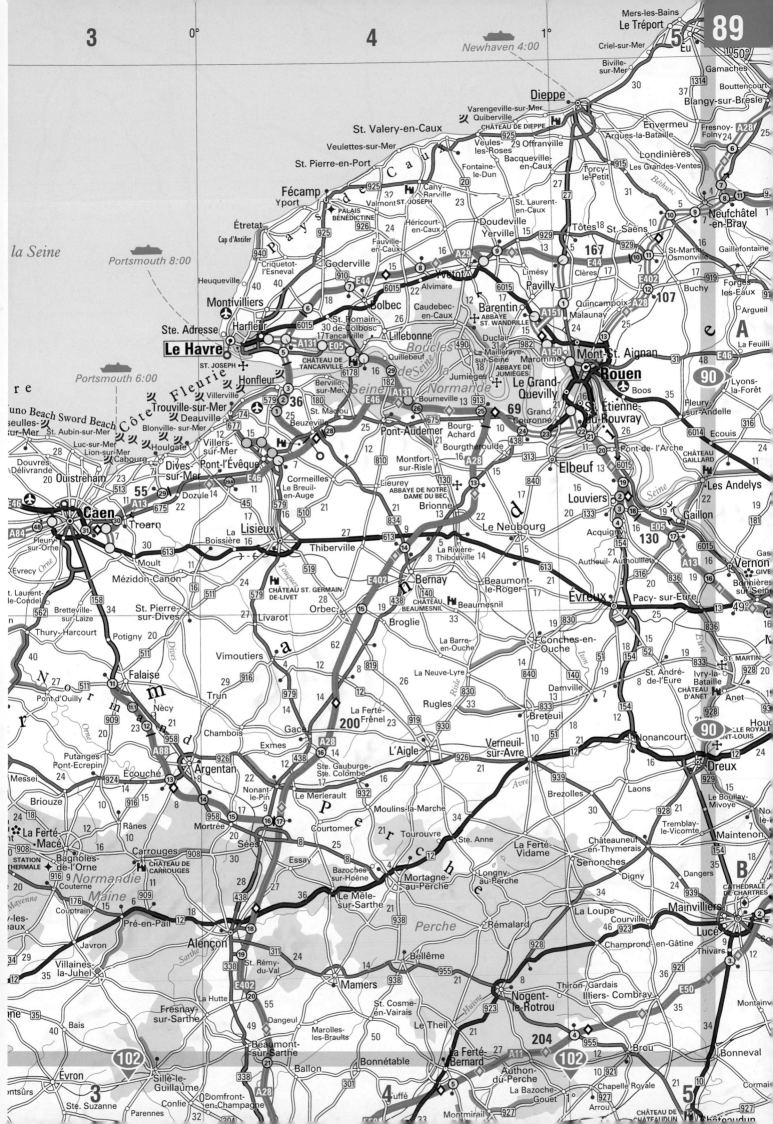

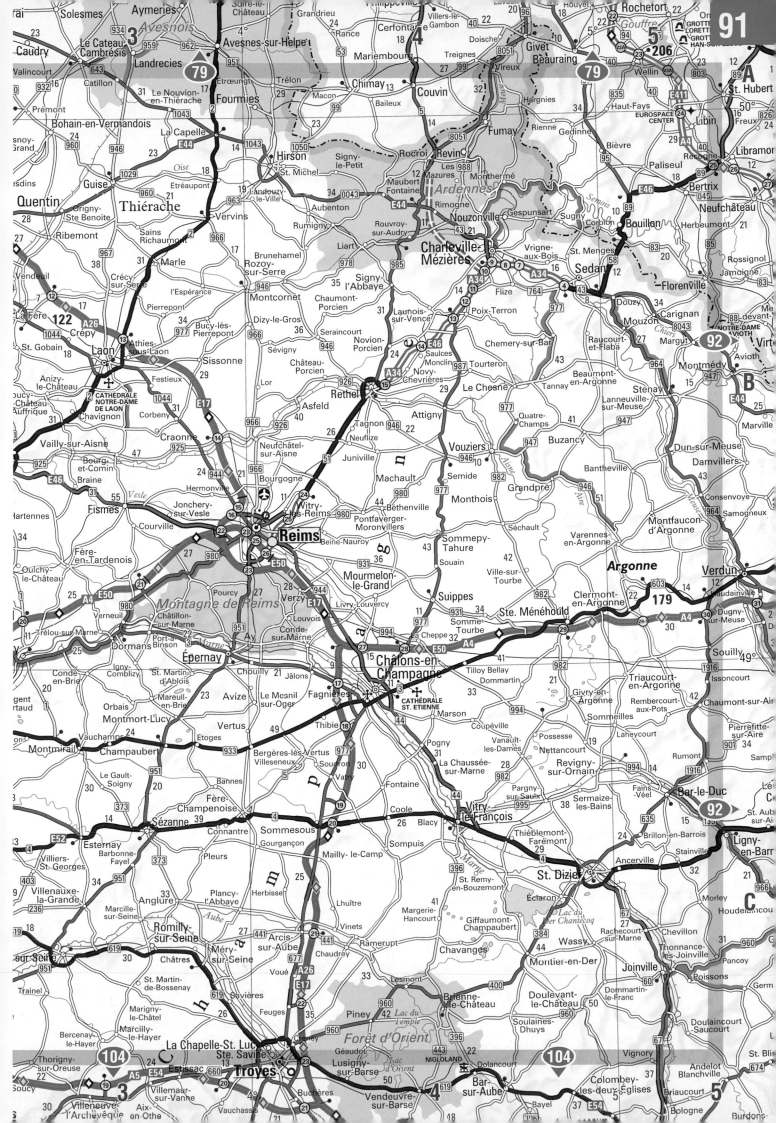

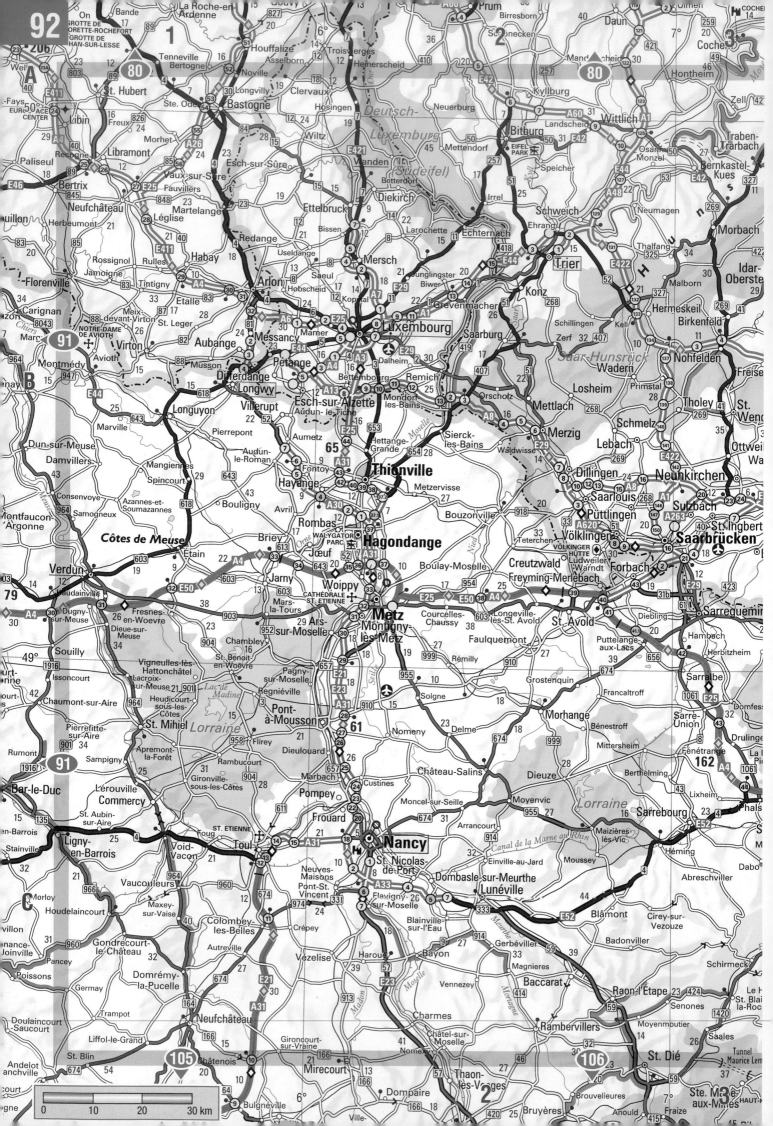

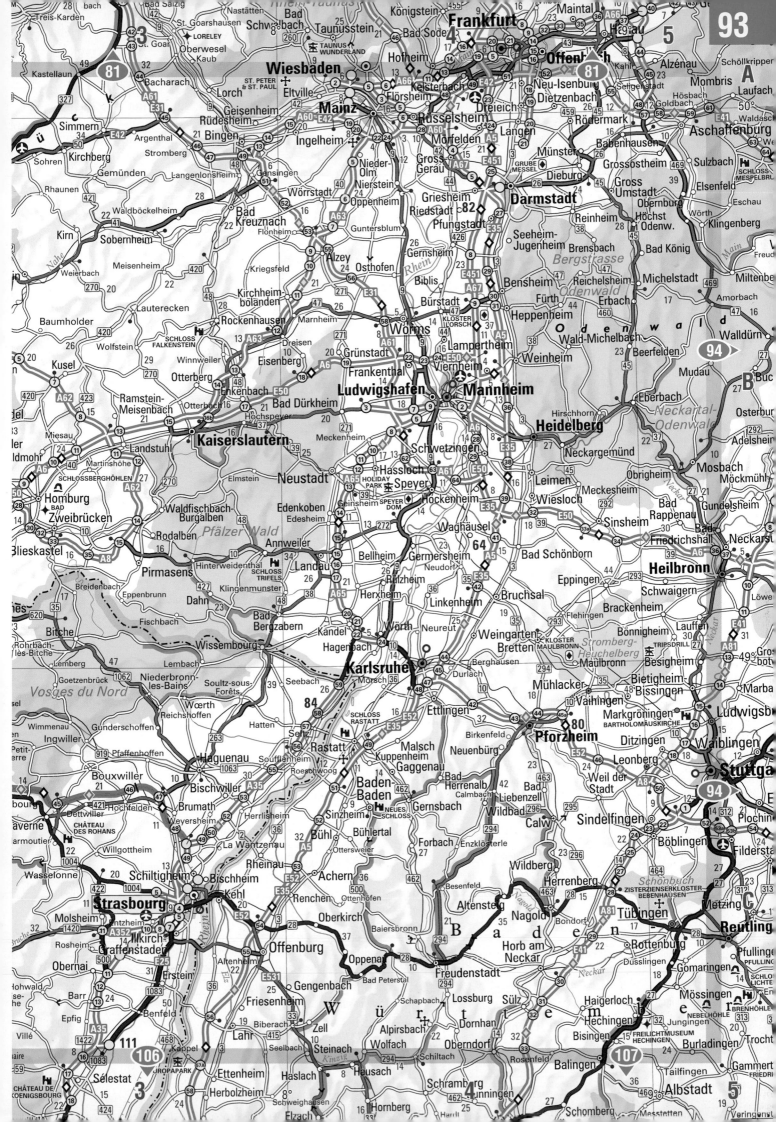

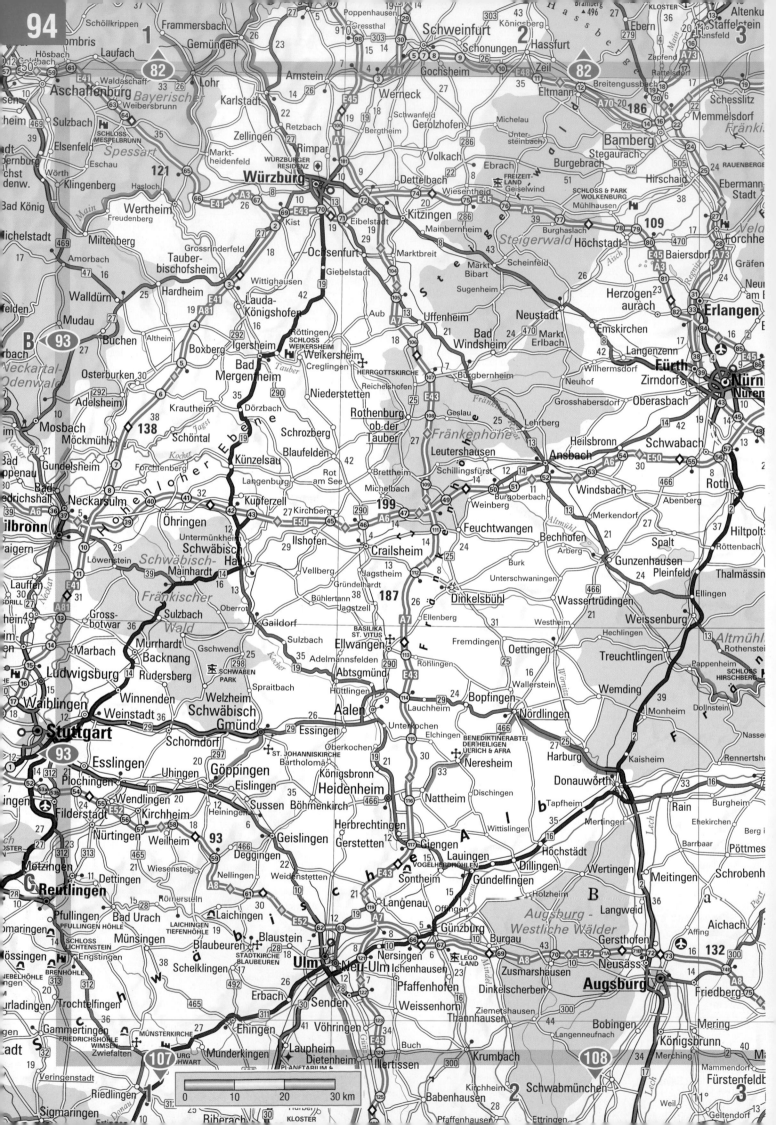

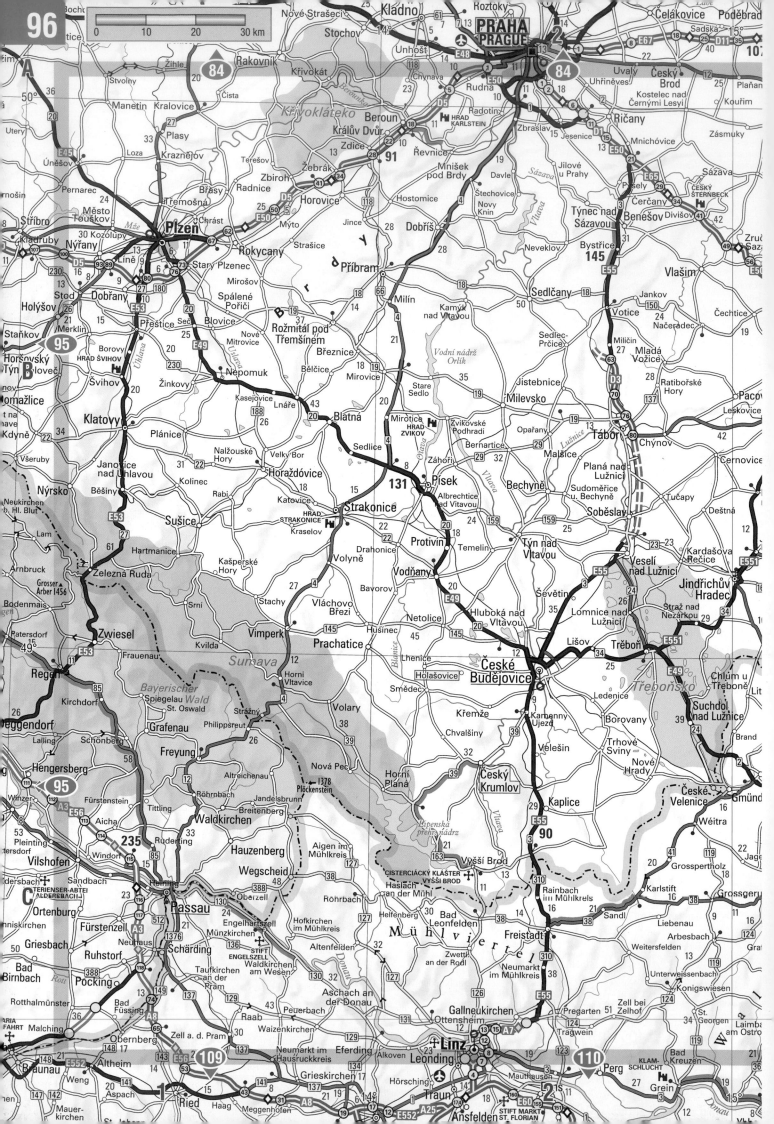

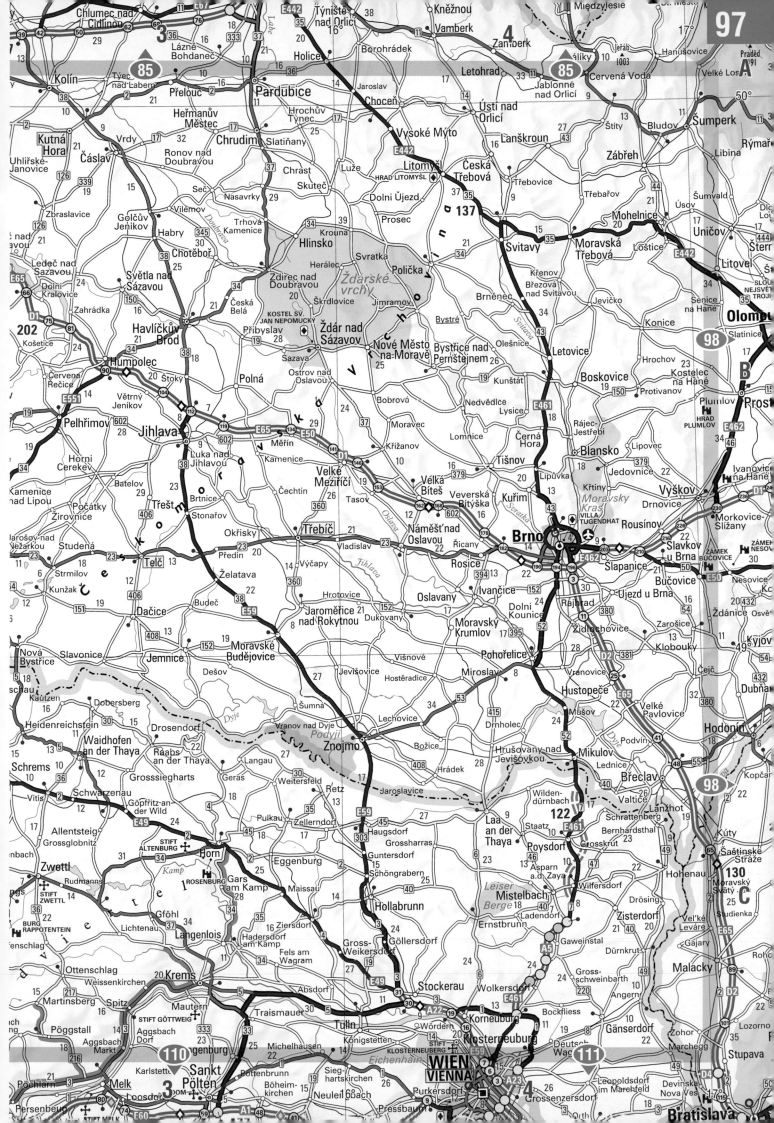

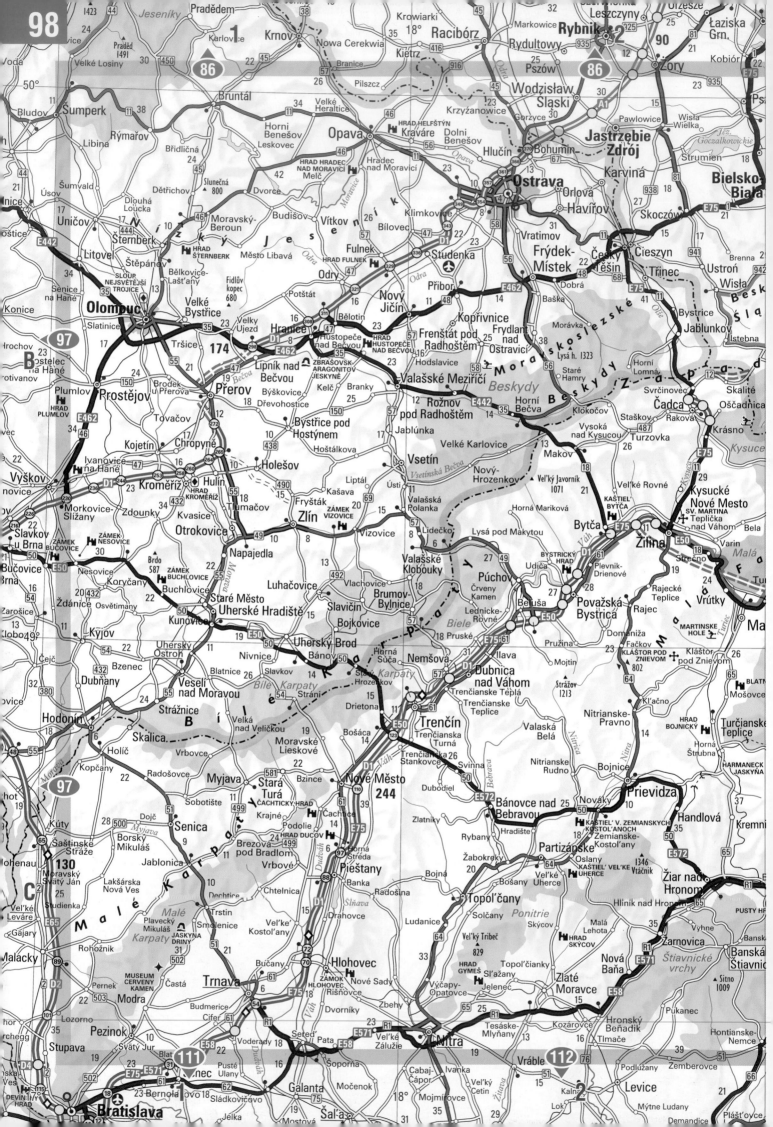

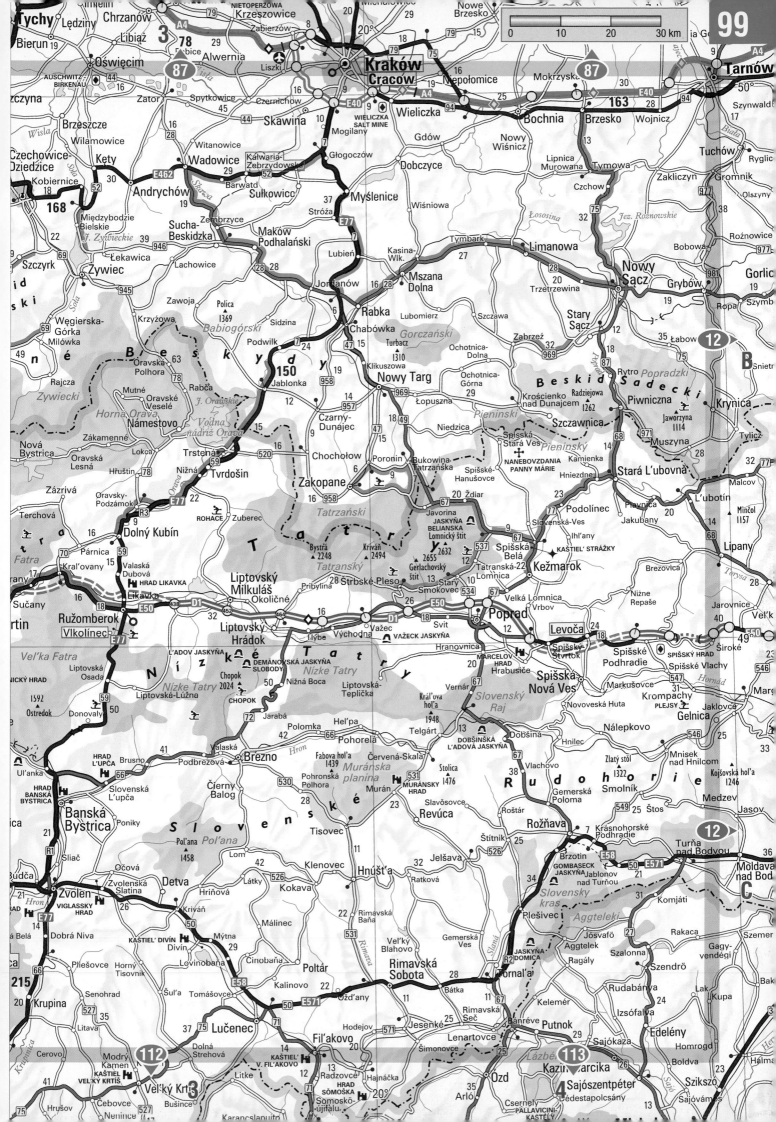

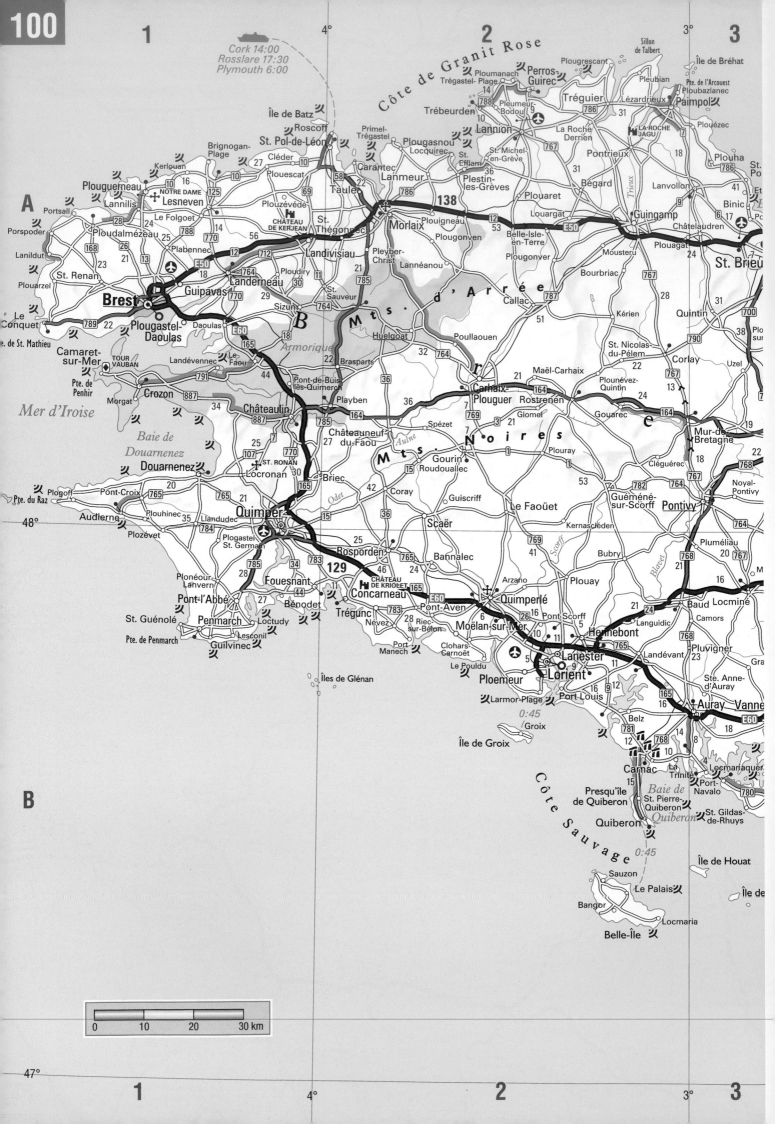

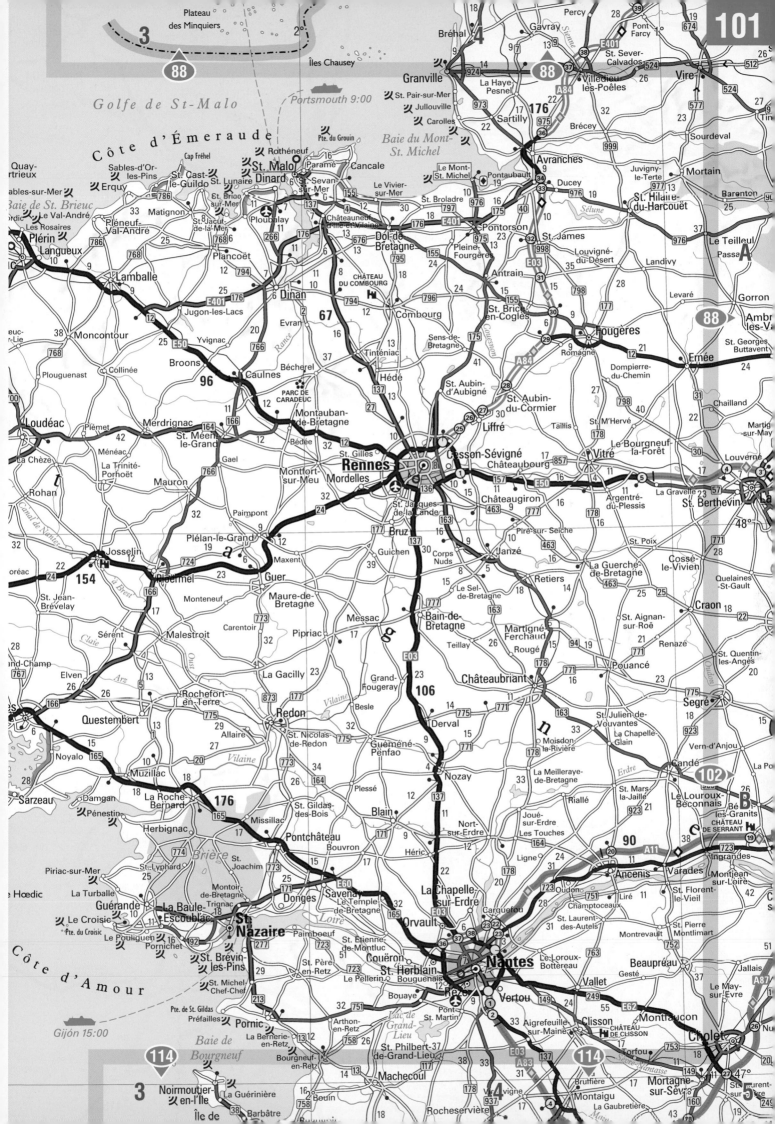

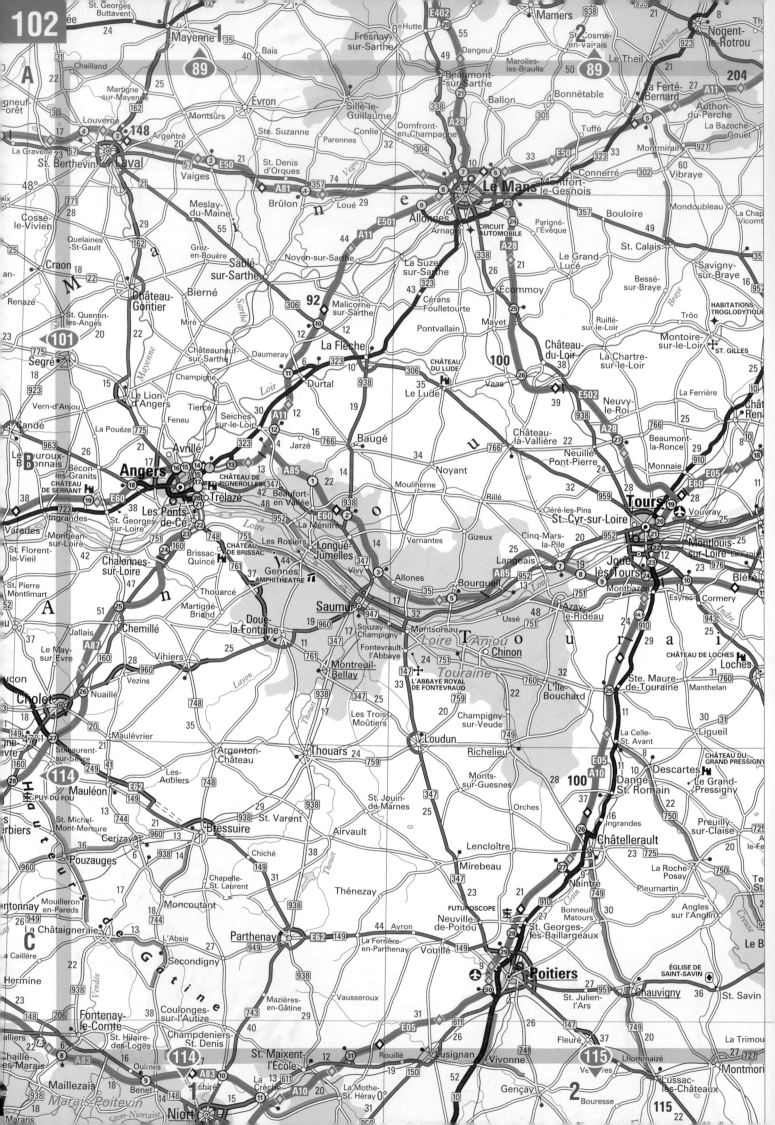

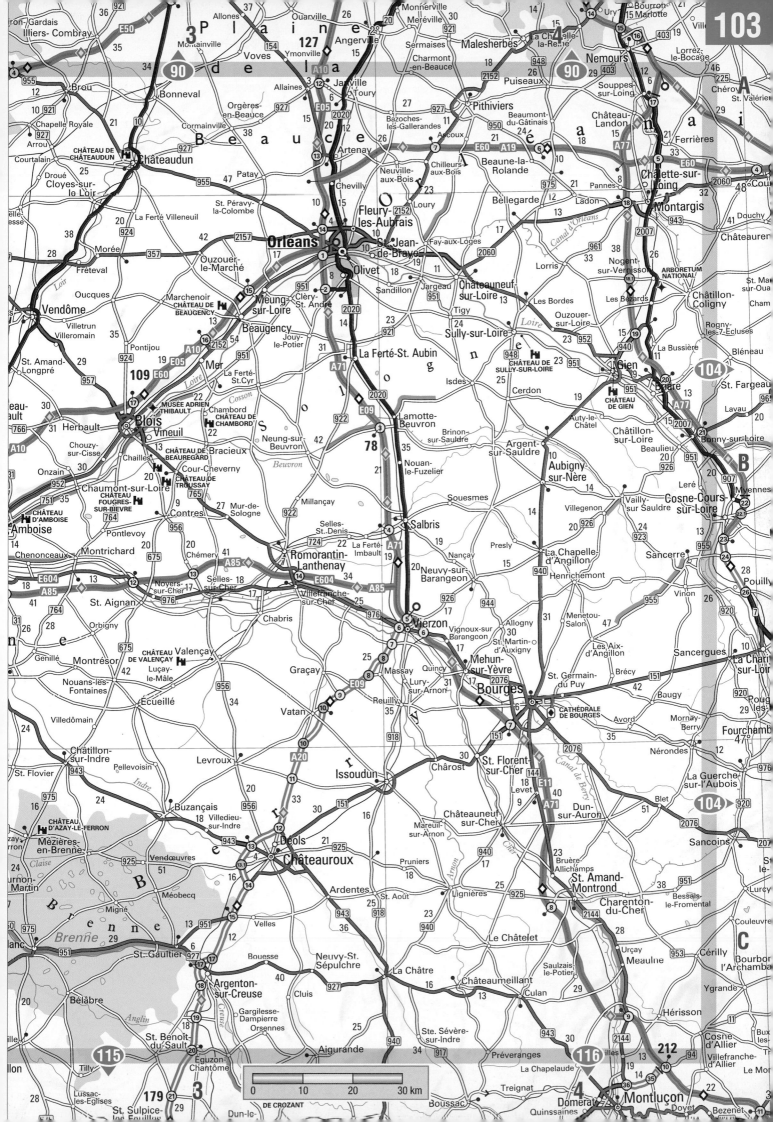

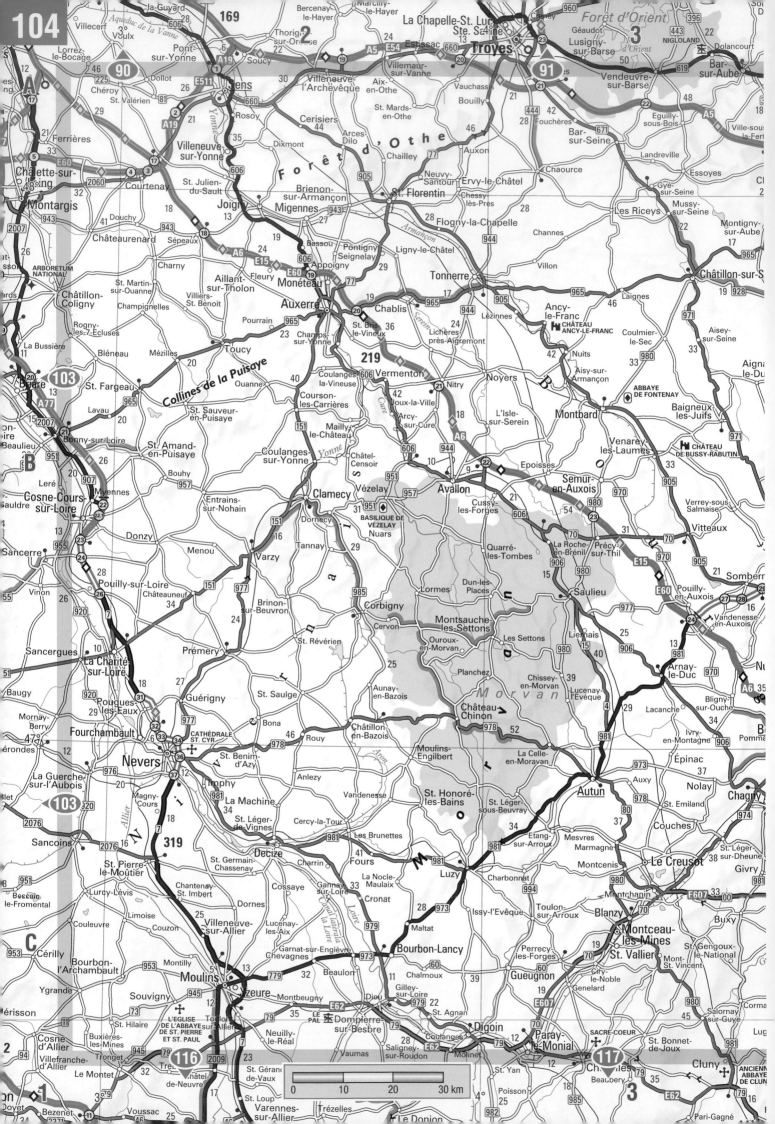

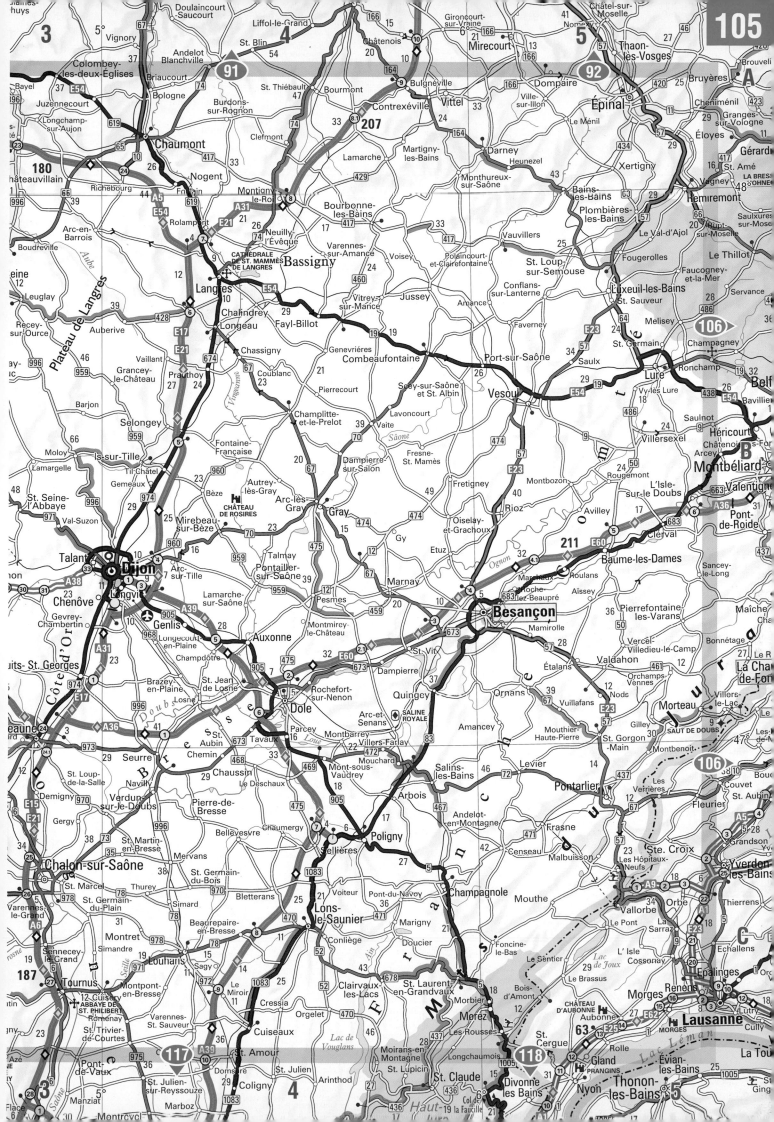

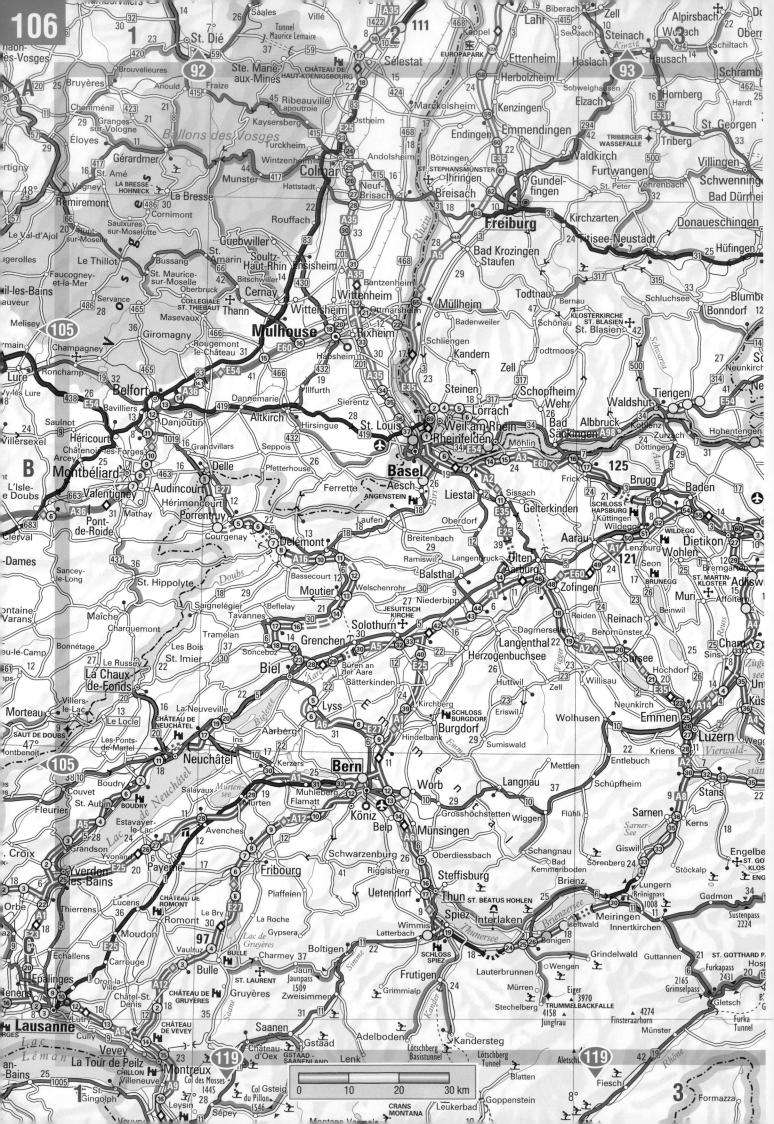

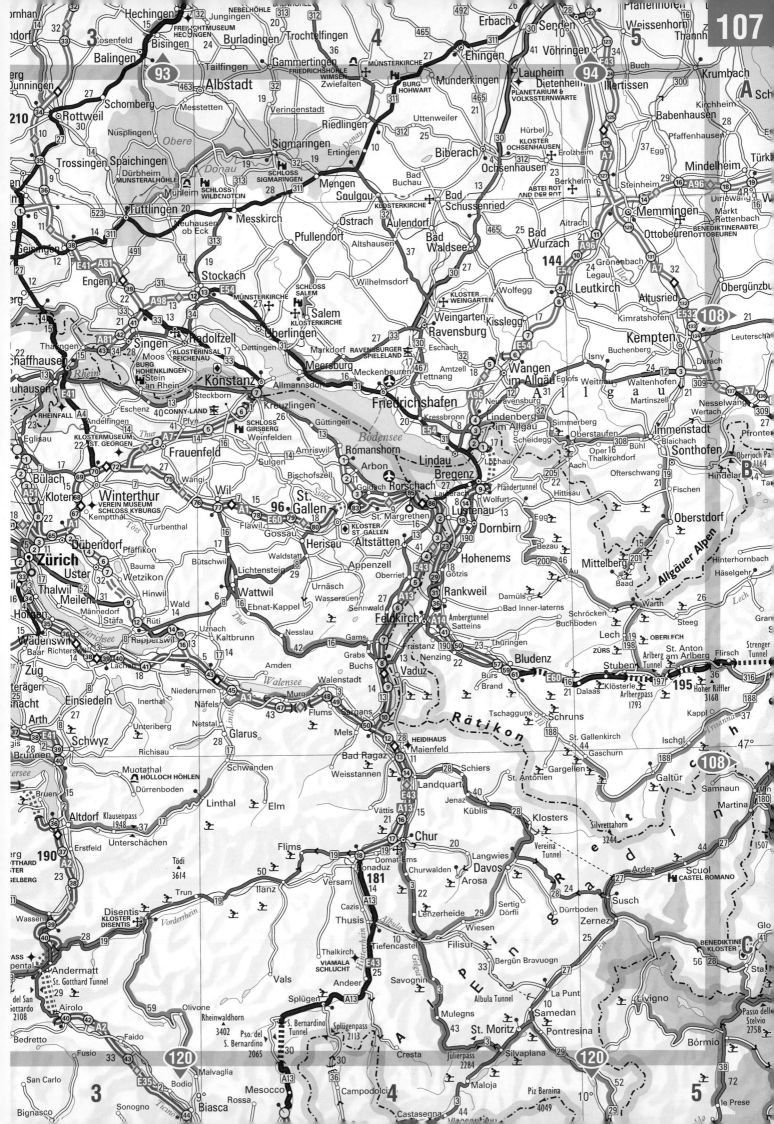

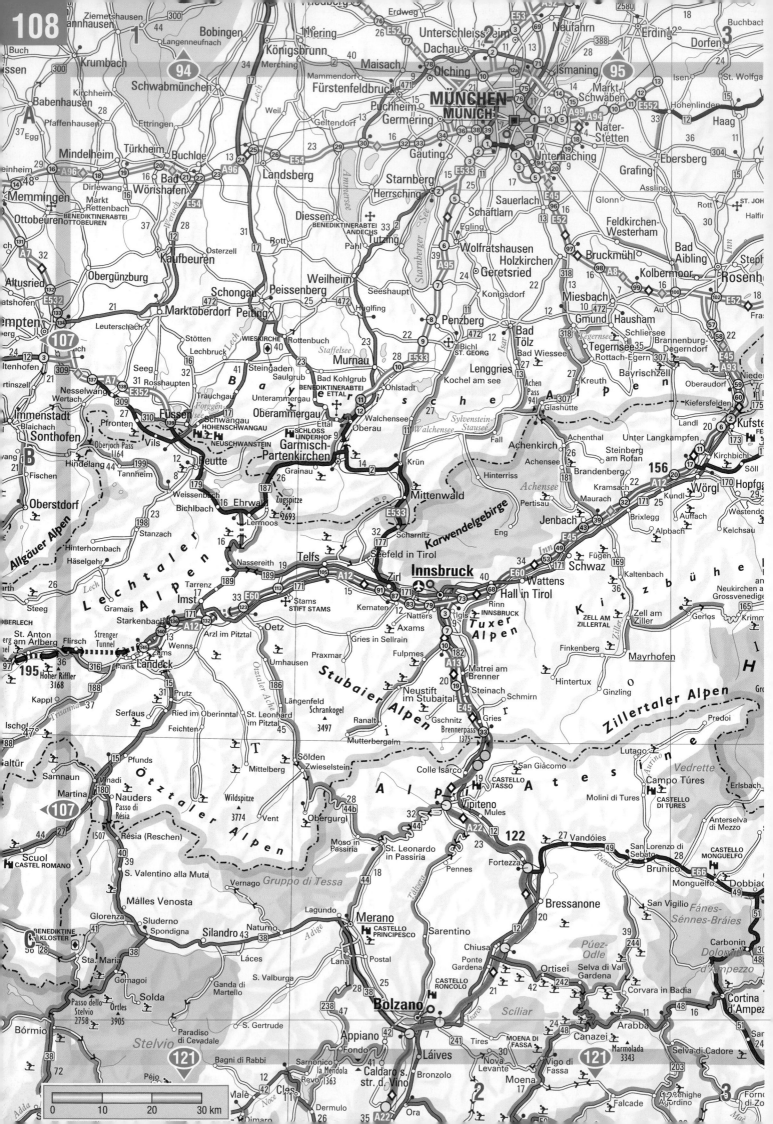

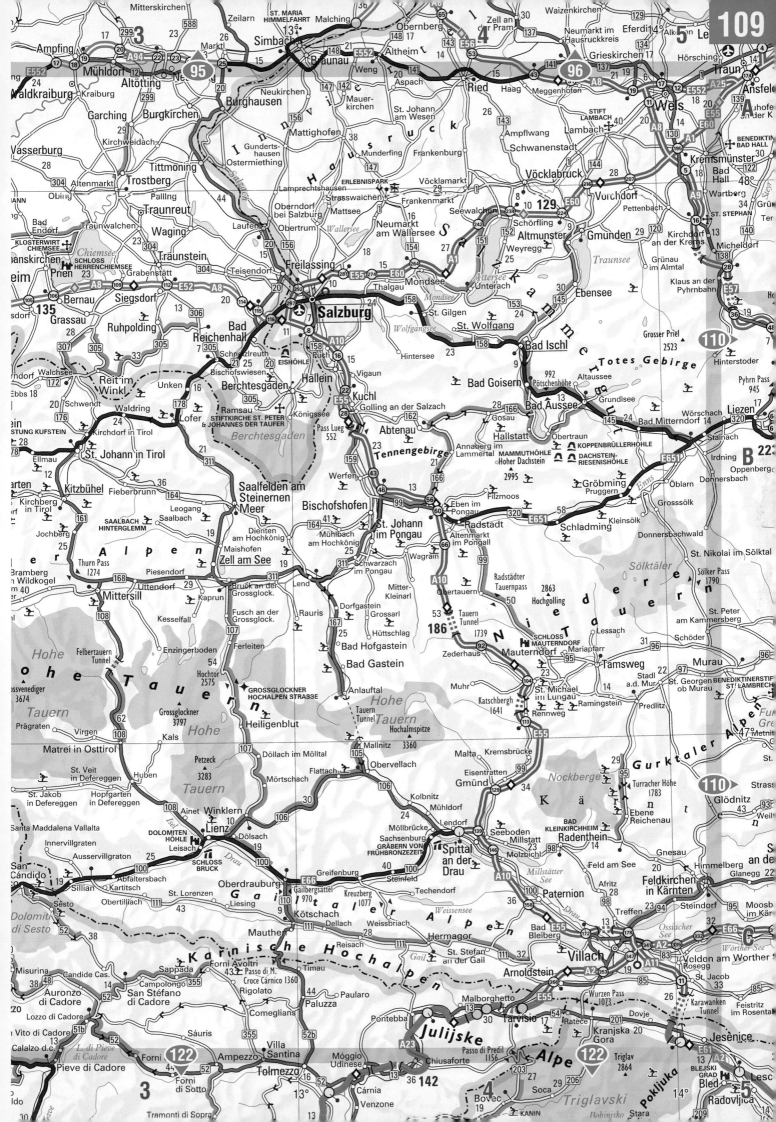

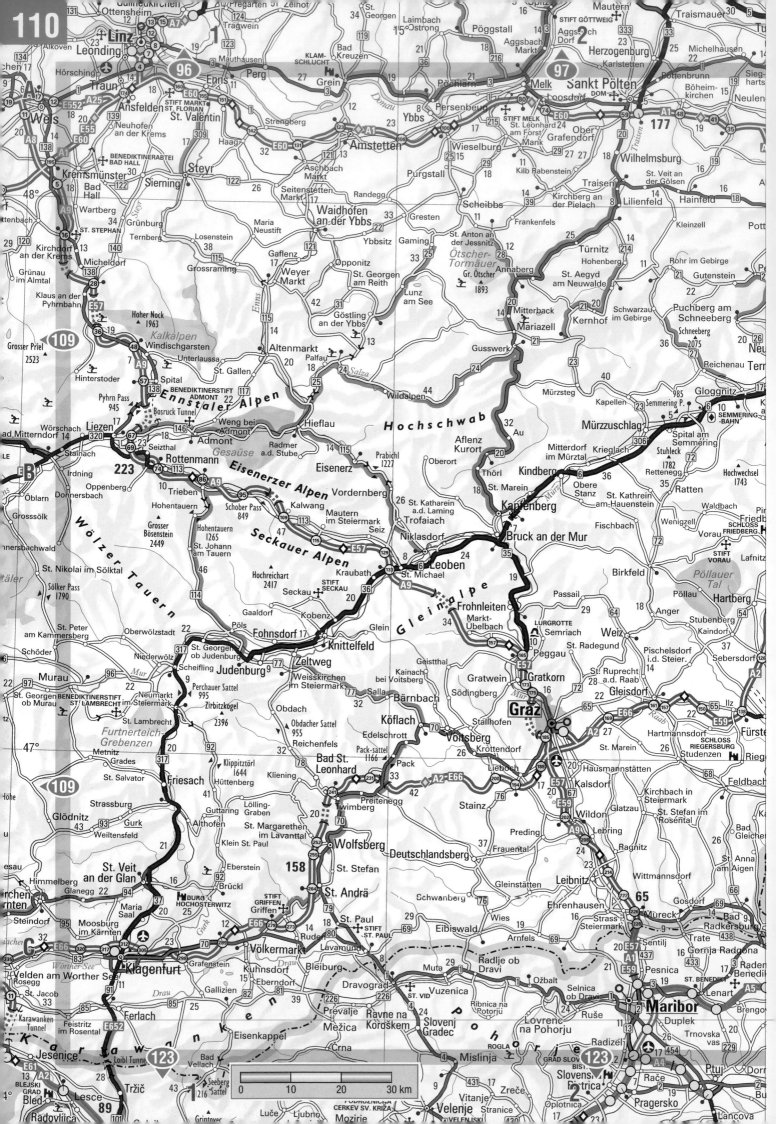

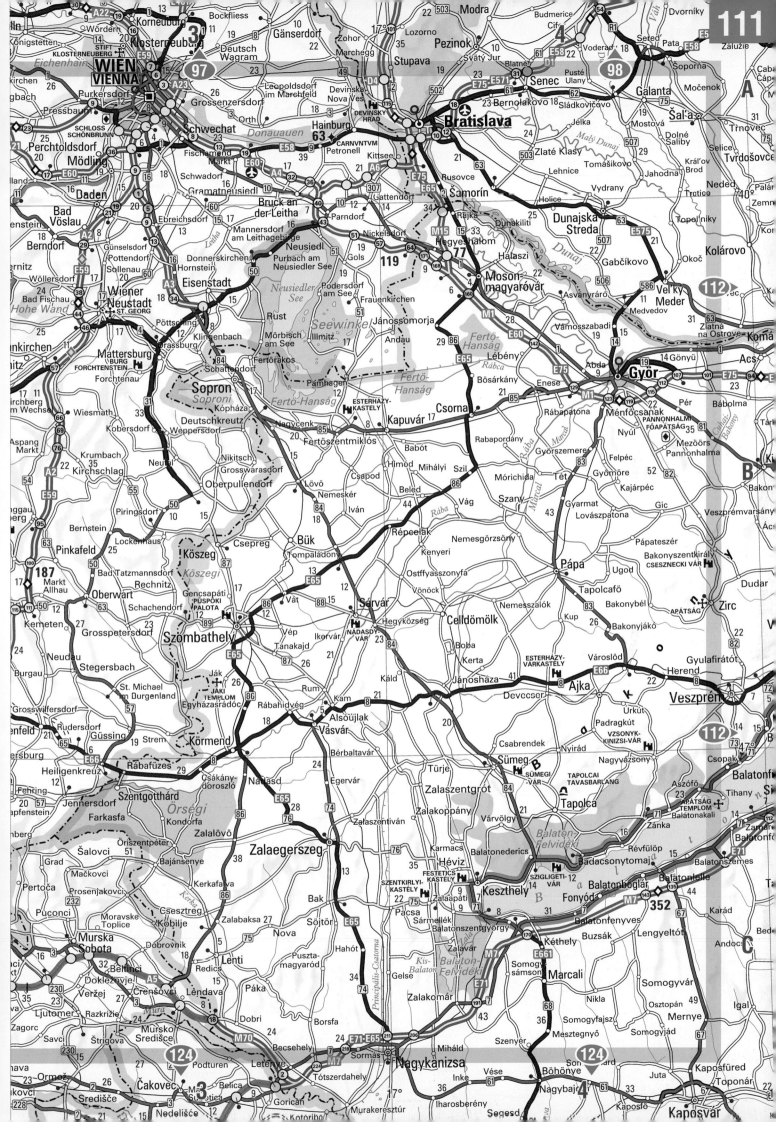

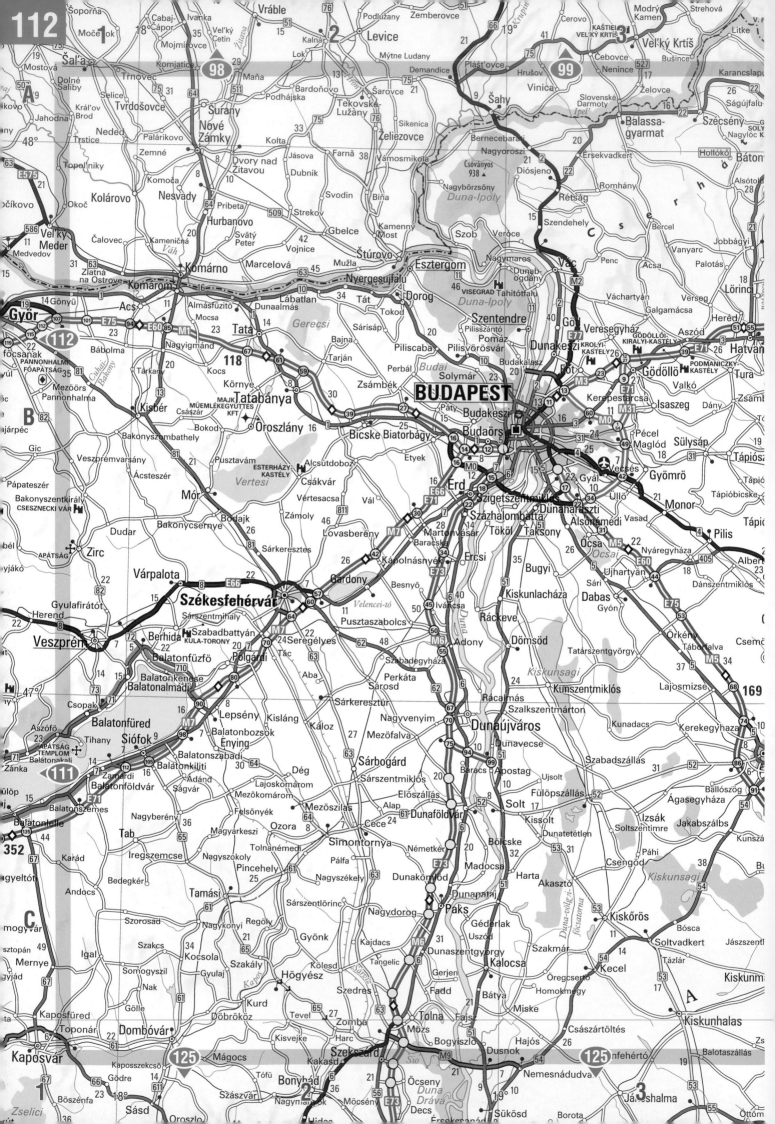

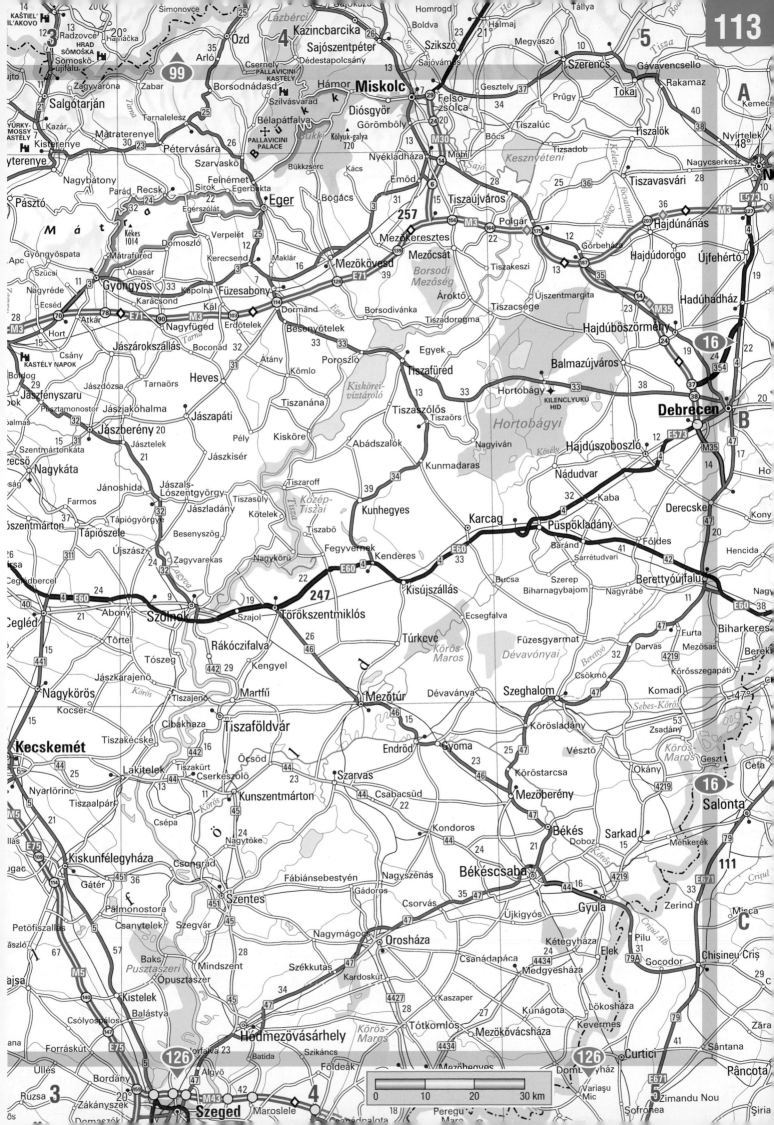

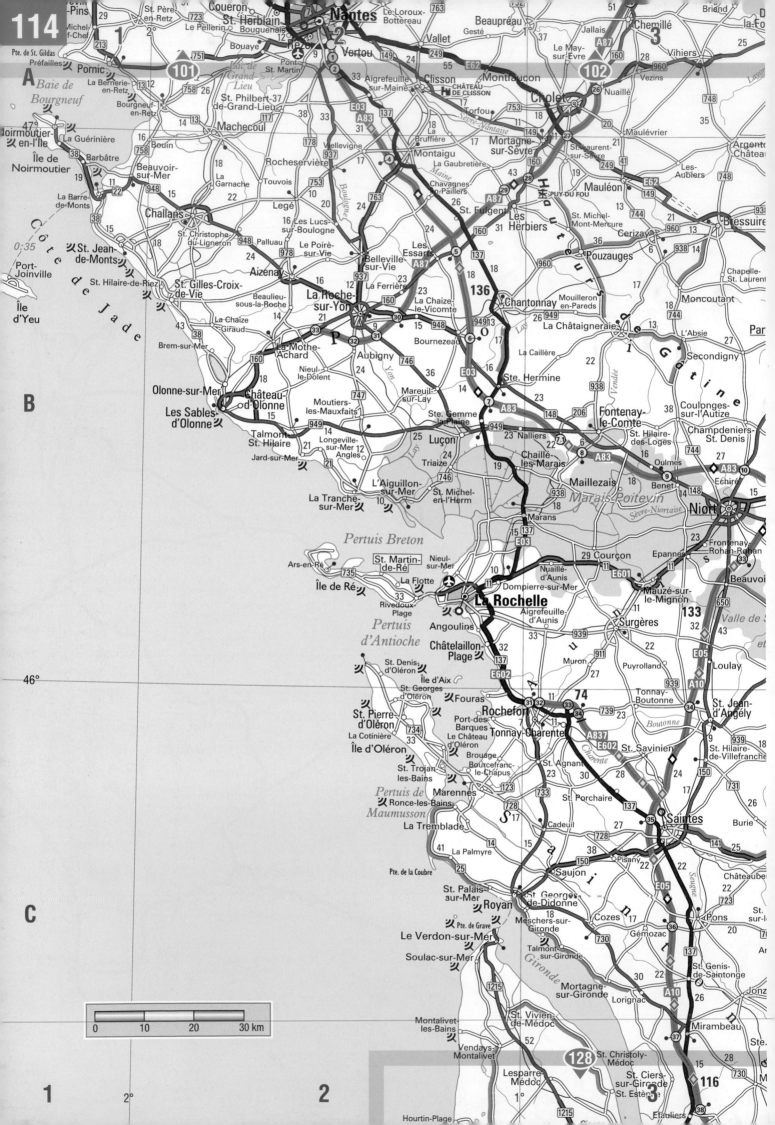

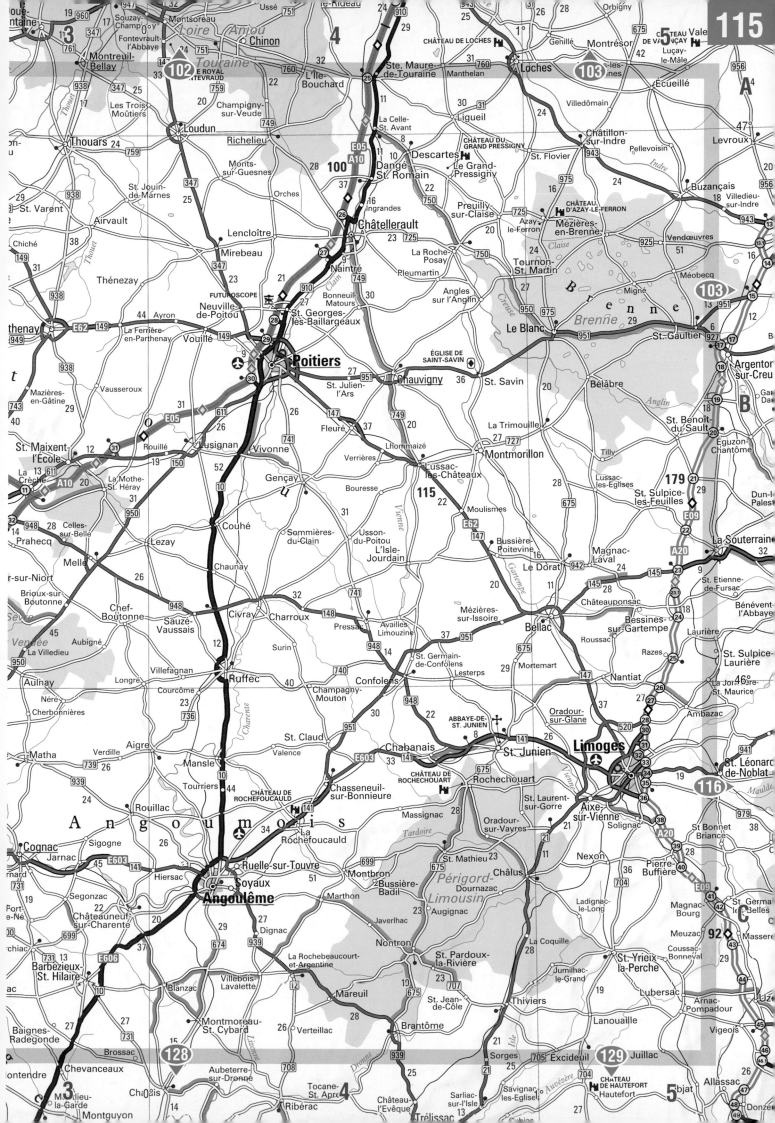

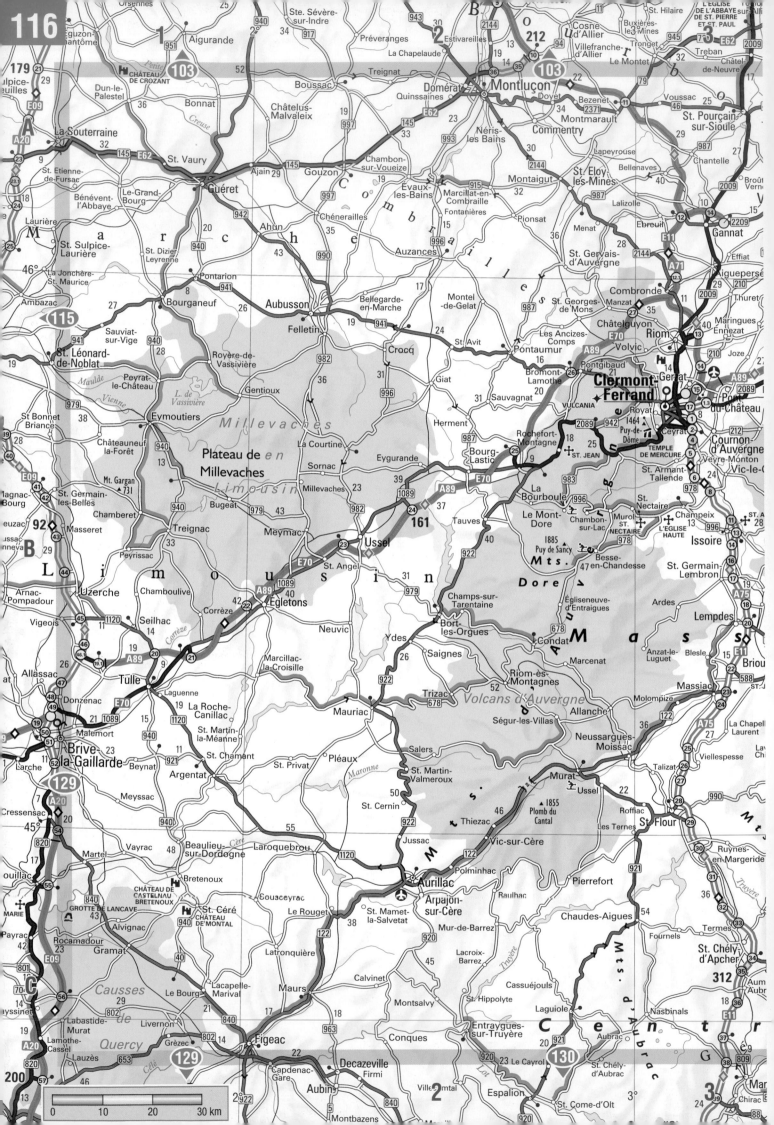

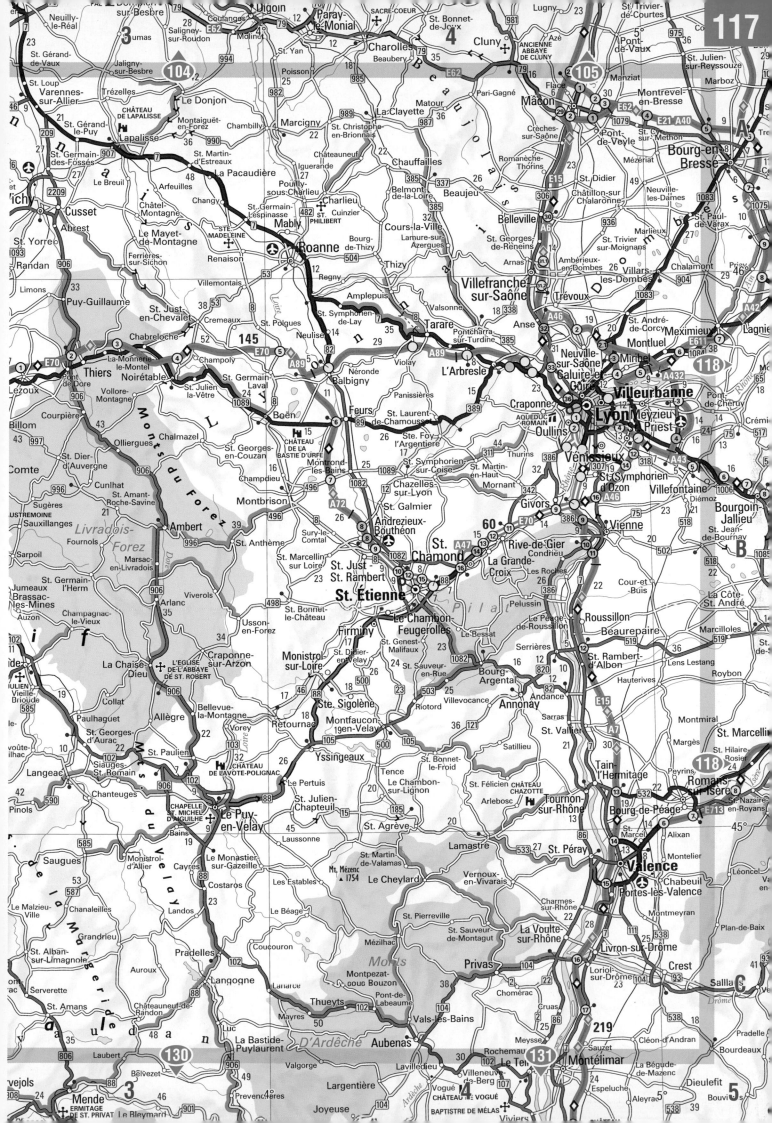

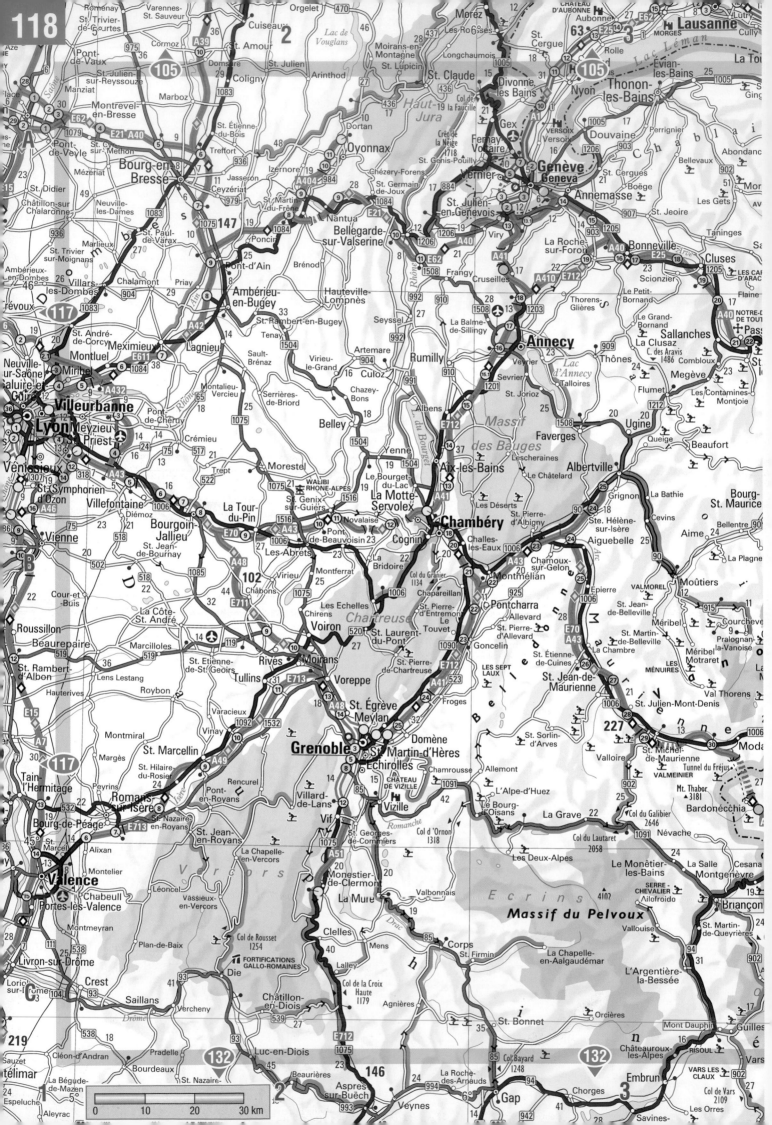

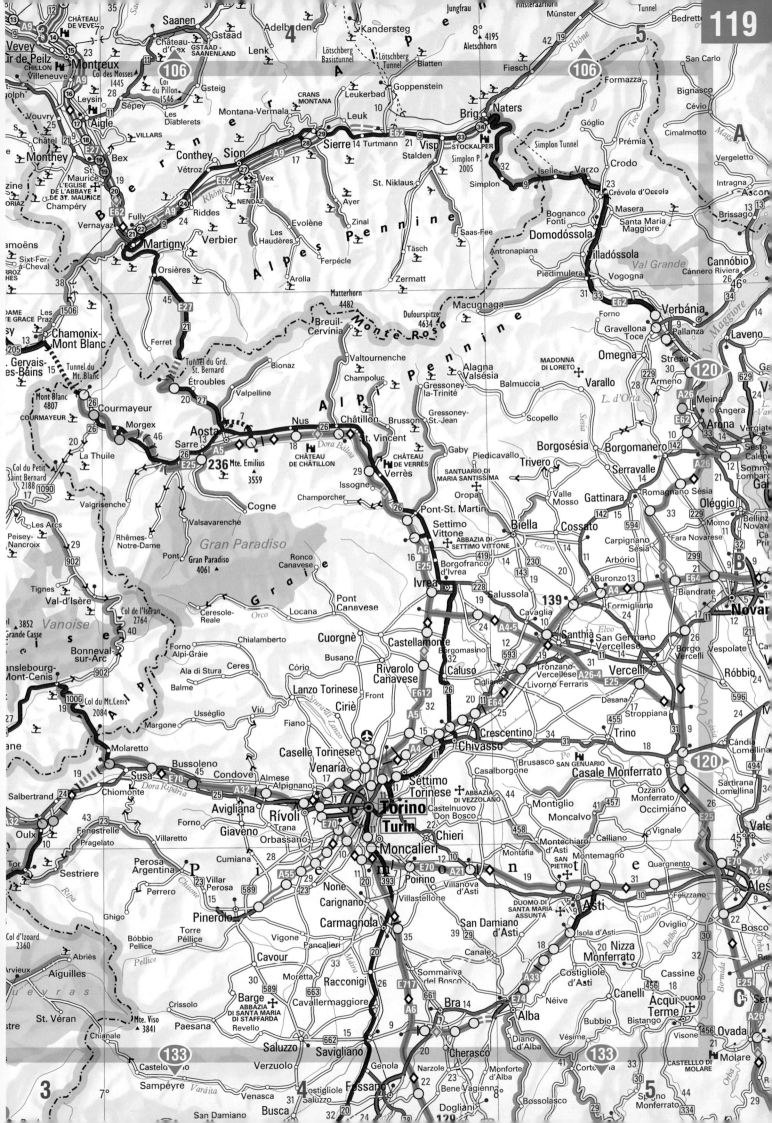

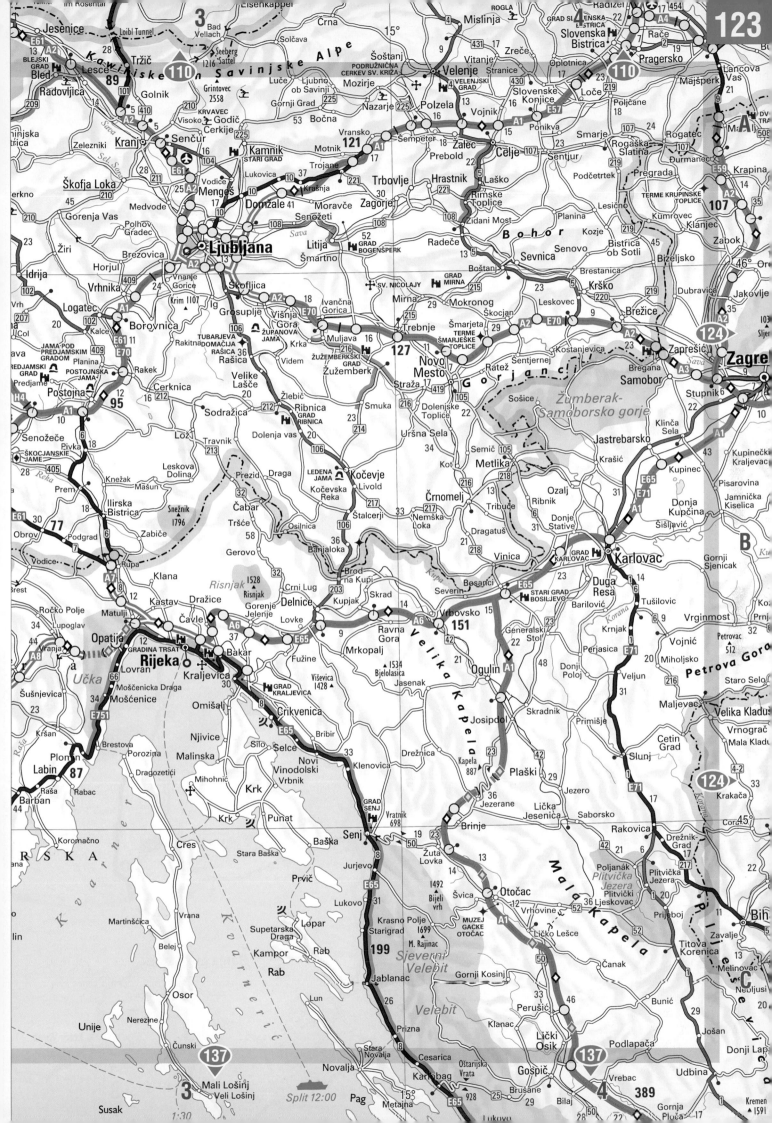

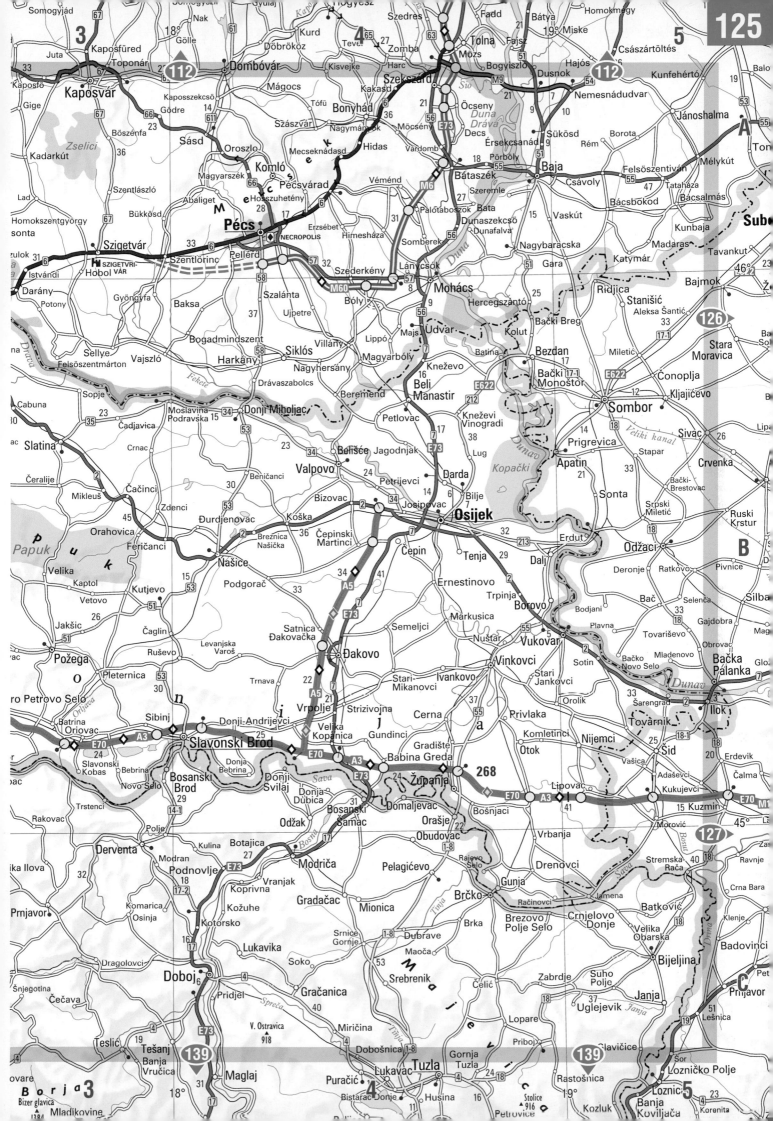

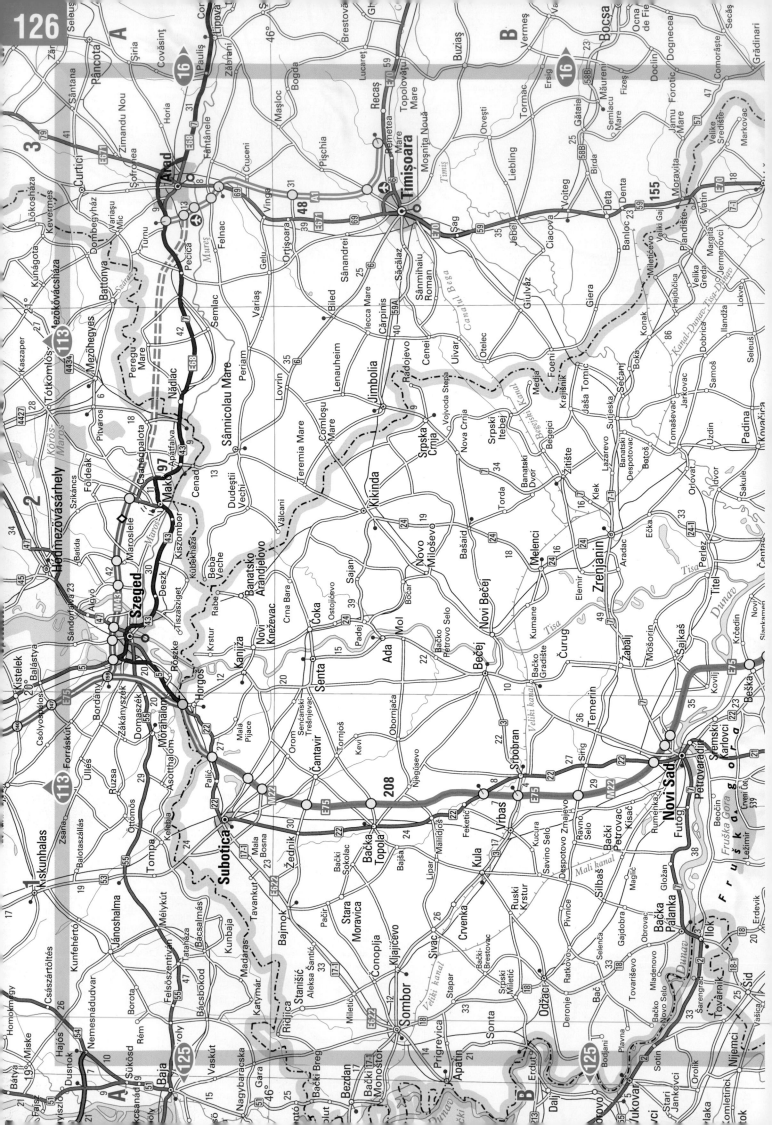

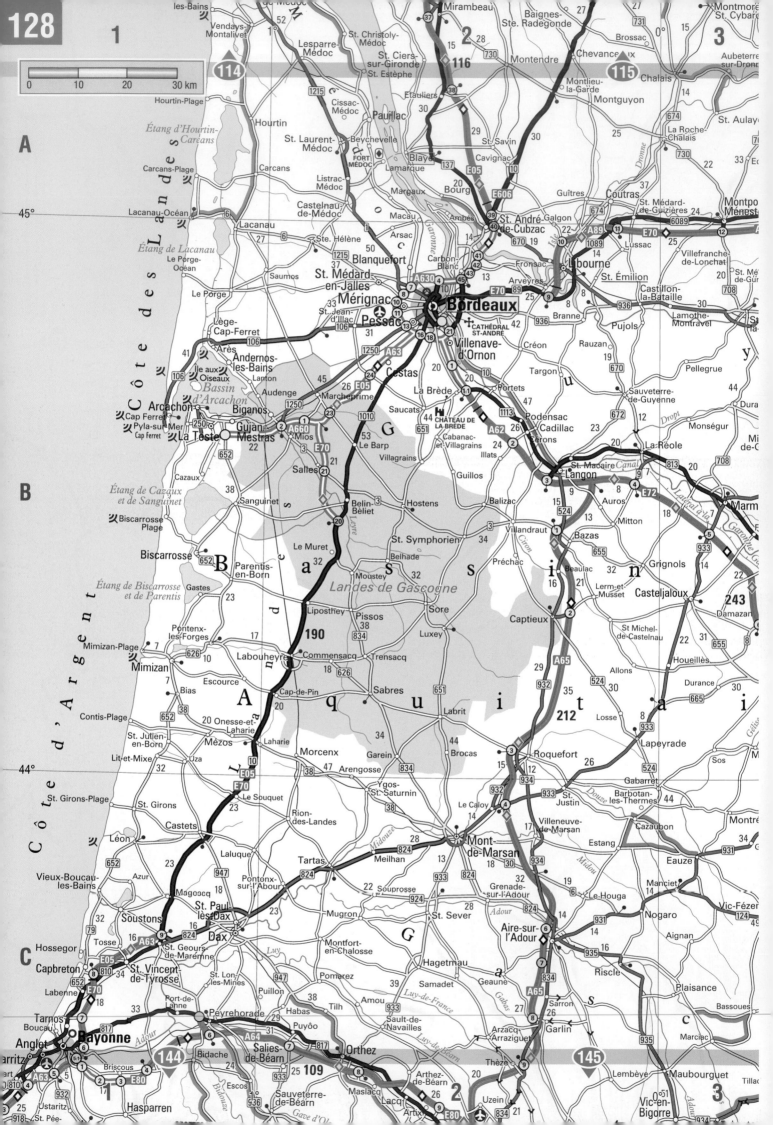

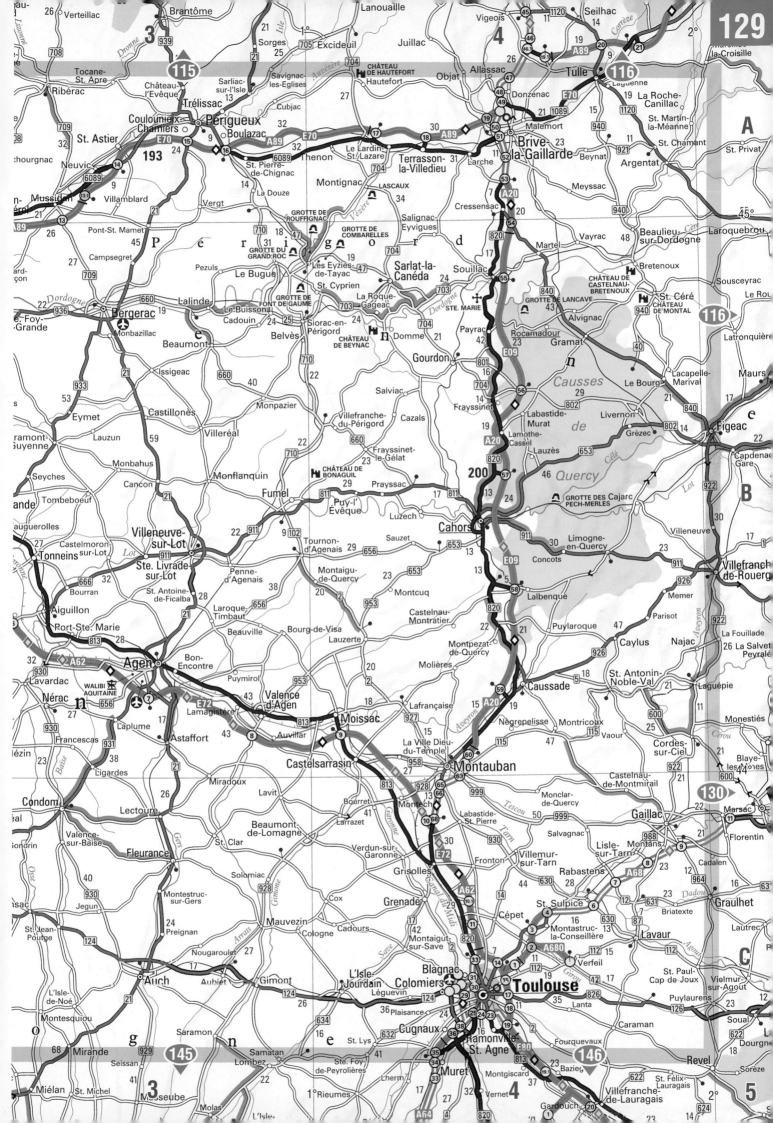

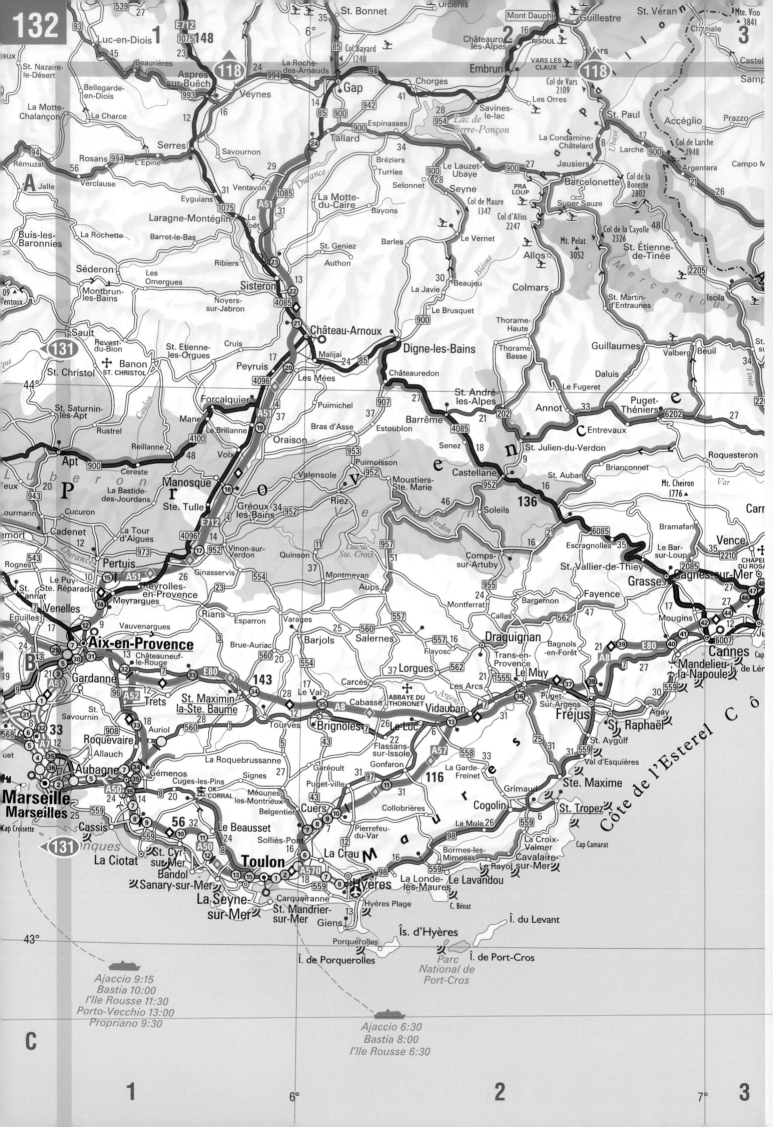

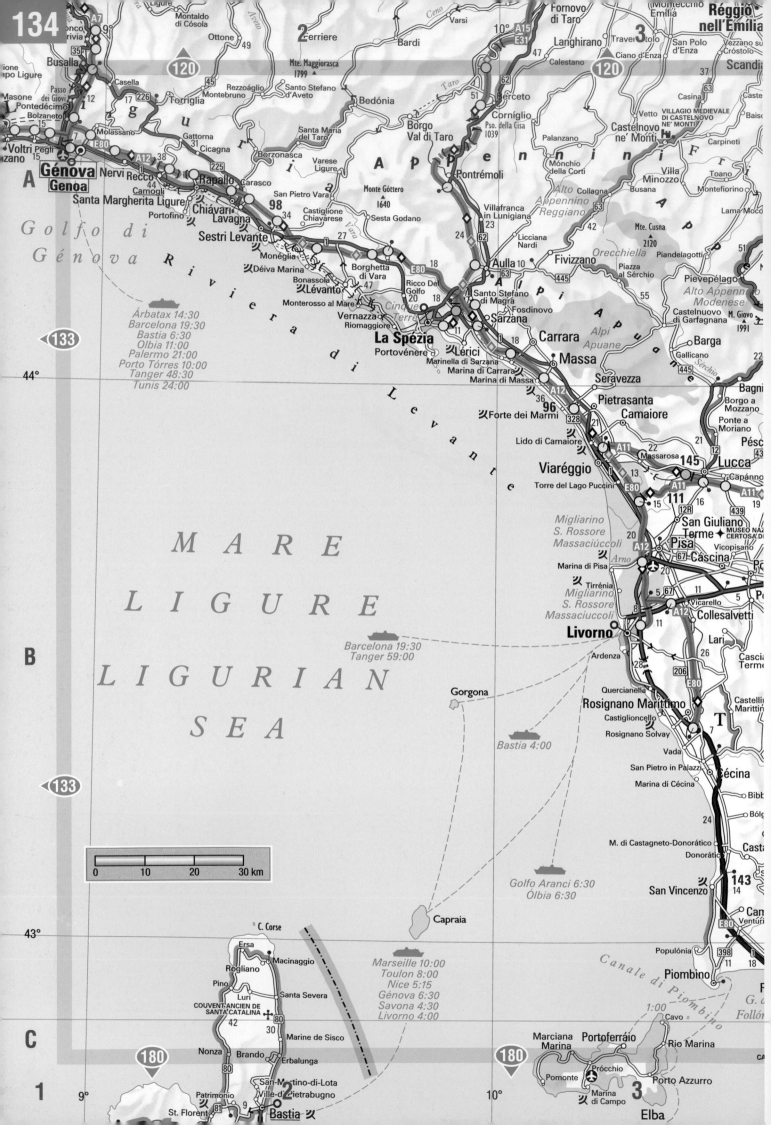

A7
35
Busalla
pone di Córsa
rivia
A7
9
Montaldo di Cósola
Ottone 49
2 Ferriere
Fornovo di Taro
Varsi
10° A15 E31 Langhirano 47
Traver stolo
Ciano d'Enza
Réggio nell'Emília
Montecchio Emília
San Polo d'Enza
Vezzano su
Scandia

120
Bardi
Berceto
Calestano
120
Casina
Castel

Masone
Passo dei Giovi
Pontedécimo
Bolzaneto
12
1
17
226
45
Casella
Rezzóaglio
Montebruno
Torriglia
Mte. Maggiorasca 1799
Santo Stefano d'Aveto
Bedónia
51
Corníglio
Pso. della Cisa 1039
Palanzano
Mónchio della Corti
VILLAGIO MEDIEVALE DI CASTELNOVO NE' MONTI
Baiso

Voltri Pegli
zano
15
Molassano
7
E80
A12 38
Gattorna
Cicagna
31
Borzonasca
Santa Maria del Taro
Borgo Val di Taro
20
Pontrémoli
Villafranca in Lunigiana
Castelnovo ne' Monti
Carpineti
Toano
Busana
Villa Minozzo
Montefiorino
Lama Mocó

Génova Genoa
Nervi Recco
Camogli
Santa Margherita Ligure
Portofino
Rapallo
Carasco
San Pietro Vara
225
Chiávari
Lavagna
98
34
Castiglione Chiavárese
Sesta Godano
Monte Góttero 1640
24
23
Licciana Nardi
Alto Appennino Reggiano
63
42
Mte. Cusna 2120
Orecchiella
Piandelagotti
Alto Appennino Modenese
M. Giovo 1991
51

Golfo di Génova
Riviera di Levante
Sestri Levante
Monéglia
Déiva Marina
Bonassola
Lévanto
Monterosso al Mare
Vernazza
Riomaggiore
27
1
Borghetta di Vara
47
Ricco Del Golfo
E80
18
18
Aulla
63
445
Fivizzano
Fosdinovo
Santo Stefano di Magrá
Piazza al Sérchio
Pievepélago
55
Castelnuovo di Garfagnana

44°
Árbatax 14:30
Barcelona 19:30
Bastia 6:30
Olbia 11:00
Palermo 21:00
Porto Tórres 10:00
Tanger 48:30
Tunis 24:00
Cinque Terre
La Spézia
Portovénere
Lérici
Marinella di Sarzana
Marina di Carrara
Marina di Massa
11
Sarzana
Carrara
Massa
Seravezza
1
18
Alpi Apuane
Barga
Gallicano
445
Sérchio
22
Pésc

A12
36
96
328
Forte dei Marmi
Pietrasanta
Camaiore
Borgo a Mozzano
Ponte a Moriano
12
21
21
Lido di Camaiore
A11
22
21
145
Lucca
Capánno
A11

133
Viaréggio
Torre del Lago Puccini
1
13
E80
A11
15
111
12R
San Giuliano Terme
MUSEO NAZ
CERTOSA DI
439
16
19

MARE
LIGURE
Migliarino S. Rossore Massaciúccoli
20
A12
Pisa
Vicopisano
67
Cáscina

Barcelona 19:30
Tanger 59:00
Marina di Pisa
Tirrénia
Migliarino S. Rossore Massaciúccoli
Livorno
Arno
5
8
67
11
Vicarello
A12
Collesalvetti
11
Po

B
LIGURIAN
Gorgona
Ardenza
28
206
E80
Lari
26
Casci
Term

SEA
Bastia 4:00
Quercianella
Castiglioncello
Rosignano Solvay
Rosignano Maríttimo
Vada
7
T
Castelli Maríttim

133
San Pietro in Palazzi
Marina di Cécina
Cécina
Bibb
Bólg

0  10  20  30 km
Golfo Aranci 6:30
Ólbia 6:30
M. di Castagneto-Donorático
Donorático
24
Casta

43°
C. Corse
Capraia
Populónia
398
11
18

Ersa
Macinaggio
Rogliano
Pino
Luri
COUVENT ANCIEN DE SANTA CATALINA
80
42
30
Santa Severa
Marseille 10:00
Toulon 8:00
Nice 5:15
Génova 6:30
Savona 4:30
Livorno 4:00
Canale di Piombino
1:00
Cavo
Piombino
G. d
Folló

C
180
Marine de Sisco
Nonza
Brando
Erbalunga
San Martino-di-Lota
Ville-di-Pietrabugno
180
Marciana Marina
Portoferráio
Rio Marina
Pomonte
Pròcchio
Porto Azzurro

1
9°
Patrimonio
St. Florent
80
81
9
Nonza
2
Bastia
10°
Marina di Campo
3
Elba

1  13°  2  14°

122  122

MARE

Marina Romea
Marina di Ravenna
Punta Marina
**Ravenna**
MIRABILANDIA
Delta del Po
Lido di Classe
Lido di Savio
Milano Marittima
**Cérvia**
Pinerella
Casemurate
Cesenático
Gatteo a Mare
**Bellária**
Igea Marina
ITALIA IN MINIATURA
Viserba
**Cesena**
Savignano sul Rubicone
Santarcángelo
di Romágna
**Rímini**
FIABILANDIA
Miramare
Sogliano
al Rubicone
Riccione
**SAN MARINO**
San Leo
San-Marino
Novaféltria
Morciano
di Romagna
Cattólica
**Pésaro**
Saludécio
Mercatino
Conca
Pennabilli
Macerata Féltria
Montécchio
**Fano**
Carpegna
Sassocorvaro
Mombaróccio
**105**
Marotta
Sestino
Lunano
Saltara
Calcinelli
San
Costanzo
Senigállia
**Urbino**
Fossombrone
Monte Porzio
Mondolfo
Badia Tedalda
Urbánia
Monte Porzio
Marzocca
Borgo Pace
Sant'Angelo
in Vado
Mondavio
Rocca
Priora
Falconara
Maríttima
Pióbbico
Corinaldo
Chiaravalle
**Ancona**
Apécchio
Cagli
Pérgola
San Lorenzo
in Campo
Ostra
Cónero
epolcro
San Marcello
SAN PIETRO
San Giustino
Montecarotto
Agugliano
Camerano
VILLAGIO
MEDIEVALE
DI SIROLO
**Città di Castello**
Cantiano
SAN GIOVANNI BATTISTA
Arcévia
Móie
**Jesi**
Sirolo
Numana
Pietralunga
Mte. Cátria
Serra
S. Quírico
Cupramontana
**Ósimo**
Igoumenitsa 16:30
Patra 22:00
SAN FRANCESCO
DI SASSOFERRATO
GROTTA DI
FRASSASSI
Castelfidardo
Schéggia
Sassoferrato
Apiro
Filottrano
Montefano
Loreto
Porto Recanati
Monte
Cucco
Cíngoli
Recanati
**Gúbbio**
Sigillo
Fabriano
Montecássiano
Potenza
Picena
Porto Potenza Picena
Camporeggiano
Cerreto d'Esi
Passo
di Tréia
Tréia
**Macerata**
Civitanova Marche
Umbértide
Branca
Fossato di Vico
Sforzacosta
SAN CLAUDIO
AL CHIENTI
Porto Sant'Elpídio
asimeno
signano sul
rasimeno
Scritto
Casa
Castalda
Matélica
San Serverino
Marche
Tolentino
Corridónia
Montegranaro
Sant'Elpídio a Mare
Piccione
Gualdo Tadino
Castelraimondo
Serrapetrona
Mogliano
Lido di Fermo
Porto San Giórgio
Ponte Felcino
Valfábbrica
Pióraco
Camerino
ABBAZIA DI
CHIARAVALLE DI
FIASTRA
Abbadia
di Fiastra
Caldarola
Montegiórgio
Fermo
**Perúgia**
Nocera Umbra
Monte
Pennino
Caldarola
San Ginésio
Monterubbiano
Pedaso
Bastia
Ponte
San Giovanni
Monte
Subásio
Serravalle
di Chienti
Múccia
Servigliano
Bettona
**Assisi**
Valtopina
Pieve
Torina
Sarnano
Cupra Maríttima
Deruta
Spello
Colfiorito
Appennino
Bolognola
Santa Vittória in
Matenano
Montalto
d. Marche
Ripatransone
**152**
Grottammare
Cannara
Casenove
Amándola
MADONNA
DEL PIANO
San Benedetto de
Collepepe
Foligno
Visso
Monte
Montefortino
Rotella
Comunanza
Acquaviva
Picena
Porto d'Áscoli
Montefalco
Sellano
Castelsantángelo
Montemónaco
Monte
Sibillini
Offida
Bevagna
Trevi
**Áscoli
Piceno**
Martinsicuro
Fratta
Todina
Bastardo
San Giácomo
Triponzo
Mte. Vettore
Balzo
Arquata
del Tronto
Sant'Egídio
alla Vibrata
Nereto
Alba Adriática
**Todi**
Massa
Martana
Piedipaterno
Nórcia
Civitella di Tronto
Tortoreto Lido
**Spoleto**
168
169
Mosciano
Sant'Angelo
Giulianova
Acquasparta
Serravalle
Accúmoli
Acquasanta
Terme
Valle
Castellana
CATTEDRALE DI
SAN BERNARDO
Campli
Montecastrilli
Monteleone
di Spoleto
Cáscia
Cívita
Gran Sasso
e Monti
della Laga
**Téramo**
Roseto
Notaresc

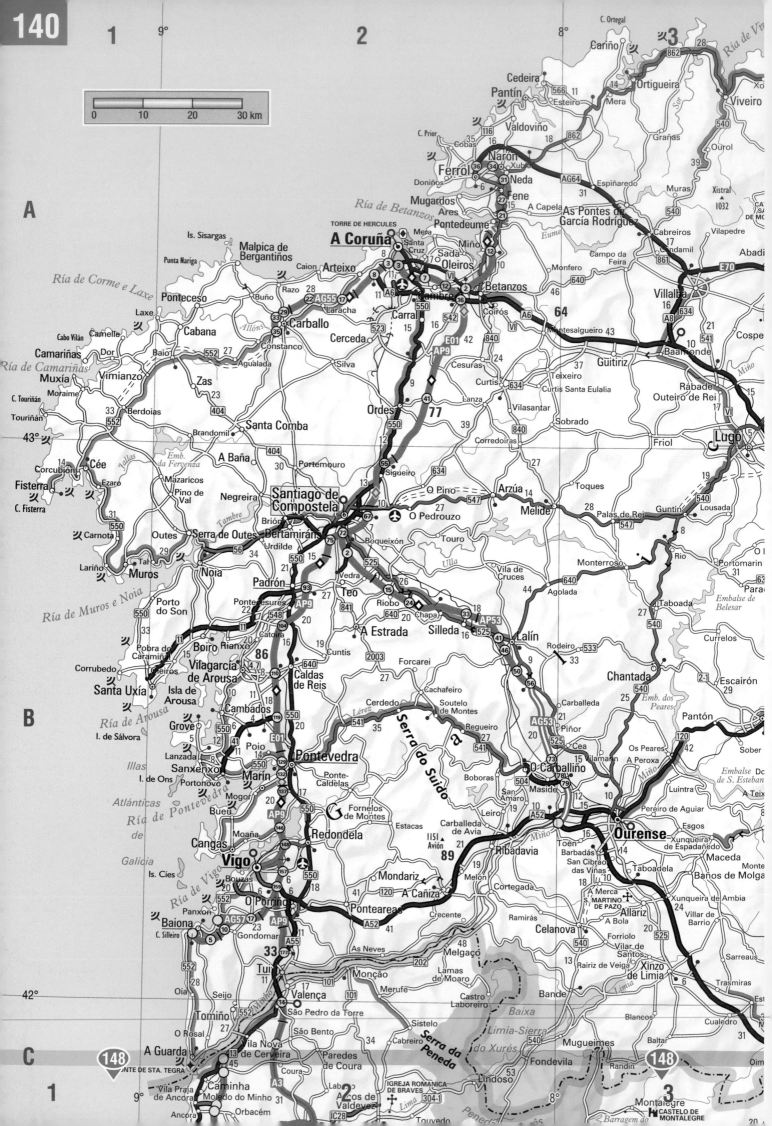

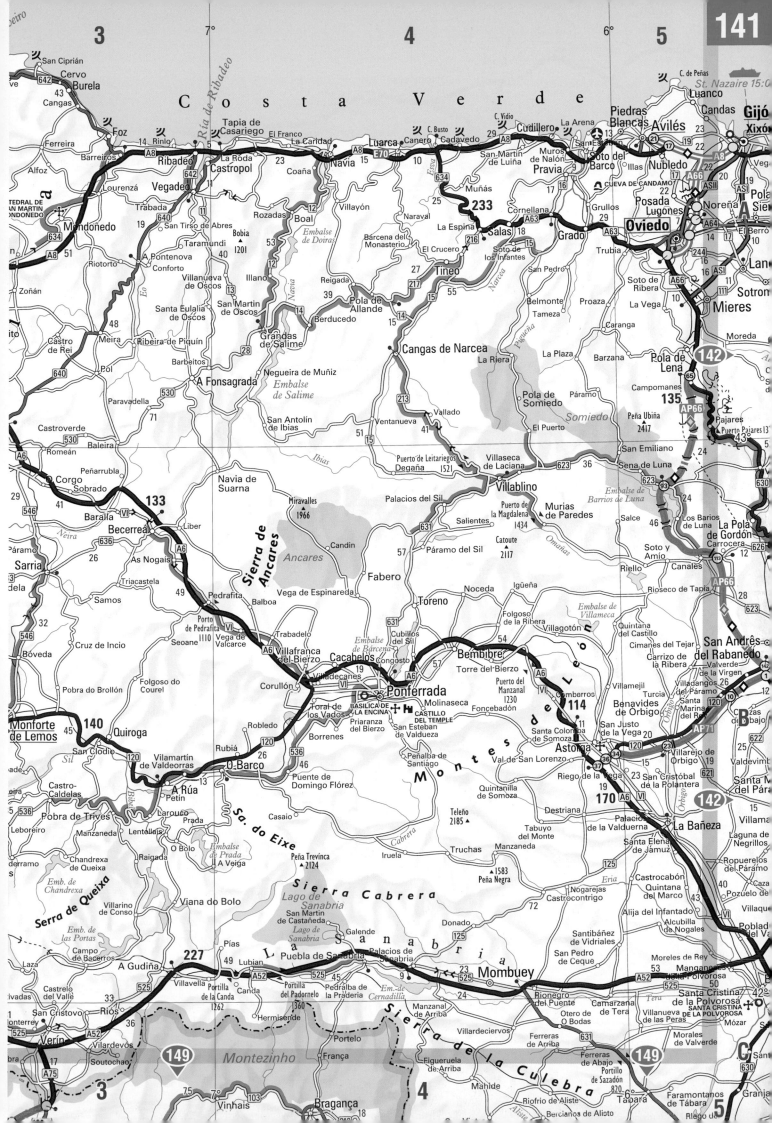

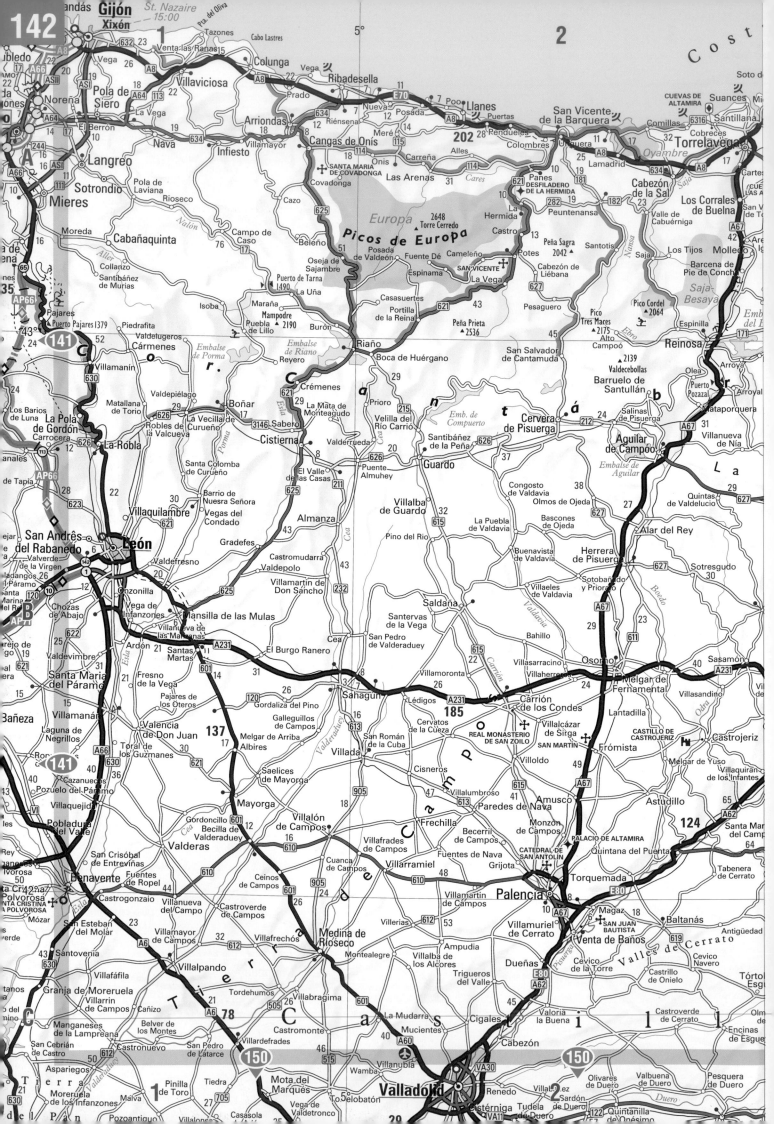

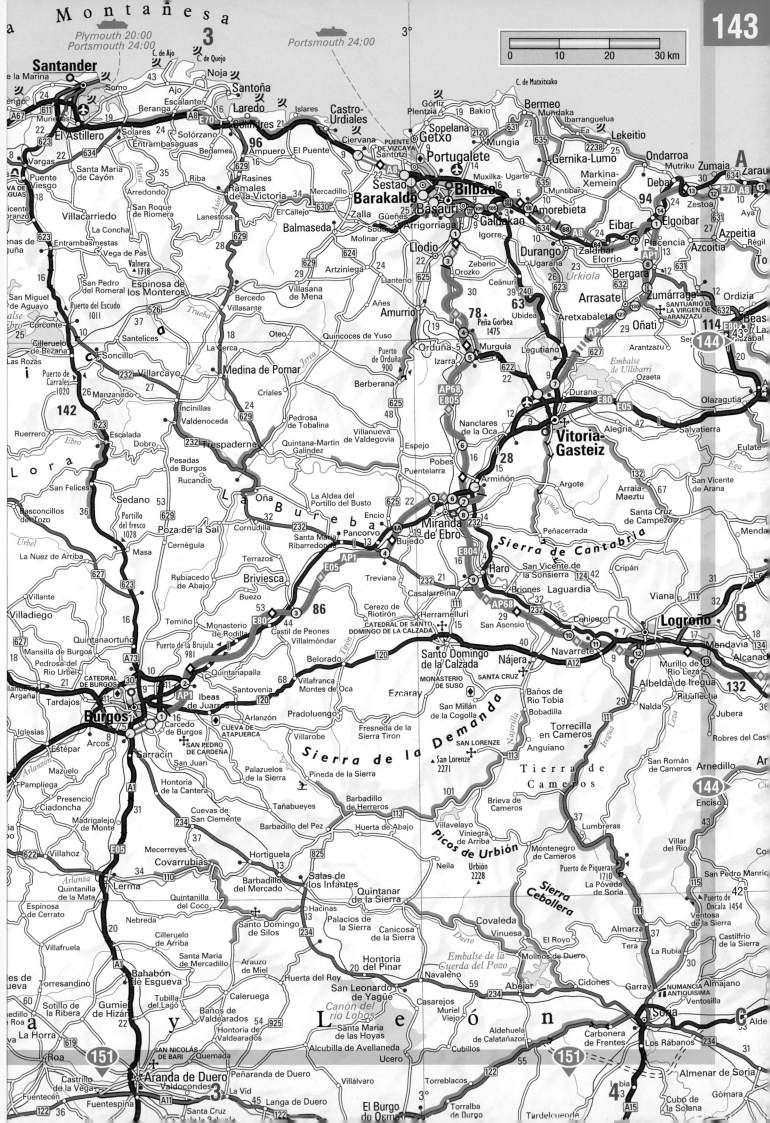

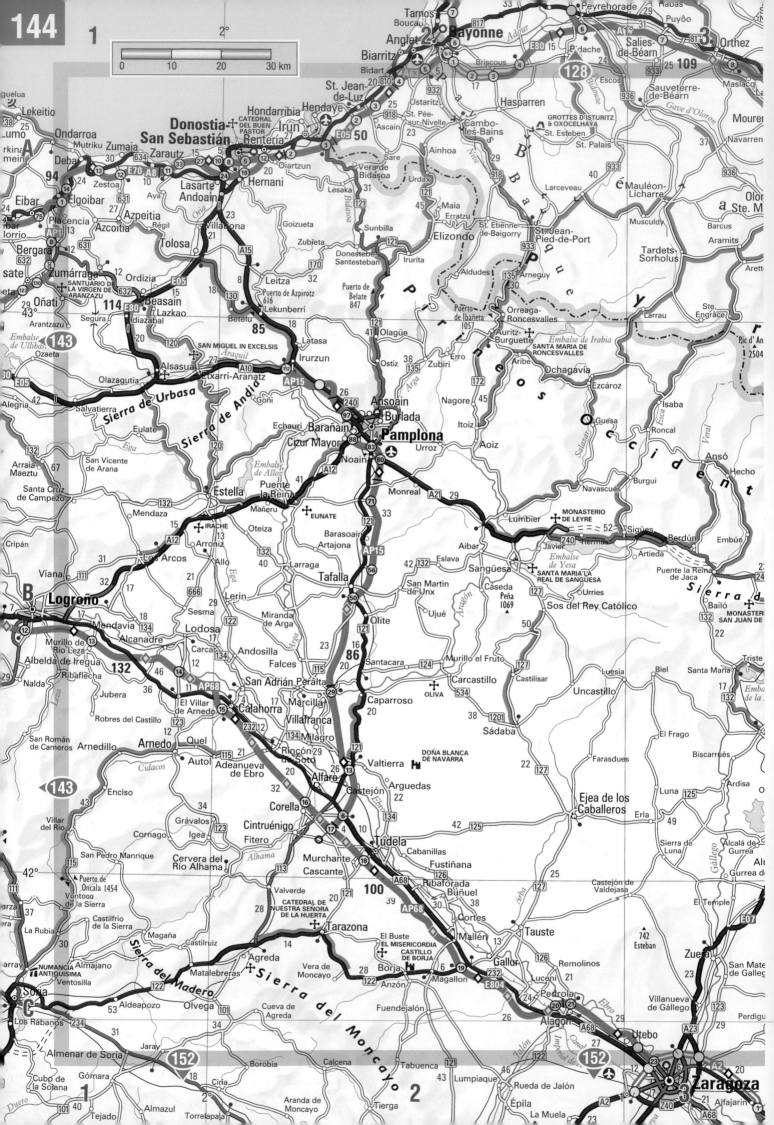

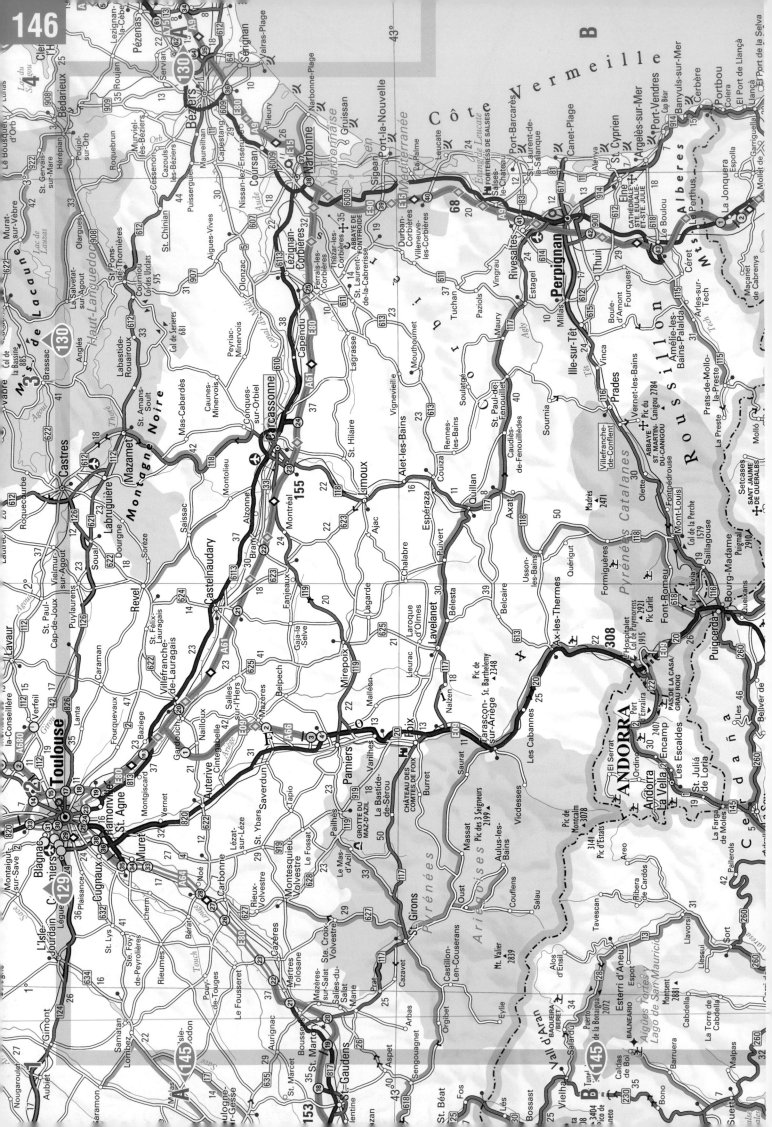

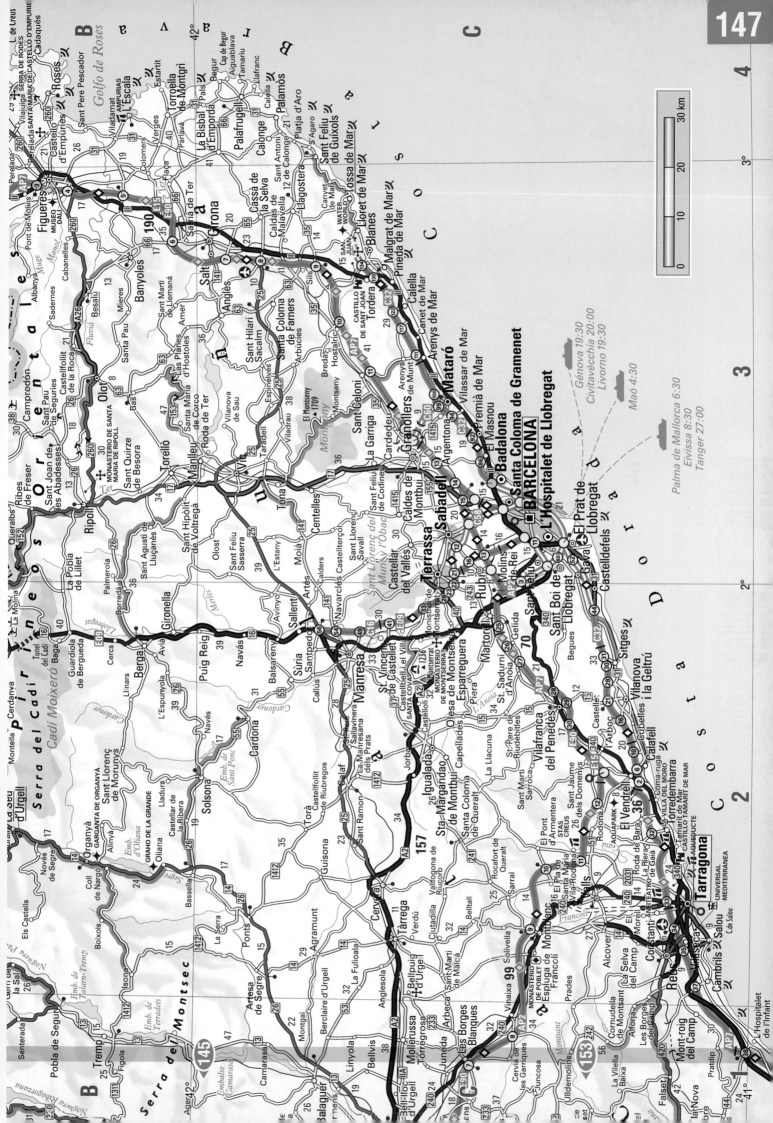

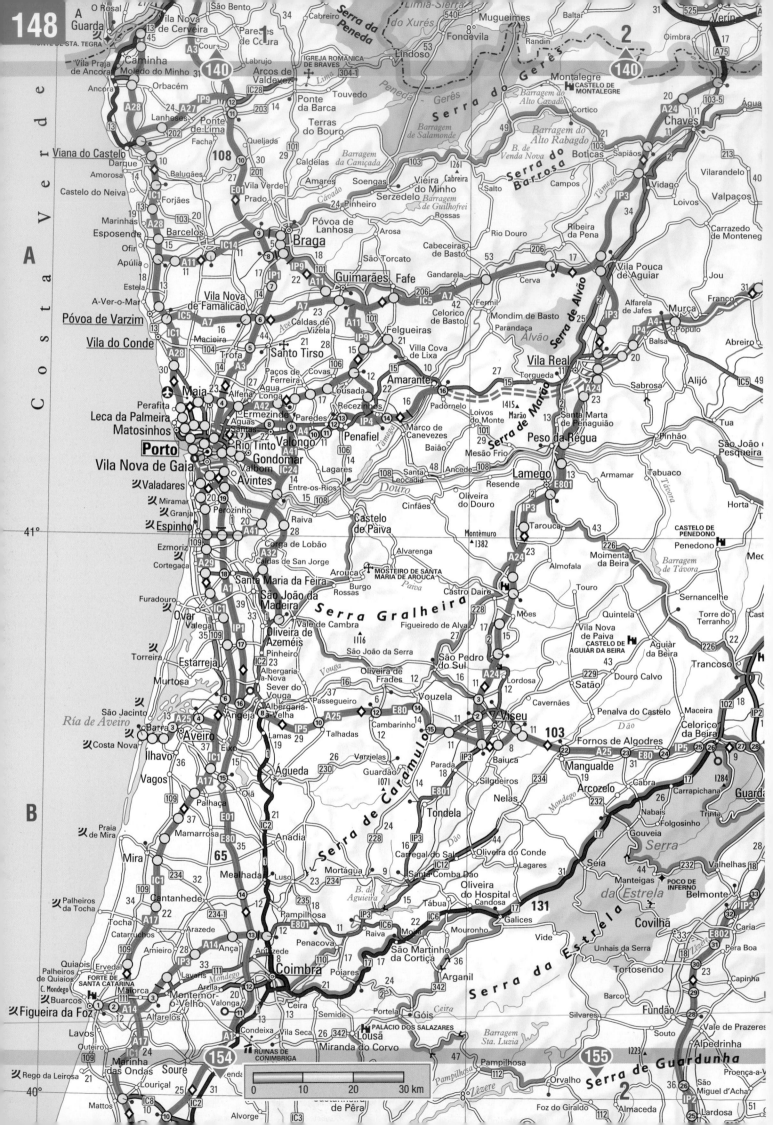

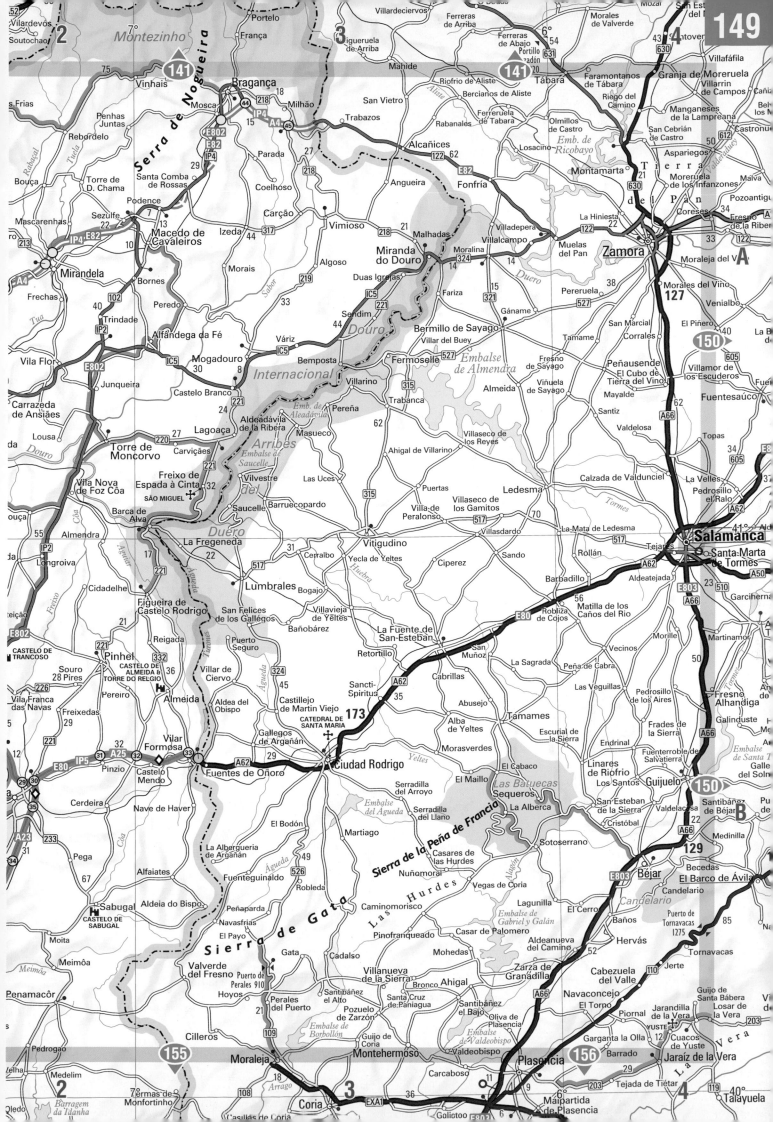

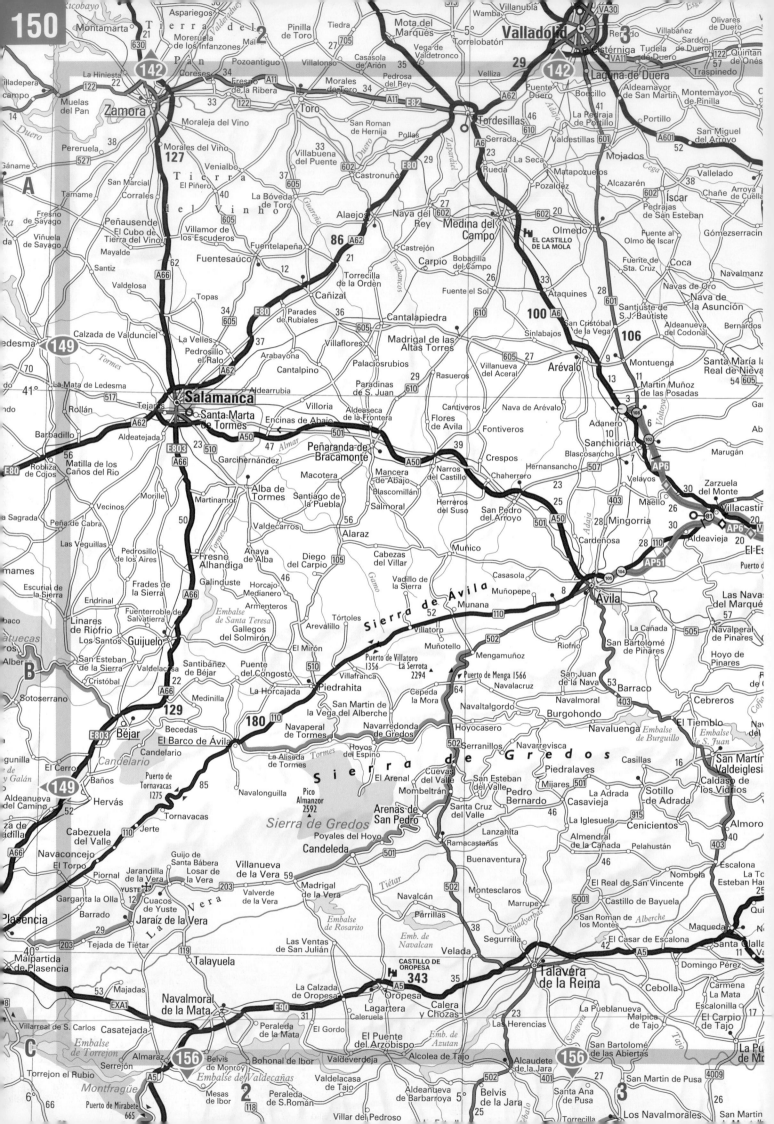

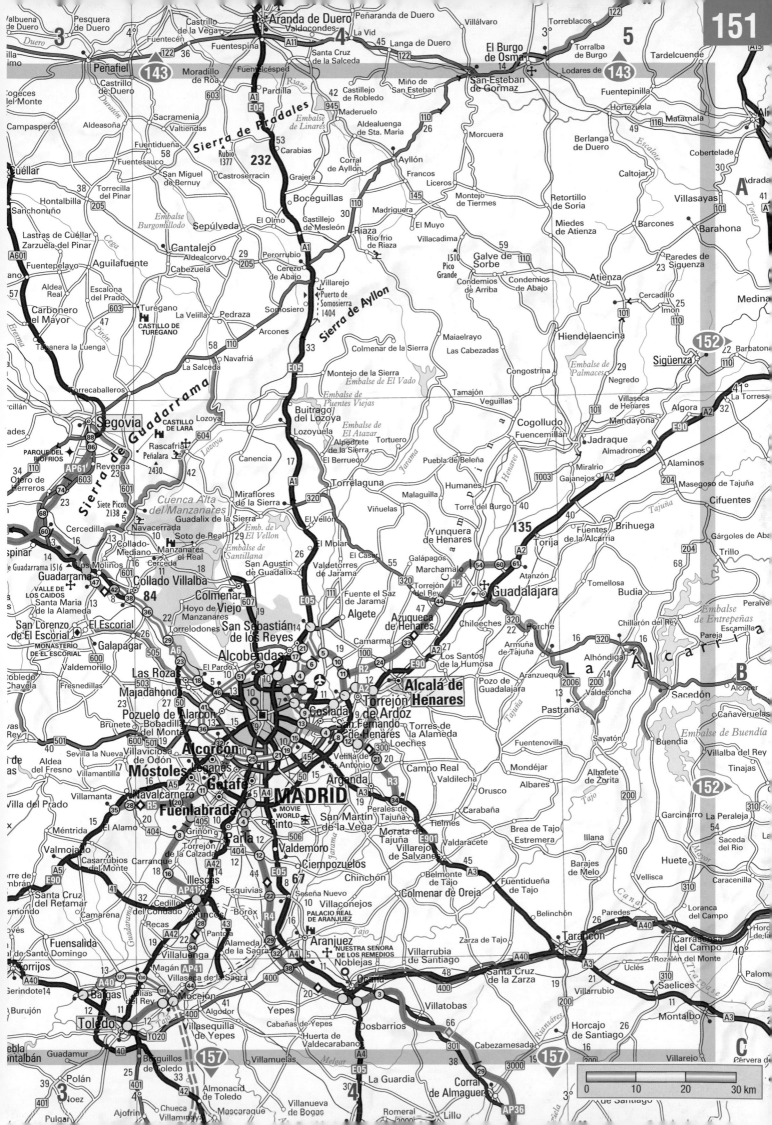

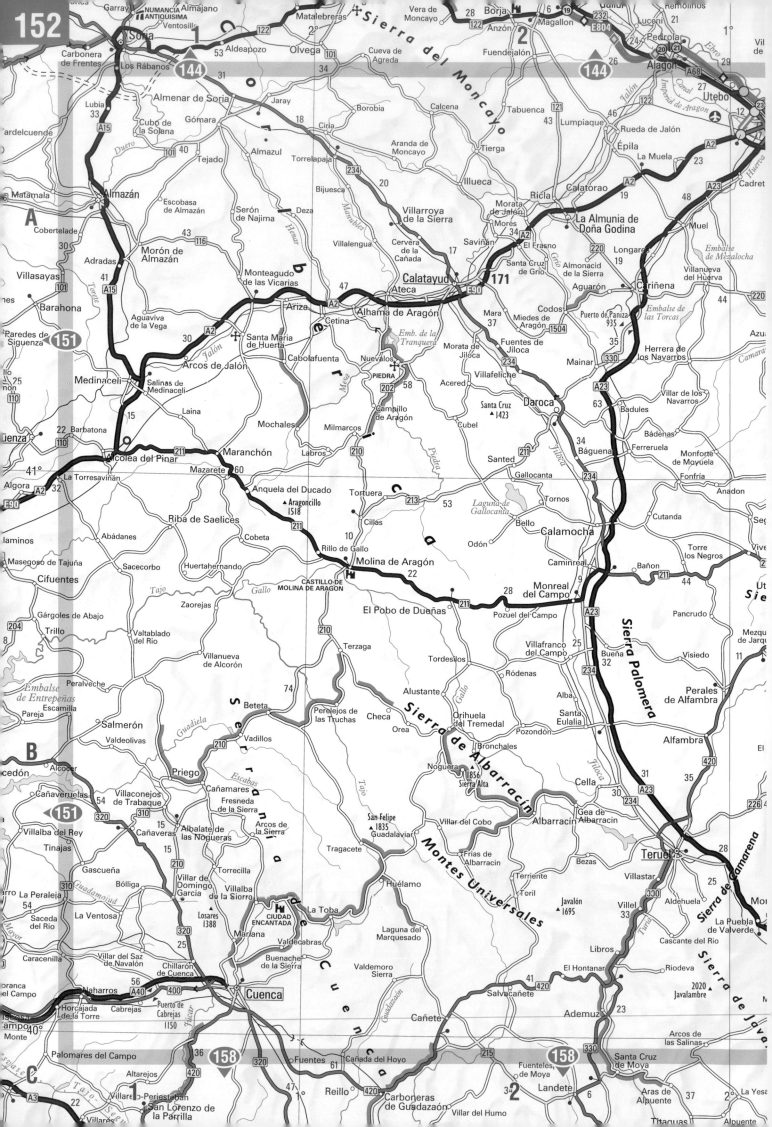

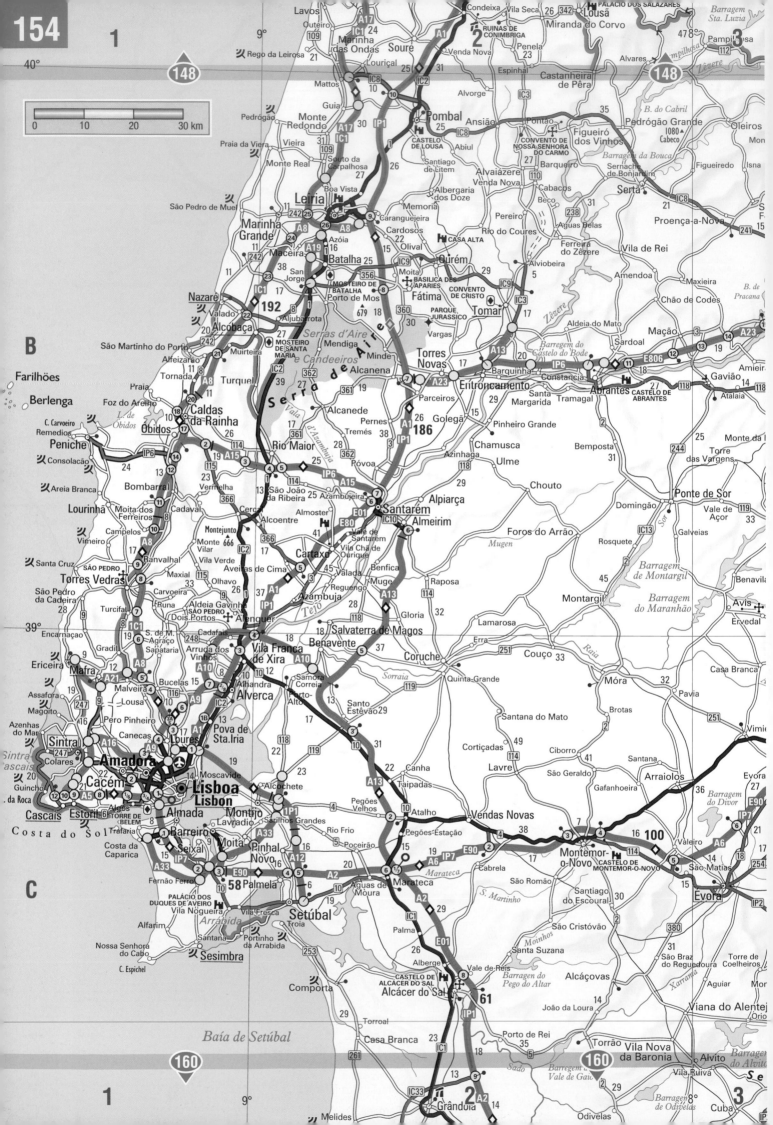

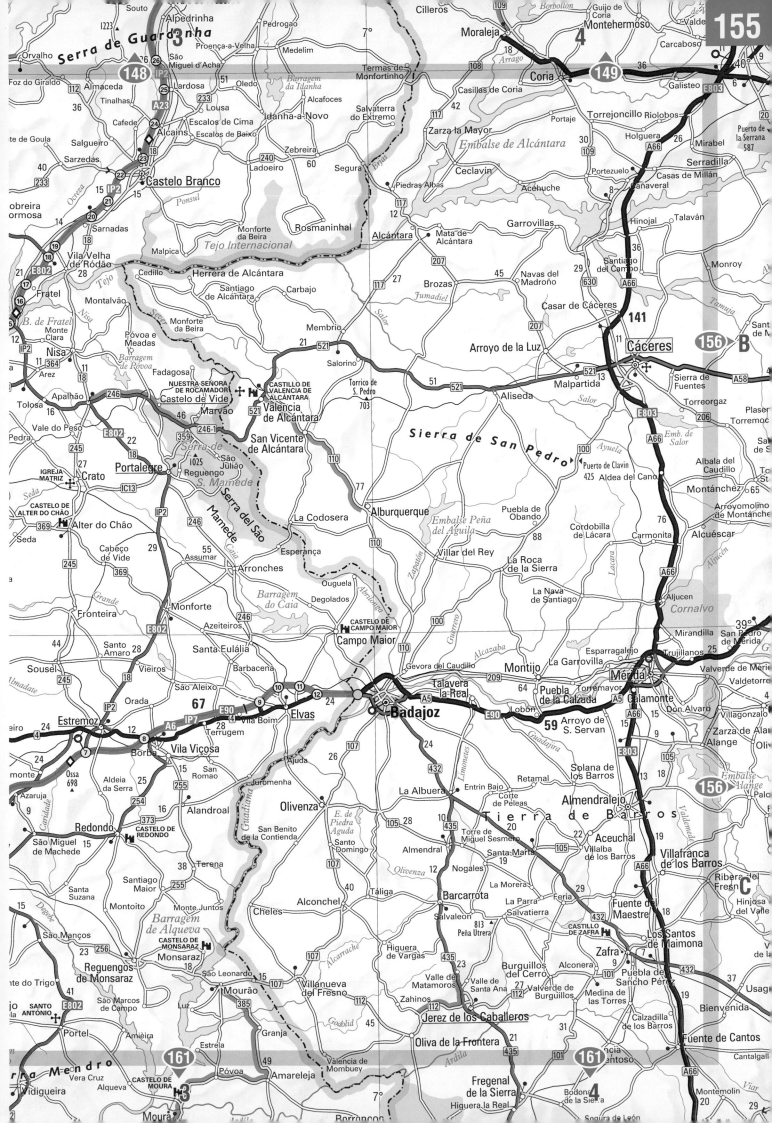

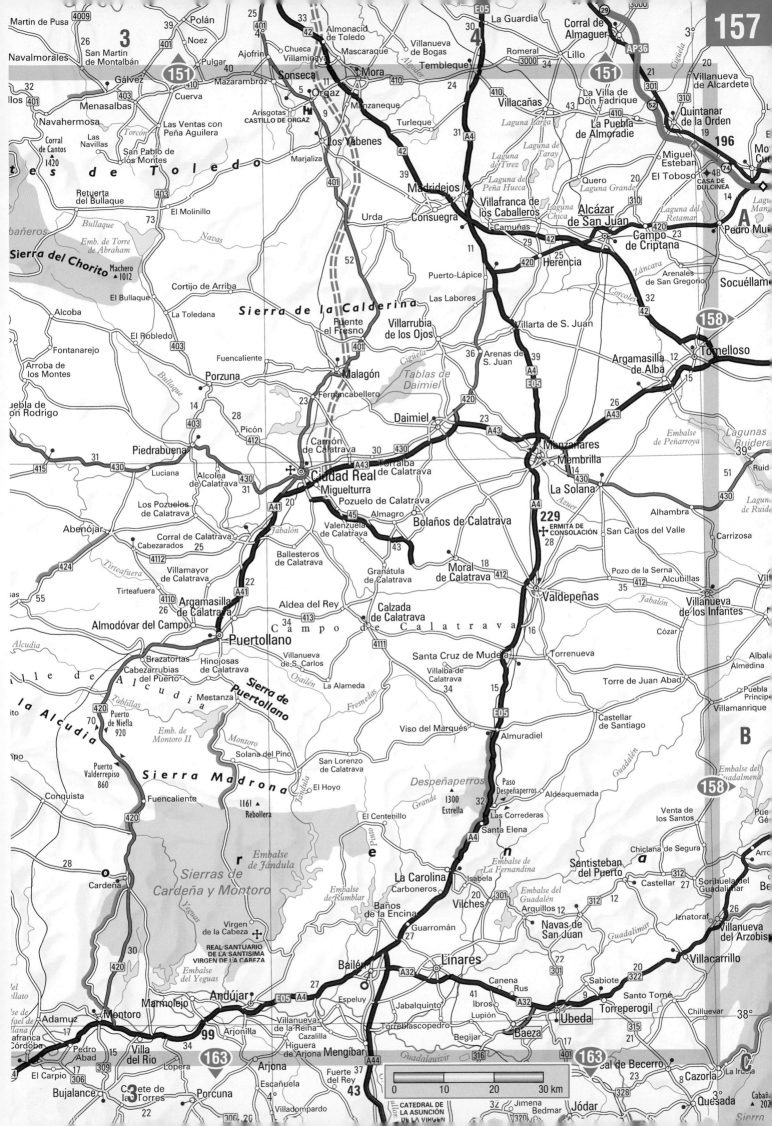

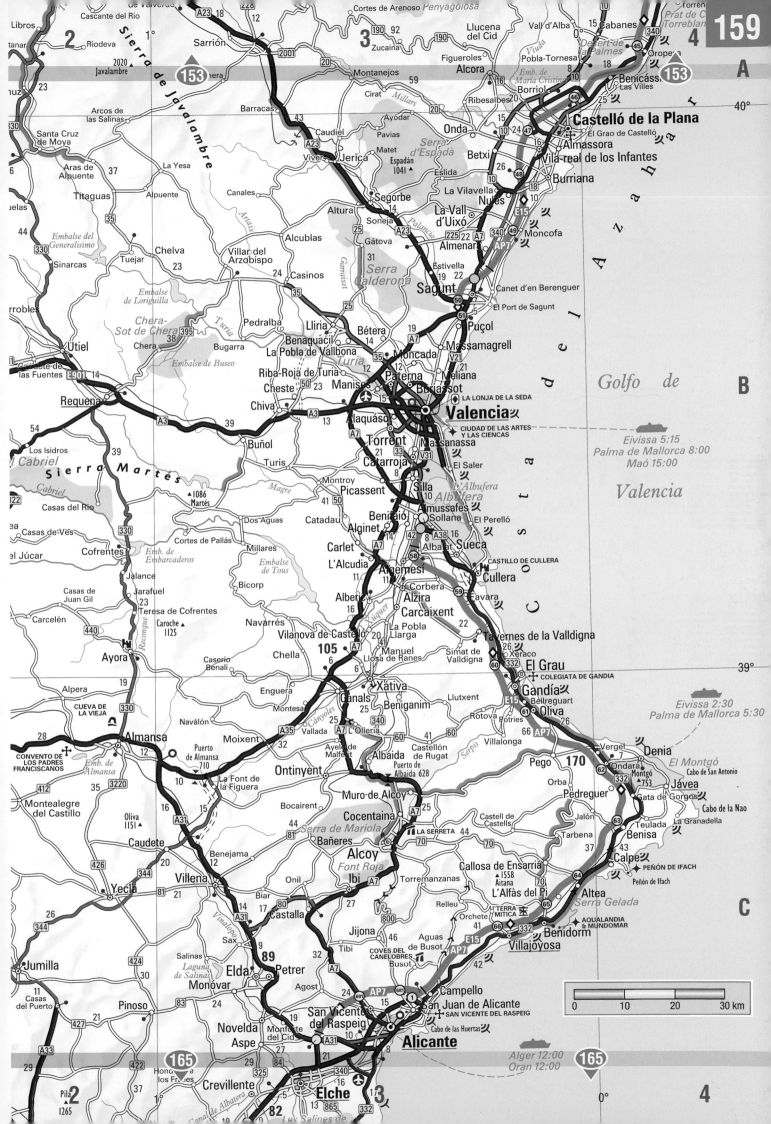

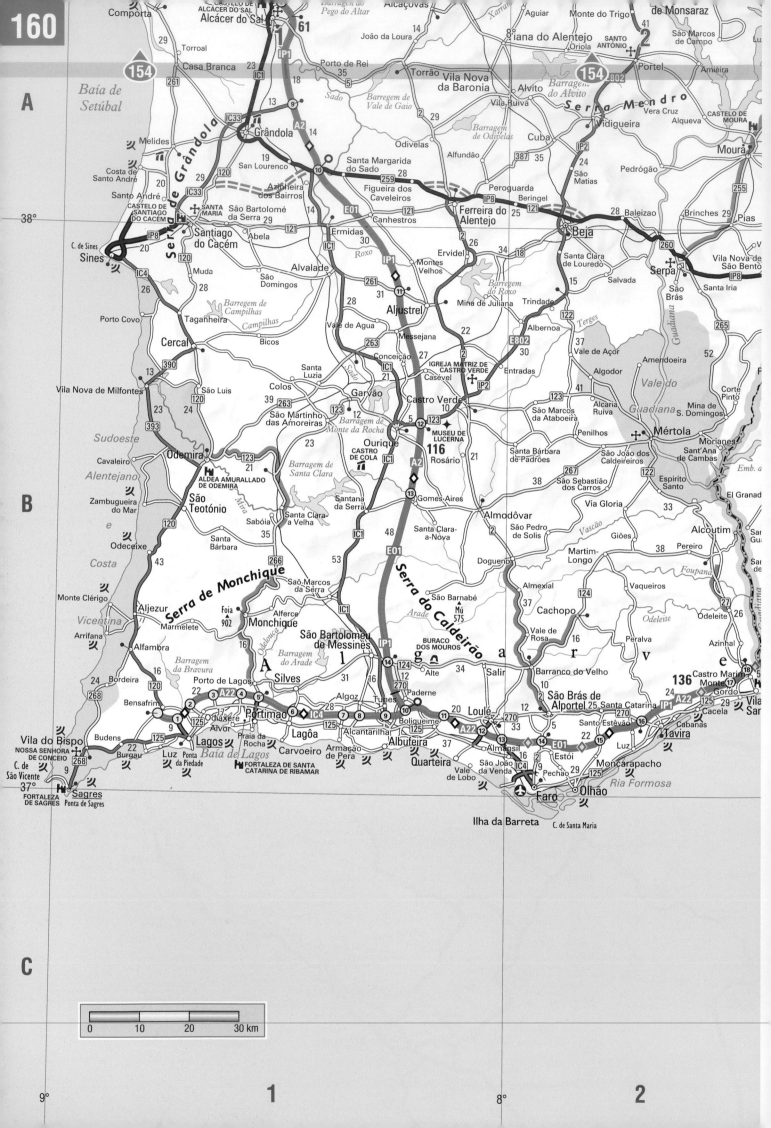

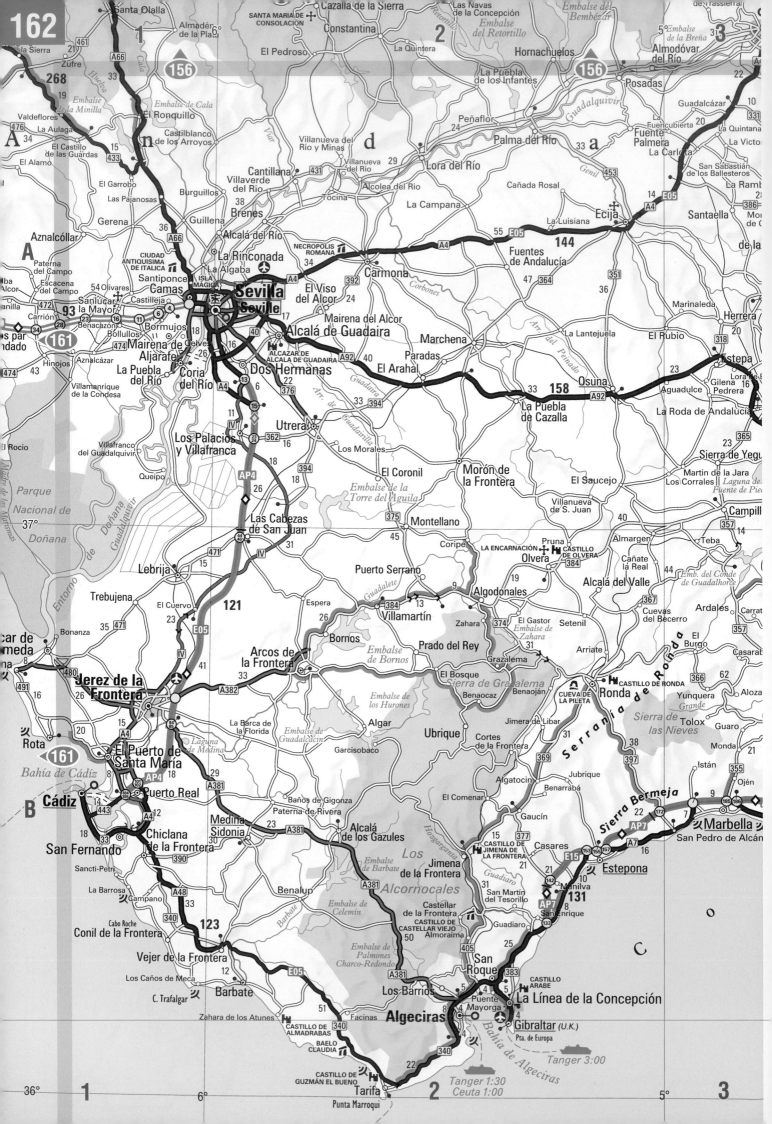

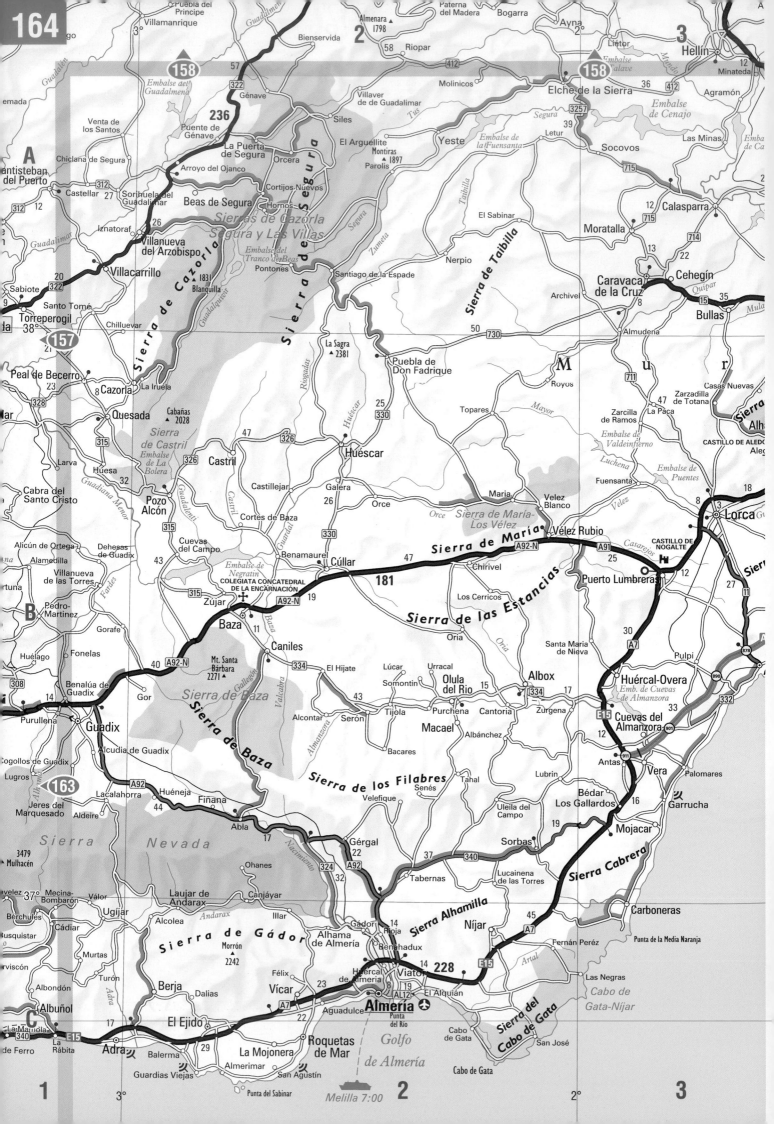

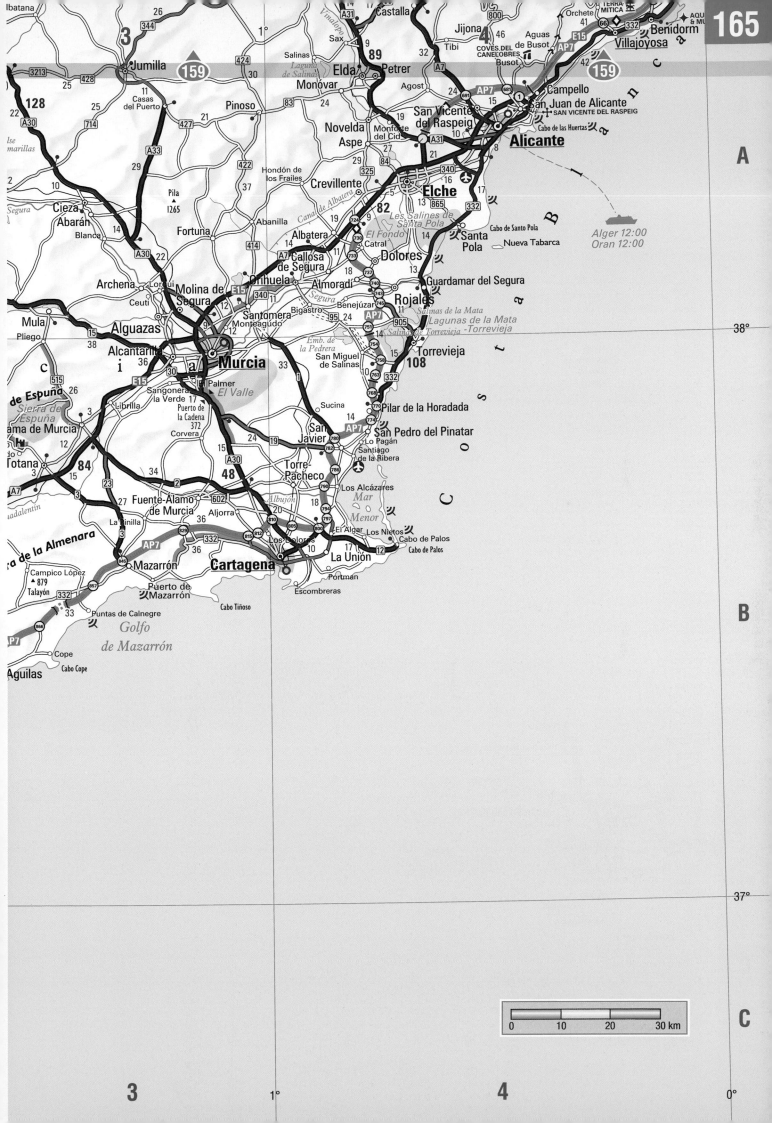

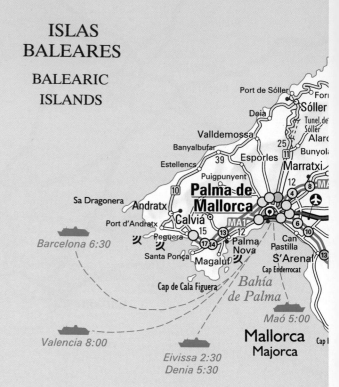

## ISLAS BALEARES

### BALEARIC ISLANDS

Port de Sóller
For
Sóller
Deià
Tunel de
Sóller
Valldemossa
Alar
Banyalbufar
25
Bunyol
Estellencs
39
Esporles
11
Puigpunyent
Marratxi
Sa Dragonera
10
Palma de
12
MA
Andratx
Mallorca
4
Calvià
MA1
Port d'Andratx
13
12
6
Peguera
Palma
Can
10
*Barcelona 6:30*
15
17 14
Nova
Pastilla
Santa Ponça
Magaluf
S'Arenal
13
Cap Enderrocat
Bahía
Cap de Cala Figuera
de Palma
*Maó 5:00*
*Valencia 8:00*
**Mallorca**
*Eivissa 2:30*
Majorca
Cap
*Denia 5:30*

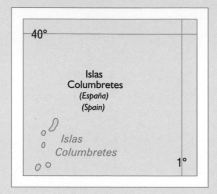

Islas
Columbretes
*(España)*
*(Spain)*

*Islas*
*Columbretes*

40°

1°

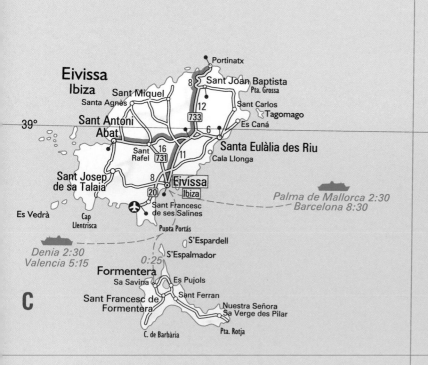

Portinatx
**Eivissa**
Sant Joan Baptista
Ibiza
Pta. Grossa
Sant Miquel
8
Santa Agnès
12
Sant Carlos
**Sant Antoni**
Tagomago
**Abat**
733
Es Caná
6
Sant
16
**Santa Eulàlia des Riu**
Rafel
731
11
Cala Llonga
**Sant Josep**
8
**de sa Talaia**
20
**Eivissa**
Ibiza
Sant Francesc
*Palma de Mallorca 2:30*
de ses Salines
*Barcelona 8:30*
Es Vedrà
Cap
Llentrisca
Punta Portás
S'Espardell
S'Espalmador
*Denia 2:30*
0:25
*Valencia 5:15*
**Formentera**
Sa Savina
Es Pujols
Sant Ferran
Sant Francesc de
Nuestra Señora
Formentera
Sa Verge des Pilar
C. de Barbària
Pta. Rotja

40°

39°

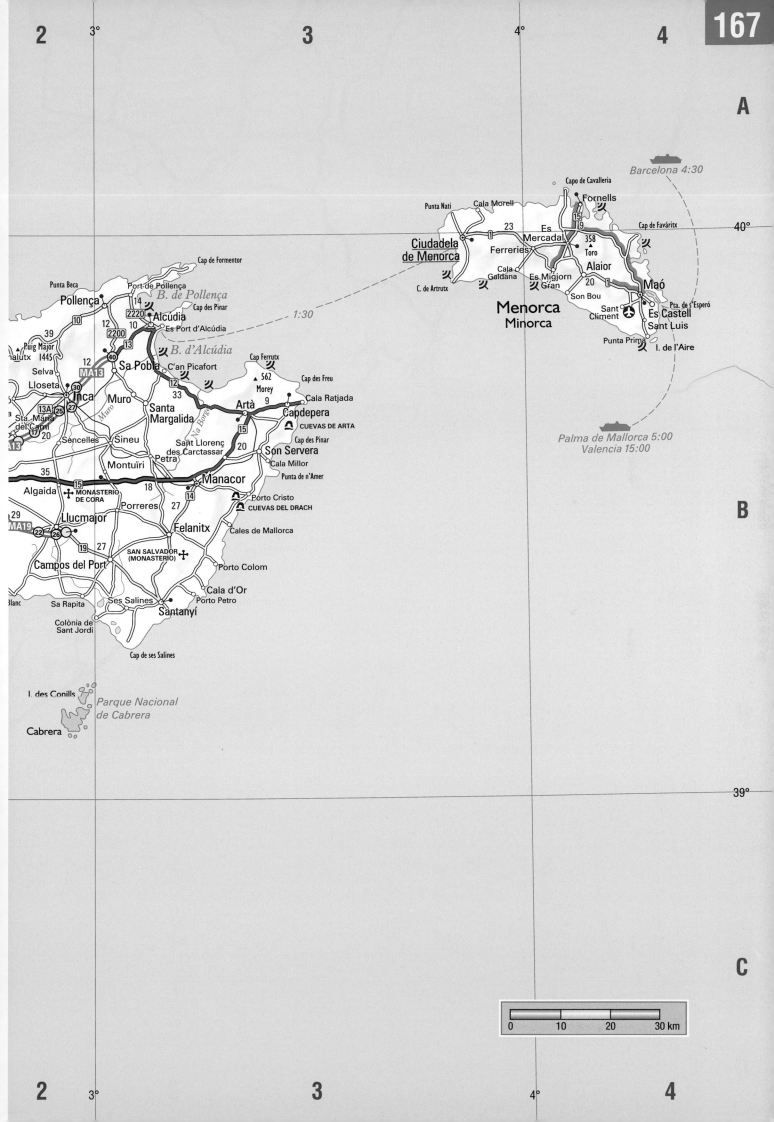

A

B

C

2    3°

3

4°    4

Barcelona 4:30

Capo de Cavalleria
Fornells
Punta Nati    Cala Morell
15
9
Cap de Faváritx
40°
23
Es
Mercadal
358
Toro
Ciudadela
de Menorca
Ferreries
Alaior
Maó
Cap de Formentor
Cala
Galdana
Es Migjorn
Gran
20
1
Pta. de s'Esperó
Punta Beca
Port de Pollença
B. de Pollença
C. de Artrutx
Son Bou
Sant
Climent
Es Castell
Pollença
14
Cap des Pinar
Menorca
Sant Luis
10
12
2220
Alcúdia
Minorca
10
2200    Es Port d'Alcúdia
Punta Prima
I. de l'Aire
39
13
1:30
Puig Major
40    B. d'Alcúdia
1445    Sa Pobla    C'an Picafort
alutx    12    Cap Ferrutx
Selva    MA13    12    562
Lloseta    33    Morey
30    Inca    Muro    Artà    Cala Ratjada
13A 25    27    Santa    9
Sta. Maria    Margalida    Capdepera
del Camí    17 20    Sencelles    Sineu    Sant Llorenç    CUEVAS DE ARTA
MA13    des Carctassar    Cap des Pinar
Petra    20    Son Servera
Montuïri    Cala Millor
35    Punta de n'Amer
Algaida    15    18    Manacor
MONASTERIO    14    Porto Cristo
DE CORA    CUEVAS DEL DRACH
Porreres    27
29    Felanitx    Cales de Mallorca
Llucmajor
MA19    SAN SALVADOR
22 26    (MONASTERIO)
19    27    Porto Colom
Campos del Port
Cala d'Or
Blanc    Ses Salines    Porto Petro
Sa Rapita    Santanyí
Colònia de
Sant Jordi
Cap de ses Salines

I. des Conills
Parque Nacional
de Cabrera

Cabrera

Palma de Mallorca 5:00
Valencia 15:00

39°

0    10    20    30 km

2    3°

3

4°    4

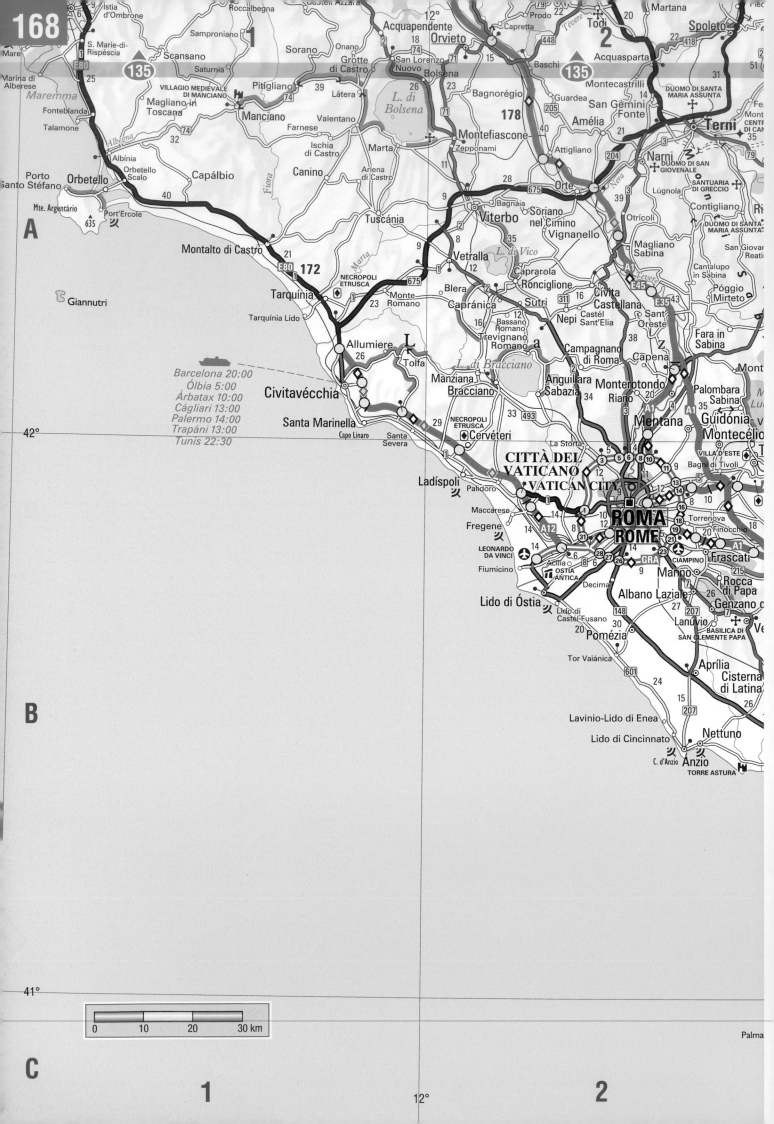

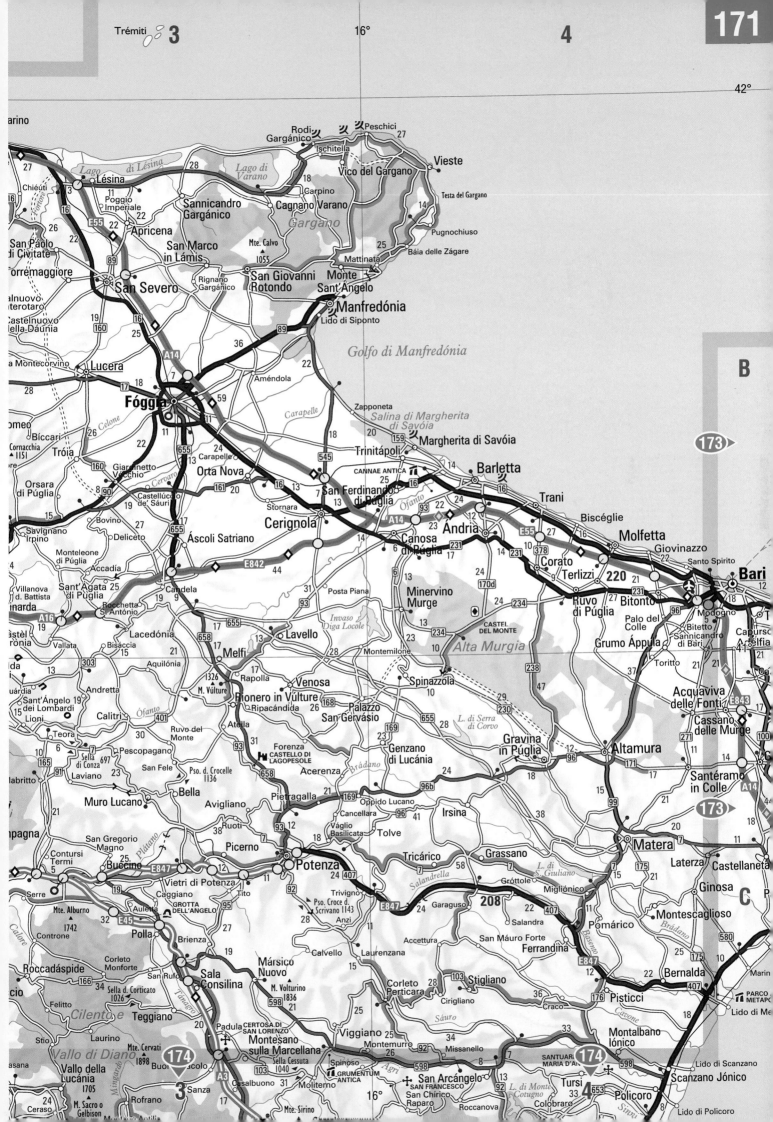

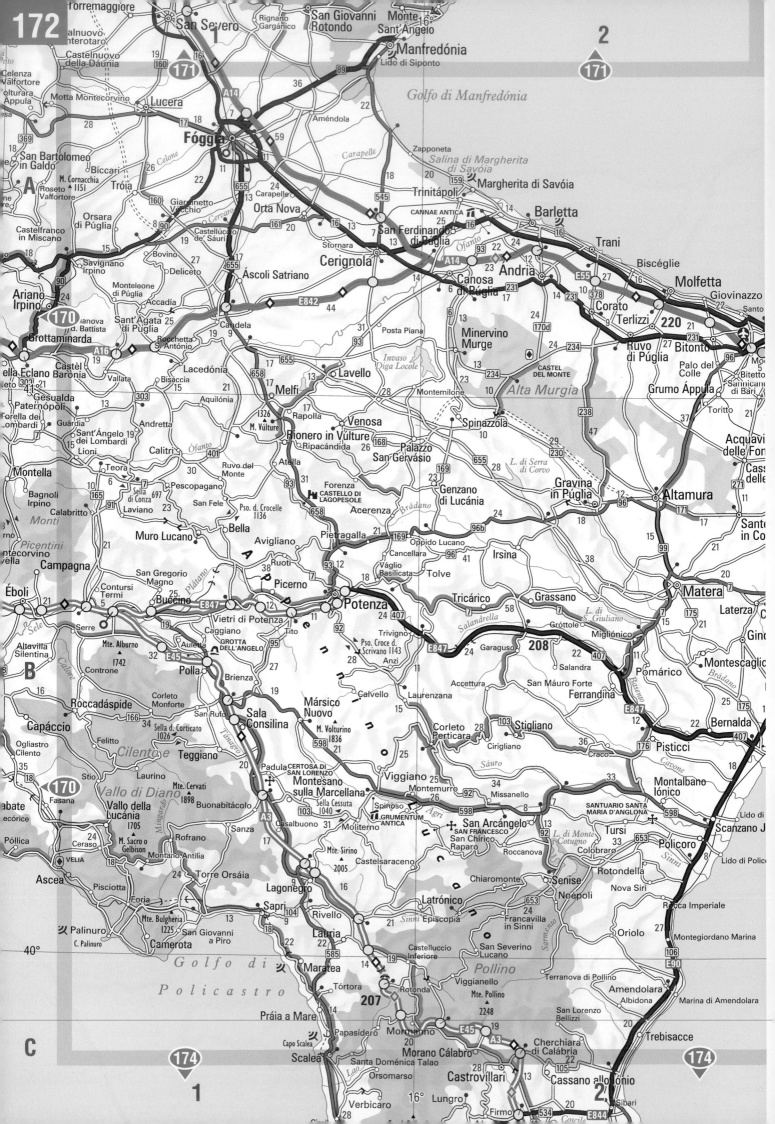

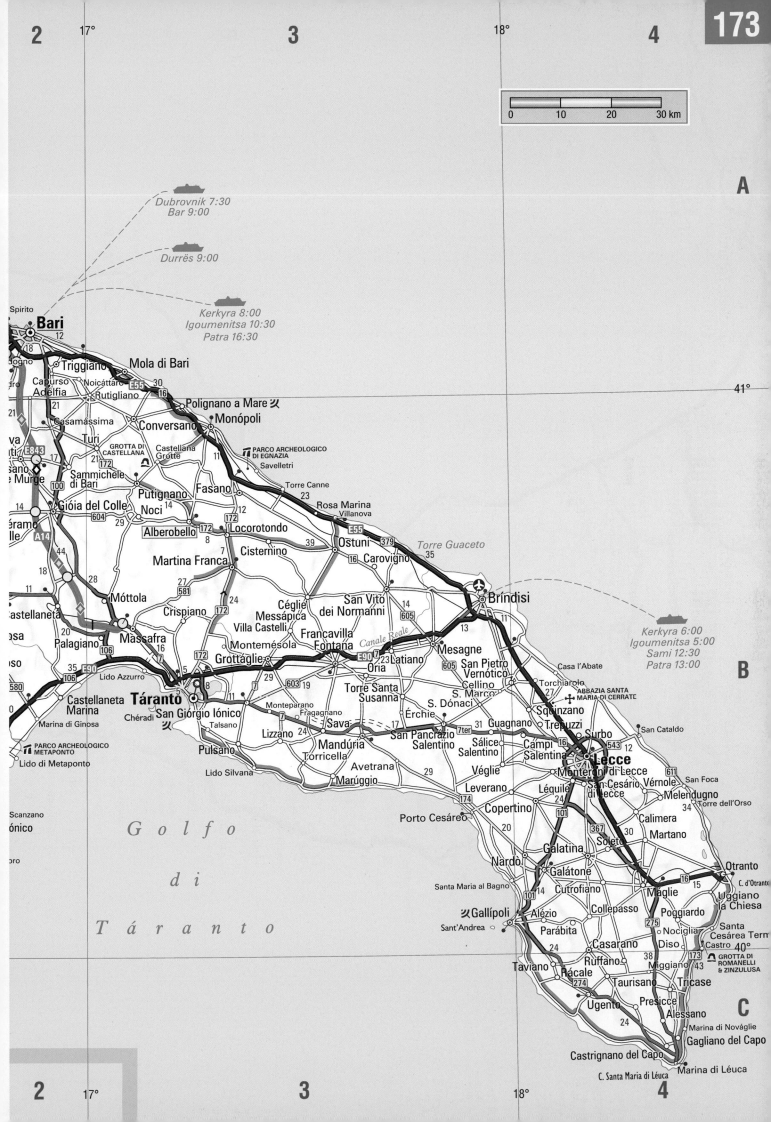

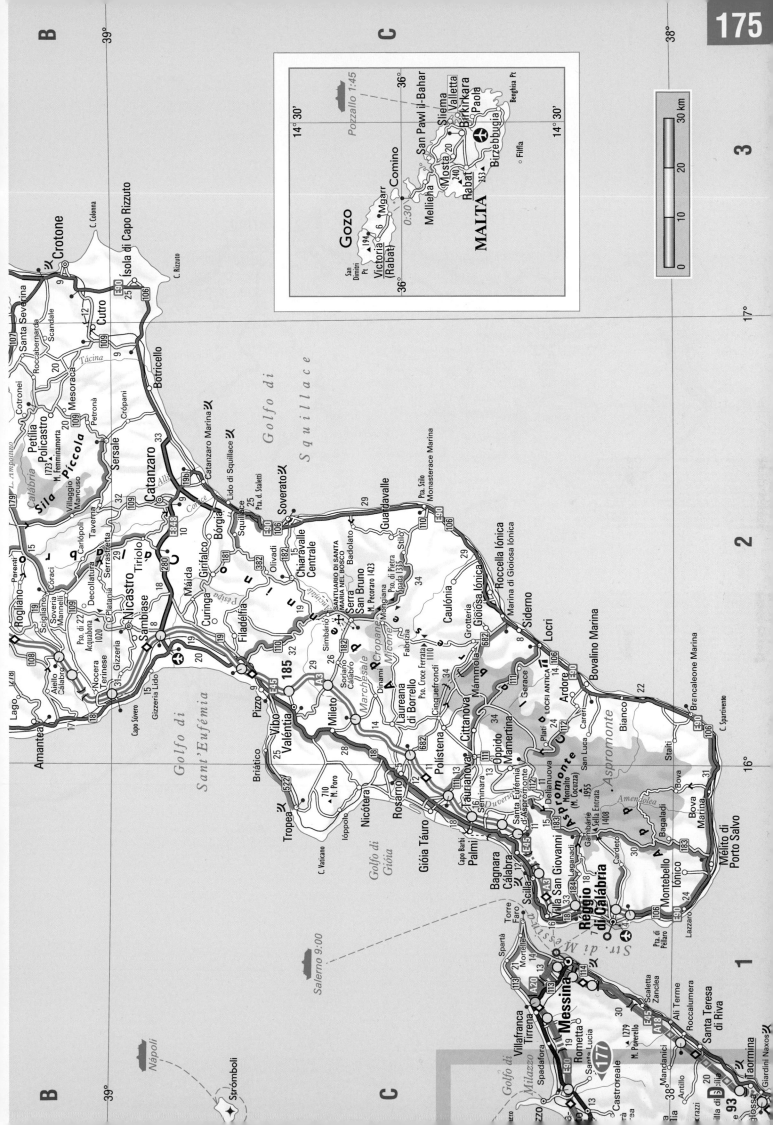

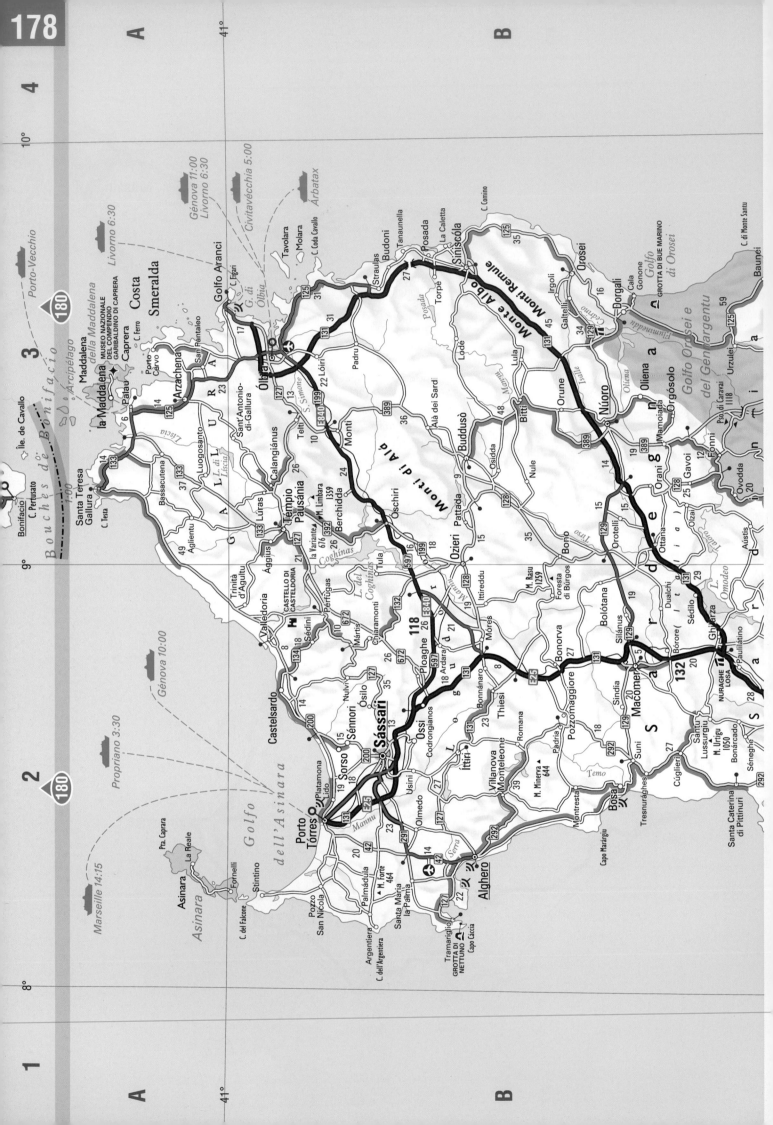

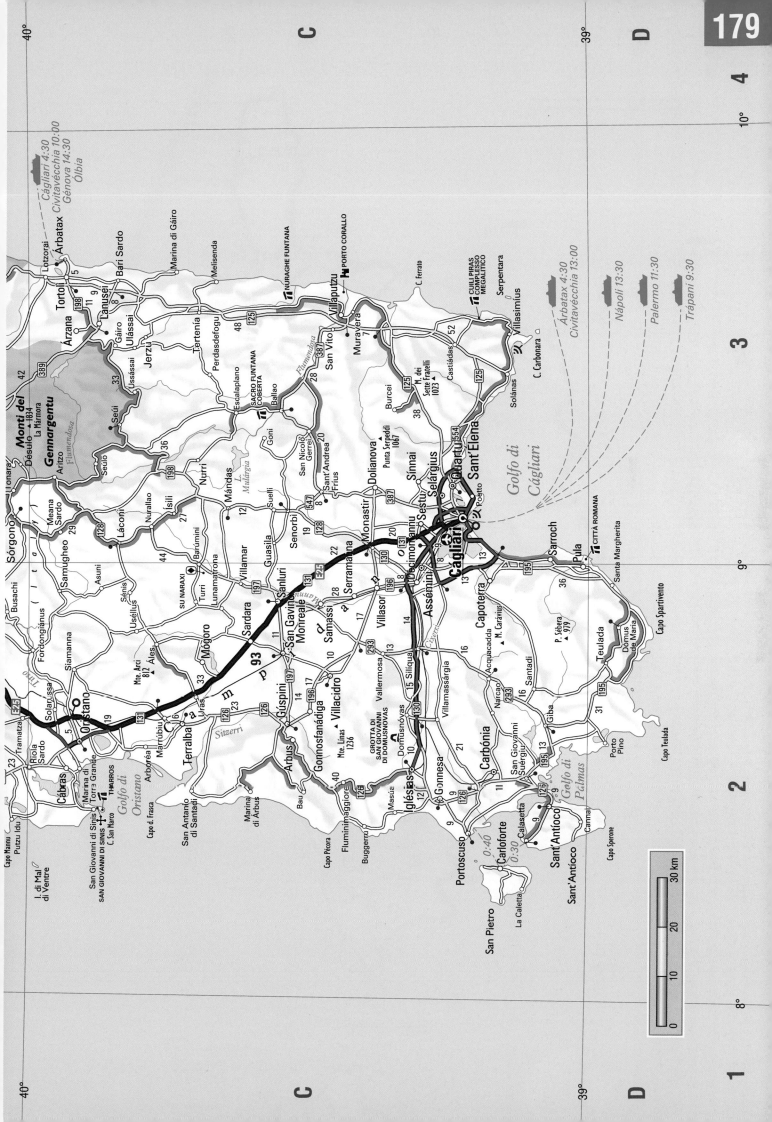

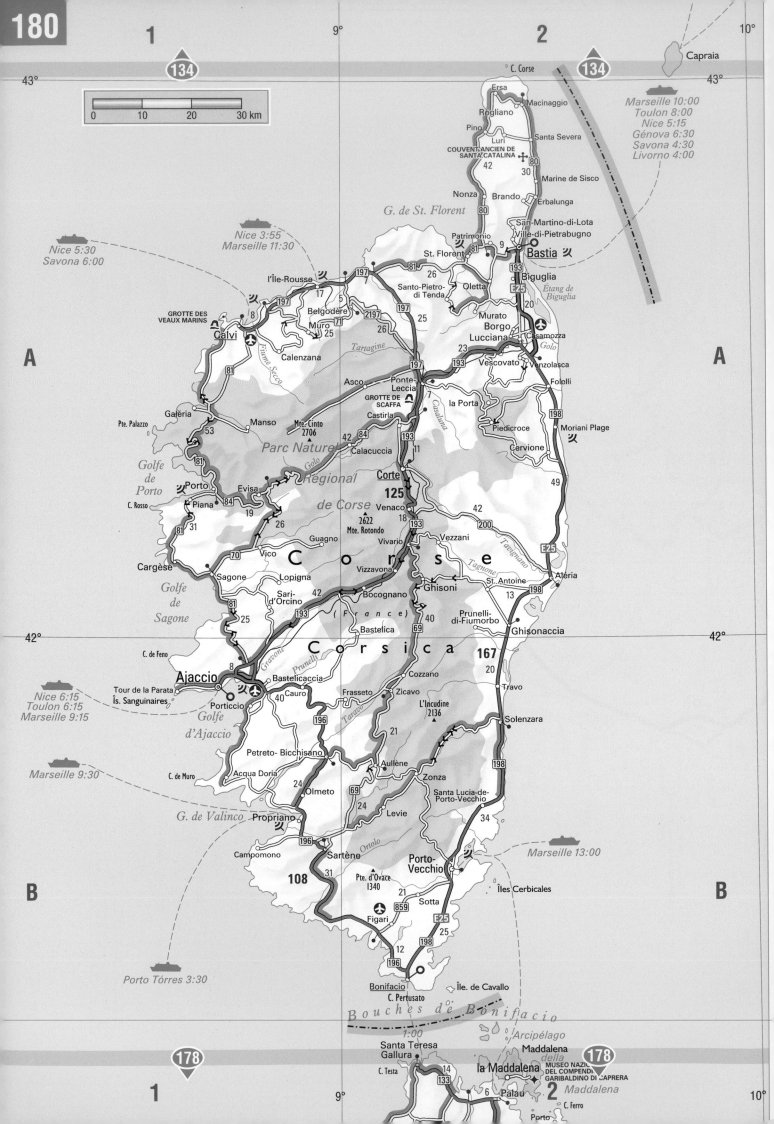

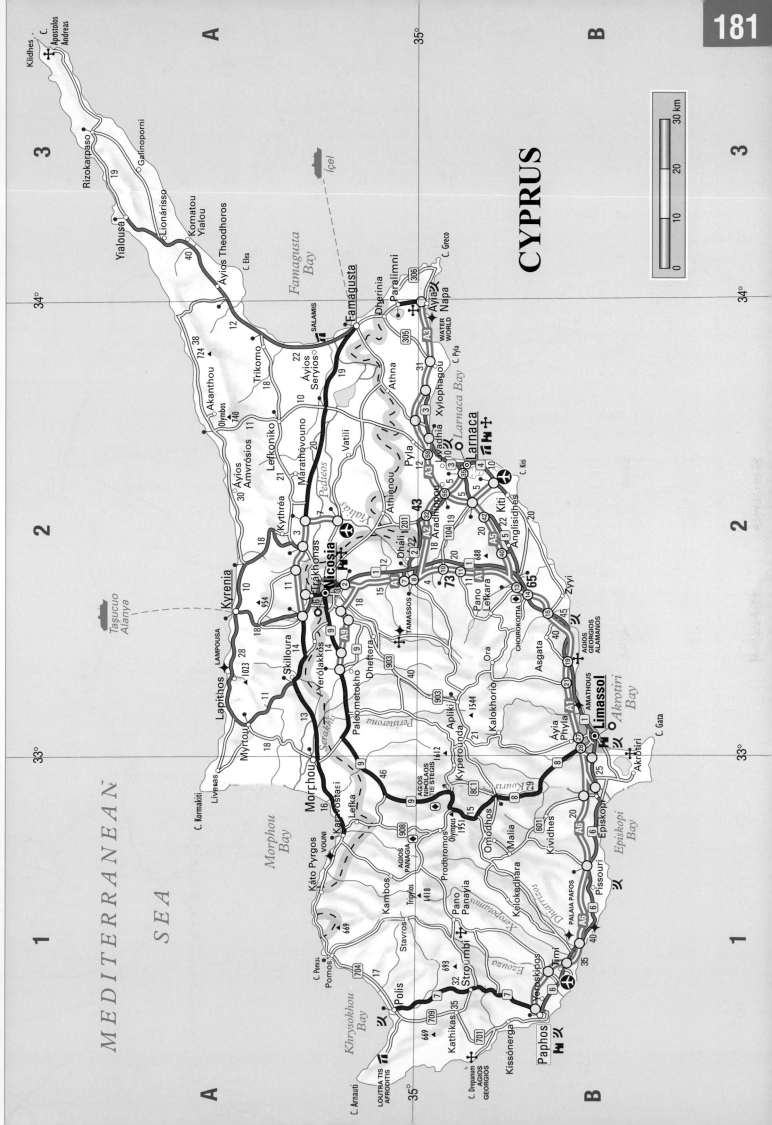

**CYPRUS**

*MEDITERRANEAN*

*SEA*

C. Apostolos Andreas
Klidhes
Rizokarpaso
Galinoporni
19
Lionárisso
Komatou Yialou
Vialousa
40
Ávios Theodhoros
12
C. Elea
Akanthou
724 38
740
Olymbos
Trikomo
Áyios Amvrósios
11
Lefkoniko
18
Áyios Servios
22
*Famagusta Bay*
SALAMIS
Famagusta
Dherinia
Paralimni
306
Áyia Napa
WATER WORLD
C. Greco
305
A3
31
Athna
Xylophagou
*Larnaca Bay*
3
Ávios Amvrósios
30
Marathóvouno
20
Vatili
Pyla
Athienou
12
A3 69
Livadhia
Larnaca
*Íçel*
Kythréa
3
21
Márathóvouno
201
32
A2
Aradhippou
104 19
5
3
35
42
C. Kiti
Skilloura
18
3
Trákhonas
Nicosia
Dháli
2
22
18
A2
888
A5
22
Kiti
Anglisidhes
20
C. Kormakiti
Liveras
Kyrenia
10
11
7
Yialás
1
12
8
4
73
11
1
A1
40
20
Zyyi
65
*Taşucu Alanya*
LAMPOUSA
1023 28
18
Verólakkos
A9
9
18
15
TAMASSOS
Pano Lefkara
14
CHOIROKOITIA
14
15
45
AGIOS GEORGIOS ALAMANOS
Lapithos
Skilloura
14
Dheftera
903
Ora
Asgata
40
19
Myrtou
18
Karavostasi
13
*Serákhis*
Paleometokho
903
40
Apliki
1544
Kalokhorió
21
AMATHOUS
Limassol
*Akrotiri Bay*
Morphou
16
Lefka
46
9
*Peristerona*
1612
Kyperounda
8
Áyia Phyla
27
28
Akrotiri
C. Gata
Káto Pyrgos
AGIOS NIKOLAOS TIS STEGIS
15
801
8
8
25
*Morphou Bay*
908
AGIOS PANAGIA
Prodhromos
Olympus 1951
Omódhos
Malia
601
Kividhes
Episkopi
*Episkopi Bay*
C. Pomos
Kambos
1418
Tripylos
Pano Panayia
*Dhiarizos*
PALAIA PAFOS
20
A6
C. Armauti
LOUTRA TIS AFRODITIS
704
17
Stavros
669
693
Stroumbi
32
*Xeropotamos*
*Ezousa*
A6
40
Pissouri
Kelokedhára
Khrysokhou Bay
Polis
Yeroskipos
7
6
Kouklia
35
*Khrysokhou Bay*
709
669
701
Kathikas 35
Kissónerga
Paphos
C. Drepanum
AGIOS GEORGIOS

30 km
20
10
0

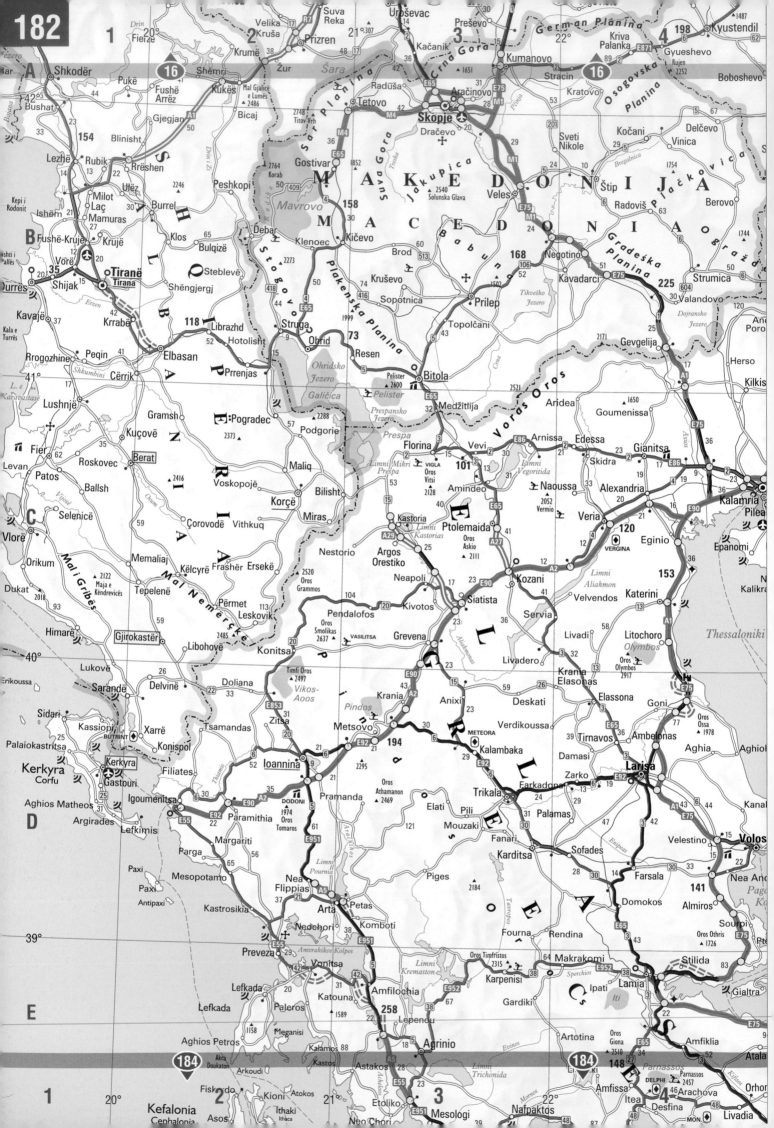

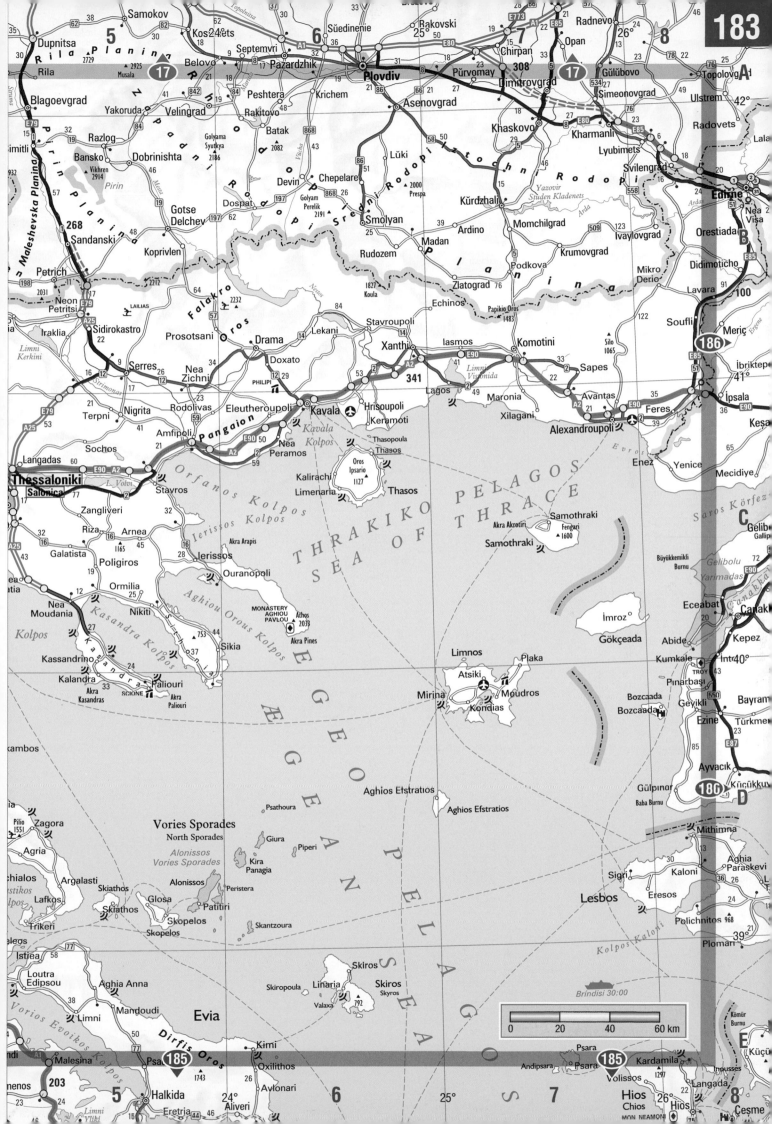

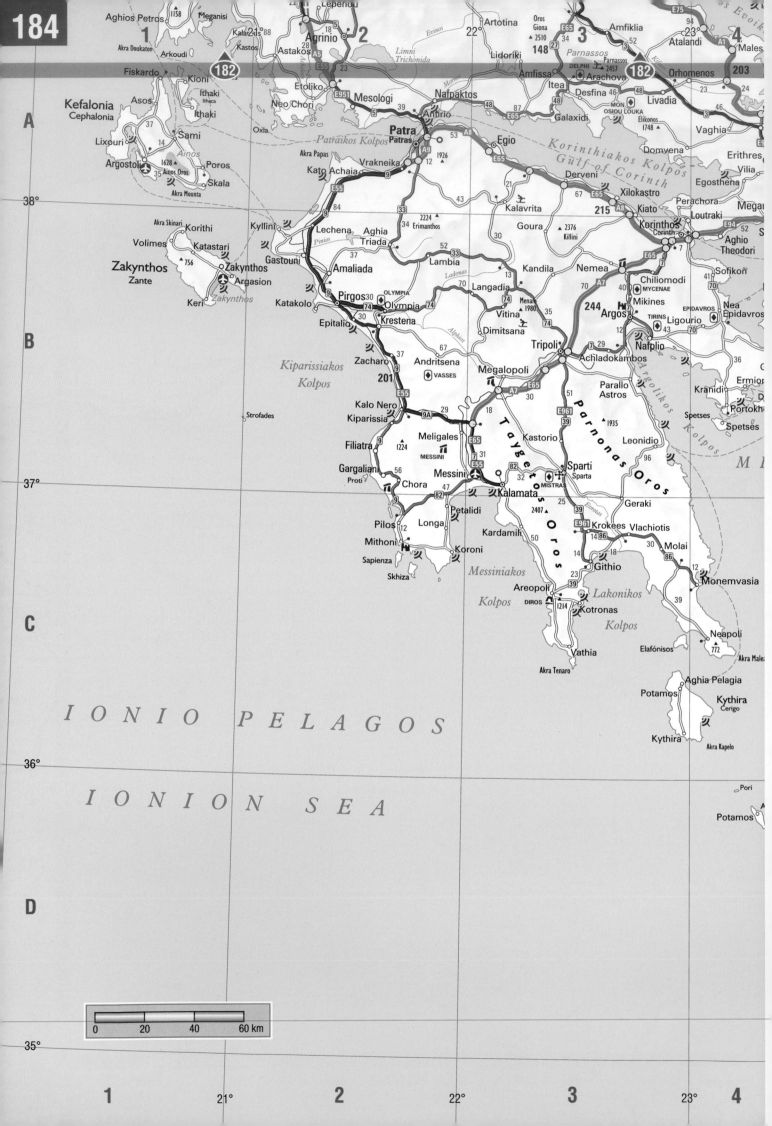

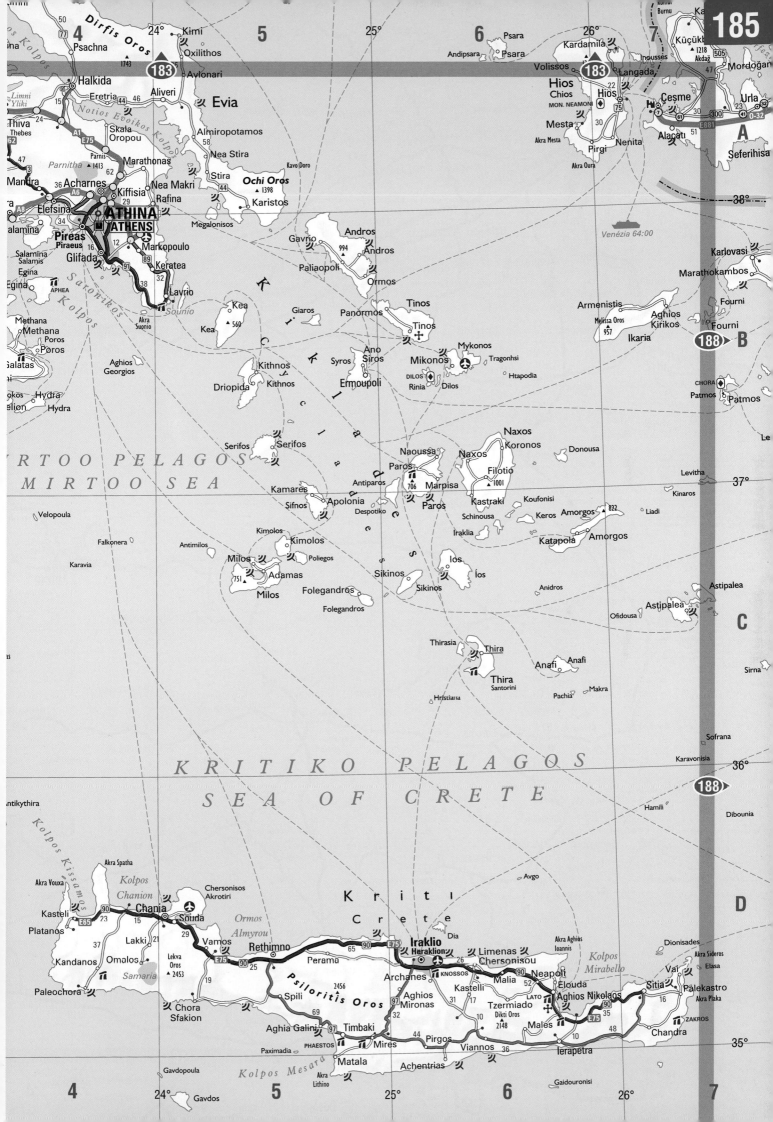

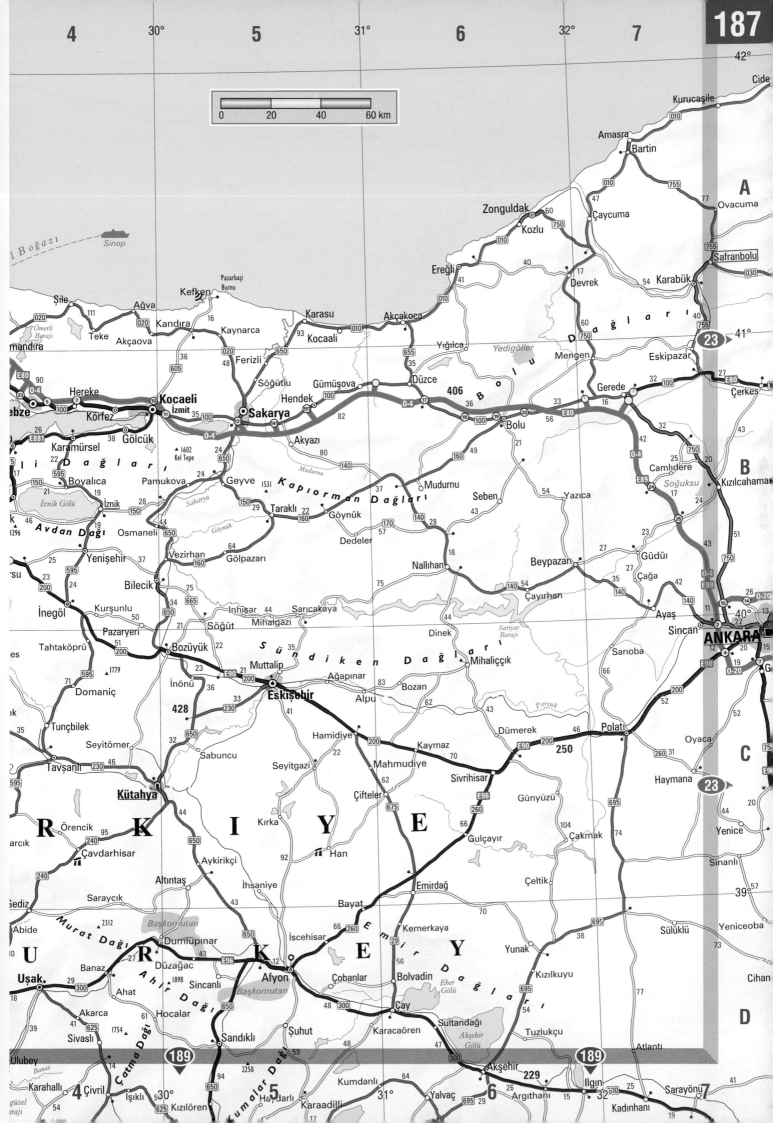

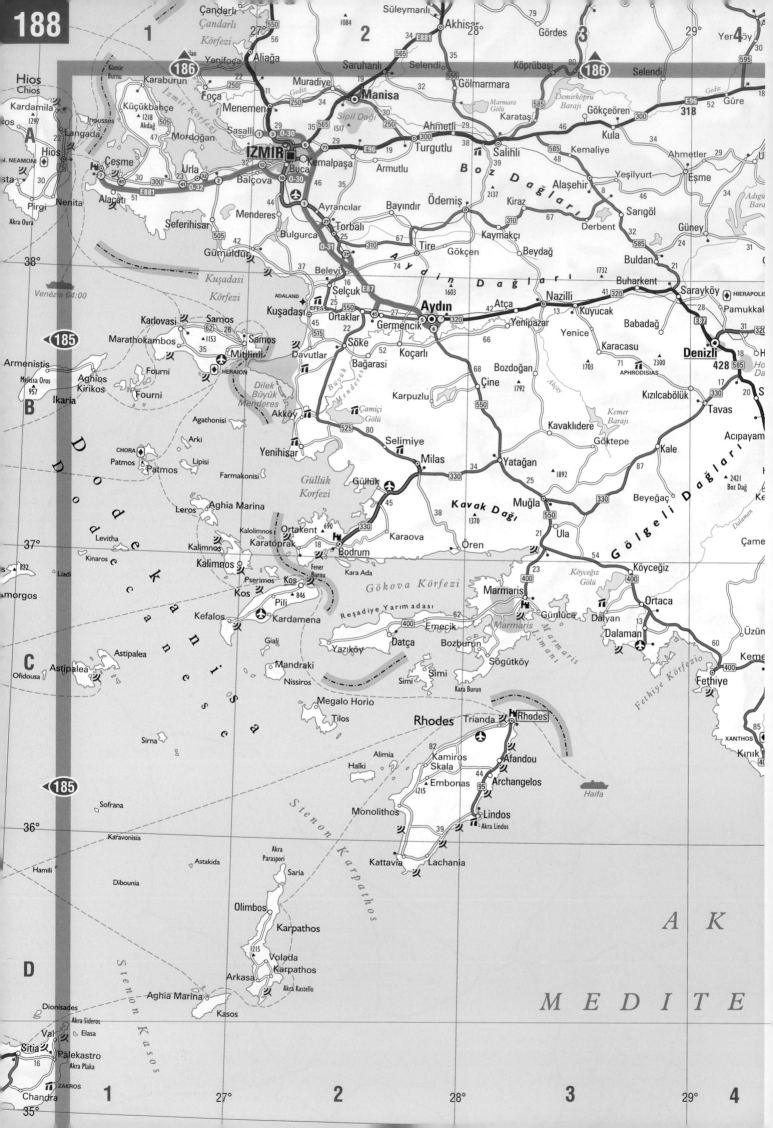

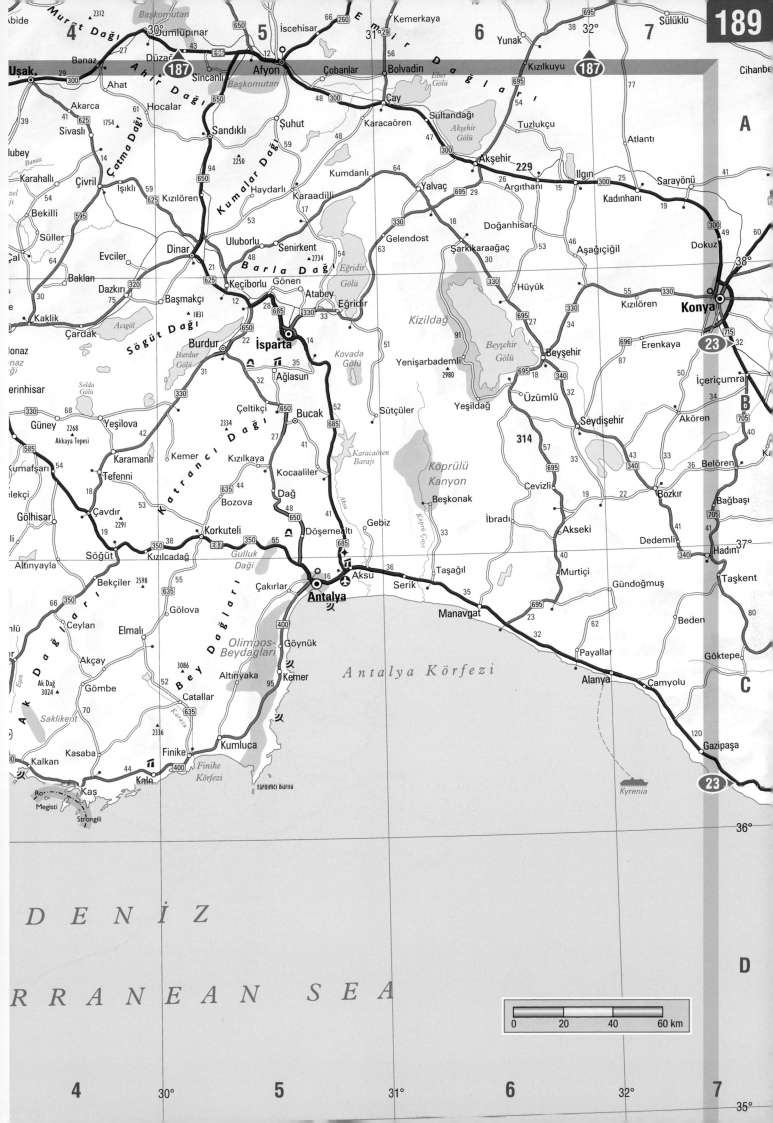

ARCTIC CIRCLE

66°30'

A

66°

B

65°

C

64°

D

63°

Grímsey

3:30

Eyjafjörður

Ólafsfjörður

Dalvík

Hauganes

82

Grenivík

Björg

Tröllaskagi

84

Akureyri

30

21

83

82

82

32

Hrafnagil

1538

Saurbær

24

34

85

Laugar

46

87

61

Húsavík

Laxamýri

75

85

Skjálfandi

Jökulsá á Fjöllum

Skjálfandafljót

Myri

Bláfjall

1222

Öðaðahraun

Herðubreið

1682

Reykjahlíð

38

Mývatn

285

Grímsstaðir

1

Möðrudalur

44

Kópasker

Öxarfjörður

Raufarhöfn

85

Svalbarð

177

Pórshöfn

Hlio

Asbygri

285

Pistilfjörður

Fontur

Digranes

Bakkafjörður

85

Bakkaflói

Vopnafjörður

Vopnafjörður

Héraðsflói

Husey

Sleðbrjótur

82

94

64

Bakkagerði

Glettinganes

Lagarfljót

77

1

23

93

Seyðisfjörður

12

92

32

Neskaupstaður

Egilsstaðir

931

92

35

Eskifjörður

Hallormsstaður

27

Reyðarfjörður

Valbjofsstaður

69

86

Fáskrúðsfjörður

96

Stöðvarfjörður

Berufjörður

Breiðdalsvík

Snæfell

1833

Djúpivogur

146

1

Tórshavn 19:00
Hirtshals 46:00

I S L A N D

1765

Hofsjökull

C E L A N D

Vatnajökull

Pórisvatn

1460

Trölladyngja

Nesjahverfi

Höfn

Stokksnes

1

Gerði

192

Hvannadalshnúkur

2119

1

Skaftafell

687

LAKAGIGAR

Búland

26

Kirkjubæjarklaustur

Skeiðarársandur

Ingólfshöfði

204

50

Langholt

1

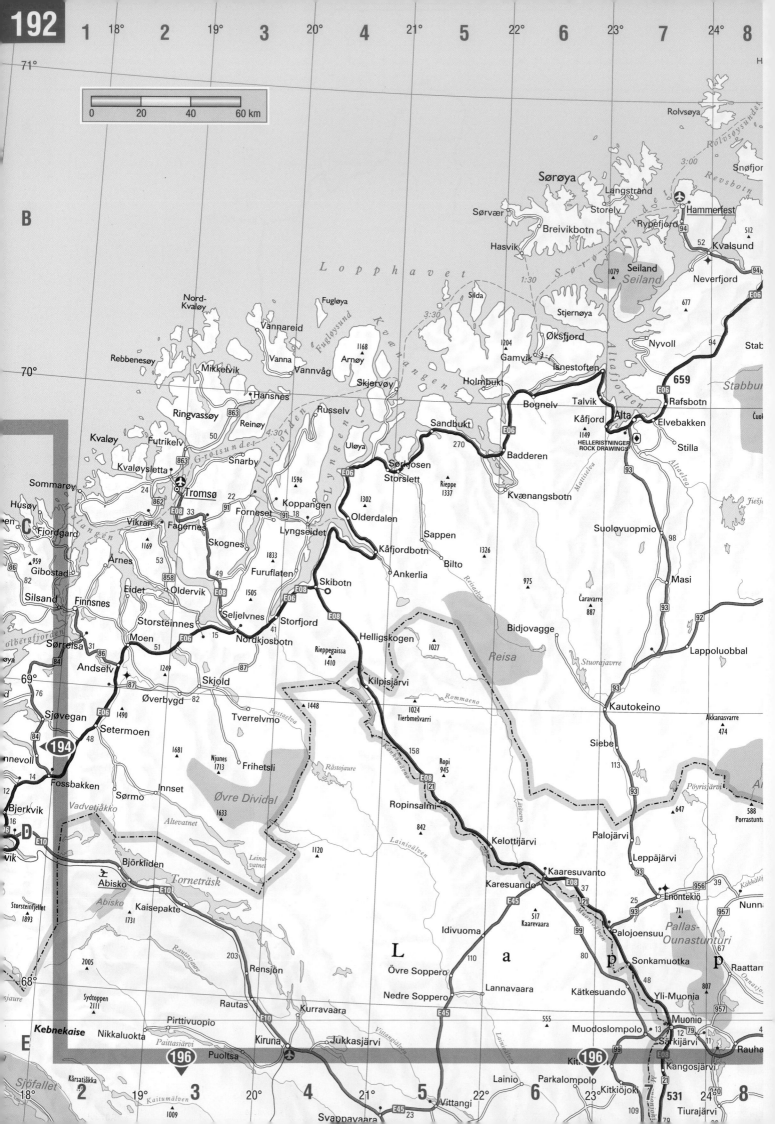

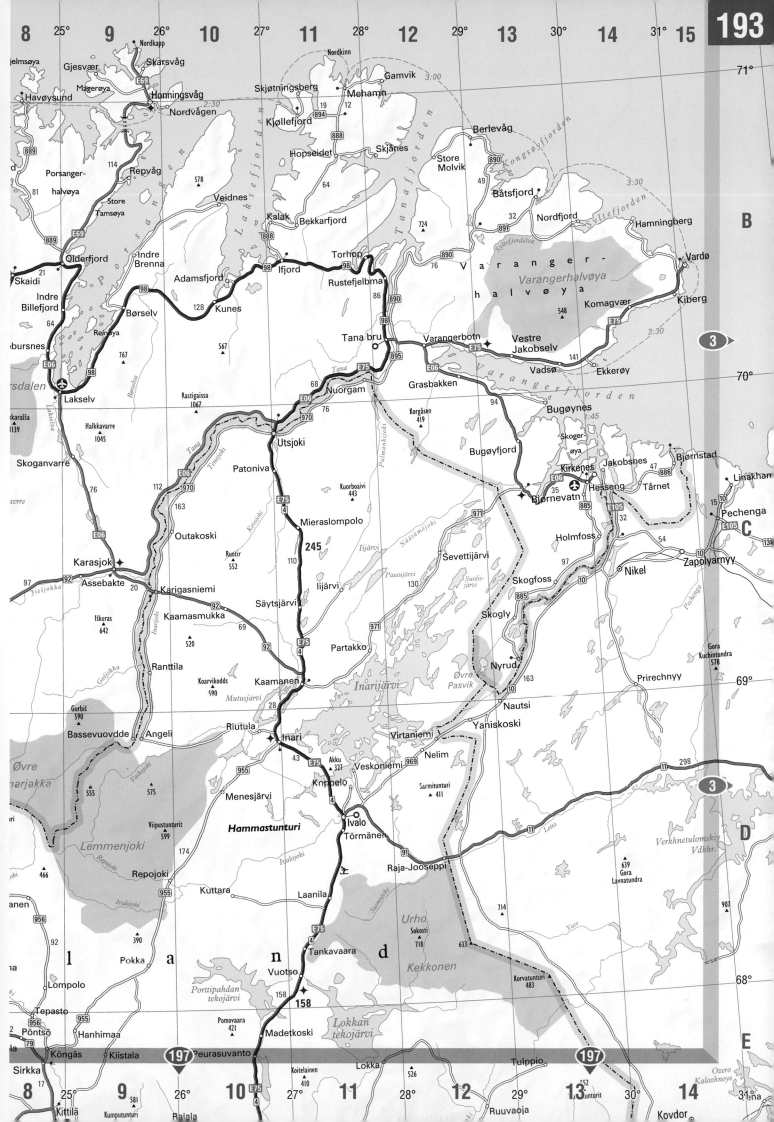

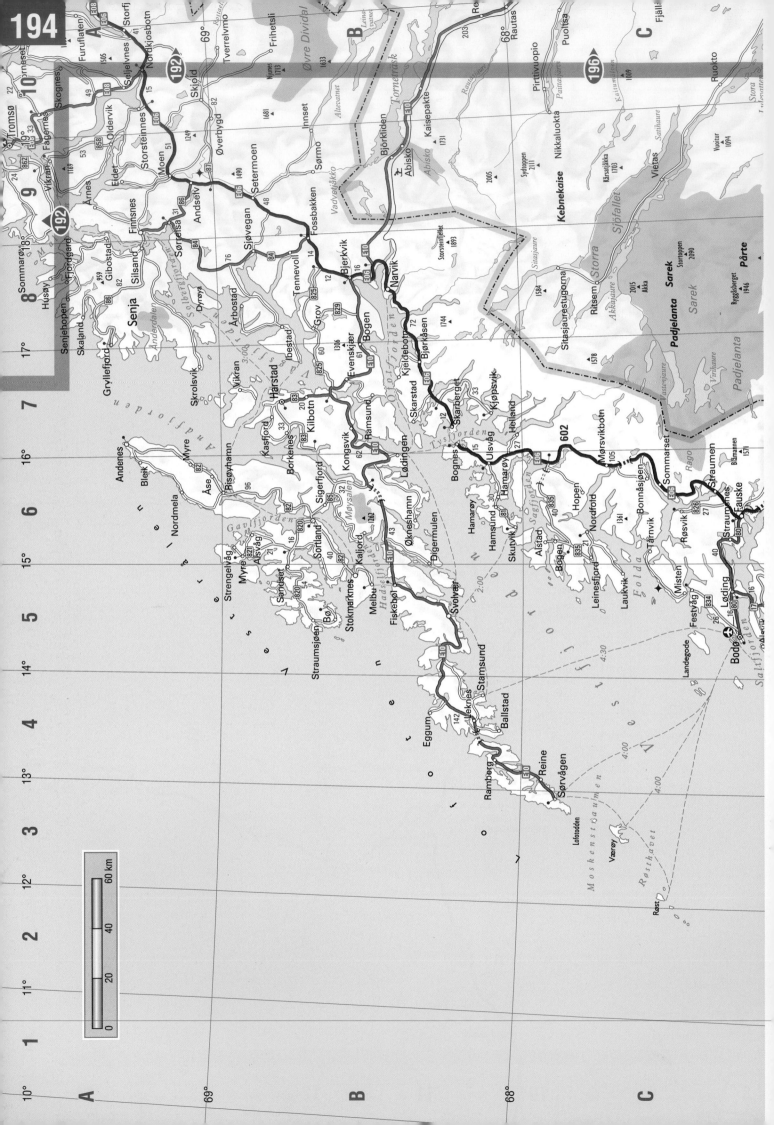

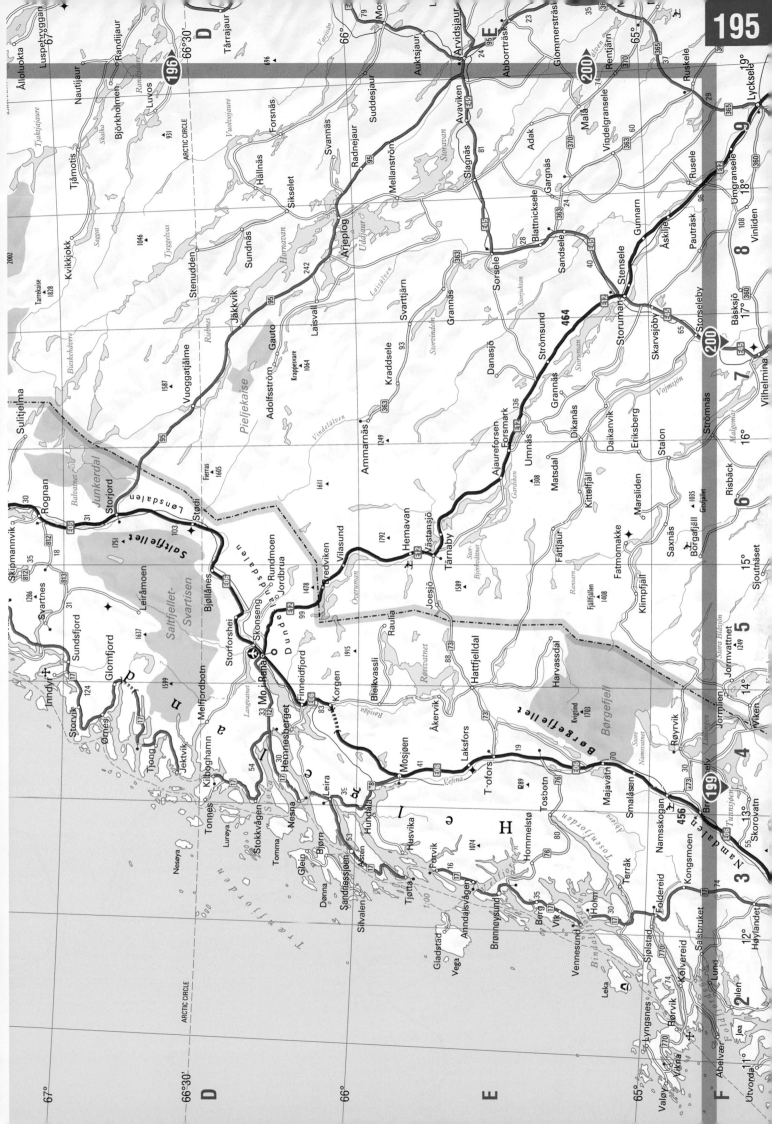

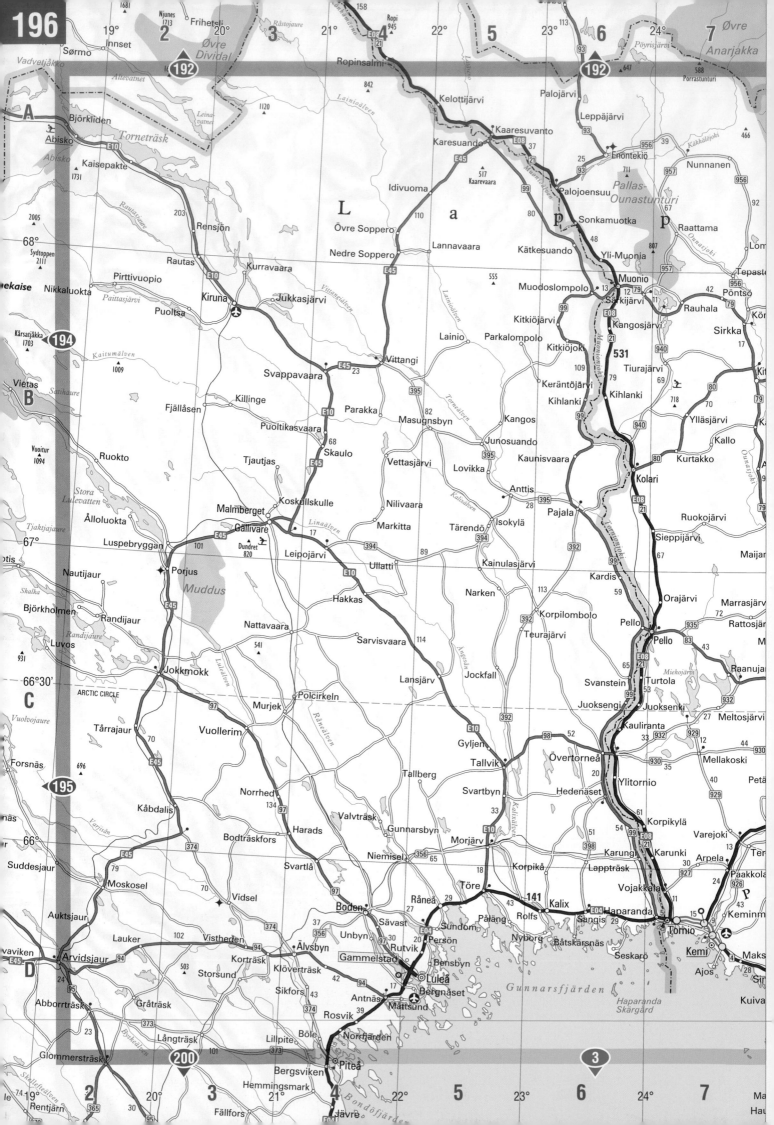

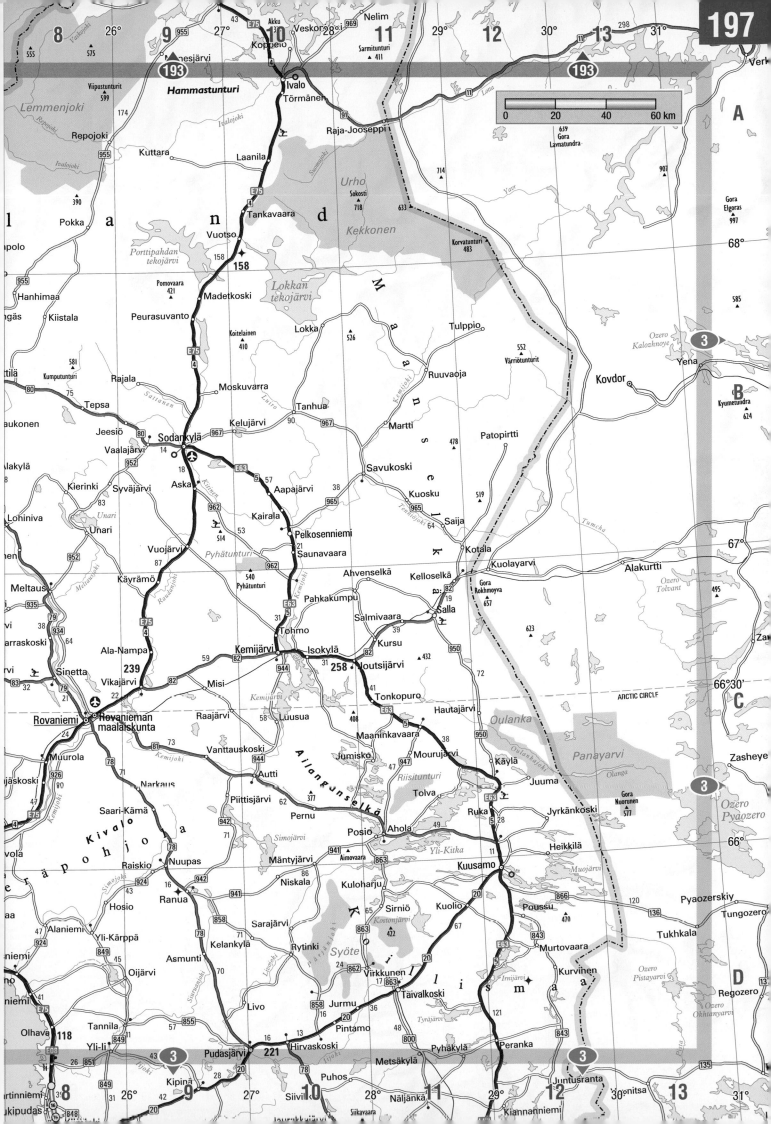

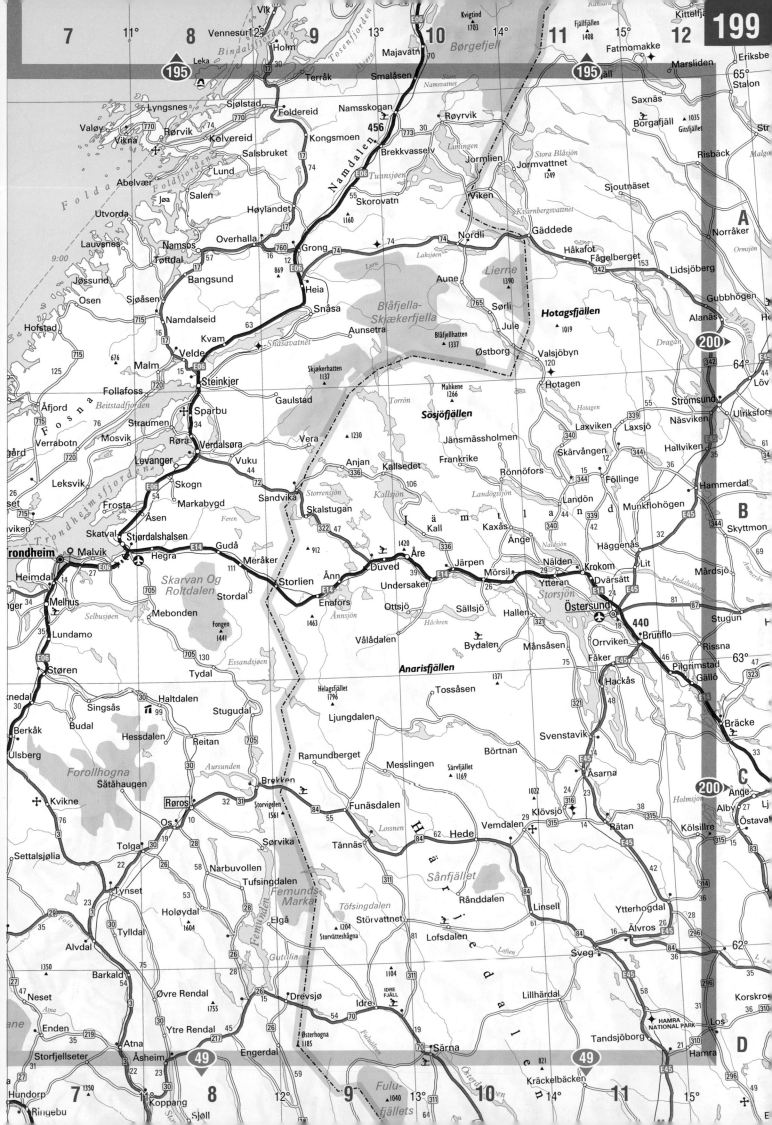

## City plans • Plans de villes
## Stadtpläne • Piante di città

| | | | |
|---|---|---|---|
| Motorway | Autoroute | Autobahn | Autostrada |
| Major through route | Route principale majeur | Hauptstrecke | Strada di grande comunicazione |
| Through route | Route principale | Schnellstrasse | Strada d'importanza regionale |
| Secondary road | Route secondaire | Nebenstrasse | Strada d'interesse locale |
| Dual carriageway | Chaussées séparées | Zweispurig Schnellstrasse | Strada a carreggiate doppie |
| Other road | Autre route | Nebenstrecke | Altra strada |
| Tunnel | Tunnel | Tunnel | Galleria stradale |
| Limited access / pedestrian road | Rue réglementée / rue piétonne | Beschränkter Zugang/ Fussgängerzone | Strada pedonale / a accesso limitato |
| One-way street | Sens unique | Einbahnstrasse | Senso unico |
| Parking | Parc de stationnement | Parkplatz | Parcheggio |
| Motorway number A7 | Numéro d'autoroute | Autobahnnummer A7 | Numero di autostrada |
| National road number 447 | Numéro de route nationale | Nationalstrassen-nummer 447 | Numero di strada nazionale |
| European road number E45 | Numéro de route européenne | Europäische Strassennummer E45 | Numero di strada europea |
| Destination GENT | Destination | Ziel GENT | Destinazione |
| Car ferry | Bac passant les autos | Autofähre | Traghetto automobili |
| Railway | Chemin de fer | Eisenbahn | Ferrovia |
| Rail/bus station | Gare / gare routière | Bahnhof / Busstation | Stazione ferrovia / pullman |
| Underground, metro station | Station de métro | U-Bahnstation | Metropolitano |
| Cable car | Téléférique | Drahtseilbahn | Funivia |
| Abbey, cathedral | Abbaye, cathédrale | Abtei, Kloster, Kathedrale | Abbazia, duomo |
| Church of interest | Église intéressante | Interessante Kirche | Chiesa da vedere |
| Synagogue | Synagogue | Synagoge | Sinagoga |
| Hospital | Hôpital | Krankenhaus | Ospedale |
| Police station | Police | Polizeiwache | Polizia |
| Post office | Bureau de poste | Postamt | Ufficio postale |
| Tourist information | Office de tourisme | Informationsbüro | Ufficio informazioni turistiche |
| Place of interest Theatre | Autre curiosité | Sonstige Sehenswürdigkeit Theatre | Luogo da vedere |

## Approach maps • Agglomérations
## Carte régionale • Regionalkarte

| | | | |
|---|---|---|---|
| Toll motorway – with motorway number A10 | Autoroute à péage – avec numéro d'autoroute | Gebührenpflichtige Autobahn – mit Autobahnnummer A10 | Autostrada a pedaggio – con numero |
| Toll-free motorway – with European road number E51 | Autoroute – avec numéro de route européenne | Gebührenfreie Autobahn – Europäische Strassennummer E51 | Autostrada – con numero di strada europea |
| Pre-pay motorway – vignette required | Autoroute – 'vignette' | Autobahn – 'vignette' | Autostrada – 'vignette' |
| Motorway services | Aire de service | Autobahnservice | Area di servizio autostradale |
| Motorway junction full access, restricted access | Échangeur d'autoroute – accès libre, accès réglementé | Autobahnkreuz – voller/begrenzter Zugang | Raccordi autostradali – completo/parziali |
| Under construction | En construction | Im Bau | In construzione |
| Tunnel | Tunnel | Tunnel | Galleria stradale |
| Major route dual carriageway single carriageway | Route principale chausées séparées chausée sans séparation | Hauptstrecke – zweispurige Schnellstrasse | Strada di grande communicazione carreggiata doppia carreggiata unica |
| Secondary route dual carriageway single carriageway | Route secondaire chausées séparées chausée sans séparation | Nebenstrasse – zweispurige Schnellstrasse | Strada d'interesse locale – carreggiata doppia carreggiata unica |
| Other road | Autre route | Nebenstrecke | Altra strada |
| Car ferry | Bac passant les autos | Autofähre | Traghetto automobili |
| Destination GIRONA | Destination | Ziel GIRONA | Destinazione |
| Railway | Chemin de fer | Eisenbahn | Ferrovia |
| Railway station Estación Central | Gare | Hauptbahnhof Estación Central | Stazione ferrovia |
| Height – in metres 234 | Altitude – en mètres | Höhe – über dem Meeresspiegel 234 | Altezza in metri |
| Airport | Aéroport principal | Flughafen | Aeroporto |
| Airfield | Autre aéroport | Flugplatz | Aerodromo/ campo d'aviazione |
| City plan coverage area | Région de plan de ville | Vom Stadtplan abgedecktes Gebiet | Area della pianta della città |

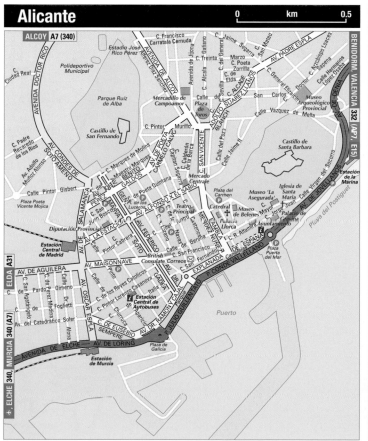

**Alicante**  0 km 0.5

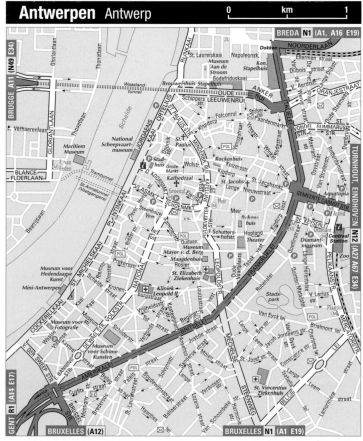

**Antwerpen** Antwerp  0 km 1

## Amsterdam

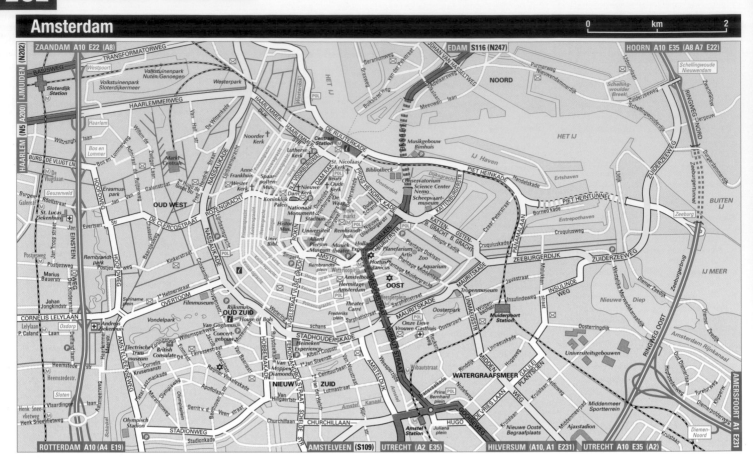

## Amsterdam

## Athina Athens

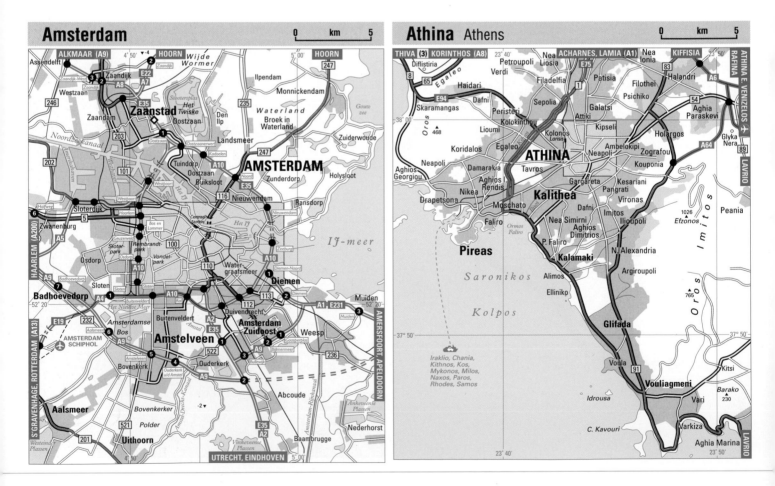

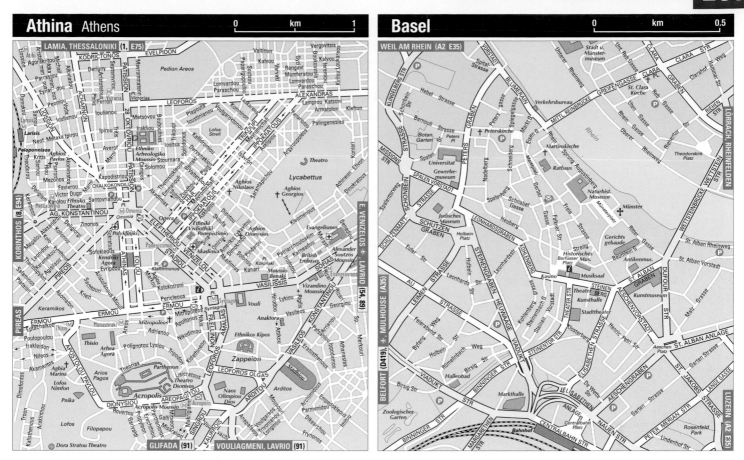

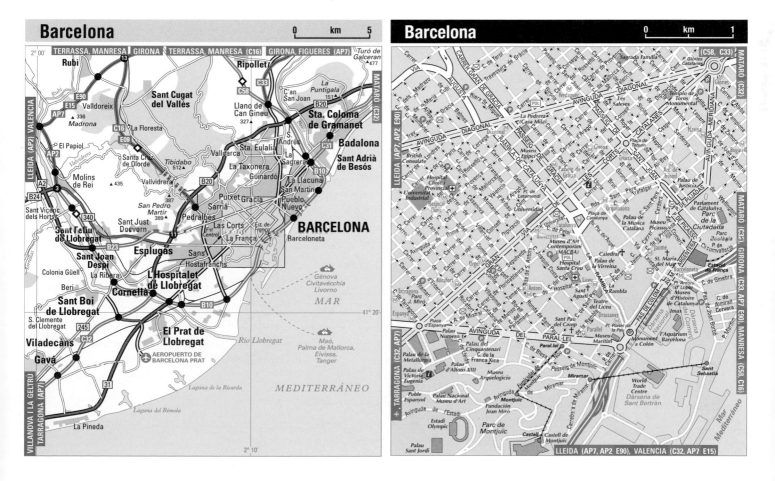

# Berlin

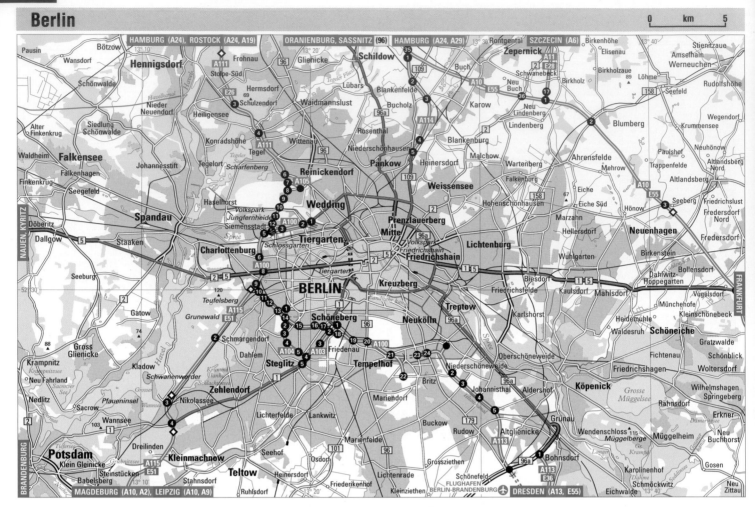

# Berlin

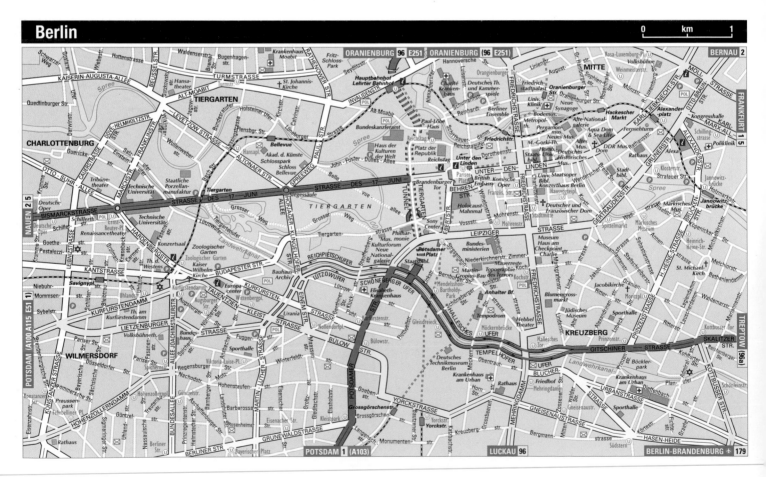

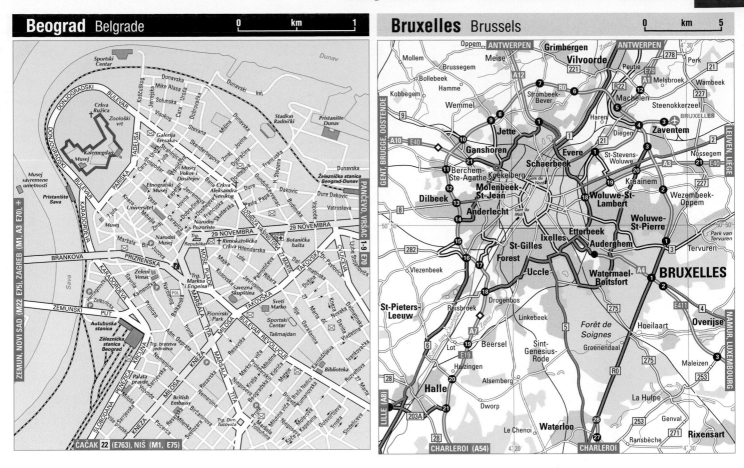

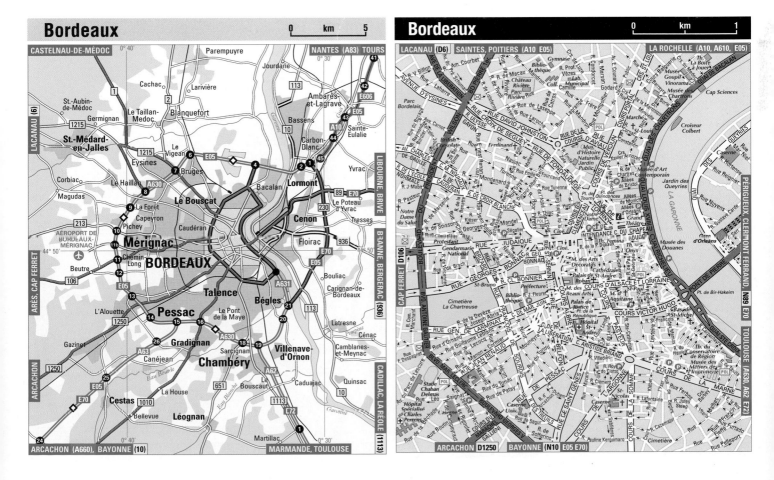

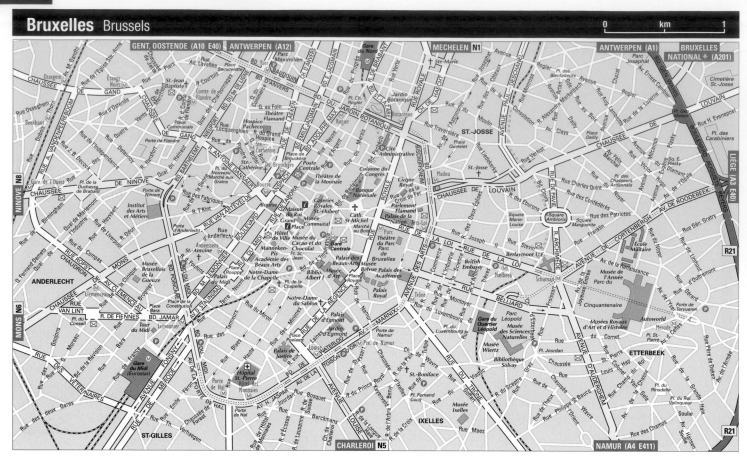

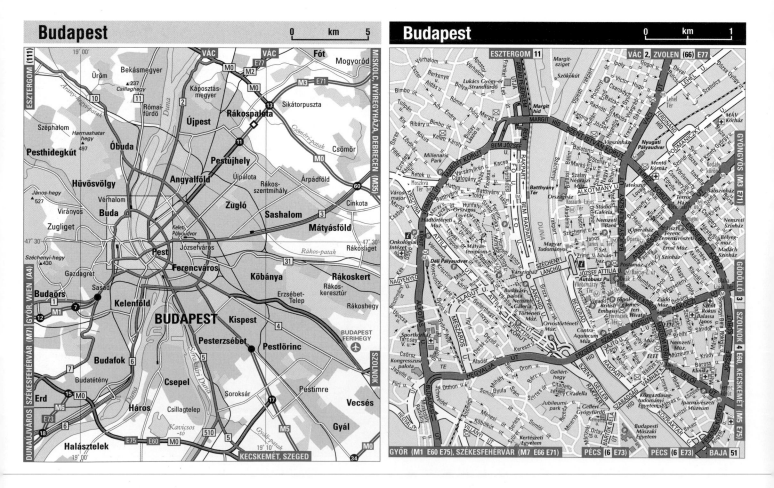

## Dublin

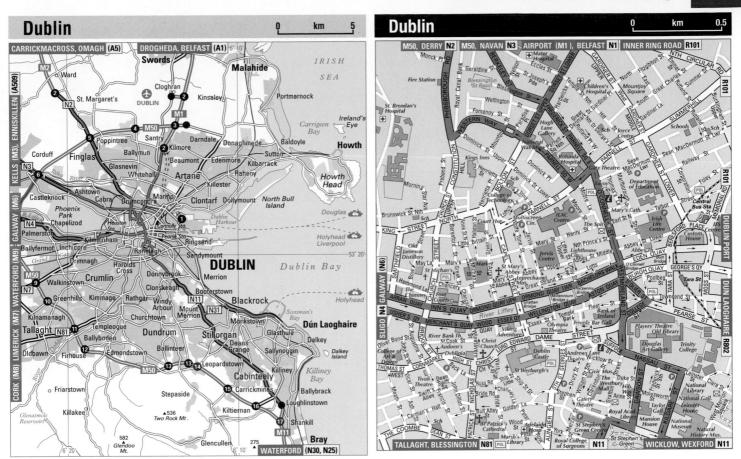

## Düsseldorf

## Edinburgh

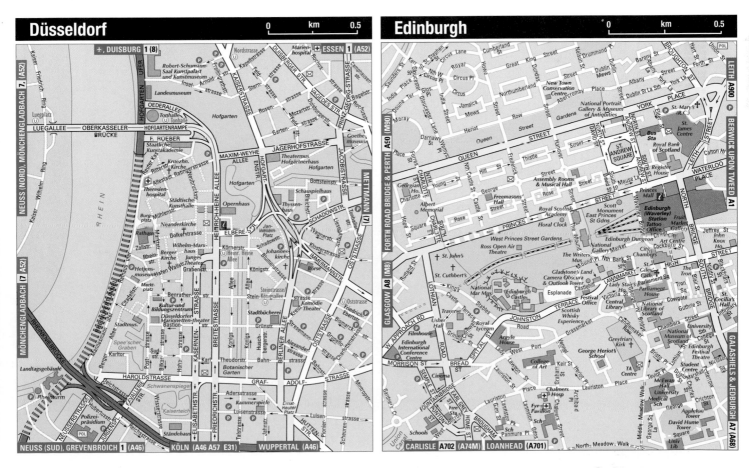

For **Cologne** see page 212

For **Copenhagen** see page 212

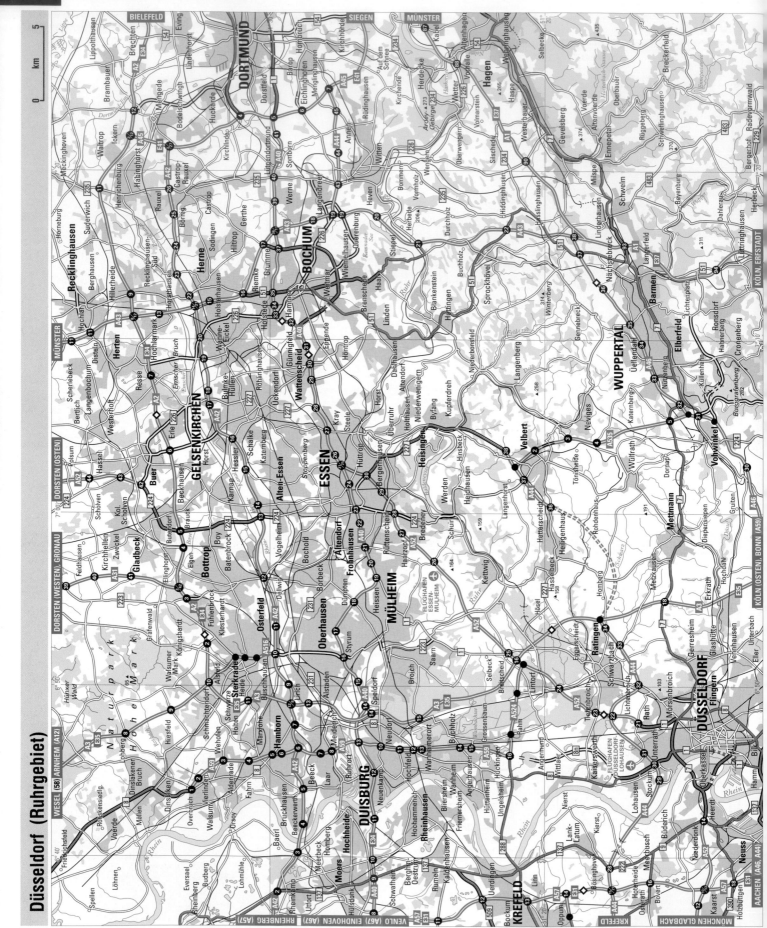

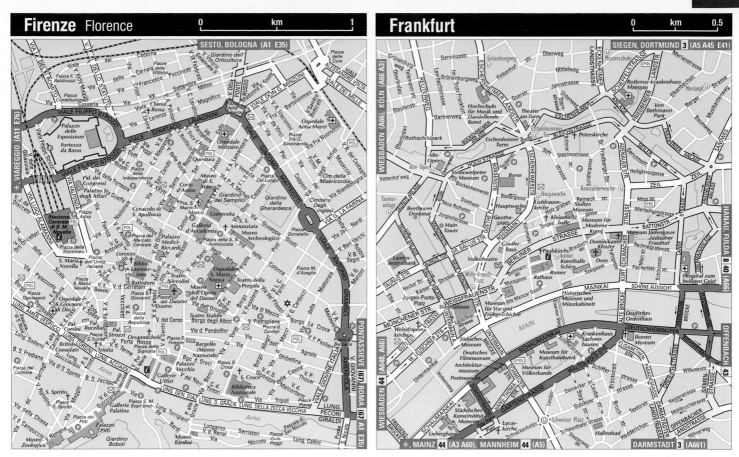

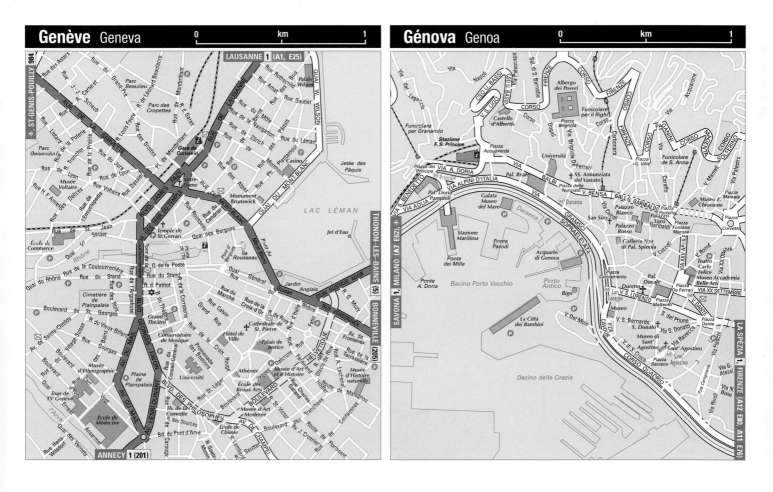

## Granada

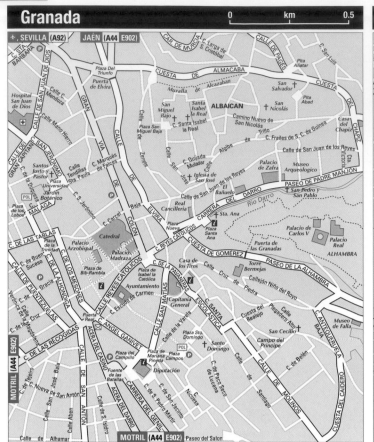

## Göteborg Gothenburg

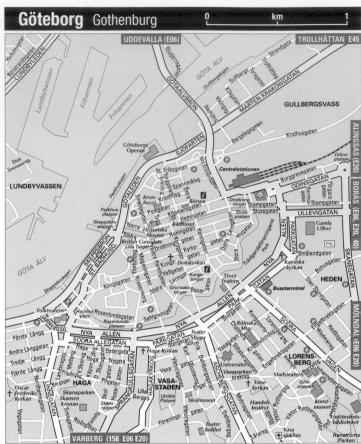

## Hamburg

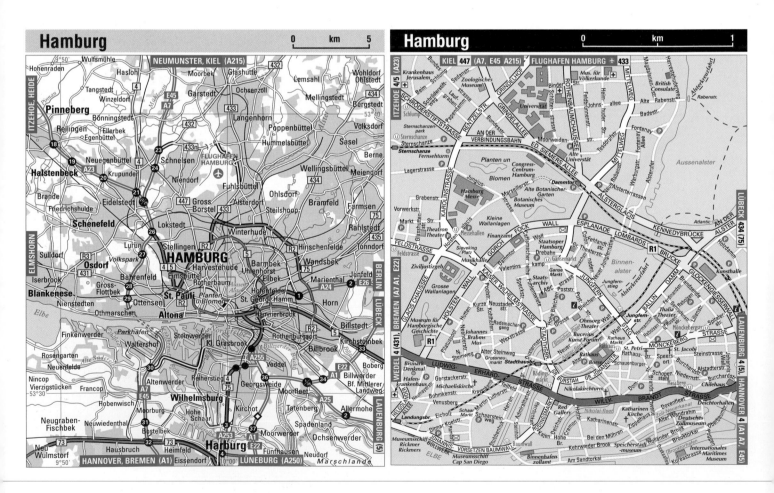

## Hamburg

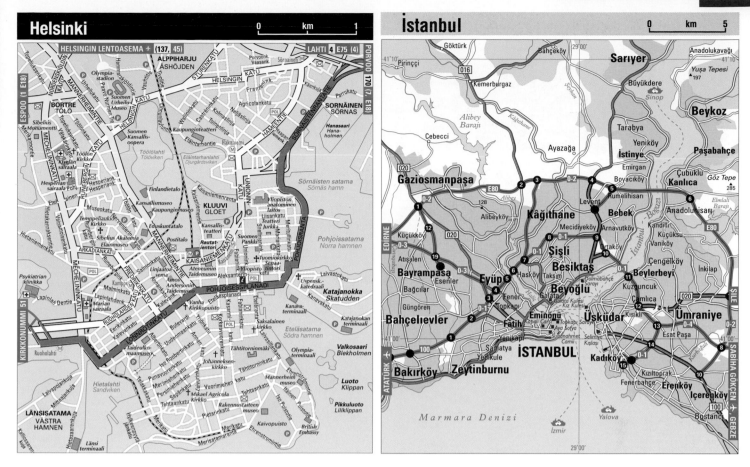

# Helsinki

# İstanbul

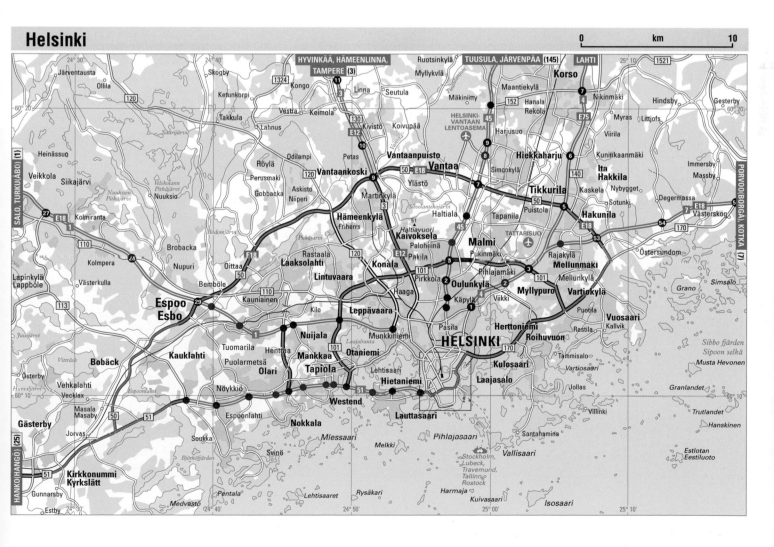

# Helsinki

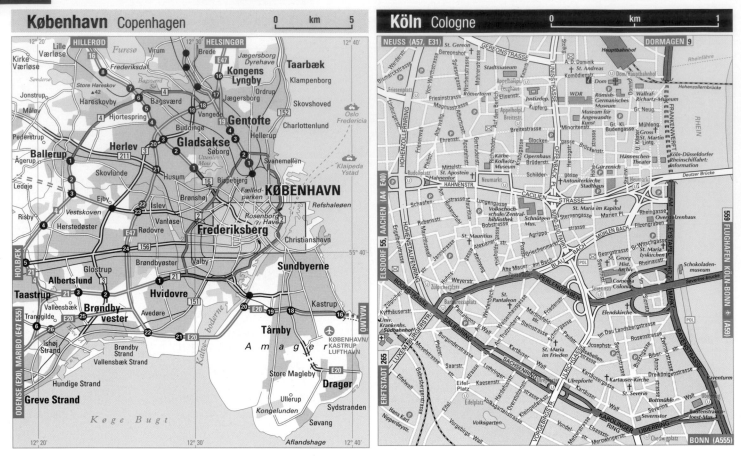

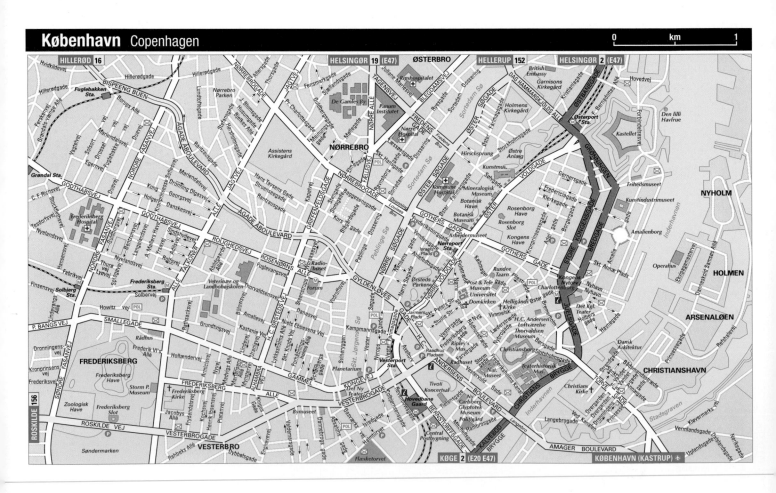

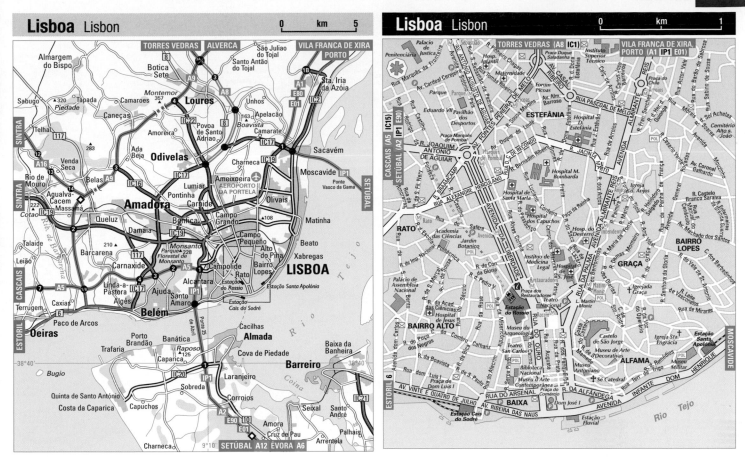

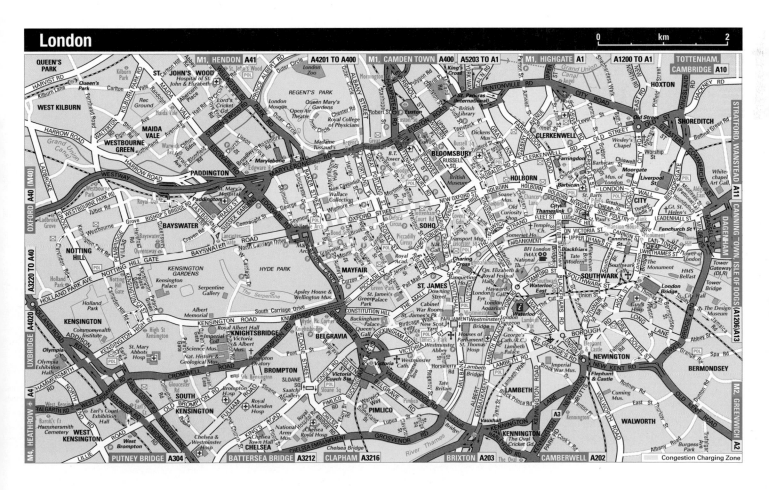

## London

0 km 10

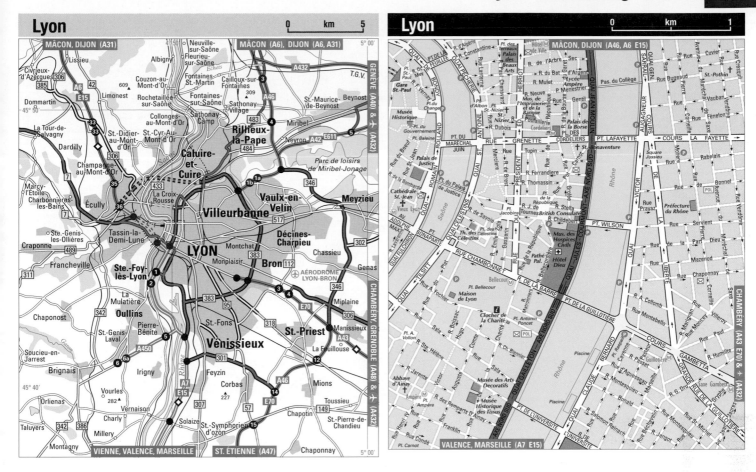

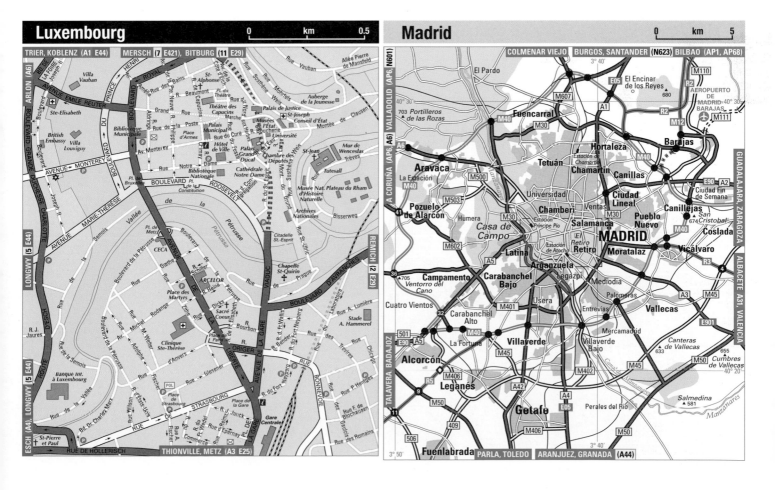

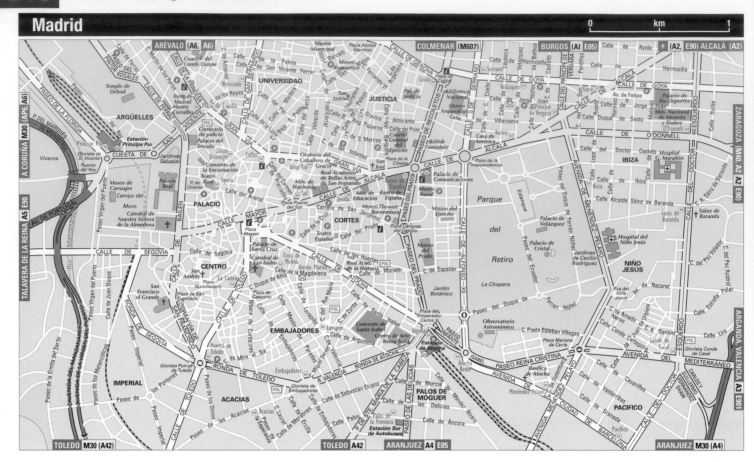

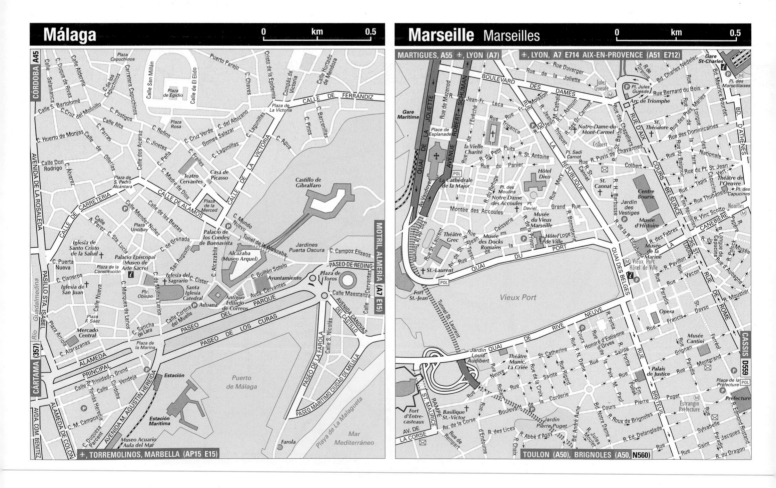

## Milano

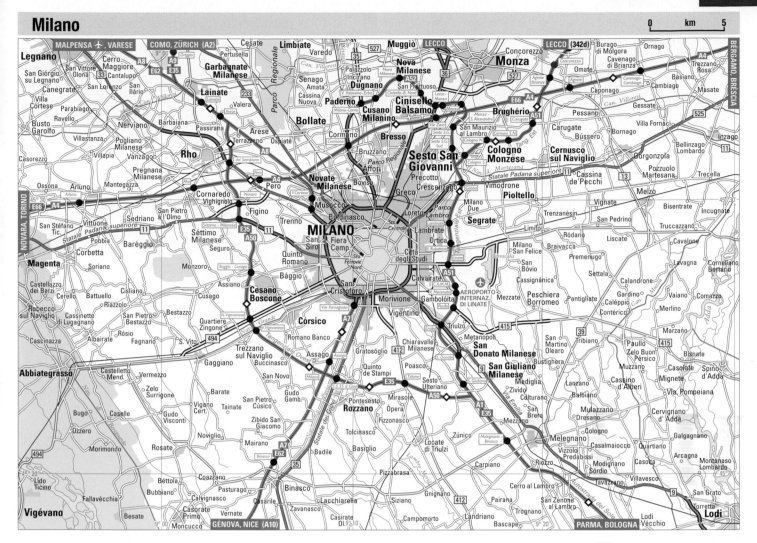

## Milano Milan

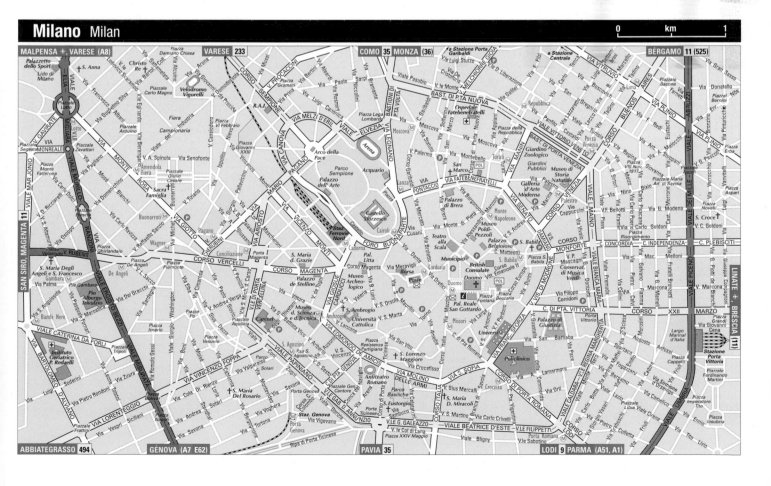

## Moskva Moscow

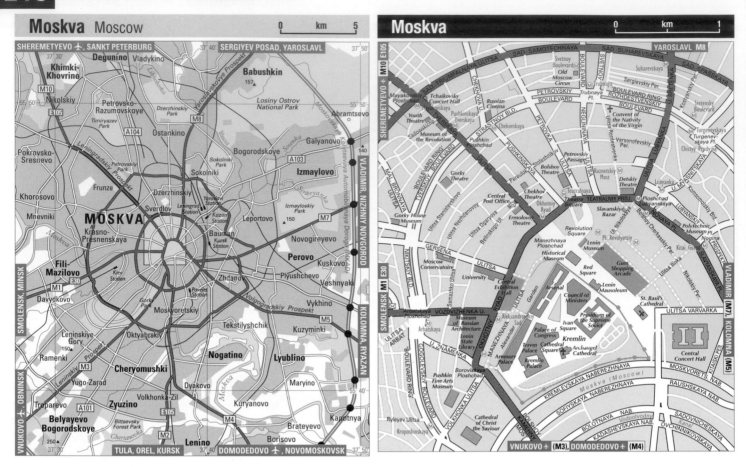

## Moskva

## München Munich

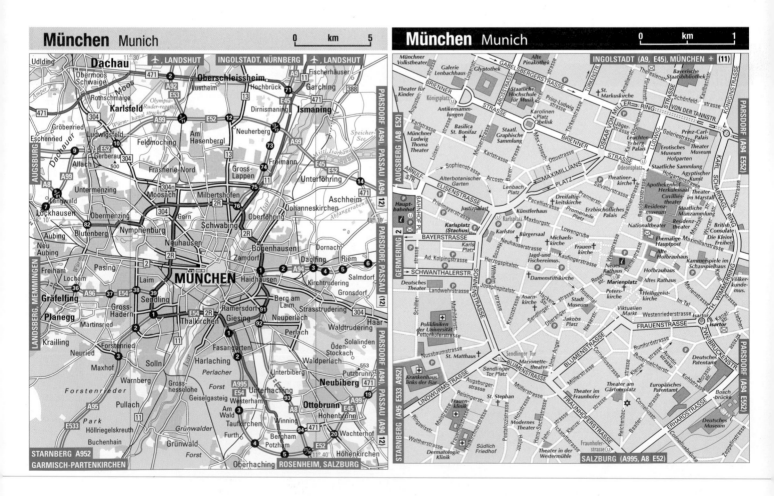

## München Munich

# Paris

0 km 5

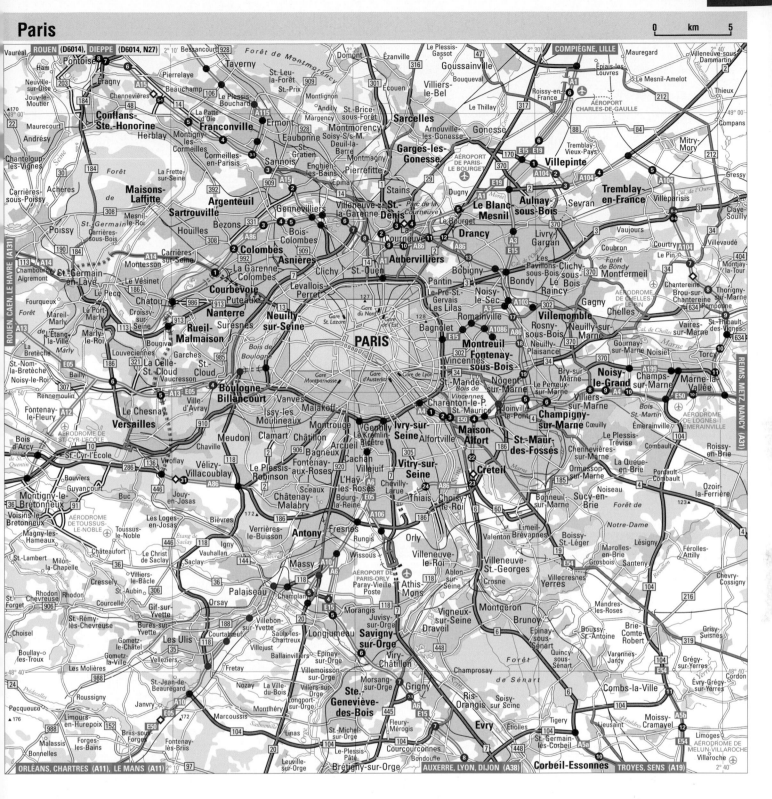

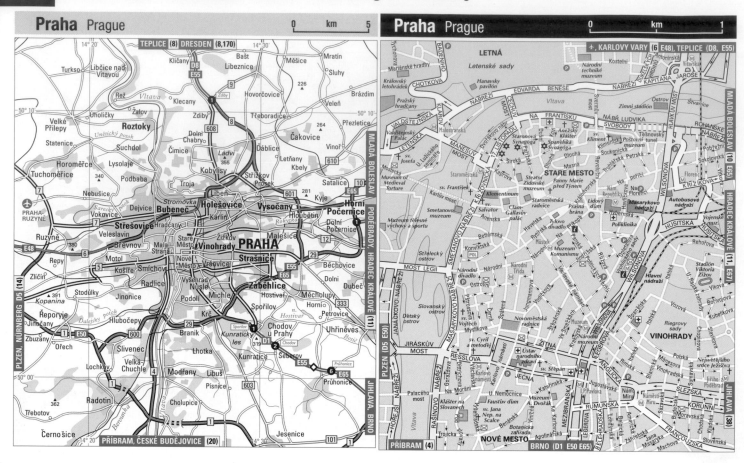

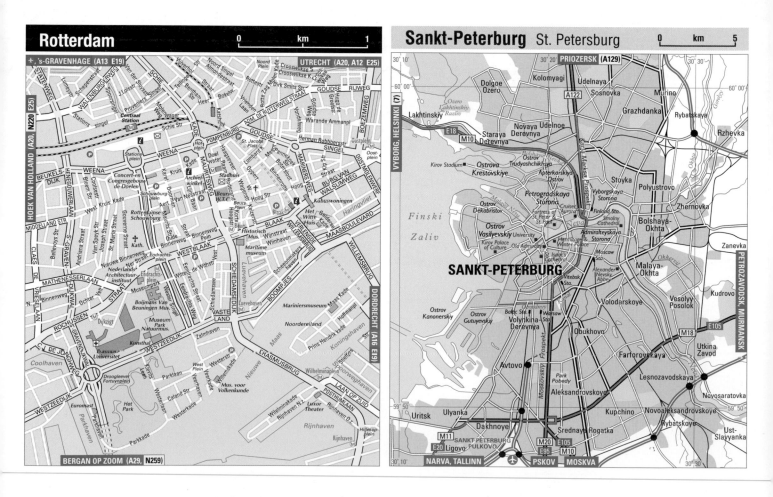

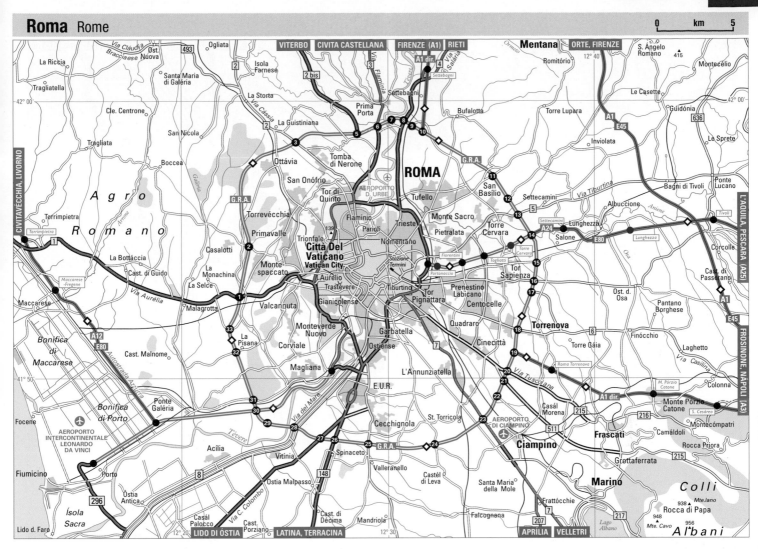

## Roma Rome

## Sevilla Seville

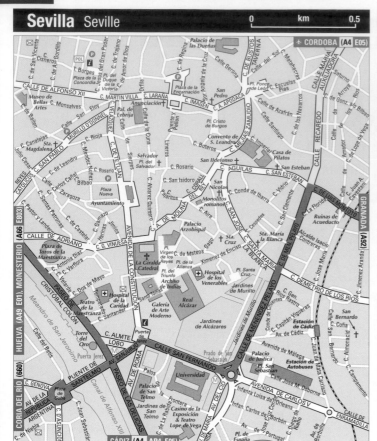

## Stuttgart

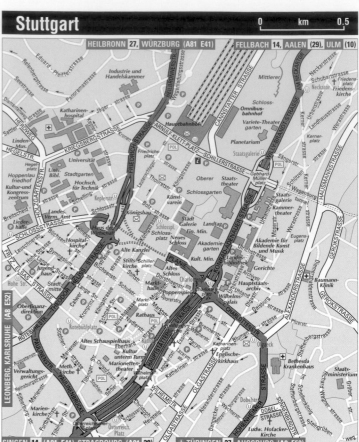

## Strasbourg

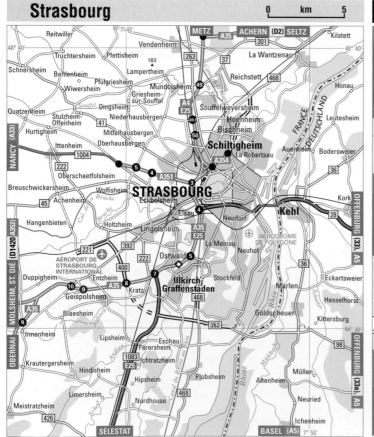

## Strasbourg

# Stockholm

0     km     5

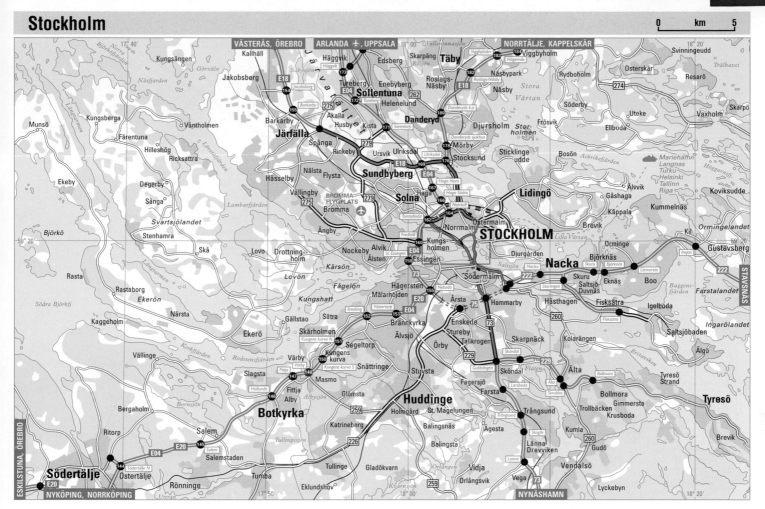

# Stockholm

0     km     1

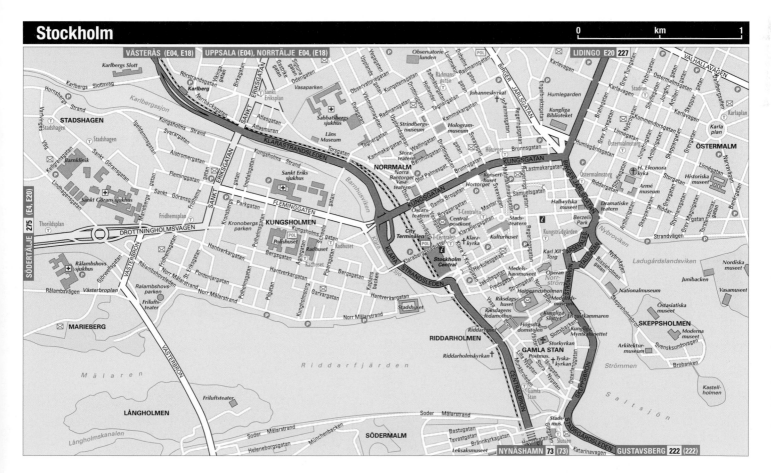

## Torino Turin

0 km 5

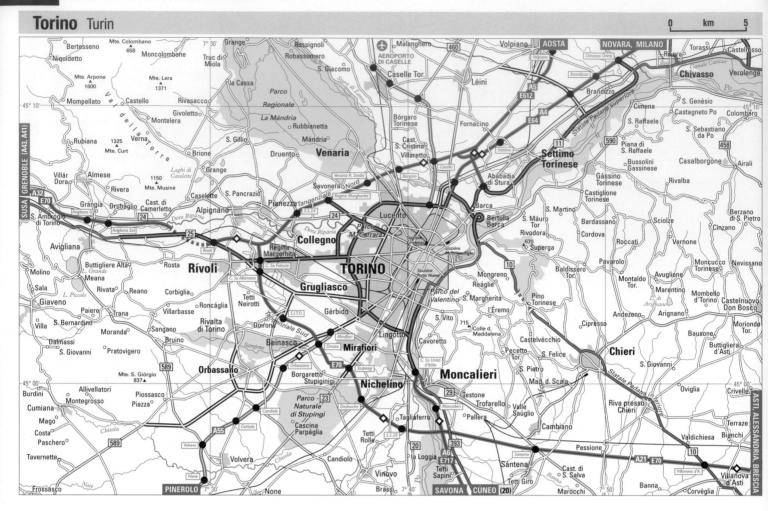

## Venézia Venice

0 km 0.5

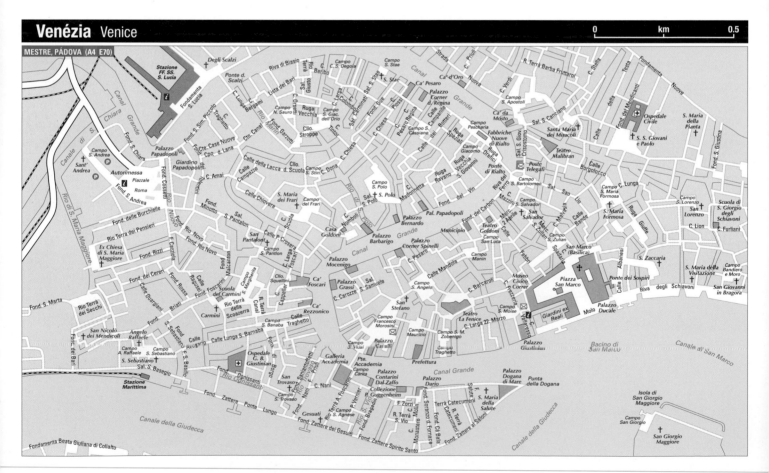

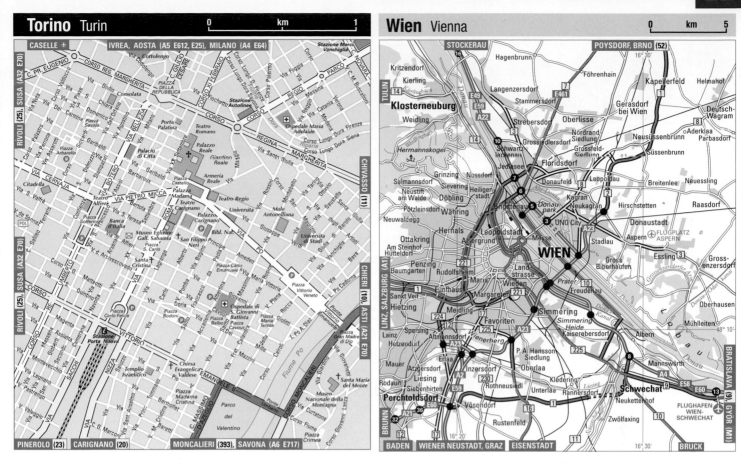

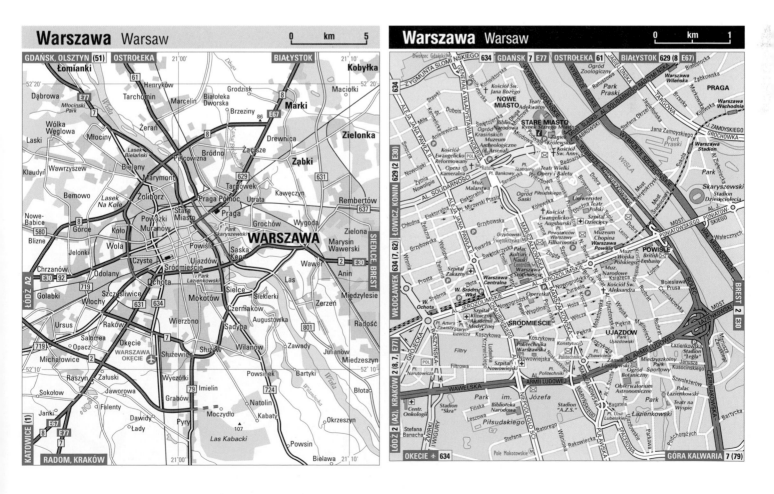

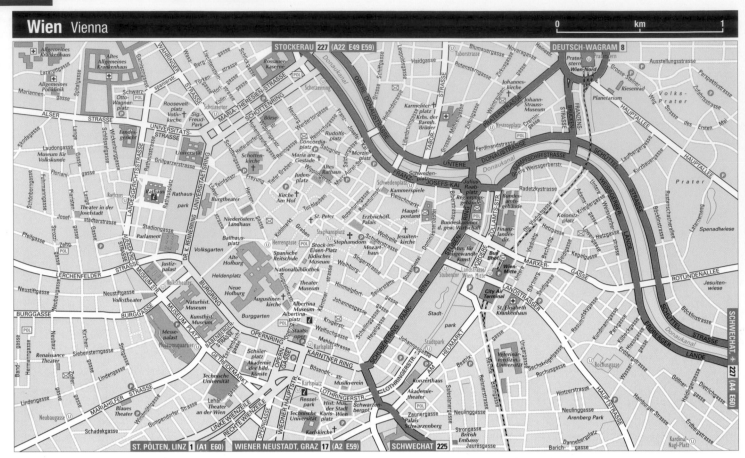

# Wien Vienna

# Zagreb

# Zürich

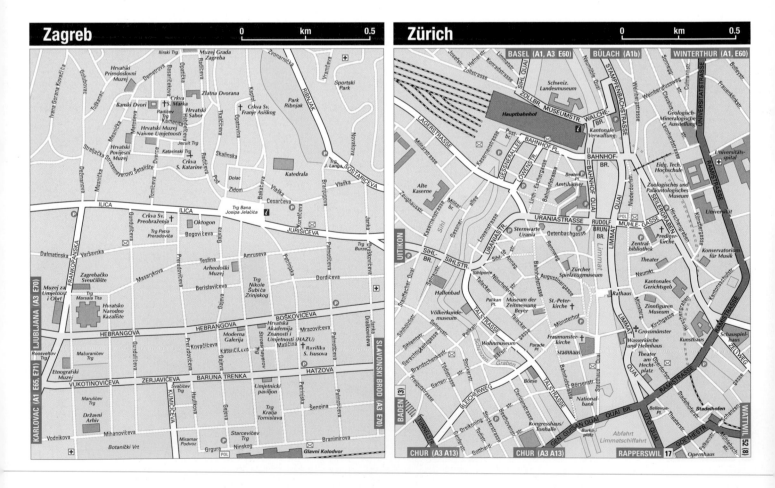

| GB | F | D | I |
|---|---|---|---|
| (A) Austria | Autriche | Österreich | Austria |
| (AL) Albania | Albanie | Albanien | Albania |
| (AND) Andorra | Andorre | Andorra | Andorra |
| (B) Belgium | Belgique | Belgien | Belgio |
| (BG) Bulgaria | Bulgarie | Bulgarien | Bulgaria |
| (BIH) Bosnia-Herzegovin | Bosnia-Herzegovine | Bosnien-Herzegowina | Bosnia-Herzogovina |
| (BY) Belarus | Belarus | Weissrussland | Bielorussia |
| (CH) Switzerland | Suisse | Schweiz | Svizzera |
| (CY) Cyprus | Chypre | Zypern | Cipro |
| (CZ) Czech Republic | République Tchèque | Tschechische Republik | Repubblica Ceca |
| (D) Germany | Allemagne | Deutschland | Germania |
| (DK) Denmark | Danemark | Dänemark | Danimarca |
| (E) Spain | Espagne | Spanien | Spagna |
| (EST) Estonia | Estonie | Estland | Estonia |
| (F) France | France | Frankreich | Francia |
| (FIN) Finland | Finlande | Finnland | Finlandia |
| (FL) Liechtenstein | Liechtenstein | Liechtenstein | Liechtenstein |
| (FO) Faeroe Islands | Îles Féroé | Färoër-Inseln | Isole Faroe |
| (GB) United Kingdom | Royaume Uni | Grossbritannien und Nordirland | Regno Unito |
| (GBZ) Gibraltar | Gibraltar | Gibraltar | Gibilterra |
| (GR) Greece | Grèce | Greichenland | Grecia |
| (H) Hungary | Hongrie | Ungarn | Ungheria |
| (HR) Croatia | Croatie | Kroatien | Croazia |

| GB | F | D | I |
|---|---|---|---|
| (I) Italy | Italie | Italien | Italia |
| (IRL) Ireland | Irlande | Irland | Irlanda |
| (IS) Iceland | Islande | Island | Islanda |
| (KOS) Kosovo | Kosovo | Kosovo | Kosovo |
| (L) Luxembourg | Luxembourg | Luxemburg | Lussemburgo |
| (LT) Lithuania | Lituanie | Litauen | Lituania |
| (LV) Latvia | Lettonie | Lettland | Lettonia |
| (M) Malta | Malte | Malta | Malta |
| (MC) Monaco | Monaco | Monaco | Monaco |
| (MD) Moldova | Moldavie | Moldawien | Moldavia |
| (MK) Macedonia | Macédoine | Makedonien | Macedonia |
| (MNE) Montenegro | Monténégro | Montenegro | Montenegro |
| (N) Norway | Norvège | Norwegen | Norvegia |
| (NL) Netherlands | Pays-Bas | Niederlande | Paesi Bassi |
| (P) Portugal | Portugal | Portugal | Portogallo |
| (PL) Poland | Pologne | Polen | Polonia |
| (RO) Romania | Roumanie | Rumanien | Romania |
| (RSM) San Marino | Saint-Marin | San Marino | San Marino |
| (RUS) Russia | Russie | Russland | Russia |
| (S) Sweden | Suède | Schweden | Svezia |
| (SK) Slovak Republic | République Slovaque | Slowak Republik | Repubblica Slovacca |
| (SLO) Slovenia | Slovénie | Slowenien | Slovenia |
| (SRB) Serbia | Serbie | Serbien | Serbia |
| (TR) Turkey | Turquie | Türkei | Turchia |
| (UA) Ukraine | Ukraine | Ukraine | Ucraina |

## A

Aabenraa DK . . . . . . 64 A2
Aabybro DK . . . . . . 58 A2
Aach D . . . . . . . . 107 B4
Aachen D . . . . . . . 80 B2
Aalborg DK . . . . . . 58 A2
Aalen D . . . . . . . . 94 C2
Aalestrup DK . . . . . 58 B2
Aalsmeer NL . . . . . 70 B1
Aalst B . . . . . . . . 79 B4
Aalten NL . . . . . . . 71 C3
Aalter B . . . . . . . . 79 A3
Äänekoski FIN . . . . . 8 A4
Aapajärvi FIN . . . 197 B10
Aarau CH . . . . . . 106 B3
Aarberg CH . . . . . . 106 B2
Aarburg CH . . . . . . 106 B2
Aardenburg NL . . . . 79 A3
Aars DK . . . . . . . . 58 B2
Aarschot B . . . . . . 79 B4
Aarup DK . . . . . . . 59 C3
Aba H . . . . . . . . . 112 B2
Abádanes E . . . . . 152 B1
Abades E . . . . . . . 151 B3
Abadin E . . . . . . . 141 A3
Abádszalók H . . . . .113 B4
Abaliget H . . . . . . 125 A4
Abana TR . . . . . . . 23 A8
A Baña E . . . . . . . 140 B2
Abanilla E . . . . . . 165 A3
Abano Terme I . . . . 121 B4
Abarán E . . . . . . . 165 A3
Abasár H . . . . . . . .113 B4
Abbadia San Salvatore
I . . . . . . . . . . . . 135 C4
Abbaue D . . . . . . . 74 A2
Abbehausen D . . . . 72 A1
Abbekås S . . . . . . 66 A2
Abbeville F . . . . . . 90 A1
Abbey IRL . . . . . . . 28 A3
Abbeydorney IRL . . 29 B2
Abbeyfeale IRL . . . . 29 B2
Abbeyleix IRL . . . . . 30 B1
Abbey Town GB . . . 36 B3
Abbiategrasso I . . . 120 B1
Abborrträsk S . . . . 196 D2
Abbots Bromley GB 40 C2
Abbotsbury GB . . . . 43 B4
Abda H . . . . . . . . .111 B4
Abejar E . . . . . . . 143 C4
Abela P . . . . . . . . 160 B1
Abelvær N . . . . . . 199 A8
Abenberg D . . . . . . 94 B2
Abenójar E . . . . . . 157 B3
Abensberg D . . . . . 95 C3
Aberaeron GB . . . . 39 B2
Abercarn GB . . . . . 39 C3
Aberchirder GB . . . 33 D4
Aberdare GB . . . . . 39 C3
Aberdaron GB . . . . 38 B2
Aberdeen GB . . . . . 33 D4
Aberdulais GB . . . . 39 C3
Aberdyfi GB . . . . . 39 B2
Aberfeldy GB . . . . . 35 B4
Aberffraw GB . . . . . 38 A2
Aberfoyle GB . . . . . 34 B3
Abergavenny GB . . . 39 C3
Abergele GB . . . . . 38 A3
Abergynolwyn GB . . 38 B3
Aberporth GB . . . . . 39 B2

Abersoch GB . . . . . 38 B2
Abertillery GB . . . . . 39 C3
Abertura E . . . . . . 156 A2
Aberystwyth GB . . . 39 B2
Abetone I . . . . . . . 135 A3
Abfaltersbach A . . . 109 C3
Abide
  Çanakkale TR . . . . .186 B1
  Kütahya TR . . . . . .187 D4
Abiego E . . . . . . . 145 B3
Abild DK . . . . . . . . 64 B1
Abingdon GB . . . . . 44 B2
Abington GB . . . . . 36 A3
Abisko S . . . . . . . 194 B9
Abiul P . . . . . . . . 154 B2
Abla E . . . . . . . . . 164 B2
A Bola E . . . . . . . 140 B3
Abondance F . . . . .118 A3
Abony H . . . . . . . .113 B4
Aboyne GB . . . . . . 33 D4
Abrantes P . . . . . . 154 B2
Abreiro P . . . . . . . 148 A2
Abreschviller F . . . .112 B1
Abrest F . . . . . . . .117 A3
Abriès F . . . . . . . 119 C3
Abrud RO . . . . . . . 17 B5
Absdorf A . . . . . . . 97 C3
Abstenau A . . . . . 109 B4
Abtsgmünd D . . . . . 94 C1
Abusejo E . . . . . . 149 B3
Åby
  Kronoberg S . . . . . .62 A2
  Östergötland S . . . .56 B2
Åbyggeby S . . . . . 51 B4
Åbytorp S . . . . . . 55 A6
A Cañiza E . . . . . . 140 B2
A Capela E . . . . . . 140 A2
Acate I . . . . . . . . 177 B3
Accadía I . . . . . . . 171 B3
Accéglio I . . . . . . . 132 A2
Accettura I . . . . . . 172 B2
Acciaroli I . . . . . . 170 C3
Accous F . . . . . . . 145 A3
Accrington GB . . . . 40 B1
Accúmoli I . . . . . . 169 A3
Acedera E . . . . . . 156 A2
Acehúche E . . . . . 155 B4
Acered E . . . . . . . 152 A2
Acerenza I . . . . . . 172 B1
Acerno I . . . . . . . 170 C3
Acerra I . . . . . . . . 170 C2
Aceuchal E . . . . . . 155 C4
Acharacle GB . . . . . 34 B2
Acharnes GR . . . . . 185 A4
Achavanich GB . . . . 32 C3
Achene B . . . . . . . 79 B5
Achenkirch A . . . . . 108 B2
Achensee A . . . . . 108 B2
Achenthal A . . . . . 108 B2
Achentrias GR . . . . 185 E6
Achern D . . . . . . . 93 C4
Acheux-en-Amienois
  F . . . . . . . . . . . 90 A2
Achiltibuie GB . . . . . 32 C1
Achim D . . . . . . . . 72 A2
Achladokambos
  GR . . . . . . . . . . 184 B3
Achnasheen GB . . . 32 D1
Achnashellach GB . 32 D1
Achosnich GB . . . . 34 B1
Aci Castello I . . . . . 177 B4
Aci Catena I . . . . . 177 B4

Acílla I . . . . . . . . 168 B2
Acıpayam TR . . . . . 189 B4
Acireale I . . . . . . . 177 B4
Acle GB . . . . . . . . 41 C5
A Coruña E . . . . . . 140 A2
Acquacadda I . . . . 179 C2
Acqua Doria F . . . . 180 B1
Acquanegra sul Chiese
  I . . . . . . . . . . . 121 B3
Acquapendente I . . 168 A1
Acquasanta Terme
  I . . . . . . . . . . . 136 C2
Acquasparta I . . . . 168 A2
Acquaviva I . . . . . 135 B4
Acquaviva delle Fonti
  I . . . . . . . . . . . 171 C4
Acquaviva Picena
  I . . . . . . . . . . . 136 C2
Acquigny F . . . . . . 89 A5
Ácqui Terme I . . . . 119 C5
Acrí I . . . . . . . . . 174 B2
Acs H . . . . . . . . . .112 B2
Acsa H . . . . . . . . .112 B3
Ácsteszér H . . . . . .112 B1
Acy-en-Multien F . . 90 B2
Ada SRB . . . . . . . 126 B2
Adak S . . . . . . . . 195 E9
Ádalsbruk N . . . . . 48 B3
Adamas GR . . . . . 185 C5
Adamsfjord N . . . . 193 B10
Adamuz E . . . . . . 157 B3
Adana TR . . . . . . . 23 C8
Ádánd H . . . . . . . 112 C2
Adanero E . . . . . . 150 B3
Adare IRL . . . . . . . 29 B3
Adaševci SRB . . . . 125 B5
Adeanueva de Ebro
  E . . . . . . . . . . . 144 B2
Adelboden CH . . . . 106 C2
Adelebsen D . . . . . 82 A1
Adélfia I . . . . . . . 173 A2
Adelmannsfelden D 94 C2
Adelsheim D . . . . . 94 B1
Adelsö S . . . . . . . 57 A3
Ademuz E . . . . . . 152 B2
Adenau D . . . . . . . 80 B2
Adendorf D . . . . . . 72 A3
Adinkerke B . . . . . . 78 A2
Adjud RO . . . . . . . 17 B7
Adliswil CH . . . . . . 107 B3
Admont A . . . . . . .110 B1
Ådneram N . . . . . . 52 A2
Adolfsström S . . . . 195 D7
Adony H . . . . . . . .112 B2
Adorf
  Hessen D . . . . . . .81 A4
  Sachsen D . . . . . .83 B4
Adra E . . . . . . . . 164 C1
Adradas E . . . . . . 152 A1
Adrall E . . . . . . . . 147 B2
Adrano I . . . . . . . 177 B3
Adria I . . . . . . . . . 121 B5
Adrigole IRL . . . . . . 29 C2
Adwick le Street GB 40 B2
Adzaneta E . . . . . . 153 B3
Afandou GR . . . . . 188 C3
Åfarnes N . . . . . . 198 C4
Affing D . . . . . . . . 94 C2
Affoltern CH . . . . . 106 B3
Affric Lodge GB . . . 32 D1
Åfjord N . . . . . . . 199 B7

Aflenz Kurort A . . . .110 B2
A Fonsagrada E . . . 141 A3
Afragóla I . . . . . . . 170 C2
Afritz A . . . . . . . . 109 C4
Afyon TR . . . . . . . 187 D5
Ágasegyháza H . . . 112 C3
Agay F . . . . . . . . 132 B2
Agazzano I . . . . . . 120 C2
Agde F . . . . . . . . 130 B2
Agdenes N . . . . . . 198 B6
Agen F . . . . . . . . 129 B3
Ager E . . . . . . . . 145 C4
Agerbæk DK . . . . . 59 C1
Agerskov DK . . . . . 64 A2
Agger DK . . . . . . . 58 B1
Aggersund DK . . . . 58 A2
Aggius I . . . . . . . . 178 B3
Aggsbach Dorf A . . . 97 C3
Aggsbach Markt A . . 97 C3
Aggtelek H . . . . . . 99 C4
Aghalee GB . . . . . . 27 B4
Aghia GR . . . . . . . 182 D4
Aghia Anna GR . . . 183 E5
Aghia Galini GR . . . 185 D5
Aghia Marina GR . . 188 D1
Aghia Paraskevi
  GR . . . . . . . . . . 186 C1
Aghia Pelagia GR . . 184 C3
Aghia Triada GR . . . 184 B2
Aghiokambos GR . . 182 D4
Aghios Efstratios
  GR . . . . . . . . . . 183 D6
Aghios Kirikos GR . 185 B7
Aghios Matheos
  GR . . . . . . . . . . 182 D1
Aghios Mironas
  GR . . . . . . . . . . 185 D6
Aghios Nikolaos
  GR . . . . . . . . . . 185 D6
Aghios Petros GR . . 182 E2
Aghio Theodori
  GR . . . . . . . . . . 184 B4
Agiči BIH . . . . . . . 124 C2
Agira I . . . . . . . . . 177 B3
Aglientu I . . . . . . . 178 A3
Agnières F . . . . . . 118 C2
Agno CH . . . . . . . 120 B1
Agnone I . . . . . . . 170 B2
Agolada E . . . . . . 140 B2
Agon Coutainville F 88 A2
Ágordo I . . . . . . . 121 A5
Agost E . . . . . . . . 165 A4
Agramón E . . . . . . 158 C2
Agramunt E . . . . . 147 C2
Agreda E . . . . . . . 144 C2
Agria GR . . . . . . . 183 D5
Agrigento I . . . . . . 176 B2
Agrinio GR . . . . . . 182 E3
Agrón E . . . . . . . . 163 A4
Agrópoli I . . . . . . . 170 C2
Aguadulce
  Almería E . . . . . .164 C2
  Sevilla E . . . . . . .162 A3
Agualada E . . . . . . 140 A2
Agua Longa P . . . . 148 A1
A Guarda E . . . . . . 140 C2
Aguarón E . . . . . . 152 A2
Aguas E . . . . . . . 145 B3
Aguas Belas P . . . . 154 B2
Aguas de Busot E . 159 C3
Aguas de Moura P . 154 C2
Águas Frias P . . . . 148 A2
Aguas Santas P . . . 148 A1

Aguaviva E . . . . . . 153 B3
Aguaviva de la Vega
  E . . . . . . . . . . . 152 A1
Agudo E . . . . . . . 156 B3
Águeda P . . . . . . . 148 B1
Aguessac F . . . . . 130 A2
Agugliano I . . . . . . 136 B2
Aguiar P . . . . . . . 154 C3
Aguiàr da Beira P . . 148 B2
Aguilafuente E . . . . 151 A3
Aguilar de Campóo
  E . . . . . . . . . . . 142 B2
Aguilar de la Frontera
  E . . . . . . . . . . . 163 A3
Águilas E . . . . . . . 164 B3
Agunnaryd S . . . . . 60 C4
Ahat TR . . . . . . . . 187 D4
Ahaus D . . . . . . . 71 B3
Åheim N . . . . . . . 198 C2
Ahigal E . . . . . . . . 149 B3
Ahigal de Villarino
  E . . . . . . . . . . . 149 A3
Ahillones E . . . . . . 156 B2
Ahlbeck
  Mecklenburg-
  Vorpommern D . . . .66 C3
  Mecklenburg-
  Vorpommern D . . . .74 A3
Ahlen D . . . . . . . . 81 A3
Ahlhorn D . . . . . . . 71 B5
Ahmetbey TR . . . . 186 A2
Ahmetler TR . . . . . 188 A4
Ahmetli TR . . . . . . 188 A2
Ahoghill GB . . . . . . 27 B4
Ahola FIN . . . . . . . 197 C11
Ahrensbök D . . . . . 65 B3
Ahrensburg D . . . . 72 A3
Ahrenshoop D . . . . 66 B1
Ahun F . . . . . . . . .116 A2
Åhus S . . . . . . . . 63 C2
Ahvenselkä FIN . . 197 C11
Aibar E . . . . . . . . 144 B2
Aich D . . . . . . . . . 95 C4
Aicha D . . . . . . . . 96 C1
Aichach D . . . . . . . 94 C3
Aidone I . . . . . . . . 177 B3
Aiello Cálabro I . . . 175 B2
Aigen im Mühlkreis
  A . . . . . . . . . . . 96 C1
Aigle CH . . . . . . . .119 A3
Aignan F . . . . . . . 128 C3
Aignay-le-Duc F . . 104 B3
Aigre F . . . . . . . . 115 C4
Aigrefeuille-d'Aunis
  F . . . . . . . . . . . .114 B3
Aigrefeuille-sur-Maine
  F . . . . . . . . . . . 101 B4
Aiguablava E . . . . . 147 C4
Aiguebelle F . . . . . .118 B3
Aigueperse F . . . . .116 A3
Aigues-Mortes F . . 131 B3
Aigues-Vives F . . . 130 B1
Aiguilles F . . . . . . 119 C3
Aiguillon F . . . . . . 129 B3
Aigurande F . . . . . 103 C3
Ailefroide F . . . . . .118 C3
Aillant-sur-Tholon
  F . . . . . . . . . . . 104 B2
Ailly-sur-Noye F . . . 90 B2
Ailly-sur-Somme F . 90 B2
Aimargues F . . . . . 131 B3
Aime F . . . . . . . . .118 B3

Aab–Aku

Ainaži LV . . . . . . . 8 D4
Ainet A . . . . . . . . 109 C3
Ainhoa F . . . . . . . 144 A2
Ainsa E . . . . . . . . 145 B4
Airaines F . . . . . . 90 B1
Aird GB . . . . . . . . 34 B2
Aird Asaig Tairbeart
  GB . . . . . . . . . . 31 B2
Airdrie GB . . . . . . . 35 C4
Aire-sur-l'Adour F . 128 C2
Aire-sur-la-Lys F . . 78 B2
Airole I . . . . . . . . 133 B3
Airolo CH . . . . . . . 107 C3
Airvault F . . . . . . . 102 C1
Aisey-sur-Seine F . 104 B3
Aïssey F . . . . . . . 105 B5
Aisy-sur-Armançon
  F . . . . . . . . . . . 104 B3
Aiterhofen D . . . . . 95 C4
Aith
  Orkney GB . . . . . .33 B4
  Shetland GB . . . . .33 A5
Aitona E . . . . . . . 153 A4
Aitrach D . . . . . . . 107 B5
Aiud RO . . . . . . . . 17 B5
Aix-en-Othe F . . . . 104 A2
Aix-en-Provence F . 131 B4
Aixe-sur-Vienne F . 115 C5
Aix-les-Bains F . . . .118 B2
Aizenay F . . . . . . .114 B2
Aizkraukle LV . . . . . 8 D4
Aizpute LV . . . . . . 8 D2
Ajac F . . . . . . . . . 146 A3
Ajaccio F . . . . . . . 180 B1
Ajain F . . . . . . . . .116 A1
Ajaureforsen S . . . 195 E6
Ajdovščina SLO . . . 122 B2
Ajka H . . . . . . . . .111 B4
Ajo E . . . . . . . . . 143 A3
Ajofrin E . . . . . . . 157 A4
Ajos FIN . . . . . . . 196 D7
Ajuda P . . . . . . . . 155 C3
Akanthou CY . . . . . 181 A2
Akarca TR . . . . . . 189 A4
Akasztó H . . . . . . .112 C3
Akçakoca TR . . . . . 187 A6
Akçaova TR . . . . . 187 A4
Akçay TR . . . . . . . 189 C4
Aken D . . . . . . . . 83 A4
Åkerby S . . . . . . . 51 B4
Åkernes N . . . . . . 52 B3
Åkersberga S . . . . 57 A4
Åkers styckebruk S 56 A3
Åkervik N . . . . . . . 195 E4
Akhisar TR . . . . . . 186 D2
Åkirkeby DK . . . . . 67 A3
Akköy TR . . . . . . . 188 B2
Akkrum NL . . . . . . 70 A2
Akören TR . . . . . . 189 B7
Akra N . . . . . . . . 52 A2
Akranes IS . . . . . . 190 C3
Åkrehamn N . . . . . 52 A2
Akrotiri CY . . . . . . 181 B1
Aksaray TR . . . . . . 23 B8
Akşehir TR . . . . . . 189 A6
Akseki TR . . . . . . 189 B6
Aksla N . . . . . . . . 46 A3
Aksu TR . . . . . . . 189 C5
Aktsyabrski BY . . . 13 B8
Akureyri IS . . . . . . 191 B7

Åkvåg N . . . . . . . . . 53 B5
Akyazı TR . . . . . . 187 B5
Ål N . . . . . . . . . . . . 47 B5
Ala I . . . . . . . . . . . 121 B4
Alaca TR . . . . . . . . 23 A8
Alacaatlı TR . . . . . 186 C3
Alaçam TR . . . . . . . 23 A8
Alaçatı TR . . . . . . 188 A1
Alàdei Sardi I . . . . . 178 B3
Ala di Stura I . . . . . 119 B4
Alaejos E . . . . . . . 150 A2
Alagna Valsésia I . . 119 B4
Alagón E . . . . . . . 144 C2
Alaior E . . . . . . . . 167 B4
Alájar E . . . . . . . . 161 B3
Alakurtti RUS . . 197 C13
Alakylä FIN . . . . . 196 B7
Alameda E . . . . . . 163 A3
Alameda de la Sagra
  E . . . . . . . . . . . . .151 B4
Alamedilla E . . . . . 163 A4
Alamillo E . . . . . . 156 B3
Alaminos E . . . . . 151 B5
Ala-Nampa FIN . . . 197 C9
Alanäs S . . . . . . 199 A12
Alandroal P . . . . . 155 C3
Alange E . . . . . . . 156 B1
Alaniemi FIN . . . . 197 D8
Alanís E . . . . . . . . 156 B2
Alanno I . . . . . . . . 169 A3
Ålansbro S . . . . . 200 D3
Alanya TR . . . . . . 189 C7
Alap H . . . . . . . . . 112 C2
Alaquàs E . . . . . . 159 B3
Alaraz E . . . . . . . 150 B2
Alarcón E . . . . . . 158 B1
Alar del Rey E . . . 142 B2
Alaró E . . . . . . . . 167 B2
Alaşehir TR . . . . . 188 A3
Alássio I . . . . . . . 133 A4
Ağlasun TR . . . . . 189 B5
Alatoz E . . . . . . . 158 B2
Alatri I . . . . . . . . . 169 B3
Alavus FIN . . . . . . . 8 A3
Alba
  E . . . . . . . . . . . . .152 B2
  I . . . . . . . . . . . . . .119 C5
Alba Adriática I . . . 136 C2
Albacete E . . . . . 158 C2
Alba de Tormes E . 150 B2
Alba de Yeltes E . . 149 B3
Albaida E . . . . . . 159 C3
Alba-Iulia RO . . . . 17 B5
Albæk DK. . . . . . . 58 A3
Albaladejo E . . . . 158 C1
Albala del Caudillo
  E . . . . . . . . . . . . 156 A1
Albalat E . . . . . . . 159 B3
Albalate de Cinca
  E . . . . . . . . . . . . 145 C4
Albalate del Arzobispo
  E . . . . . . . . . . . . 153 A3
Albalate de las
  Nogueras E . . . . 152 B1
Albalete de Zorita
  E . . . . . . . . . . . . 151 B5
Alban F . . . . . . . . 130 B1
Albánchez E . . . . . 164 B2
Albanchez de Ubeda
  E . . . . . . . . . . . . 163 A4
Albano Laziale I . . . 168 B2
Albanyà E . . . . . . 147 B3
Albaredo d'Adige I 121 B4
Albares E . . . . . . 151 B4
Albarracín E . . . . . 152 B2
Albatana E . . . . . . 158 C2
Albatàrrec E . . . . . 153 A4
Albatera E . . . . . . 165 A4
Albbruck D . . . . . 106 B3
Albedin E . . . . . . 163 A3
Albelda de Iregua
  E . . . . . . . . . . . . 143 B4
Albenga I . . . . . . 133 A4
Albens F . . . . . . . .118 B2
Alberga
  Södermanland S . .56 A2
  Södermanland S . .56 B2
Albergaria-a-Nova
  P . . . . . . . . . . . . 148 B1
Albergaria-a-Velha
  P . . . . . . . . . . . . 148 B1
Albergaria dos Doze
  P . . . . . . . . . . . . 154 B2
Alberge P . . . . . . 154 C2
Alberic E . . . . . . . 159 B3
Albernoa P . . . . . 160 B2
Alberobello I . . . . . 173 B3
Alberoni I . . . . . . . 122 B1
Albersdorf D . . . . . 64 B2
Albersloh D . . . . . . 81 A3
Albert F . . . . . . . . . 90 A2
Albertirsa H . . . . . .112 B3
Albertville F . . . . . .118 B3
Albéruela de Tubo
  E . . . . . . . . . . . . 145 C3
Albi F . . . . . . . . . 130 B1
Albidona I . . . . . . 174 B2
Albínia I . . . . . . . 168 A1
Albino I . . . . . . . . 120 B2
Albinshof D . . . . . . 66 C2
Albires E . . . . . . . 142 B1
Albisola Marina I . . 133 A4
Albocàcer E . . . . . 153 B4
Albolote E . . . . . . 163 A4
Albondón E . . . . . 164 C1

Alborea E . . . . . . 158 B2
Albox E . . . . . . . . 164 B2
Albrechtice nad Vitavou
  CZ . . . . . . . . . . . . 96 B2
Albstadt D . . . . . . 107 A4
Albufeira P . . . . . 160 B1
Albuñol E . . . . . . 164 C1
Albuñuelas E . . . . 163 B4
Alburquerque E . . 155 B3
Alby
  Öland S . . . . . . . 63 B4
  Västernorrland S . .200 D1
Alcácer do Sal P . . 154 C2
Alcáçovas P . . . . . 154 C2
Alcadozo E . . . . . 158 C2
Alcafoces P . . . . . 155 B3
Alcains P . . . . . . . 155 B3
Alcaláde Guadaira
  E . . . . . . . . . . . . 162 A2
Alcaláde Gurrea E . 144 B3
Alcaláde Henares
  E . . . . . . . . . . . . 151 B4
Alcaláde la Selva
  E . . . . . . . . . . . . 153 B3
Alcaládel Júcar E . 158 B2
Alcaládel Río E . . . 162 A2
Alcaládel Valle E . . 162 B2
Alcaládel Xivert E . 153 B4
Alcalála Real E . . . 163 A4
Alcamo I . . . . . . . 176 B1
Alcampell E . . . . . 145 C4
Alcanadre E . . . . . 144 B1
Alcanar E . . . . . . . 153 B4
Alcanede P . . . . . 154 B2
Alcanena P . . . . . 154 B2
Alcañices E . . . . . 149 A3
Alcántara E . . . . . 155 B4
Alcantarilha P . . . . 160 B1
Alcantarilla E . . . . 165 B3
Alcañz E . . . . . . . 153 A3
Alcaracejos E . . . . 156 B3
Alcara il Fusi I . . . . 177 A3
Alcaraz E . . . . . . . 158 C1
Alcaria Ruiva P . . . 160 B2
Alcarraz E . . . . . . 153 A4
Alcaudete E . . . . . 163 A3
Alcaudete de la Jara
  E . . . . . . . . . . . . 150 C3
Alcázar de San Juan
  E . . . . . . . . . . . . 157 A4
Alcazarén E . . . . . 150 A3
Alcester GB . . . . . . 44 A2
Alcoba E . . . . . . . 157 A3
Alcobaça P . . . . . . 154 B1
Alcobendas E . . . . 151 B4
Alcocer E . . . . . . . 151 B5
Alcochete P . . . . . 154 C2
Alcoentre P . . . . . 154 B2
Alcolea
  Almería E . . . . . .164 C2
  Córdoba E . . . . . .156 C3
Alcolea de Calatrava
  E . . . . . . . . . . . . 157 B3
Alcolea de Cinca E 145 C4
Alcolea del Pinar E 152 A1
Alcolea del Río E . . 162 A2
Alcolea de Tajo E . 150 C2
Alcollarin E . . . . . 156 A2
Alconchel E . . . . . 155 C3
Alconera E . . . . . . 155 C4
Alcontar E . . . . . . 164 B2
Alcora E . . . . . . . 153 B3
Alcorcón E . . . . . . 151 B4
Alcorisa E . . . . . . 153 B3
Alcossebre E . . . . 153 B4
Alcoutim P . . . . . . 160 B2
Alcover E . . . . . . . 147 C2
Alcoy E . . . . . . . . 159 C3
Alcsútdoboz H . . . .112 B2
Alcubierre E . . . . . 145 C3
Alcubilla de Avellaneda
  E . . . . . . . . . . . . 143 C3
Alcubilla de Nogales
  E . . . . . . . . . . . . 141 B5
Alcubillas E . . . . . 157 B4
Alcublas E . . . . . . 159 B3
Alcúdia E . . . . . . . 167 B3
Alcudia de Guadix
  E . . . . . . . . . . . . 164 B1
Alcuéscar E . . . . . 155 B4
Aldbrough GB . . . . 41 B3
Aldeacentenera E . 156 A2
Aldeadávila de la Ribera
  E . . . . . . . . . . . . 149 A3
Aldea del Cano E . . 155 B4
Aldea del Fresno E 151 B3
Aldea del Obispo
  E . . . . . . . . . . . . 149 B3
Aldea del Rey E . . . 157 B4
Aldea de Trujillo E . 156 A2
Aldealcorvo E . . . . 151 A4
Aldealuenga de Santa
  Maria E . . . . . . . 151 A4
Aldeamayor de San
  Martin E . . . . . . . 150 A3
Aldeanueva de
  Barbarroya E . . . 150 C2
Aldeanueva del Camino
  E . . . . . . . . . . . . 149 B4
Aldeanueva del Codonal
  E . . . . . . . . . . . . 150 A3
Aldeanueva de San
  Bartolomé E . . . . 156 A2
Aldeapozo E . . . . 144 C1
Aldeaquemada E . . 157 B4
Aldea Real E . . . . 151 A3

Aldearrubia E . . . 150 A2
Aldeaseca de la
  Frontera E . . . . . 150 B2
Aldeasoña E . . . . . 151 A3
Aldeatejada E . . . . 150 B2
Aldeavieja E . . . . . 150 B3
Aldeburgh GB . . . . 45 A5
Aldehuela E . . . . . 152 B2
Aldehuela de
  Calatañazor E . . . 143 C4
Aldeia da Serra P . 155 C3
Aldeia do Bispo P . 149 B3
Aldeia do Mato P . . 154 B2
Aldeia Gavinha P . 154 B1
Aldeire E . . . . . . . 164 B1
Aldenhoven D . . . . 80 B2
Aldersbach D . . . . 95 C5
Aldershot GB . . . . . 44 B3
Aldudes F . . . . . . 144 A2
Åled S . . . . . . . . . 60 C2
Aledo E . . . . . . . . 165 B3
Alegria E . . . . . . . 143 B4
Aleksandrovac
  SRB . . . . . . . . . 127 C3
Aleksandrów Kujawski
  PL . . . . . . . . . . . . 76 B3
Aleksandrów Łódźki
  PL. . . . . . . . . . . . 86 A3
Aleksa Šantić SRB 126 B1
Ålem S . . . . . . . . . 62 B4
Alençon F . . . . . . . 89 B4
Alenquer P . . . . . . 154 B1
Alenya F . . . . . . . 146 B3
Aléria F . . . . . . . . 180 A2
Alès F . . . . . . . . . 131 A3
Åles I . . . . . . . . . 179 C2
Alessándria I . . . . 120 C1
Alessándria della Rocca
  I . . . . . . . . . . . . . 176 B2
Alessano I . . . . . . 173 C4
Ålesund N . . . . . . 198 C3
Alet-les-Bains F . . 146 B3
Alexandria
  GB. . . . . . . . . . . .34 C3
  GR . . . . . . . . . . .182 C4
  RO . . . . . . . . . . . .17 D6
Alexandroupoli
  GR . . . . . . . . . . . 183 C7
Aleyrac F . . . . . . . 131 A3
Alézio I . . . . . . . . 173 B4
Alfacar E . . . . . . . 163 A4
Alfaiates P . . . . . . 149 B3
Alfajarin E . . . . . . 153 A3
Alfambra
  E . . . . . . . . . . . . .152 B2
  P . . . . . . . . . . . . .160 B1
Alfândega da Fé P . 149 A3
Alfarela de Jafes P 148 A2
Alfarelos P . . . . . . 148 B1
Alfarim P . . . . . . . 154 C1
Alfarnate E . . . . . . 163 B3
Alfaro E . . . . . . . . 144 B2
Alfarràs E . . . . . . 145 C4
Alfas del Pi E . . . . 159 C3
Alfedena I . . . . . . 169 B4
Alfeizarão P . . . . . 154 B1
Alfeld
  Bayern D . . . . . . .95 B3
  Niedersachsen D . .72 C2
Alfena P . . . . . . . . 148 A1
Alferce P . . . . . . . 160 B1
Alfhausen D . . . . . 71 B4
Alfonsine I . . . . . . 135 A5
Alford
  Aberdeenshire
  GB . . . . . . . . . . .33 D4
  Lincolnshire GB . .41 B4
Alforja E . . . . . . . 147 C1
Alfoz E . . . . . . . . 141 A3
Alfreton GB . . . . . . 40 B2
Alfta S . . . . . . . . . 50 A3
Alfundão P . . . . . . 160 A1
Algaida E . . . . . . . 167 B2
Algar E . . . . . . . . 162 B2
Algarinejo E . . . . . 163 A3
Algarrobo E . . . . . 163 B3
Algatocin E . . . . . 162 B2
Algeciras E . . . . . 162 B2
Algemesí E . . . . . 159 B3
Algés P . . . . . . . . 154 C1
Algete E . . . . . . . 151 B4
Alghero I . . . . . . . 178 B2
Ålghult S . . . . . . . 62 A3
Alginet E . . . . . . . 159 B3
Algodonales E . . . 162 B2
Algodor
  E . . . . . . . . . . . . 151 C4
  P . . . . . . . . . . . . 160 B2
Algora E . . . . . . . 151 B5
Algoso P . . . . . . . 149 A3
Algoz P . . . . . . . . 160 B1
Älgsjö S . . . . . . . 200 B3
Alguaire E . . . . . . 145 C4
Alguazas E . . . . . 165 A3
Algutsrum S . . . . . 63 B4
Algyö H . . . . . . . . 126 A2
Alhama de Almería
  E . . . . . . . . . . . . 164 C2
Alhama de Aragón
  E . . . . . . . . . . . . 152 A2
Alhama de Granada
  E . . . . . . . . . . . . 163 B4
Alhama de Murcia
  E . . . . . . . . . . . . 165 B3
Alhambra E . . . . . 157 B4
Alhandra P . . . . . . 154 C1

Alhaurin de la Torre
  E . . . . . . . . . . . . 163 B3
Alhaurín el Grande
  E . . . . . . . . . . . . 163 B3
Alhendin E . . . . . . 163 A4
Alhóndiga E . . . . . 151 B5
Alia E . . . . . . . . . 156 A2
Ália I . . . . . . . . . . 176 B2
Aliaga TR . . . . . . 186 D1
Aliaga E . . . . . . . 153 B3
Alibunar SRB . . . . 127 B2
Alicante E . . . . . . 165 A4
Alicún de Ortega E 164 B1
Alife I . . . . . . . . . 170 B2
Alija del Infantado
  E . . . . . . . . . . . . 141 B5
Alijó P . . . . . . . . . 148 A2
Alimena I . . . . . . . 177 B3
Alingsås S . . . . . . 60 B2
Alinyà E . . . . . . . 147 B2
Aliseda E . . . . . . . 155 B4
Ali Terme I . . . . . . 177 A4
Alixan F . . . . . . . . 117 C5
Aljaraque E . . . . . 161 B2
Aljorra E . . . . . . . 165 B3
Aljubarrota P . . . . 154 B2
Aljucen E . . . . . . . 155 B4
Aljustrel P . . . . . . 160 B1
Alken B . . . . . . . . 79 B5
Alkmaar NL . . . . . 70 B1
Alkoven A . . . . . . . 96 C2
Allaines F . . . . . . . 103 A3
Allaire F . . . . . . . . 101 B3
Allanche F . . . . . . .116 B2
Alland A . . . . . . . .111 A3
Allariz E . . . . . . . . 140 B3
Allassac F . . . . . . 129 A4
Allauch F . . . . . . . 131 B4
Alleen N . . . . . . . . 52 B3
Allègre F . . . . . . . .117 B3
Allemont F . . . . . . .118 B3
Allendale Town GB . 37 B4
Allendorf D . . . . . . 81 B4
Allentsteig A . . . . . 97 C3
Allepuz E . . . . . . . 153 B3
Allersberg D . . . . . 95 B3
Allershausen D . . . 95 C3
Alles E . . . . . . . . 142 A2
Allevard F . . . . . . .118 B3
Allgunnen S . . . . . 62 A3
Allihies IRL . . . . . . 29 C1
Allingåbro DK . . . . 58 B3
Allmannsdorf D . . . 107 B4
Allo E . . . . . . . . . 144 B1
Alloa GB. . . . . . . . 35 B4
Allogny F . . . . . . . 103 B4
Alloluokta S . . . . . 196 B2
Allones
  Eure et Loire F . .90 C1
  Maine-et-Loire F . .102 B2
Allonnes F . . . . . . 102 B2
Allons F . . . . . . . . 128 B2
Allos F . . . . . . . . . 132 A2
Allstedt D . . . . . . . 82 A3
Alltwalis GB . . . . . 39 C2
Allumiere I . . . . . . 168 A1
Almaceda P . . . . . 155 B3
Almacelles E . . . . . 145 C4
Almachar E . . . . . 163 B3
Almada P . . . . . . . 154 C1
Almadén E . . . . . . 156 B3
Almadén de la Plata
  E . . . . . . . . . . . . 161 B3
Almadenejos E . . . 156 B3
Almadrones E . . . . 151 B5
Almagro E . . . . . . 157 B4
Almajano E . . . . . . 144 C1
Almansa E . . . . . . 159 C2
Almansil P . . . . . . 160 B1
Almanza E . . . . . . 142 B1
Almaraz E . . . . . . 150 C2
Almargen E . . . . . 162 B2
Almarza E . . . . . . 143 C4
Almásfüzitö H . . . .112 B2
Almassora E . . . . . 159 B3
Almazán E . . . . . . 152 A1
Almazul E . . . . . . 152 A1
Alme D . . . . . . . . . 81 A4
Almedina E . . . . . . 158 C1
Almedinilla E . . . . 163 A3
Almeida
  E . . . . . . . . . . . . 149 A3
  P . . . . . . . . . . . . 149 B3
Almeirim P . . . . . . 154 B2
Almelo NL . . . . . . 71 B3
Almenar E . . . . . . 145 C4
Almenara E . . . . . 159 B3
Almenar de Soria
  E . . . . . . . . . . . . 152 A1
Almendra P . . . . . 149 B2
Almendral E . . . . . 155 C4
Almendral de la Cañada
  E . . . . . . . . . . . . 150 B3
Almendralejo E . . . 155 C4
Almenno San
  Bartolomeo I . . . . 120 B2
Almere NL . . . . . . 70 B2
Almería E . . . . . . 164 C2
Almerimar E . . . . . 164 C2
Almese I . . . . . . . .119 B4
Almexial P . . . . . . 160 B2
Almhult S . . . . . . . 63 B2
Almiropotamos
  GR . . . . . . . . . . . 185 A5
Almiros GR . . . . . 182 D4
Almodôvar P . . . . 160 B1

Almodóvar del Campo
  E . . . . . . . . . . . . 157 B3
Almodóvar del Pinar
  E . . . . . . . . . . . . 158 B2
Almodóvar del Río
  E . . . . . . . . . . . . 162 A2
Almofala P . . . . . . 148 B2
Almogia E . . . . . . 163 B3
Almoharin E . . . . . 156 A1
Almonacid de la Sierra
  E . . . . . . . . . . . . 152 A2
Almonacid de Toledo
  E . . . . . . . . . . . . 157 A4
Almonaster la Real
  E . . . . . . . . . . . . 161 B3
Almondsbury GB . . 43 A4
Almonte E . . . . . . 161 B3
Almoradí E . . . . . . 165 A4
Almoraima E . . . . . 162 B2
Almorox E . . . . . . 150 B3
Almoster P . . . . . . 154 B2
Almsele S . . . . . . 200 B3
Ålmsta S . . . . . . . 51 C5
Almudena E . . . . . 164 A3
Almudévar E . . . . . 145 B3
Almuñécar E . . . . . 163 B4
Almunge S . . . . . . 51 C5
Almuradiel E . . . . . 157 B4
Almussafes E . . . . 159 B3
Almvik S . . . . . . . 62 A4
Alness GB . . . . . . 32 D2
Alnmouth GB . . . . 37 A5
Alnwick GB . . . . . 37 A5
Åloppe S . . . . . . . 51 C4
Álora E . . . . . . . . 163 B3
Alos d'Ensil E . . . . 146 B2
Alosno E . . . . . . . 161 B2
Alozaina E . . . . . . 162 B3
Alpbach A . . . . . . 108 B2
Alpedrete de la Sierra
  E . . . . . . . . . . . . 151 B4
Alpedrinha P . . . . 148 B2
Alpen D . . . . . . . . 80 A2
Alpera E . . . . . . . 159 C2
Alphen aan de Rijn
  NL. . . . . . . . . . . . 70 B1
Alpiarça P . . . . . . 154 B2
Alpignano I . . . . . .119 B4
Alpirsbach D . . . . . 93 C4
Alpu TR . . . . . . . . 187 C5
Alpuente E . . . . . . 159 B2
Alqueva P . . . . . . 160 A2
Alquézar E . . . . . . 145 B4
Als DK . . . . . . . . . 58 B3
Alsasua E . . . . . . 144 B1
Alsdorf D . . . . . . . 80 B2
Alselv DK. . . . . . . 59 C1
Alsfeld D . . . . . . . 81 B5
Alsike S . . . . . . . . 57 A3
Alskog S . . . . . . . 57 C4
Alsleben D . . . . . . 83 A3
Alsónémedi H . . . . .112 B3
Alsótold H . . . . . . .112 B3
Alsóújlak H . . . . . .111 B3
Alstad N . . . . . . . 194 C6
Alstätte D . . . . . . . 71 B3
Alsterbro S . . . . . . 62 B3
Alstermo S . . . . . . 62 B3
Alston GB . . . . . . 37 B4
Alsvåg N . . . . . . . 194 B6
Alsvik N . . . . . . . 194 C5
Alta N . . . . . . . . . 192 C7
Älta S . . . . . . . . . 57 A4
Altamura I . . . . . . 172 B2
Altarejos E . . . . . . 158 B1
Altaussee A . . . . . 109 B4
Altavilla Irpina I . . . 170 B2
Altavilla Silentina I 170 C3
Altdöbern D . . . . . 84 A2
Altdorf
  CH . . . . . . . . . . . 107 C3
  D . . . . . . . . . . . . .95 C4
Altdorf bei Nürnberg
  D . . . . . . . . . . . . .95 B3
Alte P . . . . . . . . . 160 B1
Altea E . . . . . . . . 159 C3
Alteidet I . . . . . . . 121 C4
Altena D . . . . . . . 81 A3
Altenau D . . . . . . 82 A2
Altenberg D . . . . . 84 B1
Altenberge D . . . . 71 B4
Altenbruch D . . . . 64 C1
Altenburg D . . . . . 83 B4
Altenfelden A . . . . 96 C1
Altengronau D . . . . 82 B1
Altenheim D . . . . . 93 C3
Altenhundem D . . . 81 A4
Altenkirchen
  Mecklenburg-
  Vorpommern D . . . . 66 B2
  Radom S . . . . . . . .81 B3
Altenkunstadt D . . . 82 B3
Altenmarkt
  A . . . . . . . . . . . . .110 B1
  D . . . . . . . . . . . . .109 A3
Altenmarkt im Pongall
  A . . . . . . . . . . . . 109 B4
Altensteig D . . . . . 93 C4
Altentreptow D . . . 74 A2
Altenwalde D . . . . 64 C1
Alten-weddingen D . 73 B4
Alter do Chão P . . 155 B3
Altfraunhofen D . . . 95 C4
Altheim
  A . . . . . . . . . . . . 109 A4
  D . . . . . . . . . . . . .94 B1
Althofen A . . . . . . 110 C1
Altınoluk TR. . . . . 186 C1

Altınova TR . . . . . 186 C1
Altıntaş TR. . . . . . 187 C5
Altınyaka TR . . . . 189 C5
Altınyayla TR. . . . 189 B4
Altkirch F . . . . . . . 106 B2
Altlandsberg D . . . 74 B2
Altlewin D . . . . . . 74 B3
Altmannstein D . . . 95 C3
Altmorschen D . . . 82 A1
Altmunster A . . . . 109 B4
Altnaharra GB . . . . 32 C2
Alto Campoó E . . . 142 A2
Altofonte I . . . . . . 176 A2
Altomonte I . . . . . 174 B2
Alton
  Hampshire GB . . . .44 B3
  Staffordshire GB . .40 C2
Altopáscio I . . . . . 135 B3
Altötting D . . . . . . 109 A3
Altreichenau D . . . 96 C1
Alt Ruppin D . . . . . 74 B1
Altshausen D . . . . 107 B4
Altstätten CH . . . . 107 B4
Altura E . . . . . . . . 159 B3
Altusried D . . . . . . 107 B5
Alūksne LV. . . . . . . 8 D5
Alunda S . . . . . . . 51 B5
Alustante E . . . . . 152 B2
Alva GB . . . . . . . . 35 B4
Alvaiázere P. . . . . 154 B2
Alvalade P . . . . . . 160 B1
Älvängen S . . . . . . 60 B2
Alvarenga P . . . . . 148 B1
Alvares P . . . . . . . 154 A2
Ålvdal N . . . . . . . 199 C7
Älvdalen S . . . . . . 49 A6
Alverca P . . . . . . . 154 C1
Alversund N . . . . . 46 B2
Alvesta S . . . . . . . 62 B2
Alvignac F . . . . . . 129 B4
Alvignano I . . . . . . 170 B2
Ålvik N . . . . . . . . . 46 B3
Alvik S . . . . . . . . . 50 B1
Alvimare F . . . . . . 89 A4
Alviobeira P . . . . . 154 B2
Alvito P . . . . . . . . 160 A2
Älvkarleby S . . . . . 51 B4
Älvkarleöbruk S . . 51 B4
Alvor P . . . . . . . . 160 B1
Alvorge P . . . . . . . 154 B2
Alvøy N . . . . . . . . 46 B2
Älvros S . . . . . . . 199 C11
Alvsbacka S . . . . . 55 A4
Älvsbyn S . . . . . . 196 D4
Älvsered S . . . . . . 60 B2
Alwernia PL. . . . . . 86 B3
Alwinton GB . . . . . 37 A4
Alyth GB . . . . . . . 35 B4
Alytus LT . . . . . . . 13 A6
Alzénau D . . . . . . 93 A5
Alzey D . . . . . . . . 93 B4
Alzira E . . . . . . . . 159 B3
Alzonne F . . . . . . 146 A3
Amadora P. . . . . . 154 C1
Åmål S . . . . . . . . . 55 A3
Amalfi I. . . . . . . . . 170 C2
Amaliada GR . . . . 184 B2
Amance F . . . . . . 105 B5
Amancey F . . . . . . 105 B5
Amándola I . . . . . . 136 C2
Amantea I . . . . . . 175 B2
Amarante P . . . . . 148 A1
Amareleja P . . . . . 161 A2
Amares P . . . . . . . 148 A1
Amaseno I . . . . . . 169 B3
Amasra TR. . . . . . 187 A7
Amatrice I . . . . . . 169 A3
Amay B . . . . . . . . 79 B5
Ambarnyy RUS . . . 3 D13
Ambazac F . . . . . . 115 C5
Ambelonas GR . . . 182 D4
Amberg D . . . . . . 95 B3
Ambérieu-en-Bugey
  F. . . . . . . . . . . . .118 B2
Ambérieux-en-Dombes
  F. . . . . . . . . . . . .117 A4
Ambert F . . . . . . . .117 B3
Ambès F . . . . . . . 128 A2
Ambjörby S . . . . . . 49 B5
Ambjörnarp S . . . . 60 B3
Amble GB . . . . . . 37 A5
Ambleside GB . . . . 36 B4
Ambleteuse F . . . . 78 B1
Amboise F . . . . . . 102 B2
Ambrières-les-Vallées
  F. . . . . . . . . . . . . 88 B3
Amden CH . . . . . . 107 B4
Amel B . . . . . . . . . 80 B2
Amélia I . . . . . . . . 168 A2
Amélie-les-Bains-
  Palalda F . . . . . . 146 B3
Amelinghausen D . . 72 A3
Amendoa P . . . . . 154 B2
Amendoeira P . . . . 160 B2
Améndola I . . . . . . 171 B3
Amendolara I . . . . 174 B2
Amer E . . . . . . . . 147 B3
A Merca E . . . . . . 140 B3
Ameronpen NL . . . 70 B2
Amersfoort NL. . . . 70 B2
Amersham GB . . . . 44 B3
Amesbury GB . . . . 44 B2
Amfiklia GR . . . . . 182 E4
Amfilochia GR . . . 182 E3
Amfipoli GR . . . . . 183 C5
Amfissa GR . . . . . 184 A3
Amièira P . . . . . . . 155 C3
Amieira P . . . . . . . 154 B3

Amieiro P. . . . 148 B1
Amiens F . . . 90 B2
Amindeo GR . . . 182 C3
Åminne S . . . 60 B3
Åmli N . . . 53 B4
Amlwch GB . . . 38 A2
Ammanford GB . . . 39 C3
Ammarnäs S . . . 195 E7
Åmmeberg S . . . 55 B5
Amorbach D . . . 94 B1
Amorebieta E . . . 143 A4
Amorgos GR . . . 185 C6
Amorosa P . . . 148 A1
Amorosi I . . . 170 B2
Åmot
 Buskerud N . . . 48 C1
 Telemark N . . . 53 A4
 S . . . 50 B3
Åmotfors S . . . 54 A3
Åmotsdal N . . . 53 A4
Amou F . . . 128 C2
Ampezzo I . . . 122 A1
Ampfing D . . . 95 C4
Ampflwang A . . . 109 A4
Amplepuis F . . . 117 B4
Amposta E . . . 153 B4
Ampthill GB . . . 44 A3
Ampudia E . . . 142 C2
Ampuero E . . . 143 A3
Amriswil CH . . . 107 B4
Åmsele S . . . 200 B5
Amstelveen NL . . . 70 B1
Amsterdam NL . . . 70 B1
Amstetten A . . . 110 A1
Amtzell D . . . 107 B4
Amulree GB . . . 35 B4
Amurrio E . . . 143 A4
Amusco E . . . 142 B2
Anacapri I . . . 170 B2
Anadia P . . . 148 B1
Anadon E . . . 152 B2
Anafi GR . . . 185 C6
Anagni I . . . 169 B3
Anamur TR . . . 23 C7
Ananyiv UA . . . 17 B8
Anascaul IRL . . . 29 B1
Ånäset S . . . 2 D7
Åna-Sira N . . . 52 B2
Anastazewo PL . . . 76 B3
Anaya de Alba E . . . 150 B2
Ança P . . . 148 B1
Ancaster GB . . . 40 C3
Ancede P . . . 148 A1
Ancenis F . . . 101 B4
Ancerville F . . . 91 C5
Anchuras E . . . 156 A3
Ancona I . . . 136 B2
Ancora P . . . 148 A1
Ancrum GB . . . 35 C5
Ancy-le-Franc F . . . 104 B3
Andalo I . . . 121 A3
Åndalsnes N . . . 198 C4
Andance F . . . 117 B4
Andau F . . . 111 B4
Andebu N . . . 53 A6
Andeer CH . . . 107 C4
Andelfingen CH . . . 107 B3
Andelot-Blancheville
 F . . . 105 A4
Andelot-en-Montagne
 F . . . 105 C4
Andenes N . . . 194 A7
Andenne B . . . 79 B5
Anderlues B . . . 79 B4
Andermatt CH . . . 107 C3
Andernach D . . . 80 B3
Andernos-les-Bains
 F . . . 128 B1
Anderslöv S . . . 66 A2
Anderstorp S . . . 60 B3
Andijk NL . . . 70 B2
Andoain E . . . 144 A1
Andocs H . . . 112 C1
Andolsheim F . . . 106 A2
Andorra E . . . 153 B3
Andorra La Vella
 AND . . . 146 B2
Andosilla E . . . 144 B2
Andover GB . . . 44 B2
Andratx E . . . 166 B2
Andreapol RUS . . . 9 D8
Andreas GB . . . 36 B2
Andréspol PL . . . 86 A3
Andrest F . . . 145 A4
Andretta I . . . 172 B1
Andrezieux-Bouthéon
 F . . . 117 B4
Ándria I . . . 171 B4
Andrijevica MNE . . . 16 D3
Andritsena GR . . . 184 B2
Andros GR . . . 185 B5
Andrychów PL . . . 99 B3
Andselv N . . . 194 A9
Andújar E . . . 157 B3
Anduze F . . . 131 A2
Aneby N . . . 48 B2
Aneby S . . . 62 A2
Añes E . . . 143 A3
Anet F . . . 90 C1
Anfo I . . . 121 B3
Ang S . . . 62 A2
Anga S . . . 57 C4
Ånge S . . . 199 B11
Ånge S . . . 200 D1
Angeja P . . . 148 B1
Ängelholm S . . . 61 C2
Angeli FIN . . . 193 D9

Ängelsberg S . . . 50 C3
Anger A . . . 110 B2
Angera I . . . 120 B1
Angermünde D . . . 74 A3
Angern A . . . 97 C4
Angers F . . . 102 B1
Angerville F . . . 90 C2
Anghiari I . . . 135 B5
Angle GB . . . 39 C1
Anglès E . . . 147 C3
Anglés F . . . 130 B1
Angles F . . . 114 B2
Anglesola E . . . 147 C2
Angles sur l'Anglin
 F . . . 115 B4
Anglet F . . . 128 C1
Anglisidhes CY . . . 181 B2
Anglure F . . . 91 C3
Angoulême F . . . 115 C4
Angoulins F . . . 114 B2
Angsö S . . . 56 A2
Angueira P . . . 149 A3
Angües E . . . 145 B3
Anguiano E . . . 143 B4
Anguillara Sabazia
 I . . . 168 A2
Anguillara Véneta
 I . . . 121 B4
Anhée B . . . 79 B4
Anholt DK . . . 60 C1
Aniane F . . . 130 B2
Aniche F . . . 78 B3
Ånimskog S . . . 54 B3
Anina RO . . . 16 C4
Anixi GR . . . 182 D3
Anizy-le-Château F . . . 91 B3
Anjalankoski FIN . . . 8 B5
Anjan S . . . 199 B9
Ankara TR . . . 187 C7
Ankaran SLO . . . 122 B2
Ankarsrum S . . . 62 A4
Ankerlia N . . . 192 C4
Anklam D . . . 66 C2
Ankum D . . . 71 B4
Anlauftal A . . . 109 B4
Anlezy F . . . 104 C2
Ånn S . . . 199 B9
Annaberg A . . . 110 B2
Annaberg-Buchholz
 D . . . 83 B5
Annaberg im Lammertal
 A . . . 109 B4
Annaburg D . . . 83 A5
Annahütte D . . . 84 A1
Annalong GB . . . 27 B5
Annan GB . . . 36 B3
Anndalsvågen N . . . 195 E3
Anneberg
 Halland S . . . 60 B2
 Jönköping S . . . 62 A2
Annecy F . . . 118 B3
Annelund S . . . 60 B3
Annemasse F . . . 118 A3
Annenskiy Most
 RUS . . . 9 B10
Annerstad S . . . 60 C3
Annestown IRL . . . 30 B1
Annevoie-Rouillon
 B . . . 79 B4
Annonay F . . . 117 B4
Annot F . . . 132 B2
Annweiler D . . . 93 B3
Ano Poroia GR . . . 183 B5
Añora E . . . 156 B3
Ano Siros GR . . . 185 B5
Anould F . . . 106 A1
Anquela del Ducado
 E . . . 152 B1
Anröchte D . . . 81 A4
Ans DK . . . 59 B2
Ansager DK . . . 59 C1
Ansbach D . . . 94 B2
Anse F . . . 117 B4
Anseroeul B . . . 79 B3
Ansfelden A . . . 110 A1
Ansião P . . . 154 B2
Ansó E . . . 144 B3
Ansoain E . . . 144 B2
Anstruther GB . . . 35 B5
Antas E . . . 164 B3
Antegnate I . . . 120 B2
Antequera E . . . 163 A3
Anterselva di Mezzo
 I . . . 108 C3
Antibes F . . . 132 B3
Antigüedad E . . . 142 C2
Antillo I . . . 177 B4
Antirio GR . . . 184 A2
Antnäs S . . . 196 D4
An t-Ob GB . . . 31 B1
Antoing B . . . 79 B3
Antonin PL . . . 86 A1
Antrain F . . . 88 B2
Antrim GB . . . 27 B4
Antrodoco I . . . 169 A3
Antronapiana I . . . 119 A5
Anttis S . . . 196 B5
Antuzede P . . . 148 B1
Antwerp = Antwerpen
 B . . . 79 A4
Antwerpen = Antwerp
 B . . . 79 A4
Anversa d'Abruzzi
 I . . . 169 B3
Anvin F . . . 78 B2
Anzat-le-Luguet F . . . 116 B3
Anzi I . . . 172 B1

Ånzio I . . . 168 B2
Anzola d'Emilia I . . . 135 A4
Anzón E . . . 144 C2
Aoiz E . . . 144 B2
Aosta I . . . 119 B4
Apalhão P . . . 155 B3
Apátfalva H . . . 126 A2
Apatin SRB . . . 125 B5
Apatity RUS . . . 3 C13
Apc H . . . 112 B3
Apécchio I . . . 136 B1
Apeldoorn NL . . . 70 B2
Apen D . . . 71 A4
Apenburg D . . . 73 B4
Apensen D . . . 72 A2
A Peroxa E . . . 140 B3
Apiro I . . . 136 B2
Apliki CY . . . 181 B2
Apolda D . . . 82 A3
Apolonia GR . . . 185 C5
A Pontenova E . . . 141 A3
Apostag H . . . 112 C2
Äppelbo S . . . 49 B6
Appennino I . . . 136 C2
Appenzell CH . . . 107 B4
Appiano I . . . 108 C2
Appingedam NL . . . 71 A3
Appleby-in-
 Westmorland GB . . . 37 B4
Applecross GB . . . 31 B3
Appledore GB . . . 42 A2
Appoigny F . . . 104 B2
Apremont-la-Forêt
 F . . . 92 C1
Aprica I . . . 120 A3
Apricena I . . . 171 B3
Aprigliano I . . . 174 B2
Aprília I . . . 168 B2
Apt F . . . 131 B4
Apúlia P . . . 148 A1
Aquiléia I . . . 122 B2
Aquilónia I . . . 172 B1
Aquino I . . . 169 B3
Ar S . . . 57 C4
Arabayona E . . . 150 A2
Arabba I . . . 108 C2
Araç TR . . . 23 A7
Aracena E . . . 161 B3
Arachova GR . . . 184 A3
Aračinovo MK . . . 182 A3
Arad RO . . . 126 A3
Aradac SRB . . . 126 B2
Aradhippou CY . . . 181 B2
Aragnouet F . . . 145 B4
Aragona I . . . 176 B2
Aramits F . . . 144 A3
Aramon F . . . 131 B3
Aranda de Duero E . . . 143 C3
Aranda de Moncayo
 E . . . 152 A2
Arandjelovac SRB . . . 127 C2
Aranjuez E . . . 151 B4
Arantzazu E . . . 143 B4
Aranzueque E . . . 151 B4
Aras de Alpuente
 E . . . 159 B2
Arauzo de Miel E . . . 143 C3
Arazede P . . . 148 B1
Arbas F . . . 145 B4
Árbatax I . . . 179 C3
Arbeca E . . . 147 C1
Arberg D . . . 94 B2
Arbesbach A . . . 96 C2
Arboga S . . . 56 A1
Arbois F . . . 105 C4
Arbon CH . . . 107 B4
Arboréa I . . . 179 C2
Arbório I . . . 119 B5
Årbostad N . . . 194 B8
Arbrå S . . . 50 A3
Arbroath GB . . . 35 B5
Arbùcies E . . . 147 C3
Arbuniel E . . . 163 A4
Arbus I . . . 179 C2
Arcachon F . . . 128 B1
Arce I . . . 169 B3
Arcen NL . . . 80 A2
Arc-en-Barrois F . . . 105 B3
Arces-Dilo F . . . 104 A2
Arc-et-Senans F . . . 105 B4
Arcévia I . . . 136 B1
Arcey F . . . 106 B1
Archanes GR . . . 185 D6
Archangelos GR . . . 188 C3
Archena E . . . 165 A3
Archez E . . . 163 B4
Archiac F . . . 115 C3
Archidona E . . . 163 A3
Archiestown GB . . . 32 D3
Archivel E . . . 164 A3
Arcidosso I . . . 135 C4
Arcille I . . . 135 C4
Arcis-sur-Aube F . . . 91 C4
Arc-lès-Gray F . . . 105 B4
Arco I . . . 121 B3
Arcones E . . . 151 A4
Arcos E . . . 143 B3
Arcos de Jalón E . . . 152 A1
Arcos de la Frontera
 E . . . 162 B2
Arcos de la Sierra
 E . . . 152 B1
Arcos de las Salinas
 E . . . 159 B2
Arcos de Valdevez
 P . . . 148 A1
Arcozelo P . . . 148 B2
Arc-sur-Tille F . . . 105 B4

Arcusa E . . . 145 B4
Arcy-sur-Cure F . . . 104 B2
Ardagh IRL . . . 29 B2
Årdal N . . . 52 A2
Ardala S . . . 55 B4
Ardales E . . . 162 B3
Årdalstangen N . . . 47 A4
Ardara
 I . . . 178 B2
 IRL . . . 26 B2
Ardarroch GB . . . 31 B3
Ardbeg GB . . . 34 C1
Ardcharnich GB . . . 32 D1
Ardchyle GB . . . 34 B3
Ardee IRL . . . 27 C4
Arden DK . . . 58 B2
Ardentes F . . . 103 C3
Ardersier GB . . . 32 D2
Ardes F . . . 116 B3
Ardessie GB . . . 32 D1
Ardez CH . . . 107 C5
Ardfert IRL . . . 29 B2
Ardgay GB . . . 32 D2
Ardglass GB . . . 27 B5
Ardgroom IRL . . . 29 C2
Ardhasig GB . . . 31 B2
Ardino BG . . . 183 B7
Ardisa E . . . 144 B3
Ardkearagh IRL . . . 29 C1
Ardlui GB . . . 34 B3
Ardlussa GB . . . 34 B2
Ardón E . . . 142 B1
Ardooie B . . . 78 B3
Ardore I . . . 175 C2
Ardre S . . . 57 C4
Ardres F . . . 78 B1
Ardrishaig GB . . . 34 B2
Ardrossan GB . . . 34 C3
Åre S . . . 199 B10
Areia Branca P . . . 154 B1
Aremark N . . . 54 A2
Arenales de San
 Gregorio E . . . 157 A4
Arenas E . . . 163 B3
Arenas de Iguña E . . . 142 A2
Arenas del Rey E . . . 163 B4
Arenas de San Juan
 E . . . 157 A4
Arenas de San Pedro
 E . . . 150 B2
Arendal N . . . 53 B4
Arendonk B . . . 79 A5
Arengosse F . . . 128 B2
Arentorp S . . . 55 B4
Arenys de Mar E . . . 147 C3
Arenys de Munt E . . . 147 C3
Arenzano I . . . 133 A4
Areo E . . . 146 B2
Areopoli GR . . . 184 C3
Ares E . . . 140 A2
Arès F . . . 128 B1
Ares del Maestrat
 E . . . 153 B3
Aresvika N . . . 198 B5
Arette F . . . 144 A3
Aretxabaleta E . . . 143 A4
Arevalillo E . . . 150 B2
Arévalo E . . . 150 A3
Arez P . . . 155 B3
Arezzo I . . . 135 B4
Arfeuilles F . . . 117 A3
Argalasti GR . . . 183 D5
Argallón E . . . 156 B2
Argamasilla de Alba
 E . . . 157 A4
Argamasilla de
 Calatrava E . . . 157 B3
Arganda E . . . 151 B4
Arganil P . . . 148 B1
Argasion GR . . . 184 B1
Argegno I . . . 120 B2
Argelès-Gazost F . . . 145 A3
Argelès-sur-Mer F . . . 146 B4
Argenta I . . . 121 C4
Argentan F . . . 89 B3
Argentat F . . . 116 B1
Argentera I . . . 132 A2
Argenteuil F . . . 90 C2
Argenthal D . . . 93 B3
Argentiera I . . . 178 B2
Argentona E . . . 147 C3
Argenton-Château
 F . . . 102 C1
Argenton-sur-Creuse
 F . . . 103 C3
Argentré F . . . 102 A1
Argentré-du-Plessis
 F . . . 101 A4
Argent-sur-Sauldre
 F . . . 103 B4
Argirades GR . . . 182 D1
Argithanı TR . . . 189 A6
Argos GR . . . 184 B3
Argos Orestiko GR . . . 182 C3
Argostoli GR . . . 184 A1
Argote E . . . 143 B4
Arguedas E . . . 144 B2
Argueil F . . . 90 B1
Arholma S . . . 51 C6
Árhus DK . . . 59 B3
Ariano Irpino I . . . 170 B3
Ariano nel Polésine
 I . . . 121 C5
Aribe E . . . 144 B2
Aridea GR . . . 182 C4
Arienzo I . . . 170 B2

Arild S . . . 61 C2
Arileod GB . . . 34 B1
Arinagour GB . . . 34 B1
Ariño E . . . 153 A3
Arinthod F . . . 118 A2
Arisaig GB . . . 34 B2
Arisgotas E . . . 157 A4
Aritzo I . . . 179 C3
Ariza E . . . 152 A1
Årjäng S . . . 54 A3
Arjeplog S . . . 195 D8
Arjona E . . . 157 C3
Arjonilla E . . . 157 C3
Arkasa GR . . . 188 D2
Arkelstorp S . . . 63 B2
Arklow IRL . . . 30 B2
Arkösund S . . . 56 B2
Ärla S . . . 56 A2
Arlanc F . . . 117 B3
Arlanzón E . . . 143 B3
Arlebosc F . . . 117 B4
Arlena di Castro I . . . 168 A1
Arles F . . . 131 B3
Arles-sur-Tech F . . . 146 B3
Arló H . . . 113 A4
Arlon B . . . 92 B1
Armação de Pera
 P . . . 160 B1
Armadale
 Highland GB . . . 31 B3
 West Lothian GB . . . 35 C4
Armagh GB . . . 27 B4
Armamar P . . . 148 A2
Armenistis GR . . . 185 B7
Armeno I . . . 119 B5
Armenteros E . . . 150 B2
Armentières F . . . 78 B2
Armilla E . . . 163 A4
Armiñón E . . . 143 B4
Armoy GB . . . 27 A4
Armuña de Tajuña
 E . . . 151 B4
Armutlu
 Bursa TR . . . 186 B3
 İzmir TR . . . 188 A2
Arnac-Pompadour
 F . . . 115 C5
Arnafjord N . . . 46 A3
Arnage F . . . 102 B2
Arnas F . . . 117 A4
Årnäs S . . . 55 B4
Arnay-le-Duc F . . . 104 B3
Arnborg DK . . . 59 B2
Arnbruck D . . . 95 B4
Arnea GR . . . 183 C5
Arneberg
 Hedmark N . . . 48 A3
 Hedmark N . . . 49 B4
Arneburg D . . . 73 B5
Arnedillo E . . . 144 B1
Arnedo E . . . 144 B1
Arneguy F . . . 144 A2
Arnés E . . . 153 B4
Árnes IS . . . 190 A4
Årnes
 Akershus N . . . 48 B3
 Troms N . . . 194 A9
Arnfels A . . . 110 C2
Arnhem NL . . . 70 C2
Arnissa GR . . . 182 C3
Arno S . . . 56 B3
Arnold GB . . . 40 B2
Arnoldstein A . . . 109 C4
Arnsberg D . . . 81 A4
Arnschwang D . . . 95 B4
Arnsdorf D . . . 84 A1
Årnset N . . . 198 B6
Arnside GB . . . 37 B4
Arnstadt D . . . 82 B2
Arnstein D . . . 94 B1
Arnstorf D . . . 95 C4
Arnum DK . . . 59 C1
Aroche E . . . 161 B3
Árokto H . . . 113 B4
Arolla CH . . . 119 A4
Arolsen D . . . 81 A5
Arona I . . . 119 B5
Åros N . . . 54 A1
Arosa
 CH . . . 107 C4
 P . . . 148 A1
Ærøskøbing DK . . . 65 B3
Arøsund DK . . . 59 C2
Arouca P . . . 148 B1
Arøysund N . . . 54 A1
Arpajon F . . . 90 C2
Arpajon-sur-Cère
 F . . . 116 C2
Arpela FIN . . . 196 C7
Arpino I . . . 169 B3
Arquata del Tronto
 I . . . 136 C2
Arques F . . . 78 B2
Arques-la-Bataille F . . . 89 A5
Arquillos E . . . 157 B4
Arraia-Maeztu E . . . 143 B4
Arraiolos P . . . 154 C2
Arrancourt F . . . 92 C2
Arras F . . . 78 B2
Arrasate E . . . 143 A4
Årre DK . . . 59 C1
Arreau F . . . 145 B4
Arredondo E . . . 143 A3
Arrens-Marsous F . . . 145 B3
Arriate E . . . 162 B2
Arrifana P . . . 160 B1
Arrigorriaga E . . . 143 A4
Arriondas E . . . 142 A1

Arroba de los Montes
 E . . . 157 A3
Arrochar GB . . . 34 B3
Arromanches-les-Bains
 F . . . 88 A3
Arronches P . . . 155 B3
Arroniz E . . . 144 B1
Arrou F . . . 103 A3
Arroya E . . . 142 B2
Arroya de Cuéllar
 E . . . 150 A3
Arroyal E . . . 142 B2
Arroyo de la Luz E . . . 155 B4
Arroyo del Ojanco
 E . . . 164 A2
Arroyo de San Servan
 E . . . 155 C4
Arroyomolinos de León
 E . . . 161 A3
Arroyomolinos de
 Montánchez E . . . 156 A1
Arruda dos Vinhos
 P . . . 154 C1
Arsac F . . . 128 B2
Ars-en-Ré F . . . 114 B2
Arsiè I . . . 121 B4
Arsiero I . . . 121 B4
Årslev DK . . . 59 C3
Årsoli I . . . 169 A3
Ars-sur-Moselle F . . . 92 B2
Årsunda S . . . 50 B3
Artà E . . . 167 B3
Arta GR . . . 182 D3
Artajona E . . . 144 B2
Artegna I . . . 122 A2
Arteixo E . . . 140 A2
Artemare F . . . 118 B2
Arten I . . . 121 A4
Artena I . . . 169 B2
Artenay F . . . 103 A3
Artern D . . . 82 A3
Artés E . . . 147 C2
Artesa de Segre E . . . 147 C2
Arth CH . . . 107 B3
Arthez-de-Béarn F . . . 145 A3
Arthon-en-Retz F . . . 101 B4
Arthurstown IRL . . . 30 B2
Artieda E . . . 144 B3
Artix F . . . 145 A3
Artotina GR . . . 182 E4
Artsyz UA . . . 17 B8
Artziniega E . . . 143 A3
A Rúa E . . . 141 B3
Arudy F . . . 145 A3
Arundel GB . . . 44 C3
Arveyres F . . . 128 B2
Arvidsjaur S . . . 196 D2
Arvieux F . . . 118 C3
Arvika S . . . 54 A3
Åryd
 Blekinge S . . . 63 B3
 Kronoberg S . . . 62 B2
Arzachena I . . . 178 A3
Arzacq-Arraziguet
 F . . . 128 C2
Árzana I . . . 179 C3
Arzano F . . . 100 B2
Aržano HR . . . 138 B2
Arzberg D . . . 95 A4
Arzignano I . . . 121 B4
Arzila P . . . 148 B1
Arzl im Pitztal A . . . 108 B1
Arzúa E . . . 140 B2
As B . . . 80 A1
Aš CZ . . . 83 B4
Ås N . . . 54 A1
Åsa S . . . 60 B2
Asaa DK . . . 58 A3
Aşağıçiğil TR . . . 189 A6
Ašanja SRB . . . 127 C2
Åsarna S . . . 199 C11
Åsarøy N . . . 52 A2
Åsarp S . . . 55 B4
Asasp F . . . 145 A3
Åsbro S . . . 55 A6
Åsby S . . . 60 B2
Asby S . . . 62 A3
Åsbygri IS . . . 191 A9
Ascain F . . . 144 A2
Ascea I . . . 172 B1
Ascha D . . . 95 B4
Aschach an der Donau
 A . . . 96 C2
Aschaffenburg D . . . 93 B5
Aschbach Markt A . . . 110 A1
Ascheberg
 Nordrhein-Westfalen
 D . . . 81 A3
 Schleswig-Holstein
 D . . . 65 B3
Aschendorf D . . . 71 A4
Aschersleben D . . . 82 A3
Asciano I . . . 135 B4
Ascó E . . . 153 A4
Asco F . . . 180 A2
Áscoli Piceno I . . . 136 C2
Áscoli Satriano I . . . 171 B3
Ascona CH . . . 120 A1
Ascot GB . . . 44 B3
Ascoux F . . . 103 A4
Åse N . . . 194 A6
Åseda S . . . 62 A3
Åsele S . . . 200 B3
Åsen
 N . . . 199 B8

Åsen *continued*
*S* 49 A5
Asendorf D 72 B2
Asenovgrad BG 183 A6
Åsensbruk S 54 B3
Åseral N 52 B3
Asfeld F 91 B4
Åsgårdstrand N 54 A1
Ásgarður IS 190 B1
Asgate CY 181 B2
Ash
*Kent* GB 45 B5
*Surrey* GB 44 B3
Åshammar S 50 B3
Ashbourne
GB 40 B2
IRL 30 A2
Ashburton GB 43 B3
Ashby-de-la-Zouch
GB 40 C2
Ashchurch GB 44 B1
Åsheim N 199 D8
Ashford GB 45 B4
Ashington GB 37 A5
Ashley GB 38 B4
Ashmyany BY 13 A6
Ashton Under Lyne
GB 40 B1
Ashwell GB 44 A3
Asiago I 121 B4
Asipovichy BY 13 B8
Aska FIN 197 B9
Askam-in-Furness
GB 36 B3
Askeaton IRL 29 B3
Asker N 48 C2
Askersund S 55 B5
Åskilje S 200 B3
Askim N 54 A2
Askland N 53 B4
Äsköping S 56 A2
Askvoll N 46 A2
Åsljunga S 61 C3
Asmunti FIN 197 D9
Asnæs DK 61 D1
As Neves E 140 B2
As Nogais E 141 B3
Ásola I 120 B3
Asolo I 121 B4
Asos GR 184 A1
Asotthalom H 126 A1
Aspach A 109 A4
Aspang Markt A 111 B3
Aspariegos E 149 A4
Asparn an der Zaya
A 97 C4
Aspatria GB 36 B3
Aspberg S 55 A4
Aspe E 165 A4
Aspet F 145 A4
Äspö S 63 B3
As Pontes de García
Rodríguez E 140 A3
Aspres-sur-Buëch
F 132 A1
Aspsele S 200 C4
Assafora P 154 C1
Asse B 79 B4
Assebakte N 193 C9
Assel D 72 A2
Asselborn L 92 A1
Assémini I 179 C2
Assen NL 71 B3
Assenede B 79 A3
Assens
*Aarhus Amt.* DK 58 B3
*Fyns Amt.* DK 59 C2
Assesse B 79 B5
Assisi I 136 B1
Åsskard N 198 B5
Assling D 108 B3
Asso I 120 B2
Asson F 145 A3
Ássoro I 177 B3
Assumar P 155 B3
Åsta N 48 A3
Astaffort F 129 B3
Astakos GR 184 A2
Asten NL 80 A1
Asti I 119 C5
Astipalea GR 188 C1
Astorga E 141 B4
Åstorp S 61 C2
Åsträsk S 200 B5
Astudillo E 142 B2
Asuni I 170 C2
Asványráró H 111 B4
Aszód H 112 B3
Aszófő H 111 C4
Atabey TR 189 B5
Atalaia P 154 B3
Atalandi GR 182 E4
Atalho P 154 C2
Átány H 113 B4
Atanzón E 151 B4
Ataquines E 150 A3
Atarfe E 163 A4
Atça TR 188 B3
Ateca E 152 A2
A Teixeira E 141 B3
Atella I 172 B1
Atessa I 169 A4
Ath B 79 B3
Athboy IRL 30 A2
Athea IRL 29 B2
Athenry IRL 28 A3
Athens = Athina
GR 185 B4
Atherstone GB 40 C2
Athienou CY 181 A2
Athies F 90 B2
Athies-sous-Laon F 91 B3
Athina = Athens
GR 185 B4
Athleague IRL 28 A3
Athlone IRL 28 A4
Athna CY 181 A2
Athy IRL 30 B2
Atienza E 151 A5
Atina I 169 B3
Atkár H 113 B3
Atlantı TR 189 A7
Atna N 199 D7
Åtorp S 55 A5
Åtrå N 47 C5
Ätran S 60 B2
Atri I 169 A3
Atripalda I 170 C2
Atsiki GR 183 D7
Attendorn D 81 A3
Attichy F 90 B3
Attigliano I 168 A2
Attigny F 91 B4
Attleborough GB 41 C5
Åtvidaberg S 56 B1
Atzendorf D 73 C4
Au
*Steiermark* A 110 B2
*Vorarlberg* A 107 B4
*Bayern* D 95 C3
*Bayern* D 108 B2
Aub D 94 B2
Aubagne F 132 B1
Aubange B 92 B1
Aubel B 80 B1
Aubenas F 117 C4
Aubenton F 91 B4
Auberive F 105 B4
Aubeterre-sur-Dronne
F 128 A3
Aubiet F 129 C3
Aubigné F 115 B3
Aubigny F 114 B2
Aubigny-au-Bac F 78 B3
Aubigny-en-Artois F 78 B2
Aubigny-sur-Nère
F 103 B4
Aubin F 130 A1
Aubonne CH 105 C5
Aubrac F 116 C2
Aubusson F 116 B2
Auch F 129 C3
Auchencairn GB 36 B3
Auchinleck GB 36 A2
Auchterarder GB 35 B4
Auchtermuchty GB 35 B4
Auchtertyre GB 31 B3
Auchy-au-Bois F 78 B2
Audenge F 128 B1
Auderville F 88 A2
Audierne F 100 A1
Audincourt F 106 B1
Audlem GB 38 B4
Audruicq F 78 B2
Audun-le-Roman F 92 B1
Audun-le-Tiche F 92 B1
Aue
*Nordrhein-Westfalen*
D 81 A4
*Sachsen* D 83 B4
Auerbach
*Bayern* D 95 B3
*Sachsen* D 83 B4
Auffach A 108 B3
Augher GB 27 B3
Aughnacloy GB 27 B4
Aughrim IRL 30 B2
Augignac F 115 C4
Augsburg D 94 C2
Augusta I 177 B4
Augusten-borg DK 64 B2
Augustfehn D 71 A4
Augustów PL 12 B5
Aukrug D 64 B2
Auktsjaur S 196 D2
Auldearn GB 32 D3
Aulendorf D 107 B4
Auletta I 172 B1
Aulla I 134 A2
Aullène F 180 B2
Aulnay F 115 B3
Aulnoye-Aymeries
F 79 B3
Ault F 90 A1
Aultbea GB 31 B3
Aulum DK 59 B1
Aulus-les-Bains F 146 B2
Auma D 83 B3
Aumale F 90 B1
Aumetz F 92 B1
Aumont-Aubrac F 116 C3
Aunay-en-Bazois F 104 B2
Aunay-sur-Odon F 88 A3
Aune N 199 A10
Auneau F 90 C1
Auneuil F 90 B1
Auning DK 58 B3
Aunsetra N 199 A9
Aups F 132 B2
Aura D 82 B1
Auray F 100 B3
Aurdal N 47 B6
Aure N 198 B5
Aurich D 71 A4
Aurignac F 145 A4
Aurillac F 116 C2
Auriol F 132 B1
Auritz-Burguette E 144 B2
Aurlandsvangen N 47 B4
Auronzo di Cadore
I 109 C3
Auros F 128 B2
Auroux F 117 C3
Aurskog N 48 C3
Aursmoen N 48 C3
Ausónia I 169 B3
Ausservillgraton A 109 C3
Austad N 52 B3
Austbygda N 47 B5
Aústis I 178 B3
Austmarka N 49 B4
Austre Moland N 53 B4
Austre Vikebygd N 52 A1
Austrheim N 46 B1
Auterive F 146 A2
Autheuil-Authouillet
F 89 A5
Authon F 132 A2
Authon-du-Perche
F 102 A2
Autol E 144 B2
Autreville F 92 C1
Autrey-lès-Gray F 105 B4
Autti FIN 197 C10
Autun F 104 C3
Auty-le-Châtel F 103 B4
Auvelais B 79 B4
Auvillar F 129 B3
Auxerre F 104 B2
Auxi-le-Château F 78 B2
Auxon F 104 A2
Auxonne F 105 B4
Auxy F 104 C3
Auzances F 116 A2
Auzon F 117 B3
Ağva TR 187 A4
Availles-Limouzine
F 115 B4
Avaldsnes N 52 A1
Avallon F 104 B2
Avantas GR 183 C7
Avaviken S 195 E9
Avebury GB 44 B2
A Veiga E 141 B3
Aveiras de Cima P 154 B2
Aveiro P 148 B1
Avelgem B 79 B3
Avellino I 170 C2
Avenches CH 106 C2
A-Ver-o-Mar P 148 A1
Aversa I 170 C2
Avesnes-le-Comte F 78 B2
Avesnes-sur-Helpe
F 91 A3
Avesta S 50 B3
Avetrana I 173 B3
Avezzano I 169 A3
Avià E 147 B2
Aviano I 122 A1
Aviemore GB 32 D3
Avigliana I 119 B4
Avigliano I 172 B1
Avignon F 131 B3
Ávila E 150 B3
Avilés E 141 A5
Avilley F 105 B5
Avintes P 148 A1
Avinyo E 147 C2
Àvio I 121 B3
Avioth F 92 B1
Avis P 154 B3
Avize F 91 C4
Avlonari GR 185 A5
Ávola I 177 C4
Avon F 90 C2
Avonmouth GB 43 A4
Avord F 103 B4
Avranches F 88 B2
Avril F 92 B1
Avrillé F 102 B1
Avtovac BIH 139 B4
Awans B 79 B5
Axams A 108 B2
Axat F 146 B3
Axbridge GB 43 A4
Axel NL 79 A3
Ax-les-Thermes F 146 B2
Axmarby S 51 B4
Axmarsbruk S 51 A4
Axminster GB 43 B3
Axvall S 55 B4
Ay F 91 B4
Aya E 144 A1
Ayamonte E 161 B2
Ayancık TR 23 A8
Ayaş TR 187 B7
Aydın TR 188 B2
Ayelo de Malferit E 159 C3
Ayer CH 119 A4
Ayerbe E 144 B3
Ayette F 78 B2
Ayia Napa CY 181 B2
Áyia Phyla CY 181 B2
Áyios Amvrósios
CY 181 A2
Áyios Seryios CY 181 A2
Áyios Theodhoros
CY 181 A3
Aykirikçi TR 187 C5
Aylesbury GB 44 B3
Ayllón E 151 A4
Aylsham GB 41 C5
Ayna E 158 C1
Ayódar E 159 B3
Ayora E 159 B2
Ayr GB 36 A2
Ayrancı TR 23 C7
Ayrancılar TR 188 A2
Ayron F 115 B4
Aysgarth GB 37 B4
Ayton GB 35 C5
Aytos BG 17 D7
Ayvacık TR 186 C1
Ayvalık TR 186 C1
Aywaille B 80 B1
Azaila E 153 A3
Azambuja P 154 B2
Azambujeira P 154 B2
Azanja SRB 127 C2
Azannes-et-
Soumazannes F 92 B1
Azanúy-Alins E 145 C4
Azaruja P 155 C3
Azay-le-Ferron F 115 B5
Azay-le-Rideau F 102 B2
Azcoitia E 143 A4
Azé F 117 A4
Azeiteiros P 155 B3
Azenhas do Mar P 154 C1
Azinhaga P 154 B2
Azinhal P 160 B2
Azinheira dos Bairros
P 160 A1
Aznalcázar E 161 B3
Aznalcóllar E 161 B3
Azóia P 154 B2
Azpeitia E 144 A1
Azuaga E 156 B2
Azuara E 153 A3
Azuqueca de Henares
E 151 B4
Azur F 128 C1
Azzano Décimo I 122 B1


## B


Baad A 107 B5
Baamonde E 140 A3
Baar CH 107 B3
Bağarasi TR 188 B2
Baarle-Nassau B 79 A4
Baarn NL 70 B2
Babadağ TR 188 B3
Babadag RO 17 C8
Babaeski TR 186 A2
Babayevo RUS 9 C9
Babenhausen
*Bayern* D 107 A5
*Hessen* D 93 B4
Babiak PL 76 B3
Babice PL 86 B3
Babigoszcz PL 75 A3
Babimost PL 75 B4
Babina Greda HR 125 B4
Babócsa H 124 A3
Bábolma H 112 B1
Baborów PL 86 B1
Baboszewo PL 77 B5
Babót H 111 B4
Babruysk BY 13 B8
Babsk PL 87 A4
Bac GB 31 A2
Bač SRB 125 B5
Bacares E 164 B2
Bacău RO 17 B7
Baccarat F 92 C2
Bacharach D 93 A3
Backa S 50 B2
Bačka Palanka
SRB 126 B1
Backaryd S 63 B3
Bačka Topola SRB 126 B1
Backe S 200 C2
Bäckebo S 62 B4
Bäckefors S 54 B3
Bäckhammar S 55 A5
Bački Breg SRB 125 B4
Bački-Brestovac
SRB 126 B1
Bački Monoštor
SRB 125 B4
Bački Petrovac
SRB 126 B1
Bački Sokolac
SRB 126 B1
Backnang D 94 C1
Bačko Gradište
SRB 126 B2
Bačko Novo Selo
SRB 125 B5
Bačko Petrovo Selo
SRB 126 B2
Bácoli I 170 C2
Bacqueville-en-Caux
F 89 A5
Bácsalmás H 126 A1
Bácsbokod H 125 A5
Bad Abbach D 95 C4
Badacsonytomaj H 111 C4
Bad Aibling D 108 B3
Badajoz E 155 C4
Badalona E 147 C3
Badalucco I 133 B3
Bad Aussee A 109 B4
Bad Bederkesa D 72 A1
Bad Bentheim D 71 B4
Bad Bergzabern D 93 B3
Bad Berka D 82 B3
Bad Berleburg D 81 A4
Bad Berneck D 95 A3
Bad Bevensen D 73 A3
Bad Bibra D 82 A3
Bad Birnbach D 95 C5
Bad Blankenburg D 82 B3
Bad Bleiberg A 109 C4
Bad Brambach D 83 B4
Bad Bramstedt D 64 C2
Bad Breisig D 80 B3
Bad Brückenau D 82 B1
Bad Buchau D 107 A4
Bad Camberg D 81 B4
Badderen N 192 C6
Bad Doberan D 65 B4
Bad Driburg D 81 A5
Bad Düben D 83 A4
Bad Dürkheim D 93 B4
Bad Dürrenberg D 83 A4
Bad Dürrheim D 107 A3
Bad Elster D 83 B4
Bad Ems D 81 B3
Baden
A 111 A3
CH 106 B3
Bádenas E 152 A2
Baden-Baden D 93 C4
Bad Endorf D 109 B3
Badenweiler D 106 B2
Baderna HR 122 B2
Bad Essen D 71 B5
Bad Fischau A 111 B3
Bad Frankenhausen
D 82 A3
Bad Freienwalde D 74 B3
Bad Friedrichshall
D 93 B5
Bad Füssing D 96 C1
Bad Gandersheim D 82 A2
Bad Gastein A 109 B4
Bad Gleichenberg
A 110 C2
Bad Goisern A 109 B4
Bad Gottleuba D 84 B1
Bad Grund D 82 A2
Bad Hall A 110 A1
Bad Harzburg D 82 A2
Bad Herrenalb D 93 C4
Bad Hersfeld D 82 B1
Bad Hofgastein A 109 B4
Bad Homburg D 81 B4
Bad Honnef D 80 B3
Bad Hönningen D 80 B3
Badia Calavena I 121 B4
Badia Polésine I 121 B4
Badia Pratáglia I 135 B4
Badia Tedalda I 135 B5
Bad Iburg D 71 B5
Bad Innerlaterns A 107 B4
Bad Ischl A 109 B4
Bad Karlshafen D 81 A5
Bad Kemmeriboden
CH 106 C2
Bądki PL 69 B3
Bad Kissingen D 82 B2
Bad Kleinen D 65 C4
Bad Kohlgrub D 108 B2
Bad König D 93 B5
Bad Königshofen D 82 B2
Bad Köstritz D 83 B4
Badkowo PL 76 B3
Bad Kreuzen A 110 A1
Bad Kreuznach D 93 B3
Bad Krozingen D 106 B2
Bad Laasphe D 81 B4
Bad Langensalza D 82 A2
Bad Lauchstädt D 83 A3
Bad Lausick D 83 A4
Bad Lauterberg D 82 A2
Bad Leonfelden A 96 C2
Bad Liebenwerda D 83 A5
Bad Liebenzell D 93 C4
Bad Lippspringe D 81 A4
Badljevina HR 124 B3
Bad Meinberg D 81 A4
Bad Mergentheim D 94 B1
Bad Mitterndorf A 109 B4
Bad Münder D 72 B2
Bad Münstereifel D 80 B2
Bad Muskau D 84 A2
Bad Nauheim D 81 B4
Bad Nenndorf D 72 B2
Bad Neuenahr-Ahrweiler
D 80 B3
Bad Neustadt D 82 B2
Bad Oeynhausen D 72 B1
Badolato I 175 C2
Badolatosa E 163 A3
Bad Oldesloe D 65 C3
Badonviller F 92 C2
Bad Orb D 81 B5
Badovinci SRB 127 C1
Bad Peterstal D 93 C4
Bad Pyrmont D 72 C2
Bad Radkersburg
A 110 C2
Bad Ragaz CH 107 C4
Bad Rappenau D 93 B5
Bad Reichenhall D 109 B3
Bad Saarow-Pieskow
D 74 B3
Bad Sachsa D 82 A2
Bad Säckingen D 106 B2
Bad Salzdetfurth D 72 B3
Bad Salzig D 81 B3
Bad Salzuflen D 72 B1
Bad Salzungen D 82 B2
Bad Sankt Leonhard
A 110 C1
Bad Sassendorf D 81 A4
Bad Schandau D 84 B2
Bad Schmiedeberg
D 83 A4
Bad Schönborn D 93 B4
Bad Schussenried
D 107 A4
Bad Schwalbach D 81 B4
Bad Schwartau D 65 C3
Bad Segeberg D 64 C3
Bad Soden D 81 B4
Bad Soden-Salmünster
D 81 B5
Bad Sooden-Allendorf
D 82 A1
Bad Sulza D 83 A3
Bad Sülze D 66 B1
Bad Tatzmannsdorf
A 111 B3
Bad Tennstedt D 82 A2
Bad Tölz D 108 B2
Badules E 152 A2
Bad Urach D 94 C1
Bad Vellach A 110 C1
Bad Vilbel D 81 B4
Bad Vöslau A 111 B3
Bad Waldsee D 107 B4
Bad Wiessee D 108 B2
Bad Wildungen D 81 A5
Bad Wilsnack D 73 B4
Bad Windsheim D 94 B2
Bad Wörishafen D 108 A1
Bad Wurzach D 107 B4
Bad Zwesten D 81 A5
Bad Zwischenahn D 71 A5
Baells E 145 C4
Baena E 163 A3
Baesweiler D 80 B2
Baeza E 157 C4
Baflo NL 71 A3
Baga E 147 B2
Bagaladi I 175 C1
Bagenkop DK 65 B3
Baggetorp S 56 A2
Bagh a Chaisteil GB 31 C1
Bagheria I 176 A2
Bagn N 47 B6
Bagnacavallo I 135 A4
Bagnáia I 168 A2
Bagnara Cálabra I 175 C1
Bagnasco I 133 A4
Bagnères-de-Bigorre
F 145 A4
Bagnères-de-Luchon
F 145 B4
Bagni del Másino I 120 A2
Bagni di Lucca I 134 A3
Bagni di Rabbi I 121 A3
Bagni di Tivoli I 168 B2
Bagno di Romagna
I 135 B4
Bagnoles-de-l'Orne
F 89 B3
Bagnoli dei Trigno
I 170 B2
Bagnoli di Sopra I 121 B4
Bagnoli Irpino I 170 C3
Bagnolo Mella I 120 B3
Bagnols-en-Forêt
F 132 B2
Bagnols-sur-Cèze
F 131 A3
Bagnorégio I 168 A2
Bagolino I 121 B3
Bagrationovsk RUS 12 A4
Bagrdan SRB 127 C3
Báguena E 152 A2
Bahabón de Esgueva
E 143 C3
Bahillo E 142 B2
Báia delle Zágare
I 171 B4
Báia Domizia I 169 B3
Baia Mare RO 17 B5
Baiano I 170 C2
Baião P 148 A1
Baiersbronn D 93 C4
Baiersdorf D 94 B3
Baignes-Ste Radegonde
F 115 C3
Baigneux-les-Juifs
F 104 B3
Baildon GB 40 B2
Bailén E 157 B4
Băileşti RO 17 C5
Baileux B 91 A4
Bailieborough IRL 27 C4
Bailleul F 78 B2
Baillonville B 79 B5
Bailó E 144 B3
Bain-de-Bretagne
F 101 B4
Bains F 117 B3
Bains-les-Bains F 105 A5
Bainton GB 40 B3
Baio E 140 A2
Baiona E 140 B2
Bais F 89 B3
Baiso I 134 A3
Baiuca P 148 B2
Baja H 125 A4
Bajánsenye H 111 C3
Bajina Bašta SRB 127 D1
Bajmok SRB 126 B1
Bajna H 112 B2
Bajovo Polje MNE 139 B4

Bajša SRB . . . . . . 126 B1
Bak H . . . . . . . . 111 C3
Bakar HR . . . . . . . 123 B3
Bakewell GB . . . . . 40 B2
Bakio E . . . . . . . 143 A4
Bakka N . . . . . . . . 47 C6
Bakkafjörður IS . . . 191 A11
Bakkagerði IS . . . . 191 B12
Bække DK . . . . . . . 59 C2
Bakken N . . . . . . . 48 B3
Baklan TR . . . . . . 189 B4
Bækmarksbro DK . . 58 B1
Bakonybél H . . . . . 111 B4
Bakonycsernye H . 112 B2
Bakonyjákó H . . . . 111 B4
Bakonyszentkirály
  H . . . . . . . . . . 111 B4
Bakonyszombathely
  H . . . . . . . . . . 112 B1
Bakov nad Jizerou
  CZ . . . . . . . . . . 84 B2
Bąkowiec PL . . . . . 87 A5
Baks H . . . . . . . . 113 C4
Baksa H . . . . . . . 125 B4
Bakum D . . . . . . . 71 B5
Bala GB . . . . . . . . 38 B3
Bâlâ TR . . . . . . . . 23 B7
Balaguer E . . . . . . 145 C4
Balassagyarmat H .112 A3
Balástya H . . . . . . 113 C4
Balatonalmádi H . .112 B2
Balatonboglár H . .111 C4
Balatonbozsok H . 112 C2
Balatonederics H .111 C4
Balatonfenyves H .111 C4
Balatonföldvár H . 112 C1
Balatonfüred H . . . 112 C1
Balatonfüzfö H . . . .112 B2
Balatonkenese H . .112 B2
Balatonkiliti H . . . . 112 C2
Balatonlelle H . . . . 111 C4
Balatonszabadi H . 112 C2
Balatonszemes H . 111 C4
Balatonszentgyörgy
  H . . . . . . . . . . 111 C4
Balazote E . . . . . . 158 C1
Balbeggie GB . . . . 35 B4
Balbigny F . . . . . . .117 B4
Balboa E . . . . . . . 141 B4
Balbriggan IRL . . . 30 A2
Balchik BG . . . . . . 17 D8
Balçova TR . . . . . . 188 B2
Baldock GB . . . . . . 44 B3
Bale HR . . . . . . . . 122 B2
Baleira E . . . . . . . 141 A3
Baleizao P . . . . . . 160 A2
Balen B . . . . . . . . 79 A5
Balerma E . . . . . . 164 C2
Balestrand N . . . . . 46 A3
Balestrate I . . . . . . 176 A2
Balfour GB . . . . . . 33 B4
Bälganet S . . . . . . 63 B3
Balıkesir TR . . . . . 186 C2
Balıklıçeşme TR . . 186 B2
Bälinge S . . . . . . . 51 C4
Balingen D . . . . . . 107 A3
Balingsta S . . . . . . 56 A3
Balintore GB . . . . . 32 D3
Balizac F . . . . . . . 128 B2
Balk NL . . . . . . . . 70 B2
Balkbrug NL . . . . . 71 B3
Balla IRL . . . . . . . 28 A2
Ballachulish GB . . 34 B2
Ballaghaderreen
  IRL . . . . . . . . . 26 C2
Ballancourt-sur-
  Essonne F . . . . . 90 C2
Ballantrae GB . . . . 36 A2
Ballao I . . . . . . . . 179 C3
Ballasalla GB . . . . 36 B2
Ballater GB . . . . . . 32 D3
Ballen DK . . . . . . . 59 C3
Ballenstedt D . . . . 82 A3
Ballerias E . . . . . . 145 C3
Balleroy F . . . . . . . 88 A3
Ballerup DK . . . . . 61 D2
Ballesteros de Calatrava
  E . . . . . . . . . . 157 B4
Ballı TR . . . . . . . . 186 B2
Ballina IRL . . . . . . 26 B1
Ballinalack IRL . . . 30 A1
Ballinamore IRL . . . 26 B3
Ballinascarty IRL . . 29 C3
Ballinasloe IRL . . . 28 A3
Ballindine IRL . . . . 28 A3
Balling DK . . . . . . 58 B1
Ballingarry
  Limerick IRL . . . .29 B3
  Tipperary IRL . . . 30 B1
Ballingeary IRL . . . 29 C2
Ballinhassig IRL . . 29 C3
Ballinluig GB . . . . . 35 B4
Ballino I . . . . . . . . 121 B3
Ballinrobe IRL . . . . 28 A2
Ballinskelligs IRL . 29 C1
Ballinspittle IRL . . . 29 C3
Ballintra IRL . . . . . 26 B2
Ballivor IRL . . . . . . 30 A2
Ballobar E . . . . . . 153 A4
Ballon
  F . . . . . . . . . . 102 A2
  IRL . . . . . . . . . .30 B2
Ballószög H . . . . . 112 C3
Ballsh AL . . . . . . . 182 C1
Ballstad N . . . . . . 194 B4
Ballum DK . . . . . . 64 A1
Ballybay IRL . . . . . 27 B4

Ballybofey IRL . . . . 26 B3
Ballybunion IRL . . . 29 B2
Ballycanew IRL . . . 30 B2
Ballycarry GB . . . . 27 B5
Ballycastle
  GB . . . . . . . . . . .27 A4
  IRL . . . . . . . . . . 26 B1
Ballyclare GB . . . . 27 B5
Ballyconneely IRL . 28 A1
Ballycotton IRL . . . 29 C3
Ballycroy IRL . . . . . 26 B1
Ballydehob IRL . . . 29 C2
Ballyferriter IRL . . . 29 B1
Ballygawley GB . . . 27 B3
Ballygowan GB . . . 27 B5
Ballyhaunis IRL . . . 28 A3
Ballyheige IRL . . . . 29 B2
Ballyjamesduff IRL . 27 C3
Ballylanders IRL . . 29 B3
Ballylynan IRL . . . . 30 B1
Ballymahon IRL . . . 28 A4
Ballymena GB . . . . 27 B4
Ballymoe IRL . . . . . 28 A3
Ballymoney GB . . . 27 A4
Ballymore IRL . . . . 28 A4
Ballymote IRL . . . . 26 B2
Ballynacorra IRL . . 29 C3
Ballynagore IRL . . . 30 A1
Ballynahinch GB . . 27 B5
Ballynure GB . . . . . 27 B5
Ballyragget IRL . . . 30 B1
Ballysadare IRL . . . 26 B2
Ballyshannon IRL . 26 B2
Ballyvaghan IRL . . 28 A2
Ballyvourney IRL . . 29 C2
Ballywalter GB . . . 27 B5
Balmaclellan GB . . 36 A2
Balmaseda E . . . . 143 A3
Balmazújváros H . .113 B5
Balme I . . . . . . . . .119 B4
Balmedie GB . . . . . 33 D4
Balmuccia I . . . . . .119 B5
Balna-paling GB . . 32 D2
Balneario de Panticosa
  E . . . . . . . . . . 145 B3
Balotaszállás H . . . 126 A1
Balsa P . . . . . . . . 148 A2
Balsareny E . . . . . 147 C2
Balsorano-Nuovo I 169 B3
Bålsta S . . . . . . . . 57 A3
Balsthal CH . . . . . 106 B2
Balta UA . . . . . . . . 17 A8
Baltanás E . . . . . . 142 C2
Baltar E . . . . . . . . 140 C3
Baltasound GB . . . 33 A6
Bälti MD . . . . . . . . 17 B7
Baltimore IRL . . . . . 29 C2
Baltinglass IRL . . . 30 B2
Baltiysk RUS . . . . . 69 A4
Baltów PL . . . . . . . 87 A5
Balugães P . . . . . . 148 A1
Bælum DK . . . . . . 58 B3
Balve D . . . . . . . . 81 A3
Balvi LV . . . . . . . . . 8 D5
Balvicar GB . . . . . . 34 B2
Balya TR . . . . . . . 186 C2
Balzo I . . . . . . . . . 136 C2
Bamberg D . . . . . . 94 B2
Bamburgh GB . . . . 37 A5
Banatska Palanka
  SRB . . . . . . . . 127 C3
Banatski Brestovac
  SRB . . . . . . . . 127 C2
Banatski Despotovac
  SRB . . . . . . . . 126 B2
Banatski Dvor SRB 126 B2
Banatski-Karlovac
  SRB . . . . . . . . 127 B3
Banatsko Arandjelovo
  SRB . . . . . . . . 126 A2
Banatsko-Novo Selo
  SRB . . . . . . . . 127 C2
Banaz TR . . . . . . . 187 D4
Banbridge GB . . . . 27 B4
Banbury GB . . . . . 44 A2
Banchory GB . . . . . 33 D4
Bande
  B . . . . . . . . . . . .79 B5
  E . . . . . . . . . . 140 B3
Bandholm DK . . . . 65 B4
Bandırma TR . . . . . 186 B2
Bandol F . . . . . . . 132 B1
Bandon IRL . . . . . . 29 C3
Bañeres E . . . . . . 159 C3
Banff GB . . . . . . . 33 D4
Bangor
  F . . . . . . . . . . 100 B2
  Down GB . . . . . 27 B5
  Gwynedd GB . . . 38 A2
  IRL . . . . . . . . . . 26 B1
Bangsund N . . . . . 199 A8
Banie PL . . . . . . . . 74 A3
Banja Koviljača
  SRB . . . . . . . . 127 C1
Banjaloka SLO . . . 123 B3
Banja Luka BIH . . . 124 C3
Banjani SRB . . . . . 127 C1
Banja Vručica BIH . 125 C3
Banka SK . . . . . . . 98 C1
Bankekind S . . . . . 56 B1
Bankend GB . . . . . 36 A3
Bankeryd S . . . . . . 62 A2
Bankfoot GB . . . . . 35 B4
Banloc RO . . . . . . 126 B3
Bannalec F . . . . . . 100 B2
Bannes F . . . . . . . 91 C3
Bannockburn GB . . 35 B4
Bañobárez E . . . . . 149 B3

Bañon E . . . . . . . 152 B2
Banon F . . . . . . . . 132 A1
Baños E . . . . . . . . 149 B4
Baños de Gigonza
  E . . . . . . . . . . 162 B2
Baños de la Encina
  E . . . . . . . . . . 157 B4
Baños de Molgas
  E . . . . . . . . . . 140 B3
Baños de Rio Tobia
  E . . . . . . . . . . 143 B4
Baños de Valdearados
  E . . . . . . . . . . 143 C3
Bánov CZ . . . . . . . 98 C1
Banova Jaruga HR 124 B2
Bánovce nad Bebravou
  SK . . . . . . . . . . 98 C2
Banovići BIH . . . . . 139 A4
Banovići Selo BIH . 139 A4
Bánréve H . . . . . . 99 C4
Bansin D . . . . . . . 66 C3
Banská Belá SK . . . 98 C2
Banská Bystrica SK 99 C3
Banská Štiavnica
  SK . . . . . . . . . . 98 C2
Bansko BG . . . . . . 183 B5
Banstead GB . . . . 44 B3
Banteer IRL . . . . . . 29 B3
Bantheville F . . . . . 91 B5
Bantry IRL . . . . . . . 29 C2
Bantzenheim F . . . 106 B2
Banyalbufar E . . . . 166 B2
Banyoles E . . . . . . 147 B3
Banyuls-sur-Mer F 146 B4
Bapaume F . . . . . . 90 A2
Bar
  MNE . . . . . . . . .16 D3
  UA . . . . . . . . . . .13 D7
Barabhas GB . . . . . 31 A2
Barači BIH . . . . . . 138 A2
Baracs H . . . . . . . 112 C2
Baracska H . . . . . . 112 B2
Barahona E . . . . . . 151 A5
Barajes de Melo E . 151 B5
Barakaldo E . . . . . 143 A4
Baralla E . . . . . . . 141 B3
Barañain E . . . . . . 144 B2
Baranda SRB . . . . 127 B2
Baranello I . . . . . . 170 B2
Baranów Sandomierski
  PL . . . . . . . . . . 87 B5
Baraqueville F . . . . 130 A1
Barasoain E . . . . . 144 B2
Barbacena P . . . . . 155 C3
Barbadás E . . . . . . 140 B3
Barbadillo E . . . . . 149 B4
Barbadillo de Herreros
  E . . . . . . . . . . 143 B3
Barbadillo del Mercado
  E . . . . . . . . . . 143 B3
Barbadillo del Pez
  E . . . . . . . . . . 143 B3
Barban HR . . . . . . 123 B3
Barbarano Vicento
  I . . . . . . . . . . . 121 B4
Barbariga HR . . . . 122 C2
Barbaros TR . . . . . 186 B2
Barbastro E . . . . . 145 B4
Barbate E . . . . . . . 162 B2
Barbâtre F . . . . . . .114 B1
Barbazan F . . . . . . 145 A4
Barbeitos E . . . . . . 141 A3
Barbentane F . . . . 131 B3
Barberino di Mugello
  I . . . . . . . . . . . 135 A4
Barbezieux-St Hilaire
  F . . . . . . . . . . 115 C3
Barbonne-Fayel F . 91 C3
Barbotan-les-Thermes
  F . . . . . . . . . . 128 C2
Barby D . . . . . . . . 73 C4
Bárcabo E . . . . . . 145 B4
Barca de Alva P . . . 149 A3
Barcarrota E . . . . . 155 C4
Barcellona-Pozzo di
  Gotto I . . . . . . . 177 A4
Barcelona E . . . . . 147 C3
Barcelonette F . . . . 132 A2
Barcelos P . . . . . . 148 A1
Bárcena del Monasterio
  E . . . . . . . . . . 141 A4
Barcena de Pie de
  Concha E . . . . . 142 A2
Barchfeld D . . . . . . 82 B2
Barcin PL . . . . . . . 76 B2
Barcino PL . . . . . . 68 A1
Bárcis I . . . . . . . . 122 A1
Barco P . . . . . . . . 148 B2
Barcones E . . . . . . 151 A5
Barcs H . . . . . . . . 124 B3
Barcus F . . . . . . . 144 A3
Bardejov SK . . . . . 12 D4
Bårdesø DK . . . . . 59 C3
Bardi I . . . . . . . . . 120 C2
Bardney GB . . . . . 40 B3
Bardo PL . . . . . . . 85 B4
Bardolino I . . . . . . 121 B3
Bardonécchia I . . . .118 B3
Bardoñovo SK . . . . .112 A2
Barèges F . . . . . . . 145 B4
Barenstein D . . . . . 83 B5
Barentin F . . . . . . . 89 A4
Barenton F . . . . . . 88 B3
Barevo BIH . . . . . . 138 A3
Barfleur F . . . . . . . 88 A2

Barga I . . . . . . . . . 134 A3
Bargas E . . . . . . . 151 C3
Barge I . . . . . . . . . 119 C4
Bargemon F . . . . . 132 B2
Barghe I . . . . . . . . 120 B3
Bargoed GB . . . . . 39 C3
Bargrennan GB . . . 36 A2
Bargteheide D . . . . 64 C3
Barham GB . . . . . . 45 B5
Bari I . . . . . . . . . . 173 A2
Barič Draga HR . . . 137 A4
Barilović HR . . . . . 123 B4
Bari Sardo I . . . . . 179 C3
Barisciano I . . . . . . 169 A3
Barjac F . . . . . . . . 131 A3
Barjols F . . . . . . . 132 B1
Barjon F . . . . . . . . 105 B3
Bårkåker N . . . . . . 54 A1
Barkald N . . . . . . . 199 D7
Barkowo
  Dolnośląskie PL . . .85 A4
  Pomorskie PL . . . . .68 B2
Bârlad RO . . . . . . 17 B7
Bar-le-Duc F . . . . . 91 C5
Barles F . . . . . . . . 132 A2
Barletta I . . . . . . . 171 B4
Barlinek PL . . . . . . 75 B4
Barmouth GB . . . . 38 B2
Barmstedt D . . . . . 64 C2
Barnard Castle GB . 37 B5
Barnarp S . . . . . . . 62 A2
Bärnau D . . . . . . . 95 B4
Bärnbach A . . . . . . 110 B2
Barneberg D . . . . . 73 B4
Barnenitz D . . . . . . 74 B1
Barnet GB . . . . . . 44 B3
Barnetby le Wold
  GB . . . . . . . . . . 40 B3
Barneveld NL . . . . 70 B2
Barneville-Carteret
  F . . . . . . . . . . . 88 A2
Barnoldswick GB . . 40 B1
Barnowko PL . . . . . 75 B3
Barnsley GB . . . . . 40 B2
Barnstädt D . . . . . . 83 A3
Barnstaple GB . . . . 42 A2
Barnstorf D . . . . . . 72 B1
Barntrup D . . . . . . 72 C2
Baron F . . . . . . . . 90 B2
Baronissi I . . . . . . 170 C2
Barqueiro P . . . . . . 154 B2
Barquinha P . . . . . 154 B2
Barr
  F . . . . . . . . . . . .93 C3
  GB . . . . . . . . . . .36 A2
Barra P . . . . . . . . 148 B1
Barracas E . . . . . . 159 A3
Barraco E . . . . . . . 150 B3
Barrado E . . . . . . . 150 B2
Barrafranca I . . . . . 177 B3
Barranco do Velho
  P . . . . . . . . . . . 160 B2
Barrancos P . . . . . 161 A3
Barrax E . . . . . . . . 158 B1
Barrbaar D . . . . . . 94 C2
Barre-des-Cevennes
  F . . . . . . . . . . 130 A2
Barreiro P . . . . . . . 154 C1
Barreiros E . . . . . . 141 A3
Barrême F . . . . . . . 132 B2
Barret-le-Bas F . . . 132 A1
Barrhead GB . . . . . 34 C3
Barrhill GB . . . . . . 36 A2
Barrio de Nuesra
  Señora E . . . . . 142 B1
Barrowford GB . . . 40 B1
Barrow-in-Furness
  GB . . . . . . . . . . 36 B3
Barrow upon Humber
  GB . . . . . . . . . . 40 B3
Barruecopardo E . 149 A3
Barruelo de Santullán
  E . . . . . . . . . . 142 B2
Barruera E . . . . . . 145 B4
Barry GB . . . . . . . 39 C3
Bårse DK . . . . . . . 65 A4
Barsinghausen D . . 72 B2
Barssel D . . . . . . . 71 A4
Bar-sur-Aube F . . . 104 A3
Bar-sur-Seine F . . . 104 A3
Barth D . . . . . . . . 66 B1
Bartholomä D . . . . 94 C1
Bartin TR . . . . . . . 187 A7
Barton upon Humber
  GB . . . . . . . . . . 40 B3
Barúmini I . . . . . . . 179 C2
Baruth D . . . . . . . . 74 B2
Barvaux B . . . . . . . 80 B1
Barver D . . . . . . . . 72 B1
Barwatd PL . . . . . . 99 B3
Barwice PL . . . . . . 68 B1
Barysaw BY . . . . . 13 A8
Barzana E . . . . . . . 141 A5
Bârzava RO . . . . . 16 B4
Bárzio I . . . . . . . . 120 B2
Bas E . . . . . . . . . . 147 B3
Bašaid SRB . . . . . 126 B2
Basaluzzo I . . . . . . 120 C1
Basarabeasca MD . 17 B8
Basauri E . . . . . . . 143 A4
Baschi I . . . . . . . . 168 A2
Baschurch GB . . . . 38 B4
Basconcillos del Tozo
  E . . . . . . . . . . 143 B3
Bascones de Ojeda
  E . . . . . . . . . . 142 B2
Basécles B . . . . . . 79 B3
Basel CH . . . . . . . 106 B2

Basélice I . . . . . . . 170 B2
Basildon GB . . . . . 45 B4
Basingstoke GB . . . 44 B2
Baška
  CZ . . . . . . . . . . .98 B2
  HR . . . . . . . . . . .123 C3
Baška Voda HR . . . 138 B2
Bäsksjö S . . . . . . . 200 B3
Başmakçı TR . . . . . 189 B5
Basovizza I . . . . . . 122 B2
Bassacutena I . . . . 178 A3
Bassano del Grappa
  I . . . . . . . . . . . 121 B4
Bassano Romano I 168 A2
Bassecourt CH . . . 106 B2
Bassella E . . . . . . 147 B2
Bassevuovdde N . . 193 D9
Bassou F . . . . . . . 104 B2
Bassoues F . . . . . . 128 C3
Bassum D . . . . . . . 72 B1
Båstad S . . . . . . . . 61 C2
Bastardo I . . . . . . 136 C1
Bastelica F . . . . . . 180 A2
Bastelicaccia F . . . 180 B1
Bastia
  F . . . . . . . . . . 180 A2
  I . . . . . . . . . . . 136 B1
Bastogne B . . . . . . 92 A1
Baston GB . . . . . . 40 C3
Bastuträsk S . . . . . 200 B6
Bata H . . . . . . . . . 125 A4
Batajnica SRB . . . . 127 C2
Batak BG . . . . . . . 183 B6
Batalha P . . . . . . . 154 B2
Bátaszék H . . . . . . 125 A4
Batea E . . . . . . . . 153 A4
Batelov CZ . . . . . . 97 B3
Bath GB . . . . . . . . 43 A4
Bathgate GB . . . . . 35 C4
Batida H . . . . . . . . 126 A2
Batignano I . . . . . . 135 C4
Batina HR . . . . . . . 125 B4
Bátka SK . . . . . . . 99 C4
Batković BIH . . . . . 125 C5
Batley GB . . . . . . . 40 B2
Batnfjordsøra N . . . 198 C4
Batočina SRB . . . . 127 C3
Bátonyterenye H . . .113 B3
Batrina HR . . . . . . 125 B3
Båtsfjord N . . . . . . 193 B13
Båtskärsnäs S . . . . 196 D6
Battaglia Terme I . . 121 B4
Bätterkinden CH . . 106 B2
Battice B . . . . . . . . 80 B1
Battipáglia I . . . . . . 170 C2
Battle GB . . . . . . . 45 C4
Battonya H . . . . . . 126 A3
Batuša SRB . . . . . 127 C3
Bátya H . . . . . . . . 112 C2
Bau I . . . . . . . . . . 179 C2
Baud F . . . . . . . . . 100 B2
Baudour B . . . . . . . 79 B3
Baugé F . . . . . . . . 102 B1
Baugy F . . . . . . . . 103 B4
Bauma CH . . . . . . 107 B3
Baume-les-Dames
  F . . . . . . . . . . 105 B5
Baumholder D . . . . 93 B3
Baunatal D . . . . . . 81 A5
Baunei I . . . . . . . . 178 B3
Bauska LV . . . . . . . 8 D4
Bautzen D . . . . . . . 84 A2
Bavanište SRB . . . 127 C2
Bavay F . . . . . . . . 79 B3
Bavilliers F . . . . . . 106 B1
Bavorov CZ . . . . . . 96 B2
Bawdsey GB . . . . . 45 A5
Bawinkel D . . . . . . 71 B4
Bawtry GB . . . . . . 40 B2
Bayat TR . . . . . . . 187 D5
Bayel F . . . . . . . . 105 A3
Bayeux F . . . . . . . 88 A3
Bayındır TR . . . . . . 188 A2
Bayon F . . . . . . . . 92 C2
Bayonne F . . . . . . 128 C1
Bayons F . . . . . . . 132 A2
Bayramiç TR . . . . . 186 C1
Bayreuth D . . . . . . 95 B3
Bayrischzell D . . . . 108 B3
Baza E . . . . . . . . . 164 B2
Bazas F . . . . . . . . 128 B2
Baziege F . . . . . . . 146 A2
Bazoches-les-
  Gallerandes F . . 103 A4
Bazoches-sur-Hoëne
  F . . . . . . . . . . . 89 B4
Bazzano I . . . . . . . 135 A4
Beaconsfield GB . . 44 B3
Beade E . . . . . . . . 140 B2
Beadnell GB . . . . . 37 A5
Beaminster GB . . . 43 B4
Bearsden GB . . . . . 34 C3
Beas E . . . . . . . . . 161 B3
Beasain E . . . . . . . 144 A1
Beas de Segura E . 164 A2
Beattock GB . . . . . 36 A3
Beaubery F . . . . . . .117 A4
Beaucaire F . . . . . 131 B3
Beaufort
  F . . . . . . . . . . 118 B3
  IRL . . . . . . . . . . 29 B2
Beaufort-en-Vallée
  F . . . . . . . . . . 102 B1
Beaugency F . . . . . 103 B3
Beaujeu
  Alpes-de-Haute-
  Provence F . . . . . 132 A2

Beaujeu continued
  Rhône F . . . . . . . .117 A4
Beaulac F . . . . . . . 128 B2
Beaulieu
  F . . . . . . . . . . 103 B4
  GB . . . . . . . . . . .44 C2
Beaulieu-sous-la-Roche
  F . . . . . . . . . . .114 B2
Beaulieu-sur-Dordogne
  F . . . . . . . . . . 129 B4
Beaulieu-sur-Mer F 133 B3
Beaulon F . . . . . . . 104 C2
Beauly GB . . . . . . 32 D2
Beaumaris GB . . . . 38 A2
Beaumesnil F . . . . 89 A4
Beaumetz-lès-Loges
  F . . . . . . . . . . . 78 B2
Beaumont
  B . . . . . . . . . . . .79 B4
  F . . . . . . . . . . 129 B3
Beaumont-de-Lomagne
  F . . . . . . . . . . 129 C3
Beaumont-du-Gâtinais
  F . . . . . . . . . . 103 A4
Beaumont-en-Argonne
  F . . . . . . . . . . . 91 B5
Beaumont-Hague F 88 A2
Beaumont-la-Ronce
  F . . . . . . . . . . 102 B2
Beaumont-le-Roger
  F . . . . . . . . . . . 89 A4
Beaumont-sur-Oise
  F . . . . . . . . . . . 90 B2
Beaumont-sur-Sarthe
  F . . . . . . . . . . 102 A2
Beaune F . . . . . . . 105 B3
Beaune-la-Rolande
  F . . . . . . . . . . 103 A4
Beaupréau F . . . . . 101 B5
Beauraing B . . . . . 91 A4
Beaurepaire F . . . . 117 B5
Beaurepaire-en-Bresse
  F . . . . . . . . . . 105 C4
Beaurières F . . . . . 132 A1
Beauvais F . . . . . . 90 B2
Beauval F . . . . . . . 90 A2
Beauville F . . . . . . 129 B3
Beauvoir-sur-Mer
  F . . . . . . . . . . .114 B1
Beauvoir-sur-Niort
  F . . . . . . . . . . .114 B3
Beba Veche RO . . . 126 A2
Bebertal D . . . . . . 73 B4
Bebington GB . . . . 38 A3
Bebra D . . . . . . . . 82 B1
Bebrina HR . . . . . . 125 B3
Beccles GB . . . . . . 45 A5
Becedas E . . . . . . 150 B2
Beceite E . . . . . . . 153 B4
Bečej SRB . . . . . . 126 B2
Becerreá E . . . . . . 141 B3
Becerril de Campos
  E . . . . . . . . . . 142 B2
Bécherel F . . . . . . 101 A4
Bechhofen D . . . . . 94 B2
Bechyně CZ . . . . . 96 B2
Becilla de Valderaduey
  E . . . . . . . . . . 142 B1
Beckfoot GB . . . . . 36 B3
Beckingham GB . . . 40 B3
Beckum D . . . . . . . 81 A4
Beco P . . . . . . . . . 154 B2
Bécon-les-Granits
  F . . . . . . . . . . 102 B1
Bečov nad Teplou
  CZ . . . . . . . . . . 83 B4
Becsehely H . . . . . .111 C3
Bedale GB . . . . . . 37 B5
Bedames E . . . . . . 143 A3
Bédar E . . . . . . . . 164 B3
Bédarieux F . . . . . 130 B2
Bédarrides F . . . . . 131 A3
Bedburg D . . . . . . 80 B2
Beddgelert GB . . . . 38 A2
Beddingestrand S . 66 A2
Bédée F . . . . . . . . 101 A4
Bedegkér H . . . . . . 112 C2
Beden TR . . . . . . . 189 C7
Bedford GB . . . . . . 44 A3
Będków PL . . . . . . 87 A3
Bedlington GB . . . . 37 A5
Bedlno PL . . . . . . . 77 B4
Bedmar E . . . . . . . 163 A4
Bédoin F . . . . . . . . 131 A4
Bedónia I . . . . . . . 134 A2
Bedretto CH . . . . . 107 C3
Bedsted DK . . . . . . 58 B1
Bedum NL . . . . . . . 71 A3
Bedwas GB . . . . . . 39 C3
Bedworth GB . . . . . 40 C2
Beekbergen NL . . . 70 B2
Beek en Donk NL . . 80 A1
Beelen D . . . . . . . 71 C5
Beelitz D . . . . . . . . 74 B1
Beer GB . . . . . . . . 43 B3
Beerfelde D . . . . . . 74 B3
Beerfelden D . . . . . 93 B4
Beernem B . . . . . . 78 A3
Beeskow D . . . . . . 74 B3
Beetsterzwaag NL . 70 A3
Beetzendorf D . . . . 73 B4
Beflelay CH . . . . . . 106 B2
Begaljica SRB . . . . 127 C2
Bégard F . . . . . . . 100 A2

Begejci SRB . . . . . 126 B2
Begijar E . . . . . . . 157 C4
Begijnendijk B. . . . 79 A4
Begndal N . . . . . . . 48 B1
Begues E . . . . . . . 147 C2
Beguildy GB . . . . . 39 B3
Begur E . . . . . . . . 147 C4
Beho B . . . . . . . . 80 B1
Behringen D . . . . . 82 A2
Beilen NL . . . . . . . 71 B3
Beilngries D. . . . . . 95 B3
Beine-Nauroy F. . . . 91 B4
Beinwil CH. . . . . . 106 B3
Beiseförth D . . . . . 82 A1
Beith GB . . . . . . . 34 C3
Beitostølen N . . . . 47 A5
Beiuş RO . . . . . . . 16 B5
Beja P. . . . . . . . . 160 A2
Béjar E . . . . . . . . 149 B4
Bekçiler TR . . . . . 189 C4
Békés H . . . . . . . 113 C5
Békéscsaba H . . . . 113 C5
Bekilli TR . . . . . . 189 A4
Bekkarfjord N . . . .193 B11
Bela SK . . . . . . . . 98 B2
Bélâbre F . . . . . . .115 B5
Bela Crkva SRB. . . 127 C3
Belalcázar E . . . . . 156 B2
Belánad Radbuzou
  CZ . . . . . . . . . . 95 B4
Belanovica SRB . . . 127 C2
Bélapátfalva H. . . . .113 A4
Bělápod Bezdězem
  CZ . . . . . . . . . . 84 B2
Belcaire F . . . . . . 146 B2
Bełchatów PL . . . . 86 A3
Belchite E . . . . . . 153 A3
Bělčice CZ. . . . . . 96 B1
Belcoo GB . . . . . . 26 B3
Belecke D . . . . . . 81 A4
Beled H . . . . . . . .111 B4
Belej HR. . . . . . . 123 C3
Beleño E . . . . . . . 142 A1
Bélesta F . . . . . . 146 B2
Belevi TR . . . . . . 188 A2
Belfast GB . . . . . . 27 B5
Belford GB . . . . . . 37 A5
Belfort F . . . . . . . 106 B1
Belgentier F . . . . . 132 B1
Belgern D. . . . . . . 83 A5
Belgioioso I . . . . . 120 B2
Belgodère F . . . . . 180 A2
Belgooly IRL . . . . . 29 C3
Belgrade = Beograd
  SRB . . . . . . . . . 127 C2
Belhade F . . . . . . 128 B2
Belica HR . . . . . . 124 A2
Beli Manastir HR . . 125 B4
Belin-Béliet F. . . . . 128 B2
Belinchón E . . . . . 151 B4
Belišće HR . . . . . . 125 B4
Bělkovice-Lašťany
  CZ . . . . . . . . . . 98 B1
Bella I . . . . . . . . 172 B1
Bellac F . . . . . . . .115 B5
Bellágio I . . . . . . . 120 B2
Bellananagh IRL . . . 27 C3
Bellano I . . . . . . . 120 A2
Bellária I . . . . . . . 136 A1
Bellavary IRL . . . . . 26 C1
Belleau F . . . . . . . 90 B3
Belleek GB . . . . . . 26 B2
Bellegarde
  Gard F . . . . . . . .131 B3
  Loiret F . . . . . . .103 B4
Bellegarde-en-Diois
  F. . . . . . . . . . . 132 A1
Bellegarde-en-Marche
  F. . . . . . . . . . . .116 B2
Bellegarde-sur-Valserine
  F. . . . . . . . . . . .118 A2
Belle-Isle-en-Terre
  F. . . . . . . . . . . 100 A2
Bellême F. . . . . . . 89 B4
Bellenaves F. . . . . .116 A3
Bellentre F . . . . . . .118 B3
Bellevaux F . . . . . .118 A3
Bellevesvre F . . . . 105 C4
Belleville F . . . . . . .117 A4
Belleville-sur-Vie F 114 B2
Bellevue-la-Montagne
  F. . . . . . . . . . . .117 B3
Belley F . . . . . . . .118 B2
Bellheim D. . . . . . 93 B4
Bellinge DK . . . . . 59 C3
Bellingham GB . . . 37 A4
Bellinzago Novarese
  I . . . . . . . . . . . 120 B1
Bellinzona CH . . . . 120 A2
Bell-lloc d'Urgell E 153 A4
Bello E . . . . . . . . 152 B2
Bellpuig d'Urgell E 147 C2
Bellreguart E . . . . . 159 C3
Bellsbank GB . . . . 36 A2
Belltall E . . . . . . . 147 C2
Belluno I . . . . . . . 121 A5
Bellver de Cerdanya
  E. . . . . . . . . . . 146 B2
Bellvis E. . . . . . . 147 C1
Bélmez E . . . . . . . 156 B2
Belmez de la Moraleda
  E. . . . . . . . . . . 163 A4
Belmont GB. . . . . 33 A6
Belmont-de-la-Loire
  F. . . . . . . . . . . .117 A4

Belmonte
  Asturias E . . . . . 141 A4
  Cuenca E. . . . . . 158 B1
Belmonte de San José
  E. . . . . . . . . . . 153 B3
Belmonte de Tajo
  E. . . . . . . . . . . 151 B4
Belmont-sur-Rance
  F. . . . . . . . . . . 130 B1
Belmullet IRL. . . . . 26 B1
Belobreşca RO . . . 127 C3
Beloeil B . . . . . . . 79 B3
Belogradchik BG. . . 16 D5
Belokorovichi UA . . 13 C8
Belorado E. . . . . . 143 B3
Belotič SRB . . . . . 127 C1
Bělotin CZ. . . . . . 98 B1
Belovo BG . . . . . . 183 A6
Belozersk RUS . . . 9 C10
Belp CH . . . . . . . 106 C2
Belpasso I . . . . . . 177 B3
Belpech F . . . . . . 146 A2
Belper GB . . . . . . 40 B2
Belsay GB . . . . . . 37 A5
Belsk Duzy PL . . . 87 A4
Beltinci SLO . . . . .111 C3
Beltra IRL. . . . . . . 26 C1
Belturbet IRL . . . . . 27 B3
Beluša SK . . . . . . 98 B2
Belvedere Maríttimo
  I . . . . . . . . . . . 174 B1
Belver de Cinca E . 153 A4
Belver de los Montes
  E. . . . . . . . . . . 142 C1
Belvès F. . . . . . . 129 B3
Belvezet F . . . . . . 130 A2
Belvis de la Jara E 150 C3
Belvis de Monroy
  E. . . . . . . . . . . 150 C2
Belyy RUS . . . . . . 9 E8
Belz F . . . . . . . . 100 B2
Belżec PL. . . . . . . 13 C5
Belzig D . . . . . . . 73 B5
Bembibre E . . . . . 141 B4
Bembridge GB. . . . 44 C2
Bemmel NL . . . . . 80 A1
Bemposta
  Bragança P . . . . 149 A3
  Santarém P . . . . 154 B2
Benabarre E . . . . . 145 B4
Benacazón E . . . . . 161 B3
Benahadux E. . . . . 164 C2
Benalmádena E. . . . 163 B3
Benalúa de Guadix
  E. . . . . . . . . . . 164 B1
Benalúa de las Villas
  E. . . . . . . . . . . 163 A4
Benalup E . . . . . . 162 B2
Benamargosa E . . . 163 B3
Benamaurel E . . . . 164 B2
Benameji E . . . . . . 163 A3
Benamocarra E. . . . 163 B3
Benaocaz E . . . . . 162 B2
Benaoján E . . . . . . 162 B2
Benarrabá E . . . . . 162 B2
Benasque E . . . . . 145 B4
Benátky nad Jizerou
  CZ . . . . . . . . . . 84 B2
Benavente
  E. . . . . . . . . . . 142 B1
  P . . . . . . . . . . 154 C2
Benavides de Örbigo
  E. . . . . . . . . . . 141 B5
Benavila P . . . . . . 154 B2
Bendorf D . . . . . . 81 B3
Benedikt SLO . . . . 110 C2
Benejama E . . . . . 159 C3
Benejúzar E. . . . . . 165 A4
Benešov CZ. . . . . 96 B2
Bénestroff F . . . . . 92 C2
Benet F . . . . . . . .114 B3
Bene Vagienna I . . 133 A3
Bénévent-l'Abbaye
  F. . . . . . . . . . . .116 A1
Benevento I . . . . . 170 B2
Benfeld F . . . . . . . 93 C3
Benfica P . . . . . . 154 B2
Bengtsfors S . . . . 54 A3
Bengtsheden S . . . 50 B2
Beničanci HR . . . . 125 B4
Benicarló E . . . . . 153 B4
Benicássim E . . . . 153 B4
Benidorm E . . . . . 159 C3
Benifaió E . . . . . . 159 B3
Beniganim E . . . . . 159 C3
Benington GB . . . . 41 B4
Benisa E . . . . . . . 159 C4
Benkovac HR . . . . 137 A4
Benllech GB . . . . . 38 A2
Benneckenstein D . 82 A2
Bénodet F . . . . . . 100 B1
Benquerencia de la
  Serena E . . . . . . 156 B2
Bensafrim P. . . . . . 160 B1
Bensbyn S. . . . . . 196 D5
Bensdorf D . . . . . . 73 B5
Benshausen D. . . . 82 B2
Bensheim D . . . . . 93 B4
Bentley GB . . . . . . 44 B3
Bentwisch D . . . . . 65 B5
Beočin SRB . . . . . 126 B1
Beograd = Belgrade
  SRB . . . . . . . . . 127 C2
Beragh GB . . . . . . 27 B3
Beranga E . . . . . . 143 A3
Berat AL. . . . . . . 182 C1

Bérat F . . . . . . . . 146 A2
Beratzhausen D . . . 95 B3
Bérbaltavár H . . . .111 B3
Berbegal E. . . . . . 145 C3
Berbenno di Valtellina
  I . . . . . . . . . . . 120 A2
Berberana E . . . . . 143 B3
Bercedo E . . . . . . 143 A3
Bercel H . . . . . . . .112 B3
Bercenay-le-Hayer
  F . . . . . . . . . . . 91 C3
Berceto I . . . . . . . 134 A2
Berchem B. . . . . . 79 B3
Berchidda I . . . . . . 178 B3
Berching D . . . . . . 95 B3
Berchtesgaden D . 109 B4
Bérchules E . . . . . 163 B4
Bercianos de Aliste
  E. . . . . . . . . . . 149 A3
Berck F . . . . . . . . 78 B1
Berclaire d'Urgell
  E. . . . . . . . . . . 147 C1
Berdoias E. . . . . . 140 A1
Berducedo E . . . . . 141 A4
Berdún E . . . . . . . 144 B3
Berdychiv UA . . . . 13 D8
Bere Alston GB . . . 42 B2
Bereguardo I . . . . . 120 B2
Berehommen N. . . . 53 A3
Berehove UA. . . . . 16 A5
Berek BIH. . . . . . . 124 B3
Beremend H . . . . . 125 B4
Bere Regis GB . . . 43 B4
Berestechko UA . . . 13 C6
Berettyóújfalu H . . .113 B5
Berezhany UA . . . . 13 D6
Berezivka UA. . . . . 17 B9
Berezna UA . . . . . 13 C9
Berg
  D . . . . . . . . . . . 95 B3
  N . . . . . . . . . . 195 E3
  S . . . . . . . . . . . 56 B2
Berga
  Sachsen-Anhalt D . 82 A3
  Thüringen D. . . . . 83 B4
  E . . . . . . . . . . . 147 B2
  S . . . . . . . . . . . 62 A4
Bergama TR. . . . . 186 C2
Bérgamo I . . . . . . 120 B2
Bergara E . . . . . . 143 A4
Bergby S . . . . . . . 51 B4
Berge
  Brandenburg D . . . 74 B1
  Niedersachsen D. . 71 B4
  Telemark N . . . . . 53 A4
  Telemark N . . . . . 53 A4
Bergeforsen S . . . 200 D3
Bergen
  Mecklenburg-
    Vorpommern D. . . 66 B2
  Niedersachsen D. . 72 B2
  Niedersachsen D. . 73 B3
  N . . . . . . . . . . . 46 B2
  NL . . . . . . . . . . 70 B1
Bergen op Zoom NL 79 A4
Bergerac F . . . . . . 129 B3
Bergères-lés-Vertus
  F. . . . . . . . . . . . 91 C4
Bergeyk NL . . . . . 79 A5
Berghausen D . . . . 93 C4
Bergheim D . . . . . 80 B2
Berghem S . . . . . . 60 B2
Berg im Gau D. . . . 95 C3
Bergisch Gladbach
  D . . . . . . . . . . . 80 B3
Bergkamen D . . . . 81 A3
Bergkvara S. . . . . 63 B4
Berglern D . . . . . . 95 C3
Bergnäset S. . . . . 196 D5
Bergneustadt D. . . . 81 A3
Bergsäng S . . . . . 49 B5
Bergshamra S . . . . 57 A4
Bergsjö S. . . . . . . 200 E3
Bergs slussar S. . . 56 B1
Bergtheim D . . . . . 94 B2
Bergues F . . . . . . 78 B2
Bergum NL. . . . . . 70 A2
Bergün Bravuogn
  CH . . . . . . . . . . 107 C4
Bergwitz D . . . . . . 83 A4
Berhida H. . . . . . . .112 B2
Beringel P . . . . . . 160 A2
Beringen B. . . . . . 79 A5
Berja E . . . . . . . . 164 C2
Berkåk N . . . . . . . 199 C7
Berkeley GB . . . . . 43 A4
Berkenthin D . . . . . 65 C3
Berkheim D . . . . . 107 A5
Berkhof D . . . . . . 72 B2
Berkovići BIH . . . . 139 B4
Berkovitsa BG. . . . 17 D5
Berlanga E . . . . . . 156 B2
Berlanga de Duero
  E. . . . . . . . . . . 151 A5
Berlevåg N . . . . . 193 B13
Berlikum NL. . . . . 70 A2
Berlin D . . . . . . . 74 B2
Berlstedt D . . . . . . 82 A3
Bermeo E . . . . . . 143 A4
Bermillo de Sayago
  E. . . . . . . . . . . 149 A3
Bernartice
  Jihočeský CZ. . . . 96 B2

Bernartice continued
  Vychodočeský CZ . 85 B3
Bernau
  Baden-Württemberg
    D. . . . . . . . . . 106 B3
  Bayern D . . . . . . 109 B3
  Brandenburg D . . . 74 B2
Bernaville F . . . . . 90 A2
Bernay F . . . . . . . 89 A4
Bernburg D . . . . . 83 A3
Berndorf A . . . . . . .111 B3
Berne D . . . . . . . . 72 A1
Bernecebaráti H . . .112 A2
Bernhardsthal A . . . 97 C4
Bernkastel-Kues D . 92 B3
Bernolakovo SK . . .111 A4
Bernsdorf D . . . . . 84 A2
Bernstadt D . . . . . 84 A2
Bernstein A . . . . . .111 B3
Bernués E . . . . . . 145 B3
Beromünster CH . . 106 B3
Beroun CZ. . . . . . 96 B2
Berovo MK. . . . . . 182 B4
Berre-l'Etang F . . . 131 B4
Berriedale GB . . . . 32 C3
Berriew GB . . . . . . 39 B3
Berrocal E . . . . . . 161 B3
Bersenbrück D . . . 71 B4
Bershad' UA . . . . . 13 D8
Bertamiráns E . . . . 140 B2
Berthåga S . . . . . . 51 C4
Berthelming F . . . . 92 C2
Bertincourt F . . . . . 90 A2
Bertinoro I . . . . . . 135 A5
Bertogne B . . . . . . 92 A1
Bertrix B . . . . . . . 91 B5
Berufjörður IS . . . 191 C11
Berville-sur-Mer F. . 89 A4
Berwick-upon-Tweed
  GB . . . . . . . . . . 37 A4
Berzasca RO . . . . 16 C4
Berzence H . . . . . 124 A3
Berzocana E . . . . . 156 A2
Besalú E . . . . . . . 147 B3
Besançon F . . . . . 105 B5
Besenfeld D . . . . . 93 C4
Besenyötelek H . . . .113 B4
Besenyszög H. . . . .113 B4
Beshenkovichi BY. . 13 A8
Besigheim D . . . . . 93 C5
Běšiny CZ. . . . . . 96 B1
Beška SRB. . . . . . 126 B2
Beşkonak TR. . . . . 189 B6
Besle F. . . . . . . . 101 B4
Besnyö H. . . . . . . .112 B2
Bessais-le-Fromental
  F. . . . . . . . . . . 103 C4
Bessan F . . . . . . . 130 B2
Besse-en-Chandesse
  F. . . . . . . . . . . .116 B2
Bessèges F . . . . . 131 A3
Bessé-sur-Braye F 102 B2
Bessines-sur-Gartempe
  F. . . . . . . . . . . .115 B5
Best NL . . . . . . . . 79 A5
Bestorp S. . . . . . . 56 B1
Betanzos E . . . . . 140 A2
Betelu E . . . . . . . 144 A2
Bétera E . . . . . . . 159 B3
Beteta E. . . . . . . 152 B1
Béthenville F . . . . . 91 B4
Bethesda GB . . . . 38 A2
Béthune F . . . . . . 78 B2
Beton-Bazoches F . 90 C3
Bettembourg L . . . 92 B2
Betterdorf L. . . . . . 92 B2
Bettna S. . . . . . . 56 B2
Béttola I . . . . . . . 120 C2
Bettona I . . . . . . . 136 B1
Bettyhill GB . . . . . 32 C2
Betws-y-Coed GB . 38 A3
Betxi E . . . . . . . . 159 B3
Betz F . . . . . . . . 90 B2
Betzdorf D . . . . . . 81 B3
Beuil F . . . . . . . . 132 A2
Beulah GB . . . . . . 39 B3
Beuzeville F . . . . . 89 A4
Bevagna I. . . . . . . 136 C1
Bevens-bruk S . . . 56 A1
Beveren B . . . . . . 79 A4
Beverley GB . . . . . 40 B3
Bevern D . . . . . . . 81 A5
Beverstedt D . . . . 72 A1
Beverungen D . . . . 81 A5
Beverwijk NL. . . . . 70 B1
Bex CH . . . . . . . .119 A4
Bexhill GB . . . . . . 45 C4
Beyazköy TR . . . . 186 A2
Beychevelle F . . . . 128 A2
Beydağ TR. . . . . . 188 A3
Beyeğaç TR. . . . . 188 B3
Beykoz TR. . . . . . 186 A4
Beynat F . . . . . . . 129 A4
Beyoğlu TR. . . . . . 186 A4
Beypazarı TR . . . . 187 B6
Beyşehir TR. . . . . 189 B6
Bezas E . . . . . . . 152 B2
Bezau A . . . . . . . 107 B4
Bèze F . . . . . . . . 105 B4
Bezenet F. . . . . . .116 A2
Bezhetsk RUS . . . 9 D10
Bilje HR . . . . . . . 125 B4
Béziers F . . . . . . 130 B2
Bezzecca I . . . . . . 121 B3
Biadki PL. . . . . . . 85 A5
Biała
  Łódzkie PL. . . . . 77 C4
  Opolskie PL. . . . . 85 B5

Białaczów PL. . . . . 87 A4
Biała Podlaska PL. . 13 B5
Biała Rawska PL. . . 87 A4
Biale Błota PL . . . . 76 A2
Białobłoty PL. . . . . 76 B2
Białobrzegi PL. . . . 87 A4
Białogard PL . . . . . 67 C4
Bialośliwie PL. . . . . 76 A2
Białowąs PL. . . . . . 68 B1
Biały Bór PL. . . . . 68 B1
Białystok PL . . . . . 13 B5
Biancavilla I . . . . . 177 B3
Bianco I . . . . . . . 175 C2
Biandrate I . . . . . . 119 B5
Biar E. . . . . . . . . 159 C3
Biarritz F . . . . . . . 144 A2
Bias F. . . . . . . . . 128 B1
Biasca CH . . . . . . 120 A1
Biatorbágy H . . . . .112 B2
Bibbiena I . . . . . . 135 B4
Bibbona I . . . . . . . 134 B3
Biberach
  Baden-Württemberg
    D. . . . . . . . . . 93 C4
  Baden-Württemberg
    D. . . . . . . . . . 107 A4
Biograd na Moru
  HR . . . . . . . . . . 137 B4
Bibione I . . . . . . . 122 B2
Biblis D . . . . . . . . 93 B4
Bibury GB . . . . . . 44 B2
Bicaj AL . . . . . . . 182 B2
Biccari I . . . . . . . 171 B3
Bicester GB . . . . . 44 B2
Bichl D . . . . . . . . 108 B2
Bichlbach A . . . . . 108 B1
Bicorp E . . . . . . . 159 B3
Bicos E. . . . . . . . 160 B1
Bicske H . . . . . . . .112 B2
Bidache F . . . . . . 128 C1
Bidart F . . . . . . . 144 A2
Biddinghuizen NL . . 70 B2
Biddulph GB . . . . . 40 B1
Bideford GB. . . . . 42 A2
Bidford-on-Avon
  GB . . . . . . . . . . 44 A2
Bidjovagge N. . . . 192 C6
Bie S. . . . . . . . . 56 A2
Bieber D. . . . . . . 81 B5
Biebersdorf D . . . . 74 C2
Biedenkopf D . . . . 81 B4
Biel
  CH . . . . . . . . . . 106 B2
  E . . . . . . . . . . . 144 B3
Bielany Wrocławskie
  PL. . . . . . . . . . . 85 A4
Bielawa PL . . . . . . 85 B4
Bielawy PL. . . . . . 77 B4
Bielefeld D . . . . . . 72 B1
Biella I. . . . . . . . .119 B5
Bielsk PL . . . . . . . 77 B4
Bielsko-Biała PL . . 99 B3
Bielsk Podlaski PL . 13 B5
Bienenbuttel D . . . 72 A3
Bieniow PL . . . . . . 84 A3
Bienservida E . . . . 158 C1
Bienvenida E . . . . 156 B1
Bierdzany PL. . . . . 86 B2
Bierné F . . . . . . . 102 B1
Biersted DK . . . . . 58 A2
Bierun PL. . . . . . . 86 B3
Bierutów PL. . . . . . 85 A5
Bierwart B . . . . . . 79 B5
Bierzwina PL . . . . . 75 A4
Bierzwnik PL . . . . . 75 A4
Biescas E . . . . . . 145 B3
Biesenthal D . . . . . 74 B2
Biesiekierz PL . . . . 67 B5
Bietigheim-Bissingen
  D . . . . . . . . . . . 93 C5
Bièvre B. . . . . . . 91 B5
Bieżuń PL. . . . . . . 77 B4
Biga TR. . . . . . . . 186 B2
Bigadiç TR. . . . . . 186 C3
Biganos F . . . . . . 128 B2
Bigas P. . . . . . . . 148 B2
Bigastro E . . . . . . 165 A4
Biggar GB . . . . . . 36 A3
Biggin Hill GB . . . . 45 B4
Biggleswade GB . . 44 A3
Bignasco CH . . . . .119 A5
Biguglia F . . . . . . 180 A2
Bihać BIH. . . . . . . 124 C1
Biharnagybajom H .113 B5
Bijeljani BIH. . . . . 139 B4
Bijeljina BIH. . . . . 125 C5
Bijuesca E . . . . . . 152 A2
Bila Tserkva UA. . . 13 D9
Bilbao E . . . . . . . 143 A4
Bilbor RO . . . . . . 17 B6
Bilcza PL. . . . . . . 87 B4
Bildudalur IS . . . . 190 B2
Bileća BIH . . . . . . 139 C4
Bilecik TR . . . . . . 187 B4
Biled RO . . . . . . . 126 B2
Biłgoraj PL. . . . . . 12 C5
Bilhorod-Dnistrovskyy
  UA . . . . . . . . . . 17 B9
Bílina CZ . . . . . . . 84 B1
Bilisht AL. . . . . . . 182 C2
Bilje HR . . . . . . . 125 B4
Billdal S . . . . . . . 60 B1
Billdudalur IS . . . . 190 B2
Billerbeck D. . . . . 71 C4
Billericay GB. . . . . 45 B4
Billesholm S . . . . . 61 C2
Billingborough GB . 40 C3
Billinge S. . . . . . . 61 D3

Billingham GB . . . . 37 B5
Billinghay GB . . . . 41 B3
Billingsfors S . . . . 54 B3
Billingshurst GB . . 44 B3
Billom F. . . . . . . .116 B3
Billsta S . . . . . . . 200 C4
Billund DK. . . . . . 59 C2
Bilovec CZ. . . . . . 98 B2
Bilstein D. . . . . . . 81 A4
Bilthoven NL . . . . . 70 B2
Bilto N . . . . . . . . 192 C5
Bilzen B . . . . . . . 80 B1
Biňa SK. . . . . . . .112 B2
Binaced E . . . . . . 145 C4
Binasco I . . . . . . . 120 B2
Binbrook GB . . . . . 41 B3
Binche B . . . . . . . 79 B4
Bindlach D. . . . . . 95 B3
Bindslev DK. . . . . 58 A3
Binefar E . . . . . . . 145 C4
Bingen D . . . . . . . 93 B3
Bingham GB . . . . . 40 C3
Bingley GB . . . . . . 40 B2
Bingsjö S. . . . . . . 50 A2
Binic F . . . . . . . . 100 A3
Binz D . . . . . . . . 66 B2
Biograd na Moru
  HR . . . . . . . . . . 137 B4
Bionaz I . . . . . . . .119 B4
Bioska SRB . . . . . 127 D1
Birda RO . . . . . . . 126 B3
Birdlip GB . . . . . . 44 B1
Biri N . . . . . . . . . 48 B2
Birkeland N . . . . . 53 B4
Birkenfeld
  Baden-Württemberg
    D. . . . . . . . . . 93 C4
  Rheinland-Pfalz D . 92 B3
Birkenhead GB . . . 38 A3
Birkerød DK. . . . . 61 D2
Birkfeld A . . . . . . .110 B2
Birkirkara M. . . . . 175 C3
Birmingham GB . . . 40 C2
Birr IRL. . . . . . . . 28 A4
Birresborn D . . . . . 80 B2
Birstein D. . . . . . . 81 B5
Biržai LT. . . . . . . 8 D4
Birzebbugia M. . . . 175 C3
Bisáccia I. . . . . . . 172 A1
Bisacquino I . . . . . 176 B2
Bisbal de Falset E . 153 A4
Biscarosse F . . . . 128 B1
Biscarosse Plage
  F. . . . . . . . . . . 128 B1
Biscarrués E . . . . . 144 B3
Biscéglie I . . . . . . 171 B4
Bischheim F . . . . . 93 C3
Bischofsheim D . . . 82 B1
Bischofshofen A . . 109 B4
Bischofswerda D . . 84 A2
Bischofswiesen D . 109 B3
Bischofszell CH . . 107 B4
Bischwiller F . . . . 93 C3
Bisenti I . . . . . . . 169 A3
Bishop Auckland
  GB . . . . . . . . . . 37 B5
Bishop's Castle GB. 39 B4
Bishops Lydeard
  GB . . . . . . . . . . 43 A3
Bishop's Stortford
  GB . . . . . . . . . . 45 B4
Bishop's Waltham
  GB . . . . . . . . . . 44 C2
Bisignano I . . . . . . 174 B2
Bisingen D. . . . . . 93 C4
Biskupice-Oławskie
  PL. . . . . . . . . . . 85 A5
Biskupiec PL . . . . . 69 B4
Bismark D . . . . . . 73 B4
Bismo N. . . . . . . 198 D5
Bispgården S . . . . 200 C2
Bispingen D. . . . . 72 A2
Bissen L. . . . . . . 92 B2
Bissendorf D . . . . . 71 B5
Bisserup DK. . . . . 65 A4
Bistango I . . . . . . 119 C5
Bistarac Donje BIH 139 A4
Bistrica BIH . . . . . 124 C3
Bistrica ob Sotli
  SLO . . . . . . . . . 123 A4
Bistriţa RO. . . . . . 17 B6
Bitburg D . . . . . . . 92 B2
Bitche F . . . . . . . 93 B3
Bitetto I . . . . . . . 171 B4
Bitola MK. . . . . . . 182 B3
Bitonto I . . . . . . . 171 B4
Bitschwiller F . . . . 106 B2
Bitterfeld D . . . . . 83 A4
Bitti I . . . . . . . . . 178 B3
Biville-sur-Mer F . . 89 A5
Bivona I . . . . . . . 176 B2
Biwer L. . . . . . . . 92 B2
Bizeljsko SLO . . . . 123 A4
Bizovac HR . . . . . 125 B4
Bjåen N . . . . . . . 52 A3
Bjärnum S . . . . . . 61 C3
Bjärred S . . . . . . 61 D3
Bjästa S . . . . . . . 200 C4
Bjelland
  Vest-Agder N . . . 52 B3
  Vest-Agder N . . . 52 B3
Bjelovar HR . . . . . 124 B2
Bjerkreim N . . . . . 52 B2
Bjerkvik N . . . . . . 194 B8
Bjerreby DK. . . . . 65 B3
Bjerregrav DK . . . . 58 B2
Bjerringbro DK . . . 59 B2
Bjøberg N . . . . . . 47 B5

Bjøllånes N . . . . . 195 D5
Björbo S. . . . . . . . 50 B1
Bjordal N . . . . . . . . 46 A2
Björg IS . . . . . . . . 191 B8
Bjørkåsen N. . . . . . 194 B7
Björke
  *Gävleborg S.* . . . . .51 B4
  *Östergötland S.* . . . .56 B1
Bjørkelangen N . . . . 48 C3
Björketorp S . . . . . . 60 B2
Björkholmen S . . . . 196 C2
Björkliden S. . . . . . 194 B9
Björklinge S . . . . . . 51 B4
Björko S. . . . . . . . . 51 C6
Björkö S. . . . . . . . . 60 B1
Björköby S. . . . . . . 62 A2
Björkvik S . . . . . . . 56 B2
Bjørn N. . . . . . . . . 195 D3
Björna S. . . . . . . . 200 C4
Björneborg S. . . . . . 55 A5
Björnerod S. . . . . . 54 A2
Bjørnevatn N . . . . 193 C13
Björnlunda S. . . . . . 56 A3
Bjørnstad N . . . . 193 C14
Björsäter S . . . . . . 56 B2
Bjurberget S . . . . . 49 B4
Bjurholm S . . . . . 200 C5
Bjursås S. . . . . . . . 50 B2
Bjurtjärn S . . . . . . 55 A5
Bjuv S . . . . . . . . . 61 C2
Blachownia PL . . . . 86 B2
Blackburn GB . . . . 38 A4
Blackpool GB . . . . . 38 A3
Blackstad S. . . . . . 62 A4
Blackwater IRL . . . . 30 B2
Blackwaterfoot GB . 34 C2
Bladåker S. . . . . . . 51 B5
Blaenau Ffestiniog
  GB . . . . . . . . . . 38 B3
Blaenavon GB . . . . 39 C3
Blaengarw GB . . . . 39 C3
Blagaj
  BIH . . . . . . . .124 B2
  BIH . . . . . . . .139 B3
Blagdon GB . . . . . . 43 A4
Blagnac F . . . . . . . 129 C4
Blagoevgrad BG . . 183 A5
Blaichach D. . . . . . 107 B5
Blain F . . . . . . . . . 101 B4
Blainville-sur-l'Eau
  F. . . . . . . . . . . . 92 C2
Blair Atholl GB . . . . 35 B4
Blairgowrie GB . . . . 35 B4
Blajan F . . . . . . . . 145 A4
Blakeney GB . . . . . 39 C4
Blakstad N. . . . . . . 53 B4
Blåmont F . . . . . . . 92 C2
Blanca E . . . . . . . 165 A3
Blancos E . . . . . . 140 C3
Blandford Forum
  GB . . . . . . . . . . 43 B4
Blanes E . . . . . . . 147 C3
Blangy-sur-Bresle F 90 B1
Blankaholm S . . . . . 62 A4
Blankenberge B . . . 78 A3
Blankenburg D . . . . 82 A2
Blankenfelde D . . . . 74 B2
Blankenhain D. . . . . 82 B3
Blankenheim D . . . . 80 B2
Blanquefort F . . . . 128 B2
Blansko CZ . . . . . . 97 B4
Blanzac F. . . . . . . 115 C4
Blanzy F. . . . . . . . 104 C3
Blaricum NL. . . . . . 70 B2
Blarney IRL. . . . . . . 29 C3
Blascomillán E . . . 150 B2
Blascosancho E . . . 150 B3
Błaszki PL . . . . . . . 86 A2
Blatná CZ. . . . . . . . 96 B1
Blatné SK. . . . . . . 111 A4
Blatnice CZ. . . . . . . 98 C1
Blatnika BIH. . . . . . 139 A3
Blato HR . . . . . . . 138 C2
Blato na Cetini HR 138 B2
Blatten CH. . . . . . . 119 A4
Blattnicksele S . . . 195 E8
Blatzheim D. . . . . . 80 B2
Blaubeuren D . . . . . 94 C1
Blaufelden D . . . . . 94 B1
Blaustein D . . . . . . 94 C1
Blaydon GB . . . . . . 37 B5
Blaye F. . . . . . . . . 128 A2
Blaye-les-Mines F . 130 A1
Blázquez E . . . . . . 156 B2
Bleckede D . . . . . . 73 A3
Blecua E . . . . . . . 145 B3
Bled SLO . . . . . . . 123 A3
Bleiburg A . . . . . . 110 C1
Bleichenbach D. . . . 81 B5
Bleicherode D. . . . . 82 A2
Bleik N . . . . . . . . 194 A6
Bleikvassli N . . . . 195 E4
Bléneau F . . . . . . . 104 B1
Blentarp S . . . . . . 61 D3
Blera I . . . . . . . . . 168 A2
Blérancourt F . . . . . 90 B3
Bléré F . . . . . . . . . 102 B2
Blesle F . . . . . . . . 116 B3
Blessington IRL. . . . 30 A2
Blet F . . . . . . . . . 103 C4
Bletchley GB . . . . . 44 B3
Bletterans F. . . . . . 105 C4
Blidö S . . . . . . . . . 57 A4
Blidsberg S . . . . . . 60 B3
Blieskastel D. . . . . . 92 B3
Bligny-sur-Ouche
  F. . . . . . . . . . . . 104 B3
Blikstorp S. . . . . . . 55 B5
Blinisht AL. . . . . . . 182 B1
Blinja HR . . . . . . . 124 B2
Blizanówek PL. . . . . 76 C3
Bliżyn PL . . . . . . . 87 A4
Blois F . . . . . . . . . 103 B3
Blokhus DK . . . . . . 58 A2
Blokzijl NL . . . . . . . 70 B2
Blombacka S . . . . . 55 A4
Blomberg D . . . . . . 72 C2
Blomskog S . . . . . . 54 A3
Blomstermåla S . . . 62 B4
Blomvåg N. . . . . . . 46 B1
Blönduós IS. . . . . . 190 B5
Błonie PL. . . . . . . . 77 B5
Blonville-sur-Mer F . 89 A4
Blötberget S . . . . . 50 B2
Blovice CZ. . . . . . . 96 B1
Bloxham GB . . . . . 44 A2
Bludenz A. . . . . . . 107 B4
Bludov CZ. . . . . . . 97 B4
Blumberg D . . . . . . 107 B3
Blyberg S. . . . . . . . 49 A6
Blyth
  *Northumberland*
  GB . . . . . . . . .37 A5
  *Nottinghamshire*
  GB . . . . . . . . .40 B2
Blyth Bridge GB . . . 35 C4
Blythburgh GB . . . . 45 A5
Blythe Bridge GB . . 40 C1
Bø
  *Nordland N.* . . . . . .194 B5
  *Telemark N* . . . . . .53 A5
Boal E . . . . . . . . . 141 A4
Boan MNE . . . . . . 139 C5
Boario Terme I . . . . 120 B3
Boat of Garten GB . 32 D3
Boa Vista P . . . . . 154 B2
Boğazkale TR . . . . . 23 A8
Boğazlıyan TR . . . . 23 B8
Boba H . . . . . . . . .111 B4
Bobadilla
  *Logroño E* . . . . . .143 B4
  *Málaga E* . . . . . .163 A3
Bobadilla del Campo
  E. . . . . . . . . . . 150 A2
Bobadilla del Monte
  E. . . . . . . . . . . 151 B4
Bóbbio I . . . . . . . . 120 C2
Bóbbio Péllice I . . . 119 C4
Bobigny F . . . . . . . 90 C2
Bobingen D . . . . . . 94 C2
Böblingen D . . . . . . 93 C5
Bobolice PL . . . . . . 68 B1
Boboras S . . . . . . 140 B2
Boboshevo BG . . . 182 A4
Bobowa PL . . . . . . 99 B4
Bobrová CZ. . . . . . 97 B4
Bobrovitsa UA. . . . . 13 C9
Bobrowice PL . . . . . 75 C4
Bobrówko PL . . . . . 75 B4
Boca de Huérgano
  E. . . . . . . . . . . 142 B2
Bocairent E . . . . . 159 C3
Bočar SRB. . . . . . . 126 B2
Bocchigliero I . . . . 174 B2
Boceguillas E . . . . 151 A4
Bochnia PL . . . . . . 99 B4
Bocholt
  B. . . . . . . . . . .80 A1
  D. . . . . . . . . . .80 A2
Bochov CZ. . . . . . . 83 B5
Bochum D . . . . . . . 80 A3
Bockara S . . . . . . . 62 A4
Bockenem D . . . . . 72 B3
Bockfliess A. . . . . . 97 C4
Bockhorn D . . . . . . 71 A5
Bočna SLO . . . . . . 123 A3
Bocognano F. . . . . 180 A2
Boconád H. . . . . . .113 B4
Bőcs H. . . . . . . . .113 A4
Boczów PL. . . . . . . 75 B3
Boda S . . . . . . . . . 50 A2
Böda S. . . . . . . . . 62 A5
Boda
  *Stockholm S.* . . . . .51 B5
  *Värmland S* . . . . . .55 A4
  *Västernorrland S* . .200 D2
Bodafors S . . . . . . 62 A2
Boda Glasbruk S. . . 63 B3
Bodajk H . . . . . . . .112 B2
Boddam
  *Aberdeenshire*
  GB . . . . . . . . .33 D5
  *Shetland* GB . . . . .33 B5
Boddin D . . . . . . . . 73 A4
Bödefeld-Freiheit D 81 A4
Boden S . . . . . . . 196 D4
Bodenmais D. . . . . 95 B5
Bodenteich D . . . . . 73 B3
Bodenwerder D . . . . 72 C2
Bodiam GB . . . . . . 45 B4
Bodinnick GB . . . . . 42 B2
Bodio CH . . . . . . . 120 A1
Bodjani SRB . . . . . 125 B5
Bodmin GB . . . . . . 42 B2
Bodø N . . . . . . . . 194 C5
Bodonal de la Sierra
  E. . . . . . . . . . . 161 A3
Bodrum TR . . . . . . 188 B2
Bodstedt D . . . . . . 66 B1
Bodzanów PL. . . . . 77 B5
Bodzanowice PL. . . 86 B2
Bodzechów PL . . . . 87 B5
Bodzentyn PL . . . . . 87 B4
Boecillo E . . . . . . . 150 A3
Boëge F. . . . . . . . .118 A3
Boën F. . . . . . . . . .117 B3
Bogács H. . . . . . . .113 B4
Bogadmindszent H 125 B4
Bogajo E . . . . . . . 149 B3
Bogarra E . . . . . . . 158 C1
Bogarre E . . . . . . . 163 A4
Bogatić SRB. . . . . . 127 C1
Bogatynia PL. . . . . . 84 B2
Bogda RO . . . . . . 126 B3
Bogdaniec PL . . . . . 75 B4
Boge S. . . . . . . . . 57 C4
Bogen
  D. . . . . . . . . . . .95 C4
  *Nordland N.* . . . . . .194 B7
  *Nordland N.* . . . . .194 C6
  S. . . . . . . . . . .49 B4
Bogense DK . . . . . 59 C3
Bognanco Fonti I . .119 A5
Bognelv N . . . . . . 192 B6
Bognes N. . . . . . . 194 B7
Bogno CH . . . . . . 120 A2
Bognor Regis GB . . 44 C3
Bogoria C. . . . . . . . 87 B5
Bograngen S . . . . . 49 B4
Boguchwaly PL. . . . 69 B5
Bogumiłowice PL . . 86 A3
Boguslav UA . . . . . 13 D9
Boguszów-Gorce
  PL. . . . . . . . . . .85 B4
Bogyiszló H. . . . . . 112 C2
Bohain-en-Vermandois
  F. . . . . . . . . . . . 91 B3
Böheimkirchen A. . .110 A2
Bohinjska Bistrica
  SLO . . . . . . . . . 122 A2
Böhlen D . . . . . . . . 83 A4
Böhmenkirch D. . . . 94 C1
Bohmte D. . . . . . . . 71 B5
Böhönye H. . . . . . . 124 A3
Bohumin CZ . . . . . . 98 B2
Boiro E . . . . . . . . 140 B2
Bois-d'Amont F . . . 105 C5
Boisseron F. . . . . . 131 B3
Boitzenburg D . . . . 74 A2
Boizenburg D . . . . . 73 A3
Bojadła PL . . . . . . . 75 C4
Bojano I . . . . . . . . 170 B2
Bojanowo PL . . . . . 85 A4
Bojkovice CZ . . . . . 98 B1
Bojná SK . . . . . . . 98 C2
Bojnice SK. . . . . . . 98 C2
Boka SRB . . . . . . 126 B2
Böklund S . . . . . . . 64 B2
Bökönyi H . . . . . . .112 B2
Böksholm S . . . . . . 62 A2
Boksitogorsk RUS . . 9 C8
Bol HR . . . . . . . . 138 B2
Bolaños de Calatrava
  E. . . . . . . . . . . 157 B4
Bolayır TR . . . . . . 186 B1
Bolbec F . . . . . . . . 89 A4
Bölcske H . . . . . . . 112 C2
Bolderslev DK . . . . 64 B2
Boldog H. . . . . . . .112 B3
Boldva H . . . . . . . .113 A4
Bôle S . . . . . . . . 196 D4
Bolea E . . . . . . . . 145 A3
Bolekhiv UA. . . . . . 13 D5
Bolesławiec PL . . . . 84 A3
Boleszkowice PL. . . 74 B3
Bolewice PL. . . . . . 75 B5
Bólgheri I . . . . . . . 134 B3
Bolhrad UA . . . . . . 17 C8
Boliden S . . . . . . . 200 B6
Bolimów PL. . . . . . . 77 B5
Boliqueime P. . . . . 160 B1
Boljevci SRB. . . . . . 127 C2
Boljkovci SRB. . . . . 127 C2
Bolków PL. . . . . . . . 85 B4
Bollebygd S. . . . . . 60 B2
Bollène F. . . . . . . . 131 A3
Bólliga E . . . . . . . . 152 B1
Bollnäs S . . . . . . . 50 A3
Bollstabruk S . . . . 200 D3
Bollullos E . . . . . . 161 B3
Bollullos par del
  Condado E . . . . . 161 B3
Bologna I . . . . . . . 135 A4
Bologne F . . . . . . 105 A4
Bolognetta I. . . . . . 176 B2
Bolognola I . . . . . . 136 C2
Bologoye RUS. . . . . 9 D9
Bolótana I . . . . . . . 178 B2
Bolsena I . . . . . . . 168 A1
Bolshaya Vradiyevka
  UA . . . . . . . . . . 17 B9
Bolsover GB . . . . . 40 B2
Bolstad S . . . . . . . 54 B3
Bolsward NL . . . . . 70 A2
Boltaña E . . . . . . . 145 B4
Boltenhagen D . . . . 65 C4
Boltigen CH . . . . . 106 C2
Bolton GB . . . . . . . 38 A4
Bolu TR . . . . . . . . 187 B6
Bolungavík IS . . . . 190 A2
Bolvadin TR. . . . . . 187 D6
Bóly H . . . . . . . . . 125 B4
Bolzaneto I . . . . . . 133 A4
Bolzano I . . . . . . . 108 C2
Bomba I . . . . . . . . 169 A4
Bombarral P . . . . . 154 B1
Bömenzien D. . . . . 73 B4
Bomlitz D . . . . . . . 72 B2
Bømlo N. . . . . . . . . 52 A1
Bøn N. . . . . . . . . . 48 B3
Bona F . . . . . . . . . 104 B2
Bonaduz CH . . . . . 107 C4
Bonanza E . . . . . . 161 C3
Boñar E . . . . . . . . 142 B1
Bonarbridge GB . . . 32 D2
Bonárcado I. . . . . . 178 B2
Bonares E . . . . . . 161 B3
Bonäs S. . . . . . . . . 50 A1
Bonassola I . . . . . . 134 A2
Bonawe GB . . . . . . 34 B2
Bondal N . . . . . . . . 53 A4
Bondeno I . . . . . . . 121 C4
Bondorf D . . . . . . . 93 C4
Bondstorp S . . . . . 60 B3
Bon-Encontre F . . . 129 B3
Bo'ness GB . . . . . . 35 B4
Bonete E . . . . . . . 158 C2
Bonifacio F . . . . . . 180 B2
Bonigen CH. . . . . . 106 C2
Bonin PL . . . . . . . . 67 B5
Bonn D. . . . . . . . . 80 B3
Bonnánaro I. . . . . . 178 B2
Bonnåsjøen N . . . . 194 C6
Bonnat F . . . . . . . .116 A1
Bonndorf D . . . . . . 106 B3
Bonnétable F . . . . . 102 A2
Bonnétage F . . . . . 106 B1
Bonneuil-les-Eaux F 90 B2
Bonneuil-Matours
  F. . . . . . . . . . . .115 B4
Bonneval F . . . . . . 103 A3
Bonneval-sur-Arc
  F. . . . . . . . . . . .119 B4
Bonneville F. . . . . .118 A3
Bonnières-sur-Seine
  F. . . . . . . . . . . . 90 B1
Bonnieux F . . . . . . 131 B4
Bönnigheim D . . . . . 93 B5
Bönnigheim D . . . . . 93 B5
Bonnyrigg GB. . . . . 35 C4
Bonny-sur-Loire F 103 B4
Bono
  E. . . . . . . . . . . 145 B4
  I. . . . . . . . . . . .178 B3
Bonorva I . . . . . . . 178 B2
Bønsnes N. . . . . . . 48 B2
Bonyhád H . . . . . . 125 A4
Boom B . . . . . . . . 79 A4
Boos F . . . . . . . . . 89 A5
Boostedt D . . . . . . 64 B3
Bootle
  *Cumbria* GB. . . . . .36 B3
  *Merseyside* GB. . . . .38 A3
Bopfingen D . . . . . . 94 C2
Boppard D. . . . . . . 81 B3
Boqueixón E . . . . . 140 B2
Bor
  CZ. . . . . . . . . .95 B4
  S. . . . . . . . . . .62 A2
  SRB. . . . . . . . .16 C5
  TR. . . . . . . . . .23 C8
Boran-sur-Oise F . . 90 B2
Borås S . . . . . . . . . 60 B2
Borba P . . . . . . . . 155 C3
Borča SRB. . . . . . . 127 C2
Borci BIH . . . . . . . 139 B4
Borculo NL. . . . . . . 71 B3
Bordány H. . . . . . . 126 A1
Bordeaux F . . . . . . 128 B2
Bordeira P . . . . . . 160 B1
Bordesholm D . . . . 64 B3
Borðeyri IS . . . . . . 190 B4
Bordighera I . . . . . 133 B3
Bording DK . . . . . . 59 B2
Bordón E . . . . . . . 153 B3
Bore I . . . . . . . . . 120 C2
Borehamwood GB . . 44 B3
Borek Strzeliński PL 85 B5
Borek Wielkopolski
  PL. . . . . . . . . . .76 C2
Boreland GB . . . . . 36 A3
Borello I . . . . . . . . 135 A5
Borensberg S . . . . . 56 B1
Borgafjäll S . . . . . 199 A12
Borgarnes IS . . . . 190 C4
Borgentreich D. . . . 81 A5
Börger D . . . . . . . . 71 B4
Borger NL . . . . . . . 71 B3
Borggård S . . . . . . 56 B1
Borghamn S . . . . . 55 B5
Borghetto di Vara I 134 A2
Borghetto d'Arróscia
  I . . . . . . . . . . . 133 A3
Borghetto Santo Spirito
  I . . . . . . . . . . . 133 A4
Borgholm S . . . . . . 62 B4
Borghorst D . . . . . . 71 B4
Bórgia I . . . . . . . . 175 C2
Borgloon B . . . . . . 79 B5
Børglum DK . . . . . . 58 A2
Borgo F . . . . . . . . 180 A2
Borgo alla Collina I 135 B4
Borgo a Mozzano I 134 B3
Borgoforte I. . . . . . 121 B3
Borgofranco d'Ivrea
  I. . . . . . . . . . . .119 B4
Borgomanero I . . . .119 B5
Borgomasino I . . . .119 B4
Borgonovo Val Tidone
  I. . . . . . . . . . . . 120 B2
Borgo Pace I . . . . . 135 B5
Borgorose I . . . . . . 169 A3
Borgo San Dalmazzo
  I. . . . . . . . . . . .133 A3
Borgo San Lorenzo
  I. . . . . . . . . . . . 135 B4
Borgosésia I . . . . . .119 B5
Borgo Val di Taro I 134 A2
Borgo Valsugana I 121 A4
Borgo Vercelli I . . . .119 B5
Borgstena S . . . . . 60 B3
Borgue GB . . . . . . 36 B2
Borgund N . . . . . . 47 A4
Borgvik S . . . . . . . 55 A3
Borja E . . . . . . . . 144 C2
Bork D . . . . . . . . . 80 A3
Borken D . . . . . . . . 80 A2
Borkenes N . . . . . 194 B7
Børkop DK . . . . . . . 59 C2
Borkum D . . . . . . . 71 A3
Borlänge S. . . . . . . 50 B2
Borlu TR. . . . . . . . 186 D3
Bormes-les-Mimosas
  F. . . . . . . . . . . . 132 B2
Bórmio I. . . . . . . . 107 C5
Bormujos E . . . . . . 161 B3
Borna D . . . . . . . . 83 A4
Borne NL . . . . . . . 71 B3
Borne P . . . . . . . . 149 A2
Borne Sulinowo PL. 68 B1
Bornheim D . . . . . . 80 B2
Bornhöved D . . . . . 64 B3
Börnicke D . . . . . . 74 B1
Bornos E . . . . . . . 162 B2
Borobia E . . . . . . . 152 A2
Borodino RUS. . . . . 9 E9
Borohrádek CZ . . . . 85 B4
Boronów PL. . . . . . 86 B2
Bórore I . . . . . . . . 178 B2
Boroszów PL. . . . . . 86 B2
Borota H . . . . . . . 126 A1
Boroughbridge GB . 40 A2
Borovany CZ. . . . . . 96 C2
Borovichi RUS . . . . 9 C8
Borovnica SLO . . . 123 B3
Borovo HR . . . . . . 125 B4
Borovsk RUS. . . . . 9 E10
Borovy CZ . . . . . . . 96 B1
Borowa PL. . . . . . . 85 A5
Borox E . . . . . . . . 151 B4
Borrby S . . . . . . . . 66 A3
Borre
  DK. . . . . . . . . .65 B5
  N. . . . . . . . . . .54 A1
Borredá E . . . . . . . 147 B2
Borrenes E . . . . . . 141 B4
Borriol E . . . . . . . . 159 A3
Borris
  DK. . . . . . . . . .59 C1
  IRL . . . . . . . . .30 B2
Borris-in-Ossory
  IRL . . . . . . . . .28 B4
Borrisokane IRL . . . 28 B3
Borrisoleigh IRL . . . 28 B4
Borrowdale GB . . . . 36 B3
Børrud N . . . . . . . . 49 C4
Borşa RO . . . . . . . 17 B6
Borsdorf D . . . . . . . 83 A4
Børselv N. . . . . . . 193 B9
Borsfa H. . . . . . . . .111 C3
Borský Mikuláš SK . 98 C1
Borsodivánka H. . . .113 B4
Borsodnádasd H. . .113 A4
Börte N. . . . . . . . . 53 A3
Borth GB . . . . . . . . 39 B2
Bort-les-Orgues F . .116 B2
Börtnan S . . . . . . 199 C10
Børtnes N . . . . . . . 47 B6
Boruja Kościelne
  PL. . . . . . . . . . .75 B5
Borup DK . . . . . . . 61 D1
Boryslav UA . . . . . . 13 D5
Boryspil UA. . . . . . . 13 C9
Boryszyn PL . . . . . . 75 B4
Borzęciczki PL. . . . . 85 A5
Borzęcin PL. . . . . . . 77 B5
Borzonasca I . . . . . 134 A2
Borzyszkowy PL. . . . 68 A2
Borzytuchom PL. . . . 68 A2
Bosa I . . . . . . . . . 178 B2
Bošáca SK . . . . . . 98 C1
Bosanci HR . . . . . . 123 B4
Bosanska Dubica
  BIH . . . . . . . . . 124 B2
Bosanska Gradiška
  BIH . . . . . . . . . 124 B3
Bosanska Kostajnica
  BIH . . . . . . . . . 124 B2
Bosanska Krupa
  BIH . . . . . . . . . 124 C2
Bosanski Brod BIH 125 B3
Bosanski Novi BIH 124 B2
Bosanski Petrovac
  BIH . . . . . . . . . 124 C2
Bosanski Šamac
  BIH . . . . . . . . . 125 B4
Bosansko Grahovo
  BIH . . . . . . . . . 138 A2
Bošány SK. . . . . . . 98 C2
Bösárkány H . . . . . .111 B4
Bósca H . . . . . . . . 112 C3
Boscastle GB . . . . . 42 B2
Bosco I. . . . . . . . . 120 C1
Bosco Chiesanuova
  I. . . . . . . . . . . .121 B4
Bösdorf D . . . . . . . 65 B3
Bösel D . . . . . . . . 71 A4
Bosham GB. . . . . . 44 C3
Bösingfeld D . . . . . 72 B2
Bosjön S . . . . . . . . 49 C5
Boskoop NL. . . . . . 70 B1
Boskovice CZ . . . . . 97 B4
Bošnjaci HR . . . . . 125 B4
Bošnjane SRB. . . . . 127 D3
Bossast E . . . . . . . 145 B4
Bossolasco I . . . . . 133 A4
Boštanj SLO . . . . . 123 A4
Boston GB. . . . . . . 41 C3
Bostrak N. . . . . . . . 53 A4
Böszénfa H . . . . . . 125 A3
Bot E . . . . . . . . . . 153 A4
Botajica BIH. . . . . . 125 C4
Bøte By DK. . . . . . . 65 B4
Bothel GB . . . . . . . 36 B3
Boticas P . . . . . . . 148 A2
Botilsäter S . . . . . . 55 A4
Botngård N . . . . . . 198 B6
Botoš SRB. . . . . . . 126 B2
Botoşani RO . . . . . 17 B7
Botricello I. . . . . . . 175 C2
Botsmark S . . . . . . 200 B6
Bottendorf D . . . . . 81 A4
Bottesford GB . . . . 40 C3
Bottnaryd S . . . . . . 60 B3
Bottrop D. . . . . . . . 80 A2
Botunje SRB . . . . . 127 C3
Bötzingen D . . . . . 106 A2
Bouaye F . . . . . . . 101 B4
Bouça P . . . . . . . . 149 A2
Boucau F . . . . . . . 128 C1
Bouchain F . . . . . . 78 B3
Bouchoir F . . . . . . 90 B2
Boudreville F . . . . . 105 B3
Boudry CH . . . . . . 106 C1
Bouesse F . . . . . . 103 C3
Bouguenais F . . . . 101 B4
Bouhy F . . . . . . . . 104 B2
Bouillargues F . . . . 131 B3
Bouillon B . . . . . . . 91 B5
Bouilly F . . . . . . . . 104 A2
Bouin F . . . . . . . . .114 B2
Boulay-Moselle F . . 92 B2
Boulazac F . . . . . . 129 A3
Boule-d'Amont F . . 146 B3
Bouligny F . . . . . . . 92 B1
Boulogne-sur-Gesse
  F. . . . . . . . . . . .145 A4
Boulogne-sur-Mer F 78 B1
Bouloire F . . . . . . . 102 B2
Bouquemaison F . . 78 B2
Bourbon-Lancy F . 104 C2
Bourbon-l'Archambault
  F. . . . . . . . . . . . 104 C2
Bourbonne-les-Bains
  F. . . . . . . . . . . . 105 B4
Bourbourg F . . . . . 78 B2
Bourbriac F . . . . . . 100 A2
Bourcefranc-le-Chapus
  F. . . . . . . . . . . .114 C2
Bourdeaux F . . . . . 131 A4
Bouresse F . . . . . . 115 B4
Bourg F . . . . . . . . 128 A2
Bourg-Achard F . . . 89 A4
Bourganeuf F . . . . .116 B1
Bourg-Argental F . .117 B4
Bourg-de-Péage F .117 B5
Bourg-de-Thizy F . .117 A4
Bourg-de-Visa F . . 129 B3
Bourg-en-Bresse F 118 A2
Bourges F . . . . . . 103 B4
Bourg-et-Comin F . 91 B3
Bourg-Lastic F . . . .116 B2
Bourg-Madame F . 146 B2
Bourgneuf-en-Retz
  F. . . . . . . . . . . .114 A2
Bourgogne F . . . . . 91 B4
Bourgoin-Jallieu F .118 B2
Bourg-St Andéol F 131 A3
Bourg-St Maurice
  F. . . . . . . . . . . .119 B3
Bourgtheroulde F . . 89 A4
Bourgueil F . . . . . . 102 B2
Bourmont F . . . . . . 105 A4
Bourne GB . . . . . . 40 C3
Bournemouth GB . . 43 B5
Bournezeau F . . . . .114 B2
Bourran F . . . . . . . 129 B3
Bourret F . . . . . . . 129 C4
Bourron-Marlotte F . 90 C2
Bourton-on-The-Water
  GB . . . . . . . . . . 44 B2
Boussac F . . . . . . .116 A2
Boussens F . . . . . 145 A4
Boutersem B . . . . . 79 B4
Bouttencourt F . . . . 90 B1
Bouvières F . . . . . . 131 A4
Bouvron F . . . . . . . 101 B4
Bouxwiller F . . . . . . 93 C3
Bouzas E . . . . . . . 140 B2
Bouzonville F . . . . . 92 B2
Bova I . . . . . . . . . 175 D1
Bova Marina I . . . . 175 D1
Bovallstrand S . . . . 54 B2
Bované I . . . . . . . . 141 B3
Bóvegno I . . . . . . . 120 B3
Bovenau D . . . . . . 64 B2
Bovenden D. . . . . . 82 A1
Bøverdal N. . . . . . . 198 D5
Boves F . . . . . . . . 90 B2
Bóves I . . . . . . . . . 133 A3
Bovey Tracey GB . . 43 B3
Bovino I . . . . . . . . 171 B3
Bøvlingbjerg DK . . . 58 B1

Bovolenta I 121 B4
Bovolone I 121 B4
Bowes GB 37 B5
Bowmore GB 34 C1
Bowness-on-Windermere GB 36 B4
Box GB 43 A4
Boxberg
*Baden-Württemberg* D 94 B1
*Sachsen* D 84 A2
Boxholm S 55 B6
Boxmeer NL 80 A1
Boxtel NL 79 A5
Boyabat TR 23 A8
Boyalıca TR 187 B4
Boyle IRL 26 C2
Bozan TR 187 C6
Božava HR 137 A3
Bozburun TR 188 C3
Bozcaada TR 186 C1
Bozdoğan TR 188 B3
Bożepole Wielkie PL 68 A2
Boževac SRB 127 C3
Božice CZ 97 C4
Boží Dar CZ 83 B4
Bozkır TR 189 B7
Bozouls F 130 A1
Bozova TR 189 B5
Bozüyük TR 187 C5
Bózzolo I 121 B3
Bra I 119 C4
Braås S 62 A3
Brabrand DK 59 B3
Bracadale GB 31 B2
Bracciano I 168 A2
Bracieux F 103 B3
Bräcke S 199 C12
Brackenheim D 93 B5
Brackley GB 44 A2
Bracklin IRL 27 C4
Bracknell GB 44 B3
Brackwede D 72 C1
Braco GB 35 B4
Brad RO 16 B5
Bradford GB 40 B2
Bradford on Avon GB 43 A4
Bradina BIH 139 B4
Brådland N 52 B2
Brædstrup DK 59 C2
Brae GB 33 A5
Braemar GB 32 D3
Braemore GB 32 D1
Braga P 148 A1
Bragança P 149 A3
Brăila RO 17 C7
Braine F 91 B3
Braine-le-Comte B 79 B4
Braintree GB 45 B4
Braives B 79 B5
Brake D 72 A1
Brakel
B 79 B3
D 81 A5
Bräkne-Hoby S 63 B3
Brålanda S 54 B3
Bralin PL 86 A1
Brallo di Pregola I 120 C2
Bram F 146 A3
Bramafan F 132 B2
Bramberg am Wildkogel A 109 B3
Bramdrupdam DK 59 C2
Bramming DK 59 C1
Brampton GB 37 B4
Bramsche D 71 B4
Branca I 136 B1
Brancaleone Marina I 175 D2
Brancaster GB 41 C4
Brand
*Nieder Östereich* A 96 C3
*Vorarlberg* A 107 B4
Brandbu N 48 B2
Brande DK 59 C2
Brande-Hornerkirchen D 64 C2
Brandenberg A 108 B2
Brandenburg D 73 B5
Brand-Erbisdorf D 83 B5
Brandis D 83 A4
Brando F 180 A2
Brandomil E 140 A2
Brandon GB 45 A4
Brandshagen D 66 B2
Brandval N 49 B4
Brandýs nad Labem CZ 84 B2
Branice PL 98 A1
Braničevo SRB 127 C3
Braniewo PL 69 A4
Branik SLO 122 B2
Brankovina SRB 127 C1
Branky CZ 98 B1
Branne F 128 B2
Brannenburg-Degerndorf D 108 B3
Brantôme F 115 C4
Branzi I 120 A2
Bras d'Asse F 132 B2
Braskereidfoss N 48 B3
Braslaw BY 13 A7
Braşov RO 17 C6
Brasparts F 100 A2
Brassac F 130 B1
Brassac-les-Mines F 116 B3
Brasschaat B 79 A4
Brastad S 54 B2
Břasy CZ 96 B1
Brąszewice PL 86 A2
Bratislava SK 111 A4
Brattfors S 55 A5
Brattvåg N 198 C3
Bratunac BIH 127 C1
Braubach D 81 B3
Braunau A 95 C5
Braunfels D 81 B4
Braunlage D 82 A2
Braunsbedra D 83 A3
Braunschweig D 73 B3
Bray IRL 30 A2
Bray Dunes F 78 A2
Bray-sur-Seine F 90 C3
Bray-sur-Somme F 90 B2
Brazatortas E 157 B3
Brazey-en-Plaine F 105 B4
Brbinj HR 137 A4
Brčko BIH 125 C4
Brdani SRB 127 D2
Brdów PL 76 B3
Brea de Tajo E 151 B4
Brécey F 88 B2
Brechen D 81 B4
Brechin GB 35 B5
Brecht B 79 A4
Brecketfeld D 80 A3
Břeclav CZ 97 C4
Brecon GB 39 C3
Brécy F 103 B4
Breda
E 147 C3
NL 79 A4
Bredaryd S 60 B3
Bredbyn S 200 C4
Breddin D 73 B5
Bredebro DK 64 A1
Bredelar D 81 A4
Bredenfelde D 74 A2
Bredsjö S 50 C1
Bredstedt D 64 B1
Bredsten DK 59 C2
Bredträsk S 200 C4
Bredviken S 195 D5
Bree B 80 A1
Bregana HR 123 B4
Breganze I 121 B4
Bregenz A 107 B4
Bréhal F 88 B2
Brehna D 83 A4
Breiðdalsvík IS 191 C11
Breidenbach F 93 B3
Breil-sur-Roya F 133 B3
Breisach D 106 A2
Breitenbach
CH 106 B2
D 81 B5
Breitenberg D 96 C1
Breitenfelde D 73 A3
Breitengussbach D 94 B2
Breivikbotn N 192 B6
Brejning DK 59 C2
Brekke N 46 A2
Brekken N 199 C8
Brekkestø N 53 B4
Brekkvasselv N 199 A10
Brekstad N 198 B6
Breland N 53 B3
Bremanger N 198 D1
Bremen D 72 A1
Bremerhaven D 72 A1
Bremervörde D 72 A2
Bremgarten CH 106 B3
Bremsnes N 198 B4
Brem-sur-Mer F 114 B2
Brenderup DK 59 C2
Brenes E 162 A2
Brengova SLO 110 C2
Brenna PL 98 B2
Breno I 120 B3
Brénod F 118 A2
Brensbach D 93 B4
Brentwood GB 45 B4
Brescello I 121 C3
Bréscia I 120 B3
Breskens NL 79 A3
Bresles F 90 B2
Bresnica SRB 127 D2
Bressana I 120 B2
Bressanone I 108 C2
Bressuire F 102 C1
Brest
BY 13 B5
F 100 A1
HR 122 B2
Brestač SRB 127 C1
Brestanica SLO 123 A4
Brestova HR 123 B3
Brestovac HR 125 B3
Bretenoux F 129 B4
Breteuil
*Eure* F 89 B4
*Oise* F 90 B2
Brétigny-sur-Orge F 90 C2
Bretten D 93 B4
Bretteville-sur-Laize F 89 A3
Brettheim D 94 B2
Breuil-Cervínia I 119 B4
Breukelen NL 70 B2
Brevik
N 53 A5
*Stockholm* S 57 A4
*Västra Götaland* S 55 B5
Breza BIH 139 A4
Brežice SLO 123 B4
Bréziers F 132 A2
Breznica HR 124 A2
Breznica Našička HR 125 B4
Březnice CZ 96 B1
Brezno SK 99 C3
Brézolles F 89 B5
Březovánad Svitavou CZ 97 B4
Brezovápod Bradlom SK 98 C1
Brezovica
SK 99 B4
SLO 123 A3
Brezovo Polje Selo BIH 125 C4
Briançon F 118 C3
Brianconnet F 132 B2
Briare F 103 B4
Briatexte F 129 C4
Briático I 175 C2
Briaucourt F 105 A4
Bribir HR 123 B3
Bricquebec F 88 A2
Bridgend
*Argyll & Bute* GB 34 C1
*Bridgend* GB 39 C3
Bridge of Cally GB 35 B4
Bridge of Don GB 33 D4
Bridge of Earn GB 35 B4
Bridge of Orchy GB 34 B3
Bridgnorth GB 39 B4
Bridgwater GB 43 A4
Břidličná CZ 98 B1
Bridlington GB 41 A3
Bridport GB 43 B4
Briec F 100 A1
Brie-Comte-Robert F 90 C2
Brienne-le-Château F 91 C4
Brienon-sur-Armançon F 104 B2
Brienz CH 106 C3
Brienza I 172 B1
Briesen D 74 B3
Brieskow Finkenheerd D 74 B3
Brietlingen D 72 A3
Brieva de Cameros E 143 B4
Briey F 92 B1
Brig CH 119 A5
Brigg GB 40 B3
Brighouse GB 40 B2
Brightlingsea GB 45 B5
Brighton GB 44 C3
Brignogan-Plage F 100 A1
Brignoles F 132 B2
Brigstock GB 40 C3
Brihuega E 151 B5
Brijuni HR 122 C2
Brillon-en-Barrois F 91 C5
Brilon D 81 A4
Brimnes N 46 B3
Brinches P 160 A2
Bríndisi I 173 B3
Brinje HR 123 B4
Brinon-sur-Beuvron F 104 B2
Brinon-sur-Sauldre F 103 B4
Brinyan GB 33 B3
Brión E 140 B2
Briones E 143 B4
Brionne F 89 A4
Brioude F 117 B3
Brioux-sur-Boutonne F 115 B3
Briouze F 89 B3
Briscous F 144 A2
Brisighella I 135 A4
Brissac-Quincé F 102 B1
Brissago CH 120 A1
Bristol GB 43 A4
Brive-la-Gaillarde F 129 A4
Briviesca E 143 B3
Brixham GB 43 B3
Brixlegg A 108 B2
Brjánslækur IS 190 B2
Brka BIH 125 C4
Brnaze HR 138 B2
Brněnec CZ 97 B4
Brno CZ 97 B4
Bro S 57 A3
Broadclyst GB 43 B3
Broadford
GB 31 B3
IRL 28 B3
Broad Haven GB 39 C1
Broadstairs GB 45 B5
Broadstone GB 43 B4
Broadway GB 44 A2
Broager DK 64 B2
Broaryd S 60 B3
Broby S 61 C4
Brobyværk DK 59 C3
Bročanac BIH 138 B3
Brocas F 128 B2
Brock D 71 B4
Brockel D 72 A2
Brockenhurst GB 44 C2
Broczyno PL 75 A5
Brod MK 182 B3
Brodalen S 54 B2
Broddbo S 50 C3
Brodek u Přerova CZ 98 B1
Broden-bach D 80 B3
Brodick GB 34 C2
Brod na Kupi HR 123 B3
Brodnica PL 69 B4
Brodnica Graniczna PL 68 A3
Brodowe Łąki PL 77 A6
Brody
*Lubuskie* PL 75 B4
*Lubuskie* PL 84 A2
*Mazowieckie* PL 77 B5
UA 13 C6
Broglie F 89 B4
Brójce PL 75 B4
Brokind S 56 B1
Brolo I 177 A3
Brome D 73 B3
Bromley GB 45 B4
Bromölla S 63 B2
Bromont-Lamothe F 116 B2
Brömsebro S 63 B3
Bromsgrove GB 44 A1
Bromyard GB 39 B4
Bronchales E 152 B2
Bronco E 149 B3
Brønderslev DK 58 A2
Broni I 120 B2
Brønnøysund N 195 E3
Brøns DK 59 C1
Bronte I 177 B3
Bronzani Mejdan BIH 124 C2
Bronzolo I 121 A4
Broons F 101 A3
Broquies F 130 A1
Brora GB 32 C3
Brørup DK 59 C2
Brösarp S 63 C2
Brossac F 115 C3
Brostrud N 47 B5
Brotas P 154 C2
Brötjärna S 50 B2
Broto E 145 B3
Brottby S 57 A4
Brøttum N 48 A2
Brou F 103 A3
Brouage F 114 C2
Brough GB 37 B4
Broughshane GB 27 B4
Broughton GB 35 C4
Broughton-in-Furness GB 36 B3
Broumov CZ 85 B4
Broût-Vernet F 116 A3
Brouvelieures F 106 A1
Brouwershaven NL 79 A3
Brovary UA 13 C9
Brovst DK 58 A2
Brownhills GB 40 C2
Brozas E 155 B4
Brozzo I 120 B3
Brtnice CZ 97 B3
Brtonigla HR 122 B2
Bruay-la-Buissière F 78 B2
Bruchhausen-Vilsen D 72 B2
Bruchsal D 93 B4
Bruck D 95 B4
Brück D 74 B1
Bruck an der Grossglocknerstrasse A 109 B3
Bruck an der Leitha A 111 A3
Bruck an der Mur A 110 B2
Brückl A 110 C1
Bruckmühl D 108 B2
Brue-Auriac F 132 B1
Brüel D 65 C4
Bruen CH 107 C3
Bruère-Allichamps F 103 C4
Bruff IRL 29 B3
Bruflat N 47 B6
Brugg CH 106 B3
Brugge B 78 A3
Brüggen D 80 A2
Brühl D 80 B2
Bruinisse NL 79 A4
Brûlon F 102 B1
Brumano I 120 B2
Brumath F 93 C3
Brummen NL 70 B3
Brumov-Bylnice CZ 98 B2
Brumunddal N 48 B2
Brunau D 73 B4
Brunehamel F 91 B4
Brünen D 80 A2
Brunete E 151 B3
Brunflo S 199 B11
Brunico I 108 C2
Brunkeberg N 53 A4
Brunn D 74 A2
Brunnen CH 107 C3
Brunsbüttel D 64 C2
Brunssum NL 80 B1
Bruntál CZ 98 B1
Brušane HR 137 A4
Brusasco I 119 B5
Brusio CH 120 A3
Brusno SK 99 C3
Brusque F 130 B1
Brussels = Bruxelles B 79 B4
Brusson I 119 B4
Brüssow D 74 A3
Brusy PL 68 B2
Bruton GB 43 A4
Bruvno HR 138 A1
Bruvoll N 48 B3
Bruxelles = Brussels B 79 B4
Bruyères F 106 A1
Bruz F 101 A4
Bruzaholm S 62 A3
Brwinów PL 77 B5
Brynamman GB 39 C3
Bryncrug GB 39 B2
Bryne N 52 B1
Brynmawr GB 39 C3
Bryrup DK 59 B2
Brzeg PL 85 B5
Brzeg Dolny PL 85 A4
Brześć Kujawski PL 76 B3
Brzesko PL 99 B4
Brzeszcze PL 99 B3
Brzezie PL 68 B1
Brzeziny
*Łódzkie* PL 87 A3
*Wielkopolskie* PL 86 A2
Brzeźnica PL 84 A3
Brzeźnica Nowa PL 86 A3
Brzeżno PL 75 A4
Brzotin SK 99 C4
Brzozie Lubawskie PL 69 B4
Bua S 60 B2
Buarcos P 148 B1
Buaveg N 52 A1
Bubbio I 119 C5
Bubry F 100 B2
Buca TR 188 A2
Bucak TR 189 B5
Bučany SK 98 C1
Buccheri I 177 B3
Buccino I 172 B1
Bucelas P 154 C1
Buch
*Bayern* D 94 C2
*Bayern* D 95 C4
Buchach UA 13 D6
Bucharest = Bucureşti RO 17 C7
Buchbach D 95 C4
Buchboden A 107 B4
Buchen D 94 B1
Büchen D 73 A3
Buchenberg D 107 B5
Buchères F 104 A3
Buchholz D 72 A2
Buchloe D 108 A1
Buchlovice CZ 98 B1
Buchlyvie GB 34 B3
Bucholz D 73 A5
Buchs CH 107 B4
Buchy F 89 A5
Bückeburg D 72 B2
Buckfastleigh GB 42 B3
Buckhaven GB 35 B4
Buckie GB 33 D4
Buckingham GB 44 A3
Buckley GB 38 A3
Bückwitz D 73 B5
Bučovice CZ 97 B5
Bucsa H 113 B5
Bucureşti = Bucharest RO 17 C7
Bucy-lés-Pierreport F 91 B3
Buczek PL 86 A3
Bud N 198 C3
Budakalasz H 112 B3
Budakeszi H 112 B2
Budal N 199 C7
Budaörs H 112 B2
Budapest H 112 B3
Búðardalur IS 190 B4
Budča SK 99 C3
Buddusò I 178 B3
Bude GB 42 B2
Budeč CZ 97 B3
Büdelsdorf D 64 B2
Budens P 160 B1
Budia E 151 B5
Budimlić-Japra BIH 124 C2
Büdingen D 81 B5
Budinšćina HR 124 A2
Budišov CZ 98 B1
Budleigh Salterton GB 43 B3
Budmerice SK 98 C1
Budoni I 178 B3
Búdrio I 135 A4
Budva MNE 16 D3
Budyněnad Ohří CZ 84 B2
Budziszewice PL 87 A3
Budzyń PL 76 B1
Bue N 52 B1
Bueña E 152 B2
Buenache de Alarcón E 158 B1
Buenache de la Sierra E 152 B2
Buenaventura E 150 B3
Buenavista de Valdavia E 142 B2
Buendia E 151 B5
Bueu E 140 B2
Buezo E 143 B3
Bugac H 112 C3
Bugarra E 159 B3
Bugeat F 116 B1
Buggerru I 179 C2
Bugojno BIH 138 A3
Bugøyfjord N 193 C13
Bugøynes N 193 C13
Bugyi H 112 B3
Buharkent TR 188 B3
Bühl
*Baden-Württemberg* D 93 C4
*Bayern* D 107 B5
Bühlertal D 93 C4
Bühlertann D 94 B1
Buia I 122 A2
Builth Wells GB 39 B3
Buin N 47 B6
Buis-les-Baronnies F 131 A4
Buitenpost NL 70 A3
Buitrago del Lozoya E 151 B4
Bujalance E 157 C3
Bujaraloz E 153 A3
Buje HR 122 B2
Bujedo E 143 B3
Bük H 111 B3
Buk PL 75 B5
Bükkösd H 125 A3
Bükkzsérc H 113 B4
Bukovci SLO 124 A1
Bukowiec PL 75 B5
Bukowina Tatrzańska PL 99 B4
Bukownica PL 86 A2
Bukowno PL 86 B3
Bülach CH 107 B3
Búland IS 191 D7
Buldan TR 188 A3
Bulgari BG 17 D7
Bulgnéville F 105 A4
Bulgurca TR 188 A2
Bülkau D 64 C1
Bulken N 46 B3
Bulkowo PL 77 B5
Bullas E 164 A3
Bulle CH 106 C2
Büllingen B 80 B2
Bullmark S 200 B6
Bulqizë AL 182 B2
Buna BIH 139 B3
Bunahowen IRL 26 B1
Bunbeg IRL 26 A2
Bunclody IRL 30 B2
Buncrana IRL 27 A3
Bunde D 71 A4
Bünde D 72 B1
Bundoran IRL 26 B2
Bunessan GB 34 B1
Bungay GB 45 A5
Bunge S 57 C5
Bunić HR 123 C4
Bunmahon IRL 30 B1
Bunnyconnellan IRL 26 B1
Buño E 140 A2
Buñol E 159 B3
Bunratty IRL 29 B3
Bunsbeek B 79 B4
Buñuel E 144 C2
Bunyola E 166 B2
Buonabitácolo I 172 B1
Buonalbergo I 170 B2
Buonconvento I 135 B4
Buonvicino I 174 B1
Burano I 122 B1
Burbach D 81 B4
Burcei I 179 C3
Burdons-sur-Rognon F 105 A4
Burdur TR 189 B5
Bureå S 2 D7
Burela E 141 A3
Büren D 81 A4
Büren an der Aare CH 106 B2
Burford GB 44 B2
Burg
*Cottbus* D 84 A2
*Magdeburg* D 73 B4
*Schleswig-Holstein* D 64 C2
Burgas BG 17 D7
Burgau
A 111 B3
D 94 C2
P 160 B1
Burg auf Fehmarn D 65 B4
Burgbernheim D 94 B2
Burgdorf
CH 106 B2
D 72 B3
Burgebrach D 94 B2
Bürgel D 83 B3
Burgess Hill GB 44 C3
Burghaslach D 94 B2
Burghausen D 109 A3
Burghead GB 32 D3
Burgheim D 94 C3
Burgh le Marsh GB 41 B4
Búrgio I 176 B2
Burgkirchen D 109 A3
Burgkunstadt D 82 B3

Burglengenfeld D . . 95 B4
Burgo P . . . . . . . 148 B1
Burgoberbach D . . . 94 B2
Burgohondo E. . . . . 150 B3
Burgos E . . . . . . . 143 B3
Burgsinn D . . . . . . 82 B1
Burgstädt D . . . . . . 83 B4
Burgstall D . . . . . . 73 B4
Burg Stargard D . . . 74 A2
Burgsvik S. . . . . . . 57 C4
Burgui E. . . . . . . . 144 B3
Burguillos E . . . . . . 162 A2
Burguillos del Cerro
E. . . . . . . . . . . . 155 C4
Burguillos de Toledo
E. . . . . . . . . . . . 151 C4
Burhaniye TR . . . . . 186 C1
Burhave D . . . . . . . 71 A5
Burie F . . . . . . . . . 114 C3
Burjassot E . . . . . . 159 B3
Burk D . . . . . . . . . 94 B2
Burkhardtsdorf D . . 83 B4
Burlada E. . . . . . . . 144 B3
Burladingen D. . . . . 107 A4
Burlage D. . . . . . . . 71 A4
Burness GB . . . . . . 33 B4
Burnham GB . . . . . 44 B3
Burnham Market
GB . . . . . . . . . . 41 C4
Burnham-on-Crouch
GB . . . . . . . . . . 45 B4
Burnham-on-Sea
GB . . . . . . . . . . 43 A4
Burniston GB . . . . . 40 A3
Burnley GB . . . . . . 40 B1
Burntisland GB . . . . 35 B4
Burón E . . . . . . . . . 142 A1
Buronzo I. . . . . . . .119 B5
Burovac SRB. . . . . 127 C3
Burow D. . . . . . . . . 74 A2
Burravoe GB . . . . . 33 A5
Burrel AL . . . . . . . 182 B2
Burret F . . . . . . . . 146 B2
Burriana E . . . . . . . 159 B3
Burry Port GB . . . . . 39 C2
Bürs A . . . . . . . . . 107 B4
Bursa TR . . . . . . . 186 B4
Burseryd S . . . . . . 60 B3
Bürstadt D . . . . . . . 93 B4
Burton GB . . . . . . . 37 B4
Burton Agnes GB . . 41 A3
Burton Bradstock
GB . . . . . . . . . . 43 B4
Burton Latimer GB . 44 A3
Burton upon Stather
GB . . . . . . . . . . 40 B3
Burton upon Trent
GB . . . . . . . . . . 40 C2
Burträsk S . . . . . . . 200 B6
Burujón E . . . . . . . 151 C3
Burwell GB . . . . . . 45 A4
Burwick GB . . . . . . 33 C4
Bury GB . . . . . . . . 40 B1
Bury St Edmunds
GB . . . . . . . . . . 45 A4
Burzenin PL. . . . . . 86 A2
Busachi I . . . . . . . . 179 B2
Busalla I. . . . . . . . . 134 A1
Busana I. . . . . . . . . 134 A3
Busano I . . . . . . . .119 B4
Busca I. . . . . . . . . . 133 A3
Busch D . . . . . . . . . 73 B4
Buševec HR. . . . . . 124 B2
Bushat AL . . . . . . . 182 B1
Bushey GB . . . . . . 44 B3
Bushmills GB . . . . . 27 A4
Bušince SK . . . . . .112 A3
Buskhyttan S. . . . . 56 B2
Busko-Zdrój PL. . . . 87 B4
Busot E . . . . . . . . . 159 C3
Busovača BIH . . . . 139 A3
Busquistar E . . . . . 163 B4
Bussang F. . . . . . . 106 B1
Busseto I . . . . . . . 120 C3
Bussière-Badil F. . . 115 C4
Bussière-Poitevine
F. . . . . . . . . . . .115 B4
Bussolengo I. . . . . . 121 B3
Bussoleno I. . . . . . .119 B4
Bussum NL . . . . . . 70 B2
Busto Arsízio I. . . . 120 B1
Büsum D . . . . . . . . 64 B1
Butera I . . . . . . . . 177 B3
Butgenbach B . . . . 80 B2
Butler's Bridge IRL. 27 B3
Butryny PL. . . . . . . 77 A5
Bütschwil CH . . . . . 107 B4
Buttermere GB . . . . 36 B3
Buttevant IRL. . . . . 29 B3
Buttle S . . . . . . . . 57 C4
Buttstädt D . . . . . . 82 A3
Butzbach D . . . . . . 81 B4
Bützfleth D. . . . . . . 72 A2
Bützow D . . . . . . . 65 C4
Buxières-les-Mines
F. . . . . . . . . . . . 104 C1
Buxtehude D . . . . . 72 A2
Buxton GB. . . . . . . 40 B2
Buxy F . . . . . . . . . 104 C3
Büyükçekmece
TR . . . . . . . . . . 186 A3
Büyükkarıştıran
TR . . . . . . . . . . 186 A2
Büyükorhan TR. . . . 186 C3
Buzançais F . . . . . . 103 C3
Buzancy F . . . . . . . 91 B4
Buzău RO . . . . . . . 17 C7
Buzet HR . . . . . . . 122 B2

Buziaş RO . . . . . . 126 B3
Buzsák H . . . . . . . .111 C4
Buzy F . . . . . . . . . 145 A3
By S . . . . . . . . . . . 50 B3
Byala BG . . . . . . . 17 D6
Byaroza BY . . . . . . 13 B6
Byczyna PL . . . . . . 86 A2
Bydalen S . . . . . . 199 B10
Bydgoszcz PL . . . . 76 A3
Bygdin N . . . . . . . . 47 A5
Bygdsiljum S. . . . 200 B6
Bygland N . . . . . . . 53 B3
Byglandsfjord N . . 53 B3
Bygstad N . . . . . . . 46 A2
Bykhaw BY . . . . . . 13 B9
Bykle N . . . . . . . . . 52 A3
Bylderup-Bov DK . . 64 B2
Byrkjedal N . . . . . . 52 D2
Byrkjelo N . . . . . . 198 D3
Byrum DK . . . . . . . 58 A3
Byšice CZ . . . . . . . 84 B2
Byske S . . . . . . . . . 2 D7
Býškovice CZ . . . . . 98 B1
Bysław PL . . . . . . . 76 A2
Bystré CZ. . . . . . . . 97 B4
Bystřice CZ . . . . . . 96 B2
Bystrice CZ . . . . . . 98 B2
Bystřice nad
Pernštejnem CZ . . 97 B4
Bystřice pod Hostýnem
CZ . . . . . . . . . . 98 B1
Bystrzyca Kłodzka
PL. . . . . . . . . . . 85 B4
Bytča SK . . . . . . . . 98 B2
Bytnica PL . . . . . . . 75 B4
Bytom PL. . . . . . . . 86 B2
Bytom Odrzański
PL. . . . . . . . . . . 85 A3
Bytów PL . . . . . . . . 68 A2
Byxelkrok S . . . . . . 62 A5
Bzenec CZ. . . . . . . 98 C1
Bzince SK . . . . . . . 98 C1

**C**

Çağa TR . . . . . . . 187 B7
Cabacos P . . . . . . 154 B2
Cabaj-Čápor SK . . 98 C2
Cabana E . . . . . . . 140 A2
Cabanac-et-Villagrains
F. . . . . . . . . . . . 128 B2
Cabañaquinta E . . 142 A1
Cabanas P . . . . . . 160 B2
Cabañas del Castillo
E. . . . . . . . . . . . 156 A2
Cabañas de Yepes
E. . . . . . . . . . . . 151 C4
Cabanelles E . . . . 147 B3
Cabanes E . . . . . . 153 B4
Çabanillas E . . . . . 144 B2
Čabar HR . . . . . . . 123 B3
Cabasse F . . . . . . 132 B2
Cabdella E. . . . . . . 146 B2
Cabeceiras de Basto
P. . . . . . . . . . . . 148 A1
Cabeço de Vide P . 155 B3
Cabella Ligure I . . . 120 C2
Cabeza del Buey E 156 B2
Cabeza la Vaca E. . 161 A3
Cabezamesada E . 151 C4
Cabezarados E . . . 157 B3
Cabezarrubias del
Puerto E . . . . . . 157 B3
Cabezas del Villar
E. . . . . . . . . . . . 150 B2
Cabezas Rubias E. 161 B2
Cabezón E . . . . . . 142 C2
Cabezón de la Sal
E. . . . . . . . . . . . 142 A2
Cabezón de Liébana
E. . . . . . . . . . . . 142 A2
Cabezuela E . . . . . 151 A4
Cabezuela del Valle
E. . . . . . . . . . . . 149 B4
Cabo de Gata E . . 164 C2
Cabo de Palos E . . 165 B4
Cabolafuente E . . . 152 A1
Cabourg F . . . . . . . 89 A3
Cabra
E. . . . . . . . . . . .163 A3
P. . . . . . . . . . . .148 B2
Cabrach GB . . . . . . 32 D3
Cabra del Santo Cristo
E. . . . . . . . . . . . 163 A4
Cábras I . . . . . . . . 179 C2
Cabreiro P . . . . . . 140 C2
Cabreiros E . . . . . . 140 A3
Cabrejas E . . . . . . 152 B1
Cabrela P . . . . . . . 154 C2
Cabrillas E . . . . . . 149 B3
Cabuna HR . . . . . . 125 B3
Çacabelos E . . . . . 141 B4
Čačak SRB . . . . . . 127 D2
Cáccamo I . . . . . . 176 B2
Caccuri I . . . . . . . . 174 B2
Cacela P . . . . . . . . 160 B2
Cacém P. . . . . . . . 154 C1
Cáceres E . . . . . . . 155 B4
Cachafeiro E . . . . . 140 B2
Cachopo P. . . . . . . 160 B2
Cachtice SK . . . . . 98 C1
Čacin E . . . . . . . . 163 A4
Čačinci HR . . . . . . 125 B3
Cadafais P . . . . . . 154 C1
Cadalen F . . . . . . . 129 C5
Cadalso E . . . . . . . 149 B3
Cadaqués E . . . . . 147 B4

Cadaval P. . . . . . . 154 B1
Cadavedo E. . . . . . 141 A4
Čadavica BIH. . . . . 138 A2
Čadca SK. . . . . . . . 98 B2
Cadéac F . . . . . . . 145 B4
Cadelbosco di Sopra
I. . . . . . . . . . . . 121 C3
Cadenazzo CH. . . . 120 A1
Cadenberge D . . . . 64 C2
Cadenet F. . . . . . . 131 B4
Cadeuil F . . . . . . . 114 C3
Cádiar E . . . . . . . . 164 C1
Cadillac F. . . . . . . 128 B2
Cádiz E. . . . . . . . . 162 B1
Čadjavica HR. . . . . 125 B3
Cadouin F . . . . . . . 129 B3
Cadours F . . . . . . . 129 C4
Cadrete E. . . . . . . 152 A3
Caen F. . . . . . . . . . 89 A3
Caerleon GB . . . . . 39 C4
Caernarfon GB . . . . 38 A2
Caerphilly GB . . . . 39 C3
Caersws GB. . . . . . 39 B3
Cafede P . . . . . . . 155 B3
Caggiano I . . . . . . 172 B1
Cagli I . . . . . . . . . 136 B1
Cágliari I . . . . . . . 179 C3
Čaglin HR . . . . . . . 125 B3
Cagnano Varano I . 171 B3
Cagnes-sur-Mer F . 132 B3
Caher IRL. . . . . . . 29 B4
Caherciveen IRL. . . 29 C1
Caherdaniel IRL. . . 29 C1
Cahors F . . . . . . . 129 B4
Cahul MD. . . . . . . 17 C8
Caiazzo I . . . . . . . 170 B2
Caion E . . . . . . . . 140 A2
Cairndow GB. . . . . 34 B3
Cairnryan GB. . . . . 36 B1
Cairo Montenotte I 133 A4
Caister-on-Sea GB . 41 C5
Caistor GB. . . . . . . 41 B3
Caivano I . . . . . . . 170 C2
Cajarc F. . . . . . . . 129 B4
Čajniče BIH . . . . . 139 B5
Çakırlar TR . . . . . . 189 C5
Çakmak TR . . . . . 187 C6
Çal TR . . . . . . . . . 189 A4
Cala E. . . . . . . . . . 161 B3
Calabritto I. . . . . . 172 B1
Calaceite E . . . . . 153 B4
Calacuccia F . . . . 180 A2
Cala d'Or E . . . . . 167 B3
Calaf E . . . . . . . . 147 C2
Calafat RO . . . . . . 17 C5
Calafell E . . . . . . . 147 C2
Cala Galdana E . . 167 B3
Cala Gonone I. . . . 178 B3
Calahonda
Granada E. . . . . .163 B4
Málaga E . . . . . .163 B3
Calahorra E . . . . . 144 B2
Calais F . . . . . . . . 78 B1
Cala Llonga E . . . 166 C1
Calalzo di Cadore I 109 C3
Cala Millor E . . . . 167 B3
Calamocha E . . . . 152 B2
Calamonte E. . . . . 155 C4
Cala Morell E. . . . 167 A3
Calanais GB. . . . . 31 A2
Calanda E . . . . . . 153 B3
Calangiánus I . . . . 178 B3
Călărași RO . . . . . 17 C7
Cala Ratjada E . . . 167 B3
Calascibetta I . . . . 177 B3
Calasetta I . . . . . . 179 C2
Calasparra E . . . . 164 A3
Calatafimi I . . . . . . 176 B1
Calatayud E. . . . . . 152 A2
Calatorao E . . . . . 152 A2
Calau D . . . . . . . . 84 A1
Calbe D . . . . . . . . 73 C4
Calcena E . . . . . . 152 A2
Calcinelli I . . . . . . 136 B1
Calco I . . . . . . . . . 120 B2
Caldarola I . . . . . . 136 B2
Caldaro sulla strada del
Vino I . . . . . . . . 121 A4
Caldas da Rainha
P. . . . . . . . . . . . 154 B1
Caldas de Bo ì E . . 145 B4
Caldas de Malavella
E. . . . . . . . . . . . 147 C3
Caldas de Reis E. . 140 B2
Caldas de San Jorge
P. . . . . . . . . . . . 148 B1
Caldas de Vizela P 148 A1
Caldaso de los Vidrios
E. . . . . . . . . . . . 150 B3
Caldbeck GB . . . . . 36 B3
Caldearenas E. . . . 145 B3
Caldelas P . . . . . . 148 A1
Calders E . . . . . . . 147 C2
Caldes de Montbui
E. . . . . . . . . . . . 147 C3
Caldicot GB . . . . . . 39 C4
Caldirola I . . . . . . 120 C2
Caledon GB . . . . . 27 B4
Calella
Barcelona E. . . . .147 C3
Girona E. . . . . . .147 C4
Calenzana F . . . . . 180 A1
Calera de León E . 161 A3
Calera y Chozas E. 150 C3
Caleruega E . . . . . 143 C3
Caleruela E . . . . . 150 C2

Cales de Mallorca
E. . . . . . . . . . . . 167 B3
Calestano I . . . . . . 134 A3
Calfsound GB . . . . 33 B4
Calgary GB . . . . . . 34 B1
Calimera I . . . . . . 173 B4
Calitri I . . . . . . . . . 172 B1
Calizzano I . . . . . . 133 A4
Callac F. . . . . . . . . 100 A2
Callan IRL . . . . . . 30 B1
Callander GB . . . . . 35 B3
Callas F . . . . . . . . 132 B2
Calliano
Piemonte I . . . . . . 119 B5
Trentino Alto Adige
I . . . . . . . . . . . . .121 B4
Callington GB . . . . 42 B2
Callosa de Ensarriá
E. . . . . . . . . . . . 159 C3
Callosa de Segura
E. . . . . . . . . . . . 165 A4
Callús E . . . . . . . . 147 C2
Calolziocorte I . . . . 120 B2
Calonge E . . . . . . 147 C4
Čalovec SK . . . . . .112 B1
Calpe E . . . . . . . . 159 C4
Caltabellotta I . . . . 176 B2
Caltagirone I . . . . . 177 B3
Caltanissetta I . . . . 177 B3
Caltavuturo I . . . . . 176 B2
Çaltılıbük TR . . . . . 186 C3
Caltojar E . . . . . . . 151 A5
Caluire-et-Cuire F . .117 B4
Caluso I . . . . . . . .119 B4
Calvello I . . . . . . . 172 B1
Calvi F . . . . . . . . . 180 A1
Calviá E . . . . . . . . 166 B2
Calvinet F . . . . . . 116 C2
Calvisson F . . . . . . 131 B3
Calvörde D . . . . . . 73 B4
Calw D . . . . . . . . . 93 C4
Calzada de Calatrava
E. . . . . . . . . . . . 157 B4
Calzada de Valdunciel
E. . . . . . . . . . . . 150 A2
Calzadilla de los Barros
E. . . . . . . . . . . . 155 C4
Cam GB . . . . . . . . 43 A4
Camaiore I. . . . . . . 134 B3
Camarasa E . . . . . 145 C4
Camarena E . . . . . 151 B3
Camarès F . . . . . . 130 B1
Camaret-sur-Aigues
F. . . . . . . . . . . . 131 A3
Camaret-sur-Mer F 100 A1
Camarillas E . . . . . 153 B3
Camariñas E . . . . . 140 A1
Camarzana de Tera
E. . . . . . . . . . . . 141 B4
Camas E . . . . . . . 162 A1
Camastra I . . . . . . 176 B2
Cambados E . . . . . 140 B2
Cambarinho P . . . . 148 B1
Camberley GB. . . . 44 B3
Cambil E . . . . . . . 163 A4
Cambligeu F . . . . . 78 B2
Cambo-les-Bains F 144 A2
Camborne GB . . . . 42 B1
Cambrai F . . . . . . . 78 B3
Cambre E . . . . . . . 140 A2
Cambridge GB. . . . 45 A4
Cambrils E . . . . . . 147 C2
Cambs D . . . . . . . 65 C4
Camburg D . . . . . . 83 A3
Camden GB . . . . . 44 B3
Cameleño E . . . . . 142 A2
Camelford GB . . . . 42 B2
Çameli TR . . . . . . 189 B4
Camelle E . . . . . . 140 A1
Camerano I . . . . . . 136 B2
Camerino I . . . . . . 136 B2
Camerota I . . . . . . 172 B1
Camigliatello Silano
I . . . . . . . . . . . . 174 B2
Caminha P . . . . . . 148 A1
Caminomorisco E. . 149 B3
Caminreal E. . . . . . 152 B2
Camisano Vicentino
I . . . . . . . . . . . . 121 B4
Camlıdere TR. . . . . 187 B7
Cammarata I . . . . . 176 B2
Camogli I . . . . . . . 134 A2
Camors F . . . . . . . 100 B3
Camp IRL . . . . . . . 29 B2
Campagna I . . . . . 172 B1
Campagnano di Roma
I . . . . . . . . . . . . 168 A2
Campan F . . . . . . . 145 A4
Campana I . . . . . . 174 B2
Campanario E . . . . 156 B2
Campanillas E . . . . 163 B3
Campano E . . . . . . 162 B1
Campaspero E . . . 151 A3
Campbeltown GB . . 34 C2
Campello I . . . . . . 165 A4
Campelos P . . . . . 154 B1
Campi Bisénzio I . . 135 B4
Campico López E . 165 B3
Campíglia Maríttima
I . . . . . . . . . . . . 134 B3
Campillo de Altobuey
E. . . . . . . . . . . . 158 B2

Campillo de Aragón
E. . . . . . . . . . . . 152 A2
Campillo de Arenas
E. . . . . . . . . . . . 163 A4
Campillo de Llerena
E. . . . . . . . . . . . 156 B2
Campillos E. . . . . . 162 A3
Câmpina RO . . . . . 17 C6
Campi Salentina I . 173 B4
Campli I. . . . . . . . . 136 C2
Campo E . . . . . . . 145 B4
Campobasso I. . . . 170 B2
Campobello di Licata
I . . . . . . . . . . . . 176 B2
Campobello di Mazara
I . . . . . . . . . . . . 176 B1
Campo da Feira E . 140 A3
Campodarsego I . . 121 B4
Campo de Bacerros
E. . . . . . . . . . . . 141 B3
Campo de Caso E . 142 A1
Campo de Criptana
E. . . . . . . . . . . . 157 A4
Campodolcino I. . . 120 A2
Campofelice di Roccella
I . . . . . . . . . . . . 176 B2
Campofiorito I . . . . 176 B2
Campofórmido I . . 122 A2
Campofranco I . . . 176 B2
Campofrio E . . . . . 161 B3
Campogalliano I . . 121 C3
Campo Ligure I . . . 133 A4
Campolongo I . . . . 109 C3
Campo Lugar E . . . 156 A2
Campo Maior P . . . 155 B3
Campomanes E . . . 141 A5
Campomarino I . . . 170 B3
Campo Molino I . . . 133 A3
Campo Real E . . . . 151 B4
Camporeale I . . . . 176 B2
Camporeggiano I . . 136 B1
Camporrells E . . . . 145 C4
Camporrobles E . . 158 B2
Campos P . . . . . . 148 A2
Camposa P . . . . . . 148 A1
Camposampiero I . 121 B4
Camposanto I . . . . 121 C4
Campos del Port E 167 B3
Camposines E . . . . 153 A4
Campotéjar E . . . . 163 A4
Campotosto I. . . . . 169 A3
Campo Túres I . . . 108 C2
Camprodón E . . . . 147 B3
Campsegret F . . . . 129 B3
Camrose GB . . . . . 39 C1
Camuñas E . . . . . . 157 A4
Çamyolu TR. . . . . . 189 C7
Çan TR . . . . . . . . . 186 B2
Cana I . . . . . . . . . 135 C4
Cañada del Hoyo
E. . . . . . . . . . . . 158 B2
Cañadajuncosa E . 158 B1
Cañada Rosal E. . . 162 A2
Çanak TR. . . . . . . 123 C4
Çanakkale TR . . . . 186 B1
Canale I . . . . . . . .119 C4
Canales
Asturias E . . . . . .141 B5
Castellón de la Plana
E. . . . . . . . . . . . .159 B3
Canals E . . . . . . . 159 C3
Canal San Bovo I . 121 A4
Cañamares E . . . . 152 B1
Cañamero E . . . . . 156 A2
Cañar E . . . . . . . . 163 B4
Cañate la Real E . . 162 B2
Cañaveral E . . . . . 155 B4
Cañaveral de León
E. . . . . . . . . . . . 161 A3
Cañaveras E . . . . . 152 B1
Cañaveruelas E . . . 151 B5
Canazei I . . . . . . . 108 C2
Cancale F. . . . . . . 88 B2
Cancellara I . . . . . 172 B1
Cancello ed Arnone
I . . . . . . . . . . . . 170 B2
Cancon F . . . . . . . 129 B3
Canda E . . . . . . . . 141 B4
Candamil E . . . . . . 140 A3
Candanchu E. . . . . 145 B3
Çandarlı TR . . . . . 186 D1
Candas E . . . . . . . 141 A5
Candasnos E. . . . . 153 A4
Candé F . . . . . . . . 101 B4
Candela I . . . . . . . 172 A1
Candelario E . . . . . 150 B2
Candeleda E . . . . . 150 B2
Cándia Lomellina I 120 B1
Candide Casamazzano
I . . . . . . . . . . . . 109 C3
Candin E . . . . . . . 141 B4
Candosa P . . . . . . 148 B2
Canecas P . . . . . . 154 C1
Canelli I . . . . . . . .119 C5
Canena E . . . . . . . 157 B4
Canero E . . . . . . . 141 A4
Canet F . . . . . . . . 130 B2
Canet de Mar E . . 147 C3
Canet d'en Berenguer
E. . . . . . . . . . . . 159 B3
Cañete E . . . . . . . 158 A2
Cañete de las Torres
E. . . . . . . . . . . . 163 A3
Canet-Plage F . . . 146 B4
Canfranc E. . . . . . 145 B3

Cangas
Lugo E. . . . . . . .141 A3
Pontevedra E. . . .140 B2
Cangas de Narcea
E. . . . . . . . . . . . 141 A4
Cangas de Onís E . 142 A1
Canha P. . . . . . . . 154 C2
Canhestros P. . . . . 160 A1
Canicattì I . . . . . . . 176 B2
Canicattini Bagni I 177 B4
Canicosa de la Sierra
E. . . . . . . . . . . . 143 C3
Caniles E . . . . . . . 164 B2
Canillas de Aceituno
E. . . . . . . . . . . . 163 B3
Canino I . . . . . . . . 168 A1
Canisy F . . . . . . . . 88 A2
Cañizal E . . . . . . . 150 A2
Cañizo E . . . . . . . 142 C1
Canjáyar E . . . . . . 164 C2
Çankırı TR . . . . . . 23 A7
Cannai I . . . . . . . . 179 C2
Cannara I . . . . . . . 136 B1
Cánnero Riviera I . 120 A1
Cannes F . . . . . . . 132 B3
Canneto
Sicilia I . . . . . . . .177 A3
Toscana I . . . . . .135 B3
Canneto sull'Oglio
I . . . . . . . . . . . . 120 B3
Cannich GB . . . . . . 32 D2
Cannóbio I . . . . . . 120 A1
Cannock GB . . . . . 40 C1
Canonbie GB. . . . . 36 A4
Canosa di Púglia I . 171 B4
Can Pastilla E . . . . 166 B2
C'an Picafort E . . . 167 B3
Cantalapiedra E . . 150 A2
Cantalejo E . . . . . 151 A4
Cantalgallo E. . . . . 161 A3
Cantalice I . . . . . . 169 A2
Cantalpino E . . . . . 150 A2
Cantalupo in Sabina
I . . . . . . . . . . . . 168 A2
Cantanhede P . . . . 148 B1
Cantavieja E . . . . . 153 B3
Čantavir SRB. . . . . 126 B1
Canterbury GB . . . 45 B5
Cantiano I . . . . . . . 136 B1
Cantillana E . . . . . 162 A2
Cantiveros E . . . . . 150 B3
Cantoria E . . . . . . 164 B2
Cantù I . . . . . . . . . 120 B2
Cany-Barville F . . . 89 A4
Canyet de Mar E . . 147 C3
Caol GB. . . . . . . . 34 B2
Cáorle I . . . . . . . . 122 B1
Caorso I . . . . . . . . 120 B2
Capáccio I . . . . . . 172 B1
Capalbio I . . . . . . 168 A1
Capánnori I . . . . . . 134 B3
Caparde BIH . . . . . 139 A4
Caparroso E . . . . . 144 B2
Capbreton F . . . . . 128 C1
Capdenac-Gare F . 116 C2
Capdepera E . . . . 167 B3
Cap-de-Pin F . . . . 128 B2
Capel Curig GB . . . 38 A3
Capellades E . . . . 147 C2
Capena I . . . . . . . 168 A2
Capendu F. . . . . . 146 A3
Capestang F . . . . . 130 B2
Capestrano I . . . . . 169 A3
Cap Ferret F . . . . . 128 B1
Capileira E . . . . . . 163 B4
Capinha P . . . . . . 148 B2
Ca'Pisani I . . . . . . 122 C1
Capistrello I . . . . . 169 B3
Capizzi I . . . . . . . . 177 B3
Čaplje BIH . . . . . . 124 C2
Čapljina BIH . . . . . 139 B3
Capo di Ponte I . . . 120 A3
Caposile I . . . . . . . 122 B1
Capoterra I . . . . . . 179 C2
Cappamore IRL . . . 29 B3
Cappeln D . . . . . . 71 B5
Cappoquin IRL . . . 29 B4
Capracotta I . . . . . 169 B4
Capránica I . . . . . . 168 A2
Caprarola I . . . . . . 168 A2
Capretta I . . . . . . . 135 C5
Capri I . . . . . . . . . 170 C2
Capriati a Volturno
I . . . . . . . . . . . . 170 B2
Caprino Veronese
I . . . . . . . . . . . . 121 B3
Captieux F . . . . . . 128 B2
Cápua I . . . . . . . . 170 B2
Capurso I . . . . . . . 173 A2
Capvern F . . . . . . 145 A4
Carabaña E . . . . . 151 B4
Carabias E . . . . . . 151 A4
Caracal RO . . . . . . 17 C6
Caracenilla E . . . . 152 B1
Caráglio I . . . . . . . 133 A3
Caraman F. . . . . . 146 A2
Caramánico Terme
I . . . . . . . . . . . . 169 A4
Caranga E . . . . . . 141 A4
Caranguejeira P . . 154 B2
Caransebeş RO . . . 16 C5
Carantec F. . . . . . 100 A2
Carapelle I . . . . . . 171 B3

Carasco I . . . 134 A2
Carate Brianza I . . . 120 B2
Caravaca de la Cruz E . . . 164 A2
Caravággio I . . . 120 B2
Carbajal E . . . 163 B3
Carbajo E . . . 155 B3
Carballeda E . . . 140 B3
Carballeda de Avia E . . . 140 B2
Carballo E . . . 140 A2
Carbis Bay GB . . . 42 B1
Carbon-Blanc F . . . 128 B2
Carbonera de Frentes E . . . 143 C4
Carboneras E . . . 164 C3
Carboneras de Guadazón E . . . 158 B2
Carbonero el Mayor E . . . 151 A3
Carboneros E . . . 157 B4
Carbónia I . . . 179 C2
Carbonin I . . . 108 C3
Carbonne F . . . 146 A2
Carbost
  Highland GB . . . 31 B2
  Highland GB . . . 31 B2
Carcaboso E . . . 149 B3
Carcabuey E . . . 163 A3
Carcaixent E . . . 159 B3
Carcans F . . . 128 A1
Carcans-Plage F . . . 128 A1
Carção P . . . 149 A3
Carcar E . . . 144 B2
Cárcare I . . . 133 A4
Carcassonne F . . . 146 A3
Carcastillo E . . . 144 B2
Carcedo de Burgos E . . . 143 B3
Carcelén E . . . 159 B2
Carcès F . . . 132 B2
Carchelejo E . . . 163 A4
Çardak
  Çanakkale TR . . . 186 B1
  Denizli TR . . . 189 B4
Cardedeu E . . . 147 C3
Cardeña E . . . 157 B3
Cardenete E . . . 158 B2
Cardeñosa E . . . 150 B3
Cardeto I . . . 175 C1
Cardiff GB . . . 39 C3
Cardigan GB . . . 39 B2
Cardona E . . . 147 C2
Cardosos P . . . 154 B2
Carei RO . . . 16 B5
Carentan F . . . 88 A2
Carentoir F . . . 101 B3
Careri I . . . 175 C2
Carevdar HR . . . 124 A2
Cargèse F . . . 180 A1
Carhaix-Plouguer F . . . 100 A2
Caria P . . . 148 B2
Cariati I . . . 174 B2
Carignan F . . . 91 B5
Carignano I . . . 119 C4
Cariñena E . . . 152 A2
Carini I . . . 176 A2
Cariño E . . . 140 A3
Carínola I . . . 170 B1
Carisbrooke GB . . . 44 C2
Carlabhagh GB . . . 31 A2
Carlepont F . . . 90 B3
Carlet E . . . 159 B3
Carlingford IRL . . . 27 B4
Carlisle GB . . . 36 B4
Carloforte I . . . 179 C2
Carlópoli I . . . 175 B2
Carlow
  D . . . 65 C3
  IRL . . . 30 B2
Carlton GB . . . 40 C2
Carluke GB . . . 35 C4
Carmagnola I . . . 119 C4
Carmarthen GB . . . 39 C2
Carmaux F . . . 130 A1
Carmena E . . . 150 C3
Cármenes E . . . 142 B1
Carmine I . . . 133 A3
Carmona E . . . 162 A2
Carmonita E . . . 155 B4
Carmyllie GB . . . 35 B5
Carnac F . . . 100 B2
Carndonagh IRL . . . 27 A3
Çarnew IRL . . . 30 B2
Carnforth GB . . . 37 B4
Cárnia I . . . 122 A2
Carnlough GB . . . 27 B5
Carno GB . . . 39 B3
Carnon Plage F . . . 131 B2
Carnota E . . . 140 B1
Carnoustie GB . . . 35 B5
Carnwath GB . . . 35 C4
Carolei I . . . 174 B2
Carolinensiel D . . . 71 A4
Carolles F . . . 88 B2
Carona I . . . 120 A2
Caronía I . . . 177 A3
Carovigno I . . . 173 B3
Carovilli I . . . 170 B2
Carpaneto Piacentino I . . . 120 C2
Carpegna I . . . 135 B5
Carpenédolo I . . . 121 B3
Carpentras F . . . 131 A4

Carpi I . . . 121 C3
Carpignano Sésia I . . . 119 B5
Carpineti I . . . 134 A3
Carpineto Romano I . . . 169 B3
Cărpinis RO . . . 126 B2
Carpino I . . . 171 B3
Carpinone I . . . 170 B2
Carpio E . . . 150 A2
Carquefou F . . . 101 B4
Carqueiranne F . . . 132 B2
Carral E . . . 140 A2
Carranque E . . . 151 B4
Carrapichana P . . . 148 B2
Carrara I . . . 134 A3
Carraroe IRL . . . 28 A2
Carrascalejo E . . . 156 A2
Carrascosa del Campo E . . . 151 B5
Carratraca E . . . 162 B3
Carrazeda de Ansiães P . . . 148 A2
Carrazedo de Montenegro P . . . 148 A2
Carrbridge GB . . . 32 D3
Carregal do Sal P . . . 148 B1
Carreña E . . . 142 A2
Carrick IRL . . . 26 B2
Carrickart IRL . . . 26 A3
Carrickfergus GB . . . 27 B5
Carrickmacross IRL 27 C4
Carrick-on-Shannon IRL . . . 26 C2
Carrick-on-Suir IRL . 30 B1
Carrigallen IRL . . . 27 C3
Carrión E . . . 161 B3
Carrión de Calatrava E . . . 157 A4
Carrión de los Condes E . . . 142 B2
Carrizo de la Ribera E . . . 141 B5
Carrizosa E . . . 157 B5
Carro F . . . 131 B4
Carrocera E . . . 142 B1
Carros F . . . 133 B3
Carrouge CH . . . 106 C1
Carrouges F . . . 89 B3
Carrù I . . . 133 A3
Carryduff GB . . . 27 B5
Carry-le-Rouet F . . . 131 B4
Carsóli I . . . 169 A3
Carsphairn GB . . . 36 A2
Cartagena E . . . 165 B4
Cártama E . . . 163 B3
Cartaxo P . . . 154 B2
Cartaya E . . . 161 B2
Carteret F . . . 88 A2
Cartes E . . . 142 A2
Carúnchio I . . . 170 B2
Carviçães P . . . 149 A3
Carvin F . . . 78 B2
Carvoeira P . . . 154 B1
Carvoeiro P . . . 160 B1
Casabermeja E . . . 163 B3
Casa Branca
  Portalegre P . . . 154 C3
  Setúbal P . . . 154 C2
Casacalenda I . . . 170 B2
Casa Castalda I . . . 136 B1
Casais E . . . 141 B4
Casal l'Abate I . . . 173 B4
Casalarreina E . . . 143 B4
Casalbordino I . . . 169 A4
Casalborgone I . . . 119 B4
Casalbuono I . . . 174 A1
Casalbuttano ed Uniti I . . . 120 B2
Casàl di Principe I . 170 B2
Casalécchio di Reno I . . . 135 A4
Casale Monferrato I . . . 119 B5
Casalina I . . . 136 C1
Casalmaggiore I . . . 121 C3
Casalnuovo Monterotaro I . . . 170 B3
Casaloldo I . . . 121 B3
Casalpusterlengo I 120 B2
Casamássima I . . . 173 B2
Casamicciola Terme I . . . 170 C1
Casamozza F . . . 180 A2
Casarabonela E . . . 162 B3
Casarano I . . . 173 B4
Casar de Cáceres E . . . 155 B4
Casar de Palomero E . . . 149 B3
Casarejos E . . . 143 C3
Casares E . . . 162 B2
Casares de las Hurdes E . . . 149 B3
Casariche E . . . 163 A3
Casarrubios del Monte E . . . 151 B3
Casas de Don Pedro E . . . 156 A2
Casas de Fernando Alonso E . . . 158 B1
Casas de Haro E . . . 158 B1
Casas de Juan Gil E . . . 159 B2
Casas del Juan Núñez E . . . 158 B2
Casas del Puerto E . . . 159 C2

Casas del Rio E . . . 159 B2
Casas de Millán E . . . 155 B4
Casas de Reina E . . . 156 B2
Casas de Ves E . . . 159 B2
Casas-Ibáñez E . . . 158 B2
Casasimarro E . . . 158 B1
Casas Nuevas E . . . 164 B3
Casasola E . . . 150 B3
Casasola de Arión E . . . 150 A2
Casasuertes E . . . 142 A2
Casatejada E . . . 150 C2
Casavieja E . . . 150 B3
Casazza I . . . 120 B2
Cascais P . . . 154 C1
Cascante E . . . 144 C2
Cascante del Rio E 152 B2
Cáscia I . . . 169 A3
Casciana Terme I . 134 B3
Cáscina I . . . 134 B3
Cáseda E . . . 144 B2
Casekow D . . . 74 A3
Casella I . . . 134 A2
Caselle Torinese I . .119 B4
Casemurate I . . . 135 A5
Casenove I . . . 136 C1
Caseres E . . . 153 A4
Caserío Benali E . . . 159 B3
Caserta I . . . 170 B2
Casével P . . . 160 B1
Cashel IRL . . . 29 B4
Casillas E . . . 150 B3
Casillas de Coria E 155 B4
Casina I . . . 134 A3
Casinos I . . . 159 B3
Čáslav CZ . . . 97 B3
Cásola Valsénio I . 135 A4
Cásole d'Elsa I . . . 135 B4
Cásoli I . . . 169 A4
Casória I . . . 170 C2
Caspe E . . . 153 A3
Cassàde la Selva E . . . 147 C3
Cassagnas F . . . 130 A2
Cassagnes-Bégonhès F . . . 130 A1
Cassano allo Iónio I . . . 174 B2
Cassano d'Adda I . 120 B2
Cassano delle Murge I . . . 171 C4
Cassano Magnago I . . . 120 B1
Cassano Spínola I . 120 C1
Cassel F . . . 78 B2
Cassíbile I . . . 177 C4
Cassine I . . . 119 C5
Cassino I . . . 169 B3
Cassis F . . . 132 B1
Cassolnovo I . . . 120 B1
Cassuéjouls F . . . 116 C2
Castá SK . . . 98 C1
Castagnaro I . . . 121 B4
Castagneto Carducci I . . . 134 B3
Castagnola CH . . . 120 A1
Castalla E . . . 159 C3
Castañar de Ibor E 156 A2
Castanheira de Pêra P . . . 154 A2
Cástano Primo I . . . 120 B1
Castasegna CH . . . 120 A2
Castéggio I . . . 120 B2
Casteição P . . . 148 B2
Castejón E . . . 144 B2
Castejón de Monegros E . . . 153 A3
Castejón de Sos E 145 B4
Castejón de Valdejasa E . . . 144 C3
Castèl Baronia I . . . 172 A1
Castel Bolognese I 135 A4
Castelbuono I . . . 177 B3
Casteldáccia I . . . 176 A2
Castel d'Aiano I . . . 135 A3
Castel d'Ario I . . . 121 B3
Castel de Cabra E 153 B3
Casteldelfino I . . . 132 A3
Castél del Monte I . 169 A3
Castel del Piano I . 135 C4
Castel di Iúdica I . . 177 B3
Castel di Rio I . . . 135 A4
Castèl di Sangro I . 169 B4
Castél di Tora I . . . 169 A2
Castelfidardo I . . . 136 B2
Castelfiorentino I . 135 B3
Castelforte I . . . 169 B3
Castelfranco Emília I . . . 121 C4
Castelfranco in Miscano I . . . 170 B3
Castelfranco Véneto I . . . 121 B4
Castèl Frentano I . 169 A4
Casteljaloux F . . . 128 B3
Castellabate I . . . 170 C2
Castellammare del Golfo I . . . 176 A1
Castellammare di Stábia I . . . 170 C2
Castellamonte I . . .119 B4
Castellana Grotte I 173 B3
Castellane F . . . 132 B2
Castellaneta I . . . 173 B2
Castellaneta Marina I . . . 173 B2
Castellar E . . . 157 B4
Castellarano I . . . 135 A3

Castellar de la Frontera E . . . 162 B2
Castellar de la Ribera E . . . 147 B2
Castellar del Vallés E . . . 147 C3
Castellar de Santiago E . . . 157 B4
Castell Arquato I . . . 120 C2
Castell'Azzara I . . . 135 C4
Castellbell i Villar E . . . 147 C2
Castelldans E . . . 153 A4
Castell de Cabres E . . . 153 B4
Castell de Castells E . . . 159 C3
Castelldefels E . . . 147 C2
Castell de Ferro E . 163 B4
Castelleone I . . . 120 B2
Castellet E . . . 147 C2
Castelletto di Brenzone I . . . 121 B3
Castellfollit de la Roca E . . . 147 B3
Castellfollit de Riubregos E . . . 147 C2
Castellfort E . . . 153 B3
Castellina in Chianti I . . . 135 B4
Castellina Marittima I . . . 134 B3
Castellóde Farfaña E . . . 145 C4
Castellóde la Plana E . . . 159 B3
Castello d'Empúries E . . . 147 B4
Castello di Fiemme I . . . 121 A4
Castellóli E . . . 147 C2
Castellón de Rugat E . . . 159 C3
Castellote E . . . 153 B3
Castello Tesino I . 121 A4
Castellterçol E . . . 147 C3
Castellúcchio I . . . 121 B3
Castellúccio de'Sáuri I . . . 171 B3
Castelluccio Inferiore I . . . 174 B1
Castelmassa I . . . 121 B4
Castelmáuro I . . . 170 B2
Castelmoron-sur-Lot F . . . 129 B3
Castelnaudary F . 146 A2
Castelnau-de-Médoc F . . . 128 A2
Castelnau-de-Montmirail F . . . 129 C4
Castelnau-Magnoac F . . . 145 A4
Castelnau-Montratier F . . . 129 B4
Castelnovo ne'Monti I . . . 134 A3
Castelnuovo Berardenga I . . . 135 B4
Castelnuovo della Dáunia I . . . 170 B3
Castelnuovo di Garfagnana I . . . 134 A3
Castelnuovo di Val di Cécina I . . . 135 B3
Castelnuovo Don Bosco I . . . 119 B4
Castelnuovo Scrivia I . . . 120 C1
Castelo Branco
  Bragança P . . . 149 A3
  Castelo Branco P . 155 B3
Castelo de Paiva P 148 A1
Castelo de Vide P . 155 B3
Castelo do Neiva P 148 A1
Castelo Mendo P . . 149 B3
Castelraimondo I . 136 B2
Castel San Gimignano I . . . 135 B4
Castèl San Giovanni I . . . 120 B2
Castèl San Pietro Terme I . . . 135 A4
Castelsantángelo I 136 C2
Castél Sant'Elia I . 168 A2
Castelsaraceno I . . 174 A1
Castelsardo I . . . 178 B2
Castelsarrasin F . . 129 B4
Castelserás E . . . 153 B3
Casteltérmini I . . . 176 B2
Castelvecchio Subéquo I . . . 169 A3
Castelvetrano I . . . 176 B1
Castél Volturno I . . 170 B1
Castenédolo I . . . 120 B3
Castets F . . . 128 C1
Castiádas I . . . 179 C3
Castiglioncello I . . 134 B3
Castiglione I . . . 169 A3
Castiglione Chiavarese I . . . 134 A2
Castiglione d'Adda I . . . 120 B2
Castiglione dei Pepoli I . . . 135 A4
Castiglione del Lago I . . . 135 B5

Castiglione della Pescáia I . . . 135 C3
Castiglione delle Stiviere I . . . 121 B3
Castiglione di Sicília I . . . 177 B4
Castiglione d'Órcia I . . . 135 B4
Castiglione Messer Marino I . . . 170 B2
Castiglione Messer Raimondo I . . . 169 A3
Castiglion Fibocchi I . . . 135 B4
Castiglion Fiorentino I . . . 135 B4
Castilblanco E . . . 156 A2
Castilblanco de los Arroyos E . . . 161 B4
Castil de Peones E 143 B3
Castilfrio de la Sierra E . . . 144 C1
Castilgaleu E . . . 145 B4
Castilisar E . . . 144 B2
Castilleja E . . . 161 B3
Castillejar E . . . 164 B2
Castillejo de Martin Viejo E . . . 149 B3
Castillejo de Mesleón E . . . 151 A4
Castillejo de Robledo E . . . 151 A4
Castillo de Bayuela E . . . 150 B3
Castillo de Locubín E . . . 163 A4
Castillonès F . . . 129 B3
Castillon-la-Bataille F . . . 128 B2
Castillon-Len-Couserans F . . . 146 B2
Castillonroy E . . . 145 C4
Castilruiz E . . . 144 C1
Castione I . . . 120 A2
Castions di Strada I . . . 122 B2
Castirla F . . . 180 A2
Castlebar IRL . . . 28 A2
Castlebellingham IRL . . . 27 C4
Castleblaney IRL . . 27 B4
Castlebridge IRL . . 30 B2
Castle Cary GB . . . 43 A4
Castlecomer IRL . . 30 B1
Castlederg GB . . . 27 B3
Castledermot IRL . 30 B2
Castle Douglas GB . 36 B3
Castleford GB . . . 40 B2
Castleisland IRL . . 29 B2
Castlemaine IRL . . 29 B2
Castlemartyr IRL . . 29 C3
Castlepollard IRL . 30 A1
Castlerea IRL . . . 28 A3
Castleton GB . . . 40 B2
Castletown
  Highland GB . . . 32 C3
  Isle of Man GB . . . 36 B2
Castletown Bearhaven IRL . . . 29 C2
Castletownroche IRL . . . 29 B3
Castlewellan GB . . 27 B5
Casto I . . . 120 B3
Castrejón E . . . 150 A2
Castrelo del Valle E . . . 141 B3
Castres F . . . 130 B1
Castricum NL . . . 70 B1
Castries F . . . 131 B2
Castrignano del Capo I . . . 173 C4
Castril E . . . 164 B2
Castrillo de Duero E . . . 151 A4
Castrillo de la Vega E . . . 143 C3
Castrillo de Onielo E . . . 142 C2
Castro
  E . . . 142 A2
  I . . . 173 B4
Castrocabón E . . . 141 B5
Castro-Caldelas E . 141 B3
Castrocaro Terme I . . . 135 A4
Castrocontrigo E . 141 B4
Castro Daire P . . . 148 B2
Castro dei Volsci I . 169 B3
Castro del Rio E . . . 163 A3
Castro de Rey E . . 141 A3
Castrofilippo I . . . 176 B2
Castrogonzalo E . . 142 B1
Castrojeriz E . . . 142 B2
Castro Laboreiro P 140 B2
Castro Marim P . . . 160 B2
Castromonte E . . . 142 C1
Castromudarra E . 142 B1
Castronuevo E . . . 142 C1
Castronuño E . . . 150 A2
Castrópol E . . . 141 A3
Castroreale I . . . 177 A4
Castroserracín E . . 151 A4
Castro-Urdiales E . 143 A3
Castroverde E . . . 141 A3
Castro Verde P . . . 160 B1
Castroverde de Campos E . . . 142 C1

Castroverde de Cerrato E . . . 142 C2
Castrovillari I . . . 174 B2
Castuera E . . . 156 B2
Catadau E . . . 159 B3
Cataéggio I . . . 120 A2
Çatalca TR . . . 186 A3
Catallar TR . . . 189 C5
Catánia I . . . 177 B4
Catanzaro I . . . 175 C2
Catanzaro Marina I 175 C2
Catarroja E . . . 159 B3
Catarruchos P . . . 148 B1
Catcleugh GB . . . 37 A4
Catenanuova I . . . 177 B3
Caterham GB . . . 44 B3
Cati E . . . 153 B4
Čatići BIH . . . 139 A4
Catignano I . . . 169 A3
Catillon F . . . 91 A3
Catoira E . . . 140 B2
Caton GB . . . 37 B4
Catral E . . . 165 A4
Catterick GB . . . 37 B5
Cáttolica I . . . 136 B1
Cáttolica Eraclea I . 176 B2
Catton GB . . . 37 B4
Caudebec-en-Caux F . . . 89 A4
Caudete E . . . 159 C3
Caudete de las Fuentes E . . . 159 B2
Caudiel E . . . 159 B3
Caudiès-de-Fenouillèdes F . 146 B3
Caudry F . . . 91 A3
Caulkerbush GB . . 36 B3
Caulnes F . . . 101 A3
Caulónia I . . . 175 C2
Caumont-l'Evente F 88 A3
Caunes-Minervois F . . . 146 A3
Cauro F . . . 180 B1
Caussade F . . . 129 B4
Causse-de-la-Selle F . . . 130 B2
Cauterets F . . . 145 B3
Cava de Tirreni I . . 170 C2
Cavaglia I . . . 119 B5
Cavaillon F . . . 131 B4
Cavalaire-sur-Mer F . . . 132 B2
Cavaleiro P . . . 160 B1
Cavalese I . . . 121 A4
Cavallermaggiore I 119 C4
Cavallino I . . . 122 B1
Cavan IRL . . . 27 C3
Cavárzere I . . . 121 B5
Çavdarhisar TR . . . 187 C4
Çavdır TR . . . 189 B4
Cavernães P . . . 148 B2
Cavezzo I . . . 121 C4
Cavignac F . . . 128 A2
Čavle HR . . . 123 B3
Cavo I . . . 134 C3
Cavour I . . . 119 C4
Cawdor GB . . . 32 D3
Çay TR . . . 187 D6
Çaycuma TR . . . 187 A7
Cayeux-sur-Mer F . 78 B1
Cayiralan TR . . . 23 B8
Çayırhan TR . . . 187 B6
Caylus F . . . 129 B4
Cayres F . . . 117 C3
Cazalilla E . . . 157 C4
Cazalla de la Sierra E . . . 156 C2
Cazals F . . . 129 B4
Cazanuecos E . . . 142 B1
Cazaubon F . . . 128 C2
Cazaux F . . . 128 B1
Cazavet F . . . 146 A2
Cazères F . . . 146 A2
Cazin BIH . . . 124 C1
Cazis CH . . . 107 C4
Čazma HR . . . 124 B2
Cazo E . . . 142 A1
Cazorla E . . . 164 B2
Cazouls-lès-Béziers F . . . 130 B2
Cea
  León E . . .142 B1
  Orense E . . . 140 B3
Ceánuri E . . . 143 A3
Ceauce F . . . 88 B3
Cebolla E . . . 150 C3
Cebreros E . . . 150 B3
Čebovce SK . . .112 A3
Cebrones E . . . 141 B4
Ceccano I . . . 169 B3
Cece H . . . 112 C2
Cecenowo PL . . . 68 A2
Čechtice CZ . . . 96 B3
Čechtín CZ . . . 97 B3
Cécina I . . . 134 B3
Ceclavín E . . . 155 B4
Cedégolo I . . . 120 A3
Cedeira E . . . 140 A2
Cedillo E . . . 155 B3
Cedillo del Condado E . . . 151 B4
Cedrillas E . . . 153 B3
Cedynia PL . . . 74 B3
Cée E . . . 140 B1
Cefalù I . . . 177 A3
Céggia I . . . 122 B1
Ceglédh H . . . .113 B3

Ceglédbercel H 112 B3
Céglie Messápica I 173 B3
Cehegín E 164 A3
Ceilhes-et-Rocozels F 130 B2
Ceinos de Campos E 142 B1
Ceira P 148 B1
Čejč CZ 97 C4
Cekcyn PL 76 A3
Cela BIH 124 C2
Čelákovice CZ 84 B2
Celano I 169 A3
Celanova E 140 B3
Celbridge IRL 30 A2
Čelebič BIH 138 B2
Celenza Valfortore I 170 B2
Čelić BIH 125 C4
Čelinac BIH 124 C3
Celje SLO 123 A4
Cella E 152 B2
Celldömölk H 111 B4
Celle D 72 B3
Celle Ligure I 133 A4
Celles B 79 B4
Celles-sur-Belle F 115 B3
Cellino San Marco I 173 B3
Celorico da Beira P 148 B2
Celorico de Basto P 148 A1
Çeltik TR 187 C6
Çeltikçi TR 189 B5
Cemaes GB 38 A2
Cembra I 121 A4
Čemerno BIH 139 B4
Cenad RO 126 A2
Cencenighe Agordino I 121 A4
Cenei RO 126 B2
Ceneselli I 121 B4
Cenicero E 143 B4
Cenicientos E 150 B3
Censeau F 105 C5
Čenta SRB 126 B2
Centallo I 133 A3
Centelles E 147 C3
Cento I 121 C4
Centúripe I 177 B3
Cepeda la Mora E 150 B2
Cépet F 129 C4
Čepin HR 125 B4
Čepinski Martinci HR 125 B4
Cepovan SLO 122 A2
Ceprano I 169 B3
Čeralije HR 125 B3
Cerami I 177 B3
Cerano I 120 B1
Cérans Foulletourte F 102 B2
Ceraso I 172 B1
Cerbaia I 135 B4
Cerbère F 146 B4
Cercadillo E 151 A5
Cercal
*Lisboa* P 154 B1
*Setúbal* P 160 B1
Čerčany CZ 96 B2
Cerceda E 151 B4
Cercedilla E 151 B3
Cercemaggiore I 170 B2
Cercs E 147 B2
Cercy-la-Tour F 104 C2
Cerda I 176 B2
Cerdedo E 140 B2
Cerdeira P 149 B2
Cerdon F 103 B4
Cerea I 121 B4
Ceres
GB 35 B5
I 119 B4
Cerese I 121 B3
Ceresole-Reale I 119 B4
Cereste F 132 B1
Céret F 146 B3
Cerezo de Abajo E 151 A4
Cerezo de Riotirón E 143 B3
Cerfontaine B 79 B4
Cergy F 90 B2
Cerignola I 171 B3
Cérilly F 103 C4
Cerisiers F 104 A2
Cerizay F 114 B3
Çerkeş TR 23 A7
Çerkezköy TR 186 A3
Cerkije SLO 123 A3
Cerknica SLO 123 B3
Cerkno SLO 122 A2
Cerkwica PL 67 B4
Cerna HR 125 B4
Černá Hora CZ 97 B4
Cernavodă RO 17 C8
Cernay F 106 B2
Cerne Abbas GB 43 B4
Cernégula E 143 B3
Cernik HR 124 B3
Cernóbbio I 120 B2
Černošin CZ 95 B4
Cernovice CZ 96 B2
Cérons F 128 B2
Cerovlje HR 123 B3
Cerovo SK 99 C3
Cerqueto I 135 C5
Cerralbo E 149 B3
Cerreto d'Esi I 136 B1
Cerreto Sannita I 170 B2
Cerrigydrudion GB 38 A3
Cërrik AL 182 B1
Cerro Muriano E 156 B3
Certaldo I 135 B4
Certosa di Pésio I 133 A3
Cerva P 148 A2
Cervaro I 169 B3
Cervatos de la Cueza E 142 B2
Červena Řečice CZ 97 B3
Červená-Skala SK 99 C4
Cervená Voda CZ 97 A4
Cerveny Kostelec CZ 85 B4
Cervera E 147 C2
Cervera de la Cañada E 152 A2
Cervera del Llano E 158 B1
Cervera del Río Alhama E 144 B2
Cervera de Pisuerga E 142 B2
Cervéteri I 168 B2
Cérvia I 135 A5
Cerviáde les Garriques E 147 C1
Cervignano del Friuli I 122 B2
Cervinara I 170 B2
Cervione F 180 A2
Cervo E 141 A3
Cervon F 104 B2
Cesana Torinese I 119 C3
Cesarica HR 137 A4
Cesarò I 177 B3
Cesena I 135 A5
Cesenático I 135 A5
Cēsis LV 8 D4
Česká Belá CZ 97 B3
Česká Kamenice CZ 84 B2
Česká Lípa CZ 84 B2
Česká Skalice CZ 85 B4
Česká Třebová CZ 97 B4
České Budějovice CZ 96 C2
České Velenice CZ 96 C2
Český Brod CZ 96 A2
Český Dub CZ 84 B2
Český Krumlov CZ 96 C2
Český Těšín CZ 98 B2
Čeśljeva Bara SRB 127 C3
Çeşme TR 188 A1
Cessenon F 130 B2
Cesson-Sévigné F 101 A4
Cestas F 128 B2
Čestobrodica SRB 127 D2
Cesuras E 140 A2
Cetina E 152 A2
Cetin Grad HR 123 B4
Cetinje MNE 16 D3
Cetraro I 174 B1
Ceuti E 165 A3
Ceva I 133 A4
Cevico de la Torre E 142 C2
Cevico Navero E 142 C2
Cevins F 118 B3
Cévio CH 119 A5
Cevizli TR 189 B6
Cewice PL 68 A2
Ceylan TR 189 C4
Ceyrat F 116 B3
Ceyzériat F 118 A2
Chaam NL 79 A4
Chabanais F 115 C4
Chabeuil F 117 C5
Chabielice PL 86 A3
Chablis F 104 B2
Châbons F 118 B2
Chabówka PL 99 B3
Chabreloche F 117 B3
Chabris F 103 B3
Chagford GB 42 B3
Chagny F 105 C3
Chagoda RUS 9 C9
Chaherrero E 150 B3
Chailland F 88 B3
Chaillé-les-Marais F 114 B2
Chailles F 103 B3
Chailley F 104 A2
Chalabre F 146 B3
Chalais F 128 A3
Chalamont F 118 B2
Châlette-sur-Loing F 103 A4
Chalindrey F 105 B4
Challacombe GB 42 A3
Challans F 114 B2
Challes-les-Eaux F 118 B2
Chalmazel F 117 B3
Chalmoux F 104 C2
Chalonnes-sur-Loire F 102 B1
Châlons-en-Champagne F 91 C4
Chalon-sur-Saône F 105 C3
Chalupy PL 69 A3
Châlus F 115 C4
Cham
CH 106 B3
D 95 B4
Chamberet F 116 B1
Chambéry F 118 B2
Chambilly F 117 A4
Chambley F 92 B1
Chambly F 90 B2
Chambois F 89 B4
Chambon-sur-Lac F 116 B2
Chambon-sur-Voueize F 116 A2
Chambord F 103 B3
Chamborigaud F 131 A2
Chamboulive F 116 B1
Chamerau D 95 B4
Chamonix-Mont Blanc F 119 B3
Chamoux-sur-Gelon F 118 B3
Champagnac-le-Vieux F 117 B3
Champagney F 106 B1
Champagnole F 105 C4
Champagny-Mouton F 115 B4
Champaubert F 91 C3
Champdeniers-St Denis F 114 B3
Champdieu F 117 B4
Champdôtre F 105 B4
Champeix F 116 B3
Champéry CH 119 A3
Champigne F 102 B1
Champignelles F 104 B2
Champigny-sur-Veude F 102 B2
Champlitte-et-le-Prelot F 105 B4
Champoluc I 119 B4
Champoly F 117 B3
Champorcher I 119 B4
Champrond-en-Gâtine F 89 B5
Champs-sur-Tarentaine F 116 B2
Champs-sur-Yonne F 104 B2
Champtoceaux F 101 B4
Chamrousse F 118 B2
Chamusca P 154 B2
Chanac F 130 A2
Chanaleilles F 117 C3
Chandler's Ford GB 44 C2
Chandra GR 185 D7
Chandrexa de Queixa E 141 B3
Chañe E 150 A3
Changy F 117 A3
Chania GR 185 D5
Channes F 104 B3
Chantada E 140 B3
Chantelle F 116 A3
Chantenay-St Imbert F 104 C2
Chanteuges F 117 B3
Chantilly F 90 B2
Chantonnay F 114 B2
Chão de Codes P 154 B2
Chaource F 104 A3
Chapa E 140 B2
Chapareillan F 118 B2
Chapel en le Frith GB 40 B2
Chapelle Royale F 103 A3
Chapelle-St Laurent F 102 C1
Charbonnat F 104 C3
Chard GB 43 B4
Charenton-du-Cher F 103 C4
Charlbury GB 44 B2
Charleroi B 79 B4
Charlestown
GB 42 B2
IRL 26 C2
Charlestown of Aberlour GB 32 D3
Charleville IRL 29 B3
Charleville-Mézières F 91 B4
Charlieu F 117 A4
Charlottenberg S 49 C4
Charlton Kings GB 44 B1
Charly F 90 C3
Charmes F 92 C2
Charmes-sur-Rhône F 117 C4
Charmey CH 106 C2
Charminster GB 43 B4
Charmont-en-Beauce F 103 A4
Charny F 104 B2
Charolles F 117 A4
Chârost F 103 C4
Charquemont F 106 B1
Charrin F 104 C2
Charroux F 115 B4
Chartres F 90 C1
Charzykow PL 68 B2
Chasseneuil-sur-Bonnieure F 115 C4
Chassigny F 105 B4
Château-Arnoux F 132 A2
Châteaubernard F 115 C3
Châteaubourg F 101 A4
Châteaubriant F 101 B4
Château-Chinon F 104 B2
Château-d'Oex CH 106 C2
Château-d'Olonne F 114 B2
Château-du-Loir F 102 B2
Châteaudun F 103 A3
Châteaugiron F 101 A4
Château-Gontier F 102 B1
Château-Landon F 103 A4
Château-la-Vallière F 102 B2
Château-l'Evêque F 129 A3
Châteaulin F 100 A1
Châteaumeillant F 103 C4
Châteauneuf
*Nièvre* F 104 B2
*Saône-et-Loire* F 117 A4
Châteauneuf-de-Randon F 117 C3
Châteauneuf-d'Ille-et-Vilaine F 88 B2
Châteauneuf-du-Faou F 100 A2
Châteauneuf-du-Pape F 131 A3
Châteauneuf-en-Thymerais F 89 B5
Châteauneuf la-Forêt F 116 B1
Châteauneuf-le-Rouge F 132 B1
Châteauneuf-sur-Charente F 115 C3
Châteauneuf-sur-Cher F 103 C4
Châteauneuf-sur-Loire F 103 B4
Châteauneuf-sur-Sarthe F 102 B1
Châteauponsac F 115 B5
Château-Porcien F 91 B4
Châteauredon F 132 A2
Châteaurenard
*Bouches du Rhône* F 131 B3
*Loiret* F 104 B1
Château-Renault F 102 B2
Châteauroux F 103 C3
Châteauroux-les-Alpes F 118 C3
Château-Salins F 92 C2
Château-Thierry F 91 B3
Châteauvillain F 105 A3
Châtel F 119 A3
Châtelaillon-Plage F 114 B2
Châtelaudren F 100 A3
Châtel-Censoir F 104 B2
Châtel-de-Neuvre F 116 A3
Châtelet B 79 B4
Châtelguyon F 116 B3
Châtellerault F 115 B4
Châtel-Montagne F 117 A3
Châtel-St Denis CH 106 C1
Châtel-sur-Moselle F 92 C2
Châtelus-Malvaleix F 116 A2
Châtenois F 105 A4
Châtenois-les-Forges F 106 B1
Chatham GB 45 B4
Châtillon I 119 B4
Châtillon-Coligny F 103 B4
Châtillon-en-Bazois F 104 B2
Châtillon-en-Diois F 118 C2
Châtillon-sur-Chalaronne F 117 A4
Châtillon-sur-Indre F 103 C3
Châtillon-sur-Loire F 103 B4
Châtillon-sur-Marne F 91 B3
Châtillon-sur-Seine F 104 B3
Châtres F 91 C3
Chatteris GB 45 A4
Chatton GB 37 A5
Chauchina E 163 A4
Chaudes-Aigues F 116 C3
Chaudrey F 91 C4
Chauffailles F 117 A4
Chaulnes F 90 B2
Chaument Gistoux B 79 B4
Chaumergy F 105 C4
Chaumont F 105 A4
Chaumont-en-Vexin F 90 B1
Chaumont-Porcien F 91 B4
Chaumont-sur-Aire F 91 C5
Chaumont-sur-Loire F 103 B3
Chaunay F 115 B4
Chauny F 90 B3
Chaussin F 105 C4
Chauvigny F 115 B4
Chavagnes-en-Paillers F 114 B2
Chavanges F 91 C4
Chaves P 148 A2
Chavignon F 91 B3
Chazelles-sur-Lyon F 117 B4
Chazey-Bons F 118 B2
Cheadle
*Greater Manchester* GB 40 B1
*Staffordshire* GB 40 C2
Cheb CZ 83 B4
Chebsara RUS 9 C11
Checa E 152 B2
Chęciny PL 87 B4
Cheddar GB 43 A4
Cheddleton GB 40 B1
Chef-Boutonne F 115 B3
Cheles E 155 C3
Chella E 159 B3
Chelles F 90 C2
Chełm PL 13 C5
Chełmno
*Kujawsko-Pomorskie* PL 76 A3
*Wielkopolskie* PL 76 B3
Chelmsford GB 45 B4
Chelmuzhi RUS 9 A9
Chelmża PL 76 A3
Cheltenham GB 44 B1
Chelva E 159 B2
Chémery F 103 B3
Chemery-sur-Bar F 91 B4
Chemillé F 102 B1
Chemin F 105 C4
Chemnitz D 83 B4
Chénerailles F 116 A2
Cheniménil F 105 A5
Chenonceaux F 103 B3
Chenôve F 105 B3
Chepelare BG 183 B6
Chepstow GB 39 C4
Chera E 159 B3
Cherasco I 119 C4
Cherbonnières F 115 C3
Cherbourg F 88 A2
Cherchiara di Calábria I 174 B2
Cherepovets RUS 9 C10
Chernihiv UA 13 C9
Chernivtsi UA 17 A6
Chernobyl = Chornobyl UA 13 C9
Chernyakhovsk RUS 12 A4
Chéroy F 104 A1
Cherven BY 13 B8
Chervonohrad UA 13 C6
Cherykaw BY 13 B9
Chesham GB 44 B3
Cheshunt GB 44 B3
Chessy-lès-Pres F 104 A2
Cheste E 159 B3
Chester GB 38 A4
Chesterfield GB 40 B2
Chester-le-Street GB 37 B5
Chevagnes F 104 C2
Chevanceaux F 115 C3
Chevillon F 91 C5
Chevilly F 103 A3
Chew Magna GB 43 A4
Chézery-Forens F 118 A2
Chialamberto I 119 B4
Chiampo I 121 B4
Chianale I 119 C4
Chianciano Terme I 135 B4
Chiaramonte Gulfi I 177 B3
Chiaramonti I 178 B2
Chiaravalle I 136 B2
Chiaravalle Centrale I 175 C2
Chiaréggio I 120 A2
Chiari I 120 B2
Chiaromonte I 174 A2
Chiasso CH 120 B2
Chiávari I 134 A2
Chiavenna I 120 A2
Chiché F 102 C1
Chichester GB 44 C3
Chiclana de la Frontera E 162 B1
Chiclana de Segura E 164 A1
Chiddingfold GB 44 B3
Chieri I 119 B4
Chiesa in Valmalenco I 120 A2
Chieti I 169 A4
Chieti Scalo I 169 A4
Chiéuti I 171 B3
Chigwell GB 45 B4
Chiliomodi GR 184 B3
Chillarón de Cuenca E 152 B1
Chillarón del Rey E 151 B5
Chilleurs-aux-Bois F 103 A4
Chillón E 156 B3
Chilluevar E 164 B1
Chiloeches E 151 B4
Chimay B 91 A4
Chimeneas E 163 A4
Chinchilla de Monte Aragón E 158 C2
Chinchón E 151 B4
Chingford GB 45 B4
Chinon F 102 B2
Chióggia I 122 B1
Chiomonte I 119 B3
Chipiona E 161 C3
Chippenham GB 43 A4
Chipping Campden GB 44 A2
Chipping Norton GB 44 B2
Chipping Ongar GB 45 B4
Chipping Sodbury GB 43 A4
Chirac F 130 A2
Chirbury GB 39 B3
Chirens F 118 B2
Chirivel E 164 B2
Chirk GB 38 B3
Chirnside GB 35 C5
Chişinău = Khisinev MD 17 B8
Chişineu Criş RO 113 C5
Chissey-en-Morvan F 104 B3
Chiusa I 108 C2
Chiusa di Pésio I 133 A3
Chiusaforte I 122 A2
Chiusa Sclàfani I 176 B2
Chiusi I 135 B4
Chiva E 159 B3
Chivasso I 119 B4
Chlewiska PL 87 A4
Chludowo PL 75 B5
Chlumec nad Cidlinou CZ 84 B3
Chlum u Třeboně CZ 96 C2
Chmielnik PL 87 B4
Chobienia PL 85 A4
Chobienice PL 75 B4
Choceň CZ 97 A4
Choceń PL 77 B4
Chochołow PL 99 B3
Chocianów PL 85 A3
Chociw PL 86 A3
Chociwel PL 75 A4
Choczewo PL 68 A2
Chodaków PL 77 B5
Chodecz PL 77 B4
Chodov CZ 83 B4
Chodzież PL 75 B5
Chojna PL 74 B3
Chojnice PL 68 B2
Chojno
*Kujawsko-Pomorskie* PL 77 B4
*Wielkopolskie* PL 75 B5
Chojnów PL 85 A3
Cholet F 114 A3
Chomérac F 117 C4
Chomutov CZ 83 B5
Chop UA 12 D5
Chora GR 184 B2
Chora Sfakion GR 185 D5
Chorges F 132 A2
Chorley GB 38 A4
Chornobyl = Chernobyl UA 13 C9
Chortkiv UA 13 D6
Chorzele PL 77 A5
Chorzew PL 86 A2
Chorzów PL 86 B2
Choszczno PL 75 A4
Chotěboř CZ 97 B3
Chouilly F 91 B4
Chouto P 154 B2
Chouzy-sur-Cisse F 103 B3
Chozas de Abajo E 142 B1
Chrast CZ 97 B3
Chrást CZ 96 B1
Chrastava CZ 84 B2
Chřibská CZ 84 B2
Christchurch GB 44 C2
Christiansfeld DK 59 C2
Chroberz PL 87 B4
Chropyně CZ 98 B1
Chrudim CZ 97 B3
Chrzanów PL 86 B3
Chtelnica SK 98 C1
Chudovo RUS 9 C7
Chueca E 157 A4
Chulmleigh GB 42 B3
Chur CH 107 C4
Church Stretton GB 39 B4
Churriana E 163 B3
Churwalden CH 107 C4
Chvalšiny CZ 96 C2
Chwaszczyno PL 69 A3
Chynava CZ 96 A2
Chýnov CZ 96 B2
Ciacova RO 126 B3
Ciadîr-Lunga MD 17 B8
Ciadoncha E 143 B3
Cianciana I 176 B2
Ciano d'Enza I 134 A3
Ciążen PL 76 B2
Cibakhaza H 113 C4
Ciborro P 154 C2
Cicagna I 134 A2
Cicciano I 170 C2
Ciciliano I 169 B2
Cicognolo I 120 B3
Cidadelhe P 149 B2
Cide TR 23 A7
Cidones E 143 C4
Ciechanów
*Dolnośląskie* PL 85 A4
*Mazowieckie* PL 77 B5

Ciechocinek PL.... 76 B3
Cielądz PL ...... 87 A4
Ciemnik PL ...... 75 A4
Ciempozuelos E . 151 B4
Ciepielów PL ..... 87 A5
Čierny Balog SK ... 99 C3
Cierp-Gaud F.... 145 B4
Cierpice PL ...... 76 B3
Ciervana E....... 143 A3
Cierznie PL ...... 68 B2
Cieslé PL........ 77 B5
Cieszyn PL....... 98 B2
Cieutat F ....... 145 A4
Cieza E.......... 165 A3
Cifer SK ........ 98 C1
Çifteler TR ...... 187 C6
Cifuentes E ..... 151 B5
Cigales E ....... 142 C2
Cigliano I........119 B5
Cihanbeyli TR .... 23 B7
Cillas E......... 152 B2
Cilleros E........ 149 B3
Cilleruelo de Arriba
  E........... 143 C3
Cilleruelo de Bezana
  E........... 143 B3
Cimalmotto CH ....119 A5
Cimanes del Tejar
  E........... 141 B5
Ciminna I........ 176 B2
Cimişlia MD...... 17 B8
Cimoláis I........ 122 A1
Cimpulung RO .... 17 C6
Çınarcık TR ..... 186 B4
Cinctorres E ..... 153 B3
Cinderford GB.... 39 C4
Çine TR ........ 188 B3
Ciněves CZ ...... 84 B3
Ciney B ......... 79 B5
Cinfães P........ 148 A1
Cingia de Botti I .. 120 B3
Cingoli I......... 136 B2
Cinigiano I....... 135 C4
Cinobaňa SK ..... 99 C3
Cinq-Mars-la-Pile F 102 B2
Cinquefrondi I..... 175 C2
Cintegabelle F .. 146 A2
Cintruénigo E .... 144 B2
Ciółkowo PL ..... 77 B4
Ciperez E........ 149 B3
Cirat E.......... 153 B3
Cirella I......... 174 B1
Cirencester GB.... 44 B2
Cirey-sur-Vezouze
  F........... 92 C2
Ciria E.......... 152 A2
Ciriè I...........119 B4
Cirigliano I....... 174 A2
Cirò I........... 174 B3
Cirò Marina I..... 174 B3
Ciry-le-Noble F ... 104 C3
Cislău RO ....... 17 C7
Cismon del Grappa
  I........... 121 B4
Cisneros E....... 142 B2
Çissac-Médoc F .. 128 A2
Čista CZ........ 96 A1
Cisterna di Latina I 169 B2
Cistérniga E...... 150 A3
Cisternino I...... 173 B3
Cistierna E....... 142 B1
Čitluk BIH....... 139 B3
Čítov CZ........ 84 B2
Cittadella I....... 121 B4
Cittàdella Pieve I . 135 C5
Cittádel Vaticano =
  Vatican City I.... 168 B2
Città di Castello I . 135 B5
Cittaducale I..... 169 A2
Cittanova I....... 175 C2
Città Sant'Angelo I 169 A4
Ciudadela de Menorca
  E........... 167 B3
Ciudad Real E .... 157 A4
Ciudad Rodrigo E . 149 B3
Cividale del Friuli I 122 A2
Civita I.......... 169 A3
Cívita Castellana I . 168 A2
Civitanova Alta I . 136 B2
Civitanova Marche
  I........... 136 B2
Civitavécchia I.... 168 A1
Civitella di Romagna
  I........... 135 A4
Civitella di Tronto I 136 C2
Civitella Roveto I.. 169 B3
Civray F.........115 B4
Çivril TR........ 189 A4
Cizur Mayor E .. 144 B2
Cjutadilla E ..... 147 C2
Clabhach GB..... 34 B1
Clachan GB...... 31 B2
Clachan na Luib GB 31 B1
Clacton-on-Sea GB. 45 B5
Cladich GB...... 34 B2
Claggan GB...... 34 B2
Clairvaux-les-Lacs
  F........... 105 C4
Clamecy F....... 104 B2
Claonaig GB ..... 34 C2
Clarecastle IRL ... 28 B3
Claregalway IRL .. 28 A3
Claremorris IRL... 28 A2
Clarinbridge IRL .. 28 A3

Clashmore
  GB............32 D2
  IRL............ 29 B4
Claudy GB ...... 27 B3
Clausthal-Zellerfeld
  D............ 82 A2
Cláut I.......... 122 A1
Clay Cross GB.... 40 B2
Claye-Souilly F ... 90 C2
Cléder F ........ 100 A1
Cleethorpes GB... 41 B3
Clefmont F....... 105 A4
Cléguérec F...... 100 A2
Clelles F......... 118 C2
Clenze D ....... 73 B3
Cleobury Mortimer
  GB............ 39 B4
Cléon-d'Andran F . 117 C4
Cléré-les-Pins F . 102 B2
Clères F......... 89 A5
Clermont F....... 90 B2
Clermont-en-Argonne
  F........... 91 B5
Clermont-Ferrand
  F...........116 B3
Clermont-l'Hérault
  F........... 130 B2
Clerval F........ 105 B5
Clervaux L....... 92 A2
Cléry-St André F . 103 B3
Cles I.......... 121 A4
Clevedon GB..... 43 A4
Cleveleys GB..... 38 A3
Cley GB......... 41 C5
Clifden IRL...... 28 A1
Clifford GB....... 39 B3
Clisson F........ 101 B4
Clitheroe GB..... 40 B1
Clogh IRL ....... 30 B1
Cloghan
  Donegal IRL.....26 B3
  Offaly IRL..... 28 A4
Clogheen IRL..... 29 B4
Clogher GB...... 27 B3
Cloghjordan IRL .. 28 B3
Clohars-Carnoët F 100 B2
Clonakilty IRL .... 29 C3
Clonaslee IRL .... 30 A1
Clondalkin IRL.... 30 A2
Clones IRL....... 27 B3
Clonmany IRL .... 27 A3
Clonmel IRL...... 29 B4
Clonmellon IRL ... 30 A1
Clonord IRL...... 30 A1
Clonroche IRL.... 30 B2
Cloone IRL....... 26 C3
Cloppenburg D ... 71 B5
Closeburn GB .... 36 A3
Clough GB....... 27 B5
Clova GB........ 35 B4
Clovelly GB ...... 42 B2
Clowne GB....... 40 B2
Cloyes-sur-le-Loir
  F........... 103 B3
Cloyne IRL....... 29 C3
Cluis F.......... 103 C3
Cluj-Napoca RO .. 17 B5
Clun GB......... 39 B3
Clunes GB....... 34 B3
Cluny F..........117 A4
Cluses F.........118 A3
Clusone I........ 120 B2
Clydach GB...... 39 C3
Clydebank GB.... 34 C3
Coachford IRL.... 29 C3
Coagh GB....... 27 B4
Coalisland GB.... 27 B4
Coalville GB...... 40 C2
Coaña E......... 141 A4
Çobanlar TR..... 187 D5
Cobas E......... 140 A2
Cobertelade E.... 151 A5
Cobeta E........ 152 B1
Cóbh IRL........ 29 C3
Cobreces E ...... 142 A2
Coburg D........ 82 B2
Coca E.......... 150 A3
Cocentaina E..... 159 C3
Cochem D ...... 80 B3
Cockburnspath GB. 35 C5
Cockermouth GB . 36 B3
Codigoro I....... 121 C5
Codogno I....... 120 B2
Codos E......... 152 A2
Codróipo I....... 122 B1
Codrongianos I... 178 B2
Coelhoso P...... 149 A3
Coesfeld D....... 71 C4
Coevorden NL.... 71 B3
Cofrentes E...... 159 B2
Cogeces del Monte
  E........... 150 A3
Coggeshall GB.... 45 B4
Cognac F........ 115 C3
Cogne I..........119 B4
Cognin F.........118 B2
Cogolin F........ 132 B2
Cogollos de Guadix
  E........... 164 B1
Cogollos-Vega E.. 163 A4
Cogolludo E ..... 151 B4
Coimbra P....... 148 B1
Coin E.......... 163 B3
Coirós E......... 140 A2
Čoka SRB ...... 126 B2
Col SLO ........ 123 B3
Colares P........ 154 C1

Colbitz D ....... 73 B4
Colchester GB.... 45 B4
Coldingham GB... 35 C5
Colditz D ....... 83 A4
Coldstream GB ... 35 C5
Colebrooke GB ... 43 B3
Colera E......... 146 B4
Coleraine GB..... 27 A4
Colfiorito I....... 136 B1
Cólico I.......... 120 A2
Coligny F.........118 A2
Colindres E ...... 143 A3
Collado-Mediano E 151 B3
Collado Villalba E . 151 B4
Collagna I........ 134 A3
Collanzo E ....... 142 A1
Collat F..........117 B3
Coll de Nargó E .. 147 B2
Collécchio I...... 120 C3
Colledimezzo I.... 169 B4
Colle di Val d'Elsa
  I........... 135 B4
Colleferro I....... 169 B3
Colle Isarco I..... 108 C2
Collelongo I...... 169 B3
Collepasso I...... 173 B4
Collepepe I....... 136 C1
Collesalvetti I.... 134 B3
Colle Sannita I.... 170 B2
Collesano I....... 176 B2
Colli a Volturno I.. 169 B4
Collin GB........ 36 A3
Collinée F........ 101 A3
Collingham
  Nottinghamshire
  GB............40 B2
  West Yorkshire GB .40 B3
Collinghorst D..... 71 A4
Cóllio I.......... 120 B3
Collobrières F .... 132 B2
Collon IRL....... 27 C4
Collooney IRL .... 26 B2
Colmar F........ 106 A2
Colmars F....... 132 A2
Colmenar E ..... 163 B3
Colmenar de la Sierra
  E........... 151 A4
Colmenar de Oreja
  E........... 151 B4
Colmenar Viejo E . 151 B4
Colmonel GB..... 36 A2
Colne GB........ 40 B1
Colobraro I....... 174 A2
Cologna Véneta I. 121 B4
Cologne = Köln D . 80 B2
Cologne F........ 129 C3
Cologne al Serio I . 120 B2
Colombey-les-Belles
  F........... 92 C1
Colombey-les-deux-
  Églises F..... 105 A3
Colombres E ..... 142 A2
Colomera E ...... 163 A4
Colomers E ...... 147 B3
Colomiers F...... 129 C4
Colònia de Sant Jordi
  E........... 167 B3
Colorno I........ 120 C3
Colos P......... 160 B1
Cölpin D......... 74 A2
Colpy GB........ 33 D4
Colsterworth GB . 40 C3
Coltishall GB..... 41 C5
Colunga E ....... 142 A1
Colwell GB....... 37 A4
Colwyn Bay GB... 38 A3
Colyford GB...... 43 B3
Comácchio I...... 121 C5
Coma-ruga E ..... 147 C2
Combarros E..... 141 B4
Combeaufontaine
  F........... 105 B4
Comber GB...... 27 B5
Comblain-au-Pont B 80 B1
Combloux F.......118 B3
Combourg F...... 88 B2
Combronde F.....116 B3
Comeglians I..... 109 C3
Comillas E....... 142 A2
Comines F....... 78 B3
Cómiso I........ 177 C3
Comloşu Mare RO. 126 B2
Commensacq F... 128 B2
Commentry F.....116 A2
Commerau D..... 84 A2
Commercy F..... 92 C1
Como I.......... 120 B2
Cómpeta E....... 163 B4
Compiègne F..... 90 B2
Comporta P...... 154 C2
Comps-sur-Artuby
  F........... 132 B2
Comrat MD...... 17 B8
Comrie GB....... 35 B4
Comunanza I..... 136 C2
Cona
  Emilia Romagna
  I............121 C4
  Veneto I..... 121 B5
Concarneau F.... 100 B2
Conceição P..... 160 B1
Conches-en-Ouche
  F........... 89 B4
Concordia Sagittária
  I........... 122 B1
Concordia sulla Sécchia
  I........... 121 C3
Concots F........ 129 B4

Condat F.........116 B2
Condé-en-Brie F . 91 C3
Condeixa P ..... 148 B1
Condemios de Abajo
  E........... 151 A4
Condemios de Arriba
  E........... 151 A4
Condé-sur-l'Escaut
  F........... 79 B3
Conde-sur-Marne F. 91 B4
Condé-sur-Noireau
  F........... 88 B3
Condino I........ 121 B3
Condom F....... 129 C3
Condove I........119 B4
Condrieu F.......117 B4
Conegliano I..... 122 B1
Conflans-sur-Lanterne
  F........... 105 B5
Confolens F......115 B4
Conforto E....... 141 A3
Cong IRL........ 28 A2
Congleton GB.... 40 B1
Congosto E...... 141 B4
Congosto de Valdavia
  E........... 142 B2
Congostrina E.... 151 A4
Conil de la Frontera
  E........... 162 B1
Coningsby GB.... 41 B3
Coniston GB..... 36 B3
Conlie F......... 102 A1
Conliège F....... 105 C4
Conna IRL....... 29 B3
Connah's Quay GB. 38 A3
Connantre F ..... 91 C3
Connaugh IRL.... 28 B3
Connaux F....... 131 A3
Connel GB....... 34 B2
Connerré F ...... 102 A2
Cononbridge GB.. 32 D2
Čonoplja SRB.... 126 B1
Conques F.......116 C2
Conques-sur-Orbiel
  F........... 146 A3
Conquista E...... 157 B3
Conquista de la Sierra
  E........... 156 A2
Consándolo I..... 121 C4
Consélice I....... 135 A4
Conselve I....... 121 B4
Consenvoye F.... 91 B5
Consett GB...... 37 B5
Consolacão P.... 154 B1
Constancia P..... 154 B2
Constanco E..... 140 A2
Constanţa RO.... 17 C8
Constanti E....... 147 C2
Constantina E.... 162 A2
Consuegra E..... 157 A4
Consuma I....... 135 B4
Contarina I....... 122 B1
Contay F......... 90 B2
Conthey CH......119 A4
Contigliano I..... 168 A2
Contis-Plage F ... 128 B1
Contrada I....... 170 C2
Contres F........ 103 B3
Contrexéville F ... 105 A4
Controne I....... 172 B1
Contursi Termi I .. 172 B1
Conty F......... 90 B2
Conversano I..... 173 B3
Conwy GB....... 38 A3
Cookstown GB... 27 B4
Coole F......... 91 C4
Coolgreany IRL... 30 B2
Cooneen GB..... 27 B3
Cootehill IRL..... 27 B3
Cope E.......... 165 B3
Copenhagen =
  København DK ... 61 D2
Copertino I....... 173 B4
Copparo I........ 121 C4
Coppenbrugge D . 72 B2
Corabia RO...... 17 D6
Córaci I......... 175 B2
Coralići BIH...... 124 C1
Corato I......... 171 B4
Coray F......... 100 A2
Corbeil-Essonnes F 90 C2
Corbeny F....... 91 B3
Corbera E ....... 159 B3
Corbie F......... 90 B2
Corbigny F....... 104 B2
Corbion B ....... 91 B4
Corbridge GB.... 37 B4
Corby GB........ 40 C3
Corconte E....... 143 A3
Corcubión E ..... 140 B1
Corcumello I..... 169 A3
Cordenòns I...... 122 B1
Cordes-sur-Ciel F. 129 C4
Córdoba E....... 156 C3
Cordobilla de Lácara
  E........... 155 B4
Cordovado I...... 122 B1
Corella E........ 144 B2
Coreses E ....... 150 A2
Corfe Castle GB .. 43 B4
Corga de Lobão P. 148 B1
Cori I........... 169 B2
Coria E.......... 155 B4
Coria del Río E ... 162 A1
Corigliano Cálabro
  I........... 174 B2
Corinaldo I....... 136 B1

Corinth = Korinthos
  GR.......... 184 B3
Cório I..........119 B4
Coripe E......... 162 B2
Cork IRL........ 29 C3
Corlay F........ 100 A2
Corleone I....... 176 B2
Corleto Monforte I 172 B1
Corleto Perticara I. 174 A2
Çorlu TR........ 186 A2
Cormainville F.... 103 A3
Cormatin F....... 104 C3
Cormeilles F ..... 89 A4
Cormery F ....... 102 B2
Cormòns I....... 122 B2
Cormoz F........118 A2
Cornago E....... 144 B1
Cornberg D ..... 82 A1
Cornellana E..... 141 A4
Corneşti MD .... 17 B8
Corníglio I....... 134 A3
Cornimont F..... 106 B1
Corniolo I....... 135 B4
Cornuda I....... 121 B5
Cornudella de Montsant
  E........... 147 C1
Cornudilla E ..... 143 B3
Cornus F........ 130 B2
Çorovodë AL .... 182 C2
Corpach GB..... 34 B2
Corps F......... 118 C2
Corps Nuds F .... 101 B4
Corral de Almaguer
  E........... 157 A4
Corral de Ayllon E. 151 A4
Corral de Calatrava
  E........... 157 B3
Corrales E ....... 149 A4
Corral-Rubio E ... 158 C2
Corredoiras E .... 140 A2
Corréggio I....... 121 C3
Corrèze F........116 B1
Corridónia I...... 136 B2
Corris GB........ 38 B3
Corrubedo E..... 140 B1
Córsico I........ 120 B2
Corsock GB..... 36 A3
Corte F......... 180 A2
Corteconceptión E 161 B3
Corte de Peleas E. 155 C4
Cortegaca P..... 148 B1
Cortegada E ..... 140 B2
Cortegana E..... 161 B3
Cortemaggiore I . 120 B2
Cortemilia I...... 133 A4
Corte Pinto P.... 160 B2
Cortes E......... 144 C2
Cortes de Aragón
  E........... 153 B3
Cortes de Arenoso
  E........... 153 B3
Cortes de Baza E . 164 B2
Cortes de la Frontera
  E........... 162 B2
Cortes de Pallás E 159 B3
Cortiçadas P..... 154 C2
Cortico P........ 148 A2
Cortijo de Arriba E 157 A3
Cortijos Nuevos E. 164 A2
Cortina d'Ampezzo
  I........... 108 C3
Corton GB....... 41 C5
Cortona I........ 135 B4
Coruche P....... 154 C2
Corullón E ....... 141 B4
Çorum TR....... 23 A8
Corvara in Badia I . 108 C2
Corvera E........ 165 B3
Corwen GB...... 38 B3
Cosa E.......... 152 B2
Cosenza I........ 174 B2
Cosham GB...... 44 C2
Coslada E ....... 151 B4
Cosne-Cours-sur-Loire
  F........... 104 B1
Cosne d'Allier F .. 103 C4
Cospeito E....... 140 A3
Cossato I........119 B5
Cossaye F....... 104 C2
Cossé-le-Vivien F. 101 B5
Cossonay CH .... 105 C5
Costa da Caparica
  P........... 154 C1
Costa de Santo André
  P........... 160 A1
Costalpino I...... 135 B4
Costa Nova P.... 148 B1
Costaros F....... 117 C3
Costeşti RO...... 17 C6
Costigliole d'Asti I 119 C5
Costigliole Saluzzo
  I........... 133 A3
Coswig
  Sachsen.......83 A5
  Sachsen-Anhalt D .83 A4
Cotherstone GB .. 37 B5
Cotronei I....... 175 B2
Cottbus D....... 84 A2
Cottenham GB... 45 A4
Cottingham GB... 40 B3
Coublanc F...... 105 B4
Couches F....... 104 C3
Couço P......... 154 C2
Coucouron F..... 117 C3
Coucy-le-Château-
  Auffrique F..... 90 B3
Couëron F....... 101 B4
Couflens F....... 146 B2

Couhé F.........115 B4
Couiza F......... 146 B3
Coulags GB..... 31 B3
Coulanges F ..... 104 C2
Coulanges-la-Vineuse
  F........... 104 B2
Coulanges-sur-Yonne
  F........... 104 B2
Couleuvre F...... 104 C1
Coulmier-le-Sec F. 104 B3
Coulommiers F... 90 C3
Coulonges-sur-l'Autize
  F........... 114 B3
Coulounieix-Chamiers
  F........... 129 A3
Coulport GB..... 34 B3
Coupar Angus GB. 35 B4
Coupéville F..... 91 C4
Couptrain F..... 89 B3
Coura P......... 140 C2
Courcelles B ..... 79 B4
Courcelles-Chaussy
  F........... 92 B2
Courchevel F.....118 B3
Cour-Cheverny F . 103 B3
Courcôme F..... 115 C4
Courçon F.......114 B3
Cour-et-Buis F....117 B4
Courgenay CH.... 106 B2
Courmayeur I ....119 B3
Courniou F....... 130 B1
Cournon-d'Auvergne
  F........... 116 B3
Cournonterral F . 130 B2
Courpière F......117 B3
Coursan F ....... 130 B2
Courseulles-sur-Mer
  F........... 89 A3
Cours-la-Ville F...117 A4
Courson-les-Carrières
  F........... 104 B2
Courtalain F ..... 103 A3
Courtenay F..... 104 A2
Courtomer F .... 89 B4
Courville
  Eure-et-Loire F... 89 B5
  Marne F..... 91 B4
Coussac-Bonneval
  F........... 115 C5
Coutances F..... 88 A2
Couterne F...... 89 B3
Coutras F....... 128 A2
Couvet CH...... 106 C1
Couvin B ....... 91 A4
Couzon F........ 104 C2
Covadonga E..... 142 A1
Covaleda E ...... 143 C4
Covarrubias E ... 143 B3
Covas E......... 148 A1
Cove GB........ 31 B3
Coventry GB..... 44 A2
Coverack GB..... 42 B1
Covigliáio I....... 135 A4
Covilhã P........ 148 B2
Cowbridge GB.... 39 C3
Cowdenbeath GB . 35 B4
Cowes GB....... 44 C2
Cox F.......... 129 C4
Cózar E......... 157 B4
Cozes F......... 114 C3
Cozzano F....... 180 B2
Craco I.......... 174 A2
Cracow = Kraków
  PL............ 99 A3
Craibstone GB... 33 D4
Craighouse GB... 34 C2
Craignure GB.... 34 B2
Crail GB......... 35 B5
Crailsheim D..... 94 B2
Craiova RO...... 17 C5
Cramlington GB .. 37 A5
Cranleigh GB.... 44 B3
Craon F......... 101 B5
Craonne F....... 91 B3
Craponne F......117 B4
Craponne-sur-Arzon
  F........... 117 B4
Crathie GB....... 32 D3
Crato P......... 155 B3
Craughwell IRL ... 28 A3
Craven Arms GB .. 39 B4
Crawford GB..... 36 A3
Crawinkel D...... 82 B2
Crawley GB...... 44 B3
Creag Ghoraidh GB 31 B1
Crecente E....... 140 B2
Crèches-sur-Saône
  F........... 117 A4
Crécy-en-Ponthieu
  F........... 78 B1
Crécy-la-Chapelle F 90 C2
Crécy-sur-Serre F . 91 B3
Crediton GB..... 43 B3
Creeslough IRL ... 26 A3
Creetown GB..... 36 B2
Creeve GB....... 27 B4
Creglingen D..... 94 B2
Creil F.......... 90 B2
Creissels F....... 130 A2
Crema I......... 120 B2
Cremeaux F......117 B3
Crémenes E...... 142 B1
Crémieu F........118 B2
Cremlingen D..... 73 B3
Cremona I....... 120 B3
Creney F........ 91 C4
Črenšovci SLO...111 C3
Créon F......... 128 B2

Crepaja SRB . . . . . 127 B2
Crépey F . . . . . . 92 C1
Crépy F . . . . . 91 B3
Crépy-en-Valois F . . 90 B2
Cres HR . . . . . . 123 C3
Crescentino I . . . . .119 B5
Crespino I . . . . . 121 C4
Crespos E . . . . . 150 B3
Cressage GB . . . . 39 B4
Cressensac F . . . 129 A4
Cressia F . . . . . 105 C4
Crest F . . . . . . 117 C5
Cresta CH . . . . . 107 C4
Créteil F . . . . . . 90 C2
Creully F . . . . . . 88 A3
Creussen D . . . . . 95 B3
Creutzwald F . . . . 92 B2
Creuzburg D . . . . 82 A2
Crevalcore I . . . . 121 C4
Crèvecoeur-le-Grand
  F . . . . . . . . . . . 90 B2
Crevillente E . . . 165 A4
Crévola d'Ossola I .119 A5
Crewe GB . . . . . 38 A4
Crewkerne GB . . . 43 B4
Criales E . . . . . 143 B3
Crianlarich GB . . . 34 B3
Criccieth GB . . . . 38 B2
Crickhowell GB . . . 39 C3
Cricklade GB . . . . 44 B2
Crieff GB . . . . . . 35 B4
Criel-sur-Mer F . . . 90 A1
Crikvenica HR . . . 123 B3
Crillon F . . . . . . 90 B1
Crimmitschau D . . 83 B4
Crimond GB . . . . 33 D5
Crinitz D . . . . . . 84 A1
Cripán E . . . . . . 143 B4
Criquetot-l'Esneval
  F . . . . . . . . . . 89 A4
Crispiano I . . . . . 173 B3
Crissolo I . . . . . 119 C4
Cristóbal E . . . . 149 B4
Crivitz D . . . . . . 73 A4
Črna SLO . . . . . 110 C1
Crna Bara
  Srbija SRB . . . . .127 C1
  Vojvodina SRB. . . 126 B2
Crnac HR . . . . . 125 B3
Crnča SRB . . . . . 127 C1
Crni Lug
  BIH . . . . . . . .138 A2
  HR . . . . . . . . 123 B3
Črni Vrh SLO . . . 123 B3
Crnjelovo Donje
  BIH . . . . . . . 125 C5
Črnomelj SLO . . . 123 B4
Crocketford GB . . . 36 A3
Crocq F . . . . . .116 B2
Crodo I . . . . . . .119 A5
Croglin GB . . . . . 37 B4
Crolly IRL . . . . . . 26 A2
Cromarty GB . . . . 32 D2
Cromer GB . . . . . 41 C5
Cronat F . . . . . . 104 C2
Crookhaven IRL . . 29 C2
Crookstown IRL . . 29 C3
Croom IRL . . . . . 29 B3
Cropalati I . . . . . 174 B2
Crópani I . . . . . 175 C2
Crosbost GB . . . . 31 A2
Crosby GB . . . . . 38 A3
Crosía I . . . . . . 174 B2
Crossakiel IRL. . . . 27 C3
Cross-Hands GB . . 39 C2
Crosshaven IRL . . . 29 C3
Crosshill GB . . . . 36 A2
Crossmolina IRL . . 26 B1
Crotone I . . . . . . 175 B3
Crottendorf D . . . . 83 B4
Crouy F . . . . . . 90 B3
Crowborough GB . . 45 B4
Crowland GB . . . . 41 C3
Crowthorne GB . . . 44 B3
Croyde GB . . . . . 42 A2
Croydon GB . . . . . 44 B3
Crozon F . . . . . 100 A1
Cruas F . . . . . . 117 C4
Cruceni RO . . . . 126 A3
Crúcoli I . . . . . . 174 B3
Cruden Bay GB . . . 33 D5
Crudgington GB . . 38 B4
Cruis F . . . . . . 132 A1
Crumlin GB . . . . . 27 B4
Cruseilles F. . . . . .118 A3
Crusheen IRL. . . . 28 B3
Cruz de Incio E . . 141 B3
Crvenka SRB . . . 126 B1
Crveny Kamen SK. . 98 C2
Csabacsüd H. . . . 113 C4
Csabrendek H . . . .111 B4
Csákánydoroszló
  H . . . . . . . . . .111 C3
Csákvár H . . . . . .112 B2
Csanádapáca H . . 113 C4
Csanádpalota H . . 126 A2
Csány H. . . . . . .113 B3
Csanytelek H. . . . 113 C4
Csapod H. . . . . . .111 B3
Császár H . . . . . .112 B2
Császártöltés H. . . 112 C3
Csávoly H . . . . . 125 A5
Csemö H. . . . . . .113 B3
Csengöd H. . . . . . 112 C3
Csépa H. . . . . . . 113 C4
Cseprég H. . . . . .111 B3
Cserkeszölö H. . . . 113 C4
Csernely H. . . . . .113 A4

Csesztreg H. . . . . .111 C3
Csökmö H . . . . . .113 B5
Csököly H . . . . . 124 A3
Csokonyavisonta
  H . . . . . . . . . . 124 A3
Csólyospálos H. . . 113 C3
Csongrád H . . . . . 113 C4
Csopak H . . . . . 112 C1
Csorna H . . . . . .111 B4
Csorvás H . . . . . 113 C4
Csurgo H . . . . . 124 A3
Cuacos de Yuste E 150 B2
Cualedro E . . . . . 140 C3
Cuanca de Campos
  E. . . . . . . . . . . 142 B1
Cuba P . . . . . . 160 A2
Cubel E . . . . . . 152 A2
Cubelles E . . . . . 147 C2
Cubillos E . . . . . 143 C4
Cubillos del Sil E . 141 B4
Cubjac F . . . . . . 129 A3
Cubo de la Solana
  E. . . . . . . . . . . 152 A1
Cuckfield GB . . . . 44 B3
Cucuron F . . . . . 131 B4
Cudillero E . . . . . 141 A4
Cuéllar E . . . . . 151 A3
Cuenca E . . . . . 152 B1
Cuers F . . . . . . 132 B2
Cuerva E . . . . . 157 A3
Cueva de Agreda
  E. . . . . . . . . . . 144 C2
Cuevas Bajas E . . 163 A3
Cuevas del Almanzora
  E. . . . . . . . . . . 164 B3
Cuevas del Becerro
  E. . . . . . . . . . . 162 B2
Cuevas del Campo
  E. . . . . . . . . . . 164 B2
Cuevas del Valle E 150 B2
Cuevas de San
  Clemente E . . . . 143 B3
Cuevas de San Marcos
  E. . . . . . . . . . . 163 A3
Cuges-les-Pins F . 132 B1
Cúglieri I . . . . . . 178 B2
Cugnaux F . . . . . 129 C4
Cuijk NL . . . . . . 80 A1
Cuinzier F . . . . . .117 A4
Cuiseaux F . . . . 105 C4
Cuisery F . . . . . 105 C4
Culan F . . . . . . 103 C4
Culemborg NL . . . 79 A5
Cúllar E . . . . . . 164 B2
Cullaville GB . . . . 27 B4
Cullera E . . . . . 159 B3
Cullivoe GB . . . . . 33 A5
Cullompton GB . . . 43 B3
Cully CH. . . . . . 106 C1
Cults GB . . . . . . 33 D4
Cumbernauld GB . 35 C4
Cumbres de San
  Bartolomé E . . . 161 A3
Cumbres Mayores
  E. . . . . . . . . . . 161 A3
Cumiana I . . . . . 119 C4
Čumić SRB . . . . 127 C2
Cumnock GB . . . . 36 A2
Çumra TR. . . . . . 23 C7
Cúneo I . . . . . . 133 A3
Cunlhat F . . . . . .117 B3
Čunski HR . . . . . 123 C3
Cuntis E . . . . . . 140 B2
Cuorgnè I . . . . . .119 B4
Cupar GB . . . . . . 35 B4
Cupello I . . . . . . 170 A2
Cupra Maríttima I . 136 B2
Cupramontana I . . 136 B2
Čuprija SRB. . . . 127 D3
Curinga I . . . . . 175 C2
Currelos E . . . . . 140 B3
Currie GB. . . . . . . 35 C4
Curtea de Argeş RO 17 C6
Curtici RO . . . . . 126 A3
Curtis E . . . . . . 140 A2
Curtis Santa Eulalia
  E. . . . . . . . . . . 140 A2
Čurug SRB . . . . 126 B2
Cusano Mutri I. . . 170 B2
Cushendall GB . . . 27 A4
Cusset F . . . . . .117 A3
Cussy-les-Forges
  F. . . . . . . . . . . 104 B3
Custines F . . . . . 92 C2
Cutanda E . . . . . 152 B2
Cutro I . . . . . . . 175 B2
Cutrofiano I . . . . 173 B4
Cuts F . . . . . . . 90 B3
Cuvilly F . . . . . . 90 B2
Cuxhaven D. . . . . 64 C1
Cvikov CZ . . . . . 84 B2
Cwmbran GB. . . . 39 C3
Cybinka PL . . . . . 75 B3
Czacz PL . . . . . . 75 B5
Czajków PL . . . . . 86 A2
Czaplinek PL . . . . 75 A5
Czarlin PL . . . . . 69 A3
Czarna-Dąbrówka
  PL. . . . . . . . . . . 68 A2
Czarna Woda PL . . 68 B3
Czarnca PL . . . . . 87 B3
Czarne PL . . . . . 68 B1
Czarnków PL . . . . 75 B5
Czarnozyly PL . . . 76 A3
Czarny Bór PL. . . . 85 B4

Czarny-Dunajec PL. 99 B3
Czarny Las PL. . . . 86 A1
Czchow PL. . . . . . 99 B4
Czechowice-Dziedzice
  PL. . . . . . . . . . . 98 B2
Czempiń PL . . . . . 75 B5
Czermno PL. . . . . 87 A4
Czernichow PL . . . 99 B3
Czerniejewo PL . . . 76 B2
Czernikowo PL . . . 76 B3
Czersk PL. . . . . . 68 B2
Czerwieńsk PL. . . . 75 B4
Czerwionka-Leszczyny
  PL. . . . . . . . . . . 86 B2
Częstochowa PL. . . 86 B3
Czeszewo PL. . . . 76 B2
Człopa PL. . . . . . 75 A5
Człuchów PL . . . . 68 B2
Czołpino PL . . . . . 68 A2

## D

Dağ TR. . . . . . . 189 B5
Daaden D. . . . . . 81 B3
Dabas H. . . . . . .112 B3
Dąbie PL. . . . . . . 76 B3
Dąbki PL. . . . . . . 67 B5
Dabo F . . . . . . . 92 C3
Dabrowa PL. . . . . 76 B2
Dąbrowa Górnicza
  PL. . . . . . . . . . . 86 B3
Dąbrowa Tarnowska
  PL. . . . . . . . . . . 87 B4
Dąbrowice PL . . . . 77 B4
Dabrowno PL . . . . 77 A5
Dachau D . . . . . 108 A2
Dačice CZ . . . . . . 97 B3
Daday TR . . . . . . 23 A7
Dagali N . . . . . . 47 B5
Dägebüll D. . . . . . 64 B1
Dagmersellen CH . 106 B2
Dahlen D . . . . . . 83 A4
Dahlenburg D . . . 73 A3
Dahme D . . . . . . 83 A5
Dahn D . . . . . . . 93 B3
Dähre D . . . . . . 73 B3
Daikanvik S . . . . 195 E7
Dail bho Dheas GB . 31 A2
Dailly GB . . . . . . 36 A2
Daimiel E . . . . . 157 A4
Daingean IRL . . . . 30 A1
Đakovica KOS . . . 16 D4
Đakovo HR . . . . 125 B4
Dal
  Akershus N . . . . .48 B3
  Telemark N . . . . .47 C5
Dalaas A. . . . . . 107 B5
Dalabrog GB . . . . 31 B1
Dala-Floda S . . . . 50 B1
Dala-Husby S . . . . 50 B2
Dala-Järna S . . . . 50 B1
Dalaman TR. . . . 188 C3
Dalarö S . . . . . . 57 A4
Dalbeattie GB . . . 36 B3
Dalby
  DK. . . . . . . . .59 C3
  Skåne S . . . . . .61 D3
  Uppsala S . . . . .57 A3
  Värmland S . . . . .49 B4
Dale
  Pembrokeshire
    GB . . . . . . . . .39 C1
  Shetland GB . . . 33 A5
  Hordaland N. . . . 46 B2
  Sogn og Fjordane
    N. . . . . . . . . . 46 A2
Dalen
  Akershus N . . . . .48 C3
  Telemark N . . . . .53 A4
Daleszyce PL. . . . 87 B4
Dalhalvaig GB . . . 32 C3
Dalheim L. . . . . . 92 B2
Dalhem S . . . . . . 57 C4
Dalías E . . . . . . 164 C2
Dalj HR . . . . . . 125 B4
Dalkeith GB . . . . 35 C4
Dalkey IRL . . . . . 30 A2
Dalmally GB . . . . 34 B3
Dalmellington GB . 36 A2
Dalmose DK . . . . 65 A4
Dalry
  Dumfries & Galloway
    GB . . . . . . . . .34 C3
  North Ayrshire GB . 36 A2
Dalrymple GB . . . 36 A2
Dalseter N . . . . . 47 A6
Dalsjöfors S . . . . 60 B3
Dalskog S . . . . . 54 B3
Dals Langed S . . . 54 B3
Dals Rostock S . . . 54 B3
Dalston GB . . . . . 36 B4
Dalstorp S . . . . . 60 B3
Dalton-in-Furness
  GB . . . . . . . . . . 36 B3
Daluis F . . . . . . 132 A2
Dalum
  D. . . . . . . . . .71 B4
  S. . . . . . . . . .60 B3
Dalvík IS . . . . . . 191 B7
Dalwhinnie GB . . . 32 E2
Dalyan TR . . . . . 188 C3
Damasi GR . . . . 182 D4
Damasławek PL. . . 76 B2
Damazan F . . . . 129 B3
Damgan F . . . . . 101 B3
Dammarie-les-Lys F 90 C2

Dammartin-en-Goële
  F. . . . . . . . . . . 90 B2
Damme D . . . . . . 71 B5
Damnica PL . . . . . 68 A2
Dampierre F . . . . 105 B4
Dampierre-sur-Salon
  F. . . . . . . . . . . 105 B4
Damüls A . . . . . 107 B4
Damville F . . . . . 89 B5
Damvillers F . . . . 92 B1
Damwoude NL. . . . 70 A2
Danasjö S . . . . . 195 E7
Danbury GB. . . . . 45 B4
Dångebo S. . . . . . 63 B3
Dangers F . . . . . 89 B5
Dangé-St Romain
  F . . . . . . . . . . 102 C2
Dangeul F . . . . . 89 B4
Danilovgrad MNE . . 16 D3
Danischenhagen D. 64 B3
Daniszyn PL. . . . . 85 A5
Danjoutin F . . . . 106 B1
Dannas S . . . . . . 60 B3
Dannemarie F . . . 106 B2
Dannemora S . . . . 51 B4
Dannenberg D . . . 73 A4
Dánszentmiklós H. .112 B3
Dány H. . . . . . . .112 B3
Daoulas F . . . . . 100 A1
Darabani RO . . . . 17 A7
Darány H . . . . . 125 B3
Darda H . . . . . . 125 B4
Dardesheim D . . . 73 C3
Darfeld D . . . . . . 71 B4
Darfo I . . . . . . . 120 B3
Dargin PL . . . . . . 68 A1
Dargun D . . . . . . 66 C1
Darlington GB . . . 37 B5
Darłowo PL . . . . . 68 A1
Darmstadt D . . . . 93 B4
Darney F . . . . . . 105 A5
Daroca E . . . . . 152 A2
Darque P . . . . . 148 A1
Darragh IRL . . . . . 28 B2
Dartford GB. . . . . 45 B4
Dartington GB . . . 43 B3
Darton GB . . . . . 40 B2
Daruvar HR . . . . 124 B3
Darvas H . . . . . . .113 B5
Darvel GB . . . . . 36 A2
Darwen GB . . . . . 38 A4
Dassel D . . . . . . 82 A1
Dassow D . . . . . . 65 C3
Datça TR . . . . . 188 C2
Datteln D . . . . . . 80 A3
Dattenfeld D . . . . 81 B3
Daugard DK . . . . 59 C2
Daugavpils LV . . . . 8 E5
Daumeray F . . . . 102 B1
Daun D . . . . . . . 80 B2
Daventry GB . . . . 44 A2
Davle CZ . . . . . . 96 B2
Davor HR . . . . . 124 B3
Davos CH . . . . . 107 C4
Davutlar TR . . . . 188 B2
Davyd Haradok BY . 13 B7
Dawlish GB . . . . . 43 B3
Dax F . . . . . . . 128 C1
Dazkırı TR . . . . . 189 B4
Deal GB . . . . . . 45 B5
Deauville F. . . . . . 89 A4
Deba E . . . . . . 143 A4
Debar MK . . . . . 182 B2
Dębe PL . . . . . . 77 B5
Dębica PL . . . . . . 87 B5
Dębnica Kaszubska
  PL. . . . . . . . . . . 68 A2
Dębno PL . . . . . . 74 B3
Dębołeka PL . . . . 86 A2
Dębowa Łąka PL . . 69 B4
Debrc SRB. . . . . 127 C1
Debrecen H. . . . . .113 B5
Debrznica PL . . . . 75 B4
Debrzno PL . . . . . 68 B2
Debstedt D. . . . . . 72 A1
Decazeville F . . . 130 A1
Dechtice SK. . . . . 98 C1
Decima I . . . . . . 168 B2
Decimomannu I . . 179 C2
Děčín CZ . . . . . . 84 B2
Decize F . . . . . . 104 C2
De Cocksdorp NL. . 70 A1
Decollatura I . . . . 175 B2
Decs H . . . . . . . 125 A4
Deddington GB . . . 44 B2
Dedeler TR. . . . . 187 B5
Dedelow D . . . . . 74 A2
Dedemli TR . . . . 189 B7
Dedemsvaart NL . . 71 B3
Dédestapolcsány
  H . . . . . . . . . . .113 A4
Dedovichi RUS . . . 9 D6
Deeping St Nicholas
  GB . . . . . . . . . . 41 C3
Dég H . . . . . . . 112 C2
Degaña E . . . . . 141 B4
Degeberga S . . . . 61 D4
Degerby FIN . . . . 51 B7
Degerfors S . . . . 55 A5
Degerhamn S . . . . 63 B4
Degernes N . . . . . 54 A2
Deggendorf D . . . 95 C4
Deggingen D . . . . 94 C1
Dego I . . . . . . . 133 A4
Degolados P . . . . 155 B3
De Haan B . . . . . 78 A3

Dehesas de Guadix
  E . . . . . . . . . . 164 B1
Dehesas Viejas E . 163 A4
Deia I . . . . . . . 166 B2
Deining D. . . . . . . 95 B3
Deinze B. . . . . . . 79 B3
Déiva Marina I . . . 134 A2
Dej RO . . . . . . . 17 B5
Deje S. . . . . . . . 55 A4
De Koog NL . . . . . 70 A1
Delabole GB . . . . 42 B2
Delary S. . . . . . . 61 C3
Delbrück D. . . . . . 81 A4
Delčevo MK . . . . 182 B4
Delden NL . . . . . 71 B3
Deleitosa E . . . . 156 A2
Delekovec HR . . . 124 A2
Delémont CH. . . . 106 B2
Delft NL . . . . . . . 70 B1
Delfzijl NL . . . . . . 71 A3
Délia I . . . . . . . 176 B2
Delianuova I . . . . 175 C1
Deliblato SRB . . . 127 C3
Delice TR . . . . . . 23 B7
Deliceto I . . . . . 171 B3
Delitzsch D . . . . . 83 A4
Dellach A . . . . . 109 C4
Delle F . . . . . . . 106 B2
Delme F . . . . . . . 92 C2
Delmen-horst D. . . 72 A1
Delnice HR. . . . . 123 B3
Delsbo S . . . . . 200 E2
Delvin IRL . . . . . . 30 A1
Delvině AL . . . . . 182 D2
Demandice SK. . . .112 A2
Demen D . . . . . . 73 A4
Demidov RUS . . . . 13 A9
Demigny F . . . . . 105 C3
Demirci TR. . . . . 186 C3
Demirköy TR . . . . 186 A2
Demirtaş TR. . . . 186 B4
Demmin D . . . . . . 66 C2
Demonte I . . . . . 133 A3
Demyansk RUS. . . . 9 D8
Denain F . . . . . . 78 B3
Denbigh GB. . . . . 38 A3
Dender-monde B. . . 79 A4
Denekamp NL . . . 71 B4
Den Ham NL. . . . . 71 B3
Den Helder NL . . . 70 B1
Denholm GB . . . . 35 C5
Denia E . . . . . . 159 C4
Denizli TR . . . . . 188 B4
Denkendorf D . . . . 95 C3
Denklingen D. . . . . 81 B3
Denny GB . . . . . . 35 B4
Den Oever NL . . . . 70 B2
Derby GB. . . . . . . 40 C2
Derecske H . . . . .113 B5
Dereköy TR . . . . 186 A2
Derenberg D . . . . 82 A2
Derinkuyu TR . . . . 23 B8
Dermbach D . . . . 82 B2
Dermulo I . . . . . 121 A4
Deronje SRB . . . 125 B5
Derrygonnelly GB. . 26 B3
Derrylin GB . . . . . 27 B3
Derry/Londonderry
  GB . . . . . . . . . . 27 B3
Dersingham GB. . . 41 C4
Deruta I . . . . . . 136 C1
Dervaig GB. . . . . 34 B1
Derval F . . . . . . 101 B4
Derveni GR . . . . 184 A3
Derventa BIH . . . 125 C3
Dervock GB . . . . . 27 A4
Desana I . . . . . . 119 B5
Descartes F . . . . 102 C2
Desenzano del Garda
  I . . . . . . . . . . 121 B3
Deset N . . . . . . . 48 A3
Deševa BIH . . . . 139 B4
Desfina GR . . . . 184 A3
Desimirovac SRB . 127 C2
Désio I . . . . . . . 120 B2
Deskati GR . . . . 182 D3
Deskle SLO . . . . 122 A2
Desná CZ . . . . . . 84 B3
Dešov CZ . . . . . . 97 C3
Despotovac SRB. . 127 C3
Despotovo SRB. . . 126 B1
Dessau D. . . . . . . 83 A4
Deštná CZ . . . . . . 96 B2
Destriana E . . . . 141 B4
Désulo I . . . . . . 179 B3
Desvres F . . . . . . 78 B1
Deszk H . . . . . . 126 A2
Deta RO . . . . . . 126 B3
Detmold D . . . . . 72 C1
Dětřichov CZ . . . . 98 B1
Dettelbach D . . . . 94 B2
Dettingen
  Baden-Württemberg
    D. . . . . . . . . .94 C1
  Baden-Württemberg
    D. . . . . . . . . 107 B4
Dettwiller F . . . . . 93 C3
Detva SK . . . . . . 99 C3
Deurne NL . . . . . 80 A1
Deutschkreutz A. . .111 B3
Deutschlandsberg
  A. . . . . . . . . . . 110 C2

Deutsch Wagram
  A. . . . . . . . . . . .111 A3
Deva RO. . . . . . . 16 C5
Dévaványa H. . . . .113 B4
Devecikonağı TR. . 186 C3
Devecser H . . . . .111 B4
Develi TR . . . . . . 23 B8
Deventer NL . . . . 70 B3
Devil's Bridge GB . 39 B3
Devín BG . . . . . 183 B6
Devínska Nova Ves
  SK. . . . . . . . . . .111 A3
Devizes GB . . . . . 43 A5
Devonport GB . . . 42 B2
Devrek TR . . . . . 187 A6
Devrekâni TR . . . . 23 A7
Đevrske HR . . . . 137 B4
De Wijk NL . . . . . 71 B3
Dewsbury GB . . . . 40 B2
Deza E . . . . . . . 152 A1
Dežanovac HR. . . 124 B3
Dezzo I . . . . . . . 120 B3
Dhali CY . . . . . . 181 A2
Dheftera CY . . . . 181 A2
Dherinia CY . . . . 181 B2
Diamante I . . . . . 174 B1
Dianalund DK . . . . 61 D1
Diano d'Alba I . . . 119 C5
Diano Marina I . . . 133 B4
Dicomano I . . . . 135 B4
Didcot GB . . . . . . 44 B2
Didimoticho GR . . 186 A1
Die F. . . . . . . . 118 C2
Diebling F . . . . . . 92 B2
Dieburg D . . . . . . 93 B4
Diego del Carpio E 150 B2
Diekirch L. . . . . . . 92 B2
Diélette F . . . . . . 88 A2
Diémoz F . . . . . .118 B2
Dienten am Hochkönig
  A. . . . . . . . . . . 109 B3
Diepenbeck B . . . . 79 B5
Diepholz D . . . . . 71 B5
Dieppe F . . . . . . 89 A5
Dierberg D . . . . . 74 A1
Dierdorf D . . . . . . 81 B3
Dieren NL. . . . . . 70 B3
Dierhagen D . . . . 66 B1
Diesdorf D . . . . . 73 B3
Diessen D . . . . . 108 B2
Diest B . . . . . . . 79 B5
Dietenheim D . . . . 94 C2
Dietfurt D. . . . . . . 95 B3
Dietikon CH . . . . 106 B3
Dietzenbach D. . . . 93 A4
Dieue-sur-Meuse F . 92 B1
Dieulefit F . . . . . 131 A4
Dieulouard F . . . . 92 C2
Dieuze F . . . . . . 92 C2
Diever NL . . . . . . 71 B3
Diez D. . . . . . . . 81 B4
Diezma E . . . . . 163 A4
Differdange L. . . . . 92 B1
Digermulen N . . . 194 B6
Dignac F . . . . . . 115 C4
Dignano I . . . . . 122 A1
Digne-les-Bains F . 132 A2
Digny F . . . . . . . 89 B5
Digoin F . . . . . . 104 C2
Dijon F . . . . . . . 105 B4
Dikanäs S . . . . . 195 E7
Dikili TR . . . . . . 186 C1
Diksmuide B . . . . 78 A2
Dilar E . . . . . . . 163 A4
Dillenburg D . . . . 81 B4
Dillingen
  Bayern D. . . . . .94 C2
  Saarland D. . . . . 92 B2
Dilsen B . . . . . . 80 A1
Dimaro I . . . . . . 121 A3
Dimitrovgrad BG. . 183 A7
Dimitsana GR . . . 184 B3
Dinami I . . . . . . 175 C2
Dinan F . . . . . . 101 A3
Dinant B . . . . . . 79 B4
Dinar TR. . . . . . 189 A5
Dinard F . . . . . . 101 A3
Dinek TR . . . . . 187 C6
Dingden D . . . . . 80 A2
Dingelstädt D . . . . 82 A2
Dingle
  IRL . . . . . . . .29 B1
  S . . . . . . . . . 54 B2
Dingolfing D . . . . 95 C4
Dingtuna S. . . . . . 56 A2
Dingwall GB. . . . . 32 D2
Dinkelsbühl D . . . . 94 B2
Dinkelscherben D . 94 C2
Dinklage D . . . . . 71 B5
Dinslaken D . . . . . 80 A2
Dinxperlo NL . . . . 80 A2
Diö S . . . . . . . . 63 B2
Diósgyör H . . . . .113 A4
Diósjeno H. . . . . .112 B3
Diou F . . . . . . . 104 C2
Dippen GB . . . . . 34 C2
Dipperz D. . . . . . 82 B1
Dippoldiswalde D . 84 B1
Dirdal N . . . . . . . 52 B2
Dirksland NL . . . . 79 A4
Dirlewang D. . . . . 108 B1
Dischingen D. . . . . 94 C2
Disentis CH . . . . 107 C3
Diso I . . . . . . . 173 B4
Diss GB . . . . . . . 45 A5

Dissen D . . . . . . . 71 B5
Distington GB . . . . 36 B3
Ditzingen D . . . . . . 93 C5
Ditzum D . . . . . . . 71 A4
Divača SLO . . . . . . 122 B2
Dives-sur-Mer F . . . 89 A3
Divín SK. . . . . . . . 99 C3
Divion F . . . . . . . . 78 B2
Divišov CZ . . . . . . 96 B2
**Divonne les Bains**
F. . . . . . . . . . . . .118 A3
Dixmont F . . . . . . 104 A2
Dizy-le-Gros F . . . . 91 B4
Djúpivogur IS . . . . 191 C11
Djupvasshytta N . . 198 C4
Djura S. . . . . . . . . 50 B1
Djurås S. . . . . . . . 50 B2
Djurmo S. . . . . . . . 50 B2
Djursdala S . . . . . . 62 A3
Dlouhá Loucka CZ . 98 B1
Długowola PL . . . . 87 A5
Dmitrov RUS . . . . . 9 D10
Dno RUS . . . . . . . . 9 D6
Doade E . . . . . . . 141 B3
Doğanhisar TR . . . 189 A6
Dobanovci SRB. . . . 127 C2
Dobbertin D . . . . . 73 A5
Dobbiaco I . . . . . . 108 C3
Dobczyce PL . . . . . 99 B4
Dobele LV. . . . . . . 8 D3
Döbeln D . . . . . . . 83 A5
**Doberlug-Kirchhain**
D . . . . . . . . . . . . 83 A5
Dobern D . . . . . . . 84 A2
Dobersberg A . . . . 97 C3
Dobiegniew PL . . . 75 B4
Dobieszyn PL . . . . 87 A5
Doboj BIH . . . . . . 125 C4
Dobošnica BIH . . . 125 C4
Doboz H . . . . . . . 113 C5
Dobrá CZ . . . . . . . 98 B2
**Dobra**
Wielkopolskie PL . .76 C3
Zachodnio-Pomorskie
PL. . . . . . . . . . . . .74 A3
Zachodnio-Pomorskie
PL. . . . . . . . . . . . .75 A4
Dobrá Niva SK. . . . 99 C3
Dobřany CZ . . . . . 96 B1
Dobre PL . . . . . . . 76 B3
Dobre Miasto PL . . 69 B5
**Dobreta-Turnu-Severin**
RO . . . . . . . . . . . . 16 C5
Dobri H. . . . . . . . .111 C3
Dobrica SRB . . . . . 126 B2
Dobrich BG . . . . . . 17 D7
Dobrinishta BG . . . 183 B5
Dobříš CZ . . . . . . . 96 B2
Dobro E . . . . . . . . 143 B3
Dobrodzień PL. . . . 86 B2
Döbrököz H . . . . . 112 C2
Dobromierz PL . . . 85 B4
Dobrosołowo PL . . 76 B3
Dobroszyce PL . . . 85 A5
Dobrovnik SLO . . . .111 C3
Dobrush BY . . . . . . 13 B9
Dobruška CZ . . . . . 85 B4
Dobrzen Wielki PL. . 86 B1
**Dobrzyca**
Wielkopolskie PL . .75 A5
Wielkopolskie PL . .85 A5
Zachodnio-Pomorskie
PL. . . . . . . . . . . . .67 B4
**Dobrzyńnad Wisłą**
PL. . . . . . . . . . . . .77 B4
Dobšiná SK . . . . . . 99 C4
Dobwalls GB . . . . . 42 B2
Dochamps B . . . . . 80 B1
Docking GB . . . . . 41 C4
Docksta S . . . . . . 200 C4
Doddington GB . . . 37 A4
Döderhult S . . . . . . 62 A4
Doesburg NL. . . . . 70 B3
Doetinchem NL . . . 71 C3
Dogliani I . . . . . . . 133 A3
Dogueno P. . . . . . 160 B2
Doische B . . . . . . . 91 A4
Dois Portos P . . . . 154 B1
Dojč SK . . . . . . . . 98 C1
Dokka N. . . . . . . . 48 B2
Dokkedal DK . . . . . 58 B3
Dokkum NL . . . . . . 70 A2
Dokležovje SLO. . . .111 C3
Doksy CZ. . . . . . . . 84 B2
Đokuz TR . . . . . . . 189 A7
Dolancourt F . . . . . 104 A3
Dolceácqua I . . . . . 133 B3
Dol-de-Bretagne F . 88 B2
Dole F. . . . . . . . . 105 B4
Dølemo N. . . . . . . 53 B4
Dolenja vas SLO . . 123 B3
**Dolenjske Toplice**
SLO . . . . . . . . . . . 123 B4
Dolfor GB . . . . . . . 39 B3
Dolgarrog GB . . . . 38 A3
Dolgellau GB . . . . . 38 B3
Doliana GR . . . . . . 182 D2
Dolianova I . . . . . . 179 C3
Dolice PL . . . . . . . .75 A4
Doljani HR . . . . . . 138 A2
**Döllach im Mölltal**
A. . . . . . . . . . . . . 109 C3
Dolle D . . . . . . . . 73 B4
Dollnstein D. . . . . . 94 C3

Dollot F . . . . . . . 104 A2
Döllstadt D. . . . . . 82 A2
Dolná Strehová SK . 99 C3
Dolné Saliby SK . . .111 A4
Dolni Benešov CZ . 98 B2
Dolni Bousov CZ . . 84 B3
Dolni Kounice CZ . 97 B4
Dolni Kralovice CZ . 97 B3
Dolní Újezd CZ . . . 97 B4
Dolní Žandov CZ . . 95 A4
Dolný Kubín SK. . . . 99 B3
Dolo I . . . . . . . . . 121 B5
Dolores E. . . . . . . 165 A4
Dolovo SRB. . . . . . 127 C2
Dölsach A . . . . . . 109 C3
Dolsk PL. . . . . . . . 76 B2
Dolwyddelan GB . . 38 A3
Domaljevac BIH . . 125 B4
Domaniç TR . . . . . 187 C4
Domaniža SK. . . . . 98 B2
Domašov CZ . . . . . 85 B5
Domaszék H . . . . . 126 A1
Domaszków PL . . . 85 B4
Domaszowice PL. . . 86 A1
Domat-Ems CH . . . 107 C4
Domažlice CZ . . . . 95 B4
Dombås N . . . . . . 198 C6
**Dombasle-sur-Meurthe**
F . . . . . . . . . . . . 92 C2
Dombegyház H . . . 126 A3
Dombóvár H . . . . . 112 C2
Domène F . . . . . . 118 B2
Domérat F . . . . . . 116 A2
Domfessel F . . . . . 92 C3
Domfront F . . . . . . 88 B3
**Domfront-en-**
**Champagne** F . . . 102 A2
Domingão P. . . . . . 154 B2
**Domingo Pérez**
Granada E. . . . . .163 A4
Toledo E. . . . . . . .150 C3
Dömitz D . . . . . . . 73 A4
Dommartin F . . . . . 91 C4
**Dommartin-le-Franc**
F . . . . . . . . . . . . 91 C4
Domme F. . . . . . . 129 B4
Dommitzsch D. . . . 83 A4
Domodóssola I . . . .119 A5
Domoszló H. . . . . .113 B4
Dompaire F . . . . . 105 A5
**Dompierre-du-Chemin**
F. . . . . . . . . . . . . 88 B2
**Dompierre-sur-Besbre**
F. . . . . . . . . . . . . 104 C2
**Dompierre-sur-Mer**
F. . . . . . . . . . . . .114 B2
**Domrémy-la-Pucelle**
F . . . . . . . . . . . . 92 C1
Dömsöd H . . . . . . .112 B3
Domsure F. . . . . . .118 A2
Dómus de Maria I . 179 D2
Domusnóvas I. . . . 179 C2
Domvena GR. . . . . 184 A3
Domžale SLO. . . . . 123 A3
Donado E. . . . . . . 141 B4
Donaghadee GB . . 27 B5
Don Alvaro E . . . . 155 C4
Doña Mencía E . . . 163 A3
Donaueschingen D 106 B3
Donauwörth D. . . . 94 C2
Don Benito E . . . . 156 B2
Doncaster GB . . . . 40 B2
Donegal IRL. . . . . . 26 B2
**Donestebe-Santesteban**
E. . . . . . . . . . . . . 144 A2
Donges F. . . . . . . 101 B3
Dongo I . . . . . . . . 120 A2
Donington GB . . . . 41 C3
Doniños E . . . . . . 140 A2
**Donja Bebrina** HR 125 B4
**Donja Brela** HR . . 138 B2
**Donja Dubica** BIH . 125 B4
**Donja Dubrava** HR 124 A2
**Donja Kupčina** HR 123 B4
**Donja Šatornja**
SRB. . . . . . . . . . . 127 C2
**Donja Stubica** HR 124 B1
**Donje Brišnik** BIH 138 B3
**Donje Stative** HR . 123 B4
**Donji-Andrijevci**
HR . . . . . . . . . . . 125 B4
**Donji Kazanci** BIH 138 B2
**Donji Koričáni** BIH 138 A3
**Donji Malovan** BIH 138 B3
**Donji Miholjac** HR 125 B4
**Donji Mosti** I IR . . 124 A2
**Donji Poloj** HR. . . 123 B4
**Donji-Rujani** BIH . 138 B2
**Donji Srb** BIH . . . 138 A2
**Donji Svilaj** BIH . . 125 B4
**Donji Tovarnik**
SRB . . . . . . . . . . 127 C1
**Donji Vakuf** BIH . . 138 A3
Donnalucata I . . . . 177 C3
**Donnemarie-Dontilly**
F. . . . . . . . . . . . . 90 C3
Donnersbach A . . . .110 B1
**Donnersbachwald**
A. . . . . . . . . . . . . 109 B5
Donnerskirchen A. . .111 B3
Donorático I . . . . . 134 B3
**Donostia-San Sebastián**
E. . . . . . . . . . . . . 144 A2
Donovaly SK. . . . . . 99 C3
Donzenac F . . . . . 129 A4

Donzère F . . . . . . 131 A3
Donzy F . . . . . . . . 104 B2
Doonbeg IRL . . . . . 29 B2
Door E . . . . . . . . 140 A1
Dorchester GB . . . 43 B4
Dørdal N. . . . . . . . 53 B5
Dordrecht NL. . . . . 79 A4
Dörenthe D . . . . . . 71 B4
Dores GB . . . . . . . 32 D2
Dorfgastein A. . . . . 109 B4
Dorfmark D . . . . . . 72 B2
**Dorf Mecklenburg** D 65 C4
Dorgali I . . . . . . . 178 B3
Dorking GB . . . . . . 44 B3
Dormagen D . . . . . 80 A2
Dormánd H . . . . . .113 B4
Dormans F. . . . . . . 91 B3
Dornava SLO. . . . . 124 A1
Dornbirn A. . . . . . 107 B4
Dornburg D. . . . . . 83 A3
Dorndorf D. . . . . . . 82 B2
Dornecy F . . . . . . 104 B2
Dornes F . . . . . . . 104 C2
Dornhan D . . . . . . 93 C4
Dornie GB. . . . . . . 31 B3
Dornoch GB. . . . . . 32 D2
Dornum D . . . . . . . 71 A4
Dorog H . . . . . . . .112 B2
Dorohoi RO . . . . . . 17 B7
Dorotea S. . . . . . . 200 B2
Dorotowo PL . . . . . 69 B5
Dörpen D . . . . . . . 71 B4
Dorsten D . . . . . . . 80 A2
Dortan F . . . . . . . .118 A2
Dortmund D. . . . . . 80 A3
Doruchów PL. . . . . 86 A2
Dorum D . . . . . . . . 64 C1
Dörverden D . . . . . 72 B2
Dörzbach D . . . . . . 94 B1
Dos Aguas E . . . . 159 B3
Dosbarrios E . . . . . 151 C4
Döşemealtı TR. . . . 189 B5
Dos Hermanas E . . 162 A2
Dospat BG . . . . . . 183 B6
Dos-Torres E . . . . 156 B3
Dötlingen D . . . . . . 72 B1
Dottignies B. . . . . . 78 B3
Döttingen CH. . . . . 106 B3
Douai F . . . . . . . . 78 B3
Douarnenez F . . . . 100 A1
Douchy F . . . . . . . 104 B2
Douchy-les-Mines F 78 B3
Doucier F . . . . . . . 105 C4
Doudeville F . . . . . 89 A4
**Doué-la-Fontaine**
F. . . . . . . . . . . . . 102 B1
**Douglas**
Isle of Man GB. . . .36 B2
South Lanarkshire
GB . . . . . . . . . . . .36 A3
**Doulaincourt-Saucourt**
F. . . . . . . . . . . . . 91 C5
**Doulevant-le-Château**
F. . . . . . . . . . . . . 91 C4
Doullens F . . . . . . 90 A2
Dounby GB . . . . . . 33 B3
Doune GB . . . . . . . 35 B3
Dounreay GB. . . . . 32 C3
Dour B . . . . . . . . . 79 B3
Dourdan F . . . . . . . 90 C2
Dourgne F . . . . . . 146 A2
Dournazac F . . . . . 115 C4
Douro Calvo P. . . . 148 B2
Douvaine F . . . . . .118 A3
**Douvres-la-Délivrande**
F . . . . . . . . . . . . 89 A3
Douzy F . . . . . . . . 91 B5
Dover GB. . . . . . . . 45 B5
Dovje SLO . . . . . . 109 C4
Dovre N . . . . . . . . 198 D6
**Downham Market**
GB . . . . . . . . . . . 41 C4
Downhill GB . . . . . 27 A4
Downpatrick GB . . 27 B5
Dowra IRL . . . . . . . 26 B2
Doxato GR . . . . . . 183 B6
Doyet F . . . . . . . . .116 A2
Dozule F . . . . . . . . 89 A3
Drača SRB . . . . . . 127 C2
**Dračevo**
BIH . . . . . . . . . . .139 C4
MK . . . . . . . . . . . .182 B3
Drachten NL. . . . . . 70 A3
Draga SLO. . . . . . 123 B3
Drăgăşani RO . . . . 17 C6
Dragatuš SLO . . . . 123 B4
Dragichyn BY . . . . 13 B6
Draginja SRB. . . . . 127 C1
Dragocvet SRB . . . 127 D3
Dragolovci BIH . . . 125 C3
Dragoni I . . . . . . . 170 B2
Dragør DK . . . . . . . 61 D2
Dragotina HR. . . . . 124 B2
Dragotinja BIH. . . . 124 B2
Dragozetići HR . . . 123 B3
Draguignan F . . . . 132 B2
Drahnsdorf D. . . . . 74 C2
Drahonice CZ. . . . . 96 B2
Drahovce SK. . . . . 98 C1
Drama GR . . . . . . 183 B6
Drammen N. . . . . . 54 A1
Drangedal N . . . . . 53 A5
Drangsnes IS. . . . . 190 B4
Dransfeld D . . . . . . 82 A1
Dranske D. . . . . . . 66 B2
Draperstown GB . . 27 B4

Drassburg A. . . . . .111 B3
Drávaszabolcs H. . . 125 B4
Dravograd SLO . . . 110 C2
Drawno PL. . . . . . . 75 A4
**Drawsko Pomorskie**
PL. . . . . . . . . . . . 75 A4
Drayton GB . . . . . . 41 C5
Draždžewo PL . . . . 77 A6
Draženov CZ . . . . . 95 B4
Draževac SRB . . . . 127 C2
Dražice HR. . . . . . 123 B3
Drebkau D . . . . . . . 84 A2
Dreieich D . . . . . . . 93 A4
Dreisen D. . . . . . . . 93 B4
Drenovci HR . . . . . 125 C4
Drensteinfurt D . . . 81 A3
Dresden D . . . . . . . 84 A1
Dretyń PL. . . . . . . . 68 A1
Dreux F . . . . . . . . 89 B5
Drevohostice CZ. . . 98 B1
Drevsjø N . . . . . . . 199 D9
Drewitz D . . . . . . . 73 B5
Drezdenko PL . . . . 75 B4
Dřežnica HR . . . . . 123 B4
Drežnik-Grad HR. . 123 C4
Drietona SK. . . . . . 98 C1
Driffield GB . . . . . . 40 A3
Drimnin GB . . . . . . 34 B2
Drimoleague IRL . . 29 C2
Dringenberg D. . . . 81 A5
Drinić BIH . . . . . . 138 A2
Drinjača BIH . . . . . 139 A5
Drinovci BIH. . . . . 138 B3
Driopida GR . . . . . 185 B5
Drivstua N . . . . . . 198 C6
Drlače SRB . . . . . . 127 C1
Drnholec CZ . . . . . 97 C4
Drniš HR . . . . . . . 138 B2
Drnje HR . . . . . . . 124 A2
Drnovice CZ . . . . . 97 B4
Dro I . . . . . . . . . . 121 B3
Drøbak N . . . . . . . 54 A1
Drobin PL. . . . . . . . 77 B5
Drochia MD. . . . . . 17 A7
Drochtersen D. . . . 64 C2
Drogheda IRL . . . . 30 A2
Drohobych UA. . . . 13 D5
Droitwich Spa GB . 44 A1
Drołtowice PL . . . . 85 A5
Dromahair IRL. . . . 26 B2
Dromcolliher IRL. . . 29 B3
**Dromore**
Down GB . . . . . .27 B4
Tyrone GB . . . . . .27 B3
Dromore West IRL. 26 B2
Dronero I . . . . . . . 133 A3
Dronfield GB . . . . . 40 B2
Drongan GB. . . . . . 36 A2
Dronninglund DK . . 58 A3
Dronrijp NL . . . . . . 70 A2
Dronten NL . . . . . . 70 B2
Drosendorf A. . . . . 97 C3
Drösing A. . . . . . . . 97 C4
Drottningholm S . . 57 A3
Droué F . . . . . . . . 103 A3
Drulingen F . . . . . . 92 C3
Drumbeg GB . . . . . 32 C1
Drumcliff IRL . . . . . 26 B2
Drumgask GB . . . . 32 D2
Drumkeeran IRL . . 26 B2
Drummore GB . . . . 36 B2
Drumnadrochit GB . 32 D2
Drumquin GB . . . . 27 B3
Drumshanbo IRL . . 26 B2
Drumsna IRL. . . . . 26 C2
Drunen NL . . . . . . 79 A5
Druskininkai LT . . . 13 A5
Druten NL. . . . . . . 80 A1
Druya BY. . . . . . . . 13 A7
Družetići SRB . . . . 127 C2
Drvar BIH . . . . . . . 138 A2
Drvenik HR . . . . . . 138 B3
Drwalew PL . . . . . . 77 C6
Drymen GB . . . . . . 34 B3
Drynoch GB . . . . . 31 B2
Drzewce PL . . . . . . 76 B2
Drzewiany PL. . . . . 68 B1
Drzewica PL. . . . . . 87 A4
Dualchi I. . . . . . . . 178 B2
Duas Igrejas P. . . . 149 A3
Dub SRB . . . . . . . 127 D1
Dubá CZ . . . . . . . . 84 B2
Dubăsari MD . . . . . 17 B8
Duben D . . . . . . . . 74 C2
Dübendorf CH . . . . 107 B3
Dubi CZ . . . . . . . . 84 B1
Dubica HR . . . . . . 124 B2
Dublin IRL . . . . . . 30 A2
Dubna RUS . . . . . . 9 D10
Dubňany CZ . . . . . 98 C1
**Dubnica nad Váhom**
SK . . . . . . . . . . . 98 C2
Dubnik SK . . . . . . .112 B2
Dubno UA . . . . . . . 13 C6
Dubodiel SK . . . . . 98 C2
Dubona SRB . . . . . 127 C2
Dubovac SRB . . . . 127 C3
Dubovic BIH . . . . . 124 C2
Dubrava HR. . . . . . 124 B2
Dubrave BIH . . . . . 125 C4
**Dubravica**
HR. . . . . . . . . . . .123 B4
SRB . . . . . . . . . . .127 C3
Dubrovnik HR . . . . 139 C4
Dubrovytsya UA . . 13 C7
Ducey F . . . . . . . . 88 B2
Duchcov CZ. . . . . . 84 B1

Ducherow D. . . . . . 74 A2
Dučina SRB . . . . . 127 C2
Duclair F . . . . . . . . 89 A4
Dudar H . . . . . . . .112 B1
Duddington GB . . . 40 C3
Duderstadt D. . . . . 82 A2
Dudeştii Vechi RO. 126 A2
Dudley GB . . . . . . 40 C1
Dueñas E . . . . . . . 142 C2
Duesund N. . . . . . . 46 B2
Dueville I . . . . . . . 121 B4
Duffel B . . . . . . . . 79 A4
Duffield GB . . . . . . 40 C2
Dufftown GB . . . . . 32 D3
Duga Resa HR. . . . 123 B4
Dugi Rat HR. . . . . . 138 B2
Dugny-sur-Meuse F 92 B1
Dugopolje HR . . . . 138 B2
Dugo Selo HR . . . . 124 B2
Duino I . . . . . . . . 122 B2
Duisburg D. . . . . . . 80 A2
Dukat AL. . . . . . . . 182 C1
Dukovany CZ. . . . . 97 B4
Duleek IRL . . . . . . 30 A2
Dülken D . . . . . . . . 80 A2
Dülmen D. . . . . . . . 80 A3
Dulovo BG . . . . . . 17 D7
Dulpetorpet N . . . . 49 B4
Dulverton GB. . . . . 43 A3
Dumbarton GB . . . 34 C3
Dümerek TR. . . . . . 187 C6
Dumfries GB . . . . . 36 A3
Dumlupınar TR . . . 187 D4
Dümpelfeld D . . . . 80 B2
Dunaalmás H. . . . .112 B2
Dunabogdány H . .112 B3
Dunafalva H . . . . . 125 A4
Dunaföldvár H . . . .112 C2
Dunaharaszti H . . .112 B3
**Dunajská Streda**
SK . . . . . . . . . . . .111 B4
Dunakeszi H . . . . .112 B3
Dunakiliti H . . . . . .111 B4
Dunakömlöd H . . . .112 C2
Dunapataj H. . . . . .112 C2
Dunaszekcső H . . . 125 A4
**Dunaszentgyorgy**
H . . . . . . . . . . . .112 C2
Dunatetétlen H . . .112 C3
Dunaújváros H . . . .112 C2
Dunavecse H . . . . .112 C2
Dunbar GB . . . . . . 35 B5
Dunbeath GB. . . . . 32 C3
Dunblane GB. . . . . 35 B4
Dunboyne IRL . . . . 30 A2
Dundalk IRL . . . . . 27 B4
Dundee GB . . . . . . 35 B5
Dundrennan GB . . . 36 B3
Dundrum GB . . . . . 27 B5
Dunfanaghy IRL. . . 26 A3
Dunfermline GB . . . 35 B4
Dungannon GB . . . 27 B4
Dungarvan IRL . . . 29 B4
Dungiven GB. . . . . 27 A4
Dunglow IRL . . . . . 26 B2
Dungourney IRL . . 29 C3
Dunkeld GB . . . . . 35 B4
Dunker S . . . . . . . 56 A2
**Dunkerque = Dunkirk**
F. . . . . . . . . . . . . 78 A2
Dunkineely IRL . . . 26 B2
**Dunkirk = Dunkerque**
F. . . . . . . . . . . . . 78 A2
Dun Laoghaire IRL . 30 A2
Dunlavin IRL . . . . . 30 A2
Dunleer IRL . . . . . . 27 C4
Dun-le-Palestel F . .116 A1
Dun-les-Places F. . 104 B3
Dunlop GB. . . . . . . 36 A2
Dunloy GB . . . . . . 27 A4
Dunmanway IRL . . 29 C2
Dunmore IRL. . . . . 28 A3
Dunmore East IRL. 30 B2
Dunmurry GB . . . . 27 B4
Dunnet GB . . . . . . 32 C3
Dunningen D . . . . . 107 A3
Dunoon GB . . . . . . 34 C3
Duns GB . . . . . . . . 35 C5
Dunscore GB . . . . . 36 A3
Dunsford GB . . . . . 43 B3
Dunshaughlin IRL. . 30 A2
Dunstable GB. . . . . 44 B3
Dunster GB . . . . . . 43 A3
Dun-sur-Auron F. . 103 C4
Dun-sur-Meuse F . . 91 B5
Dunvegan GB . . . . 31 B2
Duplek SLO . . . . . 110 C2
Dupnitsa BG . . . . . 17 D5
Durağan TR . . . . . 23 A8
Durach D . . . . . . . 107 B5
Durak TR . . . . . . . 186 C3
Durana E . . . . . . . 143 B4
Durance F . . . . . . 128 B3
Durango E . . . . . . 143 A4
Durankulak BG . . . 17 D8
Duras F . . . . . . . . 128 B3
**Durban-Corbières**
F. . . . . . . . . . . . . 146 B3
Dürbheim D . . . . . 107 A3
Durbuy B . . . . . . . 79 B5
Dúrcal E . . . . . . . 163 B4
Đurđenovac HR . . 125 B4
Đurđevac HR . . . . 124 A3
Đurđevik BIH . . . . 139 A4
Düren D . . . . . . . . 80 B2
Durham GB . . . . . . 37 B5
Đurinci SRB . . . . . 127 C2

Durlach D. . . . . . . . 93 C4
Đurmanec HR . . . . 124 A1
Durness GB. . . . . . 32 C2
Dürnkrut A . . . . . . 97 C4
Dürrboden CH . . . . 107 C4
Dürrenboden CH . . 107 C3
Durrës AL. . . . . . . 182 B1
Durrow IRL. . . . . . . 30 B1
Durrus IRL . . . . . . 29 C2
Dursunbey TR . . . . 186 C3
Durtal F . . . . . . . . 102 B1
Đurup DK. . . . . . . . 58 B1
Durusu TR . . . . . . 186 A3
Dusina BIH. . . . . . 139 B3
Dusnok H. . . . . . . .112 C2
Dusocin PL . . . . . . 69 B3
Düsseldorf D. . . . . 80 A2
Dusslingen D. . . . . 93 C5
Duszniki PL . . . . . . 75 B5
Duszniki-Zdrój PL . 85 B4
Dutovlje SLO. . . . . 122 B2
Duvebo S . . . . . . . 55 B5
Duved S . . . . . . . 199 B9
Düzağac TR . . . . . 187 D5
Düzce TR . . . . . . . 187 B6
Dvärsätt S . . . . . . .199 B11
Dvor HR . . . . . . . . 124 B2
Dvorce CZ . . . . . . 98 B1
Dvorníky SK . . . . . 98 C1
**Dvory nad Žitavou**
SK . . . . . . . . . . . .112 B2
**Dvůr Králóvénad Labem**
CZ . . . . . . . . . . . 85 B3
Dybvad DK. . . . . . . 58 A3
Dygowo PL . . . . . . 67 B4
Dykehead GB . . . . 35 B4
Dymchurch GB . . . 45 B5
Dymer UA. . . . . . . 13 C9
Dyrnes N . . . . . . . 198 B4
Dywity PL. . . . . . . . 69 B5
Džanići BIH . . . . . 139 B3
Działdowa Kłoda PL. 86 A1
Działdowo PL. . . . . 77 A5
Działoszyce PL . . . 87 B4
Działoszyn PL . . . . 86 A2
Dziemiany PL. . . . . 68 A2
Dzierżążnia PL. . . . 77 B5
Dzierzgoń PL . . . . 69 B4
Dzierzgowo PL . . . 77 A5
Dzierżoniów PL. . . 85 B4
Dzisna BY . . . . . . 13 A8
Dziwnów PL. . . . . . 67 B3
Dźwierzuty PL . . . . 77 A5
Dzyarzhynsk BY . . 13 B7
Dzyatlava BY . . . . 13 B6

**E**

Ea E . . . . . . . . . . 143 A4
Eaglesfield GB . . . 36 A3
Ealing GB. . . . . . . 44 B3
Eardisley GB . . . . . 39 B3
Earls Barton GB . . 44 A3
Earl Shilton GB . . . 40 C2
Earlston GB . . . . . 35 C5
Easington GB . . . . 41 B4
Easky IRL. . . . . . . 26 B2
Eastbourne GB . . . 45 C4
East Calder GB . . . 35 C4
East Dereham GB . 41 C4
Easter Skeld GB . . 33 A5
East Grinstead GB . 45 B4
East Ilsley GB . . . . 44 B2
East Kilbride GB . . 36 A2
Eastleigh GB . . . . . 44 C2
East Linton GB . . . 35 C5
East Markham GB. . 40 B3
Easton GB. . . . . . . 43 B4
East Wittering GB . 44 C3
Eaton Socon GB . . 44 A3
Eaux-Bonnes F . . . 145 B3
Eauze F . . . . . . . . 128 C3
Ebberup DK. . . . . . 59 C2
Ebbs A . . . . . . . . 108 B3
Ebbw Vale GB . . . . 39 C3
Ebeleben D . . . . . . 82 A2
Ebeltoft DK . . . . . . 59 B3
**Ebene Reichenau**
A. . . . . . . . . . . . . 109 C4
Eben im Pongau A. 109 B4
Ebensee A . . . . . . 109 B4
Ebensfeld D . . . . . 94 A2
Eberbach D . . . . . . 93 B4
Ebergötzen D . . . . 82 A2
Ebermann-Stadt D . 94 B3
Ebern D . . . . . . . . 82 B2
Eberndorf A . . . . . 110 C1
Ebersbach D . . . . . 84 A2
Ebersberg D . . . . . 108 A2
**Ebersdorf**
Bayern D . . . . . . .82 B3
Niedersachsen D . .72 A2
Eberstein A . . . . . 110 C1
Eberswalde D . . . . 74 B2
Ebnat-Kappel CH . 107 B4
Éboli I . . . . . . . . . 170 C3
Ebrach D . . . . . . . 94 B2
Ebreichsdorf A . . . .111 B3
Ebreuil F . . . . . . . .116 A3
Ebstorf D. . . . . . . . 72 A3
Ecclefechan GB . . 36 A3
Eccleshall GB. . . . . 40 C1
Eceabat TR . . . . . 186 B1
Echallens CH. . . . . 106 C1
Echauri E. . . . . . . 144 B2
Echinos GR . . . . . 183 B7

Echiré F . . . . . . . 114 B3
Échirolles F . . . . . 118 B2
Echourgnac F . . . . 128 A3
Echt NL . . . . . . . 80 A1
Echte D . . . . . . . 82 A2
Echternach L . . . . 92 B2
Ecija E . . . . . . . 162 A2
Ečka SRB . . . . . . 126 B2
Eckartsberga D . . . 82 A3
Eckelshausen D . . 81 B4
Eckental D . . . . . . 94 B3
Eckernförde D . . . . 64 B2
Eckerö FIN . . . . . 51 B6
Eckington GB . . . . 40 B2
Éclaron F . . . . . . . 91 C4
Écommoy F . . . . . 102 B2
Écouché F . . . . . . 89 B3
Ecouis F . . . . . . . 90 B1
Lcsed H . . . . . . . 113 B3
Ecsegfalva H . . . . 113 B4
Écueillé F . . . . . . 103 B3
Ed S . . . . . . . . 54 B2
Eda S . . . . . . . . 49 C4
Eda glasbruk S . . . 49 C4
Edam NL . . . . . . 70 B2
Edane S . . . . . . . 55 A3
Edderton GB . . . . 32 D2
Ede NL . . . . . . . 70 B2
Edebäck S . . . . . 49 B5
Edebo S . . . . . . . 51 B5
Edelény H . . . . . . 99 C4
Edelschrott A . . . . 110 B2
Edemissen D . . . . 72 B3
Edenbridge GB . . . 45 B4
Edenderry IRL . . . 30 A1
Edenkoben D . . . . 93 B4
Edesheim D . . . . . 93 B4
Edessa GR . . . . . 182 C4
Edewecht D . . . . . 71 A4
Edgeworthstown
  IRL . . . . . . . . 30 A1
Edinburgh GB . . . . 35 C4
Edineţ MD . . . . . 17 A7
Edirne TR . . . . . . 186 A1
Edland N . . . . . . 52 A3
Edolo I . . . . . . . 120 A3
Edøy N . . . . . . . 198 B5
Edremit TR . . . . . 186 C2
Edsbro S . . . . . . 51 C5
Edsbruk S . . . . . . 56 B2
Edsbyn S . . . . . . 50 A2
Edsele S . . . . . . 200 C2
Edsleskog S . . . . 54 A3
Edsvalla S . . . . . 55 A4
Eekloo B . . . . . . 79 A3
Eemshaven NL . . . 71 A3
Eerbeek NL . . . . . 70 B3
Eersel NL . . . . . . 79 A5
Eferding A . . . . . 96 C2
Effiat F . . . . . . . 116 A3
Eftelot N . . . . . . 53 A5
Egeln D . . . . . . . 73 C4
Eger H . . . . . . . 113 B4
Egerbakta H . . . . 113 B4
Egersund DK . . . . 64 B2
Egersund N . . . . . 52 B2
Egerszólát H . . . . 113 B4
Egervár H . . . . . . 111 C3
Egg
  A . . . . . . . . . 107 B4
  D . . . . . . . . . 107 A5
Eggby S . . . . . . 55 B4
Eggedal N . . . . . . 47 B6
Eggenburg A . . . . 97 C3
Eggenfelden D . . . 95 C4
Eggesin D . . . . . . 74 A3
Eggum N . . . . . . 194 B4
Egham GB . . . . . 44 B3
Éghezée B . . . . . 79 B4
Egiertowo PL . . . . 68 A3
Egilsstaðir IS . . . . 191 B11
Egina GR . . . . . . 185 B4
Eginio GR . . . . . . 182 C4
Egio GR . . . . . . 184 A3
Égletons F . . . . . 116 B2
Egling D . . . . . . 108 B2
Eglinton GB . . . . . 27 A3
Eglisau CH . . . . . 107 B3
Égliseneuve-
  d'Entraigues F . . 116 B2
Eglofs D . . . . . . 107 B4
Egmond aan Zee NL 70 B1
Egna I . . . . . . . 121 A4
Egosthena GR . . . 184 A4
Egremont GB . . . . 36 B3
Egtved DK . . . . . . 59 C2
Eguilles F . . . . . . 131 B4
Eguilly-sous-Bois
  F . . . . . . . . . 104 A3
Éguzon-Chantôme
  F . . . . . . . . . 103 C3
Egyek H . . . . . . 113 B4
Egyházasrádóc H . 111 B3
Ehekirchen D . . . . 94 C3
Ehingen D . . . . . 94 C1
Ehra-Lessien D . . . 73 B3
Ehrang D . . . . . . 92 B2
Ehrenfriedersdorf D 83 B4
Ehrenhain D . . . . 83 B4
Ehrenhausen A . . . 110 C2
Ehringshausen D . . 81 B4
Ehrwald A . . . . . 108 B1
Eibar E . . . . . . . 143 A4
Eibelstadt D . . . . 94 B2
Eibenstock D . . . . 83 B4
Eibergen NL . . . . 71 B3
Eibiswald A . . . . . 110 C2
Eichenbarleben D . 73 B4

Eichendorf D . . . 95 C4
Eichstätt D . . . . . 95 C3
Eickelborn D . . . . 81 A4
Eide
  Hordaland N . . . . 46 B3
  Møre og Romsdal
  N . . . . . . . . 198 C4
Eidet N . . . . . . . 194 A9
Eidfjord N . . . . . . 46 B4
Eidsberg N . . . . . 54 A2
Eidsbugarden N . . 47 A5
Eidsdal N . . . . . . 198 C4
Eidsfoss N . . . . . 53 A6
Eidskog N . . . . . . 49 B4
Eidsvåg
  Hordaland N . . . . 46 B2
  Møre og Romsdal
  N . . . . . . . . 198 C5
Eidsvoll N . . . . . . 48 B3
Eikefjord N . . . . . 46 A2
Eikelandsosen N . . 46 B2
Eiken N . . . . . . . 52 B3
Eikesdal N . . . . . 198 C5
Eikstrand N . . . . . 53 A5
Eilenburg D . . . . . 83 A4
Eilsleben D . . . . . 73 B4
Eina N . . . . . . . 48 B2
Einbeck D . . . . . . 82 A1
Eindhoven NL . . . 79 A5
Einsiedeln CH . . . 107 B3
Einville-au-Jard F . 92 C2
Eisenberg
  Rheinland-Pfalz D 93 B4
  Thüringen D . . . . 83 B3
Eisenerz A . . . . . 110 B1
Eisenhüttenstadt D . 74 B3
Eisenkappel A . . . 110 C1
Eisenstadt A . . . . 111 B3
Eisentratten A . . . 109 C4
Eisfeld D . . . . . . 82 B2
Eisleben D . . . . . 82 A3
Eislingen D . . . . . 94 C1
Eitensheim D . . . . 95 C3
Eiterfeld D . . . . . 82 B1
Eitorf D . . . . . . . 80 B3
Eivindvik N . . . . . 46 B2
Eivissa = Ibiza E . 166 C1
Eixo P . . . . . . . 148 B1
Ejby DK . . . . . . . 59 C2
Ejea de los Caballeros
  E . . . . . . . . . 144 B2
Ejstrupholm DK . . 59 C2
Ejulve E . . . . . . 153 B3
Eke B . . . . . . . . 79 B3
Ekeby
  Gotland S . . . . . 57 C4
  Skåne S . . . . . . 61 D2
  Uppsala S . . . . . 51 B5
Ekeby-Almby S . . . 56 A1
Ekenäs S . . . . . . 55 B4
Ekenässjön S . . . 62 A3
Ekerö S . . . . . . . 57 A3
Eket S . . . . . . . 61 C3
Eketorp S . . . . . . 63 B4
Ekevik S . . . . . . 56 B2
Ekkerøy N . . . . . 193 B14
Ekshärad S . . . . . 49 B5
Eksingedal N . . . . 46 B2
Eksjö S . . . . . . . 62 A2
Eksta S . . . . . . . 57 C4
Ekträsk S . . . . . . 200 B5
El Alamo
  Madrid E . . . . . 151 B4
  Sevilla E . . . . . 161 B3
El Algar E . . . . . 165 B4
El Almendro E . . . 161 B2
El Alquián E . . . . 164 C2
Élancourt F . . . . . 90 C1
El Arahal E . . . . . 162 A2
El Arenal E . . . . . 150 B2
El Arguellite E . . . 164 A2
El Astillero E . . . . 143 A3
Elassona GR . . . . 182 D4
Elati GR . . . . . . 182 D3
Żelazno PL . . . . . 85 B4
El Ballestero E . . . 158 C1
El Barco de Ávila
  E . . . . . . . . . 150 B2
Elbasan AL . . . . . 182 B2
El Berrón E . . . . . 142 A1
El Berrueco E . . . 151 B4
Elbeuf F . . . . . . 89 A4
Elbingerode D . . . 82 A2
Elbląg PL . . . . . . 69 A4
El Bodón E . . . . . 149 B3
El Bonillo E . . . . . 158 C1
El Bosque E . . . . 162 B2
El Bullaque E . . . . 157 A3
El Burgo E . . . . . 162 B3
El Burgo de Ebro
  E . . . . . . . . . 153 A3
El Burgo de Osma
  E . . . . . . . . . 151 A4
El Burgo Ranero E 142 B1
El Buste E . . . . . 144 C2
El Cabaco E . . . . 149 B3
El Callejo E . . . . . 143 A3
El Campillo E . . . . 161 B3
El Campillo de la Jara
  E . . . . . . . . . 156 A2
El Cañavete E . . . 158 B1
El Carpio E . . . . . 157 C3
El Carpio de Tajo
  E . . . . . . . . . 150 C3
El Casar E . . . . . 151 B4

El Casar de Escalona
  E . . . . . . . . . 150 B3
El Castillo de las
  Guardas E . . . . 161 B3
El Centenillo E . . . 157 B4
El Cerro E . . . . . 149 B4
El Cerro de Andévalo
  E . . . . . . . . . 161 B3
Elche E . . . . . . . 165 A4
Elche de la Sierra
  E . . . . . . . . . 158 C1
Elchingen D . . . . . 94 C2
El Comenar E . . . 162 B2
El Coronil E . . . . . 162 A2
El Crucero E . . . . 141 A4
El Cubo de Tierra del
  Vino E . . . . . . 149 A4
El Cuervo E . . . . 162 B1
Elda E . . . . . . . 159 C3
Eldena D . . . . . . 73 A4
Eldingen D . . . . . 72 B3
Elefsina GR . . . . . 185 A4
El Ejido E . . . . . . 164 C2
Elek H . . . . . . . 113 C5
Elemir SRB . . . . . 126 B2
El Escorial E . . . . 151 B3
El Espinar E . . . . 151 B3
Eleutheroupoli GR . 183 C6
El Frago E . . . . . 144 B3
El Franco E . . . . . 141 A4
El Frasno E . . . . . 152 A2
Elgå N . . . . . . . 199 C8
El Garrobo E . . . . 161 B3
El Gastor E . . . . . 162 B2
Elgin GB . . . . . . 32 D3
Elgoibar E . . . . . 143 A4
Elgol GB . . . . . . 31 B2
El Gordo E . . . . . 150 C2
El Grado E . . . . . 145 B4
El Granado E . . . . 161 B2
El Grao de Castelló
  E . . . . . . . . . 159 B4
El Grau E . . . . . . 159 C3
Elgshøa N . . . . . 49 A4
El Higuera E . . . . 163 A3
El Hijate E . . . . . 164 B2
El Hontanar E . . . 152 B2
El Hoyo E . . . . . . 157 B4
Elie GB . . . . . . . 35 B5
Elizondo E . . . . . 144 A2
Ełk PL . . . . . . . 12 B5
Elkhovo BG . . . . . 17 D7
Ellenberg D . . . . . 94 B2
Ellesmere GB . . . 38 B4
Ellesmere Port GB . 38 A4
Ellezelles B . . . . . 79 B3
Ellingen D . . . . . . 94 B2
Ellmau A . . . . . . 109 B3
Ellon GB . . . . . . 33 D4
Ellös S . . . . . . . 54 B2
Ellrich D . . . . . . 82 A2
Ellwangen D . . . . 94 C2
Elm
  CH . . . . . . . . 107 C4
  D . . . . . . . . . 72 A2
Elmadağ TR . . . . 23 B7
El Madroño E . . . . 161 B3
El Maíllo E . . . . . 149 B3
Elmalı TR . . . . . . 189 C4
El Masnou E . . . . 147 C3
El Mirón E . . . . . 150 B2
El Molar E . . . . . 151 B4
El Molinillo E . . . . 157 A3
El Morell E . . . . . 147 C2
Elmshorn D . . . . . 64 C2
Elmstein D . . . . . 93 B3
El Muyo E . . . . . 151 A4
Elne F . . . . . . . 146 B3
Elnesvågen N . . . 198 C4
El Olmo E . . . . . . 151 A4
Elorrio E . . . . . . 143 A4
Előszállás H . . . . 112 C2
Elouda GR . . . . . 185 D6
Éloyes F . . . . . . 105 A5
El Palo E . . . . . . 163 B3
El Pardo E . . . . . 151 B4
El Payo E . . . . . . 149 B3
El Pedernoso E . . 158 B1
El Pedroso E . . . . 162 A2
El Peral E . . . . . . 158 B2
El Perelló
  Tarragona E . . . 153 B4
  Valencia E . . . . 159 B3
Elphin GB . . . . . . 32 C1
El Picazo E . . . . . 158 B1
El Pinell de Bray E 153 A4
El Piñero E . . . . . 150 A2
El Pla de Santa Maria
  E . . . . . . . . . 147 C2
El Pobo E . . . . . . 153 B3
El Pobo de Dueñas
  E . . . . . . . . . 152 B2
El Pont d'Armentera
  E . . . . . . . . . 147 C2
El Port de la Selva
  E . . . . . . . . . 147 B4
El Port de Llançà
  E . . . . . . . . . 146 B4
El Port de Sagunt
  E . . . . . . . . . 159 B3
El Prat de Llobregat
  E . . . . . . . . . 147 C3
El Provencio E . . . 158 B1
El Puente E . . . . . 143 A3
El Puente del Arzobispo
  E . . . . . . . . . 150 C2
El Puerto E . . . . . 141 A4

El Puerto de Santa María
  E . . . . . . . . . 162 B1
El Real de la Jara
  E . . . . . . . . . 161 B3
El Real de San Vincente
  E . . . . . . . . . 150 B3
El Robledo E . . . . 157 A3
El Rocio E . . . . . 161 B3
El Rompido E . . . . 161 B2
El Ronquillo E . . . 161 B3
El Royo E . . . . . . 143 C4
El Rubio E . . . . . 162 A3
El Sabinar E . . . . 164 A2
El Saler E . . . . . . 159 B3
El Salobral E . . . . 158 C2
El Saucejo E . . . . 162 A2
Els Castells E . . . 147 B2
Elsdorf D . . . . . . 80 B2
Elsenfeld D . . . . . 93 B5
El Serrat AND . . . 146 B2
Elsfleth D . . . . . . 72 A1
Elspeet NL . . . . . 70 B2
Elst NL . . . . . . . 70 C2
Elstead GB . . . . . 44 B3
Elster D . . . . . . . 83 A4
Elsterberg D . . . . 83 B4
Elsterwerda D . . . 83 A5
Elstra D . . . . . . . 84 A2
El Temple E . . . . 144 C3
El Tiemblo E . . . . 150 B3
Eltmann D . . . . . 94 B2
El Toboso E . . . . 157 A5
El Tormillo E . . . . 145 C3
El Torno E . . . . . 149 B4
Eltville D . . . . . . 93 A4
El Valle de las Casas
  E . . . . . . . . . 142 B1
Elvas P . . . . . . . 155 C3
Elvebakken N . . . . 192 C7
El Vellón E . . . . . 151 B4
Elven F . . . . . . . 101 B3
El Vendrell E . . . . 147 C2
Elverum N . . . . . 48 B3
El Villar de Arnedo
  E . . . . . . . . . 144 B1
Elvington GB . . . . 40 B3
El Viso E . . . . . . 156 B3
El Viso del Alcor E 162 A2
Elxleben D . . . . . 82 A2
Ely GB . . . . . . . 45 A4
Elzach D . . . . . . 106 A3
Elze D . . . . . . . 72 B2
Emådalen S . . . . 50 A1
Embleton GB . . . . 37 A5
Embonas GR . . . . 188 C2
Embrun F . . . . . . 132 A2
Embún E . . . . . . 144 B3
Emden D . . . . . . 71 A4
Emecik TR . . . . . 188 C2
Emet TR . . . . . . 186 C4
Emirdağ TR . . . . 187 C6
Emlichheim D . . . . 71 B3
Emmaboda S . . . . 63 B3
Emmaljunga S . . . 61 C3
Emmeloord NL . . . 70 B2
Emmen
  CH . . . . . . . . 106 B3
  NL . . . . . . . . 71 B3
Emmendingen D . . 106 A2
Emmer-Compascuum
  NL . . . . . . . . 71 B4
Emmerich D . . . . 80 A2
Emmern D . . . . . 72 B2
Emöd H . . . . . . . 113 B4
Émpoli I . . . . . . . 135 B3
Emsbüren D . . . . 71 B4
Emsdetten D . . . . 71 B4
Emsfors S . . . . . 62 A4
Emskirchen D . . . 94 B2
Emstek D . . . . . . 71 B5
Emsworth GB . . . 44 C3
Emyvale IRL . . . . 27 B4
Enafors S . . . . . . 199 B9
Enánger S . . . . . 51 A4
Encamp AND . . . . 146 B2
Encarnaçao P . . . 154 C1
Encinas de Abajo
  E . . . . . . . . . 150 B2
Encinas de Esgueva
  E . . . . . . . . . 142 C2
Encinasola E . . . . 161 A3
Encinas Reales E . 163 A3
Encio E . . . . . . . 143 B3
Enciso E . . . . . . 144 B1
Enden N . . . . . . 199 D7
Endingen D . . . . . 106 A2
Endrinal E . . . . . 149 B4
Endröd H . . . . . . 113 C4
Enebakk N . . . . . 54 A2
Eneryda S . . . . . 63 B2
Enese H . . . . . . 111 B4
Enez TR . . . . . . 183 C8
Enfield IRL . . . . . 30 A2
Eng A . . . . . . . 108 B2
Engelberg CH . . . 106 C3
Engelhartszell A . . 96 C1
Engen D . . . . . . 107 B3
Enger N . . . . . . 48 B2
Engerdal N . . . . . 199 D8
Engerneset N . . . 49 A4
Enge-sande D . . . 64 B1
Engesvang DK . . . 59 B2
Enghien B . . . . . 79 B4
Engstingen D . . . . 94 C1
Engter D . . . . . . 71 B5
Enguera E . . . . . 159 C3
Enguidanos E . . . 158 B2

Enkenbach D . . . . 93 B3
Enkhuizen NL . . . 70 B2
Enklinge FIN . . . . 51 B7
Enköping S . . . . . 56 A3
Enna I . . . . . . . 177 B3
Ennezat F . . . . . 116 B3
Ennigerloh D . . . . 81 A4
Enningdal N . . . . 54 B2
Ennis IRL . . . . . . 28 B3
Enniscorthy IRL . . 30 B2
Enniskean IRL . . . 29 C3
Enniskillen GB . . . 27 B3
Ennistimon IRL . . . 28 B2
Enns A . . . . . . . 110 A1
Eno FIN . . . . . . . 9 A7
Enontekiö FIN . . . 196 A6
Ens NL . . . . . . . 70 B2
Enschede NL . . . . 71 B3
Ensdorf D . . . . . . 95 B3
Ensisheim F . . . . 106 B2
Enstaberga S . . . . 56 B2
Enstone GB . . . . . 44 B2
Entlebuch CH . . . . 106 B3
Entrácque I . . . . . 133 A3
Entradas P . . . . . 160 B1
Entrains-sur-Nohain
  F . . . . . . . . . 104 B2
Entrambasaguas E 143 A3
Entrambasmestas
  E . . . . . . . . . 143 A3
Entraygues-sur-Truyère
  F . . . . . . . . . 116 C2
Entre-os-Rios P . . 148 A1
Entrevaux F . . . . 132 B2
Entrin Bajo E . . . . 155 C4
Entroncamento P . 154 B2
Entzheim F . . . . . 93 C3
Envermeu F . . . . 89 A5
Enviken S . . . . . . 50 B2
Enying H . . . . . . 112 C2
Enzingerboden A . . 109 B3
Enzklösterle D . . . 93 C4
Épagny F . . . . . . 90 B3
Epalinges CH . . . . 106 C1
Epannes F . . . . . 114 B3
Epanomi GR . . . . 182 C4
Epe
  D . . . . . . . . . 71 B4
  NL . . . . . . . . 70 B2
Épernay F . . . . . 91 B3
Épernon F . . . . . 90 C1
Epfig F . . . . . . . 93 C3
Epierre F . . . . . . 118 B3
Épila E . . . . . . . 152 A2
Épinac F . . . . . . 104 C3
Épinal F . . . . . . 105 A5
Episcopia I . . . . . 174 A2
Episkopi CY . . . . 181 B1
Epitalio GR . . . . . 184 B2
Epoisses F . . . . . 104 B3
Eppenbrunn D . . . 93 B3
Eppendorf D . . . . 83 B5
Epping GB . . . . . 45 B4
Eppingen D . . . . . 93 B4
Epsom GB . . . . . 44 B3
Epworth GB . . . . 40 B3
Eraclea I . . . . . . 122 B1
Eraclea Mare I . . . 122 B1
Erba I . . . . . . . 120 B2
Erbach
  Baden-Württemberg
  D . . . . . . . . . 94 C1
  Hessen D . . . . . 93 B5
Erbalunga F . . . . 180 A2
Erbendorf D . . . . 95 B4
Érchie I . . . . . . . 173 B3
Ercolano I . . . . . 170 C2
Ercsi H . . . . . . . 112 B2
Érd H . . . . . . . 112 B2
Erdek TR . . . . . . 186 B2
Erdemli TR . . . . . 23 C8
Erdevik SRB . . . . 126 B1
Erding D . . . . . . 95 C3
Erdötelek H . . . . . 113 B4
Erdut HR . . . . . . 125 B5
Erdweg D . . . . . . 95 C3
Ereğli
  Konya TR . . . . . 23 C8
  Zonguldak TR . . 187 A6
Erenkaya TR . . . . 189 B7
Eresfjord N . . . . . 198 C5
Eresos GR . . . . . 183 D7
Eretria GR . . . . . 185 A4
Erfde D . . . . . . . 64 B2
Erfjord N . . . . . . 52 A2
Erfstadt D . . . . . . 80 B2
Erfurt D . . . . . . . 82 B3
Érgli LV . . . . . . . 8 D4
Ergoldsbach D . . . 95 C4
Eriboll GB . . . . . . 32 C2
Érice I . . . . . . . 176 A1
Ericeira P . . . . . . 154 C1
Eğirdir TR . . . . . 189 B5
Eriksberg S . . . . . 195 E6
Eriksmåla S . . . . 62 B3
Eringsboda S . . . . 63 B3
Eriswil CH . . . . . 106 B2
Erithres GR . . . . . 185 A4
Erkelenz D . . . . . 80 A2
Erkner D . . . . . . 74 B2
Erkrath D . . . . . . 80 A2
Erla E . . . . . . . 144 B3
Erlangen D . . . . . 94 B3
Erli I . . . . . . . . 133 A4
Erlsbach A . . . . . 109 C3
Ermelo NL . . . . . 70 B2
Ermenak TR . . . . 23 C7
Ermenonville F . . . 90 B2

Ermezinde P . . . . 148 A1
Ermidas P . . . . . 160 A1
Ermioni GR . . . . . 184 B4
Ermoupoli GR . . . 185 B5
Ermsleben D . . . . 82 A3
Erndtebrück D . . . 81 B4
Ernée F . . . . . . . 88 B3
Ernestinovo HR . . 125 B4
Ernstbrunn A . . . . 97 C4
Erolzheim D . . . . 107 A5
Erquelinnes B . . . 79 B4
Erquy F . . . . . . . 101 A3
Erra P . . . . . . . 154 C2
Erratzu E . . . . . . 144 A2
Errindlev DK . . . . 65 B4
Erro E . . . . . . . 144 B2
Ersa F . . . . . . . 180 A2
Érsekcsanád H . . . 125 A4
Erseke AL . . . . . 182 C2
Érsekvadkert H . . . 112 B3
Ersmark S . . . . . 200 C6
Erstein F . . . . . . 93 C3
Erstfeld CH . . . . . 107 C3
Ertebølle DK . . . . 58 B2
Ertingen D . . . . . 107 A4
Ervedal
  Coimbra P . . . . 148 B1
  Portalegre P . . . 154 B3
Ervenik HR . . . . . 138 A1
Ervidel P . . . . . . 160 B1
Ervy-le-Châtel F . . 104 A2
Erwitte D . . . . . . 81 A4
Erxleben D . . . . . 73 B4
Erzsébet H . . . . . 125 A4
Esbjerg DK . . . . . 59 C1
Esbly F . . . . . . . 90 C2
Escacena del Campo
  E . . . . . . . . . 161 B3
Escairón E . . . . . 140 B3
Escalada E . . . . . 143 B3
Escalante E . . . . 143 A3
Escalaplano I . . . . 179 C3
Escalona E . . . . . 150 B3
Escalona del Prado
  E . . . . . . . . . 151 A3
Escalonilla E . . . . 150 C3
Escalos de Baixo
  P . . . . . . . . . 155 B3
Escalos de Cima P 155 B3
Escamilla E . . . . . 152 B1
Es Caná E . . . . . 166 B1
Escañuela E . . . . 157 C3
Es Castell E . . . . 167 B4
Escatrón E . . . . . 153 A3
Eschach D . . . . . 107 B4
Eschau D . . . . . . 94 B1
Eschede D . . . . . 72 B3
Eschenau D . . . . 95 B3
Eschenbach D . . . 95 B3
Eschenz CH . . . . 107 B3
Eschershausen D . 72 C2
Esch-sur-Alzette L . 92 B1
Esch-sur-Sûre L . . 92 B1
Eschwege D . . . . 82 A2
Eschweiler D . . . . 80 B2
Escobasa de Almazán
  E . . . . . . . . . 152 A1
Escoeuilles F . . . . 78 B1
Escombreras E . . . 165 B4
Escos F . . . . . . . 144 A2
Escource F . . . . . 128 B1
Escragnolles F . . . 132 B2
Escrick GB . . . . . 40 B2
Escurial E . . . . . 156 A2
Escurial de la Sierra
  E . . . . . . . . . 149 B4
Esgos E . . . . . . 140 B3
Esher GB . . . . . . 44 B3
Eskdalemuir GB . . 36 A3
Eskifjörður IS . . . 191 B12
Eskilhem S . . . . . 57 C4
Eskilsäter S . . . . 55 B4
Eskilstuna S . . . . 56 A2
Eskipazar TR . . . . 187 B7
Eskişehir TR . . . . 187 C5
Eslarn D . . . . . . 95 B4
Eslava E . . . . . . 144 B2
Eslida E . . . . . . 159 B3
Eslohe D . . . . . . 81 A4
Eslöv S . . . . . . . 61 D3
Eşme TR . . . . . . 188 A3
Es Mercadal E . . . 167 B4
Es Migjorn Gran E . 167 B4
Espa N . . . . . . . 48 B3
Espalion F . . . . . 130 A1
Esparragalejo E . . 155 C4
Esparragosa del
  Caudillo E . . . . 156 B2
Esparragossa de la
  Serena E . . . . . 156 B2
Esparreguera E . . 147 C2
Esparron F . . . . . 132 B1
Espe N . . . . . . . 46 B3
Espedal N . . . . . 52 B2
Espejo
  Alava E . . . . . . 143 A3
  Córdoba E . . . . 163 A3
Espeland N . . . . . 46 B2
Espelkamp D . . . . 72 B1
Espeluche F . . . . 131 A3
Espeluy E . . . . . 157 B4
Espera E . . . . . . 162 B2
Esperança P . . . . 155 B3

Espéraza F. . . . . . . . 146 B3
Espéria I. . . . . . . . . 169 B3
Espevær N. . . . . . . . 52 A1
Espiel E. . . . . . . . . 156 B2
Espinama E. . . . . . 142 A2
Espiñaredo E. . . . . 140 A3
Espinasses F. . . . . 132 A2
Espinelves E . . . . . 147 C3
Espinhal P. . . . . . . 154 A2
Espinho P . . . . . . . 148 A1
Espinilla E . . . . . . . 142 A2
Espinosa de Cerrato
E. . . . . . . . . . . . . 143 C3
Espinosa de los
Monteros E . . . . . 143 A3
Espinoso del Rey
E. . . . . . . . . . . . . 156 A3
Espirito Santo P. . . 160 B2
Espluga de Francolí
E. . . . . . . . . . . . . 147 C2
Esplús E . . . . . . . . 145 C4
Espolla E . . . . . . . . 146 B3
Espoo FIN . . . . . . . . 8 B4
Esporles E . . . . . . . 166 B2
Es Port d'Alcúdia
E. . . . . . . . . . . . . 167 B3
Esposende P. . . . . . 148 A1
Espot E . . . . . . . . . 146 B2
Es Pujols E . . . . . . 166 C1
Esquedas E . . . . . . 145 B3
Esquivias E . . . . . . 151 B4
Essay F . . . . . . . . . 89 B4
Essen
B. . . . . . . . . . . . . 79 A4
Niedersachsen D . . . 71 B4
Nordrhein-Westfalen
D. . . . . . . . . . . . . 80 A3
Essenbach D. . . . . 95 C4
Essertaux F. . . . . . 90 B2
Essingen D. . . . . . 94 C2
Esslingen D. . . . . . 94 C1
Es Soleràs E . . . . . 153 A4
Essoyes F . . . . . . . 104 A3
Estacas E. . . . . . . 140 B2
Estadilla E . . . . . . 145 B4
Estagel F . . . . . . . 146 B3
Estaires F . . . . . . . 78 B2
Estang F . . . . . . . . 128 C2
Estarreja P. . . . . . 148 B1
Estartit E . . . . . . . 147 B4
Estavayer-le-Lac
CH . . . . . . . . . . . 106 C1
Este I . . . . . . . . . . 121 B4
Esteiro E . . . . . . . 140 A2
Estela P. . . . . . . . 148 A1
Estella E . . . . . . . 144 B1
Estellencs E . . . . . 166 B2
Estepa E . . . . . . . 162 A3
Estépar E. . . . . . . 143 B3
Estepona E. . . . . . 162 B2
Esternay F . . . . . . 91 C3
Esterri d'Aneu E . . 146 B2
Esterwegen D . . . . 71 B4
Estissac F . . . . . . 104 A2
Estivadas E. . . . . . 140 B3
Estivareilles F . . . . 116 A2
Estivella E . . . . . . 159 B3
Estói P. . . . . . . . . 160 B2
Estopiñán E. . . . . . 145 C4
Estoril P. . . . . . . . 154 C1
Estoublon F. . . . . . 132 B2
Estrée-Blanche F . . 78 B2
Estrées-St Denis F . 90 B2
Estrela E . . . . . . . 155 C3
Estremera E. . . . . . 151 B4
Estremoz P . . . . . . 155 C3
Estuna S . . . . . . . 51 C5
Esyres F . . . . . . . 102 B2
Esztergom H . . . . . 112 B2
Étables-sur-Mer F. . 100 A3
Étain F . . . . . . . . . 92 B1
Étalans F . . . . . . . 105 B5
Étalle B. . . . . . . . . 92 B1
Étampes F. . . . . . . 90 C2
Étang-sur-Arroux
F. . . . . . . . . . . . . 104 C3
Étaples F. . . . . . . . 78 B1
Étauliers F . . . . . . 128 A2
Etili TR . . . . . . . . 186 C1
Etna N . . . . . . . . . 48 B1
Etne N . . . . . . . . . 52 A1
Etoges F . . . . . . . . 91 C3
Etoliko GR . . . . . . 184 A2
Eton GB . . . . . . . . 44 B3
Etréaupont F . . . . . 91 B3
Étréchy F . . . . . . . 90 C2
Étrépagny F. . . . . . 90 B1
Étretat F . . . . . . . . 89 A4
Étroeungt F . . . . . . 91 A3
Étroubles I . . . . . . 119 B4
Ettal D . . . . . . . . . 108 B2
Ettelbruck L . . . . . 92 B2
Etten NL . . . . . . . . 79 A4
Ettenheim D. . . . . 106 A2
Ettington GB . . . . . 44 A2
Ettlingen D. . . . . . 93 C4
Ettringen D . . . . . 108 A1
Etuz F . . . . . . . . . 105 B4
Etxarri-Aranatz E . 144 B1
Etyek H . . . . . . . . 112 B2
Eu F . . . . . . . . . . . 90 A1
Euerdorf D . . . . . . 82 B2
Eulate E. . . . . . . . 144 B1
Eupen B . . . . . . . . 80 B2
Europoort NL . . . . . 79 A4

Euskirchen D. . . . . 80 B2
Eutin D. . . . . . . . . 65 B3
Evanger N . . . . . . . 46 B3
Évaux-les-Bains F. . 116 A2
Evciler
Afyon TR . . . . . . . 189 A4
Çanakkale TR . . . . 186 C1
Evenskjær N . . . . . 194 B7
Evenstad N . . . . . . 48 A3
Evercreech GB . . . . 43 A4
Evergem B. . . . . . . 79 A3
Everöd S . . . . . . . . 61 D4
Eversberg D. . . . . . 81 A4
Everswinkel D . . . . 71 C4
Evertsberg S . . . . . 49 A5
Evesham GB . . . . . 44 A2
Évian-les-Bains F . . 118 A3
Evisa F . . . . . . . . . 180 A1
Evje N. . . . . . . . . . 53 B3
Evolène CH . . . . . . 119 A4
Évora P. . . . . . . . . 154 C3
Evoramonte P . . . . 155 C3
Evran F . . . . . . . . . 101 A4
Evrecy F. . . . . . . . . 89 A3
Évreux F . . . . . . . . 89 A5
Évron F . . . . . . . . . 102 A1
Évry F. . . . . . . . . . 90 C2
Ewell GB . . . . . . . . 44 B3
Ewersbach D. . . . . 81 B4
Excideuil F. . . . . . . 115 C5
Exeter GB . . . . . . . 43 B3
Exmes F. . . . . . . . . 89 B4
Exminster GB . . . . . 43 B3
Exmouth GB . . . . . . 43 B3
Eydehamn N . . . . . 53 B4
Eye
Peterborough GB. . . 41 C3
Suffolk GB . . . . . . 45 A5
Eyemouth GB . . . . . 35 C5
Eyguians F . . . . . . . 132 A1
Eyguières F . . . . . . 131 B4
Eygurande F . . . . . 116 B2
Eylie F . . . . . . . . . 145 B4
Eymet F . . . . . . . . 129 B3
Eymoutiers F . . . . . 116 B1
Eynsham GB . . . . . . 44 B2
Eyrarbakki IS. . . . . 190 D4
Eystrup D. . . . . . . . 72 B2
Ezaro E . . . . . . . . . 140 B1
Ezcaray E . . . . . . . 143 B4
Ezcároz E. . . . . . . . 144 B2
Ezine TR. . . . . . . . 186 C1
Ezmoriz P. . . . . . . . 148 B1

**F**

Fabara E . . . . . . . . 153 A4
Fábbrico I . . . . . . . 121 C3
Fåberg N . . . . . . . . 48 A2
Fabero E . . . . . . . . 141 B4
Fábiánsebestyén
H . . . . . . . . . . . . 113 C4
Fåborg DK . . . . . . . 64 A3
Fabrègues F . . . . . 130 B2
Fabriano I . . . . . . . 136 B1
Fabrizia I . . . . . . . 175 C2
Facha P . . . . . . . . 148 A1
Facinas E . . . . . . . 162 B2
Fačkov SK . . . . . . . 98 B2
Fadagosa P. . . . . . 155 B3
Fadd H . . . . . . . . . 112 C2
Faédis I . . . . . . . . 122 A2
Faenza I . . . . . . . . 135 A4
Fafe P. . . . . . . . . . 148 A1
Fagagna I . . . . . . . 122 A2
Fǎgǎras RO . . . . . . 17 C6
Fågelberget S . . . 199 A11
Fågelfors S . . . . . . 62 A3
Fågelmara S . . . . . 63 B3
Fågelsta S . . . . . . 55 B6
Fagerås S . . . . . . . 55 A4
Fagerheim N . . . . . 47 B4
Fagerhøy N . . . . . . 48 A1
Fagerhult S . . . . . . 62 A3
Fagerlund N. . . . . . 48 B2
Fagernes
Oppland N . . . . . . 47 B6
Troms N . . . . . . . 192 C3
Fagersanna S . . . . 55 B5
Fagersta S . . . . . . 50 B2
Fåglavik S . . . . . . . 55 B4
Fagnano Castello I 174 B2
Fagnières F . . . . . . 91 C4
Faido CH . . . . . . . 107 C3
Fains-Véel F . . . . . 91 C5
Fairford GB . . . . . . 44 B2
Fairlie GB. . . . . . . . 34 C3
Fajoz H . . . . . . . . . 112 C2
Fakenham GB . . . . . 41 C4
Fåker S . . . . . . . . 199 B11
Fakse DK . . . . . . . . 65 A5
Fakse Ladeplads
DK . . . . . . . . . . . 65 A5
Falaise F . . . . . . . . 89 B3
Falcade I . . . . . . . . 121 A4
Falcarragh IRL. . . . 26 A2
Falces E. . . . . . . . 144 B2
Fălciu RO. . . . . . . 17 B8
Falconara I. . . . . . 177 B3
Falconara Maríttima
I. . . . . . . . . . . . . 136 B2
Falcone I . . . . . . . 177 A4
Faldingworth GB. . . 40 B3
Falerum S . . . . . . . 56 B2
Fălești MD . . . . . . 17 B7
Falkenberg
Bayern D . . . . . . . 95 B4

Falkenberg continued
Bayern D . . . . . . . 95 C4
Brandenburg D . . . 83 A5
S. . . . . . . . . . . . . 60 C2
Falkensee D. . . . . . 74 B2
Falkenstein
Bayern D . . . . . . . 95 B4
Sachsen D . . . . . . 83 B4
Falkenthal D . . . . . 74 B2
Falkirk GB. . . . . . . 35 B4
Falkland GB. . . . . . 35 B4
Falköping S . . . . . . 55 B4
Fall D . . . . . . . . . . 108 B2
Falla S . . . . . . . . . 56 B1
Fallingbostel D . . . 72 B2
Falmouth GB . . . . . 42 B1
Falset E . . . . . . . . 147 C1
Fălticeni RO. . . . . . 17 B7
Falun S. . . . . . . . . 50 B2
Famagusta CY. . . . 181 A2
Fammestad N . . . . 46 B2
Fana N. . . . . . . . . 46 B2
Fanano I. . . . . . . . 135 A3
Fanari GR. . . . . . . 182 D3
Fanjeaux F . . . . . . 146 A3
Fano I. . . . . . . . . . 136 B2
Fântânele RO . . . . 126 A3
Fara in Sabina I. . . 168 A2
Faramontanos de
Tábara E . . . . . . 149 A4
Fara Novarese I. . . 119 B5
Farasdues E . . . . . 144 B2
Fårbo S. . . . . . . . . 62 A4
Fareham GB . . . . . 44 C2
Färentuna S. . . . . . 57 A3
Färgelanda S. . . . . 54 B2
Färila S. . . . . . . . 200 E1
Faringdon GB . . . . 44 B2
Faringe S. . . . . . . 51 C5
Farini I . . . . . . . . . 120 C2
Fariza E . . . . . . . . 149 A3
Färjestaden S . . . . 63 B4
Farkadona GR. . . . 182 D4
Farkasfa H. . . . . . . 111 C3
Farlete E . . . . . . . . 153 A3
Färlöv S . . . . . . . . 61 C4
Farmos H. . . . . . . 113 B3
Farnå SK . . . . . . . 112 B2
Färnäs S . . . . . . . 50 B1
Farnborough GB. . . 44 B3
Farnese I . . . . . . . 168 A1
Farnham GB . . . . . 44 B3
Farnroda D . . . . . . 82 B2
Faro P . . . . . . . . . 160 B2
Fåro S . . . . . . . . . 57 C5
Fårösund S . . . . . . 57 C5
Farra d'Alpago I . . 122 A1
Farranfore IRL. . . . 29 B2
Farre DK. . . . . . . . 59 B2
Farsala GR. . . . . . 182 D4
Farsø DK. . . . . . . . 58 B2
Farsund N . . . . . . . 52 B2
Farum DK. . . . . . . . 61 D2
Fårup DK . . . . . . . 58 B2
Fasana I . . . . . . . . 172 B1
Fasano I . . . . . . . . 173 B3
Fáskrúdsfjördur
IS . . . . . . . . . . . 191 C11
Fassberg D . . . . . . 72 B3
Fastiv UA . . . . . . . 13 C8
Fastnäs S. . . . . . . 49 B5
Fátima P. . . . . . . . 154 B2
Fatmomakke S . . . 195 E6
Fättjaur S . . . . . . 195 E6
Faucogney-et-la-Mer
F. . . . . . . . . . . . 105 B5
Fauguerolles F . . . 128 B3
Faulenrost D . . . . . 74 A1
Faulquemont F . . . 92 B2
Fauquembergues F 78 B2
Fauske N . . . . . . . 194 C6
Fauville-en-Caux F. 89 A4
Fauvillers B . . . . . . 92 B1
Fåvang N . . . . . . . 48 A2
Favara
E. . . . . . . . . . . . 159 B3
I. . . . . . . . . . . . 176 B2
Faverges F. . . . . . 118 B3
Faverney F. . . . . . 105 B5
Faversham GB . . . 45 B4
Favignana I . . . . . 176 B1
Fawley GB . . . . . . 44 C2
Fay-aux-Loges F. . 103 B4
Fayence F . . . . . . 132 B2
Fayet F. . . . . . . . . 130 B1
Fayl-Billot F . . . . . 105 B4
Fayón E . . . . . . . . 153 A4
Fearn GB . . . . . . . 32 D3
Fécamp F . . . . . . . 89 A4
Feda N . . . . . . . . . 52 B2
Fedje N. . . . . . . . . 46 B1
Feeny GB. . . . . . . . 27 B3
Fegen S. . . . . . . . 60 B3
Fegyvernek H . . . 113 B4
Fehrbellin D. . . . . . 74 B1
Fehring A. . . . . . . 111 C3
Feichten A. . . . . . 108 B1
Feiring N . . . . . . . 48 B3
Feistritz im Rosental
A. . . . . . . . . . . . 110 C1
Feketić SRB. . . . . 126 B1
Felanitx E. . . . . . . 167 B3
Feld am See A . . . 109 C4
Feldbach A. . . . . . 110 C2
Feldberg D. . . . . . 74 A2
Feldkirch A. . . . . . 107 B4
Feldkirchen in Kärnten
A. . . . . . . . . . . . 109 C5

Feldkirchen-Westerham
D. . . . . . . . . . . . 108 B2
Felgueiras P . . . . . 148 A1
Felitto I. . . . . . . . . 172 B1
Félix E . . . . . . . . . 164 C2
Felixstowe GB . . . . 45 B5
Felizzano I . . . . . . 119 C5
Felletin F . . . . . . . 116 B2
Fellingsbro S. . . . . 56 A1
Felnac RO. . . . . . . 126 A3
Felnémet H . . . . . . 113 B4
Felpéc H. . . . . . . . 111 B4
Fels am Wagram A. 97 C3
Felsberg D . . . . . . 81 A5
Felsönyék H . . . . . 112 C2
Felsöszentiván H . . 126 A1
Felsöszentmárton
H . . . . . . . . . . . . 125 B3
Felsözsolca H . . . . 113 A4
Felsted DK . . . . . . 64 B2
Feltre I . . . . . . . . . 121 A4
Femsjö S . . . . . . . 60 C3
Fenagh IRL . . . . . . 26 B3
Fene E . . . . . . . . . 140 A2
Fenestrelle I. . . . . 119 B4
Fénétrange F . . . . . 92 C3
Feneu F . . . . . . . . 102 B1
Fengersfors S . . . . 54 B3
Fenit IRL. . . . . . . . 29 B2
Fensmark DK. . . . . 65 A4
Fenwick GB . . . . . . 36 A2
Feolin Ferry GB. . . 34 C1
Ferbane IRL. . . . . . 28 A4
Ferdinandovac HR 124 A3
Ferdinandshof D . . 74 A2
Fère-Champenoise
F. . . . . . . . . . . . . 91 C3
Fère-en-Tardenois
F. . . . . . . . . . . . . 91 B3
Ferentillo I . . . . . . 168 A2
Ferentino I . . . . . . 169 B3
Feres GR . . . . . . . 183 C8
Feria E . . . . . . . . . 155 C4
Feričanci HR . . . . . 125 B3
Ferizli TR . . . . . . . 187 B5
Ferla I. . . . . . . . . . 177 B3
Ferlach A . . . . . . . 110 C1
Ferleiten A . . . . . . 109 B3
Fermil P . . . . . . . . 148 A2
Fermo I. . . . . . . . . 136 B2
Fermoselle E . . . . . 149 A3
Fermoy IRL . . . . . . 29 B3
Fernancaballero E 157 A4
Fernán Nuñéz E . . 163 A3
Fernán Perez E . . . 164 C2
Fernão Ferro P . . . 154 C1
Fernay-Voltaire F. . 118 A3
Ferndown GB . . . . 43 B5
Ferness GB . . . . . . 32 D3
Fernhurst GB. . . . . 44 B3
Ferns IRL. . . . . . . . 30 B2
Ferpécle CH. . . . . . 119 A4
Ferrals-les-Corbières
F. . . . . . . . . . . . 146 A3
Ferrandina I. . . . . . 172 B2
Ferrara I . . . . . . . . 121 C4
Ferrara di Monte Baldo
I . . . . . . . . . . . . 121 B3
Ferreira I. . . . . . . . 141 A3
Ferreira do Alentejo
P. . . . . . . . . . . . 160 A1
Ferreira do Zêzere
P. . . . . . . . . . . . 154 B2
Ferreras de Abajo
E. . . . . . . . . . . . 141 C4
Ferreras de Arriba
E. . . . . . . . . . . . 141 C4
Ferreries E. . . . . . . 167 B4
Ferreruela E. . . . . . 152 A2
Ferreruela de Tabara
E. . . . . . . . . . . . 149 A3
Ferret CH . . . . . . . 119 B4
Ferrette F . . . . . . . 106 B2
Ferriere I . . . . . . . . 120 C2
Ferrière-la-Grande
F. . . . . . . . . . . . . 79 B3
Ferrières
Hautes-Pyrénées
F. . . . . . . . . . . . 145 A3
Loiret F . . . . . . . 103 A4
Oise F . . . . . . . . 90 B2
Ferrières-sur-Sichon
F. . . . . . . . . . . . 117 A3
Ferrol E . . . . . . . . 140 A2
Ferryhill GB. . . . . . 37 B5
Fertörakos H . . . . . 111 B3
Fertöszentmiklós
H . . . . . . . . . . . . 111 B3
Fethard
Tipperary IRL. . . . 29 B4
Wexford IRL. . . . . 30 B2
Fethiye TR . . . . . . 188 C4
Fetsund N . . . . . . 48 C3
Fettercairn GB. . . . 35 B5
Feucht D . . . . . . . 95 B3
Feuchtwangen D. . 94 B2
Feudingen D . . . . . 81 B4
Feuges F. . . . . . . . 91 C4
Feuquières F. . . . . 90 B1
Feurs F . . . . . . . . 117 B4
Fevik N. . . . . . . . . 53 B4
Ffestiniog GB . . . . 38 B3
Fiamignano I . . . . 169 A3

Fiano I. . . . . . . . . .119 B4
Ficarazzi I . . . . . . 176 A2
Ficarolo I. . . . . . . 121 C4
Fichtelberg D. . . . . 95 A3
Ficulle I . . . . . . . . 135 C5
Fidenza I . . . . . . . 120 C3
Fidjeland N . . . . . . 52 B2
Fieberbrunn A. . . . 109 B3
Fier AL. . . . . . . . . 182 C1
Fiera di Primiero I. 121 A4
Fiesch CH . . . . . . 119 A5
Fiesso Umbertiano
I . . . . . . . . . . . . 121 C4
Figari F . . . . . . . . 180 B2
Figeac F . . . . . . . 116 C2
Figeholm S . . . . . . 62 A4
Figgjo N . . . . . . . . 52 B1
Figline Valdarno I . 135 B4
Figols E . . . . . . . . 145 B4
Figueira da Foz P . 148 B1
Figueira de Castelo
Rodrigo P . . . . . 149 B3
Figueira dos Caveleiros
P. . . . . . . . . . . . 160 A1
Figueiredo P . . . . . 154 B3
Figueiredo de Alva
P. . . . . . . . . . . . 148 B2
Figueiródos Vinhos
P. . . . . . . . . . . . 154 B2
Figueres E. . . . . . . 147 B3
Figueroles E . . . . . 153 B3
Figueruela de Arriba
E. . . . . . . . . . . . 141 C4
Filadélfia I . . . . . . 175 C2
Fil'akovo SK . . . . . 99 C3
Filderstadt D . . . . . 94 C1
Filey GB . . . . . . . . 41 A3
Filiaşi RO. . . . . . . 17 C5
Filiates GR. . . . . . 182 D2
Filiatra GR . . . . . . 184 B2
Filipstad S . . . . . . 55 A5
Filisur CH. . . . . . . 107 C4
Fillan N . . . . . . . . 198 B5
Filotio GR . . . . . . 185 B6
Filottrano I. . . . . . 136 B2
Filskov DK. . . . . . . 59 C2
Filton GB . . . . . . . 43 A4
Filtvet N . . . . . . . . 54 A1
Filzmoos A. . . . . . 109 B4
Finale Emilia I . . . 121 C4
Finale Ligure I . . . 133 A4
Fiñana E . . . . . . . 164 B2
Finby FIN. . . . . . . . 51 B7
Fincham GB. . . . . . 41 C4
Finchingfield GB. . . 45 B4
Findhorn GB . . . . . 32 D3
Findochty GB . . . . 33 D4
Finike TR . . . . . . . 189 C5
Finkenberg A. . . . . 108 B2
Finnea IRL . . . . . . 27 C3
Finneidfjord N . . . . 195 D4
Finnerödja S . . . . . 55 B5
Finnskog N . . . . . . 49 B4
Finnsnes N . . . . . 194 A9
Finntorp S . . . . . . 54 A3
Finócchio I . . . . . . 168 B2
Finsjö S . . . . . . . . 62 A4
Finsland N. . . . . . . 52 B3
Finspång S . . . . . . 56 B1
Finsterwalde D. . . . 84 A1
Finsterwolde NL. . . 71 A4
Finstown GB . . . . . 33 B3
Fintona GB . . . . . . 27 B3
Fintown GB . . . . . . 26 B2
Fionnphort GB. . . . 34 B1
Fiorenzuola d'Arda
I . . . . . . . . . . . . 120 C2
Firenze = Florence
I . . . . . . . . . . . . 135 B4
Firenzuola I . . . . . 135 A4
Firmi F. . . . . . . . . 130 A1
Firminy F . . . . . . . 117 B4
Firmo I . . . . . . . . . 174 B2
Fischamend Markt
A. . . . . . . . . . . . 111 A3
Fischbach
A. . . . . . . . . . . . 110 B2
D . . . . . . . . . . . . 93 B3
Fischbeck D . . . . . 73 B5
Fischen D . . . . . . . 107 B5
Fishbourne GB . . . 44 C2
Fishguard GB . . . . 39 C2
Fiskardo GR . . . . . 184 A1
Fiskebäckskil S . . . 54 B2
Fiskebøl N . . . . . . 194 B5
Fismes F . . . . . . . 91 B3
Fisterra E . . . . . . . 140 B1
Fitero E . . . . . . . . 144 B2
Fitjar N. . . . . . . . . 46 C2
Fiuggi I . . . . . . . . 169 B3
Fiumata I . . . . . . . 169 A3
Fiumefreddo Brúzio
I . . . . . . . . . . . . 174 B2
Fiumefreddo di Sicília
I . . . . . . . . . . . . 177 B4
Fiumicino I. . . . . . 168 B2
Fivemiletown GB. . 27 B3
Fivizzano I . . . . . . 134 A3
Fjäkinge S . . . . . . 63 B2
Fjällåsen S . . . . . 196 B3
Fjällbacka S. . . . . 54 B2
Fjæra N. . . . . . . . . 46 C3
Fjärdhundra S . . . . 56 A2
Fjellerup DK. . . . . . 58 B3
Fjerritslev DK . . . . 58 A2
Fjordgard N . . . . . 194 A8
Fjugesta S . . . . . . 55 A5
Flå N. . . . . . . . . . 47 B6
Flåbygd N . . . . . . 53 A4

Flaça E. . . . . . . . . 147 B3
Flace F. . . . . . . . . 117 A4
Fladungen D . . . . . 82 B2
Flaine F . . . . . . . . 118 A3
Flaka FIN . . . . . . . 51 B7
Flåm N . . . . . . . . . 46 B4
Flamatt CH. . . . . . 106 C2
Flamborough GB . . 41 A3
Flammersfeld D . . . 81 B3
Flassans-sur-Issole
F. . . . . . . . . . . . 132 B2
Flatdal N . . . . . . . 53 A4
Flatebø N . . . . . . . 46 B3
Flateby N. . . . . . . 48 C3
Flateland N . . . . . . 52 A3
Flateyri IS . . . . . . 190 A2
Flатøydegard N . . . 47 B6
Flatråker N. . . . . . 46 C2
Flattach A. . . . . . . 109 C4
Flatvarp S . . . . . . 62 A4
Flauenskjold DK. . . 58 A3
Flavigny-sur-Moselle
F. . . . . . . . . . . . . 92 C2
Flavy-le-Martel F . . 90 B3
Flawil CH. . . . . . . 107 B4
Flayosc F. . . . . . . 132 B2
Flechtingen D . . . . 73 B4
Fleckeby D. . . . . . . 64 B2
Fleet GB. . . . . . . . 44 B3
Fleetmark D. . . . . . 73 B4
Fleetwood GB . . . . 38 A3
Flehingen D. . . . . . 93 B4
Flekke N. . . . . . . . 46 A2
Flekkefjord N. . . . . 52 B2
Flen S . . . . . . . . . 56 A2
Flensburg D. . . . . . 64 B2
Fleringe S . . . . . . 57 C4
Flerohopp S. . . . . . 62 B3
Flers F . . . . . . . . . 88 B3
Flesberg N . . . . . . 47 C6
Fleurance F . . . . . 129 C3
Fleuré F . . . . . . . . 115 B4
Fleurier CH . . . . . . 105 C5
Fleurus B . . . . . . . 79 B4
Fleury
Hérault F . . . . . . 130 B2
Yonne F . . . . . . . 104 B2
Fleury-les-Aubrais
F. . . . . . . . . . . . 103 B3
Fleury-sur-Andelle
F. . . . . . . . . . . . . 89 A5
Fleury-sur-Orne F . 89 A3
Flieden D. . . . . . . . 81 B5
Flimby GB . . . . . . 36 B3
Flims CH . . . . . . . 107 C4
Flines-lèz-Raches F 78 B3
Flint GB . . . . . . . . 38 A3
Flirey F . . . . . . . . 92 C1
Flirsch A. . . . . . . 108 B1
Flisa N . . . . . . . . . 49 B4
Flisby S . . . . . . . . 62 A2
Fliseryd S . . . . . . 62 A4
Flix E . . . . . . . . . . 153 A4
Flixecourt F . . . . . 90 A2
Flize F . . . . . . . . . 91 B4
Flobecq B . . . . . . . 79 B3
Floby S. . . . . . . . . 55 B4
Floda S. . . . . . . . . 60 B2
Flodden GB . . . . . . 37 A4
Flogny-la-Chapelle
F. . . . . . . . . . . . 104 B2
Flöha D . . . . . . . . 83 B5
Flonheim D . . . . . . 93 B4
Florac F . . . . . . . . 130 A2
Floreffe B. . . . . . . 79 B4
Florence = Firenze
I . . . . . . . . . . . . 135 B4
Florennes B . . . . . 79 B4
Florensac F . . . . . 130 B2
Florentin F . . . . . . 129 C5
Florenville B . . . . . 91 B5
Flores de Avila E . 150 B2
Floresta I . . . . . . . 177 B3
Floreşti MD . . . . . 17 B8
Florídia I . . . . . . . 177 B4
Florina GR . . . . . . 182 C3
Florø N. . . . . . . . . 46 A2
Flörsheim D . . . . . 93 A4
Floss D. . . . . . . . . 95 B4
Fluberg N. . . . . . . 48 B2
Flúðir IS . . . . . . . 190 C5
Flühli CH. . . . . . . 106 C3
Flumet F. . . . . . . . 118 B3
Fluminimaggiore I . 179 C2
Flums CH. . . . . . . 107 B4
Flyeryd S . . . . . . . 63 B3
Flygsfors S . . . . . . 62 B3
Foča BIH. . . . . . . 139 B4
Foča TR . . . . . . . 186 D1
Fochabers GB. . . . 32 D3
Focşani RO. . . . . . 17 C7
Foel GB . . . . . . . . 38 B3
Foeni RO . . . . . . . 126 B2
Fogdö S . . . . . . . . 56 A2
Fóggia I . . . . . . . . 171 B3
Foglianise I . . . . . 170 B2
Föglö FIN. . . . . . . . 51 B7
Fohnsdorf A. . . . . .110 B1
Foiano della Chiana
I. . . . . . . . . . . . . 135 B4
Foix F . . . . . . . . . 146 B2
Fojnica
BIH. . . . . . . . . . . 139 B3
BIH. . . . . . . . . . . 139 B4
Fokstua N. . . . . . . 198 C6
Földeák H . . . . . . 126 A2
Foldereid N . . . . . 199 A9
Földes H . . . . . . . 113 B5

Folegandros GR . . 185 C5
Folelli F . . . . . . . 180 A2
Folgaria I . . . . . . . 121 B4
Folgosinho P. . . . 148 B2
Folgoso de la Ribera
  E. . . . . . . . . . . . 141 B4
Folgoso do Courel
  E. . . . . . . . . . . . 141 B3
Foligno I . . . . . . . 136 C1
Folkärna S . . . . . . 50 B3
Folkestad N. . . . . 198 C3
Folkestone GB . . . 45 B5
Follafoss N . . . . . 199 B8
Folldal N . . . . . . . 198 C6
Follebu N . . . . . . . 48 A2
Follina I . . . . . . . 121 B5
Föllinge S . . . . . .199 B11
Follónica I . . . . . 135 C3
Fölsbyn S . . . . . . 54 A3
Foncebadón E. . . . 141 B4
Foncine-le-Bas F. . 105 C5
Fondevila E . . . . . 140 C2
Fondi I . . . . . . . . 169 B3
Fondo I. . . . . . . . 121 A4
Fonelas E . . . . . . 164 B1
Fonfría
  Teruel E . . . . . . .152 B2
  Zamora E . . . . . 149 A3
Fonn N . . . . . . . . 46 A3
Fonnes N . . . . . . . 46 B1
Fonni I . . . . . . . . 178 B3
Fontaine F . . . . . . 91 C4
Fontainebleau F . . 90 C2
Fontaine de Vaucluse
  F . . . . . . . . . . . 131 B4
Fontaine-Française
  F. . . . . . . . . . . 105 B4
Fontaine-le-Dun F . 89 A4
Fontan F . . . . . . . 133 A3
Fontanarejo E . . . 157 A3
Fontane I . . . . . . . 133 A3
Fontanélice I . . . . 135 A4
Fontanières F . . . . 116 A2
Fontanosas E . . . 157 B3
Fonteblanda I . . . . 168 A1
Fontenay-le-Comte
  F . . . . . . . . . . . .114 B3
Fontenay-Trésigny
  F. . . . . . . . . . . . 90 C2
Fontevrault-l'Abbaye
  F. . . . . . . . . . . 102 B2
Fontiveros E . . . . 150 B3
Fontoy F . . . . . . . 92 B1
Fontpédrouse F . . 146 B3
Font-Romeu F . . . 146 B3
Fontstown IRL. . . . 30 A2
Fonyód H. . . . . . . 111 C4
Fonz E . . . . . . . . 145 B4
Fonzaso I. . . . . . . 121 A4
Fóppolo I . . . . . . . 120 A2
Föra S . . . . . . . . . 62 A4
Forbach
  D . . . . . . . . . . . .93 C4
  F . . . . . . . . . . . .92 B2
Forcall E . . . . . . . 153 B3
Forcalquier F. . . . . 132 B1
Forcarei E . . . . . . 140 B2
Forchheim D . . . . 94 B3
Forchtenau A. . . .111 B3
Forchtenberg D. . . 94 B1
Ford GB . . . . . . . . 34 B2
Førde
  Hordaland N. . . .52 A1
  Sogn og Fjordane
  N. . . . . . . . . . .46 A2
Förderstedt D . . . . 83 A3
Førdesfjorden N . . 52 A1
Fordham GB . . . . . 45 A4
Fordingbridge GB. . 44 C2
Fordon PL . . . . . . 76 A3
Fordongiánus I . . . 179 C2
Forenza I . . . . . . . 172 B1
Foresta di Búrgos
  I . . . . . . . . . . . . 178 B2
Forfar GB . . . . . . 35 B5
Forges-les-Eaux F . 90 B1
Foria I. . . . . . . . . 172 B1
Forío I . . . . . . . . 170 C1
Forjães P. . . . . . . 148 A1
Førland N. . . . . . . 52 B3
Forl i I. . . . . . . . . 135 A5
Forlimpopoli I . . . 135 A5
Formazza I . . . . . .119 A5
Formby GB . . . . . . 38 A3
Formerie F . . . . . . 90 B1
Fórmia I . . . . . . . 169 B3
Formígine I . . . . . 135 A3
Formigliana I . . . .119 B5
Formiguères F . . . 146 B3
Fornalutx E . . . . . 166 B2
Fornåsa S . . . . . . 56 B1
Fornelli I. . . . . . . 178 B2
Fornells E . . . . . . 167 A4
Fornelos de Montes
  E. . . . . . . . . . . . 140 B2
Fornes E . . . . . . . 163 B4
Forneset N. . . . . . 192 C3
Forni Avoltri I. . . . 109 C3
Forni di Sopra I . . 122 A1
Forni di Sotto I . . 122 A1
Forno
  Piemonte I. . . . .119 B4
  Piemonte I. . . . .119 B5
Forno Alpi-Gráie I .119 B4
Forno di Zoldo I . . 121 A5
Fornos de Algodres
  P. . . . . . . . . . . . 148 B2
Fornovo di Taro I . . 120 C3

Foros do Arrão P. . 154 B2
Forráskút H . . . . . 126 A1
Forres GB . . . . . . 32 D3
Forriolo E. . . . . . . 140 B3
Fors S . . . . . . . . . 50 B3
Forsand N . . . . . . 52 B2
Forsbacka S . . . . . 51 B3
Forserum S . . . . . 62 A2
Forshaga S . . . . . 55 A4
Forsheda S . . . . . 60 B3
Forsinain GB. . . . . 32 C3
Forslev DK. . . . . . 65 A4
Förslöv S . . . . . . . 61 C2
Forsmark
  Uppsala S . . . . . .51 B5
  Västerbotten S. . . 195 E6
Forsmo S. . . . . . . 200 C3
Forsnäs S . . . . . 195 D9
Forsnes N . . . . . . 198 B5
Forssa FIN. . . . . . . 8 B3
Forssjöbruk S . . . . 56 B2
Forst D. . . . . . . . . 84 A2
Forsvik S. . . . . . . 55 B5
Fortanete E . . . . . 153 B3
Fort Augustus GB. . 32 D2
Forte dei Marmi I. . 134 B3
Fortezza I. . . . . . . 108 C2
Forth GB . . . . . . . 35 C4
Fort-Mahon-Plage F 78 B1
Fortrie GB. . . . . . . 33 D4
Fortrose GB. . . . . . 32 D2
Fortun N. . . . . . . . 47 A4
Fortuna E . . . . . . 165 A3
Fortuneswell GB. . . 43 B4
Fort William GB. . . 34 B2
Forvik N . . . . . . . 195 E3
Fos F . . . . . . . . . 145 B4
Fosdinovo I. . . . . . 134 A3
Foss N . . . . . . . . 47 B6
Fossacésia I . . . . 169 A4
Fossano I . . . . . . 133 A3
Fossato di Vico I . . 136 B1
Fossbakken N. . . .64 C2
Fosse-la-Ville B. . . 79 B4
Fossombrone I . . . 136 B1
Fot H . . . . . . . . .112 B3
Fouchères F . . . . 104 A3
Fouesnant F . . . . 100 B1
Foug F . . . . . . . . 92 C1
Fougères F . . . . . . 88 B2
Fougerolles F . . . 105 B5
Foulain F . . . . . . 105 A4
Fountainhall GB . . . 35 C5
Fouras F . . . . . . . 114 C2
Fourchambault F . . 104 B2
Fourmies F . . . . . . 91 A4
Fourna GR . . . . . 182 D3
Fournels F . . . . . 116 C3
Fourni GR . . . . . . 188 B1
Fournols F . . . . . .117 B3
Fourques F . . . . . 146 B3
Fourquevaux F . . . 146 A2
Fours F . . . . . . . 104 C2
Fowey GB . . . . . . 42 B2
Foxdale GB. . . . . . 36 B2
Foxford IRL . . . . . 26 C1
Foyers GB . . . . . . 32 D2
Foynes IRL. . . . . . 29 B2
Foz E . . . . . . . . . 141 A3
Foza I . . . . . . . . 121 B4
Foz do Arelho P. . . 154 B1
Foz do Giraldo P. . 155 B3
Frabosa Soprana I 133 A3
Frades de la Sierra
  E. . . . . . . . . . . 149 B4
Fraga E . . . . . . . 153 A4
Fragagnano I. . . . 173 B3
Frailes E. . . . . . . 163 A4
Fraire B . . . . . . . . 79 B4
Fraize F . . . . . . . 106 A1
Framlingham GB. . . 45 A5
Frammersbach D . . 94 A1
Framnes N . . . . . . 54 A1
França P. . . . . . . 141 C4
Francaltroff F . . . . 92 C2
Francavilla al Mare
  I . . . . . . . . . . . . 169 A4
Francavilla di Sicília
  I . . . . . . . . . . . . 177 B4
Francavilla Fontana
  I . . . . . . . . . . . . 173 B3
Francavilla in Sinni
  I . . . . . . . . . . . . 174 A2
Francescas F. . . . 129 B3
Franco P . . . . . . 148 A2
Francofonte I. . . . 177 B3
Francos E . . . . . . 151 A4
Frändefors S . . . . 54 B3
Franeker NL. . . . . 70 A2
Frangy F. . . . . . . .118 A2
Frankenau D . . . . 81 A4
Frankenberg
  Hessen D. . . . . .81 A4
  Sachsen D. . . . . 83 B5
Frankenburg A. . . 109 A4
Frankenfels A. . . .110 B2
Frankenmarkt A. . . 109 B4
Frankenthal D . . . 93 B4
Frankfurt
  Brandenburg D . . 74 B3
  Hessen D. . . . . .81 B4
Frankrike S . . . . 199 B10
Františkovy Lázně
  CZ . . . . . . . . . . 83 B4
Franzburg D . . . . 66 B1
Fränsta S . . . . . . 200 D2
Frascati I . . . . . . 168 B2

Frasdorf D . . . . . . 109 B3
Fraserburgh GB . . . 33 D4
Frashër AL. . . . . . 182 C2
Frasne F. . . . . . . 105 C5
Frasnes-lez-Anvaing
  B. . . . . . . . . . . . 79 B3
Frasseto F . . . . . 180 B2
Frastanz A . . . . . 107 B4
Fratel P. . . . . . . . 155 B3
Fratta Todina I . . . 135 C5
Frauenau D . . . . . 96 C1
Frauenfeld CH. . . . 107 B3
Frauenkirchen A . .111 B3
Frauenstein D . . . 83 B5
Frauental A . . . . . 110 C2
Frayssinet F . . . . 129 B4
Frayssinet-le-Gélat
  F . . . . . . . . . . . 129 B4
Frechas P. . . . . . 149 A2
Frechen D . . . . . . 80 B2
Frechilla E . . . . . 142 B2
Freckenhorst D . . . 71 C4
Fredeburg D . . . . 81 A4
Fredelsloh D . . . . 82 A1
Fredeng N . . . . . . 48 B2
Fredensborg DK. . . 61 D2
Fredericia DK. . . . 59 C2
Frederiks DK. . . . . 59 B2
Frederiksberg S . . 50 B1
Frederikshavn DK. . 58 A3
Frederikssund DK. . 61 D2
Frederiksværk DK. . 61 D2
Fredrika S . . . . . 200 B4
Fredriksberg S . . . 50 B1
Fredriksdal S. . . . . 62 A2
Fredrikstad N . . . . 54 A1
Fregenal de la Sierra
  E . . . . . . . . . . . 161 A3
Fregene I . . . . . . 168 B2
Freiberg D . . . . . . 83 B5
Freiburg
  Baden-Württemberg
  D. . . . . . . . . . . .106 B2
  Niedersachsen D. . .64 C2
Freienhagen D . . . 81 A5
Freienhufen D . . . 84 A1
Freiensteinau D. . . 81 B5
Freihung D. . . . . . 95 B3
Freilassing D . . . . 109 B3
Freisen D. . . . . . . 92 B3
Freising D . . . . . . 95 C3
Freistadt A. . . . . . 96 C2
Freital D. . . . . . . . 84 A1
Freixedas P. . . . . 149 B2
Freixo de Espada à
  Cinta P. . . . . . . 149 A3
Fréjus F . . . . . . . 132 B2
Fremdingen D . . . . 94 C2
Frenštát pod
  Radhoštěm CZ . . 98 B2
Freren D. . . . . . . . 71 B4
Freshford IRL . . . . 30 B1
Freshwater GB . . . 44 C2
Fresnay-sur-Sarthe
  F. . . . . . . . . . . . 89 B4
Fresneda de la Sierra
  E. . . . . . . . . . . . 152 B1
Fresneda de la Sierra
  Tiron E. . . . . . . 143 B3
Fresnedillas E . . . 151 B3
Fresnes-en-Woevre
  F. . . . . . . . . . . . 92 B1
Fresne-St Mamès
  F. . . . . . . . . . . 105 B4
Fresno Alhandiga
  E. . . . . . . . . . . 150 B2
Fresno de la Ribera
  E. . . . . . . . . . . 150 A2
Fresno de la Vega
  E. . . . . . . . . . . 142 B1
Fresno de Sayago
  E. . . . . . . . . . . 149 A4
Fresnoy-Folny F . . 90 B1
Fresnoy-le-Grand F 91 B3
Fressenville F . . . . 90 A1
Fresvik N . . . . . . . 46 A3
Fréteval F . . . . . . 103 B3
Fretigney F . . . . . 105 B4
Freudenberg
  Baden-Württemberg
  D. . . . . . . . . . . .94 B1
  Nordrhein-Westfalen
  D. . . . . . . . . . . .81 B3
Freudenstadt D. . . 93 C4
Freux B . . . . . . . . 92 B1
Frévent F . . . . . . . 78 B2
Freyburg D . . . . . 83 A3
Freyenstein D . . . . 73 A5
Freyming-Merlebach
  F. . . . . . . . . . . . 92 B2
Freystadt D . . . . . 95 B3
Freyung D. . . . . . . 96 C1
Frias de Albarracin
  E. . . . . . . . . . . . 152 B2
Fribourg CH. . . . . 106 C2
Frick CH. . . . . . . 106 B3
Fridafors S. . . . . . 63 B2
Fridaythorpe GB . . 40 A3
Friedberg
  Bayern D . . . . . .94 C2
  Hessen D. . . . . .81 B4
Friedeburg D. . . . . 71 A4
Friedewald D. . . . . 82 B1
Friedland
  Brandenburg D . .74 B3
  Mecklenburg-
  Vorpommern D. . .74 A2
  Niedersachsen D. .82 A1

Friedrichroda D. . . 82 B2
Friedrichsdorf D . . 81 B4
Friedrichshafen D. 107 B4
Friedrichskoog D . . 64 B1
Friedrichstadt D . . 64 B2
Friedrichswalde D. . 74 A2
Friesach A . . . . . . 110 C1
Friesack D. . . . . . . 73 B5
Friesenheim D. . . . 93 C3
Friesoythe D . . . . 71 A4
Friggesund S. . . . 200 E2
Frigiliana E . . . . . 163 B4
Frihetsli N . . . . . . 192 D3
Frillesås S . . . . . . 60 B2
Frinnaryd S . . . . . 62 A2
Frinton-on-Sea GB . 45 B5
Friockheim GB . . . 35 B5
Friol E . . . . . . . . 140 A3
Fristad S . . . . . . . 60 B2
Fritsla S . . . . . . . 60 B2
Fritzlar D . . . . . . . 81 A5
Frizington GB . . . . 36 B3
Frödinge S. . . . . . 62 A4
Froges F . . . . . . .118 B2
Frohburg D . . . . . 83 A4
Frohnhausen D . . . 81 B4
Frohnleiten A. . . . .110 B2
Froissy F . . . . . . . 90 B2
Frombork PL . . . . 69 A4
Frome GB . . . . . . 43 A4
Frómista E . . . . . . 142 B2
Fröndenberg D . . . 81 A3
Fronsac F . . . . . . 128 B2
Front I . . . . . . . . .119 B4
Fronteira P. . . . . . 155 B3
Frontenay-Rohan-Rohan
  F. . . . . . . . . . . . .114 B3
Frontenhausen D . . 95 C4
Frontignan F . . . . 130 B2
Fronton F. . . . . . . 129 C4
Fröseke S . . . . . . 62 B3
Frosinone I . . . . . 169 B3
Frosolone I . . . . . 170 B2
Frosta N . . . . . . . 199 B7
Frøstrup DK. . . . . 58 A1
Frosunda S . . . . . 57 A4
Frouard F. . . . . . . 92 C2
Frövi S. . . . . . . . . 56 A1
Frøyset N . . . . . . . 46 B2
Fruges F . . . . . . . 78 B2
Frutigen CH. . . . . 106 C2
Frýdek-Mistek CZ . . 98 B2
Frýdlant CZ . . . . . 84 B3
Frydlant nad Ostravicí
  CZ . . . . . . . . . . 98 B2
Frygnowo PL. . . . . 77 A5
Fryšták CZ. . . . . . 98 B1
Fucécchio I . . . . . 135 B3
Fuencaliente
  Ciudad Real E . . 157 A4
  Ciudad Real E . . 157 B3
Fuencemillán E . . . 151 B4
Fuendejalón E . . . 144 C2
Fuengirola E . . . . 163 B3
Fuenlabrada E . . . 151 B4
Fuenlabrada de los
  Montes E. . . . . . 156 A3
Fuensalida E . . . . 151 B3
Fuensanta E . . . . 164 B3
Fuensanta de Martos
  E. . . . . . . . . . . . 163 A4
Fuente-Alamo E . . 158 C2
Fuente-Álamo de Murcia
  E. . . . . . . . . . . . 165 B3
Fuentealbilla E . . . 158 B2
Fuente al Olmo de Iscar
  E. . . . . . . . . . . . 150 A3
Fuentecén E . . . . 151 A4
Fuente Dé E . . . . 142 A2
Fuente de Cantos
  E. . . . . . . . . . . . 155 C4
Fuente del Arco E . 156 B2
Fuente del Conde
  E. . . . . . . . . . . . 163 A3
Fuente del Maestre
  E. . . . . . . . . . . . 155 C4
Fuente de Santa Cruz
  E. . . . . . . . . . . . 150 A3
Fuente el Fresno E 157 A4
Fuente el Saz de Jarama
  E. . . . . . . . . . . . 151 B4
Fuente el Sol E . . . 150 A3
Fuenteguinaldo E . 149 B3
Fuentelapeña E . . . 150 A2
Fuentelcésped E. . 151 A4
Fuentelespino de Haro
  E. . . . . . . . . . . . 158 B1
Fuentelespino de Moya
  E. . . . . . . . . . . . 158 B2
Fuentenovilla E . . . 151 B4
Fuente Obejuna E . 156 B2
Fuente Palmera E . 162 A2
Fuentepelayo E . . . 151 A3
Fuentepinilla E . . . 151 A5
Fuenterroble de
  Salvatierra E . . . 150 B2
Fuenterrobles E . . 158 B2
Fuentes E . . . . . . 158 B1
Fuentesaúco E . . . 150 A2
Fuentesaúco E . . . 150 A2
Fuentes de Andalucía
  E. . . . . . . . . . . . 162 A2
Fuentes de Ebro E 153 A3
Fuentes de Jiloca
  E. . . . . . . . . . . . 152 A2
Fuentes de la Alcarria
  E. . . . . . . . . . . . 151 B5
Fuentes de León E 161 A3

Fuentes de Nava E 142 B2
Fuentes de Oñoro
  E. . . . . . . . . . . . 149 B3
Fuentes de Ropel
  E. . . . . . . . . . . . 142 B1
Fuentespalda E . . . 153 B4
Fuentespina E . . . 151 A4
Fuente-Tójar E . . . 163 A3
Fuente Vaqueros E 163 A4
Fuentidueña E . . . 151 A4
Fuentidueña de Tajo
  E. . . . . . . . . . . . 151 B4
Fuerte del Rey E. . 157 C4
Fügen A . . . . . . . 108 B2
Fuglebjerg DK. . . . 65 A4
Fuglevik N . . . . . . 54 A1
Fuhrberg D . . . . . 72 B2
Fulda D. . . . . . . . 82 B1
Fulgatore I . . . . . 176 B1
Fully CH. . . . . . . .119 A4
Fulnek CZ. . . . . . . 98 B1
Fülöpszállás H . . . 112 C3
Fulpmes A . . . . . 108 B2
Fulunäs S . . . . . . 49 A5
Fumay F . . . . . . . 91 B4
Fumel F . . . . . . . 129 B3
Funäsdalen S . . . 199 C9
Fundão P . . . . . . 148 B2
Funzie GB . . . . . . 33 A6
Furadouro P . . . . 148 B1
Fure N . . . . . . . . 46 A2
Fürstenau D. . . . . 71 B4
Furstenau D. . . . . 81 A5
Fürstenberg D. . . . 74 A2
Fürstenfeld A. . . . .111 B3
Fürstenfeldbruck
  D . . . . . . . . . . . 108 A2
Fürstenstein D . . . 96 C1
Fürstenwalde D . . . 74 B3
Fürstenwerder D . . 74 A2
Fürstenzell D. . . . . 96 C1
Furta H. . . . . . . . .113 B5
Fürth
  Bayern D . . . . . .94 B2
  Hessen D. . . . . .93 B4
Furth im Wald D . . 95 B4
Furtwangen D . . . 106 A3
Furuby S . . . . . . . 62 B3
Furudal S . . . . . . 50 A2
Furuflaten N . . . . 192 C4
Furulund S. . . . . . 61 D3
Furusjö S. . . . . . . 60 B3
Fusa N . . . . . . . . 46 B2
Fuscaldo I . . . . . 174 B2
Fusch an der
  Grossglocknerstrasse
  A. . . . . . . . . . . . 109 B3
Fushë Arrëz AL. . . 182 A2
Fushë-Krujë AL. . . 182 B1
Fusina I . . . . . . . 122 B1
Fusio CH . . . . . . 107 C3
Füssen D . . . . . . 108 B1
Fustiñana E . . . . . 144 B2
Futog SRB . . . . . 126 B1
Futrikelv N . . . . . 192 C3
Füzesabony H . . . .113 B4
Füzesgyarmat H . .113 B5
Fužine HR . . . . . . 123 B3
Fyllinge S. . . . . . . 61 C2
Fynshav DK. . . . . . 64 B2
Fyresdal N . . . . . . 53 A4

G

Gaaldorf A . . . . . .110 B1
Gabaldón E . . . . . 158 B2
Gabarret F . . . . . 128 C2
Gabčíkovo SK. . . .111 B4
Gabin PL . . . . . . . 77 B4
Gabriac F . . . . . . 130 A1
Gaby I . . . . . . . . .119 B4
Gacé F . . . . . . . . 89 B4
Gacko BIH . . . . . 139 B4
Gäddede S . . . . .199 A11
Gadebusch D . . . . 65 C4
Gadmen CH. . . . . 106 C3
Gádor E . . . . . . . 164 C2
Gádoros H . . . . . 113 C4
Gael F. . . . . . . . . 101 A3
Găeşti RO . . . . . . 17 C6
Gaeta I . . . . . . . . 169 B3
Gafanhoeira P . . . 154 C2
Gaflenz A. . . . . . .110 B1
Gagarin RUS . . . . 9 E9
Gaggenau D . . . . 93 C4
Gagliano Castelferrato
  I . . . . . . . . . . . . 177 B3
Gagliano del Capo
  I . . . . . . . . . . . . 173 C4
Gagnet S . . . . . . . 50 B2
Gaibanella I . . . . . 121 C4
Gaildorf D . . . . . . 94 B1
Gaillac F. . . . . . . 129 C4
Gaillefontaine F . . . 90 B1
Gaillon F . . . . . . . 89 A5
Gainsborough GB. . 40 B3
Gairloch GB. . . . . 31 B3
Gairlochy GB. . . . . 34 B3
Gáiro I . . . . . . . . 179 C3
Gaj
  HR. . . . . . . . . . 124 B3
  SRB . . . . . . . . 127 C3
Gaja-la-Selve F . . 146 A2
Gajanejos E . . . . 151 B5
Gajary SK. . . . . . . 97 C4
Gajdobra SRB . . . 126 B1

Galan F . . . . . . . 145 A4
Galanta SK. . . . . .111 A4
Galapagar E. . . . . 151 B3
Galápagos E . . . . 151 B4
Galaroza E . . . . . 161 B3
Galashiels GB . . . 35 C5
Galatas GR . . . . . 185 B4
Galaţi RO . . . . . . 17 C8
Galatina I . . . . . . 173 B4
Galatista GR . . . . 183 C5
Galátone I . . . . . . 173 B4
Galaxidi GR . . . . . 184 A3
Galdakao E . . . . . 143 A4
Galeata I . . . . . . . 135 B4
Galende E. . . . . . 141 B4
Galera E . . . . . . . 164 B2
Galéria F . . . . . . 180 A1
Galgamácsa H. . . .112 B3
Galgate GB . . . . . 38 A4
Galgon F . . . . . . 128 B2
Galices P. . . . . . . 148 B2
Galinduste E . . . . 150 B2
Galinoporni CY . . . 181 A3
Galisteo E . . . . . . 155 B4
Galków PL . . . . . . 87 A3
Gallarate I . . . . . . 120 B1
Gallardon F . . . . . 90 C1
Gallegos de Argañán
  E. . . . . . . . . . . . 149 B3
Gallegos del Solmirón
  E. . . . . . . . . . . . 150 B2
Galleguillos de Campos
  E. . . . . . . . . . . . 142 B1
Galleno I . . . . . . . 135 B3
Galliate I . . . . . . . 120 B1
Gallicano I . . . . . 134 A3
Gállio I . . . . . . . . 121 B4
Gallipoli = Gelibolu
  TR . . . . . . . . . . 186 B1
Gallipoli I . . . . . . 173 B3
Gällivare S . . . . . 196 B3
Gallizien A . . . . . . 110 C1
Gallneukirchen A. . 96 C2
Gällö S . . . . . . . 199 C12
Gallocanta E . . . . 152 B2
Gällstad S . . . . . . 60 B3
Gallur E . . . . . . . 144 C2
Galmisdale GB . . . 31 C2
Galmpton GB. . . . . 43 B3
Galston GB . . . . . 36 A2
Galta N . . . . . . . . 52 A1
Galtelli I . . . . . . . 178 B3
Galten DK . . . . . . 59 B2
Galtür A . . . . . . . 107 C5
Galve de Sorbe E . 151 A4
Galveias P . . . . . 154 B2
Gálvez E. . . . . . . 157 A3
Galway IRL. . . . . . 28 A2
Gamaches F . . . . . 90 B1
Gámbara I . . . . . . 120 B3
Gambárie I . . . . . 175 C1
Gambassi Terme I . 135 B3
Gambatesa I . . . . 170 B2
Gambolò I . . . . . . 120 B1
Gaming A . . . . . . .110 B2
Gamla Uppsala S . 51 C4
Gamleby S . . . . . . 62 A4
Gamlingay GB. . . . 44 A3
Gammelgarn S . . . 57 C4
Gammelstad S. . . 196 D5
Gammertingen D. . 107 A4
Gams CH . . . . . . 107 B4
Gamvik
  Finnmark N . . . 192 B6
  Finnmark N . . . 193 A12
Gan F . . . . . . . . . 145 A3
Gáname E . . . . . . 149 A3
Ganda di Martello I 108 C1
Gandarela P. . . . . 148 A1
Ganddal N . . . . . . 52 B1
Ganderkesee D. . . 72 A1
Gandesa E . . . . . 153 A4
Gandia E . . . . . . 159 C3
Gandino I . . . . . . 120 B2
Gandrup DK. . . . . 58 A3
Ganges F . . . . . . 130 B2
Gånghester S . . . . 60 B3
Gangi I . . . . . . . . 177 B3
Gangkofen D . . . . 95 C4
Gannat F. . . . . . . .116 A3
Gannay-sur-Loire
  F. . . . . . . . . . . . 104 C2
Gänserdorf A. . . . . 97 C4
Ganzlin D. . . . . . . 73 A5
Gap F . . . . . . . . . 132 A2
Gara H . . . . . . . . 125 A5
Garaballa E . . . . . 158 B2
Garaguso I . . . . . 172 B2
Garbayuela E . . . 156 A2
Garbhallt GB . . . . 34 B2
Garbsen D . . . . . . 72 B2
Garching D . . . . . 109 A3
Garciaz E . . . . . . 156 A2
Garcihernández E . 150 B2
Garcillán E . . . . . 151 B3
Garcinarro E . . . . 151 B5
Garcisobaco E . . . 162 B2
Garda I . . . . . . . . 121 B3
Gardanne F . . . . . 131 B4
Gärdås S . . . . . . . 49 B5
Gårdby S . . . . . . . 63 B4
Gardeja PL. . . . . . 69 B3
Gardelegen D . . . . 73 B4
Gardermoen N. . . . 48 B3
Gardiki GR. . . . . . 182 E3

Garding D 64 B1
Gardone Riviera I 121 B3
Gardone Val Trómpia I 120 B3
Gárdony H 112 B2
Gardouch F 146 A2
Gårdsjö S 55 B5
Gårdskär S 51 B4
Gards Köpinge S 63 C2
Garein F 128 B2
Garelochhead GB 34 B3
Garéoult F 132 B2
Garešnica HR 124 B2
Garéssio I 133 A4
Garforth GB 40 B2
Gargaliani GR 184 B2
Gargaligas E 156 A2
Gargallo E 153 B3
Garganta la Olla E 150 B2
Gargantiel E 156 B3
Gargellen A 107 C4
Gargilesse-Dampierre F 103 C3
Gargnano I 121 B3
Gargnäs S 195 E8
Gárgoles de Abajo E 152 B1
Gargrave GB 40 B1
Garitz D 73 C5
Garlasco I 120 B1
Garlieston GB 36 B2
Garlin F 128 C2
Garlitos E 156 B2
Garmisch-Partenkirchen D 108 B2
Garnat-sur-Engièvre F 104 C2
Garpenberg S 50 B3
Garphyttan S 55 A5
Garray E 143 C4
Garrel D 71 B5
Garriguella E 146 B4
Garrison GB 26 B2
Garrovillas E 155 B4
Garrucha E 164 B3
Gars-am-Kamp A 97 C3
Garsås S 50 B1
Garsdale Head GB 37 B4
Gärsnäs S 63 C2
Garstang GB 38 A4
Gartow D 73 A4
Gartz D 74 A3
Gærum DK 58 A3
Garvagh GB 27 B4
Garvão P 160 B1
Garve GB 32 D2
Garwolin PL 12 C4
Garz D 66 B2
Garzyn PL 85 A4
Gąsawa PL 76 B2
Gåsborn S 49 C6
Gaschurn A 107 C5
Gascueña E 152 B1
Gasny F 90 B1
Gąsocin PL 77 B5
Gastes F 128 B1
Gastouni GR 184 B2
Gastouri GR 182 D1
Gata
E 149 B3
HR 138 B2
Gata de Gorgos E 159 C4
Gătaia RO 126 B3
Gatchina RUS 9 C7
Gatehouse of Fleet GB 36 B2
Gátér H 113 C3
Gateshead GB 37 B5
Gátova E 159 B3
Gattendorf A 111 A3
Gatteo a Mare I 136 A1
Gattinara I 119 B5
Gattorna I 134 A2
Gaucín E 162 B2
Gaulstad N 199 B9
Gaupne N 47 A4
Gautefall N 53 A4
Gauting D 108 A2
Gauto S 195 D7
Gava E 147 C3
Gavardo I 121 B3
Gavarnie F 145 B3
Gávavencsello H 113 A5
Gavi I 120 C1
Gavião P 154 B3
Gavirate I 120 B1
Gävle S 51 B4
Gavoi I 178 B3
Gavorrano I 135 C3
Gavray F 88 B2
Gavrio GR 185 B5
Gävunda S 49 B6
Gaweinstal A 97 C4
Gaworzyce PL 85 A3
Gawroniec PL 75 A5
Gaydon GB 44 A2
Gayton GB 41 C4
Gazipaşa TR 189 C7
Gazoldo degli Ippoliti I 121 B3
Gazzuolo I 121 B3
Gbelce SK 112 B2
Gdańsk PL 69 A3
Gdinj HR 138 B2
Gdov RUS 8 C5
Gdów PL 99 B4
Gdynia PL 69 A3
Gea de Albarracin E 152 B2
Geary GB 31 B2
Géaudot F 91 C4
Geaune F 128 C2
Gebesee D 82 A2
Gebiz TR 189 B5
Gebze TR 187 B4
Géderlak H 112 C2
Gedern D 81 B5
Gedinne B 91 B4
Gediz TR 187 D4
Gèdre F 145 B4
Gedser DK 65 B4
Gedsted DK 58 B2
Geel B 79 A4
Geesthacht D 72 A3
Geetbets B 79 B5
Gefell D 83 B3
Gehrden D 72 B2
Gehren D 82 B3
Geilenkirchen D 80 B2
Geilo N 47 B5
Geinsheim D 93 B4
Geisa D 82 B1
Geiselhöring D 95 C4
Geiselwind D 94 B2
Geisenfeld D 95 C3
Geisenhausen D 95 C4
Geisenheim D 93 B4
Geising D 84 B1
Geisingen D 107 B3
Geislingen D 94 C1
Geistthal A 110 B2
Geiterygghytta N 47 B4
Geithain D 83 A4
Geithus N 48 C1
Gela I 177 B3
Geldermalsen NL 79 A5
Geldern D 80 A2
Geldrop NL 80 A1
Geleen NL 80 B1
Gelembe TR 186 C2
Gelendost TR 189 A6
Gelibolu = Gallipoli TR 186 B1
Gelida E 147 C2
Gelnhausen D 81 B5
Gelnica SK 99 C4
Gelsa E 153 A3
Gelse H 111 C3
Gelsenkirchen D 80 A3
Gelsted DK 59 C2
Geltendorf D 108 A2
Gelterkinden CH 106 B2
Gelting D 64 B2
Gelu RO 126 A3
Gelves E 162 A1
Gembloux B 79 B4
Gemeaux F 105 B4
Gémenos F 132 B1
Gemerská Poloma SK 99 C4
Gemerská Ves SK 99 C4
Gemert NL 80 A1
Gemla S 62 B2
Gemlik TR 186 B4
Gemmenich B 80 B1
Gemona del Friuli I 122 A2
Gémozac F 114 C3
Gemund D 80 B2
Gemünden
*Bayern* D 94 A1
*Hessen* D 81 B4
*Rheinland-Pfalz* D 93 B3
Genappe B 79 B4
Génave E 164 A2
Genazzano I 169 B2
Gençay F 115 B4
Gencsapáti H 111 B3
Gendringen NL 80 A2
Genelard F 104 C3
Genemuiden NL 70 B3
Generalski Stol HR 123 B4
Geneva = Genève CH 118 A3
Genevad S 61 C3
Genève = Geneva CH 118 A3
Genevriéres F 105 B4
Gengenbach D 93 C4
Genillé F 103 B3
Genk B 80 B1
Genlis F 105 B4
Gennep NL 80 A1
Genner DK 64 A2
Gennes F 102 B1
Genoa = Génova I 134 A1
Genola I 133 A3
Génova = Genoa I 134 A1
Genowefa PL 76 B3
Gensingen D 93 B3
Gent = Ghent B 79 A3
Genthin D 73 B5
Gentioux F 116 B1
Genzano di Lucània I 172 B2
Genzano di Roma I 168 B2
Georgenthal D 82 B2
Georgsmarienhütte D 71 B5
Gera D 83 B4
Geraards-bergen B 79 B3
Gerace I 175 C2
Geraci Siculo I 177 B3
Geraki GR 184 C3
Gérardmer F 106 A1
Geras A 97 C3
Gerbéviller F 92 C2
Gerbini I 177 B3
Gerbstedt D 83 A3
Gerði IS 191 C9
Gerede TR 187 B7
Gerena E 161 B3
Geretsried D 108 B2
Gérgal E 164 B2
Gergy F 105 C3
Gerindote E 150 C3
Gerjen H 112 C2
Gerlos A 108 B3
Germay F 92 C1
Germencik TR 188 B2
Germering D 108 A2
Germersheim D 93 B4
Gernika-Lumo E 143 A4
Gernrode D 82 A3
Gernsbach D 93 C4
Gernsheim D 93 B4
Geroda D 82 B1
Gerola Alta I 120 A2
Geroldsgrun D 83 B3
Gerolsbach D 95 C3
Gerolstein D 80 B2
Gerolzhofen D 94 B2
Gerovo HR 123 B3
Gerpinnes B 79 B4
Gerrards Cross GB 44 B3
Gerri de la Sal E 147 B2
Gersfeld D 82 B1
Gerstetten D 94 C2
Gersthofen D 94 C2
Gerstungen D 82 B2
Gerswalde D 74 A2
Gerzat F 116 B3
Gerze TR 23 A8
Gerzen D 95 C4
Gescher D 71 C4
Geseke D 81 A4
Geslau D 94 B2
Gespunsart F 91 B4
Gesté F 101 B4
Gestorf D 72 B2
Gesualda I 170 C3
Gesunda S 50 B1
Gesztely H 113 A4
Geta FIN 51 B6
Getafe E 151 B4
Getinge S 60 C2
Getxo E 143 A4
Geversdorf D 64 C2
Gevgelija MK 182 B4
Gevora del Caudillo E 155 C4
Gevrey-Chambertin F 105 B3
Gex F 118 A3
Gey D 80 B2
Geyikli TR 186 C1
Geysir IS 190 C5
Geyve TR 187 B5
Gföhl A 97 C3
Ghedi I 120 B3
Ghent = Gent B 79 A3
Gheorgheni RO 17 B6
Ghigo I 119 C4
Ghilarza I 178 B2
Ghisonaccia F 180 A2
Ghisoni F 180 A2
Gialtra GR 182 E4
Gianitsa GR 182 C4
Giardinetto Vécchio I 171 B3
Giardini Naxos I 177 B4
Giarratana I 177 B3
Giarre I 177 B4
Giat F 116 B2
Giaveno I 119 B4
Giazza I 121 B4
Giba I 179 C2
Gibellina Nuova I 176 B1
Gibostad N 194 A9
Gibraleón E 161 B3
Gibraltar GBZ 162 B2
Gic H 111 B4
Gideå S 200 C5
Gideåkroken S 200 B3
Gidle PL 86 B3
Giebelstadt D 94 B1
Gieboldehausen D 82 A2
Gielniów PL 87 A4
Gielow D 74 A1
Gien F 103 B4
Giengen D 94 C2
Giens F 132 B2
Giera RO 126 B2
Gieselwerder D 81 A5
Giessen D 81 B4
Gieten NL 71 A3
Giethoorn NL 70 B3
Giffaumont-Champaubert F 91 C4
Gifford GB 35 C5
Gifhorn D 73 B3
Gige H 125 A3
Gignac F 130 B2
Gijón = Xixón E 142 A1
Gilena E 162 A3
Gilford GB 27 B4
Gillberga S 55 A3
Gilleleje DK 61 C2
Gilley F 105 B5
Gilley-sur-Loire F 104 C2
Gillingham
*Dorset* GB 43 A4
Gillingham *continued*
*Medway* GB 45 B4
Gilocourt F 90 B2
Gilserberg D 81 B5
Gilsland GB 37 B4
Gilze NL 79 A4
Gimåt S 200 C4
Gimo S 51 B5
Gimont F 129 C3
Ginasservis F 132 B1
Gingelom B 79 B5
Gingst D 66 B2
Ginosa I 171 C4
Ginzling A 108 B2
Giões P 160 B2
Gióia dei Marsi I 169 B3
Gióia del Colle I 173 B2
Gióia Sannitica I 170 B2
Gióia Táuro I 175 C1
Gioiosa Iónica I 175 C2
Gioiosa Marea I 177 A3
Giosla GB 31 A2
Giovinazzo I 171 B4
Girifalco I 175 C2
Giromagny F 106 B1
Girona E 147 C3
Gironcourt-sur-Vraine F 92 C1
Gironella E 147 B2
Gironville-sous-les-Côtes F 92 C1
Girvan GB 36 A2
Gislaved S 60 B3
Gislev DK 59 C3
Gisors F 90 B1
Gissi I 170 A2
Gistad S 56 B1
Gistel B 78 A2
Gistrup DK 58 B3
Giswil CH 106 C3
Githio GR 184 C3
Giugliano in Campania I 170 C2
Giulianova I 136 C2
Giulvăz RO 126 B2
Giurgiu RO 17 D6
Give DK 59 C2
Givet F 91 A4
Givors F 117 B4
Givry
B 79 B4
F 104 C3
Givry-en-Argonne F 91 C4
Givskud DK 59 C2
Giżałki PL 76 B2
Gizeux F 102 B2
Giżycko PL 12 A4
Gizzeria I 175 C2
Gizzeria Lido I 175 C2
Gjedved DK 59 C2
Gjegjan AL 182 B2
Gjendesheim N 47 A5
Gjerde N 46 B3
Gjerlev DK 58 B3
Gjermundshamn N 46 B2
Gjerrild DK 58 B3
Gjerstad N 53 B5
Gjesås N 49 B4
Gjesvær N 193 A9
Gjirokastër AL 182 C2
Gjøfjell N 54 A1
Gjøl DK 58 A2
Gjøra N 198 C6
Gjøvik N 48 B2
Gladbeck D 80 A2
Gladenbach D 81 B4
Gladstad N 195 E2
Glamis GB 35 B4
Glamoč BIH 138 A2
Glamsbjerg DK 59 C3
Gland CH 105 C5
Glandorf D 71 B4
Glanegg A 110 C1
Glanshammar S 56 A1
Glarus CH 107 B4
Glasgow GB 35 C3
Glashütte
*Bayern* D 108 B2
*Sachsen* D 84 B1
Glastonbury GB 43 A4
Glatzau A 110 C2
Glauchau D 83 B4
Glava S 54 A3
Glavatičevo BIH 139 B4
Glavičice BIH 127 C1
Gŭlŭbovo BG 183 A7
Glein
A 110 B1
N 195 D3
Gleinstätten A 110 C2
Gleisdorf A 110 B2
Glenamoy IRL 26 B1
Glenarm GB 27 B5
Glenavy GB 27 B4
Glenbarr GB 34 C2
Glenbeigh IRL 29 B2
Glenbrittle GB 31 B2
Glencoe GB 34 B2
Glencolumbkille IRL 26 B2
Glendalough IRL 30 A2
Glenealy IRL 30 B2
Glenelg GB 31 B3
Glenfinnan GB 34 B2
Glengarriff IRL 29 C2
Glenluce GB 36 B2
Glennamaddy IRL 28 A3
Glenrothes GB 35 B4
Glenties IRL 26 B2
Glesborg DK 58 B3
Glesien D 83 A4
Gletsch CH 106 C3
Glewitz D 66 B1
Glifada GR 185 B4
Glimåkra S 63 B2
Glin IRL 29 B2
Glina HR 124 B2
Glinde D 72 A3
Glinojeck PL 77 B5
Glinsk IRL 28 A2
Gliwice PL 86 B2
Glödnitz A 109 C5
Gloggnitz A 110 B2
Głogoczów PL 99 B3
Glogonj SRB 127 C2
Glogovac SRB 127 C3
Głogów PL 85 A4
Głogówek PL 86 B1
Glomel F 100 A2
Glomfjord N 195 D4
Glommen S 60 C2
Glommersträsk S 196 D2
Glonn D 108 B2
Glorenza I 108 C1
Gloria P 154 B2
Glosa GR 183 D5
Glossop GB 40 B2
Gloucester GB 39 C4
Głowaczów PL 87 A5
Główczyce PL 68 A2
Glöwen D 73 B5
Głowno PL 77 C4
Gložan SRB 126 B1
Głubczyce PL 86 B1
Głuchołazy PL 85 B5
Głuchów PL 87 A4
Głuchowo PL 75 B5
Glücksburg D 64 B2
Glückstadt D 64 C2
Glumina BIH 139 A5
Glumsø DK 65 A4
Glušci SRB 127 C1
Glusk BY 13 B8
Głuszyca PL 85 B4
Glyngøre DK 58 B1
Glyn Neath GB 39 C3
Gmünd
*Karnten* A 109 C4
*Nieder Östereich* A 96 C2
Gmund D 108 B2
Gmunden A 109 B4
Gnarp S 200 D3
Gnarrenburg D 72 A2
Gnesau A 109 C4
Gnesta S 56 A3
Gnięchowice PL 85 A4
Gniew PL 69 B3
Gniewkowo PL 76 B3
Gniezno PL 76 B2
Gnoien D 66 C1
Gnojnice BIH 139 B3
Gnojno PL 87 B4
Gnosall GB 40 C1
Gnosjö S 60 B3
Göbel TR 186 B3
Göçbeyli TR 186 C2
Goch D 80 A2
Gochsheim D 94 A2
Göd H 112 B3
Godalming GB 44 B3
Godby FIN 51 B6
Goðdalir IS 190 B6
Goddelsheim D 81 A4
Gódega di Sant'Urbano I 122 B1
Godegård S 56 B1
Godelheim D 81 A5
Goderville F 89 A4
Godiasco I 120 C2
Godič SLO 123 A3
Godkowo PL 69 A4
Godmanchester GB 44 A3
Gödöllö H 112 B3
Gödre H 125 A3
Godshill GB 44 C2
Godzikowice PL 85 B5
Godziszewo PL 69 A3
Goes NL 79 A3
Goetzenbrück F 93 C3
Góglio I 119 A5
Gogolin PL 86 B2
Göhren D 66 B2
Goirle NL 79 A5
Góis P 148 B1
Góito I 121 B3
Goizueta E 144 A2
Gojna Gora SRB 127 D2
Gójsk PL 77 B4
Gökçedağ TR 186 C3
Gökçen TR 188 A2
Gökçeören TR 188 A3
Gökçeyazı TR 186 C2
Göktepe TR 188 B3
Gol N 47 B5
Gola
HR 124 A3
N 48 A1
Gołańcz PL 76 B2
Gölbaşı TR 23 B7
Gölby FIN 51 B6
Gölcük
*Kocaeli* TR 187 B4
*Niğde* TR 23 B8
Golčův Jenikov CZ 97 B3
Gołczewo PL 67 C3
Goldach CH 107 B4
Goldbach D 93 A5
Goldbeck D 73 B4
Goldberg D 73 A5
Goldelund D 64 B2
Goldenstedt D 72 B1
Gołębiewo PL 69 A3
Golegã P 154 B2
Goleniów PL 75 A3
Golfo Aranci I 178 B3
Gölhisar TR 189 B4
Golina PL 76 B3
Gölle H 112 C2
Göllersdorf A 97 C4
Golling an der Salzach A 109 B4
Gölmarmara TR 186 D2
Golnice PL 84 A3
Golnik SLO 123 A3
Gölova TR 189 C5
Gölpazarı TR 187 B5
Gols A 111 B3
Golspie GB 32 D3
Golssen D 74 C2
Golub-Dobrzyń PL 77 A4
Golubinci SRB 127 C2
Goluchów PL 86 A1
Golymin-Ośrodek PL 77 B5
Golzow D 73 B5
Gomagoi I 108 C1
Gómara E 152 A1
Gomaringen D 93 C5
Gömbe TR 189 C4
Gömeç TR 186 C1
Gomel = Homyel BY 13 B9
Gomes Aires P 160 B1
Gómezserracin E 150 A3
Gommern D 73 B4
Gomulin PL 86 A3
Gonäs S 50 B2
Goncelin F 118 B2
Gończyce PL 87 A5
Gondomar
E 140 B2
P 148 A1
Gondrecourt-le-Château F 92 C1
Gondrin F 128 C3
Gönen
*Balıkesir* TR 186 B2
*Isparta* TR 189 B5
Gonfaron F 132 B2
Goñi E 144 B2
Goni
GR 182 D4
I 179 C3
Gonnesa I 179 C2
Gonnosfanádiga I 179 C2
Gönyü H 111 B4
Gonzaga I 121 C3
Goodrich GB 39 C4
Goodwick GB 39 B1
Gooik B 79 B4
Goole GB 40 B3
Goor NL 71 B3
Göpfritz an der Wild A 97 C3
Goppenstein CH 119 A4
Göppingen D 94 C1
Gor E 164 B2
Góra
*Dolnośląskie* PL 85 A4
*Mazowieckie* PL 77 B5
Gorafe E 164 B1
Gorawino PL 67 C4
Goražde BIH 139 B4
Gőrbeháza H 113 B5
Gordaliza del Pino E 142 B1
Gördes TR 186 D3
Gørding DK 59 C1
Górdola CH 120 A1
Gordon GB 35 C5
Gordoncillo E 142 B1
Gorebridge GB 35 C4
Gorenja Vas SLO 123 A3
Gorenje Jelenje HR 123 B3
Gorey
GB 88 A1
IRL 30 B2
Gorgonzola I 120 B2
Gorica HR 137 A4
Gorican HR 124 A2
Gorinchem NL 79 A4
Goring GB 44 B2
Goritsy RUS 9 D10
Göritz D 74 A2
Gorízia I 122 B2
Górki PL 77 B1
Gorleben D 73 A4
Gorleston-on-sea GB 41 C5
Gørlev DK 61 D1
Görlitz D 84 A2
Górliz E 143 A4
Görmin D 66 C2
Górna Grupa PL 69 B3
Gorna Oryakhovitsa BG 17 D6
Gornja Gorevnica SRB 127 D2
Gornja Ploča HR 137 A4
Gornja Radgona SLO 110 C2
Gornja Sabanta SRB 127 D3
Gornja Trešnjevica SRB 127 C2

Gornja Tuzla BIH . . 125 C4
Gornje Polje MNE . 139 C4
Gornje Ratkovo
  BIH . . . . . . . . 124 C2
Gornji Grad SLO . 123 A3
Gornji Humac HR . 138 B2
Gornji Jasenjani
  BIH . . . . . . . . 139 B3
Gornji Kamengrad
  BIH . . . . . . . . 124 C2
Gornji Kneginec
  HR . . . . . . . . 124 A2
Gornji Kosinj HR . 123 C4
Gornji Milanovac
  SRB . . . . . . . 127 C2
Gornji Podgradci
  BIH . . . . . . . . 124 B3
Gornji Ravno BIH . 138 B3
Gornji Sjenicak HR 124 B1
Gornji Vakuf BIH . 138 B3
Górno PL . . . . . . 87 B4
Görömböly H. . . .113 A4
Górowo Iławeckie
  PL. . . . . . . . . . 69 A5
Gorran Haven GB . 42 B2
Gorredijk NL . . . . 70 A3
Gorron F . . . . . . . 88 B3
Gorseinon GB . . . 39 C2
Gort IRL . . . . . . . 28 A3
Gortin GB. . . . . . 27 B3
Görzke D . . . . . . 73 B5
Gorzkowice PL . . . 86 A3
Górzno
  Kujawsko-Pomorskie
  PL. . . . . . . . . .77 A4
  Zachodnio-Pomorskie
  PL. . . . . . . . . .75 A4
Gorzów Śląski PL . 86 A2
Gorzów Wielkopolski
  PL. . . . . . . . . 75 B4
Górzyca PL . . . . 74 B3
Gorzyce PL . . . . 98 B2
Górzyn PL . . . . . 84 A2
Gorzyń PL . . . . . 75 B4
Gorzyno PL . . . . 68 A2
Gosaldo I . . . . . 121 A4
Gosau A . . . . . . 109 B4
Gosberton GB . . . 41 C3
Gościcino PL . . . 68 A3
Gościęcin PL . . . 86 B2
Gościm PL. . . . . 75 B4
Gościno PL . . . . 67 B4
Gosdorf A. . . . . 110 C2
Gosforth GB . . . . 36 B3
Goslar D. . . . . . 82 A2
Goslice PL . . . . . 77 B4
Gospič HR . . . . 137 A4
Gosport GB. . . . . 44 C2
Gössäter S. . . . . 55 B4
Gossau CH . . . . 107 B4
Goss Ilsede D . . . 72 B3
Gössnitz D . . . . . 83 B4
Gössweinstein D. . 95 B3
Gostivar MK. . . . 182 B2
Gostkow PL. . . . . 77 C4
Göstling an der Ybbs
  A. . . . . . . . . .110 B1
Gostomia PL . . . 75 A5
Gostycyn PL . . . 76 A2
Gostyń PL . . . . . 85 A5
Gostynin PL. . . . 77 B4
Goszczyn PL . . . 87 A4
Göta S . . . . . . . 54 B3
Göteborg = Gothenburg
  S. . . . . . . . . . 60 B1
Götene S . . . . . 55 B4
Gotha D . . . . . . 82 B2
Gothem S. . . . . . 57 C4
Gothenburg = Göteborg
  S. . . . . . . . . . 60 B1
Gotse Delchev BG. 183 B5
Gottersdorf D . . . . 95 C4
Göttingen D. . . . . 82 A1
Gottne S. . . . . . 200 C4
Götzis A. . . . . . 107 B4
Gouarec F . . . . . 100 A2
Gouda NL. . . . . . 70 B1
Goudhurst GB. . . . 45 B4
Goumenissa GR . 182 C4
Goura GR. . . . . . 184 B3
Gourdon F . . . . . 129 B4
Gourgançon F. . . . 91 C4
Gourin F. . . . . . 100 A2
Gournay-en-Bray F. 90 B1
Gourock GB. . . . . 34 C3
Gouveia P . . . . . 148 B2
Gouvy B. . . . . . . 80 B1
Gouzeacourt F . . . 90 A3
Gouzon F. . . . . . .116 A2
Govedari HR . . . 138 C3
Govérnolo I . . . . 121 B3
Gowarczów PL . . . 87 A4
Gowerton GB. . . . 39 C2
Gowidlino PL. . . . 68 A2
Gowran IRL . . . . 30 B1
Goyatz D . . . . . . 74 B3
Göynük
  TR. . . . . . . . .187 B5
  Antalya TR. . . .189 C5
Gozdnica PL . . . . 84 A3
Gozdowo PL . . . . 77 B4
Gozee B . . . . . . 79 B4
Graal-Müritz D. . . 65 B5
Grabenstätt D . . . 109 B3
Grabhair GB . . . . 31 A2
Gråbo S . . . . . . 60 B2
Grabovac
  HR. . . . . . . . .138 B2

Grabovac continued
  SRB . . . . . . . .127 C2
Grabovci SRB . . . 127 C1
Grabow D. . . . . . . 73 A4
Grabów PL. . . . . 77 B4
Grabow nad Pilicą
  PL. . . . . . . . . . 87 A5
Grabów nad Prosną
  PL. . . . . . . . . . 86 A2
Grabowno PL . . . 76 A2
Grabs CH. . . . . 107 B4
Gračac HR . . . . . 138 A1
Gračanica BIH . . 125 C4
Graçay F . . . . . 103 B3
Grad SLO. . . . . .111 C3
Gradac
  BIH . . . . . . . . .139 C4
  HR. . . . . . . . .130 D0
  MNE . . . . . . . .139 B5
Gradačac BIH . . 125 C4
Gradec HR. . . . 124 B2
Gradefes E . . . . 142 B1
Grades A . . . . . 110 C1
Gradil P . . . . . . 154 C1
Gradina
  HR. . . . . . . . .124 B3
  MNE . . . . . . . .139 B5
Gradisca d'Isonzo
  I . . . . . . . . . . 122 B2
Gradište HR . . . 125 B4
Grado
  E . . . . . . . . . .141 A4
  I . . . . . . . . . . 122 B2
Grafenau D . . . . . 96 C1
Gräfenberg D . . . . 95 B3
Gräfenhainichen D . 83 A4
Grafenschlag A . . 97 C3
Grafenstein A . . . 110 C1
Gräfenthal D . . . . 82 B3
Grafentonna D. . . 82 A2
Grafenwöhr D . . . 95 B3
Grafing D . . . . . 108 A2
Grafling D . . . . . 95 C4
Gräfsnäs S. . . . . 54 B3
Gragnano I. . . . . 170 C2
Grahovo SLO. . . 122 A2
Graiguenamanagh
  IRL . . . . . . . . . 30 B2
Grain GB . . . . . . 45 B4
Grainau D . . . . . 108 B2
Graja de Iniesta E . 158 B2
Grajera E . . . . . 151 A4
Gram DK . . . . . . 59 C2
Gramais A . . . . . 108 B1
Gramat F . . . . . 129 B4
Gramatneusiedl A. .111 A3
Grambow D . . . . 74 A3
Grammichele I. . . 177 B3
Gramsh AL. . . . . 182 C2
Gramzow D . . . . 74 A3
Gran N . . . . . . . 48 B2
Granada E . . . . 163 A4
Granard IRL . . . . 27 C3
Grañas E . . . . . 140 A3
Granátula de Calatrava
  E. . . . . . . . . . 157 B4
Grancey-le-Château
  F . . . . . . . . . 105 B4
Grandas de Salime
  E. . . . . . . . . . 141 A4
Grandcamp-Maisy F 88 A2
Grand-Champ F . . 100 B3
Grand Couronne F . 89 A5
Grand-Fougeray F 101 B4
Grândola P. . . . . 160 A1
Grandpré F . . . . . 91 B4
Grandrieu
  B. . . . . . . . . . .79 B4
  F . . . . . . . . . .117 C3
Grandson CH . . . 106 C1
Grandvillars F . . . 106 B1
Grandvilliers F . . . 90 B1
Grañén E . . . . . 145 C3
Grangärde S . . . . 50 B1
Grange IRL. . . . . 26 B2
Grangemouth GB . 35 B4
Grange-over-Sands
  GB. . . . . . . . . . 36 B4
Grängesberg S . . . 50 B1
Granges-de Crouhens
  F. . . . . . . . . . 145 B4
Granges-sur-Vologne
  F. . . . . . . . . . 106 A1
Gräningen D . . . . 73 B5
Granitola-Torretta I 176 B1
Granja
  Évora P . . . . . .155 C3
  Porto P. . . . . . .148 A1
Granja de Moreruela
  E. . . . . . . . . . 142 C1
Granja de Torrehermosa
  E. . . . . . . . . . 156 B2
Gränna S . . . . . . 55 B5
Grannäs
  Västerbotten S. . .195 E7
  Västerbotten S. . .195 E8
Granö S . . . . . . 200 B5
Granollers E . . . . 147 C3
Granowiec PL . . . 85 A5
Granowo PL. . . . 75 B5
Gransee D. . . . . 74 A2
Gransherad N . . . 53 A5
Grantham GB . . . 40 C3
Grantown-on-Spey
  GB . . . . . . . . . 32 D3
Grantshouse GB . 35 C5
Granville F. . . . . 88 B2
Granvin N . . . . . 46 B3

Grærup Strand DK . 59 C1
Gräsås S . . . . . . 60 C2
Grasbakken N . . 193 B12
Grasberg D . . . . . 72 A2
Grasmere GB. . . . 36 B3
Gräsmyr S . . . . . 200 C5
Grasö S . . . . . . . 51 B5
Grassano I . . . . . 172 B2
Grassau D . . . . . 109 B3
Grasse F . . . . . . 132 B2
Grassington GB . . 40 A2
Gråsten DK . . . . . 64 B2
Grästorp S. . . . . 54 B3
Gratkorn A . . . . . .110 B2
Gratwein A. . . . . .110 B2
Graulhet F . . . . . 129 C4
Graus E . . . . . . 145 B4
Grávalos E . . . . . 144 B2
Gravberget N. . . . 49 B4
Grave NL . . . . . . 80 A1
Gravedona I. . . . . 120 A2
Gravellona Toce I . .119 B5
Gravendal S. . . . . 50 B1
Gravens DK . . . . 59 C2
Gravesend GB. . . 45 B4
Graveson F. . . . . 131 B3
Gravina in Púglia I 172 B2
Gray F . . . . . . . 105 B4
Grayrigg GB . . . . 37 B4
Grays GB. . . . . . 45 B4
Grayshott GB . . . 44 B3
Graz A . . . . . . . .110 B2
Grazalema E . . . 162 B2
Grazzano Visconti
  I . . . . . . . . . . 120 C2
Greåker N . . . . . 54 A2
Great Dunmow GB . 45 B4
Great Malvern GB . 39 B4
Great Torrington
  GB . . . . . . . . . 42 B2
Great Waltham GB . 45 B4
Great Yarmouth GB. 41 C5
Grebbestad S . . . 54 B2
Grebenstein D. . . . 81 A5
Grębocice PL. . . . 85 A4
Grębocin PL. . . . . 76 A3
Greding D . . . . . . 95 B3
Gredstedbro DK . . 59 C1
Greencastle IRL. . . 27 A3
Greenhead GB. . . . 37 B4
Greenisland GB. . . 27 B5
Greenlaw GB . . . . 35 C5
Greenock GB. . . . 34 C3
Greenway GB . . . 39 C2
Greenwich GB . . . 45 B4
Grefrath D . . . . . 80 A2
Greifenburg A . . . 109 C4
Greiffenberg D . . . 74 A2
Greifswald D . . . . 66 B2
Grein A. . . . . . . .110 A1
Greipstad N . . . . 53 B3
Greiz D . . . . . . . 83 B4
Grenaa DK . . . . . 58 B3
Grenade F . . . . . 129 C4
Grenade-sur-l'Adour
  F. . . . . . . . . . 128 C2
Grenchen CH. . . . 106 B2
Grendi N . . . . . . 53 B3
Grenivík IS . . . . . 191 B7
Grenoble F. . . . . .118 B2
Gréoux-les-Bains
  F. . . . . . . . . . 132 B1
Gresenhorst D. . . . 66 B1
Gressoney-la-Trinité
  I . . . . . . . . . . .119 B4
Gressoney-St.-Jean
  I . . . . . . . . . . .119 B4
Gressthal D . . . . . 82 B2
Gresswik N . . . . . 54 A1
Gresten A. . . . . . .110 B2
Gretna GB . . . . . 36 B3
Greussen D . . . . . 82 A2
Greve in Chianti I . 135 B4
Greven
  Mecklenburg-
  Vorpommern D. .73 A3
  Nordrhein-Westfalen
  D. . . . . . . . . . .71 B4
Grevena GR. . . . 182 C3
Grevenbroich D. . . 80 A2
Grevenbrück D . . . 81 A4
Grevenmacher L. . . 92 B2
Grevesmühlen D. . . 65 C4
Grevestrand DK. . . 61 D2
Grevie S. . . . . . . 61 C2
Greystoke GB . . . . 36 B4
Greystones IRL. . . 30 A2
Grez-Doiceau B. . . 79 B4
Grèzec F . . . . . . 129 B4
Grez-en-Bouère F . 102 B1
Grezzana I . . . . . 121 B4
Grgar SLO . . . . . 122 A2
Grgurevci SRB . . 127 B1
Gries A . . . . . . . 108 B2
Griesbach D . . . . . 96 C1
Griesheim D . . . . 93 B4
Gries in Sellrain A. 108 B2
Grieskirchen A. . . 109 A4
Griffen A. . . . . . .110 C1
Grignan F. . . . . . 131 A3
Grignano I . . . . . 122 B2
Grigno I . . . . . . 121 A4
Grignols F . . . . . 128 B2
Grignon F. . . . . . .118 B3

Grijota E. . . . . . . 142 B2
Grijpskerk NL . . . . 71 A3
Grillby S. . . . . . . 56 A3
Grimaud F . . . . . 132 B2
Grimbergen B . . . . 79 B4
Grimma D . . . . . . 83 A4
Grimmen D . . . . . 66 B2
Grimmialp CH . . . 106 C2
Grimsås S. . . . . . 60 B3
Grimsby GB. . . . . 41 B3
GrimsH IS . . . . . 191 B9
Grimstad N . . . . . 53 B4
Grimstorp S. . . . . 62 A2
Grindavík IS. . . . . 190 D3
Grindelwald CH. . . 106 C3
Grindheim N . . . . 52 B3
Grindsted DK. . . . 59 C1
Griñón E . . . . . . 151 B4
Gripenberg S. . . . 62 A2
Gripsholm S . . . . 56 A3
Grisolles F . . . . . 129 C4
Grisslehamn S . . . 51 B5
Gritley GB . . . . . 33 C4
Grizebeck GB . . . 36 B3
Grndina BIH. . . . . 124 C2
Gröbming A . . . . . 109 B4
Gröbzig D . . . . . . 83 A3
Grocka SRB. . . . . 127 C2
Gröditz D. . . . . . . 83 A5
Gródki PL. . . . . . 77 A5
Grodków PL. . . . . 85 B5
Grodzisk Mazowiecki
  PL. . . . . . . . . . 77 B5
Groenlo NL . . . . . 71 B3
Groesbeek NL. . . . 80 A1
Grohote HR . . . . . 138 B2
Groitzsch D . . . . . 83 A4
Groix F. . . . . . . . 100 B2
Grójec PL. . . . . . 77 C5
Grom PL. . . . . . . 77 A5
Gromiljca BIH . . . 139 B4
Grömitz D . . . . . . 65 B3
Gromnik PL. . . . . 99 B4
Gromo I . . . . . . . 120 B2
Gronau
  Niedersachsen D. . .72 B2
  Nordrhein-Westfalen
  D. . . . . . . . . . .71 B4
Grönenbach D. . . 107 B5
Grong N. . . . . . . 199 A9
Grönhögen S. . . . 63 B4
Groningen
  D. . . . . . . . . . .73 C4
  NL . . . . . . . . . .71 A3
Grønnestrand DK . 58 A2
Grono CH. . . . . . 120 A2
Grönskåra S . . . . 62 A3
Grootegast NL. . . . 71 A3
Gropello Cairoli I. . 120 B1
Grorud N . . . . . . 48 C2
Grósio I . . . . . . . 120 A3
Grošnica SRB . . . 127 D2
Grossalmerode D . 82 A1
Grossarl A . . . . . 109 B4
Gross Beeren D. . . 74 B2
Gross Berkel D. . . 72 B2
Grossbodungen D . 82 A2
Gross-botwar D. . . 94 C1
Grossburgwedel D . 72 B2
Grosschönau D. . . 84 B2
Gross-Dölln D . . . 74 A2
Grossenbrode D. . . 65 B4
Grossenehrich D. . . 82 A2
Grossengottern D. . 82 A2
Grossenhain D . . . 83 A5
Grossenkneten D . 71 B5
Grossenlüder D. . . 81 B5
Grossensee D . . . 72 A3
Grossenzersdorf A .111 A3
Grosseto I . . . . . 135 C4
Gross-Gerau D . . . 93 B4
Grossgerungs A . . 96 C2
Grossglobnitz A . . 97 C3
Grosshabersdorf D. 94 B2
Grossharras A . . . 97 C4
Grosshartmansdorf
  D. . . . . . . . . . .83 B5
Grosshöchstetten
  CH . . . . . . . . . 106 C2
Gross Kreutz D. . . 74 B1
Grosskrut A . . . . 97 C4
Gross Lafferde D. . 72 B3
Gross Leuthen D. . 74 B3
Grosslohra D. . . . 82 A2
Grossmehring D. . 95 C3
Gross Muckrow D . 74 B3
Gross Oesingen D . 72 B3
Grossostheim D . . 93 B5
Grosspertholz A . . 96 C2
Grosspetersdorf A .111 B3
Grosspostwitz D. . 84 A2
Grossraming A . . .110 B1
Gross-Rosenburg D 83 A4
Gross Reken D . . . 80 A3
Grossrinderfeld D. . 94 B1
Grossröhrsdorf D . 84 A2
Gross Sarau D. . . 65 C3
Gross Särchen D. . 84 A2
Grossschirma D . . 83 B5
Gross Schönebeck
  D. . . . . . . . . . .74 B2
Grossschweinbarth
  A. . . . . . . . . . . 97 C4
Grosssieghartz A . 97 C3
Grosssölk A . . . . 109 B4

Gross Umstadt D . . 93 B4
Grosswarasdorf A. .111 B3
Gross Warnow D. . . 73 A4
Gross-Weikersdorf
  A. . . . . . . . . . . 97 C3
Gross-Welle D. . . . 73 A5
Grosswilfersdorf A .110 B2
Gross Wokern D . . 65 C5
Grostenquin F. . . . 92 C2
Grosuplje SLO. . . 123 B3
Grotli N . . . . . . . 198 C4
Grötlingbo S . . . . 57 C4
Grottáglie I. . . . . 173 B3
Grottaminarda I. . . 170 B3
Grottammare I . . . 136 C2
Grotte di Castro I . 168 A1
Grotteria I . . . . . 175 C2
Gröttöie I . . . . . . 172 B2
Grouw NL. . . . . . 70 A2
Grov N . . . . . . . 194 B8
Grova N . . . . . . . 53 A4
Grove D . . . . . . . 140 B2
Grua N . . . . . . . 48 B2
Grube D. . . . . . . 65 B4
Grubišno Polje HR 124 B3
Grude BIH . . . . . 138 B3
Grudusk PL . . . . . 77 A5
Grudziądz PL. . . . 69 B3
Grue N . . . . . . . 49 B4
Gruissan F. . . . . 130 B2
Grullos E . . . . . . 141 A4
Grumo Áppula I. . . 171 B4
Grums S. . . . . . . 55 A4
Grünau im Almtal
  A. . . . . . . . . . 109 B4
Grünberg D . . . . . 81 B4
Grünburg A . . . . . .110 B1
Grundarfjörður IS . 190 C2
Gründau D. . . . . . 81 B5
Gründelhardt D . . . 94 B1
Grundforsen S . . . 49 A4
Grundlsee A. . . . . 109 B4
Grundsund S. . . . 54 B2
Grunewald D . . . . 84 A1
Grungedal N . . . . 53 A3
Grünhain D. . . . . 83 B4
Grünstadt D. . . . . 93 B4
Gruvberget S. . . . 50 A3
Gruyères CH . . . . 106 C2
Gruža SRB . . . . . 127 D2
Gryazi RUS . . . . . 7 E14
Grybów PL. . . . . . 99 B4
Grycksbo S . . . . . 50 B2
Gryfino PL. . . . . . 74 A3
Gryfów Śląski PL. . 84 A3
Gryllefjord N . . . . 194 A8
Grymyr N . . . . . . 48 B2
Gryt S. . . . . . . . 56 B2
Grytgöl S . . . . . . 56 B1
Grythyttan S . . . . 55 A5
Grytnäs S. . . . . . 57 B3
Grzmiąca PL . . . . 68 B1
Grzybno PL . . . . . 74 A3
Grzywna PL . . . . 76 A3
Gschnitz A . . . . . 108 B2
Gschwend D . . . . 94 C1
Gstaad CH . . . . . 106 C2
Gsteig CH . . . . . .119 A4
Guadahortuna E . . 163 A4
Guadalajara E . . . 151 B4
Guadalaviar E . . . 152 B2
Guadalcanal E . . . 156 B2
Guadalcázar E. . . 162 A3
Guadalix de la Sierra
  E. . . . . . . . . . 151 B4
Guadálmez E. . . . 156 B3
Guadalupe E . . . . 156 A2
Guadamur E . . . . 151 C3
Guadarrama E . . . 151 B3
Guadiaro E . . . . . 162 B2
Guadix E . . . . . . 164 B1
Guagnano I . . . . 173 B3
Guagno F . . . . . . 180 A1
Guajar-Faragüit E . 163 B4
Gualchos E . . . . . 163 B4
Gualdo Tadino I. . . 136 B1
Gualtieri I . . . . . . 121 C3
Guarcino I . . . . . 169 B3
Guarda P . . . . . . 149 B2
Guardamar del Segura
  E. . . . . . . . . . 165 A4
Guardão P . . . . . 148 B1
Guardavalle I . . . . 175 C2
Guardea I. . . . . . 168 A2
Guárdia I . . . . . . 172 B1
Guardiagrele I . . . 169 A4
Guardiarégia I . . . 170 B2
Guárdia Sanframondi
  I . . . . . . . . . . 170 B2
Guardias Viejas E . 164 C2
Guardiola de Bergueda
  E. . . . . . . . . . 147 B2
Guardo E . . . . . . 142 B2
Guareña E . . . . . 156 B1
Guaro E . . . . . . . 162 B3
Guarromán E . . . . 157 B4
Guasila I . . . . . . 179 C3
Guastalla I . . . . . 121 C3
Gubbhögen S . . . 199 A12
Gúbbio I . . . . . . 136 B1
Guben D . . . . . . 74 C3
Gubin PL . . . . . . 74 C3
Gudå N . . . . . . . 199 B8
Gudavac BIH . . . . 124 C2
Guddal N . . . . . . 46 A2
Güderup DK. . . . . 64 B2
Gudhem S . . . . . 55 B4
Gudhjem DK . . . . 67 A3

Gudovac HR . . . . 124 B2
Gudow D. . . . . . . 73 A3
Güdül TR. . . . . . 187 B7
Gudvangen N . . . . 46 B3
Guebwiller F . . . . 106 B2
Guéjar-Sierra E . . 163 A4
Guémené-Penfao
  F. . . . . . . . . . 101 B4
Guémené-sur-Scorff
  F. . . . . . . . . . 100 A2
Güeñes E . . . . . . 143 A3
Guer F . . . . . . . 101 B3
Guérande F . . . . 101 B3
Guéret F. . . . . . .116 A1
Guérigny F. . . . . 104 B2
Guesa E . . . . . . 144 B2
Gueugnon F . . . . 104 C3
Guglionesi I . . . . 170 B2
Gühlen Glienicke D. 74 A1
Guia P . . . . . . . 154 B2
Guichen F . . . . . 101 B4
Guidizzolo I . . . . 121 B3
Guidónia-Montecélio
  I . . . . . . . . . . 168 B2
Guiglia I . . . . . . 135 A3
Guignes F . . . . . 90 C2
Guijo F . . . . . . . 156 B3
Guijo de Coria E . 149 B3
Guijo de Santa Bábera
  E. . . . . . . . . . 150 B2
Guijuelo E . . . . . 150 B2
Guildford GB . . . . 44 B3
Guillaumes F . . . . 132 A2
Guillena E . . . . . 162 A1
Guillestre F . . . . .118 C3
Guillos F . . . . . . 128 B2
Guilsfield GB. . . . 38 B3
Guilvinec F . . . . . 100 B1
Guimarães P . . . 148 A1
Guincho P . . . . . 154 C1
Guînes F . . . . . . 78 B1
Guingamp F. . . . . 100 A2
Guipavas F . . . . . 100 A1
Guisborough GB. . 37 B5
Guiscard F . . . . . 90 B3
Guiscriff F . . . . . 100 A2
Guise F . . . . . . . 91 B3
Guisona E . . . . . 147 C2
Guitiriz E . . . . . . 140 A3
Guîtres F . . . . . . 128 A2
Gujan-Mestras F . 128 B1
Gulbene LV . . . . . 8 D5
Gulçayir TR . . . . 187 C6
Guldborg DK . . . . 65 B4
Gullabo S . . . . . . 63 B3
Gullane GB . . . . . 35 B5
Gullbrå N . . . . . . 46 B3
Gullbrandstorp S . 61 C2
Gulleråsen S . . . . 50 A2
Gullhaug N . . . . . 53 A6
Gullringen S . . . . 62 A3
Gullspång S . . . . 55 B5
Gullstein N. . . . . 198 B5
Güllük TR . . . . . . 188 B2
Gülnar TR . . . . . 23 C7
Gülpınar TR. . . . . 186 C1
Gülşehir TR . . . . 23 B8
Gulsvik N. . . . . . 48 B1
Gumiel de Hizán E 143 C3
Gummersbach D. . 81 A3
Gümüldür TR. . . . 188 A2
Gümüshacıköy TR 23 A8
Gümüşova TR. . . 187 B5
Gundelfingen D. . . 94 C2
Gundel-fingen D . . 106 A2
Gundelsheim D . . 93 B5
Gunderschoffen F . 93 C3
Gundertshausen A 109 A3
Gundinci HR . . . . 125 B4
Gundoğmuş TR. . 189 C7
Güney
  Burdur TR . . . . .189 B4
  Denizli TR. . . . .188 A4
Gunja HR. . . . . . 125 C4
Günlüce TR . . . . 188 C3
Gunnarn S . . . . . 195 E8
Gunnarsbyn S . . . 196 C4
Gunnarskog S . . . 49 C4
Gunnebo S . . . . . 62 A4
Gunnislake GB . . 42 B2
Günselsdorf A . . . .111 B3
Guntersblum D . . 93 B4
Guntersdorf A . . . 97 C4
Guntin E . . . . . . 140 B3
Günyüzü TR. . . . 187 C6
Gunzenhausen D . 94 B2
Güre
  Balıkesir TR . . . .186 C1
  Uşak TR. . . . . .186 D4
Gurk A . . . . . . . 110 C1
Gurrea de Gállego
  E. . . . . . . . . . 144 B3
Gürsu TR . . . . . . 186 B4
Gušće HR . . . . . 124 B2
Gusev RUS . . . . 12 A5
Gúspini I . . . . . . 179 C2
Gusselby S . . . . . 56 A1
Güssing A . . . . . .111 B3
Gusswerk A . . . . .110 B2
Gustav Adolf S . . 49 B5
Gustavsberg S . . 57 A4
Gustavsfors S . . . 54 A3
Güstrow D . . . . . 65 C5
Gusum S . . . . . . 56 B2

Gutcher GB . . . . . 33 A5
Gutenstein A . . . . . .110 B2
Gütersloh D. . . . . . 81 A4
Guttannen CH . . . . 106 C3
Guttaring A . . . . . . 110 C1
Guttau D. . . . . . . . 84 A2
Güttingen CH . . . . 107 B4
Gützkow D. . . . . . . 66 C2
Guzów PL. . . . . . . . 77 B5
Gvardeysk RUS. . . . 12 A4
Gvarv N . . . . . . . . . 53 A5
Gvozd MNE . . . . . . 139 C5
Gvozdansko HR . . . 124 B2
Gwda Wielka PL . . . 68 B1
Gwennap GB . . . . . 42 B1
Gy F . . . . . . . . . . . 105 B4
Gyál H . . . . . . . . . .112 B3
Gyarmat H . . . . . . .111 B4
Gyékényes H . . . . 124 A3
Gyé-sur-Seine F . . 104 A3
Gyljen S. . . . . . . . 196 C5
Gylling DK . . . . . . . 59 C3
Gyoma H . . . . . . . 113 C4
Gyömöre H . . . . . .111 B4
Gyömrö H . . . . . . .112 B3
Gyón H. . . . . . . . . .112 B3
Gyöngyfa H . . . . . 125 B3
Gyöngyös H . . . . . .113 B3
Gyöngyöspata H. . 113 B3
Gyönk H. . . . . . . . 112 C2
Györ H . . . . . . . . .111 B4
Györszemere H . . . .111 B4
Gypsera CH. . . . . . 106 C2
Gysinge S . . . . . . . 51 B3
Gyttorp S . . . . . . . 55 A5
Gyula H . . . . . . . . 113 C5
Gyulafirátót H . . . .112 B1
Gyulaj H. . . . . . . . 112 C2

**H**

Haacht B . . . . . . . . 79 B4
Haag
 Nieder Österreich
 A. . . . . . . . . . . .110 A1
 Ober Österreich A . 109 A4
 D. . . . . . . . . . . .108 A3
Haaksbergen NL . . . 71 B3
Haamstede NL . . . . 79 A3
Haan D. . . . . . . . . . 80 A3
Haapajärvi FIN. . . . . 3 E9
Haapsalu EST . . . . . 8 C3
Haarlem NL . . . . . . 70 B1
Habas F . . . . . . . . 128 C2
Habay B . . . . . . . . . 92 B1
Habo S . . . . . . . . . . 62 A2
Håbol S . . . . . . . . . 54 B3
Habry CZ. . . . . . . . 97 B3
Habsheim F. . . . . . 106 B2
Hachenburg D. . . . . 81 B3
Hacıbektaş TR. . . . . 23 B8
Hacılar TR . . . . . . . 23 B8
Hacinas E . . . . . . . 143 C3
Hackås S . . . . . . . 199 C11
Hacketstown IRL. . . 30 B2
Hackthorpe GB . . . . 37 B4
Hadamar D. . . . . . . 81 B4
Hädanberg S . . . . 200 C4
Haddington GB. . . . 35 C5
Hadersdorf am Kamp
 A. . . . . . . . . . . . 97 C3
Haderslev DK. . . . . 59 C2
Haderup DK. . . . . . 59 B1
Hadım TR . . . . . . . 23 C7
Hadleigh
 Essex GB. . . . . .45 B4
 Suffolk GB . . . . .45 A4
Hadlow GB. . . . . . . 45 B4
Hadmersleben D . . . 73 B4
Hadsten DK. . . . . . 59 B3
Hadsund DK . . . . . . 58 B3
Hadžići BIH . . . . . 139 B4
Hafnarfjörður IS . . 190 C4
Hafnir IS. . . . . . . . 190 D3
Hafslo N. . . . . . . . 47 A4
Hagby S. . . . . . . . . 63 B4
Hage D . . . . . . . . . 71 A4
Hægebostad N . . . . 52 B3
Hægeland N. . . . . . 53 B3
Hagen
 Niedersachsen D . .72 A1
 Nordrhein-Westfalen
 D . . . . . . . . . . . . 80 A3
Hagenbach D. . . . . 93 B4
Hagenow D . . . . . . 73 A4
Hagetmau F. . . . . . 128 C2
Hagfors S . . . . . . . 49 B5
Häggenäs S. . . . . .199 B11
Hagondange F. . . . . 92 B2
Hagsta S . . . . . . . . 51 B4
Haguenau F. . . . . . 93 C3
Hahnbach D. . . . . . 95 B3
Hahnslätten D . . . . 81 B4
Hahót H . . . . . . . . .111 C3
Haiger D. . . . . . . . . 81 B4
Haigerloch D . . . . . 93 C4
Hailsham GB . . . . . 45 C4
Hainburg A. . . . . . .111 A3
Hainfeld A . . . . . . .110 A2
Hainichen D. . . . . . 83 B5
Hajdúböszörmény
 H . . . . . . . . . . . .113 B5
Hajdučica SRB . . . 126 B2

Hajdúdorogo H . . . .113 B5
Hajdúnánás H . . . .113 B5
Hajdúszoboszló H. .113 B5
Hajnáčka SK. . . . . .113 A3
Hajnówka PL . . . . . 13 B5
Hajós H . . . . . . . . 112 C3
Håkafot S. . . . . . .199 A11
Hakkas S . . . . . . . 196 C4
Håksberg S . . . . . . 50 B2
Halaszi H . . . . . . . .111 B4
Halberstadt D . . . . 82 A3
Halberton GB . . . . 43 B3
Hald Ege DK . . . . . 58 B2
Haldem D. . . . . . . . 71 B5
Halden N . . . . . . . . 54 A2
Haldensleben D. . . 73 B4
Halenbeck D . . . . . 73 A5
Halesowen GB. . . . 40 C1
Halesworth GB . . . 45 A5
Halfing D . . . . . . . 109 B3
Halhjem N . . . . . . . 46 B2
Håliden S. . . . . . . . 49 B5
Halifax GB . . . . . . 40 B2
Häljelöt S. . . . . . . . 56 B2
Halkida GR . . . . . . 185 A4
Halkirk GB . . . . . . 32 C3
Hall S . . . . . . . . . . 57 C4
Hälla S . . . . . . . . . 200 C3
Hallabro S. . . . . . . 63 B3
Hällabrottet S . . . . 56 A1
Halland S. . . . . . . . 45 C4
Hällaryd S . . . . . . . 63 B2
Hallaryd S . . . . . . . 61 C3
Hällberga S . . . . . . 56 A2
Hällbybrunn S . . . . 56 A2
Halle
 B. . . . . . . . . . . . .79 B4
 Nordrhein-Westfalen
 D. . . . . . . . . . . . .72 B3
 Sachsen-Anhalt D . .83 A3
Hålleberga S . . . . . 62 B3
Hällefors S. . . . . . . 55 A5
Hälleforsnäs S. . . . 56 A2
Hallein A. . . . . . . . 109 B4
Hällekis S. . . . . . . . 55 B4
Hallen S. . . . . . . .199 B11
Hållen S . . . . . . . . 51 B4
Hallenberg D . . . . . 81 A4
Hällestad S . . . . . . 56 B1
Hällevadsholm S. . . 54 B2
Hällevik S. . . . . . . . 63 B2
Hälleviksstrand S . . 54 B2
Hallingby N . . . . . . 48 B2
Hallingeberg S . . . . 62 A4
Hallingen N . . . . . . 47 B6
Hällnäs S . . . . . . . . 51 B4
Hällnäs S . . . . . . . 200 B5
Hallormsstaður
 IS. . . . . . . . . . . .191 B11
Hallsberg S . . . . . . 56 A1
Hällsta S . . . . . . . . 56 A2
Hallstahammar S . . 56 A2
Hallstatt A . . . . . . 109 B4
Hallstavik S . . . . . . 51 B5
Halltorp S. . . . . . . . 63 B4
Halluin F . . . . . . . . 78 B3
Hallviken S . . . . . .199 B12
Hallworthy GB. . . . . 42 B2
Halmstad S . . . . . . 61 C2
Hals DK. . . . . . . . . 58 A3
Halsa N . . . . . . . . 198 B5
Halstead GB . . . . . 45 B4
Haltdalen N . . . . . 199 C8
Haltern D. . . . . . . . 80 A3
Haltwhistle GB . . . . 37 B4
Halvarsgårdarna S . 50 B2
Halver D. . . . . . . . . 80 A3
Halvrimmen DK. . . . 58 A2
Ham F. . . . . . . . . . 90 B3
Hamar N. . . . . . . . 48 B3
Hamarhaug N . . . . 46 B2
Hamarøy N. . . . . . 194 B6
Hambach F . . . . . . 92 B3
Hambergen D . . . . 72 A1
Hambergsund S . . . 54 B2
Hambledon GB . . . 44 C2
Hambuhren D . . . . 72 B2
Hamburg D . . . . . . 72 A3
Hamdibey TR. . . . . 186 C2
Hamdorf D . . . . . . 64 B2
Hämeenlinna FIN . . 8 B4
Hameln = Hamlin D . 72 B2
Hamersleben D . . . 73 B4
Hamidiye TR . . . . . 187 C5
Hamilton GB . . . . . 36 A2
Hamina FIN . . . . . . 8 B5
Hamlagrø N . . . . . . 46 B3
Hamlin = Hameln D . 72 B2
Hamm D. . . . . . . . 81 A3
Hammar S. . . . . . . 55 B5
Hammarland FIN . . 51 B6
Hammarö S . . . . . . 55 A4
Hammarstrand S . . 200 C2
Hamme B . . . . . . . 79 A4
Hammel DK. . . . . . 59 B2
Hammelburg D . . . . 82 B1
Hammelspring D . . . 74 A2
Hammenhög S . . . . 66 A3
Hammerdal S. . . . .199 B12
Hammerfest N . . . . 192 B7
Hammershøj DK. . . 58 B2
Hammerum DK . . . . 59 B2
Hamminkeln D . . . . 80 A2
Hamnavoe GB . . . . 33 A5
Hamneda S . . . . . . 60 C3
Hamningberg N . . . 193 B14

Hamoir B . . . . . . . . 80 B1
Hamont B. . . . . . . . 80 A1
Hámor H. . . . . . . . .113 A4
Hamra
 Gävleborg S. . . . .199 D12
 Gotland S. . . . . . .57 D4
Hamrångefjärden S. 51 B4
Hamstreet GB . . . . 45 B4
Hamsund N . . . . . . 194 B6
Han TR. . . . . . . . . 187 C5
Hanaskog S . . . . . . 61 C4
Hanau D. . . . . . . . . 81 B4
Händelöp S . . . . . . 62 A4
Handlová SK. . . . . . 98 C2
Hanerau-Hademarschen
 D . . . . . . . . . . . . 64 B2
Hånger S . . . . . . . . 60 B3
Hanhimaa FIN . . . 197 B8
Hanken S. . . . . . . . 55 B5
Hankensbüttel D . . 73 B3
Han Knežica BIH . . 124 B2
Hanko FIN . . . . . . . 8 C3
Hannover D . . . . . . 72 B2
Hannut B . . . . . . . . 79 B5
Han Pijesak BIH. . 139 A4
Hansnes N . . . . . . 192 C3
Hanstedt D . . . . . . 72 A3
Hanstholm DK. . . . 58 A1
Hantsavichy BY . . . 13 B7
Hanušovice CZ. . . . 85 B4
Haparanda S . . . . 196 D7
Haradok BY . . . . . . 13 A8
Harads S . . . . . . . 196 C4
Häradsbäck S . . . . 63 B2
Häradsbygden S. . . 50 B2
Harbo S . . . . . . . . . 51 B4
Harboør DK . . . . . . 58 B1
Harburg
 Bayern D . . . . . . .94 C2
 Hamburg D . . . . . .72 A2
Hårby DK. . . . . . . . 59 C3
Harc H . . . . . . . . . 112 C2
Hardegarijp NL . . . 70 A2
Hardegsen D . . . . . 82 A1
Hardelot Plage F . . 78 B1
Hardenbeck D . . . . 74 A2
Hardenberg NL . . . 71 B3
Harderwijk NL . . . . 70 B2
Hardheim D . . . . . . 94 B1
Hardt D. . . . . . . . . 106 A3
Hareid N. . . . . . . . 198 C3
Haren
 D. . . . . . . . . . . . .71 B4
 NL. . . . . . . . . . . .71 A3
Harestua N. . . . . . . 48 B2
Harfleur F. . . . . . . . 89 A4
Harg S . . . . . . . . . . 51 B5
Hargicourt F. . . . . . 90 B3
Hargnies F. . . . . . . 91 A4
Hargshamn S . . . . 51 B5
Härja S . . . . . . . . . 55 B4
Harkány F. . . . . . . 125 B4
Härkeberga S . . . . 56 A3
Harkebrügge D . . . 71 A4
Harlech GB. . . . . . . 38 B2
Harleston GB. . . . . 45 A5
Hårlev DK. . . . . . . . 65 A5
Harlingen NL . . . . . 70 A2
Harlösa S . . . . . . . 61 D3
Harlow GB. . . . . . . 45 B4
Harmancık TR . . . . 186 C4
Harmånger S. . . . . 200 E3
Härnevi S . . . . . . . 56 A3
Härnösand S . . . . 200 D3
Haro E . . . . . . . . . 143 B4
Haroldswick GB . . . 33 A6
Háromfa H . . . . . . 124 A3
Haroué F . . . . . . . . 92 C2
Harpenden GB. . . . 44 B3
Harplinge S . . . . . . 60 C2
Harpstedt D . . . . . . 72 B1
Harrogate GB . . . . 40 A2
Harrow GB. . . . . . . 44 B3
Härryda S. . . . . . . . 60 B2
Harsefeld D . . . . . . 72 A2
Harsewinkel D. . . . . 71 C5
Hârşova . . . . . . . . 17 C7
Harstad N. . . . . . . 194 B7
Harsum D . . . . . . . 72 B2
Harsvik N. . . . . . . .199 A7
Harta H . . . . . . . . . 112 C3
Hartberg A. . . . . . .110 B2
Hartennes F. . . . . . 90 B3
Hartest GB . . . . . . 45 A4
Hartha D. . . . . . . . 83 A4
Hartland GB. . . . . . 42 B2
Hartlebury GB . . . . 37 A5
Hartlepool GB. . . . . 37 B5
Hartmanice CZ. . . . 96 B1
Hartmannsdorf A. . .110 B2
Harvassdal N . . . . 195 E5
Harwell GB. . . . . . . 44 B2
Harwich GB. . . . . . 45 B5
Harzgerode D . . . . 82 A3
Häselgehr A. . . . . . 108 B1
Haselünne D . . . . . 71 B4
Hasköy TR. . . . . . . 186 A1
Haslach D . . . . . . . 106 A3
Haslach an der Mühl
 A. . . . . . . . . . . . 96 C2
Hasle DK. . . . . . . . 67 A3
Haslemere GB. . . . 44 B3
Haslev DK. . . . . . . 65 A4
Hasloch D . . . . . . . 94 B1
Hasparren F. . . . . . 144 A2
Hassela S . . . . . . 200 D2
Hasselfelde D . . . . 82 A2
Hasselfors S . . . . . 55 A5

Hasselt
 B. . . . . . . . . . . . .79 B5
 NL. . . . . . . . . . . .70 B3
Hassfurt D . . . . . . . 94 A2
Hassleben D . . . . . 74 A2
Hässleholm S . . . . . 61 C3
Hasslö S . . . . . . . . 63 B3
Hassloch D . . . . . . 93 B4
Hästbo S . . . . . . . . 51 B4
Hastersboda FIN . . 51 B7
Hästholmen S. . . . . 55 B5
Hastière-Lavaux B . 79 B4
Hastigrow GB . . . . 32 C3
Hastings GB . . . . . 45 C4
Hästveda S . . . . . . 61 C3
Hasvik N . . . . . . . 192 B6
Hatfield
 Hertfordshire GB . .44 B3
 South Yorkshire GB. 40 B3
Hatherleigh GB . . . 42 B2
Hathersage GB . . . 40 B2
Hatlestrand N . . . . 46 B2
Hattem NL . . . . . . 70 B3
Hatten
 D. . . . . . . . . . . . .71 A5
 F. . . . . . . . . . . . .93 C3
Hattfjelldal N . . . . . 195 E4
Hatting DK. . . . . . . 59 C2
Hattingen D. . . . . . 80 A3
Hattstedt D . . . . . . 64 B2
Hatvan H . . . . . . . .112 B3
Hatvik N. . . . . . . . . 46 B2
Hau D. . . . . . . . . . 80 A2
Haudainville F. . . . . 92 B1
Hauganes IS . . . . . 191 B7
Haugastøl N. . . . . . 47 B4
Hauge N . . . . . . . . 52 B2
Haughom N . . . . . . 52 B2
Haugsdal N . . . . . . 46 B2
Haugsdorf A. . . . . . 97 C4
Haukedal N. . . . . . 46 A3
Haukeland N. . . . . . 46 B2
Haukeligrend N. . . . 52 A3
Haukeliseter N. . . . 52 A3
Haukipudas FIN . . . 3 D9
Haulerwijk NL . . . . 71 A3
Haunersdorf D. . . . 95 C4
Haus N. . . . . . . . . . 46 B2
Hausach D. . . . . . . 106 A3
Hausham D . . . . . . 108 B2
Hausmannstätten
 A. . . . . . . . . . . . 110 C2
Hausvik N . . . . . . . 52 B2
Hautajärvi FIN . . . 197 C12
Hautefort F . . . . . . 129 A4
Hauterives F. . . . . .117 B5
Hauteville-Lompnès
 F. . . . . . . . . . . . .118 B2
Haut-Fays B. . . . . . 91 A5
Hautmont F . . . . . . 79 B3
Hautrage B. . . . . . . 79 B3
Hauzenberg D . . . . 96 C1
Havant GB. . . . . . . 44 C3
Havdhem S . . . . . . 57 C4
Havdrup DK. . . . . . 61 D2
Havelange B . . . . . 79 B5
Havelberg D. . . . . . 73 B5
Havelte NL. . . . . . . 70 B3
Haverfordwest GB . 39 C2
Haverhill GB . . . . . 45 A4
Havering GB . . . . . 45 B4
Håverud S . . . . . . . 54 B3
Havířov CZ. . . . . . . 98 B2
Havixbeck D . . . . . 71 C4
Havlíčkův Brod CZ. . 97 B3
Havndal DK . . . . . . 58 B3
Havneby DK. . . . . . 64 A1
Havnebyen DK. . . . 61 D1
Havnsø DK. . . . . . . 61 D1
Havøysund N. . . . . 193 A8
Havran TR. . . . . . . 186 C2
Havrebjerg DK. . . . 61 D1
Havsa TR. . . . . . . . 186 A1
Havstenssund S . . . 54 B2
Havza TR. . . . . . . . 23 A8
Hawes GB . . . . . . 37 B4
Hawick GB. . . . . . . 35 C5
Hawkhurst GB . . . . 45 B4
Hawkinge GB. . . . . 45 B5
Haxey GB. . . . . . . . 40 B3
Hayange F. . . . . . . 92 B2
Haydarlı TR . . . . . 189 A5
Haydon Bridge GB . 37 B4
Hayle GB. . . . . . . . 42 B1
Haymana TR . . . . . 187 C7
Hay-on-Wye GB. . . 39 B3
Haywards Heath GB 44 C3
Hazebrouck F . . . . 78 B2
Hazlov CZ. . . . . . . . 83 B4
Heacham GB . . . . . 41 C4
Headcorn GB. . . . . 45 B4
Headford IRL. . . . . 28 A2
Heanor GB. . . . . . . 40 B2
Héas F . . . . . . . . . 145 B4
Heathfield GB . . . . 45 C4
Hebden Bridge GB . 40 B1
Heberg S . . . . . . . . 60 C2
Hechingen D . . . . . 93 C4
Hechlingen D . . . . . 94 C2
Hecho E . . . . . . . . 144 B3
Hechtel B. . . . . . . . 79 A5
Hechthausen D . . . 72 A2

Heckelberg D. . . . . 74 B2
Heckington GB . . . . 41 C3
Hecklingen D. . . . . 82 A3
Hed S . . . . . . . . . . 56 A1
Hedalen N . . . . . . . 48 B1
Hedared S . . . . . . . 60 B2
Heddal N . . . . . . . . 53 A5
Hédé F . . . . . . . . . 101 A4
Hede S . . . . . . . . . 199 C10
Hedekas S . . . . . . 54 B2
Hedemora S . . . . . 50 B2
Hedenäset S . . . . . 196 C6
Hedensted DK. . . . 59 C2
Hedersleben D . . . . 82 A3
Hedesunda S . . . . . 51 B4
Hedge End GB. . . . 44 C2
Hedon GB . . . . . . . 41 B3
Heede D. . . . . . . . . 71 B4
Heek D. . . . . . . . . . 71 B4
Heemstede NL. . . . 70 B1
Heerde NL. . . . . . . 70 B3
Heerenveen NL. . . . 70 B2
Heerhugowaard NL. 70 B1
Heerlen NL. . . . . . . 80 B1
Heeze NL . . . . . . . 80 A1
Heggenes N . . . . . 47 A6
Hegra N . . . . . . . . 199 B8
Hegyeshalom H . . . .111 B4
Hegyközség H . . . .111 B3
Heia N. . . . . . . . . 199 A9
Heide D . . . . . . . . . 64 B2
Heidelberg D . . . . . 93 B4
Heiden D . . . . . . . . 80 A2
Heidenau D . . . . . . 84 B1
Heidenheim D . . . . 94 C2
Heidenreichstein A . 97 C3
Heikendorf D. . . . . . 64 B3
Heikkilä FIN . . . . . 197 C12
Heilam GB . . . . . . . 32 C2
Heiland N. . . . . . . . 53 B4
Heilbad Heiligenstadt
 D . . . . . . . . . . . . 82 A2
Heilbronn D. . . . . . . 93 B5
Heiligenblut A . . . . 109 B3
Heiligendamm D . . . 65 B4
Heiligendorf D . . . . 73 B3
Heiligengrabe D . . . 73 A5
Heiligenhafen D . . . 65 B3
Heiligenhaus D . . . 80 A2
Heiligenkreuz A . . .111 C3
Heiligenstadt D . . . 94 B3
Heiloo NL. . . . . . . . 70 B1
Heilsbronn D. . . . . . 94 B2
Heim N . . . . . . . . . 198 B6
Heimburg D . . . . . . 82 A2
Heimdal N . . . . . . . 199 B7
Heinerscheid L . . . . 92 A2
Heinersdorf D . . . . 74 B3
Heining D. . . . . . . . 96 C1
Heiningen D. . . . . . 94 C1
Heinola FIN . . . . . . 8 B5
Heinsberg D . . . . . 80 A2
Heist-op-den-Berg
 B. . . . . . . . . . . . .79 A4
Hejde S . . . . . . . . . 57 C4
Hejdeby S . . . . . . . 57 C4
Hejls DK. . . . . . . . . 59 C2
Hejnice CZ. . . . . . . 84 B3
Hel PL. . . . . . . . . . 69 A3
Helchteren B . . . . . 79 A5
Heldburg D . . . . . . 82 B2
Heldrungen D . . . . . 82 A3
Helechosa E . . . . . 156 A3
Helensburgh GB . . 34 B3
Helfenberg A. . . . . 96 C2
Helgen N . . . . . . . . 53 A5
Helgeroa N . . . . . . 53 B5
Hella
 IS . . . . . . . . . . .190 D5
 N. . . . . . . . . . . . .46 A3
Helland N . . . . . . . 194 B7
Hellas S . . . . . . . . 55 B3
Helle N. . . . . . . . . . 52 B2
Helleland N . . . . . . 52 B2
Hellendoorn NL. . . . 71 B3
Hellenthal D. . . . . . 80 B2
Hellesøy N . . . . . . 46 B1
Hellesylt N . . . . . . 198 C3
Hellevoetsluis NL . . 79 A4
Helligskogen N . . . 192 C4
Hellín E . . . . . . . . 158 C2
Hellissandur IS . . . 190 C2
Hellnar IS. . . . . . . 190 C2
Hellum DK . . . . . . . 58 A3
Hellvi S. . . . . . . . . . 57 C4
Hellvik N . . . . . . . . 52 B1
Helm-brechts D. . . . 83 B3
Helmond NL. . . . . . 80 A1
Helmsdale GB . . . . 32 C3
Helmsley GB . . . . . 37 B5
Helmstedt D. . . . . . 73 B3
Hel'pa SK. . . . . . . . 99 C3
Helsa D . . . . . . . . . 82 A1
Helsby GB. . . . . . . 38 A4
Helsinge DK. . . . . . 61 C2
Helsingør DK. . . . . 61 C2
Helsinki FIN . . . . . . 8 B4
Helston GB . . . . . . 42 B1
Hemau D . . . . . . . . 95 B3
Hemavan S . . . . . . 195 E6
Hemel Hempstead
 GB . . . . . . . . . . .44 B3
Hemer D. . . . . . . . 81 A3
Héming F . . . . . . . 92 C2
Hemmet DK. . . . . . 59 C1
Hemmingstedt D . . 64 B2
Hemmoor D . . . . . . 64 C2

Hemnes N . . . . . . . 54 A2
Hemnesberget N . . 195 D4
Hemse S . . . . . . . . 57 C4
Hemsedal N . . . . . . 47 B5
Hemslingen D . . . . 72 A2
Hemsworth GB . . . . 40 B2
Hen N. . . . . . . . . . 48 B2
Henán S . . . . . . . . 54 B2
Hendaye F . . . . . . 144 A2
Hendek TR. . . . . . . 187 B5
Hendungen D . . . . . 82 B2
Henfield GB. . . . . . 44 C3
Hengelo
 Gelderland NL . . . .71 B3
 Overijssel NL. . . . .71 B3
Hengersberg D . . . 95 C5
Hengoed GB . . . . . 39 C3
Hénin-Beaumont F . 78 B2
Henley-on-Thames
 GB . . . . . . . . . . .44 B3
Hennan S . . . . . . . 200 D1
Henneberg D. . . . . 82 B2
Hennebont F . . . . . 100 B2
Henne Strand DK . . 59 C1
Hennigsdorf D. . . . . 74 B2
Hennset N . . . . . . . 198 B5
Hennstedt
 Schleswig-Holstein
 D. . . . . . . . . . . . .64 B2
 Schleswig-Holstein
 D. . . . . . . . . . . . .64 B2
Henrichemont F . . . 103 B4
Henryków PL. . . . . . 85 B5
Henrykowo PL. . . . . 69 A5
Hensås N . . . . . . . 47 A5
Henstedt-Ulzburg D 64 C2
Heppenheim D . . . . 93 B4
Herad
 Buskerud N . . . . . 47 B6
 Vest-Agder N . . . . 52 B2
Heradsbygd N . . . . 48 B3
Heraklion = Iraklio
 GR . . . . . . . . . . 185 D6
Herálec CZ. . . . . . . 97 B4
Herand N . . . . . . . 46 B3
Herbault F . . . . . . . 103 B3
Herbern D . . . . . . . 81 A3
Herbertstown IRL . . 29 B3
Herbeumont B . . . . 91 B5
Herbignac F . . . . . . 101 B3
Herbisse F . . . . . . . 91 C4
Herbitzheim F . . . . 92 B3
Herbolzheim D . . . . 106 A2
Herborn D . . . . . . . 81 B4
Herbrechtingen D . . 94 C2
Herby PL. . . . . . . . 86 B2
Herceg-Novi MNE . 16 D3
Hercegovac HR . . . 124 B3
Hercegszántó H . . . 125 B4
Herchen D. . . . . . . 80 B3
Heréd H . . . . . . . . .112 B3
Hereford GB . . . . . 39 B4
Herefoss N . . . . . . 53 B4
Hereke TR. . . . . . . 187 B4
Herencia E . . . . . . 157 A4
Herend H . . . . . . . .111 B4
Herent B . . . . . . . . 79 B4
Herentals B . . . . . . 79 A4
Hérépian F . . . . . . 130 B2
Herfølge DK. . . . . . 61 D2
Herford D . . . . . . . 72 B1
Herguijuela E. . . . . 156 A2
Héric F . . . . . . . . . 101 B4
Héricourt F. . . . . . . 106 B1
Héricourt-en-Caux
 F. . . . . . . . . . . . .89 A4
Hérimoncourt F. . . . 106 B1
Heringsdorf D . . . . 65 B4
Herisau CH . . . . . . 107 B4
Hérisson F. . . . . . . 103 C4
Herk-de-Stad B . . . 79 B5
Herlufmagle DK. . . 65 A4
Hermagor A . . . . . 109 C4
Hermannsburg D . . 72 B3
Hermansverk N . . . 46 A3
Heřmanův Městec
 CZ. . . . . . . . . . . 97 B3
Herment F. . . . . . . .116 B2
Hermeskeil D. . . . . 92 B2
Hermisende E . . . . 141 C4
Hermonville F . . . . 91 B3
Hermsdorf D . . . . . 83 B3
Hernani E. . . . . . . 144 A2
Hernansancho E . . 150 B3
Herne D . . . . . . . . 80 A3
Herne Bay GB . . . . 45 B5
Hernes N . . . . . . . 48 B3
Herning DK . . . . . . 59 B1
Heroya N . . . . . . . 53 A5
Herramelluri E . . . . 143 B3
Herräng S . . . . . . . 51 B5
Herre N . . . . . . . . . 53 A5
Herrenberg D. . . . . 93 C4
Herrera E . . . . . . . 162 A3
Herrera de Alcántara
 E. . . . . . . . . . . . 155 B3
Herrera del Duque
 E. . . . . . . . . . . . 156 A2
Herrera de los Navarros
 E. . . . . . . . . . . . 152 A2
Herrera de Pisuerga
 E. . . . . . . . . . . . 142 B2
Herreros del Suso
 E. . . . . . . . . . . . 150 B2
Herrestad S . . . . . . 54 B2
Herrhamra S . . . . . 57 B3
Herritslev DK. . . . . 65 B4
Herrlisheim F. . . . . 93 C3

Herrljunga S . . . . . . 55 B4
Herrnhut D. . . . . . . . 84 A2
Herrsching D . . . . . . 108 A2
Hersbruck D . . . . . 95 B3
Hersby S . . . . . . . . 57 A4
Herscheid D. . . . . . . 81 A3
Herselt B . . . . . . . . . 79 A4
Herso GR. . . . . . . . 182 B4
Herstal B . . . . . . . . . 80 B1
Herstmonceux GB . . 45 C4
Herten D. . . . . . . . . 80 A3
Hertford GB. . . . . . . 44 B3
Hervás E . . . . . . . 149 B4
Hervik N. . . . . . . . . . 52 A1
Herxheim D . . . . . . . 93 B4
Herzberg
  Brandenburg D . . . . 74 B1
  Brandenburg D . . . 83 A5
  Niedersachsen D. . . 82 A2
Herzebrock D . . . . . . 81 A4
Herzfelde D . . . . . . . 74 B2
Herzlake D . . . . . . . 71 B4
Herzogenaurach D . 94 B2
Herzogenbuchsee
  CH . . . . . . . . . . 106 B2
Herzogenburg A . .110 A2
Herzsprung D . . . . . 73 A5
Hesby N. . . . . . . . . . 52 A1
Hesdin F . . . . . . . . . 78 B2
Hesel D . . . . . . . . . . 71 A4
Heskestad N . . . . . . 52 B2
Hessdalen N . . . . . 199 C8
Hesselager DK . . . . 65 A3
Hesseng N. . . . . . 193 C13
Hessisch Lichtenau
  D . . . . . . . . . . . . 82 A1
Hessisch-Oldendorf
  D . . . . . . . . . . . . 72 B2
Hestra S. . . . . . . . . 60 B3
Heswall GB . . . . . . . 38 A3
Hetlevik N . . . . . . . . 46 B2
Hettange-Grande F. . 92 B2
Hetton-le-Hole GB. . 37 B5
Hettstedt D . . . . . . . 82 A3
Heuchin F . . . . . . . . 78 B2
Heudicourt-sous-les-
  Côtes F . . . . . . . . 92 C1
Heunezel F . . . . . . 105 A5
Heuqueville F . . . . . 89 A4
Heves H . . . . . . . .113 B4
Héviz H . . . . . . . .111 C4
Hexham GB . . . . . . . 37 B4
Heysham GB . . . . . . 36 B4
Heytesbury GB . . . . 43 A4
Hidas H . . . . . . . . 125 A4
Hieflau A. . . . . . . . .110 B1
Hiendelaencina E . 151 A5
Hiersac F . . . . . . . 115 C4
High Bentham GB. . 37 B4
Highclere GB. . . . . . 44 B2
High Hesket GB. . . . 37 B4
Highley GB . . . . . . . 39 B4
High Wycombe GB. 44 B3
Higuera de Arjona
  E . . . . . . . . . . . 157 C4
Higuera de Calatrava
  E . . . . . . . . . . . 163 A3
Higuera de la Serena
  E . . . . . . . . . . . 156 B2
Higuera de la Sierra
  E . . . . . . . . . . . 161 B3
Higuera de Vargas
  E . . . . . . . . . . . 155 C4
Higuera la Real E . 161 A3
Higuers de Llerena
  E . . . . . . . . . . . 156 B1
Higueruela E . . . . . 158 C2
Híjar E . . . . . . . . . 153 A3
Hilchenbach D. . . . . 81 A4
Hildburghausen D. . 82 B2
Hilden D . . . . . . . . . 80 A2
Hilders D . . . . . . . . 82 B1
Hildesheim D. . . . . . 72 B2
Hilgay GB. . . . . . . . 41 C4
Hillared S. . . . . . . . 60 B3
Hille D . . . . . . . . . . 72 B1
Hillegom NL. . . . . . . 70 B1
Hillerød D . . . . . . . . 61 D2
Hillerstorp S . . . . . . 60 B3
Hillesheim D . . . . . . 80 B2
Hillestad N . . . . . . . 53 A6
Hillmersdorf D. . . . . 83 A5
Hillsborough GB . . . 27 B4
Hillswick GB . . . . . . 33 A5
Hilpoltstein D . . . . . 95 B3
Hiltpoltstein D . . . . . 94 B3
Hilvarenbeek NL . . . 79 A5
Hilversum NL. . . . . . 70 B2
Himarë AL . . . . . . 182 C1
Himbergen D. . . . . . 73 A3
Himesháza H . . . . 125 A4
Himmelberg A . . . . 109 C5
Himmelpforten D. . . 72 A2
Himód H. . . . . . . . .111 B4
Hinckley GB. . . . . . . 40 C2
Hindås S . . . . . . . . . 60 B2
Hindelang D. . . . . . 108 B1
Hindelbank CH . . . 106 B2
Hinderavåg N . . . . . 52 A1
Hindhead GB. . . . . . 44 B3
Hinojsa del Valle E 156 B1
Hinnerup DK . . . . . . 59 B3
Hinojal E . . . . . . . 155 B4
Hinojales E . . . . . . 161 B3
Hinojos E . . . . . . . 161 B3
Hinojosa del Duque
  E . . . . . . . . . . . 156 B2

Hinojosas de Calatrava
  E. . . . . . . . . . . . 157 B3
Hinterhornbach A . 108 B1
Hinterriss A . . . . . . 108 B2
Hintersee
  A . . . . . . . . . . . 109 B4
  D. . . . . . . . . . . . .74 A3
Hinterstoder A . . . .110 B1
Hintertux A . . . . . . 108 B2
Hinterweidenthal D. 93 B3
Hinwil CH. . . . . . . 107 B3
Hios GR . . . . . . . . 185 A7
Hippolytushoef NL . 70 B1
Hirschaid D . . . . . . . 94 B2
Hirschau D. . . . . . . . 95 B3
Hirschfeld D. . . . . . . 83 A5
Hirschhorn D. . . . . . 93 B4
Hirsingue F . . . . . 106 B2
Hirson F . . . . . . . . . 91 B4
Hirtshals DK . . . . . . 58 A2
Hirvaskoski FIN. . 197 D10
Hirzenhain D . . . . . . 81 B5
Hisarcık TR . . . . . . 186 C4
Hishult S . . . . . . . . 61 C3
Hissjön S . . . . . . . 200 C6
Hitchin GB . . . . . . . 44 B3
Hitra N . . . . . . . . . 198 B5
Hittarp S. . . . . . . . . 61 C2
Hittisau A . . . . . . . 107 B4
Hittun N . . . . . . . . . 46 A1
Hitzacker D . . . . . . . 73 A4
Hjallerup DK . . . . . . 58 A3
Hjällstad S . . . . . . . 49 B5
Hjältevad S . . . . . . . 62 A3
Hjärnarp S . . . . . . . 61 C2
Hjartdal N. . . . . . . . 53 A4
Hjellestad N . . . . . . 46 B2
Hjelmeland N. . . . . . 52 A2
Hjelset N . . . . . . . . 198 C4
Hjerkinn N . . . . . . . 198 C6
Hjerm DK . . . . . . . . 58 B1
Hjerpsted DK . . . . . 64 A1
Hjerting DK . . . . . . . 59 C1
Hjo S . . . . . . . . . . . 55 B5
Hjordkær DK . . . . . . 64 A2
Hjørring DK . . . . . . . 58 A2
Hjorted S . . . . . . . . 62 A4
Hjortkvarn S . . . . . . 56 B1
Hjortnäs S . . . . . . . 50 B1
Hjukse N . . . . . . . . 53 A5
Hjuksebø N . . . . . . 53 A5
Hjulsjö S . . . . . . . . . 55 A5
Hliník nad Hronom
  SK . . . . . . . . . . . 98 C2
Hlinsko CZ. . . . . . . . 97 B3
Hlío IS . . . . . . . 191 A10
Hlubokánad Vltavou
  CZ . . . . . . . . . . . 96 B2
Hlučín CZ. . . . . . . . . 98 B2
Hlyboka UA . . . . . . . 17 A6
Hlybokaye BY . . . . 13 A7
Hniezdne SK . . . . . . 99 B4
Hnilec SK. . . . . . . . . 99 C4
Hnúšťa SK. . . . . . . . 99 C3
Hobol H . . . . . . . . 125 A3
Hobro DK. . . . . . . . . 58 B2
Hobscheid L . . . . . . 92 B1
Hocalar TR. . . . . . . 189 A4
Hochdonn D . . . . . . 64 B2
Hochdorf CH . . . . . 106 B3
Hochfelden F. . . . . . 93 C3
Hochspeyer D . . . . . 93 B3
Höchstädt D . . . . . . 94 B2
Höchstädt D . . . . . . 94 C2
Hochstenbach D . . . 81 B3
Höchst im Odenwald
  D . . . . . . . . . . . . 93 B5
Höckendorf D . . . . . 83 B5
Hockenheim D. . . . . 93 B4
Hoddesdon GB . . . . 44 B3
Hodejov SK . . . . . . . 99 C3
Hodenhagen D . . . . 72 B2
Hodkovice CZ . . . . . 84 B3
Hódmezővásárhely
  H . . . . . . . . . . . 113 C4
Hodnet GB. . . . . . . . 38 B4
Hodonín CZ. . . . . . . 98 C1
Hodslavice CZ. . . . . 98 B2
Hoedekenskerke NL 79 A3
Hoegaarden B . . . . . 79 B4
Hoek van Holland
  NL. . . . . . . . . . . . 79 A4
Hoenderlo NL . . . . . 70 B2
Hof
  D. . . . . . . . . . . . .83 B3
  N . . . . . . . . . . . . .53 A6
Hofbieber D . . . . . . 82 B1
Hoff GB . . . . . . . . . 37 B4
Hofgeismar D . . . . . 81 A5
Hofheim
  Bayern D . . . . . . . 82 B2
  Hessen D. . . . . . . 93 A4
Hofkirchen im Mühlkreis
  A. . . . . . . . . . . . . 96 C1
Höfn IS. . . . . . . . 191 C10
Hofors S. . . . . . . . . 50 B3
Hofsós IS. . . . . . . 190 B6
Hofstad N. . . . . . . 199 A7
Höganäs S. . . . . . . 61 C2
Högbo S. . . . . . . . . 51 B3
Hogdal S . . . . . . . . 54 A2
Høgebru N. . . . . . . 46 A4
Högfors S . . . . . . . . 50 C2
Högklint S . . . . . . . 57 C4
Högsäter S. . . . . . . 54 B3
Högsby S . . . . . . . . 62 A4

Högsjö S . . . . . . . . 56 A1
Hogstad S . . . . . . . 55 B6
Högyész H . . . . . 112 C2
Hohenau A . . . . . . . 97 C4
Hohenberg A . . . . .110 B2
Hohenbucko D . . . . 83 A5
Hohenburg D . . . . . 95 B3
Hohendorf D . . . . . . 66 B1
Hohenems A . . . . . 107 B4
Hohenhameln D . . . 72 B3
Hohenhausen D . . . 72 B1
Hohenkirchen D . . . 71 A4
Hohenlinden D . . . 108 A2
Hohenlockstedt D . . 64 C2
Hohenmölsen D . . . 83 A4
Hohennauen D . . . . 73 B5
Hohen Neuendorf D 74 B2
Hohenseeden D . . . 73 B5
Hohentauern A . . . .110 B1
Hohentengen D . . 106 B3
Hohenwepel D . . . . 81 A5
Hohenwestedt D . . . 64 B2
Hohenwutzen D . . . 74 B3
Hohenzieritz D. . . . . 74 A2
Hohn D. . . . . . . . . . 64 B2
Hohne D. . . . . . . . . 72 B3
Hohnstorf D. . . . . . . 73 A3
Højer DK . . . . . . . . . 64 B1
Højslev Stby DK . . . 58 B2
Hok S . . . . . . . . . . . 62 A2
Hökerum S. . . . . . . . 60 B3
Hökhuvud S. . . . . . . 51 B5
Hokksund N. . . . . . . 53 A5
Hökön S. . . . . . . . . 63 B2
Hol N . . . . . . . . . . . 47 B5
Hólar IS . . . . . . . . 190 B6
Holašovice CZ. . . . . 96 C2
Holbæk
  Aarhus Amt. DK. . . 58 B3
  Vestsjællands Amt.
  DK . . . . . . . . . . . 61 D1
Holbeach GB . . . . . 41 C4
Holdenstedt D . . . . . 73 B3
Holdhus N . . . . . . . 46 B2
Holeby DK. . . . . . . . 65 B4
Hølen N . . . . . . . . . 54 A1
Hølervasseter N . . . 47 B6
Holešov CZ . . . . . . . 98 B1
Holguera E. . . . . . . 155 B4
Holíč SK. . . . . . . . . . 98 C1
Holice
  CZ. . . . . . . . . . . .97 A3
  SK. . . . . . . . . . . 111 B4
Höljes S . . . . . . . . . 49 B4
Hollabrunn A . . . . . . 97 C4
Hollandstoun GB . . 33 B4
Høllen N . . . . . . . . . 53 B3
Hollfeld D. . . . . . . . 95 B3
Hollókő H . . . . . . . .112 B3
Hollstadt D. . . . . . . . 82 B2
Hollum NL . . . . . . . . 70 A2
Hölliviksnäs S . . . . . 66 A1
Holm N . . . . . . . . . 195 E3
Hólmavík IS. . . . . . 190 B4
Holmbukt N . . . . . . 192 B5
Holmedal S . . . . . . . 54 A2
Holmegil N. . . . . . . . 54 A2
Holmen N . . . . . . . . 48 B2
Holme-on-Spalding-
  Moor GB. . . . . . . 40 B3
Holmes Chapel GB . 38 A4
Holmestrand N . . . . 54 A1
Holmfirth GB . . . . . . 40 B2
Holmfoss N . . . . . 193 C14
Holmsbu N . . . . . . . 54 A1
Holmsjö S . . . . . . . . 63 B3
Holmsund S . . . . . 200 C6
Holmsveden S . . . . . 50 A3
Holmudden S . . . . . 57 C5
Holø S . . . . . . . . . . 57 A3
Holøydal N . . . . . . 199 C8
Holsbybrunn S . . . . 62 A3
Holseter N . . . . . . . 48 A1
Holsljunga S . . . . . . 60 B2
Holstebro DK . . . . . 59 B1
Holsted DK . . . . . . . 59 C1
Holsworthy GB . . . . 42 B2
Holt
  D. . . . . . . . . . . . .64 B2
  Norfolk GB. . . . . . .41 C5
  Wrexham GB. . . . . .38 A4
  IS . . . . . . . . . . . 190 D6
  N . . . . . . . . . . . . .53 B4
Holten NL. . . . . . . . . 71 B3
Holtwick D . . . . . . . . 71 B4
Holum N . . . . . . . . . 52 B3
Holwerd NL . . . . . . . 70 A2
Holycross IRL . . . . . 29 B4
Holyhead GB. . . . . . 38 A2
Holýsov CZ . . . . . . . 95 B5
Holywell GB. . . . . . . 38 A3
Holywood GB . . . . . 27 B5
Holzdorf D . . . . . . . . 83 A5
Holzhausen D . . . . . 72 B1
Holzheim D . . . . . . . 94 C2
Holzkirchen D . . . . 108 B2
Holzminden D . . . . . 81 A5
Holzthaleben D . . . . 82 A2
Homberg
  Hessen D. . . . . . . 81 A5
  Hessen D. . . . . . . 81 B5
Homburg D . . . . . . . 93 B3
Hommelstø N . . . . 195 E3
Hommersåk N. . . . . 52 B1
Homokmegy H . . . . 112 C3
Homokszentgyörgy
  H . . . . . . . . . . . 124 A3

Homyel = Gomel BY 13 B9
Honaz TR. . . . . . . . 188 B4
Hondarribia E . . . . 144 A2
Hondón de los Frailes
  E. . . . . . . . . . . . 165 A4
Hondschoote F . . . . 78 B2
Hönebach D. . . . . . . 82 B1
Hönefoss N . . . . . . . 48 B2
Honfleur F . . . . . . . . 89 A4
Høng DK . . . . . . . . . 61 D1
Honiton GB . . . . . . . 43 B3
Hönningen D . . . . . . 80 B2
Honningsvåg N . . . 193 B9
Hönö S . . . . . . . . . . 60 B1
Honrubia E . . . . . . 158 B1
Hontalbilla E . . . . . 151 A3
Hontheim D . . . . . . . 92 A2
Hontianske Nemce
  SK . . . . . . . . . . . 98 C2
Hontoria de la Cantera
  E. . . . . . . . . . . . 143 B3
Hontoria del Pinar
  E. . . . . . . . . . . . 143 C3
Hontoria de Valdearados
  E. . . . . . . . . . . . 143 C3
Hoofddorp NL. . . . . 70 B1
Hoogerheide NL . . . 79 A4
Hoogeveen NL. . . . . 71 B3
Hoogezand-Sappemeer
  NL. . . . . . . . . . . . 71 A3
Hoogkarspel NL. . . . 70 B2
Hoogkerk NL. . . . . . 71 A3
Hoogstede D . . . . . . 71 B3
Hoogstraten B. . . . . 79 A4
Hook GB . . . . . . . . . 44 B3
Hooksiel D. . . . . . . . 71 A5
Höör S . . . . . . . . . . 61 D3
Hoorn NL . . . . . . . . 70 B2
Hope GB . . . . . . . . . 38 A3
Hopen N. . . . . . . . . 194 C6
Hope under Dinmore
  GB . . . . . . . . . . . 39 B4
Hopfgarten A . . . . . 108 B3
Hopfgarten in
  Defereggen A . . . 109 C3
Hopseidet N. . . . . .193 B11
Hopsten D . . . . . . . . 71 B4
Hoptrup DK . . . . . . . 59 C2
Hora Svatého
  Sebestiána CZ . . . 83 B5
Horaždóvice CZ . . . 96 B1
Horb am Neckar D. . 93 C4
Horbelev DK . . . . . . 65 B5
Hørby DK. . . . . . . . . 58 A3
Hörby S . . . . . . . . . 61 D3
Horcajada de la Torre
  E. . . . . . . . . . . . 158 A1
Horcajo de los Montes
  E. . . . . . . . . . . . 156 A3
Horcajo de Santiago
  E. . . . . . . . . . . . 151 C4
Horcajo-Medianero
  E. . . . . . . . . . . . 150 B2
Horche E . . . . . . . . 151 B4
Horda S . . . . . . . . . 62 A2
Hordabø N . . . . . . . 46 B1
Hordalia N . . . . . . . 52 A2
Hordvik N. . . . . . . . . 46 B2
Hořesedly CZ . . . . . 83 B5
Horezu RO. . . . . . . . 17 C6
Horgen CH. . . . . . . 107 B3
Horgoš SRB. . . . . . 126 A1
Horia RO. . . . . . . . 126 A3
Hořice CZ. . . . . . . . . 84 B3
Horjul SLO. . . . . . . 123 A3
Horka D. . . . . . . . . . 84 A2
Hörken S . . . . . . . . . 50 B1
Horki BY. . . . . . . . . 13 A9
Hörle S. . . . . . . . . . 60 B4
Horn
  A. . . . . . . . . . . . .97 C3
  D. . . . . . . . . . . . .81 A4
  S. . . . . . . . . . . . .62 A3
Horna E . . . . . . . . 158 C2
Hornachos E . . . . . 156 B1
Hornachuelos E . . . 162 A2
Horná Mariková SK. 98 B2
Hornanes N . . . . . . 46 C2
Horná Streda SK. . . 98 C1
Horná Štrubna SK. . 98 C2
Horná Súča SK. . . . 98 C1
Hornbæk
  Aarhus Amt. DK. . . 58 B2
  Frederiksværk DK . 61 C2
Hornberg D . . . . . . 106 A3
Hornburg D . . . . . . . 73 B3
Horncastle GB. . . . . 41 B3
Horndal S. . . . . . . . 50 B3
Horndean GB. . . . . . 44 C2
Horne
  Fyns Amt. DK. . . . .64 A3
  Ribe Amt. DK. . . . .59 C1
Hornebo S. . . . . . . 55 B5
Horneburg D . . . . . . 72 A2
Hörnefors S. . . . . . 200 C5
Horní Bečva CZ. . . . 98 B2
Horní Benešov CZ. . 98 B1
Horní Cerekev CZ . . 97 B3
Horní Jiřetín CZ. . . . 83 B5
Horní Lomná CZ . . . 98 B2
Horní Maršov CZ. . . 85 B3
Horní Planá CZ . . . . 96 C2
Horní Slavkov CZ . . 83 B4
Horní Vltavice CZ . . 96 C1

Hornnes N . . . . . . . 53 B3
Horno D . . . . . . . . . 84 A2
Hornos E . . . . . . . . 164 A2
Hornoy-le-Bourg F . 90 B1
Hornsea GB. . . . . . . 41 B3
Hornsjø N . . . . . . . . 48 A2
Hornslet DK . . . . . . . 59 B3
Hornstein A . . . . . . .111 B3
Hörnum D . . . . . . . . 64 B1
Hornum DK . . . . . . . 58 B2
Horný Tisovnik SK . 99 C3
Horodenka UA. . . . . 13 D6
Horodnya UA. . . . . . 13 C9
Horodok
  Khmelnytskyy UA. . .13 D7
  Lviv UA. . . . . . . .13 D5
Horokhiv UA. . . . . . 13 C6
Horrabridge GB . . . 42 B2
Horred S . . . . . . . . . 60 B2
Hörröd S . . . . . . . . . 61 D4
Hörsching A. . . . . . .110 A1
Horsens DK . . . . . . . 59 C2
Horsham GB . . . . . . 44 B3
Hørsholm DK. . . . . . 61 D2
Horslunde DK. . . . . 65 B4
Horšovský Týn CZ . . 95 B4
Horst NL. . . . . . . . . . 80 A2
Horstel D . . . . . . . . 71 B4
Horsten D. . . . . . . . . 71 A4
Horstmar D . . . . . . . 71 B4
Hort H. . . . . . . . . . .113 B3
Horta P. . . . . . . . . . 148 A2
Hortezuela E . . . . . 151 A5
Hortiguela E . . . . . . 143 B3
Hortobágy H . . . . . .113 B5
Höör S . . . . . . . . . . 61 D3
Horton in Ribblesdale
  GB . . . . . . . . . . . 37 B4
Hørve DK. . . . . . . . . 61 D1
Hörvik S . . . . . . . . . 63 B2
Horwich GB. . . . . . . 38 A4
Hosanger N . . . . . . 46 B2
Hösbach D. . . . . . . . 93 A5
Hosena D. . . . . . . . . 84 A2
Hosenfeld D. . . . . . . 81 B5
Hosingen L . . . . . . . 92 A2
Hosio FIN. . . . . . . 197 D8
Hospental CH . . . . 107 C3
Hospital IRL . . . . . . 29 B3
Hossegor F . . . . . . 128 C1
Hosszuhétény H . . 125 A4
Hostal de Ipiés E . . 145 B3
Hošťálkova CZ . . . . 98 B1
Hostalric E . . . . . . . 147 C3
Hostens F . . . . . . . 128 B2
Hostěradice CZ . . . . 97 C4
Hostinné CZ . . . . . . 85 B3
Hostomice CZ . . . . . 96 B2
Hostouň CZ . . . . . . . 95 B4
Hotagen S . . . . . . .199 B11
Hoting S . . . . . . . . 200 B2
Hotolisht AL. . . . . . 182 B2
Hotton B. . . . . . . . . 79 B5
Houdain F . . . . . . . . 78 B2
Houdan F . . . . . . . . 90 C1
Houdelaincourt F . 92 C1
Houeillès F . . . . . . 128 B3
Houffalize B. . . . . . . 92 A1
Houghton-le-Spring
  GB . . . . . . . . . . . 37 B5
Houlberg DK . . . . . . 59 B2
Houlgate F . . . . . . . 89 A3
Hounslow GB . . . . . 44 B3
Hourtin F . . . . . . . . 128 A1
Hourtin-Plage F . . . 128 A1
Houthalen B. . . . . . . 79 A5
Houyet B . . . . . . . . . 79 B4
Hov
  DK. . . . . . . . . . . . .59 C3
  N. . . . . . . . . . . . .48 B2
Hova S . . . . . . . . . . 55 B5
Høvåg N. . . . . . . . . 53 B4
Hovborg DK. . . . . . . 59 C1
Hovda N . . . . . . . . . 47 B6
Hovden N . . . . . . . . 52 A3
Hove GB. . . . . . . . . 44 C3
Hovedgård DK. . . . . 59 C2
Hovelhof D. . . . . . . . 81 A4
Hoven DK . . . . . . . . 59 C1
Hovet N . . . . . . . . . 47 B5
Hovingham GB . . . . 40 A3
Hovmantorp S. . . . . 62 B3
Hovsta S . . . . . . . . . 56 A1
Howden GB . . . . . . 40 B3
Howe D . . . . . . . . . 72 A3
Höxter D. . . . . . . . . 81 A5
Hoya D . . . . . . . . . . 72 B2
Hoya de Santa Maria
  E. . . . . . . . . . . . 161 B3
Hoya-Gonzalo E . . 158 C2
Høyanger N . . . . . . 46 A3
Hoyerswerda D. . . . 84 A2
Høyjord N. . . . . . . . . 53 A6
Hoylake GB . . . . . . 38 A3
Høylandet N. . . . . . 199 A9
Hoym D . . . . . . . . . 82 A3
Høymyr N. . . . . . . . . 47 C6
Hoyocasero E . . . . 150 B3
Hoyo de Manzanares
  E. . . . . . . . . . . . 151 B4
Hoyo de Pinares E . 150 B3
Hoyos E. . . . . . . . . 149 B3
Hoyos del Espino
  E. . . . . . . . . . . . 150 B2
Hrabušice SK. . . . . 99 C4
Hradec Králové CZ . 85 B3
Hradec nad Moravicí
  CZ . . . . . . . . . . . 98 B1

Hrádek CZ. . . . . . . . 97 C4
Hrádek nad Nisou
  CZ . . . . . . . . . . . 84 B2
Hradiště SK . . . . . . . 98 C2
Hrafnagil IS . . . . . . 191 B7
Hrafnseyri IS . . . . . 190 B2
Hranice
  Severomoravsky
  CZ . . . . . . . . . . . .98 B1
  Západočeský CZ . .83 B4
Hranovnica SK . . . . 99 C4
Hrasnica BIH . . . . . 139 B4
Hrastnik SLO. . . . . 123 A4
Hřensko CZ . . . . . . . 84 B2
Hriňová SK . . . . . . . 99 C3
Hrisoupoli GR . . . . 183 C6
Hrochov CZ. . . . . . . 97 B4
Hrochův Tynec CZ . 97 B3
Hrodna BY . . . . . . . 13 B5
Hrodzyanka BY . . . 13 B8
Hronov CZ . . . . . . . . 85 B4
Hronský Beňadik
  SK . . . . . . . . . . . 98 C2
Hrotovice CZ. . . . . . 97 B4
Hrtkovci SRB. . . . . 127 C1
Hrun IS. . . . . . . . . 190 A5
Hrušov SK. . . . . . . .112 A3
Hrušovany nad
  Jevišovkou CZ . . . 97 C4
Hřuštin SK. . . . . . . . 99 B3
Hrvaćani BIH . . . . . 124 C3
Hrvace HR . . . . . . . 138 B2
Hrymayliv UA. . . . . . 13 D7
Huben A . . . . . . . . 109 C3
Hückel-hoven D . . . 80 A2
Hückeswagen D . . . 80 A3
Hucknall GB. . . . . . . 40 B2
Hucqueliers F . . . . . 78 B1
Huddersfield GB. . . 40 B2
Huddinge S . . . . . . 57 A3
Huddunge S . . . . . . 51 B3
Hude D. . . . . . . . . . 72 A1
Hudiksvall S . . . . . 200 E3
Huélago E . . . . . . . 163 A4
Huélamo E. . . . . . . 152 B2
Huelgoat F . . . . . . 100 A2
Huelma E . . . . . . . 163 A4
Huelva E . . . . . . . . 161 B3
Huéneja E . . . . . . . 164 B2
Huércal de Almería
  E. . . . . . . . . . . . 164 C2
Huércal-Overa E . . 164 B3
Huerta de Abajo E . 143 B3
Huerta del Rey E . . 143 C3
Huerta de
  Valdecarabanos
  E. . . . . . . . . . . . 151 C4
Huertahernando E 152 B1
Huesa E . . . . . . . . 164 B1
Huesca E . . . . . . . 145 B3
Huéscar E . . . . . . . 164 B2
Huete E . . . . . . . . 151 B5
Huétor Tájar E . . . . 163 A3
Hüfingen D . . . . . . 106 B3
Hufthamar N . . . . . . 46 B2
Hugh Town GB . . . . 42 B1
Huglfing D . . . . . . . 108 B2
Huissen NL . . . . . . . 70 C2
Huittinen FIN . . . . . . 8 B3
Huizen NL . . . . . . . . 70 B2
Hulín CZ. . . . . . . . . 98 B1
Hüls D . . . . . . . . . . 80 A2
Hulsig DK. . . . . . . . 58 A3
Hulst NL. . . . . . . . . 79 A4
Hult
  S . . . . . . . . . . . . 62 A3
Hulta S . . . . . . . . . . 56 B2
Hulteby S . . . . . . . . 55 A5
Hulterstad S . . . . . . 63 B4
Hultsfred S . . . . . . . 62 A3
Humanes E . . . . . . 151 B4
Humberston GB . . . 41 B3
Humble DK. . . . . . . 65 B3
Humenné SK . . . . . 12 D4
Humilladero E . . . . 163 A3
Humlebæk DK. . . . . 61 D2
Humlum DK. . . . . . . 58 B1
Hummelsta S . . . . . 56 A2
Humpolec CZ . . . . . 97 B3
Humshaugh GB. . . . 37 A4
Hundåla N . . . . . . . 195 E3
Hundested DK. . . . . 61 D1
Hundorp N . . . . . . . 48 A1
Hundvåg N. . . . . . . 52 A1
Hundvin N . . . . . . . 46 B2
Hunedoara RO . . . . 17 C5
Hünfeld D. . . . . . . . 82 B1
Hungen D . . . . . . . . 81 B4
Hungerford GB . . . . 44 B2
Hunndalen N. . . . . . 48 B2
Hunnebostrand S . . 54 B2
Hunstanton GB . . . . 41 C4
Huntingdon GB . . . . 44 A3
Huntley GB . . . . . . . 39 C4
Huntly GB . . . . . . . . 33 D4
Hünxe D . . . . . . . . . 80 A2
Hurbanovo SK. . . . .112 B2
Hürbel D . . . . . . . . 107 A4
Hurdal N. . . . . . . . . 48 B3
Hurezani RO . . . . . . 17 C5
Hurlford GB . . . . . . . 36 A2
Hurstbourne Tarrant
  GB . . . . . . . . . . . 44 B2
Hurstpierpoint GB. . 44 C3
Hürth D . . . . . . . . . . 80 B2
Hurum N . . . . . . . . . 47 A5

Hurup DK . . . . . . . . 58 B1
Húsafell IS . . . . . 190 C5
Húsavík IS . . . . . 191 A8
Husbands Bosworth
 GB . . . . . . . . . 44 A2
Husby
 D . . . . . . . . . 64 B2
 DK . . . . . . . . . 59 B1
Husey IS . . . . . . 191 B11
Huşi RO . . . . . . . 17 B8
Husina BIH . . . . . 139 A4
Husinec CZ . . . . . . 96 B1
Husinish GB . . . . . 31 B1
Huskvarna S . . . . . 62 A2
Husnes N . . . . . . . 46 C2
Husøy N . . . . . . 194 A8
Hustad N . . . . . . 198 C4
Hüsten D . . . . . . . 81 A3
Hustopeče CZ . . . . 97 C4
Hustopeče nad Bečvou
 CZ . . . . . . . . . 98 B1
Husum
 D . . . . . . . . . 64 B2
 S . . . . . . . . . 200 C5
Husvika N . . . . . 195 E3
Huta PL . . . . . . . 75 B5
Hutovo BIH . . . . . 139 C3
Hüttenberg A . . . . 110 C1
Hüttlingen D . . . . 94 C2
Huttoft GB . . . . . 41 B4
Hutton Cranswick
 GB . . . . . . . . . 40 B3
Hüttschlag A . . . . 109 B4
Huttwil CH . . . . . 106 B2
Huy B . . . . . . . . 79 B5
Hüyük TR . . . . . . 189 B6
Hval N . . . . . . . . 48 B2
Hvåle N . . . . . . . 47 B6
Hvaler N . . . . . . . 54 A2
Hvalpsund DK . . . . 58 B2
Hvammstangi IS . . 190 B5
Hvammur IS . . . . . 190 B6
Hvanneyri IS . . . . 190 C4
Hvar HR . . . . . . 138 B2
Hvarnes N . . . . . . 53 A5
Hveragerði IS . . . 190 D4
Hvidbjerg DK . . . . 58 B1
Hvide Sande DK . . 59 C1
Hvittingfoss N . . . 53 A6
Hvolsvöllur IS . . . 190 D5
Hybe SK . . . . . . . 99 B3
Hycklinge S . . . . . 62 A3
Hydra GR . . . . . . 185 B4
Hyen N . . . . . . . 198 D2
Hyères F . . . . . . 132 B2
Hyéres Plage F . . 132 B2
Hylestad N . . . . . 52 A3
Hylke DK . . . . . . . 59 C2
Hyllestad N . . . . . 46 A2
Hyllstofta S . . . . 61 C3
Hyltebruk S . . . . . 60 B3
Hynnekleiv N . . . . 53 B4
Hythe
 Hampshire GB . . . . 44 C2
 Kent GB . . . . . . . 45 B5
Hyvinkää FIN . . . . . . 8 B4

**I**

Iam RO . . . . . . . 127 B3
Iaşi RO . . . . . . . 17 B7
Iasmos GR . . . . . 183 B7
Ibahernando E . . 156 A2
Ibarranguelua E . 143 A4
Ibbenbüren D . . . . 71 B4
Ibeas de Juarros E 143 B3
Ibestad N . . . . . 194 B8
Ibi E . . . . . . . . 159 C3
Ibiza = Eivissa E . 166 C1
İbradı TR . . . . . 189 B6
İbriktepe TR . . . 186 A1
Ibros E . . . . . . . 157 B4
İçel TR . . . . . . . 23 C8
Ichenhausen D . . . 94 C2
Ichtegem B . . . . . 78 A3
Ichtershausen D . . 82 B2
Idanha-a-Novo P . . 155 B3
Idar-Oberstein D . 93 B3
Idd N . . . . . . . . 54 A2
Idiazábal E . . . . 144 B1
Idivuoma S . . . . . 196 A4
Idkerberget S . . . 50 B2
Idön S . . . . . . . . 51 B5
Idre Š . . . . . . . 199 D9
Idrija SLO . . . . . 123 A4
Idritsa RUS . . . . . 9 D6
Idstein D . . . . . . 81 B4
Idvor SRB . . . . . 126 B2
Iecca Mare RO . . 126 B2
Ielsi I . . . . . . . 170 B2
Ieper = Ypres B . . 78 B2
Ierapetra GR . . . 185 D6
Ierissos GR . . . . 183 C5
Ifjord N . . . . . . 193 B11
Ig SLO . . . . . . . 123 B3
Igal H . . . . . . . 112 C1
Igea E . . . . . . . 144 B1
Igea Marina I . . . 136 A1
Igelfors S . . . . . 56 B1
Igersheim D . . . . . 94 B1
Iggesund S . . . . . 200 E3
Iglésias E . . . . . 143 B3
Iglésias I . . . . . 179 C2

Igls A . . . . . . . 108 B2
Igny-Comblizy F . . 91 B3
Igorre E . . . . . . 143 A4
Igoumenitsa GR . . 182 D2
Igries E . . . . . . 145 B3
Igualada E . . . . . 147 C2
Igüeña E . . . . . . 141 B4
Iguerande F . . . . 117 A4
Iharosberény H . . 124 A3
Ihl'any SK . . . . . 99 B4
Ihlienworth D . . . 64 C1
Ihringen D . . . . . 106 A2
Ihrlerstein D . . . 95 C3
İhsaniye TR . . . . 187 C5
Ii FIN . . . . . . . 197 D8
Iijärvi FIN . . . . 193 C11
Iisalmi FIN . . . . . 3 E10
IJmuiden NL . . . . 70 B1
IJsselmuiden NL . . 70 B2
IJzendijke NL . . . 79 A3
Ikast DK . . . . . . 59 B2
Ikervár H . . . . . 111 B3
Ilandža SRB . . . . 126 B2
Ilanz CH . . . . . . 107 C4
Ilava SK . . . . . . 98 C2
Iława PL . . . . . . 69 B4
il Castagno I . . . 135 B3
Ilche E . . . . . . . 145 C4
Ilchester GB . . . . 43 B4
Ilfeld D . . . . . . 82 A2
Ilfracombe GB . . . 42 A2
Ilgaz TR . . . . . . 23 A7
Ilgın TR . . . . . . 189 A6
Ílhavo P . . . . . . 148 B1
Ilica TR . . . . . . 186 C2
Ilidža BIH . . . . . 139 B4
Ilijaš BIH . . . . . 139 B4
Ilirska Bistrica
 SLO . . . . . . . . 123 B3
Ilkeston GB . . . . 40 C2
Ilkley GB . . . . . . 40 B2
Illana E . . . . . . 151 B5
Illano E . . . . . . 141 A4
Illar E . . . . . . . 164 C2
Illas E . . . . . . . 141 A5
Illats F . . . . . . 128 B2
Illertissen D . . . 94 C2
Illescas E . . . . . 151 B4
Ille-sur-Têt F . . . 146 B3
Illfurth F . . . . . 106 B2
Illichivsk UA . . . 17 B9
Illiers-Combray F . 89 B5
Illkirch-Graffenstaden
 F . . . . . . . . . 93 C3
Illmersdorf D . . . 74 C2
Illmitz A . . . . . 111 B3
Íllora E . . . . . . 163 A4
Illueca E . . . . . 152 A2
Ilmajoki FIN . . . . 8 A3
Ilmenau D . . . . . . 82 B2
Ilminster GB . . . . 43 B4
Ilok HR . . . . . . 126 B1
Iłow PL . . . . . . . 77 B5
Iłowa PL . . . . . . 84 A3
Iłowo-Osada PL . . 77 A5
Ilsenburg D . . . . 82 A2
Ilshofen D . . . . . 94 B1
Ilz A . . . . . . . . 110 B2
Iłża PL . . . . . . . 87 A5
Imatra FIN . . . . . . 9 B6
Imielin PL . . . . . 86 B3
Imingen N . . . . . . 47 B5
Immeln S . . . . . . 63 B2
Immenhausen D . . . 81 A5
Immenstadt D . . . 107 B5
Immingham GB . . . 41 B3
Ímola I . . . . . . 135 A4
Imon E . . . . . . . 151 A5
Imotski HR . . . . . 138 B3
Impéria I . . . . . 133 B4
Imphy F . . . . . . 104 C2
İmroz TR . . . . . . 183 C7
Imsland N . . . . . . 52 A1
Imst A . . . . . . . 108 B1
Inagh IRL . . . . . . 28 B2
Inari FIN . . . . . 193 D10
Inca E . . . . . . . 167 B2
Inchnadamph GB . . 32 C2
Incinillas E . . . 143 B3
Indal S . . . . . . 200 D3
Indjija SRB . . . . 127 B2
Indre Arna N . . . . 46 B2
Indre Billefjord N . 193 B9
Indre Brenna N . . 193 B9
İğneada TR . . . . 186 A2
İnebolu TR . . . . . 23 A7
İnecik TR . . . . . 186 B2
İnegöl TR . . . . . 187 B4
Inerthal CH . . . . 107 B3
Infiesto E . . . . . 142 A1
Ingatorp S . . . . . 62 A3
Ingedal N . . . . . . 54 A2
Ingelheim D . . . . 93 B4
Ingelmunster B . . 78 B3
Ingelstad S . . . . 62 B2
Ingleton GB . . . . 37 B4
Ingolfsland N . . . 47 C5
Ingolstadt D . . . . 95 C3
Ingrandes
 Maine-et-Loire F . 101 B5
 Vienne F . . . . . 102 C2
Ingwiller F . . . . 93 C3
İnhisar TR . . . . 187 B5
Iniesta E . . . . . 158 B2
Inishannon IRL . . 29 C3
Inishcrone IRL . . 26 B1
Inke H . . . . . . . 124 A3

Inndyr N . . . . . . 195 C5
Innellan GB . . . . 34 C3
Innerleithen GB . . 35 C4
Innermessan GB . . 36 B2
Innertkirchen CH . 106 C3
Innervillgraten A . 109 C3
Innset N . . . . . . 194 B9
Innvik N . . . . . . 198 D3
İnönü TR . . . . . . 187 C5
Inowłódz PL . . . . 87 A4
Inowrocław PL . . . 76 B3
Ins CH . . . . . . . 106 B2
Insch GB . . . . . . 33 D4
Insjön S . . . . . . 50 B2
Ińsko PL . . . . . . 75 A4
Instow GB . . . . . . 42 A2
İntepe TR . . . . . 186 B1
Interlaken CH . . . 106 C2
Intragna CH . . . . 120 A1
Introbio I . . . . . 120 B2
Inveran
 GB . . . . . . . . . 32 D2
 IRL . . . . . . . . 28 A2
Inveraray GB . . . . 34 B2
Inverbervie GB . . 35 B5
Invergarry GB . . . 32 D2
Invergordon GB . . 32 D2
Invergowrie GB . . 35 B4
Inverkeilor GB . . 35 B5
Inverkeithing GB . 35 B4
Invermoriston GB . 32 D2
Inverness GB . . . . 32 D2
Inveruno I . . . . . 120 B1
Inverurie GB . . . . 33 D4
Ioannina GR . . . . 182 D2
Iolanda di Savoia I 121 C4
Ion Corvin RO . . . 17 C7
Ióppolo I . . . . . 175 C1
Ios GR . . . . . . . 185 C6
Ipati GR . . . . . . 182 E4
İpsala TR . . . . . 186 B1
Ipswich GB . . . . . 45 A5
Iraklia GR . . . . . 183 B5
Iraklio = Heraklion
 GR . . . . . . . . 185 D6
Irdning A . . . . . 110 B1
Iregszemcse H . . 112 C2
Irgoli I . . . . . . 178 B3
İrig SRB . . . . . . 127 B1
Ironbridge GB . . . 39 B4
Irpin UA . . . . . . 13 C9
Irrel D . . . . . . . 92 B2
Irsina I . . . . . . 172 B2
Irsta S . . . . . . . 56 A2
Irthlingborough GB 44 A3
Iruela E . . . . . . 141 B4
Irún E . . . . . . . 144 A2
Irurita E . . . . . 144 A2
Irurzun E . . . . . 144 B2
Irvine GB . . . . . . 36 A2
Irvinestown GB . . 27 B3
Isaba E . . . . . . 144 B3
Isabela E . . . . . 157 B4
Ísafjörður IS . . . 190 A2
Isane N . . . . . . 198 D2
Isaszeg H . . . . . 112 B3
Isbister GB . . . . 33 A5
İscar E . . . . . . 150 A3
İscehisar TR . . . 187 D5
İschgl A . . . . . . 107 B5
İschia I . . . . . . 170 C1
Ischia di Castro I . 168 A1
Ischitella I . . . 171 B3
Isdes F . . . . . . 103 B4
Ise N . . . . . . . . 54 A2
Iselle I . . . . . . 119 A5
Iseltwald CH . . . 106 C2
Isen D . . . . . . . 108 A3
Isenbüttel D . . . . 73 B3
Iseo I . . . . . . . 120 B3
Iserlohn D . . . . . 81 A3
Isérnia I . . . . . 170 B2
Isfjorden N . . . . 198 C4
İshëm AL . . . . . . 182 B1
Isigny-sur-Mer F . 88 A2
Işıklı TR . . . . . 189 A4
İsili I . . . . . . 179 C3
İskilip TR . . . . . 23 A8
İsla Canela E . . . 161 B2
Isla Cristina E . . 161 B2
Islares E . . . . . 143 A3
Isleham GB . . . . . 45 A4
Isle of Whithorn GB 36 B2
Ismaning D . . . . 108 A2
Isna P . . . . . . . 154 B3
Isnestoften N . . . 192 B6
Isny D . . . . . . . 107 B5
Isoba E . . . . . . 142 A1
Isokylä
 FIN . . . . . . . 197 C10
 S . . . . . . . . . 196 B5
Isola F . . . . . . 132 A3
Isola d'Asti I . . 119 C5
Isola del Gran Sasso
 d'Itália I . . . 169 A3
Ísola della Scala I 121 B4
Isola delle Fémmine
 I . . . . . . . . . 176 A2
Ísola del Liri I . 169 B3
Ísola di Capo Rizzuto
 I . . . . . . . . . 175 C3
Isona E . . . . . . 147 B2
Ispagnac F . . . . 130 A2
İsparta TR . . . . 189 B5
Isperikh BG . . . . 17 D7
İspica I . . . . . . 177 C3

Isselburg D . . . . 80 A2
Issigeac F . . . . 129 B3
Issogne I . . . . . 119 B4
Issoire F . . . . . 116 B3
Issoncourt F . . . 91 C5
Issoudun F . . . . 103 C4
Issum D . . . . . . 80 A2
Is-sur-Tille F . . 105 B4
Issy-l'Evêque F . 104 C2
İstán E . . . . . . 162 B3
İstanbul TR . . . . 186 A3
Istebna PL . . . . . 98 B2
Ístia d'Ombrone I . 135 C4
Istiea GR . . . . . 183 E5
Istres F . . . . . . 131 B3
Istvándi H . . . . 125 A3
Itea GR . . . . . . 184 A3
Ithaki GR . . . . . 184 A1
Itoiz E . . . . . . 144 B2
Ítrabo E . . . . . . 163 B4
Itri I . . . . . . . 169 B3
Ittireddu I . . . . 178 B2
Íttiri I . . . . . . 178 B2
Itzehoe D . . . . . 64 C2
Ivalo FIN . . . . . 193 D11
Ivan H . . . . . . . 111 B3
Ivanava BY . . . . . 13 B6
Ivančice CZ . . . . 97 B4
Ivančna Gorica
 SLO . . . . . . . 123 B3
Ivanec HR . . . . . 124 A2
Ivanić Grad HR . . 124 B2
Ivanjska BIH . . . 124 C3
Ivanka SK . . . . . 98 C2
Ivankovo HR . . . . 125 B4
Ivano-Frankivsk UA 13 D6
Ivanovice na Hané
 CZ . . . . . . . . 98 B1
Ivanska HR . . . . 124 B2
Ivatsevichy BY . . 13 B6
Ivaylovgrad BG . . 183 B8
Iveland N . . . . . 53 B3
Ivoz Ramet F . . . 79 B5
Ivrea I . . . . . . 119 B4
İvrindi TR . . . . 186 C2
Ivry-en-Montagne
 F . . . . . . . . . 104 B3
Ivry-la-Bataille F . 90 C1
Ivybridge GB . . . . 42 B3
Izarra E . . . . . . 143 B4
Izbica Kujawska PL 76 B3
Izbište SRB . . . . 127 B3
Izeda P . . . . . . 149 A3
Izegem B . . . . . . 78 B3
Izernore F . . . . 118 A2
Izmayil UA . . . . . 17 C8
İzmir TR . . . . . . 188 A2
İzmit = Kocaeli TR 187 B4
İznájar E . . . . . 163 A3
İznalloz E . . . . 163 A4
İznatoraf E . . . . 164 A1
İznik TR . . . . . . 187 B4
Izola SLO . . . . . 122 B2
Izsák H . . . . . . 112 C3
Izsófalva H . . . . 99 C4
Izyaslav UA . . . . 13 C7

**J**

Jabalquinto E . . 157 B4
Jablanac HR . . . . 123 C3
Jablanica BIH . . 139 B3
Jablonec nad Jizerou
 CZ . . . . . . . . 84 B3
Jablonec nad Nisou
 CZ . . . . . . . . 84 B3
Jablonica SK . . . 98 C1
Jablonka PL . . . . 99 B3
Jabłonna PL . . . . 77 B5
Jablonné nad Orlicí
 CZ . . . . . . . . 97 A4
Jablonne Podještědi
 CZ . . . . . . . . 84 B2
Jablonov nad Turňou
 SK . . . . . . . . 99 C4
Jabłonowo Pomorskie
 PL . . . . . . . . 69 B4
Jablúnka CZ . . . . 98 B1
Jablunkov CZ . . . 98 B2
Jabučje SRB . . . . 127 C2
Jabugo E . . . . . 161 B3
Jabuka SRB . . . . 127 C2
Jabukovac HR . . . 124 D2
Jaca E . . . . . . . 145 B3
Jáchymov CZ . . . . 83 B4
Jacobidrebber D . 72 B1
Jade D . . . . . . . 71 A5
Jäderfors S . . . . 50 B3
Jädraås S . . . . . 50 B3
Jadraque E . . . . 151 B5
Jaén E . . . . . . . 163 A4
Jagare BIH . . . . 124 C3
Jagel D . . . . . . 64 B2
Jagenbach A . . . . 96 C3
Jægerspris DK . . 61 D1
Jagodina SRB . . . 127 D3
Jagodnjak HR . . . 125 B4
Jagodzin PL . . . . 84 A3
Jagstheim D . . . . 94 B2
Jagstzell D . . . . 94 B2
Jahodna SK . . . . 111 A4
Jajce BIH . . . . . 138 A3
Ják H . . . . . . . 111 B3
Jakabszálbs H . . 112 C3
Jäkkvik S . . . . . 195 D8
Jakobsnes N . . . . 193 C14
Jakovlje HR . . . . 124 B1
Jakšic HR . . . . . 125 B3
Jakubany SK . . . . 99 B4
Jalance E . . . . . 159 B2
Jalasjärvi FIN . . . 8 A3
Jalhay B . . . . . . 80 B1
Jaligny-sur-Besbre
 F . . . . . . . . . 117 A3
Jallais F . . . . . 102 B1
Jalón E . . . . . . 159 C3
Jâlons F . . . . . . 91 C4
Jamena SRB . . . . 125 C5
Jamilena E . . . . 163 A4
Jämjö S . . . . . . 63 B3
Jamnička Kiselica
 HR . . . . . . . . 124 B1
Jamno PL . . . . . . 67 B5
Jamu Mare RO . . . 126 B3
Janakkala FIN . . . 8 B4
Jandelsbrunn D . . 96 C1
Jänickendorf D . . 74 B2
Janikowo PL . . . . 76 B3
Janja BIH . . . . . 125 C5
Janjina HR . . . . 138 C3
Janki
 Łódzkie PL . . . . 86 A3
 Mazowieckie PL . . 77 B5
Jankov CZ . . . . . 96 B2
Jankowo Dolne PL . 76 B2
Jánoshalma H . . . 126 A1
Jánosháza H . . . . 111 B4
Jánoshida H . . . . 113 B4
Jánossomorja H . . 111 B4
Janovice nad Uhlavou
 CZ . . . . . . . . 96 B1
Janów PL . . . . . . 86 B3
Janowiec Wielkopolski
 PL . . . . . . . . 76 B2
Janowo PL . . . . . 77 A5
Jänsmässholmen
 S . . . . . . . . . 199 B10
Janville F . . . . 103 A3
Janzé F . . . . . . 101 B4
Jarabá SK . . . . . 99 C3
Jaraczewo PL . . . 76 C2
Jarafuel E . . . . 159 B2
Jaraicejo E . . . . 156 A2
Jaráiz de la Vera E 150 B2
Jarak SRB . . . . . 127 C1
Jarandilla de la Vera
 E . . . . . . . . . 150 B2
Jaray E . . . . . . 152 A1
Järbo S . . . . . . 50 B3
Jard-sur-Mer F . . 114 B2
Jaren N . . . . . . 48 B2
Jargeau F . . . . . 103 B4
Jarkovac SRB . . . 126 B2
Järlåsa S . . . . . 51 C4
Jarmen D . . . . . . 66 C2
Järna
 D . . . . . . . . . 57 A3
 S . . . . . . . . . 200 C5
Jarnac F . . . . . . 115 C3
Jarny F . . . . . . 92 B1
Jarocin PL . . . . . 76 C2
Jaroměř CZ . . . . . 85 B3
Jaroměřice nad
 Rokytnou CZ . . . 97 B3
Jaroslav CZ . . . . 97 A4
Jaroslavice CZ . . 97 C4
Jarosław PL . . . . 12 C5
Jaroslawiec PL . . 68 A1
Jarošov nad Nežárkou
 CZ . . . . . . . . 96 B3
Järpås S . . . . . . 55 B3
Järpen S . . . . . . 199 B10
Jarrow GB . . . . . 37 B5
Järso FIN . . . . . 51 B6
Järvenpää FIN . . . 8 B4
Jarvornik CZ . . . 85 B4
Järvsö S . . . . . . 200 E2
Jarzé F . . . . . . 102 B1
Jaša Tomic SRB . . 126 B2
Jasenak HR . . . . 123 B4
Jasenica BIH . . . 124 C2
Jasenice HR . . . . 137 A4
Jasenovac HR . . . 124 B2
Jasenovo SRB . . . 127 C3
Jasień PL . . . . . 84 A3
Jasienica PL . . . 84 A2
Jasło PL . . . . . . 12 D4
Jásova SK . . . . . 112 B2
Jasseron F . . . . 118 A2
Jastarnia PL . . . 69 A3
Jastrebarsko HR . 123 B4
Jastrowie PL . . . 68 B1
Jastrzębia-Góra PL 68 A3
Jastrzębie Zdrój PL 98 B2
Jászals-Lószentgyörgy
 H . . . . . . . . . 113 B4
Jászapáti H . . . . 113 B4
Jászárokszállás
 H . . . . . . . . . 113 B4
Jászberény H . . . 113 B4
Jászdózsa H . . . . 113 B4
Jászfényszaru H . 113 B4
Jászkarajenő H . . 113 B4
Jászkisér H . . . . 113 B4
Jászladány H . . . 113 B4
Jászszentlászló H . 113 C3

Jásztelek H . . . . 113 B4
Játar E . . . . . . 163 B4
Jättendal S . . . . 200 E3
Jatznick D . . . . . 74 A2
Jaun CH . . . . . . 106 C2
Jausiers F . . . . 132 A2
Jávea E . . . . . . 159 C4
Jävenitz D . . . . . 73 B4
Javerlhac F . . . . 115 C4
Javier E . . . . . . 144 B2
Javorani BIH . . . 124 C3
Javorina SK . . . . 99 B4
Javron F . . . . . . 89 B3
Jawor PL . . . . . . 85 A4
Jaworzno PL . . . . 86 B3
Jaworzyna Śl. PL . 85 B4
Jayena E . . . . . . 163 B4
Jażów PL . . . . . . 84 A2
Jebel RO . . . . . . 126 B3
Jebjerg DK . . . . . 58 B2
Jedburgh GB . . . . 35 C5
Jedlinsk PL . . . . 87 A5
Jedlnia PL . . . . . 87 A5
Jedlnia Letnisko PL 87 A5
Jednorożec PL . . . 77 A6
Jedovnice CZ . . . 97 B4
Jędrychow PL . . . 69 B4
Jędrzejów PL . . . 87 B4
Jedwabno PL . . . . 77 A5
Jeesiö FIN . . . . . 197 B9
Jegłownik PL . . . 69 A4
Jegun F . . . . . . 129 C3
Jēkabpils LV . . . . 8 D4
Jektevik N . . . . . 46 C2
Jektvik N . . . . . 195 D4
Jelcz-Laskowice PL 85 A5
Jelenec SK . . . . . 98 C2
Jelenia Góra PL . . 85 B3
Jelgava LV . . . . . 8 D3
Jelka SK . . . . . . 111 A4
Jelling DK . . . . . 59 C2
Jels DK . . . . . . 59 C2
Jelsa
 HR . . . . . . . . 138 B2
 N . . . . . . . . . 52 A2
Jelšava SK . . . . . 99 C4
Jemgum D . . . . . . 71 A4
Jemnice CZ . . . . . 97 B3
Jena D . . . . . . . 82 B3
Jenaz CH . . . . . . 107 C4
Jenbach A . . . . . 108 B2
Jenikow PL . . . . . 75 A4
Jennersdorf A . . . 111 C3
Jenny S . . . . . . 62 A4
Jerchel D . . . . . 73 B4
Jeres del Marquesado
 E . . . . . . . . . 164 B1
Jerez de la Frontera
 E . . . . . . . . . 162 B1
Jerez de los Caballeros
 E . . . . . . . . . 155 C4
Jerica E . . . . . . 159 B3
Jerichow D . . . . . 73 B5
Jerka PL . . . . . . 75 B5
Jermenovci SRB . . 126 B3
Jerslev DK . . . . . 58 A3
Jerte E . . . . . . 150 B2
Jerup DK . . . . . . 58 A3
Jerxheim D . . . . . 73 B3
Jerzmanowice PL . . 87 B3
Jerzu I . . . . . . 179 C3
Jerzwałd PL . . . . 69 B4
Jesberg D . . . . . 81 B5
Jesenice
 Středočeský CZ . . 83 B5
 Středočeský CZ . . 96 B2
 SLO . . . . . . . 109 C5
Jeseník CZ . . . . . 85 B5
Jesenké SK . . . . . 99 C4
Jesi I . . . . . . . 136 B2
Jésolo I . . . . . . 122 B1
Jessen D . . . . . . 83 A4
Jessenitz D . . . . 73 A4
Jessheim N . . . . . 48 B3
Jessnitz D . . . . . 83 A4
Jesteburg D . . . . 72 A2
Jeumont F . . . . . 79 B4
Jeven-stedt D . . . 64 B2
Jever D . . . . . . 71 A4
Jevičko CZ . . . . . 97 B4
Jevišovice CZ . . . 97 C3
Jevnaker N . . . . . 48 B2
Jezerane HR . . . . 123 B4
Jezero
 BIH . . . . . . . 138 A3
 HR . . . . . . . . 123 B4
Jeżów PL . . . . . . 87 A3
Jičín CZ . . . . . . 84 B3
Jičiněves CZ . . . 84 B3
Jihlava CZ . . . . . 97 B3
Jijona E . . . . . . 159 C3
Jilemnice CZ . . . 84 B3
Jílové CZ . . . . . 84 B2
Jílové Prahy CZ . . 96 B2
Jimbolia RO . . . . 126 B2
Jimena E . . . . . . 163 A4
Jimena de la Frontera
 E . . . . . . . . . 162 B2
Jimera de Libar E . 162 B2
Jimramov CZ . . . . 97 B4
Jince CZ . . . . . . 96 B1
Jindřichovice CZ . 83 B4
Jindřichův Hradec
 CZ . . . . . . . . 96 B3
Jirkov CZ . . . . . 83 B5
Jistebnice CZ . . . 96 B2
Joachimsthal D . . 74 B2
João da Loura P . 154 C2

Jobbágyi H . . . . . .112 B3
Jochberg A . . . . . . 109 B3
Jockfall S. . . . . . . 196 C5
Jódar E . . . . . . . . . 163 A4
Jodoigne B . . . . . . . 79 B4
Joensuu FIN . . . . . . 9 A6
Joesjö S. . . . . . . . 195 E5
Joeuf F. . . . . . . . . . 92 B1
Jõgeva EST . . . . . . 8 C5
Johanngeorgenstadt
D . . . . . . . . . . . . 83 B4
Johannishus S . . . . . 63 B3
Johanniskirchen D . . 95 C4
Johansfors S. . . . . . 63 B3
John o'Groats GB . . 32 C5
Johnshaven GB . . . 35 B5
Johnstone GB . . . . 34 C3
Johnstown IRI . . . . 30 B1
Jõhvi EST . . . . . . . . 8 C5
Joigny F. . . . . . . . . 104 B2
Joinville F . . . . . . . 91 C5
Jokkmokk S. . . . . . 196 C2
Jöllenbeck D . . . . . 72 B1
Jomala FIN . . . . . . . 51 B6
Jönåker S . . . . . . . 56 B2
Jonava LT . . . . . . . 13 A6
Jonchery-sur-Vesle
F. . . . . . . . . . . . . 91 B3
Jondal N . . . . . . . . 46 B3
Jondalen N . . . . . . 53 A5
Joniškis LT . . . . . . . 8 D3
Jönköping S . . . . . . 62 A2
Jonkowo PL. . . . . . 69 B5
Jønnbu N . . . . . . . 53 A5
Jonsberg S . . . . . . 56 B2
Jonsered S . . . . . . 60 B2
Jonstorp S. . . . . . . 61 C2
Jonzac F . . . . . . . 114 C3
Jorba E . . . . . . . . 147 C2
Jordanów PL. . . . . . 99 B3
Jordanowo PL . . . . 75 B4
Jordanów Ślaski PL 85 B4
Jordbro S. . . . . . . . 57 A4
Jordbrua N . . . . . . 195 D5
Jördenstorf D . . . . . 66 C1
Jordet N. . . . . . . . . 49 A4
Jordøse DK . . . . . . 59 C3
Jork D . . . . . . . . . . 72 A2
Jörlanda S. . . . . . . 60 B1
Jormlien S . . . . . . 199 A10
Jormvattnet S . . . .199 A11
Jörn S . . . . . . . . . 200 A6
Jørpeland N . . . . . . 52 A2
Jorquera E. . . . . . . 158 B2
Jošan HR. . . . . . . . 123 C4
Jošavka BIH . . . . . 124 C3
Josipdol HR. . . . . . 123 B4
Josipovac HR . . . . 125 B4
Jössefors S. . . . . . . 54 A3
Josselin F . . . . . . . 101 B3
Jøssund N . . . . . . 199 A7
Jostedal N . . . . . . . 47 A4
Jósvafö H . . . . . . . . 99 C4
Jou P . . . . . . . . . . 148 A2
Jouarre F . . . . . . . . 90 C3
Joué-lès-Tours F. . . 102 B2
Joué-sur-Erdre F. . . 101 B4
Joure NL . . . . . . . . 70 B2
Joutseno FIN. . . . . . 9 B6
Joutsijärvi FIN. . . . 197 C10
Joux-la-Ville F . . . . 104 B2
Jouy F . . . . . . . . . . 90 C1
Jouy-le-Châtel F . . . 90 C3
Jouy-le-Potier F . . . 103 B3
Joyeuse F . . . . . . . 131 A3
Jozo F . . . . . . . . . 116 B2
Juankoski FIN . . . . . 8 A6
Juan-les-Pins F . . . 132 B3
Jübek D. . . . . . . . . 64 B2
Jubera E . . . . . . . . 144 B1
Jubrique E . . . . . . . 162 B2
Jüchsen D . . . . . . . 82 B2
Judaberg N . . . . . . 52 A1
Judenburg A . . . . . 110 B1
Juelsminde DK . . . . 59 C3
Jugon-les-Lacs F . . 101 A3
Juillac F . . . . . . . . 129 A4
Juillan F . . . . . . . . 145 A4
Juist D . . . . . . . . . 71 A4
Jukkasjärvi S. . . . . 196 B3
Jule N. . . . . . . . . . 199 A10
Julianadorp NL . . . . 70 B1
Julianstown IRL . . . 30 A2
Jülich D . . . . . . . . . 80 B2
Jullouville F. . . . . . . 88 B2
Jumeaux F. . . . . . . 117 B3
Jumièges F . . . . . . 89 A4
Jumilhac-le-Grand
F. . . . . . . . . . . . 115 C5
Jumilla E . . . . . . . . 159 C2
Jumisko FIN . . . . . 197 C11
Juncosa E . . . . . . 153 A4
Juneda E . . . . . . . 147 C1
Jung S . . . . . . . . . 55 B4
Jungingen D . . . . . 93 C5
Junglingster L. . . . . 92 B2
Juniville F . . . . . . . 91 B4
Junosuando S. . . . 196 B5
Junqueira P. . . . . . 149 A2
Junsele S. . . . . . . 200 C2
Juoksengi S . . . . . 196 C6
Juoksenki FIN . . . . 196 C6
Juprelle B . . . . . . . 80 B1
Jurata PL . . . . . . . . 69 A3
Jurbarkas LT . . . . . 12 A5
Jurjevo HR. . . . . . . 123 C3
Jūrmala LV. . . . . . . . 8 D3
Jurmu FIN . . . . . . 197 D10

Juromenha P. . . . . 155 C3
Jursla S . . . . . . . . 56 B2
Jussac F . . . . . . . 116 C2
Jussey F . . . . . . . 105 B4
Jussy F . . . . . . . . 90 B3
Juta H . . . . . . . . . 125 A3
Jüterbog D. . . . . . . 74 C2
Juuka FIN . . . . . . . 3 E11
Juuma FIN . . . . . . 197 C12
Juvigny-le-Terte F. . 88 B2
Juvigny-sous-Andaine
F. . . . . . . . . . . . . 89 B3
Juzennecourt F. . . . 105 A3
Jyderup DK . . . . . . 61 D1
Jyrkänkoski FIN . 197 C12
Jyväskylä FIN . . . . . 8 A4

### K

Kaamanen FIN. . . 193 C11
Kaamasmukka
FIN. . . . . . . . . . 193 C10
Kaaresuvanto FIN. 192 D6
Kaarssen D . . . . . . 73 A4
Kaatscheuvel NL. . 79 A5
Kaba H . . . . . . . . .113 B5
Kåbdalis S . . . . . . 196 C3
Kačarevo SRB. . . . 127 C2
Kács H . . . . . . . . .113 B4
Kadaň CZ. . . . . . . 83 B5
Kadarkút H . . . . . . 125 A3
Kadınhanı TR. . . . . 189 A7
Kaduy RUS . . . . . . 9 C10
Káfalla S . . . . . . . . 56 A1
Kåfjord N . . . . . . . 192 C7
Kåfjordbotn N . . . . 192 C4
Kågeröd S . . . . . . . 61 D3
Kahl D . . . . . . . . . . 93 A5
Kahla D . . . . . . . . . 82 B3
Kainach bei Voitsberg
A. . . . . . . . . . . . .110 B2
Kaindorf A . . . . . . .110 B2
Kainulasjärvi S . . . 196 C5
Kairala FIN. . . . . . 197 B10
Kaisepakte S . . . . 192 D3
Kaisersesch D. . . . 80 B3
Kaiserslautern D. . . 93 B3
Kaisheim D . . . . . . 94 C2
Kajaani FIN . . . . . . 3 D10
Kajárpéc H . . . . . . .111 B4
Kajdacs H . . . . . . . 112 C2
Kakanj BIH. . . . . . . 139 A4
Kakasd H . . . . . . . 125 A4
Kaklik TR. . . . . . . . 189 B4
Kakolewo PL. . . . . . 85 A4
Kál H . . . . . . . . . . .113 B4
Kalajoki FIN. . . . . . . 3 D8
Kalak N. . . . . . . . .193 B11
Kalamata GR. . . . . 184 B3
Kalambaka GR . . . 182 D3
Kalamria GR . . . . . 182 C4
Kalandra GR . . . . . 183 D5
Kälarne S . . . . . . . 200 D2
Kalavrita GR . . . . . 184 A3
Kalbe D . . . . . . . . . 73 B4
Kalce SLO . . . . . . 123 B3
Káld H . . . . . . . . . .111 B4
Kale
Antalya TR. . . . . .189 C4
Denizli TR. . . . . . 188 B3
Kalecik TR. . . . . . . 23 A7
Kalefeld D . . . . . . . 82 A2
Kalesija BIH. . . . . . 139 A4
Kalety PL. . . . . . . . 86 B2
Kalevala RUS . . . . 3 D12
Kalí HR. . . . . . . . . . 137 A4
Kalimnos GR. . . . . 188 C2
Kaliningrad RUS . . 69 A5
Kalinkavichy BY . . 13 B8
Kalinovac HR . . . . 124 A3
Kalinovik BIH. . . . . 139 B4
Kalinovo SK. . . . . . 99 C3
Kaliráchti GR . . . . 183 C6
Kaliska
Pomorskie PL . . . 68 A3
Pomorskie PL . . . 68 B3
Kalisko PL. . . . . . . 86 A3
Kalisz PL . . . . . . . . 86 A2
Kalisz Pomorski PL. 75 A4
Kaljord N . . . . . . . 194 B6
Kalkan TR . . . . . . . 189 C4
Kalkar D . . . . . . . . 80 A2
Kalkım TR . . . . . . . 186 C2
Kall
D. . . . . . . . . . . . .80 B2
S. . . . . . . . . . . .199 B10
Källby S . . . . . . . . 55 B4
Kållered S . . . . . . . 60 B2
Källerstad S. . . . . . 60 B3
Kallinge S . . . . . . . 63 B3
Kallmünz D . . . . . . 95 B3
Kallo FIN . . . . . . . 196 B7
Kallsedet S . . . . . 199 B9
Kalmar S . . . . . . . . 63 B4
Kalmthout B . . . . . 79 A4
Kalná SK . . . . . . . .112 A2
Kalocsa H . . . . . . . 112 C2
Kalokhorio CY. . . . 181 B2
Kalo Nero GR . . . . 184 B2
Kaloni GR . . . . . . . 186 C1
Kaloní GR . . . . . . . 112 C2
Kals A. . . . . . . . . . 109 B3
Kalsdorf A . . . . . . . 110 C2
Kaltbrunn CH . . . . 107 B4
Kaltenbach A. . . . . 108 B2

Kaltenkirchen D . . . 64 C2
Kaltennordheim D. . 82 B2
Kalundborg DK. . . . 61 D1
Kalush UA . . . . . . . 13 D6
Kalv S. . . . . . . . . . 60 B3
Kalvåg N . . . . . . . 198 D1
Kalvehave DK . . . . 65 A5
Kalwang A . . . . . . .110 B1
Kalwaria-Zebrzydowska
PL. . . . . . . . . . . . 99 B3
Kalyazin RUS . . . . . 9 D10
Kam H . . . . . . . . . .111 B3
Kaman TR . . . . . . . 23 B7
Kamares GR . . . . . 185 C5
Kambos CY . . . . . . 181 A1
Kamen D . . . . . . . . 81 A3
Kamenice CZ. . . . . 97 B3
Kamenice nad Lipou
CZ . . . . . . . . . . . 96 B3
Kameničná SK. . . . .112 B2
Kamenný Most SK .112 B2
Kamenny Ujezd CZ. 96 C2
Kamenska HR . . . . 124 B3
Kamensko HR . . . . 138 B2
Kamenz D . . . . . . . 84 A2
Kamičak BIH . . . . . 124 C2
Kamień PL. . . . . . . 87 A4
Kamieniec Zabk PL. 85 B4
Kamienka SK. . . . . 99 B4
Kamień Krajeński
PL. . . . . . . . . . . . 76 A2
Kamienna Góra PL . 85 B4
Kamień Pomorski
PL. . . . . . . . . . . . 67 C3
Kamieńsk PL. . . . . 86 A3
Kamiros Skala GR. 188 C2
Kamnik SLO . . . . . 123 A3
Kampen NL . . . . . . 70 B2
Kampinos PL. . . . . 77 B5
Kamp-Lintfort D . . . 80 A2
Kampor HR . . . . . . 123 C3
Kamyanets-Podil's'kyy
UA . . . . . . . . . . . 13 D7
Kamyanka-Buz'ka
UA . . . . . . . . . . . 13 C6
Kamýk nad Vltavou
CZ . . . . . . . . . . . 96 B2
Kanal SLO . . . . . . 122 A2
Kanalia GR . . . . . . 182 D4
Kandalaksha RUS. . 3 C13
Kandanos GR . . . . 185 D4
Kandel D . . . . . . . . 93 B4
Kandern D . . . . . . 106 B2
Kandersteg CH . . . 106 C2
Kandila GR . . . . . . 184 B3
Kandıra TR. . . . . . . 187 A5
Kandyty PL . . . . . . 69 A5
Kanfanar HR . . . . . 122 B2
Kangasala FIN. . . . . 3 E8
Kangos S . . . . . . . 196 B5
Kangosjärvi FIN . . 196 B6
Kaniów PL. . . . . . . 75 C3
Kanjiža SRB. . . . . . 126 A2
Kankaanpää FIN . . . 8 B3
Kannus FIN . . . . . . . 3 E8
Kanturk IRL . . . . . . 29 B3
Kapaklı TR. . . . . . . 186 A2
Kapellen
A. . . . . . . . . . . . .110 B2
B. . . . . . . . . . . . .79 A4
Kapellskär S . . . . . 57 A5
Kapfenberg A . . . . .110 B2
Kapfenstein A . . . . 110 C2
Kaplice CZ. . . . . . . 96 C2
Kapljuh BIH . . . . . . 124 C2
Kápolna H . . . . . . .113 B4
Kápolnásnyék H . . 112 B2
Kaposfö H . . . . . . . 125 A3
Kaposfüred H . . . . 125 A3
Kaposszekcsö H . . 125 A3
Kaposvár H . . . . . . 125 A3
Kapp N . . . . . . . . . 48 B2
Kappel D . . . . . . . . 93 C3
Kappeln D . . . . . . . 64 B2
Kappelshamn S. . . 57 C4
Kappl A. . . . . . . . . 107 B5
Kappstad S . . . . . . 55 A4
Kaprun A . . . . . . . 109 B3
Kaptol HR . . . . . . . 125 B3
Kapuvár H . . . . . . .111 B4
Karaadilli TR . . . . . 189 A5
Karabiğa TR. . . . . . 186 B2
Karabük TR . . . . . . 187 A7
Karaburun TR . . . . 186 D1
Karacabey TR . . . . 186 B3
Karacaköy TR . . . . 186 A3
Karacaören TR . . . . 189 A5
Karacasu TR . . . . . 188 B3
Karácsond H . . . . .113 B4
Karád H . . . . . . . . . 112 C1
Karahallı TR. . . . . . 189 A4
Karaisali TR. . . . . . 23 C8
Karaman
Balıkesir TR. . . . .186 C3
Karaman TR . . . . . . 23 C7
Karamanlı TR . . . . . 189 B4
Karamürsel TR . . . . 187 B4
Karan SRB. . . . . . . 127 D1
Karancslapujto H . .113 A3
Karaova TR . . . . . . 188 B2
Karapınar TR . . . . . 23 C7
Karasjok N . . . . . . 193 C9
Karasu TR . . . . . . . 187 A5
Karataş
Adana TR. . . . . . . .23 C8
Manisa TR . . . . . . 188 A3
Karatoprak TR. . . . 188 B2
Karavostasi CY. . . . 181 A1

Karbenning S . . . . . 50 B3
Kårberg S . . . . . . . 55 B5
Kårböle S. . . . . . . 199 D12
Karby
D. . . . . . . . . . . . .64 B2
DK. . . . . . . . . . . .58 B1
Kårby S . . . . . . . . . 62 A4
Karby S . . . . . . . . . 57 A4
Karcag H . . . . . . . .113 B4
Karczów PL. . . . . . . 86 B1
Karczowiska PL. . . 85 A4
Kardamena GR . . . 188 C2
Kardamila GR . . . . 185 A7
Kardamili GR. . . . . 184 C3
Kardašova Řečice
CZ . . . . . . . . . . . 96 B2
Kardis S . . . . . . . . 196 C6
Karditsa GR. . . . . . 182 D3
Kärdla EST. . . . . . . . 8 C3
Kardoskút H . . . . . 113 C4
Karesuando S . . . . 192 D6
Kargı TR. . . . . . . . . 23 A8
Kargopol RUS. . . . .9 B11
Kargowa PL. . . . . . 75 B4
Karigasniemi FIN . 193 C9
Karise DK. . . . . . . . 65 A5
Karistos GR. . . . . . 185 A5
Karkkila FIN. . . . . . . 8 B4
Karlholmsbruk S . . 51 B4
Karlino PL. . . . . . . . 67 B4
Karlobag HR . . . . . 137 A4
Karlovac HR . . . . . 123 B4
Karlovasi GR . . . . . 188 B1
Karlovo BG . . . . . . 17 D6
Karlovy Vary CZ . . 83 B4
Karłowice PL. . . . . . 86 B1
Karlsborg S . . . . . . 55 B5
Karlshamn S . . . . . 63 B2
Karlshöfen D . . . . . 72 A2
Karlshus N. . . . . . . 54 A1
Karlskoga S . . . . . . 55 A5
Karlskrona S . . . . . 63 B3
Karlsrud N . . . . . . . 47 B5
Karlsruhe D . . . . . . 93 B4
Karlstad S . . . . . . . 55 A4
Karlstadt D . . . . . . 94 B1
Karlstetten A . . . . .110 A2
Karlstift A . . . . . . . 96 C2
Karlstorp S . . . . . . 62 A3
Karmacs H . . . . . . .111 C4
Karmin PL . . . . . . . 85 A5
Kärna S . . . . . . . . . 60 B1
Karnobat BG . . . . . 17 D7
Karojba HR . . . . . . 122 B2
Karow D . . . . . . . . 73 A5
Karpacz PL . . . . . . 85 B3
Karpathos GR . . . . 188 D2
Karpenisi GR . . . . . 182 E3
Karpuzlu TR. . . . . . 188 B2
Kärrbo S . . . . . . . . 56 A2
Karrebaeksminde
DK. . . . . . . . . . . 65 A4
Karshult S . . . . . . . 60 B3
Karsin PL. . . . . . . . 68 B2
Kärsta S . . . . . . . . 57 A4
Karstädt D . . . . . . . 73 A4
Kartal TR. . . . . . . . 186 B4
Kartitsch A. . . . . . . 109 C3
Kartuzy PL. . . . . . . 68 A3
Karungi S. . . . . . . . 196 C6
Karunki FIN . . . . . . 196 C7
Karup DK . . . . . . . . 59 B2
Karvina CZ. . . . . . . 98 B2
Kás DK. . . . . . . . . . 58 A2
Kaş TR. . . . . . . . . . 189 C4
Kasaba TR . . . . . . . 189 C4
Kašava CZ. . . . . . . 98 B1
Káseberga S . . . . . 66 A3
Kasejovice CZ. . . . . 96 B1
Kasfjord N . . . . . . . 194 B7
Kashin RUS. . . . . . . 9 D10
Kašina HR . . . . . . . 124 B2
Kasina-Wielka PL . . 99 B4
Kaskinen FIN. . . . . . 8 A2
Kašperské Hory CZ. 96 B1
Kassandrino GR . . 183 C5
Kassel D . . . . . . . . 81 A5
Kassiopi GR . . . . . 182 D1
Kastamonu TR . . . . 23 A7
Kastav HR . . . . . . . 123 B3
Kasteli GR . . . . . . . 185 D4
Kastellaun D . . . . . 93 A3
Kastelli GR . . . . . . 185 D6
Kaštel Stari HR . . . 138 B2
Kaštel Zegarski
HR . . . . . . . . . . 138 A1
Kasterlee B . . . . . . 79 A4
Kastl D . . . . . . . . . 95 B3
Kastlösa S . . . . . . . 63 B4
Kastorf D . . . . . . . . 65 C3
Kastoria GR. . . . . . 182 C3
Kastorio GR. . . . . . 184 B3
Kastraki GR. . . . . . 185 C6
Kastrosikia GR . . . 182 D2
Kastsyukovichy
BY . . . . . . . . . . . 13 B10
Kaszaper H . . . . . . 113 C4
Katakolo GR . . . . . 184 B2
Katapola GR . . . . . 185 C6
Katastari GR . . . . . 184 B1
Katerbow D . . . . . . 74 B1
Katerini GR . . . . . . 182 C4
Kathikas CY. . . . . . 181 B1
Kätkesuando S . . . 196 A6
Katlenburg-Lindau
D. . . . . . . . . . . . 82 A2

Kato Achaia GR. . . 184 A2
Káto Pyrgos CY . . . 181 A1
Katouna GR. . . . . . 182 E3
Katovice CZ. . . . . . 96 B1
Katowice PL. . . . . . 86 B3
Katrineberg S . . . . 50 A3
Katrineholm S . . . . 56 B2
Kattarp S . . . . . . . . 61 C2
Kattavia GR . . . . . 188 D2
Katthammarsvik S . 57 C4
Kattilstorp S . . . . . 55 B4
Katwijk NL. . . . . . . 70 B1
Katy Wrocławskie
PL. . . . . . . . . . . . 85 A4
Katzenelnbogen D . 81 B3
Katzhütte D . . . . . . 82 B3
Kaub D. . . . . . . . . . 93 A3
Kaufbeuren D . . . . 108 B1
Kauhajoki FIN. . . . . 8 A3
Kauhava FIN . . . . . . 8 A3
Kaukonen FIN . . . . 196 B7
Kaulsdorf D . . . . . . 82 B3
Kaunas LT . . . . . . . 13 A5
Kaunisvaara S . . . . 196 B6
Kaupanger N . . . . . 47 A4
Kautokeino N . . . . 192 C7
Kautzen A. . . . . . . . 97 C3
Kavadarci MK . . . . 182 B4
Kavajë AL. . . . . . . . 182 B1
Kavakköy TR. . . . . 186 B1
Kavaklı TR. . . . . . . 186 A2
Kavaklıdere TR . . . 188 B3
Kavala GR . . . . . . . 183 C6
Kävlinge S . . . . . . . 61 D3
Kawczce PL. . . . . . 68 A1
Kaxås S . . . . . . . . 199 B10
Kaxholmen S. . . . . 62 A2
Käylä FIN . . . . . . . 197 C12
Kaymakçı TR . . . . . 188 A3
Kaymaz TR. . . . . . . 187 C6
Kaynarca TR . . . . . 187 A5
Käyrämö FIN . . . . . 197 C9
Kayseri TR. . . . . . . 23 B8
Kaysersberg F. . . . 106 A2
Kazanlık BG . . . . . 17 D6
Kazár H . . . . . . . . .113 A3
Kazimierza Wielka
PL. . . . . . . . . . . . 87 B4
Kazincbarcika H . . .113 A4
Kaźmierz PL. . . . . . 75 B5
Kcynia PL. . . . . . . . 76 A2
Kdyně CZ. . . . . . . . 95 B5
Kea GR. . . . . . . . . 185 B5
Keadew IRL . . . . . . 26 B2
Keady GB. . . . . . . . 27 B4
Kecel H . . . . . . . . 112 C3
Keçiborlu TR. . . . . 189 B5
Kecskemét H . . . . 113 C3
Kėdainiai LT. . . . . . 13 A5
Kędzierzyn-Koźle
PL. . . . . . . . . . . . 86 B2
Keel IRL . . . . . . . . 28 A1
Keenagh IRL . . . . . 28 A4
Keerbergen B . . . . 79 A4
Kefalos GR . . . . . . 188 C1
Kefken TR . . . . . . . 187 A5
Keflavík IS . . . . . . 190 C3
Kegworth GB. . . . . 40 C2
Kehl D . . . . . . . . . . 93 C3
Kehrigk D. . . . . . . . 74 B2
Keighley GB . . . . . 40 B2
Keila EST. . . . . . . . . 8 C4
Keillmore GB. . . . . 34 C2
Keiss GB . . . . . . . . 32 C3
Keith GB . . . . . . . . 33 D4
Kelankylä FIN . . . 197 D10
Kelberg D . . . . . . . 80 B2
Kelbra D. . . . . . . . . 82 A3
Kelč CZ . . . . . . . . . 98 B1
Kelchsau A. . . . . . 108 B3
Kelderý AL . . . . . . 182 C2
Keld GB . . . . . . . . 37 B4
Kelebia H . . . . . . . 126 A1
Kelekçi TR . . . . . . 188 B4
Kelemér H . . . . . . . 99 C4
Keles TR . . . . . . . . 186 C4
Kelheim D . . . . . . . 95 C3
Kell D . . . . . . . . . . 92 B2
Kellas GB. . . . . . . . 32 D3
Kellinghusen D . . . 64 C2
Kelloselkä FIN . . . 197 C11
Kells
GB. . . . . . . . . . . .27 B4
IRL . . . . . . . . . . .27 C4
Kelmis B . . . . . . . . 80 B2
Kelokedhara CY . . 181 B1
Kelottijärvi FIN . . . 192 D6
Kelsall GB . . . . . . . 38 A4
Kelso GB . . . . . . . 35 C5
Kelsterbach D . . . . 93 A4
Keltneyburn GB . . . 35 B4
Kelujärvi FIN . . . . 197 B10
Kemaliye TR. . . . . . 188 A3
Kemalpaşa TR. . . . 188 A2
Kematen A . . . . . . 108 B2
Kemberg D . . . . . . 83 A4
Kemer
Antalya TR. . . . . .189 C5
Burdur TR . . . . . . 189 B5
Muğla TR . . . . . . 189 C4
Kemerkaya TR. . . . 187 C6
Kemeten A . . . . . . .111 B3
Kemi FIN . . . . . . . . 196 D7
Kemijärvi FIN. . . . 197 C10
Keminmaa FIN. . . . 196 D7

### Job–Kik 251

Kemnath D. . . . . . . 95 B3
Kemnay GB . . . . . . 33 D4
Kemnitz
Brandenburg D . . .74 B1
Mecklenburg-
Vorpommern D. . .66 B2
Kempen D . . . . . . . 80 A2
Kempsey GB . . . . . 39 B4
Kempten D. . . . . . . 107 B5
Kemptthal CH . . . . 107 B3
Kendal GB . . . . . . . 37 B4
Kenderes H . . . . . .113 B4
Kengyel H . . . . . . .113 B4
Kenilworth GB. . . . 44 A2
Kenmare IRL . . . . . 29 C2
Kenmore GB . . . . . 35 B4
Kennacraig GB . . . 34 C2
Kenyeri H. . . . . . . .111 B4
Kenzingen D . . . . . 106 A2
Kepez TR. . . . . . . . 186 B1
Kepice PL. . . . . . . . 68 A1
Kępno PL. . . . . . . . 86 A2
Kepsut TR. . . . . . . 186 C3
Keramoti GR . . . . . 183 C6
Keräntöjärvi S . . . . 196 B6
Keratea GR . . . . . . 185 B4
Kerava FIN. . . . . . . . 8 B4
Kerecsend H . . . . .113 B4
Kerekegyhaza H . . 112 C3
Kerepestarcsa H . .112 B3
Keri GR . . . . . . . . . 184 B1
Kérien F . . . . . . . . 100 A2
Kerkafalva H . . . . .111 C3
Kerken D . . . . . . . . 80 A2
Kerkrade NL. . . . . . 80 B2
Kerkyra GR . . . . . . 182 D1
Kerlouan F. . . . . . . 100 A1
Kernascléden F. . . 100 A2
Kernhof A. . . . . . . .110 B2
Kerns CH . . . . . . . 106 C3
Kerpen D . . . . . . . . 80 B2
Kerrysdale GB . . . . 31 B3
Kerteminde DK . . . 59 C3
Kerzers CH . . . . . . 106 C2
Keşan TR. . . . . . . . 186 B1
Kesgrave GB . . . . . 45 A5
Kesh GB. . . . . . . . . 26 B3
Keskin TR . . . . . . . 23 B7
Kesselfall A . . . . . . 109 B3
Kestenga RUS. . . . 3 D12
Keswick GB . . . . . . 36 B3
Keszthely H. . . . . . .111 C4
Kétegyháza H . . . . 113 C5
Kéthely H. . . . . . . . .111 C4
Kętrzyn PL. . . . . . . 12 A4
Kettering GB . . . . . 44 A3
Kettlewell GB. . . . . 40 A1
Kęty PL. . . . . . . . . . 99 B3
Ketzin D . . . . . . . . 74 B1
Keula D. . . . . . . . . . 82 A2
Keuruu FIN . . . . . . . 8 A4
Kevelaer D. . . . . . . 80 A2
Kevermes H . . . . . 113 C5
Kevi SRB . . . . . . . 126 B1
Keyingham GB . . . . 41 B3
Keynsham GB . . . . 43 A4
Kežmarok SK. . . . . 99 B4
Kharmanli BG . . . . 183 B7
Khaskovo BG . . . . 183 B7
Khimki RUS. . . . . . . 9 E10
Khisinev = Chişinău
MD . . . . . . . . . . 17 B8
Khmelnik UA . . . . . 13 D7
Khmelnytskyy UA . 13 D7
Khodoriv UA . . . . . 13 D6
Kholm RUS . . . . . . 9 D7
Khotyn UA . . . . . . . 13 D7
Khoyniki BY. . . . . . 13 C8
Khust UA . . . . . . . . 17 A5
Khvoynaya RUS . . . 9 C9
Kiato GR . . . . . . . . 184 A3
Kibæk DK . . . . . . . 59 B1
Kiberg N. . . . . . . . 193 B14
Kicasalih TR . . . . . 186 A1
Kičevo MK . . . . . . 182 B2
Kidderminster GB . . 39 B4
Kidlington GB . . . . 44 B2
Kidsgrove GB . . . . 40 B1
Kidwelly GB. . . . . . 39 C2
Kiefersfelden D. . . 108 B3
Kiel D . . . . . . . . . . 64 B3
Kielce PL. . . . . . . . 87 B4
Kielczygłów PL. . . . 86 A3
Kielder GB . . . . . . 37 A4
Kiełpino PL. . . . . . . 68 A3
Kiełpiny PL. . . . . . . 77 A4
Kierinki FIN . . . . . 197 B8
Kiernozia PL. . . . . . 77 B4
Kierspe D. . . . . . . . 81 A3
Kietrz PL . . . . . . . . 86 B2
Kietz D . . . . . . . . . 74 B3
Kiev = Kyyiv UA. . . 13 C9
Kiezmark PL. . . . . . 69 A3
Kiffisia GR. . . . . . . 185 A4
Kifino Selo BIH . . . 139 B4
Kihlanki
FIN . . . . . . . . . . 196 B6
S. . . . . . . . . . . .196 B6
Kiistala FIN . . . . . . 197 B8
Kije PL . . . . . . . . . . 87 B4
Kijevo HR. . . . . . . . 138 B2
Kikallen N . . . . . . . 46 B2
Kikinda SRB . . . . . 126 B2

252 Kil–Kos


Kil N 53 B5
*Örebro* S 55 A6
*Värmland* S 55 A4
Kila S 55 A3
Kilafors S 50 A3
Kilbaha IRL 29 B2
Kilbeggan IRL 30 A1
Kilberry GB 34 C2
Kilbirnie GB 34 C3
Kilboghamn N 195 D4
Kilbotn N 194 B7
Kilb Rabenstein A 110 A2
Kilchattan GB 34 C2
Kilchoan GB 34 B1
Kilcock IRL 30 A2
Kilconnell IRL 28 A3
Kilcormac IRL 28 A4
Kilcreggan GB 34 C3
Kilcullen IRL 30 A2
Kilcurry IRL 27 B4
Kildare IRL 30 A2
Kildinstroy RUS 3 B13
Kildonan GB 32 C3
Kildorrery IRL 29 B3
Kilegrend N 53 A4
Kilen N 53 A4
Kilgarvan IRL 29 C2
Kiliya UA 17 C8
Kilkee IRL 29 B2
Kilkeel GB 27 B4
Kilkelly IRL 26 C2
Kilkenny IRL 30 B1
Kilkieran IRL 28 A2
Kilkinlea IRL 29 B2
Kilkis GR 182 B4
Killadysert IRL 29 B2
Killala IRL 26 B1
Killaloe IRL 28 B3
Killarney IRL 29 B2
Killashandra IRL 27 B3
Killashee IRL 28 A4
Killearn GB 34 B3
Killeberg S 61 C4
Killeigh IRL 30 A1
Killenaule IRL 29 B4
Killimor IRL 28 A3
Killin GB 34 B3
Killinaboy IRL 28 B2
Killinge S 196 B3
Killinick IRL 30 B2
Killorglin IRL 29 B2
Killucan IRL 30 A1
Killybegs IRL 26 B2
Killyleagh GB 27 B5
Kilmacrenan IRL 26 A3
Kilmacthomas IRL 30 B1
Kilmaine IRL 28 A2
Kilmallock IRL 29 B3
Kilmarnock GB 36 A2
Kilmartin GB 34 B2
Kilmaurs GB 36 A2
Kilmeadan IRL 30 B1
Kilmeedy IRL 29 B3
Kilmelford GB 34 B2
Kilmore Quay IRL 30 B2
Kilmuir GB 32 D2
Kilnaleck IRL 27 C3
Kilninver GB 34 B2
Kilpisjärvi FIN 192 C4
Kilrea GB 27 B4
Kilrush IRL 29 B2
Kilsmo S 56 A1
Kilsyth GB 35 C3
Kiltoom IRL 28 A3
Kilwinning GB 36 A2
Kimasozero RUS 3 D12
Kimi GR 185 A5
Kimolos GR 185 C5
Kimovsk RUS 9 E10
Kimratshofen D 107 B5
Kimry RUS 9 D10
Kimstad S 56 B1
Kinbrace GB 32 C3
Kincardine GB 35 B4
Kincraig GB 32 D3
Kindberg A 110 B2
Kindelbruck D 82 A3
Kingarrow IRL 26 B2
Kingisepp RUS 9 C6
Kingsbridge GB 43 B3
Kingsclere GB 44 B2
Kingscourt IRL 27 C4
King's Lynn GB 41 C4
Kingsteignton GB 43 B3
Kingston
*Greater London* GB 44 B3
*Moray* GB 32 D3
Kingston Bagpuize GB 44 B2
Kingston upon Hull GB 40 B3
Kingswear GB 43 B3
Kingswood GB 43 A4
Kington GB 39 B3
Kingussie GB 32 D2
Kınık
*Antalya* TR 188 C4
*İzmir* TR 186 C2
Kinloch
*Highland* GB 31 B2
*Highland* GB 32 C2
Kinlochbervie GB 32 C1
Kinlochewe GB 32 D1
Kinlochleven GB 34 B3
Kinlochmoidart GB 34 B2
Kinloch Rannoch GB 35 B3
Kinloss GB 32 D3
Kinlough IRL 26 B2
Kinn N 48 B2
Kinna S 60 B2
Kinnared S 60 B3
Kinnarp S 55 B4
Kinnegad IRL 30 A1
Kinne-Kleva S 55 B4
Kinnitty IRL 28 A4
Kinrooi B 80 A1
Kinross GB 35 B4
Kinsale IRL 29 C3
Kinsarvik N 46 B3
Kintarvie GB 31 A2
Kintore GB 33 D4
Kinvarra IRL 28 A3
Kioni GR 184 A1
Kiparissia GR 184 B2
Kipfenburg D 95 C3
Kippen GB 35 B3
Kiraz TR 188 A3
Kirazlı TR 186 B1
Kirberg D 81 B4
Kirchbach in Steiermark A 110 C2
Kirchberg
CH 106 B2
*Baden-Württemberg* D 94 B1
*Rheinland-Pfalz* D 93 B3
Kirchberg am Wechsel A 110 B2
Kirchberg an der Pielach A 110 A2
Kirchberg in Tirol A 109 B3
Kirchbichl A 108 B3
Kirchdorf
*Bayern* D 96 C1
*Mecklenburg-Vorpommern* D 65 C4
*Niedersachsen* D 72 B1
Kirchdorf an der Krems A 109 B5
Kirchdorf in Tirol A 109 B3
Kirchenlamitz D 83 B3
Kirchenthumbach D 95 B3
Kirchhain D 81 B4
Kirchheim
*Baden-Württemberg* D 94 C1
*Bayern* D 108 A1
*Hessen* D 81 B5
Kirchheimbolanden D 93 B4
Kirchhundem D 81 A4
Kirchlintein D 72 B2
Kirchschlag A 111 B3
Kirchweidach D 109 A3
Kirchzarten D 106 B2
Kircubbin GB 27 B5
Kireç TR 186 C3
Kırıkkale TR 23 B7
Kirillov RUS 9 C11
Kirishi RUS 9 C8
Kırka TR 187 C5
Kırkağaç TR 186 C2
Kirkbean GB 36 B3
Kirkbride GB 36 B3
Kirkby GB 38 A4
Kirkby Lonsdale GB 37 B4
Kirkby Malzeard GB 40 A2
Kirkbymoorside GB 37 B6
Kirkby Stephen GB 37 B4
Kirkcaldy GB 35 B4
Kirkcolm GB 36 B1
Kirkconnel GB 36 A2
Kirkcowan GB 36 B2
Kirkcudbright GB 36 B2
Kirkehamn N 52 B2
Kirke Hyllinge DK 61 D1
Kirkenær N 49 B4
Kirkenes N 193 C14
Kirkham GB 38 A4
Kirkintilloch GB 35 C3
Kirkjubæjarklaustur IS 191 D7
Kirkkonummi FIN 8 B4
Kırklareli TR 186 A2
Kirkmichael GB 35 B4
Kirk Michael GB 36 B2
Kirkoswald GB 36 A2
Kirkpatrick Fleming GB 36 A3
Kirkton of Glenisla GB 35 B4
Kirkwall GB 33 C4
Kirkwhelpington GB 37 A5
Kirn D 93 B3
Kirovsk RUS 3 C13
Kirriemuir GB 35 B5
Kırşehir TR 23 B8
Kirton GB 41 C3
Kirton in Lindsey GB 40 B3
Kirtorf D 81 B5
Kiruna S 196 B3
Kisa S 62 A3
Kisač SRB 126 B1
Kisbér H 112 B2
Kiseljak BIH 139 B4
Kisielice PL 69 B4
Kisköre H 113 B4
Kiskőrös H 112 C3
Kiskunfélegyháza H 113 C3
Kiskunhalas H 112 C3
Kiskunlacháza H 112 B2
Kiskunmajsa H 113 C3
Kisláng H 112 C2
Kisslegg D 107 B4
Kissolt H 112 C3
Kissónerga CY 181 B1
Kist D 94 B1
Kistanje HR 138 B1
Kistelek H 113 C3
Kisterenye H 113 A3
Kisújszállás H 113 B4
Kisvárda H 16 A5
Kisvejke H 112 C2
Kiszkowo PL 76 B2
Kiszombor H 126 A2
Kitee FIN 9 A7
Kithnos GR 185 B5
Kiti CY 181 B2
Kitkiöjärvi S 196 B6
Kitkiöjoki S 196 B6
Kittelfjäll S 195 E6
Kittendorf D 74 A1
Kittilä FIN 196 B7
Kittlitz D 84 A2
Kittsee A 111 A4
Kitzbühel A 109 B3
Kitzingen D 94 B2
Kiuruvesi FIN 3 E10
Kivertsi UA 13 C6
Kividhes CY 181 B1
Kivik S 63 C2
Kivotos GR 182 C3
Kıyıköy TR 186 A3
Kızılcabölük TR 188 B4
Kızılcadağ TR 189 B4
Kızılcahamam TR 23 A7
Kızılırmak TR 23 A7
Kızılkaya TR 189 B5
Kızılkuyu TR 187 D6
Kızılören
*Afyon* TR 189 A5
*Konya* TR 189 B7
Kjeldebotn N 194 B7
Kjellerup DK 59 B2
Kjellmyra N 49 B4
Kjøllefjord N 193 B11
Kjopmannskjaer N 54 A1
Kjøpsvik N 194 B7
Kl'ačno SK 98 C2
Kladanj BIH 139 A4
Kläden D 73 B4
Klädesholmen S 60 B1
Kladnice HR 138 B2
Kladno CZ 84 B2
Kladruby CZ 95 B4
Klagenfurt A 110 C1
Klågerup S 61 D3
Klagstorp S 66 A2
Klaipėda LT 8 E2
Klaistow D 74 B1
Klaksvík FO 4 A3
Klana HR 123 B3
Klanac HR 123 C4
Klanjec HR 123 A4
Klardorf D 95 B4
Klarup DK 58 A3
Klašnice BIH 124 C3
Klässbol S 55 A3
Klášterec nad Ohří CZ 83 B5
Kláštor pod Znievom SK 98 C2
Klatovy CZ 96 B1
Klaus an der Pyhrnbahn A 110 B1
Klazienaveen NL 71 B3
Kłecko PL 76 B2
Kleczew PL 76 B3
Klein Plasten D 74 A1
Klein Sankt Paul A 110 C1
Kleinsölk A 109 B4
Kleinzell A 110 B2
Klejtrup DK 58 B2
Klek SRB 126 B2
Klemensker DK 67 A3
Klenak SRB 127 C1
Klenci pod Cerchovem CZ 95 B4
Klenica PL 75 C4
Klenje SRB 127 C1
Klenoec MK 182 B2
Klenovec SK 99 C3
Klenovica HR 123 B3
Klenovnik HR 124 A2
Kleppe N 52 B1
Kleppestø N 46 B2
Kleptow D 74 A2
Kleszewo PL 77 B6
Kleve D 80 A2
Klevshult S 60 B4
Klewki PL 77 A5
Kličevac SRB 127 C3
Kliening A 110 C1
Klietz D 73 B5
Klikuszowa PL 99 B3
Klimkovice CZ 98 B2
Klimontów PL 87 B5
Klimovichi BY 13 B9
Klimpfjäll S 195 E5
Klin RUS 9 D10
Klinča Sela HR 123 B4
Klingenbach A 111 B3
Klingenberg D 93 B5
Klingenmunster D 93 B4
Klingenthal D 83 B4
Klinken D 73 A4
Klintehamn S 57 C4
Kliny PL 87 A4
Kliplev DK 64 B2
Klippan S 61 C3
Klis HR 138 B2
Klitmøller DK 58 A1
Klitten S 49 A6
Klixbüll D 64 B1
Kljajićevo SRB 126 B1
Ključ BIH 138 A2
Klobouky CZ 97 C4
Kłobuck PL 86 B2
Klockestrand S 200 D3
Kłodawa
*Lubuskie* PL 75 B4
*Wielkopolskie* PL 76 B3
Kłodzko PL 85 B4
Kløfta N 48 B3
Klokkarvik N 46 B2
Klokkerholm DK 58 A3
Klokočov SK 98 B2
Kłomnice PL 86 B3
Klonowa PL 86 A2
Kloosterzande NL 79 A4
Kłopot PL 74 B3
Klos AL 182 B2
Kloštar Ivanić HR 124 B2
Kloster
D 66 B2
DK 59 B1
Klösterle A 107 B5
Klostermansfeld D 82 A3
Klosterneuburg A 97 C4
Klosters CH 107 C4
Kloten CH 107 B3
Klötze D 73 B4
Klöverträsk S 196 D4
Klövsjö S 199 C11
Kluczbork PL 86 B2
Kluczewo PL 75 A5
Kluisbergen B 79 B3
Klundert NL 79 A4
Klutz D 65 C4
Klwów PL 87 A4
Klyetsk BY 13 B7
Knaben N 52 B2
Knaften S 200 B4
Knapstad N 54 A2
Knäred S 61 C3
Knaresborough GB 40 A2
Knarvik N 46 B2
Knebel DK 59 B3
Knebworth GB 44 B3
Knesebeck D 73 B3
Knesselare B 78 A3
Knežak SLO 123 B3
Kneževi Vinogradi HR 125 B4
Kneževo HR 125 B4
Knić SRB 127 D2
Knighton GB 39 B3
Knin HR 138 A2
Knislinge S 61 C4
Knittelfeld A 110 B1
Knivsta S 57 A3
Knock IRL 28 A3
Knocktopher IRL 30 B1
Knokke-Heist B 78 A3
Knowle GB 44 A2
Knurów PL 86 B2
Knutby S 51 C5
Knutsford GB 38 A4
Kobarid SLO 122 A2
København = Copenhagen DK 61 D2
Kobenz A 110 B1
Kobersdorf A 111 B3
Kobiernice PL 99 B3
Kobierzyce PL 85 B4
Kobilje SLO 111 C3
Kobiór PL 86 B2
Koblenz
CH 106 B3
D 81 B3
Kobryn BY 13 B6
Kobylanka PL 75 A3
Kobylin PL 85 A5
Kobylniki PL 77 B5
Kocaali TR 187 A5
Kocaaliler TR 189 B5
Kocaeli = İzmit TR 187 B4
Kočani MK 182 B4
Koçarlı TR 188 B2
Koceljevo SRB 127 C1
Kočerin BIH 138 B3
Kočevje SLO 123 B3
Kočevska Reka SLO 123 B3
Kochel am see D 108 B2
Kocs H 112 B2
Kocsér H 113 B3
Kocsola H 112 C2
Koczala PL 68 B2
Kodal N 53 A6
Kode S 60 B1
Kodersdorf D 84 A2
Kodrab PL 86 A3
Koekelare B 78 A2
Kofçaz TR 186 A2
Köflach A 110 B2
Køge DK 61 D2
Kohlberg D 95 B4
Kohtla-Järve EST 8 C5
Köinge S 60 B2
Kojetín CZ 98 B1
Kökar FIN 51 C7
Kokava SK 99 C3
Kokkola FIN 3 E8
Kokori BIH 124 C3
Kokoski PL 69 A3
Koksijde B 78 A2
Kola
BIH 124 C3
RUS 3 B13
Köla S 54 A3
Kołacin PL 87 A3
Kolari FIN 196 B6
Kolárovo SK 112 B1
Kolašin MNE 16 D3
Kolbäck S 56 A2
Kolbacz PL 75 A3
Kolbeinsstaðir IS 190 C3
Kolbermoor D 108 B3
Kolbnitz A 109 C4
Kolbotn N 54 A1
Kolbu N 48 B2
Kolby Kås DK 59 C3
Kolczewo PL 67 C3
Kolczygłowy PL 68 A2
Kolding DK 59 C2
Kölesd H 112 C2
Kolgrov N 46 A1
Kolín CZ 97 A3
Kolind DK 59 B3
Kolinec CZ 96 B1
Koljane HR 138 B2
Kølkær DK 59 B2
Kölleda D 82 A3
Kollum NL 70 A3
Köln = Cologne D 80 B2
Koło PL 76 B3
Kołobrzeg PL 67 B4
Kolochau D 83 A5
Kolomyya UA 13 D6
Kolonowskie PL 86 B2
Koloveč CZ 95 B5
Kolpino RUS 9 C7
Kolrep D 73 A5
Kölsillre S 199 C12
Kolsko PL 75 C4
Kolsva S 56 A1
Kolta SK 112 A2
Kolunič BIH 138 A2
Koluszki PL 87 A3
Kolut SRB 125 B4
Kolvereid N 199 A8
Kølvrå DK 59 B2
Komadi H 113 B5
Komagvær N 193 B14
Komarica BIH 125 C3
Komárno SK 112 B2
Komárom H 112 B2
Komatou Yialou CY 181 A3
Komboti GR 182 D3
Komen SLO 122 B2
Komin HR 138 B3
Komiža HR 138 B2
Komjáti H 99 C4
Komjatice SK 112 A2
Komletinci HR 125 B4
Komló H 125 A4
Kömlo H 113 B4
Komoča SK 112 B2
Komorniki PL 75 B5
Komorzno PL 86 A2
Komotini GR 183 B7
Konak SRB 126 B2
Konakovo RUS 9 D10
Konarzyny PL 68 B2
Kondias GR 183 D7
Kondopaga RUS 9 A9
Kondorfa H 111 C3
Kondoros H 113 C4
Konevo RUS 9 A11
Køng DK 65 A4
Konga S 63 B3
Köngäs FIN 196 B7
Kongerslev DK 58 B3
Kongsberg N 53 A5
Kongshamn N 53 B4
Kongsmark DK 64 A1
Kongsmoen N 199 A9
Kongsvik N 194 B7
Kongsvinger N 48 B3
Konice CZ 97 B4
Konie PL 77 C5
Koniecpol PL 86 B3
Königsberg D 82 B2
Königsbronn D 94 C2
Königsbrück D 84 A1
Königsbrunn D 94 C2
Konigsdorf D 108 B2
Königsee D 82 B3
Königshorst D 74 B1
Königslutter D 73 B3
Königssee D 109 B3
Königstein
*Hessen* D 81 B4
*Sachsen* D 84 B2
Königstetten A 97 C4
Königswartha D 84 A2
Konigswiesen A 96 C2
Königswinter D 80 B3
Königs Wusterhausen D 74 B2
Konin PL 76 B3
Konispol AL 182 D2
Konitsa GR 182 C2
Köniz CH 106 C2
Konjevići BIH 139 A5
Konjevrate HR 138 B2
Konjic BIH 139 B3
Konjščina HR 124 A2
Könnern D 83 A3
Konnerud N 53 A6
Konopiska PL 86 B2
Konotop PL 75 C4
Końskie PL 87 A4
Konsmo N 52 B3
Konstancin-Jeziorna PL 77 B6
Konstantynów Łódźki PL 86 A3
Konstanz D 107 B4
Kontich B 79 A4
Kontiolahti FIN 9 A6
Konya TR 189 B7
Konz D 92 B2
Kópasker IS 191 A9
Kópavogur IS 190 C4
Kopčany SK 98 C1
Koper SLO 122 B2
Kopervik N 52 A1
Kópháza H 111 B3
Kopice PL 85 B5
Kopidlno CZ 84 B3
Köping S 56 A1
Köpingebro S 66 A2
Köpingsvik S 62 B4
Köpmanholmen S 200 C4
Koppang N 48 A3
Koppangen N 192 C4
Kopparberg S 50 C1
Koppelo FIN 193 D11
Koppom S 54 A3
Koprivlen BG 183 B5
Koprivna BIH 125 C4
Koprivnica HR 124 A2
Kopřivnice CZ 98 B2
Köprübaşı TR 186 D3
Koprzywnica PL 87 B5
Kopstal L 92 B2
Kopychyntsi UA 13 D6
Kopytkowo PL 69 B3
Korbach D 81 A4
Körbecke D 81 A4
Korçë AL 182 C2
Korčula HR 138 C3
Korczyców PL 75 B3
Korenita SRB 127 C1
Korets UA 13 C7
Korfantów PL 85 B5
Körfez TR 187 B4
Korgen N 195 D4
Korinth DK 64 A3
Korinthos = Corinth GR 184 B3
Korita
BIH 138 A2
HR 139 C3
Korithi GR 184 B1
Korkuteli TR 189 B5
Körmend H 111 B3
Korne PL 68 A2
Korneuburg A 97 C4
Kornevo RUS 69 A5
Kórnik PL 76 B2
Kornsjø N 54 B2
Környe H 112 B2
Koromačno HR 123 C3
Koroni GR 184 C2
Koronos GR 185 B6
Koronowo PL 76 A2
Körösladány H 113 C5
Köröstarcsa H 113 C5
Korosten UA 13 C8
Korostyshev UA 13 C8
Korpikå S 196 D6
Korpikylä FIN 196 C6
Korpilombolo S 196 C6
Korsberga
*Jönköping* S 62 A3
*Skaraborg* S 55 B5
Korshavn N 54 A1
Korskrogen S 200 E1
Korsnäs S 50 B2
Korsør DK 65 A4
Korsun Shevchenkovskiy UA 13 D9
Korträsk S 196 D3
Kortrijk B 78 B3
Korucu TR 186 C2
Koryčany CZ 98 B1
Korzeńsko PL 85 A4
Korzybie PL 68 A1
Kos GR 188 C2
Kosakowo PL 69 A3
Kosanica MNE 139 B5
Kösching D 95 C3
Kościan PL 75 B5
Kościelec PL 76 B3
Kościerzyna PL 68 A2
Koserow D 66 B2
Košetice CZ 97 B3
Košice SK 12 D4
Kosjerić SRB 127 D1
Koška HR 125 B4
Koskullskulle S 196 B3
Kosovska Mitrovica KOS 16 D4
Kosta S 62 B3
Kostajnica HR 124 B2
Kostajnik SRB 127 C1
Kostanjevica SLO 123 B4
Kostelec nad Černými Lesy CZ 96 B2
Kostelec na Hané CZ 97 B5
Kostice CZ 84 B1
Kostkowo PL 68 A3
Kostojevići SRB 127 C1

Kostolac SRB 127 C3
Kostomłoty PL 85 A4
Kostopil UA 13 C7
Kostów PL 86 A2
Kostrzyn
*Lubuskie* PL 74 B3
*Wielkopolskie* PL 76 B2
Koszalin PL 67 B5
Koszęcin PL 86 B2
Kőszeg H 111 B3
Koszwaly PL 69 A3
Koszyce PL 87 B4
Kot SLO 123 B4
Kotala FIN 197 B11
Kötelek H 113 B4
Köthen D 83 A3
Kotka FIN 8 B5
Kotomierz PL 76 A3
Kotor MNE 16 D3
Kotoriba HR 124 A2
Kotorsko BIH 125 C4
Kotor Varoš BIH 124 C3
Kotovsk UA 17 B8
Kotronas GR 184 C3
Kötschach A 109 C3
Kötzting D 95 B4
Koudum NL 70 B2
Kouřim CZ 96 A2
Kout na Šumave CZ 95 B5
Kouvola FIN 8 B5
Kovačevac SRB 127 C2
Kovačica SRB 126 B2
Kovdor RUS 197 B13
Kovel' UA 13 C6
Kovilj SRB 126 B2
Kovin SRB 127 C2
Kowal PL 77 B4
Kowalewo Pomorskie
PL 69 B3
Kowalów PL 75 B3
Kowary PL 85 B3
Köyceğiz TR 188 C3
Kozani GR 182 C3
Kozarac
BIH 124 C2
HR 124 B1
Kozárovce SK 98 C2
Kozelets UA 13 C9
Kozica HR 138 B3
Koziegłowy PL 86 B3
Kozienice PL 87 A5
Kozina SLO 122 B2
Kozje SLO 123 A4
Kozlu TR 187 A6
Kozluk BIH 139 A5
Koźmin PL 85 A5
Koźminek PL 86 A2
Kozolupy CZ 96 B1
Kożuchów PL 84 A3
Kožuhe BIH 125 C4
Kozyatyn UA 13 D8
Kozyürük TR 186 A1
Kräckelbräken S 49 A6
Krackow D 74 A3
Kraddsele S 195 E7
Krąg PL 68 A1
Kragenæs DK 65 B4
Kragerø N 53 B5
Krągi PL 68 B1
Kragujevac SRB 127 C2
Kraiburg D 109 A3
Krajenka PL 68 B1
Krajišnik SRB 126 B2
Krajková CZ 83 B4
Krajné SK 98 C1
Krajnik Dolny PL 74 A3
Krakača BIH 124 B1
Kräklingbo S 57 C4
Kraków = Cracow
PL 99 A3
Krakow am See D 73 A5
Králíky CZ 85 B4
Kraljevica HR 123 B3
Kraljevo SRB 16 D4
Kral'ovany SK 99 B3
Kráľov Brod SK 111 A4
Kralovice CZ 96 B1
Kralupy nad Vltavou
CZ 84 B2
Králův Dvůr CZ 96 B2
Kramfors S 200 D3
Kramsach A 108 B2
Kramsk PL 76 B3
Kråmvik N 53 A4
Kranenburg D 80 A2
Krania GR 182 D3
Krania Elasonas
GR 182 D4
Kranichfeld D 82 B3
Kranidi GR 184 B4
Kranj SLO 123 A3
Kranjska Gora
SLO 109 C4
Krapanj HR 138 B1
Krapina HR 124 A1
Krapje HR 124 B2
Krapkowice PL 86 B1
Kraselov CZ 96 B1
Krašić HR 123 B4
Krāslava LV 8 E5
Kraslice CZ 83 B4
Krasna PL 87 A4
Krasna Lipa CZ 84 B2
Krasne PL 77 B5
Kraśnik PL 12 C5
Krašnja SLO 123 A3
Krásno SK 98 B2
Krásnohorské
Podhradie SK 99 C4
Krasno Polje HR 123 C4
Krasnozavodsk
RUS 9 D11
Krasnystaw PL 13 C5
Krasnyy RUS 13 A9
Krasnyy Kholm
RUS 9 C10
Krasocin PL 87 B4
Kraszewice PL 86 A2
Kraszkowice PL 86 A2
Kratigos GR 186 C1
Kratovo MK 182 A4
Kraubath A 110 B1
Krausnick D 74 B2
Krautheim D 94 B1
Kravaře CZ 84 B2
Kraváre CZ 98 B2
Kravarsko HR 124 B2
Kraznějov CZ 96 B1
Krčedin SRB 126 B2
Kŭrdzhali BG 183 B7
Krefeld D 80 A2
Kregme DK 61 D2
Krembz D 73 A4
Kremenets UA 13 C6
Kremmen D 74 B2
Kremna SRB 127 D1
Kremnica SK 98 C2
Krempe D 64 C2
Krems A 97 C3
Kremsbrücke A 109 C4
Kremsmünster A 110 A1
Křemže CZ 96 C2
Křenov CZ 97 B4
Krepa PL 76 C3
Krępa Krajeńska PL 75 A5
Krepsko PL 68 B1
Kreševo BIH 139 B4
Kressbronn D 107 B4
Krestena GR 184 B2
Kretinga LT 8 E2
Krettsy RUS 9 C8
Kreuth D 108 B2
Kreuzau D 80 B2
Kreuzlingen CH 107 B4
Kreuztal D 81 B3
Krewelin D 74 B2
Krezluk BIH 138 A3
Krichem BG 183 A6
Krieglach A 110 B2
Kriegsfeld D 93 B3
Kriens CH 106 B3
Krimml A 108 B3
Krimpen aan de IJssel
NL 79 A4
Křinec CZ 84 B3
Kristdala S 62 A4
Kristiansand N 53 B4
Kristianstad S 61 C4
Kristiansund N 198 B4
Kristiinankaupunki
FIN 8 A2
Kristinefors S 49 B4
Kristinehamn S 55 A5
Kriváň SK 99 C3
Kriva Palanka MK 182 A4
Křivokát CZ 96 A1
Kriz HR 124 B2
Křižanov CZ 97 B4
Križevci HR 124 A2
Krk HR 123 B3
Krka SLO 123 B3
Krnjača SRB 127 C2
Krnjak HR 123 B4
Krnjeuša BIH 124 C2
Krnjevo SRB 127 C3
Krnov CZ 98 A1
Krobia PL 85 A4
Kroczyce PL 86 B3
Krøderen N 48 B1
Krokees GR 184 C3
Krokek S 56 B2
Krokom S 199 B11
Krokowa PL 68 A3
Krokstad-elva N 53 A5
Kroksund N 54 A2
Kroměříž CZ 98 B1
Krommenie NL 70 B1
Krompachy SK 99 C4
Kronach D 82 B3
Kronshagen D 64 B3
Kronshtadt RUS 9 C6
Kröpelin D 65 B4
Kropp D 64 B2
Kroppenstedt D 73 C4
Kropstädt D 74 C1
Krościenko nad
Dunajcem PL 99 B4
Kröslin D 66 B2
Krośnice PL 85 A5
Krośniewice PL 77 B4
Krosno PL 12 D4
Krosno Odrzańskie
PL 75 B4
Krostitz D 83 A4
Krotoszyn PL 85 A5
Krottendorf A 110 B2
Krouna CZ 97 B4
Krowiarki PL 86 B2
Krrabë AL 182 B1
Kršan HR 123 B3
Krško SLO 123 B4
Krstac MNE 139 B4
Krstur SRB 126 A2
Křtiny CZ 97 B4
Kruft D 80 B3
Kruishoutem B 79 B3
Krujë AL 182 B1
Krulyewshchyna BY 13 A7
Krumbach
A 111 B3
D 94 C2
Krumovgrad BG 183 B7
Krün D 108 B2
Krupá CZ 84 B1
Krupa na Vrbasu
BIH 124 C3
Krupanj SRB 127 C1
Krupina SK 99 C3
Krupka CZ 84 B1
Krupki BY 13 A8
Kruså DK 64 B2
Kruščica BIH 139 A3
Kruševac SRB 16 D4
Kruševo MK 182 B3
Kruszwica PL 76 B3
Kruszyn PL 77 B4
Krychaw BY 13 B9
Krynica PL 99 B4
Krynica Morska PL 69 A4
Krzęcin PL 75 A4
Krzelów PL 85 A4
Krzepice PL 86 B2
Krzepielów PL 85 A4
Krzeszowice PL 86 B3
Krzeszyce PL 75 B4
Krzynowlaga Mała
PL 77 A5
Krzywiń PL 75 C5
Krzyżanowice PL 98 B2
Krzyżowa PL 99 B3
Krzyż Wielkopolski
PL 75 B5
Ksiaz Wielkopolski
PL 87 B4
Książ Wielkopolski
PL 76 B2
Ktębowiec PL 75 A5
Kübekháza H 126 A2
Küblis CH 107 C4
Kuchary PL 86 A1
Kuchl A 109 B4
Kucice PL 77 B5
Kuciste HR 138 C3
Kuçovë AL 182 C1
Küçükbahçe TR 188 A1
Küçükköy TR 186 C1
Küçükkuyu TR 186 C1
Kucura SRB 126 B1
Kuczbork-Osada PL 77 A5
Kuddby S 56 B2
Kudowa-Zdrój PL 85 B4
Kufstein A 108 B3
Kuggeboda S 63 B3
Kuggörana S 200 E3
Kühbach D 95 C3
Kuhmo FIN 3 D11
Kuhmoinen FIN 8 B4
Kuhnsdorf A 110 C1
Kuhstedt D 72 A1
Kuinre NL 70 B2
Kuivaniemi FIN 197 D8
Kuivastu EST 8 C3
Kukës AL 182 A2
Kuklin PL 77 A5
Kukljica HR 137 A4
Kukujevci SRB 127 B1
Kula
*Srbija* SRB 127 C3
*Vojvodina* SRB 126 B1
TR 188 A3
Kuldīga LV 8 D2
Kulen Vakuf BIH 124 C2
Kulina BIH 125 C4
Kullstedt D 82 A2
Kulmain D 95 B3
Kulmbach D 82 B3
Kuloharju FIN 197 D11
Kulu TR 23 B7
Kumachevo RUS 69 A5
Kumafşarı TR 189 B4
Kumane SRB 126 B2
Kumanovo MK 182 A3
Kumbağ TR 186 B2
Kumdanlı TR 189 A5
Kumkale TR 186 C1
Kumla S 56 A1
Kumlakyrkby S 50 C3
Kumlinge FIN 51 B7
Kumluca TR 189 C5
Kumrovec HR 123 A4
Kunadacs H 112 C3
Kunágota H 113 C5
Kunbaja H 126 A1
Kunda EST 8 C5
Kundl A 108 B2
Kunes N 193 B10
Kunfehértó H 126 A1
Kungälv S 60 B1
Kungsängen S 57 A3
Kungsäter S 60 B2
Kungsbacka S 60 B2
Kungsgården S 50 B3
Kungshamn S 54 B2
Kungs-Husby S 56 A3
Kungsör S 56 A2
Kunhegyes H 113 B4
Kunmadaras H 113 B4
Kunovice CZ 98 B1
Kunów PL 87 B5
Kunowo
*Wielkopolskie* PL 76 C2
*Zachodnio-Pomorskie*
PL 74 A3
Kunštát CZ 97 B4
Kunszállás H 113 C3
Kunszentmárton
H 113 C4
Kunszentmiklós H 112 B3
Kunžak CZ 97 B3
Künzelsau D 94 B1
Kuolayarvi RUS 197 C12
Kuolio FIN 197 D11
Kuopio FIN 8 A5
Kuosku FIN 197 B11
Kup
H 111 B4
PL 86 B1
Kupferzell D 94 B1
Kupinec HR 123 B4
Kupinečki Kraljevac
HR 124 B1
Kupinovo SRB 127 C2
Kupirovo HR 138 A2
Kupjak HR 123 B3
Kuppenheim D 93 C4
Kupres BIH 138 B3
Küps D 82 B3
Kurd H 112 C2
Küre TR 23 A7
Kuressaare EST 8 C3
Kurikka FIN 8 A3
Kuřim CZ 97 B4
Kuřivody CZ 84 B2
Kurki PL 77 A5
Kurort Oberwiesenthal
D 83 B4
Kurort Schmalkalden
D 82 B2
Kurort Stolberg D 82 A2
Kurort Wippra D 82 A3
Kurów PL 12 C5
Kurowice PL 86 A3
Kurravaara S 196 B3
Kursu FIN 197 C11
Kurşunlu
*Bursa* TR 187 B4
*Çankırı* TR 23 A7
Kurtakko FIN 196 B7
Kürten D 80 A3
Kurucaşile TR 187 A7
Kurvinen FIN 197 D12
Kurzelów PL 87 B3
Kusadak SRB 127 C2
Kuşadası TR 188 B2
Kusel D 93 B3
Kusey D 73 B4
Küsnacht CH 106 B3
Kütahya TR 187 C4
Kutenholz D 72 A2
Kutina HR 124 B2
Kutjevo HR 125 B3
Kutná Hora CZ 97 B3
Kutno PL 77 B4
Kuttara FIN 193 D10
Küttingen CH 106 B3
Kúty SK 98 C1
Kuusamo FIN 197 D12
Kuusankoski FIN 8 B5
Kuvshinovo RUS 9 D9
Kuyucak TR 188 B3
Kuzmin SRB 127 B1
Kuźnia Raciborska
PL 86 B2
Kuźnica Czarnkowska
PL 75 B5
Kuźnica Żelichowska
PL 75 B5
Kvaløysletta N 192 C2
Kvalsund N 192 B7
Kvam
*Nord-Trøndelag*
N 199 A8
*Oppland* N 198 D6
Kvamsøy N 46 A3
Kvænangsbotn N 192 C6
Kvanndal N 46 B3
Kvänum S 55 B4
Kværndrup DK 59 C3
Kvås N 52 B3
Kvasice CZ 98 B1
Kvelde N 53 A5
Kvenna N 198 C5
Kvernaland N 52 B1
Kvibille S 60 C2
Kvicksund S 56 A2
Kvidinge S 61 C3
Kvikkjokk S 195 D8
Kvikne
*Hedmark* N 199 C7
*Oppland* N 47 A6
Kvilda CZ 96 B1
Kville S 54 B2
Kvillsfors S 62 A3
Kvinesdal N 52 B2
Kvinlog N 52 B2
Kvinnherad N 46 C3
Kvissel DK 58 A3
Kvissleby S 200 D3
Kviteseid N 53 A4
Kvitsøy N 52 A1
Kwakowo PL 68 A2
Kwidzyn PL 69 B3
Kwilcz PL 75 B5
Kyjov CZ 98 C1
Kyleakin GB 31 B3
Kyle of Lochalsh
GB 31 B3
Kylerhea GB 31 B3
Kylestrome GB 32 C1
Kyllburg D 92 A2
Kyllini GR 184 B2
Kynšperk nad Ohří
CZ 83 B4
Kyperounda CY 181 B1
Kyrenia CY 181 A2
Kyritz D 73 B5
Kyrkesund S 60 A1
Kyrkhult S 63 B2
Kyrksæterøra N 198 B6
Kysucké Nové Mesto
SK 98 B2
Kythira GR 184 C3
Kythréa CY 181 A2
Kyustendil BG 16 D5
Kyyiv = Kiev UA 13 C9
Kyyjärvi FIN 8 A4


## L


Laa an der Thaya A 97 C4
La Adrada E 150 B3
Laage D 65 C5
La Alameda E 157 B4
La Alberca E 149 B3
La Alberca de Záncara
E 158 B1
La Albergueria de
Argañán E 149 B3
La Albuera E 155 C4
La Aldea del Portillo del
Busto E 143 B3
La Algaba E 162 A1
La Aliseda de Tormes
E 150 B2
La Almarcha E 158 B1
La Almolda E 153 A3
La Almunia de Doña
Godina E 152 A2
Laanila FIN 193 D11
La Antillas E 161 B2
La Arena E 141 A4
Laatzen D 72 B2
La Aulaga E 161 B3
La Balme-de-Sillingy
F 118 B3
Laban IRL 28 A3
La Bañeza E 141 B5
La Barca de la Florida
E 162 B2
La Barre-de-Monts
F 114 B1
La Barre-en-Ouche
F 89 B4
La Barrosa E 162 B1
La Barthe-de-Neste
F 145 A4
La Bassée F 78 B2
La Bastide-de-Sèrou
F 146 A2
La Bastide-des-
Jourdans F 132 B1
Labastide-Murat F 129 B4
La Bastide-Puylaurent
F 117 C3
Labastide-Rouairoux
F 130 B1
Labastide-St Pierre
F 129 C4
La Bathie F 118 B3
Lábatlan H 112 B2
La Baule-Escoublac
F 101 B3
La Bazoche-Gouet
F 102 A2
La Bégude-de-Mazenc
F 131 A3
Labenne F 128 C1
La Bernerie-en-Retz
F 114 A1
Labin HR 123 B3
La Bisbal d'Empordà
E 147 C4
Łabiszyn PL 76 B2
Lablachère F 131 A3
Lábod H 124 A3
Laboe D 64 B3
La Boissière F 89 A4
Labouheyre F 128 B2
La Bourboule F 116 B2
La Bóveda de Toro
E 150 A2
Łabowa PL 99 B4
La Brède F 128 B2
La Bresse F 106 A1
La Bridoire F 118 B2
La Brillanne F 132 B1
Labrit F 128 B2
Labros E 152 A2
La Bruffière F 114 A2
Labruguière F 130 B1
Labrujo P 148 A1
L'Absie F 114 B3
La Bussière F 103 B4
Laç AL 182 B1
La Caillère F 114 B3
Lacalahorra E 164 B1
La Caletta
*Cágliari* I 179 C2
*Núoro* I 178 B3
La Calmette F 131 B3
La Calzada de Oropesa
E 150 C2
La Campana E 162 A2
La Cañada E 150 B3
Lacanau F 128 B1
Lacanau-Océan F 128 A1
Lacanche F 104 B3
La Canourgue F 130 A2
La Capelle F 91 B3
Lacapelle-Marival
F 129 B4
Laćarak SRB 127 B1
La Cardanchosa E 156 B2
La Caridad E 141 A4
La Carlota E 162 A3
La Carolina E 157 B4
Lacaune F 130 B1
La Cava E 153 B4
La Cavalerie F 130 A2
Laceby GB 41 B3
Lacedónia I 172 A1
La Celle-en-Moravan
F 104 B3
La Celle-St Avant
F 102 B2
La Cerca E 143 B3
Láces I 108 C1
La Chaise-Dieu F 117 B3
La Chaize-Giraud
F 114 B2
La Chaize-le-Vicomte
F 114 B2
La Chambre F 118 B3
Lachania GR 188 D2
La Chapelaude F 116 A2
La Chapelle-d'Angillon
F 103 B4
La Chapelle-en-
Aalgaudémar F 118 C3
La Chapelle-en-Vercors
F 118 C2
La Chapelle-Glain
F 101 B4
La Chapelle-la-Reine
F 90 C2
La Chapelle-Laurent
F 116 B3
La Chapelle-St Luc
F 91 C4
La Chapelle-sur-Erdre
F 101 B4
La Chapelle-Vicomtesse
F 103 B3
La Charce F 132 A1
La Charité-sur-Loire
F 104 B2
La Chartre-sur-le-Loir
F 102 B2
La Châtaigneraie
F 114 B3
La Châtre F 103 C3
La Chaussée-sur-Marne
F 91 C4
La Chaux-de-Fonds
CH 106 B1
Lachen CH 107 B3
Lachendorf D 72 B3
La Cheppe F 91 B4
La Chèze F 101 A3
Lachowice PL 99 B3
La Ciotat F 132 B1
Łąck PL 77 B4
Läckeby S 62 B4
Läckö S 55 B4
La Clayette F 117 A4
La Clusaz F 118 B3
Lacock GB 43 A4
La Codosera E 155 B3
La Concha E 143 A3
La Condamine-
Châtelard F 132 A2
Láconi I 179 C3
La Contienda E 161 A3
La Coquille F 115 C4
La Coronada E 156 B2
La Côte-St André
F 118 B2
La Cotinière F 114 C2
La Courtine F 116 B2
Lacq F 145 A3
La Crau F 132 B2
La Crèche F 115 B3
La Croix F 102 B2
Lacroix-Barrez F 116 C2
Lacroix-St Ouen F 90 B2
Lacroix-sur-Meuse
F 92 C1
La Croix-Valmer F 132 B2
La Cumbre E 156 A2
Łącznik PL 86 B1
Lad H 125 A3
Ladbergen D 71 B4
Lądek-Zdrój PL 85 B4
Ladelund D 64 B2
Ladendorf A 97 C4
Ladignac-le-Long
F 115 C5
Ladíspoli I 168 B2
Ladoeiro P 155 B3
Ladon F 103 B4
La Douze F 129 A3
Ladushkin RUS 69 A5
Ladybank GB 35 B4
Laer D 71 B4
La Espina E 141 A4
La Estrella E 156 A2
La Farga de Moles
E 146 B2
La Fatarella E 153 A4
La Felipa E 158 B2
La Fère F 90 B3
La Ferrière
*Indre-et-Loire* F 102 B2

**La Ferrière** continued
Vendée F . . . 114 B2
**La Ferrière-en-Parthenay** F . . .115 B3
La-Ferté-Alais F . . 90 C2
La-Ferté-Bernard F 102 A2
La-Ferté-Frênel F. . 89 B4
La-Ferté-Gaucher F. 90 C3
La-Ferté-Imbault F. 103 B3
La-Ferté-Macé F . . 89 B3
La-Ferté-Milon F . . 90 B3
**La-Ferté-sous-Jouarre** F . . . . . . 90 C3
**La-Ferté-St-Aubin** F . . . . . 103 B3
La-Ferté-St-Cyr F. . 103 B3
La-Ferté-Vidame F. . 89 B4
**La Ferté Villeneuil** F . . . . . 103 B3
La Feuillie F . . . . 90 B1
Lafkos GR . . . . . 183 D5
La Flèche F . . . . 102 B1
La Flotte F . . . . 114 B2
Lafnitz A. . . . . . 111 B3
**La Font de la Figuera** E. . . . . . 159 C3
La Fouillade F . . 130 A1
Lafrançaise F . . . 129 B4
La Fregeneda E . . 149 B3
La Fresneda E . . . 153 B4
La Fuencubierta E . 162 A3
**La Fuente de San Esteban** E . . . . 149 B3
La Fulioala E . . . 147 C2
La Gacilly F . . . . 101 B3
La Galera E . . . . 153 B4
Lagan S . . . . . . 60 C3
Laganadi I . . . . . 175 C1
Lagarde F . . . . . 146 A2
La Garde-Freinet F 132 B2
**Lagares**
  Coimbra P . . . . 148 B2
  Porto P. . . . . . 148 A1
La Garnache F. . . 114 B2
Lagaro I . . . . . . 135 A4
La Garriga E . . . . 147 C3
La Garrovilla E . . 155 C4
Lagartera E . . . . 150 C2
La Gaubretière F. . 114 B2
Lågbol S . . . . . . 51 B5
Lage F . . . . . . . 72 C1
Lägerdorf D . . . . 64 C2
Lagg GB. . . . . . . 34 C2
Laggan GB. . . . . 32 D2
Laggartorp S . . . . 55 A5
Łagiewniki PL . . . 85 B4
La Gineta E . . . . 158 B1
Láglio I . . . . . . 120 B2
Lagnieu F . . . . . 118 B2
Lagny-sur-Marne F . 90 C2
**Lago**
  Calabria I . . . . 175 B2
  Veneto I . . . . . 121 B5
Lagôa P . . . . . . 160 B1
Lagoaça P . . . . . 149 A3
Lagonegro I . . . . 174 A1
**Lagos**
  GR . . . . . . . . 183 B7
  P . . . . . . . . . 160 B1
Lagosanto I . . . . 121 C5
**Łagów**
  Lubuskie PL . . . 75 B4
  Świętokrzyskie PL . 87 B5
**La Granadella**
  Alicante E . . . . 159 C4
  Lleida E . . . . . 153 A4
La Grand-Combe F 131 A3
La Grande-Croix F . 117 B4
La Grande-Motte F 131 B3
**La Granja d'Escarp** E. . . . . . 153 A4
La Granjuela E. . . 156 B2
Lagrasse F . . . . . 146 A3
La Grave F . . . . . 118 B3
La Gravelle F . . . 101 A4
Laguardia E . . . . 143 B4
La Guardia E . . . 151 C4
**La Guardia de Jaén** E. . . . . . 163 A4
Laguarres E . . . . 145 B4
Laguenne F . . . . 116 B1
Laguépie F. . . . . 129 B4
**La Guerche-de-Bretagne** F . . . . . 101 B4
**La Guerche-sur-l'Aubois** F . . . . . 104 C1
La Guérinière F . . 114 B1
Laguiole F . . . . . 116 C2
Laguna de Duera E 150 A3
**Laguna del Marquesado** E . . . . . . 152 B2
**Laguna de Negrillos** E . . . . . . 142 B1
Lagundo I . . . . . 108 C2
Lagunilla E . . . . 149 B3
La Haba E . . . . . 156 B2
Laharie F . . . . . 128 B1
La Haye-du-Puits F. 88 A2
La Haye-Pesnel F . 88 B2
Lahden D. . . . . . 71 B4
La Herlière F . . . 78 B2
La Hermida E . . . 142 A2
La Herrera E . . . . 158 C1
Laheycourt F . . . . 91 C5
La Higuera E . . . 158 C2

La Hiniesta E . . . 149 A4
Lahnstein D . . . . 81 B3
Laholm S . . . . . . 61 C3
La Horcajada E . . 150 B2
La Horra E . . . . . 143 C3
Lahr D . . . . . . . 93 C3
Lahti FIN . . . . . . 8 B4
La Hulpe B . . . . . 79 B4
La Hutte F . . . . . 89 B4
Laichingen D . . . . 94 C1
L'Aigle F . . . . . . 89 B4
La Iglesuela E . . . 150 B3
**La Iglesuela del Cid** E . . . . . 153 B3
Laignes F . . . . . 104 B3
Laiguéglia I . . . . 133 B4
**L'Aiguillon-sur-Mer** F. . . . . . 114 B2
**Laimbach am Ostrong** A. . . . . . 97 C3
Laina E . . . . . . 152 A1
Lainio S . . . . . . 196 B5
Lairg GB. . . . . . . 32 C2
La Iruela E . . . . 164 B2
Laissac F . . . . . 130 A1
Laisvall S . . . . . 195 D8
Láives I . . . . . . 121 A4
La Javie F . . . . . 132 A2
Lajkovac SRB . . . 127 C2
**La Jonchère-St Maurice** F . . . . . 116 A1
La Jonquera E . . . 146 B3
Lajoskomárom H . 112 C2
Lajosmizse H. . . . 112 B3
Lak H . . . . . . . 99 C4
Lakenheath GB . . 45 A4
Lakitelek H. . . . . 113 C4
Lakki GR . . . . . 185 D4
Lakolk DK . . . . . 64 A1
Łąkorz PL. . . . . . 69 B4
**Lakšárska Nová Ves** SK . . . . . 98 C1
Lakselv N . . . . . 193 B8
Laksfors N . . . . . 195 E4
Laktaši BIH . . . . 124 C3
La Lantejuela E . . 162 A2
Lalapaşa TR. . . . 186 A1
L'Albagès E . . . . 153 A4
Lalbenque F . . . . 129 B4
L'Alcudia E . . . . 159 B3
L'Aldea E . . . . . 153 B4
Lalín E . . . . . . 140 B2
**La Línea de la Concepción** E . . 162 B2
Lalizolle F . . . . . 116 A3
La Llacuna E . . . 147 C2
Lalley F . . . . . . 118 C2
Lalling D . . . . . . 95 C5
Lalm N . . . . . . 198 D6
**La Londe-les-Maures** F. . . . . . 132 B2
La Loupe F. . . . . 89 B5
La Louvière B . . . 79 B4
L'Alpe-d'Huez F . .118 B3
La Luisiana E . . . 162 A2
Laluque F . . . . . 128 C1
Lam D. . . . . . . . 95 B5
La Machine F . . . 104 C2
la Maddalena I . . 178 A3
Lama dei Peligni I . 169 A4
Lamadrid E . . . . 142 A2
Lamagistére F . . . 129 B3
**La Mailleraye-sur-Seine** F. . . . . . 89 A4
La Malène F . . . . 130 A2
Lama Mocogno I . 135 A3
La Mamola E . . . 163 B4
**La Manresana dels Prats** E . . . . . 147 C2
Lamarche F . . . . 105 A4
**Lamarche-sur-Saône** F. . . . . . 105 B4
Lamargelle F . . . 105 B3
Lamarosa P . . . . 154 B2
Lamarque F . . . . 128 A2
Lamas P. . . . . . . 148 B1
La Masadera E . . 145 C3
Lamas de Moaro P 140 B2
Lamastre F . . . . 117 C4
La Mata E . . . . . 150 C3
**La Mata de Ledesma** E . . . . . 149 A4
**La Mata de Monteagudo** E. . . . . . 142 B1
Lambach A. . . . . 109 A4
Lamballe F . . . . 101 A3
Lamberhurst GB . . 45 B4
Lambesc F . . . . 131 B4
Lambia GR. . . . . 184 B2
Lambley GB . . . . 37 B4
Lambourn GB . . . 44 B2
Lamego P. . . . . . 148 A2
**La Meilleraye-de-Bretagne** F . . . . 101 B4
Le Ménitré F . . . 102 B1
L'Ametlla de Mar E 153 B4
Lamia GR. . . . . . 182 E4
Lammhult S . . . . 62 A2
La Mojonera E . . . 164 C2
La Mole F . . . . . 132 B2
**La Monnerie-le-Montel** F. . . . . . 117 B3
La Morera E . . . . 155 C4
La Mothe-Achard F 114 B2
Lamothe-Cassel F. 129 B4

**Lamothe-Montravel** F. . . . . . 128 B3
**La Mothe-St Héray** F. . . . . . .115 B3
**Lamotte-Beuvron** F. . . . . . 103 B4
**La Motte-Chalançon** F. . . . . . 131 A4
**La Motte-du-Caire** F. . . . . . 132 A2
**La Motte-Servolex** F. . . . . . 118 B2
Lampertheim D . . 93 B4
Lampeter GB . . . 39 B2
L'Ampolla E . . . . 153 B4
**Lamprechtshausen** A. . . . . . 109 B3
Lamsfeld D . . . . 74 C3
Lamspringe D . . . 72 C3
Lamstedt D . . . . 72 A2
La Mudarra E . . . 142 C2
La Muela E . . . . 152 A2
La Mure F . . . . . 118 C2
**Lamure-sur-Azergues** F. . . . . . 117 A4
Lana I . . . . . . . 108 C2
Lanaja E. . . . . . 145 C3
Lanarce F . . . . . 117 C3
Lanark GB . . . . . 36 A3
La Nava E . . . . . 161 B3
**La Nava de Ricomalillo** E. . . . . . 156 A3
**La Nava de Santiago** E. . . . . . 155 B4
Lancaster GB . . . 37 B4
Lanchester GB . . 37 B5
Lanciano I . . . . . 169 A4
Lancing GB . . . . 44 C3
**Lançon-Provence** F. . . . . . 131 B4
Lancova Vas SLO . 124 A1
**Landau**
  Bayern D . . . . . .95 C4
  Rheinland-Pfalz D . 93 B4
Landeck A . . . . . 108 B1
Landen B . . . . . 79 B5
Landerneau F . . . 100 A1
Landeryd S . . . . 60 B3
Landesbergen D . . 72 B2
Landete E . . . . . 158 B2
Landévant F . . . . 100 B2
Landévennec F . . 100 A1
Landivisiau F . . . 100 A1
Landivy F . . . . . 88 B2
Landl A . . . . . . 108 B3
Landön S . . . . . .199 B11
Landos F . . . . . . 117 C3
Landouzy-le-Ville F. 91 B4
Landquart CH . . . 107 C4
Landrecies F . . . 91 A3
Landreville F . . . 104 A3
Landriano I . . . . 120 B2
Landsberg D . . . . 108 A1
Lands-berg D . . . 83 A4
Landsbro S . . . . 62 A2
Landscheid D . . . 92 B2
Landshut D . . . . 95 C4
Landskrona S . . . 61 D2
Landstuhl D. . . . . 93 B3
Lanesborough IRL . 28 A4
Lanester F . . . . . 100 B2
Lanestosa E . . . . 143 A3
La Neuve-Lyre F . . 89 B4
La Neuveville CH. . 106 B2
Langå DK . . . . . . 59 B2
Langada GR . . . . 185 A7
Langadas GR . . . 183 C5
Langa de Duero E . 151 A4
Langadia GR . . . . 184 B3
Langangen N . . . . 53 A5
Långared S . . . . 60 A2
Långaröd S . . . . 61 D3
Långaryd S . . . . 60 B3
Långås S . . . . . . 60 C2
Langasjö S . . . . 63 B3
Langau A . . . . . . 97 C3
Langeac F . . . . .117 B3
Langeais F . . . . 102 B2
Langedijk NL . . . 70 B1
Langeln D . . . . . 73 C3
Langelsheim D . . 72 C3
**Langemark-Poelkapelle** B. . . . . . 78 B2
**Langen**
  Hessen D . . . . . .93 B4
  Niedersachsen D . .72 A1
Langenau D . . . . 94 C2
Langenberg D . . . 81 A4
Langenbruck CH. . 106 B2
Langenburg D . . . 94 B1
Längenfeld A . . . 108 B1
Langenfeld D . . . 80 A2
Langenhorn D . . . 64 B1
Langenlois A . . . . 97 C3
Langenlonsheim D. 93 B3
Langennaudorf D . 83 A5
Langenneufnach D . 94 C2
Langenthal CH . . 106 B2
Langenzenn D . . . 94 B2
Langeoog D. . . . . 71 A4
Langeskov DK . . . 59 C3
Langesund N . . . . 53 A5
Langewiesen D . . 82 B2
Långflon S . . . . . 49 A4
Langförden D . . . 71 B5
Langhagen D . . . 73 A5
Länghem S . . . . 60 B3
Langhirano I . . . . 120 C3

Langholm GB . . . 36 A4
Langholt IS . . . . 191 D7
Långlöt S . . . . . . 62 B4
Langnau CH . . . . 106 C2
Langø DK. . . . . . 65 B4
Langogne F. . . . . 117 C3
Langon F . . . . . 128 B2
Langquaid D . . . . 95 C4
Långrådna S . . . . 56 B2
Langreo E . . . . . 142 A1
Langres F . . . . . 105 B4
Långsele S . . . . 200 C3
Långserud S . . . . 54 A3
Langset N . . . . . 48 B3
Långshyttan S . . . 50 B3
Langstrand N . . . 192 B7
Långträsk S . . . . 196 D3
Langueux F . . . . 101 A3
Languidic F. . . . . 100 B2
Längvik S. . . . . . 57 A4
Langwarden D . . . 71 A5
Langwathby GB . . 37 B4
Langwedel D . . . 72 B2
Langweid D . . . . 94 C2
Langwies CH . . . 107 C4
Lanheses E . . . . 148 A1
Lanięta PL . . . . . 77 B4
Lanildut F . . . . . 100 A1
Lanjarón E . . . . . 163 B4
Lanmeur F . . . . . 100 A2
**Lanna**
  Jönköping S . . . . 60 B3
  Örebro S . . . . . . 55 A5
Lännaholm S . . . 51 C4
Lannavaara S . . . 196 A4
Lannéanou F . . . . 100 A2
Lannemezan F. . . 145 A4
**Lanneuville-sur-Meuse** F. . . . . . 91 B5
Lannilis F . . . . . 100 A1
Lannion F . . . . . 100 A2
**La Nocle-Maulaix** F. . . . . . 104 C2
Lanouaille F . . . . 115 C5
Lansjärv S . . . . . 196 C5
**Lanslebourg-Mont-Cenis** F. . . . . . .119 B3
Lanta F . . . . . . 129 C4
Lantadilla E . . . . 142 B2
Lanton F . . . . . . 128 B1
Lantosque F . . . . 133 B3
**La Nuez de Arriba** E. . . . . . 143 B3
Lanusei I . . . . . . 179 C3
Lanúvio I . . . . . 168 B2
Lanvollon F . . . . 100 A3
Lanz D . . . . . . . 73 A4
Lanza E . . . . . . 140 A2
Lanzada E . . . . . 140 B2
Lanzahita E . . . . 150 B3
Lanzo Torinese I . .119 B4
Laole SRB . . . . . 127 C3
Laon F . . . . . . . 91 B3
Laons F . . . . . . 89 B5
La Paca E . . . . . 164 B3
La Pacaudière F . .117 A3
Lapalisse F . . . . 117 A3
La Palma d'Ebre E 153 A4
**La Palma del Condado** E . . . . . 161 B3
La Palme F . . . . 146 B4
La Palmyre F . . . 114 C2
La Parra E . . . . . 155 C4
Łapczyna Wola PL. 87 B3
**La Pedraja de Portillo** E . . . . . 150 A3
La Peraleja E . . . 152 B1
La Petit-Pierre F . . 93 C3
Lapeyrade F . . . . 128 B2
Lapeyrouse F . . . .116 A2
Lapford GB . . . . 42 B3
La Pinilla E . . . . 165 B3
Lapithos CY . . . . 181 A2
La Plagne F . . . . .118 B3
Laplume F . . . . . 129 B3
**La Pobla de Lillet** E . . . . . 147 B2
**La Pobla de Vallbona** E. . . . . . 159 B3
La Pobla Llarga E . 159 B3
**La Pola de Gordón** E. . . . . . 142 B1
la Porta F . . . . . 180 A2
La Pouèze F . . . . 102 B1
Lapoutroie F . . . . 106 A2
**La Póveda de Soria** E . . . . . 143 B4
Lapovo SRB . . . . 127 C3
Läppe S . . . . . . 56 A1
Lappenranta FIN . . 8 B6
Lappoluobbal N . . 192 C7
Lappträsk S . . . . 196 C6
La Preste F . . . . 146 B3
La Primaube F . . 130 A1
Lapseki TR. . . . . 186 B1
Lapua FIN . . . . . 8 A3
**La Puebla de Almoradie** E. . . . . . 157 A4
**La Puebla de Cazalla** E . . . . . 162 A2
**La Puebla de los Infantes** E . . . 162 A2
**La Puebla del Río** E . . . . . 162 A1

**La Puebla de Montalbán** E . . . . . 150 C3
**La Puebla de Roda** E . . . . . 145 B4
**La Puebla de Valdavia** E . . . . . 142 B2
**La Puebla de Valverde** E . . . . . 152 B3
La Pueblanueva E . 150 C3
**La Puerta de Segura** E . . . . . 164 A2
La Punt CH . . . . 107 C4
La Quintana E . . . 162 A3
La Quintera E . . . 162 A2
**La Rábita**
  Granada E . . . . .164 C1
  Jaén E . . . . . . .163 A3
Laracha E . . . . . 140 A2
Laragh IRL . . . . . 30 A2
**Laragne-Montéglin** F. . . . . . 132 A1
La Rambla E . . . . 163 A3
l'Arboç E . . . . . 147 C2
L'Arbresle F. . . . .117 B4
Lärbro S . . . . . . 57 C4
Larceveau F. . . . 144 A2
**Larche**
  Alpes-de-Haute-
    Provence F. . . .132 A2
  Corrèze F. . . . . 129 A4
Lårdal N . . . . . . 53 A4
Lærdalsøyri N . . . 47 A4
Lardosa P . . . . . 155 B3
La Reale I . . . . . 178 A2
Laredo E . . . . . . 143 A3
La Réole F . . . . . 128 B2
Largentière F . . . 131 A3
**L'Argentière-la-Bessée** F. . . . . . 118 C3
Largs GB . . . . . . 34 C3
Lari I . . . . . . . 134 B3
La Riera E . . . . . 141 A4
La Riera de Gaià E 147 C2
La Rinconada E . . 162 A1
Lariño E . . . . . . 140 B1
Larino I . . . . . . 170 B2
Larisa GR. . . . . . 182 D4
**La Rivière-Thibouville** F. . . . . . 89 A4
La Robla E . . . . 142 B1
**La Roca de la Sierra** E. . . . . . 155 B4
La Roche CH . . . 106 C2
**La Rochebeaucourt-Argentine** F . . . 115 C4
**La Roche-Bernard** F. . . . . . 101 B3
**La Roche-Canillac** F. . . . . . .116 B1
**La Roche-Chalais** F. . . . . . 128 A3
**La Roche Derrien** F. . . . . . 100 A2
**La Roche-des-Arnauds** F. . . . . . 132 A1
**La Roche-en-Ardenne** B. . . . . . 80 B1
**La Roche-en-Brénil** F. . . . . . 104 B3
**La Rochefoucauld** F. . . . . . 115 C4
La Roche-Guyon F . 90 B1
La Rochelle F . . . .114 B2
La Roche-Posay F .115 B4
**La Roche-sur-Foron** F. . . . . . .118 A3
**La Roche-sur-Yon** F. . . . . . .114 B2
**La Roda**
  Albacete E . . . .158 B1
  Oviedo E . . . . .141 A4
**La Roda de Andalucía** E. . . . . . 162 A3
Laroquebrou F . . .116 C2
**La Roquebrussanne** F. . . . . . 132 B1
Laroque d'Olmes F 146 B2
**La Roque-Gageac** F . . . . . 129 B4
**Laroque-Ste-Marguerite** F . . . 130 A2
Laroque-Timbaut F 129 B3
Larouco E . . . . . 141 B3
Larraga E . . . . . 144 B2
Larrau F . . . . . . 144 A3
Larrazet F . . . . . 129 C4
Laruns F . . . . . . 145 A3
Larva E . . . . . . 164 B1
Larvik N . . . . . . 53 A6
La Sagrada E . . . 149 B3
La Salceda E . . . 151 A4
Lasalle F . . . . . . 131 A2
La Salle I . . . . . 119 B3
**la Salute di Livenza** I . . . . . 122 B1
**La Salvetat-Peyralés** F. . . . . . 130 A1

**La Salvetat-sur-Agout** F. . . . . . 130 B1
Las Arenas E . . . 142 A2
La Sarraz CH . . . 105 C5
Lasarte E . . . . . 144 A1
Låsby DK . . . . . . 59 B2
Las Cabezadas E . 151 A4
**Las Cabezas de San Juan** E . . . . 162 B2
Las Correderas E . 157 B4
**Las Cuevas de Cañart** E. . . . . . 153 B3
La Seca E . . . . . 150 A3
**La Selva del Camp** E. . . . . . 147 C2
La Senia E . . . . 153 B4
La Serra E . . . . . 147 C2
La Seu d'Urgell E . 146 B2
**La Seyne-sur-Mer** F. . . . . . 132 B1
Las Gabias E . . . 163 A4
Las Herencias E . . 150 C3
Las Herrerias E . . 161 B2
Łasin PL. . . . . . . 69 B4
Lask PL . . . . . . 86 A3
Laska PL . . . . . . 68 B2
Łaskarzow PL . . . 87 A5
Laško SLO . . . . . 123 A4
Laskowice PL . . . 76 A3
Las Labores E . . . 157 A4
Las Mesas E . . . . 158 B1
Las Minas E . . . . 164 A3
Las Navas E . . . . 163 A3
**Las Navas de la Concepción** E . . 156 C2
**Las Navas del Marqués** E. . . . . . 150 B3
Las Navillas E . . . 157 A3
Las Negras E . . . 164 C3
La Solana E . . . . 157 B4
La Souterraine F . .116 A1
Las Pajanosas E . . 161 B3
Laspaules E. . . . . 145 B4
Las Pedroñas E . . 158 B1
La Spézia I . . . . . 134 A2
**Las Planes d'Hostoles** E . . . . . 147 B3
Laspuña E . . . . . 145 B4
**Las Rozas**
  Cantabria E . . . .142 B2
  Madrid E . . . . . .151 B4
Lassan D . . . . . . 66 C2
**Lassay-les-Châteaux** F. . . . . . 89 B3
Lasseube F . . . . 145 A3
Lassigny F . . . . . 90 B2
La Storta I . . . . . 168 B2
Lastovo HR . . . . 138 C2
**Lastras de Cuéllar** E. . . . . . 151 A3
Lästringe S . . . . 56 B3
Lastrup D. . . . . . 71 B4
Las Uces E . . . . 149 A3
**La Suze-sur-Sarthe** F. . . . . . 102 B2
Las Veguillas E . . 149 B4
**Las Ventas con Peña Aguilera** E . . . . 157 A3
**Las Ventas de San Julián** E . . . . 150 B2
Las Villes E . . . . 153 B4
Latasa E . . . . . . 144 B2
Látera I . . . . . . 168 A1
Laterza I . . . . . . 171 C4
La Teste F . . . . . 128 B1
Latheron GB . . . . 32 C3
La Thuile I . . . . .119 B3
Latiano I . . . . . . 173 B3
Latina I . . . . . . 169 B2
Latisana I . . . . . 122 B2
Látky SK . . . . . . 99 C3
La Toba E . . . . . 152 B2
La Toledana E . . . 157 A3
**La Torre de Cabdella** E . . . . . 146 B2
**La Torre de Esteban Hambrán** E . . . . 151 B3
**La Torre del l'Espanyol** E . . . . . 153 A4
La Torresaviñán E. 152 B1
La Tour d'Aigues F 132 B1
**La Tour de Peilz** CH . . . . . 106 C1
La Tour-du-Pin F . .118 B2
**La Tranche-sur-Mer** F. . . . . . .114 B2
La Tremblade F . . 114 C2
La Trimouille F . . . 115 B5
La Trinité F . . . . 100 B2
**La Trinité-Porhoët** F. . . . . . 101 A3
Latronico I . . . . 174 A2
Latronquière F . . . 116 C2
Latterbach CH . . . 106 C2
Laubach D . . . . . 81 B4
Laubert F . . . . . 117 C3
Laucha D . . . . . . 83 A3
Lauchhammer D . . 84 A1
Lauchheim D. . . . 94 C2
**Lauda-Königshofen** D . . . . . 94 B1
Laudal N . . . . . . 52 B3
Lauder GB . . . . . 35 C5
Lauenau D . . . . . 72 B2
Lauenburg D . . . . 73 A3
Lauf D . . . . . . . 95 B3

Laufach D 94 A1
Laufen
CH 106 B2
D 109 B3
Lauffen D 93 B5
Laugar IS 191 B8
Laugarás IS 190 C5
Laugarbakki IS 190 B5
Laugarvatn IS 190 C5
Laugharne GB 39 C2
Lauingen D 94 C2
Laujar de Andarax
E 164 C2
Laukaa FIN 8 A4
Lauker S 196 D2
Laukvik N 194 C5
La Uña E 142 A1
Launceston GB 42 B2
La Unión E 165 B4
Launois-sur-Vence
F 91 B4
Laupheim D 94 C1
Lauragh IRL 29 C2
Laureana di Borrello
I 175 C2
Laurencekirk GB 35 B5
Laurencetown IRL 28 A3
Laurenzana I 172 B1
Lauria I 174 A1
Laurière F 116 A1
Laurieston GB 36 B2
Laurino I 172 B1
Lausanne CH 106 C1
Laussonne F 117 C4
Lauta D 84 A2
Lautenthal D 82 A2
Lauterach A 107 B4
Lauterbach D 81 B5
Lauterbrunnen CH 106 C2
Lauterecken D 93 B3
Lauterhofen D 95 B3
Lautrec F 130 B1
Lauvsnes N 199 A7
Lauvvlk N 52 B2
Lauzerte F 129 B4
Lauzès F 129 B4
Lauzun F 129 B3
Lavagna I 134 A2
Laval F 102 A1
La Vall d'Uixó E 159 B3
Lavamünd A 110 C1
Lavara GR 186 A1
Lavardac F 129 B3
Lavaris P 148 B1
Lavarone I 121 B4
Lavau F 104 B1
Lavaur F 129 C4
La Vecilla de Curueño
E 142 B1
La Vega
*Asturias* E 141 A5
*Asturias* E 142 A1
*Cantabria* E 142 A2
Lavelanet F 146 B2
La Velilla E 151 A4
La Velles E 150 A2
Lavello I 172 A1
Lavelsloh D 72 B1
Lavenham GB 45 A4
Laveno I 120 B1
La Ventosa E 152 B1
Lavezzola I 135 A4
Laviano I 172 B1
La Victoria E 162 A3
La Vid E 151 A4
Lavik N 46 A2
La Vilavella E 159 B3
La Vilella Baixa E 147 C1
La Villa de Don Fadrique
E 157 A4
Lavilledieu F 131 A3
La Villedieu F 115 B3
La Ville Dieu-du-Temple
F 129 B4
Lavinio-Lido di Enea
I 168 B2
Lav is I 121 A4
Lavit F 129 C3
Lavoncourt F 105 B4
Lavos P 148 B1
La Voulte-sur-Rhône
F 117 C4
Lavoûte-Chilhac F 117 B3
Lavradio P 154 C1
Lavre P 154 C2
Lavrio GR 185 B5
La Wantzenau F 93 C3
Lawers GB 35 B3
Ławy PL 75 B3
Laxå S 55 B5
Laxamýri IS 191 B8
Laxe E 140 A2
Laxey GB 36 B2
Laxford Bridge GB 32 C1
Laxhall S 55 B4
Laxsjö S 199 B11
Laxtjarn S 49 B6
Laxvik S 61 C2
Laxviken S 199 B11
La Yesa E 159 B3
Laza E 141 B3
Lazarevac SRB 127 C2
Lazarevo SRB 126 B2
Lazise I 121 B3
Łaziska Grn. PL 86 B2
Lazkao E 144 A1
Lázně Bělohrad CZ 84 B3
Lázně Bohdaneč
CZ 97 A3
Lázně Kynžvart CZ 95 A4
Lazonby GB 37 B4
La Zubia E 163 A4
Łazy PL 67 B5
Lazzaro I 175 D1
Lea GB 40 B3
Leadburn GB 35 C4
Leadhills GB 36 A3
Leap IRL 29 C2
Leatherhead GB 44 B3
Łeba PL 68 A2
Lebach D 92 B2
Le Barp F 128 B2
Le Bar-sur-Loup F 132 B2
Le Béage F 117 C4
Le Beausset F 132 B1
Lebekke B 79 A4
Lébény H 111 B4
Le Bessat F 117 B4
Le Blanc F 115 B5
Le Bleymard F 130 A2
Łebno PL 68 A3
Leboreiro E 140 B3
Lębork PL 68 A2
Le Boullay-Mivoye
F 89 B5
Le Boulou F 146 B3
Le Bourg F 129 B4
Le Bourg-d'Oisans
F 118 B3
Le Bourget-du-Lac
F 118 B2
Le Bourgneuf-la-Forêt
F 101 A5
Le Bousquet d'Orb
F 130 B2
Le Brassus CH 105 C5
Le Breuil F 117 A3
Le Breuil-en-Auge F 89 A4
Lebrija E 162 B1
Lebring A 110 C2
Le Brusquet F 132 A2
Le Bry CH 106 C2
Le Bugue F 129 B3
Le Buisson F 129 B3
Lebus D 74 B3
Lebusa D 83 A5
Leca da Palmeira
P 148 A1
Le Caloy F 128 C2
Le Cap d'Agde F 130 B2
Le Cateau Cambrésis
F 91 A3
Le Caylar F 130 B2
Le Cayrol F 116 C2
Lecce I 173 B4
Lecco I 120 B2
Lécera E 153 A3
Lećevica HR 138 B2
Lech A 107 B5
Le Chambon-
Feugerolles F 117 B4
Le Chambon-sur-Lignon
F 117 B4
Le Château d'Oléron
F 114 C2
Le Châtelard F 118 B3
Le Châtelet F 103 C4
Le Chatelet-en-Brie
F 90 C2
Lechbruck D 108 B1
Lechena GR 184 B2
Le Chesne F 91 B4
Le Cheylard F 117 C4
Lechlade GB 44 B2
Lechovice CZ 97 C4
Leciñena E 145 C3
Leck D 64 B1
Le Collet-de-Deze
F 131 A2
Le Conquet F 100 A1
Le Creusot F 104 C3
Le Croisic F 101 B3
Le Crotoy F 78 B1
Lectoure F 129 C3
Łęczyca
*Łódzkie* PL 77 B4
*Zachodnio-Pomorskie*
PL 75 A4
Ledaña E 158 B2
Ledbury GB 39 B4
Lede B 79 B3
Ledečnad Sazavou
CZ 97 B3
Ledenice CZ 96 C2
Le Deschaux F 105 C4
Ledesma E 149 A3
Lédignan F 131 B3
Lédigos E 142 B2
Ledmore GB 32 C2
Lednice CZ 97 C4
Lednicke-Rovné SK 98 B2
Le Donjon F 117 A3
Le Dorat F 115 B5
Lędyczek PL 68 B1
Lędziny PL 86 B3
Leeds GB 40 B2
Leek
GB 40 B1
NL 71 A3
Leenaun IRL 28 A2
Leens NL 71 A3
Leer D 71 A4
Leerdam NL 79 A5
Leerhafe D 71 A4
Leese D 72 B2
Leeuwarden NL 70 A2
Leezen D 64 C3
Le Faou F 100 A1
Le Faoüet F 100 A2
Lefka CY 181 A1
Lefkada GR 182 E2
Lefkimis GR 182 D2
Lefkoniko CY 181 A2
Le Folgoet F 100 A1
Le Fossat F 146 A2
Le Fousseret F 146 A2
Le Fugeret F 132 A2
Leganés E 151 B4
Legau D 107 B5
Le Gault-Soigny F 91 C3
Legbąd PL 68 B2
Legé F 114 B2
Lège-Cap-Ferret F 128 B1
Legionowo PL 77 B5
Léglise B 92 B1
Legnago I 121 B4
Legnano I 120 B1
Legnaro I 121 B4
Legnica PL 85 A4
Łęgowo PL 69 A3
Legrad HR 124 A2
Le Grand-Bornand
F 118 B3
Le-Grand-Bourg F 116 A1
Le Grand-Lucé F 102 B2
Le Grand-Pressigny
F 102 C2
Le Grand-Quevilly F 89 A5
Le Grau-du-Roi F 131 B3
Léguevin F 129 C4
Legutiano E 143 B4
Le Havre F 89 A4
Lehesten D 82 B3
Lehnice SK 111 A4
Lehnin D 74 B1
Le Hohwald F 93 C3
Le Houga F 128 C2
Lehrberg D 94 B2
Lehre D 73 B3
Lehrte D 72 B2
Lehsen D 73 A4
Leibnitz A 110 C2
Leicester GB 40 C2
Leiden NL 70 B1
Leidschendam NL 70 B1
Leigh GB 38 A4
Leighlinbridge IRL 30 B2
Leighton Buzzard
GB 44 B3
Leignon B 79 B5
Leikanger N 198 C2
Leimen D 93 B4
Leinefelde D 82 A2
Leinesfjord N 194 C6
Leintwardine GB 39 B4
Leipojärvi S 196 B4
Leipzig D 83 A4
Leira
*Nordland* N 195 D4
*Oppland* N 47 B6
Leiråmoen N 195 D5
Leiria P 154 B2
Leirvassbu N 47 A5
Leirvik
*Hordaland* N 52 A1
*Sogn og Fjordane*
N 46 A2
Leisach A 109 C3
Leisnig D 83 A4
Leiston GB 45 A5
Leitholm GB 35 C5
Leitrim IRL 26 C2
Leitza E 144 A2
Leitzkau D 73 B4
Lejkowo PL 68 A1
Lekani GR 183 B6
Łękawa PL 86 A3
Łekawica PL 99 B3
Lekeitio E 143 A4
Lekenik HR 124 B2
Lekeryd S 62 A2
Leknes N 194 B4
Łęknica PL 84 A2
Leksand S 50 B1
Leksvik N 199 B7
Lekunberri E 144 A2
Lekvattnet S 49 B4
Le Lardin-St Lazare
F 129 A4
Le Lauzet-Ubaye F 132 A2
Le Lavandou F 132 B2
Le Lion-d'Angers
F 102 B1
Lelkowo PL 69 A5
Le Locle CH 106 B1
Le Loroux-Bottereau
F 101 B4
Le Louroux-Béconnais
F 101 B5
Lelów PL 86 B3
Le Luc F 132 B2
Le Lude F 102 B2
Lelystad NL 70 B2
Lem
*Ringkøbing* DK 59 B1
*Viborg Amt.* DK 58 B1
Le Malzieu-Ville F 116 C3
Le Mans F 102 A2
Le Mas-d'Azil F 146 A2
Le Massegros F 130 A2
Le Mayet-de-Montagne
F 117 A3
Le May-sur-Evre F 101 B5
Lembach F 93 B3
Lemberg F 93 B3
Lembèye F 145 A3
Lemelerveld NL 71 B3
Le Mêle-sur-Sarthe
F 89 B4
Le Ménil F 105 A5
Le Merlerault F 89 B4
Le Mesnil-sur-Oger
F 91 C4
Lemförde D 71 B5
Lemgo D 72 B1
Le Miroir F 105 C4
Lemland FIN 51 B7
Lemmer NL 70 B2
Le Molay-Littry F 88 A3
Le Monastier-sur-
Gazeille F 117 C3
Le Monêtier-les-Bains
F 118 C3
Le Mont-Dore F 116 B2
Le Montet F 116 A3
Le Mont-St Michel F 88 B2
Lempdes F 116 B3
Le Muret F 128 B2
Le Muy F 132 B2
Lemvig DK 58 B1
Lemwerder D 72 A1
Lena N 48 B2
Lenart SLO 110 C2
Lenartovce SK 99 C4
Lenauheim RO 126 B2
Lencloître F 102 C2
Lend A 109 B4
Lendalfoot GB 36 A2
Lendava SLO 111 C3
Lendery RUS 3 E12
Lendinara I 121 B4
Lendorf A 109 C4
Lendum DK 58 A3
Le Neubourg F 89 A4
Lengefeld D 83 B5
Lengerich
*Niedersachsen* D 71 B4
*Nordrhein-Westfalen*
D 71 B4
Lenggries D 108 B2
Lengyeltóti H 111 C4
Lenhovda S 62 B3
Lenk CH 106 C2
Lennartsfors S 54 A2
Lennestadt D 81 A4
Lennoxtown GB 35 C3
Leno I 120 B3
Lénola I 169 B3
Le Nouvion-en-
Thiérache F 91 A3
Lens
B 79 B3
F 78 B2
Lensahn D 65 B3
Lens Lestang F 117 B5
Lensvik N 198 B6
Lentellais E 141 B3
Lentföhrden D 64 C2
Lenti H 111 C3
Lentini I 177 B3
Lenungshammar S 54 A3
Lenzburg CH 106 B3
Lenzen D 73 A4
Lenzerheide CH 107 C4
Leoben A 110 B2
Leogang A 109 B3
Leominster GB 39 B4
León E 142 B1
Léon F 128 C1
Leonberg D 93 C5
Léoncel F 118 C2
Leonding A 96 C2
Leonessa I 169 A2
Leonforte I 177 B3
Leonidio GR 184 B3
Leopoldsburg B 79 A5
Leopoldsdorf im
Marchfeld A 111 A3
Leopoldshagen D 74 A2
Leova MD 17 B8
Le Palais F 100 B2
Le Parcq F 78 B2
Lepe E 161 B2
Le Péage-de-Roussillon
F 117 B4
Le Pellerin F 101 B4
Lepenou GR 182 E3
Le Perthus F 146 B3
Le Pertuis F 117 B4
Le Petit-Bornand F 118 B3
Lephin GB 31 B2
L'Epine F 132 A1
Le Poët F 132 A1
Lepoglava HR 124 A2
Le Poirè-sur-Vie F 114 B2
Le Pont CH 105 C5
Le Pont-de-Montvert
F 130 A2
Le Porge F 128 B1
Le Porge-Océan F 128 B1
Le Portel F 78 B1
Le Pouldu F 100 B2
Le Pouliguen F 101 B3
Leppäjärvi FIN 192 D7
Leppävirta FIN 8 A5
Leppin D 73 B4
le Prese I 120 A3
Lepsény H 112 C2
Le Puy-en-Velay F 117 B3
Le Puy-Ste Réparade
F 131 B4
Le Quesnoy F 79 B3
Léquile I 173 B4
Le Rayol F 132 B2
Lercara Friddi I 176 B2
Lerdal S 54 B2
Leré F 103 B4
Lérici I 134 A2
Lerin E 144 B2
Lerma E 143 B3
Lerm-et-Musset F 128 B2
Lermoos A 108 B1
Le Roeulx B 79 B4
Le Rouget F 116 C2
Lérouville F 92 C1
Le Rozier F 130 A2
Lerum S 60 B2
Le Russey F 106 B1
Lervik N 54 A1
Lerwick GB 33 A5
Lés E 145 B4
Les Abrets F 118 B2
Les Aix-d'Angillon
F 103 B4
Lesaka E 144 A2
Les Ancizes-Comps
F 116 B2
Les Andelys F 90 B1
Les Arcs
*Savoie* F 119 B3
*Var* F 132 B2
Les-Aubiers F 102 C1
Les Baux-de-Provence
F 131 B3
Les Bézards F 103 B4
Les Bois CH 106 B1
Les Bordes F 103 B4
Les Borges Blanques
E 147 C1
Les Borges del Camp
E 147 C2
Les Brunettes F 104 C2
Lesbury GB 37 A5
Les Cabannes F 146 B2
L'Escala E 147 B4
Lescar F 145 A3
L'Escarène F 133 B3
Lesce SLO 123 A3
Lescheraines F 118 B3
Lesconil F 100 B1
Les Contamines-
Montjoie F 118 B3
les Coves de Vinroma
E 153 B4
Les Déserts F 118 B2
Les Deux-Alpes F 118 C3
Les Diablerets CH 119 A4
Lesdins F 90 B3
Les Echelles F 118 B2
Le Sel-de-Bretagne
F 101 B4
Le Sentier CH 105 C5
Les Escaldes AND 146 B2
Les Essarts F 114 B2
Les Estables F 117 C4
Les Eyzies-de-Tayac
F 129 B4
Les Gets F 118 A3
Les Grandes-Ventes
F 89 A5
Les Haudères CH 119 A4
Les Herbiers F 114 B2
Les Hôpitaux-Neufs
F 105 C5
Lesično SLO 123 A4
Lésina I 171 B3
Lesjaskog N 198 C5
Lesjöfors S 49 C6
Leskovac SRB 16 D4
Leskova Dolina
SLO 123 B3
Leskovec
CZ 98 B1
SLO 123 B4
Leskovice CZ 97 B3
Leskovik AL 182 C2
Leslie GB 35 B4
Les Lucs-sur-Boulogne
F 114 B2
Les Mages F 131 A3
Lesmahagow GB 36 A3
Les Mazures F 91 B4
Les Mées F 132 A1
Lesmont F 91 C4
Les Mureaux F 90 C1
Leśna PL 84 A3
Lesneven F 100 A1
Leśnica PL 86 B2
Lešnica SRB 127 C1
Leśniów Wielkoplski
PL 75 C4
Lesnoye RUS 9 C9
Les Omergues F 132 A1
Les Ormes-sur-Voulzie
F 90 C3
Les Orres F 132 A2
Le Souquet F 128 C1
Lesparre-Médoc F 128 A2
l'Espérance F 91 B3
l'Esperou F 130 A2
Les Pieux F 88 A2
Lesponne F 145 A4
Les Ponts-de-Cé F 102 B1
Les Ponts-de-Martel
CH 106 C1
Les Praz F 119 B3
L'Espunyola E 147 B2
Les Riceys F 104 B3
Les Roches F 117 B4
Les Rosaires F 101 A3
Les Rosiers F 102 B1
Les Rousses F 105 C5
Les Sables-d'Olonne
F 114 B2
Lessach A 109 B4
Lessay F 88 A2
Lessebo S 62 B3
Les Settons F 104 B3
Lessines B 79 B3
L'Estany E 147 C3
Les Ternes F 116 B2
Lesterps F 115 B4
Les Thilliers en-Vexin
F 90 B1
Les Touches F 101 B4
Les Trois Moûtiers
F 102 B2
Les Vans F 131 A3
Les Verrières CH 105 C5
Les Vignes F 130 A2
Leswalt GB 36 B1
Leszno
*Mazowieckie* PL 77 B5
*Wielkopolskie* PL 85 A4
Leszno Górne PL 84 A3
Letchworth GB 44 B3
Le Teil F 131 A3
Le Teilleul F 88 B3
Le Temple-de-Bretagne
F 101 B4
Letenye H 111 C3
Le Theil F 89 B4
Le Thillot F 106 B1
Letino I 170 B2
Letohrad CZ 97 A4
Le Touquet-Paris-Plage
F 78 B1
Le Touvet F 118 B2
Letovice CZ 97 B4
Le Translay F 90 B1
Le Tréport F 90 A1
Letschin D 74 B3
Letterfrack IRL 28 A2
Letterkenny IRL 26 B3
Lettermacaward IRL 26 B2
Lettoch GB 32 D3
Letur E 164 A2
Letux E 153 A3
Letzlingen D 73 B4
Leucate F 146 B4
Leuchars GB 35 B5
Leuglay F 105 B3
Leuk CH 119 A4
Leukerbad CH 119 A4
Leumrabhagh GB 31 A2
Leuna D 83 A4
Leusden NL 70 B2
Leutenberg D 82 B3
Leuterschach D 108 B1
Leutershausen D 94 B2
Leutkirch D 107 B5
Leuven B 79 B4
Leuze-en-Hainaut B 79 B3
Le Val F 132 B2
Le Val-André F 101 A3
Le Val-d'Ajol F 105 B5
Levan AL 182 C1
Levanger N 199 B8
Levanjska Varoš
HR 125 B4
Lévanto I 134 A2
Levaré F 88 B3
Levata I 120 B3
Leveld N 47 B5
Leven
*East Yorkshire*
GB 41 B3
*Fife* GB 35 B5
Leverano I 173 B3
Le Verdon-sur-Mer
F 114 C2
Leverkusen D 80 A2
Levern D 72 B1
Le Vernet F 132 A2
Levet F 103 C4
Levice SK 112 A2
Lévico Terme I 121 A4
Levie F 180 B2
Levier F 105 C5
Le Vigan F 130 B2
Lévignen F 90 B2
le Ville I 135 B5
Levinovac HR 124 B3
Le Vivier-sur-Mer F 88 B2
Levoča SK 99 B4
Levroux F 103 C3
Lewes GB 45 C4
Lewin Brzeski PL 85 B5
Lewisham GB 44 B3
Leyburn GB 37 B5
Leyland GB 38 A4
Leysdown-on-Sea
GB 45 B4
Leysin CH 119 A4
Lezajsk PL 12 C5
Lézardrieux F 100 A2
Lézat-sur-Lèze F 146 A2
Lezay F 115 B3
Lezhë AL 182 B1
Lézignan-Corbières
F 130 B1
Lezignan-la-Cèbe
F 130 B2
Ležimir SRB 126 B1

**Lézinnes** F 104 B3
**Lezoux** F 117 B3
**Lezuza** E 158 C1
**Lhenice** CZ 96 C2
**Lherm** F 146 A2
**Lhommaizé** F 115 B4
**L'Hospitalet** F 146 B2
**L'Hospitalet de l'Infant**
E 147 D1
**L'Hospitalet de Llobregat** E 147 C3
**L'Hospitalet-du-Larzac**
F 130 B2
**Lhuître** F 91 C4
**Liancourt** F 90 B2
**Liart** F 91 B4
**Liatorp** S 63 B2
**Liatrie** GB 32 D2
**Libáň** CZ 84 B3
**Libceves** CZ 84 B1
**Liběchov** CZ 84 B2
**Liber** E 141 B3
**Liberec** CZ 84 B3
**Libiąż** PL 86 B3
**Libina** CZ 98 B1
**Libochovice** CZ 84 B2
**Libohovë** AL 182 C2
**Libourne** F 128 B2
**Libramont** B 92 B1
**Librazhd** AL 182 B2
**Librilla** E 165 B3
**Libros** E 152 B2
**Licata** I 176 B2
**Licciana Nardi** I 134 A3
**Licenza** I 169 A2
**Liceros** E 151 A4
**Lich** D 81 B4
**Lichères-près-Aigremont** F 104 B2
**Lichfield** GB 40 C2
**Lichtenau**
A 97 C3
D 81 A4
**Lichtenberg** D 83 B3
**Lichtenfels** D 82 B3
**Lichtensteig** CH 107 B4
**Lichtenstein** D 83 B4
**Lichtenvoorde** NL 71 C3
**Lichtervelde** B 78 A3
**Lička Jesenica** HR 123 B4
**Lickershamn** S 57 C4
**Lički Osik** HR 123 C4
**Ličko Lešce** HR 123 C4
**Licodía Eubéa** I 177 B3
**Licques** F 78 B1
**Lida** BY 13 B6
**Lidar** N 47 A6
**Lidečko** CZ 98 B2
**Liden** S 200 D2
**Lidhult** S 60 C3
**Lidköping** S 55 B4
**Lido** I 122 B1
**Lido Azzurro** I 173 B3
**Lido degli Estensi**
I 122 C1
**Lido degli Scacchi**
I 122 C1
**Lido della Nazioni**
I 122 C1
**Lido di Camaiore** I 134 B3
**Lido di Casalbordino**
I 169 A4
**Lido di Castél Fusano**
I 168 B2
**Lido di Cincinnato**
I 168 B2
**Lido di Classe** I 135 A5
**Lido di Fermo** I 136 B2
**Lido di Fondi** I 169 B3
**Lido di Jésolo** I 122 B1
**Lido di Lícola** I 170 C2
**Lido di Metaponto**
I 174 A2
**Lido di Óstia** I 168 B2
**Lido di Policoro** I 174 A2
**Lido di Pomposa** I 122 C1
**Lido di Savio** I 135 A5
**Lido di Scanzano** I 174 A2
**Lido di Siponto** I 171 B3
**Lido di Squillace** I 175 C2
**Lido di Volano** I 122 C1
**Lido Riccio** I 169 A4
**Lidoriki** GR 184 A3
**Lido Silvana** I 173 B3
**Lidsjöberg** S 199 A12
**Lidzbark** PL 77 A4
**Lidzbark Warmiński**
PL 69 A5
**Liebenau**
A 96 C2
D 72 B2
**Liebenwalde** D 74 B2
**Lieberose** D 74 C3
**Liebling** RO 126 B3
**Lieboch** A 110 C2
**Liège** B 80 B1
**Lieksa** FIN 3 E12
**Lienen** D 71 B4
**Lienz** A 109 C3
**Liepāja** LV 8 D2
**Lier** B 79 A4
**Lierbyen** N 54 A1
**Liernais** F 104 B3
**Liesing** A 109 C3
**Liestal** CH 106 B2
**Liétor** E 158 C2
**Lieurac** F 146 B2
**Lieurey** F 89 A4
**Liévin** F 78 B2
**Liezen** A 110 B1
**Liffol-le-Grand** F 92 C1
**Lifford** IRL 27 B3
**Liffré** F 101 A4
**Ligardes** F 129 B3
**Lignano Sabbiadoro**
I 122 B2
**Ligne** F 101 B4
**Lignières** F 103 C4
**Ligny-en-Barrois** F 92 C1
**Ligny-le-Châtel** F 104 B2
**Ligoła Polska** PL 85 A5
**Ligourio** GR 184 B4
**Ligowo** PL 77 B4
**Ligueil** F 102 B2
**Likavka** SK 99 B3
**Likenäs** S 49 B5
**Likhoslavl** RUS 9 D9
**Lild Strand** DK 58 A1
**L'Île-Bouchard** F 102 B2
**l'Île-Rousse** F 180 A1
**Lilienfeld** A 110 A2
**Lilienthal** D 72 A1
**Lilla Edet** S 54 B3
**Lilla Tjärby** S 61 C3
**Lille**
B 79 A4
F 78 B3
**Lillebonne** F 89 A4
**Lillehammer** N 48 A2
**Lillerød** DK 61 D2
**Lillers** F 78 B2
**Lillesand** N 53 B4
**Lillestrøm** N 48 C3
**Lillhärdal** S 199 D11
**Lillkyrka** S 56 A3
**Lillo** E 157 A4
**Lillögda** S 200 B3
**Lillpite** S 196 D4
**Lima** S 49 B5
**Limanowa** PL 99 B4
**Limassol** CY 181 B2
**Limavady** GB 27 A4
**Limbach-Oberfrohna**
D 83 B4
**Limbaži** LV 8 D4
**Limbourg** B 80 B1
**Limburg** D 81 B4
**Lime** DK 58 B3
**Limedsforsen** S 49 B5
**Limenaria** GR 183 C6
**Limenas Chersonisou**
GR 185 D6
**Limerick** IRL 29 B3
**Limes** I 121 B3
**Limésy** F 89 A4
**Limmared** S 60 B3
**Limni** GR 183 E5
**Limoges** F 115 C5
**Limogne-en-Quercy**
F 129 B4
**Limoise** F 104 C2
**Limone Piemonte** I 133 A3
**Limone sul Garda** I 121 B3
**Limons** F 117 B3
**Limours** F 90 C2
**Limoux** F 146 A3
**Linares** E 157 B4
**Linares de Mora** E 153 B3
**Linares de Riofrio**
E 149 B4
**Linaria** GR 183 E6
**Linas de Broto** E 145 B3
**Lincoln** GB 40 B3
**Lind** DK 59 B1
**Lindås** N 46 B2
**Lindau** D 107 B4
**Lindberget** N 48 A3
**Lindelse** DK 65 B3
**Lindenberg** D 74 B3
**Lindenberg im Allgäu**
D 107 B4
**Lindern** D 71 B4
**Linderöd** S 61 D3
**Lindesberg** S 56 A1
**Lindesnäs** S 50 B1
**Lindesnes** N 52 C3
**Lindholmen** S 57 A4
**Lindknud** DK 59 C2
**Lindlar** D 80 A3
**Lindö** S 56 B2
**Lindome** S 60 B2
**Lindos** GR 188 C3
**Lindoso** P 148 A1
**Lindow** D 74 B1
**Lindsdal** S 62 B4
**Lindshammar** S 62 A3
**Lindstedt** D 73 B4
**Lindved** DK 59 C2
**Líně** CZ 96 B1
**Lingbo** S 50 A3
**Lingen** D 71 B4
**Linghed** S 50 B2
**Linghem** S 56 B1
**Linguaglossa** I 177 B4
**Linia** PL 68 A2
**Linie** PL 74 A3
**Liniewo** PL 68 A3
**Linkenheim** D 93 B4
**Linköping** S 56 B1
**Linksness** GB 33 C3
**Linlithgow** GB 35 C4
**Linneryd** S 63 B3
**Linnes Hammarby**
S 51 C4
**Linnich** D 80 B2
**Linsell** S 199 C10
**Linslade** GB 44 B3
**Linthal** CH 107 C4
**Linyola** E 147 C1
**Linz**
A 96 C2
D 80 B3
**Liomseter** N 47 A6
**Lionárisso** CY 181 A3
**Lioni** I 172 B1
**Lion-sur-Mer** F 89 A3
**Lipany** SK 99 B4
**Lipar** SRB 126 B1
**Lipari** I 177 A3
**Lipcani** MD 17 A7
**Liperi** FIN 9 A6
**Liphook** GB 44 B3
**Lipiany** PL 75 A3
**Lipik** HR 124 B3
**Lipka** PL 68 B2
**Lipki Wielkie** PL 75 B4
**Lipnica** PL 68 B2
**Lipnica Murowana**
PL 99 B4
**Lipnik** PL 87 B5
**Lipník nad Bečvou**
CZ 98 B1
**Lipno**
*Kujawsko-Pomorskie*
PL 77 B4
*Łódzkie* PL 86 A2
**Liposthey** F 128 B2
**Lipovac** HR 125 B5
**Lipovec** CZ 97 B4
**Lipovets** UA 13 D8
**Lipovljani** HR 124 B2
**Lipowiec** PL 77 A6
**Lipowina** PL 69 A4
**Lippborg** D 81 A4
**Lippó** H 125 B4
**Lippoldsberg** D 81 A5
**Lippstadt** D 81 A4
**Lipsko** PL 87 A5
**Liptál** CZ 98 B1
**Liptovská-Lúžna**
SK 99 C3
**Liptovská Osada**
SK 99 C3
**Liptovská-Teplička**
SK 99 C4
**Liptovský Hrádok**
SK 99 B3
**Liptovský Milkuláš**
SK 99 B3
**Lipusz** PL 68 A2
**Lipůvka** CZ 97 B4
**Liré** F 101 B4
**Lisac** BIH 139 A3
**Lisbellaw** GB 27 B3
**Lisboa = Lisbon** P 154 C1
**Lisbon = Lisboa** P 154 C1
**Lisburn** GB 27 B4
**Liscannor** IRL 28 B2
**Lisdoonvarna** IRL 28 A2
**Lisewo** PL 69 B3
**Lisia Góra** PL 87 B5
**Lisięcice** PL 86 B1
**Lisieux** F 89 A4
**Lisjö** S 56 A2
**Liskeard** GB 42 B2
**L'Isle** CH 105 C5
**L'Isle-Adam** F 90 B2
**L'Isle-de-Noé** F 129 C3
**L'Isle-en-Dodon** F 145 A4
**L'Isle-Jourdain**
*Gers* F 129 C4
*Vienne* F 115 B4
**L'Isle-sur-la-Sorgue**
F 131 B4
**L'Isle-sur-le Doubs**
F 105 B5
**L'Isle-sur-Serein** F 104 B3
**Lisle-sur-Tarn** F 129 C4
**Lismore** IRL 29 B4
**Lisnaskea** GB 27 B3
**Lišov** CZ 96 B2
**Lisów**
*Lubuskie* PL 74 B3
*Śląskie* PL 86 B2
**Lisse** NL 70 B1
**Lissycasey** IRL 28 B2
**List** D 64 A1
**Listerby** S 63 B3
**Listowel** IRL 29 B2
**Listrac-Médoc** F 128 A2
**Liszki** PL 99 A3
**Liszkowo** PL 76 A2
**Lit** S 199 B11
**Litava** SK 99 C3
**Litcham** GB 41 C4
**Lit-et-Mixe** F 128 B1
**Litija** SLO 123 A3
**Litke** H 112 A3
**Litlabø** N 52 A1
**Litochoro** GR 182 C4
**Litoměřice** CZ 84 B2
**Litomyšl** CZ 97 B4
**Litovel** CZ 98 B1
**Litschau** A 96 C3
**Littlehampton** GB 44 C3
**Littleport** GB 45 A4
**Littleton** IRL 29 B4
**Little Walsingham**
GB 41 C4
**Litvinov** CZ 83 B5
**Livadero** GR 182 C3
**Livadhia** CY 181 B2
**Livadi** GR 182 C4
**Livadia** GR 184 A3
**Livarot** F 89 B4
**Liveras** CY 181 A1
**Livernon** F 129 B4
**Liverovici** MNE 139 C5
**Liverpool** GB 38 A4
**Livigno** I 107 C5
**Livingston** GB 35 C4
**Livno** BIH 138 B2
**Livo** FIN 197 D9
**Livold** SLO 123 B3
**Livorno** I 134 B3
**Livorno Ferraris** I 119 B5
**Livron-sur-Drôme**
F 117 C4
**Livry-Louvercy** F 91 B4
**Lixheim** F 92 C3
**Lixouri** GR 184 A1
**Lizard** GB 42 C1
**Lizy-sur-Ourcq** F 90 B3
**Lizzano** I 173 B3
**Lizzano in Belvedere**
I 135 A3
**Ljig** SRB 127 C2
**Ljørdalen** N 49 A4
**Ljosland** N 52 B3
**Ljubija** BIH 124 C2
**Ljubinje** BIH 139 C4
**Ljubljana** SLO 123 A3
**Ljubno ob Savinji**
SLO 123 A3
**Ljubovija** SRB 127 C1
**Ljubuški** BIH 138 B3
**Ljugarn** S 57 C4
**Ljung** S 60 B3
**Ljunga** S 56 B2
**Ljungaverk** S 200 D2
**Ljungby** S 60 C3
**Ljungbyhed** S 61 C3
**Ljungbyholm** S 63 B4
**Ljungdalen** S 199 C9
**Ljungsarp** S 60 B3
**Ljungsbro** S 56 B1
**Ljungskile** S 54 B2
**Ljusdal** S 200 E2
**Ljusfallshammar** S 56 B1
**Ljusne** S 51 A4
**Ljusterö** S 57 A4
**Ljutomer** SLO 111 C3
**Lŭki** BG 183 B6
**Lladurs** E 147 B2
**Llafranc** E 147 C4
**Llagostera** E 147 C3
**Llanaelhaiarn** GB 38 B2
**Llanarth** GB 39 B2
**Llanbedr** GB 38 B2
**Llanbedrog** GB 38 B2
**Llanberis** GB 38 A2
**Llanbister** GB 39 B3
**Llanbrynmair** GB 39 B3
**Llançà** E 146 B4
**Llandeilo** GB 39 C3
**Llandissilio** GB 39 C2
**Llandovery** GB 39 C3
**Llandrillo** GB 38 B3
**Llandrindod Wells**
GB 39 B3
**Llandudec** F 100 A1
**Llandudno** GB 38 A3
**Llandysul** GB 39 B2
**Llanelli** GB 39 C2
**Llanerchymedd** GB 38 A2
**Llanes** E 142 A2
**Llanfair Caereinion**
GB 38 B3
**Llanfairfechan** GB 38 A3
**Llanfyllin** GB 38 B3
**Llangadog** GB 39 C3
**Llangefni** GB 38 A2
**Llangollen** GB 38 B3
**Llangrannog** GB 39 B2
**Llangurig** GB 39 B3
**Llanidloes** GB 39 B3
**Llanilar** GB 39 B2
**Llanrhystud** GB 39 B2
**Llanrwst** GB 38 A3
**Llansannan** GB 38 A3
**Llansawel** GB 39 B2
**Llanstephan** GB 39 C2
**Llanteno** E 143 A3
**Llanthony** GB 39 C3
**Llantrisant** GB 39 C3
**Llantwit-Major** GB 39 C3
**Llanuwchllyn** GB 38 B3
**Llanwddyn** GB 38 B3
**Llanwrda** GB 39 C3
**Llanwrtyd Wells** GB 39 B3
**Llanybydder** GB 39 B2
**Llanymynech** GB 38 B3
**Llavorsi** E 146 B2
**Lleida** E 153 A4
**Llera** E 156 B1
**Llerena** E 156 B1
**Lles** E 146 B2
**Llessui** E 146 B2
**Llinars** E 147 B2
**Lliria** E 159 B3
**Llivia** E 146 B2
**Llodio** E 143 A4
**Lloret de Mar** E 147 C3
**Llosa de Ranes** E 159 B3
**Lloseta** E 167 B2
**Llucena del Cid** E 153 B3
**Llucmajor** E 167 B2
**Llutxent** E 159 C3
**Llwyngwril** GB 38 B2
**Llyswen** GB 39 B3
**Lnáře** CZ 96 B1
**Lniano** PL 76 A3
**Loanhead** GB 35 C4
**Loano** I 133 A4
**Loarre** E 145 B3
**Löbau** D 84 A2
**Löbejün** D 83 A3
**Löberöd** S 61 D3
**Łobez** PL 75 A4
**Löbnitz** D 66 B1
**Lobón** E 155 C4
**Loburg** D 73 B5
**Łobżenica** PL 76 A2
**Locana** I 119 B4
**Locarno** CH 120 A1
**Loccum** D 72 B2
**Loče** SLO 123 A4
**Lochailort** GB 34 B2
**Lochaline** GB 34 B2
**Lochans** GB 36 B1
**Locharbriggs** GB 36 A3
**Lochau** A 107 B4
**Loch Baghasdail**
GB 31 B1
**Lochcarron** GB 31 B3
**Lochearnhead** GB 34 B3
**Lochem** NL 71 B3
**Loches** F 102 B2
**Lochgelly** GB 35 B4
**Lochgilphead** GB 34 B2
**Lochgoilhead** GB 34 B3
**Lochinver** GB 32 C1
**Loch nam Madadh**
GB 31 B1
**Lochranza** GB 34 C2
**Ločika** SRB 127 D3
**Lockenhaus** A 111 B3
**Lockerbie** GB 36 A3
**Löcknitz** D 74 A3
**Locmaria** F 100 B2
**Locmariaquer** F 100 B3
**Locminé** F 100 B3
**Locorotondo** I 173 B3
**Locquirec** F 100 A2
**Locri** I 175 C2
**Locronan** F 100 A1
**Loctudy** F 100 B1
**Lodares de Osma**
E 151 A5
**Lodé** I 178 B3
**Lodeinoye Pole** RUS 9 B8
**Lodève** F 130 B2
**Lodi** I 120 B2
**Løding** N 194 C5
**Lødingen** N 194 B6
**Lodosa** E 144 B1
**Lödöse** S 54 B3
**Łódź** PL 86 A3
**Loeches** E 151 B4
**Løfallstrand** N 46 B3
**Lofer** A 109 B3
**Lofsdalen** S 199 C10
**Loftahammar** S 62 A4
**Lofthus** N 46 B3
**Loftus** GB 37 B6
**Loga** N 52 B2
**Logatec** SLO 123 B3
**Lögdeå** S 200 C5
**Lograto** I 120 B3
**Logroño** E 143 B4
**Logrosán** E 156 A2
**Løgstør** DK 58 B2
**Løgumgårde** DK 64 A1
**Løgumkloster** DK 64 A1
**Lohals** DK 65 A3
**Lohiniva** FIN 197 B8
**Lohja** FIN 8 B4
**Löhlbach** D 81 A4
**Lohmen**
*Mecklenburg-Vorpommern* D 65 C5
*Sachsen* D 84 B2
**Löhnberg** D 81 B4
**Lohne** D 71 B5
**Löhne** D 72 B1
**Lohr** D 94 B1
**Lohra** D 81 B4
**Lohsa** D 84 A2
**Loiano** I 135 A4
**Loimaa** FIN 8 B3
**Lóiri** I 178 B3
**Loitz** D 66 C2
**Loivos** P 148 A2
**Loivos do Monte** P 148 A2
**Loja** E 163 A3
**Lojanice** SRB 127 C1
**Løjsta** S 67 C4
**Løjt Kirkeby** DK 64 A2
**Lok** SK 112 A2
**Lokca** SK 99 B3
**Løken** N 54 A2
**Lokeren** B 79 A3
**Loket** CZ 83 B4
**Lokka** FIN 197 B10
**Løkken**
DK 58 A2
N 198 B6
**Loknya** RUS 9 D7
**Lökösháza** H 113 C5
**Lokve** SRB 126 B3
**Lollar** D 81 B4
**L'Olleria** E 159 C3
**Lölling-Graben** A 110 C1
**Lom**
BG 17 D5
N 198 D5
**Lom** *continued*
SK 99 C3
**Lombez** F 146 A1
**Lomello** I 120 B1
**Łomianki** PL 77 B5
**Lomma** S 61 D3
**Lommaryd** S 62 A2
**Lommatzsch** D 83 A5
**Lommel** B 79 A5
**Lommersum** D 80 B2
**Lomnice** CZ 97 B4
**Lomnice nad Lužnici**
CZ 96 B2
**Lomnice-nad Popelkou**
CZ 84 B3
**Lompolo** FIN 196 A7
**Łomza** PL 12 B5
**Lönashult** S 63 B2
**Lønborg** DK 59 C1
**Londerzeel** B 79 A4
**Londinières** F 89 A5
**London** GB 44 B3
**Lonevåg** N 46 B2
**Longa** GR 184 C2
**Longare** I 121 B4
**Longares** E 152 A2
**Longarone** I 122 A1
**Longastrino** I 135 A5
**Long Bennington**
GB 40 C3
**Longbenton** GB 37 A5
**Longchamp-sur-Aujon**
F 105 A3
**Longchaumois** F 118 A2
**Long Eaton** GB 40 C2
**Longeau** F 105 B4
**Longecourt-en-Plaine**
F 105 B4
**Longeville-les-St Avold**
F 92 B2
**Longeville-sur-Mer**
F 114 B2
**Longford** IRL 28 A4
**Longframlington**
GB 37 A5
**Longhope** GB 33 C3
**Longhorsley** GB 37 A5
**Longhoughton** GB 37 A5
**Longi** I 177 A3
**Long Melford** GB 45 A4
**Longny-au-Perche**
F 89 B4
**Longobucco** I 174 B2
**Long Preston** GB 40 A1
**Longré** F 115 B3
**Longridge** GB 38 A4
**Longroiva** P 149 B2
**Long Sutton** GB 41 C4
**Longtown**
*Cumbria* GB 36 A4
*Herefordshire* GB 39 C4
**Longueau** F 90 B2
**Longué-Jumelles**
F 102 B1
**Longuyon** F 92 B1
**Longvic** F 105 B4
**Longvilly** B 92 A1
**Longwy** F 92 B1
**Lonigo** I 121 B4
**Löningen** D 71 B4
**Lonja** HR 124 B2
**Lönneberga** S 62 A3
**Lönsboda** S 63 B2
**Lønset** N 198 C6
**Lons-le-Saunier** F 105 C4
**Lønstrup** DK 58 A2
**Looe** GB 42 B2
**Loone-Plage** F 78 A2
**Loon op Zand** NL 79 A5
**Loosdorf** A 110 A2
**Lo Pagán** E 165 B4
**Lopar** HR 123 C3
**Lopare** BIH 125 C4
**Lopera** E 157 C3
**Lopigna** F 180 A1
**Loppersum** NL 71 A3
**Łopuszna** PL 99 B4
**Łopuszno** PL 87 B4
**Lor** F 91 B4
**Lora** N 198 C5
**Lora de Estepa** E 162 A3
**Lora del Río** E 162 A2
**Loranca del Campo**
E 151 B5
**Lörby** S 63 B2
**Lorca** E 164 B3
**Lorch** D 93 A3
**Lørenfallet** N 48 B3
**Lørenskog** N 48 C2
**Loreo** I 122 B1
**Loreto** I 136 B2
**Lorgues** F 132 B2
**Lorica** I 174 B2
**Lorient** F 100 B2
**Lorignac** F 114 C3
**Lörinci** H 112 B3
**Loriol-sur-Drôme**
F 117 C4
**Lormes** F 104 B2
**Loro Ciuffenna** I 135 B4
**Lorqui** E 165 A3
**Lörrach** D 106 B2
**Lorrez-le-Bocage** F 103 A4
**Lorris** F 103 B4
**Lorup** D 71 B4
**Łoś** PL 77 C5
**Los** S 199 D12
**Losacino** E 149 A3

Los Alcázares E . . 165 B4
Los Arcos E . . . . . 144 B1
Losar de la Vera E . 150 B2
Los Barios de Luna
E . . . . . . . . . . . . 141 B5
Los Barrios E . . . . 162 B2
Los Caños de Meca
E . . . . . . . . . . . . 162 B1
Los Cerricos E . . . 164 B2
Los Corrales E . . . 162 A3
Los Corrales de Buelna
E . . . . . . . . . . . . 142 A2
Los Dolores E . . . 165 B3
Losenstein A . . . . .110 B1
Los Gallardos E . . 164 B3
Losheim
  Nordrhein-Westfalen
  D . . . . . . . . . . . .00 D2
  Saarland D . . . . . . .92 B2
Los Hinojosos E . . 158 B1
Los Isidros E . . . . 159 B2
Los Molinos E . . . 151 B3
Los Morales E . . . 162 A2
Los Navalmorales
E . . . . . . . . . . . . 156 A3
Los Navalucillos E 156 A3
Losne F . . . . . . . . 105 B4
Los Nietos E . . . . 165 B4
Løsning DK . . . . . 59 C2
Los Palacios y
  Villafranca E . . . . 162 A2
Los Pozuelos de
  Calatrava E . . . . 157 B3
Los Rábanos E . . . 143 C4
Los Santos E . . . . 149 B4
Los Santos de la
  Humosa E . . . . 151 B4
Los Santos de Maimona
E . . . . . . . . . . . . 155 C4
Lossburg D . . . . . . 93 C4
Losse F . . . . . . . . 128 B2
Losser NL . . . . . . 71 B4
Lossiemouth GB . . 32 D3
Lössnitz D . . . . . . 83 B4
Loštice CZ . . . . . . 97 B4
Los Tijos E . . . . . . 142 A2
Lostwithiel GB . . . 42 B2
Los Villares E . . . 163 A4
Los Yébenes E . . . 157 A4
Løten N . . . . . . . . 48 B3
Lotorp S . . . . . . . . 56 B1
Lottefors S . . . . . . 50 A3
Löttorp S . . . . . . . 62 A5
Lotyń PL . . . . . . . . 68 B1
Lotzorai I . . . . . . . 179 C3
Louargat F . . . . . . 100 A2
Loudéac F . . . . . . 101 A3
Loudun F . . . . . . . 102 B2
Loué F . . . . . . . . . 102 B1
Loughborough GB . 40 C2
Loughbrickland GB 27 B4
Loughrea IRL . . . . 28 A3
Louhans F . . . . . . 105 C4
Loukhi RUS . . . . . 3 C13
Loulay F . . . . . . . .114 B3
Loulé P . . . . . . . . 160 B1
Louny CZ . . . . . . . 84 B1
Lourdes F . . . . . . 145 A3
Lourenzá E . . . . . 141 A3
Loures P . . . . . . . 154 C1
Loures-Barousse
F . . . . . . . . . . . . 145 A4
Louriçal P . . . . . . 154 A2
Lourinhã P . . . . . . 154 B1
Lourmarin F . . . . . 131 B4
Loury F . . . . . . . . 103 B4
Lousa
  Bragança P . . . . . 149 A2
  Castelo Branco P . 155 B3
Lousã P . . . . . . . . 148 B1
Lousa P . . . . . . . . 154 C1
Lousada
E . . . . . . . . . . . . 140 B3
P . . . . . . . . . . . . 148 A1
Louth GB . . . . . . . 41 B3
Loutra Edipsou
GR . . . . . . . . . . . 183 E5
Loutraki GR . . . . . 184 B3
Loutropoli Thermis
GR . . . . . . . . . . . 186 C1
Louverné F . . . . . 102 A1
Louvie-Juzon F . . 145 A3
Louviers F . . . . . . 89 A5
Louvigné-du-Désert
F . . . . . . . . . . . . 88 B2
Louvois F . . . . . . . 91 B4
Lova I . . . . . . . . . 121 B5
Lovasberény H . . .112 B2
Lövåsen S . . . . . . 49 C5
Lovászpatona H . .111 B4
Lövberga S . . . . . 200 C1
Lovech BG . . . . . . 17 D6
Lövenich D . . . . . . 80 A2
Lóvere I . . . . . . . . 120 B3
Lövestad S . . . . . . 61 D3
Loviisa FIN . . . . . . 8 B5
Lovikka S . . . . . . 196 B5
Lovinobaňa SK . . . 99 C3
Loviste HR . . . . . 138 B3
Lovke HR . . . . . . 123 B3
Lovnäs S . . . . . . . 49 A5
Lövö H . . . . . . . . .111 B3
Lovosice CZ . . . . . 84 B2
Lovozero RUS . . . 3 C14
Lovran HR . . . . . . 123 B3
Lovreć HR . . . . . . 138 B2

Lovrenc na Pohorju
SLO . . . . . . . . . 110 C2
Lovrin RO . . . . . . 126 B2
Lövstabruk S . . . . 51 B4
Löwenberg D . . . . 74 B2
Löwenstein D . . . . 94 B1
Lowestoft GB . . . . 41 C5
Lowick GB . . . . . . 37 A5
Łowicz PL . . . . . . 77 B4
Loxstedt D . . . . . . 72 A1
Loyew BY . . . . . . 13 C9
Lož SLO . . . . . . . 123 B3
Loza CZ . . . . . . . . 96 B1
Łozina PL . . . . . . . 85 A5
Loznica SRB . . . . 127 C1
Lozničko Polje
SRB . . . . . . . . . 127 C1
Lozorno OK . . . . . .111 A4
Lozovik SRB . . . . 127 C3
Lozoya E . . . . . . . 151 B4
Lozoyuela E . . . . . 151 B4
Lozzo di Cadore I . 109 C3
Luanco E . . . . . . . 141 A5
Luarca E . . . . . . . 141 A4
Lubaczów PL . . . . 13 C5
Lubań PL . . . . . . . 84 A3
Lubanie PL . . . . . . 76 B3
Lubanów PL . . . . . 86 A3
Lubars D . . . . . . . 73 B5
Lubasz PL . . . . . . 75 B5
Lubawa PL . . . . . . 69 B4
Lubawka PL . . . . . 85 B4
Lübbecke D . . . . . 72 B1
Lübben D . . . . . . . 74 C2
Lübbenau D . . . . . 84 A1
Lubczyna PL . . . . . 74 A3
Lübeck D . . . . . . . 65 C3
Lubenec CZ . . . . . 83 B5
Lubersac F . . . . . 115 C5
Lübesse D . . . . . . 73 A4
Lubia E . . . . . . . . 152 A1
Lubian E . . . . . . . 141 B4
Lubiatowo PL . . . . 75 A4
Lubichowo PL . . . . 69 B3
Lubicz Dolny PL . . 76 A3
Lubień PL . . . . . . . 99 B3
Lubienia PL . . . . . 87 A5
Lubień Kujawski PL 77 B4
Lubiewo PL . . . . . 75 A4
Lubin
  Dolnośląskie PL . . .85 A4
  Zachodnio-Pomorskie
  PL . . . . . . . . . . .67 C3
Lublin PL . . . . . . . 12 C5
Lubliniec PL . . . . . 86 B2
Lubmin D . . . . . . . 66 B2
Lubniewice PL . . . 75 B4
Lubochnia PL . . . . 87 A4
Lubomierz
  Dolnośląskie PL . . .84 A3
  Małopolskie PL . . .99 B4
Lubomino PL . . . . 69 A5
Luboń PL . . . . . . . 76 B1
L'ubotín SK . . . . . 99 B4
Lubowidz PL . . . . . 77 A4
Łubowo
  Wielkopolskie PL . .76 B2
  Zachodnio-Pomorskie
  PL . . . . . . . . . . .68 B1
Lubraniec PL . . . . 76 B3
Lubrin E . . . . . . . 164 B2
Lubrza PL . . . . . . . 85 B5
Lubsko PL . . . . . . 84 A2
Lübtheen D . . . . . . 73 A4
Lubuczewo PL . . . 68 A2
Luby CZ . . . . . . . . 83 B4
Lübz D . . . . . . . . . 73 A5
Luc F . . . . . . . . . 117 C3
Lucainena de las Torres
E . . . . . . . . . . . . 164 B2
Lucan IRL . . . . . . 30 A2
Lučani SRB . . . . . 127 D2
Lúcar E . . . . . . . . 164 B2
Luçay-le-Mâle F . . 103 B3
Lucca I . . . . . . . . 134 B3
Lucciana F . . . . . . 180 A2
Lucé F . . . . . . . . . 90 C1
Luče SLO . . . . . . 123 A3
Lucena
  Córdoba E . . . . . .163 A3
  Huelva E . . . . . . 161 B3
Lucenay-les-Aix F . 104 C2
Lucenay-l'Evéque
F . . . . . . . . . . . . 104 B3
Luc-en-Diois F . . . 118 C2
Lučenec SK . . . . . 99 C3
Luceni E . . . . . . . 144 C2
Lucens CH . . . . . 106 C1
Lucera I . . . . . . . 171 B3
Luceram F . . . . . . 133 B3
Lüchow D . . . . . . . 73 B4
Luciana E . . . . . . 157 B3
Lucignano I . . . . . 135 B4
Lucija SLO . . . . . 122 B2
Lucka D . . . . . . . . 83 A4
Luckau D . . . . . . . 84 A1
Luckenwalde D . . . 74 B2
Lückstedt D . . . . . 73 B4
Luco dei Marsi I . . 169 B3
Luçon F . . . . . . . .114 B2
Luc-sur-Mer F . . . 89 A3
Ludanice SK . . . . 98 C2
Ludbreg HR . . . . . 124 A2
Lüdenscheid D . . . 81 A3
Lüderitz D . . . . . . 73 B4
Lüdersdorf D . . . . 65 C3
Ludgershall GB . . . 44 B2
Ludgo S . . . . . . . . 56 B3

Lüdinghausen D . . . 80 A3
Ludlow GB . . . . . . 39 B4
Ludomy PL . . . . . . 75 B5
Ludvika S . . . . . . . 50 B2
Ludweiler Warndt D 92 B2
Ludwigsburg D . . . 94 C1
Ludwigsfelde D . . . 74 B2
Ludwigshafen D . . 93 B4
Ludwigslust D . . . . 73 A4
Ludwigsstadt D . . . 82 B3
Ludza LV . . . . . . . . 8 D5
Luesia E . . . . . . . 144 B2
Luftkurort Arendsee
D . . . . . . . . . . . . . 73 B4
Lug
  BIH . . . . . . . . . . .139 C4
  HR . . . . . . . . . . . 125 B4
Luga RUS . . . . . . . 9 C6
Lugagnano Val d'Arda
I . . . . . . . . . . . . . 120 C2
Lugano CH . . . . . 120 A1
Lugau D . . . . . . . . 83 B4
Lugnas S . . . . . . . 55 B4
Lúgnola I . . . . . . . 168 A2
Lugny F . . . . . . . . 105 C3
Lugo
  E . . . . . . . . . . . . 140 A3
  I . . . . . . . . . . . . 135 A4
Lugoj RO . . . . . . . 16 C4
Lugones E . . . . . . 141 A5
Lugros E . . . . . . . 163 A4
Luhačovice CZ . . . 98 B1
Luhe D . . . . . . . . . 95 B4
Luino I . . . . . . . . . 120 B1
Luintra E . . . . . . . 140 B3
Lújar E . . . . . . . . 163 B4
Luka nad Jihlavou
CZ . . . . . . . . . . . 97 B3
Lukavac BIH . . . . 125 C4
Lukavika BIH . . . . 125 C4
Lukovë AL . . . . . . 182 D1
Lukovica SLO . . . . 123 A3
Lukovit BG . . . . . . 17 D6
Lukovo HR . . . . . 123 C3
Lukovo Šugorje
HR . . . . . . . . . . . 137 A4
Łuków PL . . . . . . . 12 C5
Łukowice Brzeskie
PL . . . . . . . . . . . 85 B5
Luksefjell N . . . . . 53 A5
Łukta PL . . . . . . . . 69 B5
Lula I . . . . . . . . . . 178 B3
Luleå S . . . . . . . . 196 D5
Lüleburgaz TR . . . 186 A2
Lumbarda HR . . . . 138 C3
Lumbier E . . . . . . 144 B2
Lumbrales E . . . . . 149 B3
Lumbreras E . . . . 143 B4
Lumbres F . . . . . . 78 B2
Lummelunda S . . . 57 C4
Lummen B . . . . . . 79 B5
Lumparland FIN . . 51 B7
Lumpiaque E . . . . 152 A2
Lumsås DK . . . . . . 61 D1
Lumsden GB . . . . 33 D4
Lumsheden S . . . . 50 B3
Lun HR . . . . . . . . 123 C3
Luna E . . . . . . . . 144 B3
Lunamatrona I . . . 179 C2
Lunano I . . . . . . . 136 B1
Lunas F . . . . . . . . 130 B2
Lund
  N . . . . . . . . . . . . .199 A8
  Skåne S . . . . . . . .61 D3
  Västra Götaland S . 54 A3
Lundamo N . . . . . 199 B7
Lunde
  DK . . . . . . . . . . . .59 C1
  Sogn og Fjordane
  N . . . . . . . . . . . .46 A3
  Sogn og Fjordane
  N . . . . . . . . . . . .46 A3
  Telemark N . . . . . .53 A5
  S . . . . . . . . . . . .200 D3
Lundebyvollen N . . 49 B4
Lunden D . . . . . . . 64 B2
Lunderseter N . . . 49 B4
Lunderskov DK . . . 59 C2
Lundsberg S . . . . . 55 A5
Lüneburg D . . . . . 72 A3
Lunel F . . . . . . . . 131 B3
Lünen D . . . . . . . . 81 A3
Lunéville F . . . . . . 92 C2
Lungern CH . . . . . 106 C3
Lungro I . . . . . . . . 174 B2
Luninyets BY . . . . 13 B7
Lünne D . . . . . . . . 71 B4
Lunner N . . . . . . . 48 B2
Lunteren NL . . . . . 70 B2
Lunz am See A . . .110 B2
Luogosanto I . . . . 178 A3
Łupawa PL . . . . . . 68 A2
Lupión E . . . . . . . 157 B4
Lupoglav HR . . . . 123 B3
Luppa D . . . . . . . . 83 A4
Luque E . . . . . . . 163 A3
Lurago d'Erba I . . 120 B2
Lúras I . . . . . . . . 178 B3
Lurcy-Lévis F . . . . 104 C1
Lure F . . . . . . . . . 105 B5
Lurgan GB . . . . . . 27 B4
Luri F . . . . . . . . . 180 A2
Lury-sur-Arnon F . 103 B4
Lušci Palanka BIH . 124 C2
Lusévera I . . . . . . 122 A2
Lusignan F . . . . . .115 B4

Lusigny-sur-Barse
F . . . . . . . . . . . . 104 A3
Lusnić BIH . . . . . . 138 B2
Luso P . . . . . . . . 148 B1
Lusówko PL . . . . . 75 B5
Luspebryggan S . . 196 B2
Luss GB . . . . . . . 34 B3
Lussac F . . . . . . . 128 B2
Lussac-les-Châteaux
F . . . . . . . . . . . . .115 B4
Lussac-les-Eglises
F . . . . . . . . . . . . .115 B5
Lussan F . . . . . . . 131 A3
Lüssow D . . . . . . . 65 C5
Lustenau A . . . . . 107 B4
Luštěnice CZ . . . . 84 B2
Luster N . . . . . . . . 47 A4
Lutago I . . . . . . . . 108 C2
Lutherstadt Wittenberg
D . . . . . . . . . . . . . 83 A4
Lütjenburg D . . . . . 65 B3
Lutnes N . . . . . . . 49 A4
Lutocin PL . . . . . . 77 B4
Lutomiersk PL . . . . 86 A3
Luton GB . . . . . . . 44 B3
Lutry CH . . . . . . . 106 C1
Lutsk UA . . . . . . . 13 C6
Lutter am Barenberge
D . . . . . . . . . . . . . 72 C3
Lutterworth GB . . . 40 C2
Lututów PL . . . . . . 86 A2
Lützen D . . . . . . . . 83 A4
Lutzow D . . . . . . . 73 A4
Luusua FIN . . . . 197 C10
Luvos S . . . . . . . 196 C1
Luxembourg L . . . . 92 B2
Luxeuil-les-Bains
F . . . . . . . . . . . . 105 B5
Luxey F . . . . . . . . 128 B2
Luz
  Évora P . . . . . . . .155 C3
  Faro P . . . . . . . . 160 B1
  Faro P . . . . . . . . 160 B2
Luzarches F . . . . . 90 B2
Luže CZ . . . . . . . . 97 B4
Luzech F . . . . . . . 129 B4
Luzern CH . . . . . . 106 B3
Luzino PL . . . . . . . 68 A3
Luz-St Sauveur F . 145 B3
Luzy F . . . . . . . . . 104 C2
Luzzi I . . . . . . . . . 174 B2
L'viv UA . . . . . . . . 13 D6
Lwówek PL . . . . . . 75 B5
Lwówek Śląski PL . 84 A3
Lyakhavichy BY . . 13 B7
Lybster GB . . . . . . 32 C3
Lychen D . . . . . . . 74 A2
Lychkova RUS . . . . 9 D8
Lyckeby S . . . . . . . 63 B3
Lycksele S . . . . . 200 B4
Lydd GB . . . . . . . 45 C4
Lydford GB . . . . . . 42 B2
Lydney GB . . . . . . 39 C4
Lyepyel BY . . . . . 13 A8
Lygna N . . . . . . . . 48 B2
Lygnsna N . . . . . . 199 A8
Lykkja N . . . . . . . . 47 B5
Lykling N . . . . . . . 52 A1
Lyme Regis GB . . . 43 B4
Lymington GB . . . . 44 C2
Lympne GB . . . . . 45 C4
Lyndhurst GB . . . . 44 C2
Lyneham GB . . . . . 43 A5
Lyness GB . . . . . . 33 C3
Lyngdal
  Buskerud N . . . . . .47 C6
  Vest-Agder N . . . . .52 B3
Lyngør N . . . . . . . 53 B5
Lyngsa DK . . . . . . 58 A3
Lyngseidet N . . . . 192 C4
Lyngsnes N . . . . . 199 A8
Lynmouth GB . . . . 42 A3
Lynton GB . . . . . . 42 A3
Lyntupy BY . . . . . . 13 A7
Lyon F . . . . . . . . .117 B4
Lyons-la-Forêt F . . 90 B1
Lyozna BY . . . . . . 13 A9
Lyrestad S . . . . . . 55 B5
Lysánad Labem CZ 84 B2
Lysápod Makytou
SK . . . . . . . . . . . 98 B2
Lysebotn N . . . . . . 52 A2
Lysekil S . . . . . . . 54 B2
Lysice CZ . . . . . . . 97 B4
Lysomice PL . . . . . 76 A3
Lysøysund N . . . . 198 B6
Lyss CH . . . . . . . 106 B2
Lystrup DK . . . . . . 59 B3
Lysvik S . . . . . . . . 49 B5
Łyszkowice PL . . . 77 C4
Lytham St Anne's
GB . . . . . . . . . . . 38 A3
Lyuban RUS . . . . . 9 C7
Lyubertsy RUS . . 9 E10
Lyubimets BG . . . 183 B8
Lyuboml' UA . . . . 13 C6
Lyubytino RUS . . . 9 C8

**M**

Maaninkavaara
FIN . . . . . . . . . 197 C11
Maarheeze NL . . . 80 A1
Maaseik B . . . . . . 80 A1
Maastricht NL . . . . 80 B1
Mablethorpe GB . . 41 B4
Mably F . . . . . . . .117 A4
Macael E . . . . . . . 164 B2

Maçanet de Cabrenys
E . . . . . . . . . . . . 146 B3
Mação P . . . . . . . 154 B2
Macau F . . . . . . . 128 A2
Maccagno-Agra I . . 120 A1
Maccarese I . . . . . 168 B2
Macclesfield GB . . 40 B1
Macduff GB . . . . . 33 D4
Maceda E . . . . . . 140 B3
Macedo de Cavaleiros
P . . . . . . . . . . . . 149 A3
Maceira
  Guarda P . . . . . . .148 B2
  Leiria P . . . . . . . .154 B2
Macelj HR . . . . . . 124 A1
Macerata I . . . . . . 136 B2
Macerata Feltria I . 136 B1
Machault F . . . . . . 91 B4
Machecoul F . . . . .114 B2
Mchowo PL . . . . . 77 A5
Machrihanish GB . 34 C2
Machynlleth GB . . 39 B3
Macieira P . . . . . . 148 A1
Maciejowice PL . . 87 A5
Macinaggio F . . . . 180 A2
Mackenrode D . . . 82 A2
Mačkovci SLO . . . .111 C3
Macomer I . . . . . . 178 B2
Macon B . . . . . . . 91 A4
Mâcon F . . . . . . . .117 A4
Macotera E . . . . . 150 B2
Macroom IRL . . . . 29 C3
Macugnaga I . . . . .119 B4
Madan BG . . . . . . 183 B6
Madängsholm S . . 55 B4
Madaras H . . . . . . 126 A1
Maddaloni I . . . . . 170 B2
Made NL . . . . . . . 79 A4
Madeley GB . . . . . 38 B4
Maderuelo E . . . . 151 A4
Madetkoski FIN . . 197 B9
Madley GB . . . . . . 39 B4
Madocsa H . . . . . 112 C2
Madona LV . . . . . . 8 D5
Madonna di Campíglio
I . . . . . . . . . . . . . 121 A3
Madrid E . . . . . . . 151 B4
Madridejos E . . . . 157 A4
Madrigal de las Altas
  Torres E . . . . . . . 150 A2
Madrigal de la Vera
E . . . . . . . . . . . . 150 B2
Madrigalejo E . . . . 156 A2
Madrigalejo de Monte
E . . . . . . . . . . . . 143 B3
Madrigueras E . . . 158 B2
Madroñera E . . . . 156 A2
Mafra P . . . . . . . . 154 C1
Magacela E . . . . . 156 B2
Magallon E . . . . . 144 C2
Magaluf E . . . . . . 166 B2
Magán E . . . . . . . 151 C4
Magaña E . . . . . . 144 C1
Magasa I . . . . . . . 121 B3
Magaz E . . . . . . . 142 C2
Magdeburg D . . . . 73 B4
Magenta I . . . . . . 120 B1
Magescq F . . . . . . 128 C1
Maghera GB . . . . . 27 B4
Magherafelt GB . . 27 B4
Maghull GB . . . . . 38 A4
Magilligan GB . . . 27 A4
Magione I . . . . . . 135 B5
Magioto P . . . . . . 154 C1
Maglaj BIH . . . . . 125 C4
Maglehem S . . . . . 63 C2
Magliano de'Marsi
I . . . . . . . . . . . . . 169 A3
Magliano in Toscana
I . . . . . . . . . . . . . 168 A1
Magliano Sabina I . 168 A2
Máglie I . . . . . . . . 173 B4
Maglód H . . . . . . .112 B3
Magnac-Bourg F . .115 C5
Magnac-Laval F . . .115 B5
Magnieres F . . . . . 92 C2
Magnor N . . . . . . . 49 C4
Magnuszew PL . . . 87 A5
Magny-Cours F . . 104 C2
Magny-en-Vexin F . 90 B1
Mágocs H . . . . . . 125 A4
Magomadas I . . . . 178 B2
Magoro E . . . . . . 158 B2
Mähring D . . . . . . . 95 B4
Maia
  E . . . . . . . . . . . . 144 A2
  P . . . . . . . . . . . . 148 A1
Maiaelrayo E . . . . 151 B4
Maials E . . . . . . . 153 A4
Maîche F . . . . . . . 106 B1
Máida I . . . . . . . . 175 C2
Maida I . . . . . . . . 175 C2
Maiden Bradley GB . 43 B4
Maidenhead GB . . . 44 B3

Maiden Newton GB . 43 B4
Maidstone GB . . . . 45 B4
Maienfeld CH . . . . 107 B4
Maignelay Montigny
F . . . . . . . . . . . . . 90 B2
Maijanen FIN . . . . 197 B8
Maillezais F . . . . . .114 B3
Mailly-le-Camp F . . 91 C4
Mailly-le-Château
F . . . . . . . . . . . . 104 B2
Mainar E . . . . . . . 152 A2
Mainbernheim D . . 94 B2
Mainburg D . . . . . . 95 C3
Mainhardt D . . . . . 94 B1
Maintal D . . . . . . . 81 B4
Maintenon F . . . . . 90 C1
Mainvilliers F . . . . 90 C1
Mainz D . . . . . . . . 93 A4
Maiorca P . . . . . . 148 B1
Mairena de Aljarafe
E . . . . . . . . . . . . 162 A1
Mairena del Alcor
E . . . . . . . . . . . . 162 A2
Maisach D . . . . . . 108 A2
Maishofen A . . . . . 109 B3
Maison-Rouge F . . 90 C3
Maissau A . . . . . . 97 C3
Maisse F . . . . . . . 90 C2
Maizières-lès-Vic F . 92 C2
Maja HR . . . . . . . 124 B2
Majadahonda E . . 151 B4
Majadas E . . . . . . 150 C2
Majs H . . . . . . . . . 125 B4
Majšperk SLO . . . 123 A4
Makarska HR . . . . 138 B3
Makkum NL . . . . . 70 A2
Maklár H . . . . . . . .113 B4
Makó H . . . . . . . . 126 A2
Makoszyce PL . . . . 85 B5
Makov SK . . . . . . 98 B2
Mąkowarsko PL . . 76 A2
Maków Mazowiecki
  PL . . . . . . . . . . . 77 B6
Maków Podhalański
  PL . . . . . . . . . . . 99 B3
Makrakomi GR . . . 182 E4
Maksniemi FIN . . 196 D7
Malå S . . . . . . . . 195 E9
Mala Bosna SRB . 126 A1
Malacky SK . . . . . 97 C5
Maladzyechna BY . 13 A7
Málaga E . . . . . . . 163 B3
Malagón E . . . . . . 157 A4
Malaguilla E . . . . . 151 B4
Malahide IRL . . . . 30 A2
Mala Kladuša BIH . 124 B1
Mala Krsna SRB . 127 C3
Malalbergo I . . . . 121 C4
Malá Lehota SK . . 98 C2
Malanów PL . . . . . 76 C3
Mala Pijace SRB . 126 A1
Mala Subotica HR . 124 A2
Malaucène F . . . . 131 A4
Malaunay F . . . . . 89 A5
Malaya Vishera RUS . 9 C8
Malborghetto I . . . 109 C4
Malbork PL . . . . . . 69 A4
Malborn D . . . . . . 92 B2
Malbuisson F . . . . 105 C5
Malcésine I . . . . . 121 B3
Malchin D . . . . . . . 74 A1
Malching D . . . . . . 96 C1
Malchow D . . . . . . 73 A5
Malcocinado E . . . 156 B2
Malczyce PL . . . . . 85 A4
Maldegem B . . . . . 79 A3
Maldon GB . . . . . . 45 B4
Małdyty PL . . . . . . 69 B4
Malè I . . . . . . . . . 121 A3
Malemort F . . . . . 129 A4
Malente D . . . . . . 65 B3
Målerås S . . . . . . 62 B3
Males GR . . . . . . 185 D6
Malesherbes F . . . 90 C2
Malesina GR . . . . 183 E5
Malestroit F . . . . . 101 B3
Maletto I . . . . . . . 177 B3
Malexander S . . . . 56 B1
Malgrat de Mar E . 147 C3
Malhadas P . . . . . 149 A3
Malia
  CY . . . . . . . . . . . 181 B1
  GR . . . . . . . . . . 185 D6
Malicorne-sur-Sarthe
F . . . . . . . . . . . . 102 B2
Malijai F . . . . . . . 132 A2
Maliljdoš SRB . . . 126 B1
Málilla S . . . . . . . 62 A3
Mali Lošinj HR . . . 137 A3
Malin IRL . . . . . . . 27 A3
Málinec SK . . . . . . 99 C3
Malingsbo S . . . . . 50 C2
Maliniec PL . . . . . 76 B3
Malinska HR . . . . 123 B3
Maliq AL . . . . . . . 182 C2
Maljevac HR . . . . 123 B4
Malkara TR . . . . . 186 B1
Malki PL . . . . . . . . 69 B4
Malko Tŭrnovo BG . 17 D7
Mallaig GB . . . . . . 34 A2
Mallaranny IRL . . . 28 A2
Mallemort F . . . . . 131 B4
Mallén E . . . . . . . 144 C2
Malléon F . . . . . . 146 A2

Mallersdorf-Pfaffenberg
D . . . . . . . . . . . . . 95 C4
Málles Venosta I . . . . 108 C1
Malling DK . . . . . . . . 59 B3
Mallnitz A . . . . . . . . 109 C4
Mallow IRL . . . . . . . . 29 B3
Mallwyd GB . . . . . . . 38 B3
Malm N . . . . . . . . . 199 A8
Malmbäck S . . . . . . . 62 A2
Malmberget S . . . . 196 B3
Malmby S . . . . . . . . 56 A3
Malmédy B . . . . . . . 80 B2
Malmesbury GB . . . . 43 A4
Malmköping S . . . . . 56 A2
Malmö S . . . . . . . . . 61 D3
Malmon S . . . . . . . . 54 B2
Malmslätt S . . . . . . . 56 B1
Malnate I . . . . . . . . 120 B1
Malo I . . . . . . . . . . 121 B4
Małogoszcz PL . . . . 87 B4
Maloja CH . . . . . . . 120 A2
Małomice PL . . . . . . 84 A3
Måløy N . . . . . . . . 198 D2
Malpartida E . . . . . 155 B4
Malpartida de la Serena
E . . . . . . . . . . . . 156 B2
Malpartida de Plasencia
E . . . . . . . . . . . . 150 C1
Malpas
E . . . . . . . . . . . . 145 B4
GB . . . . . . . . . . . . 38 A4
Malpica P . . . . . . . 155 B3
Malpica de Bergantiños
E . . . . . . . . . . . . 140 A2
Malpica de Tajo E . . 150 C3
Malsch D . . . . . . . . 93 C4
Malšice CZ . . . . . . . 96 B2
Malta A . . . . . . . . . 109 C4
Maltat F . . . . . . . . 104 C2
Maltby GB . . . . . . . 40 B2
Malung S . . . . . . . . 49 B5
Malungsfors S . . . . . 49 B5
Maluszów PL . . . . . 75 B4
Maluszyn PL . . . . . . 87 B3
Malva E . . . . . . . . 142 C1
Malvaglia CH . . . . . 120 A1
Malveira P . . . . . . . 154 C1
Malvik N . . . . . . . . 199 B7
Malyn UA . . . . . . . . 13 C8
Mamarrosa P . . . . . 148 B1
Mamer L . . . . . . . . 92 B2
Mamers F . . . . . . . . 89 B4
Mamirolle F . . . . . . 105 B5
Mammendorf D . . . . 108 A2
Mámmola I . . . . . . 175 C2
Mamoiada I . . . . . . 178 B3
Mamonovo RUS . . . 69 A4
Mamuras AL . . . . . 182 B1
Maña SK. . . . . . . . . 112 A2
Manacor E . . . . . . . 167 B3
Manavgat TR . . . . . 189 C6
Mancera de Abajo
E . . . . . . . . . . . . 150 B2
Mancha Real E . . . 163 A4
Manchester GB . . . . 40 B1
Manching D . . . . . . 95 C3
Manchita E . . . . . . 156 B1
Manciano I . . . . . . 168 A1
Manciet F . . . . . . . 128 C3
Mandal N . . . . . . . . 52 B3
Mandanici I . . . . . . 177 A4
Mándas I . . . . . . . . 179 C3
Mandatoríccio I . . . 174 B2
Mandayona E . . . . . 151 B5
Mandelieu-la-Napoule
F . . . . . . . . . . . . 132 B2
Mandello del Lário
I . . . . . . . . . . . . 120 B2
Mandelsloh D . . . . . 72 B2
Manderfeld B . . . . . 80 B2
Manderscheid D . . . 80 B2
Mandino Selo BIH . 138 B3
Mandoudi GR . . . . 183 E5
Mandra GR . . . . . . 185 A4
Mandraki GR . . . . . 188 C2
Mandúria I . . . . . . 173 B3
Mane
Alpes-de-Haute-
Provence F . . . . . 132 B1
Haute-Garonne F. . 145 A4
Manérbio I . . . . . . 120 B3
Mañeru E . . . . . . . 144 B2
Manetin CZ . . . . . . 96 B1
Manfredónia I . . . . 171 B3
Mangalia RO . . . . . 17 D8
Manganeses de la
Lampreana E. . . 149 A4
Manganeses de la
Polvorosa E . . . 141 B5
Mangen N . . . . . . . 48 C3
Manger N . . . . . . . 46 B2
Mangiennes F . . . . . 92 B1
Mangotsfield GB . . . 43 A4
Mångsbodarna S. . . . 49 A5
Mangualde P . . . . . 148 B2
Maniago I . . . . . . . 122 A1
Manilva E . . . . . . . 162 B2
Manises E . . . . . . . 159 B3
Mank A . . . . . . . . . 110 A2
Månkarbo S . . . . . . 51 B4
Manlleu E . . . . . . . 147 C3
Manna DK . . . . . . . 58 A2
Männedorf CH. . . . 107 B3

Mannersdorf am
Leithagebirge A. . 111 B3
Mannheim D . . . . . . 93 B4
Manningtree GB . . . 45 B5
Manoppello I . . . . . 169 A4
Manorbier GB . . . . . 39 C2
Manorhamilton IRL. . 26 B2
Manosque F . . . . . 132 B1
Manowo PL . . . . . . 67 B5
Manresa E . . . . . . 147 C2
Månsarp S . . . . . . . 62 A2
Månsåsen S . . . . . 199 B11
Manschnow D . . . . . 74 B3
Mansfeld D . . . . . . 82 A3
Mansfield GB . . . . . 40 B2
Mansilla de Burgos
E . . . . . . . . . . . . 143 B3
Mansilla de las Mulas
E . . . . . . . . . . . . 142 B1
Manskog S . . . . . . . 55 A3
Mansle F . . . . . . . 115 C4
Manso F . . . . . . . . 180 A1
Manteigas P . . . . . 148 B2
Mantel D. . . . . . . . . 95 B4
Mantes-la-Jolie F. . . 90 C1
Mantes-la-Ville F . . . 90 C1
Manthelan F . . . . . 102 B2
Mantorp S . . . . . . . 56 B1
Mántova I . . . . . . . 121 B3
Mänttä FIN . . . . . . . . 8 A4
Mäntyjärvi FIN . . . 197 C10
Manuel E . . . . . . . 159 B3
Manyas TR . . . . . . 186 B2
Manzanal de Arriba
E . . . . . . . . . . . . 141 B4
Manzanares E . . . . 157 A4
Manzanares el Real
E . . . . . . . . . . . . 151 B4
Manzaneda
León E . . . . . . . . 141 B4
Orense E . . . . . . 141 B3
Manzanedo E. . . . . 143 B3
Manzaneque E. . . . 157 A4
Manzanera E . . . . . 153 B3
Manzanilla E . . . . . 161 B3
Manzat F . . . . . . . 116 B2
Manziana I . . . . . . 168 A2
Manziat F . . . . . . . 117 A4
Maó E . . . . . . . . . 167 B4
Maoča BIH . . . . . . 125 C4
Maqueda E. . . . . . . 150 B3
Maramaraereğlisi
TR . . . . . . . . . . 186 B2
Maraña E . . . . . . . 142 A1
Maranchón E . . . . . 152 A1
Maranello I . . . . . . 135 A3
Marano I . . . . . . . . 170 C2
Marano Lagunare I . 122 B2
Maranos F . . . . . . . 114 B2
Maratea I . . . . . . . 174 B1
Marateca P . . . . . . 154 C2
Marathokambos
GR . . . . . . . . . . 188 B1
Marathonas GR. . . . 185 A4
Marathóvouno CY. . 181 A2
Marazion GB . . . . . . 42 B1
Marbach
Baden-Württemberg
D. . . . . . . . . . . . .94 C1
Hessen D. . . . . . . .82 B1
F. . . . . . . . . . . . . .92 C2
Marbäck S . . . . . . . 60 B3
Mårbacka S . . . . . . 55 A4
Marbella E . . . . . . 162 B3
Marboz F . . . . . . . 118 A2
Marburg D . . . . . . . 81 B4
Marcali I . . . . . . . . 111 C4
Marčana HR . . . . . 122 C2
Marcaria I . . . . . . . 121 B3
Marcelová SK . . . . 112 B2
Marcenat F . . . . . . 116 B2
March GB . . . . . . . 41 C4
Marchamalo E . . . . 151 B4
Marchaux F . . . . . . 105 B5
Marche-en-Famenne
B . . . . . . . . . . . . 79 B5
Marchegg A . . . . . 111 A3
Marchena E . . . . . 162 A2
Marchenoir F . . . . . 103 B3
Marcheprime F . . . 128 B2
Marciac F . . . . . . . 128 C3
Marciana Marina I . 134 C3
Marcianise I . . . . . 170 B2
Marcigny F . . . . . . 117 A4
Marcilla E . . . . . . . 144 B2
Marcillac-la-Croisille
F. . . . . . . . . . . . . 116 B2
Marcillac-Vallon F. . 130 A1
Marcillat-en-Combraille
F. . . . . . . . . . . . . 116 A2
Marcille-sur-Seine F 91 C3
Marcilloles F . . . . . 118 B2
Marcilly-le-Hayer F . 91 C3
Marcinkowice PL. . . 75 A5
Marciszów PL . . . . . 85 B4
Marck F . . . . . . . . 78 B1
Marckolsheim F . . . 106 A2
Marco de Canevezes
P. . . . . . . . . . . . . 148 A1
Mårdsele S. . . . . . 200 B5
Mårdsjö S. . . . . . . 200 C1
Mareham le Fen GB 41 B3
Marek S . . . . . . . . 62 A3
Marennes F . . . . . . 114 C2
Maresquel F. . . . . . 78 B1
Mareuil F . . . . . . . 115 C4
Mareuil-en-Brie F . 91 C3

Mareuil-sur-Arnon
F. . . . . . . . . . . . . 103 C4
Mareuil-sur-Lay F . .114 B2
Mareuil-sur-Ourcq F 90 B3
Margam GB . . . . . . 39 C3
Margariti GR . . . . . 182 D2
Margate GB . . . . . . 45 B5
Margaux F . . . . . . 128 A2
Margerie-Hancourt
F. . . . . . . . . . . . . 91 C4
Margès F . . . . . . . .117 B5
Margherita di Savóia
I . . . . . . . . . . . . 171 B4
Margita SRB . . . . . 126 B3
Margone I . . . . . . .119 B4
Margonin PL . . . . . . 76 B2
Marguerittes F. . . . 131 B3
Margut F . . . . . . . . 91 B5
Maria E. . . . . . . . . 164 B2
Mariager DK . . . . . . 58 B2
Mariana E. . . . . . . 152 B1
Maria Neustift A. . . .110 B1
Mariannelund S. . . . 62 A3
Mariánské Lázně
CZ . . . . . . . . . . . 95 B4
Mariapfarr A. . . . . . 109 B4
Maria Saal A. . . . . . 110 C1
Mariazell A. . . . . . .110 B2
Maribo DK . . . . . . . 65 B4
Maribor SLO . . . . . 110 C2
Marieberg S . . . . . . 56 A1
Mariefred S . . . . . . 56 A3
Mariehamn FIN . . . . 51 B6
Marieholm S . . . . . . 61 D3
Mariembourg B . . . . 91 A4
Marienbaum D. . . . . 80 A2
Marienberg D. . . . . . 83 B5
Marienheide D. . . . . 81 A3
Mariental D . . . . . . . 73 B3
Mariestad S . . . . . . 55 B4
Marieux F. . . . . . . . 90 A2
Marigliano I . . . . . . 170 C2
Marignane F . . . . . 131 B4
Marigny
Jura F . . . . . . . . 105 C4
Manche F. . . . . . . 88 A2
Marigny-le-Châtel F 91 C3
Marija Bistrica HR. . 124 A2
Marijampolė LT . . . . 13 A5
Marin E. . . . . . . . . 140 B2
Marina HR . . . . . . . 138 B2
Marina del Cantone
I . . . . . . . . . . . . 170 C2
Marina di Acquappesa
I . . . . . . . . . . . . 174 B1
Marina di Alberese
I . . . . . . . . . . . . 168 A1
Marina di Amendolara
I . . . . . . . . . . . . 174 B2
Marina di Árbus I. . . 179 C2
Marina di Campo I . 134 C3
Marina di Carrara I . 134 A3
Marina di Castagneto-
Donorático I . . . 134 B3
Marina di Cécina I . 134 B3
Marina di Gáiro I . . 179 C3
Marina di Ginosa I . 173 B2
Marina di Gioiosa Iónica
I . . . . . . . . . . . . 175 C2
Marina di Grosseto
I . . . . . . . . . . . . 135 C3
Marina di Léuca I . . 173 C4
Marina di Massa I . . 134 A3
Marina di Nováglie
I . . . . . . . . . . . . 173 C4
Marina di Pisa I . . . 134 B3
Marina di Ragusa I . 177 C3
Marina di Ravenna
I . . . . . . . . . . . . 135 A5
Marina di Torre Grande
I . . . . . . . . . . . . 179 C2
Marinaleda E . . . . . 162 A3
Marina Romea I . . . 135 A5
Marine de Sisco F . 180 A2
Marinella I . . . . . . 176 B1
Marinella di Sarzana
I . . . . . . . . . . . . 134 A3
Marineo I . . . . . . . 176 B2
Marines F. . . . . . . . 90 B1
Maringues F . . . . . .116 B3
Marinha das Ondas
P. . . . . . . . . . . . . 154 A2
Marinha Grande P. . 154 B2
Marinhas P. . . . . . . 148 A1
Marino I . . . . . . . . 168 B2
Marjaliza E . . . . . . 157 A4
Markabygd N . . . . . 199 B8
Markaryd S . . . . . . 61 C3
Markdorf D. . . . . . . 107 B4
Markelo NL . . . . . . . 71 B3
Market Deeping GB . 40 C3
Market Drayton GB . 38 B4
Market Harborough
GB . . . . . . . . . . . 40 C3
Market Rasen GB . . 40 B3
Market Warsop GB . 40 B2
Market Weighton
GB . . . . . . . . . . . 40 B3
Markgröningen D . . 93 C5
Markhausen D . . . . 71 B4
Marki PL . . . . . . . . .77 B6
Markina-Xemein E. . 143 A4
Märkische Buchholz
D . . . . . . . . . . . . . 74 B2
Markitta S . . . . . . 196 B4

Markkleeberg D. . . . 83 A4
Marklohe D . . . . . . 72 B2
Marknesse NL . . . . 70 B2
Markneukirchen D . . 83 B4
Markopoulo GR. . . . 185 B4
Markovac
Srbija SRB. . . . .127 C3
Vojvodina SRB. . . 126 B3
Markowice PL . . . . . 86 B2
Markranstädt D . . . . 83 A4
Marksuhl D . . . . . . . 82 B2
Markt Allhau A . . . .111 B3
Markt Bibart D . . . . . 94 B2
Marktbreit D. . . . . . . 94 B2
Markt Erlbach D . . . . 94 B2
Markt-heidenfeld D. . 94 B1
Markt Indersdorf D . 95 C3
Marktl D. . . . . . . . . 95 C4
Marktleuthen D . . . . 83 B3
Marktoberdorf D . . . 108 B1
Marktredwitz D . . . . 95 A4
Markt Rettenbach
D . . . . . . . . . . . . 108 B1
Markt Schwaben D 108 A2
Markt-Übelbach A. . 110 B2
Markusica HR . . . . . 125 B3
Markušovce SK. . . . 99 C4
Marl D. . . . . . . . . . . 80 A3
Marlborough
Devon GB . . . . . . 42 B3
Wiltshire GB . . . . .44 B2
Marle F . . . . . . . . . 91 B3
Marlieux F . . . . . . .117 A5
Marlow
D . . . . . . . . . . . . . 66 B1
GB . . . . . . . . . . . . 44 B3
Marma S . . . . . . . . 51 B4
Marmagne F . . . . . 104 C3
Marmande F . . . . . 128 B3
Marmara TR . . . . . 186 B2
Marmaris TR . . . . . 188 C3
Marmelete P . . . . . 160 B1
Marmolejo E . . . . . 157 B3
Marmoutier F. . . . . . 93 C3
Marnay F . . . . . . . 105 B4
Marne D . . . . . . . . . 64 C2
Marnheim D . . . . . . 93 B4
Marnitz D . . . . . . . . 73 A4
Maroldsweisach D . 82 B2
Marolles-les-Braults
F. . . . . . . . . . . . . 89 B4
Maromme F . . . . . . 89 A5
Marone I . . . . . . . . 120 B3
Maronia GR . . . . . 183 C7
Maroslele H . . . . . 126 A2
Maróstica I . . . . . . 121 B4
Marotta I . . . . . . . 136 B2
Marpisa GR . . . . . . 185 B6
Marquion F . . . . . . . 78 B3
Marquise F . . . . . . . 78 B1
Marradi I . . . . . . . 135 A4
Marrasjärvi FIN . . . 197 C8
Marraskoski FIN . . 197 C8
Marratxi E . . . . . . 166 B2
Marrúbiu I . . . . . . 179 C2
Marrum NL . . . . . . 70 A2
Marrupe E . . . . . . 150 B3
Marsac F . . . . . . . 129 C5
Marsac-en-Livradois
F. . . . . . . . . . . . .117 B3
Marságlia I . . . . . . 120 C2
Marsala I . . . . . . . 176 B1
Marsberg D . . . . . . 81 A4
Marsciano I . . . . . 135 C5
Marseillan F . . . . . 130 B2
Marseille = Marseilles
F. . . . . . . . . . . . . 131 B4
Marseille en Beauvaisis
F. . . . . . . . . . . . . 90 B1
Marseilles = Marseille
F. . . . . . . . . . . . . 131 B4
Mársico Nuovo I . . 172 B1
Marske-by-the-Sea
GB . . . . . . . . . . . 37 B5
Mars-la-Tours F. . . . 92 B1
Marslev DK. . . . . . . 59 C3
Marson F . . . . . . . . 91 C4
Märsta S . . . . . . . . 57 A3
Marstal DK . . . . . . . 65 B3
Marstrand S . . . . . . 60 B1
Marta I . . . . . . . . . 168 A1
Martano I . . . . . . . 173 B4
Martel F . . . . . . . . 129 B4
Martelange B . . . . . 92 B1
Martfeld D . . . . . . . 72 B2
Martfű H. . . . . . . . .113 B4
Martham GB . . . . . . 41 C5
Marthon F . . . . . . . 115 C4
Martiago E . . . . . . 149 B3
Martigné-Briand F. . 102 B1
Martigné-Ferchaud
F. . . . . . . . . . . . . 101 B4
Martigne-sur-Mayenne
F. . . . . . . . . . . . . 102 A1
Martigny CH . . . . . .119 A4
Martigny-les-Bains
F. . . . . . . . . . . . . 105 A4
Martigues F . . . . . . 131 B4
Martim-Longo P . . . 160 B2
Martin SK. . . . . . . . 98 B2
Martina CH. . . . . . . 108 C1
Martina Franca I . . 173 B3
Martinamor E. . . . . 150 B2
Martin de la Jara E 162 A3
Martinengo I . . . . . 120 B2
Martin Muñoz de las
Posadas E. . . . . 150 A3
Martinsberg A . . . . . 97 C3

Martinšćica HR . . . 123 C3
Martinshöhe D. . . . . 93 B3
Martinsicuro I . . . . . 136 C2
Martinszell D . . . . . 107 B5
Mártis I . . . . . . . . . 178 B2
Martofte DK . . . . . . 59 C3
Martonvásár H. . . . .112 B2
Martorell E . . . . . . 147 C2
Martos E . . . . . . . . 163 A4
Martres Tolosane
F . . . . . . . . . . . . 146 A1
Martti FIN. . . . . . . .197 B11
Marugán E . . . . . . 150 B3
Marúggio I . . . . . . 173 B3
Marvão P . . . . . . . 155 B3
Marvejols F . . . . . . 130 A2
Marville F . . . . . . . . 92 B1
Marwałd PL . . . . . . 77 A4
Marzabotto I . . . . . 135 A4
Marzahna D . . . . . . 74 C1
Marzahne D . . . . . . 73 B5
Marzamemi I . . . . . 177 C4
Marzocca I . . . . . . 136 B2
Masa E . . . . . . . . . 143 B3
Mas-Cabardès F . . 146 A3
Máscali I . . . . . . . 177 B4
Mascaraque E . . . . 157 A4
Mascarenhas P . . . 149 A2
Mascioni I . . . . . . . 169 A3
Mas de Barberáns
E . . . . . . . . . . . . 153 B4
Mas de las Matas
E . . . . . . . . . . . . 153 B3
Masegoso E. . . . . . 158 C1
Masegoso de Tajuña
E . . . . . . . . . . . . 151 B5
Masera I . . . . . . . .119 A5
Masevaux F . . . . . . 106 B1
Masfjorden N . . . . . 46 B2
Masham GB . . . . . . 37 B5
Masi N . . . . . . . . . 192 C7
Maside E . . . . . . . . 140 B2
Maslacq F . . . . . . . 144 A3
Maslinica HR . . . . . 138 B2
Maşloc RO. . . . . . . 126 B3
Maslovare BIH . . . . 138 A3
Masone I . . . . . . . . 133 A4
Massa I . . . . . . . . . 134 A3
Massa Fiscáglia I . . 121 C5
Massafra I . . . . . . . 173 B3
Massa Lombarda I . 135 A4
Massa Lubrense I . . 170 C2
Massamagrell E . . . 159 B3
Massa Marittima I . . 135 B3
Massa Martana I . . 136 C1
Massanassa E . . . . 159 B3
Massarosa I . . . . . . 134 B3
Massat F . . . . . . . . 146 B2
Massay F . . . . . . . . 103 B3
Massbach D. . . . . . . 82 B2
Massechelen B. . . . . 80 B1
Masseret F . . . . . . .116 B1
Masseube F . . . . . . 145 A4
Massiac F . . . . . . . .116 B3
Massignac F . . . . . 115 C4
Massing D . . . . . . . 95 C4
Massmechelen B. . . 80 B1
Masterud N . . . . . . 49 B4
Mästocka S . . . . . . 61 C3
Masty BY . . . . . . . . 13 B6
Masúa I . . . . . . . . . 179 C2
Masueco E. . . . . . . 149 A3
Masugnsbyn S . . . . 196 B5
Mašun SLO . . . . . . 123 B3
Maszewo
Lubuskie PL. . . . . . 75 B3
Zachodnio-Pomorskie
PL. . . . . . . . . . . . . 75 A4
Mata de Alcántara
E . . . . . . . . . . . . 155 B4
Matala GR . . . . . . 185 E5
Matalebreras E . . . 144 C1
Matallana de Torio
E . . . . . . . . . . . . 142 B1
Matamala E . . . . . 151 A5
Mataporquera E . . . 142 B2
Matapozuelos E . . . 150 A3
Mataró E . . . . . . . . 147 C3
Matarocco I . . . . . . 176 B1
Matélica I . . . . . . . 136 B2
Matera I . . . . . . . . 172 B2
Mátészalka H. . . . . 16 B5
Matet E. . . . . . . . . 159 B3
Matfors S . . . . . . . 200 D3
Matha F . . . . . . . . 115 C3
Mathay F . . . . . . . 106 B1
Matignon F . . . . . . 101 A3
Matilla de los Caños del
Rio E . . . . . . . . 149 B4
Matlock GB . . . . . . 40 B2
Matosinhos P . . . . 148 A1
Matour F . . . . . . . .117 A4
Mátrafüred H. . . . . .113 B3
Mátraterenye H. . . .113 A3
Matre
Hordaland N. . . . . 46 B2
Hordaland N. . . . . 52 A1
Matrei am Brenner
A . . . . . . . . . . . . 108 B2
Matrei in Osttirol A 109 B3
Matríce I . . . . . . . . 170 B2
Matsdal S. . . . . . . 195 E6
Mattarello I . . . . . . 121 A4
Mattersburg A . . . . 111 B3
Mattighofen A . . . . 109 A4

Mattinata I . . . . . . 171 B4
Mattos P. . . . . . . . 154 B2
Mattsee A . . . . . . . 109 B4
Mattsmyra S . . . . . 50 A2
Måttsund S . . . . . . 196 D5
Matulji HR . . . . . . . 123 B3
Maubert-Fontaine F 91 B4
Maubeuge F . . . . . . 79 B3
Maubourguet F . . . 145 A4
Mauchline GB . . . . . 36 A2
Maud GB . . . . . . . . 33 D4
Mauer-kirchen A . . 109 A4
Mauern D . . . . . . . . 95 C3
Mauguio F . . . . . . 131 B3
Maulbronn D . . . . . 93 C4
Maule F . . . . . . . . . 90 C1
Mauléon F . . . . . . .114 B3
Mauléon-Barousse
F . . . . . . . . . . . . 145 B4
Mauléon-Licharre
F . . . . . . . . . . . . 144 A3
Maulévrier F . . . . . .114 A3
Maum IRL . . . . . . . 28 A2
Maurach A . . . . . . 108 B2
Maure-de-Bretagne
F . . . . . . . . . . . . 101 B4
Maureilhan F . . . . . 130 B2
Mãureni RO . . . . . 126 B3
Mauriac F . . . . . . . .116 B2
Mauron F . . . . . . . 101 A3
Maurs F . . . . . . . . 116 C2
Maury F . . . . . . . . 146 B3
Maussane-les-Alpilles
F . . . . . . . . . . . . 131 B3
Mautern A. . . . . . . . 97 C3
Mauterndorf A . . . 109 B4
Mautern im Steiermark
A. . . . . . . . . . . . .110 B1
Mauthausen A. . . . .110 A1
Mauthen A . . . . . . 109 C3
Mauvezin F . . . . . . 129 C3
Mauzé-sur-le-Mignon
F . . . . . . . . . . . . .114 B3
Maxent F . . . . . . . 101 B3
Maxey-sur-Vaise F . 92 C1
Maxial F . . . . . . . . 154 B1
Maxieira P . . . . . . 154 B2
Maxwellheugh GB. . 35 C5
Mayalde E . . . . . . 149 A4
Maybole GB . . . . . . 36 A2
Mayen D. . . . . . . . . 80 B3
Mayenne F . . . . . . . 88 B3
Mayet F . . . . . . . . 102 B2
Maylough IRL . . . . . 28 A3
Mayorga E . . . . . . 142 B1
Mayres F . . . . . . . .117 C4
Mayrhofen A . . . . . 108 B2
Mazagón E . . . . . . 161 B3
Mazaleón E. . . . . . 153 A4
Mazamet F . . . . . . 130 B1
Mazan F . . . . . . . . 131 A4
Mazara del Vallo I . . 176 B1
Mazarambroz E . . . 157 A3
Mazarete E . . . . . . 152 B1
Mazaricos E . . . . . 140 B2
Mazarrón E . . . . . . 165 B3
Mažeikiai LT . . . . . . 8 D3
Mazères F . . . . . . . 146 A2
Mazères-sur-Salat
F . . . . . . . . . . . . 145 A4
Mazières-en-Gâtine
F . . . . . . . . . . . . .115 B3
Mazin HR . . . . . . . 138 A1
Mazuelo E . . . . . . 143 B3
Mazyr BY . . . . . . . . 13 B8
Mazzarino I . . . . . . 177 B3
Mazzarrà Sant'Andrea
I . . . . . . . . . . . . 177 A4
Mazzo di Valtellina
I . . . . . . . . . . . . 120 A3
Mdzewo PL . . . . . . . 77 B5
Mealabost GB . . . . . 31 A2
Mealhada P . . . . . . 148 B1
Méan B . . . . . . . . . 79 B5
Meana Sardo I . . . . 179 C3
Meaulne F . . . . . . 103 C4
Meaux F . . . . . . . . 90 C2
Mebonden N . . . . . 199 B8
Mecerreyes E . . . . 143 B3
Mechelen B . . . . . . 79 A4
Mechernich D . . . . . 80 B2
Mechnica PL . . . . . 86 B2
Mechowo PL . . . . . 67 C4
Mechterstädt D . . . . 82 B2
Mecidiye TR. . . . . . 186 B1
Mecikal PL . . . . . . . 68 B2
Mecina-Bombarón
E. . . . . . . . . . . . . 164 C1
Mecitözü TR . . . . . 23 A8
Meckenbeuren D. . . 107 B4
Meckenheim
Rheinland-Pfalz D . 80 B3
Rheinland-Pfalz D . 93 B4
Meckesheim D. . . . . 93 B4
Mecseknádasd H . 125 A4
Meda
I. . . . . . . . . . . . . 120 B2
P. . . . . . . . . . . . . 149 B2
Medak HR . . . . . . . 137 A4
Mede I . . . . . . . . . 120 B1
Medebach D . . . . . . 81 A4
Medelim P . . . . . . . 155 A3
Medemblik NL . . . . . 70 B2
Medena Selista
BIH. . . . . . . . . . . 138 A2
Medesano I . . . . . . 120 C3
Medevi S . . . . . . . . 55 B5
Medgidia RO . . . . . 17 C8

Medgyesháza H. . . 113 C5
Medhamn S. . . . . 55 A4
Mediaş RO. . . . . . 17 B6
Medicina I . . . . . . 135 A4
Medinaceli E . . . . 152 A1
Medina de las Torres
E. . . . . . . . . . . 155 C4
Medina del Campo
E. . . . . . . . . . . 150 A3
Medina de Pomar
E. . . . . . . . . . . 143 B3
Medina de Rioseco
E. . . . . . . . . . . 142 C1
Medina Sidonia E . 162 B2
Medinilla E . . . . . 150 B2
Medja SRB. . . . . . 126 B2
Medjedja BIH . . . . 139 B5
Medulin HR . . . . . 122 C2
Meduno I . . . . . . 122 A1
Medveda SRB . . . . 127 C3
Medvedov SK . . . 111 B4
Medvezhyegorsk
RUS . . . . . . . . . 9 A9
Medvide HR . . . . . 137 A4
Medvode SLO . . . . 123 A3
Medzev SK. . . . . . 99 C4
Medžitlija MK. . . . 182 C3
Meerane D . . . . . . 83 B4
Meerle B. . . . . . . 79 A4
Meersburg D . . . . 107 B4
Meeuwen B . . . . . 79 A5
Megalo Horio GR . . 188 C2
Megalopoli GR . . . 184 B3
Megara GR. . . . . . 185 A4
Megève F. . . . . . . 118 B3
Meggenhofen A. . . 109 A4
Megra RUS . . . . . . 9 B10
Megyaszó H. . . . . .113 A5
Mehamn N. . . . . .193 A11
Mehedeby S. . . . . . 51 B4
Méhkerék H . . . . . 113 C5
Mehun-sur-Yèvre
F. . . . . . . . . . . 103 B4
Meigle GB . . . . . . 35 B4
Meijel NL . . . . . . 80 A1
Meilen CH . . . . . . 107 B3
Meilhan F . . . . . . 128 C2
Meimôa P. . . . . . . 149 B2
Meina I . . . . . . . .119 B5
Meine D . . . . . . . 73 B3
Meinersen D . . . . 72 B3
Meinerzhagen D . . 81 A3
Meiningen D . . . . 82 B2
Meira E . . . . . . . . 141 A3
Meiringen CH . . . . 106 C3
Meisenheim D . . . 93 B3
Meissen D . . . . . . 83 A5
Meitingen D . . . . . 94 C2
Meix-devant-Virton
B. . . . . . . . . . . 92 B1
Męka PL . . . . . . . 86 A2
Meka Gruda BIH . . 139 B4
Mel I . . . . . . . . . 121 A5
Melbu N . . . . . . . 194 B5
Melč CZ . . . . . . . 98 B1
Meldal N . . . . . . . 198 B6
Méldola I . . . . . . 135 A5
Meldorf D. . . . . . . 64 B2
Melegnano I . . . . 120 B2
Melenci SRB . . . . 126 B2
Melendugno I . . . 173 B4
Melfi I . . . . . . . . 172 B1
Melfjordbotn N . . 195 D4
Melgaço P . . . . . . 140 B2
Melgar de Arriba E 142 B1
Melgar de Fernamental
E. . . . . . . . . . . 142 B2
Melgar de Yuso E . 142 B2
Melhus N . . . . . . 199 B7
Meliana E . . . . . . 159 B3
Melide
CH. . . . . . . . . .120 B1
E. . . . . . . . . . . 140 B2
Melides P. . . . . . . 160 A1
Meligales GR . . . . 184 B2
Melilli I . . . . . . . 177 B4
Melinovac HR . . . 124 C1
Melisenda I . . . . . 179 C3
Melisey F . . . . . . 105 B5
Mélito di Porto Salvo
I . . . . . . . . . . . 175 D1
Melk A. . . . . . . . .110 A2
Melksham GB . . . 43 A4
Mellakoski FIN. . . 196 C7
Mellanström S . . . 195 E9
Mellbystrand S . . . 61 C2
Melle
B. . . . . . . . . . . 79 A3
D. . . . . . . . . . . 71 B5
F. . . . . . . . . . . 115 B3
Mellendorf D . . . . 72 B2
Mellerud S. . . . . . 54 B3
Mellieha M. . . . . . 175 C3
Mellösa S . . . . . . 56 A2
Mellrichstadt D . . 82 B2
Mělnické Vtelno CZ. 84 B2
Mělník CZ. . . . . . . 84 B2
Melón E . . . . . . . 140 B2
Melrose GB . . . . . 35 C5
Mels CH . . . . . . . 107 B4
Melsungen D. . . . . 82 A1
Meltaus FIN . . . . . 197 C8
Meltham GB. . . . . 40 B2
Melton Mowbray GB 40 C3
Meltosjärvi FIN . . . 196 C7
Melun F . . . . . . . 90 C2
Melvaig GB . . . . . 31 B3
Melvich GB . . . . . 32 C3

Mélykút H. . . . . . . 126 A1
Melzo I . . . . . . . . 120 B2
Memaliaj AL. . . . . 182 C1
Membrilla E . . . . . 157 B4
Membrio E. . . . . . 155 B3
Memer F. . . . . . . . 129 B4
Memmelsdorf D. . . 94 B2
Memmingen D. . . . 107 B5
Memoria P. . . . . . 154 B2
Menággio I . . . . . 120 A2
Menai Bridge GB. . 38 A2
Menasalbas E . . . . 157 A3
Menat F. . . . . . . . .116 A2
Mendavia E . . . . . 144 B1
Mendaza E . . . . . . 144 B1
Mende F. . . . . . . . 130 A2
Menden D . . . . . . 81 A3
Menderes TR. . . . . 188 A2
Mendig D. . . . . . . 80 B3
Mendiga P . . . . . . 154 B2
Mendrisio CH . . . . 120 B1
Ménéac F . . . . . . . 101 A3
Menemen TR. . . . . 188 A2
Menen B. . . . . . . . 78 B3
Menesjärvi FIN . . . 193 D10
Menetou-Salon F. . 103 B4
Menfi I . . . . . . . . 176 B1
Ménfőcsanak H. . . .111 B4
Mengamuñoz E . . . 150 B3
Mengen
D. . . . . . . . . . . 107 A4
TR. . . . . . . . . . .187 B7
Mengeš SLO . . . . . 123 A3
Mengíbar E . . . . . 157 C4
Mengkofen D. . . . . 95 C4
Menou F. . . . . . . . 104 B2
Mens F. . . . . . . . . 118 C2
Menslage D . . . . . 71 B4
Mensträsk S . . . . . 200 A5
Mentana I . . . . . . 168 A2
Menton F . . . . . . . 133 B3
Méntrida E . . . . . . 151 B3
Méobecq F . . . . . .115 B5
Méounes-les-Montrieux
F. . . . . . . . . . . 132 B1
Meppel NL . . . . . . 70 B3
Meppen D . . . . . . 71 B4
Mequinenza E . . . 153 A4
Mer F . . . . . . . . . 103 B3
Mera
Coruña E . . . . . . 140 A2
Coruña E . . . . . . 140 A3
Meråker N . . . . . . 199 B8
Merano I . . . . . . . 108 C2
Merate I . . . . . . . 120 B2
Mercadillo E . . . . 143 A3
Mercatale I . . . . . 135 B5
Mercatino Conca I. 136 B1
Mercato San Severino
I . . . . . . . . . . . 170 C2
Mercato Saraceno
I . . . . . . . . . . . 135 B5
Merching D . . . . . 108 A1
Merchtem B. . . . . . 79 B4
Merdrignac F. . . . . 101 A3
Merdžanići BIH . . . 139 B3
Meré E . . . . . . . . 142 A2
Mere GB . . . . . . . 43 A4
Méréville F. . . . . . 90 C2
Merfeld D. . . . . . . 80 A3
Méribel F . . . . . . .118 B3
Méribel Motraret F. .118 B3
Meriç TR. . . . . . . . 186 A1
Mérida E. . . . . . . . 155 C4
Mérignac F . . . . . . 128 B2
Měřín CZ . . . . . . . . 97 B3
Mering D . . . . . . . 94 C2
Merkendorf D . . . . 94 B2
Merklin CZ. . . . . . . 96 B1
Merksplas B. . . . . . 79 A4
Merlànna S . . . . . . 56 A2
Merlimont Plage F. . 78 B1
Mern DK . . . . . . . 65 A5
Mernye H. . . . . . . .111 C4
Mersch L . . . . . . . 92 B2
Merseburg D . . . . 83 A3
Mers-les-Bains F. . . 90 A1
Merthyr Tydfil GB . 39 C3
Mertingen D. . . . . 94 C2
Mértola P. . . . . . . 160 B2
Méru F . . . . . . . . 90 B2
Merufe P. . . . . . . . 140 B2
Mervans F. . . . . . . 105 C4
Merville F. . . . . . . 78 B2
Méry-sur-Seine F . . 91 C3
Merzen D . . . . . . . 71 B4
Merzifon TR. . . . . . 23 A8
Merzig D. . . . . . . . 92 B2
Mesagne I . . . . . . 173 B3
Mesão Frio P. . . . . 148 A2
Mesas de Ibor E . . 156 A2
Meschede D. . . . . . 81 A4
Meschers-sur-Gironde
F. . . . . . . . . . . 114 C3
Meslay-du-Maine F 102 B1
Mesna N. . . . . . . . 48 A2
Mesnalien N. . . . . 48 A2
Mesocco CH . . . . 120 A2
Mésola I . . . . . . . 122 C1
Mesologi GR . . . . 184 A2
Mesopotamo GR. . 182 D2
Mesoraca I. . . . . . 175 B2
Messac F. . . . . . . 101 B4
Messancy B . . . . . 92 B1
Messdorf D . . . . . 73 B4
Messei F. . . . . . . . 88 B3
Messejana P . . . . . 160 B1
Messelt N. . . . . . . 48 A3

Messina I . . . . . . 177 A4
Messingen D . . . . . 71 B4
Messini GR . . . . . . 184 B3
Messkirch D . . . . . 107 B4
Messlingen S. . . . . 199 C9
Messtetten D . . . . 107 A3
Mesta GR. . . . . . . 185 A6
Mestanza E . . . . . 157 B3
Město Králové CZ . 84 B3
Mestlin D . . . . . . . 73 A4
Město Albrechtice
CZ. . . . . . . . . . 85 B5
Město Libavá CZ. . 98 B1
Město Touškov CZ . 96 B1
Mestre I . . . . . . . 122 B1
Mesvres F . . . . . . 104 C3
Metajna HR . . . . . 137 A4
Metelen D. . . . . . . 71 B4
Methana GR. . . . . 185 B4
Methlick GB . . . . . 33 D4
Methven GB. . . . . 35 B4
Methwold GB. . . . 41 C4
Metković HR . . . . . 139 B3
Metlika SLO . . . . . 123 B4
Metnitz A . . . . . . 110 C1
Metsäkylä FIN . . . 197 D11
Metslawier NL . . . . 70 A3
Metsovo GR. . . . . 182 D3
Metten D . . . . . . . 95 C4
Mettendorf D . . . . 92 B2
Mettet B . . . . . . . 79 B4
Mettingen D. . . . . 71 B4
Mettlach D . . . . . . 92 B2
Mettlen CH. . . . . . 106 C2
Mettmann D. . . . . 80 A2
Metz F . . . . . . . . 92 B2
Metzervisse F . . . . 92 B2
Metzingen D . . . . 94 C1
Meulan F . . . . . . . 90 B1
Meung-sur-Loire F 103 B3
Meuselwitz D. . . . . 83 A4
Meuzac F. . . . . . . 115 C5
Mevagissey GB . . . 42 B2
Mexborough GB . . 40 B2
Meximieux F . . . . .118 B2
Mey GB . . . . . . . . 32 C3
Meyenburg D. . . . . 73 A5
Meyerhöfen D . . . 71 B5
Meylan F . . . . . . . .118 B2
Meymac F. . . . . . . .116 B2
Meyrargues F . . . . 132 B1
Meyrueis F. . . . . . 130 A2
Meyssac F . . . . . . 129 A4
Meysse F . . . . . . . 117 C4
Meyzieu F . . . . . . .117 B4
Mèze F . . . . . . . . 130 B2
Mézériat F . . . . . . .117 A5
Mežica SLO . . . . . 110 C1
Mézidon-Canon F. . 89 A3
Mézières-en-Brenne
F. . . . . . . . . . . .115 B5
Mézières-sur-Issoire
F. . . . . . . . . . . .115 B4
Mézilhac F . . . . . . 117 C4
Mézilles F. . . . . . . 104 B2
Mézin F . . . . . . . . 128 B3
Mezöberény H . . . . 113 C5
Mezőcsát H . . . . . .113 B4
Mezöfalva H . . . . . 112 C2
Mezöhegyes H. . . . 126 A2
Mezökeresztes H. . .113 B4
Mezökomárom H. . 112 C2
Mezökövácsháza
H . . . . . . . . . . . 113 C4
Mezökövesd H. . . .113 B4
Mezöörs H . . . . . . .111 B4
Mézos F. . . . . . . . 128 B1
Mezöszilas H . . . . 112 C2
Mezötúr H. . . . . . .113 B4
Mezquita de Jarque
E. . . . . . . . . . . 153 B3
Mezzano
Emilia Romagna
I. . . . . . . . . . . .135 A5
Trentino Alto Adige
I. . . . . . . . . . . .121 A4
Mezzojuso I . . . . . 176 B2
Mezzoldo I . . . . . 120 A2
Mezzolombardo I . 121 A4
Mgarr M . . . . . . . 175 C3
Miajadas E . . . . . 156 A2
Mianowice PL . . . . 68 A2
Miasteczko Krajeńskie
PL. . . . . . . . . . 76 A2
Miasteczko Sl. PL. 86 B2
Miastko PL. . . . . . 68 A1
Michalovce SK. . . . 12 D4
Michałowice PL. . . 87 B3
Michelau D . . . . . 94 B2
Michelbach D . . . . 94 B2
Micheldorf A. . . . .110 B1
Michelhausen A. . . .110 A2
Michelsneukirchen
D . . . . . . . . . . . 95 B4
Michelstadt D . . . . 93 B5
Michendorf D. . . . . 74 B2
Mickleover GB. . . . 40 C2
Midbea GB. . . . . . 33 B4
Middelburg NL. . . . 79 A3
Middelfart DK. . . . 59 C2
Middelharnis NL . . 79 A4
Middelkerke B. . . . 78 A2
Middelstum NL . . . 71 A3
Middlesbrough GB . 37 B5

Middleton Cheney
GB. . . . . . . . . . 44 A2
Middleton-in-Teesdale
GB. . . . . . . . . . 37 B4
Middletown GB . . . 27 B4
Middlewich GB . . . 38 A4
Middlezoy GB . . . . 43 A4
Midhurst GB . . . . . 44 C3
Midleton IRL . . . . . 29 C3
Midlum D . . . . . . . 64 C1
Midsomer Norton
GB. . . . . . . . . . 43 A4
Midtgulen N . . . . . 198 D2
Midtskogberget N . 49 A4
Mid Yell GB . . . . . 33 A5
Miechów PL. . . . . . 87 B4
Miedes de Aragón
E. . . . . . . . . . . 152 A2
Miedes de Atienza
E. . . . . . . . . . . 151 A4
Międzybodzie Bielskie
PL. . . . . . . . . . 99 B3
Międzybórz PL. . . . 85 A5
Międzychód PL. . . 75 B4
Międzylesie PL. . . . 85 B4
Międzyrzec Podlaski
PL. . . . . . . . . . 12 C5
Międzyrzecz PL. . . 75 B4
Międzywodzie PL. . 67 B3
Międzyzdroje PL. . 67 C3
Miejska Górka PL . . 85 A4
Miélan F. . . . . . . . 145 A4
Mielec PL. . . . . . . 87 B5
Mielęcin PL. . . . . . 75 A3
Mielno
Warmińsko-Mazurskie
PL. . . . . . . . . . .77 A5
Zachodnio-Pomorskie
PL. . . . . . . . . . .67 B5
Mieraslompolo
FIN. . . . . . . . . . 193 C11
Miercurea Ciuc RO . 17 B6
Mieres
Asturias E . . . . . . 141 A5
Girona E. . . . . . . 147 B3
Mieroszów PL. . . . 85 B4
Mierzyn PL. . . . . . 86 A3
Miesau D . . . . . . . 93 B3
Miesbach D . . . . . 108 B2
Mieścisko PL. . . . . 76 B2
Mieste D. . . . . . . . 73 B4
Miesterhorst D . . . 73 B4
Mieszków PL. . . . . 76 B2
Mieszkowice PL. . . 74 B3
Mietków PL. . . . . . 85 B4
Migennes F . . . . . 104 B2
Miggiano I . . . . . . 173 C4
Migliánico I. . . . . . 169 A4
Migliarino I. . . . . . 121 C4
Migliónico I . . . . . 172 B2
Mignano Monte Lungo
I . . . . . . . . . . . 169 B3
Migné F . . . . . . . .115 B5
Miguel Esteban E . 157 A4
Miguelturra E. . . . 157 B4
Mihajlovac SRB. . . 127 C2
Miháld H. . . . . . . .111 C4
Mihalgazi TR. . . . . 187 B5
Mihaliççik TR. . . . 187 C6
Mihályi H . . . . . . .111 B4
Mihla D. . . . . . . . . 82 A2
Mihohnić HR. . . . . 123 B3
Miholjsko HR. . . . . 123 B4
Mihovljan HR. . . . 124 A1
Mijares E . . . . . . . 150 B3
Mijas E. . . . . . . . . 163 B3
Mike H . . . . . . . . 124 A3
Mikines GR . . . . . 184 B3
Mikkeli FIN. . . . . . 8 B5
Mikkelvik N . . . . . 192 B3
Mikleuš HR . . . . . 125 B3
Mikołajki Pomorskie
PL. . . . . . . . . . 69 B4
Mikołów PL. . . . . . 86 B2
Mikonos GR. . . . . 185 B6
Mikorzyn PL. . . . . 86 A2
Mikro Derio GR . . 183 B8
Mikstat PL. . . . . . 86 A1
Mikulášovice CZ. . 84 B2
Mikulov CZ. . . . . . 97 C4
Mikulovice CZ. . . . 85 B5
Milagro E . . . . . . 144 B2
Miłakowo PL. . . . . 69 A5
Milan = Milano I . . 120 B2
Miland N . . . . . . . 47 C5
Milano = Milan I . . 120 B2
Milano Marittima I . 135 A5
Milas TR. . . . . . . . 188 B2
Milazzo I . . . . . . . 177 A4
Mildenhall GB . . . 45 A4
Milejewo PL. . . . . 69 A4
Milelín CZ. . . . . . . 85 B3
Miletić SRB . . . . . 125 B5
Miletićevo SRB . . 126 B3
Mileto I . . . . . . . . 175 C2
Milevsko CZ. . . . . 96 B2
Milford IRL . . . . . . 26 A3
Milford Haven GB . 39 C1
Milford on Sea GB. 44 C2
Milhão P. . . . . . . . 149 A3
Milići BIH . . . . . . 139 A5
Miličín CZ. . . . . . . 96 B2
Milicz PL. . . . . . . 85 A5
Milín CZ. . . . . . . . 96 B2
Militello in Val di
Catánia I . . . . . . 177 B3

Miljevina BIH . . . . 139 B4
Milkowice PL. . . . . 85 A4
Millançay F . . . . . 103 B3
Millares E. . . . . . . 159 B3
Millas F . . . . . . . . 146 B3
Millau F . . . . . . . . 130 A2
Millesimo I . . . . . 133 A4
Millevaches F . . . .116 B2
Millom GB . . . . . . 36 B3
Millport GB . . . . . 34 C3
Millstatt A. . . . . . . 109 C4
Millstreet
Cork IRL. . . . . . . 29 B2
Waterford IRL. . . . 29 B4
Milltown
Galway IRL . . . . . 28 A3
Kerry IRL . . . . . . 29 B1
Milltown Malbay IRL 28 B2
Milly-la-Forêt F . . . 90 C2
Milmarcos E . . . . 152 A2
Milmersdorf D . . . 74 A2
Milna HR . . . . . . . 138 B2
Milnthorpe GB. . . . 37 B4
Milogórze PL. . . . . 69 A5
Miłomłyn PL. . . . . 69 B4
Milos GR . . . . . . . 185 C5
Miłosław PL. . . . . . 76 B2
Milot AL . . . . . . . 182 B1
Miłówka PL. . . . . . 99 B3
Miltach D . . . . . . . 95 B4
Miltenberg D . . . . 94 B1
Milton Keynes GB . 44 A3
Miltzow D. . . . . . . 66 B2
Milverton GB . . . . 43 A3
Milzyn PL. . . . . . . 76 B3
Mimice HR . . . . . . 138 B2
Mimizan F . . . . . . 128 B1
Mimizan-Plage F . . 128 B1
Mimoň CZ . . . . . . 84 B2
Mina de Juliana P . 160 B1
Mina de São Domingos
P. . . . . . . . . . . 160 B2
Minas de Riotinto
E. . . . . . . . . . . 161 B3
Minateda E . . . . . 158 C2
Minaya E . . . . . . . 158 B1
Minde P . . . . . . . 154 B2
Mindelheim D . . . 108 A1
Mindelstetten D. . . 95 C3
Minden D . . . . . . 72 B1
Mindszent H . . . . 113 C4
Minehead GB. . . . . 43 A3
Mineo I . . . . . . . . 177 B3
Minerbe I . . . . . . 121 B4
Minérbio I. . . . . . . 121 C4
Minervino Murge I. 171 B4
Minglanilla E . . . . 158 B2
Mingorria E . . . . . 150 B3
Minnesund N . . . . 48 B3
Miño E . . . . . . . . 140 A2
Miño de San Esteban
E. . . . . . . . . . . 151 A4
Minsen D . . . . . . . 71 A4
Minsk BY . . . . . . . 13 B7
Mińsk Mazowiecki
PL. . . . . . . . . . 12 B4
Minsterley GB . . . 39 B4
Mintlaw GB . . . . . 33 D4
Minturno I . . . . . . 169 B3
Mionica
BIH . . . . . . . . . .125 C4
SRB . . . . . . . . . .127 C2
Mios F . . . . . . . . 128 B2
Mira
E. . . . . . . . . . . 158 B2
I. . . . . . . . . . . . 121 B5
P. . . . . . . . . . . . 148 B1
Mirabel E . . . . . . 155 B4
Mirabel-aux-Baronnies
F. . . . . . . . . . . 131 A4
Mirabella Eclano I. 170 B3
Mirabella Imbáccari
I . . . . . . . . . . . 177 B3
Mirabello I . . . . . . 121 C4
Miradoux F . . . . . 129 B3
Miraflores de la Sierra
E. . . . . . . . . . . 151 B4
Miralrio E. . . . . . . 151 B5
Miramar P . . . . . . 148 A1
Miramare I . . . . . . 136 A1
Miramas F . . . . . . 131 B3
Mirambeau F . . . . 114 C3
Miramont-de-Guyenne
F. . . . . . . . . . . 129 B3
Miranda de Arga E 144 B2
Miranda de Ebro E 143 B4
Miranda do Corvo
P. . . . . . . . . . . 148 B1
Miranda do Douro
P. . . . . . . . . . . 149 A3
Mirande F . . . . . . 129 C3
Mirandela P . . . . . 149 A2
Mirandilla E . . . . . 155 C4
Mirándola I. . . . . . 121 C4
Miranje HR. . . . . . 137 A4
Mirano I. . . . . . . . 121 B5
Miras AL. . . . . . . . 182 C2
Miravet E. . . . . . . 153 A4
Miré F. . . . . . . . . 102 B1
Mirebeau F. . . . . . 102 C2
Mirebeau-sur-Bèze
F. . . . . . . . . . . 105 B4
Mirecourt F . . . . . 105 A5
Mirepoix F . . . . . . 146 A2
Mires GR . . . . . . . 185 D5
Miribel F. . . . . . . .117 B4
Miričina BIH . . . . . 125 C4

Mirina GR. . . . . . . 183 D7
Mirna SLO . . . . . . 123 B4
Miroslav CZ. . . . . . 97 C4
Mirosławice PL. . . . 85 B4
Mirosławiec PL . . . 75 A5
Mirošov CZ. . . . . . 96 B1
Mirotice CZ. . . . . . 96 B2
Mirovice CZ. . . . . . 96 B2
Mirow D . . . . . . . 74 A1
Mirsk PL. . . . . . . . 84 B3
Mirzec PL. . . . . . . 87 A5
Misi FIN . . . . . . . . 197 C9
Misilmeri I . . . . . . 176 A2
Miske H . . . . . . . . 112 C3
Miskolc H. . . . . . . .113 A4
Mislinja SLO . . . . . 110 C2
Missanello I . . . . . 174 A2
Missillac F . . . . . . 101 B3
Mistelbach
A. . . . . . . . . . . .97 C4
D. . . . . . . . . . . .95 B3
Misten N. . . . . . . . 194 C5
Misterbianco I . . . 177 B4
Misterhult S. . . . . . 62 A4
Mistretta I . . . . . . 177 B3
Misurina I. . . . . . . 109 C3
Mitchelstown IRL . 29 B3
Mithimna GR . . . . 186 C1
Mithoni GR . . . . . 184 C2
Mitilini GR . . . . . . 186 C1
Mitilinii GR. . . . . . 188 B1
Mittelberg
Tirol A. . . . . . . . .108 C1
Vorarlberg A. . . . . 107 B5
Mittenwald D . . . . 108 B2
Mittenwalde D . . . 74 B2
Mitterback A . . . . .110 B2
Mitterdorf im Mürztal
A. . . . . . . . . . . .110 B2
Mitter-Kleinarl A . . 109 B4
Mittersheim F . . . . 92 C2
Mittersill A . . . . . . 109 B3
Mitterskirchen D . . 95 C4
Mitterteich D . . . . 95 B4
Mitton D . . . . . . . 128 B2
Mittweida D . . . . . 83 B4
Mitwitz D . . . . . . . 82 B3
Mizhhir'ya UA . . . . 13 D5
Mjällby S . . . . . . . 63 B2
Mjåvatn N. . . . . . . 53 B4
Mjöbäck S . . . . . . 60 B2
Mjölby S . . . . . . . 56 B1
Mjølfjell N. . . . . . . 46 B3
Mjøndalen N . . . . . 53 A6
Mjørlund N . . . . . . 48 B2
Mladá Boleslav CZ . 84 B2
Mladá Vožice CZ . . 96 B2
Mladé Buky CZ . . . 85 B3
Mladenovac SRB. . 127 C2
Mladenovo SRB . . 126 B1
Mladikovine BIH . . 139 A3
Mława PL. . . . . . . 77 A5
Mlinište BIH . . . . . 138 A2
Młodzieszyn PL. . . 77 B5
Młogoszyn PL. . . . 77 B4
Młynary PL. . . . . . 69 A4
Mnichovice CZ. . . . 96 B2
Mnichovo Hradiště
CZ. . . . . . . . . . 84 B2
Mnišek nad Hnilcom
SK . . . . . . . . . . 99 C4
Mnišek pod Brdy
CZ. . . . . . . . . . 96 B2
Mniszek PL . . . . . 87 A4
Mniszków PL . . . . 87 A4
Mo
Hedmark N. . . . . .48 B3
Hordaland N. . . . . 46 B2
Møre og Romsdal
N. . . . . . . . . . . .198 C5
Telemark N . . . . . 53 A3
Gävleborg S. . . . . 51 B3
Västra Götaland S. . 54 B2
Moaña E. . . . . . . . 140 B2
Moate IRL. . . . . . . 28 A4
Mocejón E . . . . . . 151 C4
Močenok SK . . . . .111 A4
Mochales E . . . . . 152 A1
Mochowo PL. . . . . 77 B4
Mochy PL. . . . . . . 75 B5
Mockern D . . . . . . 73 B4
Mockfjärd S . . . . . 50 B1
Möckmühl D . . . . . 94 B1
Mockrehna D . . . . 83 A4
Moclin E. . . . . . . . 163 A4
Mocsa H. . . . . . . .112 B2
Möcsény H. . . . . . 125 A4
Modane F. . . . . . . .118 B3
Modbury GB . . . . . 42 B3
Módena I. . . . . . . . 121 C3
Módica I . . . . . . . 177 C3
Modigliana I . . . . . 135 A4
Modlin PL. . . . . . . 77 B5
Mödling A. . . . . . . .111 A3
Modliszewice PL. . 87 A4
Modliszewko PL . . 76 B2
Modogno I . . . . . . 171 B4
Modra SK. . . . . . . 98 C1
Modran BIH . . . . . 125 C3
Modriča BIH . . . . . 125 C4
Mõõrudalur IS . . . 191 B10
Modrý Kamen SK . 99 C3
Moëlan-sur-Mer F . 100 B2
Moelfre GB. . . . . . 38 A2

Moelv N . . . . . . . . . 48 B2
Moen N. . . . . . . . . 194 A9
Moena I . . . . . . . . . 121 A4
Moerbeke B . . . . . . 79 A3
Moers D . . . . . . . . . 80 A2
Móes P. . . . . . . . . 148 B2
Moffat GB. . . . . . . . 36 A3
Mogadouro P. . . . . 149 A3
Mogata S . . . . . . . . 56 B2
Móggio Udinese I . 122 A2
Mogielnica PL . . . . 87 A4
Mogilany PL. . . . . . 99 B3
Mogilno PL. . . . . . . 76 B2
Mogliano I . . . . . . . 136 B2
Mogliano Véneto I . 122 B1
Mogor E . . . . . . . . 140 B2
Mógoro I . . . . . . . . 179 C2
Moguer E . . . . . . . 161 B3
Mohács H. . . . . . . 125 B4
Moheda S. . . . . . . . 62 A2
Mohedas E. . . . . . 149 B3
Mohedas de la Jara
  E. . . . . . . . . . . . 156 A2
Mohelnice CZ . . . . . 97 B4
Mohill IRL . . . . . . . . 26 C3
Möhlin CH . . . . . . . 106 B2
Moholm S . . . . . . . 55 B5
Mohorn D. . . . . . . . 83 A5
Mohyliv-Podil's'kyy
  UA . . . . . . . . . . . 13 D7
Moi N . . . . . . . . . . . 52 B2
Moià E . . . . . . . . . 147 C3
Móie I . . . . . . . . . . 136 B2
Moimenta da Beira
  P. . . . . . . . . . . . 148 B2
Mo i Rana N . . . . . 195 D5
Moirans F. . . . . . . .118 B2
Moirans-en-Montagne
  F. . . . . . . . . . . . .118 A2
Moisaküla EST . . . . . 8 C4
Moisdon-la-Rivière
  F. . . . . . . . . . . . 101 B4
Moissac F . . . . . . . 129 B4
Moita
  Coimbra P . . . . . 148 B1
  Guarda P . . . . . . 149 B2
  Santarém P . . . . 154 A2
  Setúbal P . . . . . .154 C1
Moita dos Ferreiros
  P. . . . . . . . . . . . 154 B1
Moixent E. . . . . . . 159 C3
Mojacar E. . . . . . . 164 B3
Mojados E . . . . . . 150 A3
Mojmírovce SK . . . .112 A2
Mojtin SK . . . . . . . . 98 C2
Möklinta S . . . . . . . 50 B3
Mokošica HR. . . . . 139 C4
Mokronog SLO . . . 123 B4
Mokro Polje HR . . . 138 A2
Mokrzyska PL . . . . . 99 A4
Møkster N . . . . . . . 46 B2
Mol
  B. . . . . . . . . . . . .79 A5
  SRB . . . . . . . . . .126 B2
Mola di Bari I . . . . . 173 A3
Molai GR . . . . . . . . 184 C3
Molare I . . . . . . . . 133 A4
Molaretto I . . . . . . .119 B4
Molas F . . . . . . . . 145 A4
Molassano I . . . . . 134 A1
Molbergen D . . . . . . 71 B4
Mold GB . . . . . . . . . 38 A3
Molde N . . . . . . . . 198 C4
Møldrup DK . . . . . . 58 B2
Moledo do Minho
  P. . . . . . . . . . . . 148 A1
Molfetta I . . . . . . . 171 B4
Molfsee D. . . . . . . . 64 B3
Moliden S. . . . . . . 200 C4
Molières F . . . . . . 129 B4
Molina de Aragón
  E. . . . . . . . . . . . 152 B2
Molina de Segura
  E. . . . . . . . . . . . 165 A3
Molinar E . . . . . . . 143 A3
Molinaseca E. . . . . 141 B4
Molinella I . . . . . . 121 C4
Molinet F . . . . . . . 104 C2
Molinicos E . . . . . 158 C1
Molini di Tures I. . . 108 C2
Molinos de Duero
  E. . . . . . . . . . . . 143 C4
Molins de Rei E . . . 147 C3
Moliterno I . . . . . . 174 A1
Molkom S. . . . . . . . 55 A4
Möllbrücke A . . . . . 109 C4
Mölle S . . . . . . . . . 61 C2
Molledo E. . . . . . . 142 A2
Möllenbeck D . . . . . 74 A2
Mollerussa E . . . . . 147 C1
Mollet de Perelada
  E. . . . . . . . . . . . 146 B3
Mollina E . . . . . . . 163 A3
Mölln D . . . . . . . . . 73 A3
Molló E. . . . . . . . . 146 B3
Mollösund S . . . . . . 54 B2
Mölltorp S . . . . . . . 55 B5
Mölnbo S . . . . . . . . 56 A3
Mölndal S . . . . . . . 60 B2
Mölnlycke S. . . . . . 60 B2
Molompize F . . . . .116 B3
Moloy F . . . . . . . . 105 B3
Molsheim F . . . . . . 93 C3
Moltzow D . . . . . . . 73 A5
Molve HR. . . . . . . 124 A3

Molveno I. . . . . . . 121 A3
Molvizar E . . . . . . 163 B4
Molzbichl A . . . . . . 109 C4
Mombaróccio I . . . . 136 B1
Mombeltrán E . . . . 150 B2
Mombris D. . . . . . . 93 A5
Mombuey E . . . . . . 141 B4
Momchilgrad BG. . . 183 B7
Momo I. . . . . . . . . .119 B5
Monaghan IRL . . . . . 27 B4
Monar Lodge GB. . . 32 D2
Monasterace Marina
  I . . . . . . . . . . . . 175 C2
Monasterevin IRL . . 30 A1
Monasterio de Rodilla
  E. . . . . . . . . . . . 143 B3
Monastir I . . . . . . . 179 C3
Monbahus F . . . . . 129 B3
Monbazillac F . . . . 129 B3
Moncada E. . . . . . 159 B3
Moncalieri I. . . . . . .119 B4
Moncalvo I . . . . . . .119 B5
Monção P. . . . . . . 140 B2
Moncarapacho P. . . 160 B2
Moncel-sur-Seille F. 92 C2
Monchegorsk RUS . 3 C13
Mönchengladbach =
  München-Gladbach
  D . . . . . . . . . . . . 80 A2
Mónchio della Corti
  I . . . . . . . . . . . . 134 A3
Monchique P. . . . . 160 B1
Monclar-de-Quercy
  F. . . . . . . . . . . . 129 C4
Moncofa E . . . . . . 159 B3
Moncontour F . . . . 101 A3
Moncoutant F . . . . .114 B3
Monda E. . . . . . . . 162 B3
Mondariz E . . . . . . 140 B2
Mondavio I . . . . . . 136 B1
Mondéjar E . . . . . . 151 B4
Mondello I . . . . . . 176 A2
Mondim de Basto
  P. . . . . . . . . . . . 148 A2
Mondolfo I . . . . . . 136 B2
Mondoñedo E . . . . 141 A3
Mondorf-les-Bains L 92 B2
Mondoubleau F. . . . 102 B2
Mondovi I . . . . . . . 133 A3
Mondragon F. . . . . 131 A3
Mondragone I . . . . 170 B1
Mondsee A. . . . . . 109 B4
Monéglia I . . . . . . 134 A2
Monegrillo E . . . . . 153 A3
Monein F . . . . . . . 145 A3
Monemvasia GR . . 184 C4
Mónesi I . . . . . . . . 133 A3
Monesíglio I . . . . . 133 A4
Monesterio E . . . . 161 A3
Monestier-de-Clermont
  F. . . . . . . . . . . . 118 C2
Monestiés F . . . . . 130 A1
Monéteau F . . . . . 104 B2
Moneygall IRL . . . . . 28 B4
Moneymore GB. . . . 27 B4
Monfalcone I . . . . . 122 B2
Monfero E . . . . . . 140 A2
Monflanquin F. . . . . 129 B3
Monflorite E. . . . . . 145 B3
Monforte P. . . . . . . 155 B3
Monforte da Beira
  E. . . . . . . . . . . . 155 B3
  P. . . . . . . . . . . . 155 B3
Monforte d'Alba I . . 133 A3
Monforte del Cid E . 165 A4
Monforte de Lemos
  E. . . . . . . . . . . . 140 B3
Monforte de Moyuela
  E. . . . . . . . . . . . 152 A2
Monghidoro I. . . . . 135 A4
Mongiana I. . . . . . 175 C2
Monguelfo I . . . . . 108 C3
Monheim D . . . . . . 94 C2
Moniaive GB . . . . . 36 A3
Monifieth GB . . . . . 35 B5
Monikie GB . . . . . . 35 B5
Monistrol-d'Allier
  F. . . . . . . . . . . . 117 C3
Monistrol de Montserrat
  E. . . . . . . . . . . . 147 C2
Monistrol-sur-Loire
  F. . . . . . . . . . . . .117 B4
Mönkebude D . . . . . 74 A2
Monkton GB . . . . . . 36 A2
Monmouth GB. . . . . 39 C4
Monnaie F . . . . . . 102 B2
Monnerville F . . . . . 90 C2
Monnickendam NL . 70 B2
Monolithos GR . . . 188 C2
Monópoli I . . . . . . 173 B3
Monor H. . . . . . . . .112 B3
Monóvar E . . . . . . 159 C3
Monpazier F . . . . . 129 B3
Monreal
  D . . . . . . . . . . . . 80 B3
  E. . . . . . . . . . . . 144 B2
Monreal del Campo
  E. . . . . . . . . . . . 152 B2
Monreale I. . . . . . . 176 A2
Monroy E . . . . . . . 155 B4
Monroyo E . . . . . . 153 B3
Mons B. . . . . . . . . 79 B3
Monsaraz P. . . . . . 155 C3
Monschau D . . . . . . 80 B2
Monségur F . . . . . 128 B3
Monsélice I . . . . . . 121 B4
Mønshaug N . . . . . 46 B2

Monster NL . . . . . . 70 B1
Mönsterås S . . . . . 62 A4
Monsummano Terme
  I. . . . . . . . . . . . 135 B3
Montabaur D . . . . . 81 B3
Montafia I. . . . . . . .119 C5
Montagnac F . . . . . 130 B2
Montagnana I . . . . 121 B4
Montaigu F . . . . . . .114 B2
Montaigu-de-Quercy
  F. . . . . . . . . . . . 129 B4
Montaiguët-en-Forez
  F. . . . . . . . . . . . .117 A3
Montaigut F . . . . . .116 A2
Montaigut-sur-Save
  F. . . . . . . . . . . . 129 C4
Montainville F. . . . . 90 C1
Montalbán E . . . . . 153 B3
Montalbán de Córdoba
  E. . . . . . . . . . . . 163 A3
Montalbano Elicona
  I. . . . . . . . . . . . 177 A4
Montalbano Iónico
  I. . . . . . . . . . . . 174 A2
Montalbo E . . . . . . 158 B1
Montalcino I. . . . . . 135 B4
Montaldo di Cósola
  I. . . . . . . . . . . . 120 C2
Montalegre P. . . . . 148 A2
Montalieu-Vercieu
  F. . . . . . . . . . . . .118 B2
Montalivet-les-Bains
  F. . . . . . . . . . . . 114 C2
Montallegro I. . . . . 176 B2
Montalto delle Marche
  I . . . . . . . . . . . . 136 C2
Montalto di Castro
  I . . . . . . . . . . . . 168 A1
Montalto Pavese I . 120 C2
Montalto Uffugo I . . 174 B2
Montalvão P. . . . . . 155 B3
Montamarta E . . . . 149 A4
Montana BG. . . . . . 17 D5
Montana-Vermala
  CH . . . . . . . . . . .119 A4
Montánchez E . . . . 156 A1
Montanejos E . . . . 153 B3
Montano Antilia I. . . 172 B1
Montans F . . . . . . 129 C4
Montargil P . . . . . . 154 B2
Montargis F. . . . . . 103 B4
Montastruc-la-
  Conseillère F. . . . 129 C4
Montauban F . . . . . 129 B4
Montauban-de-Bretagne
  F. . . . . . . . . . . . 101 A3
Montbard F . . . . . . 104 B3
Montbarrey F . . . . . 105 B4
Montbazens F. . . . . 130 A1
Montbazon F . . . . . 102 B2
Montbéliard F . . . . 106 B1
Montbenoit F . . . . . 105 C5
Montbeugny F . . . . 104 C2
Montblanc E . . . . . 147 C2
Montbozon F . . . . . 105 B5
Montbrison F. . . . . .117 B4
Montbron F . . . . . . 115 C4
Montbrun-les-Bains
  F. . . . . . . . . . . . 131 A4
Montceau-les-Mines
  F. . . . . . . . . . . . 104 C3
Montcenis F . . . . . 104 C3
Montchanin F . . . . 104 C3
Montcornet F . . . . . 91 B4
Montcuq F . . . . . . 129 B4
Montdardier F . . . . 130 B2
Mont-de-Marsan F . 128 C2
Montdidier F . . . . . . 90 B2
Monteagudo E. . . . 165 A3
Monteagudo de las
  Vicarias E . . . . . 152 A1
Montealegre E. . . . 142 C2
Montealegre del Castillo
  E. . . . . . . . . . . . 159 C2
Montebello Iónico
  I. . . . . . . . . . . . 175 D1
Montebello Vicentino
  I. . . . . . . . . . . . 121 B4
Montebelluna I . . . . 121 B5
Montebourg F . . . . . 88 A2
Montebruno I . . . . 134 A2
Monte-Carlo MC . . 133 B3
Montecarotto I . . . . 136 B2
Montecassiano I . . . 136 B2
Montecastrilli I . . . . 168 A2
Montecatini Terme
  I. . . . . . . . . . . . 135 B3
Montécchio I . . . . . 136 B1
Montécchio Emilia
  I. . . . . . . . . . . . 121 C3
Montécchio Maggiore
  I. . . . . . . . . . . . 121 B4
Montech F . . . . . . 129 C4
Montechiaro d'Asti
  I. . . . . . . . . . . . .119 B5
Monte Clara P . . . . 155 B3
Monte Clérigo P . . 160 B1
Montecórice I . . . . 170 C2
Montecorvino Rovella
  I. . . . . . . . . . . . 170 C2
Monte da Pedra P. . 155 B3
Monte de Goula P . 155 B3
Montederramo E. . . 141 B3
Montedoro I. . . . . . 176 B2
Monte do Trigo P. . 155 C3
Montefalco I. . . . . . 136 C1
Montefalcone di Val
  Fortore I. . . . . . . 170 B3

Montefalcone nel
  Sánnio I . . . . . . . 170 B2
Montefano I. . . . . . 136 B2
Montefiascone I . . . 168 A2
Montefiorino I. . . . . 134 A3
Montefortino I . . . . 136 C2
Montefranco I . . . . 168 A2
Montefrío E . . . . . . 163 A4
Montegiordano Marina
  I . . . . . . . . . . . . 174 A2
Montegiórgio I. . . . 136 B2
Monte Gordo P . . . 160 B2
Montegranaro I . . . 136 B2
Montehermoso E . . 149 B3
Montejicar E . . . . . 163 A4
Montejo de la Sierra
  E. . . . . . . . . . . . 151 A4
Montejo de Tiermes
  E. . . . . . . . . . . . 151 A4
Monte Juntos P . . . 155 C3
Montel-de-Gelat F . .116 B2
Monteleone di Púglia
  I. . . . . . . . . . . . 171 B3
Monteleone di Spoleto
  I. . . . . . . . . . . . 135 C5
Monteleone d'Orvieto
  I. . . . . . . . . . . . 135 C5
Montelepre I . . . . . 176 A2
Montelibretti I . . . . 168 A2
Montelier F . . . . . . 117 C5
Montélimar F . . . . . 131 A3
Montella
  E. . . . . . . . . . . . 146 B2
  I. . . . . . . . . . . . 170 C3
Montellano E . . . . . 162 A2
Montelupo Fiorentino
  I. . . . . . . . . . . . 135 B4
Montemaggiore Belsito
  I. . . . . . . . . . . . 176 B2
Montemagno I . . . . 119 C5
Montemayor E. . . . 163 A3
Montemayor de Pinilla
  E. . . . . . . . . . . . 150 A3
Montemésola I. . . . 173 B3
Montemilleto I . . . . 170 B2
Montemiglione I . . . 172 A1
Montemolin E . . . . 161 A3
Montemónaco I . . . 136 C2
Montemor-o-Novo
  P. . . . . . . . . . . . 154 C2
Montemor-o-Velho
  P. . . . . . . . . . . . 148 B1
Montemurro I. . . . . 174 A1
Montendre F . . . . . 128 A2
Montenegro de Cameros
  E. . . . . . . . . . . . 143 B4
Montenero di Bisáccia
  I. . . . . . . . . . . . 170 B2
Monteneuf F . . . . . 101 B3
Monteparano I . . . . 173 B3
Montepescali I. . . . 135 C4
Montepiano I . . . . . 135 A4
Monte Porzio I . . . . 136 B2
Montepulciano I . . . 135 B4
Monte Real P. . . . . 154 B2
Montereale I. . . . . . 169 A3
Montereale Valcellina
  I. . . . . . . . . . . . 122 A1
Montereau-Faut-Yonne
  F. . . . . . . . . . . . . 90 C2
Monte Redondo P. . 154 B2
Monterénzio I . . . . 135 A4
Monte Romano I . . 168 A1
Monteroni d'Arbia
  I. . . . . . . . . . . . 135 B4
Monteroni di Lecce
  I. . . . . . . . . . . . 173 B4
Monterosso al Mare
  I. . . . . . . . . . . . 134 A2
Monterosso Almo I 177 B3
Monterosso Grana
  I. . . . . . . . . . . . 133 A3
Monterotondo I. . . . 168 A2
Monterotondo Maríttimo
  I. . . . . . . . . . . . 135 B3
Monterrey E . . . . . 141 C3
Monterroso E . . . . 140 B3
Monterrubio de la
  Serena E . . . . . . 156 B2
Monterubbiano I . . . 136 B2
Montesa E . . . . . . 159 C3
Montesalgueiro E . 140 A2
Monte San Giovanni
  Campano I . . . . . 169 B3
Montesano sulla
  Marcellana I. . . . 174 A1
Monte San Savino
  I. . . . . . . . . . . . 135 B4
Monte Sant'Ángelo
  I. . . . . . . . . . . . 171 B3
Montesárchio I . . . 170 B2
Montescaglioso I . . 171 C4
Montesclaros E. . . 150 B3
Montesilvano I. . . . 169 A4
Montespértoli I . . . 135 B4
Montesquieu-Volvestre
  F. . . . . . . . . . . . 146 A2
Montesquiou F . . . 129 C3
Montestruc-sur-Gers
  F. . . . . . . . . . . . 129 C3
Montes Velhos P. . 160 B1
Montevarchi I . . . . 135 B4
Montéveglio I . . . . 135 A4
Monte Vilar P. . . . . 154 B1
Montfaucon F . . . . 101 B4
Montfaucon-d'Argonne
  F. . . . . . . . . . . . . 91 B5

Montfaucon-en-Velay
  F. . . . . . . . . . . . .117 B4
Montferrat
  Isère F . . . . . . . 118 B2
  Var F . . . . . . . . 132 B2
Montfort-en-Chalosse
  F. . . . . . . . . . . . 128 C2
Montfort-l'Amaury F 90 C1
Montfort-le-Gesnois
  F. . . . . . . . . . . . 102 A2
Montfort-sur-Meu
  F. . . . . . . . . . . . 101 A4
Montfort-sur-Risle F 89 A4
Montgai E . . . . . . . 147 C1
Montgaillard F. . . . . 145 A4
Montgenèvre F . . . 118 C3
Montgiscard F . . . . 146 A2
Montgomery GB . . . 39 B3
Montguyon F. . . . . 128 A2
Monthermé F . . . . . 91 B4
Monthey CH. . . . . .119 A3
Monthois F . . . . . . 91 B4
Monthureux-sur-Saône
  F. . . . . . . . . . . . 105 A4
Monti I . . . . . . . . . 178 B3
Monticelli d'Ongina
  I. . . . . . . . . . . . 120 B2
Montichiari I . . . . . 120 B3
Monticiano I. . . . . . 135 B4
Montiel E . . . . . . . 158 C1
Montieri I . . . . . . . 135 B4
Montier-en-Der F. . . 91 C4
Montignac F . . . . . 129 A4
Montigny-le-Roi F . 105 B4
Montigny-lès-Metz
  F. . . . . . . . . . . . . 92 B2
Montigny-sur-Aube
  F. . . . . . . . . . . . 105 B3
Montijo
  E. . . . . . . . . . . . 155 C4
  P. . . . . . . . . . . . 154 C2
Montilla E. . . . . . . 163 A3
Montillana E . . . . . 163 A4
Montilly F . . . . . . . 104 C2
Montivilliers F. . . . . 89 A4
Montjaux F . . . . . . 130 A1
Montjean-sur-Loire
  F. . . . . . . . . . . . 102 B1
Montlhéry F . . . . . . 90 C2
Montlieu-la-Garde
  F. . . . . . . . . . . . 128 A2
Mont-Louis F . . . . . 146 B3
Montlouis-sur-Loire
  F. . . . . . . . . . . . 102 B2
Montluçon F . . . . . .116 A2
Montluel F . . . . . . .117 B5
Montmarault F . . . .116 A2
Montmartin-sur-Mer
  F. . . . . . . . . . . . . 88 B2
Montmédy F . . . . . . 92 B1
Montmélian F . . . . .118 B3
Montmeyan F . . . . 132 B2
Montmeyran F . . . . 117 C4
Montmirail
  Marne F . . . . . . . 91 C3
  Sarthe F . . . . . . 102 A2
Montmiral F . . . . . .118 B2
Montmirat F . . . . . 131 B3
Montmirey-le-Château
  F. . . . . . . . . . . . 105 B4
Montmoreau-St Cybard
  F. . . . . . . . . . . . 115 C4
Montmorency F. . . . 90 C2
Montmorillon F . . . .115 B4
Montmort-Lucy F . . 91 C3
Montoir-de-Bretagne
  F. . . . . . . . . . . . 101 B3
Montoire-sur-le-Loir
  F. . . . . . . . . . . . 102 B2
Montois P. . . . . . . 155 C3
Montolieu F . . . . . . 146 A3
Montório al Vomano
  I. . . . . . . . . . . . 169 A3
Montoro E . . . . . . 157 B3
Montpellier F . . . . . 131 B2
Montpezat-de-Quercy
  F. . . . . . . . . . . . 129 B4
Montpezat-sous-Bouzon
  F. . . . . . . . . . . . 117 C4
Montpon-Ménestérol
  F. . . . . . . . . . . . 128 A3
Montpont-en-Bresse
  F. . . . . . . . . . . . 105 C4
Montréal
  Aude F . . . . . . . 146 A3
  Gers F . . . . . . . 128 C3
Montredon-Labessonnié
  F. . . . . . . . . . . . 130 D1
Montréjeau F . . . . . 145 A4
Montrésor F . . . . . 103 B3
Montresta I . . . . . . 178 B2
Montret F . . . . . . . 105 C4
Montreuil
  Pas de Calais F . . 78 B1
  Seine St Denis F . . 90 C2
Montreuil-aux-Lions
  F. . . . . . . . . . . . . 90 B3
Montreuil-Bellay F . 102 B1
Montreux CH . . . . 106 C1
Montrevault F . . . . 101 B4
Montrevel-en-Bresse
  F. . . . . . . . . . . . .118 A2
Montrichard F . . . . 103 B3
Montricoux F . . . . . 129 B4
Mont-roig del Camp
  E. . . . . . . . . . . . 147 C1

Montrond-les-Bains
  F. . . . . . . . . . . . .117 B4
Montrose GB . . . . . 35 B5
Montroy E . . . . . . . 159 B3
Montsalvy F. . . . . . 116 C2
Montsauche-les-Settons
  F. . . . . . . . . . . . 104 B3
Montseny E . . . . . . 147 C3
Montsoreau F . . . . 102 B2
Mont-sous-Vaudrey
  F. . . . . . . . . . . . 105 C4
Monts-sur-Guesnes
  F. . . . . . . . . . . . 102 C2
Mont-St Aignan F . . 89 A5
Mont-St Vincent F . 104 C3
Montsûrs F. . . . . . 102 A1
Montuenga E . . . . 150 A3
Montuïri E . . . . . . 167 B3
Monza I. . . . . . . . . 120 B2
Monzón E. . . . . . . 145 C4
Monzón de Campos
  E. . . . . . . . . . . . 142 B2
Moorbad Lobenstein
  D . . . . . . . . . . . . 83 B3
Moordorf D . . . . . . 71 A4
Moorslede B . . . . . 78 B3
Moos D. . . . . . . . 107 B3
Moosburg D. . . . . . 95 C3
Moosburg im Kärnten
  A. . . . . . . . . . . . 110 C1
Mór H . . . . . . . . . .112 B2
Mora E . . . . . . . . . 157 A4
Móra P . . . . . . . . . 154 C2
Mora S . . . . . . . . . 50 A1
Moraby S . . . . . . . 50 B2
Mòra d'Ebre E . . . 153 A4
Mora de Rubielos
  E. . . . . . . . . . . . 153 B3
Moradillo de Roa E 151 A4
Morąg PL . . . . . . . 69 B4
Mórahalom H. . . . . 126 A1
Moraime E . . . . . . 140 A1
Morais P. . . . . . . . 149 A3
Mòra la Nova E . . . 153 A4
Moral de Calatrava
  E. . . . . . . . . . . . 157 B4
Moraleda de Zafayona
  E. . . . . . . . . . . . 163 A4
Moraleja E . . . . . . 149 B3
Moraleja del Vino
  E. . . . . . . . . . . . 150 A2
Morales del Vino E 150 A2
Morales de Toro E . 150 A2
Morales de Valverde
  E. . . . . . . . . . . . 141 C5
Moralina E . . . . . . 149 A3
Morano Cálabro I . 174 B2
Mörarp S . . . . . . . 61 C2
Morasverdes E . . . 149 B3
Morata de Jalón E . 152 A2
Morata de Jiloca E 152 A2
Morata de Tajuña
  E. . . . . . . . . . . . 151 B4
Moratalla E . . . . . . 164 A3
Moravče SLO . . . . 123 A3
Moravec CZ . . . . . . 97 B4
Moraviţa RO . . . . . 126 B3
Morávka CZ . . . . . . 98 B2
Moravská Třebová
  CZ . . . . . . . . . . . 97 B4
Moravské Budějovice
  CZ . . . . . . . . . . . 97 B3
Moravské Lieskové
  SK . . . . . . . . . . . 98 C1
Moravske Toplice
  SLO . . . . . . . . . .111 C3
Moravský-Beroun
  CZ . . . . . . . . . . . 98 B1
Moravský Krumlov
  CZ . . . . . . . . . . . 97 B4
Moravský Svätý Ján
  SK . . . . . . . . . . . 98 C1
Morawica PL . . . . . 87 B4
Morawin PL . . . . . . 86 A2
Morbach D . . . . . . 92 B3
Morbegno I . . . . . . 120 A2
Morbier F . . . . . . . 105 C5
Mörbisch am See
  A. . . . . . . . . . . . .111 B3
Mörbylånga S . . . . 63 B4
Morcenx F . . . . . . 128 B2
Morciano di Romagna
  I. . . . . . . . . . . . 136 B1
Morcone I . . . . . . . 170 B2
Morcuera E . . . . . . 151 A4
Mordelles F . . . . . 101 A4
Mordoğan TR. . . . . 188 A1
Moréac F . . . . . . . 100 B3
Morebattle GB . . . . 35 C5
Morecambe GB . . . 36 B4
Moreda
  Granada E . . . . . 163 A4
  Oviedo E . . . . . 142 A1
Morée F . . . . . . . . 103 B3
Moreles de Rey E . 141 B5
Morella E . . . . . . . 153 B3
Moreruela de los
  Infanzones E. . . . 149 A4
Morés E . . . . . . . . 152 A2
Móres I . . . . . . . . 178 B2
Morestel F . . . . . . .118 B2
Moretonhampstead
  GB . . . . . . . . . . . 43 B3
Moreton-in-Marsh
  GB . . . . . . . . . . . 44 B2
Moret-sur-Loing F . 90 C2
Moretta I. . . . . . . . 119 C4

Moreuil F . . . . . . . . 90 B2
Morez F . . . . . . . 105 C5
Mörfelden D. . . . . . 93 B4
Morgat F . . . . . . . 100 A1
Morges CH. . . . . . 105 C5
Morgex I. . . . . . . .119 B4
Morgongåva S. . . . . 51 C3
Morhange F . . . . . . 92 C2
Morhet B . . . . . . . 92 B1
Mori I . . . . . . . . . 121 B3
Morialmé B . . . . . . 79 B4
Morianes P. . . . . . 160 B2
Moriani Plage F . . . 180 A2
Mórichida H. . . . . .111 B4
Moriles E . . . . . . . 163 A3
Morille E. . . . . . . . 150 B2
Moringen D . . . . . . 82 A1
Morjärv S. . . . . . . 196 C5
Morkarla S . . . . . . 51 B4
Mørke DK. . . . . . . 59 B3
Mørkøv DK. . . . . . . 61 D1
Morkovice-Slížany
    CZ . . . . . . . . . . 98 B1
Morlaàs F. . . . . . . 145 A3
Morlaix F . . . . . . . 100 A2
Morley F. . . . . . . . 91 C5
Mörlunda S . . . . . . 62 A3
Mormanno I . . . . . 174 B1
Mormant F . . . . . . 90 C2
Mornant F . . . . . . .117 B4
Mornay-Berry F . . . 103 B4
Morón de Almazán
    E. . . . . . . . . . . 152 A1
Morón de la Frontera
    E. . . . . . . . . . . 162 A2
Morović SRB . . . . . 125 B5
Morozzo I. . . . . . . 133 A3
Morpeth GB . . . . . . 37 A5
Morphou CY . . . . . 181 A1
Mörrum S. . . . . . . 63 B2
Morsbach D . . . . . . 81 B3
Mörsch D . . . . . . . 93 C4
Mörsil S. . . . . . . 199 B10
Morsum D . . . . . . . 64 B1
Mørsvikbotn N. . . . 194 C6
Mortagne-au-Perche
    F. . . . . . . . . . . . 89 B4
Mortagne-sur-Gironde
    F. . . . . . . . . . . 114 C3
Mortagne-sur-Sèvre
    F. . . . . . . . . . . .114 B3
Mortágua P . . . . . 148 B1
Mortain F . . . . . . . 88 B3
Mortara I . . . . . . . 120 B1
Morteau F . . . . . . 105 B5
Mortegliano I. . . . . 122 B2
Mortelle I . . . . . . . 177 A4
Mortemart F. . . . . .115 B4
Mortimer's Cross
    GB . . . . . . . . . . 39 B4
Mortrée F . . . . . . . 89 B4
Mörtschach A . . . . 109 C3
Mortsel B . . . . . . . 79 A4
Morud DK. . . . . . . 59 C3
Morwenstow GB . . . 42 B2
Moryń PL . . . . . . . 74 B3
Morzeszczyn PL . . . 69 B3
Morzewo PL. . . . . . 69 B4
Morzine F. . . . . . . .118 A3
Mosbach D . . . . . . 93 B5
Mosbjerg DK . . . . . 58 A3
Mosby N. . . . . . . . 53 B3
Mosca P. . . . . . . . 149 A3
Moscavide P . . . . . 154 C1
Moščenica I IR . . . . 124 B2
Moščenice HR . . . . 123 B3
Moščenicka Draga
    HR . . . . . . . . . . 123 B3
Mosciano Sant'Ángelo
    I . . . . . . . . . . . 136 C2
Mościsko PL. . . . . . 85 B4
Moscow = Moskva
    RUS . . . . . . . . 9 E10
Mosina PL . . . . . . . 75 B5
Mosjøen N . . . . . . 195 E4
Moskog N . . . . . . . 46 A3
Moskorzew PL. . . . . 87 B3
Moskosel S . . . . . . 196 D2
Moskuvarra FIN. . . . 197 B9
Moskva = Moscow
    RUS . . . . . . . . 9 E10
Moslavina Podravska
    HR . . . . . . . . . . 125 B3
Moşniţa Nouă RO . . 126 B3
Moso in Passíria I . . 108 C2
Mosonmagyaróvár
    H . . . . . . . . . . .111 B4
Mošorin SRB . . . . . 126 B2
Mošovce SK . . . . . . 98 C2
Mosqueruela E . . . . 153 B3
Moss N. . . . . . . . . 54 A1
Mossfellsbær IS . . . 190 C4
Mössingen D. . . . . . 93 C5
Møsstrand N . . . . . 47 C5
Most CZ . . . . . . . . 83 B5
Mosta M. . . . . . . . 175 C3
Mostar BIH. . . . . . . 139 B3
Mosterhamn N. . . . . 52 A1
Mostki PL. . . . . . . . 75 B4
Most na Soči SLO . . 122 A2
Móstoles E. . . . . . . 151 B4
Mostová SK. . . . . . .111 A4
Mostowo PL. . . . . . 68 A1
Mostuéjouls F . . . . 130 A2
Mosty PL . . . . . . . . 75 A3
Mostys'ka UA . . . . . 13 D5
Mosvik N . . . . . . . 199 B7
Mota del Cuervo E . 158 B1

Mota del Marqués
    E. . . . . . . . . . . 150 A2
Motala S. . . . . . . . 55 B6
Motherwell GB. . . . . 35 C4
Möthlow D . . . . . . . 74 B1
Motilla del Palancar
    E. . . . . . . . . . . 158 B2
Motnik SLO . . . . . . 123 A3
Motovun HR . . . . . 122 B2
Motril E. . . . . . . . . 163 B4
Motta I . . . . . . . . . 121 B4
Motta di Livenza I . . 122 B1
Motta Montecorvino
    I . . . . . . . . . . . 170 B3
Motta Visconti I. . . . 120 B1
Mottisfont GB . . . . . 44 B2
Móttola I. . . . . . . . 173 B3
Mou DK. . . . . . . . . 58 B3
Mouchard F . . . . . 105 C4
Moudon CH. . . . . . 106 C1
Moudros GR . . . . . 183 D7
Mougins F . . . . . . . 132 B2
Mouliherne F . . . . . 102 B2
Moulinet F . . . . . . 133 B3
Moulins F . . . . . . . 104 C2
Moulins-Engilbert
    F. . . . . . . . . . . 104 C2
Moulins-la-Marche
    F. . . . . . . . . . . . 89 B4
Moulismes F . . . . . .115 B4
Moult F . . . . . . . . . 89 A3
Mountain Ash GB . . . 39 C3
Mount Bellew Bridge
    IRL . . . . . . . . . . 28 A3
Mountfield GB. . . . . 27 B3
Mountmellick IRL . . . 30 A1
Mountrath IRL. . . . . 30 A1
Mountsorrel GB. . . . 40 C2
Moura P . . . . . . . . 160 A2
Mourão P. . . . . . . . 155 C3
Mourenx F. . . . . . . 145 A3
Mouriés F. . . . . . . 131 B3
Mourmelon-le-Grand
    F. . . . . . . . . . . . 91 B4
Mouronho P. . . . . . 148 B1
Mourujärvi FIN . . 197 C11
Mouscron B. . . . . . 78 B3
Mousehole GB. . . . . 42 B1
Moussac F . . . . . . 131 B3
Moussey F. . . . . . . 92 C2
Mousteru F . . . . . . 100 A2
Moustey F . . . . . . . 128 B2
Moustiers-Ste Marie
    F. . . . . . . . . . . 132 B2
Mouthe F . . . . . . . 105 C5
Mouthier-Haute-Pierre
    F. . . . . . . . . . . 105 B5
Mouthoumet F . . . . 146 B3
Moutier CH . . . . . . 106 B2
Moûtiers F . . . . . . .118 B3
Moutiers-les-Mauxfaits
    F. . . . . . . . . . . .114 B2
Mouy F . . . . . . . . . 90 B2
Mouzaki GR . . . . . 182 D3
Mouzon F. . . . . . . . 91 B5
Møvik N . . . . . . . . 46 B2
Moville IRL. . . . . . . 27 A3
Moy
    Highland GB . . . . 32 D2
    Tyrone GB . . . . . 27 B4
Moycullen IRL . . . . . 28 A2
Moyenmoutier F . . . 92 C2
Moyenvic F . . . . . . 92 C2
Mózar E . . . . . . . . 141 C5
Mozhaysk RUS . . . . 9 E10
Mozirje SLO. . . . . . 123 A3
Mözs H. . . . . . . . . 112 C2
Mozzanica I . . . . . 120 B2
Mramorak SRB. . . . 127 C2
Mrčajevci SRB. . . . 127 D2
Mrkonjić Grad BIH. . 138 A3
Mrkopalj HR. . . . . . 123 B3
Mrocza PL. . . . . . . 76 A2
Mroczeń PL. . . . . . 86 A1
Mroczno PL. . . . . . 69 B4
Mrzezyno PL . . . . . 67 B4
Mšec CZ. . . . . . . . 84 B1
Mšeno CZ. . . . . . . 84 B2
Mstów PL . . . . . . . 86 B3
Mstislaw BY. . . . . . 13 A9
Mszana Dolna PL . . 99 B4
Mszczonów PL. . . . 77 C5
Muć HR . . . . . . . . 138 B2
Múccia I . . . . . . . . 136 B2
Much D . . . . . . . . . 80 B3
Mücheln D . . . . . . . 83 A3
Much Marcle GB . . . 39 C4
Muchów PL. . . . . . . 85 A4
Much Wenlock GB . . 39 B4
Mucientes E . . . . . 142 C2
Muckross IRL . . . . . 29 B2
Mucur TR. . . . . . . . 23 B8
Muda P. . . . . . . . . 160 B1
Mudanya TR . . . . . 186 B3
Mudau D . . . . . . . . 93 B5
Müden D . . . . . . . . 72 B3
Mudersbach D. . . . . 81 B3
Mudurnu TR. . . . . . 187 B6
Muel E. . . . . . . . . . 152 A2
Muelas del Pan E . . 149 A4
Muess D. . . . . . . . . 73 A4
Muff IRL . . . . . . . . 27 A3
Mugardos E. . . . . . 140 A2
Muge P. . . . . . . . . 154 B2
Mügeln
    Sachsen D . . . . . .83 A5

Mügeln continued
    Sachsen-Anhalt D . . 83 A5
Múggia I. . . . . . . . 122 B2
Múgnano I . . . . . . 135 B5
Mugron F. . . . . . . 128 C2
Mugueimes E . . . . 140 C3
Muhi H . . . . . . . . .113 B4
Mühlacker D . . . . . 93 C4
Mühlbach am
    Hochkönig A . . . 109 B4
Mühlberg
    Brandenburg D . . . 83 A5
    Thüringen D. . . . . .82 B2
Mühldorf
    A. . . . . . . . . . . .109 C4
    D. . . . . . . . . . . . .95 C4
Muhleberg CH . . . . 106 C2
Mühleim D . . . . . . 107 A3
Muhlen-Eichsen D . . 65 C4
Mühlhausen
    Bayern D . . . . . . .94 B2
    Thüringen D . . . . .82 A2
Mühltroff D . . . . . . 83 B3
Muhos FIN . . . . . . 3 D10
Muhr A . . . . . . . . 109 B4
Muine Bheag IRL . . . 30 B2
Muirkirk GB . . . . . . 36 A2
Muir of Ord GB . . . . 32 D2
Muirteira P. . . . . . 154 B1
Mukacheve UA . . . . 12 D5
Muker GB. . . . . . . . 37 B4
Mula E . . . . . . . . . 165 A3
Muğla TR . . . . . . . 188 B3
Mulben GB. . . . . . . 32 D3
Mulegns CH. . . . . . 107 C4
Mules I . . . . . . . . . 108 C2
Mülheim D. . . . . . . 80 A2
Mulhouse F . . . . . . 106 B2
Muljava SLO . . . . . 123 B3
Mullanys Cross IRL . 26 B2
Müllheim D . . . . . . 106 B2
Mullhyttan S . . . . . 55 A5
Mullinavat IRL . . . . 30 B1
Mullingar IRL. . . . . . 30 A1
Mullion GB. . . . . . . 42 B1
Müllrose D . . . . . . . 74 B3
Mullsjö S . . . . . . . . 60 B3
Mulseryd S . . . . . . 60 B3
Munaðarnes IS . . . 190 A4
Munana E . . . . . . . 150 B2
Muñás E. . . . . . . . 141 A4
Münchberg D. . . . . . 83 B3
Müncheberg D. . . . . 74 B3
München = Munich
    D . . . . . . . . . . . 108 A2
Munchen-Gladbach =
    Mönchengladbach
    D . . . . . . . . . . . . 80 A2
Münchhausen D . . . 81 B4
Mundaka E. . . . . . 143 A4
Münden D . . . . . . . 82 A1
Munderfing A . . . . 109 A4
Munderkingen D . . . 107 A4
Mundesley GB. . . . . 41 C5
Munera E . . . . . . . 158 B1
Mungia E . . . . . . . 143 A4
Munich = München
    D . . . . . . . . . . . 108 A2
Muñico E . . . . . . . 150 B2
Muniesa E . . . . . . 153 A3
Munka-Ljungby S . . 61 C2
Munkebo DK . . . . . 59 C3
Munkedal S . . . . . . 54 B2
Munkflohögen S . .199 B11
Munkfors S . . . . . . 49 C5
Munktorp S . . . . . . 56 A2
Münnerstadt D . . . . 82 B2
Muñopepe E . . . . . 150 B3
Muñotello E. . . . . . 150 B2
Münsingen
    CH. . . . . . . . . . .106 C2
    D. . . . . . . . . . . . .94 C1
Munsö S. . . . . . . . 57 A3
Münster
    CH. . . . . . . . . . .106 C3
    Hessen D. . . . . . . .93 B4
Munster D . . . . . . . 72 B3
Münster D . . . . . . . 71 C4
Munster F . . . . . . 106 A2
Muntibar E. . . . . . 143 A4
Münzkirchen A. . . . . 96 C1
Muodoslompolo S 196 B6
Muonio FIN . . . . . 196 B6
Muotathal CH . . . . 107 C3
Muradiye TR . . . . . 186 D2
Murakeresztúr H . . 124 A2
Murán SK . . . . . . . 99 C4
Murano I. . . . . . . . 122 B1
Muras E . . . . . . . . 140 A3
Murat F . . . . . . . . .116 B2
Muratlı TR . . . . . . 186 A2
Murato F . . . . . . . 180 A2
Murat-sur-Vèbre F. 130 B1
Murau A . . . . . . . . 109 B5
Muravera I . . . . . . 179 C3
Murazzano I. . . . . . 133 A4
Murça P . . . . . . . . 148 A2
Murchante E . . . . . 144 B2
Murchin D . . . . . . . 66 C2
Murcia E. . . . . . . . 165 B3
Murczyn PL. . . . . . . 76 B2
Mur-de-Barrez F . . .116 B2
Mur-de-Bretagne F . 100 A2
Mur-de-Sologne F . 103 B3
Mureck A . . . . . . . 110 C2
Mürefte TR. . . . . . 186 B2
Muret F. . . . . . . . 146 A2
Murg CH. . . . . . . . 107 B4

Murguia E . . . . . . 143 B4
Muri CH. . . . . . . . 106 B3
Murias de Paredes
    E. . . . . . . . . . . 141 B4
Muriedas E . . . . . . 143 A3
Muriel Viejo E . . . . 143 C4
Murillo de Rio Leza
    E. . . . . . . . . . . 143 B4
Murillo el Fruto E . . 144 B2
Murjek S. . . . . . . . 196 C3
Murlaggan GB . . . . 34 B2
Murmansk RUS . . . 3 B13
Murmashi RUS . . . 3 B13
Murnau D . . . . . . 108 B2
Muro
    E . . . . . . . . . . .167 B3
    F . . . . . . . . . . . .180 A1
Muro de Alcoy E . . 159 C3
Murol F. . . . . . . . .116 B2
Muro Lucano I. . . . 172 B1
Muron F. . . . . . . . .114 B3
Muros E . . . . . . . . 140 B1
Muros de Nalón E . 141 A4
Murowana Goślina
    PL. . . . . . . . . . . 76 B2
Mürren CH. . . . . . 106 C2
Murrhardt D. . . . . . 94 C1
Murska Sobota
    SLO . . . . . . . . .111 C3
Mursko Središče
    HR . . . . . . . . . .111 C3
Murtas E . . . . . . . 164 C1
Murten CH. . . . . . 106 C2
Murter HR . . . . . . 137 B4
Murtiçi TR . . . . . . 189 C6
Murtosa P . . . . . . 148 B1
Murtovaara FIN . . 197 D12
Murvica HR . . . . . 137 A4
Murviel-lès-Béziers
    F. . . . . . . . . . . 130 B2
Mürzsteg A. . . . . . .110 B2
Mürzzuschlag A. . . .110 B2
Musculdy F . . . . . 144 A3
Muskö S. . . . . . . . 57 A4
Mušov CZ . . . . . . . 97 C4
Musselburgh GB. . . 35 C4
Musselkanaal NL. . . 71 B4
Mussidan F . . . . . 129 A3
Mussomeli I . . . . . 176 B2
Musson B. . . . . . . 92 B1
Mussy-sur-Seine F 104 B3
Mustafakemalpaşa
    TR . . . . . . . . . 186 B3
Muszaki PL . . . . . . 77 A5
Muszyna PL . . . . . . 99 B4
Mut TR . . . . . . . . . 23 C7
Muta SLO. . . . . . . 110 C2
Muthill GB . . . . . . . 35 B4
Mutné SK. . . . . . . . 99 B3
Mutriku E . . . . . . . 143 A4
Muttalip TR . . . . . 187 C5
Mutterbergalm A. . . 108 B2
Muurola FIN. . . . . 197 C8
Muxía E . . . . . . . . 140 A1
Muxilka-Ugarte E . 143 A4
Muzillac F. . . . . . . 101 B3
Mužla SK . . . . . . . .112 B2
Muzzano del Turgnano
    I . . . . . . . . . . . 122 B2
Mybster GB . . . . . . 32 C3
Myckelgensjö S . . . 200 C3
Myennes F . . . . . . 104 B1
Myjava SK. . . . . . . 98 C1
Myking N . . . . . . . 46 B2
Mykland N . . . . . . 53 B4
Myra N . . . . . . . . . 53 B5
Myrdal N . . . . . . . 46 B4
Myre
    Nordland N. . . . .194 A6
    Nordland N. . . . .194 B6
Myresjö S. . . . . . . 62 A2
Mýri IS . . . . . . . . 191 B8
Myrtou CY . . . . . . 181 A2
Mysen N. . . . . . . . 54 A2
Mysłakowice PL . . . 85 B3
Myślenice PL. . . . . 99 B3
Myślibórz PL. . . . . 75 B3
Mysłowice PL. . . . . 86 B3
Myszków PL. . . . . . 86 B3
Mytishchi RUS . . . . 9 E10
Mýtna SK . . . . . . . 99 C3
Mýtne Ludany SK . .112 A2
Mýto CZ. . . . . . . . 96 B1

**N**

Nå N. . . . . . . . . . . 46 B3
Naaldwijk NL. . . . . . 79 A4
Naantali FIN. . . . . . 8 B2
Naas IRL. . . . . . . . 30 A2
Nabais P. . . . . . . . 148 B2
Nabbelund S . . . . . 62 A5
Nabburg D. . . . . . . 95 B4
Načeradec CZ . . . . 96 B2
Náchod CZ. . . . . . . 85 B4
Nacław PL . . . . . . . 68 A1
Nadarzyce PL . . . . . 75 A5
Nadarzyn PL . . . . . 77 B5
Nádasd H. . . . . . . .111 C3
Nadrljan PL . . . . . . 133 A3
Nädlac RO . . . . . . 126 A2
Nádudvar H . . . . . .113 B5
Nadvirna UA . . . . . 13 D6
Näfels CH. . . . . . . 107 B4
Nafpaktos GR . . . . 184 A2
Nafplio GR. . . . . . 184 B3
Nagel D . . . . . . . . 95 B3

Nagele NL . . . . . . . 70 B2
Naggen S. . . . . . . 200 D2
Nagłowice PL. . . . . 87 B4
Nagold D . . . . . . . 93 C4
Nagore E . . . . . . . 144 B2
Nagyatád H . . . . . 124 A3
Nagybajom H. . . . . 124 A3
Nagybaracska H . . 125 A4
Nagybátony H. . . . .113 B3
Nagyberény H . . . . 112 C2
Nagybörzsöny H. . .112 B2
Nagycenk H . . . . . .111 B3
Nagycserkesz H . . .113 B5
Nagydorog H . . . . 112 C2
Nagyfüged H . . . . .113 B4
Nagyhersány H . . . 125 B4
Nagyigmánd H . . . .112 B2
Nagyiván H. . . . . . .113 B4
Nagykanizsa H . . . .111 C3
Nagykáta H . . . . . .113 B3
Nagykonyi H . . . . . 112 C2
Nagykörös H . . . . .113 B3
Nagykörü H . . . . . .113 B4
Nagylóc H . . . . . . .112 A3
Nagymágocs H . . . 113 C4
Nagymányok H . . . 125 A4
Nagymaros H . . . . .112 B2
Nagyoroszi H . . . . .112 A3
Nagyrábé H . . . . . .113 B5
Nagyréde H . . . . . .113 B3
Nagyszékely H . . . 112 C2
Nagyszénás H . . . . 113 C4
Nagyszokoly H . . . 112 C2
Nagytöke H . . . . . .113 C4
Nagyvázsony H. . . .111 C4
Nagyvenyim H . . . . 112 C2
Naharros E . . . . . . 152 B1
Nahe D . . . . . . . . . 64 C3
Naila D. . . . . . . . . 83 B3
Nailloux F . . . . . . 146 A2
Nailsworth GB. . . . . 43 A4
Naintré F. . . . . . . .115 B4
Nairn GB . . . . . . . 32 D3
Najac F. . . . . . . . . 129 B4
Nájera E . . . . . . . 143 B4
Nak H . . . . . . . . . 112 C2
Nakksjø N . . . . . . . 53 A5
Nakło nad Notecią
    PL. . . . . . . . . . . 76 A2
Nakskov DK. . . . . . 65 B4
Nalda E . . . . . . . . 143 B4
Nälden S . . . . . . .199 B11
Nalliers F . . . . . . .114 B2
Nallıhan TR . . . . . 187 B6
Nalzen F. . . . . . . . 146 B2
Nalžouské Hory CZ. 96 B1
Namdalseid N . . . 199 A8
Náměšť nad Oslavou
    CZ . . . . . . . . . . 97 B4
Námestovo SK . . . . 99 B3
Namna N. . . . . . . . 49 B4
Namsos N . . . . . . 199 A8
Namsskogan N . . 199 A10
Namur B. . . . . . . . 79 B4
Namysłów PL. . . . . 86 A1
Nanclares de la Oca
    E. . . . . . . . . . . 143 B4
Nancy F. . . . . . . . 92 C2
Nangis F . . . . . . . 90 C3
Nannestad N . . . . . 48 B3
Nant F . . . . . . . . 130 A2
Nanterre F . . . . . . 90 C2
Nantes F . . . . . . . 101 B4
Nanteuil-le-Haudouin
    F. . . . . . . . . . . . 90 B2
Nantiat F . . . . . . . .115 B5
Nantua F . . . . . . . .118 A2
Nantwich GB . . . . . 38 A4
Naoussa
    Cyclades GR . . . 185 B6
    Imathia GR . . . . .182 C4
Napajedla CZ. . . . . 98 B1
Napiwoda PL . . . . . 77 A5
Naples = Nápoli I. . 170 C2
Nápoli = Naples I . . 170 C2
Nar S . . . . . . . . . 57 C4
Nara N. . . . . . . . . 46 A1
Naraval E . . . . . . . 141 A4
Narberth GB . . . . . 39 C2
Nærbø N . . . . . . . 52 B1
Narbonne F . . . . . 130 B1
Narbonne-Plage F . 130 B2
Narbuvollen N . . . 199 C8
Narcao I. . . . . . . . 179 C2
Nardò I . . . . . . . . 173 B4
Narkaus FIN. . . . . 197 C9
Narken S . . . . . . . 196 C5
Narmo N. . . . . . . . 48 B3
Narni I . . . . . . . . 168 A2
Naro I . . . . . . . . . 176 B2
Naro Fominsk RUS . 9 E10
Narón E . . . . . . . . 140 A2
Narros del Castillo
    E. . . . . . . . . . . 150 B2
Narta HR . . . . . . . 124 B2
Naruszewo PL. . . . . 77 B5
Narva EST . . . . . . . 8 C6
Narvik N. . . . . . . 194 B8
Narzole I. . . . . . . . 133 A3
Näs FIN . . . . . . . . 51 B7
Näs S. . . . . . . . . . 50 B1
Näs S . . . . . . . . . . 57 C4
Näsåker S . . . . . . 200 C3
Năsăud RO . . . . . . 17 B6
Nasavrky CZ . . . . . 97 B3
Nasbinals F . . . . . .116 C3

Næsbjerg DK . . . . . 59 C1
Näshull S. . . . . . . . 62 A3
Našice HR . . . . . . 125 B4
Nasielsk PL . . . . . . 77 B5
Naso I. . . . . . . . . 177 A3
Nassau D. . . . . . . . 81 B3
Nassenfels D. . . . . . 95 C3
Nassereith A . . . . . 108 B1
Nässjö S . . . . . . . . 62 A2
Nastätten D . . . . . . 81 B3
Næstved DK . . . . . . 65 A4
Näsum S . . . . . . . . 63 B2
Näsviken S . . . . . 199 B12
Natalinci SRB . . . . 127 C2
Naters CH . . . . . . .119 A5
Nater-Stetten D . . . 108 A2
Nattavaara S . . . . 196 C3
Natters A . . . . . . . 108 B2
Nattheim D. . . . . . . 94 C2
Nättraby S . . . . . . . 63 B3
Naturno I . . . . . . . 108 C1
Naucelle F . . . . . . 130 A1
Nauders A . . . . . . 108 C1
Nauen D . . . . . . . . 74 B1
Naul IRL . . . . . . . . 30 A2
Naumburg D . . . . . 83 A3
Naundorf D . . . . . . 83 B5
Naunhof D . . . . . . . 83 A4
Naustdal N. . . . . . . 46 A2
Nautijaur S. . . . . . 196 C2
Nautsi RUS . . . . . 193 D13
Nava E . . . . . . . . 142 A1
Navacerrada E . . . . 151 B3
Navaconcejo E . . . 149 B4
Nava de Arévalo E . 150 B3
Nava de la Asunción
    E. . . . . . . . . . . 150 A3
Nava del Rey E . . . 150 A2
Navafría E . . . . . . 151 A4
Navahermosa E . . . 157 A3
Navahrudak BY . . . 13 B6
Naval E . . . . . . . . 145 B4
Navalacruz E . . . . 150 B3
Navalcán E . . . . . . 150 B2
Navalcarnero E . . . 151 B3
Navaleno E . . . . . . 143 C3
Navalmanzano E . . 151 A3
Navalmoral E . . . . 150 B3
Navalmoral de la Mata
    E. . . . . . . . . . . 150 C2
Naválón E . . . . . . 159 C3
Navalonguilla E . . . 150 B2
Navalperal de Pinares
    E. . . . . . . . . . . 150 B3
Navalpino E . . . . . 157 A3
Navaltalgordo E . . . 150 B3
Navaltoril E . . . . . . 156 A3
Navaluenga E . . . . 150 B3
Navalvillar de Pela
    E. . . . . . . . . . . 156 A2
Navan IRL . . . . . . . 30 A2
Navaperal de Tormes
    E. . . . . . . . . . . 150 B2
Navapolatsk BY. . . . 13 A8
Navarclés E. . . . . . 147 C2
Navarredonda de
    Gredos E. . . . . . 150 B2
Navarrenx F . . . . . 144 A3
Navarrés E . . . . . . 159 B3
Navarrete E . . . . . 143 B4
Navarrevisca E . . . 150 B3
Navás E. . . . . . . . 147 C2
Navascués E . . . . 144 B2
Navas del Madroño
    E. . . . . . . . . . . 155 B4
Navas del Rey E . . 151 B3
Navas del Sepillar
    E. . . . . . . . . . . 163 A3
Navas de Oro E . . . 150 A3
Navas de San Juan
    E. . . . . . . . . . . 157 B4
Navasfrias E . . . . . 149 B3
Nave I . . . . . . . . . 120 B3
Nave de Haver P . . 149 B3
Nävekvarn S . . . . . 56 B2
Navelli I . . . . . . . . 169 A3
Navenby GB . . . . . 40 B3
Nærbø N . . . . . . . 52 B1
Näverkärret S . . . . 56 A1
Naverstad S . . . . . 54 B2
Navés E. . . . . . . . 147 C2
Navezuelas E. . . . . 156 A2
Navia E. . . . . . . . 141 A4
Navia de Suarna E . 141 B4
Navilly F. . . . . . . . 105 C4
Năvodari RO . . . . . 17 C8
Naxos GR . . . . . . 185 B6
Nay F. . . . . . . . . . 145 A3
Nazaré P. . . . . . . . 154 B1
Nazarje SLO. . . . . 123 A3
Nazilli TR . . . . . . 188 B3
Nazza D . . . . . . . . 82 A2
Nea Anchialos GR. 182 D4
Nea Epidavros GR . 184 B4
Nea Flippias GR . . 182 D2
Nea Kalikratia GR . 183 C5
Nea Makri GR . . . . 185 A4
Nea Moudania GR . 183 C5
Neap GB . . . . . . . . 33 A5
Nea Peramos GR. . 183 C6
Neapoli
    Kozani GR. . . . . .182 C3
    Kriti GR . . . . . . .185 D6
    Lakonia GR . . . . .184 C4
Nea Stira GR . . . . 185 A5

Neath GB 39 C3
Nea Visa GR 186 A1
Nea Zichni GR 183 B5
Nebljusi HR 124 C1
Neblo SLO 122 A2
Nebolchy RUS 9 C8
Nebra D 82 A3
Nebreda E 143 C3
Nechanice CZ 84 B3
Neckargemünd D 93 B4
Neckarsulm D 94 B1
Neda E 140 A2
Neded SK 112 A1
Nedelišće HR 124 A2
Nederweert NL 80 A1
Nedreberg N 48 B3
Nedre Gärdsjö S 50 B2
Nedre Soppero S 196 A4
Nedstrand N 52 A1
Nedvědice CZ 97 B4
Nędza PL 86 B2
Neede NL 71 B3
Needham Market
GB 45 A5
Needingworth GB 44 A3
Neermoor D 71 A4
Neeroeteren B 80 A1
Neerpelt B 79 A5
Neesen D 72 B1
Neetze D 73 A3
Nefyn GB 38 B2
Negotin SRB 16 C5
Negotino MK 182 B4
Negrar I 121 B3
Negredo E 151 A5
Negreira E 140 B2
Nègrepelisse F 129 B4
Negru Vodă RO 17 D8
Negueira de Muñiz
E 141 A4
Neheim D 81 A3
Neila E 143 B4
Néive I 119 C5
Nejdek CZ 83 B4
Nekla PL 76 B2
Neksø DK 67 A4
Nelas P 148 B2
Nelaug N 53 B4
Nelidovo RUS 9 D8
Nelim FIN 193 D12
Nellingen D 94 C1
Nelson GB 40 B1
Neman RUS 12 A5
Nemea GR 184 B3
Nemesgörzsöny H 111 B4
Nemeskér H 111 B3
Nemesnádudvar H 125 A5
Nemesszalók H 111 B4
Németkér H 112 C2
Nemours F 103 A4
Nemška Loka SLO 123 B4
Nemšová SK 98 C2
Nenagh IRL 28 B3
Nenince SK 112 A3
Nenita GR 185 A7
Nenzing A 107 B4
Neochori GR 182 D3
Neo Chori GR 184 A2
Neon Petritsi GR 183 B5
Nepi I 168 A2
Nepomuk CZ 96 B1
Nérac F 129 B3
Neratovice CZ 84 B2
Nerchau D 83 A4
Néré F 115 C3
Neresheim D 94 C2
Nereto I 136 C2
Nerezine HR 123 C3
Nerežišća HR 138 B2
Neringa LT 12 A4
Néris-les Bains F 116 A2
Nerito I 169 A3
Nerja E 163 B4
Néronde F 117 B4
Nérondes F 103 C4
Nerpio E 164 A2
Nersingen D 94 C2
Nerva E 161 B3
Nervesa della Battáglia
I 121 B5
Nervi I 134 A2
Nes
*Buskerud* N 48 B1
*Hedmark* N 48 B2
NL 70 A2
*Sogn og Fjordane*
N 46 A3
*Sør-Trøndelag* N 198 B6
Nesbyen N 47 B6
Neset N 199 D7
Nesflaten N 52 A2
Nesjahverfi IS 191 C10
Neskaupstaður IS 191 B12
Nesland N 53 A3
Neslandsvatn N 53 B5
Nesle F 90 B2
Nesna N 195 D4
Nesoddtangen N 48 C2
Nesovice CZ 98 B1
Nesselwang D 108 B1
Nesslau CH 107 B4
Nessmersiel D 71 A4
Nesso I 120 B2
Nesterov UA 13 C5
Nestorio GR 182 C3
Nesttun N 46 B2
Nesvady SK 112 B2
Nesvatnstemmen N 53 B4
Nether Stowey GB 43 A3
Netland N 52 B2
Netolice CZ 96 B2
Netphen D 81 B4
Netstal CH 107 B4
Nettancourt F 91 C4
Nettetal D 80 A2
Nettlingen D 72 B3
Nettuno I 168 B2
Neualbenreuth D 95 B4
Neubeckum D 81 A4
Neubrandenburg D 74 A2
Neubruchhausen D 72 B1
Neubukow D 65 B4
Neuburg D 94 C3
Neuchâtel CH 106 C1
Neu Darchau D 73 A3
Neudau A 111 B3
Neudietendorf D 82 B2
Neudorf D 93 B4
Neuenbürg D 93 C4
Neuenburg D 71 A4
Neuendorf D 66 B2
Neuenhagen D 74 B2
Neuenhaus D 71 B3
Neuenkirchen
*Niedersachsen* D 71 B5
*Niedersachsen* D 72 A2
*Nordrhein-Westfalen*
D 71 B4
*Nordrhein-Westfalen*
D 81 B3
Neuenrade D 81 A3
Neuenwalde D 64 C1
Neuerburg D 92 A2
Neufahrn
*Bayern* D 95 C3
*Bayern* D 95 C4
Neuf-Brisach F 106 A2
Neufchâteau
B 92 B1
F 92 C1
Neufchâtel-en-Bray
F 90 B1
Neufchâtel-sur-Aisne
F 91 B4
Neuflize F 91 B4
Neugersdorf D 84 B2
Neuhardenberg D 74 B3
Neuharlingersiel D 71 A4
Neuhaus
*Bayern* D 95 B3
*Bayern* D 96 C1
*Niedersachsen* D 64 C2
*Niedersachsen* D 73 A3
*Niedersachsen* D 81 A5
Neuhaus a Rennweg
D 82 B3
Neuhausen
CH 107 B3
D 83 B5
Neuhausen ob Eck
D 107 B3
Neuhof
*Bayern* D 94 B2
*Hessen* D 82 B1
Neuhofen an der Krems
A 110 A1
Neuillé-Pont-Pierre
F 102 B2
Neuilly-en-Thelle F 90 B2
Neuilly-le-Réal F 104 C2
Neuilly-l'Évêque F 105 B4
Neuilly-St Front F 90 B3
Neu-Isenburg D 93 A4
Neukalen D 66 C1
Neu Kaliss D 73 A4
Neukirch D 84 A2
Neukirchen
A 109 A4
*Hessen* D 81 B5
*Schleswig-Holstein*
D 64 B1
Neukirchen am Grossvenediger
A 109 B3
Neukirchen bei Heiligen
Blut D 95 B4
Neukloster D 65 C4
Neulengbach A 110 A2
Neulise F 117 B4
Neu Lübbenau D 74 B2
Neum BIH 139 C3
Neumagen D 92 B2
Neumarkt D 95 B3
Neumarkt am Wallersee
A 109 B4
Neumarkt im
Hausruckkreis A 109 A4
Neumarkt im Mühlkreis
A 96 C2
Neumarkt im Steiermark
A 110 B1
Neumarkt Sankt Veit
D 95 C4
Neumünster D 64 B2
Neunburg vorm Wald
D 95 B4
Neung-sur-Beuvron
F 103 B3
Neunkirch
*Luzern* CH 106 B3
*Schaffhausen* CH 107 B3
Neunkirchen
A 111 B3
Neunkirchen *continued*
*Nordrhein-Westfalen*
D 80 B3
*Saarland* D 92 B3
Neunkirchen am Brand
D 94 B3
Neuötting D 95 C4
Neupetershain D 84 A2
Neuravensburg D 107 B4
Neureut D 93 B4
Neuruppin D 74 B1
Neusäss D 94 C2
Neusiedl A 111 B3
Neuss D 80 A2
Neussargues-Moissac
F 116 B2
Neustadt
*Bayern* D 94 B2
*Bayern* D 95 B4
*Bayern* D 95 C3
*Brandenburg* D 73 B5
*Hessen* D 81 B5
*Niedersachsen* D 72 B2
*Rheinland-Pfalz* D 93 B4
*Sachsen* D 84 A2
*Schleswig-Holstein*
D 65 B3
*Thüringen* D 82 B3
*Thüringen* D 83 B3
Neustadt-Glewe D 73 A4
Neustift im Stubaital
A 108 B2
Neustrelitz D 74 A2
Neutal A 111 B3
Neutrebbin D 74 B3
Neu-Ulm D 94 C2
Neuves-Maisons F 92 C2
Neuvic
*Corrèze* F 116 B2
*Dordogne* F 129 A3
Neuville-aux-Bois
F 103 A4
Neuville-de-Poitou
F 115 B4
Neuville-les-Dames
F 117 A5
Neuville-sur-Saône
F 117 B4
Neuvy-le-Roi F 102 B2
Neuvy-Santour F 104 A2
Neuvy-St Sépulchre
F 103 C3
Neuvy-sur-Barangeon
F 103 B4
Neuwied D 80 B3
Neuzelle D 74 B3
Névache F 118 B3
Neveklov CZ 96 B2
Nevel RUS 9 D6
Neverfjord N 192 B7
Nevers F 104 C2
Nevesinje BIH 139 B4
Névez F 100 B2
Nevlunghavn N 53 B5
Nevşehir TR 23 B8
New Abbey GB 36 B3
New Aberdour GB 33 D4
New Alresford GB 44 B2
Newark-on-Trent
GB 40 B3
Newbiggin-by-the-Sea
GB 37 A5
Newbliss IRL 27 B3
Newborough GB 38 A2
Newbridge IRL 30 A2
Newbridge on Wye
GB 39 B3
Newburgh
*Aberdeenshire*
GB 33 D4
*Fife* GB 35 B4
Newbury GB 44 B2
Newby Bridge GB 36 B4
Newcastle GB 27 B5
Newcastle Emlyn
GB 39 B2
Newcastleton GB 37 A4
Newcastle-under-Lyme
GB 40 B1
Newcastle upon Tyne
GB 37 B5
Newcastle West IRL 29 B2
Newchurch GB 39 B3
New Costessey GB 41 C5
New Cumnock GB 36 A2
Newent GB 39 C4
New Galloway GB 36 A2
Newham GB 45 B4
Newhaven GB 45 C4
Newington GB 45 B5
Newinn IRL 29 B4
Newlyn GB 42 B1
Newmachar GB 33 D4
Newmarket
*Suffolk* GB 45 A4
*Western Isles* GB 31 A2
IRL 29 B3
Newmarket-on-Fergus
IRL 28 B3
New Mills GB 40 B2
New Milton GB 44 C2
New Pitsligo GB 33 D4
Newport
*Isle of Wight* GB 44 C2
*Newport* GB 39 C4
*Pembrokeshire* GB 39 B2
*Telford & Wrekin*
GB 38 B4
Newport *continued*
*Mayo* IRL 28 A2
*Tipperary* IRL 29 B3
Newport-on-Tay GB 35 B5
Newport Pagnell GB 44 A3
Newquay GB 42 B1
New Quay GB 39 B2
New Radnor GB 39 B3
New Romney GB 45 C4
New Ross IRL 30 B2
Newry GB 27 B4
New Scone GB 35 B4
Newton Abbot GB 43 B3
Newton Arlosh GB 36 B3
Newton Aycliffe GB 37 B5
Newton Ferrers GB 42 B2
Newtonhill GB 33 D4
Newtonmore GB 32 D2
Newton Stewart GB 36 B2
Newtown
*Herefordshire* GB 39 B4
*Powys* GB 39 B3
Newtownabbey GB 27 B5
Newtownards GB 27 B5
Newtownbutler GB 27 B3
Newtown Cunningham
IRL 27 B3
Newtown Hamilton
GB 27 B4
Newtownmountkennedy
IRL 30 A2
Newtown St Boswells
GB 35 C5
Newtown Sands IRL 29 B2
Newtownstewart GB 27 B3
Nexon F 115 C5
Neyland GB 39 C2
Nibbiano I 120 C2
Nibe DK 58 B2
Nicastro I 175 C2
Niccone I 135 B5
Nice F 133 B3
Nickelsdorf A 111 B4
Nicolosi I 177 B4
Nicosia
CY 181 A2
I 177 B3
Nicótera I 175 C1
Nidda D 81 B5
Niğde TR 23 C8
Nidzica PL 77 A5
Niebla E 161 B3
Nieborów PL 77 B5
Niebüll D 64 B1
Niechanowo PL 76 B2
Niechorze PL 67 B4
Niedalino PL 67 B5
Niederaula D 82 B1
Niederbipp CH 106 B2
Niederbronn-les-Bains
F 93 C3
Niederfischbach D 81 B3
Niedergörsdorf D 74 C1
Niederkrüchten D 80 A2
Niederndorf A 108 B3
Nieder-Olm D 93 B4
Niedersachswerfen
D 82 A2
Niederstetten D 94 B1
Niederurnen CH 107 B4
Niederwölz A 110 B1
Niedoradz PL 85 A3
Niedzica PL 99 B4
Niegosławice PL 85 A3
Nieheim D 81 A5
Niemcza PL 85 B4
Niemegk D 74 B1
Niemisel S 196 C5
Niemodlin PL 85 B5
Nienburg
*Niedersachsen* D 72 B2
*Sachsen-Anhalt* D 83 A3
Niepołomice PL 99 A4
Nierstein D 93 B4
Niesky D 84 A2
Niestronno PL 76 B2
Nieświń PL 87 A4
Nieszawa PL 76 B3
Nieul-le-Dolent F 114 B2
Nieul-sur-Mer F 114 B2
Nieuw-Amsterdam
NL 71 B3
Nieuw-Buinen NL 71 B3
Nieuwegein NL 70 B2
Nieuwe Niedorp NL 70 B1
Nieuwe-Pekela NL 71 A3
Nieuwerkerken B 79 B5
Nieuwe-schans NL 71 A4
Nieuwolda NL 71 A3
Nieuwpoort B 78 A2
Nieuw-Weerdinge
NL 71 B3
Nigrita GR 183 C5
Nigüelas E 163 B4
Níjar E 164 C2
Nijemci HR 125 B5
Nijkerk NL 70 B2
Nijlen B 79 A4
Nijmegen NL 80 A1
Nijverdal NL 71 B3
Nikel RUS 193 C14
Nikinci SRB 127 C1
Nikiti GR 183 C5
Nikitsch A 111 B3
Nikkaluokta S 196 B2
Nikla H 111 C4
Niklasdorf A 110 B2
Nikšić MNE 139 C4
Nilivaara S 196 B4
Nîmes F 131 B3
Nimis I 122 A2
Nimtofte DK 58 B3
Nin HR 137 A4
Nindorf D 64 B2
Ninemilehouse IRL 30 B1
Ninove B 79 B4
Niort F 114 B3
Niš SRB 16 D4
Nisa P 155 B3
Niscemi I 177 B3
Niskala FIN 197 D10
Nissafors S 60 B3
Nissan-lez-Ensérune
F 130 B2
Nissedal N 53 A4
Nissumby DK 58 B1
Nisterud N 53 A5
Niton GB 44 C2
Nitra SK 98 C2
Nitrianske-Pravno
SK 98 C2
Nitrianske Rudno
SK 98 C2
Nitry F 104 B2
Nittedal N 48 B2
Nittenau D 95 B4
Nittendorf D 95 B3
Nivala FIN 3 E9
Nivelles B 79 B4
Nivnice CZ 98 C1
Nižná SK 99 B3
Nižná Boca SK 99 C3
Niżne Repaše SK 99 B4
Nizza Monferrato I 119 C5
Njarðvík IS 190 D3
Njegůsevo SRB 126 B1
Njivice HR 123 B3
Njurundabommen
S 200 D3
Njutånger S 200 E3
Noailles F 90 B2
Noain E 144 B2
Noale I 121 B5
Noalejo E 163 A4
Noblejas E 151 C4
Noceda E 141 B4
Nocera Inferiore I 170 C2
Nocera Terinese I 175 B2
Nocera Umbra I 136 B1
Noceto I 120 C3
Noci I 173 B3
Nociglia I 173 B4
Nodeland N 53 B3
Nödinge S 60 B2
Nods F 105 B5
Noé F 146 A2
Noépoli I 174 A2
Noeux-les-Mines F 78 B2
Noez E 157 A3
Nogales E 155 C4
Nogara I 121 B4
Nogarejas E 141 B4
Nogaro F 128 C2
Nogent F 105 A4
Nogent l'Artaud F 90 C3
Nogent-le-Roi F 90 C1
Nogent-le-Rotrou F 89 B4
Nogent-sur-Seine F 91 C3
Nogent-sur-Vernisson
F 103 B4
Nogersund S 63 B2
Noguera E 152 B2
Noguerones E 163 A3
Nohfelden D 92 B3
Nohn D 80 B2
Noia E 140 B2
Noicáttaro I 173 A2
Noirétable F 117 B3
Noirmoutier-en-l'Île
F 114 A1
Noja E 143 A3
Nojewo PL 75 B5
Nokia FIN 8 B3
Nol S 60 B2
Nola I 170 C2
Nolay F 104 C3
Noli I 133 A4
Nolnyra S 51 B4
Nombela E 150 B3
Nomeny F 92 C2
Nomexy F 92 C2
Nonancourt F 89 B5
Nonant-le-Pin F 89 B4
Nonántola I 121 C4
Nonaspe E 153 A4
None I 119 C4
Nontron F 115 C4
Nonza F 180 A2
Noordhorn NL 71 A3
Noordwijk NL 70 B1
Noordwijkerhout NL 70 B1
Noordwolde NL 70 B3
Noppikoski S 50 A1
Nora S 55 A6
Nørager DK 58 B2
Norberg S 50 B2
Norboda S 51 B5
Nórcia I 136 C2
Nordagutu N 53 A5
Nordanås S 200 B4
Nordausques F 78 B2
Nordborg DK 64 A2
Nordby
*Aarhus Amt.* DK 59 C3
*Ribe Amt.* DK 59 C1
Norddeich D 71 A4
Norddorf D 64 B1
Norden D 71 A4
Nordenham D 72 A1
Norderhov N 48 B2
Norderney D 71 A4
Norderstapel D 64 B2
Norderstedt D 64 C3
Nordfjord N 193 B14
Nordfjordeid N 198 D3
Nordfold N 194 C6
Nordhalben D 82 B3
Nordhausen D 82 A2
Nordheim vor der Rhön
D 82 B2
Nordholz D 64 C1
Nordhorn D 71 B4
Nordingrå S 200 D4
Nordkjosbotn N 192 C3
Nordli N 199 A10
Nördlingen D 94 C2
Nordmaling S 200 C5
Nordmark S 49 C6
Nordmela N 194 A6
Nord-Odal N 48 B3
Nordre Osen N 48 A3
Nordsinni N 48 B1
Nørdstedalsseter
N 198 D4
Nordstemmen D 72 B2
Nordvågen N 193 B10
Nordwalde D 71 B4
Noreña E 142 A1
Noresund N 48 B1
Norg NL 71 A3
Norheimsund N 46 B3
Norie S 63 B2
Norma I 169 B2
Nornäs S 49 A5
Norrahammar S 62 A2
Norråker S 200 B1
Norrala S 51 A3
Norra Vi S 62 A3
Nørre Aaby DK 59 C2
Nørre Alslev DK 65 B4
Nørre Lyndelse DK 59 C3
Nørre Nebel DK 59 C1
Norrent-Fontes F 78 B2
Nørre Snede DK 59 C2
Nørresundby DK 58 A2
Nørre Vorupør DK 58 B1
Norrfjärden S 196 D4
Norrhed S 196 C3
Norrhult Klavreström
S 62 A3
Norrköping S 56 B2
Norrskedika S 51 B5
Norrsundet S 51 B4
Norrtälje S 57 A4
Nors DK 58 A1
Norsbron S 55 A4
Norsholm S 56 B1
Norsjö S 200 B5
Nörten-Hardenberg
D 82 A1
Northallerton GB 37 B5
Northampton GB 44 A3
North Berwick GB 35 B5
North Charlton GB 37 A5
Northeim D 82 A2
Northfleet GB 45 B4
North Frodingham
GB 40 B3
North Kessock GB 32 D2
Northleach GB 44 B2
North Molton GB 42 A3
North Petherton GB 43 A3
Northpunds GB 33 B5
North Somercotes
GB 41 B4
North Tawton GB 42 B3
North Thoresby GB 41 B3
North Walsham GB 41 C5
Northwich GB 38 A4
Norton GB 40 A3
Nortorf D 64 B2
Nort-sur-Erdre F 101 B4
Nörvenich D 80 B2
Norwich GB 41 C5
Norwick GB 33 A6
Nøsen N 47 B5
Nossa Senhora do Cabo
P 154 C1
Nossebro S 55 B3
Nössemark S 54 A2
Nossen D 83 A5
Notaresco I 169 A3
Noto I 177 C4
Notodden N 53 A5
Nottingham GB 40 C2
Nottuln D 71 C4
Nouan-le-Fuzelier
F 103 B4
Nouans-les-Fontaines
F 103 B3
Nougaroulet F 129 C3
Nouvion F 78 B1
Nouzonville F 91 B4
Nova H 111 C3
Nová Baňa SK 98 C2
Nová Bystrica SK 99 B3
Nová Bystřice CZ 97 B3
Nova Crnja SRB 126 B2
Novaféltria I 135 B5
Nova Gorica SLO 122 A2
Nova Gradiška HR 124 B3
Nováky SK 98 C2
Novalaise F 118 B2
Novales E 145 B3

Nov–Orb 263


Nova Levante I 108 C2
Novalja HR 137 A3
Nová Paka CZ 84 B3
Nova Pazova SRB 127 C2
Nová Pec CZ 96 C1
Novara I 120 B1
Novara di Sicília I 177 A4
Nova Siri I 174 A2
Novate Mezzola I 120 A2
Nova Topola BIH 124 B3
Novaya Ladoga RUS 9 B8
Nova Zagora BG 17 D6
Nové Hrady CZ 96 C2
Novelda E 165 A4
Novellara I 121 C3
Nové Město SK 98 C1
Nové Město nad Metují
CZ 85 B4
Nové Město na Moravě
CZ 97 B4
Nové Město pod
Smrkem CZ 84 B3
Nové Mitrovice CZ 96 B1
Noventa di Piave I 122 B1
Noventa Vicentina
I 121 B4
Novés E 151 B3
Noves F 131 B3
Nové Sady SK 98 C1
Novés de Segre E 147 B2
Nové Strašeci CZ 84 B1
Nové Zámky SK 112 B2
Novgorod RUS 9 C7
Novi Bečej SRB 126 B2
Novi di Módena I 121 C3
Novigrad
*Istarska* HR 122 B2
*Zadarsko-Kninska*
HR 137 A4
Novigrad Podravski
HR 124 A2
Novi Kneževac
SRB 126 A2
Novi Lígure I 120 C1
Noville B 92 A1
Novi Marof HR 124 A2
Novion-Porcien F 91 B4
Novi Pazar
BG 17 D7
SRB 16 D4
Novi Sad SRB 126 B1
Novi Slankamen
SRB 126 B2
Novi Travnik BIH 139 A3
Novi Vinodolski
HR 123 B3
Novohrad-Volynskyy
UA 13 C7
Novo Mesto SLO 123 B4
Novo Miloševo
SRB 126 B2
Novorzhev RUS 9 D6
Novo Selo BIH 125 B3
Novoselytsya UA 17 A7
Novosokolniki RUS 9 D6
Novoveská Huta SK 99 C4
Novovolynsk UA 13 C6
Novska HR 124 B2
Nový Bor CZ 84 B2
Nový Bydžov CZ 84 B3
Novy-Chevrières F 91 B4
Nowy Dwór Mazowiecki
PL 77 B5
Nový-Hrozenkov CZ 98 B2
Nový Jičín CZ 98 B2
Novy Knin CZ 96 B2
Nowa Cerekwia PL 86 B1
Nowa Dęba PL 87 B5
Nowa Karczma PL 68 A3
Nowa Kościoł PL 85 A3
Nowa Ruda PL 85 B4
Nowa Słupia PL 87 B5
Nowa Sól PL 85 A3
Nowa Wieś PL 69 B4
Nowa-Wieś Wielka
PL 76 B3
Nowe PL 69 B3
Nowe Brzesko PL 87 B4
Nowe Grudze PL 77 B4
Nowe Kiejkuty PL 77 A6
Nowe Miasteczko
PL 85 A3
Nowe Miasto
*Mazowieckie* PL 77 B5
*Mazowieckie* PL 87 A4
Nowe Miasto Lubawskie
PL 69 B4
Nowe Miasto nad Wartą
PL 76 B2
Nowe Skalmierzyce
PL 86 A2
Nowe Warpno PL 74 A3
Nowica PL 69 A4
Nowogard PL 75 A4
Nowogród Bobrzanski
PL 84 A3
Nowogrodziec PL 84 A3
Nowosolna PL 86 A3
Nowy Dwór Gdański
PL 69 A4
Nowy Korczyn PL 87 B4
Nowy Sącz PL 99 B4
Nowy Staw PL 69 A4
Nowy Targ PL 99 B4
Nowy Tomyśl PL 75 B5
Nowy Wiśnicz PL 99 B4
Noyalo F 101 B3
Noyal-Pontivy F 100 A3
Noyant F 102 B2
Noyelles-sur-Mer F 78 B1
Noyen-sur-Sarthe
F 102 B1
Noyers F 104 B2
Noyers-sur-Cher F 103 B3
Noyers-sur-Jabron
F 132 A1
Noyon F 90 B2
Nozay F 101 B4
Nuaillé F 102 B1
Nuaillé-d'Aunis F 114 B3
Nuars F 104 B2
Nubledo E 141 A5
Nuéno E 145 B3
Nuestra Señora Sa
Verge des Pilar E 166 C1
Nueva E 142 A2
Nueva Carteya E 163 A3
Nuevalos E 152 A2
Nuits F 104 B3
Nuits-St Georges F 105 B3
Nule I 178 B3
Nules E 159 B3
Nulvi I 178 B2
Numana I 136 B2
Numansdorp NL 79 A4
Nümbrecht D 81 B3
Nunchritz D 83 A5
Nuneaton GB 40 C2
Nunnanen FIN 196 A7
N Unnaryd S 60 B3
Nuñomoral E 149 B3
Nunspeet NL 70 B2
Nuorgam FIN 193 B11
Núoro I 178 B3
Nurallao I 179 C3
Nuremberg = Nürnberg
D 94 B3
Nurmes FIN 3 E11
Nürnberg = Nuremberg
D 94 B3
Nurri I 179 C3
Nürtingen D 94 C1
Nus I 119 B4
Nusnäs S 50 B1
Nusplingen D 107 A3
Nuštar HR 125 B4
Nuupas FIN 197 C9
Nyåker S 200 C5
Nyáregyháza H 112 B3
Nyarlörinc H 113 C3
Nyasvizh BY 13 B7
Nybble S 55 A5
Nybergsund N 49 A4
Nybøl DK 64 B2
Nyborg
DK 59 C3
S 196 D6
Nybro S 62 B3
Nybster GB 32 C3
Nyby DK 65 B5
Nye S 62 A3
Nyékládháza H 113 B4
Nyergesujfalu H 112 B2
Nyhammar S 50 B1
Nyhyttan S 55 A5
Nyirád H 111 B4
Nyirbátor H 16 B5
Nyíregyháza H 16 B4
Nyker DK 67 A3
Nykil S 56 B1
Nykirke N 48 B2
Nykøbing
*Falster* DK 65 B4
*Vestsjællands Amt.*
DK 61 D1
Nykøbing Mors DK 58 B1
Nyköping S 56 B3
Nykroppa S 55 A5
Nykvarn S 56 A3
Nykyrke S 55 B5
Nyland S 200 C3
Nylars DK 67 A3
Nymburk CZ 84 B3
Nynäshamn S 57 B3
Nyon CH 118 A3
Nyons F 131 A4
Nýřany CZ 96 B1
Nýrsko CZ 95 B5
Nyrud N 193 C13
Nysa PL 85 B5
Nysäter S 55 A3
Nyseter N 198 C5
Nyskoga S 49 B4
Nysted DK 65 B4
Nystrand N 53 A5
Nyúl H 111 B4
Nyvoll N 192 B7


## O


Oadby GB 40 C2
Oakengates GB 38 B4
Oakham GB 40 C3
Oanes N 52 B2
Obalj BIH 139 B4
Oban GB 34 B2
O Barco E 141 B4
Obbola S 200 C6
Obdach A 110 B1
Obejo E 156 B3
Oberammergau D 108 B2
Oberasbach D 94 B2
Oberau D 108 B2
Oberaudorf D 108 B3
Oberbruck F 106 B1
Oberdiessbach CH 106 C2
Oberdorf CH 106 B2
Oberdrauburg A 109 C3
Oberelsbach D 82 B2
Obere Stanz A 110 B2
Ober Grafendorf A 110 A2
Obergünzburg D 108 B1
Obergurgl A 108 C2
Oberhausen D 80 A2
Oberhof D 82 B2
Oberkirch D 93 C4
Oberkirchen D 81 A4
Oberkochen D 94 C2
Obermassfeld-
Grimmenthal D 82 B2
Ober-Morlen D 81 B4
Obermünchen D 95 C3
Obernai F 93 C3
Obernberg A 96 C1
Obernburg D 93 B5
Oberndorf D 93 C4
Oberndorf bei Salzburg
A 109 B3
Obernkirchen D 72 B2
Oberort A 110 B2
Oberpullendorf A 111 B3
Oberriet CH 107 B4
Oberröblingen D 82 A3
Oberrot D 94 B1
Oberstaufen D 107 B5
Oberstdorf D 107 B5
Obertauern A 109 B4
Obertilliach A 109 C3
Obertraubling D 95 C4
Obertraun A 109 B4
Obertrubach D 95 B3
Obertrum A 109 B4
Oberursel D 81 B4
Obervellach A 109 C4
Oberviechtach D 95 B4
Oberwart A 111 B3
Oberwesel D 93 A3
Oberwinter D 80 B3
Oberwölzstadt A 110 B1
Oberzell D 96 C1
Obice PL 87 B4
Óbidos P 154 B1
Obing D 109 B3
Objat F 129 A4
Objazda PL 68 A2
Öblarn A 109 B5
Obninsk RUS 9 E10
O Bolo E 141 B3
Oborniki PL 75 B5
Oborniki Śląskie PL 85 A4
Obornjača SRB 126 B1
Obrenovac SRB 127 C2
Obrež SRB 127 C1
Obrigheim D 93 B5
Obrov SLO 123 B3
Obrovac
HR 137 A4
SRB 126 B1
Obrovac Sinjski
HR 138 B2
Obruk TR 23 B7
Obrzycko PL 75 B5
Obudovac BIH 125 C4
Ocaña E 151 C4
O Carballiño E 140 B2
Occhiobello I 121 C4
Occimiano I 119 B5
Očevlja BIH 139 A4
Ochagavía E 144 B2
Ochiltree GB 36 A2
Ochla PL 84 A3
Ochotnica-Dolna PL 99 B4
Ochotnica-Górna
PL 99 B4
Ochsenfurt D 94 B2
Ochsenhausen D 107 A4
Ochtendung D 80 B3
Ochtrup D 71 B4
Ocieka PL 87 B5
Ockelbo S 50 B3
Öckerö S 60 B1
Ocniţa MD 17 A7
O Corgo E 141 B3
Očová SK 99 C3
Ócsa H 112 B3
Öcseny H 125 A4
Öcsöd H 113 C4
Octeville F 88 A2
Ocypel PL 69 B3
Ödåkra S 61 C2
Odby DK 58 B1
Odda N 46 B3
Odder DK 59 C3
Ödeborg S 54 B2
Odeceixe P 160 B1
Odechów PL 87 A5
Odeleite P 160 B2
Odemira P 160 B1
Ödemiş TR 188 A2
Ödensbacken S 56 A1
Odense DK 59 C3
Odensjö
*Jönköping* S 62 A2
*Kronoberg* S 60 C3
Oderberg D 74 B3
Oderzo I 122 B1
Odesa = Odessa UA 17 B9
Ödeshög S 55 B5
Odessa = Odesa UA 17 B9
Odiáxere P 160 B1
Odie GB 33 B4
Odiham GB 44 B3
Odintsovo RUS 9 E10
Odivelas P 160 A1
Odolanów PL 85 A5
Odón E 152 B2
Odorheiu Secuiesc
RO 17 B6
Odrowaz PL 87 A4
Odry CZ 98 B1
Odrzywół PL 87 A4
Ødsted DK 59 C2
Odžaci SRB 126 B1
Odžak BIH 125 B4
Oebisfelde D 73 B3
Oederan D 83 B5
Oeding D 71 C3
Oegstgeest NL 70 B1
Oelde D 81 A4
Oelsnitz D 83 B4
Oer-Erkenschwick
D 80 A3
Oerlinghausen D 72 C1
Oettingen D 94 C2
Oetz A 108 B1
Oeventrop D 81 A4
Offanengo I 120 B2
Offenbach D 81 B4
Offenburg D 93 C3
Offida I 136 C2
Offingen D 94 C2
Offranville F 89 A5
Ofir P 148 A1
Ofte N 53 A4
Ofterschwang D 107 B5
Oggiono I 120 B2
Ogihares E 163 A4
Ogliastro Cilento I 170 C3
Ogliastro Marina I 170 C2
Ogmore-by-Sea GB 39 C3
Ogna N 52 B1
Ogre LV 8 D4
Ogrodzieniec PL 86 B3
Ogulin HR 123 B4
Ögur IS 190 A3
Ohanes E 164 B2
Ohey B 79 B5
Ohlstadt D 108 B2
Ohrdorf D 73 B3
Ohrdruf D 82 B2
Ohrid MK 182 B2
Öhringen D 94 B1
Oia E 140 B2
Oiã P 148 B1
Oiartzun E 144 A2
Oijärvi FIN 197 D8
Oilgate IRL 30 B2
Oimbra E 148 A2
Oiselay-et-Grachoux
F 105 B4
Oisemont F 90 B1
Oisterwijk NL 79 A5
Öja S 57 C4
Öje S 49 B5
Ojén E 162 B3
Ojrzeń PL 77 B5
Ojuelos Altos E 156 B2
Okalewo PL 77 A4
Okány H 113 C5
Okehampton GB 42 B2
Oklaj HR 138 B2
Økneshamn N 194 B6
Okoč SK 111 B4
Okoličné SK 99 B3
Okonek PL 68 B1
Okonin PL 69 B3
Okřisky CZ 97 B3
Oksa PL 87 B4
Oksbøl DK 59 C1
Oksby DK 59 C1
Øksfjord N 192 B6
Øksna N 48 B3
Okučani HR 124 B3
Okulovka RUS 9 C8
Ólafsfjörður IS 191 A7
Ólafsvík IS 190 C2
ÖLagnö S 57 A4
Olagüe E 144 B2
Oland N 53 B4
Olargues F 130 B1
Oława PL 85 B5
Olazagutia E 144 B1
Olbernhau D 83 B5
Ólbia I 178 B3
Olching D 108 A2
Oldbury GB 43 A4
Oldcastle IRL 27 C3
Old Deer GB 33 D4
Oldeberkoop NL 70 B3
Oldeboorn NL 70 A2
Olden N 198 D3
Oldenbrok D 71 A5
Oldenburg
*Niedersachsen* D 71 A5
*Schleswig-Holstein*
D 65 B3
Oldenzaal NL 71 B3
Olderdalen N 192 C4
Olderfjord N 193 B9
Oldersum D 71 A4
Oldervik N 192 C2
Oldham GB 40 B1
Oldisleben D 82 A3
Oldmeldrum GB 33 D4
Olea E 142 B2
Oleby S 49 B5
Olechów PL 87 A5
Oledo P 155 B3
Oléggio I 120 B1
Oleiros
*Coruña* E 140 A2
Oleiros *continued*
*Coruña* E 140 B1
P 154 B3
Oleksandriya UA 13 C7
Olen B 79 A4
Ølen N 52 A1
Olenegorsk RUS 3 B13
Olenino RUS 9 D8
Olesa de Montserrat
E 147 C2
Oleśnica PL 85 A5
Olešnice CZ 97 B4
Olesno PL 86 B2
Oletta F 180 A2
Olette F 146 B3
Olevsk UA 13 C7
Olfen D 80 A3
Olgiate Comasco I 120 B1
Olginate I 120 B2
Ølgod DK 59 C1
Olgrinmore GB 32 C3
Olhão P 160 B2
Olhava FIN 197 D8
Olhavo P 154 B1
Oliana E 147 B2
Olias del Rey E 151 C4
Oliena I 178 B3
Oliete E 153 B3
Olimbos GR 188 D2
Olite E 144 B2
Oliva E 159 C3
Oliva de la Frontera
E 155 C4
Oliva de Mérida E 156 B1
Oliva de Plasencia
E 149 B3
Olivadi I 175 C2
Olival P 154 B2
Olivar E 163 B4
Olivares E 161 B3
Olivares de Duero
E 142 C2
Olivares de Júcar
E 158 B1
Oliveira de Azeméis
P 148 B1
Oliveira de Frades
P 148 B1
Oliveira do Conde
P 148 B2
Oliveira do Douro
P 148 A1
Oliveira do Hospital
P 148 B2
Olivenza E 155 C3
Olivet F 103 B3
Olivone CH 107 C3
Öljehult S 63 B3
Olkusz PL 86 B3
Ollerton GB 40 B2
Ollerup DK 65 A3
Olliergues F 117 B3
Ölmbrotorp S 56 A1
Ölme S 55 A4
Olmedilla de Alarcón
E 158 B1
Olmedillo de Roa
E 143 C3
Olmedo
E 150 A3
I 178 B2
Olmeto F 180 B1
Olmillos de Castro
E 149 A3
Olmos de Ojeda E 142 B2
Olney GB 44 A3
Ołobok PL 86 A2
Olocau del Rey E 153 B3
Olofström S 63 B2
Olomouc CZ 98 B1
Olonets RUS 9 B8
Olonne-sur-Mer F 114 B2
Olonzac F 130 B1
Oloron-Ste Marie F 145 A3
Olost E 147 C3
Olot E 147 B3
Olovo BIH 139 A4
Olpe D 81 A3
Olsberg D 81 A4
Olsene B 79 B3
Olserud S 55 A4
Olshammar S 55 B5
Olshanka UA 13 D9
Olszanica PL 85 A3
Olsztyn
*Śląskie* PL 86 B3
*Warmińsko-Mazurskie*
PL 69 B5
Olsztynek PL 77 A5
Olszyna PL 84 A3
Olszyny PL 77 A6
Oltedal N 52 B2
Olten CH 106 B2
Olteniţa RO 17 C7
Olula del Rio E 164 B2
Ølve N 46 B2
Olvega E 144 C2
Olvera E 162 B2
Olympia GR 184 B2
Olzai I 178 B3
Omagh GB 27 B3
Omalos GR 185 D4
Omegna I 119 B5
Omiš HR 138 B2
Omišalj HR 123 B3
Ommen NL 71 B3
Omodhos CY 181 B1
Omoljica SRB 127 C2
On B 79 B5
Oña E 143 B3
Onano I 168 A1
O Näsberg S 49 B5
Oñati E 143 A4
Onda E 159 B3
Ondara E 159 C4
Ondarroa E 143 A4
Onesse-et-Laharie
F 128 B1
Oneşti RO 17 B7
Onhaye B 79 B4
Onich GB 34 B2
Onil E 159 C3
Onís E 142 A2
Önnestad S 61 C4
Onsala S 60 B2
Ontinyent E 159 C3
Ontur E 158 C2
Onzain F 103 B3
Onzonilla E 142 B1
Oostburg NL 79 A3
Oostende B 78 A2
Oosterend NL 70 A2
Oosterhout NL 79 A4
Oosterwolde NL 71 B3
Oosterzele B 79 B3
Oosthuizen NL 70 B2
Oostkamp B 78 A3
Oostmalle B 79 A4
Oost-Vlieland NL 70 A2
Oostvoorne NL 79 A4
Ootmarsum NL 71 B3
Opalenica PL 75 B5
O Páramo E 140 B3
Opařany CZ 96 B2
Opatija HR 123 B3
Opatów
*Śląskie* PL 86 B2
*Świętokrzyskie* PL 87 B5
*Wielkopolskie* PL 86 A2
Opatówek PL 86 A2
Opatowiec PL 87 B4
Opava CZ 98 B1
O Pedrouzo E 140 B2
Opeinde NL 70 A3
Oper Thalkirchdorf
D 107 B5
Opglabbeerk B 80 A1
Opicina I 122 B2
O Pino E 140 B2
Oplotnica SLO 123 A4
Opmeer NL 70 B1
Opochka RUS 9 D6
Opočno CZ 85 B4
Opoczno PL 87 A4
Opole PL 86 B1
Oporów PL 77 B4
O Porriño E 140 B2
Opovo SRB 127 B2
Oppach D 84 A2
Oppdal N 198 C6
Oppeby
*Östergötland* S 56 B1
*Södermanland* S 56 B2
Oppedal N 46 A2
Oppegård N 54 A1
Oppenau D 93 C4
Oppenberg A 110 B1
Oppenheim D 93 B4
Óppido Lucano I 172 B1
Óppido Mamertina
I 175 C1
Opponitz A 110 B1
Oppstad N 48 B3
Oprtalj HR 122 B2
Opsaheden S 49 B5
Ópusztaszer H 113 C4
Opuzen HR 138 B3
Ora
CY 181 B2
I 121 A4
Orada P 155 C3
Oradea RO 16 B4
Oradour-sur-Glane
F 115 C5
Oradour-sur-Vayres
F 115 C4
Oragonja SLO 122 B2
Orah BIH 139 C4
Orahova BIH 138 A3
Orahovica HR 125 B3
Orahovo BIH 124 B3
Oraison F 132 B1
Orajärvi FIN 196 C7
Orange F 131 A3
Orani I 178 B3
Oranienbaum D 83 A4
Oranienburg D 74 B2
Oranmore IRL 28 A3
Orašac SRB 127 C2
Orašje BIH 125 B4
Oravská Lesná SK 99 B3
Oravská Polhora
SK 99 B3
Oravské Veselé SK 99 B3
Oravsky-Podzámok
SK 99 B3
Orba E 159 C3
Orbacém P 148 A1
Orbais F 91 C3
Ørbæk DK 59 C3
Orbassano I 119 B4
Orbe CH 105 C5
Orbec F 89 A4

Orbetello I . . . . . . 168 A1
Orbetello Scalo I . . 168 A1
Orbigny F. . . . . . . 103 B3
Ørby DK. . . . . . . . 59 B3
Örbyhus S . . . . . . . 51 B4
Orce E . . . . . . . . 164 B2
Orcera E. . . . . . . 164 A2
Orchamps-Vennes
 F. . . . . . . . . . . 105 B5
Orches F . . . . . . . 102 C2
Orchete E. . . . . . . 159 C3
Orchies F. . . . . . . 78 B3
Orchowo PL. . . . . . 76 B3
Orcières F . . . . . . 118 C3
Ordes E . . . . . . . 140 A2
Ordhead GB. . . . . . 33 D4
Ordino AND . . . . . 146 B2
Ordizia E . . . . . . 144 A1
Orduña E . . . . . . . 143 B4
Ore S . . . . . . . . . 50 A2
Orea E . . . . . . . . 152 B2
Orebić HR . . . . . . 138 C3
Örebro S . . . . . . . 56 A1
Öregcsertő H. . . . . 112 C3
Öregrund S . . . . . . 51 B5
Orehoved DK. . . . . 65 B4
Orellana E . . . . . . 156 A2
Orellana de la Sierra
 E. . . . . . . . . . . 156 A2
Ören TR . . . . . . . 188 B2
Örencik TR. . . . . . 187 C4
Orestiada GR. . . . . 186 A1
Organyà E . . . . . . 147 B2
Orgaz E . . . . . . . 157 A4
Orgelet F . . . . . . 105 C4
Ørgenvika N . . . . . 48 B1
Orgères-en-Beauce
 F. . . . . . . . . . . 103 A3
Orgibet F . . . . . . 145 B4
Orgnac-l'Aven F . . . 131 A3
Orgon F . . . . . . . 131 B4
Orgósolo I . . . . . . 178 B3
Orhaneli TR . . . . . 186 C3
Orhangazi TR . . . . 187 B4
Orhei MD . . . . . . 17 B8
Orhomenos GR . . . 184 A3
Oria E . . . . . . . . 164 B2
Ória I . . . . . . . . 173 B3
Origny-Ste Benoite
 F. . . . . . . . . . . 91 B3
Orihuela E . . . . . . 165 A4
Orihuela del Tremedal
 E. . . . . . . . . . . 152 B2
Orikum AL . . . . . . 182 C1
Oriola P . . . . . . . 154 C3
Oriolo I . . . . . . . 174 A2
Oriovac HR . . . . . 125 B3
Orissaare EST. . . . . 8 C3
Oristano I . . . . . . 179 C2
Öriszentpéter H. . . .111 C3
Ørje N . . . . . . . . 54 A2
Orjiva E . . . . . . . 163 B4
Orkanger N . . . . . 198 B6
Örkelljunga S . . . . 61 C3
Örkény H . . . . . . .112 B3
Orlamünde D . . . . . 82 B3
Orléans F. . . . . . . 103 B3
Orlová CZ . . . . . . 98 B2
Orlovat SRB. . . . . . 126 B2
Ormea I . . . . . . . 133 A3
Ormelet N . . . . . . 54 A1
Ormemyr N . . . . . 53 A5
Ormilia GR. . . . . . 183 C5
Ormos GR . . . . . . 185 B5
Ormož SLO . . . . . 124 A2
Ormskirk GB . . . . . 38 A4
Ornans F . . . . . . . 105 B5
Ornäs S . . . . . . . 50 B2
Ørnes N . . . . . . . 195 D4
Orneta PL. . . . . . . 69 A5
Ørnhøj DK. . . . . . 59 B1
Ornö S . . . . . . . . 57 A4
Örnsköldsvik S . . . 200 C4
Orolik HR . . . . . . 125 B4
Orom SRB . . . . . . 126 B1
Oron-la-Ville CH . . 106 C1
Oronsko PL . . . . . 87 A4
Oropa I . . . . . . . .119 B4
Oropesa
 Castellón de la Plana
  E. . . . . . . . . . .153 B4
 Toledo E. . . . . . . .150 C2
O Rosal E. . . . . . . 140 C2
Orosei I . . . . . . . 178 B3
Orosháza H . . . . . 113 C4
Oroslavje HR. . . . . 124 B1
Oroszlány H. . . . . .112 B2
Oroszlo H. . . . . . . 125 A4
Orotelli I . . . . . . 178 B3
Orozko E . . . . . . . 143 A4
Orphir GB . . . . . . 33 C3
Orpington GB . . . . 45 B4
Orreaga-Roncesvalles
 E. . . . . . . . . . . 144 A2
Orrefors S . . . . . . 62 B3
Orrviken S . . . . . . .199 B11
Orsa S . . . . . . . . 50 A1
Orsara di Púglia I . . 171 B3
Orsay F . . . . . . . 90 C2
Orscholz D. . . . . . 92 B2
Orsennes F . . . . . . 103 C3
Orserum S . . . . . . 55 B5
Orsha BY . . . . . . 13 A9
Orsières CH. . . . . .119 A4
Örsjö S . . . . . . . . 63 B3

Ørslev DK . . . . . . 65 A4
Örslösa S. . . . . . . 55 B3
Orsogna I. . . . . . . 169 A4
Orsomarso I . . . . . 174 B1
Orşova RO. . . . . . 16 C5
Ørsta N. . . . . . . . 198 C3
Ørsted DK. . . . . . . 58 B3
Örsundsbro S . . . . 56 A3
Ortaca TR. . . . . . . 188 C3
Ortakent TR . . . . . 188 B2
Ortaklar TR . . . . . 188 B2
Ortaköy TR . . . . . 23 B8
Orta Nova I. . . . . . 171 B3
Orte I . . . . . . . . 168 A2
Ortenburg D . . . . . 96 C1
Orth A. . . . . . . . .111 A3
Orthez F. . . . . . . . 128 C2
Ortigueira E. . . . . . 140 A3
Ortilla E . . . . . . . 145 B3
Ortisei I . . . . . . . 108 C2
Orţişoara RO. . . . . 126 B3
Ortnevik N. . . . . . 46 A3
Orton GB . . . . . . 37 B4
Ortona I . . . . . . . 169 A4
Ortrand D . . . . . . 84 A1
Orubica HR . . . . . 124 B3
Ørum DK . . . . . . 58 B2
Orune I. . . . . . . . 178 B3
Orusco E . . . . . . . 151 B4
Orvalho P. . . . . . . 155 A3
Orvault F . . . . . . 101 B4
Ørvella N . . . . . . 53 A5
Orvieto I . . . . . . . 168 A2
Orvínio I . . . . . . . 169 A2
Oryakhovo BG. . . . 17 D5
Orzesze PL. . . . . . 86 B2
Orzinuovi I. . . . . . 120 B2
Orzivécchi I. . . . . . 120 B2
Orzyny PL . . . . . . 77 A6
Os
 Hedmark N. . . . . . .48 B3
 Hedmark N. . . . . . .199 C8
Osann-Monzel D . . . 92 B2
Osbruk S . . . . . . . 62 A2
Øsby DK. . . . . . . 59 C2
Osby S . . . . . . . . 61 C3
Oščadnica SK. . . . . 98 B2
Oschatz D . . . . . . 83 A5
Oschersleben D . . . 73 B4
Óschiri I . . . . . . . 178 B3
Osciłowo PL . . . . . 77 B5
Osdorf D . . . . . . . 64 B3
Osečina SRB. . . . . 127 C1
Osečná CZ. . . . . . . 84 B2
Oseja de Sajambre
 E. . . . . . . . . . . 142 A1
Osek CZ. . . . . . . . 84 B1
Osen N. . . . . . . . 199 A7
Osera de Ebro E . . . 153 A3
Osidda I. . . . . . . . 178 B3
Osie PL. . . . . . . . 69 B3
Osieczna
 Pomorskie PL . . . . 68 B3
 Wielkopolskie PL . . .75 C5
Osieczno PL . . . . . 75 A4
Osiek
 Kujawsko-Pomorskie
  PL. . . . . . . . . . .76 B3
 Kujawsko-Pomorskie
  PL. . . . . . . . . . .77 A4
 Pomorskie PL . . . . 69 B3
 Świętokrzyskie PL . .87 B5
Osiek nad Notecią
 PL. . . . . . . . . . . 76 A2
Osielsko PL. . . . . . 76 A3
Osijek HR. . . . . . . 125 B4
Osilnica SLO . . . . . 123 B3
Ósilo I . . . . . . . . 178 B2
Ósimo I . . . . . . . 136 B2
Osinja BIH . . . . . . 125 C3
Osintorf BY . . . . . 13 A9
Osipaonica SRB . . . 127 C3
Oskamull GB . . . . . 34 B1
Oskarshamn S . . . . 62 A4
Oskarström S . . . . 60 C2
Oslany SK. . . . . . . 98 C2
Oslavany CZ . . . . . 97 B4
Ošlje HR. . . . . . . . 139 C3
Oslo N . . . . . . . . 48 C2
Øsløs DK . . . . . . 58 A1
Osmancık TR. . . . . 23 A8
Osmaneli TR . . . . . 187 B4
Ösmo S . . . . . . . 57 B3
Osmolin PL . . . . . 77 B4
Osnabrück D . . . . . 71 B5
Ośno Lubuskie PL . . 75 B3
Osoblaha CZ . . . . . 85 B5
Osor HR. . . . . . . . 123 C3
Osorno E . . . . . . . 142 B2
Ósoyra N . . . . . . . 46 A2
Osøyro N. . . . . . . 46 B2
Óspakseyri IS . . . . 190 B4
Os Peares E. . . . . . 140 B3
Ospedaletti I . . . . . 133 B3
Ospitaletto I. . . . . . 120 B3
Oss NL. . . . . . . . 80 A1
Ossa de Montiel E. . 158 C1
Óssi I. . . . . . . . . 178 B2
Ossjøen N . . . . . . 47 B5
Ossun F. . . . . . . . 145 A3
Ostaná S . . . . . . . 61 C4
Östanvik S. . . . . . . 50 A2
Ostashkov RUS. . . . 9 D8
Östavall S . . . . . . 200 D1
Ostbevern D. . . . . 71 B4
Østborg N . . . . . . 199 A10
Østby N . . . . . . . 49 A4

Osted DK . . . . . . 61 D1
Ostenfeld D. . . . . . 64 B2
Oster UA . . . . . . 13 C9
Øster Assels DK . . 58 B1
Osterburg D . . . . . 73 B4
Osterburken D. . . . 94 B1
Österbybruk S . . . . 51 B4
Österbyhavn DK. . . 58 A4
Österbymo S . . . . 62 A3
Ostercappeln D. . . . 71 B5
Österfärnebo S . . . . 51 B3
Osterfeld D . . . . . 83 A3
Österforse S . . . . . 200 C3
Osterhever D. . . . . 64 B1
Osterhofen D. . . . . 95 C5
Osterholz-Scharmbeck
 D. . . . . . . . . . . 72 A1
Øster Hornum DK . . 58 B2
Øster Hurup DK. . . 58 B3
Østerild DK . . . . . 58 A1
Øster Jølby DK. . . . 58 B1
Österlövsta S . . . . . 51 B4
Øster-marie DK. . . . 67 A4
Ostermiething A . . . 109 A3
Osterode am Harz D 82 A2
Ostersiel D. . . . . . 64 B1
Östersund S . . . . . .199 B11
Øster Tørslev DK. . . 58 B3
Östervåla S . . . . . . 51 B4
Östervallskog S . . . 54 A2
Øster Vrå S . . . . . 58 A3
Osterwieck D. . . . . 73 C3
Osterzell D. . . . . . 108 B1
Ostffyasszonyfa H .111 B4
Ostheim F . . . . . . 106 A2
Ostheim vor der Rhön
 D. . . . . . . . . . . 82 B2
Osthofen D . . . . . . 93 B4
Ostiano I . . . . . . . 120 B3
Ostíglia I. . . . . . . 121 B4
Ostiz E . . . . . . . . 144 B2
Östmark S . . . . . . 49 B4
Östnor S . . . . . . . 50 A1
Ostojićevo SRB. . . . 126 B2
Ostra I . . . . . . . . 136 B2
Östra Amtervik S . . 55 A4
Östraby S. . . . . . . 61 D3
Östra Husby S . . . . 56 B2
Östra Ljungby S . . . 61 C3
Östra Ryd S . . . . . 56 B2
Ostrau D . . . . . . . 83 A5
Ostrava CZ . . . . . . 98 B2
Ostritz D. . . . . . . 84 A2
Ostróda PL. . . . . . 69 B4
Ostroh UA . . . . . . 13 C7
Ostrołęka PL . . . . . 12 B4
Ostropole PL. . . . . 68 B1
Ostroróg PL. . . . . . 75 B5
Ostrošovac BIH. . . . 124 C1
Ostrov
 CZ. . . . . . . . . . .83 B4
 RUS . . . . . . . . . .8 D6
Ostrov nad Oslavou
 CZ . . . . . . . . . . 97 B3
Ostrówek PL . . . . . 86 A2
Ostrowiec PL. . . . . 68 A1
Ostrowiec-Świętokrzyski
 PL. . . . . . . . . . . 87 B5
Ostrowite PL . . . . . 77 A4
Ostrów Mazowiecka
 PL. . . . . . . . . . . 12 B4
Ostrowo PL . . . . . 76 B3
Ostrów Wielkopolski
 PL. . . . . . . . . . . 86 A1
Ostrožac BIH . . . . . 139 B3
Ostrzeszów PL . . . . 86 A1
Ostseebad
 Kühlungsborn D. . . 65 B4
Ostuni I . . . . . . . 173 B3
Osuna E . . . . . . . 162 A2
Osvětimany CZ . . . 98 B1
Oswestry GB. . . . . 38 B3
Oświęcim PL. . . . . 86 B3
Osztopán H . . . . . .111 C4
Oteiza E . . . . . . . 144 B2
Otelec RO . . . . . . 126 B2
Oteo E . . . . . . . . 143 A3
Oterbekk N . . . . . 54 A1
Otero de Herreros
 E. . . . . . . . . . . 151 B3
Otero de O Bodas
 E. . . . . . . . . . . 141 C4
Othem S . . . . . . . 57 C4
Otley GB . . . . . . . 40 B2
Otmuchów PL. . . . 85 B5
Otočac HR . . . . . . 123 C4
Otok
 Splitsko-Dalmatinska
  HR . . . . . . . . . .138 B2
 Vukovarsko-Srijemska
  HR . . . . . . . . . .125 B4
Otoka BIH . . . . . . 124 C2
Otranto I. . . . . . . 173 B4
Otrić HR. . . . . . . . 138 A2
Otrícoli I . . . . . . . 168 A2
Otrokovice CZ. . . . 98 B1
Otta N . . . . . . . . 198 D6
Ottana I . . . . . . . 178 B3
Ottaviano I . . . . . . 170 C2
Ottenby S. . . . . . . 63 B4
Ottendorf-Okrilla D. 84 A1
Ottenhöfen D. . . . . 93 C4
Ottenschlag A . . . . 97 C3

Ottensheim A. . . . . 96 C2
Otterbach D. . . . . . 93 B3
Otterbäcken S . . . . 55 B5
Otterberg D. . . . . . 93 B3
Otterburn GB. . . . . 37 A4
Otter Ferry GB . . . 34 B2
Otterndorf D . . . . . 64 C1
Ottersburg D . . . . . 72 A2
Ottersweier D . . . . 93 C4
Otterup DK. . . . . . 59 C3
Ottery St Mary GB . 43 B3
Ottignies B. . . . . . 79 B4
Ottmarsheim F . . . 106 B2
Ottobeuren D. . . . . 107 B5
Öttömös H. . . . . . 126 A1
Ottone I . . . . . . . 120 C2
Ottsjö S . . . . . . . .199 B10
Ottweiler D. . . . . . 92 B3
Ötvöskónyi H . . . . 124 A3
Otwock PL. . . . . . 12 B4
Ouanne F. . . . . . . 104 B2
Ouarville F. . . . . . 90 C1
Oucques F. . . . . . . 103 B3
Oud-Beijerland NL . 79 A4
Ouddorp NL. . . . . 79 A3
Oudemirdum NL. . . 70 B2
Oudenaarde B. . . . 79 B3
Oudenbosch NL . . . 79 A4
Oudenburg B. . . . . 78 A3
Oude-Pekela NL. . . 71 A4
Oude-Tonge NL. . . 79 A4
Oudewater NL. . . . 70 B1
Oud Gastel NL. . . . 79 A4
Oudon F. . . . . . . . 101 B4
Oughterard IRL . . . 28 A2
Ouguela P. . . . . . . 155 B3
Ouistreham F . . . . 89 A3
Oulainen FIN . . . . 3 D9
Oulchy-le-Château
 F. . . . . . . . . . . 91 B3
Oullins F. . . . . . . .117 B4
Oulmes F. . . . . . . .114 B3
Oulton GB . . . . . . 41 C5
Oulton Broad GB. . . 41 C5
Oulu FIN. . . . . . . 3 D9
Oulx I . . . . . . . . .119 B3
Oundle GB . . . . . . 40 C3
Ouranopoli GR . . . 183 C6
Ourém P. . . . . . . . 154 B2
Ourense E . . . . . . 140 B3
Ourique P. . . . . . . 160 B1
Ourol E. . . . . . . . 140 A3
Ouroux-en-Morvan
 F. . . . . . . . . . . 104 B2
Ousdale GB . . . . . 32 C3
Oust F . . . . . . . . 146 B2
Outakoski FIN . . . 193 C10
Outeiro P. . . . . . . 148 B1
Outeiro de Rei E . . 140 A3
Outes E . . . . . . . 140 B2
Outokumpu FIN. . . 9 A6
Outreau F . . . . . . 78 B1
Outwell GB . . . . . 41 C4
Ouzouer-le-Marché
 F. . . . . . . . . . . 103 B3
Ouzouer-sur-Loire
 F. . . . . . . . . . . 103 B4
Ovada I . . . . . . . 133 A4
Ovar P . . . . . . . . 148 B1
Ove DK. . . . . . . . 58 B2
Ovelgönne D . . . . . 72 A1
Overath D . . . . . . 80 B3
Overbister GB . . . . 33 B4
Øverbygd N . . . . . 192 D3
Overdinkel NL . . . . 71 B4
Överhörnäs S . . . . 56 A3
Overhalla N . . . . . 199 A8
Overijse B . . . . . . 79 B4
Over-jerstal DK . . . 59 C2
Overlade DK. . . . . 58 B2
Överlida S . . . . . . 60 B2
Överö FIN . . . . . . 51 B7
Overpelt B . . . . . . 79 A5
Overton GB . . . . . 38 B4
Övertorneå S . . . . 196 C6
Överum S . . . . . . 62 A4
Ovidiopol UA. . . . . 17 B9
Oviedo E . . . . . . . 141 A5
Óviglio I . . . . . . . 119 C5
Ovindoli I . . . . . . 169 A3
Ovodda I . . . . . . . 178 B3
Øvre Ardal N . . . . 47 A4
Øvrebygd N . . . . . 52 B2
Øvre Rendal N . . . . 199 D8
Øvre Sirdal N . . . . 52 B2
Övre Soppero S . . . 196 A4
Övre Ullerud S . . . 55 A4
Ovruch UA. . . . . . 13 C8
Ovtrup DK . . . . . . 59 C1
Owińska PL. . . . . . 76 B1
Oxaback S . . . . . . 60 B2
Oxberg S . . . . . . . 49 A6
Oxelösund S . . . . . 56 B3
Oxenholme GB . . . 37 B4
Oxford GB . . . . . . 44 B2
Oxie S . . . . . . . . 61 D3
Oxilithos GR. . . . . 185 A5
Oxted GB. . . . . . . 45 B4
Oyaca TR . . . . . . 187 C7
Øye N. . . . . . . . . 47 A5
Øyenkilen N. . . . . . 54 A1
Øyer N. . . . . . . . . 48 A2
Øyeren N . . . . . . . 49 B4
Øyfjell N. . . . . . . 53 A4
Øygärdslia N . . . . . 53 B4
Oykel Bridge GB . . 32 D2
Øymark N. . . . . . . 54 A2

Oyonnax F. . . . . . .118 A2
Øyslebø N . . . . . . 52 B3
Øystese N . . . . . . 46 B3
Oyten D . . . . . . . 72 A2
Øyuvsbu N. . . . . . 52 A3
Ozaeta E . . . . . . . 143 B4
Ozalj HR. . . . . . . . 123 B4
Ożarów PL. . . . . . 87 B5
Ożarów Maz PL. . . 77 B5
Ožbalt SLO . . . . . 110 C2
Ózd H. . . . . . . . . .113 A4
Ozieri I . . . . . . . . 178 B3
Ozimek PL. . . . . . 86 B2
Ozimica BIH. . . . . . 139 A4
Ozora H . . . . . . . 112 C2
Ozorków PL. . . . . . 77 C4
Ozzano Monferrato
 I. . . . . . . . . . . .119 B5

## P

Paakkola FIN . . . . 196 D7
Paal B. . . . . . . . . 79 A5
Pabianice PL . . . . . 86 A3
Pacanów PL. . . . . . 87 B5
Paceco I. . . . . . . . 176 B1
Pachino I . . . . . . . 177 C4
Paços de Ferreira
 P. . . . . . . . . . . 148 A1
Pacov CZ. . . . . . . 96 B3
Pacsa H. . . . . . . . 111 C4
Pacy-sur-Eure F . . 89 A5
Paczków PL. . . . . . 85 B5
Padany RUS . . . . . 3 E13
Padborg DK. . . . . . 64 B2
Padej SRB. . . . . . . 126 B2
Padene HR. . . . . . 138 A2
Paderborn D . . . . . 81 A4
Paderne P . . . . . . 160 B1
Padiham GB . . . . . 40 B1
Padina SRB. . . . . . 126 B2
Padinska Skela
 SRB . . . . . . . . . .127 C2
Padornelo P. . . . . . 148 A1
Pádova I . . . . . . . 121 B4
Padragkút H . . . . . .111 B4
Padria I . . . . . . . . 178 B2
Padrón E . . . . . . . 140 B2
Padru I . . . . . . . . 178 B3
Padstow GB . . . . . 42 B2
Padul E . . . . . . . . 163 A4
Padula I . . . . . . . 172 B1
Paduli I . . . . . . . . 170 B2
Paesana I . . . . . . . 119 C4
Paese I . . . . . . . . 121 B5
Pag HR . . . . . . . . 137 A4
Pagani I . . . . . . . 170 C2
Pagánica I. . . . . . . 169 A3
Pagánico I . . . . . . 135 C4
Pagl ieta I . . . . . . 169 A4
Pagny-sur-Moselle
 F. . . . . . . . . . . 92 C2
Páhi H . . . . . . . . 112 C3
Pahkakumpu FIN 197 C11
Pahl D . . . . . . . . 108 B2
Paide EST . . . . . . 8 C4
Paignton GB . . . . . 43 B3
Pailhès F . . . . . . . 146 A2
Paimboeuf F . . . . . 101 B3
Paimpol F . . . . . . 100 A2
Paimpont F . . . . . . 101 A3
Painswick GB . . . . 43 A4
Painten D . . . . . . 95 C3
Paisley GB. . . . . . 34 C3
Pajala S . . . . . . . 196 B6
Pajares E . . . . . . . 141 A5
Pajares de los Oteros
 E. . . . . . . . . . . 142 B1
Pajęczno PL. . . . . . 86 A2
Páka H . . . . . . . . .111 C3
Pakość PL . . . . . . 76 B3
Pakosławice PL. . . . 85 B5
Pakoštane HR . . . . 137 B4
Pakrac HR . . . . . . 124 B3
Paks H . . . . . . . . 112 C2
Palacios de la Sierra
 E. . . . . . . . . . . 143 C3
Palaciòs de la
 Valduerna E. . . . . 141 B5
Palacios del Sil E . . 141 B4
Palacios de Sanabria
 E. . . . . . . . . . . 141 B4
Palaciosrubios E. . . 150 A2
Palafrugell E . . . . . 147 C4
Palagiano I . . . . . . 173 B3
Palagonía I. . . . . . 177 B3
Paláia I. . . . . . . . 135 B3
Palaiokastritsa GR 182 D1
Palaiseau F . . . . . . 90 C2
Palamas GR. . . . . . 182 D4
Palamòs E . . . . . . 147 C4
Påläng S . . . . . . . 196 D5
Palanga LT. . . . . . 8 E2
Palanzano I . . . . . . 134 A3
Palárikovo SK . . . . 112 A2
Palas de Rei E . . . . 140 B3
Palata I . . . . . . . . 170 B2
Palau I . . . . . . . . 178 A3
Palavas-les-Flots F 131 B2
Palazuelos de la Sierra
 E. . . . . . . . . . . 143 B3
Palazzo Adriano I . . 176 B2
Palazzo del Pero I . . 135 B4

Palazzolo Acréide
 I. . . . . . . . . . . .177 B3
Palazzolo sull Oglio
 I. . . . . . . . . . . .120 B2
Palazzo San Gervásio
 I. . . . . . . . . . . .172 B1
Palazzuolo sul Senio
 I. . . . . . . . . . . .135 A4
Paldiski EST . . . . . 8 C4
Pale BIH . . . . . . . 139 B4
Palekastro GR. . . . 185 D7
Palena I . . . . . . . 169 B4
Palencia E . . . . . . 142 B2
Palenciana E . . . . . 163 A3
Paleochora GR . . . 185 D4
Paleometokho CY. 181 A2
Palermo I . . . . . . 176 A2
Paleros GR . . . . . . 182 E2
Palestrina I . . . . . . 169 B2
Pálfa H . . . . . . . . 112 C2
Palfau A . . . . . . . .110 B1
Palhaça P. . . . . . . 148 B1
Palheiros da Tocha
 P. . . . . . . . . . . 148 B1
Palheiros de Quiaios
 P. . . . . . . . . . . 148 B1
Paliaopoli GR . . . . 185 B5
Palić SRB. . . . . . . 126 A1
Palidoro I . . . . . . 168 B2
Palinuro I. . . . . . . 172 B1
Paliouri GR . . . . . 183 D5
Paliseul B. . . . . . . 91 B5
Pallanza I. . . . . . . .119 B5
Pallares E . . . . . . 161 A3
Pallaruelo de Monegros
 E. . . . . . . . . . . 153 A3
Pallas Green IRL . . 29 B3
Pallerols E. . . . . . . 146 B2
Palling D . . . . . . . 109 A3
Palluau F. . . . . . . .114 B2
Palma P . . . . . . . 154 C2
Palma Campánia I. 170 C2
Palma del Río E. . . 162 A2
Palma de Mallorca
 E. . . . . . . . . . . 166 B2
Palma di Montechiaro
 I. . . . . . . . . . . .176 B2
Palmádula I . . . . . 178 B2
Palmanova I . . . . . 122 B2
Palma Nova E . . . . 166 B2
Palmela P. . . . . . . 154 C2
Palmerola E . . . . . 147 B3
Palmi I . . . . . . . . 175 C1
Pälmonostora H . . 113 C3
Palo del Colle I . . . 171 B4
Palojärvi FIN . . . . 192 D7
Palojoensuu FIN . . 196 A6
Palomares E . . . . . 164 B3
Palomares del Campo
 E. . . . . . . . . . . 158 B1
Palomas E . . . . . . 156 B1
Palombara Sabina
 I. . . . . . . . . . . 168 A2
Palos de la Frontera
 E. . . . . . . . . . . 161 B3
Palotaboszok H. . . 125 A4
Palotás H . . . . . . .112 B3
Pals E . . . . . . . . 147 C4
Pålsboda S . . . . . . 56 A1
Paluzza I . . . . . . . 109 C4
Pamhagen A . . . . . .111 B3
Pamiers F . . . . . . 146 A2
Pamiętowo PL . . . . 76 A2
Pampaneira E . . . . 163 B4
Pamparato I . . . . . 133 A3
Pampilhosa
 Aveiro P. . . . . . . 148 B1
 Coimbra P . . . . . . 148 B2
Pamplega E . . . . . 143 B3
Pamplona E . . . . . 144 B2
Pampow D. . . . . . 73 A4
Pamukçu TR . . . . . 186 C2
Pamukkale TR . . . . 188 B4
Pamukova TR . . . . 187 B5
Panagyurishte BG. 17 D6
Pancalieri I. . . . . . 119 C4
Pančevo SRB . . . . 127 C2
Pancey F. . . . . . . 91 C5
Pancorvo E . . . . . 143 B3
Pancrudo E . . . . . 152 B2
Pandino I. . . . . . . 120 B2
Pandrup DK. . . . . . 58 A2
Panenský-Týnec
 CZ. . . . . . . . . . 84 B1
Panes E . . . . . . . 142 A2
Panevėžys LT . . . . 8 E4
Pangbourne GB . . . 44 B2
Panissières F . . . . .117 B4
Panki PL. . . . . . . 86 B2
Pannes F . . . . . . . 103 A4
Panningen NL. . . . . 80 A1
Pannonhalma H . . .111 B4
Pano Lefkara CY. . . 181 B2
Pano Panayia CY . . 181 B1
Panormos GR . . . . 185 B6
Panschwitz-Kuckau
 D. . . . . . . . . . . 84 A2
Pansdorf D. . . . . . 65 C3
Pantano de Cijara
 E. . . . . . . . . . . 156 A3
Panticosa E . . . . . 145 B3
Pantín E . . . . . . . 140 A2
Pantoja E . . . . . . . 151 B4
Pantón E . . . . . . . 140 B3
Panxon E . . . . . . . 140 B2
Páola I . . . . . . . . 174 B2
Paola M . . . . . . . 175 C3
Pápa H . . . . . . . . .111 B4

Papasídero I . . . . . 174 B1
Pápateszér H . . . . . .111 B4
Papenburg D . . . . . 71 A4
Paphos CY . . . . . . 181 B1
Pappenheim D . . . . 94 C2
Paprotnia PL . . . . . 77 B5
Parábita I . . . . . . . 173 B4
Paracín SRB . . . . . 127 D3
Parád H . . . . . . . .113 A4
Parada
  Bragança P . . . .149 A3
  Viseu P . . . . . . 148 B1
Paradas E . . . . . . 162 A2
Paradela E . . . . . . 140 B3
Parades de Rubiales
  E . . . . . . . . . . 150 B2
Paradinas de San Juan
  E . . . . . . . . . . 150 B2
Paradiso di Cevadale
  I . . . . . . . . . . 108 C1
Paradyż PL . . . . . . 87 A4
Parainen FIN . . . . . 8 B3
Parakhino Paddubye
  RUS . . . . . . . . . . 9 C8
Parakka S . . . . . 196 B4
Paralimni CY . . . . . 181 A2
Parallo Astros GR . 184 B3
Paramé F . . . . . . . 88 B2
Paramithia GR . . . . 182 D2
Páramo E . . . . . . . 141 A4
Páramo del Sil E . . 141 A4
Parandaça P . . . . . 148 A2
Paravadella E . . . . 141 A3
Paray-le-Monial F . 104 C3
Parceiros P . . . . . 154 B2
Parcey F . . . . . . . 105 B4
Parchim D . . . . . . 73 A4
Parciaki PL . . . . . . 77 A6
Parcice PL . . . . . . 86 A2
Pardilla E . . . . . . 151 A4
Pardubice CZ . . . . 97 A3
Paredes
  E . . . . . . . . . .151 B5
  P . . . . . . . . . . 148 A1
Paredes de Coura
  P . . . . . . . . . . 140 C2
Paredes de Nava E 142 B2
Paredes de Siguenza
  E . . . . . . . . . . 151 A5
Pareja E . . . . . . . 151 B5
Parennes F . . . . . . 102 A1
Parenti I . . . . . . . 175 B2
Parentis-en-Born F 128 B1
Parey D . . . . . . . . 73 B4
Parfino RUS . . . . . . 9 D7
Parga GR . . . . . . 182 D2
Pargny-sur-Saulx F . 91 C4
Pari-Gagné F . . . . .117 A4
Parigné-l'Évêque
  F . . . . . . . . . . 102 B2
Parikkala FIN . . . . . 9 B6
Paris F . . . . . . . . 90 C2
Parisot F . . . . . . . 129 B4
Parkalompolo S . . 196 B6
Parkano FIN . . . . . . 8 A3
Parknasilla IRL . . . 29 C2
Parla E . . . . . . . 151 B4
Parlavá E . . . . . . 147 A4
Parma I . . . . . . . 120 C3
Parndorf A . . . . . .111 B3
Párnica SK . . . . . 99 B3
Parnu EST . . . . . . 8 C4
Parolis E . . . . . 164 A2
Paros GR . . . . . . 185 B6
Parrillas E . . . . . 150 B2
Parsberg D . . . . . 95 B3
Parstein D . . . . . . 74 B3
Partakko FIN . . . 193 C11
Partanna I . . . . . 176 B1
Parthenay F . . . . . 102 C1
Partinico I . . . . . 176 A2
Partizani SRB . . . . 127 C2
Partizánske SK . . . 98 C2
Partney GB . . . . . 41 B4
Páryd S . . . . . . . 63 B3
Parzymiechy PL . . 86 A2
Pașcani RO . . . . . 17 B7
Pasewalk D . . . . . 74 A2
Pašina Voda MNE . 139 B5
Páskallavik S . . . . 62 A4
Pasłęk PL . . . . . . 69 A4
Pašman HR . . . . . 137 B4
Passage East IRL . 30 B2
Passail A . . . . . . .110 B2
Passais F . . . . . . 88 B3
Passau D . . . . . . 96 C1
Passegueiro P . . . . 148 B1
Passignano sul
  Trasimeno I . . . 135 B5
Passo di Tréia I . . 136 B2
Passopisciaro I . . . 177 B4
Passow D . . . . . . 74 A3
Passy F . . . . . . . .118 B3
Pastavy BY . . . . . 13 A7
Pástena I . . . . . . 170 B2
Pastrana E . . . . . 151 B5
Pastrengo I . . . . . 121 B3
Pasym PL . . . . . . 77 A5
Pásztó H . . . . . . .113 B3
Pata SK . . . . . . . 98 C1
Patay F . . . . . . . 103 A3
Pateley Bridge GB. . 40 A2
Paterek PL . . . . . . 76 A2
Paterna E . . . . . . 159 B3
Paterna del Campo
  E . . . . . . . . . . 161 B3
Paterna del Madera
  E . . . . . . . . . . 158 C1

Paterna de Rivera
  E . . . . . . . . . . 162 B2
Paternion A . . . . . 109 C4
Paternò I . . . . . . 177 B3
Paternópoli I . . . . 170 C3
Patersdorf D . . . . . 95 B4
Paterswolde NL . . . 71 A3
Patitiri GR . . . . . . 183 D5
Patmos GR . . . . . 188 B1
Patna GB . . . . . . 36 A2
Pątnow PL . . . . . . 76 B3
Patoniva FIN . . . 193 C11
Patopirtti FIN . . . 197 B12
Patos AL. . . . . . . 182 C1
Patra = Patras GR . 184 A2
Patras = Patra GR . 184 A2
Patreksfjörður IS . . 190 B2
Patrickswell IRL . . 29 B3
Patrimonio F . . . . 180 A2
Patrington GB . . . . 41 B3
Pattada I . . . . . . . 178 B3
Pattensen
  Niedersachsen D . . .72 A3
  Niedersachsen D . . .72 B2
Patterdale GB . . . . 36 B4
Patti I . . . . . . . . 177 A3
Páty H . . . . . . . . .112 B2
Pau F . . . . . . . . 145 A3
Pauillac F . . . . . . 128 A2
Paularo I . . . . . . 109 C4
Paulhaguet F . . . . .117 B3
Paulhan F . . . . . . 130 B2
Paulilátino I . . . . . 178 B2
Pauliström S . . . . . 62 A3
Paullo I . . . . . . . 120 B2
Paulstown IRL . . . . 30 B1
Pausa D . . . . . . . 83 B3
Pauträsk S . . . . . 200 B3
Pavia
  I . . . . . . . . . . .120 B2
  P . . . . . . . . . . .154 C2
Pavias E . . . . . . . 159 B3
Pavilly F . . . . . . . 89 A4
Păvilosta LV . . . . . 8 D2
Pavullo nel Frignano
  I . . . . . . . . . . .135 A3
Pawłowice PL . . . . 86 A1
Pawlowice PL . . . . 98 B2
Paxi GR . . . . . . . 182 D2
Payallar TR . . . . . 189 C6
Payerne CH . . . . . 106 C1
Paymogo E . . . . . 161 B2
Payrac F . . . . . . . 129 B4
Pazardzhik BG . . . 183 A6
Pazaryeri TR . . . . 187 B4
Pazin HR . . . . . . 122 B2
Paziols F . . . . . . 146 B3
Pčelić HR . . . . . . 124 B3
Peal de Becerro E . 164 B1
Peasmarsh GB . . . 45 C4
Peć KOS. . . . . . . 16 D4
Péccioli I . . . . . . 135 B3
Pécel H. . . . . . . .112 B3
Pechao P . . . . . . 160 B2
Pechenga RUS . . . 3 B12
Pechenizhyn UA . . 13 D6
Pecica RO . . . . . 126 A3
Pećinci SRB. . . . . 127 C1
Pecka SRB. . . . . . 127 C1
Peckelsheim D . . . 81 A5
Pečory RUS . . . . . 8 D5
Pécs H . . . . . . . 125 A4
Pécsvárad H . . . . 125 A4
Peczniew PL . . . . . 86 A2
Pedaso I . . . . . . . 136 B2
Pedavena I . . . . . 121 A4
Pedérobba I . . . . . 121 B4
Pedersker DK . . . . 67 A3
Pedescala I . . . . . 121 B4
Pedrafita E . . . . . 141 B3
Pedrajas de San
  Esteban E . . . . 150 A3
Pedralba E . . . . . 159 B3
Pedralba de la Pradería
  E . . . . . . . . . . 141 B4
Pedraza E . . . . . . 151 A4
Pedreguer E . . . . . 159 C4
Pedrera E . . . . . . 162 A3
Pedro Abad E . . . . 157 C3
Pedro Bernardo E . 150 B3
Pedroche E . . . . . 156 B3
Pedrógao P . . . . . 160 A2
Pedrogao P . . . . . 149 B2
Pedrógão P . . . . . 154 B2
Pedrógão Grande
  P . . . . . . . . . . .154 B2
Pedrola E . . . . . . 144 C2
Pedro-Martínez E . 164 B1
Pedro Muñoz E . . . 158 B1
Pedrosa del Rey E . 150 A2
Pedrosa del Rio Urbel
  E . . . . . . . . . . 143 B3
Pedrosa de Tobalina
  E . . . . . . . . . . 143 B3
Pedrosillo de los Aires
  E . . . . . . . . . . 150 B2
Pedrosillo el Ralo
  E . . . . . . . . . . 150 B2
Pędzewo PL . . . . . 76 A3
Peebles GB . . . . . 35 C4
Peel GB . . . . . . . 36 B2
Peenemünde D . . . 66 B2
Peer B . . . . . . . . 79 A5
Pega P . . . . . . . 149 B2
Pegalajar E . . . . . 163 A4
Pegau D . . . . . . . 83 A4
Peggau A . . . . . . .110 B2
Pegli I . . . . . . . . 133 A4

Pegnitz D . . . . . . 95 B3
Pego E . . . . . . . 159 C3
Pegões-Estação P . 154 C2
Pegões Velhos P . . 154 C2
Pegów PL. . . . . . 85 A4
Pegswood GB . . . . 37 A5
Peguera E . . . . . 166 B2
Pehlivanköy TR . . . 186 A1
Peine D . . . . . . . 72 B3
Peisey-Nancroix F .118 B3
Peissenberg D. . . 108 B2
Peiting D . . . . . . 108 B1
Peitz D . . . . . . . 84 A2
Péjo I . . . . . . . . 121 A3
Pelagićevo BIH . . . 125 C4
Pelahustán E . . . . 150 B3
Pełczyce PL . . . . . 75 A4
Pelkosenniemi
  FIN . . . . . . . . . 197 B10
Pellegrino Parmense
  I . . . . . . . . . . . 120 C2
Pellegrue F . . . . . 128 B3
Pellérd H . . . . . . 125 A4
Pellestrina I . . . . . 122 B1
Pellevoisin F . . . . 103 C3
Pellizzano I . . . . . 121 A3
Pello
  FIN . . . . . . . . . .196 C7
  S . . . . . . . . . . .196 C6
Peloche E . . . . . . 156 A2
Pelplin PL . . . . . . 69 B3
Pelussin F . . . . . .117 B4
Pély H . . . . . . . .113 B4
Pembroke GB . . . . 39 C2
Pembroke Dock GB 39 C2
Peñacerrada E . . . 143 B4
Penacova P . . . . . 148 B1
Peña de Cabra E . . 149 B4
Peñafiel E . . . . . . 151 A3
Penafiel P . . . . . . 148 A1
Peñaflor E . . . . . . 162 A2
Peñalba de Santiago
  E . . . . . . . . . . 141 B4
Peñalsordo E. . . . 156 B2
Penalva do Castelo
  P . . . . . . . . . . 148 B2
Penamacôr P . . . . 149 B2
Peñaparda E . . . . 149 B3
Peñaranda de
  Bracamonte E . . 150 B2
Peñaranda de Duero
  E . . . . . . . . . . 143 C3
Peñarroya de Tastavins
  E . . . . . . . . . . 153 B4
Peñarroya-Pueblonuevo
  E . . . . . . . . . . 156 B2
Peñarrubia E . . . . 141 B3
Penarth GB . . . . . 39 C3
Peñascosa E . . . . 158 C1
Peñas de San Pedro
  E . . . . . . . . . . 158 C2
Peñausende E. . . . 149 A4
Penc H . . . . . . . .112 B3
Pencoed GB . . . . . 39 C3
Pendalofos GR . . . 182 C3
Pendeen GB . . . . . 42 B1
Pendine GB . . . . . 39 C2
Pendueles E . . . . 142 A2
Penedono P . . . . . 148 B2
Penela P . . . . . . 154 A2
Pénestin F . . . . . 101 B3
Penhas Juntas P . . 149 A2
Peniche P. . . . . . 154 B1
Penicuik GB . . . . . 35 C4
Penig D . . . . . . . 83 B4
Penilhos P . . . . . 160 B2
Penkridge GB . . . . 40 C1
Penkun D . . . . . . 74 A3
Penmarch F . . . . . 100 B1
Pennabilli I . . . . . 135 B5
Penne I . . . . . . . 169 A3
Penne-d'Agenais F 129 B3
Pennes I . . . . . . 108 C2
Pennyghael GB . . . 34 B1
Peno RUS . . . . . . 9 D8
Penpont GB . . . . . 36 A3
Penrhyndeudraeth
  GB . . . . . . . . . . 38 B2
Penrith GB. . . . . . 37 B4
Penryn GB . . . . . . 42 B1
Pentraeth GB. . . . . 38 A2
Penybontfawr GB . . 38 B3
Penygroes
  Carmarthenshire
  GB . . . . . . . . . . .39 C2
  Gwynedd GB . . . .38 A2
Penzance GB . . . . 42 B1
Penzberg D . . . . . 108 B2
Penzlin D . . . . . . 74 A2
Pepinster B . . . . . 80 B1
Peqin AL. . . . . . . 182 B1
Pér H . . . . . . . . .111 B4
Pera Boa P. . . . . 148 B2
Perachora GR . . . . 184 A3
Perafita P. . . . . . 148 A1
Peraleda de la Mata
  E . . . . . . . . . . 150 C2
Peraleda del Zaucejo
  E . . . . . . . . . . 156 B2
Peraleda de San Román
  E . . . . . . . . . . 156 A2
Perales de Alfambra
  E . . . . . . . . . . 152 B2

Perales del Puerto
  E . . . . . . . . . . 149 B3
Perales de Tajuña
  E . . . . . . . . . . 151 B4
Peralta E . . . . . . 144 B2
Peralta de la Sal E . 145 C4
Peralva P . . . . . . 160 B2
Peralveche E . . . . 152 B1
Perama GR . . . . . 185 D5
Peranka FIN. . . . . 197 D12
Perbál H . . . . . . .112 B2
Perchtoldsdorf A . .111 A3
Percy F . . . . . . . 88 B2
Perdasdefogu I . . . 179 C3
Perdiguera E . . . . 145 C3
Peredo P . . . . . . 149 A3
Peregu Mare RO . . 126 A2
Pereiro
  Faro P . . . . . . .160 B2
  Guarda P . . . . .149 B2
  Santarém P . . . .154 B2
Pereiro de Aguiar
  E . . . . . . . . . . 140 B3
Perelada E . . . . . 147 B4
Perelejos de las Truchas
  E . . . . . . . . . . 152 B2
Pereña E . . . . . . 149 A3
Pereruela E . . . . . 149 A4
Pérfugas I . . . . . . 178 B2
Perg A . . . . . . . .110 A1
Pérgine Valsugana
  I . . . . . . . . . . . 121 A4
Pérgola I . . . . . . 136 B1
Pergusa I . . . . . . 177 B3
Periam RO . . . . . 126 A2
Periana E . . . . . . 163 B3
Périers F . . . . . . 88 A2
Périgueux F . . . . . 129 A3
Perino I . . . . . . . 120 C2
Perjasica HR . . . . 123 B4
Perkáta H . . . . . . .112 B2
Perković HR . . . . . 138 B2
Perleberg D . . . . . 73 A4
Perlez SRB. . . . . . 126 B2
Përmet AL . . . . . . 182 C2
Pernarec CZ . . . . . 95 B5
Pernek SK . . . . . . 98 C1
Pernes P . . . . . . 154 B2
Pernes-les-Fontaines
  F. . . . . . . . . . . 131 A4
Pernik BG . . . . . . 17 D5
Pernink CZ. . . . . . 83 B4
Pernitz A. . . . . . . .110 B2
Pernu FIN. . . . . . 197 C10
Peroguarda P . . . 160 A1
Pérols F . . . . . . . 131 B2
Péronne F . . . . . . 90 B2
Péronnes B . . . . . 79 B4
Pero Pinheiro P . . . 154 C1
Perorrubio E . . . . 151 A4
Perosa Argentina I 119 C4
Perozinho P . . . . . 148 A1
Perpignan F . . . . . 146 B3
Perranporth GB. . . 42 B1
Perranzabuloe GB. . 42 B1
Perrecy-les-Forges
  F. . . . . . . . . . . 104 C3
Perrero I . . . . . . 119 C4
Perrignier F . . . . . .118 A3
Perros-Guirec F . . 100 A2
Persan F . . . . . . 90 B2
Persberg S . . . . . 55 A5
Persenbeug A . . . . .110 A2
Pershore GB . . . . 44 A1
Persön S . . . . . . 196 D5
Perstorp S . . . . . 61 C3
Perth GB . . . . . . 35 B4
Pertisau A . . . . . . 108 B2
Pertoča SLO . . . . .111 C3
Pertuis F . . . . . . 131 B4
Perúcac SRB . . . . 127 D1
Perúgia I . . . . . . 136 B1
Perušić HR . . . . . 123 C4
Péruwelz B . . . . . 79 B3
Perwez B . . . . . . 79 B4
Pesadas de Burgos
  E . . . . . . . . . . 143 B3
Pesaguero E . . . . 142 A2
Pésaro I . . . . . . . 136 B1
Pescantina I . . . . . 121 B3
Pescara I . . . . . . 169 A4
Pescasséroli I . . . 169 B3
Peschici I . . . . . . 171 B4
Peschiera del Garda
  I . . . . . . . . . . . 121 B3
Péscia I . . . . . . . 135 B3
Pescina I . . . . . . 169 A3
Pescocostanzo I . . 169 B4
Pescopagano I . . . 172 B1
Pesco Sannita I . . 170 B2
Peshkopi AL. . . . . 182 B2
Peshtera BG . . . . 183 A6
Pesmes F . . . . . . 105 B4
Pesnica SLO . . . . 110 C2
Peso da Régua P . . 148 A2
Pesquera de Duero
  E . . . . . . . . . . 142 C2
Pessac F . . . . . . 128 B2
Pestovo RUS. . . . . 9 C9
Petäjäskoski FIN. . . 197 C8
Petalidi GR . . . . . 184 C2
Pétange L. . . . . . 92 B1
Petas GR . . . . . . 182 D3
Peteranec HR . . . . 124 A2
Peterborough GB . . 41 C3
Peterculter GB. . . . 33 D4
Peterhead GB . . . . 33 D5

Peterlee GB . . . . . 37 B5
Petersfield GB. . . . 44 B3
Petershagen
  Brandenburg D . . .74 B2
  Brandenburg D . . . .74 B3
  Nordrhein-Westfalen
  D. . . . . . . . . . . .72 B1
Petershausen D . . . 95 C3
Peterswell IRL . . . 28 A3
Pétervására H . . . .113 A4
Petília Policastro I . 175 B2
Petín E . . . . . . . 141 B3
Pětipsy CZ. . . . . . 83 B5
Petkus D . . . . . . 74 C2
Petlovac HR. . . . . 125 B4
Petlovača SRB . . . 127 C1
Petöfiszallás H . . . 113 C3
Petra I . . . . . . . 167 B3
Petralia Sottana I . . 177 B3
Petrčane HR . . . . . 137 A4
Petrella Tifernina I . 170 B2
Petrer E . . . . . . . 159 C3
Petreto-Bicchisano
  F. . . . . . . . . . . 180 B1
Petrich BG . . . . . 183 B5
Petrijevci HR . . . . 125 B4
Petrinja HR . . . . . 124 B2
Petrodvorets RUS . . 9 C6
Pétrola E . . . . . . 158 C2
Petronà I . . . . . . 175 B2
Petronell A. . . . . . .111 A3
Petroşani RO. . . . . 17 C5
Petrovac SRB . . . . 127 C3
Petrovaradin SRB . 126 B1
Petrovice
  BIH . . . . . . . . . . 139 A4
  CZ. . . . . . . . . . .84 B1
Petrovo RUS . . . . . 69 A5
Petrozavodsk RUS . . 9 B9
Pettenbach A . . . . 109 B5
Pettigo IRL . . . . . 26 B3
Petworth GB . . . . 44 C3
Peuerbach A . . . . 96 C1
Peuntenansa E . . . 142 A2
Peurasuvanto FIN . 197 B9
Pevensey Bay GB . 45 C4
Pewsey GB . . . . . 44 B2
Pewsum D . . . . . 71 A4
Peyrat-le-Château
  F. . . . . . . . . . . .116 B1
Peyrehorade F . . . 128 C1
Peyriac-Minervois
  F. . . . . . . . . . . 146 A3
Peyrins F . . . . . . .117 B5
Peyrissac F . . . . . .116 B1
Peyrolles-en-Provence
  F. . . . . . . . . . . 132 B1
Peyruis F . . . . . . 132 A1
Pézarches F . . . . . 90 C2
Pézenas F . . . . . . 130 B2
Pezinok SK . . . . . .111 A4
Pezuls F . . . . . . . 129 B3
Pfaffenhausen D . . 108 A1
Pfaffenhofen
  Bayern D . . . . . .94 C2
  Bayern D . . . . . .95 C3
Pfaffenhoffen F . . . 93 C3
Pfäffikon CH . . . . 107 B3
Pfarrkirchen D . . . 95 C4
Pfeffenhausen D . . 95 C3
Pfetterhouse F . . . 106 B2
Pforzheim D . . . . 93 C4
Pfreimd D . . . . . . 95 B4
Pfronten D . . . . . 108 B1
Pfullendorf D. . . . . 107 B4
Pfullingen D . . . . . 94 C1
Pfunds A . . . . . . 108 C1
Pfungstadt D . . . . 93 B4
Pfyn CH . . . . . . . 107 B3
Phalsbourg F. . . . . 92 C3
Philippeville B . . . . 79 B4
Philippsreut D . . . . 96 C1
Philippsthal D . . . . 82 B1
Piacenza I . . . . . 120 B2
Piacenza d'Adige I 121 B4
Piádena I . . . . . . 120 B3
Piana F . . . . . . . 180 A1
Piana Crixia I . . . . 133 A4
Piana degli Albanesi
  I . . . . . . . . . . . 176 B2
Piana di Monte Verna
  I . . . . . . . . . . . 170 B2
Piancastagnáio I . . 135 C4
Piandelagotti I . . . 134 A3
Pianella
  Abruzzi I . . . . . .169 A4
  Toscana I . . . . .135 B4
Pianello Val Tidone
  I . . . . . . . . . . . 120 C2
Pianoro I . . . . . . 135 A4
Pians A . . . . . . . 108 B1
Pías E . . . . . . . . 141 B4
Pias P . . . . . . . . 160 A2
Piaseczno PL . . . . 77 B6
Piasek PL . . . . . . 74 B3
Piaski PL . . . . . . 69 A4
Piastów PL . . . . . 77 B5
Piaszcyna PL. . . . . 68 A2
Piątek PL . . . . . . 77 B4
Piatra Neamţ RO . . 17 B7
Piazza al Sérchio I . 134 A3
Piazza Armerina I . 177 B3
Piazza Brembana I 120 B2
Piazze I . . . . . . . 135 C4
Piazzola sul Brenta
  I . . . . . . . . . . . 121 B4
Picassent E . . . . . 159 B3

Piccione I . . . . . . 136 B1
Picerno I . . . . . . 172 B1
Picher D. . . . . . . 73 A4
Pickering GB . . . . 40 A3
Pico I . . . . . . . . 169 B3
Picón E . . . . . . . 157 A3
Picquigny F . . . . . 90 B2
Piechowice PL. . . . 84 B3
Piecnik PL . . . . . 75 A5
Piedicavallo I. . . . .119 B4
Piedicroce F . . . . 180 A2
Piedimonte Etneo I 177 B4
Piedimonte Matese
  I . . . . . . . . . . . 170 B2
Piedimulera I. . . . .119 A5
Piedipaterno I . . . . 136 C1
Piedrabuena E . . . 157 A3
Piedraescrita E . . . 156 A3
Piedrafita E . . . . . 142 A1
Piedrahita E . . . . . 150 B2
Piedralaves E . . . . 150 B3
Piedras Albas E. . . 155 B3
Piedras Blancas E . 141 A5
Piegaro I . . . . . . 135 C5
Piekary ŚI. PL . . . . 86 B2
Piekoszów PL. . . . . 87 B4
Pieksämäki FIN . . . 8 A5
Pielenhofen D . . . . 95 B3
Pielgrzymka PL. . . 85 A3
Pieniężno PL . . . . 69 A5
Pieńsk PL. . . . . . 84 A3
Pienza I . . . . . . . 135 B4
Piera E . . . . . . . 147 C2
Pieranie PL . . . . . 76 B3
Pierowall GB . . . . 33 B4
Pierre-Buffière F . . 115 C5
Pierrecourt F . . . . 105 B4
Pierre-de-Bresse F 105 C4
Pierrefeu-du-Var F 132 B2
Pierrefitte-Nestalas
  F. . . . . . . . . . . 145 B3
Pierrefitte-sur-Aire
  F. . . . . . . . . . . . 92 C1
Pierrefonds F . . . . 90 B2
Pierrefontaine-les-
  Varans F . . . . . 105 B5
Pierrefort F . . . . . 116 C2
Pierrelatte F . . . . 131 A3
Pierrepont
  Aisne F. . . . . . .91 B3
  Meurthe-et-Moselle
  F. . . . . . . . . . . .92 B1
Piesendorf A . . . . 109 B3
Piešťany SK . . . . . 98 C1
Pieszkowo PL . . . . 69 A5
Pieszyce PL. . . . . 85 B4
Pietarsaari FIN . . . 3 E8
Pietragalla I . . . . . 172 B1
Pietra Ligure I . . . 133 A4
Pietralunga I . . . . 136 B1
Pietramelara I . . . 170 B2
Pietraperzía I . . . . 177 B3
Pietrasanta I . . . . 134 B3
Pietravairano I . . . 170 B2
Pieve del Cáiro I . . 120 B1
Pieve di Bono I . . . 121 B3
Pieve di Cadore I . 122 A1
Pieve di Cento I . . 121 C4
Pieve di Solígo I . . 121 B5
Pieve di Teco I . . . 133 A3
Pievepélago I . . . . 134 A3
Pieve Santo Stefano
  I . . . . . . . . . . . 135 B5
Pieve Torina I . . . . 136 B2
Piges GR . . . . . . 182 D3
Píglio I . . . . . . . 169 B3
Pigna I . . . . . . . 133 B3
Pignan F . . . . . . 130 B2
Pignataro Maggiore
  I . . . . . . . . . . . 170 B2
Piittisjärvi FIN . . . . 197 C9
Pijnacker NL . . . . 70 B1
Pikalevo RUS . . . . 9 C9
Piła PL . . . . . . . 75 A5
Pilar de la Horadada
  E . . . . . . . . . . 165 B4
Pilas E . . . . . . . 161 B3
Pilastri I . . . . . . . 121 C4
Piława Górna PL . . 85 B4
Piławki PL . . . . . . 69 B4
Pilchowice PL . . . . 86 B2
Pilea GR. . . . . . . 183 C5
Pilgrimstad S. . . . 199 C12
Pili
  Dodekanisa GR . . .188 C2
  Trikala GR . . . . .182 D3
Pilica PL . . . . . . . 86 B3
Pilis H. . . . . . . . .112 B3
Piliscaba H . . . . . .112 B2
Pilisszántó H . . . . .112 B2
Pilisvörösvár H . . . .112 B2
Pilos GR. . . . . . . 184 C2
Pilsting D . . . . . . 95 C4
Pilszcz PL . . . . . . 98 A1
Pilterud N. . . . . . 48 C2
Pilu RO. . . . . . . 113 C5
Pina de Ebro E . . . 153 A3
Piñar E . . . . . . . 163 A4
Pınarbaşı TR . . . . 186 C1
Pınarhisar TR . . . . 186 A2
Pinas F . . . . . . . 145 A4
Pincehely H. . . . . 112 C2
Pinchbeck GB . . . . 41 C3
Pińczów PL. . . . . . 87 B4

Pineda de la Sierra E . . . 143 B3
Pineda de Mar E . 147 C3
Pinerella I . . . 135 A5
Pinerolo I . . . 119 C4
Pineta Grande I . . 170 C1
Pineto I . . . 169 A4
Piney F . . . 91 C4
Pinggau A . . . 111 B3
Pinhal Novo P . . 154 C2
Pinhão P . . . 148 A2
Pinheiro
  *Aveiro* P . . . 148 A1
  *Aveiro* P . . . 148 B1
Pinheiro Grande P 154 B2
Pinhel P . . . 149 B2
Pinhoe GB . . . 43 B3
Pinilla E . . . 158 C2
Pinilla de Toro E . 150 A2
Pinkafeld A . . . 111 B3
Pinneberg D . . . 72 A2
Pinnow D . . . 74 C3
Pino F . . . 180 A2
Pino del Rio E . . 142 B2
Pino de Val E . . 140 B2
Pinofranqueado E . 149 B3
Pinols F . . . 117 B3
Piñor E . . . 140 B2
Pinos del Valle E . 163 B4
Pinoso E . . . 159 C2
Pinos Puente E . . 163 A4
Pinsk BY . . . 13 B7
Pintamo FIN . . . 197 D10
Pinto E . . . 151 B4
Pinzano al Tagliamento I . . . 122 A1
Pinzio P . . . 149 B2
Pinzolo I . . . 121 A3
Pióbbico I . . . 136 B1
Piombino I . . . 134 C3
Pionki PL . . . 87 A5
Pionsat F . . . 116 A2
Pióraco I . . . 136 B1
Piornal E . . . 150 B2
Piotrkowice PL . . 87 B4
Piotrków-Kujawski PL . . . 76 B3
Piotrków Trybunalski PL . . . 86 A3
Piotrowo PL . . . 75 B5
Piove di Sacco I . 121 B5
Piovene I . . . 121 B4
Piperskärr S . . . 62 A4
Pipriac F . . . 101 B4
Piraeus = Pireas GR . . . 185 B4
Piran SLO . . . 122 B2
Pireas = Piraeus GR . . . 185 B4
Piré-sur-Seiche F . 101 A4
Pirgi GR . . . 185 A6
Pirgos
  *Ilia* GR . . . 184 B2
  *Kriti* GR . . . 185 D6
Piriac-sur-Mer F . 101 B3
Piringsdorf A . . . 111 B3
Pirmasens D . . . 93 B3
Pirna D . . . 84 B1
Pirnmill GB . . . 34 C2
Pirot SRB . . . 16 D5
Pirovac HR . . . 137 B4
Pirttivuopio S . . 196 B2
Pisa I . . . 134 B3
Pisany F . . . 114 C3
Pisarovina HR . . . 124 B1
Pischelsdorf in der Steiermark A . . . 110 B2
Pişchia RO . . . 126 B3
Pisciotta I . . . 172 B1
Písek CZ . . . 96 B2
Pisogne I . . . 120 B3
Pissos F . . . 128 B2
Pissouri CY . . . 181 B1
Pisticci I . . . 174 A2
Pistóia I . . . 135 B3
Piteå S . . . 196 D4
Pitești RO . . . 17 C6
Pithiviers F . . . 103 A4
Pitigliano I . . . 168 A1
Pitkyaranta RUS . . 9 B7
Pitlochry GB . . . 35 B4
Pitomača HR . . . 124 B3
Pitres E . . . 163 B4
Pittentrail GB . . . 32 D2
Pitvaros H . . . 126 A2
Pivka SLO . . . 123 B3
Pivnice SRB . . . 126 B1
Piwniczna PL . . . 99 B4
Pizarra E . . . 163 B3
Pizzano I . . . 121 A3
Pizzighettone I . . 120 B2
Pizzo I . . . 175 C2
Pízzoli I . . . 169 A3
Pizzolungo I . . . 176 A1
Pjätteryd S . . . 61 C4
Plabennec F . . . 100 A1
Placencia E . . . 143 A4
Plaffeien CH . . . 106 C2
Plaisance
  *Gers* F . . . 128 C3
  *Haute-Garonne* F . 129 C4
  *Tarn* F . . . 130 B1
Plaka GR . . . 183 D7
Plan E . . . 145 B4
Planá CZ . . . 95 B4

Planánad Lužnici CZ . . . 96 B2
Plaňany CZ . . . 96 A3
Planchez F . . . 104 B3
Plancoët F . . . 101 A3
Plancy-l'Abbaye F . 91 C3
Plan-de-Baix F . . 118 C2
Plandište SRB . . . 126 B3
Plan-d'Orgon F . . 131 B3
Plánice CZ . . . 96 B1
Planina
  SLO . . . 123 A4
  SLO . . . 123 B3
Plankenfels D . . . 95 B3
Plasencia E . . . 149 B3
Plasenzuela E . . . 156 A1
Plaški HR . . . 123 B4
Plassen
  *Buskerud* N . . . 47 B4
  *Hedmark* N . . . 49 A4
Plášťovce SK . . . 112 A3
Plasy CZ . . . 96 B1
Platamona Lido I . 178 B2
Platania I . . . 175 B2
Platanos GR . . . 185 D4
Platí I . . . 175 C2
Platičevo SRB . . . 127 C1
Platja d'Aro E . . 147 C4
Plattling D . . . 95 C4
Plau D . . . 73 A5
Plaue
  *Brandenburg* D . . 73 B5
  *Thüringen* D . . . 82 B2
Plauen D . . . 83 B4
Plavecký Mikuláš SK . . . 98 C1
Plavinas LV . . . 8 D4
Plavna SRB . . . 125 B5
Plavnica SK . . . 99 B4
Plavno HR . . . 138 A2
Playben F . . . 100 A2
Pléaux F . . . 116 B2
Pleine-Fougères F . 88 B2
Pleinfeld D . . . 94 B2
Pleinting D . . . 95 C5
Plélan-le-Grand F . 101 B3
Plémet F . . . 101 A3
Pléneuf-Val-André F . . . 101 A3
Plentzia E . . . 143 A4
Plérin F . . . 101 A3
Plešivec SK . . . 99 C4
Plessa D . . . 83 A5
Plessé F . . . 101 B4
Plestin-les-Grèves F . . . 100 A2
Pleszew PL . . . 76 C2
Pleternica HR . . . 125 B3
Plettenberg D . . . 81 A3
Pleubian F . . . 100 A2
Pleumartin F . . . 115 B4
Pleumeur-Bodou F 100 A2
Pleurs F . . . 91 C3
Pleven BG . . . 17 D6
Plevnik-Drienové SK . . . 98 B2
Pleyber-Christ F . . 100 A2
Pliego E . . . 165 B3
Pliešovce SK . . . 99 C3
Plitvička Jezera HR . . . 123 C4
Plitvički Ljeskovac HR . . . 123 C4
Ploaghe I . . . 178 B2
Ploče HR . . . 138 B3
Plochingen D . . . 94 C1
Płock PL . . . 77 B4
Ploemeur F . . . 100 B2
Ploërmel F . . . 101 B3
Ploeuc-sur-Lie F . 101 A3
Plogastel St Germain F . . . 100 B1
Plogoff F . . . 100 A1
Ploiești RO . . . 17 C7
Plomari GR . . . 186 D1
Plombières-les-Bains F . . . 105 B5
Plomin HR . . . 123 B3
Plön D . . . 65 B3
Plonéour-Lanvern F . . . 100 B1
Płonia PL . . . 74 A3
Płoniawy PL . . . 77 B6
Płońsk PL . . . 77 B5
Płoskinia PL . . . 69 A4
Plössberg D . . . 95 B4
Płoty PL . . . 67 C4
Plouagat F . . . 100 A2
Plouaret F . . . 100 A2
Plouarzel F . . . 100 A1
Plouay F . . . 100 B2
Ploubalay F . . . 101 A3
Ploubazlanec F . . 100 A2
Ploudalmézeau F . 100 A1
Ploudiry F . . . 100 A1
Plouescat F . . . 100 A1
Plouézec F . . . 100 A3
Plougasnou F . . . 100 A2
Plougastel-Daoulas F . . . 100 A1
Plougonven F . . . 100 A2
Plougonver F . . . 100 A2
Plougrescant F . . 100 A2
Plouguenast F . . . 101 A3
Plouguerneau F . . 100 A1
Plouha F . . . 100 A3
Plouhinec F . . . 100 A1
Plouigneau F . . . 100 A2

Ploumanach F . . . 100 A2
Plounévez-Quintin F . . . 100 A2
Plouray F . . . 100 A2
Plouzévédé F . . . 100 A1
Plozévet F . . . 100 B1
Plumbridge GB . . 27 B3
Pluméliau F . . . 100 B3
Plumlov CZ . . . 97 B5
Plungė LT . . . 8 E2
Pluty PL . . . 69 A5
Pluvigner F . . . 100 B3
Plužine
  BIH . . . 139 B4
  MNE . . . 139 B4
Pluznica PL . . . 69 B3
Plymouth GB . . . 42 B2
Plymstock GB . . . 42 B2
Plytnica PL . . . 68 B1
Plyusa RUS . . . 9 C6
Plzeň CZ . . . 96 B1
Pniewy PL . . . 75 B5
Pobes E . . . 143 B4
Poběžovice CZ . . 95 B4
Pobiedziska PL . . 76 B2
Pobierowo PL . . . 67 B3
Pobla de Segur E . 145 B4
Pobladura del Valle E . . . 142 B1
Pobla-Tornesa E . . 153 B4
Pobra de Trives E . 141 B3
Pobra do Brollón E . . . 141 B3
Pobra do Caramiñal E . . . 140 B2
Pobudje BIH . . . 139 A5
Počátky CZ . . . 97 B3
Poceirão P . . . 154 C2
Pöchlarn A . . . 110 A2
Pociecha PL . . . 87 A4
Pockau D . . . 83 B5
Pocking D . . . 96 C1
Pocklington GB . . 40 B3
Podbořany CZ . . . 83 B5
Podbrdo SLO . . . 122 A2
Podbrezová SK . . 99 C3
Podčetrtek SLO . . 123 A4
Poděbrady CZ . . . 84 B3
Podence P . . . 149 A3
Podensac F . . . 128 B2
Podenzano I . . . 120 C2
Podersdorf am See A . . . 111 B3
Podgaje PL . . . 68 B1
Podgora HR . . . 138 B3
Podgóra PL . . . 87 A5
Podgorač HR . . . 125 B4
Podgorica MNE . . 16 D3
Podgorie AL . . . 182 C2
Podgrad SLO . . . 123 B3
Podhájska SK . . . 112 A2
Podkova BG . . . 183 B7
Podlapača HR . . . 123 C4
Podlejki PL . . . 69 B5
Podlužany SK . . . 98 C2
Podnovlje BIH . . . 125 C4
Podolie SK . . . 98 C1
Podolínec SK . . . 99 B4
Podolsk RUS . . . 9 E10
Podporozhy RUS . . 9 B9
Podromanija BIH . . 139 B4
Podturen HR . . . 111 C3
Podvin CZ . . . 97 C4
Podwilk PL . . . 99 B3
Poetto I . . . 179 C3
Poggendorf D . . . 66 B2
Poggiardo I . . . 173 B4
Poggibonsi I . . . 135 B4
Póggio a Caiano I . 135 B4
Poggio Imperiale I . 171 B3
Póggio Mirteto I . . 168 A2
Póggio Moiano I . . 169 A2
Póggio Renatico I . 121 C4
Póggio Rusco I . . 121 C4
Pöggstall A . . . 97 C3
Pogny F . . . 91 C4
Pogorzela PL . . . 85 A5
Pogorzelice PL . . 68 A2
Pogradec AL . . . 182 C2
Pogrodzie PL . . . 69 A4
Pohorelá SK . . . 99 C4
Pohořelice CZ . . . 97 C4
Pohronská Polhora SK . . . 99 C3
Poiares P . . . 148 B1
Poio E . . . 140 B2
Poirino I . . . 119 C4
Poisson F . . . 117 A4
Poissons F . . . 91 C5
Poissy F . . . 90 C2
Poitiers F . . . 115 B4
Poix-de-Picardie F . 90 B1
Poix-Terron F . . . 91 B4
Pokka FIN . . . 197 A8
Pokój PL . . . 86 B1
Pokupsko HR . . . 124 B1
Pol E . . . 141 A3
Pola RUS . . . 9 D7
Pola a Charra GB . 31 B1
Pola de Allande E . 141 A4
Pola de Laviana E . 142 A1
Pola de Lena E . . 141 A5
Pola de Siero E . . 142 A1
Pola de Somiedo E 141 A4
Polaincourt-et-Clairefontaine F . 105 B5

Połajewo PL . . . 75 B5
Polán E . . . 151 C3
Polanica-Zdrój PL . 85 B4
Połaniec PL . . . 87 B5
Polanów PL . . . 68 A1
Polatı TR . . . 187 C7
Polatsk BY . . . 13 A8
Polch D . . . 80 B3
Polcirkeln S . . . 196 C4
Pólczno PL . . . 68 A2
Połczyn-Zdrój PL . . 67 C5
Polegate GB . . . 45 C4
Poleñino E . . . 145 C3
Polesella I . . . 121 C4
Polessk RUS . . . 12 A4
Polgár H . . . 113 B5
Polgárdi H . . . 112 B2
Polhov Gradec SLO . . . 123 A3
Police PL . . . 74 A3
Police nad Metují CZ . . . 85 B4
Polichnitos GR . . . 186 C1
Polička CZ . . . 97 B4
Poličnik HR . . . 137 A4
Policoro I . . . 174 A2
Policzna PL . . . 87 A5
Poligiros GR . . . 183 C5
Polignano a Mare I 173 B3
Poligny F . . . 105 C4
Polis CY . . . 181 A1
Polístena I . . . 175 C2
Polizzi Generosa I . 176 B3
Poljana SRB . . . 127 C3
Poljanak HR . . . 123 C4
Poljčane SLO . . . 123 A4
Polje BIH . . . 125 C3
Poljice
  BIH . . . 138 A2
  BIH . . . 139 A4
Polkowice PL . . . 85 A4
Polla I . . . 172 B1
Pollas E . . . 150 A2
Pöllau A . . . 110 B2
Polleben D . . . 82 A3
Pollença E . . . 167 B3
Pollenfeld D . . . 95 C3
Polfoss N . . . 198 D4
Póllica I . . . 170 C3
Polminhac F . . . 116 C2
Polná CZ . . . 97 B3
Polna RUS . . . 8 C6
Polne PL . . . 75 A5
Polomka SK . . . 99 C3
Polonne UA . . . 13 C7
Polperro GB . . . 42 B2
Polruan GB . . . 42 B2
Pöls A . . . 110 B1
Polska Cerekiew PL 86 B2
Poltár SK . . . 99 C3
Põltsamaa EST . . . 8 C4
Polyarny RUS . . . 3 B13
Polyarnyye Zori RUS . . . 3 C13
Polzela SLO . . . 123 A4
Pomarance I . . . 135 B3
Pomarez F . . . 128 C2
Pomárico I . . . 172 B2
Pomáz H . . . 112 B3
Pombal P . . . 154 B2
Pomeroy GB . . . 27 B4
Pomézia I . . . 168 B2
Pommard F . . . 105 B3
Pommelsbrunn D . 95 B3
Pomonte I . . . 134 C3
Pomorie BG . . . 17 D7
Pomos CY . . . 181 A1
Pompei I . . . 170 C2
Pompey F . . . 92 C2
Pomposa I . . . 122 C1
Poncin F . . . 118 A2
Pondorf D . . . 95 C3
Ponferrada E . . . 141 B4
Poniec PL . . . 85 A4
Ponikva SLO . . . 123 A4
Poniky SK . . . 99 C3
Pons F . . . 114 C3
Ponsacco I . . . 134 B3
Pont I . . . 119 B4
Pont-a-Celles B . . 79 B4
Pontacq F . . . 145 A3
Pontailler-sur-Saône F . . . 105 B4
Pont-a-Marcq F . . 78 B3
Pont-à-Mousson F . 92 C2
Pontão P . . . 154 B2
Pontardawe GB . . 39 C3
Pontarddulais GB . 39 C2
Pontarion F . . . 116 B1
Pontarlier F . . . 105 C5
Pontassieve I . . . 135 B4
Pontaubault F . . . 88 B2
Pont-Audemer F . . 89 A4
Pontaumur F . . . 116 B2
Pont-Aven F . . . 100 B2
Pont Canavese I . . 119 B4
Pontcharra F . . . 118 B3
Pontcharra-sur-Turdine F . . . 117 B4
Pontchâteau F . . . 101 B3
Pont-Croix F . . . 100 A1
Pont-d'Ain F . . . 118 A2
Pont-de-Beauvoisin F . . . 118 B2
Pont-de-Buis-lès-Quimerch F . . . 100 A1
Pont-de-Chéruy F . 118 B2
Pont de Dore F . . 117 B3

Pont-de-Labeaume F . . . 117 C4
Pont-de-l'Arche F . 89 A5
Pont de Molins E . 147 B3
Pont-de-Roide F . . 106 B1
Pont-de-Salars F . . 130 A1
Pont-d'Espagne F . 145 B3
Pont de Suert E . . 145 B4
Pont-de-Vaux F . . 117 A4
Pont-de-Veyle F . . 117 A4
Pont d'Ouilly F . . 89 B3
Pont-du-Château F . . . 116 B3
Pont-du-Navoy F . . 105 C4
Ponte a Moriano I . 134 B3
Ponte Arche I . . . 121 A3
Ponteareas E . . . 140 B2
Pontebba I . . . 109 C4
Ponte Cáffaro I . . 121 B3
Pontecagnano I . . 170 C2
Ponte-Caldelas E . 140 B2
Ponteceso E . . . 140 A2
Pontecesures E . . 140 B2
Pontecorvo I . . . 169 B3
Ponte da Barca P . 148 A1
Pontedássio I . . . 133 B4
Pontedécimo I . . . 133 A4
Ponte de Lima P . . 148 A1
Ponte dell'Ólio I . . 120 C2
Pontedera I . . . 134 B3
Ponte de Sor P . . 154 B2
Pontedeume E . . . 140 A2
Ponte di Barbarano I . . . 121 B4
Ponte di Legno I . . 121 A3
Ponte di Nava I . . 133 A3
Ponte di Piave I . . 122 B1
Ponte Felcino I . . 136 B1
Pontefract GB . . . 40 B2
Ponte Gardena I . . 108 C2
Ponteginori I . . . 135 B3
Pontelagoscuro I . 121 C4
Ponteland GB . . . 37 A5
Pontelandolfo I . . 170 B2
Ponte-Leccia F . . 180 A2
Pontelongo I . . . 121 B5
Ponte nelle Alpi I . 122 A1
Pont-en-Royans F . 118 B2
Pontenure I . . . 120 C2
Pontenx-les-Forges F . . . 128 B1
Ponterwyd GB . . . 39 B3
Ponte San Giovanni I . . . 136 B1
Ponte San Pietro I . 120 B2
Pontevedra E . . . 140 B2
Pontevico I . . . 120 B3
Pont Farcy F . . . 88 B2
Pontfaverger-Moronvillers F . . 91 B4
Pontgibaud F . . . 116 B2
Ponticino I . . . 135 B4
Pontigny F . . . 104 B2
Pontijou F . . . 103 B3
Pontínia I . . . 169 B3
Pontinvrea I . . . 133 A4
Pontivy F . . . 100 A3
Pont-l'Abbé F . . . 100 B1
Pont-l'Évêque F . . 89 A4
Pontlevoy F . . . 103 B3
Pontoise F . . . 90 B2
Pontones E . . . 164 A2
Pontonx-sur-l'Adour F . . . 128 C2
Pontoon IRL . . . 26 C1
Pontorson F . . . 88 B2
Pontrémoli I . . . 134 A2
Pont-Remy F . . . 90 A1
Pontresina CH . . . 107 C4
Pontrhydfendigaid GB . . . 39 B3
Pontrieux F . . . 100 A2
Ponts E . . . 147 C2
Ponts-aux-Dames F 90 C2
Pont Scorff F . . . 100 B2
Pöntsö FIN . . . 196 B7
Pont-Ste Maxence F 90 B2
Pont-St Esprit F . . 131 A3
Pont-St Mamet F . 129 B3
Pont-St Martin
  F . . . 101 B4
  I . . . 119 B4
Pont-St Vincent F . 92 C2
Pont-sur-Yonne F . 104 A2
Pontvallain F . . . 102 B2
Pontypool GB . . . 39 C3
Pontypridd GB . . . 39 C3
Ponza I . . . 169 C2
Poo E . . . 142 A2
Poole GB . . . 43 B5
Poolewe GB . . . 31 B3
Poperinge B . . . 78 B2
Pópoli I . . . 169 A3
Popovac SRB . . . 127 D3
Popovača HR . . . 124 B2
Popow PL . . . 77 B4
Poppel B . . . 79 A5
Poppenhausen
  *Bayern* D . . . 82 B2
  *Hessen* D . . . 82 B1
Poppi I . . . 135 B4
Poprad SK . . . 99 B4
Popučke SRB . . . 127 C1
Pópulo P . . . 148 A2
Populónia I . . . 134 C3
Pörböly H . . . 125 A4
Porcuna E . . . 163 A3
Pordenone I . . . 122 B1

Pordic F . . . 100 A3
Poręba PL . . . 86 B3
Poreč HR . . . 122 B2
Pori FIN . . . 8 B2
Porjus S . . . 196 C2
Porkhov RUS . . . 9 D6
Porlezza I . . . 120 A2
Porlock GB . . . 43 A3
Pörnbach D . . . 95 C3
Pornic F . . . 101 B3
Pornichet F . . . 101 B3
Porodin SRB . . . 127 C3
Poronin PL . . . 99 B3
Poros
  *Attiki* GR . . . 185 B4
  *Kefalonia* GR . . . 184 A1
Poroszló H . . . 113 B4
Porozina HR . . . 123 B3
Porquerolles F . . . 132 C2
Porrentruy CH . . . 106 B2
Porreres E . . . 167 B3
Porretta Terme I . . 135 A3
Porsgrunn N . . . 53 A5
Porspoder F . . . 100 A1
Port-a-Binson F . . 91 B3
Portacloy IRL . . . 26 B1
Portadown GB . . . 27 B4
Portaferry GB . . . 27 B5
Portaje E . . . 155 B4
Portalegre P . . . 155 B3
Portarlington IRL . . 30 A1
Port Askaig GB . . 34 C1
Portavadie GB . . . 34 C2
Portavogie GB . . . 27 B5
Portball F . . . 88 A2
Port Bannatyne GB 34 C2
Port-Barcarès F . . 146 B4
Portbou F . . . 146 B4
Port-Camargue F . 131 B3
Port Charlotte GB . 34 C1
Port d'Andratx E . . 166 B2
Port-de-Bouc F . . 131 B3
Port-de-Lanne F . . 128 C1
Port de Pollença E . 167 B3
Port-des-Barques F . . . 114 C2
Port de Sóller E . . 166 B2
Portegrandi I . . . 122 B1
Portel P . . . 155 C3
Portela P . . . 148 B1
Port Ellen GB . . . 34 C1
Portelo P . . . 141 C4
Portemouro E . . . 140 B2
Port-en-Bessin F . . 88 A3
Port'Ercole I . . . 168 A1
Port Erin GB . . . 36 B2
Portes-lès-Valence F . . . 117 C4
Portets F . . . 128 B2
Port Eynon GB . . 39 C2
Portezuelo E . . . 155 B4
Port Glasgow GB . 34 C3
Portglenone GB . . 27 B4
Porthcawl GB . . . 39 C3
Port Henderson GB 31 B3
Porthleven GB . . . 42 B1
Porthmadog GB . . 38 B2
Porticcio F . . . 180 B1
Portici I . . . 170 C2
Portico di Romagna I . . . 135 A4
Portilla de la Reina E . . . 142 A2
Portillo E . . . 150 A3
Portimão P . . . 160 B1
Portinatx E . . . 166 B1
Portinho da Arrabida P . . . 154 C1
Port Isaac GB . . . 42 B2
Portishead GB . . . 43 A4
Port-Joinville F . . 114 B1
Portknockie GB . . 33 D4
Port-la-Nouvelle F . 130 B2
Portlaoise IRL . . . 30 A1
Portlethen GB . . . 33 D4
Port Logan GB . . 36 B2
Port Louis F . . . 100 B2
Portmage IRL . . . 29 C1
Portmahomack GB 32 D3
Portman E . . . 165 B4
Port Manech F . . 100 B2
Portnacroish GB . . 34 B2
Portnahaven GB . . 34 C1
Port Nan Giuran GB 31 A2
Port-Navalo F . . . 100 B3
Port Nis GB . . . 31 A2
Porto
  F . . . 180 A1
  P . . . 148 A1
Porto-Alto P . . . 154 C2
Porto Azzurro I . . 134 C3
Portocannone I . . 170 B3
Porto Cerésio I . . 120 B1
Porto Cervo I . . . 178 A3
Porto Cesáreo I . . 173 B3
Porto Colom E . . 167 B3
Porto Covo P . . . 160 B1
Porto Cristo E . . . 167 B3
Porto d'Áscoli I . . 136 C2
Porto de Lagos P . 160 B1
Porto de Mos P . . 154 B2
Porto de Rei P . . 154 C2
Porto do Son E . . 140 B2
Porto Empédocle I . 176 B2
Portoferráio I . . . 134 C3
Portofino I . . . 134 A2
Porto Garibaldi I . . 122 C1
Portogruaro I . . . 122 B1

Portokhelion GR . . 184 B4
Portomaggiore I . . 121 C4
Portomarin E . . . . 140 B3
Porton GB . . . . . . 44 B2
Portonovo E . . . . 140 B2
Portopalo di Capo
  Passero I . . . . . 177 C4
Porto Petro E. . . . 167 B3
Porto Pino I . . . . 179 D2
Porto Potenza Picena
  I . . . . . . . . . . . 136 B2
Portør N . . . . . . . 53 B5
Porto Recanati I . . 136 B2
Porto San Giórgio
  I . . . . . . . . . . . 136 B2
Porto Sant'Elpídio
  I . . . . . . . . . . . 136 B2
Porto Santo Stéfano
  I . . . . . . . . . . . 168 A1
Portoscuso I . . . . 179 C2
Porto Tolle I . . . . 122 C1
Porto Tórres I . . . 178 B2
Porto-Vecchio I . . 180 B2
Portovénere I . . . . 134 A2
Portpatrick GB . . . 36 B1
Portreath GB . . . . 42 B1
Portree GB . . . . . 31 B2
Portroe IRL . . . . . 28 B3
Portrush GB . . . . 27 A4
Port St Mary GB . . 36 B2
Portsall F . . . . . . 100 A1
Portsmouth GB . . . 44 C2
Portsoy GB . . . . . 33 D4
Port-Ste Marie F . 129 B3
Portstewart GB . . . 27 A4
Port-St-Louis-du-Rhône
  F . . . . . . . . . . . 131 B3
Port-sur-Saône F . 105 B5
Port Talbot GB . . . 39 C3
Portugalete E . . . . 143 A4
Portumna IRL . . . . 28 A3
Port-Vendres F . . 146 B4
Port William GB. . . 36 B2
Porvoo FIN . . . . . . 8 B4
Porzuna E . . . . . . 157 A3
Posada
  Oviedo E . . . . . . 141 A5
  Oviedo E . . . . . . 142 A2
  I . . . . . . . . . . . 178 B3
Posada de Valdeón
  E . . . . . . . . . . . 142 A2
Posadas E . . . . . . 162 A2
Poschiavo CH . . . 120 A3
Posedarje HR . . . 137 A4
Posio FIN . . . . . 197 C11
Positano I . . . . . . 170 C2
Possagno I . . . . . 121 B4
Posseck D . . . . . . 83 B4
Possesse F . . . . . 91 C4
Pössneck D . . . . . 83 B3
Posta I . . . . . . . . 169 A3
Postal I . . . . . . . 108 C2
Posta Piana I . . . . 172 A1
Postbauer-Heng D . 95 B3
Posterholt NL . . . . 80 A2
Postioma I . . . . . . 121 B5
Postira HR . . . . . . 138 B2
Postojna SLO . . . 123 B3
Postoloprty CZ . . . 84 B1
Postomino PL . . . . 68 A1
Posušje BIH . . . . 138 B3
Potamos
  Attiki GR. . . . . . .184 C3
  Attiki GR. . . . . . .184 D4
Potegowo PL . . . . 68 A2
Potenza I . . . . . . 172 B1
Potenza Picena I . . 136 B2
Potes E . . . . . . . 142 A2
Potigny F . . . . . . . 89 B3
Potočari BIH . . . . 127 C1
Potoci
  BIH . . . . . . . . .138 A2
  BIH . . . . . . . . .139 B3
Potony H . . . . . . 125 B3
Potries E . . . . . . 159 C3
Potsdam D . . . . . 74 B2
Potštát CZ . . . . . 98 B1
Pottenbrunn A . . .110 A2
Pottendorf A . . . . .111 B3
Pottenstein
  A . . . . . . . . . . . .111 B3
  D . . . . . . . . . . . .95 B3
Potters Bar GB . . . 44 B3
Pöttmes D . . . . . 94 C3
Pöttsching A . . . . .111 B3
Potworów PL . . . . 87 A4
Pouancé F . . . . . 101 B4
Pougues-les-Eaux
  F . . . . . . . . . . . 104 B2
Pouilly-en-Auxois
  F . . . . . . . . . . . 104 B3
Pouilly-sous Charlieu
  F . . . . . . . . . . . .117 A4
Pouilly-sur-Loire F 104 B1
Poujol-sur-Orb F . 130 B2
Poullaouen F . . . . 100 A2
Poulton-le-Fylde GB 38 A4
Poundstock GB . . . 42 B2
Pourcy F . . . . . . . 91 B3
Pourrain F . . . . . 104 B2
Poussu FIN . . . . 197 D12
Pouyastruc F . . . 145 A4
Pouy-de-Touges F. 146 A2
Pouzauges F . . . . .114 B3
Pova de Santa Iria
  P. . . . . . . . . . . . 154 C1
Povaźská Bystrica
  SK . . . . . . . . . . 98 B2

Povedilla E . . . . . 158 C1
Povenets RUS . . . . 9 A9
Povlja HR. . . . . . 138 B2
Povljana HR. . . . . 137 A4
Póvoa
  Beja P . . . . . . . .161 A2
  Santarém P . . . . 154 B2
Póvoa de Lanhosa
  P. . . . . . . . . . . . 148 A1
Póvoa de Varzim
  P. . . . . . . . . . . . 148 A1
Póvoa e Meadas P. 155 B3
Powidz PL . . . . . . 76 B2
Poyales del Hoyo
  E . . . . . . . . . . . 150 B2
Poynton GB . . . . . 40 B1
Poyntz Pass GB . . 27 B4
Poysdorf A. . . . . . 97 C4
Poza de la Sal E. . 143 B3
Pozaldez E . . . . . 150 A3
Pozán de Vero E . 145 B4
Pozanti TR . . . . . 23 C8
Požarevac SRB . . . 127 C3
Požega
  HR. . . . . . . . . . .125 B3
  SRB . . . . . . . . .127 D2
Poznań PL . . . . . . 76 B1
Pozo Alcón E . . . . 164 B2
Pozoantiguo E. . . . 150 A2
Pozoblanco E . . . . 156 B3
Pozo Cañada E . . . 158 C2
Pozo de Guadalajara
  E . . . . . . . . . . . 151 B4
Pozo de la Serna E 157 B4
Pozohondo E . . . . 158 C2
Pozondón E . . . . . 152 B2
Poźrzadło Wielkie
  PL. . . . . . . . . . . 75 A4
Pozuel del Campo
  E . . . . . . . . . . . 152 B2
Pozuelo de Alarcón
  E . . . . . . . . . . . 151 B4
Pozuelo de Calatrava
  E . . . . . . . . . . . 157 B4
Pozuelo del Páramo
  E . . . . . . . . . . . 142 B1
Pozuelo de Zarzón
  E . . . . . . . . . . . 149 B3
Pozzallo I . . . . . . 177 C3
Pozzomaggiore I . . 178 B2
Pozzo San Nicola I 178 B2
Pozzuoli I . . . . . . 170 C2
Pozzuolo I . . . . . . 135 B4
Prabuty PL . . . . . . 69 B4
Prača BIH. . . . . . 139 B4
Prachatice CZ . . . . 96 B1
Prada E . . . . . . . 141 B3
Pradelle F . . . . . . 118 C2
Pradelles F . . . . . 117 C3
Prades
  E . . . . . . . . . . . .147 C1
  F . . . . . . . . . . . .146 B3
Pradła PL . . . . . . 86 B3
Prado
  E . . . . . . . . . . . .142 A1
  P . . . . . . . . . . . .148 A1
Prado del Rey E . . 162 B2
Pradoluengo E . . . 143 B3
Pragelato I . . . . . .119 B3
Pragersko SLO . . . 123 A4
Prägraten A . . . . . 109 B3
Prague = Praha CZ . 84 B2
Praha = Prague CZ . 84 B2
Prahecq F . . . . . .115 B3
Praia P . . . . . . . . 154 B1
Práia a Mare I . . . 174 B1
Praia da Rocha P. . 160 B1
Praia da Viera P. . . 154 B2
Praia de Mira P . . 148 B1
Praiano I . . . . . . . 170 C2
Pralboino I . . . . . 120 B3
Pralognan-la-Vanoise
  F . . . . . . . . . . . .118 B3
Pramanda GR . . . 182 D3
Pranjani SRB . . . . 127 C2
Prapatnica HR. . . . 138 B2
Praszka PL. . . . . . 86 A2
Prat F . . . . . . . . . 146 A1
Prata I . . . . . . . . 135 B3
Prata di Pordenone
  I . . . . . . . . . . . . 122 B1
Pratau D . . . . . . . 83 A4
Prat de Compte E . 153 B4
Pratdip E . . . . . . 147 C1
Pratella I. . . . . . . 170 B2
Prato I . . . . . . . . 135 B4
Prátola Peligna I . . 169 A3
Pratola Serra I . . . 170 C2
Prats-de-Mollo-la-Preste
  F . . . . . . . . . . . .146 B3
Prauthoy F . . . . . 105 B4
Pravia E . . . . . . . 141 A4
Praxmar A . . . . . . 108 B2
Prayssac F . . . . . 129 B4
Prazzo I . . . . . . . 132 A3
Prebold SLO . . . . 123 A4
Préchac F . . . . . . 128 B2
Précy-sur-Thil F . . 104 B3
Predáppio I . . . . . 135 A4
Predazzo I . . . . . . 121 A4
Předin CZ. . . . . . . 97 B3
Preding A . . . . . . 110 C2
Predjame SLO . . . 123 B3
Predlitz A . . . . . . 109 B4
Predmeja SLO . . . 122 B2
Predoi I . . . . . . . 108 B3
Pré-en-Pail F . . . . 89 B3

Prees GB . . . . . . . 38 B4
Preetz D . . . . . . . 64 B3
Préfailles F . . . . . 101 B3
Pregarten A . . . . . 96 C2
Pregrada HR . . . . 123 A4
Preignan F. . . . . . 129 C3
Preilji LV . . . . . . . . 8 D5
Preitenegg A . . . . 110 C1
Prekaja BIH . . . . . 138 A2
Preko HR . . . . . . 137 A4
Preljina SRB . . . . 127 D2
Prelog HR . . . . . . 124 A2
Preločśica HR . . . 124 B2
Přelouč CZ. . . . . . 97 A3
Prem SLO . . . . . . 123 B3
Premantura HR . . . 122 C2
Prémery F . . . . . . 104 B2
Prémia I . . . . . . . .119 A5
Premiàde Mar E . . 147 C3
Premnitz D. . . . . . 73 B5
Prémont F . . . . . . 91 A3
Prenzlau D. . . . . . 74 A2
Preodac BIH . . . . 138 A2
Přerov CZ. . . . . . . 98 B1
Prerow D . . . . . . . 66 B1
Presencio E. . . . . 143 B3
Presicce I . . . . . . 173 C4
Presly F. . . . . . . . 103 B4
Prešov SK . . . . . . 12 D4
Pressac F. . . . . . .115 B4
Pressath D. . . . . . 95 B3
Pressbaum A. . . . .111 A3
Prestatyn GB. . . . . 38 A3
Prestebakke N. . . . 54 B2
Presteigne GB . . . 39 B3
Přeštice CZ . . . . . 96 B1
Preston
  Lancashire GB. . .38 A4
  Scottish Borders
  GB . . . . . . . . . .35 C5
Prestonpans GB . . 35 C5
Prestwick GB. . . . . 36 A2
Prettin D. . . . . . . . 83 A4
Preturo I . . . . . . . 169 A3
Pretzchendorf D . . 83 B5
Pretzier D. . . . . . . 73 B4
Pretzsch D . . . . . . 83 A4
Preuilly-sur-Claise
  F . . . . . . . . . . . .115 B4
Prevalje SLO . . . . 110 C1
Prevenchères F. . . 131 A2
Préveranges F. . . .116 A2
Preveza GR . . . . . 182 E2
Prevršac HR . . . . 124 B2
Prezid HR. . . . . . 123 B3
Priaranza del Bierzo
  E . . . . . . . . . . . 141 B4
Priay F . . . . . . . .118 A2
Pribeta SK . . . . . .112 B2
Priboj
  BIH . . . . . . . . .125 C4
  SRB . . . . . . . . .16 D3
Přibor CZ. . . . . . . 98 B2
Příbram CZ. . . . . . 96 B2
Pribylina SK. . . . . 99 B3
Přibyslav CZ . . . . 97 B3
Pričević SRB . . . . 127 C1
Pridjel BIH . . . . . 125 C4
Priego E . . . . . . . 152 B1
Priego de Córdoba
  E . . . . . . . . . . . 163 A3
Priekule LV. . . . . . . 8 D2
Prien D . . . . . . . . 109 B3
Prienai LT. . . . . . . 13 A5
Prievidza SK . . . . 98 C2
Prigradica HR . . . 138 C2
Prigrevica SRB . . 125 B5
Prijeboj HR . . . . . 123 C4
Prijedor BIH . . . . 124 C2
Prijepolje SRB . . . 16 D3
Prilep MK . . . . . . 182 B3
Priluka BIH . . . . . 138 B2
Primda CZ . . . . . . 95 B4
Primel-Trégastel F 100 A2
Primišje HR. . . . . 123 B4
Primorsk
  Kaliningrad RUS . .69 A5
  Severo-Zapadnyy
  RUS . . . . . . . . .9 B6
Primošten HR . . . 138 B1
Primstal D . . . . . . 92 B2
Princes Risborough
  GB . . . . . . . . . . 44 B3
Princetown GB . . . 42 B2
Principina a Mare I 135 C4
Priolo Gargallo I . . 177 B4
Prioro E . . . . . . . 142 B2
Priozersk RUS. . . . . 9 B7
Prirechnyy RUS . 193 C14
Prisoje BIH. . . . . 138 B3
Priština KOS . . . . 16 D4
Pritzerbe D. . . . . . 73 B5
Pritzier D . . . . . . . 73 A4
Pritzwalk D . . . . . . 73 A5
Privas F . . . . . . . .117 C4
Priverno I . . . . . . 169 B3
Privlaka
  Vukovarsko-Srijemska
  HR . . . . . . . . . .125 B4
  Zadarska HR . . . 137 A4
Prizna HR. . . . . . 123 C3
Prizren KOS. . . . . 16 D4
Prizzi I . . . . . . . . 176 B2
Prnjavor
  BIH . . . . . . . . . .125 C3
  HR. . . . . . . . . . .124 B1
  SRB . . . . . . . . .127 C1
Proaza E . . . . . . 141 A4

Probstzella D. . . . . 82 B3
Probus GB. . . . . . 42 B2
Prócchio I . . . . . . 134 C3
Prochowice PL . . . 85 A4
Prócida I . . . . . . . 170 C2
Prodhromos CY . . 181 B1
Prodo I . . . . . . . . 135 C5
Proença-a-Nova P. 154 B3
Proença-a-Velha P 155 A3
Profondeville B . . . 79 B4
Prokuplje SRB. . . . 16 D4
Prolog HR . . . . . . 138 B2
Promachi GR . . . . 182 B3
Propriano F . . . . . 180 B1
Prosec CZ. . . . . . 97 B4
Prösen D . . . . . . . 83 A5
Prosenjakovci
  SLO . . . . . . . . . .111 C3
Prosotsani GR . . . 183 B5
Prostějov CZ. . . . . 98 B1
Prószków PL. . . . . 86 B1
Proszowice PL. . . . 87 B4
Protić BIH . . . . . . 138 A2
Protivanov CZ. . . . 97 B4
Protivín CZ . . . . . . 96 B2
Prötzel D. . . . . . . 74 B2
Provins F. . . . . . . 90 C3
Prozor BIH . . . . . 139 B3
Prrenjas AL . . . . . 182 B2
Prudhoe GB . . . . . 37 B5
Prudnik PL. . . . . . 85 B1
Pruggern A. . . . . . 109 B4
Prügy H . . . . . . . .113 A5
Prüm D. . . . . . . . . 80 B2
Pruna E . . . . . . . 162 B2
Prunelli-di-Fiumorbo
  F . . . . . . . . . . . 180 A2
Prunetta I . . . . . . 135 A3
Pruniers F . . . . . . 103 C4
Prusice PL. . . . . . 85 A4
Pruské SK . . . . . . 98 B2
Pruszce PL. . . . . . 76 A3
Pruszcz Gdański PL 69 A3
Pruszków PL. . . . . 77 B5
Prutz A . . . . . . . . 108 B1
Prüzen D. . . . . . . 65 C5
Pruzhany BY . . . . 13 B6
Pružina SK . . . . . 98 B2
Půrvomay BG . . . . 183 A7
Pryłęg PL . . . . . . 75 B4
Prząsnysz PL. . . . 77 A5
Przechlewo PL . . . 68 B2
Przecław PL. . . . . 87 B5
Przedbórz PL. . . . 87 A3
Przedecz PL. . . . . 76 B3
Przejęslav PL. . . . 84 A3
Przemków PL. . . . 85 A3
Przemocze PL. . . . 75 A3
Przemyśl PL . . . . 12 D5
Przerąb PL . . . . . 87 A3
Przewodnik PL. . . . 69 B3
Przewodowo Parcele
  PL. . . . . . . . . . . 77 B5
Przewóz PL . . . . . 84 A2
Przezmark PL . . . . 69 B4
Przodkowo PL. . . . 68 A3
Przybiernów PL. . . 75 A3
Przyborowice PL. . 77 B5
Przybyszew PL. . . . 87 A4
Przybyszów PL. . . . 86 A3
Przylęg PL . . . . . 75 B4
Przysucha PL. . . . 87 A4
Przytoczna PL. . . . 75 B4
Przytyk PL . . . . . . 87 A4
Przywidz PL. . . . . 68 A3
Psachna GR . . . . 185 A4
Psara GR . . . . . . 185 A6
Psary PL. . . . . . . 76 C3
Pskov RUS . . . . . . 8 D6
Pszczew PL. . . . . 75 B4
Pszczółki PL . . . . 69 A3
Pszczyna PL . . . . 98 B2
Pszów PL . . . . . . 86 B2
Pteleos GR . . . . . 182 D4
Ptolemaida GR . . . 182 C3
Ptuj SLO. . . . . . . 124 A1
Ptusza PL. . . . . . 68 B1
Puch A . . . . . . . . 109 B4
Puchberg am
  Schneeberg A . . .110 B2
Puchevillers F. . . . 90 A2
Puchheim D. . . . . 108 A2
Púchov SK. . . . . . 98 B2
Pučišća HR . . . . . 138 B2
Puck PL . . . . . . . 69 A3
Puçol E . . . . . . . 159 B3
Puconci SLO . . . . .111 C3
Pudasjärvi FIN. . . 197 D10
Puderbach D. . . . . 81 B3
Pudozh RUS . . . . . 9 B10
Puebla de Albortón
  E . . . . . . . . . . . 153 A3
Puebla de Alcocer
  E . . . . . . . . . . . 156 B2
Puebla de Beleña
  E . . . . . . . . . . . 151 B4
Puebla de Don Fadrique
  E . . . . . . . . . . . 164 B2
Puebla de Don Rodrigo
  E . . . . . . . . . . . 156 A3
Puebla de Guzmán
  E . . . . . . . . . . . 161 B2
Puebla de la Calzada
  E . . . . . . . . . . . 155 C4
Puebla de la Reina
  E . . . . . . . . . . . 156 B1
Puebla de Lillo E. . 142 A1
Puebla del Maestre
  E . . . . . . . . . . . 161 A3

Puebla del Principe
  E . . . . . . . . . . . 158 C1
Puebla de Obando
  E . . . . . . . . . . . 155 B4
Puebla de Sanabria
  E . . . . . . . . . . . 141 B4
Puebla de Sancho Pérez
  E . . . . . . . . . . . 155 C4
Puente Almuhey E 142 B2
Puente de Domingo
  Flórez E . . . . . . 141 B4
Puente de Génave
  E . . . . . . . . . . . 164 A2
Puente del Congosto
  E . . . . . . . . . . . 150 B2
Puente de Montañana
  E . . . . . . . . . . . 145 B4
Puente Duero E . . 150 A3
Puente-Genil E . . . 162 A3
Puente la Reina E . 144 B2
Puente la Reina de Jaca
  E . . . . . . . . . . . 144 B3
Puentelarra E . . . 143 B3
Puente Mayorga E. 162 B2
Puente Viesgo E . . 143 A3
Puertas
  Asturias E . . . . . .142 A2
  Salamanca E . . . 149 A3
Puerto de Mazarrón
  E . . . . . . . . . . . 165 B3
Puerto de Santa Cruz
  E . . . . . . . . . . . 156 A2
Puerto de San Vicente
  E . . . . . . . . . . . 156 A2
Puerto-Lápice E . 157 A4
Puertollano E . . . 157 B3
Puerto Lumbreras
  E . . . . . . . . . . . 164 B3
Puerto Moral E . . 161 B3
Puerto Real E . . . 162 B1
Puerto Rey E . . . 156 A2
Puerto Seguro E . 149 B3
Puerto Serrano E . 162 B2
Puget-Sur-Argens
  F . . . . . . . . . . . 132 B2
Puget-Théniers F . 132 B2
Puget-ville F . . . . 132 B2
Pugnochiuso I . . . 171 B4
Puigcerdà E . . . . 146 B2
Puigpunyent E . . . 166 B2
Puig Reig E . . . . 147 C2
Puillon F . . . . . . 128 C2
Puimichel F . . . . 132 B2
Puimoisson F . . . 132 B2
Puiseaux F . . . . . 103 A4
Puisieux F . . . . . . 90 A2
Puisserguier F . . . 130 B2
Puivert F . . . . . . 146 B3
Pujols F . . . . . . . 128 B2
Pukanec SK . . . . 98 C2
Pukavik S. . . . . . 63 B2
Pukë AL . . . . . . . 182 A1
Pula
  HR. . . . . . . . . . .122 C2
  I . . . . . . . . . . . . .179 C2
Puławy PL . . . . . . 12 C4
Pulborough GB . . . 44 C3
Pulfero I . . . . . . . 122 A2
Pulgar E . . . . . . . 157 A3
Pulheim D . . . . . . 80 A2
Pulkau A . . . . . . . 97 C3
Pulpi E . . . . . . . . 164 B3
Pulsano I . . . . . . 173 B3
Pulsnitz D . . . . . . 84 A2
Pułtusk PL. . . . . . 77 B6
Pumpsaint GB . . . 39 B3
Punat HR . . . . . . 123 B3
Punta Marina I . . . 135 A5
Punta Prima E . . . 167 B4
Punta Sabbioni I . . 122 B1
Puntas de Calnegre
  E . . . . . . . . . . . 165 B3
Punta Umbria E. . . 161 B3
Puolanka FIN. . . . . 3 D10
Puoltikasvaara S. . 196 B4
Puoltsa S. . . . . . 196 B2
Puračić BIH . . . . 125 C4
Purbach am Neusiedler
  See A . . . . . . . . .111 B3
Purchena E . . . . . 164 B2
Purfleet GB . . . . . 45 B4
Purgstall A. . . . . .110 A2
Purkersdorf A . . . .111 A3
Purmerend NL. . . . 70 B1
Purullena E . . . . . 164 B1
Pushkin RUS. . . . . 9 C7
Pushkino RUS. . . . 9 D10
Puśle Ulany SK. . .111 A4
Pustoshka RUS. . . 9 D6
Puszcza Mariańska
  PL. . . . . . . . . . . 77 C5
Puszczykowo PL. . 76 B1
Pusztamagyaród
  H . . . . . . . . . . . .111 C3
Pusztamonostor H .113 B3
Pusztaszabolcs H .112 B2
Pusztavám H. . . . .112 B2
Putanges-Pont-Ecrepin
  F . . . . . . . . . . . . 89 B3
Putbus D . . . . . . . 66 B2
Putignano I . . . . . 173 B3
Putlitz D . . . . . . . 73 A5
Putnok H . . . . . . . 99 C4
Putte B . . . . . . . . 79 A4
Puttelange-aux-Lacs
  F . . . . . . . . . . . . 92 B2
Putten NL. . . . . . . 70 B2

Puttgarden D. . . . . 65 B4
Püttlingen D . . . . . 92 B2
Putzu Idu I . . . . . 179 B2
Puy-Guillaume F . .117 B3
Puy-l'Évêque F . . 129 B3
Puymirol F. . . . . . 129 B3
Puyôo F . . . . . . . 128 C2
Puyrolland F . . . . .114 B3
Pwllheli GB . . . . . 38 B2
Pyetrikaw BY . . . . 13 B8
Pyhäjärvi FIN . . . . . 3 E9
Pyhäkylä FIN . . . 197 D11
Pyla CY . . . . . . . 181 A2
Pyla-sur-Mer F . . 128 B1
Pyrzyce PL . . . . . 75 A3
Pysely CZ . . . . . . 96 B2
Pyskowice PL . . . 86 B2
Pytalovo RUS . . . . 8 D5
Pyzdry PL. . . . . . 76 B2

Quakenbrück D. . . 71 B4
Quargnento I . . . . 119 C5
Quarré-les-Tombes
  F . . . . . . . . . . . 104 B2
Quarteira P . . . . . 160 B1
Quartu Sant'Élena
  I . . . . . . . . . . . . 179 C3
Quatre-Champs F . 91 B4
Quedlinburg D. . . . 82 A3
Queensferry
  Edinburgh GB . . .35 C4
  Flintshire GB . . . 38 A3
Queige F . . . . . . .118 B3
Queipo E . . . . . . 161 B3
Queixans E . . . . . 146 B2
Quel E . . . . . . . . 144 B1
Quelaines-St-Gault
  F . . . . . . . . . . . 102 B1
Queljada P. . . . . . 148 A1
Quemada E . . . . . 143 C3
Queralbs E . . . . . 147 B3
Quercianella I . . . 134 B3
Querfurt D. . . . . . 82 A3
Quérigut F . . . . . 146 B3
Quero
  E . . . . . . . . . . . .157 A4
  I . . . . . . . . . . . . .121 B4
Querqueville F. . . . 88 A2
Quesada E . . . . . 164 B1
Questembert F . . . 101 B3
Quettehou F . . . . . 88 A2
Quevauvillers F. . . 90 B2
Quevy B . . . . . . . 79 B4
Quiaios P . . . . . . 148 B1
Quiberon F . . . . . 100 B2
Quiberville F . . . . 89 A4
Quickborn D . . . . 64 C2
Quiévrain B . . . . . 79 B3
Quillan F . . . . . . 146 B3
Quillebeuf F . . . . . 89 A4
Quimper F. . . . . . 100 A1
Quimperlé F . . . . 100 B2
Quincampoix F . . . 89 A5
Quincoces de Yuso
  E . . . . . . . . . . . 143 B3
Quincy F . . . . . . 103 B4
Quinéville F . . . . . 88 A2
Quingey F . . . . . 105 B4
Quinson F . . . . . 132 B2
Quinssaines F . . .116 A2
Quinta-Grande P . 154 C2
Quintana de la Serena
  E . . . . . . . . . . . 156 B2
Quintana del Castillo
  E . . . . . . . . . . . 141 B4
Quintana del Marco
  E . . . . . . . . . . . 141 B5
Quintana del Puente
  E . . . . . . . . . . . 142 B2
Quintana-Martin
  Galindez E . . . . 143 B3
Quintanaortuño E . 143 B3
Quintanapalla E . . 143 B3
Quintanar de la Orden
  E . . . . . . . . . . . 157 A4
Quintanar de la Sierra
  E . . . . . . . . . . . 143 C3
Quintanar del Rey
  E . . . . . . . . . . . 158 B2
Quintanilla de la Mata
  E . . . . . . . . . . . 143 C3
Quintanilla del Coco
  E . . . . . . . . . . . 143 C3
Quintanilla de Onésimo
  E . . . . . . . . . . . 150 A3
Quintanilla de Somoza
  E . . . . . . . . . . . 141 B4
Quintas de Valdelucio
  E . . . . . . . . . . . 142 B2
Quintela P . . . . . 148 B2
Quintin F . . . . . . 100 A3
Quinto E . . . . . . 153 A3
Quinzano d'Oglio I 120 B3
Quiroga E . . . . . . 141 B3
Quismondo E . . . 150 B3
Quissac F . . . . . 131 B2
Quistello I . . . . . 121 B3

## R


Raab A 96 C1
Raabs an der Thaya A 97 C3
Raahe FIN 3 D9
Raajärvi FIN 197 C9
Raalte NL 71 B3
Raamsdonksveer NL 79 A4
Raanujarvi FIN 196 C7
Raattama FIN 196 A7
Rab HR 123 C3
Rabac HR 123 B3
Rábade E 140 A3
Rábafüzes H 111 C3
Rábahidvég H 111 B3
Rabanales E 149 A3
Rábapatona H 111 B4
Rabapordány H 111 B4
Rabastens F 129 C4
Rabastens-de-Bigorre F 145 A4
Rabat = Victoria M 175 C3
Rabat M 175 C3
Rabča SK 99 B3
Rabe SRB 126 A2
Rabi CZ 96 B1
Rabino PL 67 C4
Rabka PL 99 B3
Rabrovo SRB 127 C3
Rača SRB 127 C3
Rácale I 173 C4
Rácalmás H 112 B2
Racalmuto I 176 B2
Racconigi I 119 C4
Rače SLO 123 A4
Rachecourt-sur-Marne F 91 C5
Raciąż PL 77 B5
Racibórz PL 86 B2
Račinovci HR 125 C4
Ráckeve H 112 B2
Racławice PL 87 B4
Racławice Śląskie PL 86 B1
Racot PL 75 B5
Råda
*Skaraborg* S 55 B4
*Värmland* S 49 B5
Radalj SRB 127 C1
Rădăuţi RO 17 B6
Radda in Chianti I 135 B4
Raddusa I 177 B3
Radeberg D 84 A1
Radebeul D 84 A1
Radeburg D 84 A1
Radeče SLO 123 A4
Radekhiv UA 13 C6
Radenci SLO 111 C3
Radenthein A 109 C4
Radevormwald D 80 A3
Radicófani I 135 C4
Radicóndoli I 135 B4
Radišići BIH 138 B3
Radizel SLO 110 C2
Radków PL 85 B4
Radlje ob Dravi SLO 110 C2
Radlów PL 87 B4
Radmer an der Stube A 110 B1
Radnejaur S 195 E9
Radnice CZ 96 B1
Radohova BIH 138 A3
Radojevo SRB 126 B2
Radolfzell D 107 B3
Radom PL 87 A5
Radomice PL 77 B4
Radomin PL 77 A4
Radomsko PL 86 A3
Radomyshl UA 13 C8
Radomyśl Wielki PL 87 B5
Radošina SK 98 C1
Radošovce SK 98 C1
Radoszewice PL 86 A2
Radoszyce PL 87 A4
Radotin CZ 96 B2
Radovets BG 186 A1
Radoviš MK 182 B4
Radovljica SLO 123 A3
Radowo Wielkie PL 75 A4
Radstadt A 109 B4
Radstock GB 43 A4
Raduc HR 137 A4
Raduša MK 182 A3
Radviliškis LT 8 E3
Radzanów
*Mazowieckie* PL 77 B5
*Mazowieckie* PL 87 A4
Radziejów PL 76 B3
Radziejowice PL 77 B5
Radzovce SK 113 A3
Radzyń Chełmiński PL 69 B3
Raeren B 80 B2
Raesfeld D 80 A2
Raffadali I 176 B2
Rafina GR 185 A4
Rafsbotn N 192 B7
Ragachow BY 13 B9
Ragály H 99 C4
Rågeleje DK 61 C2
Raglan GB 39 C4
Ragnitz A 110 C2
Ragusa I 177 C3
Rahden D 72 B1
Råholt N 48 B3
Raiano I 169 A3
Raigada E 141 B3
Rain D 94 C2
Rainbach im Mühlkreis A 96 C2
Rainham GB 45 B4
Rairiz de Veiga E 140 B3
Raisdorf D 64 B3
Raisio FIN 8 B3
Raiskio FIN 197 D9
Raiva
*Aveiro* P 148 A1
*Coimbra* P 148 B1
Raja-Jooseppi FIN 193 D12
Rajala FIN 197 B9
Rajcza PL 99 B3
Rajec SK 98 B2
Rájec-Jestřebi CZ 97 B4
Rajecké Teplice SK 98 B2
Rajevo Selo HR 125 C4
Rajhrad CZ 97 B4
Rajić HR 124 B3
Rajka H 111 B4
Rakaca H 99 C4
Rakamaz H 113 A5
Rakek SLO 123 B3
Rakhiv UA 17 A6
Rakitna SLO 123 B3
Rakitovo BG 183 B6
Rakkestad N 54 A2
Rákóczifalva H 113 B4
Rakoniewice PL 75 B5
Rakoszyce PL 85 A4
Raková SK 98 B2
Rakovac BIH 125 B3
Rakovica HR 123 C4
Rakovník CZ 96 A1
Rakow D 66 B2
Raków PL 87 B5
Rakvere EST 8 C5
Ralja SRB 127 C2
Rälla S 62 B4
Ramacastañas E 150 B2
Ramacca I 177 B3
Ramales de la Victoria E 143 A3
Ramberg N 194 B4
Rambervillers F 92 C2
Rambouillet F 90 C1
Rambucourt F 92 C1
Ramdala S 63 B3
Ramerupt F 91 C4
Ramingstein A 109 B4
Ramirás E 140 B2
Ramiswil CH 106 B2
Ramkvilla S 62 A2
Ramme DK 58 B1
Rämmen S 49 B6
Ramnäs S 56 A2
Ramnes N 54 A1
Râmnicu Vâlcea RO 17 C6
Ramonville-St Agne F 129 C4
Rampside GB 36 B3
Ramsau D 109 B3
Ramsbeck D 81 A4
Ramsberg S 56 A1
Ramsele S 200 C2
Ramsey
*Cambridgeshire* GB 44 A3
*Isle of Man* GB 36 B2
Ramseycleuch GB 36 A3
Ramsgate GB 45 B5
Ramsjö S 200 D1
Ramstein-Meisenbach D 93 B3
Ramsund N 194 B7
Ramundberget S 199 C9
Ramvik S 200 D3
Ranalt A 108 B2
Rånäs S 51 C5
Rånåsfoss N 48 B3
Rance B 91 A4
Ránchio I 135 B5
Randaberg N 52 A1
Randalstown GB 27 B4
Randan F 117 A3
Randazzo I 177 B3
Rånddalen S 199 C10
Randegg A 110 A1
Randers DK 58 B3
Randijaur S 196 C2
Randin E 140 C3
Randsverk N 198 D6
Råneå S 196 D5
Rânes F 89 B3
Rångedala S 60 B3
Ranis D 82 B3
Rankweil A 107 B4
Rånnaväg S 60 B3
Ränneslöv S 61 C3
Rannoch Station GB 34 B3
Ranovac SRB 127 C3
Ransäter S 55 A4
Ransbach-Baumbach D 81 B3
Ransta S 56 A2
Ranttila FIN 193 C9
Ranua FIN 197 D9
Ranum DK 58 B2
Ranvalhal P 154 B1
Raon-l'Étape F 92 C2
Ráossi I 121 B4
Rapallo I 134 A2
Rapla EST 8 C4
Rapness GB 33 B4
Rapolano Terme I 135 B4
Rapolla I 172 B1
Raposa P 154 B2
Rapperswil CH 107 B3
Raša HR 123 B3
Rasal E 145 B3
Rascafria E 151 B4
Rasdorf D 82 B1
Raseiniai LT 13 A5
Rašica SLO 123 B3
Rasines E 143 A3
Rasquera E 153 A4
Rássina I 135 B4
Rastatt D 93 C4
Rastede D 71 A5
Rastenberg D 82 A3
Rastošnica BIH 125 C4
Rastovac MNE 139 C4
Rasueros E 150 A2
Rasy PL 86 A3
Raszków PL 86 A1
Rätan S 199 C11
Rateče SLO 109 C4
Ratekau D 65 C3
Ratež SLO 123 B4
Rathangan IRL 30 A2
Rathcoole IRL 30 A2
Rathcormack IRL 29 B3
Rathdrum IRL 30 B2
Rathebur D 74 A2
Rathenow D 73 B5
Rathfriland GB 27 B4
Rathkeale IRL 29 B3
Rathmelton IRL 27 A3
Rathmolyon IRL 30 A2
Rathmore IRL 29 B2
Rathmullan IRL 27 A3
Rathnew IRL 30 B2
Rathvilly IRL 30 B2
Ratibořské Hory CZ 96 B2
Ratingen D 80 A2
Ratková SK 99 C4
Ratkovo SRB 126 B1
Ratne UA 13 C6
Rattelsdorf D 94 A2
Ratten A 110 B2
Rattosjärvi FIN 196 C7
Rattray GB 35 B4
Rättvik S 50 B2
Ratvika N 199 B7
Ratzeburg D 65 C3
Rätzlingen D 73 B4
Raucourt-et-Flaba F 91 B4
Raudeberg N 198 D2
Raufarhöfn IS 191 A10
Raufoss N 48 B2
Rauhala FIN 196 B7
Rauland N 53 A4
Raulhac F 116 C2
Raulia N 195 E5
Rauma FIN 8 B2
Raundal N 46 B3
Raunds GB 44 A3
Rauris A 109 B4
Rautas S 196 B2
Rautavaara FIN 3 E11
Rauville-la-Bigot F 88 A2
Rauzan F 128 B2
Ravanusa I 176 B2
Rava-Rus'ka UA 13 C5
Ravča HR 138 B3
Ravels B 79 A4
Rävemåla S 63 B3
Ravenglass GB 36 B3
Ravenna I 135 A5
Ravensburg D 107 B4
Rävlanda S 60 B2
Ravna Gora HR 123 B3
Ravne na Koroškem SLO 110 C1
Ravnje SRB 127 C1
Ravno BIH 139 C3
Ravno Selo SRB 126 B1
Rawa Mazowiecka PL 87 A4
Rawicz PL 85 A4
Rawtenstall GB 40 B1
Rayleigh GB 45 B4
Ražana SRB 127 C1
Ražanac HR 137 A4
Razboj BIH 124 B3
Razes F 115 B5
Razgrad BG 17 D7
Razkrižie SLO 111 C3
Razlog BG 183 B5
Razo E 140 A2
Reading GB 44 B3
Réalmont F 130 B1
Rebais F 90 C3
Reboly RUS 3 E12
Rebordelo P 149 A2
Recanati I 136 B2
Recas E 151 B4
Recco I 134 A2
Recess IRL 28 A2
Recey-sur-Ource F 105 B3
Recezinhos P 148 A1
Rechnitz A 111 B3
Rechytsa BY 13 B9
Recke D 71 B4
Recklinghausen D 80 A3
Recoaro Terme I 121 B4
Recogne B 92 B1
Recoules-Prévinquières F 130 A1
Recsk H 113 B4
Recz PL 75 A4
Reda PL 69 A3
Redalen N 48 B2
Redange L 92 B1
Redcar GB 37 B5
Redditch GB 44 A2
Redefin D 73 A4
Redhill GB 44 B3
Redics H 111 C3
Redkino RUS 9 D10
Redland GB 33 B3
Redlin D 73 A5
Redon F 101 B3
Redondela E 140 B2
Redondo P 155 C3
Red Point GB 31 B3
Redruth GB 42 B1
Redzikowo PL 68 A2
Reepham GB 41 C5
Rees D 80 A2
Reeth GB 37 B5
Reetz D 73 A4
Reftele S 60 B3
Regalbuto I 177 B3
Regen D 95 C5
Regensburg D 95 B4
Regenstauf D 95 B4
Reggello I 135 B4
Réggio di Calábria I 175 C1
Reggiolo I 121 C3
Réggio nell'Emilia I 121 C3
Reghin RO 17 B6
Régil E 144 A1
Regna S 56 B1
Regniéville F 92 C1
Regny F 117 B4
Rego da Leirosa P 154 A2
Regöly H 112 C2
Regueiro E 140 B2
Reguengo
*Portalegre* P 155 B3
*Santarém* P 154 B2
Reguengos de Monsaraz P 155 C3
Rehau D 83 B4
Rehburg D 72 B2
Rehden D 72 B1
Rehna D 65 C4
Reichelsheim D 93 B4
Reichelshofen D 94 B2
Reichenau A 110 B2
Reichenbach
*Sachsen* D 83 B4
*Sachsen* D 84 A2
Reichenfels A 110 B1
Reichensachsen D 82 A2
Reichertshofen D 95 C3
Reichshoffen F 93 C3
Reiden CH 106 B2
Reigada
E 141 A4
P 149 B3
Reigate GB 44 B3
Reillanne F 132 B1
Reillo E 158 B2
Reims F 91 B4
Reinach CH 106 B3
Reinbek D 72 A3
Reinberg D 66 B2
Reine N 194 C4
Reinfeld D 65 C3
Reinheim D 93 B4
Reinli N 47 B6
Reinosa E 142 A2
Reinstorf D 65 C4
Reinsvoll N 48 B2
Reisach A 109 C4
Reiss GB 32 C3
Reitan N 199 C8
Reit im Winkl D 109 B3
Rejmyre S 56 B1
Rekavice BIH 124 C3
Rekovac SRB 127 D3
Relleu E 159 C3
Rém H 125 A5
Remagen D 80 B3
Rémalard F 89 B4
Rembercourt-aux-Pots F 91 C5
Remedios P 154 B1
Remels D 71 A4
Remetea Mare RO 126 B3
Remich L 92 B2
Rémilly F 92 B2
Remiremont F 105 A5
Remolinos E 144 C2
Remoulins F 131 B3
Remscheid D 80 A3
Rémuzat F 131 A4
Rena N 48 A3
Renaison F 117 A3
Renazé F 101 B4
Renchen D 93 C4
Rencurel F 118 B2
Rende I 174 B2
Rendina GR 182 D3
Rendsburg D 64 B2
Renedo E 150 A3
Renens CH 105 C5
Renfrew GB 34 C3
Rengsjö S 50 A3
Reni UA 17 C8
Rennebu N 198 C6
Rennerod D 81 B4
Rennertshofen D 94 C3
Rennes F 101 A4
Rennes-les-Bains F 146 B3
Rennweg A 109 B4
Rens DK 64 B2
Rensjön S 196 A2
Rentería E 144 A2
Rentjärn S 200 A4
Répcelak H 111 B4
Repojoki FIN 193 D9
Repvåg N 193 B9
Requena E 159 B2
Réquista F 130 A1
Rerik D 65 B4
Resana I 121 B4
Resarö S 57 A4
Reschen = Résia I 108 C1
Resen MK 182 B3
Resende P 148 A2
Résia = Reschen I 108 C1
Reşiţa
RO 16 C4
RO 126 B3
Resko PL 67 C4
Resnik SRB 127 C2
Ressons-sur-Matz F 90 B2
Restábal E 163 B4
Resuttano I 177 B3
Retamal E 155 C4
Retford GB 40 B3
Rethel F 91 B4
Rethem D 72 B2
Rethimno GR 185 D5
Retie B 79 A5
Retiers F 101 B4
Retortillo E 149 B3
Retortillo de Soria E 151 A4
Retournac F 117 B4
Rétság H 112 B3
Rettenegg A 110 B2
Retuerta del Bullaque E 157 A3
Retz A 97 C3
Retzbach D 94 B1
Reuden D 73 B5
Reuilly F 103 B4
Reus E 147 C2
Reusel NL 79 A5
Reuterstadt Stavenhagen D 74 A1
Reuth D 95 B4
Reutlingen D 94 C1
Reutte A 108 B1
Reuver NL 80 A2
Revel F 146 A2
Revello I 119 C4
Revenga E 151 B3
Revest-du-Bion F 132 A1
Révfülöp H 111 C4
Revigny-sur-Ornain F 91 C4
Revin F 91 B4
Řevnice CZ 96 B2
Řevničov CZ 84 B1
Revo I 121 A4
Revsnes N 47 A4
Revúca SK 99 C4
Rewa PL 69 A3
Rewal PL 67 B4
Rexbo S 50 B2
Reyðarfjörður IS 191 B11
Reyero E 142 B1
Reykhólar IS 190 B3
Reykholt
*Árnessýsla* IS 190 C5
*Borgarfjarðarsýsla* IS 190 C4
Reykjahlið IS 191 B9
Reykjavík IS 190 C4
Rezé F 101 B4
Rēzekne LV 8 D5
Rezovo BG 17 E8
Rezzato I 120 B3
Rezzoáglio I 134 A2
Rhade D 72 A2
Rhaunen D 93 B3
Rhayader GB 39 B3
Rheda-Wiedenbrück D 81 A4
Rhede
*Niedersachsen* D 71 A4
*Nordrhein-Westfalen* D 80 A2
Rheinau D 93 C3
Rheinbach D 80 B2
Rheinberg D 80 A2
Rheine D 71 B4
Rheinfelden D 106 B2
Rheinsberg D 74 A1
Rhêmes-Notre-Dame I 119 B4
Rhenen NL 70 C2
Rhens D 81 B3
Rheydt D 80 A2
Rhiconich GB 32 C2
Rhinow D 73 B5
Rhiw GB 38 B2
Rho I 120 B2
Rhoden D 81 A5
Rhodes GR 188 C3
Rhondda GB 39 C3
Rhosllanerchrugog GB 38 A3
Rhosneigr GB 38 A2
Rhossili GB 39 C2
Rhubodach GB 34 C2
Rhuddlan GB 38 A3
Rhyl GB 38 A3
Rhynie GB 33 D4
Riala S 57 A4
Riallé F 101 B4
Riaño E 142 B1
Riano I 168 A2
Rians F 132 B1
Rianxo E 140 B2
Riaza E 151 A4
Riba E 143 A3
Ribadavia E 140 B2
Ribadeo E 141 A3
Riba de Saelices E 152 B1
Ribadesella E 142 A1
Ribaflecha E 143 B4
Ribaforada E 144 C2
Ribare SRB 127 C3
Riba-roja d'Ebre E 153 A4
Riba-Roja de Turia E 159 B3
Ribe DK 59 C1
Ribeauvillé F 106 A2
Ribécourt-Dreslincourt F 90 B2
Ribeira da Pena P 148 A2
Ribeira de Piquín E 141 A3
Ribemont F 91 B3
Ribera I 176 B2
Ribérac F 129 A3
Ribera de Cardós E 146 B2
Ribera del Fresno E 156 B1
Ribesalbes E 159 A3
Ribes de Freser E 147 B3
Ribiers F 132 A1
Ribnica
BIH 139 A4
SLO 123 B3
Ribnica na Potorju SLO 110 C2
Ribnik HR 123 B4
Rîbniţa MD 17 B8
Ribnitz-Damgarten D 66 B1
Ribolla I 135 C4
Říčany CZ 97 B4
Říčany CZ 96 B2
Riccia I 170 B2
Riccione I 136 A1
Ricco Del Golfo I 134 A2
Richebourg F 105 A4
Richelieu F 102 B2
Richisau CH 107 B3
Richmond
*Greater London* GB 44 B3
*North Yorkshire* GB 37 B5
Richtenberg D 66 B1
Richterswil CH 107 B3
Rickling D 64 B3
Rickmansworth GB 44 B3
Ricla E 152 A2
Riddarhyttan S 50 C2
Ridderkerk NL 79 A4
Riddes CH 119 A4
Ridjica SRB 125 B5
Riec-sur-Bélon F 100 B2
Ried A 109 A4
Riedenburg D 95 C3
Ried im Oberinntal A 108 B1
Riedlingen D 107 A4
Riedstadt D 93 B4
Riegersburg A 110 C2
Riego de la Vega E 141 B5
Riego del Camino E 149 A4
Riello E 141 B5
Riemst B 80 B1
Rienne B 91 B4
Riénsena E 142 A2
Riesa D 83 A5
Riese Pio X I 121 B4
Riesi I 177 B3
Riestedt D 82 A3
Rietberg D 81 A4
Rieti I 169 A2
Rietschen D 84 A2
Rieumes F 146 A2
Rieupeyroux F 130 A1
Rieux-Volvestre F 146 A2
Riez F 132 B2
Rīga LV 8 D4
Riggisberg CH 106 C2
Rignac F 130 A1
Rignano Gargánico I 171 B3
Rigolato I 109 C3
Rigside GB 36 A3
Rigutino I 135 B4
Riihimäki FIN 8 B4
Rijeka HR 123 B3
Rijen NL 79 A4
Rijkevorsel B 79 A4
Rijssen NL 71 B3
Rila BG 183 A5
Rilić BIH 138 B3
Rilievo I 176 B1
Rillé F 102 B2
Rillo de Gallo E 152 B2

Rimavská Baňa SK . 99 C3
Rimavská Seč SK . . 99 C4
Rimavská Sobota
SK . . . . . . . . . 99 C4
Rimbo S . . . . . . . . 57 A4
Rimforsa S . . . . . . . 56 B1
Rímini I . . . . . . . . 136 A1
Rîmnicu Sărat RO . . 17 C7
Rimogne F . . . . . . . 91 B4
Rimpar D . . . . . . . 94 B1
Rimske Toplice
SLO . . . . . . . . 123 A4
Rincón de la Victoria
E . . . . . . . . . . 163 B3
Rincón de Soto E . 144 B2
Rindal N . . . . . . . 198 B6
Rinde N . . . . . . . . 46 A3
Ringarum S . . . . . . 56 B2
Ringaskiddy IRL . . 29 C3
Ringe DK . . . . . . . 59 C3
Ringebu N . . . . . . 48 A2
Ringkøbing DK . . . 59 B1
Ringsaker N . . . . . 48 B2
Ringsted DK . . . . . 61 D1
Ringwood GB . . . . 44 C2
Rinkaby S . . . . . . . 63 C2
Rinkabyholm S . . . 63 B4
Rinlo E . . . . . . . . 141 A3
Rinn A . . . . . . . . 108 B2
Rinteln D . . . . . . . 72 B2
Rio E . . . . . . . . . 140 B3
Riobo E . . . . . . . 140 B2
Riodeva E . . . . . . 152 B2
Rio do Coures P . 154 B2
Rio Douro P . . . . 148 A2
Riofrio E . . . . . . . 150 B3
Rio Frío P . . . . . . 154 C2
Riofrío de Aliste E . 149 A3
Rio frío de Riaza E 151 A4
Riogordo E . . . . . 163 B3
Rioja E . . . . . . . 164 C2
Riola I . . . . . . . . 135 A4
Riola Sardo I . . . . 179 C2
Riolobos E . . . . . 155 B4
Riom F . . . . . . . . 116 B3
Riomaggiore I . . . . 134 A2
Rio Maior P . . . . . 154 B2
Rio Marina I . . . . 134 C3
Riom-ès-Montagnes
F . . . . . . . . . . 116 B2
Rion-des-Landes F 128 C2
Rionegro del Puente
E . . . . . . . . . . 141 B4
Rionero in Vúlture
I . . . . . . . . . . 172 B1
Riopar E . . . . . . . 158 C1
Riós E . . . . . . . . 141 C3
Rioseco E . . . . . . 142 A1
Rioseco de Tapia
E . . . . . . . . . . 141 B5
Rio Tinto P . . . . . 148 A1
Riotord F . . . . . . 117 B4
Riotorto E . . . . . . 141 A3
Rioz F . . . . . . . . 105 B5
Ripač BIH . . . . . . 124 C1
Ripacándida I . . . . 172 B1
Ripanj SRB . . . . . 127 C2
Ripatransone I . . . . 136 C2
Ripley GB . . . . . . 40 B2
Ripoll E . . . . . . . 147 B3
Ripon GB . . . . . . 40 A2
Riposto I . . . . . . . 177 B4
Ripsa S . . . . . . . . 56 B2
Risan MNE . . . . . 16 D3
Risbäck S . . . . . . 200 B1
Risca GB . . . . . . . 39 C3
Rischenau D . . . . 81 A5
Riscle F . . . . . . . 128 C2
Risebo S . . . . . . . 56 B2
Risnes N . . . . . . . 46 A2
Rišňovce SK . . . . 98 C1
Risør N . . . . . . . . 53 B5
Risøyhamn N . . . 194 B6
Rissna S . . . . . . 199 B12
Ritsem S . . . . . . 194 C8
Ritterhude D . . . . 72 A1
Riutula FIN . . . . 193 D10
Riva del Garda I . . 121 B3
Riva Lígure I . . . . 133 B3
Rivanazzano I . . . . 120 C2
Rivarolo Canavese
I . . . . . . . . . . 119 B4
Rivarolo Mantovano
I . . . . . . . . . . 121 B3
Rive-de-Gier F . . . 117 B4
Rivedoux-Plage F . 114 B2
Rivello I . . . . . . . 174 A1
Rivergaro I . . . . . 120 C2
Rives F . . . . . . . 118 B2
Rivesaltes F . . . . 146 B3
Rivignano I . . . . . 122 B2
Rivne UA . . . . . . 13 C7
Rívoli I . . . . . . . 119 B4
Rivolta d'Adda I . . 120 B2
Rixheim F . . . . . . 106 B2
Rixo S . . . . . . . . 54 B2
Riza GR . . . . . . . 183 C5
Rizokarpaso CY . . 181 A3
Rjukan N . . . . . . 47 C5
Rø DK . . . . . . . . 67 A3
Rö S . . . . . . . . . 57 A4
Roa
E . . . . . . . . . . 143 C3
N . . . . . . . . . . 48 B2
Roade GB . . . . . . 44 A3
Roager DK . . . . . 59 C1
Roaldkvam N . . . . 52 A2
Roanne F . . . . . . 117 A4

Röbäck S . . . . . . 200 C6
Robakowo PL . . . 69 B3
Róbbio I . . . . . . . 120 B1
Röbel D . . . . . . . 73 A5
Roberton GB . . . . 35 C5
Robertsfors S . . . 200 B6
Robertville B . . . . 80 B2
Robin Hood's Bay
GB . . . . . . . . . 37 B6
Robleda E . . . . . 149 B3
Robledillo de Trujillo
E . . . . . . . . . . 156 A2
Robledo
Albacete E . . . . 158 C1
Orense E . . . . . 141 B4
Robledo de Chavela
E . . . . . . . . . . 151 B3
Robledo del Buey
E . . . . . . . . . . 156 A3
Robledo del Mazo
E . . . . . . . . . . 156 A3
Robledollano E . . 156 A2
Robles de la Valcueva
E . . . . . . . . . . 142 B1
Robliza de Cojos E 149 B4
Robres E . . . . . . 145 C3
Robres del Castillo
E . . . . . . . . . . 144 B1
Rocafort de Queralt
E . . . . . . . . . . 147 C2
Rocamadour F . . . 129 B4
Roccabernarda I . . 175 B2
Roccabianca I . . . 120 B3
Roccadáspide I . . 172 B1
Rocca di Mezzo I . 169 A3
Rocca di Papa I . . 168 B2
Roccagorga I . . . . 169 B3
Rocca Imperiale I . 174 A2
Roccalbegna I . . . 135 C4
Roccalumera I . . . 177 B4
Roccamena I . . . . 176 B2
Roccamonfina I . . 170 B1
Roccanova I . . . . 174 A2
Roccapalumba I . . 176 B2
Roccapassa I . . . 169 A3
Rocca Priora I . . . 136 B2
Roccaraso I . . . . 169 B4
Rocca San Casciano
I . . . . . . . . . . 135 A4
Roccasecca I . . . . 169 B3
Rocca Sinibalda I . 169 A2
Roccastrada I . . . 135 B4
Roccatederighi I . . 135 B4
Roccella Iónica I . 175 C2
Rocchetta Sant'António
I . . . . . . . . . . 172 A1
Rocester GB . . . . 40 C2
Rochdale GB . . . . 40 B1
Rochechouart F . . 115 C4
Rochefort
B . . . . . . . . . . 79 B5
F . . . . . . . . . . 114 C3
Rochefort-en-Terre
F . . . . . . . . . . 101 B3
Rochefort-Montagne
F . . . . . . . . . . 116 B2
Rochefort-sur-Nenon
F . . . . . . . . . . 105 B4
Roche-lez-Beaupré
F . . . . . . . . . . 105 B5
Rochemaure F . . . 131 A3
Rocheservière F . . 114 B2
Rochester
Medway GB . . . 45 B4
Northumberland GB . 37 A4
Rochlitz D . . . . . 83 A4
Rociana del Condado
E . . . . . . . . . . 161 B3
Rockenhausen D . 93 B3
Rockhammar S . . 56 A1
Rockneby S . . . . 62 B4
Ročko Polje HR . . 123 B3
Ročov CZ . . . . . 84 B1
Rocroi F . . . . . . . 91 B4
Rodach D . . . . . . 82 B2
Roda de Bara E . . 147 C2
Roda de Ter E . . . 147 C3
Rodalben D . . . . 93 B3
Rødberg N . . . . . 47 B5
Rødby DK . . . . . 65 B4
Rødbyhavn DK . . 65 B4
Rødding
Sonderjyllands Amt.
DK . . . . . . . . 59 C2
Viborg Amt. DK . 58 B1
Rödeby S . . . . . . 63 B3
Rodeiro E . . . . . 140 B3
Rødekro DK . . . . 64 A2
Roden NL . . . . . 71 A3
Ródenas E . . . . 152 B2
Rodenkirchen D . . 72 A1
Rödental D . . . . . 82 B3
Rödermark D . . . 93 B4
Rodewisch D . . . 83 B4
Rodez F . . . . . . 130 A1
Rodi Gargánico I . 171 B3
Roding D . . . . . . 95 B4
Rödjebro S . . . . 51 B4
Rødkærsbro DK . . 59 B2
Rodolivas GR . . . 183 C5
Rodoñá E . . . . . 147 C2
Rødvig DK . . . . . 65 A5
Roermond NL . . . 80 A1
Roesbrugge B . . . 78 B2
Roeschwoog F . . 93 C4
Roeselare B . . . . 78 B3
Roetgen D . . . . . 80 B2
Roffiac F . . . . . . 116 B3

Röfors S . . . . . . . 55 B5
Rofrano I . . . . . . 172 B1
Rogač HR . . . . . 138 B2
Rogačica SRB . . . 127 C1
Rogalinek PL . . . . 76 B1
Rogaška Slatina
SLO . . . . . . . . 123 A4
Rogatec SLO . . . 123 A4
Rogatica BIH . . . . 139 B5
Rogatyn UA . . . . 13 D6
Rogätz D . . . . . . 73 B4
Roggendorf D . . . 65 C4
Roggiano Gravina
I . . . . . . . . . . 174 B2
Roghadal GB . . . 31 B2
Rogliano
F . . . . . . . . . . 180 A2
I . . . . . . . . . . 175 B2
Rognan N . . . . . 195 C6
Rogne N . . . . . . 47 A6
Rognes F . . . . . . 131 B4
Rogny-les-7-Ecluses
F . . . . . . . . . . 103 B4
Rogowo PL . . . . 76 B2
Rogoznica HR . . . 138 B1
Rogoźnica PL . . . 85 A4
Rogoźno PL . . . . 76 B1
Rohan F . . . . . . 101 A3
Röhlingen D . . . . 94 C2
Rohožnik SK . . . 98 C1
Rohr D . . . . . . . 82 B2
Rohrbach A . . . . 96 C1
Rohrbach-lès-Bitche
F . . . . . . . . . . 92 B3
Rohrberg D . . . . 73 B4
Rohr im Gebirge A . 110 B2
Röhrnbach D . . . 96 C1
Roisel F . . . . . . 90 B3
Roja LV . . . . . . . 8 D3
Rojales E . . . . . 165 A4
Röjeråsen S . . . . 50 B1
Rojewo PL . . . . . 76 B3
Rokiciny PL . . . . 87 A3
Rokietnica PL . . . 75 B5
Rokiškis LT . . . . 8 E4
Rokitki PL . . . . . 85 A3
Rokycany CZ . . . 96 B1
Rolampont F . . . 105 B4
Rold DK . . . . . . 58 B2
Røldal N . . . . . . 52 A2
Rolde NL . . . . . . 71 B3
Rolfs S . . . . . . 196 D6
Rollag N . . . . . . 47 B6
Rollán E . . . . . . 149 B4
Rolle CH . . . . . . 105 C5
Roma = Rome I . . 168 B2
Roma S . . . . . . . 57 C4
Romagnano Sésia
I . . . . . . . . . . 119 B5
Romagné F . . . . 88 B2
Romakloster S . . . 57 C4
Roman RO . . . . . 17 B7
Romana I . . . . . 178 B2
Romanèche-Thorins
F . . . . . . . . . . 117 A4
Romano di Lombardia
I . . . . . . . . . . 120 B2
Romanshorn CH . 107 B4
Romans-sur-Isère
F . . . . . . . . . . 118 B2
Rombas F . . . . . 92 B2
Rome = Roma I . . 168 B2
Romeán E . . . . . 141 B3
Romenay F . . . . 105 C4
Romeral E . . . . . 157 A4
Römerstein D . . . 94 C1
Rometta I . . . . . 177 A4
Romford GB . . . . 45 B4
Romhány H . . . . 112 B3
Römhild D . . . . . 82 B2
Romilly-sur-Seine F 91 C3
Romont CH . . . . 106 C1
Romorantin-Lanthenay
F . . . . . . . . . . 103 B3
Romrod D . . . . . 81 B5
Romsey GB . . . . 44 C2
Rømskog N . . . . 54 A2
Rønbjerg DK . . . 58 B1
Roncal E . . . . . . 144 B3
Ronce-les-Bains F 114 C2
Ronchamp F . . . 106 B1
Ronchi dei Legionari
I . . . . . . . . . . 122 B2
Ronciglione I . . . 168 A2
Ronco Canavese I . 119 B4
Ronco Scrivia I . . 120 C1
Ronda E . . . . . . 162 B2
Rønde DK . . . . . 59 B3
Rone S . . . . . . . 57 C4
Ronehamn S . . . 57 C4
Rong N . . . . . . . 46 B1
Rönnäng S . . . . 60 B1
Rønne DK . . . . . 67 A3
Ronneburg D . . . 83 B4
Ronneby S . . . . 63 B3
Rönneshytta S . . 55 B6
Rönninge S . . . . 57 A3
Rönnöfors S . . . 199 B10
Rönö S . . . . . . . 56 B2
Ronse B . . . . . . 79 B3
Roosendaal NL . . 79 A4
Roosky IRL . . . . 26 C3
Ropczyce PL . . . 87 B5
Ropeid N . . . . . . 52 A2
Ropinsalmi FIN . . 192 D5

Ropuerelos del Páramo
E . . . . . . . . . . 141 B5
Roquebilière F . . . 133 A3
Roquebrun F . . . 130 B2
Roquecourbe F . . 130 B1
Roquefort F . . . . 128 B2
Roquemaure F . . 131 A3
Roquesteron F . . 132 B3
Roquetas de Mar E 164 C2
Roquetes E . . . . 153 B4
Roquevaire F . . . 132 B1
Røra N . . . . . . . 199 B8
Rosal de la Frontera
E . . . . . . . . . . 161 B2
Rosalina Mare I . . 122 B1
Rosa Marina I . . . 173 B3
Rosans F . . . . . . 132 A1
Rosário P . . . . . 160 B1
Rosarno I . . . . . 175 C1
Rosbach D . . . . . 81 B3
Rosche D . . . . . 73 B3
Rościszewo PL . . 77 B4
Roscoff F . . . . . 100 A2
Roscommon IRL . . 28 A3
Roscrea IRL . . . . 28 B4
Rosdorf D . . . . . 82 A1
Rose I . . . . . . . 174 B2
Rosegg A . . . . . 109 C5
Rosehall GB . . . . 32 D2
Rosehearty GB . . 33 D4
Rosel GB . . . . . . 88 A1
Rosell E . . . . . . 153 B4
Roselló E . . . . . 153 A4
Rosendal N . . . . 46 C3
Rosenfeld D . . . . 93 C4
Rosenfors S . . . . 62 A3
Rosenheim D . . . 108 B3
Rosenow D . . . . 74 A2
Rosenthal D . . . . 81 A4
Rosersberg S . . . 57 A3
Roses E . . . . . . 147 B4
Roseto degli Abruzzi
I . . . . . . . . . . 169 A4
Roseto Valfortore I 170 B3
Rosheim F . . . . . 93 C3
Rosía I . . . . . . . 135 B4
Rosice CZ . . . . . 97 B4
Rosières-en-Santerre
F . . . . . . . . . . 90 B2
Rosignano Maríttimo
I . . . . . . . . . . 134 B3
Rosignano Solvay
I . . . . . . . . . . 134 B3
Roşiori-de-Vede RO 17 C6
Roskhill GB . . . . 31 B2
Roskilde DK . . . . 61 D2
Roskovec AL . . . 182 C1
Röslau D . . . . . 83 B3
Roslev DK . . . . . 58 B1
Rosmaninhal P . . 155 B3
Rosnowo PL . . . 67 B5
Rosolini I . . . . . 177 C3
Rosova MNE . . . 139 B5
Rosoy F . . . . . . 104 A2
Rosporden F . . . 100 B2
Rosquete P . . . . 154 B2
Rosrath D . . . . . 80 B3
Rossa CH . . . . . 120 A2
Rossano I . . . . . 174 B2
Rossas
Aveiro P . . . . . 148 B1
Braga P . . . . . 148 A1
Rossdorf D . . . . 82 B2
Rossett GB . . . . 38 A4
Rosshaupten D . . 108 B1
Rossiglione I . . . 133 A4
Rossignol B . . . . 92 B1
Rossla D . . . . . . 82 A3
Rosslare IRL . . . 30 B2
Rosslare Harbour
IRL . . . . . . . . 30 B2
Rosslau D . . . . . 83 A4
Rosslea GB . . . . 27 B3
Rossleben D . . . 82 A3
Rossön S . . . . . 200 C2
Ross-on-Wye GB . 39 C4
Rossoszyca PL . . 86 A2
Rosswein D . . . . 83 A5
Röstånga S . . . . 61 C3
Roštár SK . . . . . 99 C4
Rostock D . . . . . 65 B5
Rostrenen F . . . . 100 A2
Røsvik N . . . . . . 194 C6
Rosvik S . . . . . . 196 D4
Rosyth GB . . . . . 35 B4
Röszke H . . . . . 126 A2
Rot S . . . . . . . . 49 A6
Rota E . . . . . . . 161 C3
Rota Greca I . . . 174 B2
Rot am See D . . . 94 B2
Rotberget N . . . . 49 B4
Rotella I . . . . . . 136 C2
Rotenburg
Hessen D . . . . 82 B1
Niedersachsen D . 72 A2
Roth
Bayern D . . . . 94 B3
Rheinland-Pfalz D . 81 B3

Rothbury GB . . . . 37 A5
Rothemühl D . . . 74 A2
Röthenbach D . . . 95 B3
Rothenburg D . . . 84 A2
Rothenburg ob der
Tauber D . . . . . 94 B2
Rothéneuf F . . . . 88 B2
Rothenklempenow
D . . . . . . . . . 74 A3
Rothenstein D . . . 94 C3
Rotherham GB . . 40 B2
Rothes GB . . . . . 32 D3
Rothesay GB . . . 34 C2
Rothwell GB . . . . 44 A3
Rotnes N . . . . . 48 B2
Rotonda I . . . . . 174 B2
Rotondella I . . . . 174 A2
Rötsee I . . . . . . 159 C3
Rott
Bayern D . . . . 108 B1
Bayern D . . . . 108 B3
Rottach-Egern D . 108 B2
Röttenbach D . . . 94 B3
Rottenbuch D . . . 108 B1
Rottenburg
Baden-Württemberg
D . . . . . . . . 93 C4
Bayern D . . . . 95 C4
Rottenmann A . . 110 B1
Rotterdam NL . . . 79 A4
Rotthalmünster D . 96 C1
Rottingdean GB . . 44 C3
Röttingen D . . . . 94 B1
Rottleberode D . . 82 A2
Rottne S . . . . . . 62 A2
Rottneros S . . . . 55 A4
Rottofreno I . . . . 120 B2
Rottweil D . . . . . 107 A3
Rötz D . . . . . . . 95 B4
Roubaix F . . . . . 78 B3
Roudnice nad Labem
CZ . . . . . . . . 84 B2
Roudouallec F . . . 100 A2
Rouen F . . . . . . 89 A5
Rouffach F . . . . . 106 B2
Rougé F . . . . . . 101 B4
Rougemont F . . . 105 B5
Rougemont le-Château
F . . . . . . . . . . 106 B1
Rouillac F . . . . . 115 C3
Rouillé F . . . . . . 115 B4
Roujan F . . . . . . 130 B2
Roulans F . . . . . 105 B5
Roundwood IRL . . 30 A2
Rousínov CZ . . . 97 B4
Roussac F . . . . . 115 B5
Roussennac F . . . 130 A1
Rousses F . . . . . 130 A2
Roussillon F . . . . 117 B4
Rouvroy-sur-Audry
F . . . . . . . . . . 91 B4
Rouy F . . . . . . . 104 B2
Rovaniemen
maalaiskunta FIN 197 C8
Rovaniemi FIN . . 197 C8
Rovato I . . . . . . 120 B2
Rovensko pod Troskami
CZ . . . . . . . . 84 B3
Roverbella I . . . . 121 B3
Rovereto I . . . . . 121 B4
Rövershagen D . . 65 B5
Roverud N . . . . . 49 B4
Rovigo I . . . . . . 121 B4
Rovinj HR . . . . . 122 B2
Rovišce HR . . . . 124 B2
Röw PL . . . . . . . 74 B3
Rowy PL . . . . . . 68 A2
Royal Leamington Spa
GB . . . . . . . . 44 A2
Royal Tunbridge Wells
GB . . . . . . . . 45 B4
Royan F . . . . . . 114 C2
Royat F . . . . . . 116 B3
Roybon F . . . . . 118 B2
Roybridge GB . . . 34 B3
Roye F . . . . . . . 90 B2
Royère-de-Vassivière
F . . . . . . . . . . 116 B1
Røykenvik N . . . 48 B2
Royos E . . . . . . 164 B2
Røyrvik N . . . . 199 A10
Royston GB . . . . 44 A3
Rozadas E . . . . 141 A4
Rozalén del Monte
E . . . . . . . . . . 151 C5
Różańsko PL . . . 75 B3
Rozay-en-Brie F . 90 C2
Roždalovice CZ . . 84 B3
Rozdilna UA . . . . 17 B9
Rozental PL . . . . 69 B4
Rozhyshche UA . . 13 C6
Rožmitál pod
Třemšínem CZ . 96 B1
Rožňava SK . . . . 99 C4
Rozoy-sur-Serre F 91 B4
Rozprza PL . . . . 86 A3
Rozvadov CZ . . . 95 B4
Rozzano I . . . . . 120 B2
Rrëshen AL . . . . 182 B1
Rrogozhinë AL . . 182 B1

Rubiacedo de Abajo
E . . . . . . . . . . 143 B3
Rubielos Bajos E . 158 B1
Rubielos de Mora
E . . . . . . . . . . 153 B3
Rubiera I . . . . . . 121 C3
Rubik AL . . . . . . 182 B1
Rucandio E . . . . 143 B3
Rud
Akershus N . . . 48 B3
Buskerud N . . . 48 B2
Ruda
PL . . . . . . . . 86 A2
S . . . . . . . . . 62 A4
Rudabánya H . . . 99 C4
Ruda Maleniecka PL 87 A4
Ruda Pilczycka PL . 87 A4
Ruda Śl. PL . . . . 86 B2
Ruddervorde B . . 78 A3
Ruden A . . . . . . 110 C1
Rudersberg D . . . 94 C1
Rudersdorf A . . . 111 B3
Rüdersdorf D . . . 74 B2
Ruderting D . . . . 96 C1
Rüdesheim D . . . 93 B3
Rudkøbing DK . . . 65 B3
Rudmanns A . . . 97 C3
Rudna
CZ . . . . . . . . 96 A2
PL . . . . . . . . 85 A4
Rudnik SRB . . . . 127 C2
Rudniki
Opolskie PL . . . 86 A2
Śląskie PL . . . . 86 B3
Rudno
Dolnośląskie PL . . 85 A4
Pomorskie PL . . 69 B3
Rudnya RUS . . . 13 A9
Rudolstadt D . . . 82 B3
Rudowica PL . . . 84 A3
Rudozem BG . . . 183 B6
Rudskoga S . . . . 55 A5
Rudston GB . . . . 40 A3
Ruds Vedby DK . . 61 D1
Rudy PL . . . . . . 86 B2
Rue F . . . . . . . . 78 B1
Rueda E . . . . . . 150 A3
Rueda de Jalón E . 152 A2
Ruelle-sur-Touvre
F . . . . . . . . . . 115 C4
Ruerrero E . . . . . 143 B3
Ruffano I . . . . . . 173 C4
Ruffec F . . . . . . 115 B4
Rufina I . . . . . . 135 B4
Rugby GB . . . . . 44 A2
Rugeley GB . . . . 40 C2
Ruggstrop S . . . . 62 B4
Rugles F . . . . . . 89 B4
Rugozero RUS . . 3 D13
Rühen D . . . . . . 73 B3
Ruhla D . . . . . . 82 B2
Ruhland D . . . . . 84 A1
Ruhle D . . . . . . 71 B4
Ruhpolding D . . . 109 B3
Ruhstorf D . . . . . 96 C1
Ruidera E . . . . . 158 C1
Ruillé-sur-le-Loir F 102 B2
Ruinen NL . . . . . 71 B3
Ruiselede B . . . . 78 A3
Ruka FIN . . . . . 197 C12
Rulles B . . . . . . 92 B1
Rülzheim D . . . . 93 B4
Rum H . . . . . . . 111 B3
Ruma SRB . . . . 127 B1
Rumboci BIH . . . 138 B3
Rumburk CZ . . . 84 B2
Rumenka SRB . . 126 B1
Rumia PL . . . . . 69 A3
Rumigny F . . . . . 91 B4
Rumilly F . . . . . 118 B2
Rumma S . . . . . 56 B2
Rumney GB . . . . 39 C3
Rumont F . . . . . 91 C5
Runa P . . . . . . 154 B1
Runcorn GB . . . . 38 A4
Rundmoen N . . . 195 D5
Rungsted DK . . . 61 D2
Runhällen S . . . . 51 B3
Runowo PL . . . . 69 A5
Ruokojärvi FIN . . 196 B7
Ruokolahti FIN . . 9 B6
Ruokto S . . . . . 196 B2
Ruoms F . . . . . . 131 A3
Ruoti I . . . . . . . 172 B1
Rupa HR . . . . . . 123 B3
Ruppichteroth D . . 80 B3
Rupt-sur-Moselle F 106 B1
Rus E . . . . . . . 157 B4
Ruse BG . . . . . . 17 D7
Ruše SLO . . . . . 110 C2
Rusele S . . . . . 200 B4
Ruševo HR . . . . 125 B4
Rush IRL . . . . . 30 A2
Rushden GB . . . . 44 A3
Rusiec PL . . . . . 86 A2
Rusinowo
Zachodnio-Pomorskie
PL . . . . . . . . 67 C4
Zachodnio-Pomorskie
PL . . . . . . . . 75 A5
Ruskele S . . . . . 200 B4
Ruski Krstur SRB . 126 B1
Ruskington GB . . 40 B3
Rusovce SK . . . . 111 A4
Rüsselsheim D . . 93 B4

Russelv N 192 C4
Russi I 135 A5
Rust A 111 B3
Rustefjelbma N 193 B12
Rustrel F 131 B4
Ruszki PL 77 B5
Ruszów PL 84 A3
Rute E 163 A3
Rüthen D 81 A4
Rutherglen GB 35 C3
Ruthin GB 38 A3
Ruthven GB 32 D2
Ruthwell GB 36 B3
Rüti CH 107 B3
Rutigliano I 173 A3
Rutledal N 46 A2
Rutuna S 56 B3
Rutvik S 196 D5
Ruurlo NL 71 B3
Ruuvaoja FIN 197 B11
Ruvo del Monte I 172 B1
Ruvo di Púglia I 171 B4
Ruynes-en-Margeride F 116 C3
Ružic HR 138 B2
Ružomberok SK 99 B3
Ruzsa H 126 A1
Ry DK 59 B2
Rybany SK 98 C2
Rybina PL 69 A4
Rybnik PL 86 B2
Rychliki PL 69 B4
Rychlocice PL 86 A2
Rychnov nad Kněžnou CZ 85 B4
Rychnowo PL 77 A5
Rychtal PL 86 A1
Rychwał PL 76 B3
Ryczywół PL 87 A5
Ryczywól PL 75 B5
Ryd S 63 B2
Rydaholm S 62 B2
Rydal S 60 B2
Rydbo S 57 A4
Rydboholm S 60 B2
Ryde GB 44 C2
Rydöbruk S 60 C3
Rydsgård S 66 A2
Rydsnäs S 62 A3
Rydultowy PL 86 B2
Rydzyna PL 85 A4
Rye GB 45 C4
Rygge N 54 A1
Ryjewo PL 69 B3
Rykene N 53 B4
Rymań PL 67 C4
Rýmařov CZ 98 B1
Rynarzewo PL 76 A2
Ryomgård DK 59 B3
Rypefjord N 192 B7
Rypin PL 77 A4
Rysjedalsvika N 46 A2
Ryssby S 60 C4
Rytel PL 68 B2
Rytinki FIN 197 D10
Rytro PL 99 B4
Rywociny PL 77 A5
Rzeczenica PL 68 B2
Rzeczniów PL 87 A5
Rzeczyca PL 87 A4
Rzęgnowo PL 77 A5
Rzejowice PL 87 A3
Rzemień PL 87 B5
Rzepin PL 75 B3
Rzesznikowo PL 67 C4
Rzeszów PL 12 C4
Rzgów PL 86 A3
Rzhev RUS 9 D9

## S

Saal
*Bayern* D 82 B2
*Bayern* D 95 C3
Saalbach A 109 B3
Saalburg D 83 B3
Saales F 92 C3
Saalfeld D 82 B3
Saalfelden am Steinernen Meer A 109 B3
Saanen CH 106 C2
Saarbrücken D 92 B2
Saarburg D 92 B2
Saarijärvi FIN 8 A4
Saari-Kämä FIN 197 C9
Saarlouis D 92 B2
Saas-Fee CH 119 A4
Šabac SRB 127 C1
Sabadell E 147 C3
Sabáudia I 169 B3
Sabbioneta I 121 C3
Sabero E 142 B1
Sabiñánigo E 145 B3
Sabiote E 157 B4
Sables-d'Or-les-Pins F 101 A3
Sablé-sur-Sarthe F 102 B1
Sabóia P 160 B1
Saborsko HR 123 B4
Sæbøvik N 52 A1
Sabres F 128 B2
Sabrosa P 148 A2
Sabugal P 149 B2
Sabuncu TR 187 C5
Sæby DK 58 A3
Săcălaz RO 126 B3
Sacecorbo E 152 B1
Saceda del Rio E 151 B5
Sacedón E 151 B5
Săcele RO 17 C6
Saceruela E 156 B3
Sachsenburg A 109 C4
Sachsenhagen D 72 B2
Sacile I 122 B1
Sacramenia E 151 A4
Sada E 140 A2
Sádaba E 144 B2
Saddell GB 34 C2
Sadernes E 147 B3
Sadki PL 76 A2
Sadkowice PL 87 A4
Sadlinki PL 69 B3
Sadów PL 75 B3
Sadská CZ 84 B2
Saelices E 151 C5
Saelices de Mayorga E 142 B1
Saerbeck D 71 B4
Saeul L 92 B1
Safaalan TR 186 A3
Safara P 161 A2
Säffle S 55 A3
Saffron Walden GB 45 A4
Safranbolu TR 187 A7
Säfsnäs S 50 B1
Şag RO 126 B3
Sagard D 66 B2
S'Agaro E 147 C4
Sågmyra S 50 B2
Sagone F 180 A1
Sagres P 160 C1
Ságújfalu H 113 A3
Sagunt E 159 B3
Sagvåg N 52 A1
Ságvár H 112 C2
Sagy F 105 C4
Sahagún E 142 B1
Šahy SK 112 A2
Saignelégier CH 106 B1
Saignes F 116 B2
Saija FIN 197 B11
Saillagouse F 146 B3
Saillans F 118 C2
Sains Richaumont F 91 B3
St Abb's GB 35 C5
St Affrique F 130 B1
St Agnan F 104 C2
St Agnant F 114 C3
St Agnes GB 42 B1
St Agrève F 117 B4
St Aignan F 103 B3
St Aignan-sur-Roë F 101 B4
St Albans GB 44 B3
St Alban-sur-Limagnole F 117 C3
St Amand-en-Puisaye F 104 B2
St Amand-les-Eaux F 79 B3
St Amand-Longpré F 103 B3
St Amand-Montrond F 103 C4
St Amans F 117 C3
St Amans-Soult F 130 B1
St Amant-Roche-Savine F 117 B3
St Amarin F 106 B1
St Ambroix F 131 A3
St Amé F 106 A1
St Amour F 118 A2
St André-de-Corcy F 117 B4
St André-de-Cubzac F 128 B2
St André-de-l'Eure F 89 B5
St André-de-Roquepertuis F 131 A3
St André-de-Sangonis F 130 B2
St Andre-de-Valborgne F 130 A2
St André-les-Alpes F 132 B2
St Andrews GB 35 B5
St Angel F 116 B2
St Anthème F 117 B3
St Antoine F 180 A2
St Antoine-de-Ficalba F 129 B3
St Antönien CH 107 C4
St Antonin-Noble-Val F 129 B4
St Août F 103 C3
St Armant-Tallende F 116 B3
St Arnoult F 90 C1
St Asaph GB 38 A3
St Astier F 129 A3
St Athan GB 39 C3
St Auban F 132 B2
St Aubin
CH 106 C1
F 105 B4
GB 88 A1
St Aubin-d'Aubigne F 101 A4
St Aubin-du-Cormier F 101 A4
St Aubin-sur-Aire F 92 C1
St Aubin-sur-Mer F 89 A3
St Aulaye F 128 A3
St Austell GB 42 B2
St Avit F 116 B2
St Avold F 92 B2
St Aygulf F 132 B2
St Bauzille-de-Putois F 130 B2
St Béat F 145 B4
St Beauzély F 130 A1
St Bees GB 36 B3
St Benim-d'Azy F 104 C2
St Benoît-du-Sault F 115 B5
St Benoit-en-Woëvre F 92 C1
St Berthevin F 102 A1
St Blaise-la-Roche F 92 C3
St Blazey GB 42 B2
St Blin F 105 A4
St Bonnet F 118 C3
St Bonnet Briance F 115 C5
St Bonnet-de-Joux F 104 C3
St Bonnet-le-Château F 117 B4
St Bonnet-le-Froid F 117 B4
St Brévin-les-Pins F 101 B3
St Briac-sur-Mer F 101 A3
St Brice-en-Coglès F 88 B2
St Brieuc F 101 A3
St Bris-le-Vineux F 104 B2
St Broladre F 88 B2
St Calais F 102 B2
St Cannat F 131 B4
St Cast-le-Guildo F 101 A3
St Céré F 129 B4
St Cergue CH 118 A3
St Cergues F 118 A3
St Cernin F 116 B2
St Chamant F 116 B1
St Chamas F 131 B4
St Chamond F 117 B4
St Chély-d'Apcher F 116 C3
St Chély-d'Aubrac F 116 C2
St Chinian F 130 B1
St Christol F 131 A4
St Christol-lès-Alès F 131 A3
St Christoly-Médoc F 114 C3
St Christophe-du-Ligneron F 114 B2
St Christophe-en-Brionnais F 117 A4
St Ciers-sur-Gironde F 128 A2
St Clair-sur-Epte F 90 B1
St Clar F 129 C3
St Claud F 115 C4
St Claude F 118 A2
St Clears GB 39 C2
St Columb Major GB 42 B2
St Come-d'Olt F 130 A1
St Cosme-en-Vairais F 89 B4
St Cyprien
*Dordogne* F 129 B4
*Pyrenées-Orientales* F 146 B4
St Cyr-sur-Loire F 102 B2
St Cyr-sur-Mer F 132 B1
St Cyr-sur-Methon F 117 A4
St David's GB 39 C1
St Denis F 90 C2
St Denis-d'Oléron F 114 B2
St Denis d'Orques F 102 A1
St Didier F 117 A4
St Didier-en-Velay F 117 B4
St Dié F 92 C2
St Dier-d'Auvergne F 117 B3
St Dizier F 91 C4
St Dizier-Leyrenne F 116 A1
St Dogmaels GB 39 B2
Ste Adresse F 89 A4
Ste Anne F 89 B4
Ste Anne-d'Auray F 100 B3
Ste Croix CH 105 C5
Ste Croix-Volvestre F 146 A2
Ste Engrâce F 144 A3
Ste Enimie F 130 A2
St Efflam F 100 A2
Ste Foy-de-Peyrolières F 146 A2
Ste Foy-la-Grande F 128 B3
Ste Foy l'Argentiere F 117 B4
Ste Gauburge-Ste Colombe F 89 B4
Ste Gemme la Plaine F 114 B2
Ste Geneviève F 90 B2
St Égrève F 118 B2
Ste Hélène F 128 B2
Ste Hélène-sur-Isère F 118 B3
Ste Hermine F 114 B2
Ste Jalle F 131 A4
Ste Livrade-sur-Lot F 129 B3
St Eloy-les-Mines F 116 A2
Ste Marie-aux-Mines F 106 A2
Ste Marie-du-Mont F 88 A2
Ste Maure-de-Touraine F 102 B2
Ste Maxime F 132 B2
Ste Ménéhould F 91 B4
Ste Mère-Église F 88 A2
St Emiland F 104 C3
St Émilion F 128 B2
St Enoder GB 42 B2
Sainteny F 88 A2
Ste Ode B 92 A1
Saintes F 114 C3
Ste Savine F 91 C4
Ste Sévère-sur-Indre F 103 C4
Ste Sigolène F 117 B4
St Esteben F 144 A2
St Estèphe F 128 A2
Ste Suzanne F 102 A1
St Étienne F 117 B4
St Etienne-de-Baigorry F 144 A2
St Étienne-de-Cuines F 118 B3
St Etienne-de-Fursac F 116 A1
St Etienne-de-Montluc F 101 B4
St Etienne-de-St Geoirs F 118 B2
St Étienne-de-Tinée F 132 A2
St Étienne-du-Bois F 118 A2
St Étienne-du-Rouvray F 89 A5
St Etienne-les-Orgues F 132 A1
Ste Tulle F 132 B1
St Fargeau F 104 B2
St Félicien F 117 B4
St Felix-de-Sorgues F 130 B1
St Félix-Lauragais F 146 A2
Saintfield GB 27 B5
St Fillans GB 35 B3
St Firmin F 118 C3
St Florent F 180 A2
St Florentin F 104 B2
St Florent-le-Vieil F 101 B4
St Florent-sur-Cher F 103 C4
St Flour F 116 B3
St Flovier F 103 C3
St Fort-sur-le-Né F 115 C3
St Fulgent F 114 B2
St Galmier F 117 B4
St Gaudens F 145 A4
St Gaultier F 115 B5
St Gély-du-Fesc F 130 B2
St Genest-Malifaux F 117 B4
St Gengoux-le-National F 104 C3
St Geniez F 132 A2
St Geniez-d'Olt F 130 A1
St Genis-de-Saintonge F 114 C3
St Genis-Pouilly F 118 A3
St Genix-sur-Guiers F 118 B2
St Georges Buttavent F 88 B3
St Georges-d'Aurac F 117 B3
St Georges-de-Commiers F 118 B2
St Georges-de-Didonne F 114 C3
St Georges-de-Luzençon F 130 A1
St Georges-de Mons F 116 B2
St Georges-de-Reneins F 117 A4
St Georges d'Oléron F 114 C2
St Georges-en-Couzan F 117 B3
St Georges-lès-Baillargeaux F 115 B4
St Georges-sur-Loire F 102 B1
St Georges-sur-Meuse B 79 B5
St Geours-de-Maremne F 128 C1
St Gérand-de-Vaux F 117 A3
St Gérand-le-Puy F 117 A3
St Germain F 105 B5
St Germain-Chassenay F 104 C2
St Germain-de-Calberte F 130 A2
St Germain-de-Confolens F 115 B4
St Germain-de-Joux F 118 A2
St Germain-des-Fossés F 117 A3
St Germain-du-Bois F 105 C4
St Germain-du-Plain F 105 C3
St Germain-du Puy F 103 B4
St Germain-en-Laye F 90 C2
St Germain-Laval F 117 B4
St Germain-Lembron F 116 B3
St Germain-les-Belles F 116 B1
St Germain-Lespinasse F 117 A3
St Germain-l'Herm F 117 B3
St Gervais-d'Auvergne F 116 A2
St Gervais-les-Bains F 118 B3
St Gervais-sur-Mare F 130 B2
St Gildas-de-Rhuys F 100 B3
St Gildas-des-Bois F 101 B3
St Gilles
*Gard* F 131 B3
*Ille-et-Vilaine* F 101 A4
St Gilles-Croix-de-Vie F 114 B2
St Gingolph F 119 A3
St Girons
*Ariège* F 146 B2
*Landes* F 128 C1
St Girons-Plage F 128 C1
St Gobain F 91 B3
St Gorgon-Main F 105 B5
St Guénolé F 100 B1
St Harmon GB 39 B3
St Helens GB 38 A4
St Helier GB 88 A1
St Herblain F 101 B4
St Hilaire
*Allier* F 104 C2
*Aude* F 146 A3
St Hilaire-de-Riez F 114 B2
St Hilaire-des-Loges F 114 B3
St Hilaire-de-Villefranche F 114 C3
St Hilaire-du-Harcouët F 88 B2
St Hilaire-du-Rosier F 118 B2
St Hippolyte
*Aveyron* F 116 C2
*Doubs* F 106 B1
St Hippolyte-du-Fort F 130 B2
St Honoré-les-Bains F 104 C2
St Hubert B 92 A1
St Imier CH 106 B2
St Issey GB 42 B2
St Ives
*Cambridgeshire* GB 44 A3
*Cornwall* GB 42 B1
St Izaire F 130 B1
St Jacques-de-la-Lande F 101 A4
St Jacut-de-la-Mer F 101 A3
St James F 88 B2
St Jaume d'Enveja E 153 B4
St Jean-Brévelay F 101 B3
St Jean-d'Angély F 114 C3
St Jean-de-Belleville F 118 B3
St Jean-de-Bournay F 118 B2
St Jean-de-Braye F 103 B3
St Jean-de-Côle F 115 C4
St Jean-de-Daye F 88 A2
St Jean de Losne F 105 B4
St Jean-de-Luz F 144 A2
St Jean-de-Maurienne F 118 B3
St Jean-de-Monts F 114 B1
St Jean-d'Illac F 128 B2
St Jean-du-Bruel F 130 A2
St Jean-du-Gard F 131 A2
St Jean-en-Royans F 118 B2
St Jean-la-Riviere F 133 B3
St Jean-Pied-de-Port F 144 A2
St Jean-Poutge F 129 C3
St Jeoire F 118 A3
St Joachim F 101 B3
St Johnstown IRL 27 B3
St Jorioz F 118 B3
St Joris Winge B 79 B4
St Jouin-de-Marnes F 102 C1
St Juéry F 130 B1
St Julien F 118 A2
St Julien-Chapteuil F 117 B4
St Julien-de-Vouvantes F 101 B4
St Julien-du-Sault F 104 A2
St Julien-du-Verdon F 132 B2
St Julien-en-Born F 128 B1
St Julien-en-Genevois F 118 A3
St Julien-l'Ars F 115 B4
St Julien la-Vêtre F 117 B3
St Julien-Mont-Denis F 118 B3
St Julien-sur-Reyssouze F 118 A2
St Junien F 115 C4
St Just
F 131 A3
GB 42 B1
St Just-en-Chaussée F 90 B2
St Just-en-Chevalet F 117 B3
St Justin F 128 C2
St Just-St Rambert F 117 B4
St Keverne GB 42 B1
St Lary-Soulan F 145 B4
St Laurent-d'Aigouze F 131 B3
St Laurent-de-Chamousset F 117 B4
St Laurent-de-Condel F 89 A3
St Laurent-de-la-Cabrerisse F 146 A3
St Laurent-de-la-Salanque F 146 B3
St Laurent-des-Autels F 101 B4
St Laurent-du-Pont F 118 B2
St Laurent-en-Caux F 89 A4
St Laurent-en-Grandvaux F 105 C4
St Laurent-Médoc F 128 A2
St Laurent-sur-Gorre F 115 C4
St Laurent-sur-Mer F 88 A3
St Laurent-sur-Sèvre F 114 B3
St Leger B 92 B1
St Léger-de-Vignes F 104 C2
St Léger-sous-Beuvray F 104 C3
St Léger-sur-Dheune F 104 C3
St Léonard-de-Noblat F 116 B1
St Leonards GB 45 C4
St Lô F 88 A2
St Lon-les-Mines F 128 C1
St Louis F 106 B2
St Loup F 117 A3
St Loup-de-la-Salle F 105 C3
St Loup-sur-Semouse F 105 B5
St Lunaire F 101 A3
St Lupicin F 118 A2
St Lyphard F 101 B3
St Lys F 146 A2
St Macaire F 128 B2
St Maclou F 89 A4
St Maixent-l'École F 115 B3
St Malo F 88 B1
St Mamet-la-Salvetat F 116 C2
St Mandrier-sur-Mer F 132 B1
St Marcel
*Drôme* F 117 C4
*Saône-et-Loire* F 105 C3
St Marcellin F 118 B2
St Marcellin sur Loire F 117 B4
St Marcet F 145 A4
St Mards-en-Othe F 104 A2
St Margaret's-at-Cliffe GB 45 B5
St Margaret's Hope GB 33 C4
St Mars-la-Jaille F 101 B4
St Martin-d'Ablois F 91 C3
St Martin-d'Auxigny F 103 B4
St Martin-de-Belleville F 118 B3

St Martin-de-Bossenay
F . . . . . . 91 C3
St Martin-de-Crau
F . . . . . . 131 B3
St Martin-de-Londres
F . . . . . . 130 B2
St Martin-d'Entraunes
F . . . . . . 132 A2
St Martin-de-Queyrières
F . . . . . . 118 C3
St Martin-de-Ré F . 114 B2
St Martin des Besaces
F . . . . . . 88 A3
St Martin-d'Estreaux
F . . . . . . 117 A3
St Martin-de-Valamas
F . . . . . . 117 C4
St Martin-d'Hères
F . . . . . . 118 B2
St Martin-du-Frêne
F . . . . . . 118 A2
St Martin-en-Bresse
F . . . . . . 105 C4
St Martin-en-Haut
F . . . . . . 117 B4
St Martin-la-Méanne
F . . . . . . 116 B1
St Martin-Osmonville
F . . . . . . 90 B1
St Martin-sur-Ouanne
F . . . . . . 104 B2
St Martin-Valmeroux
F . . . . . . 116 B2
St Martin-Vésubie
F . . . . . . 133 A3
St Martory F . . 145 A4
St Mary's GB . . . 33 C4
St Mathieu F . . 115 C4
St Mathieu-de-Tréviers
F . . . . . . 131 B2
St Maurice CH . . 119 A3
St Maurice-Navacelles
F . . . . . . 130 B2
St Maurice-sur-Moselle
F . . . . . . 106 B1
St Mawes GB . . . 42 B1
St Maximin-la-Ste
Baume F . . . . 132 B1
St Méard-de-Gurçon
F . . . . . . 128 B3
St Médard-de-Guizières
F . . . . . . 128 A2
St Médard-en-Jalles
F . . . . . . 128 B2
St Méen-le-Grand
F . . . . . . 101 A3
St Menges F . . 91 B4
St Merløse DK . . 61 D1
St Město CZ . . . 85 B4
St M'Hervé F . . . 101 A4
St Michel
Aisne F . . . . . 91 B4
Gers F . . . 145 A4
St Michel-Chef-Chef
F . . . . . . 101 B3
St Michel-de-Castelnau
F . . . . . . 128 B2
St Michel-de-Maurienne
F . . . . . . 118 B3
St Michel-en-Grève
F . . . . . . 100 A2
St Michel-enl'Herm
F . . . . . . 114 B2
St Michel-Mont-Mercure
F . . . . . . 114 B3
St Mihiel F . . . 92 C1
St Monance GB . . 35 B5
St Montant F . . 131 A3
St Moritz CH . . 107 C4
St Nazaire F . . 101 B3
St Nazaire-en-Royans
F . . . . . . 118 B2
St Nazaire-le-Désert
F . . . . . . 131 A4
St Nectaire F . . 116 B2
St Neots GB . . . 44 A3
St Nicolas-de-Port F 92 C2
St Nicolas-de-Redon
F . . . . . . 101 B3
St Nicolas-du-Pélem
F . . . . . . 100 A2
St Niklaas B . . 79 A4
St Omer F . . . 78 B2
St Pair-sur-Mer F . . 88 B2
St Palais F . . 144 A2
St Palais-sur-Mer
F . . . . . . 114 C2
St Pardoux-la-Rivière
F . . . . . . 115 C4
St Paul-Cap-de-Joux
F . . . . . . 129 C4
St Paul-de-Fenouillet
F . . . . . . 146 B3
St Paul-de-Varax F . 118 A2
St Paulien F . . 117 B3
St Paul-le-Jeune F . 131 A3
St Paul-lès-Dax F . 128 C1
St Paul-Trois-Châteaux
F . . . . . . 131 A3
St Pé-de-Bigorre F 145 A3
St Pée-sur-Nivelle
F . . . . . . 144 A2
St Péravy-la-Colombe
F . . . . . . 103 B3
St Péray F . . 117 C4
St Père-en-Retz F . 101 B3
St Peter Port GB . 88 A1

St Petersburg = Sankt-
Peterburg RUS . . . 9 C7
St Philbert-de-Grand-
Lieu F . . . . . 114 A2
St Pierre F . . . 130 B1
St Pierre-d'Albigny
F . . . . . . 118 B3
St Pierre-d'Allevard
F . . . . . . 118 B3
St Pierre-de-Chartreuse
F . . . . . . 118 B2
St Pierre-de-Chignac
F . . . . . . 129 A3
St Pierre-de-la-Fage
F . . . . . . 130 B2
St Pierre-d'Entremont
F . . . . . . 118 B2
St Pierre-d'Oléron
F . . . . . . 114 C2
St Pierre-Eglise F . 88 A2
St Pierre-en-Port F . 89 A4
St Pierre-le-Moûtier
F . . . . . . 104 C2
St Pierre Montlimart
F . . . . . . 101 B4
St Pierre-Quiberon
F . . . . . . 100 B2
St Pierre-sur-Dives
F . . . . . . 89 A3
St Pierreville F . . 117 C4
St Pieters-Leeuw B . 79 B4
St Plancard F . . 145 A4
St Poix F . . 101 B4
St Pol-de-Léon F . 100 A2
St Polgues F . . 117 B3
St Pol-sur-Ternoise
F . . . . . . 78 B2
St Pons-de-Thomières
F . . . . . . 130 B1
St Porchaire F . . 114 C3
St Pourçain-sur-Sioule
F . . . . . . 116 A3
St Priest F . . 117 B4
St Privat F . . 116 B2
St Quay-Portrieux
F . . . . . . 100 A3
St Quentin F . . 90 B3
St Quentin-la-Poterie
F . . . . . . 131 A3
St Quentin-les-Anges
F . . . . . . 102 B1
St Rambert-d'Albon
F . . . . . . 117 B4
St Rambert-en-Bugey
F . . . . . . 118 B2
St Raphaël F . . 132 B2
St Rémy-de-Provence
F . . . . . . 131 B3
St Rémy-du-Val F . 89 B4
St Remy-en-Bouzemont
F . . . . . . 91 C4
St Renan F . . 100 A1
St Révérien F . . 104 B2
St Riquier F . . 90 A1
St Romain-de-Colbosc
F . . . . . . 89 A4
St Rome-de-Cernon
F . . . . . . 130 A1
St Rome-de-Tarn F 130 A1
St Sadurní-d'Anoia
E . . . . . . 147 C2
St Saëns F . . 89 A5
St Sampson GB . . 88 A1
St Samson-la-Poterie
F . . . . . . 90 B1
St Saturnin-de-Lenne
F . . . . . . 130 A2
St Saturnin-lès-Apt
F . . . . . . 131 B4
St Sauflieu F . . 90 B2
St Saulge F . . 104 B2
St Sauveur
Finistère F . . 100 A2
Haute-Saône F . . 105 B5
St Sauveur-de-Montagut
F . . . . . . 117 C4
St Sauveur-en-Puisaye
F . . . . . . 104 B2
St Sauveur-en-Rue
F . . . . . . 117 B4
St Sauveur-Lendelin
F . . . . . . 88 A2
St Sauveur-le-Vicomte
F . . . . . . 88 A2
St Sauveur-sur-Tinée
F . . . . . . 132 A3
St Savin
Gironde F . . 128 A2
Vienne F . . 115 B4
St Savinien F . . 114 C3
St Savournin F . 131 B4
St Seine-l'Abbaye
F . . . . . . 105 B3
St Sernin-sur-Rance
F . . . . . . 130 B1
St Sevan-sur-Mer F . 88 B1
St Sever F . . 128 C2
St Sever-Calvados
F . . . . . . 88 B2
St Sorlin-d'Arves F 118 B3
St Soupplets F . . 90 B2
St Sulpice F . . 129 C4
St Sulpice-Laurière
F . . . . . . 116 A1
St Sulpice-les-Feuilles
F . . . . . . 115 B5
St Symphorien F . 128 B2

St Symphoriende-Lay
F . . . . . . 117 B4
St Symphorien d'Ozon
F . . . . . . 117 B4
St Symphoriensur-Coise
F . . . . . . 117 B4
St Teath GB . . 42 B2
St Thégonnec F . . 100 A2
St Thiébault F . . 105 A4
St Trivier-de-Courtes
F . . . . . . 118 A2
St Trivier sur-Moignans
F . . . . . . 117 A4
St Trojan-les-Bains
F . . . . . . 114 C2
St Tropez F . . 132 B2
St Truiden B . . 79 B5
St Vaast-la-Hougue
F . . . . . . 88 A2
St Valérien F . . 104 A2
St Valery-en-Caux F 89 A4
St Valéry-sur-Somme
F . . . . . . 78 B1
St Vallier
Drôme F . . 117 B4
Saône-et-Loire F . 104 C3
St Vallier-de-Thiey
F . . . . . . 132 B2
St Varent F . . 102 C1
St Vaury F . . 116 A1
St Venant F . . 78 B2
St Véran F . . 119 C3
St Vincent F . . 119 B4
St Vincent-de-Tyrosse
F . . . . . . 128 C1
St Vit F . . 105 B4
St Vith B . . 80 B2
St Vivien-de-Médoc
F . . . . . . 114 C2
St Yan F . . 117 A4
St Ybars F . . 146 A2
St Yorre F . . 117 A3
St Yrieix-la-Perche
F . . . . . . 115 C5
Saissac F . . 146 A3
Saja E . . 142 A2
Sajan SRB . . 126 B2
Šajkaš SRB . . 126 B2
Sajókaza H . . 99 C4
Sajószentpéter H . 113 A4
Sajóvámos H . . 113 A4
Sakarya TR . . 187 B5
Šakiai LT . . 13 A5
Saksköbing DK . . 65 B4
Sakule SRB . . 126 B2
Sala S . . 50 C3
Šal'a SK . . 111 A4
Sala Baganza I . . 120 C3
Sala Consilina I . 172 B1
Salakovac SRB . . 127 C3
Salamanca E . . 150 B2
Salamina GR . . 185 B4
Salandra I . . 172 B2
Salaparuta I . . 176 B1
Salar E . . 163 A3
Salardú E . . 145 B4
Salas E . . 141 A4
Salas de los Infantes
E . . 143 B3
Salau F . . 146 B2
Salavaux CH . . 106 C2
Salbertrand I . . 119 B3
Salbohed S . . 50 C3
Salbris F . . 103 B4
Salbu N . . 46 A2
Salce E . . 141 B4
Salching D . . 95 C4
Salcombe GB . . 43 B3
Saldaña E . . 142 B2
Saldus LV . . 8 D3
Sale I . . 120 C1
Saleby S . . 55 B4
Salem D . . 107 B4
Salemi I . . 176 B1
Salen
Argyll & Bute GB . 34 B2
Highland GB . . 34 B2
N. . . 199 A8
Sälen S . . 49 A5
Salernes F . . 132 B2
Salerno I . . 170 C2
Salers F . . 116 B2
Salford GB . . 40 B1
Salgótarján H . . 113 A3
Salgueiro P . . 155 B3
Salhus N . . 46 B2
Sali HR . . 137 B4
Sálice Salentino I . 173 B3
Salientes E . . 141 B4
Salies-de-Béarn F . 144 A3
Salies-du-Salat F . 145 A4
Salignac-Eyvigues
F . . . . . . 129 B4
Saligney-sur-Roudon
F . . . . . . 104 C2
Salihli TR . . 188 A3
Salihorsk BY . . 13 B7
Salinas
Alicante E . . 159 C3
Huesca E . . 145 B4
Salinas de Medinaceli
E . . 152 A1
Salinas de Pisuerga
E . . 142 B2
Salindres F . . 131 A3
Saline di Volterra I . 135 B3
Salins-les-Bains F . 105 C4
Salir P . . 160 B1

Salisbury GB . . 44 B2
Salla
A. . . 110 B1
FIN . . 197 C11
Sallachy GB . . 32 C2
Sallanches F . . 118 B3
Sallent E . . 147 C2
Sallent de Gállego
E. . . 145 B3
Salles F . . 128 B2
Salles-Curan F . 130 A1
Salles-sur-l'Hers F . 146 A2
Sallins IRL . . 30 A2
Sällsjö S . . 199 B10
Salmerón E . . 152 B1
Salmiech F . . 130 A1
Salmivaara FIN . 197 C11
Salmoral E . . 150 B2
Salo FIN . . 8 B3
Salò I . . 121 B3
Salobreña E . . 163 B4
Salon-de-Provence
F . . . . . . 131 B4
Salonica = Thessaloniki
GR . . 182 C4
Salonta RO . . 16 B4
Salorino E . . 155 B3
Salornay-sur-Guye
F . . . . . . 104 C3
Salorno I . . 121 A4
Salou E . . 147 C2
Šalovci SLO . . 111 C3
Salsbruket N . . 199 A8
Salses-le-Chateau
F . . . . . . 146 B3
Salsomaggiore Terme
I . . . . . . 120 C2
Salt E . . 147 C3
Saltaire GB . . 40 B2
Saltara I . . 136 B1
Saltash GB . . 42 B2
Saltburn-by-the-Sea
GB . . 37 B6
Saltcoats GB . . 34 C3
Saltfleet GB . . 41 B4
Saltrød N . . 53 B4
Saltsjöbaden S . . 57 A4
Saltvik
FIN . . 51 B7
S . . 62 A4
Saludécio I . . 136 B1
Salussola I . . 119 B5
Saluzzo I . . 119 C4
Salvacañete E . 152 B2
Salvagnac F . . 129 C4
Salvaleon E . . 155 C4
Salvaterra de Magos
P . . . . . . 154 B2
Salvaterra do Extremo
P . . . . . . 155 B4
Salvatierra
Avila E . . 143 B4
Badajoz E . . 155 C4
Salvatierra de Santiago
E . . 156 A1
Salviac F . . 129 B4
Salzburg A . . 109 B4
Salzgitter D . . 72 B3
Salzgitter Bad D . 72 B3
Salzhausen D . . 72 A3
Salzhemmendorf D . 72 B2
Salzkotten D . . 81 A4
Salzmünde D . . 83 A3
Salzwedel D . . 73 B4
Samadet F . . 128 C2
Samandıra TR . . 186 B4
Samassi I . . 179 C2
Samatan F . . 146 A1
Sambiase I . . 175 C2
Sambir UA . . 13 D5
Samborowo PL . . 69 B4
Sambuca di Sicília
I . . . . . . 176 B2
Samedan CH . . 107 C4
Samer F . . 78 B1
Sami GR . . 184 A1
Şamlı TR . . 186 C2
Sammichele di Bari
I . . . . . . 173 B2
Samnaun CH . . 107 C5
Samobor HR . . 123 B4
Samoëns F . . 118 A3
Samogneux F . . 92 B1
Samokov BG . . 17 D5
Samora Correia P . 154 C2
Samos
E . . . . . . 141 B3
GR . . 188 B1
Samoš SRB . . 126 B2
Samothraki GR . . 183 C7
Samper de Calanda
E . . 153 A3
Sampéyre I . . 133 A3
Sampigny F . . 92 C1
Samplawa PL . . 69 B4
Samproniano I . . 168 A1
Samtens D . . 66 B2
Samugheo I . . 179 C2
San Adrián E . . 144 B2
San Agustín E . . 144 B2
San Agustin de Guadalix
E . . 151 B4

San Amaro E . . 140 B2
Sânandrei RO . . 126 B3
San Andrés del
Rabanedo E . . 142 B1
San Antanio di Santadi
I . . . . . . 179 C2
San Antolín de Ibias
E. . . 141 A4
San Arcángelo I . . 174 A2
Sanary-sur-Mer F . 132 B1
San Asensio E . . 143 B4
San Bartoloméde las
Abiertas E . . 150 C3
San Bartoloméde la
Torre E . . 161 B2
San Bartoloméde
Pinares E . . 150 B3
San Bartolomeo in
Galdo I . . 170 B3
San Benedetto del
Tronto I . . 136 C2
San Benedetto in Alpe
I . . . . . . 135 B4
San Benedetto Po
I . . . . . . 121 B3
San Benito E . . 156 B3
San Benito de la
Contienda E . . 155 C3
San Biágio Plátani
I . . . . . . 176 B2
San Biágio Saracinisco
I . . . . . . 169 B3
San Bonifacio I . . 121 B4
San Calixto E . . 156 C2
San Cándido I . . 109 C3
San Carlo
CH . . 119 A5
I . . . . . . 176 B2
San Carlos del Valle
E . . 157 B4
San Casciano dei Bagni
I . . . . . . 135 C4
San Casciano in Val di
Pesa I . . 135 B4
San Cataldo
Puglia I . . 173 B4
Sicília I . . 176 B2
San Cebrián de Castro
E . . 149 A4
Sancergues F . . 104 B1
Sancerre F . . 103 B4
San Cesário di Lecce
I . . . . . . 173 B4
Sancey-le-Long F . 105 B5
Sanchiorian E . . 150 B3
San Chírico Raparo
I . . . . . . 174 A2
Sanchonuño E . . 151 A3
San Cibrao das Viñas
E . . 140 B3
San Cipirello I . . 176 B2
San Ciprián E . . 141 A3
San Clemente E . . 158 B1
San Clodio E . . 141 B3
Sancoins F . . 104 C1
San Colombano al
Lambro I . . 120 B2
San Costanzo I . . 136 B2
San Crisóbal de
Entreviñas E . . 142 B1
San Cristóbal de la
Polantera E . . 141 B5
San Cristóbal de la
Vega E . . 150 A3
San Cristovo E . . 141 C3
Sancti-Petri E . . 162 B1
Sancti-Spíritus E . . 149 B3
Sand
Hedmark N . . 48 B3
Rogaland N . . 52 A2
Sanda S . . 57 C4
San Damiano d'Asti
I . . . . . . 119 C5
San Damiano Macra
I . . . . . . 133 A3
Sandane N . . 198 D3
San Daniele del Friuli
I . . . . . . 122 A2
Sandanski BG . . 183 B5
Sandared S . . 60 B2
Sandarne S . . 51 A4
Sandau D . . 73 B5
Sandbach
D. . . 96 C1
GB. . . 38 A4
Sandbank GB . . 34 C3
Sandbanks GB . . 43 B5
Sandbukt N . . 192 C5
Sandby DK . . 65 B4
Sande
D. . . 71 A5
Sogn og Fjordane
N. . . 46 A2
Vestfold N . . 54 A1
Sandefjord N . . 54 A1
Sandeid N . . 52 A1
San Demétrio Corone
I . . . . . . 174 B2
San Demétrio né Vestini
I . . . . . . 169 A3
Sandersleben D . . 82 A3
Sanderstølen N . . 47 B6
Sandes N . . 53 B3
Sandesneben D . . 65 C3
Sandhead GB . . 36 B2
Sandhem S . . 60 B3
Sandhorst D . . 71 A4
Sandhurst GB . . 44 B3

Sandıklı TR . . 189 A5
Sandillon F . . 103 B4
Sandl A. . . 96 C2
Sandnes N . . 52 B1
Sandness GB . . 33 A5
Sandnessjøen N . 195 D3
Sando E . . 149 B3
Sandomierz PL . . 87 B5
San Dónaci I . . 173 B3
San Donàdi Piave
I . . . . . . 122 B1
San Donato Val di
Comino I . . 169 B3
Sándorfalva H . . 126 A2
Sandown GB . . 44 C2
Sandøysund N . . 54 A1
Sandrigo I . . 121 B4
Sandsele S . . 195 E8
Sandset N . . 194 B5
Sandsjöfors S . . 62 A2
Sandstad N . . 198 B6
Sandvatn N . . 52 B2
Sandvig-Alinge DK . 67 A3
Sandvika
Akershus N . . 48 C2
Hedmark N . . 48 B3
Nord-Trøndelag N . 199 B9
Sandviken S . . 51 B3
Sandvikvåy N . . 46 C2
Sandwich GB . . 45 B5
Sandy GB . . 44 A3
San Emiliano E . . 141 B5
San Enrique E . . 162 B2
San Esteban E . . 141 A4
San Esteban de Gormaz
E . . 151 A4
San Esteban de la Sierra
E . . 149 B4
San Esteban de Litera
E . . 145 C4
San Esteban del Molar
E . . 142 C1
San Esteban del Valle
E . . 150 B3
San Esteban de
Valdueza E . . 141 B4
San Fele I . . 172 B1
San Felice Circeo I . 169 B3
San Felices E . . 143 B3
San Felices de los
Gallégos E . . 149 B3
San Felice sul Panaro
I . . . . . . 121 C4
San Ferdinando di
Púglia I . . 171 B4
San Fernando E . . 162 B1
San Fernando de
Henares E . . 151 B4
San Fili I . . 174 B2
San Foca I . . 173 B4
San Fratello I . . 177 B3
Sangatte F . . 78 B1
San Gavino Monreale
I . . . . . . 179 C2
San Gémini Fonte
I . . . . . . 168 A2
Sangerhausen D . . 82 A3
San Germano Vercellese
I . . . . . . 119 B5
San Giácomo
Trentino Alto Adige
I . . . . . . 108 C2
Umbria I . . 136 C1
San Gimignano I . . 135 B4
San Ginésio I . . 136 B2
Sangineto Lido I . . 174 B1
San Giórgio a Liri I . 169 B3
San Giorgio della
Richinvelda I . . 122 A1
San Giórgio del Sánnio
I . . . . . . 170 B2
San Giórgio di
Lomellina I . . 120 B1
San Giórgio di Nogaro
I . . . . . . 122 B2
San Giorgio di Piano
I . . . . . . 121 C4
San Giórgio Iónico
I . . . . . . 173 B3
San Giovanni a Piro
I . . . . . . 172 B1
San Giovanni Bianco
I . . . . . . 120 B2
San Giovanni di Sinis
I . . . . . . 179 C2
San Giovanni in Croce
I . . . . . . 120 B3
San Giovanni in Fiore
I . . . . . . 174 B2
San Giovanni in
Persiceto I . . 121 C4
San Giovanni Reatino
I . . . . . . 169 A2
San Giovanni Rotondo
I . . . . . . 171 B3
San Giovanni Suérgiu
I . . . . . . 179 C2
San Giovanni Valdarno
I . . . . . . 135 B4
Sangis S . . 196 D6
San Giuliano Terme
I . . . . . . 134 B3
San Giustino I . . 135 B5
San Godenzo I . . 135 B4

272 San–San

Sangonera la Verde E 165 B3
San Gregorio Magno I 172 B1
Sangüesa E 144 B2
Sanguinet F 128 B1
San Guiseppe Jato I 176 B2
Sanica BIH 124 C2
Sanitz D 65 B5
San Javier E 165 B4
San Jorge P 154 B2
San José E 164 C2
San Juan E 143 B3
San Juan de Alicante E 165 A4
San Juan de la Nava E 150 B3
San Justo de la Vega E 141 B4
Sankt Aegyd am Neuwalde A 110 B2
Sankt Andrä A 110 C1
Sankt Andreasberg D 82 A2
Sankt Anna S 56 B2
Sankt Anna am Aigen A 110 C2
Sankt Anton am Arlberg A 107 B5
Sankt Anton an der Jessnitz A 110 B2
Sankt Augustin D 80 B3
Sankt Blasien D 106 B3
Sankt Englmar D 95 B4
Sankt Gallen
A 110 B1
CH 107 B4
Sankt Gallenkirch A 107 B4
Sankt Georgen
A 96 C2
D 106 A3
Sankt Georgen am Reith A 110 B1
Sankt Georgen ob Judenburg A 110 B1
Sankt Georgen ob Murau A 109 B5
Sankt Gilgen A 109 B4
Sankt Goar D 81 B3
Sankt Goarshausen D 81 B3
Sankt Ingbert D 92 B3
Sankt Jacob A 109 C5
Sankt Jakob in Defereggen A 109 C3
Sankt Johann am Tauern A 110 B1
Sankt Johann am Wesen A 109 A4
Sankt Johann im Pongau A 109 B4
Sankt Johann in Tirol A 109 B3
Sankt Katharein an der Laming A 110 B2
Sankt Kathrein am Hauenstein A 110 B2
Sankt Lambrecht A 110 B1
Sankt Leonhard am Forst A 110 A2
Sankt Leonhard im Pitztal A 108 B1
Sankt Lorenzen A 109 C3
Sankt Marein
*Steiermark* A 110 B2
*Steiermark* A 110 B2
Sankt Margarethen im Lavanttal A 110 C1
Sankt Margrethen CH 107 B4
Sankt Michael A 110 B2
Sankt Michael im Burgenland A 111 B3
Sankt Michael im Lungau A 109 B4
Sankt Michaelisdonn D 64 C2
Sankt Niklaus CH 119 A4
Sankt Nikolai im Sölktal A 109 B5
Sankt Olof S 63 C2
Sankt Oswald D 96 C1
Sankt Paul
A 110 C1
F 132 A2
Sankt Peter D 106 A3
Sankt Peter am Kammersberg A 110 B1
Sankt-Peterburg = St Petersburg RUS 9 C7
Sankt Peter-Ording D 64 B1
Sankt Pölten A 110 A2
Sankt Radegund A 110 B2
Sankt Ruprecht an der Raab A 110 B2
Sankt Salvator A 110 C1
Sankt Stefan A 110 C1
Sankt Stefan an der Gail A 109 C4
Sankt Stefan im Rosental A 110 C2
Sankt Valentin A 110 A1
Sankt Veit an der Glan A 110 C1
Sankt Veit an der Gölsen A 110 A2
Sankt Veit in Defereggen A 109 C3
Sankt Wendel D 92 B3
Sankt Wolfgang
A 109 B4
D 108 A3
San Lazzaro di Sávena I 135 A4
San Leo I 135 B5
San Leonardo de Yagüe E 143 C3
San Leonardo in Passiria I 108 C2
San Lorenzo al Mare I 133 B3
San Lorenzo a Merse I 135 B4
San Lorenzo Bellizzi I 174 B2
San Lorenzo de Calatrava E 157 B4
San Lorenzo de El Escorial E 151 B3
San Lorenzo de la Parrilla E 158 B1
San Lorenzo di Sebato I 108 C2
San Lorenzo in Campo I 136 B1
San Lorenzo Nuovo I 168 A1
San Lourenco P 160 A1
San Luca I 175 C2
Sanlúcar de Barrameda E 161 C3
Sanlúcar de Guadiana E 160 B2
Sanlúcar la Mayor E 161 B3
San Lúcido I 174 B2
Sanluri I 179 C2
San Marcello I 136 B2
San Marcello Pistoiese I 135 A3
San Marcial E 149 A4
San Marco I 170 C2
San Marco Argentano I 174 B2
San Marco dei Cavoti I 170 B2
San Marco in Lámis I 171 B3
San Marino RSM 136 B1
San Martin de Castañeda E 141 B4
San Martin de la Vega E 151 B4
San Martin de la Vega del Alberche E 150 B2
San Martin del Tesorillo E 162 B2
San Martin de Luiña E 141 A4
San Martin de Montalbán E 157 A3
San Martin de Oscos E 141 A4
San Martin de Pusa E 150 C3
San Martin de Unx E 144 B2
San Martín de Valdeiglesias E 150 B3
San Martino di Campagna I 122 A1
San Martino di Castrozza I 121 A4
San-Martino-di-Lota F 180 A2
San Martino in Pénsilis I 170 B3
San Mateo de Gallego E 144 C3
San Máuro Forte I 172 B2
San Michele all'Adige I 121 A4
San Michele di Ganzaria I 177 B3
San Michele Mondovì I 133 A3
San Miguel de Aguayo E 142 A2
San Miguel de Bernuy E 151 A4
San Miguel del Arroyo E 150 A3
San Miguel de Salinas E 165 B4
Sânmihaiu Roman RO 126 B3
San Millán de la Cogolla E 143 B4
San Miniato I 135 B3
San Muñoz E 149 B3
Sänna S 55 B5
Sannazzaro de'Burgondi I 120 B1
Sanne D 73 B4
Sannicandro di Bari I 171 B4
Sannicandro Gargánico I 171 B3
San Nicola del'Alto I 174 B2
San Nicolás del Puerto E 156 C2
Sânnicolau Mare RO 126 A2
San Nicolò I 121 C4
San Nicolò Gerrei I 179 C3
Sannidal N 53 B5
Sanniki PL 77 B4
Sanok PL 12 D5
San Pablo de los Montes E 157 A3
San Pancrázio Salentino I 173 B3
San Pantaleo I 178 A3
San Páolo di Civitate I 171 B3
San Pawl il-Bahar M 175 C3
San Pedro
*Albacete* E 158 C1
*Oviedo* E 141 A4
San Pedro de Alcántara E 162 B3
San Pedro de Ceque E 141 B4
San Pedro del Arroyo E 150 B3
San Pedro de Latarce E 142 C1
San Pedro del Pinatar E 165 B4
San Pedro del Romeral E 143 A3
San Pedro de Merida E 156 B1
San Pedro de Valderaduey E 142 B2
San Pedro Manrique E 144 B1
San Pellegrino Terme I 120 B2
San Piero a Sieve I 135 B4
San Piero in Bagno I 135 B4
San Piero Patti I 177 A3
San Pietro I 177 B3
San Pietro in Casale I 121 C4
San Pietro in Gu I 121 B4
San Pietro in Palazzi I 134 B3
San Pietro in Volta I 122 B1
San Pietro Vara I 134 A2
San Pietro Vernótico I 173 B3
San Polo d'Enza I 121 C3
Sanquhar GB 36 A3
San Quírico d'Órcia I 135 B4
San Rafael del Rio E 153 B4
San Remo I 133 B3
San Román de Cameros E 143 B4
San Roman de Hernija E 150 A2
San Román de la Cuba E 142 B2
San Roman de los Montes E 150 B3
San Romao P 155 C3
San Roque E 162 B2
San Roque de Riomera E 143 A3
San Rufo I 172 B1
San Sebastián de los Ballesteros E 162 A3
San Salvador de Cantamuda E 142 B2
San Salvo I 170 A2
San Salvo Marina I 170 A2
San Sebastián de los Reyes E 151 B4
San Sebastiano Curone I 120 C2
San Secondo Parmense I 120 C3
Sansepolcro I 135 B5
San Serverino Marche I 136 B2
San Severino Lucano I 174 A2
San Severo I 171 B3
San Silvestre de Guzmán E 161 B2
Sanski Most BIH 124 C2
San Sosti I 174 B2
San Stéfano di Cadore I 109 C3
San Stino di Livenza I 122 B1
Santa Agnès E 166 B1
Santa Amalia E 156 A1
Santa Ana
*Cáceres* E 156 A2
*Jaén* E 163 A4
Santa Ana de Pusa E 150 C3
Santa Barbara E 153 B4
Santa Bárbara P 160 B1
Santa Barbara de Casa E 161 B2
Santa Bárbara de Padrões P 160 B2
Santacara E 144 B2
Santa Catarina P 160 B2
Santa Caterina di Pittinuri I 178 B2
Santa Caterina Villarmosa I 177 B3
Santa Cesárea Terme I 173 B4
Santa Clara-a-Nova P 160 B1
Santa Clara-a-Velha P 160 B1
Santa Clara de Louredo P 160 B2
Santa Coloma de Farners E 147 C3
Santa Coloma de Gramenet E 147 C3
Santa Coloma de Queralt E 147 C2
Santa Colomba de Curueño E 142 B1
Santa Colomba de Somoza E 141 B4
Santa Comba E 140 A2
Santa Comba Dáo P 148 B1
Santa Comba de Rossas P 149 A3
Santa Cristina I 120 B2
Santa Cristina de la Polvorosa E 141 B5
Santa Croce Camerina I 177 C3
Santa Croce di Magliano I 170 B2
Santa Cruz
E 140 A2
P 154 B1
Santa Cruz de Alhama E 163 A4
Santa Cruz de Campezo E 143 B4
Santa Cruz de Grio E 152 A2
Santa Cruz de la Salceda E 151 A4
Santa Cruz de la Sierra E 156 A2
Santa Cruz de la Zarza E 151 C4
Santa Cruz del Retamar E 151 B3
Santa Cruz del Valle E 150 B2
Santa Cruz de Moya E 159 B2
Santa Cruz de Mudela E 157 B4
Santa Cruz de Paniagua E 149 B3
Santadi I 179 C2
Santa Doménica Talao I 174 B1
Santa Doménica Vittória I 177 B3
Santa Elena E 157 B4
Santa Elena de Jamuz E 141 B5
Santaella E 162 A3
Santa Eufemia E 156 B3
Santa Eufémia d'Aspromonte I 175 C1
Santa Eulalia E 152 B2
Santa Eulália P 155 C3
Santa Eulalia de Oscos E 141 A3
Santa Eulàlia des Riu E 166 C1
Santa Fe E 163 A4
Santa Fiora I 135 C4
Sant'Ágata dei Goti I 170 B2
Sant'Ágata di Ésaro I 174 B1
Sant'Ágata di Puglia I 171 B3
Sant'Agata Feltria I 135 B5
Sant'Ágata Militello I 177 A3
Santa Gertrude I 108 C1
Santa Giustina I 121 A5
Sant Agust ide Lluçanès E 147 B3
Santa Iria P 160 B2
Santa Leocadia P 148 A1
Santa Lucia del Mela I 177 A4
Santa Lucia-de-Porto-Vecchio F 180 B2
Santa Luzia P 160 B1
Santa Maddalena Vallalta I 108 C3
Santa Magdalena de Polpis E 153 B4
Santa Margalida E 167 B3
Santa Margarida P 154 B2
Santa Margarida do Sado P 160 A1
Santa Margaridao de Montbui E 147 C2
Santa Margherita I 179 D2
Santa Margherita di Belice I 176 B2
Santa Margherita Ligure I 134 A2
Santa Maria
CH 108 C1
E 144 B3
Santa Maria al Bagno I 173 B3
Santa Maria Cápua Vétere I 170 B2
Santa Maria da Feira P 148 B1
Santa Maria de Cayón E 143 A3
Santa Maria de Corco E 147 B3
Santa Maria de Huerta E 152 A1
Santa Maria de la Alameda E 151 B3
Santa Maria de las Hoyas E 143 C3
Santa Maria del Camí E 167 B2
Santa Maria del Campo E 143 B3
Santa Maria del Campo Rus E 158 B1
Santa Maria della Versa I 120 C2
Santa Maria del Páramo E 142 B1
Santa Maria del Taro I 134 A2
Santa Maria de Mercadillo E 143 C3
Santa Maria de Nieva E 164 B3
Santa Maria de Trassierra E 156 C3
Santa Maria di Licodia I 177 B3
Santa Maria-di-Rispéscia I 168 A1
Santa Maria la Palma I 178 B2
Santa María la Real de Nieva E 150 A3
Santa Maria Maggiore I 119 A5
Santa Maria Ribarredonda E 143 B3
Santa Marina del Rey E 141 B5
Santa Marinella I 168 A1
Santa Marta
*Albacete* E 158 B1
*Badajoz* E 155 C4
Santa Marta de Magasca E 156 A1
Santa Marta de Penaguião P 148 A2
Santa Marta de Tormes E 150 B2
Santana
*Évora* P 154 C2
*Setúbal* P 154 C1
Sântana RO 126 A3
Santana da Serra P 160 B1
Sant'Ana de Cambas P 160 B2
Santana do Mato P 154 C2
Sant'Anastasia I 170 C2
Santander E 143 A3
Sant'Andrea Frius I 179 C3
Sant'Ángelo dei Lombardi I 172 B1
Sant'Angelo in Vado I 136 B1
Sant'Angelo Lodigiano I 120 B2
Santa Ninfa I 176 B1
Sant'Antíoco I 179 C2
Sant Antoni Abat E 166 C1
Sant Antoni de Calonge E 147 C4
Sant'Antonio-di-Gallura I 178 B3
Santanyí E 167 B3
Santa Olalla
*Huelva* E 161 B3
*Toledo* E 150 B3
Santa Pau E 147 B3
Santa Pola E 165 A4
Santa Ponça E 166 B2
Santarcángelo di Romagna I 136 A1
Santarém P 154 B2
Santa Severa
F 180 A2
I 168 A1
Santa Severina I 175 B2
Santas Martas E 142 B1
Santa Sofia I 135 B4
Santa Suzana
*Évora* P 155 C3
*Setúbal* P 154 C2
Santa Teresa di Riva I 177 B4
Santa Teresa Gallura I 178 A3
Santa Uxía E 140 B2
Santa Valburga I 108 C1
Santa Vittória in Matenano I 136 B2
Sant Boi de Llobregat E 147 C3
Sant Carles de la Ràpita E 153 B4
Sant Carlos E 166 B1
Sant'Caterina I 135 C4
Sant Celoni E 147 C3
Sant Climent E 167 B4
Santed E 152 A2
Sant'Egidio alla Vibrata I 136 C2
Sant'Elia a Pianisi I 170 B2
Sant'Elia Fiumerapido I 169 B3
Santelices E 143 A3
San Telmo E 161 B3
Sant'Elpídio a Mare I 136 B2
Santéramo in Colle I 171 C4
Santervas de la Vega E 142 B2
Sant Feliu E 147 C3
Sant Feliu de Codines E 147 C3
Sant Feliu de Guíxols E 147 C4
Sant Feliu Sasserra E 147 C3
Sant Ferran E 166 C1
Sant Francesc de Formentera E 166 C1
Sant Francesc de ses Salines E 166 C1
Santhià I 119 B5
Sant Hilari Sacalm E 147 C3
Sant Hipòlit de Voltregà E 147 B3
Santiago de Alcántara E 155 B3
Santiago de Calatrava E 163 A3
Santiago de Compostela E 140 B2
Santiago de la Espade E 164 A2
Santiago de la Puebla E 150 B2
Santiago de la Ribera E 165 B4
Santiago del Campo E 155 B4
Santiago de Litem P 154 B2
Santiago do Cacém P 160 B1
Santiago do Escoural P 154 C2
Santiago Maior P 155 C3
Santibáñez de Béjar E 150 B2
Santibáñez de la Peña E 142 B2
Santibáñez de Murias E 142 A1
Santibáñez de Vidriales E 141 B4
Santibáñez el Alto E 149 B3
Santibáñez el Bajo E 149 B3
Santillana E 142 A2
Santiponce E 162 A1
San Tirso de Abres E 141 A3
Santisteban del Puerto E 157 B4
Santiuste de San Juan Bautiste E 150 A3
Santiz E 149 A4
Sant Jaume dels Domenys E 147 C2
Sant Joan Baptista E 166 B1
Sant Joan de les Abadesses E 147 B3
Sant Jordi E 153 B4
Sant Josep de sa Talaia E 166 C1
Sant Juliáde Loria AND 146 B2
Sant'Ilario d'Enza I 121 C3
Sant Llorençde Morunys E 147 B2
Sant Llorençdes Carctassar E 167 B3
Sant Llorenç Savall E 147 C3
Sant Luis E 167 B4
Sant Mart ide Llemaná E 147 B3
Sant Marti de Maldá E 147 C2
Sant Marti Sarroca E 147 C2
Sant Mateu E 153 B4
Sant Miquel E 166 B1
Santo Aleixo P 161 A2
Santo Amado P 161 A2
Santo Amaro P 155 C3
Santo André P 160 A1
Santo Domingo E 155 C3
Santo Domingo de la Calzada E 143 B4
Santo Domingo de Silos E 143 C3
Santo Estêvão
*Faro* P 160 B2
*Santarém* P 154 C2
Santok PL 75 B4
Santomera E 165 A3
Santoña E 143 A3

Santo-Pietro-di Tenda F. . . . 180 A2
Sant'Oreste I . . . . 168 A2
Santo Spirito I . . . . 171 B4
Santo Stefano d'Aveto I . . . . 134 A2
Santo Stéfano di Camastra I . . . . 177 A3
Santo Stefano di Magra I . . . . 134 A2
Santo Stéfano Quisquina I . . . . 176 B2
Santo Tirso P. . . . . 148 A1
Santotis E . . . . . 142 A2
Santo Tomé E . . . . 164 A1
Santovenia
  Burgos E . . . . . . .143 B3
  Zamora E . . . . . . .142 C1
Sant Pau de Seguries E. . . . 147 B3
Santpedor E . . . . . 147 C2
Sant Pere de Riudebitles E. . . . 147 C2
Sant Pere Pescador E. . . . 147 B4
Sant Pere Sallavinera E. . . . 147 C2
Sant Quirze de Besora E. . . . 147 B3
Sant Rafel E . . . . 166 C1
Sant Ramon E . . . . 147 C2
Santu Lussurgiu I . 178 B2
Santutzi E . . . . . . 143 A3
Sant Vincençde Castellet E . . . . 147 C2
San Valentino alla Muta I . . . . 108 C1
San Venanzo I . . . 135 C5
San Vicente de Alcántara E . . . . 155 B3
San Vicente de Arana E. . . . 144 B1
San Vicente de la Barquera E . . . . 142 A2
San Vicente de la Sonsierra E . . . . 143 B4
San Vicente de Toranzo E. . . . 143 A3
San Vietro E . . . . 149 A3
San Vigilio I . . . . . 108 C2
San Vincente del Raspeig E . . . . 165 A4
San Vincenzo I . . 134 B3
San Vito I . . . . . . 179 C3
San Vito al Tagliamento I . . . . 122 B1
San Vito Chietino I 169 A4
San Vito dei Normanni I . . . . 173 B3
San Vito di Cadore I . . . . 108 C3
San Vito lo Capo I . 176 A1
San Vito Romano I 169 B2
Sanxenxo E . . . . . 140 B2
Sanza I . . . . . . . . 172 B1
São Aleixo P . . . . . 155 C3
São Barnabé P . . . 160 B1
São Bartoloméda Serra P. . . . 160 A1
São Bartolomeu de Messines P . . . . 160 B1
São Bento P. . . . . . 140 C2
São Brás P . . . . . . 160 B2
São Brás de Alportel P. . . . 160 B2
São Braz do Reguedoura P. . . 154 C2
São Cristóvão P . . 154 C2
São Domingos P . . 160 B1
São Geraldo P . . . 154 C2
São Jacinto P . . . . 148 B1
São João da Madeira P. . . . 148 B1
São João da Pesqueira P. . . . 148 A2
São João da Ribeira P. . . . 154 B2
São João da Serra P. . . . 148 B1
São João da Venda P. . . . 160 B2
São João dos Caldeireiros P . . . 160 B2
São Julião P . . . . . 155 B3
São Leonardo P . . 155 C3
São Luis P . . . . . . 160 B1
São Manços P . . . . 155 C3
São Marcos da Ataboeira P. . . . 160 B2
Saõ Marcos da Serra P. . . . 160 B1
São Marcos de Campo P. . . . 155 C3
São Martinho da Cortiça P. . . . 148 B1
São Martinho das Amoreiras P . . . . 160 B1
São Martinho do Porto P. . . . 154 B1
São Matias
  Beja P . . . . . . . 160 A2
  Évora P . . . . . .154 C2
São Miguel d'Acha P. . . . 155 A3
São Miguel de Machede P. . . . 155 C3
São Pedro da Torre P. . . . 140 C2

São Pedro de Cadeira P. . . . 154 B1
São Pedro de Muel P. . . . 154 B1
São Pedro de Solis P. . . . 160 B2
São Pedro do Sul P. . . . 148 B1
Saorge F . . . . . . . 133 B3
São Romão P. . . . . 154 C2
São Sebastião dos Carros P . . . . 160 B2
São Teotónio P . . . 160 B1
São Torcato P . . . . 148 A1
Sapataria P . . . . . 154 C1
Sapes GR. . . . . . . 183 B7
Sapiãos P. . . . . . . 148 A2
Sa Pobla E . . . . . . 167 B3
Sappada I. . . . . . . 109 C3
Sappen N. . . . . . . 192 C5
Sapri I. . . . . . . . . 174 A1
Sarajärvi FIN . . . . 197 D10
Sarajevo BIH . . . . 139 B4
Saramon F. . . . . . 129 C3
Sarandë AL . . . . . 182 D2
Saranovo SRB. . . . 127 C2
Saraorci SRB. . . . . 127 C3
Sa Rapita E . . . . . 167 B3
Saray TR . . . . . . . 186 A2
Saraycık TR . . . . . 187 C4
Sarayköy TR . . . . . 188 B3
Saraylar TR . . . . . 186 B2
Sarayönü TR . . . . . 189 A7
Sarbia PL . . . . . . . 75 B5
Sarbinowo
  Zachodnio-Pomorskie PL. . . . .67 B4
  Zachodnio-Pomorskie PL. . . . .74 B3
Sárbogárd H . . . . . 112 C2
Sarcelles F. . . . . . . 90 B2
Sarche I . . . . . . . . 121 A3
Sardara I . . . . . . . 179 C2
Sardoal P. . . . . . . 154 B2
Sardón de Duero E. . . . 150 A3
Sare F. . . . . . . . . 144 A2
S'Arenal E . . . . . . 166 B2
Šarengrad HR . . . . 125 B5
Sarentino I . . . . . . 108 C2
Sarezzo I . . . . . . . 120 B3
Sargans CH . . . . . 107 B4
Sári H. . . . . . . . . 112 B3
Sarıbeyler TR. . . . . 186 C2
Sarıcakaya TR. . . . 187 B5
Sari-d'Orcino F . . . 180 A1
Sarıgöl TR . . . . . . 188 A3
Sarıkaya TR . . . . . 23 B8
Sarıköy TR . . . . . . 186 B2
Sarilhos Grandes P. . . . 154 C2
Sariñena E . . . . . . 145 C3
Sarıoba TR. . . . . . 187 C7
Sárisáp H. . . . . . . 112 B2
Sariyer TR . . . . . . 186 A4
Sarkad H . . . . . . . 113 C5
Sárkeresztes H . . . .112 B2
Sárkeresztúr H . . . .112 B2
Särkijärvi FIN. . . . . 196 B6
Şarkikaraağaç TR . 189 A6
Şarköy TR . . . . . . 186 B2
Sarlat-la-Canéda F 129 B4
Sarliac-sur-l'Isle F . 129 A3
Sármellék H. . . . . .111 C4
Särna S . . . . . . . 199 D10
Sarnadas P . . . . . 155 B3
Sarnano I . . . . . . . 136 B2
Sarnen CH . . . . . . 106 C3
Sarnesfield GB . . . 39 B4
Sárnico I . . . . . . . 120 B2
Sarno I. . . . . . . . . 170 C2
Sarnonico I . . . . . . 121 A4
Sarnow D . . . . . . . 74 A2
Sarny UA . . . . . . . 13 C7
Särö S . . . . . . . . . 60 B1
Saronno I . . . . . . . 120 B2
Sárosd H. . . . . . . .112 B2
Šarovce SK . . . . . .112 A2
Sarpoil F . . . . . . . .117 B3
Sarpsborg N . . . . . 54 A2
Sarracín E . . . . . . 143 B3
Sarral E . . . . . . . . 147 C2
Sarralbe F . . . . . . . 92 B3
Sarrancolin F. . . . . 145 B4
Sarras F. . . . . . . . .117 B4
Sarre I . . . . . . . . . 119 B4
Sarreaus E. . . . . . 140 B3
Sarrebourg F . . . . . 92 C3
Sarreguemines F . . 92 B3
Sárrétudvari H. . . . .113 B5
Sarre-Union F . . . . 92 C3
Sarria E . . . . . . . . 141 B3
Sarriàde Ter E . . . 147 B3
Sarrión E . . . . . . . 153 B3
Sarroca de Lleida E. . . . 153 A4
Sarroch I . . . . . . . 179 C3
Sarron F. . . . . . . . 128 C2
Šársina I. . . . . . . . 135 B5
Særslev DK . . . . . . 59 C3
Sarstedt D . . . . . . . 72 B2
Sárszentlörinc H. . . 112 C2
Sárszentmihaly H . .112 B2
Sárszentmiklós H . . 112 C2
Sarteano I . . . . . . . 135 C4
Sartène F . . . . . . . 180 B1
Sartilly F . . . . . . . . 88 B2

Sartirana Lomellina I . . . . 120 B1
Saruhanlı TR . . . . . 186 D2
Sárvár H. . . . . . . . 111 B3
Sarvisvaara S . . . . 196 C4
Sarzana I . . . . . . . 134 A2
Sarzeau F. . . . . . . 101 B3
Sarzedas P. . . . . . 155 B3
Sasalli TR. . . . . . . 188 A1
Sasamón E . . . . . . 142 B2
Sa Savina E . . . . . 166 C1
Sásd H . . . . . . . . 125 A4
Sasino PL. . . . . . . 68 A2
Sássari I . . . . . . . . 178 B2
Sassello I. . . . . . . 133 A4
Sassenberg D . . . 71 C5
Sassetta I . . . . . . 134 B3
Sassnitz D . . . . . . 66 B2
Sassocorvaro I . . . 136 B1
Sasso d'Ombrone I . . . . 135 C4
Sassoferrato I . . . . 136 B1
Sassoleone I . . . . . 135 A4
Sasso Marconi I . . . 135 A4
Sassuolo I . . . . . . 135 A3
Šaštinske Stráže SK . . . . 98 C1
Sas van Gent NL . . 79 A3
Såtåhaugen N . . . . 199 C7
Satão P. . . . . . . . 148 B2
Sätenäs S . . . . . . 55 B3
Säter S. . . . . . . . . 50 B2
Satillieu F . . . . . . .117 B4
Satnica Đakovačka HR . . . . 125 B4
Sátoraljaújhely H . . 16 A4
Satow D . . . . . . . . 65 C4
Sätra-brunn S . . . . 50 C3
Sætre N . . . . . . . . 54 A1
Satrup D. . . . . . . . 64 B2
Satteins A. . . . . . . 107 B4
Satu Mare RO . . . . 17 B5
Saturnia I . . . . . . . 168 A1
Saucats F. . . . . . . 128 B2
Saucelle E . . . . . . 149 A3
Sauda N. . . . . . . . 52 A2
Sauðarkrókur IS . . 190 B6
Saudasjøen N . . . . 52 A2
Sauerlach D . . . . . 108 B2
Saugues F . . . . . . 117 C3
Sauherad N . . . . . 53 A5
Saujon F . . . . . . . 114 C3
Sauland N . . . . . . 53 A4
Saulces Monclin F . 91 B4
Saulgau D . . . . . . 107 A4
Saulgrub D . . . . . . 108 B2
Saulieu F . . . . . . . 104 B3
Saulnot F . . . . . . . 106 B1
Sault F . . . . . . . . 131 A4
Sault-Brénaz F . . . .118 B2
Sault-de-Navailles F. . . . 128 C2
Saulx F. . . . . . . . . 105 B5
Saulxures-sur-Moselotte F. . . . 106 B1
Saulzais-le-Potier F. . . . 103 C4
Saumos F . . . . . . 128 B1
Saumur F. . . . . . . 102 B1
Saunavaara FIN. . . 197 B10
Saundersfoot GB . . 39 C2
Saurat F . . . . . . . 146 B2
Saurbær
  Borgarfjarðarsýsla IS . . . . .190 B4
  Dalasýsla IS. . . . .190 B4
  Eyjafjarðarsýsla IS . . . . .191 B7
Sáuris I. . . . . . . . . 109 C3
Sausset-les-Pins F 131 B4
Sauteyrargues F . . 131 B2
Sauvagnat F . . . . .116 B2
Sauve F . . . . . . . . 131 B2
Sauveterre-de-Béarn F. . . . 144 A3
Sauveterre-de-Guyenne F. . . . 128 B2
Sauviat-sur-Vige F .116 B1
Sauxillanges F . . . .117 B3
Sauzet
  Drôme F. . . . . . .117 C4
  Lot F. . . . . . . . .129 B4
Sauzé-Vaussais F .115 B4
Sauzon F . . . . . . . 100 B2
Sava I . . . . . . . . . 173 B3
Sävar S . . . . . . . 200 C6
Sævareid N . . . . . 46 B2
Savarsin RO . . . . . 16 B5
Sävast S. . . . . . . . 196 D4
Savaştepe TR . . . . 186 C2
Savci SLO . . . . . . .111 C3
Säve S . . . . . . . . . 60 B1
Savelletri I . . . . . . 173 B3
Savelli I . . . . . . . . 174 B2
Savenay F . . . . . . 101 B4
Saverdun F . . . . . . 146 A2
Saverne F . . . . . . . 93 C3
Savières F . . . . . . 91 C3
Savigliano I . . . . . . 119 C4
Savignac-les-Eglises F. . . . 129 A3
Savignano Irpino I . 171 B3
Savignano sul Rubicone I . . . . 136 A1
Savigny-sur-Braye F. . . . 102 B2

Saviñán E . . . . . . . 152 A2
Savines-le-lac F . . 132 A2
Savino Selo SRB. . 126 B1
Savio I . . . . . . . . . 135 A5
Sävja S. . . . . . . . . 51 C4
Šavnik MNE. . . . . . 139 C5
Savognin CH . . . . . 107 C4
Savona I. . . . . . . . 133 A4
Savonlinna FIN . . . 9 B6
Savournon F . . . . . 132 A1
Sævråvåg N . . . . . 46 B2
Sävsjö S . . . . . . . . 62 A2
Sävsjön S . . . . . . . 50 C1
Sävsjöström S. . . . 62 A3
Savudrija HR . . . . . 122 B2
Savukoski FIN. . . .197 B11
Sawbridgeworth GB 45 B4
Sawtry GB . . . . . . 44 A3
Sax E . . . . . . . . . 159 C3
Saxdalen S . . . . . . 50 B1
Saxilby GB . . . . . . 40 B3
Saxmundham GB . . 45 A5
Saxnäs S . . . . . . .195 F6
Saxthorpe GB . . . . 41 C5
Sayalonga E . . . . . 163 B3
Sayatón E . . . . . . 151 B5
Sayda D . . . . . . . . 83 B5
Säytsjärvi FIN . . . . 193 C11
Šazava CZ . . . . . . . 97 B3
Sázava CZ . . . . . . 96 B2
Scaër F. . . . . . . . . 100 A2
Scafa I . . . . . . . . . 169 A4
Scalasaig GB . . . . 34 B1
Scalby GB . . . . . . 40 A3
Scalea I . . . . . . . . 174 B1
Scaletta Zanclea I . 177 A4
Scalloway GB . . . . 33 A5
Scamblesby GB . . . 41 B3
Scandale I . . . . . . 175 B2
Scandiano I . . . . . 121 C3
Scandicci I. . . . . . . 135 B4
Scandolara Ravara I . . . . 120 B3
Scanno I. . . . . . . . 169 B3
Scansano I . . . . . . 168 A1
Scanzano Jónico I . 174 A2
Scarborough GB. . . 40 A3
Scardovari I . . . . . 122 C1
Scardoy GB . . . . . 32 D2
Scarperia I . . . . . . 135 B4
Scarriff IRL. . . . . . 28 B3
Scey-sur-Saône et St Albin F. . . . 105 B4
Schachendorf A. . . .111 B3
Schaffhausen CH . 107 B3
Schafstädt D . . . . . 83 A3
Schafstedt D . . . . . 64 B2
Schagen NL. . . . . . 70 B1
Schalkau D . . . . . . 82 B3
Schangnau CH . . . 106 C2
Schapbach D . . . . . 93 C4
Scharbeutz D . . . . 65 B3
Schärding A . . . . . . 96 C1
Scharnitz A . . . . . . 108 B2
Scharrel D . . . . . . 71 A4
Schattendorf A . . . .111 B3
Scheemda NL . . . . 71 A3
Scheessel D . . . . . 72 A2
Schéggia I . . . . . . 136 B1
Scheibbs A. . . . . . .110 A2
Scheidegg D . . . . . 107 B4
Scheifling A. . . . . . .110 B1
Scheinfeld D . . . . . 94 B2
Schelklingen D . . . 94 C1
Schenefeld
  Schleswig-Holstein D. . . . .64 B2
  Schleswig-Holstein D. . . . .72 A2
Schenkenzell D . . . 93 C4
Schenklengsfeld D . 82 B1
Scherfede D . . . . . 81 A5
Schermbeck D . . . . 80 A2
Scherpenzeel NL. . . 70 B2
Schesslitz D . . . . . 94 B3
Scheveningen NL . . 70 B1
Schiedam NL. . . . . 79 A4
Schieder-Schwalenberg D . . . . 72 C2
Schierling D. . . . . . 95 C4
Schiers CH . . . . . . 107 C4
Schildau D . . . . . . 83 A4
Schillingen D . . . . . 92 B2
Schillingsfürst D . . . 94 B2
Schilpario I . . . . . . 120 A3
Schiltach D . . . . . . 93 C4
Schiltigheim F . . . . 93 C3
Schio I . . . . . . . . . 121 B4
Schirmeck F . . . . . 92 C3
Schirnding D . . . . . 83 B4
Schkeuditz D . . . . . 83 A4
Schkölen D . . . . . . 83 A3
Schladen D . . . . . . 73 B3
Schladming A . . . . 109 B4
Schlangen D . . . . . 81 A4
Schleiden D . . . . . . 80 B2
Schleiz D . . . . . . . 83 B3
Schleswig D . . . . . 64 B2
Schleusingen D. . . . 82 B2
Schlieben D . . . . . . 83 A5
Schliengen D . . . . . 106 B2
Schliersee D . . . . . 108 B2
Schlitz D . . . . . . . . 81 B5
Schloss Neuhans D 81 A4
Schlossvippach D. . 82 A3
Schlotheim D . . . . . 82 A2

Schluchsee D . . . . 106 B3
Schlüchtern D. . . . . 81 B5
Schmallenberg D . . 81 A4
Schmelz D. . . . . . . 92 B2
Schmidmühlen D . . 95 B3
Schmiedeberg D . . 84 B1
Schmiedefeld D. . . . 82 B2
Schmirn A . . . . . . . 108 B2
Schmölln
  Brandenburg D . . .74 B3
  Sachsen D. . . . . . .83 B4
Schnaittach D . . . . 95 B3
Schneeberg D . . . . 83 B4
Schneizlreuth D . . . 109 B3
Schneverdingen D . 72 A2
Schöder A . . . . . . 109 B5
Schoenburg B . . . . 80 B2
Schollene D. . . . . . 73 B5
Schöllkrippen D . . . 81 B5
Schomberg D . . . . 107 A3
Schönach D. . . . . . 95 C4
Schönau
  Baden-Württemberg D. . . . .106 B2
  Bayern D . . . . . .95 C4
Schönbeck D. . . . . 74 A2
Schönberg
  Bayern D . . . . . .96 C1
  Mecklenburg-Vorpommern D. . . .65 C3
  Schleswig-Holstein D. . . . .65 B3
Schönebeck D . . . . 73 B4
Schöneck D . . . . . . 83 B4
Schönecken- D . . . 80 B2
Schönermark D . . . 74 A2
Schönewalde D. . . . 83 A5
Schongau D . . . . . 108 B1
Schöngrabern A . . . 97 C4
Schönhagen D . . . . 81 A5
Schönhausen D . . . 73 B5
Schöningen D . . . . 73 B3
Schönkirchen D . . . 64 B3
Schönsee D . . . . . . 95 B4
Schöntal D . . . . . . 94 B1
Schönthal D. . . . . . 95 B4
Schonungen D . . . . 94 A2
Schönwalde D . . . . 65 B3
Schoondijke NL. . . . 79 A3
Schoonebeek NL. . . 71 B3
Schoonhoven NL . . 79 A4
Schopfheim D. . . . . 106 B2
Schöppenstedt D . . 73 B3
Schörfling A . . . . . 109 B4
Schorndorf D. . . . . 94 C1
Schortens D . . . . . 71 A4
Schotten D . . . . . . 81 B5
Schramberg D . . . . 106 A3
Schraplau D . . . . . 83 A3
Schrattenberg A . . . 97 C4
Schrecksbach D . . . 81 B5
Schrems A . . . . . . 96 C3
Schrobenhausen D . 95 C3
Schröcken A . . . . . 107 B5
Schrozberg D . . . . 94 B1
Schruns A . . . . . . 107 B4
Schüpfheim CH. . . . 106 C3
Schüttorf D . . . . . . 71 B4
Schwaan D . . . . . . 65 C5
Schwabach D . . . . 94 B3
Schwäbisch Gmünd D . . . . 94 C1
Schwäbisch Hall D . 94 B1
Schwabmünchen D . . . . 108 A1
Schwadorf D . . . . .111 A3
Schwagstorf D . . . . 71 B4
Schwaigern D . . . . 93 B5
Schwalmstadt D . . . 81 B5
Schwanberg A . . . . 110 C2
Schwanden CH . . . 107 C4
Schwandorf D . . . . 95 B4
Schwanebeck D . . . 73 C4
Schwanenstadt A . 109 A4
Schwanewede D . . 72 A1
Schwanfeld D . . . . 94 B2
Schwangau D . . . . 108 B1
Schwarmstedt D . . 72 B2
Schwarza D . . . . . 82 B2
Schwarzach im Pongau A. . . . 109 B4
Schwarzau im Gebirge A. . . . .110 B2
Schwarzenau A . . . 97 C3
Schwarzenbach D. . 83 B3
Schwarzenbach am Wald D. . . . 83 B3
Schwarzenbek D . . 72 A3
Schwarzenberg D . . 83 B4
Schwarzenburg CH . . . . 106 C2
Schwarzenfeld D . . 95 B4
Schwarz-heide D . . 84 A1
Schwaz A . . . . . . . 108 B2
Schwechat A . . . . .111 A3
Schwedt D . . . . . . 74 A3
Schwei D . . . . . . . 71 A5
Schweich D . . . . . . 92 B2
Schweighausen D . 106 A2
Schweinfurt D . . . . 94 A2
Schweinitz D . . . . . 83 A5
Schweinrich D . . . . 74 A1
Schwelm D . . . . . . 80 A3
Schwemsal D . . . . 83 A4
Schwendt A . . . . . 109 B3
Schwenningen D . . 107 A3
Schwepnitz D . . . . 84 A1
Schwerin D . . . . . . 73 A4

Schwerte D . . . . . . 81 A3
Schweskau D . . . . 73 B4
Schwetzingen D . . . 93 B4
Schwyz CH . . . . . . 107 B3
Sciacca I . . . . . . . 176 B2
Scicli I . . . . . . . . . 177 C3
Ściechów PL . . . . . 75 B3
Scigliano I . . . . . . 175 B2
Scilla I . . . . . . . . . 175 C1
Ścinawa PL. . . . . . 85 A4
Scionzier F . . . . . .118 A3
Scoglitti I . . . . . . . 177 C3
Scole GB . . . . . . . 45 A5
Sconser GB . . . . . 31 B2
Scopello
  Piemonte I . . . . .119 B5
  Sicilia I . . . . . . . .176 A1
Scordia I . . . . . . . 177 B3
Scorzè I . . . . . . . . 121 B5
Scotch Corner GB. . 37 B5
Scotter GB . . . . . . 40 B3
Scourie GB . . . . . . 32 C1
Scousburgh GB . . . 33 B5
Scrabster GB. . . . . 32 C3
Screeb IRL . . . . . . 28 A2
Scremerston GB . . 37 A5
Scritto I . . . . . . . . 136 B1
Scunthorpe GB . . . 40 B3
Scúrcola Marsicana I . . . . 169 A3
Seaford GB . . . . . . 45 C4
Seaham GB . . . . . 37 B5
Seahouses GB . . . 37 A5
Seascale GB . . . . . 36 B3
Seaton GB . . . . . . 43 B3
Sebazac-Concourès F. . . . 130 A1
Seben TR. . . . . . . 187 B6
Sebersdorf A . . . . .110 B2
Sebezh RUS . . . . . 8 D6
Sebnitz D . . . . . . . 84 B2
Seborga I . . . . . . . 133 B3
Seby S . . . . . . . . . 63 B4
Seč
  Vychodočeský CZ . . . . .97 B3
  Západočeský CZ . .96 B1
Sečanj SRB . . . . . 126 B2
Secemin PL . . . . . . 87 B3
Séchault F . . . . . . . 91 B4
Seckau A . . . . . . . .110 B1
Seclin F . . . . . . . . 78 B3
Secondigny F . . . . .114 B3
Seda P . . . . . . . . . 155 B3
Sedan F . . . . . . . . 91 B4
Sedano E . . . . . . . 143 B3
Sedbergh GB. . . . . 37 B4
Sedella E . . . . . . . 163 B3
Séderon F . . . . . . 131 A4
Sedgefield GB . . . . 37 B5
Sedico I . . . . . . . . 121 A5
Sédilo I . . . . . . . . 178 B2
Sédini I . . . . . . . . 178 B2
Sedlarica HR . . . . . 124 B3
Sedlčany CZ . . . . . 96 B2
Sedlec-Prčice CZ . . 96 B2
Sedlice CZ . . . . . . 96 B1
Sędziejowice PL. . . 86 A3
Sędziszów PL . . . . 87 B4
Sędziszów Małapolski PL. . . . 87 B5
Seebach F . . . . . . 93 C3
Seeboden A . . . . . 109 C4
Seefeld
  Brandenburg D . . .74 B2
  Niedersachsen D . .71 A5
Seefeld in Tirol A. . 108 B2
Seeg D . . . . . . . . 108 B1
Seehausen
  Sachsen-Anhalt D . 73 B4
  Sachsen-Anhalt D . 73 B4
Seeheim-Jugenheim D . . . . 93 B4
Seelbach D . . . . . . 93 C3
Seelow D . . . . . . . 74 B3
Seelze D . . . . . . . 72 B2
Seerhausen D . . . . 83 A5
Sées F . . . . . . . . . 89 B4
Seesen D . . . . . . . 82 A2
Seeshaupt D . . . . . 108 B2
Seewalchen A . . . . 109 B4
Seferihisar TR . . . . 188 A1
Sefkerin SRB . . . . 127 B2
Segård N . . . . . . . 48 B2
Segerstad S . . . . . 55 A4
Segesd H . . . . . . . 124 A3
Seglinge FIN . . . . . 51 B7
Segmon S . . . . . . 55 A4
Segonzac F . . . . . 115 C3
Segorbe E . . . . . . 159 B3
Segovia E . . . . . . . 151 B3
Segré F . . . . . . . . 101 B5
Segura
  E. . . . . . . . . . .144 B1
  P. . . . . . . . . . .155 B3
Segura de León E . 161 A3
Segura de los Baños E. . . . 152 B3
Ségur-les-Villas F . .116 B2
Segurrilla E . . . . . . 150 B3
Sehnde D . . . . . . . 72 B2
Seia P. . . . . . . . . . 148 B2
Seiches-sur-le-Loir F. . . . 102 B1

Seifhennersdorf D . 84 B2
Seignelay F . . . . . 104 B2
Seijo E . . . . . . . . . 140 C2
Seilhac F . . . . . . . .116 B1
Seilles B. . . . . . . . . 79 B5
Seim N. . . . . . . . . . 46 B2
Seinäjoki FIN . . . . . . 8 A3
Seissan F . . . . . . . 145 A4
Seitenstetten Markt
   A. . . . . . . . . . . .110 A1
Seixal P . . . . . . . . 154 C1
Seiz A . . . . . . . . . .110 B1
Seizthal A. . . . . . . .110 B1
Sejerslev DK . . . . . 58 B1
Seksna RUS . . . . . 9 C11
Selárdalur IS . . . . 190 B1
Selárgius I . . . . . . 179 C3
Selb D . . . . . . . . . . 83 B4
Selby GB. . . . . . . . 40 B2
Selca HR . . . . . . . 138 B2
Selce HR . . . . . . . 123 B3
Selçuk TR . . . . . . . 188 B2
Selde DK . . . . . . . . 58 B2
Selenča SRB . . . . . 126 B1
Selendi
   Manisa TR . . . . .186 D2
   Manisa TR . . . . .186 D3
Selenicë AL . . . . . 182 C1
Sélestat F. . . . . . . 106 A2
Seleuš SRB . . . . . 126 B2
Selevac SRB . . . . . 127 C2
Selfoss IS . . . . . . 190 D5
Selgua E . . . . . . . 145 C4
Selice SK . . . . . . . .112 A1
Seligenstadt D. . . . . 93 A4
Seligenthal D. . . . . . 82 B2
Selimiye TR . . . . . . 188 B2
Selizharovo RUS. . . . 9 D8
Selja S . . . . . . . . . . 50 A1
Selje N . . . . . . . . 198 C2
Seljelvnes N . . . . . 192 C3
Seljord N . . . . . . . . 53 A4
Selkirk GB . . . . . . . 35 C5
Sellano I. . . . . . . . 136 C1
Selles-St Denis F . . 103 B3
Selles-sur-Cher F . . 103 B3
Sellières F . . . . . . 105 C4
Sellin D . . . . . . . . . 66 B2
Sellye H . . . . . . . . 125 B3
Selm D . . . . . . . . . 80 A3
Selnica ob Dravi
   SLO . . . . . . . . . 110 C2
Selongey F . . . . . . 105 B4
Selonnet F . . . . . . 132 A2
Selow D . . . . . . . . . 65 C4
Selsey GB . . . . . . . 44 C3
Selsingen D. . . . . . . 72 A2
Selters D . . . . . . . . 81 B3
Seltz F . . . . . . . . . . 93 C4
Selva E. . . . . . . . . 167 B2
Selva di Cadore I. . . 108 C2
Selva di Val Gardena
   I . . . . . . . . . . . . 108 C2
Selvik
   Sogn og Fjordane
   N. . . . . . . . . . . .46 A2
   Vestfold N . . . . . .54 A1
Selvino I. . . . . . . . 120 B2
Selyatyn UA. . . . . . 17 B6
Sem N . . . . . . . . . . 54 A1
Semeljci HR. . . . . . 125 B4
Semič SLO. . . . . . . 123 B4
Semide
   F. . . . . . . . . . . . .91 B4
   P. . . . . . . . . . . . 148 B1
Semily CZ . . . . . . . 84 B3
Seminara I . . . . . . 175 C1
Semlac RO. . . . . . 126 A2
Semlacu Mare RO. . 126 B3
Semmen-stedt D . . . 73 B3
Šempeter SLO . . . . 123 A4
Semriach A . . . . . . .110 B2
Semur-en-Auxois
   F. . . . . . . . . . . . 104 B3
Sena E. . . . . . . . . 145 C3
Sena de Luna E . . . 141 B5
Senarpont F. . . . . . . 90 B1
Sénas F . . . . . . . . 131 B4
Senčanski Trešnjevac
   SRB . . . . . . . . . 126 B1
Sencelles E . . . . . 167 B2
Senčur SLO. . . . . . 123 A3
Senden
   Bayern D . . . . . . .94 C2
   Nordrhein-Westfalen
   D. . . . . . . . . . . .80 A3
Sendenhorst D . . . . 81 A3
Sendim P . . . . . . . 149 A3
Senec SK . . . . . . . .111 A4
Seneffe B . . . . . . . . 79 B4
Séneghe I . . . . . . . 178 B2
Senés E . . . . . . . . 164 B2
Senez F . . . . . . . . 132 B2
Senftenberg D . . . . . 84 A1
Sengouagnet F . . . 145 B4
Sengwarden D. . . . . 71 A5
Senica SK . . . . . . . 98 C1
Senice na Hané CZ . 98 B1
Senigállia I . . . . . . 136 B2
Senirkent TR . . . . . 189 A5
Sénis I . . . . . . . . . 179 C2
Senise I . . . . . . . . 174 A2
Senj HR . . . . . . . . 123 C3
Senje SRB . . . . . . 127 D3
Senjehopen N . . . . 194 A8

Senjski Rudnik
   SRB . . . . . . . . . 127 D3
Senlis F. . . . . . . . . 90 B2
Sennan S . . . . . . . . 60 C2
Sennecey-le-Grand
   F. . . . . . . . . . . . 105 C3
Sennen GB . . . . . . 42 B1
Senno BY. . . . . . . . 13 A8
Sénnori I . . . . . . . 178 B2
Sennwald CH. . . . . 107 B4
Sennybridge GB . . . 39 C3
Senohrad SK. . . . . . 99 C3
Senonches F. . . . . . 89 B5
Senones F. . . . . . . . 92 C2
Senorbì I . . . . . . . 179 C3
Senovo SLO . . . . . 123 A4
Senožeče SLO. . . . 123 B3
Senožeti SLO. . . . . 123 A3
Sens F . . . . . . . . . 104 A2
Sens-de-Bretagne
   F. . . . . . . . . . . . 101 A4
Senta SRB . . . . . . 126 B2
Senterada E. . . . . . 145 B4
Sentilj SLO. . . . . . . 110 C2
Šentjernej SLO . . . 123 B4
Šentjur SLO. . . . . . 123 A4
Senumstad N. . . . . 53 B4
Seoane E . . . . . . . 141 B3
Seon CH. . . . . . . . 106 B3
Sépeaux F . . . . . . 104 B2
Sépey CH. . . . . . . .119 A4
Sepino I . . . . . . . . 170 B2
Sępólno Krajeńskie
   PL. . . . . . . . . . . . 76 A2
Seppenrade D . . . . . 80 A3
Seppois F . . . . . . . 106 B2
Septemvri BG . . . . 183 A6
Septeuil F . . . . . . . 90 C1
Sepúlveda E . . . . . 151 A4
Sequals I . . . . . . . 122 A1
Sequeros E . . . . . . 149 B3
Seraincourt F . . . . . 91 B4
Seraing B. . . . . . . . 80 B1
Seravezza I . . . . . . 134 B3
Sered' SK . . . . . . . . 98 C1
Seredka RUS. . . . . . 8 C6
Şereflikoçhisar TR . 23 B7
Seregélyes H . . . . .112 B2
Seregno I . . . . . . . 120 B2
Sérent F. . . . . . . . 101 B3
Serfaus A. . . . . . . 108 B1
Sergiyev Posad
   RUS . . . . . . . . . . 9 D11
Seriate I . . . . . . . . 120 B2
Sérifontaine F. . . . . 90 B1
Serifos GR. . . . . . . 185 B5
Sérignan F . . . . . . 130 B2
Serik TR . . . . . . . . 189 C6
Serina I. . . . . . . . . 120 B2
Serinhisar TR . . . . 188 B4
Sermaises F. . . . . . 90 C2
Sermaize-les-Bains
   F. . . . . . . . . . . . . 91 C4
Sérmide I . . . . . . . 121 C4
Sermoneta I . . . . . 169 B2
Sernache de Bonjardim
   P. . . . . . . . . . . . 154 B2
Sernancelhe P. . . . 148 B2
Serock PL . . . . . . . 77 B6
Serón E . . . . . . . . 164 B2
Serón de Najima E . 152 A1
Serooskerke NL. . . . 79 A3
Seròs E . . . . . . . . 153 A4
Serpa P . . . . . . . . 160 B2
Serracapriola I. . . . 171 B3
Serrada E. . . . . . . 150 A3
Serra de Outes E. . 140 B2
Serradifalco I. . . . . 176 B2
Serradilla E . . . . . . 155 B4
Serradilla del Arroyo
   E. . . . . . . . . . . . 149 B3
Serradilla del Llano
   E. . . . . . . . . . . . 149 B3
Serramanna I . . . . 179 C2
Serramazzoni I . . . 135 A3
Serranillos E . . . . . 150 B3
Serrapetrona I . . . . 136 B2
Serra San Bruno I . 175 C2
Serra San Quírico I 136 B2
Serrastretta I . . . . 175 B2
Serravalle
   Piemonte I . . . . . 119 B5
   Umbria I . . . . . . 136 C2
Serravalle di Chienti
   I. . . . . . . . . . . . . 136 B1
Serravalle Scrívia I 120 C1
Serre I . . . . . . . . . 172 B1
Serrejón E . . . . . . 150 C2
Serres
   F. . . . . . . . . . . . 132 A1
   GR . . . . . . . . . . 183 B5
Serrières F. . . . . . .117 B4
Serrières-de-Briord
   F. . . . . . . . . . . . .118 B2
Sersale I . . . . . . . 175 B2
Sertã P . . . . . . . . . 154 B2
Sertig Dörfli CH. . . 107 C4
Servance F . . . . . . 106 B1
Serverette F. . . . . .117 C3
Servia GR . . . . . . . 182 C4
Servian F. . . . . . . . 130 B2
Serviers F . . . . . . . 131 A3
Servigliano I . . . . . 136 B2
Serzedelo P. . . . . . 148 A1
Seseña Nuevo E . . 151 B4
Sesimbra P . . . . . . 154 C1
Seskarö S . . . . . . 196 D6
Seskinore GB . . . . . 27 B3

Sesma E. . . . . . . . 144 B1
Sessa Aurunca I . . 170 B1
Ses Salines E . . . . 167 B3
Sesta Godano I . . . 134 A2
Šestanovac HR . . . 138 B2
Sestao E . . . . . . . 143 A4
Sestino I. . . . . . . . 135 B5
Sesto I . . . . . . . . . 109 C3
Sesto Calende I . . . 120 B1
Sesto Fiorentino I . 135 B4
Séstola I . . . . . . . . 135 A3
Sesto San Giovanni
   I . . . . . . . . . . . . 120 B2
Sestriere I . . . . . . . 119 C3
Sestri Levante I . . . 134 A2
Sestroretsk RUS. . . . 9 B7
Sestu I . . . . . . . . . 179 C3
Sesvete HR . . . . . . 124 B2
Setcases E . . . . . . 146 B3
Sète F . . . . . . . . . 130 B2
Setenil E . . . . . . . . 162 B2
Setermoen N . . . . . 194 B9
Šetonje SRB . . . . . 127 C3
Setskog N . . . . . . . 54 A2
Settalsjølia N . . . . . 199 C7
Séttimo Torinese I . .119 B4
Settimo Vittone I . . .119 B4
Settle GB . . . . . . . . 40 A1
Setúbal P . . . . . . . 154 C2
Seubersdorf D. . . . . 95 B3
Seúi I . . . . . . . . . . 179 C3
Seúlo I . . . . . . . . . 179 C3
Seurre F . . . . . . . . 105 C4
Sevel DK . . . . . . . . 58 B1
Sevenoaks GB. . . . . 45 B4
Sévérac-le-Château
   F. . . . . . . . . . . . 130 A2
Sever do Vouga P . 148 B1
Severin HR . . . . . . 123 B4
Severomorsk RUS . . 3 B13
Séveso I . . . . . . . . 120 B2
Ševětin CZ. . . . . . . 96 B2
Sevettijärvi FIN . . . 193 C12
Sévigny F. . . . . . . . 91 B4
Sevilla = Seville E . 162 A2
Sevilla la Nueva E . 151 B3
Seville = Sevilla E . 162 A2
Sevilleja de la Jara
   E. . . . . . . . . . . . 156 A3
Sevlievo BG. . . . . . 17 D6
Sevnica SLO . . . . . 123 A4
Sevojno SRB . . . . . 127 D1
Sevrier F. . . . . . . . .118 B3
Sexdrega S . . . . . . 60 B3
Seyches F . . . . . . 129 B3
Seyda D . . . . . . . . 83 A4
Seydişehir TR . . . . 189 B6
Seyðisfjörður IS . 191 B12
Seyitgazi TR . . . . . 187 C5
Seyitömer TR. . . . . 187 C4
Seymen TR . . . . . . 186 A2
Seyne F . . . . . . . . 132 A2
Seynes F . . . . . . . 131 A3
Seyssel F . . . . . . .118 B2
Sežana SLO . . . . . 122 B2
Sézanne F . . . . . . . 91 C3
Sezulfe P . . . . . . . 149 A2
Sezze I . . . . . . . . . 169 B3
Sfântu Gheorghe
   RO. . . . . . . . . . . 17 C6
Sforzacosta I. . . . . 136 B2
Sgarasta Mhor GB. . 31 B1
's-Gravendeel NL. . . 79 A4
's-Gravenhage = The
   Hague NL. . . . . . . 70 B1
's-Gravenzande NL . 79 A4
Shaftesbury GB. . . . 43 A4
Shalkiy RUS . . . . . . 9 B9
Shanagolden IRL. . . 29 B2
Shanklin GB . . . . . . 44 C2
Shap GB. . . . . . . . . 37 B4
Sharpness GB. . . . . 43 A4
Shawbury GB . . . . . 38 B4
's-Heerenberg NL . . 80 A2
Sheerness GB. . . . . 45 B4
Sheffield GB. . . . . . 40 B2
Shefford GB. . . . . . 44 A3
Shëmri AL . . . . . . . 182 A2
Shenfield GB. . . . . . 45 B4
Shëngjergj AL. . . . . 182 B2
Shepshed GB . . . . . 40 C2
Shepton Mallet GB . 43 A4
Sherborne GB . . . . . 43 B4
Shercock IRL. . . . . . 27 C4
Sheringham GB. . . . 41 C5
's-Hertogenbosch
   NL. . . . . . . . . . . . 79 A5
Shiel Bridge GB. . . . 32 D1
Shieldaig GB . . . . . . 31 B3
Shijak AL . . . . . . . 182 B1
Shillelagh IRL . . . . . 30 B2
Shimsk RUS . . . . . . 9 C7
Shipston-on-Stour
   GB. . . . . . . . . . . 44 A2
Shklow BY . . . . . . . 13 A9
Shkodër AL . . . . . . 182 A1
Shoeburyness GB. . 45 B4
Shoreham-by-Sea
   GB. . . . . . . . . . . 44 C3
Shotley Gate GB . . . 45 B5
Shrewsbury GB. . . . 38 B4
Shugozero RUS . . . . 9 C9
Shumen BG. . . . . . . 17 D7
Siabost GB . . . . . . 31 A2
Siamanna I. . . . . . 179 C2
Sianów PL . . . . . . . 67 B5

Siatista GR . . . . . . 182 C3
Siauges-St Romain
   F. . . . . . . . . . . . .117 B3
Šiauliai LT . . . . . . . . 8 E3
Sibari I . . . . . . . . . 174 B2
Sibbhult S . . . . . . . 63 B2
Silvi Marina I . . . . . 169 A4
Sibinj HR . . . . . . . 125 B3
Sibiu RO. . . . . . . . . 17 C6
Sibnica SRB . . . . . 127 C2
Sibsey GB . . . . . . . 41 B4
Siculiana I . . . . . . . 176 B2
Šid SRB . . . . . . . . 125 B5
Sidari GR. . . . . . . . 182 D1
Siddeburen NL . . . . 71 A3
Sidensjö S . . . . . . 200 C4
Siderno I . . . . . . . . 175 C2
Sidirokastro GR . . . 183 B5
Sidmouth GB. . . . . . 43 B3
Sidzina PL . . . . . . . 99 B3
Siebe N . . . . . . . . 192 D7
Siebenlehn D. . . . . . 83 A5
Siedlce PL. . . . . . . . 12 B5
Siedlice PL. . . . . . . 75 A4
Siedlinghausen D . . 81 A4
Siedlisko PL. . . . . . 75 B5
Siegburg D . . . . . . . 80 B3
Siegen D . . . . . . . . 81 B4
Siegenburg D . . . . . 95 C3
Sieghartskirchen A 111 A3
Siegsdorf D . . . . . . 109 B3
Siekierki PL. . . . . . . 74 B3
Sielpia PL. . . . . . . . 87 A4
Siemiany PL. . . . . . 69 B4
Siena I . . . . . . . . . 135 B4
Sieniawa PL. . . . . . 84 B2
Sienno PL . . . . . . . 87 A5
Sieppijärvi FIN. . . . 196 B7
Sieradz PL. . . . . . . 86 A2
Sieraków
   Śląskie PL. . . . . . 86 B2
   Wielkopolskie PL . . 75 B5
Sierakowice PL. . . . 68 A2
Sierck-les-Bains F . 92 B2
Sierentz F . . . . . . . 106 B2
Sierning A . . . . . . . .110 A1
Sierpc PL. . . . . . . . 77 B4
Sierra de Fuentes
   E. . . . . . . . . . . . 155 B4
Sierra de Luna E . . 144 B3
Sierra de Yeguas E 162 A3
Sierre CH. . . . . . . .119 A4
Siestrzeń PL . . . . . 77 B5
Sietamo E . . . . . . . 145 B3
Siewierz PL . . . . . . 86 B3
Sigdal N. . . . . . . . . 48 B1
Sigean F. . . . . . . . 130 B1
Sigerfjord N . . . . . . 194 B6
Sighetu-Marmatiei
   RO. . . . . . . . . . . 17 B5
Sighişoara RO. . . . . 17 B6
Sigillo I . . . . . . . . . 136 B1
Siglufjörður IS. . . . 191 A7
Sigmaringen D . . . 107 A4
Signa I . . . . . . . . . 135 B4
Signes F. . . . . . . . 132 B1
Signy-l'Abbaye F . . 91 B4
Signy-le-Petit F . . . 91 B4
Sigogne F . . . . . . .115 C3
Sigri GR. . . . . . . . . 183 D7
Sigtuna S . . . . . . . 57 A3
Sigueiro E . . . . . . 140 B2
Sigüenza E . . . . . . 151 A5
Sigües E . . . . . . . . 144 B2
Sigulda LV . . . . . . . . 8 D4
Sihlea RO. . . . . . . . 17 C7
Siikainen FIN . . . . . . 8 A5
Siilinjärvi FIN. . . . . . . 8 A5
Sikenica SK . . . . . .112 A2
Sikfors S . . . . . . . 196 D4
Sikia GR. . . . . . . . 183 C5
Sikinos GR. . . . . . . 185 C6
Sikkilsdalseter N . . 47 A6
Siklós H . . . . . . . . 125 B4
Sikórz PL. . . . . . . . 77 B4
Sikselet S . . . . . . . 195 D8
Silandro I. . . . . . . 108 C1
Silánus I . . . . . . . . 178 B2
Silbaš SRB . . . . . . 126 B1
Silberstedt D. . . . . . 64 B2
Sile TR . . . . . . . . . 187 A4
Siles E . . . . . . . . . 164 A2
Silgueiros P. . . . . . 148 B2
Silifke TR . . . . . . . . 23 C7
Siliqua I . . . . . . . . 179 C2
Silistra BG. . . . . . . 17 C7
Siljan N . . . . . . . . . 53 A5
Siljansnäs S. . . . . . 50 B1
Silkeborg DK. . . . . . 59 B2
Silla E. . . . . . . . . . 159 B3
Sillamäe EST. . . . . . 8 C5
Silleda E. . . . . . . . 140 B2
Sillé-le-Guillaume
   F. . . . . . . . . . . . 102 A1
Sillenstede D . . . . . 71 A4
Sillerud S . . . . . . . 54 A3
Silloth GB . . . . . . . 36 B3
Silno PL . . . . . . . . . 68 B2
Silnowo PL. . . . . . . 68 B1
Silo HR. . . . . . . . . 123 B3
Sils E . . . . . . . . . . 147 C3
Silsand N . . . . . . . 194 A8
Šilte S. . . . . . . . . . 57 C4
Siluté LT. . . . . . . . . 12 A4
Silvalen N . . . . . . . 195 E3
Silvaplana CH . . . . 107 C4
Silvares P. . . . . . . 148 B2
Silvberg S . . . . . . . 50 B2

Silverdalen S. . . . . 62 A3
Silvermines IRL. . . . 28 B3
Silverstone GB . . . . 44 A2
Silverton GB . . . . . 43 B3
Silves P. . . . . . . . . 160 B1
Simandre F . . . . . . 105 C3
Šimanovci SRB . . . 127 C2
Simard F . . . . . . . 105 C4
Simat de Valldigna
   E. . . . . . . . . . . . 159 B3
Simav TR. . . . . . . . 186 C3
Simbach
   Bayern D . . . . . . .95 C4
   Bayern D . . . . . . .95 C5
Simbário I . . . . . . 175 C2
Simeonovgrad BG 183 A7
Simeria RO. . . . . . . 17 C5
Simi GR . . . . . . . . 188 C2
Simićevo SRB . . . . 127 C3
Simitli BG. . . . . . . . 183 B5
Simlångsdalen S. . . 60 C3
Simmerath D. . . . . . 80 B2
Simmerberg D. . . . 107 B4
Simmern D. . . . . . . 93 B3
Simo FIN . . . . . . . 197 D8
Šimonovce SK. . . . . 99 C4
Simonsbath GB. . . . 43 A3
Simonstorp S . . . . . 56 B2
Simontornya H . . . .112 C2
Simplon CH . . . . . .119 A5
Simrishamn S . . . . 63 C2
Sinaia RO. . . . . . . . 17 C6
Sinalunga I . . . . . . 135 B4
Sinarcas E . . . . . . 159 B2
Sincan TR . . . . . . . 187 C7
Sincanlı TR . . . . . . 187 D5
Sindal DK. . . . . . . . 58 A3
Sindelfingen D . . . . 93 C5
Sindia I. . . . . . . . . 178 B2
Sındırgı TR. . . . . . . 186 C3
Sinekli TR . . . . . . . 186 A3
Sines P . . . . . . . . 160 B1
Sinetta FIN . . . . . . 197 C8
Sineu E . . . . . . . . 167 B3
Singen D . . . . . . . 107 B3
Singleton GB. . . . . . 44 C3
Singsås N . . . . . . 199 C7
Siniscóla I . . . . . . 178 B3
Sinj HR. . . . . . . . . 138 B2
Sinlabajos E . . . . . 150 A3
Sinn D . . . . . . . . . . 81 B4
Sínnai I. . . . . . . . . 179 C3
Sinnes N . . . . . . . . 52 B2
Sinop TR . . . . . . . . 23 A8
Sins CH . . . . . . . . 106 B3
Sinsheim D . . . . . . 93 B4
Sint Annaland NL . . 79 A4
Sint Annaparochie
   NL. . . . . . . . . . . . 70 A2
Sint Athonis NL . . . 80 A1
Sint Nicolaasga NL . 70 B2
Sint Oedenrode NL . 79 A5
Sintra P . . . . . . . . 154 C1
Sinzheim D . . . . . . 93 C4
Sinzig D . . . . . . . . 80 B3
Siófok H . . . . . . . . .112 C2
Sion CH . . . . . . . . .119 A4
Sion Mills GB . . . . . 27 B3
Siorac-en-Périgord
   F. . . . . . . . . . . . 129 B3
Šipanska Luka HR 139 C3
Šipovo BIH. . . . . . . 138 A3
Sira N . . . . . . . . . . 52 B2
Siracusa I. . . . . . . 177 B4
Siret RO. . . . . . . . . 17 B7
Sirevåg N . . . . . . . . 52 B1
Sirig SRB . . . . . . . 126 B1
Sirkka FIN . . . . . . . 196 B7
Sirmione I . . . . . . 121 B3
Sirniö FIN. . . . . . . 197 D11
Sirok H . . . . . . . . . .113 B4
Siroke SK. . . . . . . . 99 C4
Široki Brijeg BIH . . 139 B3
Sirolo I . . . . . . . . . 136 B2
Siruela E . . . . . . . 156 B2
Sisak HR . . . . . . . 124 B2
Sisante E . . . . . . . 158 B1
Šišljavić HR. . . . . . 123 B4
Sissach CH . . . . . . 106 B2
Sissonne F . . . . . . . 91 B3
Sistelo P. . . . . . . . 140 C2
Sisteron F . . . . . . . 132 A1
Sistiana I . . . . . . . 122 B2
Sistranda N . . . . . . 198 B5
Sitasjaurestugorna
   S. . . . . . . . . . . . 194 C8
Sitges E . . . . . . . . 147 C2
Sitia GR. . . . . . . . . 185 D7
Sittard NL. . . . . . . . 80 A1
Sittensen D . . . . . . 72 A2
Sittingbourne GB . . 45 B4
Sitzenroda D . . . . . 83 A4
Sivac SRB . . . . . . 126 B1
Sivaslı TR. . . . . . . 189 A4
Siverić HR . . . . . . 138 B2
Sivrihisar TR . . . . . 187 C6
Sixt-Fer-á-Cheval
   F. . . . . . . . . . . . .119 A3
Siziano I . . . . . . . . 120 B2
Sizun F . . . . . . . . . 100 A1
Sjenica SRB. . . . . . 16 D3
Sjoa N . . . . . . . . . 198 D6
Sjøåsen N . . . . . . 199 A8
Sjöbo S . . . . . . . . . 61 D3
Sjøenden
   Hedmark N. . . . . .48 A3
   Hedmark N. . . . . .48 B3

Sjøholt N . . . . . . . 198 C3
Sjøli N . . . . . . . . . . 48 A3
Sjølstad N . . . . . . 199 A9
Sjölunda S . . . . . . . 56 A1
Sjømarken S . . . . . . 60 B2
Sjørring DK . . . . . . 58 B1
Sjötofta S . . . . . . . . 60 B3
Sjötorp S . . . . . . . . 55 B4
Sjoutnäset S . . . . .199 A11
Sjøvegan N . . . . . . 194 B8
Sjuntorp S . . . . . . . 54 B3
Skåbu N . . . . . . . . 47 A6
Skafså N . . . . . . . . 53 A4
Skaftafell IS . . . . . 191 D9
Skagaströnd IS . . . 190 B5
Skagen DK. . . . . . . 58 A3
Skagersvik S . . . . . 55 B5
Skaiå N . . . . . . . . . 53 B3
Skaidi N . . . . . . . . 193 B8
Skala GR . . . . . . . 184 A1
Skała PL . . . . . . . . 87 B3
Skaland N . . . . . . . 194 A8
Skala Oropou GR . 185 A4
Skala-Podilska UA . 13 D7
Skalat UA. . . . . . . . 13 D6
Skalbmierz PL. . . . . 87 B4
Skålevik N . . . . . . . 53 B4
Skalica SK . . . . . . . 98 C1
Skalité SK . . . . . . . 98 B2
Skällinge S . . . . . . 60 B2
Skalná CZ . . . . . . . 83 B4
Skals DK . . . . . . . . 58 B2
Skælskør DK . . . . . 65 A4
Skalstugan S . . . . 199 B9
Skanderborg DK . . 59 B2
Skånes-Fagerhult S 61 C3
Skåne-Tranås S . . . 61 D3
Skånevik N . . . . . . 52 A1
Skänninge S . . . . . 55 B6
Skanör med Falsterbo
   S. . . . . . . . . . . . . 66 A1
Skåpafors S . . . . . . 54 A3
Skąpe PL . . . . . . . . 75 B4
Skara S . . . . . . . . . 55 B4
Skærbæk DK . . . . . 64 A1
Skarberget N . . . . . 194 B7
Skärblacka S . . . . . 56 B1
Skarø IS . . . . . . . . 190 B3
Skarda S . . . . . . . 200 B4
Skare N . . . . . . . . . 46 C3
Skåre S . . . . . . . . . 55 A4
Skärhamn S . . . . . . 60 B1
Skarnes N . . . . . . . 48 B3
Skärplinge S . . . . . 51 B4
Skarpnatö FIN . . . . 51 B6
Skarp Salling DK. . . 58 B2
Skarrild DK . . . . . . 59 C1
Skarstad N. . . . . . . 194 B7
Skärstad S . . . . . . . 62 A2
Skarsvåg N . . . . . . 193 A9
Skarszewy PL . . . . 69 A3
Skårup DK . . . . . . . 65 A3
Skärvången S . . . .199 B11
Skarvsjöby S . . . . .195 F8
Skaryszew PL . . . . 87 A5
Skarżysko-Kamienna
   PL. . . . . . . . . . . . 87 A4
Skarzysko Ksiazece
   PL. . . . . . . . . . . . 87 A4
Skatøy N . . . . . . . . 53 B5
Skattkärr S . . . . . . . 55 A4
Skattungbyn S . . . . 50 A1
Skatval N . . . . . . . 199 B7
Skaulo S . . . . . . . 196 B4
Skave DK. . . . . . . . 59 B1
Skawina PL . . . . . . 99 B3
Skebobruk S . . . . . 51 C5
Skebokvarn S . . . . . 56 A2
Skedala S. . . . . . . . 61 C2
Skedevi S. . . . . . . . 56 B1
Skedsmokorset N . . 48 B3
Skee S . . . . . . . . . 54 B2
Skegness GB . . . . . 41 B4
Skei N. . . . . . . . . . 46 A3
Skela SRB . . . . . . 127 C2
Skelani BIH . . . . . . 127 D1
Skellefteå S . . . . . . . 2 D7
Skelleftehamn S . . . 2 D7
Skelmersdale GB . . 38 A4
Skelmorlie GB . . . . 34 C3
Skelund DK. . . . . . . 58 B3
Skender Vakuf BIH 138 A3
Skene S . . . . . . . . . 60 B2
Skępe PL . . . . . . . . 77 B4
Skepplanda S . . . . . 60 B2
Skeppshult S . . . . . 60 B3
Skerries IRL. . . . . . 30 A2
Ski N. . . . . . . . . . . 54 A1
Skiathos GR . . . . . 183 D5
Skibbereen IRL . . . 29 C2
Skibotn N. . . . . . . 192 C4
Skidra GR . . . . . . . 182 C4
Skien N . . . . . . . . . 53 A5
Skierniewice PL. . . . 77 C5
Skillingaryd S . . . . . 60 B4
Skillinge S . . . . . . . 63 C2
Skillingmark S . . . . 49 C4
Skilloura CY . . . . . 181 A2
Skinnardai S . . . . . 57 A4
Skinnskatteberg S . 50 C2
Skipmannvik N . . . 195 C6
Skipness GB . . . . . 34 C2
Skipsea GB . . . . . . 41 B3
Skipton GB . . . . . . 40 B1
Skiptvet N. . . . . . . . 54 A2
Skiros GR . . . . . . . 183 E6
Skivarp S . . . . . . . . 66 A2
Skive DK . . . . . . . . 58 B2

Skjånes N . . . . . . 193 B12
Skjærhalden N . . . . 54 A2
Skjeberg N. . . . . . . . 54 A2
Skjeggedal N. . . . . . 46 B3
Skjeljanger N. . . . . . 46 B1
Skjeljavik N . . . . . . 46 C2
Skjern DK. . . . . . . . 59 C1
Skjervøy N . . . . . . 192 B4
Skjold
  Rogaland N . . . . . 52 A1
  Troms N . . . . . . . 192 C3
Skjoldastraumen N . 52 A1
Skjolden N . . . . . . . 47 A4
Skjønhaug N . . . . . . 54 A2
Skjøtningsberg N .193 A11
Škocjan SLO . . . . . 123 B4
Skoczów PL. . . . . . . 98 B2
Skodborg DK. . . . . . 60 C2
Škofja Loka SLO . . . 123 A3
Škofljica SLO. . . . . 123 B3
Skog S . . . . . . . . . . 51 A3
Skoganvarre N . . . . 193 C9
Skogen S . . . . . . . . 54 A1
Skogfoss N . . . . . 193 C13
Skoghall S . . . . . . . 55 A4
Skogly N . . . . . . . 193 C13
Skogn N . . . . . . . . 199 B8
Skognes N . . . . . . 192 C3
Skogstorp
  Halland S. . . . . . . 60 C2
  Södermanland S . . 56 A2
Skoki PL. . . . . . . . . 76 B2
Skokloster S . . . . . . 57 A3
Sköldinge S . . . . . . 56 A2
Skole UA . . . . . . . . 13 D5
Skollenborg N . . . . . 53 A5
Sköllersta S . . . . . . 56 A1
Skomlin PL . . . . . . . 86 A2
Skonseng N . . . . . . 195 D5
Skopelos GR . . . . . 183 D5
Skopje MK. . . . . . . 182 A3
Skoppum N . . . . . . 54 A1
Skórcz PL. . . . . . . . 69 B3
Skorogoszcz PL . . . . 86 B1
Skoroszów PL. . . . . . 85 A5
Skorovatn N . . . . 199 A10
Skorped S . . . . . . . 200 C3
Skørping DK. . . . . . . 58 B2
Skotfoss N. . . . . . . 53 A5
Skotniki PL . . . . . . . 87 A3
Skotselv N . . . . . . . 48 C1
Skotterud N . . . . . . 49 C4
Skottorp S . . . . . . . 61 C2
Skovby DK. . . . . . . . 64 B2
Skövde S . . . . . . . . 55 B4
Skovsgård DK. . . . . . 58 A2
Skrad HR . . . . . . . 123 B3
Skradin HR . . . . . . 138 B1
Skradnik HR . . . . . 123 B4
Skråmestø N . . . . . . 46 B1
Škrdlovice CZ . . . . . 97 B3
Skrea S . . . . . . . . . 60 C2
Skreia N . . . . . . . . 48 B2
Skrolsvik N . . . . . . 194 A7
Skruv S . . . . . . . . . 63 B3
Skrwilno PL. . . . . . . 77 A4
Skrydstrup DK. . . . . . 59 C2
Skucani BIH. . . . . . 138 B2
Skudeneshavn N. . . . 52 A1
Skui N . . . . . . . . . . 48 C2
Skulsk PL. . . . . . . . 76 B3
Skultorp S . . . . . . . 55 B4
Skultuna S . . . . . . . 56 A2
Skuodas LT . . . . . . . 8 D2
Skurup S . . . . . . . . 66 A2
Skute N . . . . . . . . . 48 B2
Skuteč CZ . . . . . . . 97 B3
Skutskär S . . . . . . . 51 B4
Skutvik N . . . . . . . 194 B6
Skvyra UA . . . . . . . 13 D8
Skwierzyna PL. . . . . 75 B4
Skýcov SK. . . . . . . . 98 C2
Skyllberg S . . . . . . . 55 B5
Skyttmon S . . . . . . 200 C1
Skyttorp S . . . . . . . 51 B4
Sládkovičovo SK. . .111 A4
Slagelse DK. . . . . . . 61 D1
Slagharen NL. . . . . . 71 B3
Slagnäs S . . . . . . . 195 E9
Slaidburn GB. . . . . . 40 B1
Slane IRL . . . . . . . . 30 A2
Slangerup DK . . . . . 61 D2
Slano HR . . . . . . . 139 C3
Slantsy RUS . . . . . . . 8 C6
Slaný CZ . . . . . . . . 84 B2
Slap SLO . . . . . . . 122 A2
Šlapanice CZ. . . . . . 97 B4
Slåstad N . . . . . . . . 48 B3
Slatina
  BIH . . . . . . . . . . .139 B3
  HR . . . . . . . . . . .125 B3
  RO . . . . . . . . . . . 17 C6
Slatiňany CZ . . . . . . 97 B3
Slatinice CZ. . . . . . . 98 B1
Slåttberg S. . . . . . . 50 A1
Slattum N . . . . . . . . 48 C2
Slavičín CZ . . . . . . . 98 B1
Slavkov CZ . . . . . . . 98 C1
Slavkovica SRB. . . . 127 C2
Slavkov u Brna CZ . . 97 B4
Slavonice CZ . . . . . . 97 C3
Slavonski Brod HR 125 B4
Slavonski Kobas
  HR . . . . . . . . . . .125 B3
Slavošovce SK . . . . 99 C4
Slavskoye RUS. . . . . 69 A5
Slavuta UA. . . . . . . 13 C7

Sława
  Lubuskie PL. . . . . .85 A4
  Zachodnio-Pomorskie
  PL. . . . . . . . . . . .67 C4
Slawharad BY . . . . 13 B9
Sławków PL. . . . . . . 86 B3
Sławno
  Wielkopolskie PL . .76 B2
  Zachodnio-Pomorskie
  PL. . . . . . . . . . . .68 A1
Sławoborze PL . . . . 67 C4
Sľ'ažany SK . . . . . . 98 C2
Sleaford GB. . . . . . 40 C3
Sleðbrjótur IS . . .191 B11
Sledmere GB . . . . . 40 A3
Sleights GB. . . . . . 37 B6
Slemmestad N . . . . 54 A1
Ślesin PL . . . . . . . . 76 B3
Sliač SK . . . . . . . . 99 C3
Sliema M . . . . . . . 175 C3
Sligo IRL . . . . . . . . 26 B2
Slite S . . . . . . . . . 57 C4
Slitu N . . . . . . . . . 54 A2
Sliven BG. . . . . . . . 17 D7
Śliwice PL . . . . . . . 68 B3
Slobozia RO . . . . . 17 C7
Slochteren NL. . . . . 71 A3
Slöinge S . . . . . . . 60 C2
Słomniki PL . . . . . . 87 B4
Slonim BY . . . . . . . 13 B6
Słońsk PL. . . . . . . . 75 B3
Slootdorp NL. . . . . . 70 B1
Slottsbron S . . . . . . 55 A4
Slough GB. . . . . . . 44 B3
Slövag N . . . . . . . . 46 B2
Slovenj Gradec
  SLO . . . . . . . . . .110 C2
Slovenska Bistrica
  SLO . . . . . . . . . .123 A4
Slovenská Ľupča
  SK . . . . . . . . . . . 99 C3
Slovenská-Ves SK. . 99 B4
Slovenské Darmoty
  SK . . . . . . . . . . .112 A3
Slovenske Konjice
  SLO . . . . . . . . . .123 A4
Słubice PL . . . . . . . 74 B3
Sluderno I . . . . . . 108 C1
Sluis NL . . . . . . . . 78 A3
Šluknov CZ . . . . . . 84 A2
Slunj HR. . . . . . . . 123 B4
Słupca PL . . . . . . . 76 B2
Słupia PL . . . . . . . . 87 A3
Słupiec PL . . . . . . . 85 B4
Słupsk PL. . . . . . . . 68 A2
Slutsk BY. . . . . . . . 13 B7
Smålandsstenar S . 60 B3
Smalåsen N . . . . . 195 E4
Smardzewo PL . . . . 75 B4
Smarhon BY . . . . . 13 A7
Smarje SLO . . . . . 123 A4
Šmarjeta SLO . . . . 123 B4
Šmartno SLO. . . . . 123 A3
Smečno CZ . . . . . . 84 B2
Smedby S . . . . . . . 63 B4
Smědec CZ . . . . . . 96 C2
Smederevo SRB . . 127 C2
Smederevska Palanka
  SRB . . . . . . . . . .127 C2
Smedjebacken S . . 50 B2
Smeland N . . . . . . 53 B4
Smidary CZ . . . . . . 84 B3
Śmigiel PL . . . . . . . 75 B5
Smilde NL . . . . . . . 71 B3
Smiřice CZ. . . . . . . 85 B3
Smithfield GB . . . . 36 B4
Śmitowo PL. . . . . . . 75 A5
Smögen S . . . . . . . 54 B2
Smogulec PL. . . . . . 76 A2
Smołdzino PL . . . . . 68 A2
Smolenice SK . . . . 98 C1
Smolensk RUS. . . . 13 A10
Smolník SK . . . . . . 99 C4
Smolyan BG . . . . . 183 B6
Smuka SLO . . . . . 123 B3
Smygehamn S . . . . 66 A2
Smykow PL. . . . . . . 87 A4
Snainton GB. . . . . . 40 A3
Snaith GB . . . . . . . 40 B3
Snaptun DK. . . . . . . 59 C3
Snarby N . . . . . . . 192 C3
Snarum N . . . . . . . 48 B1
Snåsa N . . . . . . . . 199 A9
Snedsted DK. . . . . . 58 B1
Sneek NL . . . . . . . 70 A2
Sneem IRL . . . . . . 29 C2
Snejbjerg DK. . . . . . 59 B1
Snillfjord N . . . . . . 198 B6
Šnjegotina BIH . . . 125 C3
Snøde DK. . . . . . . . 65 A3
Snøfjord N . . . . . . 193 B8
Snogebaek DK . . . . 67 A4
Snyatyn UA. . . . . . . 13 D6
Soave I . . . . . . . . . 121 B4
Sober E . . . . . . . . 140 B3
Sobernheim D . . . . 93 B3
Soběslav CZ . . . . . 96 B2
Sobota
  Dolnośląskie PL. . .85 A3
  Łódzkie PL. . . . . . .77 B4
Sobótište SK . . . . . 98 C1
Sobotka CZ . . . . . . 84 B3
Sobótka
  Dolnośląskie PL. . .85 B4
  Wielkopolskie PL. . .86 A1
Sobra HR . . . . . . . 139 C3

Sobrado
  Coruña E . . . . . . 140 A2
  Lugo E . . . . . . . . 141 B3
Sobral da Adica P . 161 A2
Sobral de Monte Agraço
  P. . . . . . . . . . . . 154 C1
Sobreira Formosa
  P. . . . . . . . . . . . 154 B3
Søby DK. . . . . . . . . 64 B3
Sochaczew PL. . . . . 77 B5
Sochos GR . . . . . . 183 C5
Socodor RO. . . . . . 113 C5
Socol RO. . . . . . . . 127 C3
Socovos E . . . . . . 164 A3
Socuéllamos E . . . . 158 B1
Sodankylä FIN . . . . 197 B9
Soderåkra S . . . . . 63 B4
Söderala S . . . . . . 51 A3
Söderås S . . . . . . . 50 B2
Söderbärke S . . . . . 50 B2
Söderby-Karl S . . . . 51 C5
Söderfors S . . . . . . 51 B4
Söderhamn S . . . . . 51 A4
Söderköping S . . . . 56 B2
Söderö S . . . . . . . . 56 B1
Södertälje S . . . . . . 57 A3
Södingberg A. . . . . .110 B2
Södra Finnö S . . . . 56 B2
Södra Ny S. . . . . . . 55 A4
Södra Råda S . . . . . 55 A5
Södra Sandby S . . . 61 D3
Södra Vi S . . . . . . . 62 A3
Sodražica SLO . . . 123 B3
Sodupe E . . . . . . . 143 A3
Soengas P. . . . . . . 148 A1
Soest
  D. . . . . . . . . . . . .81 A4
  NL. . . . . . . . . . . .70 B2
Sofades GR . . . . . 182 D4
Sofia = Sofiya BG . . 17 D5
Sofikon GR . . . . . . 184 B4
Sofiya = Sofia BG . . 17 D5
Şofronea RO . . . . . 126 A3
Sögel D . . . . . . . . 71 B4
Sogliano al Rubicone
  I . . . . . . . . . . . . 135 A5
Sogndalsfjøra N . . . 46 A4
Søgne N . . . . . . . . 53 B3
Sögütköy TR . . . . . 188 C3
Soham GB . . . . . . 45 A4
Sohland D . . . . . . . 84 A2
Sohren D . . . . . . . . 93 B3
Soignies B. . . . . . . 79 B4
Soissons F . . . . . . 90 B3
Söjtör H . . . . . . . . .111 C3
Sokal' UA . . . . . . . 13 C6
Söke TR . . . . . . . . 188 B2
Sokna N . . . . . . . . 48 B1
Sokndal N . . . . . . . 52 B2
Soknedal N . . . . . . 199 C7
Soko BIH . . . . . . . 125 C4
Sokolac BIH. . . . . . 139 B4
Sokółka PL. . . . . . . 13 B5
Sokolov CZ . . . . . . 83 B4
Sokołowo PL. . . . . . 76 B3
Sokołów Podlaski
  PL. . . . . . . . . . . . 12 B5
Sola N . . . . . . . . . 52 B1
Solana de los Barros
  E. . . . . . . . . . . . 155 C4
Solana del Pino E . 157 B3
Solánas I . . . . . . . 179 C3
Solares E . . . . . . . 143 A3
Solarino I . . . . . . . 177 B4
Solarussa I . . . . . . 179 C2
Solas GB . . . . . . . 31 B1
Solberg S . . . . . . . 200 C3
Solberga S . . . . . . 62 A2
Solber-gelva N . . . . 48 C2
Solbjørg N . . . . . . . 46 B2
Solčany SK . . . . . . 98 C2
Solčava SLO . . . . . 123 A3
Solda I . . . . . . . . . 108 C1
Sölden A. . . . . . . . 108 C2
Solec Kujawski PL . 76 A3
Soleils F. . . . . . . . 132 B2
Solenzara F . . . . . 180 B2
Solera E . . . . . . . . 163 A4
Solesmes F . . . . . . 79 B3
Soleto I. . . . . . . . . 173 B4
Solgne F . . . . . . . . 92 C2
Solheim N . . . . . . . 46 B2
Solheimsvik N . . . . 52 A2
Solignac F . . . . . . . 115 C5
Solihull GB. . . . . . . 44 A2
Solin HR. . . . . . . . 138 B2
Solingen D. . . . . . . 80 A3
Solivella E . . . . . . . 147 C2
Solkan SLO . . . . . . 122 B2
Söll A . . . . . . . . . . 108 B3
Sollana E . . . . . . . 159 B3
Sollebrunn S . . . . . 54 B3
Sollefteå S . . . . . . 200 C3
Sollenau A . . . . . . .111 B3
Sollen-tuna S . . . . . 57 A3
Sóller E . . . . . . . . 166 B2
Sollerön S . . . . . . . 50 B1
Søllested DK . . . . . 65 B4
Solliès-Pont F . . . . 132 B2
Sollihøgda N . . . . . 48 C2
Solnechnogorsk
  RUS . . . . . . . . . .9 D10
Solnice CZ. . . . . . . 85 B4
Solofra I . . . . . . . . 170 C2
Solomiac F . . . . . . 129 C3
Solopaca I . . . . . . . 170 B2
Solórzano E . . . . . . 143 A3

Solothurn CH . . . . 106 B2
Solre-le-Château F . 79 B4
Solsona E . . . . . . . 147 C2
Solsvik N . . . . . . . . 46 B1
Solt H . . . . . . . . . . 112 C3
Soltau D . . . . . . . . 72 B2
Soltsy RUS . . . . . . . 9 C7
Soltszentimre H . . . 112 C3
Soltvadkert H . . . . . 112 C3
Solumsmoen N . . . . 48 C1
Solund N . . . . . . . . 46 A1
Solva GB . . . . . . . . 39 C1
Sölvesborg S . . . . . 63 B2
Solymár H . . . . . . . .112 B2
Soma TR . . . . . . . . 186 C2
Somain F . . . . . . . . 78 B3
Somberek H . . . . . . 125 A4
Sombernon F . . . . . 104 B3
Sombor SRB . . . . . 125 B5
Sombreffe B . . . . . . 79 B4
Someren NL. . . . . . . 80 A1
Somero FIN . . . . . . . 8 B3
Somersham GB. . . . 44 A3
Somerton GB. . . . . . 43 A4
Sominy PL . . . . . . . 68 A2
Somma Lombardo
  I . . . . . . . . . . . . 120 B1
Sommariva del Bosco
  I . . . . . . . . . . . . 119 C4
Sommarøy N . . . . . 192 C2
Sommarset N . . . . . 194 C6
Sommatino I . . . . . . 176 B2
Sombernon F . . . . . 91 C4
Sommen S . . . . . . . 55 B5
Sommepy-Tahure F 91 B4
Sömmerda D . . . . . 82 A3
Sommerfeld D . . . . . 74 B2
Sommersted DK. . . . 59 C2
Sommesous F . . . . . 91 C4
Somme-Tourbe F . . 91 B4
Sommières F . . . . . 131 B3
Sommières-du-Clain
  F . . . . . . . . . . . . 115 B4
Somo E . . . . . . . . . 143 A3
Somogyfajsz H . . . .111 C4
Somogyjád H . . . . .111 C4
Somogysámson H .111 C4
Somogysárd H . . . . 125 A3
Somogyszil H . . . . . 112 C2
Somogyszob H . . . . 124 A3
Somogyvár H . . . . .111 C4
Somontin E . . . . . . 164 B2
Somosierra E . . . . . 151 A4
Somosköújifalu H .113 A3
Sompolno PL. . . . . . 76 B3
Sompuis F . . . . . . . 91 C4
Son N . . . . . . . . . . 54 A1
Son Bou E . . . . . . . 167 B4
Sonceboz CH . . . . . 106 B2
Soncillo E . . . . . . . 143 B3
Soncino I. . . . . . . . 120 B2
Sóndalo I . . . . . . . 120 A3
Søndeled N . . . . . . 53 B5
Sønder Bjert DK . . . 59 C2
Sønderborg DK. . . . 64 B2
Sønderby DK. . . . . . 64 B2
Sønder Felding DK . 59 C1
Sønderho DK. . . . . . 59 C1
Sønder Hygum DK . 59 C1
Sønder Omme DK. . 59 C1
Sondershausen D . . 82 A2
Søndersø DK . . . . . 59 C3
Søndervig DK. . . . . 59 B1
Søndre Enningdal
  Kappel N . . . . . . . 54 B2
Sóndrio I . . . . . . . . 120 A2
Soneja E . . . . . . . . 159 B3
Son en Breugel NL . 80 A1
Songe N . . . . . . . . 53 B5
Songeons F . . . . . . 90 B1
Sonkamuotka FIN . 196 A6
Sonkovo RUS . . . . . 9 D10
Sönnarslöv S . . . . . 61 D4
Sonneberg D . . . . . 82 B3
Sonnefeld D . . . . . . 82 B3
Sonnewalde D . . . . 84 A1
Sonnino I . . . . . . . . 169 B3
Sonogno CH . . . . . 120 A1
Sonsbeck D . . . . . . 80 A2
Sonseca E . . . . . . . 157 A4
Son Servera E . . . . 167 B3
Sønsterud N . . . . . . 49 B4
Sonstorp S . . . . . . . 56 B1
Sonta SRB . . . . . . 125 B5
Sontheim D . . . . . . 94 C2
Sonthofen D . . . . . 107 B5
Sontra D. . . . . . . . . 82 A1
Sopelana E . . . . . . 143 A4
Sopje HR . . . . . . . 125 B3
Šoporňa SK . . . . . .111 A4
Sopot
  PL. . . . . . . . . . . . .69 A3
  SRB . . . . . . . . . .127 C2
Sopotnica MK . . . . 182 B3
Sopron H . . . . . . . .111 B3
Šor SRB . . . . . . . . 127 C1
Sora I . . . . . . . . . . 169 B3
Soragna I . . . . . . . 120 C3
Söråker S . . . . . . . 200 D3
Sorano I . . . . . . . . 168 A1
Sorbara I . . . . . . . . 121 C4
Sórbolo I . . . . . . . . 121 C3
Sörbygden S . . . . . 200 D2
Sordal N. . . . . . . . . 52 B3
Sordale GB . . . . . . 32 C3
Sore F . . . . . . . . . 128 B2
Sörenberg CH . . . . 106 C3

Soresina I . . . . . . . 120 B2
Sorèze F. . . . . . . . 146 A3
Sörforsa S . . . . . . . 200 E3
Sorges F . . . . . . . . 115 C4
Sórgono I . . . . . . . 179 B3
Sorgues F . . . . . . . 131 A3
Sorgun TR . . . . . . . 23 B8
Soria E . . . . . . . . . 143 C4
Soriano Cálabro I . . 175 C2
Soriano nel Cimino
  I . . . . . . . . . . . . 168 A2
Sorihuela del
  Guadalimar E . . . 164 A1
Sorisdale GB. . . . . . 34 B1
Sörjkosen N. . . . . . 192 C4
Sørli N . . . . . . . . . 199 A10
Sormás H . . . . . . . .111 C3
Sörmjöle S. . . . . . . 200 C6
Sørmo N . . . . . . . . 194 B9
Sornac F . . . . . . . . .116 B2
Sorø DK . . . . . . . . 61 D1
Soroca MD. . . . . . . 17 A8
Sørreisa N . . . . . . . 194 A9
Sorrento I . . . . . . . 170 C2
Sorsele S . . . . . . . 195 E8
Sörsjön S . . . . . . . . 49 A5
Sorso I . . . . . . . . . 178 B2
Sort E . . . . . . . . . . 146 B2
Sortavala RUS . . . . . 9 B7
Sortino I . . . . . . . . 177 B4
Sortland N . . . . . . 194 B6
Sørum N . . . . . . . . 48 B2
Sørumsand N . . . . . 48 C3
Sørvågen N . . . . . . 194 C3
Sørvær N . . . . . . . 192 B6
Sorvik S . . . . . . . . . 50 B2
Sørvika N . . . . . . . 199 C8
Sos F . . . . . . . . . . 128 B3
Sösdala S . . . . . . . 61 C3
Sos del Rey Católico
  E . . . . . . . . . . . . 144 B2
Sošice HR . . . . . . . 123 B4
Sośnica PL. . . . . . . 75 A5
Sośnicowice PL. . . . 86 B2
Sośno PL. . . . . . . . 76 A2
Sosnovyy Bor RUS. . 9 C6
Sosnowiec PL. . . . . 86 B3
Sospel F. . . . . . . . 133 B3
Šoštanj SLO . . . . . 123 A4
Sotaseter N . . . . . . 198 D4
Sotillo de Adrada
  E. . . . . . . . . . . . 150 B3
Sotillo de la Ribera
  E. . . . . . . . . . . . 143 C3
Sotin HR . . . . . . . . 125 B5
Sotkamo FIN . . . . . . 3 D11
Sotobañado y Priorato
  E . . . . . . . . . . . . 142 B2
Soto de la Marina
  E . . . . . . . . . . . . 143 A3
Soto del Barco E . . 141 A4
Soto de los Infantes
  E . . . . . . . . . . . . 141 A4
Soto de Real E . . . 151 B4
Soto de Ribera E . . 141 A5
Sotoserrano E . . . . 149 B3
Soto y Amío E . . . . 141 B5
Sotresgudo E . . . . . 142 B2
Sotrondio E . . . . . . 142 A1
Sotta F . . . . . . . . . 180 B2
Sottomarina I . . . . . 122 B1
Sottrum D . . . . . . . 72 A2
Sottunga FIN . . . . . 51 B7
Sotuelamos E . . . . 158 B1
Souain F . . . . . . . . 91 B4
Soual F . . . . . . . . . 146 A3
Soucy F . . . . . . . . 104 A2
Souda GR . . . . . . . 185 D5
Soudron F . . . . . . . 91 C4
Souesmes F . . . . . 103 B4
Soufflenheim F . . . . 93 C3
Soufli GR . . . . . . . 186 A1
Souillac F. . . . . . . 129 B4
Souilly F . . . . . . . . 91 B5
Soulac-sur-Mer F . 114 C2
Soulaines-Dhuys F . 91 C4
Soulatgé F . . . . . . 146 B3
Soultz-Haut-Rhin F 106 B2
Soultz-sous-Forêts
  F . . . . . . . . . . . . 93 C3
Soumagne B . . . . . 80 B1
Soumoulou F . . . . . 145 A3
Souppes-sur-Loing
  F . . . . . . . . . . . . 103 A4
Souprosse F . . . . . 128 C2
Sourdeval F . . . . . . 88 B3
Soure P . . . . . . . . 154 A2
Sournia F . . . . . . . 146 B3
Souro Pires P . . . . 149 B2
Sourpi GR . . . . . . . 182 D4
Sours F . . . . . . . . . 90 C1
Sousceyrac F . . . . .116 C2
Sousel P. . . . . . . . 155 C3
Soustons F . . . . . . 128 C1
Söğüt
  Bilecik TR. . . . . . 187 B5
  Burdur TR . . . . . 189 B4
Souteo de Montes
  E. . . . . . . . . . . . 140 B2
Southam GB . . . . . 44 A2
Southampton GB . . 44 C2
Southborough GB. . 45 B4
South Brent GB. . . . 42 B3
South Cave GB . . . 40 B3
Southend GB . . . . . 34 C2

Southend-on-Sea
  GB . . . . . . . . . . . 45 B4
South Hayling GB. . 44 C3
South Molton GB. . . 42 A3
South Ockendon
  GB . . . . . . . . . . . 45 B4
South Petherton GB 43 B4
Southport GB . . . . . 38 A3
South Shields GB . . 37 B5
South Tawton GB . . 42 B3
Southwell GB . . . . . 40 B3
Southwold GB . . . . 45 A5
South Woodham Ferrers
  GB . . . . . . . . . . . 45 B4
Souto P . . . . . . . . 148 B2
Soutochao E . . . . . 141 C3
Souto da Carpalhosa
  P. . . . . . . . . . . . 154 B2
Souvigny F . . . . . . 104 C2
Souzay-Champigny
  F. . . . . . . . . . . . 102 B1
Soverato I . . . . . . . 175 C2
Soveria Mannelli I . 175 B2
Sövestad S . . . . . . 66 A2
Sovetsk RUS . . . . . 12 A4
Sovići BIH . . . . . . . 138 B3
Sovicille I . . . . . . . 135 B4
Søvik N . . . . . . . . 198 C3
Sowerby GB . . . . . 37 B5
Soyaux F . . . . . . . 115 C4
Søyland N . . . . . . . 52 B1
Sozopol BG . . . . . . 17 D7
Spa B . . . . . . . . . . 80 B1
Spadafora I . . . . . . 177 A4
Spaichingen D. . . . 107 A3
Spakenburg NL. . . . 70 B2
Spalding GB . . . . . 41 C3
Spálené Poříčí CZ. . 96 B1
Spalt D . . . . . . . . . 94 B2
Spangenberg D. . . . 82 A1
Spangereid N . . . . . 52 B3
Spantekow D . . . . . 74 A2
Sparanise I . . . . . . 170 B2
Sparbu N . . . . . . . 199 B8
Sparkær DK. . . . . . 58 B2
Sparkford GB . . . . . 43 A4
Sparreholm S . . . . . 56 A2
Sparta = Sparti GR 184 B3
Spartà I . . . . . . . . 177 A4
Sparti = Sparta GR 184 B3
Spean Bridge GB . . 34 B3
Speicher D. . . . . . . 92 B2
Speichersdorf D . . . 95 B3
Speke GB. . . . . . . . 38 A4
Spello I . . . . . . . . 136 C1
Spenge D. . . . . . . . 72 B1
Spennymoor GB . . . 37 B5
Spentrup D . . . . . . 58 B3
Sperenberg D . . . . 74 B2
Sperlinga I . . . . . . 177 B3
Sperlonga I . . . . . . 169 B3
Spetalen N . . . . . . . 54 A1
Spetses GR . . . . . 184 B4
Speyer D . . . . . . . 93 B4
Spézet F . . . . . . . . 100 A2
Spezzano Albanese
  I . . . . . . . . . . . . 174 B2
Spezzano della Sila
  I . . . . . . . . . . . . 174 B2
Spiddle IRL . . . . . . 28 A2
Spiegelau D. . . . . . 96 C1
Spiekeroog D . . . . . 71 A4
Spiez CH . . . . . . . 106 C2
Spigno Monferrato
  I . . . . . . . . . . . . 133 A4
Spijk NL . . . . . . . . 71 A3
Spijkenisse NL . . . . 79 A4
Spilamberto I . . . . . 135 A4
Spili GR . . . . . . . . 185 D5
Spilimbergo I . . . . . 122 A1
Spilsby GB . . . . . . . 41 B4
Spinazzola I . . . . . 172 B2
Spincourt F . . . . . . 92 B1
Spind N. . . . . . . . . 52 B2
Spindleruv-Mlyn CZ 84 B3
Špinoso I . . . . . . . 174 A1
Špišić Bukovica
  HR . . . . . . . . . . .124 B3
Spišská Belá SK . . . 99 B4
Spišská Nová Ves
  SK . . . . . . . . . . . 99 C4
Spisska Stará Ves
  SK . . . . . . . . . . . 99 B4
Spišské-Hanušovce
  SK . . . . . . . . . . . 99 B4
Spišské Podhradie
  SK . . . . . . . . . . . 99 C4
Spišské Vlachy SK. 99 C4
Spišský-Štvrtok SK. 99 C4
Spital A. . . . . . . . .110 B1
Spital am Semmering
  A. . . . . . . . . . . . .110 B2
Spittal an der Drau
  A. . . . . . . . . . . . 109 C4
Spittle of Glenshee
  GB . . . . . . . . . . . 35 B4
Spitz A . . . . . . . . . 97 C3
Spjald DK. . . . . . . . 59 B1
Spjærøy N . . . . . . . 54 A1
Spjelkavik N . . . . . 198 C3
Spjutsbygd S. . . . . 63 B3
Split HR . . . . . . . . 138 B2
Splügen CH . . . . . 107 C4
Spodsbjerg DK . . . . 65 B3

Spofforth GB 40 B2
Spohle D 71 A5
Spoleto I 136 C1
Spoltore I 169 A4
Spondigna I 108 C1
Sponvika N 54 A2
Spornitz D 73 A4
Spotorno I 133 A4
Spraitbach D 94 C1
Sprakensehl D 72 B3
Spręcowo PL 69 B5
Spremberg D 84 A2
Spresiano I 122 B1
Sprimont B 80 B1
Springe D 72 B2
Sproatley GB 41 B3
Spydeberg N 54 A2
Spytkowice PL 99 B3
Squillace I 175 C2
Squinzano I 173 B4
Sračinec HR 124 A2
Srbac BIH 124 B3
Srbobran SRB 126 B1
Srebrenica BIH 127 C1
Srebrenik BIH 125 C4
Sredets BG 17 D7
Središče SLO 124 A2
Śrem PL 76 B2
Sremska Mitrovica SRB 127 C1
Sremski Karlovci SRB 126 B1
Srní CZ 96 B1
Srnice Gornje BIH 125 C4
Srock PL 86 A3
Środa Śląska PL 85 A4
Środa Wielkopolski PL 76 B2
Srpska Crnja SRB 126 B2
Srpski Itebej SRB 126 B2
Srpski Miletić SRB 125 B5
Staatz A 97 C4
Stabbursnes N 193 B8
Staberdorf D 65 B4
Stabroek B 79 A4
Stachy CZ 96 B1
Staðarfell IS 190 B3
Stade D 72 A2
Staden B 78 B3
Stadl an der Mur A 109 B4
Stadskanaal NL 71 B3
Stadtallendorf D 81 B5
Stadthagen D 72 B2
Stadtilm D 82 B3
Stadtkyll D 80 B2
Stadtlauringen D 82 B2
Stadtlengsfeld D 82 B2
Stadtlohn D 71 C3
Stadtoldendorf D 82 A1
Stadtroda D 83 B3
Stadtsteinach D 82 B3
Stäfa CH 107 B3
Staffanstorp S 61 D3
Staffelstein D 82 B2
Staffin GB 31 B2
Stafford GB 40 C1
Stainach A 110 B1
Staindrop GB 37 B5
Staines-upon-Thames GB 44 B3
Stainville F 91 C5
Stainz A 110 C2
Staithes GB 37 B6
Staiti I 175 D2
Stäket S 57 A3
Stakroge DK 59 C1
Štalcerji SLO 123 B3
Stalden CH 119 A4
Stalham GB 41 C5
Stalheim N 46 B3
Stallarholmen S 56 A3
Ställberg S 50 C1
Ställdalen S 50 C1
Stallhofen A 110 B2
Stalon S 195 F6
Stalowa Wola PL 12 C5
Stamford GB 40 C3
Stamford Bridge GB 40 B3
Stamnes N 46 B2
Stams A 108 B1
Stamsried D 95 B4
Stamsund N 194 B4
Stanford le Hope GB 45 B4
Stånga S 57 C4
Stange N 48 B3
Stanghella I 121 B4
Stanhope GB 37 B4
Stanišić SRB 125 B5
Staňkov CZ 95 B5
Stankovci HR 137 B4
Stanley GB 37 B5
Stans CH 106 C3
Stansted Mountfitchet GB 45 B4
Stanzach A 108 B1
Stapar SRB 125 B5
Staphorst NL 70 B3
Staplehurst GB 45 B4
Stąporków PL 87 A4
Stara Baška HR 123 C3
Starachowice PL 87 A5
Stara Fužina SLO 122 A2
Stara Kamienica PL 84 B3
Stara Kiszewa PL 68 B3
Stará L'ubovnă SK 99 B4
Stara Moravica SRB 126 B1
Stara Novalja HR 137 A3
Stara Pazova SRB 127 C2
Stará Turá SK 98 C1
Staraya Russa RUS 9 D7
Stara Zagora BG 17 D6
Stärbsnäs S 51 C6
Starčevo SRB 127 C2
Stare Dłutowo PL 77 A4
Staré Hamry CZ 98 B2
Stare Jabłonki PL 69 B5
Staré Město CZ 98 B1
Stare Pole PL 69 A4
Stare Sedlo CZ 96 B2
Stare Strącze PL 85 A4
Stargard Szczeciński PL 75 A4
Stårheim N 198 D2
Stari Banovci SRB 127 C2
Starigrad / *Ličko-Senjska* HR 123 C3 / *Splitsko-Dalmatinska* HR 138 B2
Stari Gradac HR 124 B3
Starigrad-Paklenica HR 137 A4
Stari Jankovci HR 125 B4
Stari Majdan BIH 124 C2
Stari-Mikanovci HR 125 B4
Staritsa RUS 9 D9
Starkenbach A 108 B1
Starnberg D 108 B2
Starogard PL 75 A4
Starogard Gdański PL 69 B3
Starokonstyantyniv UA 13 D7
Staro Petrovo Selo HR 124 B3
Staro Selo / HR 124 B1 / SRB 127 C3
Stary Brzozów PL 77 B5
Stary Dzierzgoń PL 69 B4
Starý Hrozenkov CZ 98 C1
Stary Jaroslaw PL 68 A1
Stary Plzenec CZ 96 B1
Stary Sącz PL 99 B4
Starý Smokovec SK 99 B4
Staryy Chartoriysk UA 13 C6
Staškov SK 98 B2
Stassfurt D 82 A3
Staszów PL 87 B5
Stathelle N 53 A5
Staufen D 106 B2
Staunton GB 39 C4
Stavang N 46 A2
Stavanger N 52 B1
Stavåsnäs S 49 B4
Stavby S 51 B5
Staveley GB 40 B2
Stavelot B 80 B1
Stavenisse NL 79 A4
Stavern N 53 B6
Stavnäs S 55 A3
Stavoren NL 70 B2
Stavros / CY 181 A1 / GR 183 C5
Stavroupoli GR 183 B6
Stavseng N 47 A6
Stavsiø N 48 B2
Stavsnäs S 57 A4
Stawiszyn PL 76 C3
Steane N 53 A4
Steblevë AL 182 B2
Stechelberg CH 106 C2
Štěchovice CZ 96 B2
Stechow D 73 B5
Steckborn CH 107 B3
Stede Broek NL 70 B2
Steeg A 107 B5
Steenbergen NL 79 A4
Steenvoorde F 78 B2
Steenwijk NL 70 B3
Štefanje HR 124 B2
Steffisburg CH 106 C2
Stegaurach D 94 B2
Stege DK 65 B5
Stegelitz D 74 A2
Stegersbach A 111 B3
Stegna PL 69 A4
Steimbke D 72 B2
Stein GB 31 B2
Steinach / A 108 B2 / *Baden-Württemberg* D 106 A3 / *Bayern* D 82 B2 / *Thüringen* D 82 B3
Stein an Rhein CH 107 B3
Steinau / *Bayern* D 81 B5 / *Niedersachsen* D 64 C1
Steinbeck D 74 B2
Steinberg am Rofan A 108 B2
Steindorf A 109 C5
Steine N 46 B2
Steinen D 106 B2
Steinfeld / A 109 C4
Steinfeld *continued* / D 71 B5
Steinfurt D 71 B4
Steingaden D 108 B1
Steinhagen D 72 B1
Steinheid D 82 B3
Steinheim / *Bayern* D 107 A5 / *Nordrhein-Westfalen* D 81 A5
Steinhöfel D 74 B3
Steinhorst D 72 B3
Steinigtwolmsdorf D 84 A2
Steinkjer N 199 A8
Steinsholt N 53 A5
Stekene B 79 A4
Stelle D 72 A3
Stellendam NL 79 A4
Stenåsa S 63 B4
Stenay F 91 B5
Stenberga S 62 A3
Stendal D 73 B4
Stenhammar S 55 B4
Stenhamra S 57 A3
Stenhousemuir GB 35 B4
Stenløse DK 61 D2
Stensätra S 50 B3
Stensele S 195 E8
Stenstorp S 55 B4
Stenstrup DK 65 A3
Stenudden S 195 D8
Stenungsund S 54 B2
Štěpánov CZ 98 B1
Stephanskirchen D 108 B3
Stepnica PL 74 A3
Stepojevac SRB 127 C2
Stepping DK 59 C2
Sterbfritz D 82 B1
Sternberg D 65 C4
Šternberk CZ 98 B1
Sterup D 64 B2
Stes Maries-de-la-Mer F 131 B3
Stęszew PL 75 B5
Štětí CZ 84 B2
Stevenage GB 44 B3
Stewarton GB 36 A2
Steyerburg D 72 B2
Steyning GB 44 C3
Steyr A 110 A1
Stężyca PL 68 A2
Stezzano I 120 B2
Stia I 135 B4
Stibb Cross GB 42 B2
Sticciano Scalo I 135 C4
Stidsvig S 61 C3
Stiens NL 70 A2
Stige DK 59 C3
Stigen S 54 B3
Stigliano I 174 A2
Stigtomta S 56 B2
Stilida GR 182 E4
Stilla N 192 C7
Stillington GB 40 A2
Stilo I 175 C2
Stintino I 178 B2
Stio I 172 B1
Štip MK 182 B4
Stira GR 185 A5
Stirling GB 35 B4
Štítnik SK 99 C4
Štíty CZ 97 B4
Stjärnhov S 56 A3
Stjärnsund S 50 B3
Stjørdalshalsen N 199 B7
Stobnica PL 87 A3
Stobno PL 75 A5
Stobreč HR 138 B2
Stochov CZ 84 B1
Stockach D 107 B4
Stöckalp CH 106 C3
Stockaryd S 62 A2
Stockbridge GB 44 B2
Stockerau A 97 C4
Stockheim D 82 B3
Stockholm S 57 A4
Stockport GB 40 B1
Stocksbridge GB 40 B2
Stockton-on-Tees GB 37 B5
Stod CZ 96 B1
Stöde S 200 D2
Stødi N 195 D6
Stöðvarfjörður IS 191 C12
Stoer GB 32 C1
Stoholm DK 58 B2
Stoke Ferry GB 41 C4
Stoke Fleming GB 43 B3
Stoke Mandeville GB 44 B3
Stoke-on-Trent GB 40 B1
Stokesley GB 37 B5
Stokke N 54 A1
Stokkemarke DK 65 B4
Stokken N 53 B4
Stokkseyri IS 190 D4
Stokkvågen N 195 D4
Stokmarknes N 194 B5
Štoky CZ 97 B3
Stolac BIH 139 B3
Stølaholmen N 46 A3
Stolberg D 80 B2
Stolin BY 13 C7
Stollberg D 83 B4
Stöllet S 49 B5
Stollhamm D 71 A5
Stolno PL 76 A3
Stolpen D 84 A2
Stolzenau D 72 B2
Stompetoren NL 70 B1
Ston HR 139 C3
Stonařov CZ 97 B3
Stone GB 40 C1
Stonehaven GB 33 E4
Stonehouse GB 36 A3
Stongfjorden N 46 A2
Stonndalen N 47 B4
Stony Stratford GB 44 A3
Stopnica PL 87 B4
Storå S 56 A1
Storås N 198 B6
Storby FIN 51 B6
Stordal / *Møre og Romsdal* N 198 C4 / *Nord-Trøndelag* N 199 B8
Store GB 33 B4
Storebø N 46 B2
Storebro S 62 A3
Store Damme DK 65 B5
Store Heddinge DK 65 A5
Store Herrestad S 66 A2
Store Levene S 55 B3
Storelv N 192 B6
Store Molvik N 193 B12
Støren N 199 B7
Store Skedvi S 50 B2
Store Vika S 57 B3
Storfjellseter N 199 D7
Storfjord N 192 C3
Storfjorden N 198 C3
Storfors S 55 A5
Storforshei N 195 D5
Storhøliseter N 47 A6
Storjord N 195 D6
Storkow / *Brandenburg* D 74 B2 / *Mecklenburg-Vorpommern* D 74 A3
Storli N 198 C6
Storlien S 199 B9
Stornara I 171 B3
Stornoway GB 31 A2
Storo I 121 B3
Storozhynets UA 17 A6
Storrington GB 44 C3
Storseleby S 200 B2
Storsjön S 50 A3
Storslett N 192 C5
Storsteinnes N 192 C3
Storsund S 196 D3
Storuman S 195 E8
Störvattnet S 199 C9
Storvik / N 195 D4 / S 50 B3
Storvreta S 51 C4
Štos SK 99 C4
Stössen D 83 A3
Stotel D 72 A1
Stötten D 108 B1
Stotternheim D 82 A3
Stouby DK 59 C2
Stourbridge GB 40 C1
Stourport-on-Severn GB 39 B4
Støvring DK 58 B2
Stow GB 35 C5
Stowbtsy BY 13 B7
Stowmarket GB 45 A5
Stow-on-the-Wold GB 44 B2
Straach D 73 C5
Strabane GB 27 B3
Strachan GB 33 D4
Strachur GB 34 B2
Stracin MK 182 A4
Strackholt D 71 A4
Stradbally IRL 29 B1
Stradella I 120 B2
Straelen D 80 A2
Stragari SRB 127 C2
Strakonice CZ 96 B1
Strålsnäs S 55 B6
Stralsund D 66 B2
Strand N 48 A3
Stranda N 198 C3
Strandby DK 58 A3
Strandebarm N 46 B3
Strandhill IRL 26 B2
Strandlykkja N 48 B3
Strandvik N 46 B2
Strangford GB 27 B5
Strängnäs S 56 A3
Strångsjö S 56 B2
Stráni CZ 98 C1
Stranice SLO 123 A4
Stranorlar IRL 26 B3
Stranraer GB 36 B1
Strasatti I 176 B1
Strasbourg F 93 C3
Strasburg D 74 A2
Strašice CZ 96 B1
Stråssa S 56 A1
Strassburg A 110 C1
Strass im Steiermark A 110 C2
Strasskirchen D 95 C4
Strasswalchen A 109 B4
Stratford-upon-Avon GB 44 A2
Strathaven GB 36 A2
Strathdon GB 32 D3
Strathkanaird GB 32 D1
Strathpeffer GB 32 D2
Strathy GB 32 C3
Strathyre GB 34 B3
Stratinska BIH 124 C2
Stratton GB 42 B2
Straubing D 95 C4
Straulas I 178 B3
Straume N 53 A5
Straumen / *Nordland* N 194 C6 / *Nord-Trøndelag* N 199 B8
Straumsjøen N 194 B5
Straumsnes N 194 C6
Straupitz D 74 C3
Strausberg D 74 B2
Straussfurt D 82 A3
Strawczyn PL 87 B4
Straža / SLO 123 B4 / SRB 127 C3
Stražnad Nezárkou CZ 96 B2
Strážnice CZ 98 C1
Strážný CZ 96 C1
Stráž Pod Ralskem CZ 84 B2
Štrbské Pleso SK 99 B4
Strečno SK 98 B2
Street GB 43 A4
Strehla D 83 A5
Strekov SK 112 B2
Strem A 111 B3
Stremska-Rača SRB 127 C1
Strengberg A 110 A1
Strengelvåg N 194 B6
Stresa I 119 B5
Streufdorf D 82 B2
Strib DK 59 C2
Striberg S 55 A5
Stříbro CZ 95 B4
Strichen GB 33 D4
Strigno I 121 A4
Štrigova HR 111 C3
Strijen NL 79 A4
Strizivojna HR 125 B4
Strmica HR 138 A2
Strmilov CZ 97 B3
Ströhen D 72 B1
Strokestown IRL 28 A3
Stromberg / *Nordrhein-Westfalen* D 81 A4 / *Rheinland-Pfalz* D 93 B3
Stromeferry GB 31 B3
Strömnäs S 200 B2
Stromness GB 33 C3
Strömsberg S 51 B4
Strömsbruk S 200 E3
Strömsfors S 56 B2
Strömsnäsbruk S 61 C3
Strömstad S 54 B2
Strömsund / *Jämtland* S 199 B12 / *Västerbotten* S 195 E7
Stronachlachar GB 34 B3
Stróngoli I 174 B3
Stronie Ślaskie PL 85 B4
Strontian GB 34 B2
Stroppiana I 119 B5
Stroud GB 43 A4
Stroumbi CY 181 B1
Stróża PL 99 B3
Strücklingen D 71 A4
Struer DK 58 B1
Struga MK 182 B2
Strugi Krasnyye RUS 9 C6
Strumica MK 182 B4
Strumien PL 98 B2
Struy GB 32 D2
Stružec HR 124 B2
Stryków PL 77 C4
Stryn N 198 D3
Stryy UA 13 D5
Strzałkowo PL 76 B2
Strzegocin PL 77 B5
Strzegom PL 85 B4
Strzegowo PL 77 B5
Strzelce PL 77 B4
Strzelce Krajeńskie PL 75 B4
Strzelce Kurowo PL 75 B4
Strzelce Opolskie PL 86 B2
Strzelin PL 85 B5
Strzelno PL 76 B3
Strzepcz PL 68 A3
Strzybnica PL 86 B2
Strzygi PL 77 A4
Stubbekøbing DK 65 B5
Stuben A 107 B5
Stubenberg A 110 B2
Stubline SRB 127 C2
Studená CZ 97 B3
Studenci HR 138 B3
Studenka CZ 98 B2
Studenzen A 110 B2
Studienka SK 98 C1
Studland GB 43 B5
Studley GB 44 A2
Studzienice PL 68 A2
Stuer D 73 A5
Stugudal N 199 C8
Stugun S 200 C1
Stuhr D 72 A1
Stukenbrock D 81 A4
Stülpe D 74 B2
Stupava SK 111 A4
Stupnik HR 124 B1
Stupsk PL 77 A5
Sturkö S 63 B3
Sturminster Newton GB 43 B4
Štúrovo SK 112 B2
Sturton GB 40 B3
Stuttgart D 94 C1
Stvolny CZ 96 A1
Stykkishólmur IS 190 B3
Styri N 48 B3
Stysö S 60 B1
Suances E 142 A2
Subbiano I 135 B4
Subiaco I 169 B3
Subotica SRB 126 A1
Subotište SRB 127 C1
Sučany SK 98 B2
Suceava RO 17 B7
Sucha-Beskidzka PL 99 B3
Suchacz PL 69 A4
Suchań PL 75 A4
Suchdol nad Lužnice CZ 96 C2
Suchedniów PL 87 A4
Suchorze PL 68 A2
Suchteln D 80 A2
Sucina E 165 B4
Suckow D 73 A4
Sućuraj HR 138 B3
Súðavík IS 190 A3
Sudbury GB 45 A4
Suddesjaur S 195 E10
Suden D 64 B1
Süderbrarup D 64 B2
Süderlügum D 64 B1
Sudoměřice u Bechyně CZ 96 B2
Sudovec HR 124 A2
Suðureyri IS 190 A2
Sueca E 159 B3
Suelli I 179 C3
Sugenheim D 94 B2
Sugères F 117 B3
Sugny B 91 B4
Suhl D 82 B2
Suhlendorf D 73 B3
Suhopolje HR 124 B3
Suho Polje BIH 125 C5
Şuhut TR 189 A5
Šuica BIH 138 B3
Suippes F 91 B4
Sukošan HR 137 A4
Sükösd H 125 A4
Suków PL 87 B4
Šul'a SK 99 C3
Suldalsosen N 52 A2
Suldrup DK 58 B2
Sulechów PL 75 B4
Sulęcin PL 75 B4
Sulęczyno PL 68 A2
Sulejów PL 87 A3
Süleymanlı TR 186 D2
Sulgen CH 107 B4
Sulibórz PL 75 A4
Sulina RO 17 C8
Sulingen D 72 B1
Suliszewo PL 75 A4
Sulitjelma N 195 C7
Sułkowice PL 99 B3
Süller TR 189 A4
Sully-sur-Loire F 103 B4
Sulmierzyce / *Łódzkie* PL 86 A3 / *Wielkopolskie* PL 85 A5
Sulmona I 169 A3
Süloğlu TR 186 A1
Sułoszowa PL 87 B3
Sulów PL 85 A5
Sulsdorf D 65 B4
Sultandağı TR 189 A6
Sülüklü TR 187 D7
Suluova TR 23 A8
Sulvik S 54 A3
Sülysáp H 112 B3
Sülz D 93 C4
Sulzbach / *Baden-Württemberg* D 94 B1 / *Baden-Württemberg* D 94 C1 / *Bayern* D 93 B5 / *Saarland* D 92 B3
Sulzbach-Rosenberg D 95 B3
Sülze D 72 B3
Sulzfeld D 82 B2
Sumartin HR 138 B2
Sumburgh GB 33 B5
Sümeg H 111 C4
Sumiswald CH 106 B2
Šumná CZ 97 C3
Šumperk CZ 97 B4
Šumvald CZ 98 B1
Sunbilla E 144 A2
Sünching D 95 C4
Sund / FIN 51 B7 / S 54 A2
Sundborn S 50 B2
Sundby DK 58 B1
Sunde N 46 C2
Sunde bru N 53 B5
Sunderland GB 37 B5
Sundern D 81 A4
Sundhultsbrunn S 62 A2
Sundnäs S 195 D8

Sundom S . . . . . . . 196 D5
Sunds DK . . . . . . . . 59 B2
Sundsfjord N . . . . . 195 D5
Sundsvall S . . . . . . 200 D3
Sungurlu TR . . . . . . 23 A8
Suni I . . . . . . . . . . 178 B2
Sunja HR . . . . . . . 124 B2
Sunnansjö S . . . . . . 50 B1
Sunnaryd S . . . . . . 60 B3
Sunndalsøra N . . . 198 C5
Sunne S . . . . . . . . . 49 C5
Sunnemo S . . . . . . 49 C5
Sunnersberg S . . . . 55 B4
Suolovuopmio N . . 192 C7
Suomussalmi FIN . 3 D11
Suoyarvi RUS . . . . . . 9 A8
Super Sauze F . . . . 132 A2
Supetar HR . . . . . . 138 B2
Supetarska Draga
  HR . . . . . . . . . . 123 C3
Supino I . . . . . . . . 169 B3
Šuplja Stijena MNE 139 B5
Surahammar S . . . . 56 A2
Šurany SK . . . . . . . 112 A2
Surazh BY . . . . . . . 13 A9
Surbo I . . . . . . . . . 173 B4
Surčin SRB . . . . . . 127 C2
Surgères F . . . . . . . 114 B3
Surhuisterveen NL . 70 A3
Sùria E . . . . . . . . . 147 C2
Surin F . . . . . . . . . 115 B4
Surka N . . . . . . . . . 48 B2
Surnadalsøra N . . . 198 C5
Sursee CH . . . . . . 106 B3
Surte S . . . . . . . . . 60 B2
Surwold D . . . . . . . 71 B4
Sury-le-Comtal F . . 117 B4
Susa I . . . . . . . . . . 119 B4
Šušara SRB . . . . . . 127 C3
Susch CH . . . . . . . 107 C5
Susegana I . . . . . . 122 B1
Süsel D . . . . . . . . . 65 B3
Sušice CZ . . . . . . . 96 B1
Šušnjevica HR . . . . 123 B3
Sussen D . . . . . . . . 94 C1
Susurluk TR . . . . . 186 C3
Susz PL . . . . . . . . . 69 B4
Sütçüler TR . . . . . . 189 B5
Sutivan HR . . . . . . 138 B2
Sutjeska SRB . . . . 126 B2
Sutri I . . . . . . . . . . 168 A2
Sutton GB . . . . . . . 44 B3
Sutton Coldfield GB 40 C2
Sutton-in-Ashfield
  GB . . . . . . . . . . . 40 B2
Sutton-on-Sea GB . 41 B4
Sutton-on-Trent GB 40 B3
Sutton Scotney GB . 44 B2
Sutton Valence GB . 45 B4
Suvaja BIH . . . . . . 124 C2
Suvereto I . . . . . . . 135 B3
Suwałki PL . . . . . . . 12 A5
Suze-la-Rousse F . . 131 A3
Suzzara I . . . . . . . . 121 C3
Svabensverk S . . . . 50 A2
Svalbarð IS . . . . . 191 A10
Svalöv S . . . . . . . . 61 D3
Svanabyn S . . . . . . 200 B2
Svanberga S . . . . . . 51 C5
Svaneke DK . . . . . . 67 A4
Svanesund S . . . . . 54 B2
Svängsta S . . . . . . 63 B2
Svannäs S . . . . . . 195 D9
Svanskog S . . . . . . 54 A3
Svanstein S . . . . . 196 C6
Svappavaara S . . . 196 B4
Svärdsjö S . . . . . . . 50 B2
Svarstad N . . . . . . . 53 A5
Svartå S . . . . . . . . . 55 A5
Svärta S . . . . . . . . . 56 B3
Svartå S . . . . . . . . . 55 A4
Svartbyn S . . . . . . 196 C5
Svärtinge S . . . . . . 56 B2
Svartlå S . . . . . . . 196 D4
Svartnäs S . . . . . . . 50 B3
Svartnes N . . . . . . 195 C5
Svarttjärn S . . . . . 195 E7
Svatsum N . . . . . . . 48 A1
Svätý Jur SK . . . . . 111 A4
Svätý Peter SK . . . 112 B2
Svedala S . . . . . . . 61 D3
Sveg S . . . . . . . . 199 C11
Sveindal N . . . . . . . 52 B2
Sveio N . . . . . . . . . 52 A1
Svejbæk DK . . . . . . 59 B2
Svelgen N . . . . . . 198 D2
Svelvik N . . . . . . . . 54 A1
Svendborg DK . . . . 65 A3
Svene N . . . . . . . . . 53 A5
Svenljunga S . . . . . 60 B3
Svennevad S . . . . . 56 A1
Svenstavik S . . . . 199 C11
Svenstrup DK . . . . . 58 B2
Švermov CZ . . . . . . 84 B2
Sveti Ivan Zabno
  HR . . . . . . . . . . 124 B2
Sveti Ivan Zelina
  HR . . . . . . . . . . 124 B2
Sveti Nikole MK . . 182 B3
Sveti Rok HR . . . . 137 A4
Světlá nad Sázavou
  CZ . . . . . . . . . . . 97 B3
Svetlyy RUS . . . . . 69 A5
Svetvinčenat HR . . 122 B2
Švica HR . . . . . . . 123 C4
Svidník SK . . . . . . . 12 D4
Svihov CZ . . . . . . . 96 B1
Svilajnac SRB . . . . 127 C3

Svilengrad BG . . . . 183 B8
Svindal N . . . . . . . . 54 A2
Svinhult S . . . . . . . 62 A3
Svinna SK . . . . . . . 98 C2
Svinninge
  DK . . . . . . . . . . . 61 D1
  S . . . . . . . . . . . . 57 A4
Svíritsa RUS . . . . . . 9 B8
Svishtov BG . . . . . 17 D6
Svislach BY . . . . . . 13 B6
Svit SK . . . . . . . . . 99 B4
Svitavy CZ . . . . . . . 97 B4
Svodin SK . . . . . . 112 B2
Svolvær N . . . . . . 194 B5
Svortemyr N . . . . . . 46 A2
Svortland N . . . . . . 52 A1
Svratka CZ . . . . . . . 97 B4
Svrčinovec SK . . . . 98 B2
Svullrya N . . . . . . . 49 B4
Svyetlahorsk BY . . . 13 B8
Swadlincote GB . . . 40 C2
Swaffham GB . . . . . 41 C4
Swanage GB . . . . . 43 B5
Swanley GB . . . . . . 45 B4
Swanlinbar IRL . . . 26 B3
Swansea GB . . . . . 39 C3
Swarzędz PL . . . . . 76 B2
Swatragh GB . . . . . 27 B4
Świątki PL . . . . . . . 69 B5
Świdnica
  Dolnośląskie PL . . 85 B4
  Lubuskie PL . . . . 84 A3
Świdnik PL . . . . . . . 12 C5
Świdwin PL . . . . . . 67 C4
Świebodzice PL . . . 85 B4
Świebodzin PL . . . . 75 B4
Świecie PL . . . . . . . 76 A3
Świedziebnia PL . . 77 A4
Świeradów Zdrój
  PL . . . . . . . . . . . 84 B3
Świerki PL . . . . . . . 85 B4
Świerzawa PL . . . . 85 A3
Świerzno PL . . . . . . 67 C3
Święta PL . . . . . . . 74 A3
Święta Anna PL . . . 86 B3
Świętno PL . . . . . . 75 B5
Swifterbant NL . . . 70 B2
Swindon GB . . . . . . 44 B2
Swineshead GB . . . 41 C3
Swinford IRL . . . . . 26 C2
Świnoujście PL . . . 66 C3
Swinton GB . . . . . . 35 C5
Swobnica PL . . . . . 74 A3
Swords IRL . . . . . . 30 A2
Swornegacie PL . . . 68 B2
Sya S . . . . . . . . . . 56 B1
Syasstroy RUS . . . . 9 B8
Sycewice PL . . . . . 68 A1
Sychevka RUS . . . . 9 E9
Syców PL . . . . . . . . 86 A1
Sycowice PL . . . . . 75 B4
Sydnes N . . . . . . . 52 A1
Syfteland N . . . . . . 46 B2
Syke D . . . . . . . . . 72 B1
Sykkylven N . . . . . 198 C3
Sylling N . . . . . . . . 48 C2
Sylte N . . . . . . . . 198 C4
Symbister GB . . . . . 33 A5
Symington GB . . . . 36 A3
Symonds Yat GB . . 39 C4
Sypniewo
  Kujawsko-Pomorskie
    PL . . . . . . . . . . 76 A2
  Wielkopolskie PL . 68 B1
Syserum S . . . . . . . 62 A4
Sysslebäck S . . . . . 49 B4
Syväjärvi FIN . . . . 197 B8
Szabadbattyán H . 112 B2
Szabadegyháza H . 112 B2
Szabadszállás H . . 112 C3
Szadek PL . . . . . . . 86 A2
Szajol H . . . . . . . . 113 B4
Szakály H . . . . . . . 112 C2
Szakcs H . . . . . . . 112 C2
Szakmár H . . . . . . 112 C3
Szalánta H . . . . . . 125 B4
Szałas PL . . . . . . . . 87 A4
Szalkszentmárton
  H . . . . . . . . . . . 112 C3
Szalonna H . . . . . . 99 C4
Szamocin PL . . . . . 76 A2
Szamotuły PL . . . . . 75 B5
Szany H . . . . . . . . 111 B4
Szarvas H . . . . . . . 113 C4
Szarvaskö H . . . . . 113 B4
Szászvár H . . . . . . 125 A4
Százhalombatta H . 112 B2
Szczawa PL . . . . . . 99 B4
Szczawnica PL . . . . 99 B4
Szczecin PL . . . . . . 74 A3
Szczecinek PL . . . . 68 B1
Szczekociny PL . . . 87 B3
Szczerców PL . . . . 86 A3
Szczucin PL . . . . . . 87 B5
Szczuczarz PL . . . . 75 A5
Szczuki PL . . . . . . . 77 B5
Szczurowa PL . . . . 87 B4
Szczyrk PL . . . . . . . 99 B3
Szczytna PL . . . . . . 85 B4
Szczytno PL . . . . . . 77 A5
Szczyty PL . . . . . . . 86 A2
Szécsény H . . . . . . 112 A3
Szederkény H . . . . 125 B4
Szedres H . . . . . . . 112 C2
Szeged H . . . . . . . 126 A2
Szeghalom H . . . . . 113 B5
Szegvár H . . . . . . . 113 C4
Székesfehérvár H . 112 B2

Székkutas H . . . . . 113 C4
Szekszárd H . . . . . 125 A4
Szemplino Czarne
  PL . . . . . . . . . . . 77 A5
Szemud PL . . . . . . 68 A3
Szendehely H . . . . 112 B3
Szendrö H . . . . . . . 99 C4
Szentes H . . . . . . . 113 C4
Szentendre H . . . . 112 B3
Szentgotthárd H . . 111 C3
Szentlászló H . . . . 125 A3
Szentlörinc H . . . . 125 A3
Szentmártonkáta
  H . . . . . . . . . . . 113 B3
Szenyér H . . . . . . . 111 C4
Szeremle H . . . . . . 125 A4
Szerencs H . . . . . . 113 A5
Szerép H . . . . . . . 113 B5
Szigetszentmiklós
  H . . . . . . . . . . . 112 B3
Szigetvár H . . . . . . 125 A3
Szikáncs H . . . . . . 126 A2
Szikszó H . . . . . . . 113 A4
Szil H . . . . . . . . . . 111 B4
Szilvásvárad H . . . 113 A4
Szklarska Poreba
  PL . . . . . . . . . . . 84 B3
Szlichtyngowa PL . . 85 A4
Szob H . . . . . . . . . 112 B2
Szolnok H . . . . . . . 113 B4
Szombathely H . . . 111 B3
Szorosad H . . . . . . 112 C2
Szpetal Graniczny
  PL . . . . . . . . . . . 77 B4
Szprotawa PL . . . . 84 A3
Szreńsk PL . . . . . . 77 A5
Sztum PL . . . . . . . . 69 B4
Sztutowo PL . . . . . 69 A4
Szubin PL . . . . . . . 76 A2
Szücsi H . . . . . . . . 113 B3
Szulmierz PL . . . . . 77 B5
Szulok H . . . . . . . . 124 A3
Szumanie PL . . . . . 77 B4
Szwecja PL . . . . . . 75 A5
Szydłów
  Łódzkie PL . . . . . 86 A3
  Świętokrzyskie PL . 87 B5
Szydłowiec PL . . . . 87 A4
Szydlowo PL . . . . . 77 A5
Szydłowo PL . . . . . 75 A5
Szymanów PL . . . . 77 B5
Szynkielów PL . . . . 86 A2

**T**

Taastrup DK . . . . . 61 D2
Tab H . . . . . . . . . . 112 C2
Tabanera la Luenga
  E . . . . . . . . . . . 151 A3
Tabaqueros E . . . . 158 B2
Tábara E . . . . . . . 149 A4
Tabenera de Cerrato
  E . . . . . . . . . . . 142 B2
Taberg S . . . . . . . . 62 A2
Tabernas E . . . . . . 164 B2
Tabiano Bagni I . . . 120 C3
Taboada E . . . . . . 140 B3
Taboadela E . . . . . 140 B3
Tábor CZ . . . . . . . . 96 B2
Táborfalva H . . . . . 112 B3
Taborište HR . . . . . 124 B2
Tábua P . . . . . . . . 148 B1
Tabuaco P . . . . . . 148 A2
Tabuenca E . . . . . . 152 A2
Tabuyo del Monte
  E . . . . . . . . . . . 141 B4
Täby S . . . . . . . . . 57 A4
Tác H . . . . . . . . . . 112 B2
Tachov CZ . . . . . . . 95 B4
Tadcaster GB . . . . . 40 B2
Tadley GB . . . . . . . 44 B2
Tafalla E . . . . . . . . 144 B2
Tafjord N . . . . . . . 198 C4
Taganheira P . . . . 160 B1
Tågarp S . . . . . . . . 61 D2
Tággia I . . . . . . . . 133 B3
Tagliacozzo I . . . . . 169 A3
Táglio di Po I . . . . . 121 B5
Tagnon F . . . . . . . . 91 B4
Tahal E . . . . . . . . . 164 B2
Tahitótfalu H . . . . . 112 B3
Tahtaköprü TR . . . 187 C4
Tailfingen D . . . . . 107 A4
Taillis F . . . . . . . . 101 A4
Tain GB . . . . . . . . 32 D2
Tain-l'Hermitage F . 117 B4
Taipadas P . . . . . . 154 C2
Taivalkoski FIN . . 197 D11
Takene S . . . . . . . 55 A4
Takovo SRB . . . . . 127 C2
Taksony H . . . . . . 112 B3
Tal E . . . . . . . . . . 140 B2
Talachyn BY . . . . . 13 A8
Talamello I . . . . . . 135 B5
Talamone I . . . . . . 168 A1
Talant F . . . . . . . . 105 B4
Talarrubias E . . . . 156 A2
Talaván E . . . . . . . 155 B4
Talavera de la Reina
  E . . . . . . . . . . . 150 C3
Talavera la Real E . 155 C4
Talayuela E . . . . . 150 C2
Talayuelas E . . . . . 159 B2
Talgarth GB . . . . . . 39 C3
Talgje N . . . . . . . . 52 A1
Talhadas P . . . . . . 148 B1
Táliga E . . . . . . . . 155 C3

Talizat F . . . . . . . . 116 B3
Tálknafjörður IS . . 190 B2
Talla I . . . . . . . . . 135 B4
Talladale GB . . . . . 31 B3
Tallaght IRL . . . . . . 30 A2
Tallard F . . . . . . . . 132 A2
Tällberg S . . . . . . . 50 B1
Tallberg S . . . . . . . 196 C5
Tallinn EST . . . . . . . 8 C4
Talloires F . . . . . . . 118 B3
Tallow IRL . . . . . . . 29 B3
Tallsjö S . . . . . . . . 200 B4
Tallvik S . . . . . . . . 196 C5
Talmay F . . . . . . . 105 B4
Talmont-St Hilaire
  F . . . . . . . . . . . 114 B2
Talmont-sur-Gironde
  F . . . . . . . . . . . 114 C3
Talne UA . . . . . . . . 13 D9
Talsano I . . . . . . . 173 B3
Talsi LV . . . . . . . . . 8 D3
Talvik N . . . . . . . . 192 B6
Talybont GB . . . . . . 39 B3
Tal-Y-Llyn GB . . . . 38 B3
Tamajón E . . . . . . 151 B4
Tamame E . . . . . . 149 A4
Tamames E . . . . . . 149 B3
Tamarit de Mar E . . 147 C2
Tamarite de Litera
  E . . . . . . . . . . . 145 C4
Tamariu E . . . . . . . 147 C4
Tamási H . . . . . . . 112 C2
Tambach-Dietharz
  D . . . . . . . . . . . . 82 B2
Tameza E . . . . . . . 141 A4
Tammisaari FIN . . . . 8 B3
Tampere FIN . . . . . . 8 B3
Tamsweg A . . . . . . 109 B4
Tamurejo E . . . . . . 156 B3
Tamworth GB . . . . . 40 C2
Tana bru N . . . . . 193 B12
Tañabueyes E . . . . 143 B3
Tanakajd H . . . . . . 111 B3
Tananger N . . . . . . 52 B1
Tanaunella I . . . . . 178 B3
Tancarville F . . . . . 89 A4
Tandsjöborg S . . . 199 D11
Tånga S . . . . . . . . 61 C2
Tangelic H . . . . . . 112 C2
Tangen N . . . . . . . 48 B3
Tangerhütte D . . . . 73 B4
Tangermünde D . . . 73 B4
Tanhua FIN . . . . . 197 B10
Taninges F . . . . . . 118 A3
Tankavaara FIN . . 197 A10
Tann D . . . . . . . . . 82 B2
Tanna D . . . . . . . . 83 B3
Tannadice GB . . . . 35 B5
Tannåker S . . . . . . 60 C3
Tännäs S . . . . . . . 199 C9
Tannay
  Ardennes F . . . . . 91 B4
  Nièvre F . . . . . . . 104 B2
Tannenbergsthal D . 83 B4
Tännesberg D . . . . 95 B4
Tannheim A . . . . . . 108 B1
Tannila FIN . . . . . 197 D8
Tanowo PL . . . . . . 74 A3
Tanum S . . . . . . . . 54 B2
Tanumshede S . . . . 54 B2
Tanus F . . . . . . . . 130 A1
Tanvald CZ . . . . . . 84 B3
Taormina I . . . . . . 177 B4
Tapa EST . . . . . . . . 8 C4
Tapfheim D . . . . . . 94 C2
Tapia de Casariego
  E . . . . . . . . . . . 141 A4
Tapio F . . . . . . . . 146 A2
Tápióbicske H . . . . 112 B3
Tápiógyörgye H . . . 113 B3
Tápióság H . . . . . . 112 B3
Tápiószecsö H . . . . 112 B3
Tápiószele H . . . . . 113 B3
Tápiószentmárton
  H . . . . . . . . . . . 113 B3
Tapolca H . . . . . . . 111 C4
Tapolcafő H . . . . . . 111 B4
Tar HR . . . . . . . . . 122 B2
Tarabo S . . . . . . . . 60 B2
Taradell E . . . . . . . 147 C3
Taraklı TR . . . . . . . 187 B5
Taramundi E . . . . . 141 A3
Tarancón E . . . . . . 151 B4
Táranto I . . . . . . . 173 B3
Tarare F . . . . . . . . 117 B4
Tarascon F . . . . . . 131 B3
Tarascon-sur-Ariège
  F . . . . . . . . . . . 146 B2
Tarashcha UA . . . . 13 D9
Tarazona E . . . . . . 144 C2
Tarazona de la Mancha
  E . . . . . . . . . . . 158 B2
Tarbena E . . . . . . . 159 C3
Tarbert
  GB . . . . . . . . . . . 34 C2
  IRL . . . . . . . . . . 29 B2
Tarbes F . . . . . . . . 145 A4
Tarbet GB . . . . . . . 34 B3
Tarbolton GB . . . . . 36 A2
Tarcento I . . . . . . . 122 A2
Tarčin BIH . . . . . . 139 B4
Tarczyn PL . . . . . . . 77 C5
Tardajos E . . . . . . 143 B3
Tardelcuende E . . . 151 A5
Tardets-Sorholus
  F . . . . . . . . . . . 144 A3
Tardienta E . . . . . . 145 C3
Táliga E . . . . . . . . 155 C3

Targon F . . . . . . . . 128 B2
Târgoviște RO . . . . 17 C6
Târgu-Jiu RO . . . . . 17 C5
Târgu Mureş RO . . 17 B6
Târgu Ocna RO . . . 17 B7
Târgu Secuiesc RO. 17 C7
Tarifa E . . . . . . . . 162 B2
Tariquejas E . . . . . 161 B2
Tárkany H . . . . . . . 112 B2
Tarland GB . . . . . . 33 D4
Tarłów PL . . . . . . . 87 A5
Tarm DK . . . . . . . . 59 C1
Tarmstedt D . . . . . 72 A2
Tärnaby S . . . . . . 195 E6
Tarnalelesz H . . . . 113 A4
Tarnaörs H . . . . . . 113 B4
Tárnet N . . . . . . . 193 C14
Tarnobrzeg PL . . . . 87 B5
Tarnos F . . . . . . . . 128 C1
Tarnów
  Lubuskie PL . . . . 75 B3
  Małopolskie PL . . 87 B4
Tarnowo Podgórne
  PL . . . . . . . . . . . 75 B5
Tarnowskie Góry
  PL . . . . . . . . . . . 86 B2
Tarouca P . . . . . . . 148 A2
Tarp D . . . . . . . . . . 64 B2
Tarquínia I . . . . . . 168 A1
Tarquínia Lido I . . . 168 A1
Tarragona E . . . . . 147 C2
Tàrrajaur S . . . . . . 196 C2
Tàrrega E . . . . . . . 147 C2
Tarrenz A . . . . . . . 108 B1
Tårs
  Nordjyllands DK . . 58 A3
  Storstrøms DK . . . 65 B4
Tarsia I . . . . . . . . . 174 B2
Tarsus TR . . . . . . . 23 C8
Tartas F . . . . . . . . 128 C2
Tartu EST . . . . . . . . 8 C5
Tarves GB . . . . . . . 33 D4
Tarvísio I . . . . . . . 109 C4
Taşağıl TR . . . . . . 189 C6
Tasch CH . . . . . . . 119 A4
Taşköprü TR . . . . . 23 A8
Tasov CZ . . . . . . . . 97 B4
Tasovčiči BIH . . . . 139 B3
Taşucuo TR . . . . . . 23 C7
Tát H . . . . . . . . . . 112 B2
Tata H . . . . . . . . . 112 B2
Tatabánya H . . . . . 112 B2
Tataháza H . . . . . . 126 A1
Tatarbunary UA . . . 17 C8
Tatárszentgyörgy
  H . . . . . . . . . . . 112 B3
Tatranská-Lomnica
  SK . . . . . . . . . . . 99 B4
Tau N . . . . . . . . . . 52 A1
Taucha D . . . . . . . . 83 A4
Taufkirchen D . . . . 95 C4
Taufkirchen an der Pram
  A . . . . . . . . . . . . 96 C1
Taulé F . . . . . . . . 100 A2
Taulignan F . . . . . 131 A3
Taulov DK . . . . . . . 59 C2
Taunton GB . . . . . . 43 A3
Taunusstein D . . . . 81 B4
Tauragė LT . . . . . . 12 A5
Taurianova I . . . . . 175 C2
Taurisano I . . . . . . 173 C4
Tauste E . . . . . . . . 144 C2
Tauves F . . . . . . . . 116 B2
Tavankut SRB . . . . 126 A1
Tavannes CH . . . . 106 B2
Tavarnelle val di Pesa
  I . . . . . . . . . . . . 135 B4
Tavas TR . . . . . . . 188 B4
Tavaux F . . . . . . . 105 B4
Tävelsås S . . . . . . 62 B2
Taverna I . . . . . . . 175 B2
Taverne CH . . . . . 120 A1
Tavernelle I . . . . . . 135 B5
Tavernes de la Valldigna
  E . . . . . . . . . . . 159 B3
Tavérnola Bergamasca
  I . . . . . . . . . . . . 120 B3
Taverny F . . . . . . . 90 B2
Tavescan E . . . . . . 146 B2
Tavira P . . . . . . . . 160 B2
Tavistock GB . . . . . 42 B2
Tavşanlı TR . . . . . . 187 C4
Tayinloan GB . . . . . 34 C2
Taynuilt GB . . . . . . 34 B2
Tayport GB . . . . . . 35 B5
Tázlár H . . . . . . . . 112 C3
Tazones E . . . . . . . 142 A1
Tczew PL . . . . . . . 69 A3
Tczów PL . . . . . . . 87 A5
Teangue GB . . . . . . 31 B3
Teano I . . . . . . . . . 170 B2
Teba E . . . . . . . . . 162 B3
Tebay GB . . . . . . . 37 B4
Techendorf A . . . . 109 C4
Tecklenburg D . . . . 71 B4
Tecko-matorp S . . . 61 D3
Tecuci RO . . . . . . . 17 C7
Tefenni TR . . . . . . 189 B4
Tegelsmora S . . . . 51 B4
Tegernsee D . . . . . 108 B2
Teggiano I . . . . . . 172 B1

**Sun–Tes 277**

Tegoleto I . . . . . . . 135 B4
Teichel D . . . . . . . . 82 B3
Teignmouth GB . . . 43 B3
Teillay F . . . . . . . . 101 B4
Teillet F . . . . . . . . 130 B1
Teisendorf D . . . . . 109 B3
Teistungen D . . . . . 82 A2
Teixeiro E . . . . . . . 140 A2
Tejada de Tiétar E . 150 B2
Tejado E . . . . . . . . 152 A1
Tejares E . . . . . . . 150 B2
Tejn DK . . . . . . . . . 67 A3
Teke TR . . . . . . . . 187 A4
Tekirdağ TR . . . . . 186 B2
Tekovské-Luzany
  SK . . . . . . . . . . 112 A2
Telavåg N . . . . . . . 46 B1
Telč CZ . . . . . . . . . 97 B3
Telese Terme I . . . . 170 B2
Telford GB . . . . . . . 38 B4
Telfs A . . . . . . . . . 108 B2
Telgárt SK . . . . . . . 99 C4
Telgte D . . . . . . . . 71 C4
Tellingstedt D . . . . 64 B2
Telšiai LT . . . . . . . . 8 E3
Telti I . . . . . . . . . . 178 B3
Teltow D . . . . . . . . 74 B2
Tembleque E . . . . . 157 A4
Temelin CZ . . . . . . 96 B2
Temerin SRB . . . . 126 B1
Temiño E . . . . . . . 143 B3
Témpio Pausánia I . 178 B3
Templederry IRL . . 28 B3
Templemore IRL . . 28 B4
Temple Sowerby
  GB . . . . . . . . . . . 37 B4
Templin D . . . . . . . 74 A2
Temse B . . . . . . . . 79 A4
Tenay F . . . . . . . . 118 B2
Ten Boer NL . . . . . 71 A3
Tenbury Wells GB . 39 B4
Tenby GB . . . . . . . 39 C2
Tence F . . . . . . . . 117 B4
Tende F . . . . . . . . 133 A3
Tenhult S . . . . . . . 62 A2
Tenja HR . . . . . . . 125 B4
Tenneville B . . . . . . 92 A1
Tennevoll N . . . . . 194 B8
Tensta S . . . . . . . . 51 B4
Tenterden GB . . . . 45 B4
Teo E . . . . . . . . . . 140 B2
Teora I . . . . . . . . . 172 B1
Tepasto FIN . . . . . 196 B7
Tepelenë AL . . . . . 182 C2
Teplá CZ . . . . . . . . 95 B4
Teplice CZ . . . . . . . 84 B1
Teplička nad Váhom
  SK . . . . . . . . . . . 98 B2
Tepsa FIN . . . . . . 197 B8
Tera E . . . . . . . . . 143 C4
Téramo I . . . . . . . . 169 A3
Ter Apel NL . . . . . . 71 B4
Terborg NL . . . . . . 71 C3
Terchová SK . . . . . 99 B3
Terebovlya UA . . . . 13 D6
Teremia Mare RO . 126 B2
Terena P . . . . . . . 155 C3
Teresa de Cofrentes
  E . . . . . . . . . . . 159 B2
Terešov CZ . . . . . . 96 B1
Terezín CZ . . . . . . 84 B2
Terezino Polje HR . 124 B3
Tergnier F . . . . . . . 90 B3
Teriberka RUS . . . . 3 B14
Terlizzi I . . . . . . . . 171 B4
Termas de Monfortinho
  P . . . . . . . . . . . 155 A4
Terme di Súio I . . . 169 B3
Terme di Valdieri I . 133 A3
Termens E . . . . . . 145 C4
Termes F . . . . . . . 116 C3
Términi Imerese I . 176 B2
Terminillo E . . . . . 169 A2
Térmoli I . . . . . . . 170 B3
Termonfeckin IRL . 27 C4
Ternberg A . . . . . . 110 B1
Terndrup DK . . . . . 58 B3
Terneuzen NL . . . . 79 A3
Terni I . . . . . . . . . 168 A2
Ternitz A . . . . . . . 111 B3
Ternopil UA . . . . . . 13 D6
Terpni GR . . . . . . 183 C5
Terracina I . . . . . . 169 B3
Terråk N . . . . . . . 195 E3
Terralba I . . . . . . . 179 C2
Terranova di Pollino
  I . . . . . . . . . . . . 174 B2
Terranova di Sibari
  I . . . . . . . . . . . . 174 B2
Terras do Bouro P . 148 A1
Terrasini I . . . . . . 176 A2
Terrassa E . . . . . . 147 C3
Terrasson-la-Villedieu
  F . . . . . . . . . . . 129 A4
Terrazos E . . . . . . 143 B3
Terriente E . . . . . . 152 B2
Terrugem P . . . . . 155 C3
Tertenía I . . . . . . . 179 C3
Teruel E . . . . . . . . 152 B2
Tervola FIN . . . . . 196 C7
Tervuren B . . . . . . 79 B4
Terzaga E . . . . . . . 152 B2
Tešanj BIH . . . . . . 125 C3
Tešáske-Mlyňany
  SK . . . . . . . . . . . 98 C2

Teslić BIH 125 C3
Tessin D 66 B1
Tessy-sur-Vire F 88 B2
Tét H 111 B4
Tetbury GB 43 A4
Teterchen F 92 B2
Teterow D 65 C5
Teteven BG 17 D6
Tetiyev UA 13 D8
Tetovo MK 182 A2
Tettau D 82 B3
Tettnang D 107 B4
Teublitz D 95 B4
Teuchern D 83 A4
Teulada
E 159 C4
I 179 D2
Teupitz D 74 B2
Teurajärvi S 196 C5
Teutschenthal D 83 A3
Tevel H 112 C2
Teviothead GB 36 A4
Tewkesbury GB 39 C4
Thale D 82 A3
Thalfang D 92 B2
Thalgau A 109 B4
Thalkirch CH 107 C4
Thalmässing D 95 B3
Thalwil CH 107 B3
Thame GB 44 B3
Thann F 106 B2
Thannhausen D 94 C2
Thaon-les-Vosges
F 105 A5
Tharandt D 83 B5
Tharsis E 161 B2
Thasos GR 183 C6
Thatcham GB 44 B2
Thaxted GB 45 B4
Thayngen CH 107 B3
Theale GB 44 B2
The Barony GB 33 B3
Thebes = Thiva GR 185 A4
Theding-hausen D 72 B2
Theessen D 73 B5
The Hague = 's-Gravenhage NL 70 B1
Themar D 82 B2
The Mumbles GB 39 C3
Thénezay F 102 C1
Thenon F 129 A4
Therouanne F 78 B2
Thessaloniki = Salonica
GR 182 C4
Thetford GB 45 A4
Theux B 80 B1
Thézar-les-Corbières
F 146 A3
Thèze F 145 A3
Thiberville F 89 A4
Thibie F 91 C4
Thiéblemont-Farémont
F 91 C4
Thiendorf D 84 A1
Thiene I 121 B4
Thierrens CH 106 C1
Thiers F 117 B3
Thiesi I 178 B2
Thiessow D 66 B2
Thiezac F 116 B2
Þingeyri IS 190 B2
Þingvellir IS 190 C4
Thionville F 92 B2
Thira GR 185 C6
Thiron-Gardais F 89 B4
Thirsk GB 37 B5
Thisted DK 58 B1
Thiva = Thebes GR 185 A4
Thivars F 90 C1
Thiviers F 115 C4
Thizy F 117 A4
Tholen NL 79 A4
Tholey D 92 B3
Thomas Street IRL 28 A3
Thomastown IRL 30 B1
Thônes F 118 B3
Thonnance-les-Joinville
F 91 C5
Thonon-les-Bains
F 118 A3
Thorame-Basse F 132 A2
Thorame-Haute F 132 A2
Thorens-Glières F 118 A3
Thorigny-sur-Oreuse
F 91 C3
Thörl A 110 B2
Þorlákshöfn IS 190 D4
Thornaby on Tees
GB 37 B5
Thornbury GB 43 A4
Thorne GB 40 B3
Thornhill
*Dumfries & Galloway* GB 36 A3
*Stirling* GB 35 B3
Thornthwaite GB 36 B3
Thornton-le-Dale
GB 40 A3
Þórshöfn IS 191 A10
Thouarcé F 102 B1
Thouars F 102 C1
Thrapston GB 44 A3
Threlkeld GB 36 B3
Thrumster GB 32 C3
Thueyts F 117 C4
Thuin B 79 B4
Thuir F 146 B3
Thumau D 95 A3
Thun CH 106 C2
Thuret F 116 B3
Thurey F 105 C4
Thüringen A 107 B4
Thurins F 117 B4
Thürkow D 65 C5
Thurles IRL 29 B4
Thurmaston GB 40 C2
Thurø By DK 65 A3
Thursby GB 36 B3
Thurso GB 32 C3
Thury-Harcourt F 89 B3
Thusis CH 107 C4
Thyborøn DK 58 B1
Þykkvibær IS 190 D5
Thyregod DK 59 C2
Tibi E 159 C3
Tibro S 55 B5
Tidaholm S 55 B4
Tidan S 55 B5
Tidersrum S 62 A3
Tiedra E 150 A2
Tiefenbach D 95 B4
Tiefencastel CH 107 C4
Tiefenort D 82 B2
Tiefensee D 74 B2
Tiel NL 79 A5
Tielmes E 151 B4
Tielt B 78 A3
Tienen B 79 B4
Tiengen D 106 B3
Tiercé F 102 B1
Tierga E 152 A2
Tiermas E 144 B2
Tierp S 51 B4
Tierrantona E 145 B4
Tighina MD 17 B8
Tighnabruaich GB 34 C2
Tignes F 119 B3
Tigy F 103 B4
Tihany H 112 C1
Tijnje NL 70 A2
Tijola E 164 B2
Tikhvin RUS 9 C8
Tilburg NL 79 A5
Til Châtel F 105 B4
Tilh F 128 C2
Tillac F 145 A4
Tillberga S 56 A2
Tille F 90 B2
Tillicoultry GB 35 B4
Tilloy Bellay F 91 B4
Tilly F 115 B5
Tilly-sur-Seulles F 88 A3
Tim DK 59 B1
Timau I 109 C4
Timbaki GR 185 D5
Timi CY 181 B1
Timişoara RO 126 B3
Timmele S 60 B3
Timmendorfer Strand
D 65 C3
Timmernabben S 62 B4
Timmersdala S 55 B4
Timoleague IRL 29 C3
Timolin IRL 30 B2
Timrå S 200 D3
Timsfors S 61 C3
Timsgearraidh GB 31 A1
Tinajas E 152 B1
Tinalhas P 155 B3
Tinchebray F 88 B3
Tincques F 78 B2
Tineo E 141 A4
Tinglev DK 64 B2
Tingsryd S 63 B2
Tingstäde S 57 C4
Tingvoll N 198 C5
Tinlot B 79 B5
Tinnoset N 53 A5
Tinos GR 185 B6
Tintagel GB 42 B2
Tinténiac F 101 A4
Tintern GB 39 C4
Tintigny B 92 B1
Tione di Trento I 121 A3
Tipperary IRL 29 B3
Tiptree GB 45 B4
Tirana = Tiranë AL 182 B1
Tiranë= Tirana AL 182 B1
Tirano I 120 A3
Tiraspol MD 17 B8
Tire TR 188 A2
Tires I 108 C2
Tiriez E 158 C1
Tirig E 153 B4
Tiriolo I 175 C2
Tirnavos GR 182 D4
Tirrénia I 134 B3
Tirschenreuth D 95 B4
Tirstrup DK 59 B3
Tirteafuera E 157 B3
Tisno HR 137 B4
Tišnov CZ 97 B4
Tisovec SK 99 C3
Tisselskog S 54 B3
Tistedal N 54 A2
Tistrup DK 59 C1
Tisvildeleje DK 61 C2
Tiszaalpár H 113 C3
Tiszabö H 113 B4
Tiszacsége H 113 B5
Tiszadorogma H 113 B4
Tiszaföldvár H 113 C4
Tiszafüred H 113 B4
Tiszajenö H 113 B4
Tiszakécske H 113 C4
Tiszakeszi H 113 B4
Tiszakürt H 113 C4
Tiszalök H 113 A5
Tiszalúc H 113 A5
Tiszanána H 113 B4
Tiszaörs H 113 B4
Tiszaroff H 113 B4
Tiszasüly H 113 B4
Tiszasziget H 126 A2
Tiszaszőlős H 113 B4
Tiszaújváros H 113 B5
Tiszavasvári H 113 B5
Titaguas E 159 B2
Titel SRB 126 B2
Titisee-Neustadt D 106 B3
Tito I 172 B1
Titova Korenica
HR 123 C4
Titran N 198 B5
Tittling D 96 C1
Tittmoning D 109 A3
Titz D 80 A2
Tiurajärvi FIN 196 B7
Tived S 55 B5
Tiverton GB 43 B3
Tivisa E 153 A4
Tivoli I 168 B2
Tizsadob H 113 A5
Tjällmo S 56 B1
Tjåmotis S 195 D9
Tjæreborg DK 59 C1
Tjautjas S 196 B3
Tjøme N 54 A1
Tjong N 195 D4
Tjonnefoss N 53 B4
Tjörn IS 190 B5
Tjörnarp S 61 D3
Tjøtta N 195 E3
Tkon HR 137 B4
Tleń PL 68 B3
Tlmače SK 98 C2
Tłuchowo PL 77 B4
Tlumačov CZ 98 B1
Tóalmas H 112 B3
Toano I 134 A3
Toba D 82 A2
Tobarra E 158 C2
Tobercurry IRL 26 B2
Tobermore GB 27 B4
Tobermory GB 34 B1
Toberonochy GB 34 B2
Tobha Mor GB 31 B1
Tobo S 51 B4
Tocane-St Apre F 129 A3
Tocha P 148 B1
Tocina E 162 A2
Töcksfors S 54 A2
Tocón E 163 A4
Todal N 198 C5
Todi I 136 C1
Todmorden GB 40 B1
Todorici BIH 138 A3
Todtmoos D 106 B3
Todtnau D 106 B2
Toén E 140 B3
Tofta
*Gotland* S 57 C4
*Skaraborg* S 55 B4
Toftbyn S 50 B2
Tofte N 54 A1
Töftedal S 54 B2
Tofterup DK 59 C1
Toftlund DK 59 C2
Tőfü H 125 A4
Tohmo FIN 197 C10
Tokaj H 113 A5
Tokarnia PL 87 B4
Tokary PL 76 C3
Tokod H 112 B2
Tököl H 112 B2
Tolastadh bho Thuath
GB 31 A2
Toledo E 151 C3
Tolentino I 136 B2
Tolfa I 168 A1
Tolg S 62 A2
Tolga N 199 C8
Tolkmicko PL 69 A4
Tollarp S 61 D3
Tollered S 60 B2
Tølløse DK 61 D1
Tolmachevo RUS 9 C6
Tolmezzo I 122 A2
Tolmin SLO 122 A2
Tolna H 112 C2
Tolnanémedi H 112 C2
Tolob GB 33 B5
Tolosa
E 144 A1
P 155 B3
Tolox E 162 B3
Tolpuddle GB 43 B4
Tolva
E 145 B4
FIN 197 C11
Tolve I 172 B2
Tomar P 154 B2
Tomaševac SRB 126 B2
Tomašica BIH 124 C2
Tomášikovo SK 111 A4
Tomašouka BY 13 C5
Tomášovce SK 99 C3
Tomaszów Mazowiecki
PL 87 A4
Tomatin GB 32 D3
Tombeboeuf F 129 B3
Tomdoun GB 32 D1
Tomelilla S 66 A2
Tomellosa E 151 B5
Tomelloso E 157 A4
Tomiño E 140 C2
Tomintoul GB 32 D3
Tomislavgrad BIH 138 B3
Tomisław PL 84 A3
Tomisławice PL 76 B3
Tomnavoulin GB 32 D3
Tompa H 126 A1
Tompaládony H 111 B3
Tomra N 198 C3
Tomter N 54 A1
Tona E 147 C3
Tonara I 179 B3
Tonbridge GB 45 B4
Tondela P 148 B1
Tønder DK 64 B1
Tongeren B 79 B5
Tongue GB 32 C2
Tönisvorst D 80 A2
Tønjum N 47 A4
Tonkopuro FIN 197 C11
Tonnay-Boutonne
F 114 C3
Tonnay-Charente
F 114 C3
Tonneins F 129 B3
Tonnerre F 104 B2
Tonnes N 195 D4
Tönning D 64 B1
Tonsåsen N 47 B6
Tønsberg N 54 A1
Tonstad N 52 B2
Toomyvara IRL 28 B3
Toormore IRL 29 C2
Topares E 164 B2
Topas E 150 A2
Toplița RO 17 B6
Topola SRB 127 C2
Topolčani MK 182 B3
Topol'čany SK 98 C2
Topol'čianky SK 98 C2
Topolje HR 124 B2
Topólka PL 76 B3
Topol'niky SK 111 B4
Topolovățu Mare
RO 126 B3
Toponár H 125 A3
Toporów PL 75 B4
Topsham GB 43 B3
Topusko HR 124 B1
Toques E 140 B3
Torà E 147 C2
Toral de los Guzmanes
E 142 B1
Toral de los Vados
E 141 B4
Torbalı TR 188 A2
Torbjörntorp S 55 B4
Torbole I 121 B3
Torchiarolo I 173 B4
Torcross GB 43 B3
Torcy-le-Petit F 89 A5
Torda SRB 126 B2
Tørdal N 53 A4
Tordehumos E 142 C1
Tordera E 147 C3
Tordesillas E 150 A2
Tordesilos E 152 B2
Töre S 196 D5
Töreboda S 55 B5
Toreby DK 65 B4
Torekov S 61 C2
Torella dei Lombardi
I 170 C3
Torellò E 147 B3
Toreno E 141 B4
Torfou F 114 A2
Torgau D 83 A5
Torgelow D 74 A3
Torgueda P 148 A2
Torhamn S 63 B3
Torhop N 193 B11
Torhout B 78 A3
Torigni-sur-Vire F 88 A3
Torija E 151 B4
Toril E 152 B2
Torino = Turin I 119 B4
Toritto I 171 C4
Torkovichi RUS 9 C7
Torla E 145 B3
Tormac RO 126 B3
Törmänen FIN 193 D11
Tormestorp S 61 C3
Tórmini I 121 B3
Tornada P 154 B1
Tornal'a SK 99 C4
Tornavacas E 150 B2
Tornby DK 58 A2
Tornesch D 72 A2
Torness GB 32 D2
Torniella I 135 B4
Tornimparte I 169 A3
Torning DK 59 B2
Tornio FIN 196 D7
Tornjoš SRB 126 B1
Tornos E 152 B2
Toro E 150 A2
Törökszentmiklós
H 113 B4
Toropets RUS 9 D7
Torpa S 61 C3
Torpè I 178 B3
Torphins GB 33 D4
Torpo N 47 B5
Torpoint GB 42 B2
Torpsbruk S 62 A2
Torquay GB 43 B3
Torquemada E 142 B2
Torralba de Burgo
E 151 A5
Torralba de Calatrava
E 157 A4
Torrão P 154 C2
Torre Annunziata I 170 C2
Torreblacos E 143 C4
Torreblanca E 153 B4
Torreblascopedro
E 157 B4
Torrecaballeros E 151 A3
Torrecampo E 156 B3
Torre Canne I 173 B3
Torre Cardela E 163 A4
Torrecilla E 152 B1
Torrecilla de la Jara
E 156 A3
Torrecilla de la Orden
E 150 A2
Torrecilla del Pinar
E 151 A3
Torrecilla en Cameros
E 143 B4
Torrecillas de la Tiesa
E 156 A2
Torre das Vargens
P 154 B3
Torre de Coelheiros
P 154 C3
Torre de Dom Chama
P 149 A2
Torre de Juan Abad
E 157 B4
Torre de la Higuera
E 161 B3
Torre del Bierzo E 141 B4
Torre del Burgo E 151 B4
Torre del Campo E 163 A4
Torre del Greco I 170 C2
Torre del Lago Puccini
I 134 B3
Torre dell'Orso I 173 B4
Torre del Mar E 163 B3
Torredembarra E 147 C2
Torre de Miguel Sesmero E 155 C4
Torre de Moncorvo
P 149 A2
Torre de Santa Maria
E 156 A1
Torredonjimeno E 163 A4
Torre do Terranho
P 148 B2
Torre Faro I 177 A4
Torregrosa E 147 C1
Torreira P 148 B1
Torrejoncillo E 155 B4
Torrejón de Ardoz
E 151 B4
Torrejón de la Calzada
E 151 B4
Torrejón del Rey E 151 B4
Torrejon el Rubio
E 156 A1
Torrelaguna E 151 B4
Torrelapaja E 152 A2
Torre la Ribera E 145 B4
Torrelavega E 142 A2
Torrelobatón E 150 A2
Torrelodones E 151 B4
Torre los Negros E 152 B2
Torremaggiore I 171 B3
Torremanzanas E 159 C3
Torremayor E 155 C4
Torremezzo di Falconara
I 174 B2
Torremocha E 156 A1
Torremolinos E 163 B3
Torrenieri I 135 B4
Torrenostra E 153 B4
Torrenova I 168 B2
Torrent E 159 B3
Torrente de Cinca
E 153 A4
Torrenueva
*Ciudad Real* E 157 B4
*Granada* E 163 B4
Torreorgaz E 155 B4
Torre Orsáia I 172 B1
Torre-Pacheco E 165 B4
Torre Péllice I 119 C4
Torreperogil E 157 B4
Torres E 163 A4
Torresandino E 143 C3
Torre Santa Susanna
I 173 B3
Torres-Cabrera E 163 A3
Torres de la Alameda
E 151 B4
Torres Novas P 154 B2
Torres Vedras P 154 B1
Torrevieja E 165 B4
Torricella I 173 B3
Torri del Benaco I 121 B3
Torridon GB 31 B3
Torriglia I 134 A2
Torrijos E 151 C3
Tørring DK 59 C2
Torrita di Siena I 135 B4
Torroal P 154 C2
Torroella de Montgr i
E 147 B4
Torrox E 163 B4
Torrskog S 54 A3
Torsåker S 50 B3
Torsang S 50 B2
Torsås S 63 B4
Torsby S 49 B4
Torsetra N 48 B2
Torshälla S 56 A2
Tórshavn FO 4 A3
Torslanda S 60 B1
Torsminde DK 59 B1
Torsnes N 46 B3
Törtel H 113 B3
Tórtoles E 150 B2
Tórtoles de Esgueva
E 142 C2
Tortol i I 179 C3
Tortona I 120 C1
Tórtora I 174 B1
Tortoreto Lido I 136 C2
Tortorici I 177 A3
Tortosa E 153 B4
Tortosendo P 148 B2
Tortuera E 152 B2
Tortuero E 151 B4
Toruń PL 76 A3
Torup S 60 C3
Tor Vaiánica I 168 B2
Torver GB 36 B3
Tørvikbygde N 46 B3
Torviscón E 163 B4
Torzhok RUS 9 D9
Torzym PL 75 B4
Tosbotn N 195 E3
Toscelanor-Maderno
I 121 B3
Tosno RUS 9 C7
Tossa de Mar E 147 C3
Tossåsen S 199 C10
Tosse F 128 C1
Tösse S 54 B3
Tossicía I 169 A3
Tostedt D 72 A2
Tosya TR 23 A8
Tószeg H 113 B4
Toszek PL 86 B2
Totana E 165 B3
Totebo S 62 A4
Tôtes F 89 A5
Tótkomlós H 113 C4
Totland N 198 D2
Tøtlandsvik N 52 A2
Totnes GB 43 B3
Tótszerdahely H 124 A2
Tøttdal N 199 A8
Totton GB 44 C2
Touça P 149 A2
Toucy F 104 B2
Toul F 92 C1
Toulon F 132 B1
Toulon-sur-Allier F 104 C2
Toulon-sur-Arroux
F 104 C3
Toulouse F 129 C4
Tourcoing F 78 B3
Tour de la Parata F 180 B1
Tourlaville F 88 A2
Tournai B 78 B3
Tournan-en-Brie F 90 C2
Tournay F 145 A4
Tournon-d'Agenais
F 129 B3
Tournon-St Martin
F 115 B4
Tournon-sur-Rhône
F 117 B4
Tournus F 105 C3
Touro
E 140 B2
P 148 B2
Tourouvre F 89 B4
Tourriers F 115 C4
Tours F 102 B2
Tourteron F 91 B4
Tourves F 132 B1
Toury F 103 A3
Touvedo P 148 A1
Touvois F 114 B2
Toužim CZ 83 B4
Tovačov CZ 98 B1
Tovariševo SRB 126 B1
Tovarnik HR 125 B5
Tovdal N 53 B4
Towcester GB 44 A3
Town Yetholm GB 35 C5
Tråastølen N 47 B4
Trabada E 141 A3
Trabadelo E 141 B4
Trabanca E 149 A3
Trabazos E 149 A3
Traben-Trarbach D 92 B3
Trabia I 176 B2
Tradate I 120 B1
Trädet S 60 B3
Trafaria P 154 C1
Tragacete E 152 B2
Tragwein A 96 C2
Traiguera E 153 B4
Trainel F 91 C3
Traisen A 110 A2
Traismauer A 97 C3
Traitsching D 95 B4
Trákhonas CY 181 A2
Tralee IRL 29 B2
Tramacastilla de Tena
E 145 B3
Tramagal P 154 B2
Tramariglio I 178 B2
Tramatza I 179 B2
Tramelan CH 106 B2

**Tramonti di Sopra**
I . . . . . . . . . . . 122 A1
Tramore IRL . . . . . . 30 B1
Trampot F . . . . . . . 92 C1
Trana I . . . . . . . . .119 B4
Tranås S . . . . . . . . 55 B5
Tranbjerg DK . . . . . 59 B3
Tranby N . . . . . . . . 54 A1
Trancoso P . . . . . . 148 B2
Tranebjerg DK . . . . . 59 C3
Tranekær DK . . . . . 65 B3
Tranemo S . . . . . . . 60 B3
Tranent GB . . . . . . . 35 C5
Tranevåg N . . . . . . 52 B2
Trängslet S . . . . . . 49 A5
Tranhult S . . . . . . . 60 B3
Trani I . . . . . . . . . 171 B4
Trans-en-Provence
F . . . . . . . . . . . 132 B2
Transtrand S . . . . . . 49 A5
Tranum DK . . . . . . . 58 A2
Tranvik S . . . . . . . . 57 A4
Trápani I . . . . . . . . 176 A1
Trappes F . . . . . . . . 90 C2
Traryd S . . . . . . . . . 61 C3
Trasacco I . . . . . . . 169 B3
Trasierra E . . . . . . . 156 B1
Träslövsläge S . . . . 60 B2
Trasmiras E . . . . . . 140 B3
Traspinedo E . . . . . 150 A3
Trate SLO . . . . . . . 110 C2
Trauchgau D . . . . . 108 B1
Traun A . . . . . . . . .110 A1
Traunreut D . . . . . . 109 B3
Traunstein D . . . . . . 109 B3
Traunwalchen D . . . 109 B3
Tråvad S . . . . . . . . . 55 B4
Travemünde D . . . . . 65 C3
Traversétolo I . . . . 120 C3
Travnik
BIH . . . . . . . . . . .139 A3
SLO . . . . . . . . . . .123 B3
Travo
F . . . . . . . . . . . .180 B2
I . . . . . . . . . . . . 120 C2
Trawsfynydd GB . . . 38 B3
Trbovlje SLO . . . . . 123 A4
Trbušani SRB . . . . . 127 D2
Treban F . . . . . . . . .116 A3
Třebařov CZ . . . . . . 97 B4
Trebatsch D . . . . . . 74 B3
Trebbin D . . . . . . . . 74 B2
Třebechovice pod
Orebem CZ . . . . . 85 B3
Trebel D . . . . . . . . . 73 B4
Třebenice CZ . . . . . 84 B1
Trébeurden F . . . . . 100 A2
Třebíč CZ . . . . . . . . 97 B3
Trebinje BIH . . . . . . 139 C4
Trebisacce I . . . . . . 174 B2
Trebitz D . . . . . . . . 83 A4
Trebnje SLO . . . . . . 123 B4
Třeboň CZ . . . . . . . 96 B2
Třebovice CZ . . . . . 97 B4
Trebsen D . . . . . . . . 83 A4
Trebujena E . . . . . . 161 C3
Trecastagni I . . . . . 177 B4
Trecate I . . . . . . . . 120 B1
Trecenta I . . . . . . . 121 B4
Tredegar GB . . . . . . 39 C3
Tredózio I . . . . . . . 135 A4
Treffen A . . . . . . . . 109 C4
Treffort F . . . . . . . .118 A2
Treffurt D . . . . . . . . 82 A2
Trefnant GB . . . . . . 38 A3
Tregaron GB . . . . . . 39 B3
Trégastel-Plage F . 100 A2
Tregnago I . . . . . . . 121 B4
Tregony GB . . . . . . 42 B2
Tréguier F . . . . . . . 100 A2
Trégunc F . . . . . . . 100 B2
Treharris GB . . . . . . 39 C3
Trehörningsjö S . . 200 C4
Tréia I . . . . . . . . . . 136 B2
Treignac F . . . . . . .116 B1
Treignat F . . . . . . . .116 A2
Treignes B . . . . . . . . 91 A4
Treis-Karden D . . . . 80 B3
Trekanten S . . . . . . 63 B4
Trélazé F . . . . . . . . 102 B1
Trelech GB . . . . . . . 39 C2
Trélissac F . . . . . . . 129 A3
Trelleborg S . . . . . . 66 A2
Trélon F . . . . . . . . . 91 A4
Trélou-sur-Marne F . 91 B3
Tremblay-le-Vicomte
F . . . . . . . . . . . . 89 B5
Tremés P . . . . . . . . 154 B2
Tremezzo I . . . . . . 120 B2
Třemošná CZ . . . . . 96 B1
Tremp E . . . . . . . . 145 B4
Trenčianska Stankovce
SK . . . . . . . . . . . 98 C1
Trenčianska Turná
SK . . . . . . . . . . . 98 C2
Trenčianske Teplá
SK . . . . . . . . . . . 98 C2
Trenčianske Teplice
SK . . . . . . . . . . . 98 C2
Trenčín SK . . . . . . . 98 C2
Trendelburg D . . . . 81 A5
Trengereid N . . . . . 46 B2
Trensacq F . . . . . . 128 B2
Trent D . . . . . . . . . . 66 B2
Trento I . . . . . . . . . 121 A4
Treorchy GB . . . . . . 39 C3
Trept F . . . . . . . . . .118 B2
Trepuzzi I . . . . . . . 173 B4

**Trescore Balneário**
I . . . . . . . . . . . 120 B2
Tresenda I . . . . . . 120 A3
Tresfjord N . . . . . 198 C4
Tresigallo I . . . . . 121 C4
Trešnjevica SRB . . 127 D3
Tresnurághes I . . . 178 B2
Trespaderne E . . . 143 B3
Třešt CZ . . . . . . . 97 B3
Trestina I . . . . . . 135 B5
Tretower GB . . . . . 39 C3
Trets F . . . . . . . . 132 B1
Tretten N . . . . . . . 48 A2
Treuchtlingen D . . 94 C2
Treuen D . . . . . . . 83 B4
Treuenbrietzen D . 74 B1
Treungen N . . . . . 53 A4
Trevélez E . . . . . . 163 B4
Trevi I . . . . . . . . 136 C1
Treviana E . . . . . . 143 B3
Treviglio I . . . . . . 120 B2
Trevignano Romano
I . . . . . . . . . . . 168 A2
Trevi nel Lázio I . . 169 B3
Treviso I . . . . . . . 122 B1
Trévoux F . . . . . . .117 B4
Treysa D . . . . . . . 81 B5
Trézelles F . . . . . .117 A3
Trezzo sull'Adda I . 120 B2
Trhová Kamenice
CZ . . . . . . . . . . . 97 B3
Trhové Sviny CZ . . 96 C2
Triacastela E . . . . 141 B3
Triaize F . . . . . . . .114 B2
Trianda GR . . . . . 188 C3
Triaucourt-en-Argonne
F . . . . . . . . . . . . 91 C5
Tribanj Krušcica
HR . . . . . . . . . . 137 A4
Triberg D . . . . . . 106 A3
Tribsees D . . . . . . 66 B1
Tribuče SLO . . . . . 123 B4
Tricárico I . . . . . . 172 B2
Tricase I . . . . . . . 173 C4
Tricésimo I . . . . . 122 A2
Trieben A . . . . . . .110 B1
Triebes D . . . . . . 83 B4
Triepkendorf D . . . 74 A2
Trier D . . . . . . . . 92 B2
Trieste I . . . . . . . 122 B2
Trie-sur-Baïse F . . 145 A4
Triggiano I . . . . . 173 A2
Triglitz D . . . . . . 73 A5
Trignac F . . . . . . 101 B3
Trigueros E . . . . . 161 B3
Trigueros del Valle
E . . . . . . . . . . . 142 C2
Trikala GR . . . . . 182 D3
Trikeri GR . . . . . . 183 D5
Trikomo CY . . . . . 181 A2
Trilj HR . . . . . . . 138 B2
Trillo E . . . . . . . . 152 B1
Trilport F . . . . . . 90 C2
Trim IRL . . . . . . . 30 A2
Trimdon GB . . . . . 37 B5
Trindade
Beja P . . . . . . . 160 B2
Bragança P . . . . 149 A2
Třinec CZ . . . . . . 98 B2
Tring GB . . . . . . . 44 B3
Trinità d'Agultu I . 178 B2
Trinitápoli I . . . . . 171 B4
Trino I . . . . . . . . .119 B5
Trinta P . . . . . . . 148 B2
Triora I . . . . . . . . 133 B3
Tripoli GR . . . . . . 184 B3
Triponzo I . . . . . . 136 C1
Triptis D . . . . . . . 83 B3
Triste E . . . . . . . . 144 B3
Trittau D . . . . . . . 72 A3
Trivento I . . . . . . 170 B2
Trivero I . . . . . . . .119 B5
Trivigno I . . . . . . 172 B1
Trn BIH . . . . . . . 124 C3
Trnava HR . . . . . . 125 B4
SK . . . . . . . . . . .98 C1
Trnovec SK . . . . . .112 A1
Trnovo BIH . . . . . 139 B4
Trnovska vas SLO . 110 C2
Troarn F . . . . . . . 89 A3
Trochtelfingen D . . 94 C1
Trödje S . . . . . . . 51 B4
Troense DK . . . . . 65 A3
Trofa P . . . . . . . . 148 A1
Trofaiach A . . . . . .110 B2
Trofors N . . . . . . 195 E4
Trogir HR . . . . . . 138 B2
Trøgstad N . . . . . . 54 A2
Tróia I . . . . . . . . 171 B3
Troia P . . . . . . . . 154 C2
Troina I . . . . . . . 177 B3
Troisdorf D . . . . . 80 B3
Trois-Ponts B . . . . 80 B1
Troisvierges L . . . . 92 A2
Trojane SLO . . . . . 123 A3
Troldhede DK . . . . 59 C1
Trollhättan S . . . . 54 B3
Trolog BIH . . . . . 138 B2
Tromello I . . . . . . 120 B1
Tromøy N . . . . . . 53 B4
Tromsø N . . . . . . 192 C3
Trondheim N . . . . 199 B7
Tronget F . . . . . . .116 A3
Trönningeby S . . . 60 B2
Trönö S . . . . . . . . 51 A3
Tronzano-Vercellese
I . . . . . . . . . . . .119 B5

**Trôo F** . . . . . . . . 102 B2
Troon GB . . . . . . . 36 A2
Tropea I . . . . . . . 175 C1
Tropy Sztumskie PL 69 B4
Trosa S . . . . . . . . 57 B3
Trösken S . . . . . . 50 B3
Trosly-Breuil F . . . 90 B3
Trossingen D . . . . 107 A3
Trostberg D . . . . . 109 A3
Trouville-sur-Mer F . 89 A4
Trowbridge GB . . . 43 A4
Troyes F . . . . . . . 104 A3
Trpanj HR . . . . . . 138 B3
Trpinja HR . . . . . 125 B4
Tršće HR . . . . . . . 123 B3
Tršice CZ . . . . . . 98 B1
Trstená SK . . . . . . 99 B3
Trstenci BIH . . . . . 125 B3
Trsteno HR . . . . . 139 C3
Trstice SK . . . . . . .111 A4
Trstin SK . . . . . . . 98 C1
Trubia E . . . . . . . 141 A5
Trubjela MNE . . . . 139 C4
Truchas E . . . . . . 141 B4
Trujillanos E . . . . 155 C4
Trujillo E . . . . . . . 156 A2
Trumieje PL . . . . . 69 B4
Trun
CH . . . . . . . . . . 107 C3
F . . . . . . . . . . . . 89 B4
Truro GB . . . . . . . 42 B1
Trusetal D . . . . . . 82 B2
Truskavets' UA . . . 13 D5
Trustrup DK . . . . . 59 B3
Trutnov CZ . . . . . 85 B3
Tryserum S . . . . . 56 B2
Trysil N . . . . . . . . 49 A4
Tryszczyn PL . . . . 76 A2
Trzcianka PL . . . . 75 A5
Trzciel PL . . . . . . 75 B4
Trzcińsko Zdrój PL . 74 B3
Trzebiatów PL . . . . 67 B4
Trzebiel PL . . . . . . 84 A2
Trzebielino PL . . . . 68 A2
Trzebień PL . . . . . . 84 A3
Trzebiez PL . . . . . 74 A3
Trzebinia PL . . . . . 86 B3
Trzebnica PL . . . . . 85 A5
Trzebnice PL . . . . . 85 A4
Trzeciewiec PL . . . 76 A3
Trzemeszno PL . . . 76 B2
Trzemeszno-Lubuskie
PL . . . . . . . . . . . 75 B4
Trzetrzewina PL . . . 99 B4
Tržič SLO . . . . . . 123 A3
Tsamandas GR . . . 182 D2
Tschagguns A . . . 107 B4
Tschernitz D . . . . . 84 A2
Tsebrykove UA . . . 17 B9
Tsyelyakhany BY . . 13 B6
Tua P . . . . . . . . . 148 A2
Tuaim IRL . . . . . . 28 A3
Tuam IRL . . . . . . 28 A3
Tubbergen NL . . . . 71 B3
Tubilla del Lago E . 143 C3
Tübingen D . . . . . 93 C5
Tubize B . . . . . . . 79 B4
Tučapy CZ . . . . . . 96 B2
Tučepi HR . . . . . . 138 B3
Tuchan F . . . . . . . 146 B3
Tüchen D . . . . . . . 73 A5
Tuchola PL . . . . . . 76 A2
Tuchomie PL . . . . . 68 A2
Tuchów PL . . . . . . 99 B5
Tuczno PL . . . . . . 75 A5
Tuddal N . . . . . . . 53 A4
Tudela E . . . . . . . 144 B2
Tudela de Duero E . 150 A3
Tudweiliog GB . . . 38 B2
Tuejar E . . . . . . . 159 B2
Tuffé F . . . . . . . . 102 A2
Tufsingdalen N . . . 199 C8
Tuhaň CZ . . . . . . . 84 B2
Tui E . . . . . . . . . 140 B2
Tukhkala RUS . . . 197 D13
Tukums LV . . . . . . 8 D3
Tulcea RO . . . . . . 17 C8
Tul'chyn UA . . . . . 13 D8
Tulette F . . . . . . . 131 A3
Tuliszków PL . . . . 76 B3
Tulla IRL . . . . . . . 28 B3
Tullamore IRL . . . . 30 A1
Tulle F . . . . . . . . .116 B1
Tullins F . . . . . . . .118 B2
Tulln A . . . . . . . . 97 C4
Tullow IRL . . . . . . 30 B2
Tułowice PL . . . . . 85 B5
Tulppio FIN . . . . . 197 B12
Tulsk IRL . . . . . . . 28 A3
Tumba S . . . . . . . 57 A3
Tummel Bridge GB . 35 B3
Tun S . . . . . . . . . 55 B3
Tuna
Kalmar S . . . . . . 62 A4
Uppsala S . . . . . 51 B5
Tuna Hästberg S . . 50 B2
Tunçbilek TR . . . . 187 C4
Tunes P . . . . . . . 160 B1
Tungelsta S . . . . . 57 A4
Tunnerstad S . . . . 55 B5
Tunnhovd N . . . . . 47 B5
Tunstall GB . . . . . 45 A5
Tuohikotti FIN . . . . 8 B5
Tuoro sul Trasimeno
I . . . . . . . . . . . 135 B5
Tupadły PL . . . . . . 76 B3
Tupanari BIH . . . . 139 A4
Tupik RUS . . . . . . 9 E8

**Tuplice PL** . . . . . . 84 A2
Tura H . . . . . . . . .112 B3
Turanj HR . . . . . . 137 B4
Turany SK . . . . . . 99 B3
Turbe BIH . . . . . . 139 A3
Turbenthal CH . . . 107 B3
Turcia E . . . . . . . 141 B5
Turčianske Teplice
SK . . . . . . . . . . 98 C2
Turcifal P . . . . . . 154 B1
Turckheim F . . . . . 106 A2
Turda RO . . . . . . . 17 B5
Turégano E . . . . . 151 A4
Turek PL . . . . . . . 76 B3
Tŭrgovishte BG . . . 17 D7
Turgutlu TR . . . . . 188 A2
Turi I . . . . . . . . . 173 B3
Turis E . . . . . . . . 159 B3
Türje H . . . . . . . . .111 C4
Türkeve H . . . . . . .113 B4
Türkheim D . . . . . 108 A1
Türkmenli TR . . . . 186 C1
Turku FIN . . . . . . . 8 B3
Turleque E . . . . . . 157 A4
Turňa nad Bodvou
SK . . . . . . . . . . 99 C4
Turnberry GB . . . . 36 A2
Turnhout B . . . . . . 79 A4
Türnitz A . . . . . . .110 B2
Turnov CZ . . . . . . 84 B3
Turnu RO . . . . . . 126 A3
Turnu Măgurele RO. 17 D6
Turón E . . . . . . . 164 C1
Turoszów PL . . . . . 84 B2
Turowo PL . . . . . . 77 A5
Turquel P . . . . . . 154 B1
Turri I . . . . . . . . 179 C2
Turries F . . . . . . . 132 A2
Turriff GB . . . . . . 33 D4
Tursi I . . . . . . . . 174 A2
Turtmann CH . . . .119 A4
Turtola FIN . . . . . 196 C6
Turze PL . . . . . . . 86 A1
Turzovka SK . . . . 98 B2
Tusa I . . . . . . . . 177 B3
Tuscánia I . . . . . . 168 A1
Tuse DK . . . . . . . 61 D1
Tušilovic HR . . . . 123 B4
Tutow D . . . . . . . 66 C2
Tutrakan BG . . . . . 17 C7
Tuttlingen D . . . . . 107 B3
Tutzing D . . . . . . 108 B2
Tuzla
BIH . . . . . . . . . .125 C4
TR . . . . . . . . . . .23 C8
Tvååker S . . . . . . . 60 B2
Tväråbäck S . . . . 200 B5
Tvärskog S . . . . . . 63 B4
Tvedestrand N . . . . 53 B4
Tveit
Hordaland N . . . . 47 B4
Rogaland N . . . . .52 A2
Tver RUS . . . . . . . 9 D9
Tverrelvmo N . . . 192 D3
Tversted DK . . . . . 58 A3
Tving S . . . . . . . . 63 B3
Tvrdošin SK . . . . . 99 B3
Tvrdošovce SK . . .112 A2
Twardogóra PL . . . 85 A5
Twatt GB . . . . . . . 33 B3
Twello NL . . . . . . 70 B3
Twimberg A . . . . . 110 C1
Twist D . . . . . . . . 71 B4
Twistringen D . . . . 72 B1
Tworóg PL . . . . . . 86 B2
Twyford
Hampshire GB . . .44 B2
Wokingham GB . . .44 B3
Tyachiv UA . . . . . . 17 A5
Tychówka PL . . . . 67 C5
Tychowo PL . . . . . 67 C5
Tychy PL . . . . . . . 86 B2
Tydal N . . . . . . . 199 B8
Týec nad Labem CZ 97 A3
Tyfors S . . . . . . . 49 B6
Tygelsjö S . . . . . . 61 D2
Tylldal N . . . . . . 199 C7
Tylstrup DK . . . . . 58 A2
Tymbark PL . . . . . 99 B4
Tymowa PL . . . . . 99 B4
Týnec nad Sázavou
CZ . . . . . . . . . . 96 B2
Tynemouth GB . . . 37 A5
Tyngsjö S . . . . . . 49 B5
Týništěnad Orlicí
CZ . . . . . . . . . . 85 B4
Týn nad Vltavou CZ 96 B2
Tyresö S . . . . . . . 57 A4
Tyringe S . . . . . . 61 C3
Tyristrand N . . . . . 48 B2
Tyrrellspass IRL . . . 30 A1
Tysnes N . . . . . . . 46 B2
Tysse N . . . . . . . . 46 B2
Tyssebotn N . . . . 46 B2
Tyssedal N . . . . . . 46 B3
Tystberga S . . . . . 56 B3
Tysvær N . . . . . . . 52 A1
Tywyn GB . . . . . . 39 B2
Tzermiado GR . . . 185 D6
Tzummarum NL . . 70 A2

**Ub SRB** . . . . . . . 127 C2
Ubby DK . . . . . . . 61 D1
Úbeda E . . . . . . . 157 B4
Überlingen D . . . . 107 B4
Ubidea E . . . . . . . 143 A4
Ubli HR . . . . . . . 138 C2
Ubrique E . . . . . . 162 B2
Ucero E . . . . . . . 143 C3
Uchaud F . . . . . . 131 B3
Uchte D . . . . . . . 72 B1
Uckerath D . . . . . 80 B3
Uckfield GB . . . . . 45 C4
Ucklum S . . . . . . 54 B2
Uclés E . . . . . . . 151 C5
Ucria I . . . . . . . . 177 A3
Udbina HR . . . . . 137 A4
Uddebo S . . . . . . 60 B3
Uddeholm S . . . . . 49 B5
Uddevalla S . . . . . 54 B2
Uddheden S . . . . . 49 C4
Uden NL . . . . . . . 80 A1
Uder D . . . . . . . . 82 A2
Udiča SK . . . . . . . 98 B2
Údine I . . . . . . . . 122 A2
Udvar H . . . . . . . 125 B4
Ueckermünde D . . 74 A3
Uelsen D . . . . . . . 71 B3
Uelzen D . . . . . . . 73 B3
Uetendorf CH . . . 106 C2
Uetersen D . . . . . 72 A2
Uetze D . . . . . . . 72 B3
Uffculme GB . . . . 43 B3
Uffenheim D . . . . 94 B2
Ugarana E . . . . . . 143 A4
Ugento I . . . . . . . 173 C4
Ugerløse DK . . . . 61 D1
Uggdal N . . . . . . 46 B2
Uggerby DK . . . . . 58 A3
Uggerslev DK . . . . 59 C3
Uggiano la Chiesa
I . . . . . . . . . . . 173 B4
Ugíjar E . . . . . . . 164 C1
Ugine F . . . . . . . .118 B3
Uglejevik BIH . . . . 125 C5
Uglenes N . . . . . . 46 B2
Uglich RUS . . . . . . 9 D11
Ugljane HR . . . . . 138 B2
Ugod H . . . . . . . .111 B4
Uherské Hradiště
CZ . . . . . . . . . . 98 B1
Uherský Brod CZ . . 98 B1
Uherský Ostroh CZ. 98 C1
Uhingen D . . . . . . 94 C1
Uhliřské-Janovice
CZ . . . . . . . . . . 96 B3
Uhřiněves CZ . . . . 96 A2
Uhyst D . . . . . . . . 84 A2
Uig GB . . . . . . . . 31 B2
Uitgeest NL . . . . . 70 B1
Uithoorn NL . . . . . 70 B1
Uithuizen NL . . . . 71 A3
Uithuizermeeden NL 71 A3
Uivar RO . . . . . . 126 B2
Ujazd
Łódzkie PL . . . . .87 A3
Opolskie PL . . . . .86 B2
Ujezd u Brna CZ . . 97 B4
Ujhartyán H . . . . .112 B3
Újkigyós H . . . . . .113 C5
Ujsolt H . . . . . . . .112 C3
Újszász H . . . . . . .113 B4
Újszentmargita H . .113 B5
Ujué E . . . . . . . . 144 B2
Ukanc SLO . . . . . 122 A2
Ukmergé LT . . . . . 13 A6
Ukna S . . . . . . . . 56 B2
Ula TR . . . . . . . . 188 B3
Ul'anka SK . . . . . . 99 C3
Ulaş TR . . . . . . . 186 A2
Ulássai I . . . . . . . 179 C3
Ulbjerg DK . . . . . 58 B2
Ulbster GB . . . . . . 32 C3
Ulceby GB . . . . . . 40 B3
Ulcinj MNE . . . . . 16 E3
Uldum DK . . . . . . 59 C2
Ulefoss N . . . . . . 53 A5
Uleila del Campo
E . . . . . . . . . . . 164 B2
Ulëz AL . . . . . . . 182 B1
Ulfborg DK . . . . . 59 B1
Uljma SRB . . . . . 127 B3
Ullånger S . . . . . 200 C4
Ullapool GB . . . . . 32 D1
Ullared S . . . . . . . 60 B2
Ullatti S . . . . . . . 196 B4
Ullatun N . . . . . . 52 A2
Ulldecona E . . . . 153 B4
Ulldemolins E . . . 147 C1
Ullerslev DK . . . . . 59 C3
Ullervad S . . . . . . 55 B4
Üllés H . . . . . . . 126 A1
Ullited S . . . . . . . 63 B2
Ursa Sela SLO . . 123 B4
Ulm D . . . . . . . . . 94 C1
Ulme P . . . . . . . . 154 B2
Ulmen D . . . . . . . 80 B2
Ulnes N . . . . . . . 47 B6
Ulog BIH . . . . . . . 139 B4
Ulricehamn S . . . . 60 B3
Ulrichstein D . . . . 81 B5
Ulrika S . . . . . . . 56 B1
Ulriksfors S . . . . . 200 C1
Ulrum NL . . . . . . 71 A3
Ulsberg N . . . . . . 198 C6

**Ulsta GB** . . . . . . . 33 [?]
Ulsted DK . . . . . . 58 [?]
Ulsteinvik N . . . . . 198 [?]
Ulstrup
Vestsjællands Amt.
DK . . . . . . . . . .59 C[?]
Viborg Amt. DK . . 59 B[?]
Ulsvåg N . . . . . . 194 B6
Ulubey TR . . . . . . 188 A4
Uluborlu TR . . . . . 189 A5
Ulukışla TR . . . . . 23 C8
Ulverston GB . . . . 36 B3
Ulvik N . . . . . . . . 46 B3
Umag HR . . . . . . 122 B2
Uman UA . . . . . . 13 D9
Umba RUS . . . . . . 3 C14
Umbértide I . . . . . 135 B5
Umbriático I . . . . . 174 B2
Umčari SRB . . . . . 127 C2
Umeå S . . . . . . . 200 C6
Umgransele S . . . 200 B4
Umhausen A . . . . 108 B1
Umka SRB . . . . . 127 C2
Umljanovic HR . . . 138 B2
Umnäs S . . . . . . 195 E7
Umurbey TR . . . . 186 B1
Unaðsdalur IS . . . 190 A3
Unapool GB . . . . . 32 C1
Unari FIN . . . . . . 197 B8
Unbyn S . . . . . . . 196 D4
Uncastillo E . . . . . 144 B2
Undenäs S . . . . . . 55 B5
Undersaker S . . . 199 B10
Undredal N . . . . . 46 B4
Unešić HR . . . . . 138 B2
Úněšov CZ . . . . . 96 B1
Ungheni MD . . . . . 17 B7
Unhais da Serra P . 148 B2
Unhošt CZ . . . . . . 84 B2
Unichowo PL . . . . 68 A2
Uničov CZ . . . . . . 98 B1
Uniejów PL . . . . . 76 C3
Unisław PL . . . . . 76 A3
Unkel D . . . . . . . 80 B3
Unken A . . . . . . . 109 B3
Unna D . . . . . . . . 81 A3
Unnaryd S . . . . . . 60 C3
Unquera E . . . . . . 142 A2
Unterach A . . . . . 109 B4
Unterägeri CH . . . 107 B3
Unterammergau D 108 B2
Unterhaching D . . 108 A2
Unteriberg CH . . . 107 B3
Unterkochen D . . . 94 C2
Unter Langkampfen
A . . . . . . . . . . 108 B3
Unterlaussa A . . . .110 B1
Unterlüss D . . . . . 72 B3
Untermünkheim D. . 94 B1
Unterschächen
CH . . . . . . . . . 107 C3
Unterschleissheim
D . . . . . . . . . . . 95 C3
Unterschwaningen
D . . . . . . . . . . . 94 B2
Untersiemau D . . . 82 B2
Unter-steinbach D . 94 B2
Unterweissenbach
A . . . . . . . . . . . 96 C2
Unterzell D . . . . . 95 B4
Upavon GB . . . . . 44 B2
Úpice CZ . . . . . . . 85 B4
Upiłka PL . . . . . . 68 B2
Upphärad S . . . . . 54 B3
Uppingham GB . . . 40 C3
Upplands-Väsby S . 57 A3
Uppsala S . . . . . . 51 C4
Uppsjøhytta N . . . 48 A1
Upton-upon-Severn
GB . . . . . . . . . . 39 B4
Ur F . . . . . . . . . . 146 B2
Uras I . . . . . . . . . 179 C2
Uraz PL . . . . . . . . 85 A4
Urbánia I . . . . . . 136 B1
Urbino I . . . . . . . 136 B1
Urçay F . . . . . . . 103 C4
Urda E . . . . . . . . 157 A4
Urdax E . . . . . . . 144 A2
Urdilde E . . . . . . 140 B2
Urdos F . . . . . . . 145 B3
Urk NL . . . . . . . . 70 B2
Úrkút H . . . . . . . .111 B4
Urla TR . . . . . . . . 188 A1
Urlingford IRL . . . . 30 B1
Urnäsch CH . . . . 107 B4
Urnes N . . . . . . . 47 A4
Uroševac KOS . . . 16 D4
Urracal E . . . . . . 164 B2
Urries E . . . . . . . 144 B2
Urroz E . . . . . . . 144 B2
Ursensollen D . . . 95 B3
Urshult S . . . . . . 63 B2
Uršna Sela SLO . . 123 B4
Urszulewo PL . . . . 77 B4
Ury F . . . . . . . . . 90 C2
Urziceni RO . . . . . 17 C7
Urzulei I . . . . . . . 178 B3
Usagre E . . . . . . 156 B1
Uşak TR . . . . . . . 187 D4
Usedom D . . . . . . 66 C2
Useldange L . . . . 92 B1
Uséllus I . . . . . . . 179 C2
Ushakovo RUS . . . 69 A5
Usingen D . . . . . . 81 B4
Usini I . . . . . . . . 178 B2

. . . . . . A5
. . . . . . A3
. . . . . . C2
. . . . . . . . C4
. . . . . ó C2
. . . . . 6 A4
. . . . . 82 A1
. . . . . 97 B5
. . . . . 71 A3
. . . . . 179 C3
. . . . . 102 B2
. . . . . 119 B4
. . . . . 116 B2
. . . . . 116 B2
. . . oitou F 115 B4
. . . Forez F . 117 B3
. . . -Bains F 146 B3
. . . t N. . . . 47 B5
. . . F . . . 144 A2
. . . CZ . . . 84 B2
. . . CH . . . 107 B3
. . . CZ . . . 98 B1
. . . ikolina BIH . . 139 B4
. . stínad Labem CZ 84 B2
. . stínad Orlicí CZ. . 97 B4
Ústipračá BIH . . . 139 B5
Ustka PL. . . . . 68 A1
Ust Luga RUS . . . . 8 C6
Ustroń PL. . . . . 98 B2
Ustronie Morskie PL 67 B4
Ustyuzhna RUS. . . 9 C10
Uszód H. . . . . . 112 C2
Utåker N. . . . . . 52 A1
Utansjö S. . . . . 200 D3
Utebo E. . . . . . 152 A3
Utena LT. . . . . 13 A6
Utery CZ. . . . . 95 B5
Uthaug N. . . . . 198 B6
Utiel E. . . . . . 159 B2
Utne N. . . . . . 46 B3
Utö S. . . . . . 57 B4
Utrecht NL. . . . . 70 B2
Utrera E. . . . . . 162 A2
Utrillas E. . . . . 153 B3
Utsjoki FIN. . . . 193 C11
Utstein kloster N. . . 52 A1
Uttendorf A. . . . 109 B3
Uttenweiler D. . . . 107 A4
Utterslev DK. . . . 65 B4
Uttoxeter GB. . . . 40 C2
Utvälinge S. . . . 61 C2
Utvorda N. . . . . 199 A7
Uusikaarlepyy FIN . . 3 E8
Uusikaupunki FIN. . . 8 B2
Uvaly CZ. . . . . 96 A2
Uvdal N. . . . . . 47 B5
Uza F. . . . . . . 128 B1
Uzdin SRB. . . . . 126 B2
Uzdowo PL. . . . . 77 A5
Uzein F. . . . . . 145 A3
Uzel F. . . . . . 100 A3
Uzerche F. . . . . 116 B1
Uzès F. . . . . . 131 A3
Uzhhorod UA. . . . 12 D5
Uzhok UA. . . . . 12 D5
Užice SRB. . . . . 127 D1
Uznach CH. . . . . 107 B3
Üzümlü
  Konya TR. . . . . 189 B6
  Muğla TR. . . . . 188 C4
Uzunköprü TR. . . . 186 A1

**V**

Vaalajärvi FIN . . . 197 B9
Vaas F. . . . . . . 102 B2
Vaasa FIN. . . . . 8 A2
Vaasen NL. . . . . 70 B2
Vabre F. . . . . . 130 B1
Vác H. . . . . . . 112 B3
Vacha D. . . . . . 82 B2
Váchartyán H. . . . 112 B3
Väckelsång S. . . . 63 B2
Vacqueyras F. . . . 131 A3
Vad S. . . . . . . 50 B2
Vada I. . . . . . . 134 B3
Väddö S. . . . . . 51 C5
Väderstad S. . . . 55 B5
Vadheim N. . . . . 46 A2
Vadillo de la Sierra
  E. . . . . . . 150 B2
Vadillos E. . . . . 152 B1
Vadla N. . . . . . 52 A2
Vado I. . . . . . . 135 A4
Vado Ligure I. . . . 133 A4
Vadsø N. . . . . 193 B13
Vadstena S. . . . . 55 B5
Vadum DK. . . . . 58 A2
Vaduz FL. . . . . 107 B4
Vafos N. . . . . . 53 B5
Vág H. . . . . . . 111 B4
Vågåmo N. . . . . 198 D6
Væggerløse DK. . . 65 B4
Vaggeryd S. . . . . 62 A2
Vaghia GR. . . . . 184 A4
Vaglia I. . . . . . 135 B4
Váglio Basilicata I. . 172 B1
Vagney F. . . . . . 106 A1
Vagnhärad S. . . . 57 B3
Vagnsunda S. . . . 57 A4
Vagos P. . . . . . 148 B1
Vai GR. . . . . . 185 D7
Vaiano I. . . . . . 135 B4
Vaiges F. . . . . . 102 A1
Vaihingen D. . . . . 93 C4
Vaillant F. . . . . 105 B4

Vailly-sur-Aisne F . . 91 B3
Vailly-sur Sauldre
  F. . . . . . . 103 B4
Vairano Scalo I . . . 170 B2
Vaison-la-Romaine
  F. . . . . . . 131 A4
Vaite F. . . . . . 105 B4
Väjern S. . . . . . 54 B2
Vajszló H. . . . . 125 B3
Vaksdal N. . . . . 46 B2
Vál H. . . . . . . 112 B2
Valaam RUS. . . . . 9 B7
Valada P. . . . . . 154 B2
Vålådalen S. . . . 199 B10
Valadares P. . . . . 148 A1
Valado P. . . . . . 154 B1
Valandovo MK. . . . 182 B4
Valaská SK. . . . . 99 C3
Valaská Belá SK . . 98 C2
Valaská Dubová SK. 99 B3
Valašská Polanka
  CZ. . . . . . . 98 B1
Valašské Klobouky
  CZ. . . . . . . 98 B2
Valašské Meziříčí
  CZ. . . . . . . 98 B1
Valberg F. . . . . 132 A2
Vålberg S. . . . . 55 A4
Valbo S. . . . . . 51 B4
Valbom P. . . . . . 148 A1
Valbondione I. . . . 120 A3
Valbonnais F. . . . 118 C2
Valbuena de Duero
  E. . . . . . . 142 C2
Vălcani RO. . . . . 126 B2
Valdagno I. . . . . 121 B4
Valdahon F. . . . . 105 B5
Valdaracete E. . . . 151 B4
Valday RUS. . . . . 9 D8
Valdealgorfa E. . . . 153 B3
Valdecaballeros E. . 156 A2
Valdecabras E. . . . 152 B1
Valdecarros E. . . . 150 B2
Valdeconcha E. . . . 151 B5
Valdeflores E. . . . 161 B3
Valdefresno E. . . . 142 B1
Valdeganga E. . . . 158 B2
Valdelacasa E. . . . 150 B2
Valdelacasa de Tajo
  E. . . . . . . 156 A2
Valdelarco E. . . . 161 B3
Valdelosa E. . . . . 149 A4
Valdeltormo E. . . . 153 B4
Valdelugeros E. . . . 142 B1
Valdemanco de Esteras
  E. . . . . . . 156 B3
Valdemarsvik S. . . 56 B2
Valdemorillo E. . . . 151 B3
Valdemoro E. . . . . 151 B4
Valdemoro Sierra
  E. . . . . . . 152 B2
Valdenoceda E. . . . 143 B3
Valdeobispo E. . . . 149 B3
Valdeolivas E. . . . 152 B1
Valdepeñas E. . . . 157 B4
Valdepeñas de Jaén
  E. . . . . . . 163 A4
Valdepiélago E. . . . 142 B1
Valdepolo E. . . . . 142 B1
Valderas E. . . . . 142 B1
Valdérice I. . . . . 176 A1
Valderrobres E. . . . 153 B4
Valderrueda E. . . . 142 B2
Val de San Lorenzo
  E. . . . . . . 141 B4
Val de Santo Domingo
  E. . . . . . . 150 B3
Val d'Esquières F. . 132 B2
Valdestillas E. . . . 150 A3
Valdetorres E. . . . 156 B1
Valdetorres de Jarama
  E. . . . . . . 151 B4
Valdeverdeja E. . . . 150 C2
Valdevimbre E. . . . 142 B1
Valdieri I. . . . . 133 A3
Valdilecha E. . . . . 151 B4
Val-d'Isère F. . . . 119 B3
Valdobbiádene I. . . 121 B4
Valdocondes E. . . . 143 C3
Valdoviño E. . . . . 140 A2
Valea lui Mihai RO. . 16 B5
Vale de Açor
  Beja P. . . . . 160 B2
  Portalegre P. . . 154 B3
Vale de Agua P . . . 160 B1
Vale de Cambra P . . 148 B1
Vale de Lobo P . . . 160 B1
Vale de Prazeres P 148 B2
Vale de Reis P . . . 154 C2
Vale de Rosa P . . . 160 B2
Vale de Santarém
  P. . . . . . . 154 B2
Vale de Vargo P . . 160 B2
Vale do Peso P . . . 155 B3
Valega P. . . . . . 148 B1
Valéggio sul Mincio
  I. . . . . . . 121 B3
Valeiro P. . . . . . 154 C2
Valença P. . . . . . 140 B2
Valençay F. . . . . 103 B3
Valence
  Charente F. . . . 115 C4
  Drôme F. . . . . 117 C4
Valence d'Agen F . . 129 B3
Valence d'Albigeois
  F. . . . . . . 130 A1
Valence-sur-Baïse
  F. . . . . . . 129 C3

Valencia E. . . . . 159 B3
Valencia de Alcántara
  E. . . . . . . 155 B3
Valencia de Don Juan
  E. . . . . . . 142 B1
Valencia de las Torres
  E. . . . . . . 156 B1
Valencia del Ventoso
  E. . . . . . . 161 A3
Valencia de Mombuey
  E. . . . . . . 161 A2
Valenciennes F . . . 79 B3
Valensole F. . . . . 132 B1
Valentano I. . . . . 168 A1
Valentigney F. . . . 106 B1
Valentine F. . . . . 145 A4
Valenza I. . . . . . 120 B1
Valenzuela E. . . . 163 A3
Valenzuela de Calatrava
  E. . . . . . . 157 B4
Våler
  Hedmark N. . . . 48 B3
  Østfold N. . . . 54 A1
Valera de Abajo E . 158 B1
Valeria E. . . . . . 158 B1
Valestrand N. . . . 52 A1
Valestrandsfossen
  N. . . . . . . 46 B2
Valevåg N. . . . . 52 A1
Valfabbrica I. . . . 136 B1
Valflaunes F. . . . 131 B2
Valga EST. . . . . 8 D5
Valgorge F. . . . . 131 A3
Valgrisenche I. . . . 119 B4
Valguarnera Caropepe
  I. . . . . . . 177 B3
Valhelhas P. . . . . 148 B2
Valjevo SRB. . . . . 127 C1
Valka LV. . . . . . 8 D4
Valkeakoski FIN. . . 8 B4
Valkenburg NL. . . . 80 B1
Valkenswaard NL . . 79 A5
Valkó H. . . . . . 112 B3
Valla S. . . . . . 56 A2
Vallada E. . . . . . 159 C3
Vallado E. . . . . . 141 A4
Valladolid E. . . . . 150 A3
Vallákra S. . . . . 61 D2
Vallata I. . . . . . 172 A1
Vallberga S. . . . . 61 C3
Vall d'Alba E. . . . 153 B3
Valldemossa E. . . . 166 B2
Valle N. . . . . . . 52 A3
Valle Castellana I. . 136 C2
Valle de Abdalajís
  E. . . . . . . 163 B3
Valle de Cabuérniga
  E. . . . . . . 142 A2
Valle de la Serena
  E. . . . . . . 156 B2
Valle de Matamoros
  E. . . . . . . 155 C4
Valle de Santa Ana
  E. . . . . . . 155 C4
Valledolmo I. . . . . 176 B2
Valledoria I. . . . . 178 B2
Valleiola E. . . . . 150 A3
Vallelunga Pratameno
  I. . . . . . . 176 B2
Valle Mosso I. . . . 119 B5
Vallendar D. . . . . 81 B3
Vallentuna S. . . . 57 A4
Vallerås S. . . . . 49 B5
Valleraugue F. . . . 130 A2
Vallermosa I. . . . . 179 C2
Vallet F. . . . . . 101 B4
Valletta M. . . . . 175 C3
Valley GB. . . . . 38 A2
Vallfogona de Riucorb
  E. . . . . . . 147 C2
Valli del Pasúbio I. 121 B4
Vallo della Lucánia
  I. . . . . . . 172 B1
Valloire F. . . . . 118 B3
Vallombrosa I. . . . 135 B4
Valls E. . . . . . . 147 C2
Vallset N. . . . . . 48 B3
Vallsta S. . . . . . 50 A3
Vallstena S. . . . . 57 C4
Valmadrid E. . . . . 153 A3
Valmiera LV. . . . . 8 D4
Valmojado E. . . . . 151 B3
Valmont F. . . . . . 89 A4
Valmontone I. . . . 169 B2
Valö S. . . . . . . 51 B5
Valognes F. . . . . 88 A2
Valonga P. . . . . . 148 B1
Valongo P. . . . . . 148 A1
Válor E. . . . . . . 164 C1
Valoria la Buena E. 142 C2
Valøy N. . . . . . 199 A7
Valpaços P. . . . . 148 A2
Valpelline I. . . . . 119 B4
Valpiana I. . . . . . 135 B3
Valpovo HR. . . . . 125 B4
Valras-Plage F. . . . 130 B2
Valréas F. . . . . . 131 A3
Vals CH. . . . . . 107 C4
Valsavarenche I. . . 119 B4
Vålse DK. . . . . . 65 B4
Valsequillo E. . . . 156 B2
Valsjöbyn S. . . . 199 A11
Vals-les-Bains F . . 117 C4

Valsonne F. . . . . .117 B4
Valstagna I. . . . . 121 B4
Val-Suzon F. . . . . 105 B3
Valtablado del Rio
  E. . . . . . . 152 B1
Valþjofsstaður IS .191 B11
Val Thorens F. . . .118 B3
Valtice CZ. . . . . 97 C4
Valtiendas E. . . . . 151 A4
Valtierra E. . . . . 144 B2
Valtopina I. . . . . 136 B1
Valtorta I. . . . . . 120 B2
Valtournenche I. . .119 B4
Valverde E. . . . . 144 C2
Valverde de Burguillos
  E. . . . . . . 155 C4
Valverde de Júcar
  E. . . . . . . 158 B1
Valverde de la Vera
  E. . . . . . . 150 B2
Valverde de la Virgen
  E. . . . . . . 142 B1
Valverde del Camino
  E. . . . . . . 161 B3
Valverde del Fresno
  E. . . . . . . 149 B3
Valverde de Llerena
  E. . . . . . . 156 B2
Valverde de Mérida
  E. . . . . . . 156 B1
Valvträsk S. . . . . 196 C4
Vamberk CZ. . . . . 85 B4
Vamdrup DK. . . . . 59 C2
Våmhus S. . . . . . 50 A1
Vamlingbo S. . . . . 57 D4
Vammala FIN. . . . . 8 B3
Vámosmikola H. . . .112 B2
Vámosszabadi H. . .111 B4
Vamos GR. . . . . . 185 D5
Vanault-les-Dames
  F. . . . . . . 91 C4
Vandel DK. . . . . 59 C2
Vandenesse F. . . . 104 C2
Vandenesse-en-Auxois
  F. . . . . . . 104 B3
Vandóies I. . . . . 108 C2
Väne-Åsaka S. . . . 54 B3
Vänersborg S. . . . 54 B3
Vänersnäs S. . . . . 54 B3
Vang N. . . . . . . 47 A5
Vänge S. . . . . . 51 C4
Vangsnes N. . . . . 46 A3
Vänjaurbäck S. . . . 200 B4
Vännacka S. . . . . 54 A3
Vannareid N. . . . . 192 B3
Vännäs S. . . . . . 200 C5
Vannes F. . . . . . 101 B3
Vannsätter S. . . . 51 A3
Vannvåg N. . . . . 192 B3
Vansbro S. . . . . 49 B6
Vanse N. . . . . . 52 B2
Vantaa FIN. . . . . 8 B4
Vanttauskoski FIN. 197 C9
Vanviken N. . . . . 199 B7
Vanyarc H. . . . . .112 B3
Vaour F. . . . . . . 129 B4
Vapnyarka UA . . . 13 D8
Vaprio d'Adda I. . . 120 B2
Vaqueiros P. . . . . 160 B2
Vara S. . . . . . . 55 B3
Varacieux F. . . . .118 B2
Varades F. . . . . . 101 B4
Varages F. . . . . . 132 B1
Varaldsøy N. . . . . 46 B2
Varallo I. . . . . . .119 B5
Varangerbotn N. . . 193 B12
Varano de'Melegari
  I. . . . . . . 120 C3
Varaždin HR. . . . . 124 A2
Varaždinske Toplice
  HR. . . . . . . 124 A2
Varazze I. . . . . . 133 A4
Varberg S. . . . . . 60 B2
Vardal N. . . . . . 48 B2
Varde DK. . . . . . 59 C1
Vårdö FIN. . . . . . 51 B7
Vardø N. . . . . . 193 B15
Vardomb H. . . . . 125 A4
Varejoki FIN. . . . . 196 C7
Varel D. . . . . . . 71 A5
Varena LT. . . . . . 13 A6
Vårenes N. . . . . 52 A1
Varengeville-sur-Mer
  F. . . . . . . 89 A4
Varenna I. . . . . . 120 A2
Varennes-en-Argonne
  F. . . . . . . 91 B5
Varennes-le-Grand
  F. . . . . . . 105 C3
Varennes-St Sauveur
  F. . . . . . . 105 C4
Varennes-sur-Allier
  F. . . . . . . .117 A3
Varennes-sur-Amance
  F. . . . . . . 105 B4
Vareš BIH. . . . . . 139 A4
Varese I. . . . . . 120 B1
Varese Ligure I. . . 134 A2
Vårfurile RO. . . . . 16 B5
Vårgårda S. . . . . 60 A2
Vargas
  E. . . . . . .143 A3
  P. . . . . . .154 B2
Vargón S. . . . . . 54 B3
Varhaug N. . . . . 52 B1
Variaş RO. . . . . . 126 A2
Variaşu Mic RO. . . 126 A3
Varilhes F. . . . . . 146 A2

Varin SK. . . . . . 98 B2
Väring S. . . . . . 55 B4
Váriz P. . . . . . . 149 A3
Varkaus FIN. . . . . 8 A5
Varmahlíð IS. . . . 190 B6
Varmaland IS. . . . 190 C4
Värmlands Bro S. . . 55 A4
Värmskog S. . . . . 55 A3
Varna
  BG. . . . . . .17 D7
  SRB. . . . . . .127 C1
Värnamo S. . . . . 60 B4
Varnhem S. . . . . 55 B4
Varnsdorf CZ. . . . 84 B2
Värö S. . . . . . . 60 B2
Varoška Rijeka
  BIH. . . . . . 124 B2
Városlöd H. . . . . .111 B4
Várpalota H. . . . .112 B2
Varreddes F. . . . . 90 C2
Vars F. . . . . . . 118 C3
Varsi I. . . . . . . 120 C2
Varsseveld NL. . . . 71 C3
Vårsta S. . . . . . 57 A3
Vartdal N. . . . . . 198 C3
Vartofta S. . . . . 55 B4
Vårvik S. . . . . . 54 A3
Várvölgy H. . . . . .111 C4
Varzi I. . . . . . . 120 C2
Varzjelas P. . . . . 148 B1
Varzo I. . . . . . .119 A5
Varzy F. . . . . . . 104 B2
Vasad H. . . . . . .112 B3
Väse S. . . . . . . 55 A4
Vašica SRB. . . . . 125 B5
Vasilevichi BY. . . . 13 B8
Väskinde S. . . . . 57 C4
Vaskút H. . . . . . 125 A4
Vaslui RO. . . . . . 17 B7
Vassbotn N. . . . . 53 B4
Vassenden N. . . . . 47 A6
Vassieux-en-Vercors
  F. . . . . . . 118 C2
Vassmolösa S. . . . 63 B4
Vassy F. . . . . . . 88 B3
Västansjö S. . . . . 195 E6
Västanvik S. . . . . 50 B1
Västerås S. . . . . 56 A2
Västerby S. . . . . 50 B2
Västerfärnebo S . . 50 C3
Västergarn S. . . . 57 C4
Västerhaninge S. . . 57 A4
Västervik S. . . . . 62 A4
Västra Ämtervik S. . 55 A4
Västra-Bodarne S. . 60 B2
Västra Karup S. . . 61 C2
Vasvár H. . . . . . .111 B3
Vasylkiv UA. . . . . 13 C9
Vát H. . . . . . . .111 B3
Vatan F. . . . . . . 103 B3
Väte S. . . . . . . 57 C4
Vathia GR. . . . . . 184 C3
Vatican City = Cittádel
  Vaticano I. . . . 168 B2
Vatili CY. . . . . . 181 A2
Vatin SRB. . . . . . 126 B3
Vatland N. . . . . . 52 B3
Vatnar N. . . . . . 53 A5
Vatnås N. . . . . . 48 C1
Vatne N. . . . . . . 53 B4
Vatnestrøm N. . . . 53 B4
Vätö S. . . . . . . 51 C5
Vatra-Dornei RO . . 17 B6
Vatry F. . . . . . . 91 C4
Vattholma S. . . . . 51 B4
Vättis CH. . . . . . 107 C4
Vauchamps F. . . . 91 C3
Vauchassis F. . . . 104 A2
Vaucouleurs F. . . . 92 C1
Vaudoy-en-Brie F . . 90 C3
Vaulen N. . . . . . 52 B1
Vaulruz CH. . . . . 106 C1
Vaulx Vraucourt F . . 90 A2
Vaumas F. . . . . . 104 C2
Vausseroux F. . . . 115 B3
Vauvenargues F . . . 132 B1
Vauvert F. . . . . . 131 B3
Vauvillers F. . . . . 105 B5
Vaux-sur-Sure B . . 92 B1
Vawkavysk BY. . . . 13 B6
Vaxholm S. . . . . 57 A4
Växjö S. . . . . . . 62 B2
Våxtorp S. . . . . . 61 C3
Vayrac F. . . . . . 129 B4
Važec SK. . . . . . 99 B3
Veberöd S. . . . . 61 D3
Vechelde D. . . . . 72 B3
Vechta D. . . . . . 71 B5
Vecinos E. . . . . . 149 B4
Vecsés H. . . . . . .112 B3
Vedavågen N. . . . 52 A1
Veddige S. . . . . . 60 B2
Vedersø DK. . . . . 59 B1
Vedeseta I. . . . . 120 B2
Vedevåg S. . . . . 56 A1
Vedra E. . . . . . . 140 B2
Vedum S. . . . . . 55 B3
Vega
  Asturias E. . . . 142 A1
  Asturias E. . . . 142 A1
Vega de Espinareda
  E. . . . . . . 141 B4
Vega de Infanzones
  E. . . . . . . 142 B1
Vegadeo E. . . . . 141 A3

Vega de Pas E. . . . 143 A3
Vega de Valcarce
  E. . . . . . . 141 B4
Vega de Valdetronco
  E. . . . . . . 150 A2
Vegårshei N. . . . . 53 B4
Vegas de Coria E. . 149 B3
Vegas del Condado
  E. . . . . . . 142 B1
Vegby S. . . . . . 60 B3
Vegger DK. . . . . 58 B2
Veggli N. . . . . . 47 B6
Veghel NL. . . . . . 80 A1
Veglast D. . . . . . 66 B1
Véglie I. . . . . . . 173 B3
Veguillas E. . . . . 151 B4
Vegusdal N. . . . . 53 B4
Veidholmen N. . . . 198 B4
Veidnes N. . . . . 193 B10
Veikåker N. . . . . 48 B1
Veinge S. . . . . . 61 C3
Vejbystrand S. . . . 61 C2
Vejen DK. . . . . . 59 C2
Vejer de la Frontera
  E. . . . . . . 162 B2
Vejle DK. . . . . . 59 C2
Vejprty CZ. . . . . 83 B5
Velada E. . . . . . 150 B3
Vela Luka HR. . . . 138 C2
Velayos E. . . . . . 150 B3
Velbert D. . . . . . 80 A3
Velburg D. . . . . . 95 B3
Velde N. . . . . . 199 A8
Velden
  Bayern D. . . . . 95 B3
  Bayern D. . . . . .95 C4
Velden am Worther See
  A. . . . . . . 109 C5
Velefique E. . . . . 164 B2
Velen D. . . . . . . 80 A2
Velenje SLO. . . . . 123 A4
Veles MK. . . . . . 182 B3
Velesevec HR. . . . 124 B2
Velešín CZ. . . . . 96 C2
Velestino GR. . . . 182 D4
Velez Blanco E. . . 164 B2
Vélez de Benaudalla
  E. . . . . . . 163 B4
Vélez-Málaga E. . . 163 B3
Vélez Rubio E. . . . 164 B2
Veliki Radinci
  SRB. . . . . . . 127 B1
Velika HR. . . . . . 125 B3
Velika Gorica HR. . 124 B2
Velika Grdevac HR 124 B3
Velika Greda SRB . 126 B3
Velika Ilova BIH. . . 125 C3
Velika Kladuša BIH 124 B1
Velika Kopanica
  HR. . . . . . . 125 B4
Velika Krsna SRB . 127 C2
Velika Obarska
  BIH. . . . . . . 125 C5
Velika Pisanica HR 124 B3
Velika Plana SRB. . 127 C3
Velika Zdenci HR. . 124 B3
Velike Lašče SLO. . 123 B3
Velike Središte
  SRB. . . . . . . 126 B3
Veliki Gaj SRB. . . 126 B3
Veliki Popović
  SRB. . . . . . . 127 C3
Velikiye Luki RUS . . 9 D7
Veliko Gradište
  SRB. . . . . . . 127 C3
Veliko Orašje SRB. 127 C3
Veliko Selo SRB. . . 127 C3
Veliko Tǔrnovo BG . 17 D6
Velilla del Río Carrió
  E. . . . . . . 142 B2
Velilla de San Antonio
  E. . . . . . . 151 B4
Veli Lošinj HR. . . . 137 A3
Velingrad BG. . . . 183 A5
Velizh RUS. . . . . 9 E7
Veljun HR. . . . . . 123 B4
Velká Bíteš CZ. . . 97 B4
Velka Hled'scbe CZ 95 B4
Velká Lomnica SK. . 99 B4
Velkánad Veličkou
  CZ. . . . . . . 98 C1
Velké Bystřice CZ. . 98 B1
Velké Heraltice CZ. 98 B1
Velké Karlovice CZ. 98 B2
Vel'ke'Kostol'any
  SK. . . . . . . 98 C1
Vel'ké Leváre SK. . 97 C5
Velké Losiny CZ. . 98 A1
Velké Meziříčí CZ. . 97 B4
Velké Pavlovice CZ. 97 C4
Vel'ké Rovné SK. . 98 B2
Vel'ké Uherce SK. . 98 C2
Vel'ké Zálužie SK. . 98 C1
Velky Bor CZ. . . . 96 B1
Vel'ký Cetin SK. . .112 A2
Vel'ký Krtiš SK. . .112 A3
Vel'ký Meder SK. . .111 B4
Velky Ujezd CZ. . . 98 B1
Vellahn D. . . . . . 73 A3
Vellberg D. . . . . 94 B1
Velles F. . . . . . 103 C3
Velletri I. . . . . . 168 B2
Vellinge S. . . . . 66 A2
Vellisca E. . . . . . 151 B5
Velliza E. . . . . . 150 A3
Vellmar D. . . . . . 81 A5
Velp NL. . . . . . . 70 B2

Velten D . . . . . . . . 74 B2
Velvary CZ . . . . . . . 84 B2
Velvendos GR . . . . 182 C4
Vemb DK . . . . . . . . 59 B1
Vemdalen S . . . . 199 C10
Veme N. . . . . . . . . . 48 B2
Véménd H . . . . . . . 125 A4
Vemmedrup DK . . . . 61 D2
Vena S . . . . . . . . . . 62 A3
Venaco F . . . . . . . 180 A2
Venafro I . . . . . . . . 169 B4
Venarey-les-Laumes
  F. . . . . . . . . . . . . 104 B3
Venaría I. . . . . . . . .119 B4
Venasca I. . . . . . . . 133 A3
Venčane SRB. . . . 127 C2
Vence F . . . . . . . . 132 B3
Venda Nova
  Coimbra P . . . . . .154 A2
  Leiria P. . . . . . . .154 B2
Vendas Novas P . . 154 C2
Vendays-Montalivet
  F. . . . . . . . . . . . . 114 C2
Vendel S. . . . . . . . . 51 B4
Vendelso S . . . . . . . 57 A4
Vendeuil F . . . . . . . 91 B3
Vendeuvre-sur-Barse
  F. . . . . . . . . . . . . 104 A3
Vendoeuvres F . . .115 B5
Vendôme F . . . . . . 103 B3
Venelles F . . . . . . 131 B4
Veness GB. . . . . . . 33 B4
Venézia = Venice I . 122 B1
Venialbo E . . . . . . 150 A2
Venice = Venézia I . 122 B1
Vénissieux F. . . . . .117 B4
Venjan S. . . . . . . . . 49 B5
Venlo NL. . . . . . . . . 80 A2
Vennesla N . . . . . . 53 B3
Vennesund N. . . . . 195 E3
Vennezey F . . . . . . 92 C2
Venn Green GB . . . . 42 B2
Venosa I. . . . . . . . . 172 B1
Venray NL . . . . . . . 80 A1
Vent A. . . . . . . . . . 108 C1
Venta de Baños E . . 142 C2
Venta del Moro E . . 158 B2
Venta de los Santos
  E. . . . . . . . . . . . . 157 B4
Venta las Ranas E . 142 A1
Ventanueva E . . . . 141 A4
Ventas de Huelma
  E. . . . . . . . . . . . . 163 A4
Ventas de Zafarraya
  E. . . . . . . . . . . . . 163 B3
Ventavon F . . . . . . 132 A1
Ventimíglia I. . . . . . 133 B3
Ventnor GB . . . . . . 44 C2
Ventosa de la Sierra
  E. . . . . . . . . . . . . 143 C4
Ventosilla E . . . . . . 143 C4
Ventspils LV. . . . . . 8 D2
Venturina I. . . . . . . 134 B3
Venzolasca F. . . . . 180 A2
Venzone I. . . . . . . . 122 A2
Vép H . . . . . . . . . . .111 B3
Vera
  E. . . . . . . . . . . . . 164 B3
  N. . . . . . . . . . . . . 199 B9
Vera Cruz P . . . . . . 160 A2
Vera de Bidasoa E. 144 A2
Vera de Moncayo
  E. . . . . . . . . . . . . 144 C2
Verbánia I. . . . . . . .119 B5
Verberie F . . . . . . . 90 B2
Verbicaro I. . . . . . . 174 B1
Verbier CH . . . . . . .119 A4
Vercelli I. . . . . . . . .119 B5
Vercel-Villedieu-le-Camp
  F. . . . . . . . . . . . . 105 B5
Verchen D . . . . . . . 66 C1
Vercheny F . . . . . . 118 C2
Verclause F . . . . . . 131 A4
Verdalsøra N . . . . . 199 B8
Verden D . . . . . . . . 72 B2
Verdens Ende N . . . 54 A1
Verdikoussa GR . . 182 D3
Verdille F . . . . . . . 115 C3
Verdú E . . . . . . . . . 147 C2
Verdun F . . . . . . . . 92 B1
Verdun-sur-Garonne
  F. . . . . . . . . . . . . 129 C4
Verdun-sur-le-Doubs
  F. . . . . . . . . . . . . 105 C4
Veresegyház H . . .112 B3
Verfeil F . . . . . . . . 129 C4
Vergato I . . . . . . . . 135 A4
Vergel E . . . . . . . . 159 C4
Vergeletto CH . . . . 120 A1
Verges F . . . . . . . . 147 B4
Vergiate I . . . . . . . 120 B1
Vergt F . . . . . . . . . 129 A3
Veria GR. . . . . . . . 182 C4
Verín E . . . . . . . . . 141 C3
Veringenstadt D . . . 107 A4
Verl D . . . . . . . . . . . 81 A4
Verma N. . . . . . . . . 198 C5
Vermand F . . . . . . . 90 B3
Vermelha P . . . . . . 154 B1
Vermenton F . . . . . 104 B2
Vernago I . . . . . . . . 108 C1
Vernante I . . . . . . . 133 A3
Vernantes F. . . . . . 102 B2
Vernár SK. . . . . . . . 99 C4
Vernasca I. . . . . . . 120 C2
Vernayaz CH . . . . .119 A4
Vernazza I. . . . . . . 134 A2
Vern-d'Anjou F . . . . 102 B1

Verneřice CZ . . . . . 84 B2
Vernet F. . . . . . . . . 146 A2
Vernet-les-Bains F 146 B3
Verneuil F . . . . . . . 91 B3
Verneuil-sur-Avre F. 89 B4
Vernier CH . . . . . . .118 A3
Vérnio I . . . . . . . . . 135 A4
Vérnole I . . . . . . . . 173 B4
Vernon F . . . . . . . . 90 B1
Vernoux-en-Vivarais
  F. . . . . . . . . . . . . 117 C4
Veróce H . . . . . . . .112 B3
Verolanuova I . . . . 120 B3
Véroli I. . . . . . . . . . 169 B3
Verona I . . . . . . . . 121 B4
Verpelét H . . . . . . .113 B4
Verrabotn N . . . . . 199 B7
Verrès I. . . . . . . . . .110 D4
Verrey-sous-Salmaise
  F. . . . . . . . . . . . . 104 B3
Verrières F . . . . . . .115 B4
Versailles F . . . . . . 90 C2
Versam CH. . . . . . . 107 C4
Verseg H . . . . . . . .112 B3
Versmold D . . . . . . 71 B5
Versoix CH. . . . . . .118 A3
Verteillac F . . . . . . 115 C4
Vértesacsa H. . . . . .112 B2
Vertou F. . . . . . . . . 101 B4
Vertus F . . . . . . . . . 91 C3
Verviers B . . . . . . . 80 B1
Vervins F. . . . . . . . 91 B3
Verwood GB . . . . . . 43 B5
Veryan GB . . . . . . . 42 B2
Veržej SLO. . . . . . . 111 C3
Verzuolo I. . . . . . . . 133 A3
Verzy F. . . . . . . . . . 91 B4
Vescovato F. . . . . . 180 A2
Vése H . . . . . . . . . . 124 A3
Veselí nad Lužnicí
  CZ. . . . . . . . . . . . 96 B2
Veselí nad Moravou
  CZ. . . . . . . . . . . . 98 C1
Veseliy BG . . . . . . . 17 D7
Vésime I . . . . . . . . 119 C5
Veskoniemi FIN. . 193 D11
Vesoul F . . . . . . . . 105 B5
Vespolate I. . . . . . . 120 B1
Vessigebro S. . . . . 60 C2
Vestbygd N . . . . . . 52 B2
Vestenanova I . . . . 121 B4
Vester Husby S . . . 56 B2
Vester Nebel DK . . 59 C2
Vesterøhavn DK . . . 58 A3
Vester Torup DK . . 58 A2
Vester Vedsted DK . 59 C1
Vestervig DK. . . . . 58 B1
Vestfossen N. . . . . 53 A5
Vestmannaeyjar IS 190 D5
Vestmarka N . . . . . 48 C3
Vestnes N . . . . . . . 198 C4
Vestone I. . . . . . . . 120 B3
Vestre Gausdal N . . 48 A2
Vestre Jakobselv
  N . . . . . . . . . . . . 193 B13
Vestre Slidre N . . . . 47 A5
Vesyegonsk RUS . . 9 C10
Veszprém H . . . . . .112 B1
Veszprémvarsány
  H . . . . . . . . . . . . .112 B1
Vésztő H . . . . . . . . 113 C5
Vetlanda S . . . . . . . 62 A3
Vetovo HR . . . . . . . 125 B3
Vetralla I. . . . . . . . 168 A2
Větrný Jeníkov CZ . 97 B3
Vétroz CH . . . . . . .119 A4
Vetschau D . . . . . . 84 A2
Vettasjärvi S . . . . . 196 B4
Vetto I. . . . . . . . . . 134 A3
Vetulónia I . . . . . . . 135 C3
Veules-les-Roses F. 89 A4
Veulettes-sur-Mer F 89 A4
Veum N . . . . . . . . . 53 A4
Veurne B . . . . . . . . 78 A2
Veverská Bítýška
  CZ. . . . . . . . . . . . 97 B4
Vevey CH . . . . . . . 106 C1
Vevi GR . . . . . . . . . 182 C3
Vevring N. . . . . . . . 46 A2
Vex CH . . . . . . . . . .119 A4
Veynes F . . . . . . . . 132 A1
Veyre-Monton F. . . .116 B3
Veyrier F . . . . . . . . .118 B3
Vézelay F . . . . . . . 104 B2
Vézelise F . . . . . . . 92 C2
Vézenobres F . . . . 131 A3
Vezins F. . . . . . . . . 102 B1
Vézins-de-Lévézou
  F. . . . . . . . . . . . . 130 A1
Vezirhan TR. . . . . . 187 B5
Vezirköprü TR . . . . 23 A8
Vezza di Óglio I . . . 120 A3
Vezzani I. . . . . . . . 180 A2
Vezzano I. . . . . . . . 121 A4
Vezzano sul Cróstolo
  I . . . . . . . . . . . . . 121 C3
Vi S . . . . . . . . . . . . 200 D3
Viadana I . . . . . . . . 121 C3
Via Gloria P . . . . . . 160 B2
Viana E. . . . . . . . . 143 B4
Viana do Alentejo
  P. . . . . . . . . . . . . 154 C2
Viana do Bolo E. . . 141 B3
Viana do Castelo P 148 A1
Vianden L. . . . . . . . 92 B2
Viannos GR . . . . . . 185 D6
Viaréggio I. . . . . . . 134 B3
Viator E . . . . . . . . . 164 C2

Vibble S . . . . . . . . . 57 C4
Viborg DK . . . . . . . 58 B2
Vibo Valéntia I . . . . 175 C2
Vibraye F . . . . . . . . 102 A2
Vic E. . . . . . . . . . . 147 C3
Vícar E . . . . . . . . . 164 C2
Vicarello I. . . . . . . . 134 B3
Vicari I. . . . . . . . . . 176 B2
Vicchio I . . . . . . . . 135 B4
Vicdesses F. . . . . . 146 B2
Vic-en-Bigorre F . . 145 A4
Vicenza I . . . . . . . . 121 B4
Vic-Fézensac F . . . 129 C3
Vichy F. . . . . . . . . .117 A3
Vickan S. . . . . . . . . 60 B2
Vickerstown GB . . . 36 B3
Vico F. . . . . . . . . . . 180 A1
Vico del Gargano I 171 B3
Vico Equense I . . . 170 C2
Vicopisano I. . . . . . 134 B3
Vicosoprano CH . . 120 A2
Vicovaro I. . . . . . . . 169 A2
Vic-sur-Aisne F . . . 90 B3
Vic-sur-Cère F . . . . 116 C2
Victoria = Rabat M. 175 C3
Vidago P . . . . . . . . 148 A2
Vidauban F . . . . . . 132 B2
Vide P. . . . . . . . . . 148 B2
Videbæk DK. . . . . . 59 B1
Videm SLO. . . . . . . 123 B3
Videseter N . . . . . . 198 D4
Vidigueira P. . . . . . 160 A2
Vidin BG. . . . . . . . . 16 D5
Vidlin GB. . . . . . . . 33 A5
Vidsel S . . . . . . . . 196 D3
Vidzy BY. . . . . . . . . 13 A7
Viechtach D. . . . . . 95 B4
Vieille-Brioude F . .117 B3
Vieira P. . . . . . . . . 154 B2
Vieira do Minho P . 148 A1
Vieiros P. . . . . . . . 155 C3
Vielha E. . . . . . . . . 145 B4
Vielle-Aure F. . . . . 145 B4
Viellespesse F. . . . .116 B3
Viellevigne F. . . . . .114 B2
Vielmur-sur-Agout
  F. . . . . . . . . . . . . 130 B1
Vielsalm B . . . . . . . 80 B1
Viels Maison F. . . . 91 C3
Vienenburg D . . . . 73 C3
Vienna = Wien A . . .111 A3
Vienne F. . . . . . . . .117 B4
Vieritz D . . . . . . . . 73 B5
Viernheim D. . . . . . 93 B4
Vierraden D . . . . . . 74 A3
Viersen D. . . . . . . . 80 A2
Vierville-sur-Mer F . 88 A3
Vierzon F . . . . . . . 103 B4
Vieselbach D. . . . . 82 B3
Vieste I. . . . . . . . . . 171 B4
Vietas S. . . . . . . . . 194 C9
Vieteren B . . . . . . . 78 B2
Vietri di Potenza I . 172 B1
Vietri sul Mare I . . . 170 C2
Vieux-Boucau-les-Bains
  F. . . . . . . . . . . . . 128 C1
Vif F . . . . . . . . . . . .118 B2
Vig DK . . . . . . . . . . 61 D1
Vigásio I . . . . . . . . 121 B3
Vigaun A. . . . . . . . 109 B4
Vigeland N. . . . . . . 52 B3
Vigeois F . . . . . . . .116 B1
Vigévano I . . . . . . . 120 B1
Viggianello I. . . . . . 174 B2
Viggiano I. . . . . . . . 174 A1
Vigliano I . . . . . . . . 169 A3
Vigmostad N . . . . . 52 B3
Vignale I . . . . . . . . .119 B5
Vignanello I . . . . . . 168 A2
Vigneulles-lès-
  Hattonchâtel F . . 92 C1
Vignevieille F. . . . . 146 B3
Vignola I . . . . . . . . 135 A4
Vignory F. . . . . . . . 105 A4
Vignoux-sur Barangeon
  F. . . . . . . . . . . . . 103 B4
Vigo E. . . . . . . . . . 140 B2
Vigo di Fassa I. . . . 121 A4
Vigone I . . . . . . . . . 119 C4
Vigrestad N . . . . . . 52 B1
Vihiers F. . . . . . . . . 102 B1
Viitasaari FIN. . . . . 8 A4
Vík IS . . . . . . . . . . 190 D6
Vik
  Nordland N. . . . . 195 E3
  Rogaland N . . . . . 52 B1
  Sogn og Fjordane
    N. . . . . . . . . . . . 46 A3
  S. . . . . . . . . . . . . 63 C2
Vika S . . . . . . . . . . 50 B2
Vikajärvi FIN . . . . . 197 C9
Vikane N. . . . . . . . . 54 A1
Vikarbyn S. . . . . . . 50 B2
Vike N. . . . . . . . . . . 46 B2
Vikedal N. . . . . . . . 52 A1
Vikeland N. . . . . . . 53 B3
Viken
  Jämtland S. . . . . 199 A10
  Skåne S. . . . . . . .61 C2
Viker N . . . . . . . . . . 48 B2
Vikersund N. . . . . . 48 C1
Vikeså N. . . . . . . . . 52 B2
Vikevåg N. . . . . . . . 52 A1
Vikingstad S . . . . . 56 B1
Vikmanshyttan S. . 50 B2
Vikna N. . . . . . . . . 199 A7
Vikøy N. . . . . . . . . . 46 B3

Vikran
  Troms N . . . . . . . 192 C2
  Troms N . . . . . . . 194 B7
Viksjö S . . . . . . . . 200 D3
Viksøyri N . . . . . . . 46 A3
Viksta S . . . . . . . . . 51 B4
Vila Boim P . . . . . . 155 C3
Vila Chã de Ourique
  P. . . . . . . . . . . . . 154 B2
Viladamat E . . . . . . 147 B4
Vila de Cruces E . . 140 B2
Vila de Rei P . . . . . 154 B2
Vila do Bispo P . . . 160 B1
Vila do Conde P. . . 148 A1
Viladrau E . . . . . . . 147 C3
Vila Flor P . . . . . . . 149 A2
Vila Franca das Navas
  P. . . . . . . . . . . . . 149 B2
Vilafranca del Maestrat
  E. . . . . . . . . . . . . 153 B3
Vilafranca del Penedès
  E. . . . . . . . . . . . . 147 C2
Vila Franca de Xira
  P. . . . . . . . . . . . . 154 C1
Vila Fresca P . . . . . 154 C1
Vilagarcía de Arousa
  E. . . . . . . . . . . . . 140 B2
Vilajuiga E . . . . . . . 147 B4
Vilamarin E . . . . . . 140 B3
Vilamartín de Valdeorras
  E. . . . . . . . . . . . . 141 B3
Vila Nogueira P. . . 154 C1
Vila Nova da Baronia
  P. . . . . . . . . . . . . 154 C2
Vilanova de Castelló
  E. . . . . . . . . . . . . 159 B3
Vila Nova de Cerveira
  P. . . . . . . . . . . . . 140 C2
Vila Nova de Famalicão
  P. . . . . . . . . . . . . 148 A1
Vila Nova de Foz Côa
  P. . . . . . . . . . . . . 149 A2
Vila Nova de Gaia
  P. . . . . . . . . . . . . 148 A1
Vila Nova de Milfontes
  P. . . . . . . . . . . . . 160 B1
Vila Nova de Paiva
  P. . . . . . . . . . . . . 148 B2
Vila Nova de São Bento
  P. . . . . . . . . . . . . 161 B2
Vilanova de Sau E. 147 C3
Vilanova i la Geltrú
  E. . . . . . . . . . . . . 147 C2
Vilapedre E . . . . . . 140 A3
Vila Pouca de Aguiar
  P. . . . . . . . . . . . . 148 A2
Vila Praja de Ancora
  P. . . . . . . . . . . . . 148 A1
Vilarandelo P. . . . . 148 A2
Vilar de Santos E. . 140 B3
Vilardevós E . . . . . 141 C3
Vila Real P . . . . . . 148 A2
Vila-real de los Infantes
  E. . . . . . . . . . . . . 159 B3
Vila Real de Santo
  António P . . . . . . 160 B2
Vilar Formoso P . . 149 B3
Vila-Rodona E . . . . 147 C2
Vila Ruiva P . . . . . . 160 A2
Vilasantar E . . . . . . 140 A2
Vilaseca E . . . . . . . 147 C2
Vila Seca P. . . . . . . 148 B1
Vilassar de Mar E . 147 C3
Vilasund S . . . . . . . 195 D5
Vila Velha de Ródão
  P. . . . . . . . . . . . . 155 B3
Vila Verde
  Braga P. . . . . . . .148 A1
  Lisboa P. . . . . . . .154 B1
Vila Verde de Filcalho
  P. . . . . . . . . . . . . 161 B2
Vila Viçosa P . . . . . 155 C3
Vileabre E. . . . . . . . 156 B3
Vilémov CZ. . . . . . . 97 B3
Vileyka BY. . . . . . . 13 A7
Vilhelmina S . . . . . 200 B2
Vílio GR . . . . . . . . 184 A4
Viljandi EST. . . . . . 8 C4
Villabáñez E. . . . . . 150 A3
Villablanca E . . . . . 161 B2
Villablino E . . . . . . 141 B4
Villabona E . . . . . . 144 A1
Villabragima E. . . . 142 C1
Villabuena del Puente
  E. . . . . . . . . . . . . 150 A2
Villacadima E . . . . 151 A4
Villacañas E. . . . . . 157 A4
Villacarriedo E. . . . 143 A3
Villacarrillo E . . . . . 164 A1
Villa Castelli I . . . . 173 B3
Villacastín E . . . . . 150 B3
Villa del Prado E . . 150 B3
Villa del Río E . . . . 157 C3
Villadepera E. . . . . 149 A3
Villa de Peralonso
  E. . . . . . . . . . . . . 149 A3

Villa di Chiavenna
  I . . . . . . . . . . . . . 120 A2
Villadiego E . . . . . . 142 B2
Villadompardo E . . 163 A3
Villadóssola I. . . . . .119 A5
Villaeles de Valdavia
  E. . . . . . . . . . . . . 142 B2
Villaescusa de Haro
  E. . . . . . . . . . . . . 158 B1
Villafáfila E . . . . . . 142 C1
Villafeliche E. . . . . 152 A2
Villaflores E . . . . . . 150 A2
Villafrades de Campos
  E. . . . . . . . . . . . . 142 B2
Villafranca
  Avila E . . . . . . . .150 B2
  Navarra E. . . . . . .144 B2
Villafranca de Córdoba
  E. . . . . . . . . . . . . 157 C3
Villafranca del Bierzo
  E. . . . . . . . . . . . . 141 B4
Villafranca de los Barros
  E. . . . . . . . . . . . . 155 C4
Villafranca de los
  Caballeros E . . . 157 A4
Villafranca di Verona
  I . . . . . . . . . . . . . 121 B3
Villafranca in Lunigiana
  I . . . . . . . . . . . . . 134 A2
Villafranca-Montes de
  Oca E. . . . . . . . . 143 B3
Villafranca Tirrena
  I . . . . . . . . . . . . . 177 A4
Villafranco del Campo
  E. . . . . . . . . . . . . 152 B2
Villafranco del
  Guadalquivir E . . 161 B3
Villafrati I. . . . . . . . 176 B2
Villafrechós E. . . . . 142 C1
Villafruela E . . . . . . 143 C3
Villagarcia de las Torres
  E. . . . . . . . . . . . . 156 B1
Villaggio Mancuso
  I . . . . . . . . . . . . . 175 B2
Villagonzalo E. . . . 156 B1
Villagotón E. . . . . . 141 B4
Villagrains F . . . . . 128 B2
Villaharta E . . . . . . 156 B3
Villahermosa E . . . 158 C1
Villaherreros E . . . 142 B2
Villahoz E. . . . . . . . 143 B3
Villaines-la-Juhel F. 89 B3
Villajoyosa E . . . . . 159 C3
Villala I. . . . . . . . . . 169 B3
Villalba
  E. . . . . . . . . . . . .140 A3
  I. . . . . . . . . . . . . .176 B2
Villalba de Calatrava
  E. . . . . . . . . . . . . 157 B4
Villalba de Guardo
  E. . . . . . . . . . . . . 142 B2
Villalba del Alcor E 161 B3
Villalba de la Sierra
  E. . . . . . . . . . . . . 152 B1
Villalba de los Alcores
  E. . . . . . . . . . . . . 142 C2
Villalba de los Barros
  E. . . . . . . . . . . . . 155 C4
Villalba del Rey E . 151 B5
Villalcampo E . . . . 149 A3
Villalcázar de Sirga
  E. . . . . . . . . . . . . 142 B2
Villalengua E . . . . . 152 A2
Villalgordo del Júcar
  E. . . . . . . . . . . . . 158 B1
Villalgordo del
  Marquesado E. . . 158 B1
Villalmóndar E . . . 143 B3
Villalón de Campos
  E. . . . . . . . . . . . . 142 B1
Villalonga E . . . . . . 159 C3
Villalonso E . . . . . . 150 A2
Villalpando E . . . . . 142 C1
Villaluenga E . . . . . 151 B4
Villalumbroso E. . . 142 B2
Villálvaro E . . . . . . 143 C3
Villamalea E . . . . . 158 B2
Villamañán E . . . . . 142 B1
Villamanín E . . . . . 142 B1
Villamanrique E . . 157 B5
Villamanrique de la
  Condesa E . . . . . 161 B3
Villamanta E . . . . . 151 B3
Villamantilla E . . . . 151 B3
Villamar I . . . . . . . . 179 C2
Villamartín E . . . . . 162 B2
Villamartín de Campos
  E. . . . . . . . . . . . . 142 B2
Villamartín de Don
  Sancho E. . . . . . 142 B1
Villamassárgia I . . 179 C2
Villamayor E . . . . . 142 A1
Villamayor de Calatrava
  E. . . . . . . . . . . . . 157 B3
Villamayor de Campos
  E. . . . . . . . . . . . . 142 C1
Villamayor de Santiago
  E. . . . . . . . . . . . . 157 A5
Villamblard F . . . . . 129 A3
Villamejil E . . . . . . 141 B4
Villamesías E . . . . 156 A2
Villaminaya E . . . . 157 A4
Villa Minozzo I. . . . 134 A3
Villamor de los
  Escuderos E . . . 150 A2
Villamoronta E. . . . 142 B2
Villamuelas E. . . . . 151 C4

Villamuriel de Cerrato
  E. . . . . . . . . . . . . 142 B2
Villandraut F . . . . . 128 B2
Villanova I . . . . . . . 173 B3
Villanova d'Asti I . . 119 C4
Villanova del Battista
  I . . . . . . . . . . . . . 171 B3
Villanova Mondov ì
  I . . . . . . . . . . . . . 133 A3
Villanova Monteleone
  I . . . . . . . . . . . . . 178 B2
Villante E . . . . . . . . 143 B3
Villantério I . . . . . . 120 B2
Villanubla E . . . . . . 142 C2
Villanueva de Alcardete
  E. . . . . . . . . . . . . 157 A4
Villanueva de Alcorón
  E. . . . . . . . . . . . . 152 B1
Villanueva de Algaidas
  E. . . . . . . . . . . . . 163 A3
Villanueva de Argaña
  E. . . . . . . . . . . . . 143 B3
Villanueva de Bogas
  E. . . . . . . . . . . . . 157 A4
Villanueva de Córdoba
  E. . . . . . . . . . . . . 156 B3
Villanueva de Gállego
  E. . . . . . . . . . . . . 144 C3
Villanueva del Aceral
  E. . . . . . . . . . . . . 150 A3
Villanueva de la
  Concepcion E . . 163 B3
Villanueva de la Fuente
  E. . . . . . . . . . . . . 158 C1
Villanueva de la Jara
  E. . . . . . . . . . . . . 158 B2
Villanueva de la Reina
  E. . . . . . . . . . . . . 157 B4
Villanueva del
  Arzobispo E . . . 164 A2
Villanueva de la Serena
  E. . . . . . . . . . . . . 156 B2
Villanueva de la Sierra
  E. . . . . . . . . . . . . 149 B3
Villanueva de las
  Manzanas E . . . . 142 B1
Villanueva de las Peras
  E. . . . . . . . . . . . . 141 C5
Villanueva de las Torres
  E. . . . . . . . . . . . . 164 B1
Villanueva de la Vera
  E. . . . . . . . . . . . . 150 B2
Villanueva del Campo
  E. . . . . . . . . . . . . 142 C1
Villanueva del Duque
  E. . . . . . . . . . . . . 156 B3
Villanueva del Fresno
  E. . . . . . . . . . . . . 155 C3
Villanueva del Huerva
  E. . . . . . . . . . . . . 152 A2
Villanueva de los
  Castillejos E . . . . 161 B2
Villanueva de los
  Infantes E . . . . . 157 B5
Villanueva del Rey
  E. . . . . . . . . . . . . 156 B2
Villanueva del Rio
  E. . . . . . . . . . . . . 162 A2
Villanueva del Río y
  Minas E. . . . . . . 162 A2
Villanueva del Rosario
  E. . . . . . . . . . . . . 163 A3
Villanueva del Trabuco
  E. . . . . . . . . . . . . 163 A3
Villanueva de Mesia
  E. . . . . . . . . . . . . 163 A4
Villanueva de Nía
  E. . . . . . . . . . . . . 142 B2
Villanueva de Oscos
  E. . . . . . . . . . . . . 141 A4
Villanueva de San
  Carlos E . . . . . . 157 B4
Villanueva de San Juan
  E. . . . . . . . . . . . . 162 A2
Villanueva de Tapia
  E. . . . . . . . . . . . . 163 A3
Villanueva de
  Valdegovia E. . . . 143 B3
Villány H . . . . . . . . 125 B4
Villaputzu I. . . . . . . 179 C3
Villaquejida E . . . . 142 B1
Villaquilambre E . . 142 B1
Villaquiran de los
  Infantes E . . . . . 142 B2
Villaralto E . . . . . . 156 B3
Villarcayo E . . . . . . 143 B3
Villard-de-Lans F . .118 B2
Villar de Barrio E . . 140 B3
Villar de Cañas E . 158 B1
Villar de Chinchilla
  E. . . . . . . . . . . . . 158 C2
Villar de Ciervo E . 149 B3
Villardeciervos E. . 141 C4
Villar de Domingo
  Garcia E. . . . . . . 152 B1
Villardefrades E. . . 142 C1
Villar del Arzobispo
  E. . . . . . . . . . . . . 159 B3
Villar del Buey E . . 149 A3
Villar del Cobo E . . 152 B2
Villar del Humo E . 158 B2
Villar de los Navarros
  E. . . . . . . . . . . . . 152 A2
Villar del Pedroso
  E. . . . . . . . . . . . . 156 A2

B4
B4
52 B1
156 A2
151 A4
es
158 B1
go
141 B5
lvanes
151 B4
iesteban
158 B1
l Saz E 158 B1
119 B4
rdo del Cabriel
158 B2
no E 149 A3
ino de Conso
141 B3
arluengo E 153 B3
larobe E 143 B3
llarosa I 177 B3
Villar Perosa I 119 C4
Villarramiel E 142 B2
Villarrasa E 161 B3
Villarreal de San Carlos
E 150 C1
Villarrin de Campos
E 142 C1
Villarrobledo E 158 B1
Villarroya de la Sierra
E 152 A2
Villarroya de los Pinares
E 153 B3
Villarrubia de los Ojos
E 157 A4
Villarrubia de Santiago
E 151 C4
Villarrubio E 151 C5
Villars-les-Dombes
F 117 A5
Villarta E 158 B2
Villarta de los Montes
E 156 A3
Villarta de San Juan
E 157 A4
Villasana de Mena
E 143 A3
Villasandino E 142 B2
Villa San Giovanni
I 175 C1
Villa Santa Maria I 169 B4
Villasante E 143 A3
Villa Santina I 122 A1
Villasarracino E 142 B2
Villasayas E 151 A5
Villasdardo E 149 A3
Villaseca de Henares
E 151 B5
Villaseca de Laciana
E 141 B4
Villaseca de la Sagra
E 151 C4
Villaseco de los Gamitos
E 149 A3
Villaseco de los Reyes
E 149 A3
Villasequilla de Yepes
E 151 C4
Villasimíus I 179 C3
Villasmundo I 177 B4
Villasor I 179 C2
Villastar E 152 B2
Villastellone I 119 C4
Villatobas E 151 C4
Villatorp E 150 B2
Villatoya E 158 B2
Villavaliente E 158 B2
Villavelayo E 143 B4
Villavella E 141 B3
Villaver de de
Guadalimar E 158 C1
Villaverde del Rio
E 162 A2
Villaviciosa E 142 A1
Villaviciosa de Córdoba
E 156 B3
Villaviciosa de Odón
E 151 B4
Villavieja de Yeltes
E 149 B3
Villayón E 141 A4
Villé F 93 C3
Villebois-Lavalette
F 115 C4
Villecerf F 90 C2
Villecomtal F 130 A1
Villedieu-les-Poêles
F 88 B2
Villedieu-sur-Indre
F 103 C3
Ville-di-Pietrabugno
F 180 A2
Villedômain F 103 B3
Villefagnan F 115 B4
Villefontaine F 118 B2
Villefort F 131 A2
Villefranche-d'Albigeois
F 130 B1
Villefranche-d'Allier
F 116 A2
Villefranche-de-
Lauragais F 146 A2
Villefranche-de-Lonchat
F 128 B3
Villefranche-de-Panat
F 130 A1
Villefranche-de-
Rouergue F 130 A1
Villefranche-du-Périgord
F 129 B4
Villefranche-sur-Cher
F 103 B3
Villefranche-sur-Mer
F 133 B3
Villefranche-sur-Saône
F 117 A4
Villegenon F 103 B4
Villel E 152 B2
Villemaur-sur-Vanne
F 104 A2
Villemontais F 117 B3
Villemur-sur-Tarn
F 129 C4
Villena E 159 C3
Villenauxe-la-Grande
F 91 C3
Villenave-d'Ornon
F 128 B2
Villeneuve
CH 119 A3
F 129 B5
Villeneuve-d'Ascq F 78 B3
Villeneuve-de-Berg
F 131 A3
Villeneuve-de-Marsan
F 128 C2
Villeneuve-de-Rivière
F 145 A4
Villeneuve-la-Guyard
F 90 C3
Villeneuve-l'Archevêque
F 104 A2
Villeneuve-le-Comte
F 90 C2
Villeneuve-lès-Avignon
F 131 B3
Villeneuve-les-Corbières
F 146 B3
Villeneuve-St Georges
F 90 C2
Villeneuve-sur-Allier
F 104 C2
Villeneuve-sur-Lot
F 129 B3
Villeneuve-sur-Yonne
F 104 A2
Villeréal F 129 B3
Villerias E 142 C2
Villeromain F 103 B3
Villers-Bocage
*Calvados* F 88 A3
*Somme* F 90 B2
Villers-Bretonneux
F 90 B2
Villers-Carbonnel F 90 B2
Villers-Cotterêts F 90 B3
Villersexel F 105 B5
Villers-Farlay F 105 C4
Villers-le-Gambon B 79 B4
Villers-le-Lac F 106 B1
Villers-sur-Mer F 89 A3
Villerupt F 92 B1
Villerville F 89 A4
Villeseneux F 91 C4
Ville-sous-la-Ferté
F 105 A3
Ville-sur-Illon F 105 A5
Ville-sur-Tourbe F 91 B4
Villetrun F 103 B3
Villetta Barrea I 169 B3
Villeurbanne F 117 B4
Villeveyrac F 130 B2
Villevocance F 117 B4
Villiers-St Benoit F 104 B2
Villiers-St Georges
F 91 C3
Villingen D 106 A3
Villmar D 81 B4
Villoldo E 142 B2
Villon F 104 B3
Villoria E 150 B2
Vilnes N 46 A1
Vilnius LT 13 A6
Vils
A 108 B1
DK 58 B1
Vilsbiburg D 95 C4
Vilseck D 95 B3
Vilshofen D 96 C1
Vilshult S 63 B2
Vilusi MNE 139 C4
Vilvestre E 149 A3
Vilvoorde B 79 B4
Vimeiro P 154 B1
Vimercate I 120 B2
Vimianzo E 140 A1
Vimieiro P 154 C3
Vimioso P 149 A3
Vimmerby S 62 A3
Vimoutiers F 89 B4
Vimperk CZ 96 B1
Vimy F 78 B2
Vinadi CH 108 C1
Vinadio I 133 A3
Vinaixa E 147 C1
Vinarós E 153 B4
Vinäs S 50 B1
Vinay F 118 B2
Vinberg S 60 C2
Vinca F 146 B3
Vinča SRB 127 C2
Vinchiaturo I 170 B2
Vinci I 135 B3
Vindeby DK 65 A3
Vindelgransele S 195 E9
Vindeln S 200 B5
Vinderup DK 58 B1
Vindsvik N 52 A2
Vinets F 91 C4
Vineuil F 103 B3
Vinga RO 126 A3
Vingåker S 56 A1
Vingnes N 48 A2
Vingrau F 146 B3
Vingrom N 48 A2
Vinhais P 149 A3
Vinica
HR 124 A2
MK 182 B4
SK 112 A3
SLO 123 B4
Viniegra de Arriba
E 143 B4
Vinje
*Hordaland* N 46 B3
*Sør-Trøndelag* N 198 B6
*Telemark* N 53 A3
Vinkovci HR 125 B4
Vinliden S 200 B3
Vinninga S 55 B4
Vinnytsya UA 13 D8
Vinon F 103 B4
Vinon-sur-Verdon
F 132 B1
Vinslöv S 61 C3
Vinstra N 48 A1
Vintjärn S 50 B3
Vintrosa S 55 A5
Viñuela E 163 B3
Viñuela de Sayago
E 149 A4
Viñuelas E 151 B4
Vinuesa E 143 C4
Vinzelberg D 73 B4
Viöl D 64 B2
Viola I 133 A3
Violay F 117 B4
Vipava SLO 122 B2
Vipiteno I 108 C2
Vipperow D 74 A1
Vir
BIH 138 B3
HR 137 A4
Vira CH 120 A1
Vire F 88 B3
Vireda S 62 A2
Vireux F 91 A4
Virgen A 109 B3
Virgen de la Cabeza
E 157 B3
Virginia IRL 27 C3
Virieu F 118 B2
Virieu-le-Grand F 118 B2
Virje HR 124 A2
Virkkunen FIN 197 D10
Virklund DK 59 B2
Virovitica HR 124 B3
Virsbo S 50 C3
Virserum S 62 A3
Virtaniemi FIN 193 D12
Virton B 92 B1
Virtsu EST 8 C3
Viry F 118 A3
Vis HR 138 B2
Visbek D 71 B5
Visby
DK 64 A1
S 57 C4
Visé B 80 B1
Višegrad BIH 139 B5
Viserba I 136 A1
Viseu P 148 B2
Visiedo E 152 B2
Viskafors S 60 B2
Visland N 52 B2
Vislanda S 62 B2
Visnes N 52 A1
Višnja Gora SLO 123 B3
Višnjan HR 122 B2
Višnové CZ 97 C4
Visnums-Kil S 55 A5
Viso del Marqués
E 157 B4
Visoko
BIH 139 B4
SLO 123 A3
Visone I 119 C5
Visp CH 119 A4
Vissefjärda S 63 B3
Visselhövede D 72 B2
Vissenbjerg DK 59 C3
Visso I 136 C2
Vistabella del Maestrat
E 153 B3
Vistheden S 196 D3
Vita I 176 B1
Vitanje SLO 123 A4
Vitebsk = Vitsyebsk
BY 13 A9
Viterbo I 168 A2
Vitez BIH 139 A3
Vithkuq AL 182 C2
Vitigudino E 149 A3
Vitina
BIH 138 B3
GR 184 B3
Vitis A 97 C3
Vitkov CZ 98 B1
Vitoria-Gasteiz E 143 B4
Vitré F 101 A4
Vitrey-sur-Mance F 105 B4
Vitry-en-Artois F 78 B2
Vitry-le-François F 91 C4
Vitry-sur-Seine F 90 C2
Vitsand S 49 B4
Vitsyebsk = Vitebsk
BY 13 A9
Vittangi S 196 B4
Vittaryd S 60 C3
Vitteaux F 104 B3
Vittel F 105 A4
Vittinge S 51 C4
Vittória I 177 C3
Vittório Véneto I 122 B1
Vittsjö S 61 C3
Viù I 119 B4
Viul N 48 B2
Vivario F 180 A2
Viveiro E 140 A3
Vivel del Rio Martin
E 152 B3
Viver E 159 B3
Viverols F 117 B3
Viveros E 158 C1
Viviers F 131 A3
Vivonne F 115 B4
Vivy F 102 B1
Vize TR 186 A2
Vizille F 118 B2
Viziñada HR 122 B2
Viziru RO 17 C7
Vizovice CZ 98 B1
Vizvár H 124 A3
Vizzavona F 180 A2
Vizzini I 177 B3
Vlachiotis GR 184 C3
Vlachovice CZ 98 B1
Vlachovo SK 99 C4
Vláchovo Březi CZ 96 B1
Vladimirci SRB 127 C1
Vladimirovac SRB 127 B2
Vladislav CZ 97 B3
Vlagtwedde NL 71 A4
Vlajkovac SRB 127 B3
Vlasenica BIH 139 A4
Vlašim CZ 96 B2
Vlatkovići BIH 138 A3
Vledder NL 70 B3
Vlissingen NL 79 A3
Vlkolínec SK 99 B3
Vlorë AL 182 C1
Vlotho D 72 B1
Vnanje Gorice SLO 123 B3
Vobarno I 121 B3
Voćin HR 124 B3
Vöcklabruck A 109 A4
Vöcklamarkt A 109 B4
Vodanj SRB 127 C2
Voderady SK 98 C1
Vodice
*Istarska* HR 123 B3
*Šibenska* HR 137 B4
SLO 123 A3
Vodňany CZ 96 B2
Vodnjan HR 122 C2
Vodskov DK 58 A3
Voe GB 33 A5
Voerså DK 58 A3
Voghera I 120 C2
Vogogna I 119 A5
Vogošća BIH 139 B4
Vogué F 131 A3
Vohburg D 95 C3
Vohenstrauss D 95 B4
Vöhl D 81 A4
Vöhrenbach D 106 A3
Vöhringen D 94 C2
Void-Vacon F 92 C1
Voiron F 118 B2
Voise F 90 C1
Voisey F 105 B4
Voiteg RO 126 B3
Voiteur F 105 C4
Voitsberg A 110 B2
Vojakkala FIN 196 D7
Vojens DK 59 C2
Vojka SRB 127 C2
Vojlovica SRB 127 C2
Vojnić HR 123 B4
Vojnice SK 112 B2
Vojnik SLO 123 A4
Vojvoda Stepa
SRB 126 B2
Volada GR 188 D2
Volargne I 121 B3
Volary CZ 96 C1
Volče SLO 122 A2
Volda N 198 C3
Volendam NL 70 B2
Volga RUS 9 C11
Volimes GR 184 B1
Volissos GR 185 A6
Volkach D 94 B2
Völkermarkt A 110 C1
Volkhov RUS 9 C8
Völklingen D 92 B2
Volkmarsen D 81 A5
Voll N 198 C4
Vollenhove NL 70 B2
Vollore-Montagne
F 117 B3
Vollsjö S 61 D3
Volodymyr-Volyns'kyy
UA 13 C6
Volokolamsk RUS 9 D9
Volos GR 182 D4
Volosovo RUS 9 C6
Volovets UA 13 D5
Voltággio I 120 C1
Volta Mantovana I 121 B3
Volterra I 135 B3
Voltri I 133 A4
Volturara Áppula I 170 B3
Volturara Irpina I 170 C2
Volvic F 116 B3
Volx F 132 B1
Volyně CZ 96 B1
Vonitsa GR 182 E2
Vönöck H 111 B4
Vonsild DK 59 C2
Voorschoten NL 70 B1
Vopnafjörður IS 191 B11
Vorau A 110 B2
Vorbasse DK 59 C2
Vorchdorf A 109 B4
Vorden
D 71 B5
NL 71 B3
Vordernberg A 110 B1
Vordingborg DK 65 A4
Vorë AL 182 B1
Voreppe F 118 B2
Vorey F 117 B3
Vorgod DK 59 B1
Vormsund N 48 B3
Võru EST 8 D5
Voskopojë AL 182 C2
Voss N 46 B3
Votice CZ 96 B2
Voué F 91 C4
Vouillé F 115 B4
Voulx F 90 C2
Voussac F 116 A3
Vouvray F 102 B2
Vouvry CH 119 A3
Vouzela P 148 B1
Vouziers F 91 B4
Voves F 103 A3
Voxna S 50 A2
Voy GB 33 B3
Voynitsa RUS 3 D12
Voznesenye RUS 9 B9
Vrå
DK 58 A2
S 60 C3
Vráble SK 98 C2
Vračenovići MNE 139 C4
Vračev Gaj SRB 127 C3
Vraćevsnica SRB 127 C2
Vrådal N 53 A4
Vrakneika GR 184 A2
Vrana HR 123 C3
Vranduk BIH 139 A3
Vrångö S 60 B1
Vrani RO 127 B3
Vranić SRB 127 C2
Vraniči BIH 139 B4
Vranja HR 123 B3
Vranjak BIH 125 C4
Vranje SRB 16 D4
Vranovice CZ 97 C4
Vranov nad Dyje CZ 97 C3
Vransko SLO 123 A3
Vrapčići BIH 139 B3
Vratimov CZ 98 B2
Vratsa BG 17 D5
Vrbanja HR 125 C4
Vrbanjci BIH 124 C3
Vrbas SRB 126 B1
Vrbaška BIH 124 B3
Vrbnik
*Primorsko-Goranska*
HR 123 B3
*Zadarsko-Kninska*
HR 138 A2
Vrbno pod Pradědem
CZ 85 B5
Vrboska HR 138 B2
Vrbov SK 99 B4
Vrbovce SK 98 C1
Vrbové SK 98 C1
Vrbovec HR 124 B2
Vrbovski SRB 127 C2
Vrbovsko HR 123 B4
Vrchlabí CZ 84 B3
Vrčin SRB 127 C2
Vrdy CZ 97 B3
Vrebac HR 137 A4
Vreden D 71 B3
Vreoci SRB 127 C2
Vretstorp S 55 A5
Vrginmost HR 124 B1
Vrgorac HR 138 B3
Vrhnika SLO 123 B3
Vrhovine HR 123 C4
Vrhpolie SRB 127 C1
Vriezenveen NL 71 B3
Vrigne-aux-Bois F 91 B4
Vrigstad S 62 A2
Vrlika HR 138 B2
Vrnograč BIH 124 B1
Vron F 78 B1
Vroomshoop NL 71 B3
Vroutek CZ 83 B5
Vrpolje HR 125 B4
Vršac SRB 126 B3
Vrsar HR 122 B2
Vrsi HR 137 A4
Vrtoče BIH 124 C2
Vrútky SK 98 B2
Všeruby CZ 95 B4
Všestary CZ 85 B3
Vsetín CZ 98 B1
Vučkovica SRB 127 D2
Vught NL 79 A5
Vuillafans F 105 B5
Vukovar HR 125 B5
Vuku N 199 B8
Vulcan RO 17 C5
Vulcănești MD 17 C8
Vuoggatjålme S 195 D7
Vuojärvi FIN 197 B9
Vuolijoki FIN 3 D10
Vuollerim S 196 C3
Vuotso FIN 197 A10
Vuzenica SLO 110 C2
Vyartsilya RUS 9 A7
Vyborg RUS 9 B6
Výčapy CZ 97 B3
Výčapy-Opatovce
SK 98 C2
Východna SK 99 B3
Vydrany SK 111 A4
Vyerkhnyadzvinsk
BY 13 A7
Vyhne SK 98 C2
Vy-lès Lure F 105 B5
Vylkove UA 17 C8
Vynohradiv UA 17 A5
Vyshniy Volochek
RUS 9 D9
Vyškov CZ 97 B5
Vysokánad Kysucou
SK 98 B2
Vysoké Mýto CZ 97 B4
Vysokovsk RUS 9 D10
Vyšší Brod CZ 96 C2
Vytegra RUS 9 B10


## W


Waabs D 64 B2
Waalwijk NL 79 A5
Waarschoot B 79 A3
Wabern D 81 A5
Wąbrzeźno PL 69 B3
Wąchock PL 87 A5
Wachow D 74 B1
Wachów PL 86 B2
Wächtersbach D 81 B5
Wackersdorf D 95 B4
Waddington GB 40 B3
Wadebridge GB 42 B2
Wadelsdorf D 84 A2
Wädenswil CH 107 B3
Wadern D 92 B2
Wadersloh D 81 A4
Wadlew PL 86 A3
Wadowice PL 99 B3
Wagenfeld D 72 B1
Wageningen NL 70 C2
Waghäusel D 93 B4
Waging D 109 B3
Wagrain A 109 B4
Wagrowiec PL 76 B2
Wahlsdorf D 74 C2
Wahlstedt D 64 C3
Wahrenholz D 73 B3
Waiblingen D 94 C1
Waidhaus D 95 B4
Waidhofen an der Thaya
A 97 C3
Waidhofen an der Ybbs
A 110 B1
Waimes B 80 B2
Wainfleet All Saints
GB 41 B4
Waizenkirchen A 96 C1
Wakefield GB 40 B2
Wałbrzych PL 85 B4
Walchensee D 108 B2
Walchsee A 109 B3
Wałcz PL 75 A5
Wald CH 107 B3
Waldaschaff D 94 B1
Waldbach A 110 B2
Waldböckelheim D 93 B3
Waldbröl D 81 B3
Waldeck D 81 A5
Waldenburg D 83 B4
Waldfischbach-
Burgalben D 93 B3
Waldheim D 83 A5
Waldkappel D 82 A1
Waldkirch D 106 A2
Waldkirchen D 96 C1
Waldkirchen am Wesen
A 96 C1
Waldkraiburg D 109 A3
Wald-Michelbach D 93 B4
Waldmohr D 93 B3
Waldmünchen D 95 B4
Waldring A 109 B3
Waldsassen D 95 A4
Waldshut D 106 B3
Waldstatt CH 107 B4
Waldwisse F 92 B2
Walenstadt CH 107 B4
Walentynów PL 87 A5
Walichnowy PL 86 A2
Walincourt F 90 A3
Walkenried D 82 A2
Walkeringham GB 40 B3
Wallasey GB 38 A3
Walldürn D 94 B1
Wallenfells D 82 B3
Wallenhorst D 71 B5
Wallers F 78 B3
Wallersdorf D 95 C4
Wallerstein D 94 C2
Wallingford GB 44 B2

Wallitz D . . . . . . . . 74 A1
Walls GB . . . . . . . 33 A5
Wallsbüll D . . . . . . 64 B2
Walmer GB. . . . . . . 45 B5
Walsall GB . . . . . . . 40 C2
Walshoutem B . . . . . 79 B5
Walsrode D . . . . . . 72 B2
Waltenhofen D . . . 107 B5
Waltershausen D. . 82 B2
Waltham Abbey GB . 45 B4
Waltham on the Wolds
 GB . . . . . . . . . . . . 40 C3
Walton-on-Thames
 GB . . . . . . . . . . . . 44 B3
Walton-on-the-Naze
 GB . . . . . . . . . . . . 45 B5
Wamba E . . . . . . . 142 C2
Wanderup D. . . . . . 64 B2
Wandlitz D . . . . . . . 74 B2
Wanfried D. . . . . . . 82 A2
Wangen im Allgäu
 D . . . . . . . . . . . . 107 B4
Wangerooge D . . 71 A4
Wangersen D. . . . . 72 A2
Wängi CH. . . . . . . 107 B3
Wanna D . . . . . . . . 64 C1
Wansford GB. . . . . 40 C3
Wantage GB. . . . . . 44 B2
Wanzleben D . . . . . 73 B4
Waplewo PL. . . . . . 77 A5
Wapnica PL. . . . . . 75 A4
Wapno PL. . . . . . . 76 B2
Warburg D . . . . . . 81 A5
Wardenburg D . . . . 71 A5
Ware GB . . . . . . . . 44 B3
Waregem B . . . . . . 79 B3
Wareham GB . . . . . 43 B4
Waremme B . . . . . . 79 B5
Waren D. . . . . . . . 74 A1
Warendorf D . . . . . 71 C4
Warga NL. . . . . . . . 70 A2
Warin D . . . . . . . . 65 C4
Wark GB. . . . . . . . 37 A4
Warka PL. . . . . . . 87 A5
Warkworth GB. . . . 37 A5
Warlubie PL. . . . . . 69 B3
Warminster GB . . . 43 A4
Warnemünde D . . . 65 B5
Warnow D . . . . . . 65 C4
Warnsveld NL . . . . 70 B3
Warrenpoint IRL . . 27 B4
Warrington GB . . . 38 A4
Warsaw = Warszawa
 PL. . . . . . . . . . . 77 B6
Warsingsfehn D . . 71 A4
Warsow D. . . . . . 73 A4
Warstein D. . . . . . 81 A4
Warszawa = Warsaw
 PL. . . . . . . . . . . 77 B6
Warta PL. . . . . . . 86 A2
Wartberg A. . . . . 110 B1
Warth A. . . . . . . . 107 B5
Warwick GB . . . . . 44 A2
Warza D. . . . . . . . 82 B2
Wasbister GB . . . . 33 B3
Washington GB. . . 37 B5
Wąsosz PL. . . . . . 85 A4
Wasselonne F . . . 93 C3
Wassen CH . . . . 107 C3
Wassenaar NL. . . . 70 B1
Wasserauen CH . . 107 B4
Wasserburg D . . . 108 A3
Wassertrüdingen D. 94 B2
Wassy F. . . . . . . . 91 C4
Wasungen D . . . . . 82 B2
Watchet GB . . . . . 43 A3
Waterford IRL . . . . 30 B1
Watergrasshill IRL. 29 B3
Waterloo B . . . . . . 79 B4
Waterville IRL . . . . 29 C1
Watford GB . . . . . . 44 B3
Wathlingen D. . . . . 72 B3
Watten
 F. . . . . . . . . . . . . 78 B2
 GB. . . . . . . . . . . . 32 C3
Wattens A. . . . . . 108 B2
Watton GB . . . . . . 41 C4
Wattwil CH . . . . . 107 B4
Waunfawr GB . . . . 38 A2
Wavignies F. . . . . . 90 B2
Wavre B . . . . . . . . 79 B4
Wearhead GB . . . . 37 B4
Węchadłow PL. . . 87 B4
Wedel D . . . . . . . . 72 A2
Wedemark D . . . . . 72 B2
Weedon Bec GB . . 44 A2
Weener D . . . . . . 71 A4
Weert NL. . . . . . . . 80 A1
Weesp NL. . . . . . . 70 B2
Weeze D. . . . . . . . 80 A2
Weferlingen D . . . . 73 B4
Wegeleben D . . . . 82 A3
Weggis CH. . . . . 106 B3
Węgierska-Górka
 PL. . . . . . . . . . . 99 B3
Węgliniec PL. . . . . 84 A3
Węgorzyno PL . . . 75 A4
Węgrzynice PL. . . 75 B4
Wegscheid D . . . . 96 C1
Wehdel D . . . . . . 72 A1
Wehr D. . . . . . . . 106 B2
Weibersbrunn D . . 94 B1
Weichering D. . . . . 95 C3
Weida D . . . . . . . 83 B4
Weiden D . . . . . . 95 B4
Weidenberg D . . . 95 B3
Weidenhain D . . . . 83 A4
Weidenstetten D . . 94 C1

Weierbach D . . . . . 93 B3
Weikersheim D . . . 94 B1
Weil D. . . . . . . . . 108 A1
Weil am Rhein D . . 106 B2
Weilburg D. . . . . . 81 B4
Weil der Stadt D . . 93 C4
Weilerswist D . . . . 80 B2
Weilheim
 Baden-Württemberg
 D. . . . . . . . . . . . .94 C1
 Bayern D . . . . . 108 B2
Weilmünster D. . . . 81 B4
Weiltensfeld A . . . 110 C1
Weimar D . . . . . . 82 B3
Weinberg D . . . . . . 94 B2
Weinfelden CH . . . 107 B4
Weingarten
 Baden-Württemberg
 D. . . . . . . . . . . . .93 B4
 Baden-Württemberg
 D. . . . . . . . . . . 107 B4
Weinheim D . . . . . 93 B4
Weinstadt D. . . . . . 94 C1
Weismain D . . . . . 82 B3
Weissbriach A . . . 109 C4
Weissenbach A . . . 108 B1
Weissenberg D . . . 84 A2
Weissenbrunn D . . 82 B3
Weissenburg D . . . 94 B2
Weissenfels D . . . . 83 A3
Weissenhorn D . . . 94 C2
Weissenkirchen A . 97 C3
Weissensee D . . . . 82 A3
Weissenstadt D. . . 83 B3
Weisskirchen im
 Steiermark A . . . .110 B1
Weisstannen CH . . 107 C4
Weisswasser D . . . 84 A2
Weitendorf D . . . . 65 C5
Weitersfeld A . . . . 97 C3
Weitersfelden A . . 96 C2
Weitnau D . . . . . 107 B5
Wéitra A. . . . . . . . 96 C2
Weiz A. . . . . . . . .110 B2
Wejherowo PL. . . . 68 A3
Welkenraedt B . . . 80 B1
Wellaune D . . . . . 83 A4
Wellin B . . . . . . . 91 A5
Wellingborough GB 44 A3
Wellington
 Somerset GB. . . .43 B3
 Telford & Wrekin
 GB . . . . . . . . . . 38 B4
Wellingtonbridge
 IRL . . . . . . . . . . 30 B2
Wells GB . . . . . . . 43 A4
Wells-next-the-Sea
 GB . . . . . . . . . . . 41 C4
Wels A . . . . . . . . 109 A5
Welschenrohr CH . 106 B2
Welshpool GB . . . . 38 B3
Welver D . . . . . . . 81 A3
Welwyn Garden City
 GB . . . . . . . . . . 44 B3
Welzheim D . . . . . 94 C1
Welzow D. . . . . . . 84 A2
Wem GB . . . . . . . . 38 B4
Wembury GB. . . . . 42 B2
Wemding D . . . . . 94 C2
Wenden D . . . . . . 81 B3
Wendisch Rietz D . 74 B3
Wendlingen D . . . . 94 C1
Weng A . . . . . . . 109 A4
Weng bei Admont
 A. . . . . . . . . . . .110 B1
Wengen CH . . . . 106 C2
Wenigzell A . . . . .110 B2
Wennigsen D . . . . 72 B2
Wenns A. . . . . . . 108 B1
Wenzenbach D . . . 95 B4
Weppersdorf A. . . .111 B3
Werben D. . . . . . . 73 B4
Werbig D . . . . . . . 74 C2
Werdau D. . . . . . . 83 B4
Werder D. . . . . . . 74 B1
Werdohl D . . . . . . 81 A3
Werfen A . . . . . . . 109 B4
Werkendam NL. . . . 79 A4
Werl D . . . . . . . . . 81 A3
Werlte D . . . . . . . 71 B4
Wermelskirchen D . 80 A3
Wermsdorf D . . . . 83 A4
Werne D . . . . . . . . 81 A3
Werneck D . . . . . . 94 B2
Werneuchen D. . . . 74 B2
Wernigerode D. . . . 82 A2
Wertach D . . . . . . 108 B1
Wertheim D . . . . . 94 B1
Wertingen D . . . . . 94 C2
Weseke D . . . . . . . 80 A2
Wesel D . . . . . . . . 80 A2
Wesenberg D . . . . 74 A1
Wesendorf D . . . . . 73 B3
Wesołowo PL. . . . . 77 A5
Wesselburen D . . . 64 B1
Wesseling D . . . . . 80 B2
West Bridgford GB . 40 C2
West Bromwich GB. 40 C2
Westbury
 Shropshire GB . . . 38 B4
 Wiltshire GB. . . . 43 A4
Westbury-on-Severn
 GB . . . . . . . . . . . 39 C4
Westendorf A. . . . 108 B3
Westensee D . . . . . 64 B2
Westerbork NL . . . 71 B3
Westerburg D . . . . 81 B3

Westerhaar NL. . . . 71 B3
Westerholt D . . . . . 71 A4
Westerkappeln D. . . 71 B4
Westerland D. . . . . 64 B1
Westerlo B. . . . . . . 79 A4
Westerstede D. . . . 71 A4
West Haddon GB. . . 44 A2
Westheim D . . . . . 94 B2
Westhill GB . . . . . . 33 D4
Westkapelle
 B. . . . . . . . . . . . .78 A3
 NL . . . . . . . . . . . .79 A3
West Kilbride GB . . 34 C3
West Linton GB . . . 35 C4
West Lulworth GB . 43 B4
West Mersea GB . . 45 B4
Westminster GB . . 44 B3
Weston GB. . . . . . 40 C1
Weston-super-Mare
 GB . . . . . . . . . . . 43 A4
Westport IRL . . . . 28 A2
Westruther GB . . . 35 C5
West-Terschelling
 NL. . . . . . . . . . . 70 A2
Westward Ho! GB . . 42 A2
West Woodburn GB 37 A4
Wetheral GB . . . . . 37 B4
Wetherby GB . . . . . 40 B2
Wetter
 Hessen D. . . . . . .81 B4
 Nordrhein-Westfalen
 D. . . . . . . . . . . . .80 A3
Wetteren B. . . . . . . 79 A3
Wettin D . . . . . . . . 83 A3
Wettringen D . . . . . 71 B4
Wetzikon CH . . . . 107 B3
Wetzlar D . . . . . . . 81 B4
Wewelsfleth D . . . . 64 C2
Wexford IRL. . . . . . 30 B2
Weybridge GB . . . . 44 B3
Weyerbusch D. . . . 81 B3
Weyer Markt A . . . .110 B1
Weyersheim F . . . . 93 C3
Weyhe D. . . . . . . . 72 B1
Weyhill GB. . . . . . . 44 B2
Weymouth GB . . . . 43 B4
Weyregg A . . . . . 109 B4
Wezep NL . . . . . . . 70 B2
Węzyska PL. . . . . . 75 B3
Whalton GB . . . . . . 37 A5
Whauphill GB . . . . 36 B2
Wheatley GB . . . . . 44 B2
Whickham GB . . . . 37 B5
Whipsnade GB . . . . 44 B3
Whitburn GB . . . . . 35 C4
Whitby GB . . . . . . . 37 B6
Whitchurch
 Hampshire GB. . . .44 B2
 Herefordshire GB. . 39 C4
 Shropshire GB . . . 38 B4
White Bridge GB . . 32 D2
Whitegate IRL . . . . 29 C3
Whitehaven GB. . . . 36 B3
Whitehead GB . . . . 27 B5
Whithorn GB. . . . . . 36 B2
Whitley Bay GB . . . 37 A5
Whitstable GB . . . . 45 B5
Whittington GB . . . 38 B4
Whittlesey GB . . . . 41 C3
Wiązów PL. . . . . . . 85 B5
Wick GB. . . . . . . . . 32 C3
Wickede D . . . . . . . 81 A3
Wickford GB . . . . . 45 B4
Wickham GB . . . . . 44 C2
Wickham Market GB 45 A5
Wicklow IRL. . . . . . 30 B2
Wicko PL. . . . . . . . 68 A2
Widawa PL. . . . . . . 86 A2
Widdrington GB . . . 37 A5
Widecombe in the Moor
 GB . . . . . . . . . . . 42 B3
Widemouth GB . . . . 42 B2
Widnes GB. . . . . . . 38 A4
Widuchowo PL. . . . 74 A3
Więcbork PL. . . . . . 76 A2
Wiefelstede D . . . . 71 A5
Wiehe D. . . . . . . . 82 A3
Wiehl D . . . . . . . . 81 B3
Wiek D . . . . . . . . . 66 B2
Większyce PL. . . . . 86 B1
Wielbark PL. . . . . . 77 A5
Wiele PL. . . . . . . . 68 B2
Wieleń PL . . . . . . . 75 B5
Wielgie
 Kujawsko-Pomorskie
 PL. . . . . . . . . . . .77 B4
 Łódzkie PL. . . . . .86 A2
 Mazowieckie PL. . .87 A5
Wielgomłyny PL . . . 87 A3
Wielichowo PL. . . . 75 B5
Wieliczka PL. . . . . . 99 B4
Wielka Łąka PL . . . 76 A3
Wielowies PL. . . . . 86 B2
Wieluń PL. . . . . . . . 86 A2
Wien = Vienna A . . .111 A3
Wiener Neustadt A .111 B3
Wiepke D. . . . . . . . 73 B4
Wierden NL. . . . . . . 71 B3
Wieren D . . . . . . . 73 B3
Wieruszów PL. . . . . 86 A2
Wierzbica
 Mazowieckie PL. . .77 B6
 Mazowieckie PL. . .87 A5
Wierzbie PL. . . . . . 86 A2
Wierzbięcin PL. . . . 75 A4
Wierzchowo PL. . . . 75 A5
Wierzchucino PL. . . 68 A3
Wierzchy PL. . . . . . 86 A2
Wies A . . . . . . . . .110 C2

Wiesau D . . . . . . . 95 B4
Wiesbaden D . . . . . 93 A4
Wieselburg A . . . . .110 A2
Wiesen CH . . . . . 107 C4
Wiesenburg D . . . . 73 B5
Wiesenfelden D . . . 95 B4
Wiesensteig D. . . . 94 C1
Wiesentheid D . . . . 94 B2
Wiesloch D . . . . . . 93 B4
Wiesmath A . . . . . .111 B3
Wiesmoor D . . . . . 71 A4
Wietmarschen D . . 71 B4
Wietze D . . . . . . . 72 B2
Wigan GB. . . . . . . 38 A4
Wiggen CH . . . . . 106 C2
Wigston GB. . . . . . 40 C2
Wigton GB . . . . . . 36 B3
Wigtown GB. . . . . . 36 B2
Wijchen NL . . . . . . 80 A1
Wijhe NL. . . . . . . . 70 B3
Wijk bij Duurstede
 NL. . . . . . . . . . . 70 C2
Wil CH . . . . . . . . 107 B4
Wilamowice PL. . . . 99 B3
Wilczęta PL. . . . . . 69 A4
Wilczkowice PL. . . . 77 B4
Wilczna PL. . . . . . . 76 B3
Wilczyn PL. . . . . . . 76 B3
Wildalpen A . . . . . .110 B1
Wildbad D . . . . . . . 93 C4
Wildberg
 Baden-Württemberg
 D. . . . . . . . . . . . .93 C4
 Brandenburg D . . .74 B1
Wildegg CH . . . . . 106 B3
Wildendürnbach A . 97 C4
Wildeshausen D . . 72 B1
Wildon A . . . . . . .110 C2
Wilfersdorf A . . . . . 97 C4
Wilhelmsburg
 A. . . . . . . . . . . .110 A2
 D. . . . . . . . . . . . .74 A2
Wilhelmsdorf D . . 107 B4
Wilhelmshaven D . . 71 A5
Wilków PL. . . . . . . 77 B5
Willebadessen D . . 81 A5
Willebroek B . . . . . 79 A4
Willgottheim F . . . . 93 C3
Willich D . . . . . . . 80 A2
Willingen D . . . . . . 81 A4
Willington GB . . . . 37 B5
Willisau CH . . . . . 106 B3
Wilmslow GB. . . . . 40 B1
Wilsdruff D . . . . . . 83 A5
Wilster D . . . . . . . 64 C2
Wilsum D . . . . . . . 71 B3
Wilton GB . . . . . . . 44 B2
Wiltz L . . . . . . . . . 92 B1
Wimborne Minster
 GB . . . . . . . . . . . 43 B5
Wimereux F . . . . . . 78 B1
Wimmenau F . . . . . 93 C3
Wimmis CH . . . . . 106 C2
Wincanton GB . . . . 43 A4
Winchcombe GB. . . 44 B2
Winchelsea GB . . . 45 C4
Winchester GB . . . . 44 B2
Windermere GB. . . . 36 B4
Windischeschenbach
 D . . . . . . . . . . . . 95 B4
Windischgarsten A .110 B1
Windorf D. . . . . . . 96 C1
Windsbach D . . . . . 94 B2
Windsor GB. . . . . . 44 B3
Wingene B. . . . . . . 78 A3
Wingham GB . . . . . 45 B5
Winkleigh GB . . . . 42 B3
Winklern A . . . . . . 109 C3
Winnenden D . . . . . 94 C1
Winnica PL. . . . . . . 77 B5
Winnigstedt D . . . . 73 B3
Winnweiler D. . . . . 93 B3
Winschoten NL. . . . 71 A4
Winsen
 Niedersachsen D. . 72 A3
 Niedersachsen D. . 72 B2
Winsford GB. . . . . 38 A4
Wińsko PL. . . . . . . 85 A4
Winslow GB. . . . . . 44 B3
Winsum
 Friesland NL . . . . 70 A2
 Groningen NL . . . .71 A3
Winterberg D . . . . . 81 A4
Winterfeld D . . . . . 73 B4
Winterswijk NL . . . 71 C3
Winterthur CH . . . 107 B3
Wintzenheim F . . . 106 A2
Winzer D . . . . . . . 95 C5
Wipperdorf D . . . . 82 A2
Wipperfürth D . . . . 80 A3
Wirksworth GB . . . 40 B2
Wisbech GB. . . . . . 41 C4
Wischhafen D . . . . 64 C2
Wishaw GB . . . . . . 35 C4
Wisła PL. . . . . . . . 98 B2
Wisła Wielka PL. . . 98 B2
Wiślica PL. . . . . . . 87 B4
Wismar D. . . . . . . 65 C4
Wisniewo PL. . . . . 77 A5
Wiśniowa PL. . . . . . 99 B4
Wissant F. . . . . . . 78 B1
Wissembourg F . . . 93 B3
Wissen D . . . . . . . 81 B3
Witanowice PL. . . . 99 B3
Witham GB . . . . . . 45 B4
Withern GB . . . . . . 41 B4
Withernsea GB . . . 41 B4

Witkowo PL . . . . . . 76 B2
Witmarsum NL. . . . 70 A2
Witney GB . . . . . . . 44 B2
Witnica PL. . . . . . . 75 B3
Witonia PL. . . . . . . 77 B4
Wittdün D. . . . . . . . 64 B1
Wittelsheim F . . . . 106 B2
Witten D . . . . . . . . 80 A3
Wittenberge D . . . . 73 A4
Wittenburg D . . . . . 73 A4
Wittenheim F . . . . 106 B2
Wittichenau D . . . . 84 A2
Wittighausen D . . . 94 B1
Wittingen D . . . . . . 73 B3
Wittislingen D . . . . 94 C2
Wittlich D. . . . . . . . 92 B2
Wittmannsdorf A . .110 C2
Wittmund D . . . . . . 71 A4
Wittorf D . . . . . . . . 72 A2
Wittstock D . . . . . . 73 A5
Witzenhausen D . . . 82 A1
Wiveliscombe GB . . 43 A3
Wivenhoe GB. . . . . 45 B4
Władysławowo PL. . 69 A3
Wleń PL . . . . . . . . 84 A3
Włocławek PL . . . . 77 B4
Włodawa PL. . . . . . 13 C5
Włodzimierzów PL . 87 A3
Włosień PL. . . . . . . 84 A3
Włostow PL. . . . . . . 87 B5
Włoszakowice PL . . 75 C5
Włoszczowa PL. . . . 87 B3
Wöbbelin D . . . . . . 73 A4
Woburn GB. . . . . . 44 B3
Wodzisław PL . . . . 87 B4
Wodzisław Śląski
 PL. . . . . . . . . . . 98 B2
Woerden NL. . . . . . 70 B1
Woerth F . . . . . . . 93 C3
Wohlen CH. . . . . . 106 B3
Woippy F . . . . . . . 92 B2
Wojcieszów PL. . . . 85 B3
Wojkowice Kościelne
 PL. . . . . . . . . . . 86 B3
Wojnicz PL. . . . . . . 99 B4
Woking GB. . . . . . . 44 B3
Wokingham GB . . . 44 B3
Wola Jachowa PL. . 87 B4
Wola Niechcicka PL 86 A3
Wolbórz PL . . . . . . 87 A3
Wolbrom PL. . . . . . 87 B3
Wołczyn PL. . . . . . 86 A2
Woldegk D . . . . . . 74 A2
Wolfach D . . . . . . . 93 C4
Wolfegg D . . . . . 107 B4
Wolfen D . . . . . . . 83 A4
Wolfenbüttel D . . . 73 B3
Wolfersheim D. . . . 81 B4
Wolfhagen D . . . . . 81 A5
Wolfratshausen D . 108 B2
Wolfsberg A . . . . . 110 C1
Wolfsburg D . . . . . 73 B3
Wolf's Castle GB . . 39 C2
Wolfshagen D . . . . 74 A2
Wolfstein D . . . . . . 93 B3
Wolfurt A . . . . . . 107 B4
Wolgast D . . . . . . 66 B2
Wolhusen CH . . . 106 B3
Wolin PL. . . . . . . . 67 C3
Wolka PL. . . . . . . . 87 A4
Wolkenstein D . . . . 83 B5
Wolkersdorf A . . . . 97 C4
Wöllersdorf A. . . . .111 B3
Wollin D . . . . . . . . 73 B5
Wöllstadt D . . . . . . 81 B4
Wolmirstedt D . . . . 73 B4
Wolnzach D . . . . . . 95 C3
Wołów PL. . . . . . . . 85 A4
Wolsztyn PL. . . . . . 75 B5
Wolvega NL . . . . . . 70 B2
Wolverhampton GB 40 C1
Wolverton GB . . . . 44 A3
Wombwell GB . . . . 40 B2
Woodbridge GB. . . 45 A5
Woodhall Spa GB . 41 B3
Woodstock GB . . . 44 B2
Wookey Hole GB. . 43 A4
Wool GB. . . . . . . . 43 B4
Woolacombe GB . . 42 A2
Wooler GB . . . . . . 37 A4
Woolwich GB. . . . . 45 B4
Wooperton GB . . . 37 A5
Worb CH . . . . . . . 106 C2
Worbis D . . . . . . . 82 A2
Worcester GB . . . . 39 B4
Wördern A . . . . . . 97 C4
Wörgl A . . . . . . . . 108 B3
Workington GB . . . 36 B3
Worksop GB . . . . . 40 B2
Workum NL . . . . . . 70 B2
Wörlitz D . . . . . . . 83 A4
Wormer NL. . . . . . 70 B1
Wormhout F. . . . . . 78 B2
Wormit GB. . . . . . . 35 B5
Worms D . . . . . . . 93 B4
Worpswede D . . . . 72 A1
Wörrstadt D . . . . . 93 B4
Wörschach A . . . . 110 B1
Worsley GB . . . . . 38 A4
Wörth
 Bayern D . . . . . . 93 B5
 Bayern D . . . . . . 95 B4
 Bayern D . . . . . . 95 C4
 Rheinland-Pfalz D . 93 B4
Worthing GB . . . . . 44 C3
Woudsend NL . . . . 70 B2
Woumen B. . . . . . . 78 A2

Woźniki PL. . . . . . . . 86 B3
Wragby GB . . . . . . . 41 B3
Wrangle GB . . . . . . 41 B4
Wręczyca Wlk. PL. . . 86 B2
Wredenhagen D . . . 73 A5
Wremen D . . . . . . . 72 A1
Wrentham GB . . . . . 45 A5
Wrexham GB . . . . . 38 A3
Wriedel D . . . . . . . . 72 A3
Wriezen D . . . . . . . 74 B3
Wrist D. . . . . . . . . . 64 C2
Wróblewo
 Mazowieckie PL. . .77 B5
 Wielkopolskie PL. . 75 B5
Wrocki PL . . . . . . . . 69 B4
Wrocław PL . . . . . . 85 A5
Wronki PL. . . . . . . . 75 B5
Wroxham GB. . . . . . 41 C5
Września PL . . . . . . 76 B2
Wrzosowo PL. . . . . 67 B4
Wschowa PL. . . . . . 85 A4
Wulfen D . . . . . . . . 80 A3
Wülfen D . . . . . . . . 83 A3
Wulkau D . . . . . . . 73 B5
Wünnenberg D . . . . 81 A4
Wünsdorf D . . . . . . 74 B2
Wunsiedel D . . . . . 95 A4
Wunstorf D . . . . . . 72 B2
Wuppertal D. . . . . . 80 A3
Wurmannsquick D . 95 C4
Würselen D . . . . . . 80 B2
Wurzbach D . . . . . 82 B3
Würzburg D . . . . . . 94 B1
Wurzen D. . . . . . . . 83 A4
Wust D . . . . . . . . . 74 B1
Wusterhausen D . . 73 B5
Wusterwitz D . . . . . 73 B5
Wustrau-Altfriesack
 D . . . . . . . . . . . . 74 B1
Wustrow D . . . . . . 66 B1
Wuustwezel B . . . . 79 A4
Wye GB . . . . . . . . . 45 B4
Wygiełdów PL. . . . . 87 A5
Wyk D. . . . . . . . . . 64 B1
Wykroty PL . . . . . . 84 A3
Wylye GB . . . . . . . 43 A5
Wymiarki PL . . . . . 84 A3
Wymondham GB . . 41 C5
Wyrzysk PL . . . . . . 76 A2
Wyśmierzyce PL. . . 87 A4
Wysoka
 Dolnośląskie PL. . . 85 A3
 Wielkopolskie PL. . 76 A2
Wyszanów PL . . . . 86 A2
Wyszogród PL. . . . . 77 B5

**X**

Xanten D . . . . . . . . 80 A2
Xanthi GR . . . . . . 183 B6
Xarrë AL . . . . . . . 182 D2
Xàtiva E. . . . . . . . 159 C3
Xeraco E . . . . . . . 159 B3
Xert E . . . . . . . . . 153 B4
Xerta E . . . . . . . . 153 B4
Xertigny F . . . . . . 105 A5
Xilagani GR . . . . . 183 C7
Xilokastro GR . . . 184 A3
Xinzo de Limia E . . 140 B3
Xixón = Gijón E . . . 142 A1
Xove E . . . . . . . . 140 A3
Xubia E . . . . . . . . 140 A2
Xunqueira de Ambia
 E. . . . . . . . . . . . 140 B3
Xunqueira de
 Espadañedo E . . 140 B3
Xylophagou CY . . . 181 B2

**Y**

Yablanitsa BG . . . . 17 D6
Yağcılar TR . . . . . 186 C3
Yahyalı TR . . . . . . 23 B8
Yakoruda BG . . . . 183 A5
Yalova TR. . . . . . . 187 B4
Yalvaç TR. . . . . . . 189 A6
Yambol BG. . . . . . . 17 D7
Yampil UA . . . . . . 13 D8
Yaniskoski RUS . 193 D12
Yantarnyy RUS . 69 A4
Yarbasan TR . . . . 186 D3
Yarcombe GB . . . . 43 B3
Yaremcha UA. . . . . 13 D6
Yarm GB. . . . . . . . 37 B5
Yarmouth GB. . . . . 44 C2
Yarrow GB . . . . . . 35 C4
Yasinya UA . . . . . . 17 A6
Yatağan TR . . . . . 188 B3
Yate GB . . . . . . . . 43 A4
Yatton GB . . . . . . . 43 A4
Yaxley GB . . . . . . 41 C3
Yazıca TR. . . . . . . 187 B6
Yazıköy TR. . . . . . 188 C2
Ybbs A . . . . . . . . .110 A2
Ybbsitz A. . . . . . . .110 B1
Ydby DK. . . . . . . . 58 B1
Yddal N . . . . . . . . 46 B2
Ydes F . . . . . . . . .116 B2
Yealmpton GB. . . . 42 B3
Yebra de Basa E . . 145 B3
Yecla E. . . . . . . . . 159 C2
Yecla de Yeltes E . . 149 B3

Yelsk BY ... 13 C8
Yelverton GB ... 42 B2
Yena RUS ... 197 B14
Yenice
  Ankara TR ... 23 B7
  Aydın TR ... 188 B3
  Çanakkale TR ... 186 C2
  Edirne TR ... 183 C8
Yenifoça TR ... 186 D1
Yenihisar TR ... 188 B2
Yeniköy TR ... 186 D4
Yeniköy Plaji TR ... 186 B3
Yenipazar TR ... 188 B3
Yenişarbademli TR ... 189 B6
Yenişehir TR ... 187 B4
Yenne F ... 118 B2
Yeovil GB ... 43 B4
Yepes E ... 151 C4
Yerköy TR ... 23 B8
Yerólakkos CY ... 181 A2
Yeroskipos CY ... 181 B1
Yerseke NL ... 79 A4
Yerville F ... 89 A4
Yeşildağ TR ... 189 B6
Yeşilhisar TR ... 23 B8
Yeşilköy TR ... 186 B3
Yeşilova TR ... 189 B4
Yeşilyurt TR ... 188 A3
Yeste E ... 164 A2
Yezerishche BY ... 9 E6
Y Felinheli GB ... 38 A2
Ygos-St Saturnin F ... 128 C2
Ygrande F ... 104 C1
Yialousa CY ... 181 A3
Yığılca TR ... 187 B6
Yli-Ii FIN ... 197 D8
Yli-Kärppä FIN ... 197 D8
Yli-Muonio FIN ... 196 A6
Ylitornio FIN ... 196 C6
Ylivieska FIN ... 3 D9
Ylläsjärvi FIN ... 196 B7
Ymonville F ... 103 A3
Yngsjö S ... 63 C2
York GB ... 40 B2
Youghal IRL ... 29 C4
Yoğuntaş TR ... 186 A2
Yozgat TR ... 23 B8
Yport F ... 89 A4
Ypres = Ieper B ... 78 B2
Yssingeaux F ... 117 B4
Ystad S ... 66 A2
Ystalyfera GB ... 39 C3
Ystebrød N ... 52 B1
Ystradgynlais GB ... 39 C3
Ytre Arna N ... 46 B2
Ytre Enebakk N ... 54 A2
Ytre Rendal N ... 199 D8
Ytteran S ... 199 B11
Ytterhogdal S ... 199 C11
Yttermalung S ... 49 B5
Yunak TR ... 187 D6
Yuncos E ... 151 B4
Yunquera E ... 162 B3
Yunquera de Henares
  E ... 151 B4
Yushkozero RUS ... 3 D13
Yverdon-les-Bains
  CH ... 106 C1
Yvetot F ... 89 A4
Yvignac F ... 101 A3
Yvoir B ... 79 B4
Yvonand CH ... 106 C1
Yxnerum S ... 56 B2
Yzeure F ... 104 C2

**Z**

Zaamslag NL ... 79 A3
Zaanstad NL ... 70 B1
Žabalj SRB ... 126 B2
Zabar H ... 113 A4
Žabari SRB ... 127 C3
Zabiče SLO ... 123 B3
Zabierzów PL ... 87 B3
Ząbki PL ... 77 B6
Ząbkowice Śląskie
  PL ... 85 B4

Zablaće HR ... 138 B1
Žabljak MNE ... 139 B5
Žabno PL ... 87 B4
Zabok HR ... 124 A1
Žabokreky SK ... 98 C2
Zabor PL ... 75 C4
Zabowo PL ... 75 A4
Zabrdje BIH ... 125 C4
Zábřeh CZ ... 97 B4
Zabrežje SRB ... 127 C2
Ząbrowo PL ... 67 C4
Zabrze PL ... 86 B2
Zabrzeź PL ... 99 B4
Zacharo GR ... 184 B2
Zadar HR ... 137 A4
Zadzim PL ... 86 A2
Zafarraya E ... 163 B3
Zafferana Etnea I ... 177 B4
Zafra E ... 155 C4
Žaga SLO ... 122 A2
Zagajica SRB ... 127 C3
Žagań PL ... 84 A3
Zaglav HR ... 137 B4
Zaglavak SRB ... 127 D1
Zagnansk PL ... 87 B4
Zagora GR ... 183 D5
Zagorc SLO ... 110 C2
Zagorićani BIH ... 138 B3
Zagorje SLO ... 123 A4
Zagórów PL ... 76 B2
Zagradje SRB ... 127 C2
Zagreb HR ... 124 B1
Zagrilla E ... 163 A3
Zagvozd HR ... 138 B3
Zagwiżdzie PL ... 86 B1
Zagyvarekas H ... 113 B4
Zagyvaróna H ... 113 A3
Zahara E ... 162 B2
Zahara de los Atunes
  E ... 162 B2
Zahinos E ... 155 C4
Zahna D ... 83 A4
Záhoří CZ ... 96 B2
Záhrádka CZ ... 97 B3
Zahrensdorf D ... 73 A3
Zaidin E ... 153 A4
Zaječar SRB ... 16 D5
Zákamenné SK ... 99 B3
Zákány H ... 124 A2
Zákányszék H ... 126 A1
Zakliczyn PL ... 99 B4
Zakopane PL ... 99 B3
Zakroczym PL ... 77 B5
Zakrzew PL ... 87 A5
Zakrzewo PL ... 76 B3
Zakupy CZ ... 84 B2
Zakynthos GR ... 184 B1
Zalaapáti H ... 111 C4
Zalabaksa H ... 111 C3
Zalaegerszeg H ... 111 C3
Zalakomár H ... 111 C4
Zalakoppány H ... 111 C4
Zalalövö H ... 111 C3
Zalamea de la Serena
  E ... 156 B2
Zalamea la Real
  E ... 161 B3
Zalaszentgrót H ... 111 C4
Zalaszentiván H ... 111 C3
Zalău RO ... 17 B5
Zalavár H ... 111 C4
Zalcsie PL ... 86 A3
Zaldibar E ... 143 A4
Žalec SLO ... 123 A4
Zalesie PL ... 77 A5
Zalewo PL ... 69 B4
Zalishchyky UA ... 13 D6
Zalla E ... 143 A3
Zaltbommel NL ... 79 A5
Zamárdi H ... 112 C1
Zamarte PL ... 68 B2
Zambugueira do Mar
  P ... 160 B1
Zámoly H ... 112 B2
Zamora E ... 149 A4
Zamość PL ... 13 C5
Zamoście PL ... 86 A3
Zams A ... 108 B1
Zandhoven B ... 79 A4

Žandov CZ ... 84 B2
Zandvoort NL ... 70 B1
Zangliveri GR ... 183 C5
Zánka H ... 111 C4
Zaorejas E ... 152 B1
Zaovine SRB ... 127 D1
Zapadnaya Dvina
  RUS ... 9 D8
Zapfend D ... 94 A2
Zapole PL ... 86 A2
Zapolyarnyy
  RUS ... 193 C14
Zapponeta I ... 171 B3
Zaprešić HR ... 124 B1
Zaragoza E ... 153 A3
Zarautz E ... 144 A1
Zarcilla de Ramos
  E ... 164 B3
Zaręby PL ... 77 A6
Żarki PL ... 86 B3
Zarko GR ... 182 D4
Žarnovica SK ... 98 C2
Zarnow PL ... 87 A4
Zarnowiec PL ... 68 A3
Zarošice CZ ... 97 B4
Żarów PL ... 85 B4
Zarren B ... 78 A2
Zarrentin D ... 73 A3
Žary PL ... 84 A3
Zarza Capilla E ... 156 B2
Zarza de Alange E ... 156 B1
Zarza de Granadilla
  E ... 149 B3
Zarza de Tajo E ... 151 B4
Zarzadilla de Totana
  E ... 164 B3
Zarza la Mayor E ... 155 B4
Zarzuela del Monte
  E ... 150 B3
Zarzuela del Pinar
  E ... 151 A3
Zas E ... 140 A2
Zasavica SRB ... 127 C1
Zasieki PL ... 84 A2
Zásmuky CZ ... 96 B3
Žatec CZ ... 83 B5
Zaton HR ... 139 C4
Zatonie PL ... 84 A3
Zator PL ... 99 A3
Zauchwitz D ... 74 B2
Zavala BIH ... 139 C3
Zavalje BIH ... 124 C1
Zavattarello I ... 120 C2
Zavidovići BIH ... 139 A4
Zavlaka SRB ... 127 C1
Zawady PL ... 77 C5
Zawadzkie PL ... 86 B2
Zawdy PL ... 86 A2
Zawidów PL ... 84 A3
Zawidz PL ... 77 B4
Zawiercie PL ... 86 B3
Zawoja PL ... 99 B3
Zawonia PL ... 85 A5
Žažina HR ... 124 B2
Zázrivá SK ... 99 B3
Zbarazh UA ... 13 D6
Zbąszyń PL ... 75 B4
Zbąszynek PL ... 75 B4
Zbehy SK ... 98 C2
Zbiersk PL ... 76 C3
Zbiroh CZ ... 96 B1
Zblewo PL ... 69 B3
Zbójno PL ... 77 A4
Zbrachlin PL ... 76 A3
Zbraslav CZ ... 96 B2
Zbraslavice CZ ... 97 B3
Ždala HR ... 124 A3
Ždánice CZ ... 98 B1
Žďár nad Sázavou
  CZ ... 97 B3
Zdbice PL ... 75 A5
Zdenci HR ... 125 B3
Ždiar SK ... 99 B4
Zdice CZ ... 96 B1
Zdirec nad Doubravou
  CZ ... 97 B3
Zdolbuniv UA ... 13 C7
Zdounky CZ ... 98 B1
Ždrelo SRB ... 127 C3
Zduńska Wola PL ... 86 A2

Zduny
  Łódzkie PL ... 77 B4
  Wielkopolskie PL ... 85 A5
Żdżary PL ... 87 A4
Zdziechowice
  Opolskie PL ... 86 A2
  Wielkopolskie PL ... 76 B2
Zdziszowice PL ... 86 B2
Zeberio E ... 143 A4
Žebrák CZ ... 96 B1
Zebreira P ... 155 B3
Zebrzydowa PL ... 84 A3
Zechlin D ... 74 A1
Zechlinerhütte D ... 74 A1
Zederhaus A ... 109 B4
Žednik SRB ... 126 B1
Zeebrugge B ... 78 A3
Zegrze PL ... 77 B6
Zehdenick D ... 74 B2
Zehren D ... 83 A5
Zeil D ... 94 A2
Zeilarn D ... 95 C4
Zeist NL ... 70 B2
Zeithain D ... 83 A5
Zeitz D ... 83 A4
Želatava CZ ... 97 B3
Zelazno PL ... 68 A2
Zele B ... 79 A4
Zelenoborskiy RUS ... 3 C13
Zelenogorsk RUS ... 9 B6
Zelenograd RUS ... 9 D10
Zelenogradsk RUS ... 12 A4
Železná Ruda CZ ... 96 B1
Železnice CZ ... 84 B3
Železnik SRB ... 127 C2
Železniki SLO ... 123 A3
Železny Brod CZ ... 84 B3
Zelhem NL ... 71 B3
Želiezovce SK ... 112 A2
Želkowo PL ... 68 A2
Zell
  CH ... 106 B2
  Baden-Württemberg
  D ... 93 C4
  Baden-Württemberg
  D ... 106 B2
  Rheinland-Pfalz D ... 92 A3
Zella-Mehlis D ... 82 B2
Zell am See A ... 109 B3
Zell am Ziller A ... 108 B2
Zell an der Pram A ... 96 C1
Zell bei Zellhof A ... 96 C2
Zellerndorf A ... 97 C3
Zellingen D ... 94 B1
Želovce SK ... 112 A3
Zelów PL ... 86 A3
Zeltweg A ... 110 B1
Zelzate B ... 79 A3
Zemberovce SK ... 98 C2
Zembrzyce PL ... 99 B3
Zemianske-Kostol'any
  SK ... 98 C2
Zemitz D ... 66 C2
Zemné SK ... 112 B1
Zemst B ... 79 B4
Zemun SRB ... 127 C2
Zemunik Donji HR ... 137 A4
Zenica BIH ... 139 A3
Zennor GB ... 42 B1
Žepce BIH ... 139 B5
Žepče BIH ... 139 A4
Zeppornami I ... 168 A2
Zerbst D ... 73 C5
Zerf D ... 92 B2
Zerind RO ... 113 C5
Žerków PL ... 76 B2
Zermatt CH ... 119 A4
Zernez CH ... 107 C5
Zerpen-schleuse D ... 74 B2
Zestoa E ... 144 A1
Zetel D ... 71 A4
Zeulenroda D ... 83 B3
Zeven D ... 72 A2
Zevenaar NL ... 70 C3
Zevenbergen NL ... 79 A4
Zévio I ... 121 B4
Zeytinbaği TR ... 186 B3
Zeytindağ TR ... 186 D2
Zgierz PL ... 86 A3
Zgorzelec PL ... 84 A3
Zgošča BIH ... 139 A4

Zhabinka BY ... 13 B6
Zharkovskiy RUS ... 9 E8
Zhashkiv UA ... 13 D9
Zhlobin BY ... 13 B9
Zhmerynka UA ... 13 D8
Zhodzina BY ... 13 A8
Zhytomyr UA ... 13 C8
Žiar nad Hronom
  SK ... 98 C2
Zicavo F ... 180 B2
Zickhusen D ... 65 C4
Zidani Most SLO ... 123 A4
Ziddorf D ... 73 A5
Židlochovice CZ ... 97 B4
Ziębice PL ... 85 B5
Ziegendorf D ... 73 A4
Ziegenrück D ... 83 B3
Zieleniec
  Dolnośląskie PL ... 85 B4
  Warmińsko-Mazurskie
  PL ... 77 A6
  Zachodnio-Pomorskie
  PL ... 75 A4
Zielona PL ... 77 A4
Zielona Góra PL ... 75 C4
Zieluń-Osada PL ... 77 A4
Ziemetshausen D ... 94 C2
Zierenberg D ... 81 A5
Zierikzee NL ... 79 A3
Ziersdorf A ... 97 C3
Zierzow D ... 73 A4
Ziesar D ... 73 B5
Ziesendorf D ... 65 C5
Ziethen D ... 74 B2
Žihle CZ ... 96 A1
Žilina SK ... 98 B2
Ziltendorf D ... 74 B3
Zimandu Nou RO ... 126 A3
Zimna Woda PL ... 77 A5
Zimnicea RO ... 17 D6
Zinal CH ... 119 A4
Zinasco I ... 120 B2
Zingst D ... 66 B1
Zinkgruvan S ... 55 B6
Zinkovy CZ ... 96 B1
Zinnowitz D ... 66 B2
Zirc H ... 112 B1
Žiri SLO ... 123 A3
Zirl A ... 108 B2
Zirndorf D ... 94 B2
Žirovnica SRB ... 127 C3
Žirovnice CZ ... 97 B3
Zisterdorf A ... 97 C4
Žitište SRB ... 126 B2
Zitsa GR ... 182 D2
Zittau D ... 84 B2
Živaja HR ... 124 B2
Živinice BIH ... 139 A4
Zlatar HR ... 124 A2
Zlatar Bistrica HR ... 124 A2
Zlate Hory CZ ... 85 B5
Zlaté Klasy SK ... 111 A4
Zlaté Moravce SK ... 98 C2
Zlatniky SK ... 98 C2
Zlatograd BG ... 183 B7
Žlebič SLO ... 123 B3
Zlín CZ ... 98 B1
Złocieniec PL ... 75 A5
Złoczew PL ... 86 A2
Zlonice CZ ... 84 B2
Złotniki Kujawskie
  PL ... 76 B3
Złotoryja PL ... 85 A3
Złotów PL ... 68 B2
Złoty Stok PL ... 85 B4
Zlutice CZ ... 83 B5
Zmajevac BIH ... 124 C2
Zmajevo SRB ... 126 B1
Żmigród PL ... 85 A4
Žminj HR ... 122 B2
Znin PL ... 76 B2
Znojmo CZ ... 97 C4
Zöblitz D ... 83 B5
Zocca I ... 135 A3
Zoetermeer NL ... 70 B1
Zofingen CH ... 106 B2
Zogno I ... 120 B2
Zohor SK ... 111 A3

Zolling D ... 95 C3
Zolochiv UA ... 13 D6
Zomba H ... 112 C2
Zomergem B ... 79 A3
Zoñán E ... 141 A3
Zonguldak TR ... 187 A6
Zonhoven B ... 79 B5
Zonza F ... 180 B2
Zörbig D ... 83 A4
Zorita E ... 156 A2
Żory PL ... 98 A3
Zossen D ... 74 B2
Zottegem B ... 79 B3
Zoutkamp NL ... 71 A3
Zovi Do BIH ... 139 B4
Zreče SLO ... 123 A4
Zrenjanin SRB ... 126 B2
Žrnovica HR ... 138 B2
Zručnad Sazavou
  CZ ... 97 B3
Zsadány H ... 113 C5
Zsámbék H ... 112 B2
Zsámbok H ... 112 B3
Zsana H ... 126 A1
Zschopau D ... 83 B5
Zuberec SK ... 99 B3
Zubieta E ... 144 A2
Zubiri E ... 144 B2
Zubtsov RUS ... 9 D9
Zucaina E ... 153 B3
Zudar D ... 66 B2
Zuera E ... 144 C3
Zufre E ... 161 B3
Zug CH ... 107 B3
Zuheros E ... 163 A3
Zuidhorn NL ... 71 A3
Zuidlaren NL ... 71 A3
Zuidwolde NL ... 71 B3
Zújar E ... 164 B2
Żukowo PL ... 69 A3
Žuljana HR ... 138 C3
Žulová CZ ... 85 B5
Zülpich D ... 80 B2
Zumaia E ... 144 A1
Zumárraga E ... 143 A4
Zundert NL ... 79 A4
Županja HR ... 125 B4
Zurgena E ... 164 B2
Zürich CH ... 107 B3
Żuromin PL ... 77 A4
Zurzach CH ... 106 B3
Zusmarshausen D ... 94 C2
Zusow D ... 65 C4
Züssow D ... 66 C2
Žuta Lovka HR ... 123 C4
Zutphen NL ... 70 B3
Žužemberk SLO ... 123 B3
Zvenyhorodka UA ... 13 D9
Zvikovské Podhradi
  CZ ... 96 B2
Zvolen SK ... 99 C3
Zvolenská Slatina
  SK ... 99 C3
Zvornik BIH ... 139 A5
Zwartsluis NL ... 70 B3
Zweibrücken D ... 93 B3
Zweisimmen CH ... 106 C2
Zwettl A ... 97 C3
Zwettl an der Rodl
  A ... 96 C2
Zwickau D ... 83 B4
Zwiefalten D ... 107 A4
Zwieryn PL ... 75 B4
Zwierzno PL ... 69 A4
Zwiesel D ... 96 B1
Zwieselstein A ... 108 C2
Zwoleń PL ... 87 A5
Zwolle NL ... 70 B3
Zwönitz D ... 83 B4
Zychlin PL ... 77 B4
Zydowo
  Wielkopolskie PL ... 76 B2
  Zachodnio-Pomorskie
  PL ... 68 A1
Żyrardów PL ... 77 B5
Żytno PL ... 86 B3
Żywiec PL ... 99 B3
Zyyi CY ... 181 B2